The Concise Encyclopedia of Orthodox Christianity

The Concise Encyclopedia of Orthodox Christianity

Edited by

John Anthony McGuckin

WILEY Blackwell

This paperback edition first published 2014
© 2014 John Wiley & Sons, Ltd.

First published in hardback as *The Encyclopedia of Eastern Orthodox Christianity* (Blackwell Publishing Ltd, 2011)

Registered Office
John Wiley & Sons, Ltd, The Atrium, Southern Gate, Chichester, West Sussex, PO19 8SQ, UK

Editorial Offices
350 Main Street, Malden, MA 02148–5020, USA
9600 Garsington Road, Oxford, OX4 2DQ, UK
The Atrium, Southern Gate, Chichester, West Sussex, PO19 8SQ, UK

For details of our global editorial offices, for customer services, and for information about how to apply for permission to reuse the copyright material in this book please see our website at www.wiley.com/wiley-blackwell.

Library of Congress Cataloging-in-Publication Data

The concise encyclopedia of Orthodox Christianity/edited by John Anthony McGuckin.
     p.   cm.
  Includes bibliographical references and index.
  ISBN 978-1-4051-8539-4 (cloth) – ISBN 978-1-118-75933-2 (pbk.)
1. Orthodox Eastern Church–Encyclopedias.   I. McGuckin, John Anthony.
  BX230.E53 2011
  281′.503–dc22

                                        2010029190

A catalogue record for this book is available from the British Library.

Cover image: (L to R) Contemporary Icon of the Divine Trinity (after Rublev); Mother of Tenderness; Contemporary Icon of Christ the Divine Wisdom; St. Matthew the Evangelist, all by Eileen McGuckin, The Icon Studio: www.sgtt.org
Cover design by Nicki Averill Design & Illustration

Set in 10/12pt Bembo by SPi Publisher Services, Pondicherry, India
Printed in Malaysia by Ho Printing (M) Sdn Bhd

1   2014

Contents

List of Entries

List of Illustrations

Editors and Contributors

Editor

John Anthony McGuckin, *Union Theological Seminary, New York, USA*

Associate Editors

Julia Konstantinovsky, *Wolfson College, Oxford, UK*
Justin M. Lasser, *Columbia University, USA*

Contributors

Stamenka E. Antonova, *Columbia University, USA*
Antonia Atanassova, *Boston College, USA*
Gordon N. Bardos, *Columbia University, USA*
Timothy J. Becker, *Pittsburgh Theological Seminary, USA*
Nicholas Birns, *New School, New York, USA*
Peter C. Bouteneff, *St Vladimir's Seminary, USA*
Kenneth Carveley, *University of Oxford, UK*
Augustine Casiday, *University of Wales, Lampeter, UK*
John Chryssavgis, *Theological Advisor to the Ecumenical Patriarch, USA*
Dimitri Conomos, *University of Oxford and University of London, UK*
Theodor Damian, *Metropolitan College of New York, USA*
George E. Demacopoulos, *Fordham University, USA*
Edward Epsen, *Champlain College, USA*
Thomas FitzGerald, *Holy Cross Greek Orthodox School of Theology, USA*
Bruce Foltz, *Eckerd College, Florida, USA*
Todd E. French, *Columbia University, USA*
Konstantin Gavrilkin, *Christ the Savior Orthodox Church
   (The Orthodox Church of America), USA*
Paul Gavrilyuk, *University of St. Thomas, USA*
Paschalis Gkortsilas, *Aristotle University of Thessaloniki, Greece*
Tamara Grdzelidze, *World Council of Churches, Switzerland*
Perry T. Hamalis, *North Central College, USA*
Chad Hatfield, *St. Vladimir's Seminary, USA*
Susan R. Holman, *Harvard School of Public Health, USA*

Andrei I. Holodny, *Weill Medical College of Cornell University, USA*
Cyril Hovorun, *Metropolitan's Administration, Kiev Caves Lavra, Ukraine*
Brenda Llewellyn Ihssen, *Pacific Lutheran University, USA*
Valentina Izmirlieva, *Columbia University, USA*
Metropolitan Kallistos, *Bishop of Diokleia, UK*
Evangelos Katafylis, *University of Cambridge, UK*
Scott M. Kenworthy, *Miami University, USA*
Thomas Kitson, *Columbia University, USA*
Julia Konstantinovsky, *Wolfson College, University of Oxford, UK*
Justin M. Lasser, *Columbia University, USA*
Andrew Louth, *University of Durham, UK*
Maria Gwyn McDowell, *Boston College, USA*
John A. McGuckin, *Columbia University, USA*
Samuel Nedelsky, *Monastery of St. Job of Pochaev, Germany*
Wendy Paula Nicholson, *University of Southampton, UK*
Irina Paert, *Tallinn University, Estonia*
Aristotle Papanikolaou, *Fordham University, USA*
Eugen J. Pentiuc, *Holy Cross School of Theology, USA*
Matthew J. Pereira, *Columbia University, USA*
Jeffrey B. Pettis, *Fordham University, USA*
Marcus Plested, *Institute for Orthodox Christian Studies, Cambridge, UK*
Andrei Psarev, *St. Tikhon's Orthodox Seminary, Pennsylvania*
Dan Sandu, *Alexandru Ioan Cuza University of Iasi, Romania*
Vera Shevzov, *Smith College, USA*
A. Edward Siecienski, *Richard Stockton College of New Jersey, USA*
James C. Skedros, *Holy Cross School of Theology, USA*
M. C. Steenberg, *Trinity and All Saints, Leeds, UK*
Theodore G. Stylianopoulos, *Holy Cross Greek Orthodox School of Theology, USA*
Stephen Thomas, *Southampton, UK*
Tenny Thomas, *Union Theological Seminary, USA*
Tarmo Toom, *Catholic University of America, USA*
Sergey Trostyanskiy, *Columbia University, USA*
Niki J. Tsironis, *The National Hellenic Research Foundation, Greece*
Sotirios A. Vlavianos, *Aristotle University of Thessaloniki, Greece*
Monica M. White, *University of Nottingham, UK*
Philip Zymaris, *Holy Cross Greek Orthodox School of Theology, USA*

Preface and Acknowledgments

Orthodoxy is old Christianity, but not antique; for it retains a freshness about it which belies all attempts (by its enemies and some of its supporters) to render it into a sustained exercise in antiquarianism. It is old in wisdom, we like to think, but fresh in its evangelical spirit: renewed by that Omega which is also the Alpha, the beginning, not simply the end. It is a Christian experience that many think they know, and often characterize in terms of its "traditionalism," its slowness to react to many things. This of course can often be a good thing. Being dogged, for example, allowed Orthodoxy to outlive, and more than outlive, its persecutors of the 20th century who greatly outmatched the ferocity of the ancient persecutors of the church; for the 20th century was (by any account) the age of the greatest persecutions the Church of Christ has ever endured. No Nero, Diocletian, or Galerius could ever match up to the oppressions put upon the Eastern Church by the Stalins, Hoxhas, or Ceaușescus of the age of totalitarians. In this gloomy herding together of the Eastern Orthodox world by communist authorities, the witness had to be one of the most basic facts of endurance. Those who know Orthodoxy more intimately than simply seeing its quaintness or its traditionalism will recognize its heroic witness in the course of the 20th century.

Today, after the irreversible fall into the dust of so many of these tyrants, who once thought they would rule forever, the intoxicating sense of joyful liberation has often passed away too, in much of Soviet-zone Eastern Europe, and the colder breezes of reality coming after the heady 1990s have been felt. Serious economic and social disorders are still to be dealt with as a long-lasting legacy of the destruction communism left behind itself. For the Orthodox Church, which suffered the purging of so many of its leaders over so many decades, and the wholesale destruction of its social mission, its church buildings, and its educational system, a similar scale of traumatic damage is undoubtedly going to be a legacy that will continue for a few generations to come. After such levels of trauma, recovery takes longer than after simple setbacks. It is perhaps the destiny of our times to see Orthodoxy climbing back up from its knees once more, while at the same time Christian practice and culture in Western Europe seems to enter into a new bleak era, neglected and despised by an alleged new humanism which mocks its own ancestral religious tradition as well as its ancient and inseparable moral and intellectual heritage: things which be token long-term social problems in terms of the transmission of societal civilized values and ethico-social cohesion in western societies.

Orthodoxy, while always having a robust sense of its theological identity, is in the course of this present era in a constant state of flux; involving growth, but also drawing the Eastern Church into areas of indeterminate conditions: strange environments it has not yet been fully able to parallel with familiar ancient precedents so as to help it navigate towards a new hermeneutic. Sometimes western commentators, however unbalanced they may be, have been given a hearing as they attempted to draw the boundaries of civilization as concomitant with the western political and religious borders of the Mediterranean, excluding the Orthodox nations as if they were of little or no importance. This position (which in my mind is a cleverly masked form of prejudice) conveniently forgets that Orthodoxy has had its schools smashed by hostile conquerors or oppressive totalitarians not only for the last seventy years, but for the last five hundred. How many centuries does it take to reestablish an intellectual tradition? A life of the mind to match the élan of a cultural and artistic fabric? While the West was establishing the Renaissance on the base of its late medieval university cities, the Christian East was falling relentlessly before ascendant Islamic military might. It was a submergence into a forcibly imposed Sharia law, a twilight existence for a conquered *ethnos*, that permitted partial cultic existence to the Orthodox Church but certainly not an independently continuing intellectual life. The schools, seminaries, printing presses, and caucuses of intellectuals belonging to the Orthodox were mostly doomed and soon were almost all entirely extinguished except for symbolic residues – those few able to secure their independence from the power of the Ottomans, or to pay for a limited degree of autonomy. After the fall of Constantinople in 1453, Russia continued on, and Ukraine, Romania, Athos, and Sinai became, at various times, fortresses of Orthodox culture under immense external pressures. But even so, Orthodoxy lost its university ethos definitively; lost its broadly spread intelligentsia, its sponsoring aristocracy; lost therefore its grasp on the tiller of culture-making – a role it had so clearly excelled in for its first millennium. Instead, it had to, by force of hostile circumstance, turn more inward towards cultural and ecclesiastic preservation. Nothing replaced the university and aristocratic caucuses (the leavening effect of the imperial court and its ability to attract international talent to the Orthodox center) and monastic culture took up the fallen crown. Monastic leadership has guided and safeguarded Orthodoxy ever since, and made a faithful job of it; but the wider intellectual culture of the Eastern Church was inevitably narrowed into slower and more mystical channels than Orthodoxy had known as part of its vital fabric in earlier, more independent and more flourishing political circumstances. Those who in recent centuries have often scorned or mocked the alleged inability of Orthodox theologians and church leaders to match the intellectual sophistication of the West, are often laughing, albeit unwittingly, at the sorrows

of conquered peoples – in a manner like the Queen of France who thought cake would substitute sufficiently well for the lack of bread.

Orthodox Christian intellectual life, however, once shone radiantly in so many periods past, and just as at times its radiance seemed self-assured, so too, just as often, historic reversals and disasters have dimmed it, sometimes crushed it for many generations. The schools of Byzantium were once a model to the world, reformulating the glories of patristic eloquence and extending their spirit of biblical interpretation so as to make a sustained set of variations on Roman Law and Civilization, such that the ages of Byzantium truly became a monument of world Christian culture. But even at their height these cultural achievements were cut short. Long before the last emperor fell in the Saint Romanos gate at Constantinople in 1453, the eastern Roman capital's intellectual life was a shadow of its former vitality. It was falling prey to the temptation to live in a virtual reality (a temptation the Orthodox Church must resist in all generations). To take one example: the medieval scholar Theodore Metochites, a leading Byzantine astronomer, Grand Logothete of the Empire, and the builder of that exquisite Constantinopolitan church St. Savior in Chora, used the newly invented Arabian astrolabe for all his practical navigational computations, but continued to comment at length upon Ptolemy. He looked and touched, but did not see. Constantinople towards the end of its glory had, for several centuries, nurtured the exiles from other major Christian centers of learning, such as Edessa, Alexandria, Antioch, Caesarea, or Jerusalem, all of which themselves had once shone bright with the flash of Greek Fire as schools of Christian learning in Antiquity but which, one by one, had fallen to the ravages of enemies or time, and often ceased to exist as Christian centers at all. After the collapse of Byzantium the Russian tsars saw themselves as the inheritors of the duty to protect Orthodoxy, calling their nation "The Third Rome."

Today, although Russian Orthodoxy is by far the largest power bloc of the world Orthodox families, no one seriously expects a Christian tsar to reemerge; and not all have happy memories about the tsar's effect on the church when he was master of the Russian Empire. The patriarchate of Constantinople was used by the Ottoman sultans in a way that gave it, through the late medieval period and through to the end of the 19th century, an international prestige as leader of all Eastern Christians in the Ottoman imperial domains. But today the Phanar suffers, and its local Christians have dwindled to the point of vanishing. Its ecclesial and political base now effectively resides in North America and Australia. However, it retains its ancient prestige among world Orthodoxy, in a way excelling the other ancient patriarchates such as Alexandria or Antioch or Jerusalem, who retain more of a ceremonial role in world Orthodox affairs. By the grace of God the patriarch of Constantinople has not dwindled to the status of a canonical "virtual reality" and still exercises a high moral authority above and beyond his role in specific legal church affairs. Other Orthodox patriarchs who were once long silenced, or degraded by oppressors, have again come into freedom. The presence of learned and insightful leaders in these high patriarchal sees will continue to be of critical importance in this age of mass media. But as articulators of world Orthodoxy the collective *Sobor* of these national patriarchs increasingly has to look beyond their nations and national interests, to wider and more inclusive horizons. The reemergence of the large Eastern European Orthodox Churches has changed the world scene definitively as the 21st century now progresses; and what world Orthodoxy will do in the coming century remains to be seen. But the prospects look good, and hopeful, as new and highly educated leaders emerge, and the schools and monasteries, theological academies and church social projects slowly come back into existence across the former communist world.

Orthodoxy also started to come of age in the New World in the latter part of the 20th century. It developed a significant body of theologians who are at once contemporary and yet rooted in past precedents, and commonly joined together in a spiritual harmony bearing a deep respect for tradition. In this, modern Orthodoxy has, in a real sense, an advantage that its theologians and spiritual teachers, its bishops, and patriarchs are all, genuinely, bonded together in the faith, and share that faith with the laity, intelligent or simple, in a way that many other ecclesial groups in the West cannot any longer sustain. These things will prove to be great resources for an intellectual flowering of Orthodox intellectual life in the 21st century.

Orthodoxy's spiritual resources, its monastic centers, its continued central focus on liturgy and prayer, on the fidelity to the gifts of the Spirit, remain at its core; and as long as they do the inner life and spirit of the church will itself remain evergreen.

Today, unarguably so, there are also numerous international signs of a reviving intellectual life among the Orthodox Greeks, Russians, Romanians, Serbs, and many other Orthodox church families. Several historic theological faculties have reopened or have been newly founded, all promising signs for the future. Throughout the English-speaking world, Orthodoxy is beginning to be represented in several secular schools of higher learning, and engaging with Protestant and Catholic iterations of theology on its own terms, offering its distinctive voice in the expression of Christian theological concern on matters of doctrine, ethics, ecumenicity, and worship.

This encyclopedia has been written, almost entirely so, out of the talents of English-speaking Orthodox thinkers, across a wide international spectrum. It is therefore one of the few existing resources, of the highest intellectual standard, that allow Orthodoxy to speak with its own voice, in its own intonations, no longer as a subaltern. What has emerged is authentically Orthodox scholarship in full engagement with historic and theological evidences, open in mentality and aspect, and at the same time deeply rooted in its values and spiritual traditions and proud to articulate them. The encyclopedia is itself one bright sign of the emerging revival of Orthodox intellectual life at the highest levels of the Academy, offering a reference resource for the life and culture of Eastern Christianity which will, on publication, be the largest and one of the most authoritative reference works in the English language for world Orthodoxy.

It has been a privilege and a pleasure working with all the contributors who are acknowledged national and international experts in their own fields. It has also been a delight to have worked with Wiley-Blackwell's team of professionals. The press not only sponsored and encouraged this work from the outset, but have been at pains to make it appear in the most artistic way possible; aligning their skill in technology with a clear eye for the beautiful (*to kalon*). In hard copy, this is a lovely set of volumes that will grace any study and enhance any academic library as an indispensable study tool. In its electronic form this is destined to be a worldwide resource that will illuminate matters of the Eastern Christian tradition at the touch of a button – something that the ancient Orthodox theologians and mystics would surely have wondered at. Special thanks are due to Wiley-Blackwell's Executive Commissioning Editor, Rebecca Harkin, whose enthusiasm moved the project towards the light of day. Thanks too are owed to Sophie Oliver for her indefatigable work in putting the materials together on the Web, to Brigitte Lee Messenger and Jack Messenger for copyediting, and to Barbara Duke and Jane Taylor for their labors in production and image management.

The encyclopedia benefited notably from the wisdom and critical insight of Revd. Dr. Konstantin Gavrilkin, who also contributed many of the articles relating to Slavic Orthodoxy. The Assistant Editors are both young Orthodox intellectuals whose research has already broken new ground. The first, the Revd. Dr. Julia (Seraphima) Konstantinovsky, a monastic of the community of Fr. Sophronios in Essex and now a tutor in the Oxford University Faculty of Theology, is an expert in early Christian studies, and a world-class *perita* in matters relating to the spiritual tradition of early monastic communities, especially the Greek and Syriac circles around Evagrios Pontike. Dr. Justin Lasser has worked in fields as disparate as the Nag Hammadi Gnostic texts, Proto-Syrian Christianity (with a doctoral dissertation from Union Theological Seminary on the Thomas tradition), and Ethiopian Orthodoxy, learning Ge'ez along with Coptic, Greek, and Syriac to enable him better to understand the world of the early fathers and mothers. It has been a delight to work alongside them both, and to feel that with such a "Cloud of Witnesses" as these, and the splendid array of writers that we amassed for this project, the appearance of this encyclopedia is not an errant swallow, but a further sign of what a great patristic divine, John Henry Newman, himself once called (in a different time and circumstance) a "Second Spring."

It is with pleasure, and a sense of a very large and important scholarly task brought to a fine completion, that I can now put this work before the reading public, more than confident too that it will serve the affairs of Church and Academy luminously for many decades to come.

V. Revd. Prof. John A. McGuckin
Priest of the Romanian Orthodox Church
Feast of the Learned Hierarch St. Grigorie Dascalui,
Metropolitan of the Romanians

Maps

Map 1 The Early Christian world.

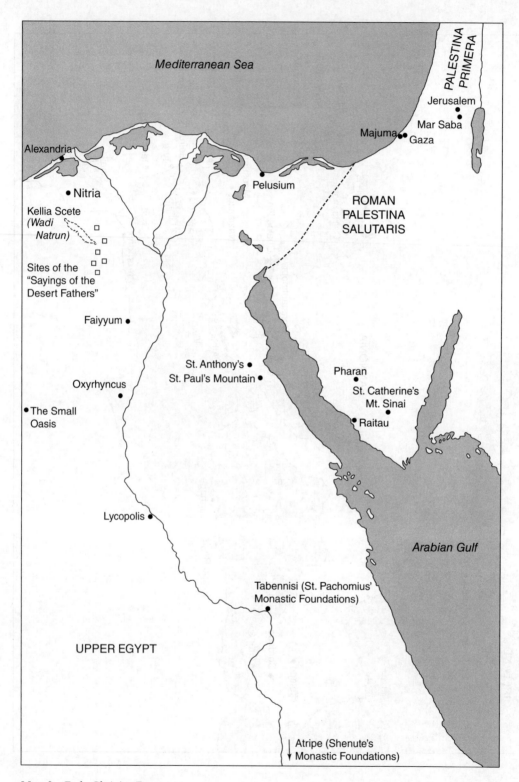

Map 2 Early Christian Egypt.

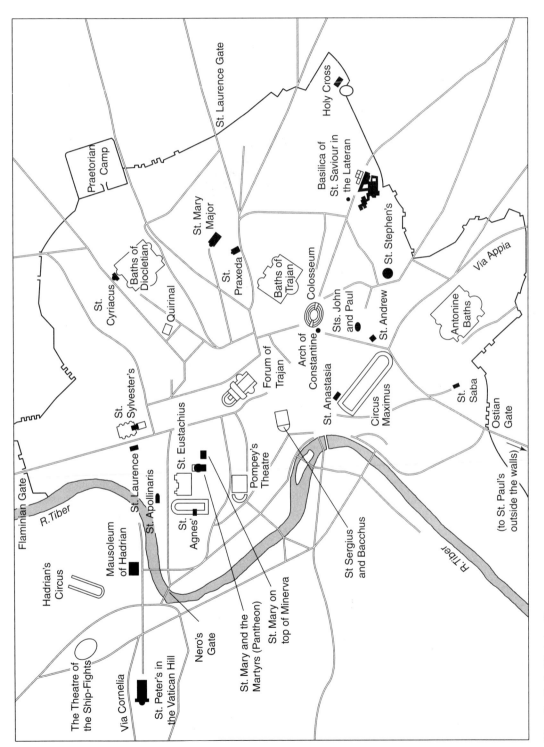

Map 3 Early Christian Rome.

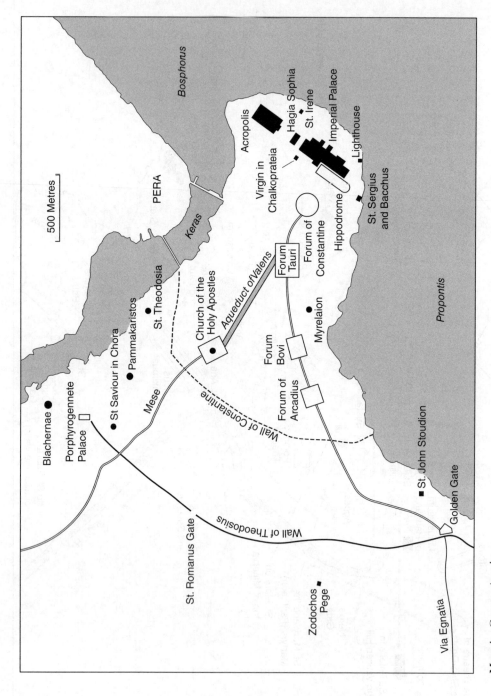

Map 4 Constantinople.

A

Afanasiev, Nicholas (1893–1966)
see Contemporary Orthodox
Theology

Africa, Orthodoxy in

JUSTIN M. LASSER

Christianity on the African continent begins its story, primarily, in four separate locales: Alexandrine and Coptic Egypt, the North African region surrounding the city of Carthage, Nubia, and the steppes of Ethiopia. The present synopsis will primarily address the trajectories of the North African Church, the Ethiopian Orthodox Church, and the Nubian Orthodox Church. The affairs of Christian Alexandria and the Coptic regions have their own treatments elsewhere in the encyclopedia.

Roman-colonial North Africa

After the Romans sacked the city of Carthage in 146 during the Third Punic War, they began a sustained colonizing campaign that slowly transformed the region (modern Tunisia and Libya) into a partially "Romanized" society. In most instances, however, the cultural transformations were superficial, affecting predominantly the trade languages and local power structures. It was Julius Caesar who laid the plans for Carthage's reemergence as *Colonia Junonia* in 44 BCE. This strong colonial apparatus made North African Christians especially susceptible to persecution by the Roman authorities on the Italian Peninsula. Because the economic power of Carthage was an essential ingredient in the support of the citizens in the city of Rome, the Romans paid careful attention to the region. The earliest extant North African Christian text, the *Passion of the Scillitan Martyrs* (180 CE), reflects a particularly negative estimation of the Roman authorities. Saturninus, the Roman proconsul, made this appeal to the African Christians: "You can win the indulgence of our ruler the Emperor, if you return to a sensible mind." The Holy Martyr Speratus responded by declaring: "The empire of this world I know not; but rather I serve that God, whom no one has seen, nor with these eyes can see. I have committed no theft; but if I have bought anything I pay the tax; because I know my Lord, the King of kings and Emperor of all nations." This declaration was a manifestation of what the Roman authorities feared most about the Christians – their proclamation of a "rival" emperor, Jesus Christ, King of kings. The Holy Martyr Donata expressed that sentiment most clearly: "Honor to Caesar as Caesar: but fear to God." Within the Roman imperial fold such declarations were not merely interpreted as "religious" expressions, but political challenges. As a result the

The Concise Encyclopedia of Orthodox Christianity, First Edition. Edited by John Anthony McGuckin.
© 2014 John Wiley & Sons, Ltd. Published 2014 by John Wiley & Sons, Ltd.

Plate 1 Ethiopian Orthodox clergy celebrating at the rock-carved church of St. George Lalibela. Photo by Sulaiman Ellison.

Plate 2 Pilgrims gathered around the Ethiopian Orthodox Church of Holy Emmanuel. Photo Sulaiman Ellison.

Roman authorities executed the Scillitan Christians, the proto-martyrs of Africa. Other such persecutions formed the character and psyche of North African Christianity. It became and remained a "persecuted" church in mentality, even after the empire was converted to Christianity.

By far the most important theologian of Latin North Africa was Augustine of Hippo (354–430). His profound theological works established the foundations of later Latin theology and remain today as some of the most important expressions of western literary culture. His articulation of Christian doctrine represents the pinnacle of Latin Christian ingenuity and depth (see especially, *On Christian Doctrine*, *On the Holy Trinity*, and *City of God*). It also should be noted

that Augustine, to a certain degree, "invented" the modern genre of the autobiography in his masterful work, the *Confessions*. However, Augustine drew on a long-established tradition of Latin theology before him as expressed in the writings of Tertullian, Minucius Felix, Optatus of Milevis, Arnobius, and Lactantius, among others, in the period of the 2nd through the 4th centuries.

Tertullian

Quintus Septimius Florens Tertullianus' (ca. 160–225) masterful rhetorical skill manifests the sentiments of the North African population in regard to the Roman authorities and various "heretical" groups. His terse rhetoric also represents the flowering of Latin rhetorical

Plate 3 Orthodox clergy at celebrations for the Feast of the Ark of the Covenant (Timkat). Photo by Sulaiman Ellison.

dexterity. Tertullian created many of the most memorable proclamations and formulae of early Christianity, several of which characterize his negative estimation of philosophical "innovators" – "What has Athens to do with Jerusalem?" he asked, casting aspersions on the utility of philosophy in the formulation of church teachings. His heresiological works laid the groundwork for many of the Orthodox responses to the Gnostics, Monarchians, and Marcionites, among others (*The Apology, Against Marcion, Against Praxeas, Against Hermogenes*). Tertullian also provided the Latin Church with much of its technical theological vocabulary (terms such as "person," "nature," and "sacrament").

Lactantius

Lactantius (ca. 250–325) differs from Tertullian in a variety of ways, but none is as clear as his different style of writing. Lactantius, to a certain degree, represents the first Christian "systematic" theology. This

genre was markedly different from the apologetic treatises which were more common in the 2nd century. His is a highly eschatological vision, but allied with a deep sense that Christianity has the destiny to emerge as the new system for Rome, and his thought is colored by his legal training. He manifests a unique window into ancient patterns of pre-Nicene western Christian thought in philosophical circles around the Emperor Constantine. However, as we shall see, the contributions of North African Christianity cannot simply be limited to the intelligentsia and the cities. Much of its unique Christian expression was manifested outside Carthage.

Cyprian of Carthage

The great rhetorician Cyprian of Carthage (ca. 200–58) represents the Orthodox response to the crises in the North African Church resulting from the Roman persecutions. He was a leading Romano-African rhetorician, and became a convert to the Christian faith under the tutelage of Bishop Caecilius, a noted "resister." Cyprian found himself at the center of the competing positions in the face of Roman persecution. In 250 the Emperor Decius demanded that all citizens should offer sacrifices to the Roman gods. Cyprian, in response, chose to flee the city and take refuge. There were many Christians in Carthage who looked upon this flight with great disdain. While Cyprian was in hiding, many of his faithful confessed their faith and died as martyrs, while others elected to offer sacrifices to the gods. These circumstances led to the controversy over whether or not lapsed Christians should be readmitted into the church. With the potential onslaught of new persecutions, Cyprian advocated reconciliation. This crisis produced some of the most profound expositions of Christian ecclesiology (see especially, *Unity of the Catholic Church* and *On the Lapsed*). In 258 Cyprian was martyred under Galerius Maximus during the reign of Emperor Valerian. His writings have had a deep effect on the ecclesiological thought of the Eastern Orthodox world, though in many instances they have been superseded, for the West, by the ecclesiological writings Augustine would produce after his encounter with the Donatists. Cyprian's theology and noble leadership bear witness to the fact that the Donatist controversy was not a disagreement between enemies, but brothers.

Augustine and the Donatists

The history of the church in the shadow of the great trade city of Carthage and the hill country of Numidia is greatly obscured by ancient rhetorical devices and the rhetoric of privilege in the classical Roman social structure. As much as the history of Christian Numidia has been characterized by the Donatist schism, it is more a story of the clash between village and city, or colonized and colonizer. It would be easy to approach African Christianity through the rhetorical prism of the capital cities alone, but that would be less than half the story. Indeed, the Christianity of Carthage was very different from the Christianity in the hill country and villages of Numidia. In classical definition (largely the manner in which St. Augustine classified

them, his major opponents), the Donatists were a schismatical group that insisted on absolute purity of the clergy and the Orthodox communion. They became emboldened by their perseverance during persecution and demanded the same of every Christian. They also expressed a remarkable literalness in exegetical interpretation and renounced those who turned over the sacred Scriptures to the authorities as *traditores* (traitors). Traditionally, they also expressed a strange eagerness for the "second baptism" of martyrdom. The memory of the Numidian Donatists has been greatly overshadowed by Augustine of Hippo's writings and his international reputation. Augustine successfully characterized the Donatists as "elitists," but this has partly occluded the more correct view of the movement as chiefly a village phenomenon, closer, perhaps, to the poorer life of the countryside than that known by Augustine, who clearly lived far more happily in the Roman colonial establishment. Augustine's friend Alypius described the Numidian Donatists thus: "All these men are bishops of estates [*fundi*] and manors [*villae*] not towns [*civitates*]" (*GestaColl. Carthage* I.164, quoted in Frend 1952: 49). The charge of sectarian elitism was a means to delegitimize the rural bishops, as the city bishops assumed that the ecclesiastical hierarchy should reflect the Roman imperial hierarchy, and they considered the Donatist flocks too small to have a significant say. In the Roman world, power was centralized in the cities, not in the manors. The estates (*fundi*) existed only as a means of supplying the cities, not as autonomous entities in themselves. The Numidian Christians challenged this social structure with the ethical tenets expressed in the teachings of Christ against wealth.

Catholic Christians in North Africa were primarily Latin and Punic speaking peoples. Many of the Donatists were primarily speakers of the various Berber languages, which still exist today in North Africa (Frend 1952: 52). The segregation of the Catholic-Donatist controversy along these ethnic lines may demonstrate that theology was not necessarily the primary reason for the schism. In fact the Numidian Donatists represent the first sustained counter-imperial operation within Christian history. It was in many instances a rural movement against the colonial cities and outposts of the Romans in the north. The schism, nevertheless, undoubtedly weakened

North African Christianity in the years before the advent of the "barbarian" invasions, followed by the ascent of Islam: events which more or less wholly suppressed Christianity in the Northern Mediterranean littoral. Augustine's theology of church unity stressed wider international aspects of communion (catholic interaction of churches) and was highly influential on later Latin ecclesiological structures. He also elevated high in his thought the conception of *caritas* (brotherly love) as one of the most important of all theological virtues.

The many internal disagreements in the North African Church and the success of the Donatist martyrs led to an increased isolation of the region. The gradual collapse of Roman authority is reflected in Augustine's *City of God*. Soon after he wrote the work, the king of the Vandals, Gaiseric, sacked Carthage and the wider region in 439. The loss of North Africa sent shock waves through the Christian world. Emperor Justinian led one final attempt at reannexing North Africa in 534, and actually succeeded for a period of time. However, the continuing internal divisions, the economic deterioration, and the failing colonial apparatus, all made it difficult to keep the region within the Romano-Byzantine fold. The last flickers of North African theological expression were witnessed by Sts. Fulgentius of Ruspe, Facundus of Hermiane, and Vigilius of Thapsus. In 698 Carthage was sacked by the invading Islamic armies, sealing the fate of the North African Christians and ending their once colorful history.

Ethiopia

The beginnings of the church in Ethiopia are difficult to decipher given the ancient confusion over the location of Ethiopia. In ancient texts India was often confused with Ethiopia and vice versa. In classical parlance "India" and "Ethiopia" merely suggest a foreign land sitting at the edge of the world, existing as the last bastion of civilization before the "tumultuous chaos of the barbarians." Their great distance away from Greece was also meant to convey a world of innocence and wonder: a "magic land." This hardly tells us much about the actual life of the Ethiopians in Africa. The very term *Ethiopia* derives from a hegemonic Greek racial slur delineating the land of "the burnt-faces" or "fire-faces." But a closer look reveals something very different, for the cultural achievements of the peoples of the Ethiopian highlands (in ancient times more of the coastal hinterland was under Ethiopian control than later on after the rise of Islam) are both astounding and utterly beautiful. A visit to the rock-hewn churches of Lalibela or an encounter with the haunting chants of the Christians at prayer is quite unforgettable. Ethiopia presents itself to the visitor as another "land of milk and honey," a second Eden indeed, since the hills of Ethiopia, along with Kenya, were the first places that humans ever walked on the face of the earth. Modern Ethiopia and Eritrea are composed of a very diverse group of people. The same doubtless could be said of ancient Ethiopia.

The history of the church here is difficult to tell in a chronological order, so many have been the devastations and loss of records that there are large holes in the evidence, and much legend replaces them. Most scholars investigating the origins of Ethiopian civilization begin their stories with the South Arabian immigrants that began to settle in the coastal city of Adulis on the Red Sea and the northern city of Aksum (Axum) in search of trade in the 5th century BCE. While it is true that South Arabian settlers partly altered some of the indigenous racial elements of the Ethiopian lands, a focus on colonial influences as explaining the distinct Ethiopic-African characteristics masks the fact that Ethiopian civilization was already far older and much more established than anything these colonial visitors brought. Christianity, however, probably came in with trade movements, as it did elsewhere. The majority of the Ethiopian populace have been categorized by a common root language called "Kushitic." This language is perhaps related to the biblical people mentioned in Genesis as the Kushites. Ancient Kushite elements are still exhibited in the unique architecture of the earliest Orthodox churches in the region and the healing and dancing ceremonies that still dominate the Ethiopian Orthodox experience; though the greatest contribution was the eclectic and rhythmic language known as Ge'ez (Ethiopic). Indeed, the best place to begin a history of the Ethiopian and Kushitic peoples is the analysis of their poetic language. Ge'ez exhibits South

Semitic roots related to the Sabaic language as well as Kushitic roots. Biblically speaking, then, Ethiopia was the land of Kush, and the story concerning the emergence of the Orthodox Church in Ethiopia is really the continuing story of the cultural eclecticism in the North of Ethiopia (the mixing of Southern Arab and native African peoples) and in the South, the negotiation of differing spiritual perspectives with a peculiar form of Judaism; relations between Ethiopia and Jerusalem comprising one of the most ancient routes known to the Africans by sea and land. Church history in this case is also a story of an imperial campaign to unite the South with the North and its newly adopted religion of Christianity, a movement that entailed the destruction of indigenous religions in the environs of the kingdom of Aksum.

This strong element of synthesis is what unifies the Ethiopian peoples. The earliest suggestion of a kingdom in the land of Kush derives from the Azbi-Dera inscription on a large altar dedicated to the god Almouqah, which was a South Arabian deity. As the South Arabian traders moved into the interior of the Ethiopian highlands, they brought with them a lucrative trade market. It seems the first group to profit from this trade was the city of Aksum in the North. Earlier Eurocentric scholars working from unexamined racist premises viewed the expansion of Aksum as a Semitic victory of the forces of "civilization" in Ethiopia, as if the indigenous groups were not civilized at all before this. The historical and cultural record simply does not support such a reconstruction. The Ethiopian highland was already home to a diverse array of indigenous cultures, but little is known about them as archeological work has barely been initiated in the region outside of Aksum and other Christian holy sites. The kingdom of Aksum, however, is the first cultural group to succeed in edging its way into considerable power and cultural influence. This was made possible by the apparent conquest of the neighboring kingdom of Meroe in the 4th century BCE. The earliest mention of the kingdom of Aksum was in the 2nd century CE by Ptolemy. An anonymous text called the *Periplos* is the first to describe the boundaries of the Aksumite territories, which are closely related to the modern state of Eritrea along the coast, extending into Northern Ethiopia.

Beyond the historic-archeological record, the Ethiopian Orthodox faithful have a variety of "foundation stories" of their own. The best known is the story of the Ethiopian eunuch in the Acts of the Apostles (8.26–40). On this occasion an Ethiopian eunuch serving in the royal court of the queen (the *Candace*) of Ethiopia (which St. Luke mistakes for a personal name) was baptized by the Apostle Philip and sent on a mission to preach the gospel in Ethiopia. This tells us, at least, that the presence of Ethiopian "Godfearers" in Jerusalem was already an established fact in the time of Jesus. The most historically substantial foundation story is that of the Syrian brothers Frumentius and Aedesius in the 4th century. There may well have been various forms of Christianity present in Ethiopia before Frumentius and Aedesius, but they were the first to convert a royal Ethiopian court to the new faith. This seems to have been a common missionary strategy of the church at this time: convert the royal courts and the countryside would follow. This strategy had the advantage of rapidity, but often failed to establish indigenous forms of Christianity that could survive future religious sways of the royal courts themselves. The defect of this strategy is exemplified in the rapid demise of the Nubian Orthodox Church, to the south, after eleven hundred years, when the royal court went over to Islam.

According to the histories, Frumentius and Aedesius arrived because of a shipwreck and were strangely asked by the recently widowed queen of Aksum to govern the kingdom until her young son was experienced enough to rule the kingdom himself. Once the young Ezana became king, the Syrian brothers left the kingdom. Aedesius returned to Tyre and Frumentius traveled to Alexandria where the great Bishop Athanasius insisted on appointing him as the first bishop of Ethiopia, and sent him back to minister to the court. This story contains much historically viable material (Syrian traders who are co-opted as state councilors) but is colored with numerous legendary flourishes. The story about Frumentius and Athanasius may well indicate more evidence of the very active campaign by St. Athanasius to establish a politically important support center for his struggle against Arianism in the Roman Empire to the far north. This is substantiated by a letter of Emperor Constantius to King Ezana and Shaizana. In this letter

Constantius informed them that Frumentius was an illegitimate bishop, as he had been consecrated by the "unorthodox" incumbent, St. Athanasius, and that Frumentius should return to Alexandria to be consecrated under the "orthodox" (Arian) bishop, George of Cappadocia (Kaplan 1984: 15).

The conversion of the royal court at Aksum was of great interest to the Romans, since Ethiopia was of great strategic importance for the empire in the North. The lucrative trade from the Southern Arabian Peninsula and exotic luxuries from sub-Saharan Africa provided much incentive for the Romans to want to control the region. Additionally, the strategic location of Ethiopia ensured a more secure buffer for Egypt from the East, the bread basket of the empire. For the Aksumites, establishing the favor and support of the empire to the north established their kingdom as the main cultural and political force in the Ethiopian highlands. This was especially important for the Aksumites given their delicate political state in the time of Athanasius and Emperor Constantius. Even so, the sudden change in religious allegiance happening in the 4th-century royal court was hardly embraced by the population as a whole. Beyond the court, Christianity was scarcely in existence and lacked the appropriate catechetical structures to instill the Christian religion. The young King Ezana also struggled to balance the needs of his diverse kingdom with his newly adopted religion. In contemporary Greek inscriptions, which were obviously illegible to most of the indigenous peoples, Ezana referred to the Blessed Trinity and declared his status as a believer in Christ. However, in Ge'ez (Ethiopic) inscriptions he uses the vaguer term "Lord of Heaven" when addressing God (Kaplan 1984: 16). In this manner Ezana spoke to and for both the Christian and indigenous communities of his kingdom without offending either.

The consecration of Frumentius in Alexandria for the Ethiopian people established a hegemonic tradition of the ecclesiastical precedence of Alexandrian Egypt that afterwards dominated much of Ethiopian Orthodox history. This occasion was seen as the paradigm for all future consecrations of the Ethiopian hierarchs, and this state of affairs lasted until 1959. Too often, the senior Ethiopian hierarch who was nominated was not even Ethiopian. In the time of the

Islamic domination of Egypt, these foreign bishops were often compromised by their Muslim overlords and by the interests of local politics in Alexandria, and sometimes adopted policies that were not always in the primary interests of the Ethiopian peoples. Sometimes the appointment of Alexandrian Coptic clergy was meant as a way of getting rid of troublesome rivals or delinquent clerics from the Egyptian Church (Kaplan 1984: 29–31). This paradigm also led to a consistent shortage of priests and bishops in Ethiopia. When a senior bishop died, there were often inter-regnum lapses of several years. After the time of Frumentius the Ethiopian Orthodox Church developed slowly, due to the strength of the indigenous faiths and the considerable lack of catechetical, clerical, and literary resources. After the Council of Chalcedon in 451, however, the strategic importance of Ethiopia emerged once again as far as the empire was concerned. As Constantinople lost control over Syria and Egypt, the condition of Ethiopian Orthodoxy became much more significant. The great pro- and anti-Chalcedonian conflicts of Alexandria were reflected in the Ethiopian highlands. Ethiopia became a battle ground for which party would win the ascendancy. The Monophysite clergy of Alexandria initiated dynamic missionary programs, focused on the winning of the Ethiopian people to the anti-Chalcedonian Coptic cause. To their efforts, already aided by the existing institutional links with Cairo and Alexandria, was added the influx of Monophysite missionaries displaced from Syria, Cappadocia, Cilicia, and other regions. This new impetus to evangelize Ethiopia arrived in the form of the Nine Saints (known as the *Tsedakan* or "righteous ones") who remain of high importance in the later church history of Ethiopia. The nine saints (Abba Za-Mika'ēl (or Abba Aregawi), Abba Pantelewon, Abba Gerima (or Yeshaq), Abba Aftse, Abba Guba, Abba Alef, Abba Yem'ata, Abba Libanos, and Abba Sehma) established numerous monasteries in the Tigre region as well as the areas outside Aksum, working mainly in the northern regions of Ethiopia. The most famous of these monasteries is certainly that of Dabra Damo, which still thrives today. The most celebrated of the Nine Saints is Abba Za-Mika'ēl, who composed an important Ethiopian monastic rule. Abba Libanos is credited with establishing the great monastic center of

Dabra Libanos. The importance and influence of these two groups cannot be overstated. They are responsible for the formation of the Ethiopian biblical canon, the translation of many Christian texts from Greek and Syriac into Ge'ez, and establishing a strong monastic base which would stand the test of time.

During the reigns of King Kalēb and his son Gabra Masqal in the 6th century, the monastic communities were generously supported and the territories of the Christian kingdom expanded. However, much of this progress was greatly inhibited by the advent of Islam on the Arabian Peninsula. The extended period between the 8th and 12th centuries lends the scholar very few sources for Christian Ethiopia beyond the Coptic *History of the Patriarchs* (Kaplan 1984: 18). However, an estimate of conditions is certainly indicated by the fact that the Ethiopians operated without an archbishop for over a half a century at one point (Budge 1928: 233–4).

After the crisis of the Council of Chalcedon in 451 the Ethiopians, who recognized no ecumenical validity to conciliar meetings in the Byzantine world after Ephesus in 431, were more and more isolated from the wider Christian world, but with the advent of Islam and the many subsequent incursions into their territory, constantly eroding their hold on the littoral lands, the Ethiopians soon found themselves isolated from the entire Christian world, save for the occasional communications with the Coptic Orthodox in the distant North, by means of the difficult land and river route. Although this isolation proved problematic in some ways, in others it served to provide the space necessary for Ethiopia to develop and create its unique expression of Orthodoxy.

Towards the end of the 11th century the Aksumite Empire declined rapidly, which led to a gradual relocation of the central authorities into the central plateau (Tamrat 1972: 53–4). The Agaw people already populated this region and the Aksumite descendants started a concentrated campaign to Christianize the area. The Agaw leaders soon embraced Christianity and were integrated into the royal court so intimately that they eventually established their own successful dynasty known as the Zagwē, which ruled Ethiopia from 1137 to 1270. However, the Zagwē suffered from their apparent lack of legitimacy. Earlier Aksumite rulers had established the tradition of "Solomonic" descent in the legendary *Kebra Negast* (*Glory of the Kings*). The Zagwē were considered illegitimate by the Tigrē and Amhara peoples in the North. The Zagwē dynasty is responsible for that jewel of Ethiopian church architecture, the city of Lali Bela. This incredible conglomeration of rock-hewn churches was meant to reproduce the sites of the holy land and established, for the Zagwē, a rival pilgrimage site opposed to Aksum in the North.

The Zagwē, however, were never able to unify the Ethiopian peoples under their banner. This inability to secure a wider consensus regarding their legitimacy as a royal line, despite the incredible accomplishments of the dynasty, fractured Christian Ethiopia; a fracture that still exists today in the painful animosities between the Tigrean people in Eritrea and the peoples of Ethiopia. In the late 12th and mid-13th centuries the expansion of Muslim trading posts channeling trade from the African interior to the wealthy Arabian Peninsula greatly strengthened the Amhara Ethiopian leaders who initiated this trade route (Kaplan 1984: 21). In time the weakened Zagwē dynasty gave way to the ambitious Amharic King Yekunno Amlak. However, during this period of rapid Islamic expansion, the Ethiopian rulers continued to splinter and struggle with problems of the succession. This inherent weakness later threatened the very continued existence of the Ethiopian "state."

It was with Yekunno Amlak's son, King Amda Şeyon, that the fortunes of the Ethiopian state turned. Amda Şeyon was a shrewd military genius. He turned the tide of internal Ethiopian divisions by creating a centralized military force. Rather than depending on the countryside for local militia, he decided to unite mercenaries and local conscripts under commanders loyal to the royal court (Kaplan 1984: 22–3). In doing this he undercut the power of the local warlords. After subduing the resistant chieftains in the Aksumite and Tigrē regions there was little further challenge to Amda Şeyon's legitimacy as an Amhara usurper. Having crushed his antagonists, he claimed the Solomonic line for himself. It was at this stage (14th century) that the great founding myth in the *Kebra Negast* became so central to Ethiopian Orthodox consciousness generally. It was first advanced by the rival Tigrean ruler Ya'ebika Egzi', but was soon shrewdly co-opted by Amda

Şeyon. Prior to his rule the Ethiopian provinces were subjected to constant Islamic incursions. Aware of their isolated status, they followed a policy of appeasement. Under Amda Şeyon the Ethiopians, with a more centralized military force, were now able to pursue a policy of aggressive reconquest, and actually succeeded in forcing certain Islamic regions into becoming vassal states. Additionally, the conquest and control of the lucrative trade route between the Arabian South and the African interior brought immense wealth to the new dynasty, which helped to solidify its political position.

The success and expansion of the medieval Ethiopian state was not without severe negative consequences. The church had become so inalienably married to the state by this time that the Christian mission began to include the subjugation of alien peoples. The *Kebra Negast* established a link between the line of King Solomon and the Ethiopian kings which granted them divine favor and a perceived duty to Christianize the region through force, if necessary. The *Feteha Negast* instructed the kings in the proper treatment of their pagan neighbors in terms redolent of the Qur'an. The *Feteha Negast* reads: "If they accept you and open their gates the men who are there shall become your subjects and shall give you tributes. But if they refuse the term of peace and after the battle fight against you, go forward to assault and oppress them since the Lord your God will give them to you."

In this emerging colonial expansion of the Ethiopian state a form of feudalism was imposed on the conquered peoples. Churches were often guarded by the military, a fact that exposes something of the unpopularity of the church's mission in the newly conquered tribal areas. The attempted Christianization of the Oromo peoples in the South, for example, brought with it rampant pillaging and extensive confiscation of lands. The Orthodox clergy and Ethiopian nobles were often given the confiscated lands to rule over as feudal lords, whereas the unfortunate Oromo were reduced to the plight of serfdom. This is a condition that Ethiopia never remedied and many ramifications from it still present themselves today as important human rights issues.

The feudal stage of Ethiopian history reached its pinnacle in the Gondar period between 1632 and 1855. During this period the country became deeply fragmented between the competing nobles, a condition that invited numerous incursions on the part of their Muslim neighbors. With the rise of Emperor Menelik II (ca. 1889) the country overthrew many of the feudal lords and moved toward a new and extensive form of political and social reunification. This was all halted during the reign of Emperor Haile Selassie I, when the Italian Army invaded and occupied Ethiopia in 1935. When the Italians left Ethiopia in 1941, Haile Selassie I was returned to power. However, the restored imperial period was not to last long. In 1974 a brutal communist regime took control of the country, inaugurating one of the most severe persecutions of Christians in Orthodox memory in those lands.

The Ethiopians have created and sustained one of the most unique expressions of world Christian Orthodoxy. One of the most intriguing aspects of the Ethiopian Church is its peculiar Jewish characteristics, the origins of which remain quite mysterious. The Ethiopian Orthodox still observe the Sabbath and continue to circumcise their male children as well as to baptize them. Moreover, they believe wholeheartedly that the original Ark of the Covenant was brought to their lands before the destruction of the Jerusalem Temple. Today, the Ark is believed to be housed in a small chapel in the city of Aksum and guarded by a lone hermit monk guardian who lives alongside it. Once a year an exact copy of the Ark is taken out of the chapel and venerated ecstatically by the faithful. The Ark plays such an important role within Ethiopian Orthodoxy that the Eucharist is celebrated over a miniature copy of the Ark (called a *Tabot*) in every Ethiopian church. The continued existence of Ethiopian and Eritrean Orthodoxy amid a sea of hostile neighbors is a testament to their zealous faith and deep roots.

Today, while having a separate patriarch, the Ethiopian Church continues with the closest of friendly relations with Coptic Alexandria. The Eritrean and Ethiopian faithful have moved apart following the divisive civil war of the late 20th century. Both Ethiopian families belong to the Oriental (Non-Chalcedonian) Orthodox family of churches, but rarely involve themselves in any form of international ecumenical discussions.

Christian Nubia

In 1960 the Islamic Egyptian authorities in the North flooded, as part of the Aswan project, many of the last vestiges of Nubian Christian antiquity. The construction of the Aswan dam devastated the archeological prospects of the region. Despite these trying circumstances there were many emergency archeological digs done at this time (mainly privileging Pharaonic remains) and some significant Nubian Christian artifacts emerged to give a slightly better shading to the obscure history of this once extensive sub-Saharan form of Orthodox Christianity. As with ancient Ethiopia, the exact geographical location of the Kingdom of Nubia is often obscured by geographical imprecisions in the ancient texts. Ibn Salīm al-Aswānī (975–96 CE), an important source for the later historian al-Maqrīzi, spent a significant amount of time among the Nubians and their royal court. To the Egyptians in the North, the Fourth Cataract along the Nile River marked the beginning of Nubian territory. The Egyptians to the north rarely ventured beyond the Fifth Cataract near the ancient city of Berber. The temperate climate to the south of the Fourth and Fifth Cataracts as well as less frequent Egyptian incursions allowed for the development of the African Kingdom of Meroe, on Meroe Island situated between the Atbara, Nile, and Blue Nile rivers. In this region dwelt the Kushites, Nubians, and Ethiopians. According to the Greek historian Strabo: "The parts on the left side of the course of the Nile are inhabited by Nubae, a large tribe, who, beginning at Meroe, extend as far as the bends of the river, and are not subject to the Aethiopians but are divided into several separate kingdoms" (Kirwan 1974: 46). The composition of what these separate kingdoms might be is very difficult to sort out historically and geographically. Generally, it seems the Nubian tribes settled between the Kingdom of Meroe in the South and Egypt in the North. The Nubians were perceived by their neighbors as "piratical" marauding tribes disrupting the trade between Egypt and the lucrative sub-Saharan world represented by the Kingdoms of Meroe and Aksum.

A 5th-century Greek inscription of the Nubian King Silko describes his campaigns into Lower Nubia against the Blemmyes, another tribe regarded by the wider world (especially the Roman Empire) as "brigands." After sacking a series of former Roman forts used by the Blemmyes, King Silko incorporated them into his kingdom and claimed the title of "King of the Nobades and of all the Ethiopians." This campaign ensured the continued existence of the Nubian Kingdom for centuries to come. It would endure as a Christian reality until the 15th century. Because the Nubian Kingdom controlled the trade route between Roman Egypt and the sub-Saharan world in Late Antiquity, it also became a very important piece of the global puzzle within the later Byzantine and Islamic political strategies. Empress Theodora, Justinian's wife, recognized the importance of the trade route and sent a series of Christian missions to the Nubian Kingdom. The success of these missions, as described by John of Ephesus, converted the Nubians to the non-Chalcedonian cause. As in Ethiopia, the Nubians were ecclesiastically related to the jurisdiction of the Coptic Egyptian authorities in the North, and the patriarch of Alexandria appointed their bishops. The vitality of this Christian tradition is evinced by their beautiful frescoes and ornate churches. Even with the decline of Christian civilization in the North, and with only the Nile as a tentative route of connection, the Christian Nubians persevered for centuries. Their increasing isolation from the rest of the Christian world made them more vulnerable to Islamic incursions in the 12th and 13th centuries. When the royal court at Dongola finally converted to Islam, the isolated condition of the Nubians, their ecclesial dependence on Egypt, and the manner in which the church had always been so heavily sustained by the power of the royal court created the climate for a rapid dissolution. In a relatively short time the Christian Nubian Kingdom faded away into nothing more than a memory, and a few alluring fragments of art history from the site at Faras (Vantini 1970).

Orthodox Christianity in Africa is an ancient and complex story: a confluence of many peoples, languages, and cultures. It was deeply rooted before ever the western colonial powers thought of mounting missions and has endured long after the colonial powers have themselves fallen.

SEE ALSO: Alexandria, Patriarchate of; Coptic Orthodoxy; Council of Chalcedon (451); Monophysitism (including Miaphysitism); St. Constantine the Emperor (ca. 271–337)

References and Suggested Readings

Brown, P. (2000) *Augustine of Hippo: A Biography*, 2nd edn. Los Angeles: University of California Press.

Budge, E. A. W. (1906) *The Life and Miracles of Takla Haymanot*. London: Methuen.

Budge, E. A. W. (1922) *The Queen of Sheba and Her Only Son Menyelek*. London: Methuen.

Budge, E. A. W. (1928a) *The Book of the Saints of the Ethiopian Church*. London: Methuen.

Budge, E. A. W. (1928b) *A History of Ethiopia: Nubia and Abyssinia*, 2 vols. London: Methuen.

Frend, W. H. C. (1952) *The Donatist Church: A Movement of Protest in Roman North Africa*. Oxford: Clarendon Press.

Kaplan, S. (1984) *The Monastic Holy Man and the Christianization of Early Solomonic Ethiopia*. Frankfurt: Franz Steiner.

Kirwan, L. P. (1974) "Nubia and Nubian Origins," *Geographical Journal* 140, 1: 43–51.

Leslau, W. (1945) "The Influence of Cushitic on the Semitic Languages of Ethiopia: A Problem of Substratum," *Word* 1: 59–82.

Phillipson, D. W. (ed.) (1997) *The Monuments of Aksum: An Illustrated Account*. Addis Ababa: University of Addis Ababa Press.

Shinnie, P. L. (1978) "Christian Nubia," in J. D. Fage (ed.) *The Cambridge History of Africa*, Vol. 2. Cambridge: Cambridge University Press.

Tamrat, T. (1972) *Church and State in Ethiopia 1270–1527*. Oxford: Clarendon Press.

Vantini, J. (1970) *The Excavations at Faras: A Contribution to the History of Christian Nubia*. Bologna: Editrice Nigrizia.

Akathistos

DIMITRI CONOMOS

The most famous of all surviving Byzantine *kontakia*. This anonymous work, which celebrates the annunciation of the Virgin and the nativity of Christ, consists of two *prooemia* (introductory hymns) and 24 strophes bound by an alphabetic acrostic. The *Akathistos* (Gk. "not seated") was, and still is, performed while the congregation stands. The even-numbered stanzas carry an alleluia refrain, whereas the odd-numbered *oikoi* include a set of Salutations to the Virgin: 12 lines in metrically matching pairs, each line beginning with "Hail!" Each *oikos* ends with the refrain "Hail, Bride Unwedded!"

Metrically, this poem is unique, as its central part is formed of alternating strophes of two different lengths. The texts of the first 12 *oikoi* elaborate on the incarnation and the infancy of Christ, whereas the last 12 alternate praise of God with praises to the Virgin. The whole coalesces to create a subtly interwoven tapestry of images that is one of the high points of Byzantine poetry. Syriac elements are evident in the deliberate use of rhyme found in the pairs of lines of equal length of the longer strophes. This and the kontakion *On Judas*, attributed to Romanos the Melodist, are the only examples in the whole of Greek poetry of the use of rhyme before the conquest of Greek lands by the Franks during the Fourth Crusade (1204–61).

Like most Byzantine kontakia, the *Akathistos* draws extensively on the Scriptures and on a number of famous prose sermons, but it retains a striking individuality. With bold similes the poet succeeds in blending the overwhelming mystery of the incarnation of the Word with the softer note of praise to Mary; the varied and intricate rhythms employed are enhanced by the music of the words.

This was originally a chant for the Feast of the Annunciation (March 25), but is now sung at the vigil of the fifth Saturday in Great Lent. According to the *Synaxarion*, it was chosen by Patriarch Sergius as the thanksgiving hymn to the Mother of God for saving the city of Constantinople from the Avars in 626. The entire work was thus turned into a hymn of victory and deliverance, and it is repeatedly used as such to this day. The literary qualities of the poem and the wide popularity of veneration to the Virgin in the East explain the far-reaching influence that the hymn has had upon subsequent Greek (and indeed worldwide Orthodox) literature. It was quoted to satiety, copied and recast in iambic trimesters and political 15-syllable lines; modern Greek paraphrases of it exist; and it even influenced Byzantine and post-Byzantine art, especially between the 14th and 16th centuries, as is evident from the paintings of Mistra, Mount Athos and even frescoes as far north as Moldavia. It is possible that Romanos wrote the *Akathistos* hymn, but its authorship has, in the past, also been ascribed to Sergios, Germanos, and even Photios the Great.

The *Akathistos* existed in a Latin version by the late 8th or early 9th century; thereafter, its rhetoric and imagery appear as the inspiration for a considerable repertory of Latin hymns.

SEE ALSO: Kontakion; St. Romanos the Melodist (6th c.)

References and Suggested Readings

Carpenter M. (ed.) (1970–3) *Kontakia of Romanos, Byzantine melodist*, 2 vols. Columbia: University of Missouri Press.

Chrêstou, P. (1974) "Hê genesis tou kontakiou," *Kleronomia* 6: 273–349.

Conomos, D. (1984) *Byzantine Hymnography and Byzantine Chant*. Brookline, MA: Hellenic College Press.

Turilov, A. A. et al. (2000) "Akafist," in *Pravoslavnaia Entsiklopediia*, vol. 1. Moscow: Pravoslavnaia entsiklopediia, pp. 371–81.

Wellesz E. (ed.) (1957) *The Akathistos Hymn*. Monumenta Musicae Byzantinae, *Transcripta* 9. Copenhagen: Munksgaard.

Albania, Orthodox Church of

JOHN A. MCGUCKIN

Christianity came to Albania in the 4th century from the north and south of the country, in the form of Byzantine as well as Latin missionaries. The country's borderland status, poised between the ancient Latin and Greek empires, gave it a liminal status, and the Christian tradition of the land has always tended to represent both Eastern and Western Christian aspects. Albania is today a religiously mixed country. About 20 percent of the population are Orthodox and 10 percent are Roman Catholic. This Christian land underwent extensive Islamicization after the fall of Byzantium to the Ottomans in 1453. The leadership, and much of the general populace, quickly converted to the religion of their new masters. The current Islamic population now numbers 70 percent of the total.

The Orthodox of this land historically leaned to the Byzantine church, and in its golden age the metropolitanate of Ohrid was a provincial rival to Constantinople in the excellence of its liturgical and intellectual life. The Byzantine archeological remains there are still highly impressive and the metropolitan-

ate's leadership was often staffed by significant Byzantine clergy and intellectuals.

In 1767, pressured by its Ottoman political masters, the patriarchate of Constantinople absorbed the church under its direct ecclesiastical rule and thereafter directly appointed Albania's metropolitan archbishops, all of whom until 1922 were Phanariot Greeks. The local church in the 20th century began to press for more independence; first in 1908 when the Young Turk movement disrupted Ottoman political control of the imperial provinces, and again after the Balkan Wars of 1912–13. The figure of the priest Fan Noli figures significantly in this latter period. He was one of the first to produce an Albanian language version of the divine liturgy for use in a newly envisioned autocephalous Albanian Orthodox Church. He first circulated (and used) this on his tour of the USA in 1908, and from that time onward advocated autocephaly strongly, especially when he returned to the country in 1912. Fan Noli eventually was ordained bishop and became prime minister of Albania for a brief time in 1924, before being forced into exile.

In 1922 the majority of the synod of the Albanian church demanded the grant of autocephaly, and the Greek-born bishops among the hierarchy collectively left the country. By 1926 the Phanar had agreed to afford Albania autocephaly under certain terms, but the head of state, Amadh Zoghu, refused to countenance them. He would later assume the title of King Zog of Albania and (though a Muslim) patronized the Orthodox, confirming by state decree the hierarchy's right to officiate as bishops, just like the sultans had before him, and the Byzantine emperors before them.

In 1929 the local Albanian synod proclaimed autocephaly independently of the Phanar, and was excommunicated for its pains by the patriarchate – a state of affairs which brought about the immediate state-ordered exile of the exarch of Constantinople, Metropolitan Hierotheos, then resident in the country. The patriarch of Serbia recognized the autocephaly in due course and eventually fostered a reconciliation with the Phanar. Constantinople accepted the state of autocephaly in 1937, from which date it is customarily recorded.

In the years after World War II, Albania fell under the heavy hand of a communist oppression which was intense in its severity. There was bitter persecution in the years after 1945, with several leading Orthodox hierarchs murdered by the communists; notably Archbishop Christophoros, whose death in mysterious circumstances was widely seen as state-sanctioned murder in the Stalinist mode. The Albanian leader at this time, Enver Hoxha, was particularly keen to please his Russian communist masters and ordered the state confiscation of all land owned by religious institutions (Muslim or Christian). The Albanian communist state policy during the 1950s was focused on bringing the surviving elements of the Orthodox Church under the jurisdictional care of the Moscow Patriarchate, and several Albanian hierarchs who resisted that policy were forcibly deposed. In 1967 Hoxha's government, now looking to communist China's Cultural Revolution for its inspiration, declared the complete and final closure of all Christian places of worship as the state was now to be a model atheist country; an empty statement, but one that was to produce many murders and imprisonments of clergy and imams, and to so exhaust the church's resources that at the collapse of communism there were said to be only twenty or so priests still functioning in the country.

The Orthodox currently represent about half a million faithful, worshipping in 909 parishes. The senior hierarch is his Beatitude the Metropolitan of Tirana and Durazzo, Archbishop of All Albania. The current incumbent is the noted Greek Orthodox theologian Anastasios Yannoulatos. His appointment in 1992 by the Phanar was greeted with skepticism in some circles, anxious in case the struggle for Albanian ecclesiastical self-determination had been in vain, but his ministry has been marked by such energetic creativity that the archbishop is now recognized as having presided over a successful policy to restore an authentic Albanian church life. Under his care more than 250 churches have been restored or built, a national seminary established, and more than 100 clergy ordained.

The Albanian diaspora (chiefly those who had fled the motherland in order to escape communist oppression) continues under the jurisdictional protection of the patriarchate of Constantinople. The communist rule, as was usual elsewhere, succeeded in bringing a poor country down further onto its knees, and the Orthodox Church in Albania, like the rest of its people, is only now beginning to emerge from the chaos of its recent nightmare.

SEE ALSO: Constantinople, Patriarchate of; Russia, Patriarchal Orthodox Church of

References and Suggested Readings

Hall, D. (1994) *Albania and the Albanians*. London: Pinter.
Pollo, S. and Puto, A. (1981) *The History of Albania from its Origins to the Present Day*. London: Routledge and Kegan Paul.
Skendi, S. (1967) *The Albanian National Awakening*. Princeton: Princeton University Press.

Alexandria, Patriarchate of

MATTHEW J. PEREIRA

The patriarchate of Alexandria flourished as one of the premier centers of Eastern Christian intellectual, ecclesial, and political life until the middle of the 7th century. Initially, the patriarchate of Alexandria was ranked second to Rome in ecclesial priority. In 381 the third canon of the Second Ecumenical Council declared that the patriarchate of Constantinople would henceforth rank higher than Alexandria and thus it assumed precedence in the whole East, a state of affairs initially resisted in Egypt. In 451 the 28th canon of the Fourth Ecumenical Council reaffirmed the priority of the patriarchate of Constantinople over that of Alexandria. Despite being overshadowed by the sees of Rome and Constantinople, the patriarchate of Alexandria undoubtedly set the foundational framework and trajectory for Christian theology. For example, the Logos theologians of Alexandria, most notably Clement (ca. 150–215) and Origen (ca. 185–ca. 251), significantly shaped future patristic reflections upon the person and nature of Jesus Christ. Also, Alexandrian hierarchs such as St. Athanasius of Alexandria (ca. 293–373) and St. Cyril of Alexandria (ca. 378–444) advanced what would become the classical Orthodox expression of the mystery of the incarnate Lord. Within the Roman Empire, theological and political allegiances often aligned together in ways that could either strengthen or weaken any given patriarchate, whether Rome, Constantinople, or another major see. In this volatile context, the patriarchate of Alexandria managed to grow into a significant political force. Further, in the 3rd century, Egyptian monasticism developed into a burgeoning movement that indelibly shaped Alexandrian Christianity (Chitty 1999). In brief, the convergence of the ecclesial, political, theological, and monastic streams into one dynamic confluence infused Alexandrian Christianity with long-lasting vitality. The following summary begins with a brief historical sketch of the city of Alexandria, followed by a list of the patriarchs of Alexandria from the 1st century up to the 8th. There then follows an overview of the most influential bishops, pivotal councils, and exceptional theological and spiritual movements that bear witness to the enduring significance of the patriarchate of Alexandria.

The City of Alexandria

Alexandria, founded by Alexander the Great (356–323 BCE), is strategically situated at the mouth of the Nile. The city boasted two harbors and was a hub of trade routes that provided access to the Mediterranean and Southeast Asia. As an international commercial port city, Alexandria attracted merchants from all over the known world, who in turn brought their religious and philosophical traditions into the Hellenistic city. Upon his conquest of Egypt, between 332 and 331 BCE, Alexander drew up plans for the layout of a new metropolis. Alexandria was divided into five neighborhoods, identified by the Greek letters A to E. The indigenous Egyptians (known by the Greek abbreviation of Copts) lived in the section called Rakotis, which was located in the southwest section of Alexandria. The native Egyptians usually belonged to one of the Hellenistic religions and likely participated in the rites of one of the nearby pagan temples. The great Temple of Serapis (founded by the early Ptolemies) was located in the heart of Rakotis. The Jews predominantly inhabited a separate sector in Alexandria. Since the Jewish quarter was afforded a significant amount of autonomy, the Jews were able to maintain, at a high level, a distinct cultural and religious identity (Haas 1977: 91–127). Jewish intellectuals, most notably Philo of Alexandria (20 BCE–50 CE), were Influential forerunners that shaped later Christianity, especially through the persons of

Clement and Origen of Alexandria. Alexander the Great's successor was his childhood friend and general, Ptolemy I Soter (ca. 367–ca. 283 BCE). Under Ptolemy's governance, Alexandria grew into a great Hellenistic center. Hellenism continued to blossom under Ptolemy Philadelphus (309–246 BCE), his son. Ptolemy Philadelphus founded the Great Library in Alexandria, which was first burned in 48 BCE when Caesar defeated Antony and Cleopatra. In 391 the second iteration of the Great Library was partially destroyed during the tenure of the anti-Origenist Patriarch Theophilus (384–412). Rather than seeking the total annihilation of the library, Theophilus only ordered the destruction of the pagan library holdings associated with the Temple of Sarapis. Consequently, many of the larger cultural Hellenistic writings remained extant after the anti-Origenist movement of the 4th century. In 641 Islamic invaders captured Alexandria and possibly destroyed some of the holdings within the Alexandrian library, but undoubtedly (since the Byzantine emperor arranged a year-long truce to allow cultural and religious artifacts to be shipped to Rome and Constantinople for safe keeping) the vast majority of materials were safely transferred. In brief, the Alexandrian library was one of the finest collections in all Antiquity. The existence of the Great Library positioned Alexandria to be the leading Hellenistic intellectual center. Origen, the first internationally respected philosopher among the Christians, based his exegetical mission on the literary tradition of the library (McGuckin 2001).

Hellenism was a significant intellectual and cultural force that, to one degree or another, influenced Christianity, Judaism, and other religious movements of Late Antiquity. Ancient Alexandria has been described as a multicultural milieu, where Judaism, Christianity, Gnosticism, and the Egyptian indigenous religions coexisted with one another in an international milieu. According to some ancient observers, the lines between one religion and another were often blurred in Alexandria. In a letter attributed to Hadrian (*Vita Saturnini* 8), Christian worshippers are depicted as if they were giving reverence to Sarapis, the popular Egyptian God. Further, Hadrian observed pagans who worshipped Sarapis in a style that resembled the Christians. The blurring of lines is further revealed by Alexandrian religious leaders, whether

Christians, Jews, or others, who experimented in astrology (*Vita Saturnini* 8). The so-called multiculturalism of Alexandria was complex and dynamic; consequently, it is difficult to fully depict the overall situation in a comprehensive manner. At times, the various religious groups coexisted in a symbiosis wherein Hellenism provided an overarching matrix that promoted assimilation among the religious subcultures. Yet, on numerous other occasions, religious enclaves asserted their group identities over and against one another and the dominant Hellenistic culture (Haas 1977: 45–90).

The Gnostic Christian Basilides was the first notable Alexandrian biblical exegete, who blossomed into a prominent figure during the reigns of the Emperors Adrian and Antoninus Pius (ca. 120–40). Basilides probably studied with Glaukios, reputed to be a confidant and translator for the Apostle Peter. Following Basilides, the influential Alexandrian Gnostic Valentinus (ca. 100–ca. 160) was almost installed as a bishop of Rome. From what we know of inchoate Alexandrian Christianity, Pantaenus was the first orthodox pedagogue residing in Alexandria. According to the church historian Eusebius of Caesarea (*H.E.* 10), sometime around 180 Pantaenus founded the first Alexandrian catechetical school. Clement of Alexandria succeeded Pantaenus as the leading Christian pedagogue in Alexandria. Clement was one of the first formidable early philosopher-theologians to develop Christian doctrine through reading the Holy Scriptures, adhering to the rule of faith (*regula fidei*), and strategically appropriating Hellenistic thought and culture. Clement advanced Logos theology while at the same time highlighting a spiritual culture of knowledge (*gnōsis*) that would have been resonant with his Gnostic contemporaries. Origen of Alexandria further developed the Logos theology of his antecedents. Without a doubt, Origen stands as the most influential theologian of the early church. Origen, even more so than Clement, was keenly aware of the usefulness and apparent dangers inherent within Greek philosophy. In Origen's *Letter to Theodore* (also known as his *Letter to Gregory*), he explains his approach to his disciple Gregory Thaumatourgos, the later apostle of Cappadocia. In this correspondence Origen admonishes Gregory carefully to employ Greek philosophy in the spirit of the Exodus Jews spoiling the Egyptians. Christian theologians should take from the Greeks whatever is useful for the worship of God and the interpretation of Scripture. However, Christians need to be prayerful and diligent, or else they may easily become infected by the "poisons" of paganism (see Origen, *Letter to Theodore*). Origen's strategic appropriation of Greek philosophy became paradigmatic for future generations of Christian theologians.

The Patriarchate of Alexandria

There is little information regarding the patriarchate of Alexandria from the first two centuries of the Common Era. The shared tradition of both the Greek East and Latin West affirms that St. Mark the Evangelist founded the Church of Alexandria. In a letter attributed to Clement of Alexandria, we are told that St. Mark's witness and theology became influential in Alexandria by the 2nd century. The first attestation of Mark's connection with Alexandria is not explicitly recorded until the 4th century (Eusebius, *H.E.* 2.16). In his *Ecclesiastical History*, Eusebius provides a list of the early Alexandrian patriarchs. However, Eusebius's list provides minimal information about the early patriarchs other than simply providing their names; further, the accuracy of his early account is controverted. Apart from Eusebius, Jerome's *Chronicle* also provides information concerning the patriarchate of Alexandria. In chronological order, with the approximate dates of each tenure set in parentheses, these early leaders of the Alexandrian Church are as follows: Mark the apostle (?); Annianus (62–84/85); Avilius (84/85–98); Cerdon (98–110), who was a presbyter ordained by Saint Mark; Primus (110–22), also called Ephraim; Justus (122–30/32); Eumenes (132–43); Mark II (143–53); Celadion (153–67); Agrippinus (167–79); Julian (179–89/90). After Julian, Eusebius provides a little more detail concerning the Alexandrian bishops; the successive list of bishops comprises Demetrius (189/190–233); Heraclas (233–47); Dionysius (247–64); Maximus (264–82). Following Maximus, the Alexandrian bishops, with verifiable dates of tenure, are Theonas (282–300); Peter the Martyr (300–11); Achillas (311–12); Alexander (312–28); Athanasius (328–73); Peter II

(373–80); Timothy I (380–4); Theophilus (384–412); Cyril (412–44); Dioscorus (444–51); Proterius (451–7); Timothy II Aelurus (457–60), a Miaphysite; Timothy II Salofaciolos (460–75), a Chalcedonian; Timothy II Aelurus (475–7), his second time as bishop; Peter III Mongus (477), a Miaphysite; Timothy II Salofaciolos (477–82), his second time as bishop; John I Talaia (482), a Chalcedonian; Peter III Mongus (482–9), his second tenure; Athanasius II Keletes (489–96), a Miaphysite; John I (496–505), a Miaphysite; John II (505–16); Dioscorus II (516–17); and Timothy III (517–35), a Miaphysite.

After the Council of Chalcedon in 451, a schism erupted between the Miaphysite and the Chalcedonian theologians. As a result of the schism, from 535 up through the Arab conquests of Alexandria, there existed two lines of Alexandrian patriarchs. The Melkite (Greek Byzantine) party supported Chalcedonian Christology; conversely, the Coptic party supported proto-Cyrilline or Miaphysite Christology. The Melkite patriarchal line runs as follows: Paul of Tabenn (537–40); Zoile (540–1); Apollinarius (541–70); John II (570–80); Eulogius (580–608); Theodore the Scribe (608–9); John III the Almoner (609–19); George (620–30); Cyrus (630/631–43/44); Peter III (643/644–51); uncertain gap in the patriarchate; Theodore (655 Synod); Peter IV (680 Council); Theophylact (695 Council); Onophes (711); Eusebius (?); Cosmas I (742–68); and Politian (768–813).

The Coptic patriarchal line (with Julianists noted) runs as follows: Theodosius (535–66); the Julianists: Gaianus (535); Elpidius (?–565); Dorotheus (565–ca. 580); Theodore (575–85), who was not received by the majority; Peter IV (575–8); Damien (578–607); Anastasius (607–19); Andronicus (619–26); Benjamin (626–65); Julianists: Menas (634); Agathon (665–81); John III (681–9); Isaac (689–92); Simon I (692–700); Julianist: Theodore (695); vacancy for three years; Alexander II (704–29); Cosmas (729–30); Theodore II (730–42); one year vacancy; Michael I (743–67); Menas (767–75); and John IV (776–99).

Under the episcopate of Demetrius (189/190–233) the Alexandrian see increased in power and prestige. At this time, every other Egyptian bishop was subordinated to the see of Alexandria. Beyond extending control over his suffragan bishops, Demetrius seized internal control within the city of Alexandria. His well-known conflict with Origen eventually led to the dismissal of the controversial Alexandrian theologian, and his relocation to Caesarea of Palestine. Without a doubt, the Church of Alexandria increased in power on account of Demetrius' astuteness and energetic zeal. Demetrius' successor, Origen's disciple Heraclas (233–47), continued to advance the unity and prestige of the Egyptian Church through his disciplinary action. Heraclas deposed Ammonius the bishop of Thmuis, and refused to reconcile Origen. Dionysius (249–65) succeeded Heraclas as the leader of the Alexandrian Church. From Dionysius onward, the Alexandrian Church and its powerful bishop served in the dual role of both ecclesial and political leader in Eastern Christian affairs (Hardy 1952: 19).

Under the Edict of Decius, delivered in January 250, the Alexandrian Church endured harsh persecution. Many citizens, or at the very least those citizens suspected of being Christian, were required to show their certificate (*libelli*) in order to prove they had sacrificed to the Egyptian gods. The Decian persecution (250–1) was shortlived; nonetheless it significantly impacted the Christian imagination, Christian self-understanding, and the Egyptian ecclesiology specifically. The Decian persecution produced Alexandrian martyrs who served as models of piety for their fellow Christians. Following the cessation of hostilities, the Alexandrian Church needed to develop a strategy for readmitting those Christians who lapsed under the weight of the Decian persecution. Ultimately, the Patriarch Dionysius adopted a moderate position, whereby he permitted the receiving back of the lapsed after they had served an appropriate penance. Furthermore, the Christian confessors, who had often endured imprisonment and punishment during the Decian persecution, were significant actors in the reconciliation of the lapsed. In order to usher in the reconciliation of the lapsed, Christian confessors prayed on behalf of their weaker co-religionists. Archbishop Maximus (265–82) succeeded Dionysius; and Theonas (292–301) assumed the see of Alexandria after Maximus. By the end of the 3rd century, the Coptic language was used widely throughout Christian Egypt in preference to Greek (Hardy 1952: 34). The 4th century ushered in the momentous age of Constantine's Christian Roman Empire.

The Arian crisis was probably the most significant theological controversy of the 4th century. It derived its name from Arius (ca. 250/256–336), a priest of Baukalis, the dockland district of Alexandria, a charismatic presbyter who gained numerous followers throughout the city during the early decades of the 4th century. Arius' Christology was an outgrowth of the earlier Alexandrian Logos theology which failed to declare the full equality of the Logos with the Father, the supreme God. Arius and those who shared similar theological leanings subordinated the Logos (and *de facto* Jesus) below the Father, who alone was confessed as the true God. The Patriarch Alexander (322–8) declared Arius guilty of heresy and excommunicated the popular Alexandrian presbyter. In 325, at the Council of Nicea, Arius was officially condemned. However, the condemnation of Arius only signaled the beginning of the series of ongoing theological debates that dominated the 4th-century ecclesial landscape. In 328 Athanasius of Alexandria succeeded Alexander and soon emerged as the leading proponent of Nicene theology. Athanasius's adherence to the Nicene confession (though his own preference was not for *homoousion* but for the more explicit *tautotes tes ousias* – identity of essence between Father and Son) would eventually emerge as the international definitive statement of Orthodox Christology. However, before the victory of Nicenism at the Council of Constantinople in 381, there was intense debate throughout the era over the Orthodox expression of the mystery of Jesus Christ. In all the debates Alexandrian theologians set the tone. Following the Council of Nicea, Athanasius's steadfast refusal to compromise adherence to the *homoousion*, in the face of imperial changes of policy, led to his expulsion from Alexandria on several occasions. In 335 Athanasius was condemned and deposed at the Council of Tyre. He returned from exile after Constantine's death in 337. Athanasius soon fled again, this time to Rome, where he was welcomed as a defender of Orthodoxy. In 346 Athanasius was received back into the Alexandrian Church under the protection of the western Emperor Constans. However, in the same year, Emperor Constantius exiled Athanasius, who this time chose to live in the Egyptian desert. In 362, after the death of Constantius, Athanasius returned to Alexandria and presided over a synod of Alexandria which set the terms for reconciling all the disparate pro-Nicean groups of the Eastern Church. He was exiled once again by the pagan Emperor Julian (361–3), but in 363, after Julian's death, Athanasius returned to Alexandria. From 365 to 366 Athanasius endured his final expulsion.

Beyond the Arian controversy, the Council of Nicea attempted to reconcile the Melitians with the rest of the church. Melitius, bishop of Lycopolis, was leader of a Christian sect that refused to receive back into communion those Christians who had lapsed during the Decian persecution. Melitius was accused of ordaining bishops into churches where he had no legitimate authority. The Melitian account of the Decian persecution depicted Archbishop Peter of Alexandria (300–11) as one of the "lapsed" because he evaded persecution and thus forfeited the honor of martyrdom. This account of Peter's actions led to questions concerning the legitimacy of his elevation as archbishop. The Melitians, who had the support of a synod of 28 bishops, formed their own sectarian party in Alexandria. Ultimately, the Council of Nicea was unsuccessful in reconciling the Melitians. Throughout his ecclesial career, Athanasius was often accused of being a tyrannical leader. In 335, at the Synod of Tyre, Athanasius answered those who accused him of unfair treatment of the Arians and Melitians. Eusebius of Nicomedia, a leading Arian who led the eastern anti-Nicene party, concluded the Synod of Tyre with the deposition of Athanasius. On November 6, 335, Constantine met with both parties who participated in the Synod of Tyre, before deciding to exile Athanasius on account of allegations that he was threatening to block the export of grain from Alexandria.

From the Synod of Alexandria (362) onward, Athanasius shifted from a rather unyielding christological position towards a more open view, whereby precise vocabulary became not as important as the basic affirmation of the full divinity of the Logos. Consequently, following the Synod of Alexandria, the majority of western and eastern bishops reached a consensus. They collectively aimed to eradicate Arianism, which was officially condemned by ecumenical decision at the Council of Constantinople in 381. After Athanasius became more open to compromise, he ultimately emerged victorious when the *homoousion* definition was received as the Orthodox expression of the status of the Divine Logos. St. Gregory of Nazianzus vindicated St. Athanasius posthumously when he employed *homoousion* theology in order to explicate orthodox trinitarian dogma (*Orations* 27–31). Further, in his *Panegyric on Athanasius*, Gregory of Nazianzus canonized Athanasius by depicting him as the father of Orthodoxy (*Oration* 21). Days before his death, Athanasius consecrated his successor Peter of Alexandria (Peter II, 373–80) to the Alexandrian see. After the death of Athanasius, imperial forces provided the Arian Bishop Lucius safe passage to Alexandria. Soon after Lucius's arrival in Alexandria, Peter fled to Rome. The Arian overthrow of Alexandria was shortlived. A couple of years later, Emperor Valens became preoccupied with the Gothic invasion from the north, and thus left the Arian cause with minimal support. In 375–6 Lucius withdrew from Alexandria and traveled to Constantinople. Thereafter, Peter returned to Alexandria in order to reclaim the see. Upon the death of the pro-Arian Emperor Valens in 378, the western Emperor Gratian installed the Nicene General Theodosius as emperor of the East. This political appointment had significant ramifications for Orthodoxy. From the reign of Emperor Theodosius onward, the Nicene faith became the official religion of the Roman Empire.

In the 3rd century, St. Anthony the Great (ca. 251–356) began to organize groups of Egyptian Christians that fled Alexandria for the desert, where they practiced solitude and prayerful worship. By the 4th century, Egyptian monasticism had grown into a powerful Christian movement. Egyptian monasticism originated as an ascetical movement in the desert, but eventually its spirituality and theology entered into the very heart of Alexandrian Christianity and subverted even the episcopate. On account of their burgeoning success, the patriarchate of Alexandria was compelled to engage and control the monastic communities. The relevance of monasticism is evident in Athanasius' *Life of Anthony*, which praises the virtuous life of the eminent monk St. Anthony (Chitty 1999: 1–16). The monks (*monachoi*) who imitated Anthony's life of solitary asceticism were called anchorites (*anchoretes*) or hermits (*eremites*). These solitaries primarily lived in northern Egypt. On the other hand, Pachomius (ca. 292–348), according to tradition,

founded Coenobitic monasticism, which emphasized communal living. Coenobitic ("common life") monasticism was at first predominantly a southern Egyptian phenomenon, but it soon became the most popular type of monastic organization. In the 370s a Pachomian community called the Metanoia, or Monastery of Penitence, was founded near Alexandria (Hardy 1952: 89). Monastic communities continued to spread throughout Egypt, eventually reaching as far north as Nitria and Scete. However, after decades of growth, the Origenistic controversy seriously weakened the coherence of Egyptian monasticism. Initially, Origenistic asceticism had spread from Palestine and Nitria to Alexandria and Constantinople. Evagrios of Pontike (345–99) was one of the leading representatives of this new monastic approach that blended asceticism and Origenistic intellectualism (Clark 1992: 43–84). In short time this novel form of monasticism fell under suspicion. In Alexandria the Patriarch Theophilus (384–412) excommunicated his one-time confidant Isidore the Hospitaller of Alexandria on the charge of being an Origenist. Furthermore, Theophilus accused the Tall Brothers of heresy on account of their Origenistic tendencies. The Tall Brothers consisted of four Egyptian monks: Dioscorus (a bishop), Ammonius, Eusebius, and Euthymius. In Nitria, Origenist monks were imprisoned; thereafter, Isidore and the Tall Brothers relocated with some eighty monks to Palestine. At this time, Theophilus convoked a synod that condemned Isidore and the Tall Brothers on account of their extravagant asceticism and their heretical speculations. In 401 John Chrysostom (ca. 347–407), who had been serving as the patriarch of Constantinople for three years, received the appeal of Isidore and the Tall Brothers who came to him in the imperial city. John's hospitality angered Theophilus. Consequently, in a shrewd political move, serving the whims of the emperor, Theophilus procured the condemnation and banishment of John at the Synod of Oak at Constantinople in 403. Immediately afterwards Theophilus reconciled with Isidore and two of the Tall Brothers. After his initial expulsion, John Chrysostom was soon reinstalled as the patriarch of Constantinople. Theophilus, however, remained resolute in his opposition towards John Chrysostom. On Easter of 404, Theophilus secured the final banishment of John from Constantinople. From Rome, Pope Innocent supported

Chrysostom and for a short time the patriarch of Rome broke communion with the Eastern Churches. The discord between Alexandria and the Western Churches would continue throughout the ensuing centuries. By the middle of the 5th century, Egyptian monasticism had lost much of its former energy, while simultaneously becoming an institutionalized part of the Egyptian Church.

The patriarchs Theophilus and Cyril of Alexandria (the nephew and successor of Theophilus) continued the defense and advancement of Nicene theology (McGuckin 2001). The early years of Cyril's patriarchate were marked with political unrest. Cyril engaged in disputes with the Alexandrian civil authorities; most notably, he battled with the civil Prefect Orestes. In this volatile environment, Cyril's first significant measure was the closing of the Novatian Church, which the Alexandrians perceived as a sectarian import from Constantinople (Hardy 1952: 104). In 415 Alexandrian civil disorder reached a crescendo. In the midst of ongoing strife, Orestes tortured Cyril's faithful supporter, the pedagogue Hierax. In this same period, Cyril expelled a number of the Jews from the city of Alexandria in retaliation for church burnings in areas adjacent to the Jewish quarter. On another occasion, monks, who arrived from Nitria, attacked Orestes. Fortunately, Orestes was rescued before enduring much harm. The conflict finally eased up after the scandalous murder of the pagan intellectual Hypatia, who had been accused of stirring up dissension between Cyril and Orestes (Hardy 1952: 104). From 428 onward, the newly appointed patriarch of Constantinople, Nestorius, engaged in an ongoing christological dispute with Cyril. Nestorius's Christology reflected the Antiochene tradition, which emphasized (in its doctrine of the "Assumed Man") the two natures of Christ rather than the unity of the one divine person Jesus Christ. Further, Nestorius denied the designation of *Theotokos* for the Virgin Mary. In opposition to Nestorius, Cyril affirmed the validity of the *Theotokos* title and insisted on the unity of Christ, on terms wherein the single subjectivity of the Logos resided in the one divine person of Jesus, the Logos incarnate. In 431 Cyril presided over the Third Ecumenical Council at Ephesus. The final outcome of Ephesus was reached before Nestorius's supporters had arrived

from Antioch. As might be suspected, the ecumenical verdict entailed the condemnation of Nestorius and the official reception of Cyril's Christology. However, rather than signaling any sustained consensus at this period, Cyril's Christology served as a reference point for the ongoing christological controversy, which would rage for several centuries to come. Cyril's early Christology was amended at the Council of Chalcedon (451) and thereafter stirred further christological debate. It was under Cyril's leadership that the see of Alexandria grew into the largest and one of the most powerful ecclesial networks of churches throughout the eastern part of the Roman Empire. In Cyril's tenure the patriarch of Alexandria usually consecrated all his bishops in a suffragan status. Under Cyril's leadership the Alexandrian Church accrued great wealth through various gifts and government grants, which were intended for charitable work.

Following Cyril's death, the patriarchate of Alexandria decreased in scope and significance. The christological controversy sparked a deep-seated division of the Eastern Church, which in turn facilitated the weakening of the patriarchate of Alexandria. Following Cyril, the Patriarch Dioscorus (444–51) staunchly defended the early Cyrilline Miaphysite theology, a Christology which tended to emphasize the Lord's one united nature (reality as incarnate God-Man) so strongly that it verged towards a deemphasis of his real humanity. The christological controversy extended well beyond Alexandria; for example, in Constantinople, the Archimandrite Eutyches resolutely upheld monist Christology in opposition to Flavian, the patriarch of Constantinople. In 449 Dioscorus convoked the so-called Robber Synod or *Latrocinium*, which met at Ephesus. The Latin Church provided Pope Leo's *Tome* (letter) for the consideration of the ecclesial leaders at the Council of Ephesus II. However, Leo's *Tome* seemed to provide support to Flavian, patriarch of Constantinople; consequently, it was not well received by the Egyptian bishops at Ephesus, led by Dioscorus, who all thought they had come there to vindicate Cyril's memory. In short order, Ephesus II reaffirmed Cyril's theology without the compromises Cyril himself had adopted in the aftermath of Ephesus 431. In 451 the Council of Chalcedon censured Ephesus II by accepting the western christological affirmation from Leo's *Tome* that Christ exists "in two natures, without confusion, without change, without division or separation." Furthermore, Chalcedon reversed the Robber Synod (as Ephesus 449 came to be called) and expelled Dioscorus on account of uncanonical practices.

The divisive nature of the christological debates is illuminated by the fact that four of Dioscorus's most outspoken opponents were clerics within the Alexandrian Church, which he had governed prior to his condemnation. The patriarchate of Alexandria became more and more marginalized over the next two centuries. Patriarch Proterius (451–7), who succeeded Dioscorus, was viewed with suspicion because many believed his installation was simply a political move. Many Alexandrians believed Proterius hardly reflected the Alexandrian ecclesial tradition.

After 451 the Alexandrian Proterians, named after their allegiance to Proterius, supported Chalcedonian Christology. Beyond his Alexandrian disciples, Proterius was supported by only a handful of Egyptian bishops, fewer than twelve in all, with the Pachomian monks living in Canopus (Hardy 1952: 115). Ultimately, the Proterians failed to gain enough support from the general populace. Upon the death of Emperor Marcian in 457, anti-Chalcedonian exiles were permitted to return to Alexandria, including some of Dioscorus's original allies. When the Byzantine duke and his forces vacated Alexandria, the anti-Proterians, led by the bishops Gregory of Pelusium and Peter the Iberian (bishop of Maiouma, near Gaza), installed their own rival bishop, Timothy II Aelurus. Timothy (nicknamed the Cat or Weasel) was a priest from Alexandria and one of the main advocates of Miaphysite theology. He held the office of patriarch for two terms (457–60; 475–7). Following Ephesus II (449), where he was a participant, Timothy assumed the leadership of the anti-Chalcedonian party. He adopted a more balanced Miaphysite position than his predecessor, partly serving as a theological bridge between Cyril of Alexandria and the later Christology of Severus of Antioch. Soon after, Proterius was formally restored as the patriarch of Alexandria even though he clearly was an unpopular choice. On Good Friday an Alexandrian mob killed him at the baptistery and dragged his body through the city streets (Hardy 1952: 116). Thereafter, Timothy the Cat was unable to reconcile the various Alexandrian parties. In short order, Emperor Leo expelled Timothy from Alexandria, and after Timothy's expulsion fourteen Chalcedonian bishops served as interim authorities for the Church of Egypt. Eventually, another Timothy, nicknamed Salofaciolos ("Wobble-hat" or "White-cap"), was consecrated as the patriarch of Alexandria. After his shortlived tenure, Timothy returned once more to the see of Alexandria.

For the next couple of centuries the christological controversy continued to divide and weaken the Alexandrian Church, separating it into Chalcedonian and anti-Chalcedonian factions. In the second decade of the 6th century, Bishop Dioscorus II (516–17) advanced Miaphysite Christology by recruiting allies throughout the Christian world. In 537 Emperor Justinian (483–565) installed the Chalcedonian Paul of Tabenn (537–40) to the patriarchate of Alexandria. While Paul was committed to Chalcedonian Christology, the vast majority of Alexandrian clergy remained loyal to the Miaphysite position. Following Paul's condemnation and expulsion, other Chalcedonian supporters, such as John II (570–80), presided as the patriarch of Alexandria. However, the Alexandrian clergy and churches predominantly remained committed to the Miaphysite Christology, which they saw as the tradition of their ancestors. In the 7th century Arab Islamic invasions separated the patriarchate of Alexandria, along with the rest of Egyptian churches, from almost all of their Christian allies throughout the Roman Empire. However, there was ongoing dialogue between the patriarchate of Alexandria and nearby African churches. For example, Nubian Christianity (in the area now occupied by the Sudan) survived from the 4th well into the 15th century. Furthermore, the patriarch of Alexandria remained in contact with segments of the Ethiopian Church. The Ethiopian Orthodox Church remained a daughter church of the patriarchate of Alexandria until Cyril VI, the patriarch of All Africa and Coptic pope of Alexandria, granted the Ethiopians their ecclesiastical autonomy in the 20th century.

Today, nearly 95 percent of Egyptian Christians identify themselves as members of the Coptic Orthodox Church of Alexandria. Pope Shenouda III is the current leader of the Coptic Church. Shenouda III carries the title of Pope of Alexandria and Patriarch of All Africa under the Holy See of St. Mark. The Orthodox

Chalcedonian Church in Alexandria (now a minority of the Christians surviving there) gives its allegiance to the Greek patriarch, who for many years of Islamic rule had found refuge in Constantinople, and eventually came to be a virtual bureau appointment of the Constantinopolitan phanar. In the 20th century some eminent holders of the Greek Orthodox patriarchal office have advanced Orthodox–Islamic dialogue in an attempt to broker peace between the religions in an often tense environment of Arab nationalism. There have also been extraordinary representatives among the Coptic patriarchs of Alexandria, whose church has witnessed a renaissance in the latter part of the 20th century.

SEE ALSO: Apostolic Succession; Arianism; Cappadocian Fathers; Ecumenical Councils; Gnosticism; Heresy; Judaism, Orthodoxy and; Logos Theology; Monasticism; Nestorianism; Philosophy; Pontike, Evagrios (ca. 345–399); St. Athanasius of Alexandria (ca. 293–373); St. Cyril of Alexandria (ca. 378–444); Theotokos, the Blessed Virgin

References and Suggested Readings

Bagnall, R. S. (1993) *Egypt in Late Antiquity*. Princeton: Princeton University Press.

Chitty, D. J. (1999) *The Desert A City: An Introduction to the Study of Egyptian and Palestinian Monasticism under the Christian Empire*. Crestwood, NY: St. Vladimir's Seminary Press.

Clark, E. A. (1992) *The Origenist Controversy: The Cultural Construction of an Early Christian Debate*. Princeton, NJ: Princeton University Press.

Fraser, P. M. (1972) *Ptolemaic Alexandria*, 3 vols. Oxford: Clarendon Press.

Griggs, C. W. (1990) *Early Egyptian Christianity: From Its Origins to 451 CE*. Leiden: E. J. Brill.

Haas, C. (1977) *Alexandria in Late Antiquity: Topography and Social Conflict*. Baltimore: Johns Hopkins University Press.

Hardy, E. R. (1952) *Christian Egypt, Church and People: Christianity and Nationalism in the Patriarchate of Alexandria*. New York: Oxford University Press.

Hinske, N. (1981) *Alexandrien: Kulturbegegnungen dreier Jahrtausende im Schmelztiegel einer mediterranen Grossstadt*. Mainz am Rhein: P. von Zabern.

McGuckin, J. A. (2001) *St. Cyril of Alexandria: The Christological Controversy, Its History, Theology and Texts*. Crestwood, NY: St. Vladimir's Seminary Press.

McGuckin, J. A. (2003) "Origen as Literary Critic in the Alexandrian Tradition," in L. Perrone (ed.) *Origeniana Octava*. Leuven: Peeters, pp. 121–35.

n.a. (1987) *Alexandrina: Hellénisme, Judaisme, et Christianisme à Alexandrie; mélanges offerts au P. Claude Mondésert*. Paris: Cerf.

Pearson, B. A. and Goehring, J. E. (eds.) (1986) *The Roots of Egyptian Christianity*. Philadelphia: Fortress Press.

Roberts, C. H. (1979) *Manuscript, Society, and Belief in Early Christian Egypt*. Oxford: Oxford University Press.

Ambo

JOHN A. MCGUCKIN

The Ambo (Gk. "crest of a hill") was the raised platform in the middle of church from which the scriptures and litanies were read. In early times it was not often used for preaching, though St. John Chrysostom was an exception to the rule (Socrates, *Church History* 6.5). In the Eastern Christian world a pathway (*Solea*) from the sanctuary (*Bema*) to the Ambo was often established, which eventually came to be similarly raised. Several examples of Byzantine Ambo remain (e.g., Byzantine Museum, Athens; the gardens of Hagia Sophia Cathedral, Istanbul) which are polygonal raised platforms with steps leading up (in the Middle Ages it became the western "pulpit"). The Ambo in St. Mark's Venice is a rare late-Byzantine "double-decker," where the gospel was read from the upper section and the epistle from the lower. Byzantine emperors, after the 6th century, were crowned from the Ambo of Hagia Sophia church, a lost masterpiece described by the poet Paul the Silentiary. In the modern presentation of most Orthodox churches the Ambo shrank back and was conflated with the smaller area of raised *Solea* immediately in front of the Iconostasis.

References and Suggested Readings

Delvoye, C. (1966) "Ambo." In K. Wessel (ed.) *Reallexicon zur byzantinischer Kunst*, vol. 1, cols. 126–33. Stuttgart: Hiersemann.

Hickley, D. (1966) "The Ambo in Early Liturgical Planning: A Study with Special Reference to the Syrian Bema," *Heythrop Journal* 7: 407–27.

Krautheimer, R. (1979) *Early Christian and Byzantine Architecture*. London: Penguin.

Leclercq, H. (1904) "Ambon." In F. Cabrol and H. Leclercq (eds.) *Dictionnaire d'archéologie chrétienne et de liturgie*, vol. 1. Paris, pp. 1330–47.

Amnos

JOHN A. MCGUCKIN

The word derives from the Greek for "Lamb" (Slavonic: *Agnets*) and signifies the central square of bread that is cut and lifted out of *prosfora* (altar) loaves at the eucharistic liturgy of preparation (*Proskomide*). It is also referred to as the "Seal" in this early part of the preparations, since it is stamped with the letters IC XC NIKA, or "Jesus Christ Conquers." The separation of the Amnos from the prosfora, by the priest's liturgical knife (Lance), is accompanied by the recitation of the "lamb-related" sacrificial verses of Isaiah 53.7. In the Proskomide the Lamb is placed centrally on the *Diskos* (paten) and, like the wine in the chalice, it is veiled until the time of the consecratory prayers of the Anaphora, when it is sanctified so as to become the Holy Eucharist. By extension, therefore, the "Lamb" is shorthand for the Eucharist itself, especially as used to connote the very presence of the Lord in the Mystery. The term originates from the words of John the Forerunner (Jn. 1.29, 36; see also Rev. 5.2).

References and Suggested Readings

McGuckin, J. A. (2008) *The Orthodox Church: An Introduction to its History, Doctrine and Spiritual Culture*. Oxford: Wiley-Blackwell, pp. 288–300.

Ware, T. (1987) *The Orthodox Church*. London: Penguin, pp. 286–95.

Anagnostes (Reader)

DIMITRI CONOMOS

The term identifies the penultimate position within the minor orders of clergy. The Anagnostes' primary role is to read the lessons from Scripture during the services. The office of a reader subsumes that of a taper-bearer (Acolyte), and the service of tonsuring mentions both. The Apostolic Constitutions indicate that the reader stands on "something high" in the middle of the congregation. Icons often show readers wearing a sticharion or cassock and a pointed hat with the brim pulled out to the sides. It appears that until the 4th century the reader also led the singing, since the office of cantor is first noted only after ca. 380.

Analogion

JEFFREY B. PETTIS

In the Orthodox Church the *analogion* is the lectern used to support the gospel, the service book, or an icon. Originally, churches used only one analogion for Scripture, although later two were used, one for the gospel and one for the epistle reading. The analogion is sometimes shaped in the form of an open-winged dove, representative of the Holy Spirit. Normally, a decorative cloth (*antipendia*) fully or partially covers it. Some analogia have a simple design and can be folded up for portability. Others are made of intricately carved wood. Certain analogia are designed to stand in the choir section (*kliros*) of the church and are used by the chanters. This style has a top that usually turns on a spindle to allow easy access to the various service books being used. The *tetrapodion*, a piece of furniture which is similar to the analogion, is a four-legged table which may stand in the center of the church. A cloth covers its surface, which is used to support special ritual objects.

References and Suggested Readings

Parry, K. et al. (eds.) (1999) *The Blackwell Dictionary of Eastern Christianity*. Oxford: Blackwell.

Patrinacos, N. D. (1984) *A Dictionary of Greek Orthodoxy*. Pleasantville, NY: Hellenic Heritage Publications.

Anaphora

JOHN A. MCGUCKIN

The Greek (Septuagintal) biblical word for "lifting up" in the sense of making an offering of prayer or sacrifice, especially that part of sacrificial ritual where the ancient priest took and offered the victim (LXX Lev. 2.14; see also 1 Peter 2.5). In Orthodox usage it is the technical term referring to the solemn and central consecratory prayer of the divine liturgy that culminates in the consecration of the gifts of bread and wine and their sacred transfiguration (some writers use the Latin term *transubstantiation*) into the body and blood of the Lord, at the words of Institution and the Epiclesis prayer for descent of the Holy Spirit to effect the change. The Anaphora begins immediately after the Creed, with the invitational words: "Let us attend that we may offer the holy oblation in peace." It continues with the Preface and Hagios (Sanctus), the Dominical words of institution, the Elevation of the holy gifts, the Epiclesis asking for the descent of the Holy Spirit, and then the intercessory prayers for all the church, especially the Holy Theotokos. It concludes with a blessing: "And the mercies of our great God and Savior Jesus Christ shall be with you all," which in turn leads into the Litany before the Lord's Prayer, and the common recitation of the Our Father itself, so as to prepare the congregation for Communion. There have been some debates whether the Anaphora alone is the central aspect of the "consecration" ritual surrounding the Holy Eucharist, but the general sense among Orthodox writers is that while it is the most solemn and sacred core of the Liturgy, the whole action ought rather to be seen as indissolubly connected and mutually related. Three different Anaphoras are in use among the Orthodox: those of St. Chrysostom, St. Basil, and St. James. The Liturgy of St. Gregory the Dialogist is really a Lenten Vesperal communion service of gifts pre-sanctified at the previous Sunday liturgy.

SEE ALSO: Divine Liturgy, Orthodox; Epiclesis; Eucharist

References and Suggested Readings

Dix, G. (1945) *The Shape of the Liturgy*. London: Dacre Press.
Gelsi, D. (1992) "Anaphora." In A. di Berardino (ed.) *Encyclopedia of the Early Church*. Cambridge: Clarke, pp. 33–5.

Anastasimatarion

DIMITRI CONOMOS

A liturgical book containing musical settings in each of the eight modes (tones) of the Resurrection or Sunday hymnody (each Sunday being a commemoration of the resurrection: *anastasis*) for Great Vespers and Matins, together with other supplementary chants. There are three types of *Anastasimatarion*: (1) *argon* ("slow") or *palaion* ("old") melodies that are highly melismatic and extended; (2) *argosyntomon* (literally, "slow-fast") melodies which are moderately ornate; and (3) *syntomon* ("fast") melodies that are syllabic and simple. The composers, editors and arrangers of the editions of the *Anastasimatarion* currently in use are Petros Peloponnesios (1730–78) and Ioannes Protopsaltes (d. 1770).

Angels

JOHN A. MCGUCKIN

Angel is the Greek biblical term for "messenger" of God (*angelos*) and in most of the many scriptural references to the angels (Gen. 16.7, 32.1; Judg. 6.11; Dan. 7.10) they appear as heavenly beings, sometimes radiant in light and power, but on earth usually in human form (called "Sons of Men" or "Sons of God"), made present as intermediaries who serve God's will by mediating with humankind. In the biblical texts the angels are especially the deliverers of revelation and, as such, play a large role in the New Testament stories of the annunciation, the nativity, and the resurrection (Mt. 28.2–7; Jn. 20.12). The late inter-testamental (especially the Apocalyptic) texts saw the angels chiefly in the court of God, attending on the divine will for earth and supervising human affairs as his ministers of providential care. This influenced the thinking of the early Christian literature (especially the Book of Revelation and the Letter to the Hebrews) and this aspect of angelic attendance at the divine court developed among the earliest churches into a vision of the angelic host as the preeminent singers of God's glory, the liturgical choir of divine praise, which was also thought to be specially attracted to the church Eucharistic liturgies, so as to join in with them. Jesus referred to angels on several occasions, teaching that they always enjoyed the presence and vision of the Father (Mt. 18.10), and that they would form the accompanying army of God which would return with the Son of Man at the Second Glorious Coming (*Parousia*; Mt. 16.27). Some very early Jewish Christian sects developed an angelology which saw Christ as a high archangel who had come to earth to deliver a salvific gospel. That theological trend to use angels as a synonym for divine presence and action, and to hypostatize the divine presence by an angelic reference, was already advanced in Hellenistic Judaism, as can be seen in the instance of Philo and in elements of some Christian gnostics. The trend imagined the angelic mediators as "manifestations" (*hypostases*) of the divine on earth; thus, the Law was seen to be given through angels, not directly by an epiphany of God to Moses. It is a doctrine that is clearly rebutted in several parts of the New Testament (the pastoral letters and the Epistle to the Hebrews) which insist that Jesus Christ is "far superior" to the angels (Col. 2.18; Heb. 1.4).

Irenaeus insisted that the angels were distinct creatures of God, not a system of divine emanations as Gnosticism imagined and, like humanity, they had a destiny to serve and worship the deity (*Adversus Haereses* 2.30.6–9). Origen greatly extended the patristic understanding of the angelic orders with his doctrine (later condemned at the ecumenical council of 553) of the preexistence of souls. The angels, in Origen's scheme, were the original souls created by God, who retained their heavenly dignity and ethereal status. Humanity had once been angelic, but had fallen into corporeality because of premundane sins; although one day the faithful soul could ascend back to become transfigured once more into angelic glory. It was Origen who brought the widespread belief in guardian angels into church life, with his teaching that God had appointed angels to watch over the destiny of nations, but also others to care for the safe journey of each soul on earth, until it returned to its original heavenly family. The Origenian scheme of preexistence was highly attractive to the Christian mystics, such as Evagrius, but was never accepted by the larger church.

In the 4th century St. Gregory of Nazianzus rescued the doctrine of angels from the implication of Origenian preexistence doctrine, and laid out a system that would become authoritative for the wider Orthodox tradition. God, Gregory argued, had made three creations. The first was the angelic order. The second was the material and animal creation, and the third was humanity. The two first creations were simple and coherent in their ontology: spiritual and fleshly, respectively. Humankind alone was a "mixed creation" (flesh and spirit). By faithful obedience, and a constant "ascent" of soul, human beings could attain to the glory of angelic status in the afterlife (*Carmina* 1.1.7).

Two scriptural passages caught the imagination of the early church, where the "ranks" of the angels were described with some differences (Col. 1.16; Eph. 1.21). The early patristic writers, putting them together, came up with an enumeration of five different ranks. Dionysius the Areopagite added to that list of five the separate ranks of Angel, Archangel, Seraph, and Cherubim, and thus set out the definitive list of the "Nine Orders" of the angels which would form the basic understanding of both the Latin and Eastern churches ever after (in ascending order: Angels, Archangels, Principalities, Powers, Virtues, Dominions, Thrones, Cherubim, and Seraphim). The Seraphim occupied the seventh heaven alongside God, and their proximity to the Divine Presence resulted in their eruption into pure fire (in such a way are they always depicted in iconography). The Cherubim were the living throne of God (a prayer recalling this is said by the priest as he moves to the high place during the divine liturgy in the course of the singing of the Trisagion hymn). The angels were seen to be endowed with almost infinite mobility and vast powers. From the Byzantine-era liturgy onwards, the deacons often assumed a role of symbolizing the angelic orders attendant on the liturgy, and the imperial eunuchs (sexless, as Jesus had said the angels were in heaven: Mk. 12.25) had the special task of singing the Cherubic hymn at the time of the Great Entrance: "We who in a mystery represent the Cherubim, and sing the thrice holy hymn to the life-creating trinity, now lay aside all earthly cares, that we may receive the King of all who comes escorted by the ranks of unseen angels."

Devotion to the angels in the Orthodox Church has always been strong, and continues to this day as a marked aspect of normal Christian life. They are referred to as the "Bodiless Powers," and several feasts in the course of the year are dedicated to them, especially to Michael and Gabriel, known as the Taxiarchs (leader of heavenly hosts). Ordinary Mondays in the Orthodox week are dedicated to them. The Sticheron for Vespers dedicated to the bodiless powers reads as follows: "Most radiant attendants of the triune Godhead; you angels who serve as supreme commanders, with all the powers on high you cry out rejoicing – Holy are you O Co-Eternal Word; Holy are you the Holy Spirit; one glory, one kingdom, one nature, one Godhead and power."

SEE ALSO: Cherubikon; Communion of Saints; Divine Liturgy, Orthodox

References and Suggested Readings

Daniélou, J. (1952) "Les anges et leurs mission d'après les Pères de l'Église," *Irenikon* 5.
Frank, K. S. (1964) *Angelikos Bios*. Munster: Graumann.

Anglicanism, Orthodoxy and

NICHOLAS BIRNS

The historic friendliness felt by Anglicans for the Orthodox found expression in 1677, when Bishop Henry Compton of London licensed a church for Orthodox refugees from Ottoman tyranny (Greek Street in Soho – though he did not care for the liturgy once he had a firsthand encounter with it). Serious Anglican-Orthodox dialogue in the early 17th century became stillborn when Cyril Lukaris, the patriarch of Alexandria, who corresponded with Anglican bishops, was censured for Protestant leanings. The fall of Lukaris associated Anglicanism with heresy for most Orthodox, though the "Non-jurors" who severed relations with Canterbury after 1689 found sanction within Orthodoxy, attempting to work through Peter the Great for a reunion of all "Catholic" Christians, although this ended when the Orthodox found out the Non-jurors did not hold ecclesiastical power in England. Dialogue intensified with the Oxford Movement of the 1840s with its emphasis on liturgy and Catholicity. Anglican churchmen like the hymnodist and translator John Mason Neale and the theologian William Palmer helped found the Anglican and Eastern Churches Association, which became an official forum for interchurch solidarity.

J. J. Overbeck went as far as to see Orthodoxy as "the only true Church" and believed full ecclesiastical reunion could only be accomplished on Orthodox terms. Isabel Florence Hapgood translated the Orthodox Service Book into English, while, later, E. S. Almedingen wrote historical novels that familiarized juvenile readers with church history. Athelstan Riley was also an important figure, virtually inaugurating a tradition of English pilgrimages to Mount Athos. Several autocephalous Orthodox communions, such as the churches of Cyprus and Romania, as well as the ecumenical patriarchate itself, considered and issued statements on the validity of Anglican holy orders.

Anglican thinkers, seeing apostolic succession as the prerequisite for a meaningful ecclesiology, have tended to be more optimistic than Orthodox about the possibility of restoring full communion. The great appeal of Anglicanism to Orthodoxy was that it was seen as Catholicism not of a Roman papal type, and that it saw the discussion about restoring intercommunion with Western Christendom as a matter of dialogue, rather than potential hegemony. The Russian theologian Aleksey Khomyakov was excited by the potential of an Anglican-Orthodox reunion; he was influenced by the writings of Yevgeny Ivanovich Popov, the first official Orthodox representative in England. Increasing Orthodox immigration and the US acquisition of Alaska brought Orthodox priests into more frequent contact with Anglicans. The Syrian Orthodox Bishop (now saint) Raphael Hawaweeny of Brooklyn saw cooperation with Anglicans as a way of serving the church needs of his people who lacked priests (despite his awareness of doctrinal differences).

The aftermath of the Russian Revolution brought many Orthodox émigrés to the West and separated dialogue with the church from the question of relations with the Russian state. Orthodox membership in the World Council of Churches as well as the Fellowship of St. Alban and St. Sergius, a Protestant-Orthodox dialogue group, facilitated these links. Notable Anglican converts to Orthodoxy such as

Stephen Hatherly and Timothy (Kallistos) Ware served as a bridge between the communions. Fr. Alexander Schmemann taught at General Theological Seminary, where J. Robert Wright trained Episcopalian seminarians in Orthodox ecclesiastical history and iconology. The Dublin Agreed Statement (1984) established key terminological similarities and differences between the two churches, while the Cyprus Agreement Statement (2006) concentrated on defining the Trinity as understood by the two communions, broadening the dialogue associated with the discussion of the Filioque.

In the aftermath of the collapse of the Soviet Union, the Anglican Communion abjured proselytizing in Orthodox "territory." Despite continuing tensions over points of ecclesiastical doctrine and discipline still to be resolved, the 21st-century relationship is still able to build upon a foundation of basic concord and respect.

SEE ALSO: Apostolic Succession; Cyril Lukaris, Patriarch of Constantinople (1572–1638); *Filioque*

References and Suggested Readings

Elder, E. R. (2006) "Anglican-Orthodox Relations: A Long Overview," in M. Dutton and E. R. Elder (eds.) *One Lord, One Faith, One Baptism*. Grand Rapids, MI: Eerdmans.

Litvack, L. (1994) *John Mason Neale and the Quest for Sobornost*. Oxford: Oxford University Press.

Pinnington, J. (2003) *Anglicans and Orthodox: Unity and Subversion (1559–1725)*. Leominster, UK: Gracewing.

Anointing of the Sick

SERGEY TROSTYANSKIY

The use of oil for healing purposes was well known in Antiquity. Both Jewish and pagan practices of healing are marked by the use of oil, the element which was symbolically associated with joy, gladness, peace, and happiness. In Christian practice, when blessed or accompanied by prayer, oil became a symbol of the Holy Spirit, a mystery of the energy of divine grace, and thus a means of sanctification.

The perception of a person as a holistic unity and the assumption that physical sickness, suffering, and death were signs of spiritual not only physical trouble were deeply rooted in the Old Testament tradition. Thus, Genesis described humanity as created to inhabit paradise, to be in perfect communion with God, and to contemplate God. There are no signs of sickness or death associated with paradise. However, the original Fall, the sin committed by Adam and Eve, caused a temporary exile from paradise, a break in communion with God, and, as a consequence, the subjection of humanity to sickness, suffering, and death. For the fathers, the devil stood directly behind this catastrophe, and accordingly this triad of woes is the result of the works of the forces of evil. Moreover, sin, a spiritual disorder, is widely seen among the fathers as the root of physical disorders. Thus, the close, almost causal connection between sin and sickness is clearly affirmed both in the Scriptures themselves and throughout most of patristic commentary on the healings of Jesus. Healing narratives in the Scriptures are viewed and presented as a divine prerogative; the direct result of the work of divine power, and of the forgiveness of sin.

Jesus' ministry adopted healing as an important aspect of his mission, and a symbol (in the form of exorcism) of the advent of the Kingdom of God. Moreover, the Scriptures present Jesus as the ultimate healer of the world, who removes the powers of evil, including sin and sickness, from the world. The apostles' ministry was also associated with healing. "They expelled many demons, and anointed with oil many that were sick and healed them" (Mk. 6.13). The Epistle of James provided a theological basis for the sacramental power of anointing of the sick:

Is any among you suffering? Let him pray. Is any cheerful? Let him sing praise. Is any among you sick? Let him call for the elders of the Church, and let them pray over him, anointing him with oil in the name of the Lord; and the prayer of faith will save the sick man, and the Lord will raise him up; and if he has committed sins, he will be forgiven. Therefore confess your sins to one another, and pray for one another, that you may be healed. (James 5.13–16)

Here the presbyters of the church are commanded to serve those who are ill in terms of a sacramental ritual of anointing of the sick accompanied by prayer. Sin, sickness, and the forgiveness of sins are once again affirmed in conjuncture.

In the early church the traditional practice of the use of oil for healing purposes accompanied by prayer became distinctively Christianized. The Orthodox Church defines the anointing of the sick as one of the major sacraments of the church, instituted by Jesus Christ himself. Its sacramental significance arises from the fact that its purpose is the removal of sins, the restoration of communion between humanity and God, and (only last in that series) the restoration of health. Sacred oil in the church's understanding conveys the presence and operation of the healing power of the Holy Spirit.

Jesus himself, who is the sacrament, the visible presence of God and divine grace in the world, did not use oil for healing purposes in his ministry; but his apostles elevated sacred anointing as a major part of their healing ministry, and so it has been used in the Orthodox Church ever since. Holy oil is central to the sacrament of anointing of the sick, as well as being used in association with the exorcism and strengthening ritual of baptismal candidates in the early stages of the rite (Oil of Gladness).

The early church's ritual for healing using blessed oil can be seen in the *Apostolic Tradition* of Hippolytus, a work of the early 3rd century. It describes a procedure of blessing oil for the sick during the Eucharistic liturgy. Another early text, the *Apostolic Constitution*, dating to the late 4th century, mirrors this earlier description of the blessing of oil. The *Prayer Book of Serapion*, compiled in the 4th century by an Egyptian bishop and disciple of St. Athanasius, gives us a concrete example of the prayer over the oil. Aphrahat, a Syrian theologian of the 4th century, also provides a description of various sacramental uses of consecrated oil, among which we can find the anointing of the sick. Later, in the 11th century, a Byzantine manuscript (reflecting the background of the Letter of St. James) describes how the sacrament ought to be celebrated by seven presbyters on seven consecutive days. Even so, already by the 11th century the service of anointing the sick had been shortened for practical reasons, was performed in one day and generally separated from its original liturgical context (although confession and reception of the Eucharist are still closely associated with the rite, albeit celebrated more often than not in the home of the sick person today). Finally, by the 14th century the sacrament of anointing of the sick acquired its final form, as still reflected in the Orthodox service books. Seven priests are still regarded as an ideal number to celebrate this sacrament (when the various prayers, gospel readings, and anointings are distributed among them), but a lesser number can also proceed with the sacrament.

There is a large variety of elements involved in the celebration of the sacrament, but it is possible to mark two constant factors: the prayer of blessing over the oil and the prayer of actual anointing. It should be noted that the sacrament of anointing has never become a part of a regular cycle of services in the church (even though a related service is celebrated on the Wednesday evening of Great Week), but rather was accomplished according to particular needs and customs. Although today's form of the service is much simpler and shorter than in the past, it still can take several hours. The sick person is not expected to be actively responsive, although he or she bears the gospel book, lying on it if necessary.

The rite of anointing includes beautiful physical as well as spiritual dimensions. Its ultimate goal is the forgiveness of sins and the restoration of communion with God for the sick person, and thus spiritual healing. However, the physical aspect of healing is also of great concern. Due to a holistic image of the human being as a psychosomatic unity, these two aspects of healing are always in a conjunction, in which the priority is, as usual in the church, given to the spiritual aspect of healing. The ritual always recognizes and calls upon the Lord of Mercies who gave us our close unity of body and soul, and whose word can cast out our sins as well as our diseases.

References and Suggested Readings

Cuschieri, A. (1993) *Anointing of the Sick: A Theological and Canonical Study*. Lanham: University Press of America.

Dudley, M. and Rowell, G. (eds.) (1993) *The Oil of Gladness: Anointing in the Christian Tradition*. London: SPCK; Collegeville: Liturgical Press.

Empereur, J. L. (1982) *Prophetic Anointing*. Wilmington: Michael Glazier.

McGuckin, J. A. (2008) *The Orthodox Church: An Introduction to Its History, Doctrine and Spiritual Culture*. Oxford: Wiley-Blackwell, pp. 306–8.

Meyendorff, P. (2009) *The Anointing of the Sick*. Crestwood, NY: St. Vladimir's Seminary Press.

Antidoron

M. C. STEENBERG

Antidoron (lit. "instead of the gifts") is bread blessed during the course of the divine liturgy and distributed to the faithful at its conclusion. In practice it is normally the excess portions of the *prosphora* used in the Proskomedie. In the Greek Orthodox traditions it is blessed by the priest after the consecration of the gifts.

Antidoron is not to be confused with the consecrated bread (the Lamb) received in Communion. Traditionally, it was given to those who did not receive Communion at the service; however, today it is often received by all. Differing traditions hold to different practices on whether antidoron may be received by non-Orthodox, and whether one must fast in order to receive it.

SEE ALSO: Divine Liturgy, Orthodox; Eucharist; Fasting; Proskomedie (Prothesis)

Antimension

JOHN A. MCGUCKIN

The word means "in place of the altar table" and denotes the cloth that is used in the Divine Liturgy (similar to the western Corporal) on which the Chalice and Diskos will stand after the Great Entrance. It is kept on the holy table, folded, underneath the gospel book until the time of the Litany of the Faithful, at which point it is unfolded for the Anaphora. The cloth is normally about two square feet in dimension and bears a printed icon of the Body of the Savior taken down from the cross. It has relics of the saints sewn into it and bears the authorizing signature of the ruling diocesan bishop. If a new church is consecrated the bishop sanctifies the Antimension at the same time by wiping it over the sacred chrism that has been spread over the altar stone. Divine Liturgy cannot be celebrated without an Antimension, but in times of emergency the Antimension can substitute for the altar itself.

SEE ALSO: Anaphora; Divine Liturgy, Orthodox

References and Suggested Readings

Izzo, J. M. (1975) *The Antimension in the Liturgical and Canonical Tradition of the Byzantine and Latin Churches: An Inter-Ritual and Inter-Confessional Study*. Rome: Pontifical Athenaeum Antonianum.

Antioch, Patriarchate of

JOHN A. MCGUCKIN

Antioch has a glorious Christian past. It was here that one of the most vibrant Christian communities in the apostolic age sprang up, and here that the first tentative workings out of the relation between Jewish and Gentile disciples of Jesus took place. The Apostle Peter was based here as a leader of the church community before he moved towards his martyrdom at Rome, and many scholars believe that it was in this church also that the Gospel of Matthew received its final editing and arrangement in the Greek text. It was one of the main cities of the international Christian world, third-ranking city of the Roman Empire (after Rome and Alexandria), site of great achievements and momentous struggles, with several martyrdoms during the time of the Roman persecutions, that made it feature high in the calendar of the saints. But the advances of Islam from the 7th century onwards left Antioch's Christian civilization in a state of slow suffocation. It was also vulnerable to sociopolitical changes because of the way its ecclesiastical territories (those churches that looked to Antioch for guidance and which followed its traditions) were so widely scattered and into such impassable mountain territory, which made communication so hard to sustain but so easily disrupted.

Several of Antioch's greatest theologians have left their mark on the church's universal patristic tradition: writers such as Mar Theodore the Interpreter (of Mopsuestia), St. John Chrysostom, Mar John of Antioch, Theodoret of Cyr, and numerous ascetics and saints such as Sadhona, or Isaac of Niniveh. The cultural and theological sphere of influence exercised by the Syrian Church in its time of glory was much greater than the (very large) extent of its ancient territories. The Syrian ritual gave the substructure to the Byzantine liturgical rite, for example. It was also the

Syrians who perfected the art of setting poetic synopses of Scripture to sung melodies. The church's greatest poets such as Ephrem and Romanos the Melodist were Syrians who taught this theological style to Byzantium and prepared the way for the glories of medieval Orthodox liturgical chant. The Syrian Church, especially in its Golden Age between the 4th and 6th centuries, generously organized missions to Ethiopia, Persia, India, and China. Its presence in China historically has tended to be occluded because of the extensive burning of Syriac Christian literature by the later Renaissance missionaries who claimed the origination of Christianity in that continent, but there are stones from ancient times recording the arrival of the Syrian missionaries, and Chinese Christian folk elements show the ancient Syrian traces. The patriarchate of Antioch influenced the whole of ancient Cappadocia in its time, and it in turn influenced Armenia and Georgia. Patristic church leaders such as Basil the Great and Gregory the Theologian were mentored by Syrian hierarchs such as Meletios of Antioch or Eusebius of Samosata, the great defenders of the Nicene faith at the time of the Second Council of Constantinople. It was Meletios and Eusebius who summoned Gregory the Theologian to preach the *Five Theological Orations* at Constantinople, and although Eusebius was assassinated before he could make his presence felt there, Gregory only assumed the presidency of the Second Council of Constantinople in 381 after Meletios, unanimously acclaimed as its first president, had died unexpectedly.

In its time of glory, the Christian orators of Syria spoke and wrote the finest Greek in the Roman world. The schools of Antioch were renowned for the purity of their Greek eloquence. Writers such as Gregory the Theologian and John Chrysostom have left behind a memorial of work that reaches to the standards of the greatest of all Greek rhetoric. Gregory, for example, has been favorably compared to Demosthenes himself. John gained his epithet "Golden Mouth" because of the limpid quality of his Greek, but he was a Syrian by birth. This outpost, at Antioch, of pure Greek culture on the banks of the Orontes was a bubble that broke before the advance of Islam; and from the 7th century the flourishing of Christianity in the Antiochene patriarchate gave way to a long and slow twilight, with the

monasteries holding on the longest, often in inaccessible valleys and rock outcrops: an unknown treasure of the Christian world still, barely, surviving to this day. As the patriarchate of Constantinople flourished and grew in stature in the ambit of the Byzantine Empire, so did Antioch, almost by antithesis, decline in prestige and influence.

The first major land mass to go from Antioch's ecclesiastical territories of supervision was Asia Minor, which was assigned to the purview of the rising capital of Constantinople in the early 5th century. Then the Church of Cyprus successfully asserted its independence from Antioch between 431 and 488, using the cause of the christological tensions between Alexandria and Antioch to press its claims on the wider Christian churches. The vast territory of Persia asserted its independence in 424, after which point it refused its assent to the Council of Ephesus of 431 and fell away from communion with the Byzantine Orthodox. The theological divisions, represented in the Syrian territories first by pro-Nestorian theologians, then by (diametrically opposed) radical Cyrilline theologians, not only weakened Syrian Christianity by cutting it off from the Byzantine world, but heavily disrupted it internally, even to the extent of dividing the Syrian language itself (always a predominantly Christian affair) into two distinct groups of Serta and Estrangela. The continuing energy of the Persian anti-Cyrilline communities for many centuries afterwards drew away the allegiance of many Assyrian Christians from the patriarchate of Antioch. The continuing prevalence of the Miaphysite resistance to the Council of Chalcedon after the 6th century also drew away many other Syrians from the communion of the patriarch. Jerusalem became a separate patriarchate in 451 and took with it, out of the purview of Christian Antioch, the territory of Palestine. In later times the scattered state of the Syrian Christian communities and their appalling vulnerability to the forces of an increasingly hostile Islamic majority led to large numbers of the Syrian Christian communities fleeing for protection to the arms of a strong and missionary active Rome. Between 1600 and 1720 six patriarchs of Antioch made professions of allegiance to the pope. The result is that there are now large communities of Syrian Eastern Catholics. At the beginning of the 20th century there were no fewer than seven distinct Eastern Catholic communities in the Syrian

Church, all representing another historic fragmentation of the ancient patriarchate of Antioch, and seven senior hierarchs, all claiming the right to be, and be designated as, the Antiochene patriarch. The Orthodox patriarch chose to reside at Damascus, the newer capital, the Latin patriarch of Antioch used to reside at Rome, the anti-Chalcedonian patriarch at Mardin, and in addition there were the four Eastern Catholic Syrian communities: those of the Greek Melkites, the Armenians at Antioch, the Maronites, and the Syrians. The Latin patriarch was created and installed as the incumbent hierarch by the Crusaders in 1098, and the office lasted at Rome until the mid-20th century although it had become merely an honorific title from the 14th century onwards. The various residences of the hierarchs are now more disparate. The Orthodox patriarch of Antioch has traditionally been the one ancient see among the Orthodox to have sustained the closest and oldest ecumenical ties with Rome since the era of the Great Schism, even though in recent times the patriarchate of Constantinople has had the most publicized dealings with Rome.

The Orthodox recognize only one "patriarch of Antioch," who is in communion with the other ancient patriarchates and autocephalous churches of the Orthodox Church, and who still resides at Damascus. The ancient city of Antioch is now Antakya, a small, provincial, and overwhelmingly Islamic town. The remaining jurisdictional territory presided over by the Orthodox patriarch is Syria and the Asiatic Roman provinces of Cilicia, Mesopotamia, and Isauria. Most of his faithful today are Arabic-speaking Christians. From 1724 to 1899 the Orthodox patriarch of Antioch was always a Phanariot Greek. Since that time Arabs have generally occupied the office. Today, there are just over a million Syriac-speaking Christians in the world and half a million Arabic speakers, who belong to the Antiochene patriarchate. The Orthodox patriarch's flock currently consists of fewer than half a million faithful, centered largely in Syria, the Lebanon, and Iraq, with the rest, a considerable diaspora, largely in America. The patriarch's title is "His Blessedness the Patriarch of Antioch the City of God, of Cilicia, Iberia, Syria, Arabia and All the East": in short, the Roman Imperial Province of the *Oriens*.

In America the hierarchs of the Antiochene patriarchate have proved to be immensely creative and open to the new situations presented by life in the New World. The Antiochene Orthodox there throughout the 20th century had a large degree of autonomy afforded to them by the patriarch and proved particularly ready to engage in evangelical mission. As well as being important pillars of support for their suffering church in the homelands, they have sponsored several highly valuable translations of the liturgical texts and prayer books in English, and in recent times have encouraged numbers of Evangelical Christians who have made their way into the Orthodox Church, both in America and England, and established them within their jurisdictional care.

SEE ALSO: Africa, Orthodoxy in; Assyrian Apostolic Church of the East; China, Autonomous Orthodox Church of

References and Suggested Readings

Atiya, A. S. (1991) *A History of Eastern Christianity*. Millwood, NY: Kraus Reprints.
Wallace-Hadrill, D. A. (1982) *Christian Antioch: A Study of Early Christian Thought in the East*. Cambridge: Cambridge University Press.

Apocalyptic *see* Eschatology

Apodeipnon

JOHN A. MCGUCKIN

The word signifies "after supper" in the Greek, and denotes the monastic office of night prayer corresponding in some senses to western Compline, although in the Orthodox daily offices there is also a later service of the late night called Mesonyktikon (lit. "the middle of the night"). Great Apodeipnon is prescribed for services in the Lent period, but a smaller service is in daily use. After the Trisagion prayers, Apodeipnon is composed of Psalms 50, 69, and 142, the Doxology and Creed. A Canon may be inserted at that point, and this is usually the time when Orthodox recite the Canon of Preparation for Communion before receiving the divine mysteries on the next day.

The service concludes with an alternating series of very fine prayers to Christ and the Blessed Virgin, with a prayer to the angels and a final litany of intercession.

Apodosis
JOHN A. MCGUCKIN

Greek term meaning "giving away," signifying the liturgical "leave-taking" of a great feast. The major festivals in Byzantine times lasted for many days with a variety of celebrations, both in the churches and in the streets. The first and last day of the festival were especially marked in church services by the main liturgical hymns and poetic compositions being performed that explained the theological significance of the events being celebrated. The Apodosis was almost like the last recapitulation of festivities before the festival was drawn to a close and "ordinary liturgical time" resumed.

Apolysis
JOHN A. MCGUCKIN

Greek term for "Dismissal," the short series of prayers and repeated blessings that end an Orthodox service. The Apolysis of the Sunday Divine Liturgy commences with the extended blessing that invokes the resurrected Christ ("May he who rose from the dead, Christ our true God, through the prayers of …") and goes on to name a whole list of saints, including the Theotokos, the apostles, the saint who composed the liturgy that is being used (St. Chrysostom, Basil, or James, for example), the church's patronal saint, and the saints commemorated that day in the calendar. Shorter forms of Dismissal are found in other services of the hours. On weekdays the Apolysis begins without invoking the resurrection as such ("May Christ our true God …").

Apolytikion
DIMITRI CONOMOS

The principal troparion of the day, chanted at the end of Vespers (hence its name, which means "dismissal hymn"), and celebrating the particular feast or saint being commemorated. It is also known as the "troparion of the feast" or the "troparion of the day." On Great Feasts it is sung three times at the end of Vespers, four times at Matins: three times after "The Lord is God," and once at the end of Matins, immediately after the Great Doxology; once at the Liturgy, after the Little Entrance and the Introit; at Great Compline and at all the Hours.

SEE ALSO: Troparion

Apophaticism
JUSTIN M. LASSER

The Greek term *apophasis* denotes a manner of doing theology by "not speaking." As the alpha-privative prefix suggests, the term is concerned with a negating function. In some forms apophaticism exists as a check on *kataphatic* or assertive theology or philosophy. The style of apophatic theology was first developed by the Platonic school philosophers, and creatively used by Plotinus, as well as appearing in some of the Gnostic literature (*Apocryphon of John*, *Trimorphic Protennoia*). Apophaticism, stressing that God exceeds the boundaries of all terms that can be applied to the divinity by human mind or language, is above all else a means of preserving mystery amid a world of theological assertions. Apophaticism preserves the religious apprehension of the mystical in a more sophisticated way than the simple asseveration of dogmatic utterances.

The Nag Hammadi writings (recovered in 1945) exhibit the earliest forms of Christian apophaticism. Clement and Origen of Alexandria both developed early Orthodox forms of apophaticism which were inherited and developed especially by St. Gregory of Nazianzus (*Orations* 27–8) and St. Gregory of Nyssa (*Contra Eunomium*) in their controversy with the Arian logicians Eunomius and Aetius. The theology of these radical Arians (Heterousiasts) against which the Cappadocians asserted apophaticism as a way of refuting their deductions about God's nature (which Aetius had affirmed was simple and directly knowable through logical method and literal exegesis) was itself a form of apophaticism, since they posited the negation "un-originate" (*agenētos*) as the first principle of their doctrine of God.

Evagrius of Ponticus, disciple of the Cappadocians, transformed Christian apophaticism into a theology of prayer, encouraging his disciples to pray without using any mental images. The first Orthodox Christian writer to employ apophaticism systematically was the great 5th-century Syrian theologian Pseudo-Dionysius the Areopagite. His treatises on the *Divine Names* and the *Mystical Theology* stand at the very pinnacle of Orthodox apophatic theology. Dionysius believed that the descriptive (affirmative or positive-utterance) elements in revelation were intended to provide a ladder by which the initiate would climb by negating each descriptive assertion about God. Dionysius' writings, considering the theological controversies that preceded them, were astoundingly thought provoking. Concerning the divinity, Dionysius wrote: "It is not a substance [*ousia*], nor is it eternity or time. … It is not Sonship or Fatherhood … it falls neither within the predicate of non-being nor of being" (*Mystical Theology*, in Rorem 1987: 141). Even so, Dionysius could still begin his treatise praying to the divine Trinity and would develop all his thought in the matrix of the divine liturgy. Such are the paradoxes of the apophatic approach.

In the modern era, Orthodox theologians such as Vladimir Lossky have used apophaticism as a means of distinguishing a "proper" form of Orthodox theology from what they often described as "Western theology" that they found to be too assertive or *kataphatic* (scholastic) in character. This school has often described Orthodox theology's "Great Captivity" by scholastic forms after the 18th century, and believed a renewal of apophaticism would release it. This sweeping generalization of western thought neglected the truth that Orthodox theological tradition itself was and is highly kataphatic in terms of its dogmatic tradition, and uses philosophical categories of discourse just as readily as have Catholicism and Protestantism in times past. The enduringly valuable aspect of the Orthodox apophatic tradition is the manner in which it guards the mystery of the divine revelation in its theological traditions.

SEE ALSO: Gnosticism; Lossky, Vladimir (1903–1958); St. Dionysius the Areopagite

References and Suggested Readings

Dionysius the Areopagite (1987) *Pseudo-Dionysius: The Complete Works*, trans. P. Rorem. New York: Paulist Press.

Lossky, V. (2002) *The Mystical Theology of the Eastern Church*. Crestwood, NY: St. Vladimir's Seminary Press.

Pelikan, J. (1993) *Christianity and Classical Culture: The Metamorphosis of Natural Theology in the Christian Encounter with Hellenism*. New Haven: Yale University Press.

Aposticha

SOTIRIOS A. VLAVIANOS

The Aposticha ('Απόστιχα in Greek) are sets of hymns accompanied by verses from the Old Testament. They belong to the family of liturgical hymns called *Stichera* and are chanted towards the end of Vespers and weekday Orthros (Matins) in the Orthodox Church. Depending on the day of the week or the feast, their content may refer to themes concerning the resurrection, crucifixion, apostles, martyrs, compunction of soul, or those who have fallen asleep.

SEE ALSO: Hymnography; Idiomelon; Orthros (Matins); Sticheron; Vespers (Hesperinos)

References and Suggested Readings

Monks of New Skete (1987) "Introduction," in *Hymns of Entreaty*. Cambridge, MA: New Skete.

Taft, R. F. (1997) *Beyond East and West: Problems in Liturgical Understanding*, 2nd edn. Rome: Pontifical Oriental Institute.

Apostolic Succession

JUSTIN M. LASSER

Orthodoxy begins not with definition or argumentation, but with an intimate and revelatory encounter with its Lord. It is this awe-inspiring engagement that the Orthodox Church yearns to preserve in all it does. Whether it is like the woman who reached out to touch Christ's garment, the rich man that went away in shame, or the disciples trembling before their transfigured Lord, the church's primary function has been

Plate 4 St. Matthew the Evangelist. By Eileen McGuckin. The Icon Studio: www.sgtt.org.

to preserve and hand on the "Tradition" of these revelatory moments, as continuing gateways of grace for his present disciples.

The Orthodox preserve and enact the occasion of Jesus' sending-out (*apostellein*) of his followers to proclaim the good news to all who would listen. Indeed, for the Orthodox, this "sending-out," this mission of Christ, never ended. The term "apostolic succession" derives from the Greek word *apostolos* which can be translated as "a sent-one." This term marks an important transition in the Christian experience. The *mathētēs*, the follower, takes on a new role as one who is sent-out not merely to proclaim the Kingdom of God, but to *enact* the Kingdom of God; in other words, to bring the reality of Christ to those seeking. The apostles were not sent-out so much to *prove* the Christian faith as to *live* as Christ, teach Christ's message, and to establish a space where those seeking might encounter Christ.

The essence of the apostolic preaching is captured in St. Peter's paradigmatic proclamation, "You are the Christ, the Son of the Living God" (Mt. 16.16). This *kerygma* was and remains the substance of all that apostolicity means. It is this mystery and stunning realization that the apostolic preaching is intended to impart and enact. Because the apostolic mission never ended, the Orthodox affirm that this *kerygma*, this living proclamation of the Kingdom of God, was passed on to the successors of the apostles.

In the 2nd century the church encountered a variety of novel expressions of the Christian faith which were, for many, foreign to the faith they were taught as catechumens. These circumstances provided the stimulus behind the emergence of an ecclesiastical conservatism that was consolidated in the office of the bishop. This conservative ecclesiastical oversight of the bishops served as means to protect, preserve, and transmit the simple and profound Tradition of the Apostles. This Tradition was preserved in a variety of forms, including the Canon of Holy Scripture, the liturgical creeds, and the Eucharistic assembly. This tradition is not understood as a mere historical "narrative," but a concrete historical reality.

The works of St. Justin the Martyr and St. Clement of Alexandria, among many others, demonstrate Orthodox appropriation of the wider philosophical vocabulary in an effort to proclaim Christian truth. However, when the "different" or heretical articulations of the *kerygma* infringed upon the experience of Christ, the Orthodox reacted immediately. These reactions came in the form of demonstrations of apostolicity. One of the first to offer an Orthodox response to alien or wildly innovative articulations of the Christian faith was St. Irenaeus of Lyons (ca. 135–200) in his *Demonstration of the Apostolic Preaching* and *Against Heresies* (*Adversus Haereses*). According to Irenaeus, his own grasp of authentic apostolic teaching was demonstrated by his relation (and obedience) to the teachings he derived from the martyr Polycarp in Smyrna, whom he knew and recognized as a teacher, and who had himself received his doctrine both from Ignatius of Antioch and from St. John the Apostle. This formulation of a lineage of known and revered authoritative teachers, which could be publicly demonstrated (as in the lists of episcopal successions of local churches demonstrably in communion with other local churches, all of whom could point to a commonality of spiritual life and teachings), was important in establishing what the Orthodox meant by apostolic succession – that is, the transmission of the sacred Tradition from Jesus to the apostles, and from the apostles to the bishops, and from the bishops to the faithful in each local church. Apostolicity, for Irenaeus, above all meant consonance with the canonical scriptural tradition (what he called the apostolic faith); and a method of exegeting those scriptures where the historical concreteness and open meaning were given preference over secret gnostic speculations.

Another important early witness to apostolic succession is Hippolytus of Rome (ca. 170–236), who wrote the *Apostolic Tradition*. Hippolytus bears witness to early practices of liturgical celebration, ordination, baptism, and prayers. Both Hippolytus and an early 2nd-century text, the *Didache* (or the *Teaching of the Twelve Apostles*), preserve a snapshot of the early consolidation of the office of the bishop and the church consolidating around the Eucharist. The early writings (known from the 17th century as the "Apostolic Fathers") of the mainly 2nd-century theologians (including Clement of Rome, Ignatius of Antioch, Papias, and others) also demonstrate the spirit of Orthodox apostolic succession, exhibiting again the importance of the figure of the bishop, the centrality of harmonious inter-church unity, and the preservation of an authentic encounter with Christ as revealed in the canonical scriptures.

The Orthodox Church preserves, as an extremely important mechanism of its enduring apostolicity, the coming together of its spiritual leaders in council or synod. This process is based upon the archetype of the Apostolic Council recorded in Acts 15. As the apostles themselves gathered harmoniously to debate certain issues that could potentially divide the church, so the later bishops established synods (the Greek means "to come together") and from the 2nd century in Asia Minor there is evidence that this became a normal way of the local churches to ensure commonality of doctrine and practice in the larger domain. This practice of joining together to decide important issues is continued even today in the Orthodox Church. As heirs of the apostles it is believed that the inspiration of the Holy Spirit especially attends the important deliberations of the hierarchs gathered in prophetic assembly for the teaching

and preservation of faith and good order in the churches. In this manner, the joining together of the successors of the apostles affirms the living experience of Christ in his church, an experience that is both ancient and contemporary. The attendant inspiration of the Holy Spirit is seen as preeminently present in the ecumenical councils of the church, to which the highest level of authority is given by the Orthodox in terms of maintaining the authentic Christian faith of the apostles in different ages and different circumstances.

While it may seem that the complex theological formulations of the later councils move away from the simplicity of the earliest apostolic witness, as given in the simpler statements of Holy Scripture, it is important to remember that these conciliar declarations (which make confident use of philosophy and subtle doctrine) are not definitions of the intimate encounter with Christ, as much as they are the *responses* to that experience – they defend and preserve that experience. In other words they are not new statements replacing the scriptural record of the apostles, rather they are commentaries upon the biblical faith of the apostles. They uncover and proclaim again in new ages the depth of the mystical meeting with Christ. The profundity of the philosophical-theological language of the councils (introducing such terms as *homoousion* or *hypostasis*) serves to reflect the profundity of the Christ experience. Though this experience always extends beyond exact articulation in words, since it is greater than any words, and cannot be contained by them, it is nonetheless understood by the most simple-hearted Orthodox Christian, even by the youngest child, who can have as authentic a faith in Christ as a learned sage. Everything in the Orthodox Church – from its dogmas, to its icons, to its liturgy – serves to recreate, reenact, and make real the simple, yet awesome, experience of the living Christ: the same Lord who moves in his church today who once spoke to the original apostles in Galilee. This selfsame Christ is the core experience of the apostles, and it is the experience which the successors of the apostles, the bishops, are entrusted to preserve. It is in this way that the Orthodox faithful proclaim every Sunday: "I believe in One, Holy, Catholic, and Apostolic Church." The Orthodox

Christians preserve and encounter that ancient apostolic experience of meeting Christ, while recognizing that this "meeting" is not only a matter of ancient truth, but a challenge and invitation made available in the present moment of grace: the *Kairos* that extends from the incarnation to the eschaton.

SEE ALSO: Apophaticism; Ecumenical Councils; Episcopacy; Heresy

References and Suggested Readings

Bakhuizen, J. N. (1966) "Tradition and Authority in the Early Church," *Studia Patristica* 7 (TU 92): 3–22.

Behr, J. (2001) *The Formation of Christian Theology, Vol. 1: The Way to Nicaea*. Crestwood, NY: St. Vladimir's Seminary Press.

Irenaeus of Lyons (1997) *On the Apostolic Preaching*. Crestwood, NY: St. Vladimir's Seminary Press.

McGuckin, J. A. (1998) "Eschaton and Kerygma: The Future of the Past in the Present Kairos: The Concept of Living Tradition in Orthodox Theology," *St. Vladimir's Theological Quarterly* 42, 3–4: 225–71.

von Campenhausen, H. (1947–8) "Le concept d'Apotre dans le Christianisme primitif," *Studia Theologica* 1: 96–130.

Zizioulas, J. D. (2001) *Eucharist, Bishop, Church: The Unity of the Church in the Divine Eucharist and the Bishop During the First Three Centuries*. Brookline, MA: Holy Cross Orthodox Press.

Archdeacon

MARIA GWYN MCDOWELL

A rank of the diaconate. Historically the archdeacon is a title of honor given to chief deacons who are also monastics. In contemporary practice the archdeacon is an administrative rank designating the deacon attached to the person of a bishop who holds primary responsibility and honor among the episcopal staff. The archdeacon is elevated, not ordained, to the new rank. An archdeacon can be married, celibate, or monastic.

SEE ALSO: Deacon; Deaconess; Ordination; Protodeacon

Architecture, Orthodox Church

JOHN A. MCGUCKIN

Today, it is almost impossible to determine anything about the architecture of the very earliest Christian communities. Our picture of the condition of church buildings in the first two centuries is generally provided by the missionary situation of the New Testament communities. The first believers shared table fellowship "from house to house" (Acts 2.46; 5.42). Paul mentions whole households being converted at once (as the master converted so did their *oikoi*, or households) and he often sends greetings to the "Church in the house" of various people (1 Cor. 16.19; Rom. 16.5; Phlm. 2; Cols. 4.15). The New Testament and other early literature mentions Christian assemblies in "Upper Rooms" that were probably hired (Acts 20.7), lecture rooms (Acts 19.19), and warehouses (*Passion of Paul* 1).

It is generally thought that from the end of the 1st century, villas of the wealthier members of the church increasingly were adapted and used for the purposes of the liturgical assembly, but no solid evidence is available, and much relies on deduction from a very small number of cases. It seems a reasonable supposition that the fluid arrangements of the earliest Christian generations increasingly gave way to specifically ordered church buildings. A rare example of a so-called "house church" from this later period of consolidation exists in Dura Europos, a Roman border town in Syria. Discovered in 1920, excavations in 1939 revealed a small mid-2nd-century Christian building that had been remodeled from a normal house. The exterior remained the same as other houses in the street, but the interior walls had been extensively redesigned to make a large rectangular assembly hall. Another small room was made into a dedicated baptistery, with a canopied font set into the floor and wall frescoes illustrating gospel scenes. From the 3rd century onwards, some of the houses of famous martyrs also became places of worship, such as the house of John and Paul on the Caelian hill in Rome which in its elaboration into a church assimilated an adjacent apartment block. Other private villas were given to the church by wealthy patrons for the purposes of worship. In the time of the Diocletianic persecution of the early 4th century, Lactantius notes in his

Plate 5   Holy Trinity Church, Sergiev Posad. Hulton-Deutsch Collection/Corbis.

Divine Institutes that the Christian church at Nicomedia was a notable public building, and was deliberately burned by imperial troops. Several prestigious churches at Constantinople took their origin from the donation of senatorial villas to church use in the 4th century, a practice which had begun with grants of imperial property and civic basilicas in the time of Constantine (who had commenced this practice to afford some form of reparation of property to the Christians who had suffered confiscation of buildings and goods in the persecutions of the preceding centuries). The Lateran Basilica is one example of such a gift. Other churches were custom-built by Constantine, including the Anastasis (Holy Sepulchre) in Jerusalem, and the shrine of Peter on the Vatican hill at Rome. Both were basilical-style buildings with adjoining martyria.

After emerging from the era of persecutions, Christians increasingly built their own churches, as well as adapting basilicas gifted to them by the emperor. Some of the best ancient basilicas, least adapted, that remain are in Orthodox use: the Church of Transfiguration at St. Catherine's Monastery, Sinai, and the Nativity Church at Bethlehem, given as a donation of Constantine in the 4th century. After the 5th century, many pagan temples were also taken over for use as Christian churches. Some of the most dramatic examples are the Pantheon in Rome, the Parthenon in Athens, and the Serapeum in Alexandria.

The donation of basilicas had a strong impact on later Christian architecture. This was substantially a rectangular hall, with an apsidal benched end (originally for magistrates) and was to become one of the most common formats of Christian building, in which case the apse was oriented to the East (an aspect not usually observed in pre-Christian basilicas that were taken over from the pagans). Churches built

Plate 6 Interior of St. Catherine's Monastery, 19th-century print, the Basilica of the Transfiguration. Holy Land Art/Alamy.

over special sites or holy places were often marked by a distinctive architectural shape. Martyria (the tomb-shrines of martyrs that developed into churches) were often octagonal or rotunda in shape. Octagonal church building in the East also usually designated a particular commemoration of a site: biblical holy places or the like being enclosed in a clear geometric design, with surrounding colonnades to allow pilgrims access to the holy place. The great Church of the Anastasis built by Constantine at Jerusalem combined a rotunda over the site of Christ's death, with a large basilica attached to the holy place by colonnaded porticoes. The design of the buildings in Jerusalem had a powerful effect on the determination of liturgical rites (such as processions or circumambulations) in many other churches of Christendom.

In the Greek East after the 5th century a new form of Christian architecture came into favor and was pat-ronised by powerful emperors. Justinian's churches of Saints Sergius and Bacchus, later to be followed by his monumental Hagia Sophia at Constantinople (replacing a basilica-type predecessor church on the site), used the idea of a squared cross floor plan set under a central dome (frequently with extra apsidal half-domes added on). This "Byzantine" style soon superseded the basilica in the Greek speaking and Slavic East, but the Armenian churches combined elements of both the squared Byzantine cross and the western basilica and formed their own distinctive synthesis.

One of the common determinants in all matters relating to church architecture was the relative wealth of the local church. Ethiopia and the Coptic Churches retained a simplicity of architectural forms in marked contrast to the burgeoning of building that was characteristic of the Latin and Byzantine Churches in their imperial expansions. After the 3rd century almost all Christian churches were fashioned to reflect a biblical typology of the Jerusalem Temple as fulfilled in the Christian mysteries. The altar area (sanctuary) was occupied by the priestly ministers, and was increasingly marked off from the main body of the church (the nave) occupied by the faithful, and from the portico (narthex) which was given over to the catechumens and those undergoing penitential discipline. The Eastern liturgies witnessed a regular movement backwards and forwards between the two areas by the deacons who had charge of public prayers.

The development of the Byzantine iconographic tradition, especially after the 8th-century iconoclastic crisis, also stimulated reflection on the shape of church buildings as an earthly mirror of the heavenly cosmos. The pattern of depicting prophets and saints, with Christ in Judgment typically occupying the central dome, and the Virgin with liturgical saints in the sanctuary area, attempted to mark a linearly progressive movement (from the narthex frescoes of Old Testament saints one entered deeper into the church with New Testament scenes until one arrived at Christ in glory), and also a vertically progressive movement (from the lower walls where ascetics and other saints gave way in an upwards sweep to great martyrs, angels, and the Mother of God).

Declining economic conditions after the 8th century made the typical village church in Orthodox lands usually a small and intimate affair (in marked contrast to Hagia Sophia, which still served as a style model). In the West the basilical form proved to be a fertile matrix for a number of stylistic developments and variations, such as Romanesque and, in the medieval period, Gothic and Perpendicular. In Orthodoxy the church building (as distinct from the Church considered as the redeemed body of Christ's elect, the *Ekklesia*) is designated with a completely separate name: the Temple (Greek: *Naos*; Slavonic: *Kram*), deliberately drawing typological resonances with the biblical Temple, which Christ himself said he had "fulfilled" by his self-identification with the concept of the holy place on earth where God dwelt among humankind (Mt. 12.6; Jn. 1.51, 2.19).

SEE ALSO: Iconography, Styles of; St. Constantine the Emperor (ca. 271–337); Sinai, Autocephalous Church of

References and Suggested Readings

Filson, F. V. (1939) "The Significance of Early Christian House-Churches," *Journal of Biblical Literature* 58: 105–12.

Kraeling, C. H. (1967) *The Christian Building*. New Haven: Yale University Press.

Krauthheimer, R. (1979) *Early Christian and Byzantine Architecture*, 3rd edn. London: Penguin.

Mango, C. (1985) *Byzantine Architecture*. New York: Oxford University Press.

Rodley, L. (1999) *Byzantine Art and Architecture: An Introduction*. Cambridge: Cambridge University Press.

Arianism

M. C. STEENBERG

"Arianism" refers to the theological doctrines emerging out of the dispute between the presbyter Arius of Alexandria (ca. 250–336) and his bishop, Alexander of Alexandria (d. 326). Their clash centered on the person of the Son and his relationship to the Father; namely, whether the Son and the Father are divine in the same manner and degree. Arius' famous claims that "before he [the Son] was begotten, or created, or purposed, or established, he was not" (*Letter to Eusebius of Nicomedia*) and "[the Son is] a perfect creature of God, but not as one of the creatures" (*Letter to Alexander*), encapsulate the central tenets of what would come to be known as Arianism: that the Son came into being at the will of the Father (and therefore that he is not eternal in the same way as the Father), and that he is therefore a creature fashioned by the Father – though one of "divine" stature, distinct from all other creation. The teachings of Arius were officially condemned by way of the creed and anathema of the First Ecumenical Council (Council of Nicea, 325), called, at least in part, specifically to respond to what scholars have called the "Arian problem"; yet the proliferation of theological systems built upon these foundations carried on through the 4th century and beyond, particularly through the so-called "Neo-Arian" (Anhomoian) movements of the 360s–380s.

"Arianism" is, however, a term prone to wide generalization and with a long history of polemical misuse. Furthermore, the abundance of systems collectively called Arian, but which in fact may have little or no direct connection to the life or thought of Arius himself, make a right understanding of the historical situation especially relevant.

Arius' dispute with Bishop Alexander began ca. 318, when he, having heard the bishop's homilies pronounce such statements as "Always God [the Father], always Son" and "the Son coexists unbegotten with God" (as recounted by Arius, *Letter to Eusebius*), began publically to question whether these in fact authentically expressed the scriptural confession of the church. Scholars hotly debate whether Arius' primary impulses, in fashioning his critique, were philosophical, textual, or soteriological; but whichever of these may have been his motivations (most likely, a combination of all three), he asserted that the scriptural language of the Son as "begotten" by the Father clearly indicated a beginning to the Son's existence, "before which, he was not." To the mind of the presbyter, Alexander's seeming dismissal of the genuine coming-into-being of a "begotten" Son threatened to mix up the divinity of Son and Father, resulting either in a conflated godhead, or a duality of Gods. Arius' assertion, then, was that the Son's existence is categorically distinct from that of the Father: the one Creator, the other creature. And yet, the creatureliness of the Son (Arius used the Greek *ktisma* for "creature," assigned to the divine wisdom in the Scriptures – Prov. 8.1, 22) was not meant by him as a denigration, nor a denial of divinity. Arius expressly asserted that the Son *is* divine (*Letter to Eusebius*: "he has subsisted for all time … as perfect God"), but in a manner distinct from the divinity of the Father. It was precisely this concept of "created divinity" that allowed the Son, in Arius' understanding, to be both Creator and Savior of all else in creation, while at the same time not being a "second god" coordinate to the Father.

Despite his intention to defend older scriptural confessions, and indeed his great influence upon numerous theologians and ecclesiastical figures of the day (many of whom felt his expression better reflected the straightforward meaning of the Scriptures than Alexander's elevated *Logos* theology of the eternal birth), the church's ultimate determination was that a "divinity" to the Son such as Arius described was inauthentic to Christian confession and failed to articulate a truly co-equal divinity of Father and Son.

The core concept of "created divinity" was rejected as contradictory. This response came first in the context of Nicea's creedal statement, in which the Son is described as "begotten not made" (refuting Arius' assertion that the Son's being "begotten" equated to his "being a creature") and "*homoousios* with the Father" – that is, of the same *ousia* or divine essence as the Father. While the introduction of the latter term would spark intense debate even among Nicea's supporters (on the grounds that it was new to Christian theological discussion, was not a term found in the Scriptures, and to many was unclear in its positive meaning), the combination of these two phrases at Nicea effectively ruled out Arius' mode of expression; and the anathema found at the end of the creed made the refutation of Arius' own phrasing yet more explicit. Nonetheless, confusion over the terminology of Nicea, as well as the abiding propensity towards adopting a logical position similar to Arius' own, meant that the disputes did not end with the First Ecumenical Council.

The thought of Arius grew into a broader movement in the decades following Nicea, and particularly from the 350s (some fifteen years after Arius' death), when St. Athanasius the Great and others began to argue for a centralization of the Nicene conciliar expressions in the face of mounting "Arian" activity. It is then that we begin to see descriptions of the movement as "Arianism" (though Athanasius' preferred term for his opponents is "Ariomaniacs" – a pun with the sense of "foolish war-mongers"), and the decades leading to the Second Ecumenical Council (Constantinople, 381) would involve some of the most significant figures of the early church in reacting to various "Arian" groups: St. Basil of Caesarea, St. Gregory the Theologian, St. Gregory of Nyssa, and many others.

Today, "Arianism" is often used in a general sense to indicate any theological system in which the divinity of the Son is downplayed or denied, or in which the Son is considered temporal or creaturely, rather than eternal and uncreated. In this it in part reflects the teachings once put forward by Arius, but also incorporates aspects of the theological disputes that did not emerge until well after his time. The legacy of Arius and earliest Arianism was ultimately to spur on the precise terms of the articulation of the Holy Trinity by the church's theologians and councils, both in the denunciation of his teaching specifically, but also through the realization, occasioned by the broader Arian disputes, of just how much variation in trinitarian expression existed in the various 4th-century church communities.

SEE ALSO: Cappadocian Fathers; Christ; Council of Constantinople I (381); Council of Nicea I (325); Council of Nicea II (787); Deification; Ecumenical Councils; Fatherhood of God; Heresy; Holy Trinity; St. Athanasius of Alexandria (ca. 293–373)

References and Suggested Readings

Ayres, L. (2006) *Nicaea and Its Legacy: An Approach to Fourth-Century Trinitarian Theology*. Oxford: Oxford University Press.

Behr, J. (2001) *The Way to Nicaea*. Crestwood, NY: St. Vladimir's Seminary Press.

Steenberg, M. C. (2009) *Of God and Man: Theology as Anthropology from Irenaeus to Athanasius*. Edinburgh: T&T Clark.

Armenian Christianity

JOHN A. MCGUCKIN

Although there may have been missionaries working in Armenia from earlier times (Dionysius of Alexandria speaks in a letter of 260 CE about Bishop Meruzanes of Armenia [Eusebius, *H.E.* 6.46.2] and also tells that the Armenians were Christian in the time of Maximin's persecution in 312: *H.E.* 9.8.2.), the Armenian Church symbolically traces its evangelization to the work of St. Gregory the Illuminator, who was ordained by the archbishop of Cappadocia in Caesarea in 314 and who baptized the Armenian King Trdat IV (Tiridates, r. 298–330). Later traditions also speak of the mission of the apostles Bartholomew and Thaddeus in the country. The Armenian relationship with Cappadocia was always close in ancient times, which itself was a see that had strong links with Syrian Church traditions. The history of the Church of Georgia was at times also closely bound up with it, until divergences over the Council of Chalcedon in

the 6th century drove them apart. The chief see of the new Armenian Church was settled by Gregory at Ashtishat near Lake Van, and for a considerable time after him the office of senior bishop, or *Catholicos*, was held in succession by members of his own family. In 390 the Byzantine and Persian empires subjugated Armenia, which lay at the critical juncture between both of them (a liminal fate which accounted for many of its later vicissitudes) and divided its territories among themselves, in the ratio of 20 percent western regions falling to Byzantine control, and 80 percent enclosed in the Persian Empire. At this time the primatial see was removed to Etchmiadzin near Mount Ararat, as recounted in the history of Agathangelos. The name derives from the Armenian for "Descent place of the Only Begotten" and relates to a story that St. Gregory the Illuminator had once had a vision of the Lord and an instruction that this site would one day become important for the church. The impressive cathedral built at this site was erected on the base of an ancient Zoroastrian fire temple.

After its inclusion in the two world empires of the day, the Armenian kingly line in the Byzantine (western) territories of Armenia was suppressed first, followed by the forced ending of the kingly line in the Persian territories in 428. Since that time Armenia has been the subject of a long line of subjugations: to the Persians, Arabs, Turks, and most recently the Russians. The first three overlords had no regard for the Christian traditions of the people, and the last had little desire for any cultural independence or (in communist times) for any religious renaissance. The religious literary and political aspirations of the Armenians have been sustained through long centuries of endurance in extraordinary ways. In the 20th century this involved the survival of genocide under Turkish rule (1915–22) and political suffocation under the Soviets. The reestablishment of a free political base in the modern Republic of Armenia (much diminished in territorial size from Antiquity) and the well-developed Armenian diaspora in the United States have proven to be bright lights in the turn of Armenian fortunes in modern times.

Among many outstanding Armenian Christian leaders throughout the ages must be counted St. Nerses (d. 373), who was the sixth catholicos and a direct descendant of St. Gregory. He was educated in

Cappadocian Caesarea and served at the royal Armenian court before becoming a priest after the death of his wife. After his election as catholicos ca. 363, he initiated a large-scale reform of the church; issuing many canons after the Council of Ashtishat in 365, concerning fasting regulations, and the forbidding of marriages in kindred degrees. His stand against the Arians, the resistance of many of the court nobles to the spread of Christianity, and the use of monastics in the evangelization process, are described in the 5th-century historical writings of P'awstos Buzand. Nerses founded hospitals and orphanages set under church supervision. King Arshak III deposed him after being the focus of Nerses' criticism for a dissolute life. His successor King Pap restored him in 369, but in turn decided to dispose of him when he too was criticized for immorality; which he did by the expedient of poisoning Nerses during a banquet. He was succeeded by his son, St. Isaac (*Sahak*) the Great, who was catholicos between ca. 397 and 438 and who was the last descendant of the bloodline of Gregory the Illuminator. It was during the reign of Pap that Armenia first stopped seeking the recognition of the metropolitans of Cappadocian Caesarea for the appointment of its catholicoi, and thus assumed an autonomous ecclesiastical existence.

St. Mesrob Mashtots (ca. 361–439) was for a long time the assistant bishop to St. Isaac and became the *locum tenens* after his death, for six months before his own death. He invented the distinctive national Armenian script, which was widely adopted after 406, as part of his lifelong concern to remove Syrian dependence in Armenian church life and establish national traditions and styles. From the 5th century onwards there was a large effort led by St. Mesrob and his disciples to translate Christian literature from other cultures into it, chief among which were the translations of the Bible in 410 (using Syriac manuscripts and later Greek exemplars) as well as key liturgical texts. In patristic times many of the church's writings were translated into Armenian, and as a result some theological texts now survive only in the Armenian versions that were made in Antiquity. Important examples of this are the *Demonstration of the Apostolic Preaching* of St. Irenaeus and several of the *opera* of St. Ephrem the Syrian. Armenia first entered international Christian debate in the time of Mesrob, whose disciples had been to Melitene to study Greek, and who were well aware that the city's bishop, Acacius of Melitene, had written in the strongest terms after the Ephesine council of 431 to protest the Constantinopolitan and Alexandrian denigration of the works of Mar Theodore Mopsuestia, a leading light of the Syrian Church. Proclos, patriarch of Constantinople 434–46, wrote a *Tome to the Armenians* which became an important standard of christological orthodoxy in Armenia and was long used afterwards as a significant reason to negate the influence of Chalcedon.

Because of the political unrest in the country during a rebellion of 451, there were no Armenian representatives at the Council of Chalcedon, though the Armenian Church authorities were kept apprized of developments and approved the *Henoticon* of Emperor Zeno at the Council of Dvin in 506. In 518 the Byzantine Church condemned the *Henoticon*, but it was not until 555, two years after Justinian's revisionist christological council, that the Armenian hierarchy decided that it would not endorse Chalcedon as a significant, ecumenical synod, nor adopt the "two-nature after the Union" theology which it had proposed as a standard. At that time the Armenian synod issued a censure of the Byzantine Church, explicitly condemning the theological errors of "both poles" of the debate: namely, Severus of Antioch, and Eutyches, on the one hand, and Theodore Mopsuestia, Nestorius, and the Council of Chalcedon, on the other. Since that time Armenian Christianity has often been categorized by commentators in the Byzantine Orthodox tradition as among the "Oriental Orthodox" anti-Chalcedonians, or "Monophysites," but this is a misleading oversimplification on both fronts. The formal christological position of the church is to endorse the Christology of the first three ecumenical councils, prioritizing St. Cyril of Alexandria's early formula: "One Physis of the Word of God Incarnate" (Miaphysitism, which meant in Cyril's hands "One concrete reality of the Incarnate Word of God," not so much an endorsement of a "singularity of nature" which is often meant by the later term "Monophysitism"). Seventh-century Byzantine emperors tried to reconcile the ecclesiastical division with Armenia, but their efforts were hindered by the Arab Islamic over-running of the regions after the late 8th century. The ecumenical moves to rapprochement from this time are described in a very important Armenian Church history known as the *Narratio de rebus Armeniae* (Garitte 1952).

Although Persian followed by Arab suzerainty covered the country for most of the next 700 years, the Bagratids managed to establish an independent Christian kingdom in Armenia from the end of the 9th century until the 11th. In the 10th century the Byzantine Empire regained control over much former Armenian territory and began to consecrate Chalcedonian bishops, but this did not have much effect in bringing about church union. This renewed political influence from the empire came to an end after the devastating Byzantine defeat by the Turks at Manzikert in 1072. After that time increasing contacts with the Crusader forces in Asia Minor and Cilicia, where large Armenian settlements had been established, caused the Armenian Church to look more than it had done hitherto to the Latin Christian world.

St. Nerses IV (1102–73), known as Nerses Snorhali the Graceful, was catholicos in 1166 at Cilicia and is one of the most renowned Armenian Church writers, producing lyrical poetry on the events of salvation history, including a masterpiece widely known in Armenia from its opening lines: "Jesus Only Son of the Father." In his lifetime St. Nerses was a strong advocate of union between the Armenian and Byzantine Orthodox. His negotiations with the emperors Manuel and Michael I were continued after his death by Catholicos Gregory IV (1173–93), who summoned a council at Hromkla in 1179 where Armenian bishops from Greater Armenia, Cilicia, Syria, and Asia Minor responded favorably to the prospect of reunion. Nerses the Graceful's nephew, Nerses of Lambron, another of the great ecclesiastic poets of Armenia, also advocated the idea of union.

The Armenian Prince Leo was instrumental, however, in seeking closer ties with the West, hoping that Armenian political independence, and a kingly line, might be reestablished with western military assistance. Leo was crowned, with the support of the Holy Roman Emperor Henry VI and Pope Celestine III, on January 6, 1198, and this small independent kingdom, known as Little Armenia, lasted from the end of the 12th century until 1375. The Latinization process led by the king and the catholicos, chiefly in the Cilician

region, met with considerable opposition from the churches in Greater Armenia. Knights Templars and the Teutonic Knights supplied military protection to Armenia against the Turks, but the Mamluk Muslims won a decisive victory in 1260 and, when Hromkla, the ecclesiastic center, was captured in 1292, Catholicos Stephen moved to exile in Egypt. His successor, Catholicos Gregory VII, transferred the central seat of the catholicate to Sis (Antelias in Lebanon) and summoned a council there in 1307 which accepted many of the terms Rome had dictated for union. Resulting schisms among the Armenians over this issue caused among other things the institution of a separate Armenian patriarchate of Jerusalem, which has had a distinguished history up to present times in the Armenian quarter of the Old City. In the later 14th and early 15th centuries there was a flowering of Armenian theology and philosophy, especially among pro-Roman Armenian writers, seen most notably in the works of Gregory Tat'evaci and his *Book of Questions*, which has a similar status in Armenian Church literature that John of Damascus had among the Byzantines, summing up a long tradition synthetically.

In 1307 the hierarchy of Little Armenia entered into formal relations with the patriarchate of Rome following the Council of Sis, a union that was reaffirmed at the Council of Florence (1438–9), though this settlement was not endorsed at the time by any Armenian council. The clergy and people of Greater Armenia, however, did not accept the union, and after their experience of discussions at the Council of Florence, where the westerners had set out a program for sacramental observance by the Armenians (the text of the *Pro Armenis*), they decided to reestablish the line of independent catholicoi at Etchmiadzin in 1441. The catholicate at Sis entered a long period of relative political decline. The site was destroyed after the genocide in the early 20th century, and from the 1930s Antelias in Lebanon became the administrative center of the catholicate of Cilicia.

The Armenian Church in the period after the Middle Ages continued to be influenced by both Latin and Byzantine currents. After the fall of Constantinople in 1453 the Armenian bishop of the city rose in importance. After the 18th century he was recognized by the sultans as ethnarch of all the Armenian peoples in the Ottoman Empire. By this time Constantinople had become a major city where Armenian culture flourished. Venice, too, which provided printing presses for Armenian literature, was particularly significant in the 16th and 18th centuries in consolidating the Armenian religious and literary culture anew. After the Ottoman collapse, Constantinople quickly dwindled in significance, although Jerusalem remained until the 20th century as a significant center of Armenian affairs and pilgrimage center until demographic changes reduced its Armenian population drastically.

The issue of having disparate catholicates continued into the modern era, providing a polarized "sense of belonging" in the affairs of the Armenian Church, which has only had the occasion of being addressed more strenuously among the Armenians in very recent times. Apart from the Catholic Armenian communities, the Armenian Orthodox Church currently has the catholicate of Etchmiadzin in the Armenian Republic, as the dominant leadership center, and the catholicate of the Great House of Cilicia (currently with a jurisdictional remit over Lebanon, Syria, Cyprus, Greece, Iran, and parts of Canada and the Americas), along with two subordinate patriarchates (Constantinople and Jerusalem).

Armenian Church art used the fresco extensively, but the cult of icons was never developed as significantly as in Byzantium, and the cross (especially in the form of distinctive stone carvings) received a higher focal symbolism. Armenian Church building styles are very distinctive. The balance of pro-Roman Armenians to the Greater Armenian Church (sometimes called the "Gregorian Armenians" by Latin commentators) is now estimated as in the ratio of approximately 100,000 to something over 5 million.

The Armenian clergy are divided into two classes, the *vardapets* (doctors) from whose ranks the bishops are normally selected, who are easily recognized from their high-pointed cowls, and the parish priests who marry before ordination unless they chose the monastic lifestyle. Liturgically, they follow the ancestral liturgical tradition of the Church of Cappadocia, following the Gregorian calendar since 1923 (except at Jerusalem) and using St. Basil's Liturgy in Armenian. Unleavened bread is used and communion is given under two species by intinction. There are several later Latin influences in the ritual. The common priestly vestment is the *shurjar*, which is reminiscent of the Latin cope, and the bishops wear the pointed mitre. In accordance with the earliest level of Eastern Christian liturgical observances, Christmas is not celebrated in late December as a separate festival, but is part of the Theophany celebrations that last over the week following January 6. The catholicate of Etchmiadzin operates two seminaries at present, one at Lake Van and the other at Etchmiadzin; while the Great House of Cilicia organizes a seminary in Lebanon. There are other seminaries at Jerusalem and in New York State (St. Nerses, at New Rochelle, which collaborates in its instructional program with St. Vladimir's Orthodox Seminary).

SEE ALSO: Georgia, Patriarchal Orthodox Church of

References and Suggested Readings

Arpee, L. (1946) *A History of Armenian Christianity from the Beginning to Our Own Time*. New York: Armenian Missionary Association of America.

Cross, F. L. and Livingstone, E. A. (eds.) (1997) The Oxford Dictionary of the Christian Church. Oxford: Oxford University Press.

Garitte, G. (ed.) (1952) *Narratio de Rebus Armeniae: Corpus Scriptorum Ecclesiasticorum Orientalium. Vol. 132, Subsidia. 4.* Rome.

Ormanian, M. (1910) L'Église arménienne: son histoire, sa doctrine, son régime, sa discipline, sa liturgie, son présent. Paris: E. Leroux.

Sarkissian, K. (1975) *The Council of Chalcedon and the Armenian Church*, 2nd edn. New York: Armenian Prelacy Press.

Artoklasia

PHILIP ZYMARIS

The Artoklasia (lit. "breaking of bread") is a service for the blessing of loaves celebrated at Vespers, recalling the gospel text of the multiplication of loaves (Mt. 14.15–21). Its original purpose was to bless and distribute food at monastic vigils to strengthen the monks, although it is presently celebrated at any service. It is performed before a table placed on the solea upon which five round loaves, wheat, wine, and oil are placed.

SEE ALSO: Vespers (Hesperinos)

References and Suggested Readings

Christodoulou, T. (2002) *He akolouthia tes artoklasias*. Athens: Ekdoseis Homologia.

Day, P. (1993) "Artoklasia," in *The Liturgical Dictionary of Eastern Christianity*. Collegeville: Liturgical Press, pp. 24–5.

Artophorion

THOMAS KITSON

The Artophorion (Greek for "bread carrier") is a container reserved in the altar area of an Orthodox church (usually on the holy table itself) that holds the consecrated Eucharist, preserved for the seriously ill and dying. Usually made from a non-corrosive or gilded metal in the form of a church (sometimes called "Zion" or "Jerusalem" in the Russian tradition), it symbolizes the presence of the New Covenant, by analogy with the Old Testament Ark of the Covenant in Moses' tabernacle and Solomon's temple (Mt. 26.28; Mk. 14.27; Jn. 16.32; Heb. 9.1–12). A small box called the "tomb" within the larger vessel holds the actual elements.

Asceticism

M. C. STEENBERG

Asceticism is understood in Orthodoxy as that way of life which prepares one for the Kingdom of God through the training and conditioning of the whole human person – body and soul – towards a Godly life, and its exercise in virtue. The Greek word *askesis* from which it derives means "exercise" or "training" and comes from an ancient sporting vocabulary used to indicate the various labors in which an athlete would engage in order to prepare himself for effective competition. In the spiritual life, it retains the notions of preparation that the term's sporting heritage provides, as well as the associated concepts of self-sacrifice, struggle, and battle against the will, habits, and passions that such exercise and training require.

The injunction towards asceticism comes from the gospel, with Christ's statement that "the Kingdom of Heaven suffers violence, and the violent take it by force' (Mt. 11.12) chief among its scriptural imperatives. The "violence" mentioned is of course not that of aggressive relationships (passionate violence), but the intentional and unrelenting work of the person against the impulses and desires of the fallen will, together with the corrupt body. Asceticism is this working against what is fallen in the human person, towards its correction, reformation, and purification, disavowing oneself of no means – however intense a struggle they may pose – by which this aim may be accomplished. It is, then, an approach to the advance in Christian virtue that follows the Lord's command: "Whosoever wishes to become my disciple, let him deny himself, take up his cross, and follow me" (Mt. 16.24; Lk. 9.23).

Orthodox Christian asceticism manifests itself in many ways, the common bond between all being their value as tools by which the conditioning and training of the heart and body may take place. The most familiar ascetical struggles are fasting, which may tame the impulses of the body and the gluttony of will; the keeping of vigils, which may bridle the impulse toward indulgent rest and focus the mind and heart on God; and the attention to physical labors, which may orient the work of body and mind toward the remembrance of God. Other common ascetical practices include the lengthening of prayer rules; permanent abstention from certain foods (as with monastics, who refrain altogether from eating meat); increased participation in divine services; prostrations; increased use of the prayer rope (Jesus Prayer), and so on. In all cases, the acts in and of themselves are not considered the end products or indications of spiritual attainment; rather, they are the means by which such attainment becomes accessible to Christian struggle.

Asceticism goes beyond specific acts, however, in the Orthodox injunction to live an ascetical *life* – that is, a whole life oriented around self-sacrifice, willing labors toward the kingdom, and the bearing of one's cross in order to draw nearer to the Lord.

Plate 7   An Ethiopian hermit cave-dweller and his two deacon assistants. Photo Sulaiman Ellison.

SEE ALSO: Confession; Fasting: Monasticism; Repentance; Sexual Ethics

References and Suggested Readings

Colliander, T. (1985) *Way of the Ascetics*. Crestwood, NY: St. Vladimir's Seminary Press.

Spidlik, T. (1986) *The Spirituality of the Christian East*. Kalamazoo: Cistercian Publications.

Assyrian Apostolic Church of the East

JOHN A. MCGUCKIN

The Assyrian Apostolic Church of the East belongs to the Oriental Orthodox family of churches in the Syrian tradition. The word "Assyrian" was applied to them by the English (Anglican) missionaries of the 19th century (1885–1915) who first established a western mission among them (Coakley 1992), and wished to avoid the pejorative term "Nestorian" that had often been applied to them, so as to signal their different theological stance from both the Non-Chalcedonian Orthodox Miaphysite Churches (pejoratively called the Monophysites) and the Eastern Orthodox Chalcedonians. After this importation of the term by the Anglicans, many among them started to use the word to designate themselves, although an earlier and more common designation had been the "Church of the East." A. H. Layard, who first excavated the archeological remains of Niniveh, was the first to suggest that the local Syrian Christians were the descendants of the ancient Assyrians, and the idea gained currency among the Anglican missionaries (Wigram 2002). Later, the title "Assyrian" was imported and used among the Syrian Orthodox diaspora, especially in America, as a way to distance themselves as Syriac-speaking Christians from the Islamic State of Syria. The church regards itself not as "Nestorian," but Christian, while holding Mar Nestorius in honor as a continuator of the teachings of the Syrian saints Mar Theodore of Mopsuestia and Mar Diodore of Tarsus, whose theological teachings are regarded as authoritative expositions. It thus departs from the colloquium of the ecumenical councils, regarding Nicea I (325) as the only authoritative standard. The Council of Ephesus (431) was the occasion of the ancient rupture. But the Council of Chalcedon and Constantinople II deepened the fracture; the latter anathematizing Theodore and Diodore posthumously.

After the great christological arguments following on the heels of the Council of Ephesus (431) it was obvious to the imperial court at Constantinople that the task of reconciling the differing approaches to the christological problem would not be as easy as simply declaring and promulgating the "Ephesine" solution. At the council of 431 St. Cyril of Alexandria himself had been proposed as a suitable case for ecclesiastical trial by Nestorius, the archbishop of Constantinople. While it is not known whether Nestorius ever succeeded in persuading John, archbishop of Antioch of the utility of this approach, it is clear enough that he had persuaded several other Syrian theologians, including Theodoret of Cyr, that this was the right way to proceed. In their estimation, Cyril had so violently reacted to their own traditional Syrian language of "Two Sons" (the divine Son of God, the human Son of Man) that he had proposed to stand against it the Christology of the single hypostasis of the divine Lord. Many Syrians of his day heard these (relatively new) technical terms coming out of Alexandria as tantamount to what would later be classed as Monophysitism. "Hypostasis," which later came to be clearly recognized as a term connoting "Person," began life as a technical term for "Nature," and so the grounds for inter-provincial confusion in the ancient church were immense. The continuing prevalence of the schisms show that they remain so. Many at the time thought Cyril was simply teaching an incredibly naïve view that Godhead and Manhood were "mixed up together" so as to make for a hybrid presence of the God-man Jesus. Believing that he had attacked their traditional Syrian teachers (Theodore of Mopsuestia and Diodore of Tarsus) out of ignorance, and believing that Nestorius was simply a straightforward reiterator of the traditional Syrian language (not someone who turned it to new directions), both of which were questionable propositions, they were looking forward to Ephesus 431 as a chance to put Cyril on trial as a defendant. The Alexandrian and Roman Churches, on the other hand, went to Ephesus thinking that this was the occasion to put Nestorius on trial. The very late arrival of the Syrian representation, under John of Antioch's leadership, allowed the Cyrilline version of what Ephesus was to be about to win the day. Despite the protests of Nestorius and the imperial representatives, the council of 431 opened and condemned Nestorius' doctrine on several points, especially his rejection of the legitimacy of the *Theotokos* title, and his preference for the language of christological union as based on "graceful association" of the divine and human, and on *Prosopon* as a term of union, a term that could in certain circumstances be "plural" (the *prosopon* of Jesus, of the Christ, and of the Son of God). Soon after this, however, the Syrian delegation arrived, and hearing Nestorius' complaints, proceeded to condemn Cyril on the basis of alleged Monophysitism as contained in the 12 Anathemas attached to his *Third Letter to Nestorius*. The anathema demanding their assent to the phrase "One of the Trinity suffered in the flesh" was read, unsympathetically, in the most literal way as an unskilled theologian teaching a mythic "avatar" Christology, and deserving of censure.

The aftermath of Ephesus 431, therefore, was that divisions existing beforehand had been even more exacerbated. The emperor first enforced the condemnations of both Ephesine synods, and put Nestorius and Cyril under house arrest before eventually finding for Cyril's majority council, and sending Nestorius into retirement. The Alexandrian and Antiochene Churches, however (that major two way split which at that time more or less comprised the whole of the eastern provinces of the church), were left in great disarray. The Antiochene hierarchs only proclaimed their Ephesine synod, not news of Cyril's; and in Alexandria and Rome, Ephesus 431 was taken solely as a great triumph for Cyril and Rome, never paying attention to the theological issues raised by the easterners. So it was that in 433 the imperial court sponsored a reconciliation based around a form of compromise between the radical Syrian (Two Sons) language and the terms of Cyril's mono-hypostatic language. This *Formula of Reunion* was probably composed in Syria (some have suggested Theodoret was the author), but was agreed to by Cyril and historically has been contained in his corpus of *Letters* as "Let the Heavens Rejoice." For the first time the two great church centers in Syria and Egypt began to see clearly the points of divergence between them, and were pressured by Constantinople to come to a resolution, which proved to be possible on the assertion that "two natures" in the one Lord were not confused. Syria was content that the two natures (Godhead and Manhood) should be discretely respected, while Alexandria was content that the principle of the single (divine) hypostasis of the One Christ (possessed of his divinity and humanity) should be affirmed.

Although this settlement in 433 restored communion between Alexandria and Antioch, it did not end the bad feelings. For the last years of his life, St. Cyril researched the writings of Mar Theodore and Mar Diodore and other leading Syrian christologians, and asserted to all who would listen that in his opinion they were reprehensible. In Syria, of course, they were regarded as the church's great and historic luminary saints. A further struggle was clearly brewing. It was abetted by the fact that Cyril's chief assistant, Dioscorus, regarded his archbishop's signing of the *Formula of Reunion* as a senile lapse, and determinedly reversed the policy after the death of Cyril in 444. Dioscorus wanted to return to Ephesus 431 and reassert the earlier Cyril who had put forward the mono-hypostatic Christology most forcefully and provocatively by advancing the formula *Mia Physis* (One *Nature – Reality* of God the Word made flesh). This dense Christology, although Orthodox in scope, could be (and certainly was) heard as out-and-out Monophysitism in Syria, because while the early Alexandrian usage of *Physis* meant "Concrete Reality" in more or less every other language zone, it had developed a restricted sense of "Nature"; and the whole point of the Syrian Church's objections was that there was not simply "One Nature" in Christ, but two.

Dioscorus and the Syrian Church were thus set upon a collision course that happened in 449, after the Monophysite teachings of Eutyches were censured at Constantinople and the old archimandrite was deposed. He appealed to Dioscorus, who supported him. Rome and Constantinople condemned him. Emperor Theodosius II realized another council had to be called and symbolically appointed Ephesus to be the place of decision, allowing Dioscorus to be the president of events (and thus showing he expected a resolution in line with former precedent). Unfortunately, the violent behavior of many at the council, abetted as many saw by Dioscorus' determination not to allow open debate (the *Tome of Leo* was prevented from being read out) or tolerate the slightest deviance from "early Cyril," made the Council of Ephesus (449) a thing far different from all who attended it had hoped for. There was a widespread sense of scandal when Flavian, archbishop of Constantinople, died, from what was widely seen as complications following his rough treatment at Ephesus. The heavy handedness of Dioscorus set the stage for calls for a fuller debate of the issues once more, although the emperor was loathe to allow this despite appeals from many sides. His accidental death in 451 allowed the Augusta Pulcheria and Marcian, the new emperor, to summon a reconciliation council at Constantinople (the suburb of Chalcedon) with the specific aim of bringing together a resolution of the different tendencies of Roman, Alexandrian, and Syrian Christology. The Formula of Chalcedon (451) is clearly a carefully balanced synthesis of Pope Leo's *Tome* and the later form of St. Cyril's theology (as it took cognisance of the legitimate Syrian calls for the protection of the two natures).

As history shows, however, far from being a reconciliation synod, Chalcedon itself became the cause of more and more strenuous divisions in the Eastern Church, involving the Byzantines, the Egyptians, the Armenians, and Syrians. Syria, which at first had been strongly for the "Two Nature" emphasis, soon moved its ground to be the home for the most zealous defenders of the early Cyrilline theology, and thus represented two polarizing views which to outsiders in Byzantium came to be commonly synopsized as the "Nestorian faction" and the "Monophysite" or "Jacobite faction." The censure of the Roman and

Byzantine Churches on both poles drove them out of the ambit of the empire, a distance from the center that was deeply exacerbated after the rise of Islam cut them off from regular contact with the wider Orthodox world. The missionaries of the Church of the East tended to go further eastwards, from Iraq and Iran along the Silk Road into China, where they established a historic mission and a lasting presence. Some also settled in India, although their heartland was until modern times Iraq and Syria. The opposing elements (Miaphysite or Jacobite Chaldeans) tended to missionize in India and Ethiopia, where they too left long-enduring traces. In the course of a long history under the yoke of Islamic forces, many "Assyrian," "Syrian," or "Chaldean" churches in the Ottoman domains came into the remit of the practical protection of Rome, and ecclesiastical reconciliations were not unknown, making the present state of the Syrian-speaking churches a particularly complex mosaic. The Assyrian Church of the East in ancient times was centered around the ancient school of Nisibis, and held in particular honor its theologian Babai the Great (d. 628), who synthesized its christological position in his *Book of the Union*. The church in the 7th century issued official statements that Christ is possessed of two natures (*qenome*) and one person (*prosopon*); with the old technical difficulties enduring (for in Syriac the term *qenome* is associated with the Greek *hypostasis*) and thus asserting duality where Chalcedon taught singularity; though leaving aside technical terms it is also clear that this is not what is meant in church history by "Nestorianism." Chief among the church's many ascetical writers are the great Isaac of Niniveh, John Saba, and Joseph the Visionary.

The ancient seat of the senior hierarch, the catholicos, was at Seleucia-Ctesiphon, on the river Tigris. Its liturgical language is Syriac, and three Anaphora are customarily used: those of Mar Theodore, Mar Nestorius, and Addai and Mari. Under the generally tolerant Islamic Abbasid dynasty (749–1258) the seat of the patriarch moved to Baghdad, where its theologians were among the first seriously to engage in dialogue with Islam (such as Patriarch Timothy of Baghdad) and its scholars served as significant channels for the translation and transmission of Greek learning to the Arab world (Fiey 1980). In the early 13th century the church suffered severe losses under Mongol domination. By the 16th century the church was centered in the mountains of Kurdistan, and weakened by internal divisions as part seceded to the jurisdiction of Rome, and accepted Chalcedonian Christology (Chaldean Eastern Catholics). The 20th century proved disastrous for the Assyrian Christians. Partly through British influence, the Christians of Kurdistan supported the Allied cause under Russian protection in World War I and suffered reprisals for it in the aftermath from both sides: the Turkish state and the Kurds. After the murder of the catholicos, many Assyrian Christians fled to Iraq, claiming the protection of the British Administration there. When this political mandate was terminated (1933) the agitation that resulted led to the deportation of the catholicos, who finally settled in North America, where the largest diaspora grew up. The indigenous Assyrians of the Middle East (Iraq, Syria, Lebanon, and Iran) have been increasingly eroded by the ascent of Arab nationalism and fundamentalist Islam throughout the latter part of the 20th century. In 1968 a major internal division occurred, leaving two catholicoi, one in the USA and one in Baghdad.

SEE ALSO: Antioch, Patriarchate of; Council of Chalcedon (451); Council of Constantinople II (553); Council of Ephesus (431); Islam, Orthodoxy and; Monophysitism (including Miaphysitism); Nestorianism; St. Cyril of Alexandria (ca. 378–444); St. Ephrem the Syrian (ca. 306–373/379); St. Isaac the Syrian (7th c.); Syrian Orthodox Churches; Theotokos, the Blessed Virgin

References and Suggested Readings

Brock, S. P. (1985) "The Christology of the Church of the East in the Synods of the 5th to Early 7th Centuries," in G. D. Dragas (ed.) *Aksum-Thyateira: A Festschrift for Archbishop Methodios of Thyateira and Great Britain*. London: Thyateira House.

Coakley, J. F. (1992) *The Church of the East and the Church of England: A History of the Archbishop of Canterbury's Assyrian Mission*. Oxford: Oxford University Press.

Fiey, J. M. (1980) *Chrétiens syriaques sous les abbasides, surtout à bagdad (749–1258)*. Beirut: Institut des Lettres Orientales.

Joseph, J. (1961) *The Nestorians and Their Muslim Neighbors*. Princeton Oriental Studies Vol. 20. Princeton: Princeton University Press.

Tisserant, E. and Amann, E. (1931) "Nestorius. 2. L'Église Nestorienne," in *Dictionnaire de Théologie Catholique*, vol. 11, part 1, cols. 157–323. Paris: Letouzey et Ané.

Wigram, W. A. (2002) *The Assyrians and Their Neighbours*. Piscataway, NJ: Gorgias Press.

Young, W. G. (1974) *Patriarch, Shah and Caliph: A Study of the Relationships of the Church of the East with the Sassanid Empire and the Early Caliphates up to 820 AD*. Rawalpindi: Christian Study Center.

Asterisk

THOMAS KITSON

The asterisk (or "star") consists of two crossed metal brackets joined so as to fold together and which are laid over the prepared Lamb on the diskos (paten) in the Proskomedie to keep the cloth veils from touching it and the other particles of bread. St. John Chrysostom is said to have introduced it, and it symbolically represents Christ's two natures and the cross. The earliest recorded evidence for its use is from Kiev in the 11th century. The priest completes the Proskomedie, characterized by nativity symbolism, by placing the asterisk on the diskos while reciting verses that recall the star of Bethlehem (Mt. 2.9). During the Holy Anaphora, the asterisk symbolizes the heavenly powers (especially the four mysterious beasts surrounding God's throne in Revelation 4.6–9), whose "triumphal hymn" the priest introduces as he makes the sign of the cross over the diskos (often tapping it loudly as he does so) with the asterisk's four ends.

Australasia, Orthodox Church in

JOHN CHRYSSAVGIS

While Australia counts among the most expansive countries in the world, comprising the fifth continent and being only slightly smaller in geographical territory than the USA, it is nonetheless sparsely populated, mostly barren desert (albeit extraordinarily attractive red-sand wilderness), and settled primarily in the few state capitals scattered on the coastline. The largest Christian denomination is the Roman Catholic Church, with the Anglican Church being the most dominant in the early years, the Uniting Church constituting the principal Protestant group, and Orthodox Christians forming a significant fraction of the overall population of 20 million (with numbers ranging from just over half to three quarters of a million, predominantly Greeks).

While there were probably no Orthodox Christians among the penal colonies or even the crew and passengers of the First Fleet, the earliest mention of Greeks dates to around 1818, probably referring to immigrants transported from Greece for misdemeanors related to piracy during the period of British hegemony. Earliest records indicate that the Russian wife of a British military officer arrived in Australia in 1810, possibly the first Orthodox resident in the country's history; however, there are no explicit indications of her religious background. Around 1820 a Russian Antarctic expedition from St. Petersburg to Alaska landed in Sydney, where a Hieromonk Dionisii celebrated liturgy at Kirribilli Point (to this day called "Russian Point") only days after Orthodox Easter, possibly on the Saturday of Thomas. Documents attest to another Russian naval vessel, whose chaplain was a Fr. Jerome, landing in Melbourne in 1862. By 1868 a certain Fr. Christophoros Arsenios had reportedly settled in Queensland, though no records survive of any liturgical services conducted.

By the middle of the 19th century, Greek immigrants began arriving in Australia and the first regular celebration of liturgical services occurred around 1895. Although precise details remain unclear or unknown, the first resident Orthodox priest was a Greek named Archimandrite Dorotheos Bakaliaros, who served communities in both Melbourne and Sydney. The foundations of the first Greek Orthodox parish were laid on May 29, 1898, for the Church of the Holy Trinity in Surry Hills, Sydney, and, two years later, in 1900, for the Church of the Annunciation in East Melbourne.

Like elsewhere in the diaspora, the canonical jurisdiction over the early communities is not entirely clear. What is abundantly clear, however, is that the communities were originally "mixed" – comprised of Greeks, Syrians, and Slavs – and so it is not surprising that clergy themselves were initially imported from the multi-ethnic patriarchate of Jerusalem. Such polyglot community leaders included the first duly assigned priest in Sydney, Fr. Seraphim Phokas, and the first priest specifically appointed for Melbourne, Fr. Athanasios Kantopoulos. Later Greek clergy knew no Arabic, and so the Syrians – arriving as immigrants in the 1880s – soon broke away to form their own communities in Melbourne and Sydney, the latter with Fr. Nicholas Shehadie, sent to Australia as official exarch of the patriarchate of Antioch in 1913. Brief jurisdiction of the Greeks in diaspora was initially transferred by the ecumenical patriarchate to the Church of Greece in 1908, but afterwards soon revoked with the formal issue of the Patriarchal Tomes establishing the metropolis of America in 1922 and the metropolis of Australia and New Zealand in 1924, under Ecumenical Patriarch Meletios IV. Thus, the Greek Orthodox metropolis of Australia and New Zealand was established "for the better organization of the Orthodox Church" in Australasia.

The first Serb priest, Fr. Svetozar Seculic, arrived in Sydney in 1948; the first Serb church was erected in Flemington, New South Wales, in 1953. From that period, the Serbian community – the largest after the Greeks – was administered by the patriarchate of Serbia until 1963, when two separate dioceses were created, currently functioning in parallel since 1992. A number of Russians migrated to Australia from Manchuria, and the first Russian parish was created in Brisbane as early as 1925. Under the Russian Orthodox Church Outside of Russia, the first bishop of Australia and New Zealand was Theodor, appointed in 1948. More recently, the Russian diocese was involved in the act, signed in 2007, of reentering canonical communion with the patriarchate of Moscow. The first Antiochian parish was established in Sydney in 1920, while the Antiochian Australasian diocese was formed in 1970, with Bishop Gibran as its first hierarch, and elevated to archdiocesan status in 1999. The first Romanian parish was established in Sydney in 1972, while the Romanian Orthodox episcopate of Australia and New Zealand was created in 2008. The first Bulgarian parish was created in 1950, with the few existing parishes administered by the ruling hierarch for the United States, Canada, and Australia.

The first Greek Orthodox metropolitan was Christophoros (1871–1959), fluent in English after graduate studies in St. Andrew's (Scotland) and Oxford (England). Christophoros served only until 1929 and was succeeded by Metropolitan Timotheos (1880–1949), elected in 1931 and serving until 1947. In 1949 Timotheos was elected archbishop of America to replace Athenagoras, but died before assuming that position. Metropolitan Theophylaktos (1891–1958), an Athonite monk, was elected and ordained in 1947; his tenure tragically ended with a car accident. Bishop Ezekiel (1913–87), formerly serving in the United States (as priest and, thereafter, as bishop and sub-dean at Holy Cross Seminary), was elected metropolitan in 1959, promoted that same year to archbishop with the elevation of the metropolis to archdiocese. His tenure proved turbulent, leading to the appointment of a patriarchal exarch in Metropolitan Iakovos from 1969 until 1970, when Archbishop Ezekiel returned until 1974. While Metropolitan Theophylaktos and Archbishop Ezekiel were in office, the Greek community grew rapidly, the result of unprecedented waves of emigration from wartorn Greece and Europe. In 1970 the ecumenical patriarchate separated New Zealand, creating a distinct metropolis, which later assumed responsibility for missions in Southeast Asia. The present Archbishop Stylianos (b. 1935) was elected in 1975 after serving as abbot of the Patriarchal Monastery of Vlatadon in Thessaloniki, where he also taught as university lecturer of systematic theology.

While the early years of Orthodox presence in Australia are characterized by a rudimentary sense of practical cooperation and unity, and whereas the original *Tome of the Ecumenical Patriarchate* specifically stated that it was intended to cover all Orthodox in Australia, it was not long before the various ethnic groups pursued their individual directions. A significant move toward greater cooperation occurred in September 1979, at the initiative of Archbishop Stylianos, with the formation of the Standing Council of Canonical Orthodox Churches in Australia (SCCOCA) in accordance with the SCOBA model in the United States. Archbishop Stylianos was appointed permanent chairman, while founding members included the Greek, Antiochian, Bulgarian, Romanian, and Serbian patriarchal groups, as well as the Russian Church Abroad, since almost all Russian Orthodox in Australasia belonged to this group. SCCOCA has been fraught with internal tensions and is yet to reach its full potential of expressing a common mind or pan-Orthodox consensus, beyond liturgical and doctrinal unity.

Similar discord gradually colored some of these constituent Orthodox groups internally, particularly the Greeks and the Serbs. The Greeks, for example, were first divided by more political and regional loyalties, later by overseas allegiances of Venizelists and Royalists, and then by patriarchal adherence and "community" opposition. The last of these divisions – originating under Christophoros and critically inflamed under Ezekiel – persists to this day, although its intensity has substantially dwindled.

Most Orthodox jurisdictions have some form of educational and welfare system, including retirement homes. However, as the largest and most efficiently organized among Orthodox jurisdictions, the Greek archdiocese possesses over one hundred parishes as well as a number of bilingual day-schools (from elementary through high school) in the major cities and a variety of impressive philanthropic institutions for the elderly (St. Basil's Homes) and disabled (Estia Foundation). Established in 1969, St. Basil's Homes has progressed exponentially to provide residential and daycare community-based services for the aged throughout Australia. Moreover, most jurisdictions also boast traditional monastic communities, whether larger or smaller, both male and female.

Several Orthodox clergy contributed to the scholarly world through the years. Fr. Seraphim Phokas published the first Orthodox book in Australia, the translation in 1905 of a religious novel. Metropolitan Christophoros had a thesis published in an English journal. The first local church magazine appeared under Metropolitan Timotheos. Metropolitan Iakovos authored a book entitled *Australia 1969*. With the tenure of Metropolitan Ezekiel, the church in Australia was organized more efficiently along the lines of the Greek Orthodox archdiocese in America. Thus, Archbishop Ezekiel introduced the Clergy-Laity Conferences (held in 1961, 1965, and 1972). Moreover, it came as no surprise that, as former professor and administrator at Holy Cross Seminary, Archbishop Ezekiel planned from the outset, as articulated in the archdiocesan *Yearbooks*, to establish a theological school. Under the present archbishop, who holds a doctoral degree from Germany and has published widely on theological as well as literary subjects,

Clergy-Laity Conferences are held with greater regularity every four years. Indeed, following a resolution at the Fourth Clergy-Laity Conference in Sydney in 1981, the dream of a theological school materialized and, in 1984, Archbishop Stylianos appointed an exploratory committee to determine the possibility of opening such an institution. Thus, in February 1986, St. Andrew's Theological College officially opened its doors as a fully accredited institute of the Sydney College of Divinity, through which students are today also able to pursue graduate degrees. The opening was attended by Metropolitan Maximos of Stavroupolis, dean of Halki, while the present Ecumenical Patriarch Bartholomew paid a visit to the college during the first official patriarchal journey to Australasia in 1996. The college publishes an annual entitled *Phronema*. It will take some time before the church in Australia begins to reap the benefits of a locally educated clergy; nevertheless, the bold step to create a theological school is already manifesting results inasmuch as its first graduates now staff administrative and teaching positions.

Of course, the bloodline of the church lies in its parishioners, clergy and laity, namely the hard-working pioneers, men and women, who constructed temples and donated halls, who developed the vision and supported the programs. Indeed, one of the peculiar features of the development of the Orthodox Church in Australia has been that lay people often preceded the clergy in movements of immigration and construction of communities. While (much like appointments in America) the ecumenical patriarchate has blessed Australia with uniquely enlightened hierarchs since the establishment of the church, the ministry of most metropolitans or archbishops in Australia (unlike the situation in America) has proved more conservative and less prophetic. In many ways this has reflected the different development of the communities in the two continents, where integration of the Orthodox Church into the local culture is less apparent than in the United States and more comparable to the migrant Orthodox communities in Canada.

Nevertheless, church history is often written on the marginal, less institutional levels, such as in the unassuming creativity of individual parish priests. Many of the early priests were well educated and bilingual, some emigrating from Asia Minor, and many introducing

English-language celebrations of the divine liturgy from the 1910s, when they also contributed religious articles in publications such as *To Vema* (now owned by the Greek Orthodox archdiocese); later clergy created the first bilingual day-schools (with seeds planted as early as the 1950s and full-fledged schools established in the 1970s), held broadcasts on radio and television as early as the 1950s, produced the first English-speaking journals, such as the *Australian Hellenic Youth Association* in the 1940s or *Enquiry* in the 1970s, or else established government-sponsored welfare centers in the 1970s. Such enterprising ministry undoubtedly provided the sound basis for later expressions in the form of university chaplaincies in the mid-1970s or prison chaplaincies in the 1980s, as well as the Archdiocesan Translation Committee for the translation of liturgical services in the 1990s. The question remains whether the newly established St. Andrew's Press will some day include publications at the cutting edge of visionary and critical theological thought. Certainly, however, what was once considered to be a Church of the Antipodes is today hailed as a vibrant and promising community.

SEE ALSO: Constantinople, Patriarchate of; Greece, Orthodox Church of

References and Suggested Readings

Gilchrist, H. (1992–7) *Australians and Greeks*, 3 vols. Rushcutters Bay, NSW: Halstead Press.
Simmons, H. L. N. (1986) *Orthodoxy in Australia*. Brookline, MA: Hellenic College Press.

Autocephaly *see* United States of America, Orthodoxy in the

Automelon *see* Idiomelon

B

Baptism

SERGEY TROSTYANSKIY

Baptism is the first sacrament of the Orthodox Church. In the Early Christian centuries this mystery was known under various names, including "the washing of regeneration," Illumination (*photismos*) and "the sacrament of water." In Christianity baptism is also considered the most important sacrament of the church, as it initiates one into mystical communion with Christ. Therefore, it is also called "the door" that leads peoples into the Christian Church. Baptism completely releases the believer from ancestral sin and personal sins committed up until that time. It is rebirth into new life, justification, and restoration of communion with God.

The theological significance of baptism in Orthodox Christianity is summed up in its primary sacramental symbols: water, oil, and sacred chrism. As Fr. Alexander Schmemann noted, water is the most ancient and universal of religious symbols. It has multiple, in some cases contradictory, scriptural significations attached to it. On the one hand, it is the principle of life, the primal matter of the world, a biblical symbol of the Divine Spirit (Jn. 4.10–14; 7.38–39); on the other, it is a symbol of destruction and death (the Flood, the drowning of the pharaoh), and of the irrational and demonic powers of the world (as in the icon of Jesus' baptism in the river Jordan). Sacramentally,

the use of water symbolizes purification, regeneration, and renewal. It has an extraordinary significance in the Creation narrative of the Old Testament, and is also a key symbol in the Exodus story. In the New Testament it is associated with St. John the Baptist and his washing of repentance and forgiveness. These three biblical types are combined powerfully in the Orthodox ritual of baptism.

In Christianity water became a symbol that incorporated the entire content of the Christian faith. It stands for creation, fall, redemption, life, death, and resurrection. St. Paul the Apostle in his Epistle to the Romans (6.3–11) gives a foundational account of this mystical symbolism. St. Cyril of Jerusalem, in his 4th-century homilies on the "awe-inspiring rites of initiation" (*Mystagogic Catecheses*) described what takes place during baptism as "an iconic imitation" of Christ's sufferings, death, and resurrection that constitutes our true salvation. Thus, here a believer dies and rises again "after the pattern" of Christ's death and resurrection. Death symbolizes sin, rejection of God, and the break of communion with God. Christ, however, destroyed death by removing sin and corruption. Here death becomes a passage into communion, love, and joy. Baptism dispenses divine grace which is given in the Spirit to humankind through Christ's mediation.

From Antiquity the rite of baptism started with lengthy preparations (shortened in later times when

The Concise Encyclopedia of Orthodox Christianity, First Edition. Edited by John Anthony McGuckin.
© 2014 John Wiley & Sons, Ltd. Published 2014 by John Wiley & Sons, Ltd.

infant baptism became a norm). The first preparatory step was enrollment, an inscription of the catechumen's name in the registration book of the local church. It signified that Christ took possession over this catechumen, and now included his or her name in "the book of life." The next step was exorcism, a serious and solemn set of rituals which were meant to liberate the catechumen from demonic powers and to restore his or her freedom. The catechumen renounced Satan. In the ritual today they still turn to the West, the symbolic dominion of Satan, and spit lifting up hands to appeal to God. Then the catechumen turns to the East, which symbolizes reorientation to the Paradise offered through Christ, and bows down, keeping the hands lowered to indicate surrender and submission. The priest then repeatedly asks the catechumen to confirm that he or she is united to Christ and believes in him as God. The catechumen confirms an unconditional commitment, faithfulness to Christ, and recites the Niceno-Constantinopolitan creed. At this point baptism itself begins with a solemn blessing of the waters. There are several elements of Orthodox Baptism: the anointing of the catechumen with blessed oil, the triple immersion in the sanctified water, the simultaneous baptismal formula of the invocation of the divine names of the Holy Trinity, and the "completion" of the water baptism with the "Seal of the Holy Spirit" in the Chrismation of the candidate with consecrated *myron*. The candidate is robed in white (the original meaning of the word *candidatus*) after the immersion, and their hair is cut (tonsured) as a sign of their vow (dedication to God). The ritual blessing of water starts with the solemn doxology: "Blessed is the Kingdom of the Father, and of the Son, and of the Holy Spirit." Then a long litany follows: "that this water may be sanctified with the power and effectual operation and the descent of the Holy Spirit." The power of the Holy Spirit visible through the sacrament is understood to recreate the fallen world, symbolized by the water, transforming it into the waters of redemption. Baptism makes the catechumen a partaker of the Kingdom of God through their sharing in the death and resurrection of Christ: their mystical embodiment with him. Through the blessing, the water of creation, corrupted by the Fall, now turns into the water of Jordan, the water of sanctification, the remission of sins, and salvation. Then the

baptismal water is anointed by the pouring in of blessed oil which here symbolizes healing, joy, and reconciliation. The triple immersion follows, symbolizing the three-day burial and resurrection of Christ, and the passing of the Israelites through the Red Sea, which is always performed in the name of the Holy Trinity. There are certain exceptions to this strict rule of immersion; for instance, those who are sick can be baptized by aspersion – that is, they have water poured over their heads – but this is never relaxed so as to become a standard alternative form in Orthodoxy.

The early church described another type of baptism when the catechumens were persecuted and suffered martyrdom in the name of Christ before their formal initiation. Those martyrs were said to have been admitted to Paradise by the baptism of blood. In the early Christian centuries most Christian catechumens

Plate 8   Baptism of a baby. Aristidis Vafeiadakis/Alamy.

were baptized in their adulthood. In the 4th century the fathers (such as St. Gregory the Theologian preaching *Orations on the Lights* in Constantinople in 380) had to encourage people not to leave their baptism until their deathbeds. Nevertheless, the baptism of infants was justified by all the early fathers. In 253 the Council of Carthage made it a recommended practice of the church. Baptism is never repeated. If a convert wishes to enter the Orthodox Church from another Christian communion it is the majority practice of the Greek and Russian traditions to chrismate a believer who has already been baptized by threefold washing in the name of the Trinity. If there is doubt over the form of liturgy that had been used, or if the convert is coming from no church background, the full service of baptism is always performed.

SEE ALSO: Catechumens; Chrismation; Exorcism; Grace; Holy Spirit; Mystery (Sacrament); Original Sin

References and Suggested Readings

Cyril of Jerusalem, St. (2008) *The Holy Sacraments of Baptism, Chrismation and Holy Communion: The Five Mystagogical Catechisms of St. Cyril of Jerusalem.* Rollinsford, NH: Orthodox Research Institute.

McGuckin, J. A. (2008) *The Orthodox Church: An Introduction to Its History, Doctrine, and Spiritual Practices.* Oxford: Wiley-Blackwell, pp. 277–88.

Sava-Popa, G. (1994) *Le Baptême dans la tradition orthodoxe et ses implications œcuméniques.* Fribourg: Editions Universitaires.

Schmemann, A. (1964) *For the Life of the World.* New York: National Student Christian Federation.

Schmemann, A. (1974) *Of Water and the Spirit.* Crestwood, NY: St. Vladimir's Seminary Press.

Barlaam of Calabria (ca. 1290–1348)

JOHN A. MCGUCKIN

Barlaam of Calabria (Bernardo Massari before he entered religion) was a 14th-century Italo-Byzantine Orthodox monk and cleric. He was the main intellectual opponent of St. Gregory Palamas and an instigator of the latter's defense of the Athonite Hesychast school. Moving from Byzantine-dominated Southern Italy, Barlaam came to Constantinople around 1330 and was part of the court of Emperor Andronikos Palaeologos, who sponsored him to become a university teacher in the capital (Aristotelian philosophy, and astronomy) and also promoted him as the higumen of the Savior Akataleptos Monastery. He was a leading theologian in the imperially sponsored attempts to broker a union with the Latin Church. In 1333–4 Barlaam was part of the mission negotiating terms of union with theologians of Pope John XXII, and in 1339 he was also sent to the royal courts of Naples and Paris, and came to Avignon on that occasion to talk with the exiled Pope Benedict XII. It was in the course of this visit that he met with, and taught some Greek to, the Renaissance poet Petrarch. Barlaam has often been elevated by subsequent Orthodox thought as a "rationalist" foil to the mystical approach of St. Gregory and the Athonite Hesychasts. He has sometimes had to play this role to excess, a parody of the "bad theologian" who uses Aristotelian syllogisms instead of the simple teachings of the fishermen; but he certainly privileged Aristotelian method and logic in his theological discourse, although the grounds for the argument were also rooted in the city-based schools of philosophical theology resisting the insistence of the monastics (especially the Athonites) that theology was now closed to new insights and had to follow only patristic precedent, as that was mediated predominantly through the ascetical lens. He attacked the Athonites in a very sarcastic *apologia* that focused on their "experiential" claim to be able to see the divine light (a theme found already in the 11th-century writings of St. Symeon the New Theologian, who advances it as a powerful pneumatological claim of the type that those who do not experience the living grace of the Spirit, consciously in their own lifetimes, are not truly Christian at all). Barlaam dismissed the monastics as ill-informed "navel-gazers" (*omphalopsychoi* – those who think their soul is in their belly-button), and used syllogistic logic to argue that if any "light" was seen in prayer it had to be a created light, being a material phenomenon that the eyes could relate to, and thus was certainly not the "Uncreated Light" of the Godhead.

St. Gregory Palamas was asked by the Athonites to mount a series of responses to Barlaam's attacks (conducted in a fraught political time) and Gregory did so in an extended series of works, chiefly the *Triads in Defence of the Hesychasts*, which laid down the intellectual basis for late Byzantine Hesychasm out of patristic cloth and personal experience in prayer. It has sometimes (but dismissively) been called Palamism in some studies. It has distinctive themes of spiritual transfiguration and the core distinction of the *essence* and *energies* of God: the divine essence being unapproachable and incomprehensible to all creatures, yet the divine energies being immanent and intimately near, and as themselves being divine, capable of allowing a mortal creature to access and experience the divine directly in this lifetime. The issue of Palamas' conflict with Barlaam turned around symbolic themes such as those related to the exegesis of the transfiguration story of the gospel. Patristic thought (for example, St. Maximos the Confessor or John of Damascus) (see McGuckin 1987) had indicated that the light of Thabor was a mystical apprehension in which the eyes of the apostles were given a supermaterial capacity. They saw the deity and were transfigured by its deifying radiance. Barlaam demanded a primacy of logic in the statements of theology, and a sharper (if not radically separate) distinction of creaturely and uncreated natures; perhaps unaware of the extent to which sophisticated theology of the Alexandria school had already articulated deification theology from the 5th century onwards. The battle was soon set over methods of discourse. The local Council of Constantinople in 1341 (two sessions known as the "Sophia synods") considered his works and ruled against them; after which he was forced to issue a retractation of his views, and his anti-hesychastic works were publicly burned. Barlaam left Constantinople soon afterwards, and was warmly received by the pope at Avignon (despite his having written twelve anti-Latin treatises against papal primacy and the *filioque* doctrine). The pope appointed him to the bishopric of Gerace in Calabria, where he lived the remainder of his life (1342–8). In 1351 another synod at the Blachernae palace in Constantinople anathematized him and his doctrine, and gave Hesychasm an official authorization as authentic Orthodox doctrine.

SEE ALSO: Deification; Hesychasm; St. Gregory Palamas (1296–1359)

References and Suggested Readings

Barlaam of Calabria (1857–1861) Works. In J. P. Migne (ed.) *Patrologia Graeca*, vol. 151, cols. 1255–82. Paris.

Jugie, M. (1932) "Barlaam de Seminara," in *Dictionnaire d'histoire et de géographie ecclésiastiques*, vol. 6, cols. 817–34. Paris.

McGuckin, J. A. (1987) *The Transfiguration of Christ in Scripture and Tradition*. Lewiston, NY: Edwin Mellen Press.

Meyendorff, J. (1987) *Byzantine Theology: Historical Trends and Doctrinal Themes*. New York: Fordham University Press.

Sinkewicz, R. E. (1982) "The Doctrine of the Knowledge of God in the Early Writings of Barlaam the Calabrian," *Medieval Studies* 44: 181–242.

Behr-Sigel, Elisabeth (1907–2005)

see Contemporary Orthodox Theology

Belarus *see* Lithuania, Orthodoxy in; Ukraine, Orthodoxy in the

Berdiaev, Nikolai A. (1874–1948)

KONSTANTIN GAVRILKIN

Nikolai Berdiaev (also spelled Nicholas Berdyaev) was one of the foremost representatives of a generation of Russian intellectuals, many of whom, after a shortlived interest in Marxism and socialism, embraced Orthodox Christianity in the 1900s and gave birth to the so-called Russian Religious Renaissance of the 20th century (Zernov 1963). Exiled from Russia by the Bolshevik regime in 1922, Berdiaev, after a short stay in Berlin, moved to France, where he spent the rest of his life (1924–48), playing a key role in uniting the intellectual forces of the Russian diaspora both as promoter of various academic and cultural institutions and editor-in-chief of the journal *Put'* which, under his leadership (1925–40), became the most significant Russian intellectual periodical of the time.

From the early books, *Philosophy of Freedom* (1911) and *The Meaning of Creativity* (1916), to the philosophic autobiography, published posthumously (1949), Berdiaev was preoccupied with the problems of freedom, creativity, and the dialectic of divine and human. Berdiaev believed that a static concept of God needed to be replaced with a dynamic one in order to provide an adequate understanding of human life and history. He argued that freedom was ontologically prior to God, who was bound by it himself. The creation of the world – of something that never existed before – was a unique act of freedom, the archetype of creativity. Human beings received from God the gift of freedom: it is reflected in personhood and creativity, the true image and likeness of God. However, human existence in the world is tragic, since freedom allows individuals to choose evil which cannot be eradicated except by the same free will. Furthermore, existence in the world is dualistic at its core: as a free and creative person, the human being belongs to the noumenal world of spirit, freedom, and creativity; as an individual, he or she is immersed in the phenomenal world of objectification through body, society, politics, culture, and economy.

According to Berdiaev, all human institutions, including the church, carry in themselves the threat of enslaving human spirit and freedom when they cease to encourage and promote creativity. The Russian revolutions, the collapse of the Romanov Empire, the two world wars, and the rise of totalitarian regimes in the Soviet Union and Nazi Germany – all of which he personally witnessed and experienced – he understood as the revolt of human spirit against the institutions that enslaved freedom in the name of false ideas. But the revolt itself led to a greater tragedy still. Berdiaev believed that the most tragic problem of modern history was the inherent dualism, the opposition between the church and the world. He was hopeful that the church of the Third Testament – the Testament of the Spirit – would embrace creativity and freedom, and that theosis and transfiguration of the world, rather than its damnation and curse, would again inspire the church in her path through history.

SEE ALSO: Russia, Patriarchal Orthodox Church of

References and Suggested Readings

Berdiaev, N. (1950) *Dream and Reality: An Essay in Autobiography*, trans. R. M. French. London: G. Bles.
Vallon, M. A. (1960) *An Apostle of Freedom: Life and Teachings of Nicolas Berdyaev*. New York: Philosophical Library.
Zernov, N. (1963) *The Russian Religious Renaissance of the Twentieth Century*. London: Darton, Longman, and Todd.

Bible

THEODORE G. STYLIANOPOULOS

The Bible, composed of the Old and New Testaments, is a rich and diverse library of sacred writings or scriptures derived from the Jewish and Christian traditions. "Bible" (from the Greek *biblos* meaning "document" or "book") points to the authority of the Bible as *the* book of divine revelation. "Scripture" (Greek *graphe*, meaning "what is written") signifies the actual content of the books proclaiming the authoritative message of salvation – the word of God. In a process lasting nearly four centuries, the ancient church preserved, selected, and gradually formed these sacred texts into two official lists or canons of the Old and New Testaments, respectively, a significant achievement that along with the shaping of the episcopacy and creed contributed to the growth and unity of the church. In Orthodox perspective, the Bible or Holy Scripture is the supreme record of God's revelation and therefore the standard of the church for worship, theology, spirituality, ethics, and practice.

The Bible is above all a book of God and about God – God himself being the primary author and the subject matter of the scriptures. The Bible bears testimony to who God is, what great acts of salvation God has accomplished, and what God's revealed will for humanity is, communicated through inspired men and women "in many and various ways" (Heb. 1.1). These "ways" include words, deeds, rites, laws, visions, symbols, parables, wisdom, ethical teachings, and commandments. The overall message of the Bible is the narrative of salvation about creation, fall, covenant, prophecy, exile, redemption, and hope of final world renewal. The supreme revelation of the mystery of God is through the life, ministry, death, and resurrection of Jesus Christ, "the Lord of glory" (1 Cor. 2.8), who constitutes the center of biblical revelation and marks the unity of the Old and New Testaments.

However, insofar as divine revelation occurred not in a vacuum but in relationship to free, willing, thinking, and acting human beings, the Bible also reflects a human and historical side which accounts for the variety of books, authors, language, style, customs, ideas, theological perspectives, numerous discrepancies in historical details, and sometimes substantial differences in teaching, especially between the Old and New Testaments. The word of God was revealed by divine condescension (*synkatabasis*) to human beings who, although inspired, wrote at different times, changing cultures, and by their own degree of understanding and literary skills. The paradox of the divine and human aspects of the Bible is to some extent comparable to the mystery of the incarnation itself, the divine and human natures of Jesus Christ. Both aspects of the Bible, the divine and the human, must be taken seriously in working out a balanced dynamic view of divine revelation and of the inspiration of the Bible, in order to pass clear of the Scylla of fundamentalism and the Charybdis of historicism.

By its origins and character, the Bible is also a book of the church. The biblical message or word of God is addressed to responsive human beings and summons them to a covenant relationship and personal communion with God. Before the writing of texts, God's revelation by word and deed was received by elect persons – leaders, priests, prophets, apostles, and others – who proclaimed God's message to a sustained community of faith, first Israel and then also the church. It was within the ongoing life of this community of faith that the ancient oral traditions and new divine interventions were celebrated, preserved, and eventually committed to writing. The community of faith was always the living and discerning context of the proclamation, reception, interpretation, transmission, and application of divine revelation in both its oral and written forms. Therefore, an organic bond exists between the church and its Bible because the community of faith, itself a result of divine initiative, is an integral part of God's revelation and stands behind the entire Bible which is shaped, transmitted, and utilized in various ways over the millennia by the church.

The Orthodox Church holds to the Greek *Septuagint* version of the Old Testament in its wider canon as the authoritative text. The church also follows closely the presuppositions and perspectives of the church fathers in interpretation pertaining to the entire Bible. The patristic theological heritage is fundamentally a biblical legacy richly enshrined in the prayers, hymnology, rites, theological writings, and doctrines of the church, an achievement of astonishing theological coherence and normative value. Chief among these critical principles are the following: (1) the unity, primacy, and centrality of the Bible; (2) Christ as the decisive criterion of salvation and of the interpretation of the Old Testament; (3) the interdependence of church, Bible, and tradition; and (4) the hermeneutical role of tradition, including the living witness of the church in every age, as the final authority over disputed interpretations of the Bible, expressed through ecumenical councils and the process of reception in the church.

The church fathers from Justin Martyr to St. Gregory the Theologian were erudite figures, intellectually open and conversant with the cultural currents and methodologies of their contemporary world. For example, in their study of the Bible, they did not invent but rather adapted the grammatical, allegorical, and typological methods of interpretation inherited from the Greek and Jewish traditions. In parallel, Orthodox scholars today countenance modern biblical studies and seek, with creative tensions, to define a genuinely Orthodox approach to biblical interpretation, being both faithful to the church's tradition and open to modern challenges and insights. The essential aim of Orthodox biblical interpretation remains the same: to give voice to the liberating and renewing witness of the scriptures, not only by explaining their contents, but also by facilitating an encounter with the living God within the context of the life of the church and its witness to the world.

SEE ALSO: Christ; Church (Orthodox Ecclesiology); Gospel; Patristics; Tradition

References and Suggested Readings

Allert, C. D. (2007) *A High View of Scripture? The Authority of the Bible and the Formation of the New Testament Canon.* Grand Rapids, MI: Baker Academic.

Breck, J. (2001) *Scripture in Tradition: The Bible and Its Interpretation in the Orthodox Church*. Crestwood, NY: St. Vladimir's Seminary Press.

Hall, C. A. (1998) *Reading Scripture with the Church Fathers*. Downers Grove, IL: InterVarsity Press.

Hopko, T. (1995) "The Church, the Bible, and Dogmatic Theology." In C. E. Braaten and R. W. Jenson (eds.) *Reclaiming the Bible for the Church*. Grand Rapids, MI: Eerdmans, pp. 107–18.

Louth, A. (1983) *Discerning the Mystery: An Essay on the Nature of Theology*. Oxford: Clarendon Press.

Metzger, B. M. (2001) *The Bible in Translation: Ancient and English Versions*. Grand Rapids, MI: Baker Academic.

Stylianopoulos, T. G. (1997) *The New Testament: An Orthodox Perspective, Vol. 1: Scripture, Tradition, Hermeneutics*. Brookline, MA: Holy Cross Orthodox Press.

Stylianopoulos, T. G. (ed.) (2006) *Sacred Text and Interpretation: Perspectives in Orthodox Biblical Studies*. Brookline, MA: Holy Cross Orthodox Press.

Stylianopoulos, T. G. (2008) "Scripture and Tradition in the Church." In M. Cunningham and E. Theokritoff (eds.) *The Cambridge Companion to Orthodox Christian Theology*. Cambridge: Cambridge University Press, pp. 21–34.

Bioethics, Orthodoxy and

PERRY T. HAMALIS

The term "bioethics" refers to a subset of the discipline of "ethics" that assesses and develops normative responses to issues at the intersection of health, medicine, and the life sciences. Bioethics emerged as a discrete academic discipline in the 1960s and has since developed into the most specialized field within applied ethics. While bioethics tends to focus on moral issues faced by single human persons and their families within a medical context (e.g., organ transplantation, reproductive technologies, abortion, and end-of-life care), it may also be understood in a broader sense that includes moral reflection upon communal dimensions of health (e.g., the provision of healthcare and the funding of stem cell research) as well as upon issues pertaining to non-human species and the environment (e.g., animal testing, genetic modification of plants, and climate change).

Throughout its history the Eastern Orthodox Church has engaged bioethical issues by articulating a vision for humanity's proper relationship toward non-human creation and by offering pastoral guidance and care to physicians, nurses, and Orthodox Christian patients who are making decisions about appropriate medical treatments. As the field of bioethics has grown over the past several decades, Orthodox thinkers have drawn from the church's tradition to develop guidelines and ethical principles with which to critique problematic tendencies in secular bioethics and construct more authentically Orthodox stances on specific issues confronted by the faithful (Breck 1998, 2005; Engelhardt 2000; Harakas 1990, 1992). In addition, representatives of Orthodoxy have worked collaboratively, through synodal statements (e.g., the "Bases of the Social Concept of the Russian Orthodox Church," 2000), ecclesial institutions (e.g., the Bioethics Committee of the Church of Greece, established 1998), and ecumenical efforts (e.g., the National Council of Churches' document on biotechnologies, "Fearfully and Wonderfully Made," 2006), in order to provide faithful responses to bioethical challenges.

As one of its subsets, Orthodox bioethics works within the same theological framework, serves the same ultimate aim, and employs the same methodology as Orthodox ethics broadly understood. Thus, Orthodox bioethics starts with the church's understanding of God as Holy Trinity, of human persons as being created in the "divine image and likeness" (Gen. 1:26), and of the goodness of God's creation. Since, from an Orthodox perspective, all of creation fell into a condition of corruption, sickness, suffering, and death, the ultimate purpose of Orthodox bioethics is to guide human thinking and acting so as to promote, through the grace of the Holy Trinity, the resurrection or deification of human persons and the healing, sanctification, and salvation of the whole cosmos.

Methodologically, the church's bioethical tradition draws from a wide range of sources, including Scripture, creeds, dogmas, liturgy, ascetical practices, hagiographies, canons, and icons, as well as from the best available scientific knowledge when developing normative principles and expressing stances. Particularly relevant to Orthodox bioethics are the church's teachings on (1) the natural world's creation and ordering by God; (2) human beings as unities of body and spirit who are utterly unique and eternally valuable; (3) the goodness of physical health and the philanthropic call to care for one's neighbor, as reflected in the lives and teachings of physician saints and in the divine services for healing;

(4) the potentially redemptive role of physical suffering and of ascetic and faithful responses to pain and illness; and (5) the value of rightly utilized science and technology, as exemplified in patristic authors who were steeped in the science of their day and who incorporated scientific claims into their responses to people's specific needs.

Since so many of the issues that arise in bioethics were never addressed directly in the church's traditional sources (e.g., the procurement and use of stem cells), Orthodox bioethicists must strive to "acquire the mind of the church" so as to relate Orthodoxy's universal and ancient ethical teachings to the particular and new situations confronted today (Breck 2005; Engelhardt 2000; Harakas 1992). Toward this end, Orthodox bioethicists immerse themselves in the church's liturgical ethos, study the tradition's sources, seek the assistance of natural scientists, and strive to acquire the virtue of discernment (Greek, *diakrisis*) so that teachings they express support the ultimate aim of bringing human persons and the natural world into saving communion with each other and God.

In its approach to issues ranging from fertility treatments to euthanasia to abortion and genetic engineering, Orthodoxy reflects a freedom and flexibility that takes personal circumstances into account, as well as several strong normative tendencies. Among these tendencies are an insistence upon the sacredness of every human being, an affirmation of humanity's call to responsible stewardship of nature, a reverence for sacramental marriage between one man and one woman as the proper context for procreation, a preference for respecting and restoring natural processes as opposed to artificially manipulating or creating new processes for transmitting life, and an eschatological viewpoint that does not place absolute value on earthly existence, but rather venerates earthly life as a gift oriented ultimately toward God's eternal kingdom.

SEE ALSO: Death (and Funeral); Ethics; Humanity; Marriage; Sexual Ethics

References and Suggested Readings

Breck, J. (1998) *The Sacred Gift of Life: Orthodox Christianity and Bioethics*. Crestwood, NY: St. Vladimir's Seminary Press.

Breck, J. (2005) *Stages on Life's Way: Orthodox Thinking on Bioethics*. Crestwood, NY: St. Vladimir's Seminary Press.

Engelhardt, H.T. (2000) *The Foundations of Christian Bioethics*. Lisse, Netherlands: Swets and Zeitlinger.

Guroian, V. (1996) *Life's Living Toward Dying: A Theological and Medical-Ethical Study*. Grand Rapids, MI: Eerdmans.

Harakas, S. (1990) *Health and Medicine in the Eastern Orthodox Tradition*. New York: Crossroad.

Harakas, S. (1992) *Living the Faith: The Praxis of Eastern Orthodox Ethics*. Minneapolis: Light and Life.

Hatzinikolaou, N. (2003) "Prolonging Life or Hindering Death? An Orthodox Perspective on Death, Dying and Euthanasia," *Christian Bioethics* 9: 187–201.

Larchet, J.-C. (2002) *The Theology of Illness*, trans. J. Breck. Crestwood, NY: St. Vladimir's Seminary Press.

LeMasters, P. (2008) *The Goodness of God's Creation*. Salisbury, MA: Regina Orthodox Press.

Blessing Rituals

JEFFREY B. PETTIS

In the Scriptures the concept "to bless" means to give favor. For example, in Genesis 27.11 Isaac receives the favor or blessing (Hebrew, *brch*) of his father Jacob. In Numbers 24.1 Balaam prayed and "saw that it pleased the Lord to bless Israel." With both of these examples blessings occur as an automatic action apart from moral conditions or expectation. There also occurs the liturgical blessing of persons (Num. 6.22ff.) and of food (1 Sam. 9.13; cf. Matt. 14.19). The Greek Septuagint and the New Testament translates this concept of blessing as *eulogeō* ("to speak well of"). In Luke 1.64 the mouth of the dumb Zachariah was opened and he "spoke praises" (*elalei eulogōn*) to God (also Acts 3.26). *Eulogeō* may also mean to ask for the bestowal of special favor, especially by the act of calling down God's gracious power. In Hebrews 7.1 the high priest Melchizedek, the King of Salem, meets Abraham returning from battle and blesses him (see also Luke 24.50f.; cf. Gen. 14.19; 1 Clem. 15.3).

Rooted in the biblical tradition, the Orthodox Church continues the tradition of offering blessings on persons and objects associated with the life in Christ (icons, worship-related objects such as holy water or crosses, or objects related to the believer's lifestyle), and reserves the "sacramental" character of the blessing by

Plate 9   Russian priest monk blessing Paschal kulich cake. RIA Novosti/AKG.

seeing it as appropriately given by a bishop or a priest. A believer approaches for a blessing with a gesture of the hands in cupped shape. The bishop or priest signs the believer's head with the sign of the cross and invokes the name of God over them. Ritual objects are blessed with special priestly prayers and the making of the sign of the cross over the article three times with the sprinkling of holy water. Many times during the liturgy the celebrant blesses the people with the cross or with the hand held in the shape of the name of Jesus: again delineating that the blessing is "In the Name" of the Lord. The Orthodox Service Book contains many priestly blessings; for guarding someone from evil influence, to secure a home and a family's godly endeavors, for the blessing of houses, farms, schools, wells, and so forth. The blessing ceremony of a foundation of a new church is of an especially solemn character, its ritual prescribed in the bishops' service book.

In many cultures of Eastern Orthodoxy parents also bless the young, laying their hands on their heads and using the simple declarative: "God bless you." In daily prayers the believer can often call upon God's blessing, as for example in this commonly used nighttime prayer: "Into thy hands, O Lord, I commend my soul and my body. Do thou thyself bless me, have mercy upon me, and grant me life eternal. Amen."

SEE ALSO: Chrismation; Confession

References and Suggested Readings

Bromily, G.W. and Barrett, D.B. (eds.) (1999) *The Encyclopedia of Christianity*. Grand Rapids, MI: Brill.

Patrinacos, N. E. (1984) *A Dictionary of Greek Orthodoxy*. Pleasantville, NY: Hellenic Heritage Publications.

Bogomils

AUGUSTINE CASIDAY

"In the reign of the good Christian Tsar Peter [927–69] there was a priest called Bogomil, (meaning: worthy of God's compassion) but in reality Bogunemil (unworthy of God's compassion), who started for the first time to preach heresy in the country of Bulgaria" – thus, Cosmas the Presbyter describes the matter in his 10th-century *Discourse* (Hamilton and Hamilton 1998: 114–34). But a problem immediately confronted Cosmas and other observers, and it continues to confront modern scholars, because in order to evaluate and criticize Bogomil's heresy, Cosmas and others instinctively turned to categories that derived from classical denunciations of earlier heresies. The framework of those denunciations will be considered before we turn to evidence about Bogomil's teachings, and then to the history of Bogomil's communities.

The major heresy invoked to understand the Bogomils was dualism, a pronounced insistence on the substantial existence of two fundamental and opposed principles: good and evil. A typical dualist identifies evil with matter and good with spirit, and so regards creation as a domain in which evil and good intersect. The best-known dualist movement was Manichaeism, with the result that Byzantine Christians used the word "Manichaean" indiscriminately to describe any and every sort of dualistic spirituality. We can see this process at work in the *Synodikon of Orthodoxy*, where Bogomil is anathematized in these terms: "Anathema to papa Bogomil who, in the reign of Peter of Bulgaria, stirred up this Manichaean heresy and spread it through every town and countryside." Another dualist Christianity known as Paulicianism was a recent precursor of Bogomil's teachings that originated in Armenia and moved into Bulgaria (Runciman 1947: 26–62; Hamilton and Hamilton 1998: 5–25). The extent to which Bogomil's teachings are actually related to Manichaeism and Paulicianism is debatable and one's position in that debate will largely determine how historical details are integrated in the attempt to describe Bogomilism.

Similarly, a common label attached by the Byzantines to any form of Christian asceticism that was deemed suspect is "Messalian." This term signals a rejection of the institutional church and its sacraments in favor of intense prayer leading to a personal relationship with God, often cultivated privately within a monastery (Obolensky 1948: 48–52). The 12th-century commentator Euthymius Zigabenus asserts the connection between Messalianism and Bogomilism in his *Dogmatic Panoply* (Hamilton and Hamilton 1998: 180–207): "The heresy of the Bogomils … is part of the Messalian heresy, and for the most part shares their doctrines, but with some additional points which increase the pollution." It is interesting to note that, when Bogomilism made its appearance on Mount Athos, both the Bogomils and the Hesychasts were accused of Messalianism (Rigo 1989). In any case, because Bogomilism is refracted in the earliest records through other rejected systems of belief and practice, a high degree of prudence is needed in any attempt to account for Bogomil's actual teachings.

What does seem reasonably clear is that Bogomils were pacifist ascetics, unlike the war-like Paulicians. According to Cosmas, Euthymius, and Anna Comnena, the Bogomils rejected the cult of saints, did not venerate the cross or icons, and disavowed Orthodox liturgical prayers, using exclusively the Our Father. They had no use for clerical orders, heavily reinterpreted key passages used in Orthodox tradition to validate the sacraments, and practiced confession to one another without regard to gender or clergy. But they were willing to feign Orthodox devotions to avoid detection: "They do not baptize in faith, but make game of holy baptism … saying to their disciples that it is water and oil" (Hamilton and Hamilton 1998: 149). Dissenting from traditional worship is a straightforward option in religious nonconformity. What is more surprising is that the Bogomils identify Satan as the brother of God the Word. As Euthymius reports, "They say that the demon whom the Saviour called Satan is himself also a son of God the Father, called Satanael; he came before the Son, the Word, and is stronger, as befits the first-born; that they are brothers one of the other" (Hamilton and Hamilton 1998: 183). Euthymius also relates how the Bogomils identify Satan(ael) as creator of the visible world.

The subjugation of Satan to God the Father has led some scholars to conclude that Bogomil theology evolved from strict dualism into a Monarchian theology in which God the Father is the ultimate source of all and Satan is, so to speak, a fallen prince (thus, Runciman

1947: 74–5, 81–6; but see the critique in Obolensky 1948: 158–62, 271–4). Whether such a message, delivered some two centuries after Bogomil's death, is true to Bogomil's original preaching cannot be said with certainty. But what is clear is that the movement bearing his name spread from Bulgaria into Constantinople and Rus' to the East and also found an audience in Bosnia and further west along the Mediterranean basin. Again, the historical connection between the Paterenes of Italy and the Cathars or Albigensians of France on the one hand and the Bogomils on the other cannot be established with precision. But it is at the very least suggestive that the Cathars' Council of Saint-Félix (ca. 1170), which settled the boundaries of dioceses in Italy and France and attempted to bring those dioceses to a strict dualist theology, was presided over by Niquinta or Nicetas, the "Pope of Constantinople," who is traditionally identified as a Bogomil (Hamilton and Hamilton 1998: 250–3).

Because Bogomil preached during the very early days of organized Christianity in Bulgaria, it seems likely that his message spoke to disenfranchised and poor Christians (perhaps by retrieving themes from pre-Christian belief, though this is by no means certain). Like other forms of medieval dualist Christianity, Bogomilism attempted a reform of the church in a direction that was popularly accessible on the basis of apocryphal texts and a deep instinct that something is profoundly wrong in the world. For those reasons and for its aberrant theological perspective on matter, the Bogomil church was regularly condemned by the relevant Orthodox authorities and its members were on occasion legally persecuted by the secular arm. However, it was less this rejection that brought about the end for the Bogomils. Instead, prevalent social circumstances that gave rise to and made sense of that message were wiped away in the East by the advances of the Turks.

SEE ALSO: Asceticism; Bulgaria, Patriarchal Orthodox Church of; Confession; Hesychasm; Icons

References and Suggested Readings

Hamilton, B. and Hamilton, J. (1998) *Christian Dualist Heresies in the Byzantine World, c. 650–c. 1450: Selected Sources*. Manchester: Manchester University Press.

Obolensky, D. (1948) *The Bogomils: A Study in Balkan Neo-Manichaeism*. Cambridge: Cambridge University Press.

Rigo, A. (1989) *Monaci esicasti e monaci bogomili*. Florence: Olschki.

Runciman, S. (1947) *The Medieval Manichee*. Cambridge: Cambridge University Press.

Bulgakov, Sergius (Sergei) (1871–1944)

PAUL GAVRILYUK

Bulgakov combines many aspects in his life: Orthodox priest, theologian, religious philosopher, and economist. As a thinker he was interested in all major questions of human existence, offering a comprehensive religious vision of the world, particularly in light of the concept of *Sophia*, or "Godmanhood."

Born into the family of a provincial priest at Livny in Russia, Bulgakov began his education at church-run schools. Having experienced a crisis of faith and being attracted to Marxism, he went on to study law and economics at the University of Moscow (1890–4). On the completion of his studies, he taught economics at Moscow (1895–1901) and Kiev (1901–6). During these years he became disillusioned with Marxist theory and gradually embraced a form of religious idealism, an intellectual evolution which he traced in a collection of essays entitled *From Marxism to Idealism* (1896–1903).

Upon his return to Moscow in 1906, Bulgakov rose to prominence as a public intellectual, participating in the Russian religious and cultural renaissance known as the "Silver Age." In 1909 Bulgakov cooperated with Nikolai Berdiaev, Semen L. Frank, and others in a collection of programmatic essays entitled *Landmarks*, which warned the Russian intelligentsia against the devastating consequences of the socialist revolution. Bulgakov construed revolutionary socialism as a form of surrogate religion, mimicking various features of apocalyptic Judaism and Orthodox Christianity. In his doctoral thesis, *Philosophy of Economy* (1912), Bulgakov offered an economic theory that moved further away from Marxism and was informed by philosophical idealism. *The Unfading Light* (1918), written during 1911–16, provides a first sketch of Bulgakov's sophiological system, focusing on such issues as the nature of religion, apophatic theology, metaphysical problems of the relationship between God and creation, and human nature.

Bulgakov played a leading role at the All-Russian Council of the Russian Orthodox Church of 1917–18. He was ordained an Orthodox priest in June 1918. With the Bolsheviks in power, Bulgakov was forced to resign from his post as a professor of economics at the University of Moscow and moved to Crimea (1919–22). Expelled from the Soviet Union in early 1923, Bulgakov eventually settled in Paris, where he became the first dean of the newly established St. Sergius Theological Institute. Outside Russia Bulgakov wrote the so-called "minor trilogy" consisting of *The Burning Bush* (1927), which develops Orthodox teaching regarding Theotokos and offers a critique of the Roman Catholic dogma of the Immaculate Conception; *The Friend of the Bridegroom* (1928), which discusses the role of John the Baptist in the history of salvation; and *Jacob's Ladder* (1929), which develops Orthodox angelology. Bulgakov developed a comprehensive sophiological system in his second trilogy, *On Godmanhood*, comprising *The Lamb of God* (kenotic Christology and a sophiological interpretation of the Chalcedonian Christology); *The Comforter* (pneumatology); and *The Bride of the Lamb* (ecclesiology, universalist eschatology, anthropology, and hamartology). While Bulgakov's sophiology was criticized by Vladimir Lossky and condemned by some church hierarchs as heretical, attention to his work continues to increase both in post-Perestroika Russia and in the West, where his fuller corpus continues to appear in English translation.

SEE ALSO: Florovsky, Georges V. (1893–1979); Lossky, Vladimir (1903–1958); Sophiology

References and Suggested Readings

Bulgakov, S. (1997) *The Orthodox Church*. Crestwood, NY: St. Vladimir's Seminary Press.
Bulgakov, S. (2001) *The Bride of the Lamb*. Grand Rapids, MI: Eerdmans.
Bulgakov, S. (2003) *The Friend of the Bridegroom: On the Orthodox Veneration of the Forerunner*. Grand Rapids, MI: Eerdmans.
Bulgakov, S. (2004) *The Comforter*. Grand Rapids, MI: Eerdmans.
Bulgakov, S. (2007) *The Lamb of God*. Grand Rapids, MI: Eerdmans.
Valliere, P. (2000) *Modern Russian Theology*. Edinburgh: T&T Clark.

Bulgaria, Patriarchal Orthodox Church of

STAMENKA E. ANTONOVA

The Bulgarian state was established in 681 CE by Khan Asparuch (681–700) on the territory of the Roman imperial provinces of Thrace and Illyria to the south of the Danube river. Khan Asparuch was the leader of the Bulgars, who were Turanian nomads originating from Central Asia, who first led his people across the Danube into territory of the Roman Empire, and then established a long line of successors. In addition to the Bulgars, who possessed warlike tendencies and initiated later expeditions and territorial expansions, there were also Slavs who had been gradually immigrating and settling in the same region from the beginning of the 6th century. In spite of the fact that the Slavs were more numerous than the Bulgars, the latter gained hegemony due to their more aggressive policies. In 681 the Byzantine Empire was compelled to negotiate a peace treaty with Khan Asparuch and to legitimize the claims to power and territory by the immigrant population. In spite of the fact that a peace treaty was made, however, the Bulgars continued to pose a challenge to Byzantine authority. In 811 Khan Krum (803–14) defeated and killed the Byzantine Emperor Nicephorus I (802–11), after an unsuccessful attempt on the part of the emperor to vanquish the new state. In 813 Khan Krum defeated Emperor Michael I, in addition to sacking the city of Adrianople and advancing as far as the walls of the city of Constantinople. After the sudden death of Kahn Krum, his successors Khan Omurtag (814–31) and Khan Malamir (831–52) agreed terms with the Byzantine Empire, and stopped the expansion of the Bulgar state to the east, turning instead to Macedonia and territories westward.

Although there were pockets of Christians in the new Bulgar state from its inception, they were not only marginal in number but were also suspected by the political leaders as having allegiance to the emperor at Constantinople. In addition to the local Christians (who were indeed under the influence of Byzantine Christian civilization at the time), the Bulgars and the Slavs followed ancestral religious practices and worshipped the sky-god Tengri. Most of the hostile attitude toward Christianity in this era was primarily due to the Bulgars' fear of Byzantine imperialism and the possibility of strengthening Byzantine influence among the more numerous Slavs. As a result, when Khan Omurtag's son Enravotas converted to Christianity, he was executed publicly along with others in 833. In order to protect the political and religious integrity of the Bulgar state, Khan Omurtag also formed an alliance with the Frankish Kingdom against Byzantium.

In the 9th century the problem of conversion to Christianity became more pronounced, as a greater number of the Khan's subjects, including members of the ruling elite, decided to accept the Christian religion. Furthermore, internal divisions along ethnic and religious lines undermined the centralizing efforts of the Bulgars, as well as their ability to conduct diplomatic relations with other states. Although the nominal date of 865 for the conversion of Khan Boris is taken as the marker of the acceptance of Christianity by the Bulgar state, it is clear that long before that time Christian influence was both present and significant among the Bulgars. During the official process of Christianization initiated in 865, Khan Boris faced not merely external problems and challenges, but also internal ones with regard to the ethnic and religious diversity within the state. In spite of concerted efforts to bring about a greater unity, ethnic and cultural divisions between the Slavs and Bulgars persisted and prevented any complete integration of the population. In the unifying force of the Christian religion, Khan Boris perceived the possibility of bringing together the different ethnic groups constituting the population, in order to consolidate and to strengthen the nation. He perceived that in order to achieve diplomatic acceptance and legitimation of the Bulgar state, as well as to convince the majority Slav population to accept Bulgar authority, the best way forward was to introduce Christianity as the official state religion.

With the baptism and conversion of Khan Boris and the Christianization of the Bulgar state, however, the problem of political dependency on the Byzantine Empire came to the fore, as the (feared) Byzantinization process seemed inevitable. Khan Boris and the Bulgarian royal family wanted to maintain the independence of the state from the political and religious hegemony of the Byzantine Empire after the fact of the Christianization of the people. In order to accomplish this purpose, Khan Boris met in 862 with Louis, King of the Franks, with whom Khan Omurtag had formed a political alliance earlier, to discuss military and religious collaboration and to ask for Latin clergy to be sent to teach and convert the Bulgarian people. As a reaction against Khan Boris's attempt to accept Latin Christianity, Byzantium urged its Christian sympathizers in the state to vanquish the state leader. After being pressed on three sides and stricken with natural disasters of earthquake and famine at the same time, Khan Boris decided to sign a peace treaty. The terms of the agreement stipulated that Bulgaria would terminate its relations with the Franks and accept only Orthodox Christianity from Constantinople. As a result of this treaty, Khan Boris was compelled to accept the faith of the Byzantines and to affirm the overall suzerainty of the Byzantine emperor. Yet, even after this agreement, Khan Boris attempted to appeal to the West, as he feared the political and religious hegemony of the Byzantines, and thus a fierce battle for ecclesiastical jurisdiction ensued for many years afterwards, between Rome and Constantinople, the two greatest, yet competing, centers of Christian evangelization at the time. For a considerable time Khan Boris tried to maneuver between Rome and Constantinople in order to obtain ecclesiastic independence for his nation, but these attempts were denied independently by both Patriarch Photius and Pope Nicholas I. Khan Boris was finally satisfied when the question of Bulgarian ecclesiastic allegiance was formally discussed at a council in 869–70 and it was determined that its jurisdiction should lie with the patriarchate of Constantinople; when it was then also granted an archbishop of its own.

The first major task undertaken by Khan Boris was the baptism of his subjects and for this purpose he appealed for help to Byzantine priests between 864 and 866, after which point he also turned for assistance to Latin priests. Even so, the process of the conversion of the population took much longer than he had imagined. In 885 when the disciples of Cyril and

Methodios were expelled from Moravia, they were welcomed in the Bulgarian Khanate and put to the task of baptizing Macedonian Slavs. Although Khan Boris's efforts were concentrated on the gradual baptism and conversion of the people, he also faced the major problem of educating his subjects and informing them about the basic tenets and the outward forms of Christian faith and worship. Realizing eventually that the complete independence of the Bulgarian Church was out of the question, Khan Boris took steps to increase the number of indigenous clergy towards the end of his rule by sending large numbers of Bulgarians to Constantinople for education. Khan Boris's own son Simeon was also sent to Constantinople to become a monk in 878 in order to obtain a solid monastic training.

Regardless of the religio-political conflicts, it is clear that by the 9th century Christianity had penetrated to the very center of the Bulgarian state and even into Khan Boris's own family. Boris's sister became a convert to Christianity, as did his cousin Khavkhan Petur, who was sent later as an envoy to Rome and to Constantinople. Khan Boris himself abdicated in 889 in order to enter a monastery. It should also be noted that at the same time when Christianity had become more visible and significant, there was also fierce opposition from the upholders of the indigenous religious traditions, some of whom saw conversion to Christianity as a sign of national treason. Khan Boris vanquished a revolt of the boyars in 865 by brutally crushing the rebels in a battle near the capital Pliska and killing fifty-two members of the pagan aristocracy, who were the leaders of the rebellion. Furthermore, with the introduction of the new religion, the khan no longer was content to be *primus inter pares* among the boyars, but accepted the Byzantine title of prince (tsar/caesar) over them.

Missionary Activity of St. Constantine-Cyril (CA. 826–869) and St. Methodios (815–885)

These two brothers were born in Thessalonica and came from a family that was part of the highly educated Byzantine elite. Methodios held a high administrative post of an *archon* in one of the Slav provinces and later became a monk and an abbot on Mount Olympus. Constantine, the younger brother, who excelled as a scholar, held a chair of philosophy at the University of Constantinople during the 850s. He left his academic post and became ordained as a deacon before joining his brother Constantine on Mount Olympus. Upon the request of the Moravian Prince Rostislav, who expressed the need for teachers to explain to the people the tenets of the Christian faith in their own language, Cyril and Methodios embarked on lengthy missionary activity among the Slavic population. Before departing for Moravia in the autumn of 863, the brothers created an alphabet suitable for the Slavonic language. The success of their mission among the Slavic population in Moravia and elsewhere was due to the fact that they were able to communicate in the Slavonic language and provide written Slavonic translations of the Scriptures and of the liturgy that were instrumental in the training of local clergy. They were sent to Moravia with the blessing of the Byzantine patriarch, but they were supported during their activity there mainly by the Latin Church and only to a limited degree. In fact, the two brothers were ordained by the Latin Church in 868, Cyril as a monk and Methodios as an archbishop of Pannonia. After the death of Cyril in 869, the mission to the Moravian people led by Methodios encountered increasing opposition at the hands of Frankish priests and by the Latin-German clergy, which claimed that only three languages were worthy of expressing God's word, namely Hebrew, Greek, and Latin. In the course of this struggle between the Byzantine and the Frankish clergy, the activity of the two brothers and their disciples was eventually suppressed and marginalized. After the death of Methodios in 885, their disciples were finally driven out of Moravia and forced to cease their missionary activity to the Slavic people in that territory.

The Slavonic Mission in Bulgaria

Kliment, Naum, and Angelarius, three of Cyril and Methodios' closest disciples, consequently fled from Moravia down the Danube river to Bulgarian territory and were warmly welcomed by Khan Boris. The khan, who had been seeking ways to oppose Byzantine supremacy, perceived the importance of the mission to the Slavonic-speaking population by the followers of Cyril and Methodios. In order to bring the Macedonian Slavs under his rule, who were the most recent converts to Christianity, Khan Boris was at last able to offer to them a Slavonic version of Christianity, thereby being able to unite his subjects by a common Christian faith and a common religious language. The missionaries were instrumental in the conversion and the education of indigenous clergy, as they were able to train many individuals and to multiply greatly the number of Slavonic liturgical and other religious texts. Kliment was especially commissioned by Khan Boris to become the mission leader and teacher of the Slavs and he dedicated the remainder of his life teaching, preaching, and writing in Macedonia. Kliment's activity as a teacher was both successful and influential in the process of conversion and education of the elite. At this same time, Khan Boris decided to replace Greek with Slavonic as the official language of both the state and the church. By the end of Khan Boris's rule in 894, when he abdicated his throne and designated his son Simeon as his successor, the mission of Cyril and Methodios' disciples had produced a large body of Slavonic literature and a considerable number of indigenously trained clergy, thereby strengthening the position of the Christian Church in the Bulgar tsardom and increasing its independence from Byzantium. It is hardly surprising, therefore, that the first act of Khan Simeon was to promote Kliment to the rank of metropolitan of the Ohrid diocese in keeping with the political and religious trajectory of his father. By the time of Boris's death in 907, the Bulgarian Church had clearly evolved substantially from its inception and reflected the agenda for unification and independence that the khan had pursued from the very beginning.

Rise of Bogomilism

After the conversion of the Slavs and Bulgars and the acceptance of Byzantine Christianity by the state, the rise of the dualistic Christian movement known as Bogomilism in the 10th century became important for the development of the Bulgarian Church. This movement gained a wide popular currency and stood in stark opposition to the official church's hierarchical institutional structures. This dualistic heterodox movement preached the value of poverty, simplicity, and asceticism and came to challenge directly the claims to worldly power and wealth advanced by the church establishment. The Bulgarian priest, Father Bogomil, who is considered to be the originator of the movement, encouraged his disciples to live as monks, to meet for prayer at regular times, to remain celibate, and to abstain from eating meat and drinking alcohol in order to achieve Christian perfection. While other Christians would give up the same things as a temporary ascetic practice of self-discipline, the Bogomils rejected them as being inherently and ontologically evil and therefore incompatible with the Christian life. In contrast to the church's teaching that God was the creator of the world and the source of perfection and goodness, the Bogomils believed that moral evil, physical suffering, cruelty, decay, and death were the creation of the "Evil One" rather than God, who cannot be the source of any evil. The spread and the success of Bogomilism was also due to the fact that the Cyrillic alphabet was used to great effect for the propagation and popularization of their ideas.

Given the political, economic, and religious circumstances of the 10th century, as is exemplified by the reign of the Bulgarian Tsar Peter (927–69), who made an alliance with the Byzantine Emperor Romanos I Lecapenos and was granted the title of *Basileus* (King), the heterodox teachings of the Bogomils gained the attention and support of many of the ordinary people. In 925 Tsar Peter was successful in gaining the grant of autocephaly for the Bulgarian Church, after his marriage to Maria Lecapena, the emperor's granddaughter, and he thereafter followed a strong policy of the Byzantinization of the Bulgarian Kingdom. Byzantine influence was present not only in Peter's court but also in the Bulgarian Church with respect to music, literature, church architecture and decoration. As the church grew rapidly in wealth and prosperity, there was increasing alienation of the general populace from the expanding power of the ruling elite, which also gave rise to a revolt in the 10th century. In the midst of these new socioeconomic and religio-political circumstances in the Bulgarian state, the popular appeal of Bogomilism as an oppositional movement against the growing authority and prosperity of the Byzantine Church has to be contextualized. In his treatise *Against the Bogomils* the Bulgarian priest Cosmas suggests that the rise of the heresy can be attributed to the fact that the clergy had not only turned into greedy and wealthy landowners, oppressing the peasantry, but had also exhibited a corruption of morals by widespread vices, such as drunkenness and sloth. Cosmas criticized the clergy and the monks, complaining that the latter lived worldly lives, reneged on their monastic vows, engaged in financial transactions, and traveled freely under the guise of pilgrimages. From the writings of Cosmas the Presbyter, it seems that the Bulgarian Church had ceased to meet the spiritual and practical aspirations of the population, thus leaving a vacuum in which the Bogomil movement flourished very successfully. In spite of repeated attempts to rid the territory of the Bogomils, the state leaders and the church encountered a strongly rooted following of Bogomilism and were unable to exterminate it. There were periods when it grew or subsided, in accordance with the levels of toleration or opposition shown by the authorities. It was only in 1211, however, that the Council of Turnovo was convened by Tsar Boril in order to legislate officially against Bogomilism, although this movement had already been anathematized long before by both the Byzantine and the Latin churches.

Ottoman Period

Bulgaria experienced one of its richest cultural periods during the reign of Tsar Ivan Alexander (1331–71), when numerous churches and monasteries were built, and literary production and religious art flourished in the forms of illuminated manuscripts, icons, and frescoes. Nonetheless, the kingdom devolved, as it was divided into three regional states governed by Tsar Ivan Shishman (1371–93), Ivan Stratismir, the tsar's half-brother, and Ivanko, a rebel boyar. Unfortunately, the political division and disunity in Bulgaria, coupled with the inability of the other Balkan states to form an alliance against the Ottoman expansion, led to the easy conquest of the Balkan territories. After an unsuccessful attempt by Shishman to

check the advance of the Ottomans in the battle of Chernomen, close to Adrianople, in 1371, the Ottomans started a process of the gradual subjugation of all the Bulgarian territories. The Bulgarian Patriarch Evtimi and the ecclesiastic leadership in Turnovo attempted to resist the Ottoman onslaught even after Tsar Ivan Shishman fled from the city, but they were forced to surrender on July 17, 1393. The expulsion of the Bulgarian patriarch from Turnovo marked the end of an independent Bulgarian Church, as well as the complete collapse of the Bulgarian Kingdom. In 1394 Patriarch Anthony IV of Constantinople appointed Metropolitan Jeremias of Moldavia as patriarchal exarch over Turnovo, thus marking the dissolution of the independent Bulgarian patriarchate of Turnovo. By 1369 Bulgaria had succumbed completely to the rule of the Ottoman Empire and lost its political and religious independence for the next five centuries. During the time of Ottoman rule in the Bulgarian territories, the Muslim population increased as a result of (often) coercive conversion to Islam. Although the historical evidence regarding the mass conversion of Christians is inconclusive and complex with respect to the numbers, it is beyond any doubt that the years immediately following the conquest were characterized by the use of violence and torture as methods of Islamicization.

Alongside the political and cultural domination of the Ottomans and the weakening of the Bulgarian Church, the authority of the Greek Church grew ever stronger in the Bulgarian territories during this time. After the conquest of Constantinople in 1453, Byzantine political influence was effectively ended, but the prerogatives of the Greek Church remained and were amalgamated by the sultans. What this meant for the Bulgarian Church was that it was directly subjugated to the authority of the patriarch of Constantinople. In 1454 Sultan Mehmet II officially recognized the patriarch of Constantinople as the representative leader (ethnarch) of all Christians in the Ottoman Empire, realizing that offering toleration and limited (heavily taxed) support to the Orthodox Church would serve as a means of opposition to the West and could ensure the loyalty of the Christian populations. In his attempt to demonstrate his support for the Greek Orthodox Church, Sultan Mehmet II granted it jurisdictional powers that it had not possessed even under Byzantine rule. As a result, the patriarch of Constantinople was granted authority in both civil and spiritual matters throughout the entire Christian population of the Ottoman Empire. He assumed a position equivalent to that of an Ottoman vizier. From this time onwards Orthodox Greeks, Bulgarians, Serbs, and Romanians were all under the jurisdiction of the ecumenical patriarch of Constantinople, in spite of their differences in language, culture, and tradition. The period of Ottoman rule in Bulgaria, therefore, brought about not merely political and social subjugation by the Ottoman Empire, but also a process of Byzantinization of the Christian Church by the introduction of Greek clergy and Greek language in the church services. It was the time of the great ascendancy of the Phanariots. This systematic campaign of Hellenization undertaken by the Ottoman-era Greek patriarchate, in both ecclesiastical and secular matters, led to the progressive erosion of Bulgarian identity and culture. The Bulgarian populace was subjected to a regime of double taxation by the Ottoman state, on the one hand, and the Greek clergy, on the other, and was increasingly alienated from both hegemonic structures of its foreign domination.

Bulgarian National Revival

In spite of the strong forces of domination and control, there were a number of attempts to resist the double yoke imposed upon the Bulgarian people during the Ottoman period, especially in the era of the national revival in the 18th and 19th centuries. Paisii of Hilandar (1722–98), a monk on Mount Athos, was the first Bulgarian to write a history during the centuries of Islamic rule and Phanariot dominance. In 1762 he wrote his celebrated work *Slavo-Bulgarian History*. Paisii was born in Bansko and he entered Hilandar Monastery in 1745, remaining there until 1761, when he moved to the Bulgarian Zographou Monastery on Mount Athos for a period of thirty years. In 1791 he returned to Hilandar Monastery, where he stayed until the end of his life. On Mount Athos Paisii was exposed to new educational and cultural ideas that influenced and shaped him. The Athonite monasteries had virtually become the only

independently surviving centers of Balkan Christian spirituality and intellectual formation. In 1753 the Greek reformer Eugenius Bulgaris founded the Athonite Academy where students were able to study secular philosophy and science and become exposed to western ideas. As a result of its establishment, new ideals were propagated among the monastic communities which gave rise in turn to a renewal of national sentiments. Paisii most likely began to work on his book when he became a deputy abbot of Hilandar Monastery in 1760 and was allowed to travel freely and collect information necessary for his research. In his narrative Paisii highlighted major events in Bulgarian history and especially moments of cultural accomplishment and military glory. As he remembered the times of national grandeur, he also pointed to the fact that such acts of national self-determination might be possible to achieve in the future as well. Paisii's patriotic voice not only exposed the fact of the spiritual enslavement of the Bulgarian people, along with their loss of cultural memory, but also provided hope for future generations that a change was indeed not to be ruled out. In his history Paisii identifies both the Greek patriarchate and the Ottoman government as oppressors and as enemies of the Bulgarian people and the idea of national freedom. He provides an intellectual map for future struggle and for the overthrow of the political and religious authorities, rather than hoping for a peaceful conciliation with existing structures. According to Paisii, by getting to know their history and their past, the Bulgarian people could regain their sense of cultural identity and national dignity, and must eventually strive to achieve freedom from foreign oppression. As a result of achieving self-knowledge and acquiring a new-found self-esteem, the Bulgarian intelligentsia and the people at large would be emboldened to believe that they could govern themselves, as they had done in centuries past, and would be able ultimately to achieve independence and self-governance once more. Due to the limited financial resources of the Bulgarian population, Paisii's book was often copied manually, rather than published in print in the Cyrillic alphabet. His work was circulated widely in manuscript form for more than a century afterwards and became profoundly influential on the Bulgarian national liberation movement of the 19th century.

What Paisii expressed in theory was to a great extent expressed by the life of his contemporary Sofroni of Vratsa (1739–1814), who visited Mount Athos in 1759 and acquainted himself with Paisii's ideas and writings. Three years later, in 1762, Stoiko Vladislavov of Kotel was ordained as a priest and met with Paisii during the latter's visit to Kotel. Stoiko Vladislavov was deeply impressed by Paisii's *Slavo-Bulgarian History* and he copied it and made it available at his church. In addition to being under the influence of Paisii's work, Stoiko Vladislavov was also exposed to Russian ideas that spread in the wake of the Russo-Turkish War (1768–74) encouraging the cause of Bulgarian liberation from Ottoman rule. Many Bulgarians, including members of Stoiko Vladislavov's parish, decided to volunteer in the Russo-Turkish War, as a result of the promise that Russia made that it would liberate Bulgaria from foreign domination. Yet, after the surrender of the Ottomans in 1774, Russian troops simply withdrew from Bulgarian territory, leaving the Christian population to the mercy of the Turkish Army, who thereafter inflicted a cruel retribution for their insurgence. During this period of massive devastation of villages in the region, Stoiko left Kotel to visit Mount Athos. His stay on Mount Athos and his communication with Paisii affected him profoundly and inspired him to return to Kotel and to initiate a reform within the church. After going back to Kotel, he began an educational program, whereby he started to teach students to read and write in the vernacular Slavic rather than the standard Greek. His educational activity, social work, and patriotic preaching made him a target for the local Ottoman officials and for the Greek clergy who wanted to punish him for his insubordination. He was sentenced to a period of imprisonment and endured harsh conditions, which he later described in his autobiography. In 1794 Stoiko Vladislavov was ordained as a bishop in the diocese of Vratsa and he took the name Sofroni. The choice of a Bulgarian bishop for this diocese was unusual and was due to the fact that it was unsafe for any Greek, as it was then terrorized by the armed bandits known as *kurdzhali*, who were disaffected Ottoman troops who had taken over control of many parts of the wilder Ottoman territory. Both Bulgarian and Ottoman sources from the period between 1792 and 1815 attest to the fact that *kurdzhali* inflicted enormous cruelties

on the population and were virtually free to act in any way that they saw fit. In his autobiography Sofroni of Vratsa described the many hardships the *kurdzhali* inflicted upon his own life, as well as that of others. The lawlessness spoke eloquently of the waning of Ottoman power and served as the spur for the Bulgarian liberation movement. The effect of the Russo-Turkish War and of the *kurdzhaliistvo* were also such that a wave of emigration occurred in the 1790s and 1820s, when nearly half a million Bulgarians left in order to settle in Romania, Ukraine, and Russia. Sofroni of Vratsa was among those emigrants, after being subject to repeated persecution and imprisonment and being forced to flee Bulgarian territory. Sofroni found security in Bucharest, where he was welcomed by the Bulgarian émigré community. In exile, he composed his autobiographical work entitled *The Life and Sufferings of the Sinful Sofroni*, where he described in great detail the lived realities of political, economic, and religious oppression in the Bulgarian territories. His autobiography was published in 1806 and was the first printed Bulgarian book, sponsored by Bulgarian merchants living in Bucharest. Between 1806 and 1809 Sofroni of Vratsa continued his educational activity by translating and publishing a number of works into Bulgarian. He also insisted on the importance of publishing books in the vernacular language, rather than only in the old Church Slavonic or Greek, which were accessible to very few. For instance, he not only copied Paisii's history but also cast the original into a vernacular Bulgarian edition, allowing it to be read more widely. In addition to his literary projects, Sofroni of Vratsa contacted the Russian authorities on the issue of cooperation between the two peoples. After the third Russo-Turkish War (1806–12) broke out, Sofroni sent a letter to the Russian government pleading for the liberation of Bulgaria by the Russian Army. The role of Sofroni of Vratsa in the actualization of the ideas for national self-determination and independence articulated by Paisii of Hilandar cannot be overestimated.

Bulgarian Cultural Renaissance

After the abolition of the Bulgarian patriarchate, in the period between the 14th and the 18th centuries, there were significant changes that occurred in the church as a result of the Ottoman conquest. In the 14th century there was a massive loss of monastic institutions, which had served as centers of intellectual and educational activity, and scholars were either killed or deported abroad. In the second half of the 15th century, however, there was a gradual revival of Bulgarian education in the form of "cell schools" throughout the Balkans. This was the only kind of education offered to Bulgarian Christians and they were primarily found in monasteries and churches, as well as private homes, and the teachers were usually monks or priests. The existence of cell schools for the best part of three centuries contributed to the continuation of Christian religious education among the people and it is not surprising, therefore, that the number and popularity of such schools increased over time. The curriculum was based on religious texts, such as the Psalter, the gospels, and the Book of Hours, along with other church literature. Fundamentally, the cell schools, which were small in size, followed a medieval model of religious and scholastic training and most of the students were prepared to become priests or monks. Additionally, they served as centers of both social activity and spiritual restoration during this era. With the expansion of cell schools in the 18th century, there began to be a felt need for higher and for secular education, which could be obtained only in other parts of the Ottoman Empire and was accessible to only very few Bulgarians. It was precisely in the context of secular schools abroad, however, that new western ideas of the European Enlightenment were introduced among the Bulgarian intellectuals and where the national revival movement began in the second half of the 18th century. The educational model of secular schools inspired many Bulgarians, as it offered an alternative to the Greek versions which propagated the idea of Hellenic superiority and suppressed local nationalist ideas. In the beginning of the 19th century new schools began to be created that affected a reform in the Bulgarian educational system and were instrumental for the deeper cultural and spiritual revival of Bulgaria. The existence of these schools was partly due to the rise of a patriotic class of wealthy businessmen and merchants who supported the reform of traditional education and also sponsored the creation of new buildings. In the midst of this educational reform emerged individuals such as Vassil Aprilov, Ilarion Makariopolski, Georgy Rakovski, and Peter Beron, among many others, who also became the leaders of the movement for Bulgarian religious and political independence.

Second Bulgarian Ecclesiastic Independence

The struggle for an independent Bulgarian Church became particularly acute in the 19th century as a result of the activity of the new intelligentsia which had been exposed to both western, non-Greek, educational models and to Russian ideas of a pan-Slavic alliance. In 1844 Neofit Bozveli, who had been exiled from the Greek patriarchate at Turnovo and forced to go back to Mount Athos, along with Ilarion Makariopolski, who was ordained in the Hilandar Monastery on Mount Athos, presented an official petition to the Ottoman authorities demanding that the Bulgarian Christians be given rights to elect Bulgarian bishops to their eparchies, as well as asking for permission to publish newspapers in the Bulgarian language and to extend the Bulgarian network of schools. Furthermore, the petition stipulated, there must be established a mixed system of law courts in Bulgaria, so as to protect Bulgarians from Greek hegemony. In addition, the petition requested permission to form a purely Bulgarian delegation which would henceforth represent Bulgarian interests to the Sublime Porte, altogether independently of the Greek patriarchate. In spite of the initial interest of the Ottoman authorities to consider these demands, the pressure from the patriarchate and the fear of the anti-Greek activities of Bozveli and Makariopolski annulled their early efforts for gaining independence.

The Bulgarian movement for ecclesiastic independence was also supported by Russia, especially as it expanded its economic, territorial, and political foothold in the Ottoman Empire with the victory of the fourth Russo-Turkish War (1828–9). Russia signed treaties with the Ottomans and was recognized officially as the protector of Christians within the Ottoman Empire. Imperial Russia emphasized its kinship with the old Byzantium and argued its right to oversee and protect all Christians, not only Slavs, who lay under the yoke of Ottoman dominion. In 1865, with the intervention of the Russian ambassador Nikolai Ignatiev, Patriarch Sophronius III (1863–6) promised the leaders of the Bulgarian Church movement that he would henceforward strive to replace Greek bishops with Bulgarian ones, even though he refused the demand for a permanent representation on the patriarchal synod. After the resignation of Sophronius III, Patriarch Gregory VI (1867–71) was more open to negotiate with the Russian ambassador and the Bulgarian Church leadership, and he approved the proposal for the creation of an independent Bulgarian exarchate in the Danube Vilayet. This proposal, however, was met with strong opposition both by Greek Phanariots and the Ottoman authorities, on the one hand, and, on the other, by some Bulgarian leaders who considered Ohrid to be the proper center of the Bulgarian Church and caused a division within the Bulgarian community on this significant issue. As a result of consultations that were arranged by Ambassador Ignatiev between the moderate Bulgarian faction and Patriarch Gregory VI, a compromise was finally reached in 1868. On March 12, 1870 the Ottoman government issued a Firman authorizing the establishment of a separate Bulgarian Church, which would not be completely autocephalous, but which was recognized as an exarchate subordinated to the ecumenical patriarch in spiritual matters, while being fully independent in matters of internal administration. The establishment of a Bulgarian exarchate necessitated the creation of a church synod and an administrative council. On March 13, 1870, therefore, the bishops and the most eminent Bulgarians in Constantinople decided to elect ten lay people and five bishops to the Temporary Council, without making a formal distinction (in terms of membership) between lay people and clergy, as the two groups were equally influential in shaping the reformed Bulgarian Church. The National Church Council opened in 1871 under the leadership of Bishop Ilarion of Lovech and was composed of fifty Bulgarians (eleven clergy and thirty-nine laity), who represented every Bulgarian community. In 1872 the National Council elected as Exarch Antim I, the former metropolitan of Vidin, who soon afterwards obtained official recognition from the sultan in Constantinople. The exarchate

constituted a legal institution which allowed the first official representation of the Bulgarian people at the Sublime Porte. Nonetheless, the new Constantinopolitan Patriarch Anthimus refused to approve of the appointment of Antim I as exarch, and went on to denounce the exarchate as schismatic on September 16, 1872. The pronouncement of schism by the ecumenical patriarch actually confirmed to all the Bulgarians involved that church independence could only be achieved as a result of political independence gained by means of revolutionary uprising. The Bulgarian revolutionary movement had already been underway with the activity of prominent figures such as Georgy Rakovski (1821–67) and Vassil Levski (1837–73). The April Uprising of 1876 was one of the more significant attempts to overthrow the Ottoman rule, although it was devastatingly crushed. Exarch Antim I intervened in the revolt, instructing the clergy to be loyal to the sultan and to preach cooperation with the Ottoman government. The brutal suppression of the uprising, however, drew international attention to the predicament of the Bulgarian Orthodox and made it clear to all observers that peaceful coexistence under Ottoman rule was impossible to maintain. Compelled to rethink their strategy, the church's exarchate made changes to its policies between the time following the April Uprising (1876) and the War of Liberation (1878), chiefly as a result of seeing the massive destruction inflicted on the people after the revolt. In 1877 the new Exarch Josef I was elected after the retirement of Antim I. When the Russian Army crossed the Danube on June 15, 1878, the actual liberation of Bulgaria had effectively begun, and the continuing anxiety of the exarchate to appease the sultans was rendered obsolete. After the Russian Army marched through San Stefano, a town less than 7 miles from Constantinople, the Sublime Porte pleaded for peace, resulting in the signing of the San Stefano Peace Treaty on February 19, 1878. The treaty between the Ottomans and the Russian Tsar Alexander II was viewed very unfavorably by the European powers, who perceived the expansion of a Russian sphere of influence in the Balkans and the creation of a Bulgarian independent state as a potential threat to the stability of the region. All interested parties met at the Congress of Berlin in June 1878 and agreed to reduce drastically the territory given to the Bulgarian state (from 176,000 to 96,000 sq. km.) in order to decrease its dominance in the Balkan peninsula. This agreement forced on them by the Great Powers came as a deep disappointment to the newly liberated Bulgarian people.

Bulgarian Orthodox Church, 1878–1948

The creation of the Bulgarian state in 1878 started a process of a highly complex relationship between the church and the state. It was decided that the exarchate and the holy synod would operate as two independent entities, the former remaining in Constantinople and the latter based in Sofia, where there was established a representation of the exarchate. An added complication was the fact that after the Berlin settlement, the Bulgarian synod lost ecclesiastic jurisdiction over Bulgarians outside the principality and it lamented that more Bulgarian Christians were living outside the borders of the state than within. The exarch ruled the remaining church territories with the help of a separate synod of metropolitans from Rumelia, Macedonia, and Thrace appointed in accordance with Ottoman law. Consequently, the leadership of the Bulgarian Church was divided into two different political regions and functioned under two systems of laws.

In 1879 the Bulgarian National Assembly conferred the title Prince of Bulgaria upon Alexander, who had served as an officer in the Russian Army during the War of Liberation. He accepted the title, even though he considered the newly drafted Bulgarian constitution to be too liberal and to grant him too little power. This choice of Alexander was opposed by the Russian Tsar Alexander III, who had political ambitions of his own in Bulgaria; a stand-off that resulted in a deteriorating relationship between the two states. The fault lines of this reflected internal divisions within Bulgarian society between Russophiles, who embraced pro-Russian, pro-Slavic, and anti-western ideology maintaining that Russia was the protector of Eastern Orthodoxy, and Russophobes, who saw the Russian religious and political system as backward feudalism. Even so, the longstanding connections with Russia that had been strengthened by the missionary activity

of the Moscow Slavonic Charitable Committee in the years before the liberation, from 1858 to 1876, as well as by the military assistance the Russian Army gave in the Liberation War itself, persisted and remained influential in Bulgarian society.

In spite of later efforts to overthrow Ottoman rule and to reunify the Bulgarian territories in Macedonia and Thrace during the Serbian-Bulgarian War in 1885 and the Ilinden Uprising in 1903, the integrity of the state as outlined in the San Stefano Peace agreement was not achieved. Furthermore, in the period between 1912 and 1945, Bulgaria was involved in three Balkan wars and two world wars, all of which did not end favorably for the country and came at a high cost for the Bulgarian population. Whereas the separation of church and state was firmly established and the secular government had complete control over internal affairs and military alliances, the Bulgarian Orthodox Church was granted a preferential position and exerted significant influence in the larger society. For example, when the Bulgarian government signed a treaty with Hitler's regime and allowed access to German troops in Bulgaria proper and in the newly annexed territories in Macedonia, the deportation of Jews from the Bulgarian territories was opposed by the church authorities, whereas the deportation of Jews from Thrace and Macedonia went on unchecked. The metropolitan of Sofia, at this time, solemnly warned the Bulgarian king that God was observing his every action, while the metropolitan of Plovdiv directly contacted the Bulgarian government in order to intercede for the Bulgarian Jews targeted in Plovdiv, threatening that he would lie down on the railway track in front of the trains attempting to deport any Jews. On the major Christian holiday of Sts. Cyril and Methodios on May 24, 1943, the Bulgarian Orthodox Church organized a large public demonstration against the government's anti-Jewish policies. No similar attempts were made to save the Jews of Macedonia and Thrace, which involved the death of over 20,000 people.

Communist Regime, 1944–1989

The Soviet Red Army entered Bulgaria on September 8, 1944 in order to crush the German forces there and to inaugurate a new political regime, which further distanced the Bulgarian Orthodox Church from the state and undermined its position in Bulgarian society dramatically. The new Bulgarian government which was established with the help of the Soviets embraced atheistic and materialistic ideology and opposed claims for any public expression or societal influence by the Bulgarian Orthodox Church. In the aftermath of the successful communist *coup d'état* on September 9, the Bulgarian Orthodox Church and its clergy were accused of being fascist sympathizers and enemies of the new state regime. Many members of the clergy, as well as of the intellectual elite, were imprisoned and killed during the process of purging the state. They were charged with collaboration with the fascists and a great number of church buildings and monasteries were destroyed outright.

After the signing of the Paris Peace Treaty in 1947, a totalitarian one-party communist system was solidified in the country under the leadership of Georgy Dimitrov, who was inspired by the Stalinist model of political regime marked by the radical separation of church and state. In 1945 Exarch Stefan was elected as the new leader of the Bulgarian Orthodox Church with the approval of the Russian Orthodox Church and was later appointed as the chair of the holy synod, after the resignation of Metropolitan Neofit of Vidin. In the years following 1949, when members of the clergy were legally required to pledge allegiance to the communist regime, relations between the Bulgarian and Russian Orthodox Church became much more pronounced. In 1944 religious instruction was legally banned from the Bulgarian school system by an act of the ministry of education, despite the opposition expressed by Exarch Stefan in an official letter to the prime minister. There were several subsequent waves of repression initiated against the clergy between 1944 and 1953, when anti-fascist purges were undertaken and public trials were staged by Dimitrov's government for the sake of further marginalizing the church and spreading communist propaganda. Following an increased and intrusive surveillance of the Bulgarian Orthodox Church, Exarch Stefan was forced to "retire" in 1948, after being classed as an enemy of the Communist Party.

In spite of the fact that the Bulgarian Orthodox Church was constantly targeted by the communist regime, the government decided to support the proposal of the holy synod for the restoration of patriarchal status and title in 1953. The decision to reinstate the Bulgarian patriarchate was a purely political act, which was recognized universally by 1961, for it did not reflect any strengthening of the church's institutions; indeed, the church remained at this time completely subordinated to its hostile communist government. In the years following the introduction of the patriarchate (at first denounced by Constantinople as canonically illegitimate) and the election of Kiril as the new patriarch in 1953, the cooperation between the Communist Party and the Orthodox Church grew to such an extent that the Bulgarian Orthodox Church virtually became one of the instruments of communist control and propaganda. After the death of Kiril in 1971, Maxim Metropolitan of Lovech was appointed as the patriarch with the approval of the Communist Party and he too followed the model of subservient cooperation adopted by his predecessor. In an effort to ensure the continued existence of the Bulgarian Orthodox Church during the communist period, its leadership and clergy accepted that it was a legitimate role of the church to propound socialist and nationalist ideas in alignment with the official state policy.

Democratic Period after 1989

After the demise of the communist system in Bulgaria in 1989, the Bulgarian Orthodox Church gained greater visibility after a long period of marginalization and subordination. The new democratic regime allowed freedom of religious expression, which had been suppressed before, a policy that was at the time met with enthusiasm and which led to a gradual revival of religious life in Bulgaria. However, the major obstacle for the restoration of the Bulgarian Orthodox Church to its previous position of importance as a religious and a cultural force in wider society was its large-scale infiltration during the communist period and its forced collaboration with the Communist Party. The many compromises that generations of church authorities had reached with the communist regime in order to secure its existence (albeit a very peripheral one) had undermined its intellectual credibility and its moral standing in society.

Furthermore, the situation was exacerbated when a dissenting faction from within the church led by Christopher Subev, a member of the clergy and a prominent political figure in the coalition of the United Democratic Front, demanded the resignation of the incumbent Bulgarian Patriarch Maxim and initiated a schism within the church. In 1991 a new democratic government was elected and Christopher Subev was appointed as a chairman to the Commission for Religious Affairs. Subev and his supporters sought to eliminate the holy synod and the patriarch as a punishment for their involvement with, and acquiescence to, the communist regime. In 1992 the government released an official statement declaring that the election of Patriarch Maxim in 1971 had been in breach of the statutes of the Bulgarian Orthodox Church and thus he had to be removed from his post and replaced by another person. This statement was supported by four Bulgarian metropolitans: Pimen of Nevrokop, Pankrati of Stara Zagora, Kalanik of Vratsa, and Stefan of Veliko Turnovo. Pimen, Pankrati, and Kalanik proclaimed that they now constituted the legitimate holy synod of the Bulgarian Orthodox Church, and were joined by five other bishops and by Christopher Subev. On May 25, 1992 the newly founded holy synod appointed Pimen as the new patriarch and *de facto* led to the creation of a schism within the Bulgarian Orthodox Church, now with two rival patriarchs and two synods vying for control of the church. The conflict and opposition between the two patriarchs and their followers led to major conflicts over the correct disposition of church funds and property, to violent actions on both sides, and to severe erosion of the authority of the Bulgarian Orthodox Church both domestically and internationally. Later, in 2004, the police, with the sanction of the office of the supreme prosecutor, tried to enforce violently the reunification of the Bulgarian Orthodox Church under Patriarch Maxim and it entered church buildings in order to remove dissident clergy, who were replaced by new priests. In the face of the fierce struggle for legitimation between the two synods, the general public and the laity have become generally disillusioned with the institution of the Bulgarian Orthodox Church, as well as the two opponent political parties that came to support the two opposing synods. Instead, the people have tended to focus their efforts on initiatives such as the Pokrov Foundation, that are based primarily on the lay people, rather than relying on the clergy and monastics. To this day, the Bulgarian Orthodox Church is still trying to rid itself of the specter of the communist period and to reenvision its role in a democratic and pluralistic modern society, which poses new challenges for its transition and future development. Of all the Orthodox countries which lay under the communist yoke, Bulgaria has perhaps had the hardest transition, and still struggles to find a new and inspiring role and mission in the wider society.

SEE ALSO: Constantinople, Patriarchate of; Russia, Patriarchal Orthodox Church of

References and Suggested Readings

Hopkins, J. L. (2009) *The Bulgarian Orthodox Church: A Socio-Historical Analysis of the Evolving Relationship Between Church, Nation and State in Bulgaria.* New York: Columbia University Press.

Kalakandjieva, D. (2002) *The Bulgarian Orthodox Church and "People's Democracy" 1944–1953.* Silistra: Demos Press.

MacDermott, M. (1982) *History of Bulgaria 1393–1885.* London: Jessica Kingsley.

Obolensky, D. (1971) *The Byzantine Commonwealth: Eastern Europe 500–1453.* London: Phoenix Press.

Simeonova, L. (1998) *Diplomacy of the Letter and the Cross: Photius, Bulgaria and the Papacy.* Amsterdam: A. M. Hakkert.

Todorov, G. (2003) *Bulgaria, Orthodoxy, History.* Sofia: Foundation St. Prince Boris Press.

Todorov, T. (1999) *The Fragility of Goodness: Why Bulgaria's Jews Survived the Holocaust.* Princeton: Princeton University Press.

Todorova, O. (1987) *The Orthodox Church and the Bulgarian Nation through the 15th–third quarter of the 18th Century.* Sofia.

Zeiller, J. (1918) *Les Origines chretiennes dans les provinces danubienne.* Paris: Boccard.

C

Caerularios, Michael (d. 1059)

A. EDWARD SIECIENSKI

Michael Caerularios was the patriarch of Constantinople (1043–58) whose exchange of excommunications with Cardinal Humbert of Silva Candida (d. 1061) in 1054 helped to formalize the "Great Schism" between East and West. Caerularios entered monastic life after an unsuccessful plot against the Paphlagonian Michael IV (1034–41), and was later appointed patriarch by Constantine IX Monomachos (1042–55). Many of Caerularios's contemporaries noted the patriarch's ambitious and volatile nature, which often brought him into conflict both with the Western Church and with political leadership in the East.

In 1054 Pope Leo IX (1049–54) sent Cardinals Humbert and Frederick of Lorraine (later Pope Stephen IX) to Constantinople in order to secure the emperor's help against the Normans and to deal with recent Eastern complaints about Western ecclesiastical customs. Humbert, like Caerularios an unbending and often intolerant character, insisted that the East accept Roman practices as both orthodox and universally binding. After a series of unsuccessful negotiations, on July 16 Humbert entered Hagia Sophia attempting to place a bull of excommunication on the altar against Patriarch Michael and his followers, citing their many crimes and errors (e.g., omission of the *filioque* from the creed). The canonical validity of Humbert's action has long been in doubt, especially since Pope Leo had died in April, a fact probably known to Humbert at the time. Caerularios, with the emperor's consent, then issued a response to Humbert, attacking a number of Latin practices, including their use of the *filioque*, and anathematizing all those who had issued the excommunication. Although often dated as the beginning of the Great Schism, contemporaries (e.g., Peter of Antioch) regarded this exchange of anathemas as a localized matter between Rome and Constantinople and not (as later history would remember it) a church-dividing schism. In December of 1965 these excommunications were symbolically lifted by both Pope Paul VI and Patriarch Athenagoras I.

Initially very popular for his stand against the West, Patriarch Michael later came into conflict with the imperial household; especially with Empress Theodora (1055–6), Emperor Michael VI (1056–7), and Emperor Isaac I Comnenos (1057–9). Isaac eventually moved against him, exiling Caerularios to Madytus and calling a synod to depose him. The charges against the patriarch (which included treason, heresy, and witchcraft) were drawn up by Michael Psellos, although Caerularios died before the trial could begin. His body was then brought back to Constantinople and buried with honors in the Church of the Holy Angels, with Psellos himself delivering the eulogy.

The Concise Encyclopedia of Orthodox Christianity, First Edition. Edited by John Anthony McGuckin.
© 2014 John Wiley & Sons, Ltd. Published 2014 by John Wiley & Sons, Ltd.

SEE ALSO: Ecumenism, Orthodoxy and; *Filioque*; Papacy

References and Suggested Readings

Kolbaba, T. (2003) "The Legacy of Humbert and Cerularius: The Tradition of the Schism of 1054 in Byzantine Texts and Manuscripts of the Twelfth and Thirteenth Centuries," in C. Dendrinos, J. Harris, and J. Herrin (eds.) *Porphyrogenita: Essays in Honour of Julian Chrysostomides.* Aldershot: Ashgate Press, pp. 47–61.

Michel, A. (ed.) (1924–30) *Humbert und Kerularios: Quellen und Studien zum Schisma des XI. Jahrhunderts*, 2 vols. Paderborn: Schöningh.

Will, C. (ed.) (1963) *Acta et scripta quae de controversiis ecclesiae Graecae et Latinae saeculo undecimo composita extant.* Frankfurt: Minerva.

Calendar

JOHN A. MCGUCKIN

The calendar, in Orthodox usage, signifies the manner in which the yearly cycle of liturgical feasts is arranged in the church. From the very beginnings of the Christian Church there was a marked desire among believers to celebrate liturgically that central moment of salvation history: the monumental events surrounding the Lord's death and resurrection, the great Paschal Mystery which included his cross and his glory as one. Liturgically separated out, so as to provide pause and meditative space for the faithful to "ponder these things" (Lk. 2.19), the Paschal Mystery itself refuses to be divided up by aspect or human chronology. It is one living reality, not a series of disparate events. So, to that extent, it is impossible to set apart the Lord's ministry from his sufferings, for they make a seamless weave. It is impossible to separate Great Friday from Pascha Sunday, or to divide out the mystery of Ascension and Pentecost. It is only a time-bounded chronological mindset that sets them in different chronological sequences. In God's work of salvation it is not *Chronos* (time sequence) that matters but *Kairos* (the timeless moment of the opportunity of Grace). Pentecost and Pascha are not just things of the past, they are things of the present moment of God's glory, and of the church's future hope – its eschatological

reality. The calendar, therefore, is a meditative aid to realize the complexity of the eschatological *Kairos* which the church senses as profound Mystery of Christ. It is not meant to be a ground plan, objectively real and definitive, as much as a cycle of recurring and elliptical reflections on the central mystery of the Word's redemption of his people.

Liturgically, the calendar revolves around Pascha. The Paschal cycle begins four weeks before Lent opens, with the Sunday of the Prodigal Son (announcing the overarching theme of repentance). Prior to Pascha come the Sundays of Great Lent, each with their own theme and motif, announced in the gospel of the day as well as in certain "saints of repentance" who are commemorated (Mary of Egypt, for example, or John of the Ladder), and also the Entry to Jerusalem. Following after it come the great feasts of that cycle, Ascension day and Pentecost. This is called the movable cycle, in the sense that it revolves around Pascha, which is itself a variable feast: not the same each year but following after a lunar calendar according to rules (the *Paschalion*) laid down at the Council of Nicea. Because of the canon that states the last days of Great Lent should not precede or fall on the same day as the Jewish Passover, Orthodox Pascha is often later than the western date which follows the lead of Rome. In the Renaissance era, Rome also moved to reform the civic calendar (the Julian calendar, so named from its ancient reformation by Julius Caesar) and repaired the 13 days' dissonance that had crept in over the centuries (caused by the fact that 365 days is not a completely accurate measurement of the earth's rotation) by omitting them, so as to bring into effect the so-called Gregorian calendar. This papally inspired "Gregorian reform" was at first resisted by Anglican England (until the time of George II) and by much of Protestant Europe, and at first by all the Orthodox, but gradually it gained acceptance throughout Western Europe, and increasingly in parts of the Orthodox world. Mount Athos, and many of the Slavic Churches (following Russia's lead), however, refused to accept the Gregorian calendar. They now appear (at least in regard to church usage) to celebrate feasts on "different days." In Russia the nativity of Christ seems to fall on January 7, 13 days after other churches have observed it on December 25. What many fail to realize, of course, it that for the Slavs, this festival does not fall in January at all, but on December 25, as they reckon it, observed under the Julian system. The patriarchate of Constantinople, after a consultative synod at Constantinople in 1923 (a time during which the Russian Church was under great duress), led the way for several Orthodox Churches to partly adopt the Gregorian calendar, but because this was not a common consensus, and in order to ensure that all Eastern Orthodox observed Pascha on the same day (that is, on the same calendar) those churches wanting to follow the Gregorian calendar for everything else reverted to the Julian calendar for things relating to the Paschal cycle. In this way all the Orthodox observe Pascha together and all things related to that cycle, while the rest of the calendar can diverge between the Old Calendarists, more properly called the Julian Calendarists (or "Old Style"), and the New Calendarists following the system which has gone under the nomenclature of "New Style" or "Revised Julian."

Apart from the Paschal cycle, the rest of the liturgical year is the fixed cycle, based upon the solar calendar. The church year begins in September, following Jewish and Byzantine precedent. The necessary space for adjustment in calendrical terms (several different cycles interweaving with one another) is provided by a varied number of Sundays "intercalated" after Pentecost to make up the varying shortfall of the way Pascha comes earlier or later in the course of a given year. These intercalated Sundays typically are placed in the interval before Lent begins the Paschal cycle all over again. The whole calendrical movement is balanced, like parts of a watch, between five revolving parts in a given year: the daily cycle of commemorations, the weekly cycle (Sundays after Pentecost, or of Lent, or after Nativity, for example), the cycle of the Eight Tones (provided by the relevant "tone" of the week as stated for the given Sunday), the Paschal cycle, and the cycle of the fixed feasts. The latter includes the Twelve Great Feasts (Nativity of the Theotokos, Exaltation of the Cross, Presentation of the Virgin in the Temple, Nativity of Christ, Theophany or Baptism of the Lord, Presentation of Christ in the Temple, Annunciation, Entry to Jerusalem, Ascension, Pentecost, Transfiguration, and Dormition. Three of these (Entry to Jerusalem, Ascension, and Pentecost) vary in the year according the Paschal cycle, while the rest are fixed.

The calendar controversy (moving from Julian to "Reformed Julian," since none of the Orthodox ever adopted the Gregorian fully) was often a bitter one in the early and mid-20th century, and some traditionalist Orthodox hierarchs looked upon it as a "faithless" reform, seeing in it a sign of lamentable "Modernism" (a term borrowed from Roman Catholic controversies of the opening of the 20th century). It was soon connected with issues of the patriarchate of Constantinople calling for a "dialogue of love" with other churches. "Ecumenism" was denounced by this minority as a wholesale "Pan-Heresy" and a secessionist movement began, notable in parts of Greece, Cyprus, and Romania, which has increasingly been called the Old Calendarists.

SEE ALSO: Cross; Dormition; Ecumenism, Orthodoxy and; Feasts; Greece, Orthodox Church of; Liturgical Books; *Oktoechos*; *Paraklitike*; Romania, Patriarchal Orthodox Church of

References and Suggested Readings

Monk of the Eastern Church (1980) *The Year of Grace of the Lord: A Scriptural and Liturgical Commentary on the Calendar of the Orthodox Church.* Crestwood, NY: St. Vladimir's Seminary Press.

Seabury, S. (1872) *The Theory and Use of the Church Calendar in the Measurement and Distribution of Time: Being An Account of the Origin and Use of the Calendar, of Its Reformation from the Old to the New Style, and of Its Adaptation to the Use of the English Church by the British Parliament under George the Second.* New York: Pott, Young.

Canon (Liturgical)

DIMITRI CONOMOS

The third major form of Byzantine hymnody after the troparion and kontakion. In its fully developed arrangement (8th century), this is a hymn cycle of nine odes (the second was usually omitted) sung after the reading of the Psalter at Matins. The canon replaced the singing of the nine scriptural canticles that were normally sung, with a short refrain inserted between their verses, in the Byzantine Morning Office. The canon therefore constitutes a highly sophisticated poetic genre. It is essentially a hymnodic complex of considerable length with a variety of themes (the feast of the day), which paraphrase in verse specific sub-themes (the ancient canticle) and musical diversity (a different melody for each ode). In some canons the initial letters of each stanza form an acrostic relevant to the day on which the hymn was to be sung. Unlike the kontakion, the music for canons was slightly more ornamented, making use of two or three notes set to a single syllable of the text.

The term *heirmos* (Gk. "link") is applied to the opening model stanza for each ode of the canon. As such, the *heirmoi* act as "link" verses joining together the theme of suppressed biblical canticles, which the odes of the canon were originally designed to accompany, and the theme of the feast or commemoration of the day, which is developed in the stanzas that followed.

For the *heirmoi*, the classical chants in syllabic style are collected in a book called the *Heirmologion*, which may contain as many as 2,000 model stanzas. Like the Western Tonary, the *Heirmologion* is divided into one section per mode.

The nine canticles are:

1 The song of Moses (Exodus 15.1–19)
2 The song of Moses (Deuteronomy 32.1–43)
3 The prayer of Hannah (I Kings 2.1–10)
4 The prayer of Habbakuk (Habbakuk 3.1–19)
5 The prayer of Isaiah (Isaiah 26.9–20)
6 The prayer of Jonah (Jonah 2.3–10)
7 The prayer of the Three Children (the Benedicite, *Apoc.* Daniel 3.26–56)
8 The prayer of the Three Children (*Apoc.* Daniel 3.57–88)
9 The Magnificat and the Benedictus (Luke 1.46–55 and 68–79)

Whatever the object of a canon may be (the celebration of a feast of the Lord or of the Virgin, or the commemoration of a saint or martyr), the hymn writer had to allude in each of the nine odes to its scriptural model.

Church traditions (wrongly) attribute the invention of the canon to St. Andrew of Crete (ca. 660–740) and his famous Great Kanon of mid-Lent contains the exceptional number of 250 stanzas. But canon composition reached its peak in the 8th and 9th centuries, first in Palestine with examples by St. John Damascene (ca. 675–ca. 749) and St. Kosmas of Jerusalem (also known as St. Kosmas the Melodist or Kosmas of Maiuma; first half of the 8th century), then in Constantinople with St. Theodore, abbot of the Studion Monastery (759–826), and his brother Joseph (d. 833), the two Sicilians Methodios (d. 846) and Joseph the Hymnographer (d. 883), and the nun Cassia (ca. 810–65).

SEE ALSO: Kontakion; Liturgical Books; Music (Sacred); Orthros (Matins)

References and Suggested Readings

Grosdidier de Matons, J. (1980–1) "Liturgie et hymnographie: Kontakion et Canon," *Dumbarton Oaks Papers* 34–5: 31–43.

Hannick, C. (1990) "The Performance of the Kanon in Thessaloniki in the 14th Century," in D. Conomos (ed.) *Studies in Eastern Chant*, vol. 5. Crestwood, NY: St. Vladimir's Seminary Press, pp. 137–52.

Harris, S. (2004) "The Kanon and the Heirmologion," *Music and Letters* 85: 175–97.

Velimirovic, M. (1973) "The Byzantine Heirmos and Heirmologion," in W. Arlt et al. (eds.) *Gattungen der Musik in Einzeldarstellungen: Gedenkschrift Leo Schrade*. Berne: Francke, pp. 192–244.

Canon Law

ANDREI PSAREV

Canon law is the sum of ecclesiastical regulations recognized by church authorities; the discipline, study, or practice of church jurisprudence. The term derives from the ancient Greek word *kanon*, meaning "yardstick" or "standard." It has been used since the time of the early church for the rule of faith (*regula fidei*) established by Christ and the apostles (Gal. 6.16; Phil. 3.16).

The Tasks of Canon Law

As a field, canon law deals with the following issues: the sources of canon law, church order, the foundation of new Orthodox churches, the canonization of saints, the ecclesiastical calendar, control for the execution of justice, the ecclesiastical court, marriage regulations, reception of converts from other confessions, the church's relations with civil authorities, the correlation of church law with civil law, finances, and ownership relations. Canon law includes the subjects and methods of other theological disciplines: critical analysis (church history), doctrinal teaching (dogmatics), canons of the holy fathers (patristics), baptism, and reception into the church (liturgics).

The New Testament is the disclosure of the essence of the "Covenant of the Law" contained in the Old Testament Pentateuch: "Not of the letter but of the Spirit; for the letter kills, but the Spirit gives life" (2 Cor. 3.6); thus, for Christian Orthodox: "In Christ Jesus neither circumcision nor uncircumcision means anything, but rather faith working through love" (Gal. 5.6). The Decalogue and all the commandments of Christ and his apostles have received in the Christian Church the status of law. Every church regulation is supposed to be based on them as on a source. From the very beginning, Christian society had to deal with a diversity of opinions. In order to establish consensus as to whether or not the proselytes had to observe Mosaic Law, a council of apostles was convened in Jerusalem (Acts 15). This principle of conciliarity, the convention of church representatives for an open competition of views, became one of the main mechanisms that the Orthodox Church applied, and still uses, to establish consensus.

The edicts of councils on non-doctrinal issues have historically been called canons and listed as appendices to the doctrinal decisions of the councils. The commentaries of a few revered ancient bishops on certain issues have also been accorded the status of canon law (Canonical Epistles). Observance of the canons is mandatory for all Orthodox Christians. The canons do not act by themselves, but they serve the bishops as authoritative guidelines in adjudicating specific cases. The canons are based on precedent and do not envisage hypothetical circumstances. The spectrum of the canons coincides largely with the above-mentioned range of subjects. One may liken the application of the canons to the prescription of medical remedies of differing potency. In some instances a practitioner may decide to follow literally (i.e., according to *akriveia*, a Greek term meaning

"exactness") the recommendations of a canon regarding penance. In other cases, strict interpretation of canon law might pastorally be adjudged counterproductive. Canons must serve *oikonomia* (a Greek term meaning "judicious economy"), the wise implementation of strategies designed to assure salvation (cf. Eph. 3.2–3; 1 Cor. 4.1). The majority of the canons were issued during the time of the Byzantine Empire, and therefore the canons do not provide a guide for the perplexed in extraordinary circumstances. In all extraordinary cases, the faithful should follow the spirit of the canonical tradition. According to the first canon of the Council of Chalcedon (451), it is imperative that the entire Orthodox Church obey all previously formulated canons. Fidelity to the canons was once more confirmed by the first canon of the Second Council of Nicea (787). At the time of his consecration, a bishop solemnly declares his allegiance to the holy canons (Council of Nicea II, Canon 2). A council that sets out to modify certain canons put forth by another council must be of the same status as the earlier council. A local council, for example, cannot modify the decrees of an ecumenical council.

The canons are not self-explanatory. One cannot interpret canons divorced from their doctrinal context, praxis, and the tradition of piety. In order to examine canons adequately a canonist should apply a historical and dogmatic method. Five key aspects are important in this regard:

1 Establish the purpose of the issuer of the canon.
2 Make sure that all terminology is understood adequately.
3 Identify the evolution of the topic of the canon.
4 Establish the quintessence of the canon.
5 Recommend specific application of the canon according to contemporary circumstances.

The acts of the Council of Nicea (325) from Antiquity had universal importance due to their significance and imperial support. They signified the beginning of the epoch of written ecclesiastical law, which has not, however, replaced customary law (*synetheia*): certain traditions, such as the election only of monastic bishops, are widely revered although no council has ever formalized them.

Canonical Collections

Among the diversity of disciplinary collections of the first centuries of Christianity, the *Apostolic Constitutions* (*AC*) enjoyed special veneration. This manual probably appeared in Antioch about 380. Book Eight of *AC* contains 85 Canons of the Apostles, which have become a key part of the Orthodox canonical tradition. The *Collection of Pontus* (*CP*, ca. 343) is the first known collection of church canons. It was included in the *Corpus Antiochenum* (ca. 380). The Greek originals of both collections have been lost. Nevertheless, since their expanded version was used by the Council of Chalcedon (451), we know that they listed, in chronological order, the canons of the 4th-century councils. These canons are still part of Orthodox canon law, and they were added to the compilation known as the *Synagoge in 50 Titles*, which is the oldest extant collection of canons possibly composed by Patriarch John III Scholastikos while he was still a presbyter in Antioch (ca. 550). In this collection the canons were organized both chronologically and by subjects. The *Epitome Synopsis*, begun by Stephen of Ephesus in the 6th or 7th centuries and completed by Symeon Magistros in the 10th, lists the canons in abbreviated form. The earliest recensions of this collection may be among the oldest extant Greek canonical sources. The Byzantine collection known as the *Nomokanon in 50 Titles* signifies a new type of thematic collection – the genre of *nomokanon* which contained both civil laws (*nomoi*) and also church laws (*kanones*). The *Nomokanon in 50 Titles* utilized an older civil-law appendix, the *Collectio 87 Capitulorum*, as taken from the *Synagoge in 50 Titles*. These additional 87 chapters were originally taken from Novel 123 of Emperor Justinian, who completed his codification of church and civil laws in 534. Nomokanons became a characteristic feature of the state church in the Byzantine Empire since they facilitated the work of bureaucrats. This term was also used to designate collections of penitential remedies (*Epitimia*).

The Council of Constantinople (Synod in Trullo, 691) represented the entire Orthodox Church of the Eastern Roman Empire in the late 7th century. In its second conciliar canon the council listed the following canons as mandatory for the whole Orthodox Church: the Canons of the Apostles; the Canons of the Ecumenical Councils (Nicea (325), Constantinople (381), Ephesus (431), Chalcedon (451)); the Canons of significant local councils (Ancyra (314), Neo-Caesarea (ca. 314), Gangra (ca. 340), Antioch (ca. 330), Laodicea (between 342 and 381), Sardica (343), Carthage (419), Constantinople (394)); Major Canons of the Holy Fathers (St. Cyprian of Carthage (d. 258), St. Dionysius of Alexandria (d. 265), St. Gregory of Neo-Caesarea (d. 270), St. Peter of Alexandria (d. 311), St. Athanasius of Alexandria (d. 373), St. Basil of Caesarea (d. 379), St. Gregory of Nazianzen (d. ca. 390), St. Gregory of Nyssa (d. ca. 394), St. Amphilochios of Ikonion (d. after 394), Timothy of Alexandria (d. 385), Theophilos of Alexandria (d. 412), St. Cyril of Alexandria (d. 444), and Gennadios of Constantinople (d. 471)).

The collection known as the *Corpus of Synagoge in 50 Titles* was rearranged in Constantinople around 580 and thereafter received the title *Syntagma in 14 Titles*, since it was structurally composed in 14 chapters. Another important civil collection known today as the *Collectio Tripartita* was probably appended to it. In the early 7th century canons from the *Syntagma in 14 Titles* and civil material (mostly the *Tripartita* materials) were incorporated into the collection known as the *Nomokanon in 14 Titles*. The content of this edition in turn became the basis of that of Canon 2 of the Synod in Trullo. In 883 under St. Patriarch Photios the canons encompassed by this collection were expanded with material drawn from the Council of Trullo, together with the edicts of the Seventh Ecumenical Council (787), and also of the 861 and 879 Synods of Constantinople, and along with the Epistle of St. Tarasios (d. 806). This 883 corpus later came to be, by general consensus, accepted as the core canonical corpus of the Orthodox Church.

Later Development of Canonical Tradition: Byzantium, the Ottoman Empire, and Greece

During the course of Byzantine history, numerous imperial laws supporting canonical regulations were issued. The description of the ideal harmonious coexistence of church and state (*symphonia*) set out in Emperor Justinian's Sixth Novella (534) had an important influence on Orthodox canon law. In the 11th century, Emperor Constantine IX Monomachos founded a law school in Constantinople. One duty of its senior professor, the *Nomophylax* (literally, "law guardian"), was to act as authoritative interpreter of law. Alexis Aristenos, who was *Nomophylax* and deacon of Hagia Sophia cathedral, is venerated as the first of three "Classical Commentators" of the Orthodox tradition of canon law (the others are Zonaras and Balsamon). The commentaries and opinions (*scholia*) of these three leading lawyers became part of the Orthodox canonical tradition. In 1130, at the request of Emperor John II Komnenos, Aristenos, basing himself on the *Synopsis*, wrote the first concise *scholia*, notes on the canons of the local and ecumenical councils. The commentaries on the canons by monk John Zonaras (d. after 1159) are notable for the academic integrity and audacity he brought to the task. Zonaras attempted to explain not just the literal meaning of the canons, but also their very essence. The last of the classical commentators was Theodore Balsamon, Patriarch of Antioch. In the 12th century, Balsamon was commissioned by Emperor Manuel Komnenos and Patriarch Michael Angelos to compile a comprehensive exegesis of the entire corpus of *Nomokanon in 14 Titles*. In his approach Balsamon largely follows Zonaras; however, Balsamon was more interested than Zonaras in harmonizing conflicts of interest between church and state.

The last notable authority in canon law belonging to the Byzantine period was the Priestmonk Matthew Blastares, who based his famous *Alphabetical Syntagma* (1335) on the *Nomokanon in 14 Titles*. The canons and civil laws are here organized by topics and arranged in alphabetical order. Blastares contributed very few comments of his own and did not distinguish those he added from the *scholia* of the classical commentators. He has an interesting personal expertise on the status of the ecumenical patriarchate within the Orthodox world.

The *Nomokanon* of the lawyer Manuel Malaxos became the preeminent canonical collection of the Ottoman period. For the 19th century and beyond, the publication of the *Pedalion* (*Rudder of the Church*) in 1800 was an important step in the development of canon law. St. Nikodemos the Hagiorite was the main author of this treatise and compilation. St. Nikodemos wrote his commentary around the *Nomokanon in 14 Titles*, omitting the imperial ecclesiastic legislation. St. Nikodemos published canons with parallel exposition in contemporary Greek. The commentaries of St. Nikodemos consist primarily of theological and philological analysis, with instructions for clergy and monastics. This collection is still very reputable, and its English translation was published in 1957 under the title *The Rudder*.

For all Greek speaking churches the six-volume *Syntagma of the Divine and Sacred Canons* (1852–9) became the standard anthology of canons. This comprehensive collection was composed by two prominent Greek scholars: Michael Potlis, professor of law at Athens University, and George Rallis, chief justice of the Supreme Court of Greece. The so-called *Athenian Syntagma* contains the *Nomokanon* of Photios, Blastares' *Syntagma*, and exegeses of the classical commentators and Byzantine authoritative canonists, the most important decrees of the *Endemousae* (Patriarchal) *Synods* of Constantinople (911–1835), as well as the ecclesiastical laws of the emperors. According to the Greek constitution, the Orthodox Church is the established religion of the state. It is therefore not surprising that Greece has had more canonists than all other Orthodox churches combined. There are chairs of canon law at the theological departments of the universities of Athens (est. 1855) and Thessaloniki (est. 1951). There is a distinction between the canon law that is taught at the theological faculties and ecclesiastical law as taught in departments of jurisprudence. The accomplishments of the following canonists should be singled out from the many works on canon law published in Greece: Melitios Sakellaropulos, who authored the first academic textbooks on canon law (1898); Constantine Rallis (d. 1942), who authored textbooks on canon and church criminal law, and also wrote about the right of asylum in the Orthodox Church; Manuel Gedeon (d. 1939), a specialist in Byzantine church law; Panagiotis Panagiotakos (d. 1966), who founded *Archives of Canon Law and Church Law* in 1947; Hamilcar Alivizatos (d. 1969), the author of an important work on *Oikonomia*, which was also translated into German; Jerome Kotsonis, archbishop of Athens (d. 1988), author of (among other works) a treatise on the Orthodox laity; Metropolitan Maxim Christopoulos, an expert on the status of the ecumenical patriarchate; Anastasios Christophilopoulos (d. 1998), whose textbook on canon law was also published in French; Metropolitan Panteleimon Karanikolas (d. 2006), the author of several concordances on the canons; Constantine Mouratides, an expert on canon law dealing with monasticism; Protopresbyter Evangelos Mantzouneas, who codified canons arranged by subjects; Bartholomew Archondonis, patriarch of Constantinople, a specialist in the codification of canons; Spyros Troianos, an expert on the sources of Byzantine church law and on church-state relations; Metropolitan Panteleimon Rhodopoulos, whose textbook has also been recently published in English; Vlasios Phydas, an expert on Pentarchy; John Konidaris, whose textbook on church law (updated in 2008), reflects the problems of the church-state interaction within the context of the European Union; Archimandrite Gregory Papathomas, who wrote on issues of "post-ecclesiological" canonical identity and who edited the series *Nomokanonike Bibliotheke*; Theodore Giangou, a specialist in liturgical-canonical matters; and finally Constantine Pitsakis, a specialist in Byzantine legal history and gender issues.

Russia

In the Slavic lands the *Nomokanon* was known as the *Kormchaia*. In the 9th century St. Methodios of Macedonia translated the *Synagoge in 50 Titles* by Emperor Leo III and the *Ecloga* of Constantine V from Greek into Slavonic. The best sample of this group is *Efremovskaia Kormchaia* (12th century) Also in the 12th century the *Synopsis* of Stephan of Ephesus, with commentaries by Aristinos, and the laws of the Byzantine emperors, were translated on Mount Athos, apparently by St. Sava of Serbia. In 1272 the Council of Vladimir approved this *Kormchaia* for use in the Russian Church. It was copied many times, and the first printed edition appeared in 1649. In 1839 a committee under the supervision of St. Filaret Drozdov published *Kniga Pravil*, which is the main canonical collection of the Russian Church. Unlike the *Kormachaia*, the *Kniga Pravil* contains only canons

from the *Nomokanon in 14 Titles*, though no imperial edicts are included. The *Kniga Pravil* reflects the influence of the *Pedalion*. In 1876–80 the Society of Lovers of Religious Instruction in Moscow published the canons with parallel texts in Greek and Slavonic, along with both the classical commentaries and those taken from *Kormchaia*. Since 1810 church law has been taught at theological schools, and from 1835 until 1917 it was taught at the universities too. In 1851 Bishop John Sokolov published the first Russian textbook of church law.

The major developments in Russian canon law are connected with the works of the following university academics: Alexis Pavlov (d. 1898), an expert on sources of canon law, who authored the best prerevolutionary textbook; Elijah Berdinkov (d. 1915), Pavlov's adversary, whose textbook focuses on the theological meaning of the canons; Nicholas Suvorov (d. 1909), whose textbook stresses the importance of imperial authority for the church. The dynamic advance of scholarship in canon law was interrupted by the Bolshevik revolution. Vladimir Beneshevich, a victim in 1938 of Stalin's purges, is known to Byzantinists and canonists throughout the world, due especially to his work on the *Synagoge in 50 Titles* and *Syntagma in 14 Titles*. Serge Troitskii died in exile in Yugoslavia in 1972. The last of the pleiad of canonists trained before the revolution, he wrote on a variety of topics, ranging from the acceptability of remarriage for clergy to the canonical organization of church life in diaspora.

The only new department of canon law in post-Soviet Russia was that established at St. Tikhon's Orthodox Humanitarian University in Moscow, which is headed by Cyrill Maksimovich, a specialist on the sources of the Slavic canon law, together with his deputy, Fr. Dimitrii Pashkov. Archpriest Vladislav Tsypin is currently the leading Russian church authority on canon law. His textbook, republished most recently in 2002, is the standard manual for the field. Fr. Vladislav took into account the latest church regulations along with the achievements of pre-revolutionary textbooks. Canonists Iaroslav Shchapov and Elena Beliakova also work on the sources of Slavic canon law and Albert Bondach works on various topics, from Byzantine canonical sources to canons dealing with suicide. The Russian *Orthodox*

Encyclopedia, which has been issued in regular fascicules since 1997, is growing into a comprehensive reference resource that also covers various particular issues of Orthodox canon law.

Serbia, Romania, Bulgaria, and Georgia

After its completion in the 12th century, St. Sava's *Kormchaia* became the main canonical collection of the Serbian Church. Centuries later the first academic textbook on canon law was published by Bishop Nikanor Ruzicich (d. 1916). His contemporary, Bishop Nikodim Milas (d. 1915), became one of the most respected canon law authorities in Serbia, Greece, Bulgaria, and Russia. He translated the canons from the *Syntagma* of Rallis and Potlis and placed his commentaries in the context of previous hermeneutic works. Canonists Branko Cisarz (d. 1982) and Fr. Dimsho Peric (d. 2007) published textbooks on canon law after World War II. Fr. Dimsho wrote studies on the history of church-state relations in Serbia. In 2002 Bishop Athanasios Evtic published the new translation of canons in Serbian with his commentaries.

In Romania the *Syntagma* of Matthew Blastares was the official church collection from the 15th century until the publication of the *Indreptarea Legii* in 1652. In 1844 Metropolitan Veniamin Costachi (d. 1846) translated the *Pedalion* into Romanian. Metropolitan Andrei Saguna (d. 1873) authored the first textbook and commentaries on the canons. More recently, Liviu Stan (d. 1973) has contributed significantly to Orthodox canon law. Among other subjects, he wrote on the role of laity in the church, on ecclesiastical autocephaly and autonomy, the Orthodox diaspora, canonization, and the future Pan-Orthodox Synod. Other modern canonical experts include Ioan Floca, a specialist in Romanian canon law; Constantine Rus, who wrote on early church standards for clergy candidates; and Nicholas Dura, a specialist in Ethiopian canon law.

In Bulgaria St. Sava's *Kormchaia* has been the main canonical collection since 1221, although the *Pedalion*, *Kniga Pravil*, and the *Syntagma of Rallis and Potlis* have also been circulated. The work of translating the *Corpus Canonum* into Bulgarian, which began in 1878, remains unfinished. In 1912 and 1913 the most prominent Bulgarian canonist, Protopresbyter Stephan Tsankov (d. 1965), published annotated Bulgarian versions of the canons of all the ecumenical and half of the local councils. His works on the constitutional law of the Bulgarian Church and on church administration are of particular importance. Today, the field of canon law is represented by Protopresbyter Radko Poptodorov, who has published important works on autocephaly and the organization of the early church, among other topics; and Dilian Nikochev, historian of church law, particularly of Byzantine and Bulgarian matrimonial law.

In the Georgian Church, St. Arseni of Ikalto translated the *Nomokanon in 14 Titles* into Georgian at the end of the 11th century. This collection received the name *Didi Sjuliskanoni*. Various texts were subsequently added to this translation, some of them written before the 11th century and some later. This is the only canonical collection formally adopted by the Georgian Church.

Canonists in the West

The edition of the Orthodox Church canons issued by the Anglican scholar and clergyman William Beveridge, known as the *Synodicon sive Pandecta* (1672), had a strong impact on St. Nikodemos the Hagiorite. The publication of *Iuris ecclesiastici Graecorum historia et monumenta* by Cardinal Jean-Baptiste François Pitra (d. 1889) includes apocrypha in addition to the entire Orthodox canonical corpus; its critical apparatus is more thorough than that of any previous collection. The *Discipline Générale Antique* by Pericles-Pierre Joannou (d. 1972) is the latest critical edition of all the canons.

The number of scholars interested in the canon law of the Eastern Church increased notably in the 19th and 20th centuries. The German scholar Zacharia von Lingenthal (d. 1894) contributed to our knowledge of the sources. The Austrian scholar Joseph Ritter von Zhishman (d. 1894) wrote on marriage and patronage law. The Russian émigré Protopresbyter Nicholas Afanasiev (d. 1966) highlighted the importance of distinguishing inner truths of the canons from their mutable historical contexts. Several Jesuits have also contributed to the scholarship on canon law. Rev. Ivan Zuzek (d. 2004) wrote on the *Kormchaia* and Rev. Francis Dvornik (d. 1995) has explored the history of the see of Constantinople based on the earliest Latin canonical collections. The transformation of the European political map in the 20th century raised many questions about canonical order for refugees and immigrants in Orthodox and non-Orthodox countries. Alexander Bogolepov (d. 1980) and Bishop Gregory Grabbe (d. 1995) wrote respectively from the perspectives of the Russian metropolia in America and the Russian Church Abroad on the issues of the canonical organization of the Russian diaspora. The monograph of Archbishop Peter L'Huillier (d. 2007) of the Orthodox Church in America, *The Church of the Ancient Councils: The Disciplinary Work of the First Four Ecumenical Councils*, contains exhaustive commentaries on the canons of these councils, and deserves to be mentioned alongside the work of such earlier illustrious commentators as St. Nikodemos the Hagiorite and Bishop Nikodim Milas. The study of canon law has also been enhanced by a number of living non-Orthodox scholars: Heinz Ohme, a specialist in the Quinisext Council (Synod of Trullo); Eva Synek, a specialist in early church law and gender issues; Andreas Schminck, a specialist in Byzantine canon law; Richard Potz, an expert on the legislations of the ecumenical patriarchate and co-author with Eva Synek of an introductory manual on Orthodox canon law in German. The Society of Canon Law of the Eastern Churches, which serves as a forum for the interconfessional cooperation of expert canonists, is based in Vienna and publishes the periodical *Kanon*. Outside traditional Orthodox countries, the field of canon law is quite significantly represented in America by Lewis Patsavos, professor of canon law at the Holy Cross Greek Orthodox School of Theology, Boston, whose *Spiritual Dimension of the Holy Canons* is required reading for anyone who wishes to study the Orthodox canons; Fr. John Erickson, a student of Fr. John Meyendorff, and a specialist on sacramental *Oikonomia*, who was succeeded as professor of canon law at St. Vladimir's Orthodox Seminary by Fr. Alexander Rentel, who currently works there on the theology of canon law; Fr. Patrick Viscuso represents the Orthodox exegetical tradition of canon law and is a specialist in gender issues; Protodeacon Stanimir

Spasovic is currently the professor of canon law at St. Sava Serbian Orthodox College of Theology.

SEE ALSO: Apostolic Succession; Canonization; Church (Orthodox Ecclesiology); Communion of Saints; Ecumenical Councils; Excommunication; Quinisext Council (Council in Trullo) (692); Repentance; St. Nikodemos the Hagiorite (1749–1809); St. Photios the Great (ca. 810–ca. 893); Tradition

References and Suggested Readings

Afanasiev, N. (1969) "The Canons of the Church: Changeable or Unchangeable?" *St. Vladimir's Theological Quarterly* 11: 54.

Burgmann, L. et al. (eds.) (1992) *Bibliographie zur Rezeption des byzantinischen Rechts im alten Rußland sowie zur Geschichte des armenischen und georgischen Rechts*, in *Forschungen zur Byzantinischen Rechtsgeschichte*, vol. 18. Frankfurt am Main: Vittorio Klostermann.

Erickson, J. H. (1987) "Nomocanon," in *The Dictionary of the Middle Ages*, vol. 9. New York: Charles Scribner's Sons.

Erickson, J. H. (1991) *The Challenge of Our Past*. Crestwood, NY: St. Vladimir's Seminary Press.

Gallagher, C. (2002) *Church Law and Church Order in Rome and Byzantium*. Aldershot: Ashgate Variorum.

Hartmann, W. and Pennington, K. (eds.) (2010) *History of Medieval Canon Law: Eastern Canon Law to 1500 AD*. Washington, DC: Catholic University Press.

Kalogeras, D. (2000) "Canon Law," in *Encyclopedia of Greece and Hellenic Tradition*. Chicago: Fitzroy Dearborn, pp. 287–90.

L'Huillier, P. (1983) "L'économie dans la tradition de l'Eglise Orthdoxe," in *Kanon: Yearbook of the Society of the Law of the Oriental Churches*. 19.

L'Huillier, P. (1997) "The Making of Written Law in the Church," *Studia Canonica* 31: 117.

Macrides, R. (1986) "Nomos and Kanon on Paper and in Court," in *Church and People in Byzantium*. Birmingham: University of Birmingham Press.

Meyendorff, J. (1983) "Ecclesiology: Canonical Sources," in *Byzantine Theology: Historical Trends and Doctrinal Trends*. New York: Fordham University Press.

Pacurariu, M. (1996) *Dicționarul teologilor Români*. Bucharest: Univers Enciclopedic.

Percival, H. R. (ed.) (1956) *The Seven Ecumenical Councils of the Undivided Church: A Select Library of Nicene and Post-Nicene Fathers of the Christian Church*, 2nd Series, 14. Grand Rapids: Eerdmans.

Pheidas, V. (1998) "Droit Canon – Une Perspective Orthodoxe," in *Analecta Chambesiana*, vol. 1. Geneva: Graduate Institute of Orthodox Theology, Center of the Ecumenical Patriarchate in Chambesy.

Pheidas, V. (1998) "Principles for the Interpretation of the Holy Canons," *Sourozh* 74: 16.

Schminck, A. (1991) "Canon Law," in A. P. Kazhdan (ed.) *The Oxford Dictionary of Byzantium*. Oxford: Oxford University Press.

Thomson, F. J. (1965) "Economy: An Examination of the Various Theories of Economy Held within the Orthodox Church, with Special Reference to the Economical Recognition of the Validity of Non-Orthodox Sacraments," *Journal of Theological Studies* n.s. 16: 401.

Troianos, S. (1999) *Hoi peges tu byzantinu dikaiou*, 2nd edn. Athens.

Viscuso, P. (2006) *Orthodox Canon Law: A Casebook for Study*. Berkeley: Inter-Orthodox Press.

Canonization

ANDREI PSAREV

The act or process by which the church formally determines and ratifies that a particular deceased person is a saint and, as such, belongs to the canon (or list) of saints. It is also known as glorification. The need to examine the cult of martyrs produced Canons 9 and 34 of the Council of Laodicea (4th century) and Canon 83 (86) of the Council of Carthage (419). These canons were the earliest precursor of the investigation that later became a part of the canonization process.

In the 4th century CE, Emperor Constantine the Great constructed churches on the Roman burial sites of the apostles Peter and Paul, and Emperor Constantius II completed the Mausoleum of the twelve apostles in Constantinople and moved there relics of three of the apostles. These acts, therefore, which might be seen as the official canonization of the apostles, clearly follow after a widespread public cult, and are closely related to veneration of the relics in a shrine or place of pilgrimage. Before the 11th century a church or monastery affiliated with a saint might preserve accounts of the saint's life and works in hagiographical (*Synaxarion*) and liturgical traditions (*Menaion*). Names of the most honored holy people of the local church were added to the list of commemorated saints and this was their glorification (*anagnorisis*).

The glorification of ancient bishops was often based on a perfunctory screening procedure. With the retrospective exception of heretics and violators of church discipline, for example, all patriarchs of Constantinople from 315 until 1025 were added to the catalogue of saints immediately after they died. After the 11th century the Synod of Constantinople set up a more formal process of examining the life of a reposed hierarch and the extent of his veneration before his glorification. Considering that the institutional formalization of a canonization process had been developing in the Church of Rome since the 10th century, it seems reasonable to suspect that it might have been the Crusaders who, directly or indirectly, introduced it to Byzantium. The categories of saints continued to expand beyond the early classic types of martyrs, ascetics, and hierarchs. Later, the concept of protectors of the faith arose and monarchs and sovereigns were also canonized at the discretion of senior hierarchs, based on the quality of their service to the church.

In current Orthodox practice the manifestation of a new saint is achieved by means of a local or general canonization. A fairly widespread veneration of reposed monastics, hierarchs, or other righteous individuals, and the occurrence of supernatural signs, are considered as indications that these persons are already active in the choir of saints. When the bishops, having studied the life, writings, and influence of a candidate, approve a canonization, there is sometimes an examination of the mortal remains prior to the announcement of a decision. In most cases of canonization, a memorial service is performed on the anniversary of the saint's death day. The saint's relics might be transferred to a new shrine, a specially designed icon is often unveiled, and a church service is composed in their honor and celebrated publicly. The names of newly glorified saints are added to the calendar of an Orthodox church by decision of its synod of governing bishops, and notified to other churches.

SEE ALSO: Communion of Saints; Constantinople, Patriarchate of; Hagiography; Icons; *Menaion*; New Martyrs; Newly Revealed Saints; Passion Bearers; Relics; St. Constantine the Emperor (ca. 271–337)

References and Suggested Readings

Galatariotou, C. (1991) *The Making of the Saint: The Life, Time and Sanctification of Neophytos the Recluse*. Cambridge: Cambridge University Press.

McGuckin, J. A. (2003) "The Legacy of the 13th Apostle: Origins of the East Christian Conceptions of Church and State Relation," *St. Vladimir's Theological Quarterly* 3–4: 276.

Pomazansky, Protopresbyter M. (1996) "The Glorification of Saints," in *Selected Essays*. Jordanville, NY: Print shop of St. Job of Pochaev.

Talbot, A.-M. (1991) "Canonization," in *The Oxford Dictionary of Byzantium*. Oxford: Oxford University Press.

Cappadocian Fathers

JOHN A. MCGUCKIN

This is the collective name given to the leading Neo-Nicene theologians of the patristic era who took on the direction of the Nicene movement after the death of St. Athanasius of Alexandria. They were closely related by family bonds or ties of close friendship, and came from the same upper echelon of ancient society, most of them demonstrating advanced rhetorical and philosophical skills which they put to the service of the church in fighting against the second generation Arians (especially Aetios and Eunomios), and thus emerged as among the greatest of all the church fathers. They have traditionally been designated as the "Three Cappadocian Fathers": St. Basil the Great of Caesarea (330–79), St. Gregory the Theologian (of Nazianzus: 329–90) who was Basil's lifelong and close friend, and St. Gregory of Nyssa, Basil's younger brother (ca. 331–95). But there was also a wider circle that ought to expand the designation to include St. Macrina (a Cappadocian "Mother" who did not leave any extant writings of her own but who educated and formed her younger brother, Gregory of Nyssa, decisively and who was an important monastic founder in her own right) and also St. Amphilokios of Ikonium, who was St. Gregory the Theologian's relative and a disciple of St. Basil, who has left important writings and canonical letters. They all came from the region of Cappadocia – present-day eastern Turkey near the Syrian border – especially the towns of Guzelyurt where Gregory Nazianzen lived; Kaisariye, the home of Basil; and Nevsehir, which was the base of St. Gregory of Nyssa. In all three places colonies of monastics grew up, many of which survived intact from the early Middle Ages until the exchange of populations after the Greek-Turkish War of 1922.

St. Basil was a major influence on the developing monastic movement and, along with Sts. Antony and Pachomius, has been regarded as the "father of monasticism" in the Eastern Church. The divine liturgy attributed to his name was the standard one used in the East before that of St. John Chrysostom (an abbreviated version) superseded it. It remains the common liturgy in use during Lent, and reflects elements of his lofty theology and spirituality. In his lifetime he was renowned as a vigorous church leader, organizer of philanthropy, and profound theologian. Today, he is perhaps best known for his treatise *On the Holy Spirit*. The two St. Gregories went to Constantinople for the occasion of the ecumenical council there in 338, and were leading architects of the Nicene theology it promulgated. St. Gregory the Theologian, one of the most learned men in the whole of Antiquity, composed in advance of the council his renowned *Five Theological Orations* (Orations 27–31) which have been called, ever afterwards, the synopsis of the trinitarian dogma of the Orthodox Church. St. Gregory of Nyssa assisted him on that occasion and continued the struggle against radical Arianism with an array of impressive theological and spiritual works. Two of the Cappadocians, Sts. Basil and Gregory the Theologian, are included among the "Three Holy Hierarchs" (the third being St. John Chrysostom), who were seen by the Byzantines as the brightest lights among all the fathers.

SEE ALSO: Arianism; Council of Constantinople 1 (381); Council of Nicea I (325); St. Athanasius of Alexandria (ca. 293–373)

References and Suggested Readings

McGuckin, J. A. (2001) *St. Gregory of Nazianzus: An Intellectual Biography*. Crestwood, NY: St. Vladimir's Seminary Press.

Meredith, A. (1995) *The Cappadocians*. Crestwood, NY: St. Vladimir's Seminary Press.

Meredith, A. (1999) *Gregory of Nyssa.* London: Routledge.
Rousseau, P. (1994) *Basil of Caesarea.* Berkeley: University of California Press.

Cassia the Poet *see* Women in Orthodoxy

Catechumens

MARIA GWYN MCDOWELL

Catechumens (the word means "those being taught") are candidates preparing for reception into the Orthodox Church, usually through baptism or chrismation. Preparation includes participation in liturgical services and instruction from a qualified clergy or lay teacher. The modern catechumenate lasts for six months to a year, unlike the ancient practice of up to three years. Also unlike ancient practice, catechumens remain for the whole of the divine liturgy rather than leaving at the litany of the catechumens, a dismissal often removed to reflect the change in custom. No universally applicable formal catechism exists, though a rich literature is available specifically for the neophyte.

SEE ALSO: Confession; Eucharist

Charity

JUSTIN M. LASSER

The Orthodox response to poverty is manifested in a variety of ways. Charity (*eleēmosyne*, almsgiving) in the form of a "coin in the coffer" represents but one of the church's responses. The Orthodox Church inherited the Old Testament's witness to God's defense of the poor and disenfranchised. One of the earliest testimonies given by the Lord of Christ is his reading from the Book of Isaiah: "The Spirit of the Lord is upon me, because he has anointed me to bring good news to the poor; He has sent me to proclaim release to the captives" (Lk. 4.18–19). The terms of the first apostolic mission ordained by Jesus instructed them to go through the towns of Galilee carrying nothing for the journey but trusting in the hospitality of those sympathetic to their cause. If a house received them, they were to eat whatever was put before them and heal the sick among them and proclaim that the Kingdom of God had come near (Mt. 10.5–14; Mk. 6.6–13; Lk. 9.1–6). In this early period the apostles did not donate money to the poor but offered an exchange. The apostles would heal the sick and proclaim the kingdom, and their hosts would provide a meal, "for laborers deserve their food" (Mt. 10.10b). In this sign of the "healing exchange" the Kingdom of God was made manifest.

The gospels also speak of the Lord instituting a common purse among the disciples out of which poor relief was disbursed (Jn. 12.5–6; 13.29). However, he strictly instructed that when one offered charitable assistance, one was to do it quietly (Mt. 6.1–4). This apostolic model of forgiving indebtedness and sharing the wherewithal to have enough to eat daily is also reflected in the prayer that Jesus taught the church. There the faithful beseech the common Father to grant them daily bread and to forgive the debts (*opheleimata*) that drive a person into poverty, just as those who hold accounts against debtors also forgive them. The symbol of shared meal in the Orthodox Church thus not only represents the kingdom, it manifests it. In the Lord's Prayer the faithful are not taught to operate on the basis of "charitable giving," but on a more substantive and radical concept of debt alleviation. Almsgiving, in this sense, is a more temporary measure. It does not correct injustices, merely alleviates the pain associated with them. Hospitality is also one of the church's primary forms of active charity. Hospitality permeates many of the teachings of Christ, as in Luke 14.13–14: "When you give a banquet, invite the poor, the crippled, the lame and the blind. And you will be blessed, because they cannot repay you."

In the post-Pentecost era an ideal state of the church is evoked as when "no one claimed private ownership of any possessions, but everything they owned was in common.... There was not a needy person among them, for as many as owned lands and houses sold them and brought them the proceeds of what was sold. They laid it at the apostles' feet, and it was distributed to those in need" (Acts 4.32–34). This foundational vision provided the Orthodox Church with certain principles which were manifested in the office of the bishop and the institution of coenobitic monasticism. In Orthodox thought the bishop oversees the wealth of the faithful and through his deacons distributes it to those in need. From the 4th century onwards bishops were known as *Philoptochoi* ("friends of the poor"). "Distributed wealth" remains a guiding principle in Orthodoxy in so far as it believes that all benefits that humans enjoy (wealth and property included) belong to the Lord, just as the Promised Land in the Old Testament was the Lord's property.

The rise of imperial Orthodoxy occasioned a clash with Classical Greek ethics. According to Aristotle's *Nicomachean Ethics*, citizens were encouraged to show love to their cities through their lavish gifts. This was a public service or *leitourgia*. The primary forms of *leitourgia* were public feasts, the giving of wine, and the establishment of gymnasia. The *leitourgia* was a way of procuring favor and establishing patronclient relationships. The ancient economy was essentially a whimsical beneficence economy. Into this system the gospel came as a radical new voice. The demands of Christ now required the governing bodies of the Roman world to care for the poor as icons of God (see St. Gregory the Theologian, Oration 14, "On the Care of the Poor"). From now on the ideal aristocrat was not a "lover of the city" but a "lover of the poor."

The fathers of the church established an obligation to give to the poor, not out of civic pride, but as a way of earning the intercessory power of prayer that the poor could command. The Christianization of the empire succeeded in creating hospitals and similar institutions to alleviate the effects of poverty. The church also owned many bakeries and lands with which it aided the poor. There were even occasions in Egypt when the bishops distributed wine to widows (one of the most influential groups in the ancient church).

The pre-Christian attitude toward poverty is best exemplified in the words of Plautus: "He does the beggar bad service who gives him meat and drink, for what he gives is lost, and the lives of the poor are merely prolonged to their own misery" (*Trinummus* 339). In marked contrast the great St. Gregory of Nyssa responded by pleading: "Do not despise those who are stretched out on the ground as if they merit no respect. Consider who they are and you will discover their worth" (*On the Love of the Poor*). Orthodox charity is exemplified most clearly in such words and in the lives of the countless saints over the ages who have embraced Christ's call to alleviate the conditions of the poor through selfless giving and charitable actions; in so doing offering to those who suffer an icon of the love of God for humankind.

SEE ALSO: St. John Chrysostom (349–407); Wealth

References and Suggested Readings

Chrysostom, St. John (1984) *On Wealth and Poverty*, trans. C. P. Roth. Crestwood, NY: St. Vladimir's Seminary Press.

Holman, S. R. (2001) *The Hungry are Dying: Beggars and Bishops in Roman Cappadocia*. Oxford: Oxford University Press.

Holman, S. R. (ed.) (2008) *Wealth and Poverty in Early Church and Society*. Grand Rapids, MI: Baker Academic.

Chastity

M. C. STEENBERG

Chastity is a condition of spiritual and bodily purity in which the Christian person retains control over his or her impulses and desires, presenting a life to God that reflects and realizes the condition of humanity's first innocent formation. It refers, most often, to the restraining of the specifically sexual appetites of the body, reflecting the word's Latin root, *castus* ("pure"), which also has from ancient times retained a meaning of abstinence from sexual and other sensual activities. St. Paul employs the term in this context of sexual purity, which yet goes beyond simple sexuality, in his exhortation to the Corinthians: "I have betrothed you to one husband, that I may present you as a chaste virgin to Christ" (2 Cor. 11.2).

With respect to sexual purity, chastity may refer in practical terms either to a complete abstention from all sexual activity (as in the case of monastics, or as the Orthodox Church expects of all persons prior to marriage), or to the right ordering and sacred engagement of the sexual appetites within the sacramental bond of married life. But chastity as a notion is often employed in relation to the whole spiritual and bodily demeanor of purity before God, and is not simply referring to the sexual appetites. The curbing of any and all passionate impulses may be enjoined under the call to chastity (which is why, for example, it is included as the first positive petition in the famous prayer attributed to St. Ephrem and used throughout the Great Fast); thus chastity may relate to a right practice of patience, godly conversation, the fostering of right social attitudes and activities, the refraining from gossip and slander, etc. Such was certainly what St. John of the Ladder had in mind when he wrote that "chastity is the name common to all the virtues" (*Ladder of Divine Ascent*, Step 15).

Fundamental to the Christian call to chastity is the scriptural assertion that the human body is the dwelling place of God, and should be accorded due honor and respect (so 1 Cor. 6.19, 20). This is also made explicit in a saying attributed to St. Ephrem of Syria: "Everyone who loves purity and chastity becomes the temple of God"; a saying that draws attention to the relationship between purity and the living out of creation as the making of dwelling places for the Creator. Chastity may therefore be seen as the overarching virtue of rightly ordering one's life and activities, bodily as well as spiritually, so that the other virtues might be realized and God's temple, the human person, made a fitting home for its King.

SEE ALSO: Ethics; Fasting; Repentance; Sexual Ethics; Virgins; Widows

References and Suggested Readings

Evdokimov, P. (1985) *The Sacrament of Love*. Crestwood, NY: St. Vladimir's Seminary Press.
Harakas, S. (1983) *Toward Transfigured Life: The Theoria of Eastern Orthodox Ethics*. Minneapolis: Light and Life.

Cheesefare (Sunday of)

JOHN A. MCGUCKIN

The Sunday immediately preceding Great Lent in the Orthodox Church. It is so named because it is the last occasion (ending at Vespers that day) when dairy products are eaten until Pascha. It follows after the preceding Sunday of Meatfare (the last occasion meats are consumed) and offers a gradual entrance into the full austerities of the fast. At the end of the week occurs the Sunday of Forgiveness, a liturgical commemoration of the expulsion of Adam and Eve from paradise and the occasion, after the divine liturgy, of the ceremony in Orthodox churches of the giving and receiving of mutual forgiveness.

Cherubikon

DIMITRI CONOMOS

The troparion that accompanies the Great Entrance in the divine liturgy. For ordinary celebrations the hymn "We who represent the cherubim," a 6th-century addition to the service, is used. During Lent and Holy Week proper hymns are used such as "Now the powers of heaven" for the Presanctified Liturgy (perhaps the earliest ordinary Cherubikon, later replaced by the Cherubic chant); "At your mystic supper" on Holy Thursday (introduced ca. 574); and "Let all mortal flesh keep silent" (borrowed from the Liturgy of Saint James) for Holy Saturday. The earliest melodies for these chants exist in 13th- and 14th-century Byzantine choir books.

SEE ALSO: Troparion

References and Suggested Readings

Conomos, D. (1974) *Byzantine Trisagia and Cheroubika of the 14th and 15th Centuries*. Thessaloniki.
Taft, R. (2004) *A History of the Liturgy of St. John Chrysostom, Vol. 2: The Great Entrance. A History of the Transfer of Gifts and Other Preanaphoral Rites*. Rome: Edizioni Orientalia.

China, Autonomous Orthodox Church of

JOHN A. MCGUCKIN

The presence of Christianity in China dates back to Antiquity. It is mentioned in church traditions that the Apostle Thomas preached the gospel there in the first century. Concrete historical evidence shows that it was a lively missionary field of the Byzantine-era patriarchate of Antioch. Artifacts from this ancient missionary enterprise along the Silk Road (once part of a wider Antiochene outreach to Ethiopia, India, and Persia) can now only be found rarely, such as the surviving stele of Xian, set up by Nestorian missionaries in 635 to mark their work in China. The Tang dynasty enacted repressive measures against foreign religions in 845, and the Christian Chinese missions must have suffered extensively then. The records that would have clarified how expansive this Eastern Christian mission was were extensively burned in a much later period (even by Renaissance western missionaries) – a profound loss to the history of Christianity in China.

The modern history of the Orthodox in China begins again with the Russians. In 1685 the Qing emperor resettled in the capital a group of some thirty or so cossacks who entered his service after his capture of several Siberian border towns along the Amur river. Among the group of hostages was the priest Maxim Leontiev, who subsequently served at the first Orthodox church in Beijing, gifted to the Orthodox community who elected to stay in China after the armistice by the Kangxi emperor. He gave over a Guandi temple (the Chinese god of war) which was reconsecrated as the Hagia Sophia Church with the blessing of the metropolitan of Tobolsk, and later refounded as Holy Dormition. The Chinese emperor recognized Fr. Leontiev by awarding him the title of "imperial official of the seventh rank."

In 1715, after Fr. Leontiev's death, the Russian Archimandrite Hilarion (Lezhaisky) was sent as replacement priest, together with a deacon and other church staff, as part of an agreement reached between Tsar Peter the Great and the Chinese emperor, thus establishing a formal Russian Orthodox mission in Beijing, which appears in official records after 1727. Its main purpose was to provide religious services to Russian diplomatic staff in the Chinese capital. An estimate of the mid-19th century suggested there were still only about 200 Orthodox faithful in Beijing, most of whom were career diplomats or ethnic Russian descendants. The latter part of the 19th century witnessed a notable revival, following on the cultural work of the priest Hyacinth Bichurin and the monk Archimandrite Palladios, who both became masters of the Chinese language and initiated many translations of Orthodox literature, as well as a sensitive outreach to the indigenous population.

The Boxer rebellion of 1898–1900, where Christian converts became a specific target for violence, saw 222 Orthodox Christians martyred for their faith. The library of the Beijing Orthodox mission was burned to the ground. Nevertheless by 1902 there were an estimated 32 Orthodox parishes in China with a total of between 5,000 and 6,000 faithful. By 1949 this had risen to about 106 Orthodox parishes in China. There was also a seminary and several Chinese parish priests. The 1917 Russian Revolution increased the missionary activity in so far as many fleeing the political turmoil came east by way of Siberia, but the fall of the tsar also meant the church's official source of funding dried up. After the revolution the Orthodox bishops in China came under the ecclesiastical jurisdiction of the Karlovci Synod of Russian Bishops Outside Russia, but the Moscow patriarchate resumed effective jurisdiction in China after an agreement reached with both state powers in the late 1940s. By 1939 there were estimated to be as many as 200,000 Orthodox in China, with five bishops and an Orthodox college operating at Harbin. By the end of the 1930s dioceses had been established in Shanghai and Tianjin, as well as in Harbin and Beijing.

Most of the clergy and people were then still ethnic Russians. The advent of repressive communist masters to China after the fall of Chang Kai Shek in the civil war altered this situation of slow growth. The communist government ordered the repatriation of all "foreign" missionaries working in China. Many of the ethnic Russian clergy were sent back at that time to the USSR, though others fled to America and Australia. With the increasing exit of the Russian community the numbers of Orthodox in China dropped precipitately. The later Cultural Revolution would also savagely crush all visibly surviving forms of the Chinese Orthodox Church. In 1956 Archbishop Viktor, the last serving Russian hierarch in China, returned to Russia following an agreement reached between Khruschev and Mao Tse-tung, and the next year the Chinese Orthodox Church was granted autonomous status by the Moscow patriarchate. This occurred despite its tiny size and its struggling condition, because of the political necessity of having verifiable independence from all "foreign powers."

Today, Orthodoxy is not among the official forms of Christianity acknowledged and legally sanctioned by the Chinese Communist State, but, even so, a small body of the Orthodox continues bravely. There are Orthodox parishes in Beijing and Northeastern China, as well as parishes operating in Shanghai, Guangdong province, Hong Kong, and Taiwan. The Russian Orthodox church of Sts. Peter and Paul recently resumed services in Hong Kong, and the oecumenical patriarchate has sent a bishop there. The Orthodox mission church in Taiwan has operated freely for many decades. The Chinese Orthodox have had an immensely difficult time, laboring under a heavy yoke that still has not lifted. Their story is not yet over, perhaps has hardly begun, but their significance as being the originating form of Eastern Christianity in the Far East merits more than a passing consideration when one considers the immense problems facing the church if it can come into freedom and leave behind its colonial legacy of a recent mission history heavily marked by intra-Christian strife.

SEE ALSO: Russia, Patriarchal Orthodox Church of

References and Suggested Readings

Baker, K. (2006) *A History of the Orthodox Church in China, Korea, and Japan.* Lewiston, NY: Edwin Mellen Press.

Barrett, D., Kurian, G., and Johnson, T. (2001) *World Christian Encyclopedia*, vol. 1, 2nd edn. Oxford: Oxford University Press.

Jenkins, P. (2008) *The Lost History of Christianity: The Thousand-Year Golden Age of the Church in the Middle East, Africa, and Asia: And How it Died.* New York: HarperOne.

Chorepiscopos

JEFFREY B. PETTIS

The term *chorepiscopos* referred in the early church to the leading cleric of a small church in the countryside (*Chora*), a bishop of unimportant rural regions who had been appointed to oversee churches located outside the metropolitan city where the ruling bishop resided. Generally, he was in episcopal orders, but sometimes the word also seems to indicate a priest who has been given extensive authorization by the diocesan. One of the earliest *chorepiscopoi* is a certain Zoticus, a 2nd-century bishop of Cumana, a Phrygian village. By the 4th century, chorepiscopoi were quite numerous, especially in Asia Minor. They generally appeared to exercise all of the functions of the bishop except for higher ordinations. Fifteen of them signed in their own right at the Council of Nicea. Even so, the chorepiscopos seems to have been distinct from both bishops and presbyters (Athanasius, *Second Apology* 85; PG.25.400B), being wholly subject to the direction of the diocesan. Over time there still developed concern that the chorepiscopoi had too much freedom to exercise their office apart from the ruling bishop. In Canon 13 of the Council of Ancyra (341) the powers of the chorepiscopos were restricted, and he was authorized to ordain only the lower ranks of the clergy. Canon 10 of the Dedication Synod of Antioch (341) also made it clear that a chorepiscopos stands under the immediate jurisdiction of the local bishop. He could ordain priests or deacons only with the bishop's written permission, and could officiate in a city church only in the presence of the city bishop and the council of presbyters (Council of Neo-Caesarea, *Canons* 13–14). The Council of Sardica (342/343) determined that no chorepiscopos should be consecrated in a place where an ordinary bishop presides. The Council of Laodicea (380) started the process whereby chorepiscopoi were phased out in favor of "visiting priests" (*periodeutai*) specially delegated as supervisory agents of the bishop. Such an archpriest was authorized to sit and vote in councils (Council of Ephesus 431). Several chorepiscopoi signed as representatives of their diocesans at the Council of Chalcedon (451), but the office was destined to disappear in favor of a system of delegated senior priests, or alternatively co-adjutor bishops, who extended the administrative reach of a ruling diocesan bishop.

SEE ALSO: Episcopacy; Priesthood

References and Suggested Readings

Langford-James, R. (ed.) (1975) *A Dictionary of the Eastern Orthodox Church.* New York: Burt Franklin.

Parry, K. et al. (eds.) (1999) *The Blackwell Dictionary of Eastern Christianity.* Oxford: Blackwell.

Chrismation

SERGEY TROSTYANSKIY

Chrismation is the second sacrament of the Orthodox Church, part of the initiation (baptismal) mysteries. Through Chrismation one is anointed with specially consecrated oil of myrrh (Ex. 30.25) in order to receive the gift of the "Seal of the Holy Spirit." In Orthodoxy Chrismation normally takes place immediately after the baptism of water. It is an organic part of the baptismal mystery and is performed as its fulfillment. Chrismation conforms the initiate to Christ, "the anointed one" and opens the door to deification, in Christ, by the transfiguring grace of the Holy Spirit, who is the Illuminator and Sanctifier. St. Cyril of Jerusalem, in his baptismal catecheses of the 4th century, noted that by becoming partakers of Christ we are called "Christs," since we receive the anti-type of the gift of the Holy Spirit. Thus, after being baptized with the sanctified waters, one receives this anti-type in the form of Chrismation, the same Holy Spirit with which the Savior was anointed in his earthly ministry by the Father. The sealing of the believer with Holy Chrism renders them into prophets, priests, and kings.

The ancients widely practiced two types of anointing: social anointing and symbolic anointing. The Scriptures present the first type of anointing as being performed primarily as a sign of hospitality. In addition it was performed for healing purposes and also for the preparation of the dead for burial. In the two evangelical stories of the anointing of Jesus, the first concerning Jesus in the house of Simon the Pharisee (Lk. 7.38–50) and the other relating the sign Mary of Bethany gave (Jn. 12.3), we can see several of these strands coming together (also with allusions to the other type of anointing symbol). The sinful woman anoints Jesus when his host has neglected that honor, and he accepts it as a symbol of the redemption God brings through love. The anointing Mary offers (which carries overtones of messianic status) is rebuffed as a messianic symbol and accepted as a symbol of burial precisely because the evangelist knows that no human can ever anoint Jesus as the Messiah, rather it is a gift of the Father. For this reason, when the

myrrh-bearing women come to anoint the Lord, they are unable to achieve their goal: in his resurrection the mysteries of glorification have already taken place.

The messianic anointing in the Scriptures was a sign of divine election and divine authority. It was restricted exclusively to high priests, kings, and prophets who were chosen by God to convey his will (Ex. 28.41; Num. 35.25; 1 Sam. 16.13). The Scriptures gives us examples of Aaron, Saul, and David being anointed by the extraordinary command of God. In fulfillment of the Old Testament prophecies Jesus is manifested through both types of anointing. Moreover, Jesus promised to his disciples that he will "Ask the Father, and He will give you another Paraclete, Who will be with you forever, the Spirit of Truth" (Jn. 14.16). And the Holy Spirit "Will teach you all things, and bring all things to your mind, whatsoever I have said to you" (Jn. 24.49). This promise was fulfilled on the day of Pentecost when the Holy Spirit descended upon the disciples. After that great gift, the disciples bestowed it to the faithful through the mysteries.

In the early church two means of the bestowal of the Holy Spirit on peoples of faith were practiced: the laying on of hands and anointing with oil. Thus, "They laid their hands upon them and they received the Holy Spirit" (Acts 8.14–17). Later on, the consecrated oil, as a sacramental sign of the bestowal of the Holy Spirit, tended to replace the rite of baptismal laying on of hands, but the apostolic charism of passing on this initiation is reserved in the church in so far as only the senior bishop of each region can consecrate the holy *myron*. In earliest times only bishops celebrated this sacrament, but eventually its administration also passed to priests, using the previously consecrated *myron*. In the 2nd century Valentinian Gnostics practiced Chrismation as a sacrament, but they detached it from the liturgical matrix of water baptism and affirmed it to be superior, as the name *Christ* was derived from "chrism." The earliest testimony of the sacramental use of Chrismation in the Orthodox Church comes from Tertullian at the beginning of the 3rd century. The Orthodox response to the early controversies was to insist on the close relation of the two parts of the initiation rite. If a convert to Orthodoxy is received after having received trinitarian baptism in another Christian communion, then Chrismation can be celebrated on its own (as a completion of the mystery of baptism), and if persons who have publicly apostatized from the Orthodox faith return, then they too receive Chrismation alone as a sign of the healing of the original mystery of baptism; but otherwise it is always celebrated with water immersion as a single mystery of initiation. Later Christian history saw the controversy renewed when the Roman Catholic Church separated Chrismation from the liturgical cycle and placed it as "Confirmation" (after Holy Communion) to strengthen the adult in the Christian faith and make him or her a full member of the church. Orthodoxy rejected that approach since baptism and Chrismation have to be followed immediately by the reception of the Eucharist, as the baptized person is made by the mysteries a full member of Christ's body by the mystical gift of the Holy Spirit – even from infancy. Protestantism, on the other hand, tended to reject Chrismation from the number of their sacraments for the reason that it appeared to them to diminish the self-sufficiency of water baptism. Orthodoxy points out that the original command was twofold: to baptize with "Water and the Holy Spirit."

Fr. Alexander Schmemann attributed those controversies to the growing divorce that sprang up between the liturgical traditions of the church and theological speculation. The scholastic approach took its starting point from definitions rather than from liturgical tradition. These definitions were tied to a particular understanding of grace and of the means of grace. They led theologians to an unavoidable dilemma: either baptismal grace makes a new gift unnecessary, or the grace received in Chrismation differs from the one received in baptism, and thus creates conditions for the detachment of Chrismation from baptism. The first position marks the Protestant approach, the second, the Roman Catholic. However, from the Orthodox perspective the entire dilemma is misguided. It arises out of a misreading of the sacramental formula which uses the gift of the Spirit, *dorea* in the singular, rather than the plural: the gifted graces, *charismata*. The dispensation of the particular gift of cleansing and reconciliation takes place during

baptism. The uniqueness of the mystery of Chrismation arises out of the fact that it bestows on the believer the royal gift of the Holy Spirit himself. Chrismation thus takes the initiate beyond the fundamental redemption and reconciliation of baptism and opens the door to the mystery of deification, which is the life in Christ through the Spirit which is to develop from the time of initiation onwards into the glory of Christ's heavenly communion of saints. After baptism, then, the initiate stands in the church dressed in white robes and with bare feet. The gateways of the human senses are marked with chrism in the form of the cross: forehead, eyes, nostrils, lips, ears, breast, hands back and front, and the feet. At each of the several anointings the priest says: "The seal of the gift of the Holy Spirit."

The ritual of preparation and consecration of Holy Chrism is of extraordinary importance and is performed by patriarchs and other most senior hierarchs of the autocephalous churches. It starts during the fourth week of Great Lent with the preparation of necessary components which may include as many as twenty ingredients. Among those ingredients are various oils, wine, fragrant herbs, and incense. The final compound, Chrism, is consecrated on the altar during the first day of Holy Week. In the Kremlin, near the Ouspensky church, one can still see the patriarchal building containing the great vats where the *myron* was mixed.

SEE ALSO: Baptism

References and Suggested Readings

Cyril of Jerusalem, St. (2008) *The Holy Sacraments of Baptism, Chrismation and Holy Communion: The Five Mystagogical Catechisms of St. Cyril of Jerusalem.* Rollinsford, NH: Orthodox Research Institute.

Golubov, A. (1994) "The Seal of the Gift of the Holy Spirit," *Sourozh* 55: 30–40.

McGuckin, J. A. (2008) *The Orthodox Church: An Introduction to Its History, Doctrine and Spiritual Culture.* Oxford: Wiley-Blackwell, pp. 285–8.

Schmemann, A. (1964) *For the Life of the World.* New York: National Student Christian Federation.

Schmemann, A. (1974) *Of Water and the Spirit.* Crestwood, NY: St. Vladimir's Seminary Press.

Christ

JOHN A. McGUCKIN

The confession of the Christ by the Orthodox Church is inspired by the Spirit of God. Its acclamation of Jesus as Lord, Son of God, and Savior largely rises within and out of doxology (in which all the titles of acclamation are joined seamlessly so as to present varieties of "aspects" – *epinoiai* – on a mystery that transcends the limits of all titles and earthly words), but that confession is also present in the controversial refutation of those whom the Orthodox Church, throughout history, has withstood as falsifying his name and message with sectarian or heretical views. The first repository of the church's confession of Christ is thus found in the Scriptures it prays from and the liturgical songs and texts it composes and sings from (its liturgical books); and the second is chiefly found in its doctrinal tradition, especially as

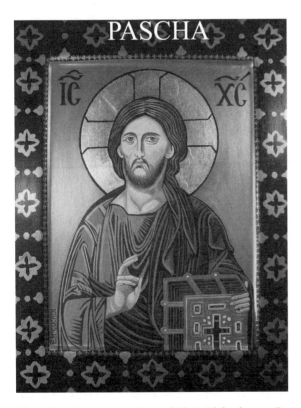

Plate 10 Contemporary icon of Christ Philanthropos. By Eileen McGuckin. The Icon Studio: www.sgtt.org.

preserved in the seven ecumenical councils which, taken together, constitute a monument of Orthodox Christology. This is the sacred *Paradosis* which the Lord has delivered to the Orthodox Church by the medium of the Spirit (as promised in Jn. 14.26; 15.26; 16.13–14), and which is marked by three distinctive characters: first, spiritual enlightenment and discernment; second, biblical rootedness; third, ecclesial conciliar consensus.

The predominant "tone" of the evangelical picture of the Lord, which Orthodoxy has always closely adhered to, is one of Christ's obedient confidence in God, culminating in the absolute trust of the Son who follows the path of ministry and service even to the point of the cross. The predominant tone of the apostolic letters, alongside the gospels, is one of triumphant victory: Christ the Lord of Life and Death. Both the confession of the Lord as Suffering Servant, and as Victor, are equally canticles of glory, and together make up the rich harmony of the whole New Testament *corpus* in terms of its "Song of Christ"; for this is a rich weave, rather than a simplistic or monolithic picture. For this reason Orthodoxy understands that the icon of the suffering and humiliated Lord which the gospels offer is no less glorious than the Savior who appears resplendent on Thabor or the Mount of Ascension. For Orthodoxy, the Christ of St. Mark is the same as the Lord of St. John's Gospel. The church follows the Evangelist John's understanding that the *Katabasis* (the descent, or "coming down") of the Word is not simply a *Kenosis*, but an epiphany of condescension. And the *Anabasis*, or exaltation of the Lord, is not merely a prophet's reward of blessing (like Elijah in the *Merkabah*), but a return to the "bosom of the Father" which the *Logos* had left only "economically" to complete the incarnate ministry. The Exalted Lord is the Servant of God: the Humble Servant is the Lord of Glory. They are one and the same: "One Lord, One Christ" has been a motif of the church from the first generation (1 Cor. 8.6; Eph. 4.5).

The formal Christology of the Orthodox Church (as distinct from its liturgical, confessional, songs and canticles which have a great poetic beauty of their own) is a long story of elaborating a defense of the evangelical icon of the Lord against a series of alternative pictures proposed, but which have been rejected by Orthodoxy as heretical, that is, not conducive to salvation and not in harmony with the "truth" of Christ which the Lord and the apostles spiritually communicated. Accuracy, historical speculation, and good biblical concordances are, therefore, not at all enough to ensure an "accurate" synopsis of biblical or early Christian Christology: for what matters and what transpires in "seeing" Orthodox Christology is first and foremost a matter of spiritual discernment transmitted through the *phronema* of the church (what the Latins called *mens ecclesiae* – the "mind of the Church" – or the *sensus fidelium* – the "spiritual instinct" that governs the faithful across time as inspired in them by the Spirit of God who is the animator of the church's confession of Jesus). The controversy surrounding each of these numerous christological debates in Antiquity, as they succeeded one another, has left behind a vast body of literature. Much of it is very complex, yet, even at its most rhetorically "precise," the patristic language about the Lord Jesus retains the spirit of the gospels and letters, and in two strong senses. First, it is a literature that confesses the power of the Lord. That is, it is soteriological in concern. It does not speculate about Christ for the sake of intellectual curiosity. It only makes statements about the Lord to clarify aspects of how his saving power has been experienced. To that extent it is a christological language of action, and even when speaking what seems to be "very high" theory, the patristic theology is always one of *praxis*. From the beginning to the present we know Christ immediately in his *energeia*, and that *energeia* is communicated so as to be universally accessible even in the contemporary world by the presence of his Spirit. Doctrinally speaking, this is why the Orthodox Church holds strongly to the confession that the head of the church is the Lord himself. Christ has not abdicated his regnant power over the community. He remains among it, needing no earthly vicar. The Orthodox Church has always insisted that to know Christ, one begins from the salvific effect he has on his world and his church. The "what" he has done, reveals the "who" the Master is. For the Orthodox Church, therefore, Christ is first and foremost the Savior.

The second way in which the patristic confession of Christ retains the evangelical spirit is the manner in which it constantly reverts to doxology. The confession of the great deeds of the Lord for the liberation and purification of his people, and their ultimate *theosis* (deification), is essentially about praise of the energy of the Trinity's life-giving revelation among humans and their social history. This language of *praxis*, for all its complexity, therefore, retained the essential character of doxology. This is how it could so easily enter into the fabric of the Orthodox liturgy at an early stage and why the Eucharistic anaphoras are full of profound christological discourses.

The Nicene-Constantinopolitan Creed expresses the fundamentals of necessary christological belief for all the Orthodox:

> [We believe] in One Lord, Jesus Christ, the only-begotten Son of God, begotten from the Father before all ages, Light of Light, True God of True God, Begotten not made, of one essence with the Father, Through whom all things were made; who for us and for our salvation came down from heaven and was incarnate of the Holy Spirit and the Virgin Mary, and became man. He was crucified for us under Pontius Pilate, suffered and was buried. On the third day he rose again, in accordance with the scriptures, and ascended into heaven. He sits at the right hand of the Father, and he will come again in glory to judge the living and the dead: of his Kingdom there shall be no end.

Orthodoxy confesses "One Lord Jesus Christ." What this means simply is that Jesus, and the Lord, and the Christ, are one and the same person. He who was the humble Son of Man, who suffered and died, is the self-same subject who was "with God in the beginning" as Word and Wisdom of the Father. It is this simple axiom that marks the heart of Orthodox Christology. It has always been a matter of great tension in Christian history, as almost all sectarian heresy has wished to reverse it and underscore a profound distinction between "the Lord" and "Jesus," finding it a difficult matter to ascribe the honor of divine adoration to such an apparently humble earthly figure. The "separatists" of the past have been the Docetists, the Gnostics, the Photinians (Psilanthropists), the Arians, the Nestorians, the Eutychian Monophysites, the Monothelites … the list goes on and is still active to this day. But the Orthodox Church worships and adores one Lord, who has perfectly united his humanity and his divinity. As the great Irenaeus said: "God became man, and it was the Lord himself who saved us" (*Against the Heresies* 3.21.1). As consubstantial with God the Father, the Son is born timelessly, eternally, from God (St. Athanasius of Alexandria, *Against the Arians* 1.24–25; 3.63, 66; St. Gregory the Theologian, *Oration* 29.2; 39.12; St. Gregory of Nyssa, *Against Eunomius* 1.26, 42), and is united to the Father in the totality of the single and self-same divine essence, as well as in the irrefragably united will and love that constitutes the union of the Son and the Spirit in the being of the Father. It is this same eternal Son who is, within history, incarnated as Jesus Christ, the Son of God on Earth, making the humanity his own; "going into the far country" (Lk. 15.13) for our salvation, while never leaving the Father's side.

It is obvious, of course, that there is some christological distinction to be made between statements which are appropriate to the earthly incarnate economy of the Lord and those which apply to his state as divine pre-incarnate Wisdom (the divine *Logos*, or *Sophia*), or to his current glory as Enthroned Savior (bearing the glorified flesh still) sitting at the right hand of the Father. But this distinction is not one of person or identity; only of the economic manner of the revelation to the church. All the attributes of the divine Word apply to the Son, in all times and states; except that a proper acknowledgment ought to be made of the self-emptying undertaken by the Word, "in the days of his flesh" (Heb. 5.7).

It was St. Cyril of Alexandria, above all other fathers, who insisted that the Orthodox belief in the christological union meant exactly that: a union (*henosis*) having taken place in Christ, of two previously disparate realities: divinity and humanity. For St. Cyril, the fact that Christ confers deification on the human race through his incarnation is a reality that first happens in the Lord's assumption of a human body. He speaks of the deification of Christ's own flesh through the power of the indwelling Godhead. Many of his own contemporaries (and many critics of Orthodox Christology following their steps to this day) have complained that this "transfiguration of the humanity" must have meant the annihilation of authentic manhood. St. Cyril argued consistently that not only was this a false conclusion, but that his opponents' premise (that the divinity and humanity remained untouched by one another in Christ, per-

fectly and mutually "intact" after the incarnation) was a meaningless and dead theology that took no account of the basic motive for the entire incarnation; namely, to render a dying race immortal. The natures, in the incarnate person, enter, on the contrary, into such a dynamic and energized relationship of intimacy that it can be described as no less than a "union." In presenting this robust sense of transfigurational power at the heart of the mystery of the incarnation, St. Cyril swept to the side those (such as Nestorius) who wanted to keep to a weak view of the incarnation union of natures, preferring to call it instead "an association" (*synapheia*).

St. Cyril pressed the conclusion (and his thought remains central to all Orthodox theology, affirmed as such at the councils of Ephesus (431), Chalcedon (451), and Constantinople II and III (553 and 681)) that while the divine and human natures preserve their integrity in complete fullness, their interaction is the whole power behind the dynamic force of the incarnation's soteriological effect (*Against Nestorius* 1.1; Letter 17; *Letters to Succensus*). St. Cyril often speaks of the *henosis* (or dynamic union) of the natures in Christ in terms that emphasize its total perfection. The natures are one in the way the perfume of a lily is one with its shape; or the way the Holy Eucharist is both earthly material (bread) and yet the life-giving power of God; or the way in which a human being's soul is "one" with their flesh. Time and again, however, he insists that a monolithic understanding of "being one with" in the sense of "being changed into" is certainly not what he means. He wishes to connote what the earlier fathers had celebrated as the glory of the incarnation, namely its transfigurative effect on the humanity, which is thereby raised to new potentialities. The fathers of the Second Council of Constantinople (553) summed up the matter once more in the tersest of terms:

> If anyone says that the Word of God who worked miracles was someone other than the Christ who suffered, or that the divine Word was joined with the Christ who had been born of woman, or that he was in him as one person within another; and does not rather say that he who was made flesh and became man is the one, selfsame, Jesus Christ our Lord, the Word of God; and that both the miracles and the sufferings which he voluntarily endured

in his humanity are his: let such a one be anathema. (*Acts of the Council of Constantinople: Anathematisms Against the Three Chapters*, Section 3)

The same council, again with an eye for the terse synopsis, affirmed this principle of the christological union in the memorably dramatic phrase of Cyril of Alexandria's: "One of the Trinity suffered in the flesh" (*Third Letter to Nestorius*, *Anathema* 10). It is therefore the faith of the Orthodox Church that the divinity of the *Logos* (eternally "God from God, and Light from Light") is just as present in the *Logos*-made-flesh in the person of Jesus the Christ. Jesus is thus the "Word made man," to demonstrate the power and presence of God to humanity in the making of a new and decisive covenant. The entire presence and power of the divinity is in Jesus (the *Logos* "hominified," as Athanasius liked to describe him in *Against the Arians* 3.30), in a direct and unlimited manner. It is precisely because of this that the Orthodox insist that one of the most succinct confessions of ecumenical faith in Jesus is the admission that the Blessed Virgin is rightly called the "Mother of God" (*Theotokos*) (St. Cyril of Alexandria, *Epistle 17*; *Against Nestorius* 1.1; St. Gregory the Theologian, *Epistle 101.5. To Cledonius*).

Because of the immense scope of the work of redemption that Christ accomplished through his incarnate ministry, it follows as something fundamental, and basic to Orthodox Christology, that the Son is not in the ranks of the creatures (St. Athanasius of Alexandria, *On the Synods* 23); neither in his pre-incarnate state, nor in his earthly economy, when he bore the flesh that he himself had made. But the Lord's is not a separate deity, as if alongside the Father's. It is the single Godhead of the Father which is given to the Son-*Logos* in the "mystical begetting" that constitutes the life of the Trinity. St. Basil described it in this way: "There is one source, and one being derived from that source; one archetype, and one image. Thus the principle of unity is preserved. The Son exists as begotten from the Father, and in himself naturally representing the Father. As the Father's image, he shows a perfect likeness; as an offspring, he safeguards the consubstantiality" (*Homily* 24.3; see also St. Gregory of Nazianzus, *Oration* 29.2; St. Gregory of Nyssa, *Against Eunomius* 1.36). The sharing of the same being is why the Son and Father do not constitute two gods, but are one power and being of God manifested in distinct *hypostases*. St. Gregory the Theologian explained it thus:

> The Father is the principle of unity; for from him the hypostases of the Son and Spirit derive their being, and in him they are drawn together: not so as to be fused together, but so as to cohere. There is no separation in the Trinity, in terms of time, or will, or power. These factors make human beings a plurality, each individual at odds with one another and even with themselves. But unity properly belongs to those who have a single nature and whose essential being is the same. (*Oration* 42.15)

St. Cyril of Jerusalem expressed it simply to his 4th-century catechumens as follows:

> He who has seen the Son, has seen the Father, for the Son is in all things like him who begot him. He is begotten Life of Life, and Light of Light, Power of Power, God of God; and the characteristics of the Godhead are unchangeable in the Son. Whoever is found worthy to behold the Son's Godhead, attains the fullness of the Father. (*Catechetical Oration* 11.18)

Already in the 2nd century St. Irenaeus had put it even more memorably: "The Father is the invisible of the Son, the Son the visible of the Father" (*Against the Heresies* 4.6.5; see also 4.4.2).

The Son comes to work on creation not merely to teach humanity. The incarnation of the Son-*Logos* was for the repair and healing of a damaged world. This is one of the reasons why the mystery of salvation was accomplished in obedience under suffering. The pain of the world in its alienation from the love of God was met and "spent" in the person of the crucified and victorious one. But it is also clear that the Orthodox Church's Christology is an aspect of its trinitarian faith, and can never be separated from this.

The fathers understood that this fundamental repair of the cosmos was quintessentially the role of the Son-*Logos*, who had first designed the created order (putting into all things the "seeds" of "*Logos*-purposes" in their root being). All things were designed to accumulate to the glory of God; and this was sufficient to their ontological fulfillment. When it ceased to be so, the harmony of the world was tilted. For all the fathers, and the Orthodox tradition of Christology which follows them, the *Logos* stooped down to his own broken world in order to heal it. Since the source of human pain had been felt most intimately in the flesh, and in the suffering of death, the incarnation of the Word of God was seen as the "stooping down" of a surgeon to a sick patient (*synkatabasis*). The very act of assuming flesh, living as a man within time, was understood as a personal remaking of humanity's being: now as a new Christ-being which was forged in the person of Jesus himself, God made man, and passed on to the church as Christ's new creation. This was the origin of the disciple's destiny, which meant to live henceforward in the potentialities of the incarnation's grace, and thereby in a "New Humanity," namely assimilation to Christ, the victor over death (e.g., see St. Cyril of Alexandria, *Letter to Succensus* 9). The motive of healing resonates in St. Athanasius who speaks of the incarnation as the embodiment of God's pity:

> Our guilt was the cause of the descent of the Word, and our transgression called forth his loving-kindness, and this was why he came to us, and why the Lord was manifest among humans. Our trouble was the reason for his embodiment. Because of our salvation, he went so far in his love for humankind as to be born and be manifest in a human body. (*On the Incarnation* 4; see also St. Cyril of Alexandria, *Letter to Succensus* 9)

For St. Irenaeus, this restoration the *Logos* effects is felt particularly in the return of humanity to the knowledge of God, and the consequent breaking of the power of corruption that had resulted from our alienation from the divine. For almost all the fathers, the loss of the divine knowledge intrinsically brings with it a loss of the power of life (St. Athanasius of Alexandria, *On the Incarnation* 4–5); an enslavement to *Ptharsia*, or corruption of existence, since the vision of God is the "proper" ontological source of life for all human and angelic being. For Orthodox theology, therefore, the great victory of Christ is manifested above all in the restoration of life given to the redeemed race. This "life" (no mere symbol, but a powerful reality) is culminated in the gift of resurrection, and in the transfigured life of the

communion of the saints, but it is manifested even here and now in the church, in the form of many charisms: the conquering of the fear of death; the willingness of the saints to prefer heavenly things for earthly; cheerful self-sacrifice for the sake of others; the offering of the warm joy and simplicity of Christ to those one meets; in an overarching philanthropy that constantly seeks out the poor to "hear" them and lift them up to the common table from which they have been pushed away; in the love of poverty and humility for the sake of Christ; in the charisms of celibacy and chastity: things which St. Athanasius describes as "unnatural" in the common world order, but as signs of "new life" in Christ (*On the Incarnation* 27; 29; 47–8; 51). These are, each one singly, great signs of the power of life in a human being. Taken collectively, within the body of Christ's disciples, they are the witness of the enduring power of the resurrection in the world.

For the fathers, beginning with Irenaeus and Athanasius, and cascading into a major soteriological theme in all of their successors (especially the Cappadocians, St. Cyril of Alexandria, and the Byzantine fathers), the Word's redemption of humanity through the assumed body can be exactly epitomized as the "Deification of the Race." The incarnation is thus fundamentally a life-giving paradox and mystery. In Christ, the church is caught up into the very life of the Trinity, and shares in its power of life.

Orthodox Christology is also highly eschatological in character. The presence of the resurrection is felt even now. That Jesus will come again as Judge of the world, his elect faithful believe in and hope on. This living belief is the sure sign that the eschatological flame of the Spirit burns in their hearts, and leads them to cry out still: "Maranatha! Lord Jesus come!" (Rev. 22.20). This continuing trust that the Lord is active for justice over the world (he will come as Judge to vindicate righteousness on earth), and also actively present for the continuance of his mercy on earth (for he will not leave us orphans – Jn. 14.18, 27), is the power of belief that activates the spiritual life of all the Orthodox faithful, their moral life, and their passion for mercy and justice.

The Mystery of the Christ is not simply a matter of discourse, however; even if it is necessary to sketch out the form and shape of Orthodox teaching "about Christ" for the sake of clarifying the Tradition. Far more so, Christ is the love and heart's joy of the Orthodox Church; its delight, its inspiration, its renewal; its endless renewal, and goal. Christ is the gift of spiritual life and illumination. It has been so from the beginning. It shall be so until the end of time; for the Lord who is the bridegroom of the church is the Alpha and the Omega, the beginning and end of all things. Poised in between, as an eschatological tension, his church reflects the whole cosmic sweep of time, knowing it lives in the interim, and yet impatient for the fulfillment, by its two most distinctive prayers: the first being the Jesus Prayer: "Lord Jesus Christ, Son of God, have mercy on us"; the second being its eschatological acclamation: "Maranatha!"

We shall leave the final words on the Lord Jesus to the great Syrian saint, Mar Isaac of Niniveh:

O Christ who are "covered with light as though with
    garment," (Ps. 104.2)
Who for my sake stood naked in front of Pilate,
Clothe me with that power which you caused to overshadow
    the saints,
And with which they triumphed in this conflicted world.
Divine Lord, be gracious to me, and lead me above this world
    to be with you.

                                   (*The Second Part* (II) 5.22–3)

SEE ALSO: Arianism; Cappadocian Fathers; Council of Chalcedon (451); Council of Constantinople II (553); Council of Constantinople III (680–681); Council of Ephesus (431); Deification; Ecumenical Councils; Fatherhood of God; Holy Spirit; Holy Trinity; Liturgical Books; Parousia; St. Cyril of Alexandria (ca. 378–444); St. Isaac the Syrian (7th c.); Theotokos, the Blessed Virgin; Tradition

References and Suggested Readings

Behr, J. (2001) *The Way to Nicaea: Formation of Christian Theology* vol. 1. Crestwood, NY: St. Vladimir's Seminary Press.
Behr, J. (2004) *The Nicene Faith: Formation of Christian Theology* vol. 2, part 2. Crestwood, NY: St. Vladimir's Seminary Press.
Gavrilyuk, P. (2004) *The Suffering of the Impassible God: The Dialectics of Patristic Thought*. Oxford Early Christian Studies. Oxford: Oxford University Press.
McGuckin, J. A. (1995) *St. Cyril of Alexandria: On The Unity of Christ (That the Christ Is One)*. Crestwood, NY: St. Vladimir's Seminary Press.
McGuckin, J. A. (2004) *St. Cyril of Alexandria and the Christological Controversy: Its History, Theology, and Texts*. Crestwood, NY: St. Vladimir's Seminary Press.
Mantzaridis, G. I. (1984) *The Deification of Man*. Crestwood, NY: St. Vladimir's Seminary Press.
Nellas, P. (1987) *Deification in Christ: The Nature of the Human Person*. Crestwood, NY: St. Vladimir's Seminary Press.
Stăniloae, D. (1976) *The Victory of the Cross*. Oxford: Fairacres Press.

Church (Orthodox Ecclesiology)

TAMARA GRDZELIDZE

The Purpose of the Church

The purpose of the church is to restore fallen humanity and thereby reconcile the whole creation to God. Its sacramental life is the means to fulfill this purpose. The divine economy of salvation is the foundational principle of the church. The mystery of human salvation leads to the mystery of the salvation of the whole creation which is God's ultimate goal. In this life the church bears witness to a new existence revealed through the incarnation and the resurrection of Jesus Christ – "The Church has been planted in the world as a Paradise," says St. Irenaeus (*Adv. Haer.* 5.20.2) – and this new reality already proclaimed is destined finally to attain the status of the new creation.

The nature of the church, as Orthodoxy understands it, is deeply experiential and accordingly it is difficult to describe it by any single formula that carries an overwhelming authority. The early church knew no such single doctrinal definition and the reason for this is that, according to Fr. Georges Florovsky (1972: 57), the reality of the church was only made manifest to the "spiritual vision" of the church fathers. The nature of the church can thus be experienced and described, but never fully defined. The closest approximation to a doctrinal definition within Orthodoxy is the clause in the Creed, which affirms that the church is "One, Holy, Catholic and Apostolic."

Plate 11   The Monastery of the Holy Trinity, now known as Troitse-Sergieva Lavra, Sergiev Posad, founded by St. Sergius of Radonezh. The most important monastery in Russia. Photo by John McGuckin.

The church is the place *par excellence* of a believer's participation in the mysteries of God. The faithful participate in the divine mysteries from the very beginning of their life in Christ through the sacrament of baptism and reach the height of that participation in the Eucharistic celebration. The very essence of this participation is experiential, something that can be readily observed in the case of children whose love exceeds their understanding, or Orthodox people of little knowledge but great faith. The love of God manifested to human beings and creation is reciprocated in faith by the church's constant returning the love of God through the praise of the faithful. This human participation in the divine mysteries is nurtured always by the belief and knowledge that "God is love" (1 John 4.8), and this movement of praise that constitutes the church's inner life is the height of creation – its meaning and fulfillment.

A Church Trinitarian and Christocentric

The Apostle Paul speaks about the church and Christ in this way: "This is a great mystery" (Eph. 5.32). Christ is the foundation of the church: "For no one can lay any foundation other than the one that has been laid; that foundation is Jesus Christ" (1 Cor. 3.11). The mystery of the incarnation and the mystery of the resurrection lie at the heart of that mystery which is the church; for, as Metropolitan Kallistos puts it, "The Church is the extension of the Incarnation, the place where the Incarnation perpetuates itself" (Ware 1993: 241). At the same time, in the words of Olivier Clément, "The Church is the power of resurrection to us; the sacrament of the Risen One who imparts his resurrection to us" (1995: 95). The

Scriptures describe the church as the body of Christ (Eph. 1.23; 2.13–14; Rom. 2.5; 1 Cor. 12.4–30) and the Temple of the Holy Spirit (Acts 2.1–4; Eph. 2.21–22). The church is christocentric, yet it is charismatic, a restless energy led by and inspired with the Holy Spirit of God. The fullness of the triune God resides in the incarnate and resurrected Son of God. It is through the Spirit that Christians are united in Christ, incorporated into his body, and all partake of the same body of the resurrected Christ (1 Cor. 10.17). It is through the Holy Spirit also that the faithful become partakers of the body of the resurrected Christ. As St. Basil describes it:

> Through the Holy Spirit comes our restoration to Paradise, our ascension to the Kingdom of heaven, our adoption as God's sons, our freedom to call God our Father, our becoming partakers of the grace of Christ, being called children of light, sharing in eternal glory, and in a word, our inheritance of the fullness of blessing, both in this world and the world to come. (*On the Holy Spirit* 36)

A Church Divine and Human, Visible and Invisible

The church as a *theandric* entity is like Christ in that it shares two natures, two wills, two realities – the divine and human; therefore, what can be said about Christ can be applied in an analogous way to the church. In this (christological) sense, the church cannot sin and the human sinfulness of its members evident within it cannot affect its holy nature. The church in its earthly existence witnesses to a certain tension because it is already the holy body of Christ (in other words it is sinless), but at the same time it gathers into its embrace members who are fallible and sinful. Even so, the element of human sinfulness cannot affect the essential nature of the church. The church, in Orthodox understanding, is at once visible and invisible: it is one, and is not divided into a visible and an invisible church. The church exists in this world, and for this world, but it cannot be reduced to this earthly existence since it can never be considered separately from Christ and the Holy Spirit. The church thus embraces at once the body of Christ and the fullness of the Holy Spirit. In

this sense, the church extends from an assembly of the gathered faithful to the assembly of saints: both realities gathered together around the throne of God.

The communion of saints denotes the continuity between the two worlds, that of the living and of the departed, a unity of present and future in the fullness of the one body of Christ. The names of the departed are read out together with the names of the living during every Eucharistic celebration, and the faithful who pray for the health and spiritual prosperity of the living also pray for those who "have fallen asleep in the true faith, and in hope of the Resurrection, and of life everlasting." Most honored among the saints is the Mother of God and Ever-Virgin Mary, "More honorable than the cherubim and incomparably more glorious than the seraphim," as a *troparion* of the church services describes her. The Orthodox adopted the early patristic heritage about the church as Virgin Mother. Such documents as the *Shepherd of Hermas* (2nd century) and the *Second Epistle of Clement* (late 2nd century), and the works of St. Irenaeus of Lyon, Clement of Alexandria (2nd–3rd centuries), Tertullian (3rd century), St. Cyprian of Carthage (3rd century), and later works from the 4th century onwards also developed the image of Mary as a symbol of the church. As St. Ephrem the Syrian expressed it: "Three angels were seen at the tomb: these three announced that he was risen on the third day. Mary, who saw him, is the symbol of the Church which will be the first to recognize the signs of his second coming" (Behr 2006: 119–34). In Orthodox iconography, Mary is symbolized in this ecclesial role with upraised hands – "Orans" praying as the symbol of Christ's church, as his truest disciple.

A Sacramental Church

The structure of worship in the Orthodox Church also reveals its true nature: Matins (Orthros), followed by 1st, 3rd, 6th, 9th Hours, the divine liturgy, Vespers, Compline, and Midnight Prayer. The church is shown in the liturgical cycle to be an unceasing prayer itself, an instrument of giving thanks to God for our life, by letting the faithful participate in the mystery of sharing the body and blood of Christ in anticipation of the kingdom and for the salvation of the whole creation. But worship is not an end to itself, for the church enters into the life of the faithful by the sacraments which spread out dynamically into the rest of their actual life. If understood otherwise, the church can seem to be a place of occultism. The participation of the faithful in the mysteries (sacraments) of the church unfolds in different ways. In the early church, in anticipation of the Eucharistic celebration, the faithful brought many products, fruits of their labor such as wheat, bread, oil, and wine, and they were used in the church services, thus offering back to God what had been given to them. Nowadays, in some places, especially in rural areas, one can still see the faithful bringing the actual fruits of their labor for use in church services. In other places this remains now only as a symbolic part of Orthodox ritual. The participation of the laity in Orthodox services is always dialogical, deliberately responsorial: clergy and laity are in dialogue throughout the worship, whether it is a question of the reciting of prayers, or the singing of *troparia*, jointly hearing Old and New Testament readings, assenting to the priestly intercessions by a corporate "Amen" or shouting out *Axios*, as a sign of assent during the rites of ordination and canonization. Sacramental operations in the church reveal the mystery by using material elements such as bread, water, and oil, thus disclosing at once the reality of this life and of the new life that is in Christ.

Sacramental life in the church is the pathway to salvation for a believer for, as Lossky puts it (1991: 181), "In the Church and through the sacraments our nature enters into union with the divine nature in the hypostasis of the Son, the Head of His mystical body." By means of the sacred mysteries, the faithful are born, formed, and united to the Savior, so that "in him we live, and move, and have our being" (Acts 17.28). Orthodox catechisms today usually list seven sacraments or mysteries of the church: baptism, chrismation, Eucharist (the sacrament of sacraments), repentance or confession, holy orders, marriage, holy unction or the anointing of the sick; but this sevenfold enumeration is a late (17th century) development, made under the influence of western scholastic theology. Different church fathers and theologians have counted them in different ways (John of Damascus referred to two, Dionysius the Areopagite to six). Although the Orthodox tradition avoids labeling the sacraments in terms of what are the most or the least important, baptism and the Eucharist remain the cornerstone of the sacramental life of the church. Baptism confers being and existence in Christ and leads the faithful into life, while the Eucharist continues this life. Nicholas Cabasilas describes this in the following terms: "Through the sacred mysteries, as through windows, the Sun of Righteousness enters this dark world ... and the Light of the World overcomes this world" (1974: 49–50).

A Eucharistic Church

It is the sacrament of the Eucharist that constantly builds up the church as the body of Christ. As St. John Chrysostom maintains: "We become a single body, according to Scripture, members of his flesh and bone of his bones. This is what is brought about by the food that he gives us. He blends himself with us so that we may all become one single entity in the way the body is joined to the head" (*Hom. Jn.* 46; PG. 59. 260). The sacrament of the Eucharist is the main key for approaching Orthodox teaching on ecclesiology. As St. Irenaeus says: "Our teaching is conformed to the Eucharist, and the Eucharist confirms our teaching" (*Adv. Haer.* 1.10.2). The Holy Eucharist expresses all the major defining ecclesiological characteristics: unity, holiness, catholicity, and apostolicity. In the Orthodox Church the celebration of the Eucharist incorporates several of the other mysteries too (baptism, marriage, holy orders, funerals), because the partaking of the holy gifts was always seen as the summit of a liturgical celebration. The eschatological dimension of the Eucharist has also indicated and expressed the very nature of the church. The Eucharistic mystery is the eschatological moment *par excellence*, a remembrance of the kingdom which is centered on the Presence (*Parousia*) of Christ. In fact, as Metropolitan John Zizioulas reminds us, there is no real unity of the church without a vision of the last days (1985: 187). Liturgical anamnesis and commemoration are understood eschatologically: every moment in the liturgy is related to the past and the coming kingdom. This is the living reality of the church which embraces all times and all places at once; which recognizes the presence of faithful in prayer together with commemorated saints and the departed. This is the living church celebrating the Eucharist of which the faithful become partakers. The Eucharist is thus the sacrament *par excellence*, but it cannot exist on its own, without the wholeness of the wider sacramental life and teaching of the church. The entire life of the mysteries is a preparation or a pretext to participation in the Eucharistic celebration and all is brought into the human gift of salvation, which is the attaining of deification.

There are extreme cases such as martyrdom by which someone may acquire all the depth and meaning of the sacramental life at once; but these exceptions attain meaning only in the general context of a believer's continual formation and transformation in and by the sacramental life of the church. Twentieth-century Orthodox theology has certainly witnessed a movement (seen in Catholicism also) for the rediscovery of Eucharistic theology. The remembrance that *lex credendi* must derive from *lex orandi* led to the "rediscovery" of the church as "the Sacrament of Christ." Fr. Alexander Schmemann was one of the leading lights in this revival. This rediscovery emphasized that sacramental life must not be seen as confined to the church, but embraces the whole of a human existence, a lifelong growth into Christ. The church does not view its faithful as spectators or attendants of church services, but rather as participants who, after being sanctified in the church, bring the church back to their everyday life.

The Church as a Temple

Obviously, when we refer to the church, for the Orthodox the particular building also comes to mind. This is a secondary meaning (the church in its iconic architectural form as temple), but it is none the less important. Since the time of the official recognition of Christianity as a licit religion in the Roman Empire (Edict of Milan, 313), the church has been more a place than an action conducted at different locations such as memorials at the grave of the martyr or prayers in the home, as it was in the earliest practices of the Christians (and in modern times too, when we consider how many modern confessors in gulags have secretly celebrated the Eucharist). The primary

importance of the action compared to the place has been preserved in the Orthodox tradition of having liturgies in the open air, or "stational" liturgies. However, the Byzantine commentaries on the liturgy (by Germanos the patriarch of Constantinople d. 733 or Maximos the Confessor d. 662) also emphasize the importance of the church as a specific, and hallowed, place. Going to the church for other occasions apart from the liturgy is also significant, says Maximos the Confessor in his *Mystagogia* (PG 91. 701–4), as the holy angels remain there even after the *synaxis* and the grace of the Holy Spirit always invisibly is present in the church. For this reason it is a marked aspect of Orthodoxy how much the faithful love their churches, care for them with great affection, and visit them often for private prayer as well as for public services.

The Church as one, Holy, Catholic, and Apostolic

The Nicene-Constantinopolitan Creed speaks about the four marks of the church. Orthodoxy understands the unity of the church as being something true and absolute, a unity provided in one sense by the communion of all the local churches in the sameness of faith in Christ, yet a unity also that is the one promised by Christ (Jn. 10.16; 17.11, 21–22), which cannot be defined according to worldly concepts of unity because it is part of the divine mystery of communion in the Trinity. As Archbishop Antony Khrapovitsky put it: "The Church is the likeness of the existence of the Holy Trinity, a likeness in which many become one" (1911: 17–18). The church is also called to be holy. From the creation until the accomplishment of all the works of God the church will guard its holiness, which in the world is the most striking manifestation of God. Orthodox tradition sees the Holy Spirit as hypostasized holiness. Various aspects of the sacramental life in the church witness to different degrees of consecration and sanctification flowing out from the divine holiness. Like the burning bush at Sinai, "this place is hallowed" because of God's presence within it; all the marks of holiness coinhere within it. The "kiss of peace" the church uses to recognize its communion is holy because it marks the fellowship of those who exchange it in Christ. The prophets and apostles are holy because of the *charism* of their ministry, and each baptized person is sealed with the gifts of the Holy Spirit and thus participates in none other than "the very holiness of God" (Heb. 12.10). The Eucharistic celebration speaks most explicitly of holiness. The Epiclesis, the invocation of the Holy Spirit during the Anaphora, consecrates not only the holy gifts but also the entire people of God; its words declare as much, saying: "Send down your Holy Spirit upon us and upon these gifts here presented."

The holy unity of the church also signifies its unifying power for divided humanity, and this characteristic is directly related to the third mark of the church – its catholicity. The Orthodox Church is called and known as catholic because it extends over all the world, from one end of the earth to the other; and because it teaches universally and completely each and all of the saving doctrines which must come to humankind's knowledge, concerning things both visible and invisible, heavenly and earthly. As St. Cyril of Jerusalem said: "The Church is rightly named Ecclesia, because it calls forth and joins together all mankind" (*Catechetical Lectures* 18.23). Catholicity (known also in its Slavonic translation as *Sobornost*) is the wholeness and integrity of the church's life rather than a simple geographical extension. The unity of the church is extended into the catholicity of the church: the church is one but it is manifested in many places, it operates with a plurality in unity and unity in plurality; and as Afanasiev put it: "In the Church, unity and plurality are not only overcome: the one also contains the other." (1992: 109). By virtue of this catholicity each member of the church on earth lives in union with the heavenly church entire, which maintains an uninterrupted union of love and faith with the visible church. This is why, in Orthodoxy, the concept of catholicity is associated with a profound sense of the church as a *body* of which every member is an integral part, endowed with profound responsibility for the whole.

Exegeting how the church can be called "the fullness of him who fills all in all" (Eph. 1.23), St. John Chrysostom says:

> The Church is the fulfillment of Christ in the same manner as the head completes the body and the body is completed by the head. Thus we understand why the Apostle sees that Christ, as the Head needs all His members. Because if many of us were not, one the hand, one the foot, one yet another member, His body would not be complete. Thus His body is formed of all the members. (*Hom Ephes.* 3.2)

Finally, the strong guardian of the unity of the church is its apostolicity. St. Irenaeus gives the classic exposition of this concept:

> Those who wish to see the truth can observe in every Church the tradition of the Apostles made manifest in the whole world.... This tradition the Church holds from the Apostles, and this faith has been proclaimed to all, and has come down to our own day through the succession of bishops. (*Adv. Haer.* 3.1)

The purity of apostolic succession, which Orthodoxy cherishes as one of its great glories, binds the entire history of church life into the unity of catholicity, bringing together the faithful of all generations, transcending limitations of time and space. Apostolic succession is a matter of fidelity to the Lord's teaching, but also involves the threefold ministry in the church: that of bishops, priests, and deacons. Ordained ministry is the manifesting of the charismatic principle, the gift of the Holy Spirit, continued in the church through the apostolic succession. The priest, the celebrant of the Eucharist, safeguards the unity within the local community, but the bishop safeguards the catholic unity of the local ekklesia, and their synodical communion defends the unity of the whole church throughout time and space. This is why the church's apostolicity is fully manifested in the celebration of the Eucharist. The structure of the Orthodox Church with its threefold ministry and collegiality unfolds the theology of the early church with a bishop presiding as the head of the Eucharistic celebration, surrounded by presbyters and deacons who facilitated a link between bishop and laity. As Fr. John Meyendorff expressed it, Orthodoxy's "maintenance of the apostolic structure of the Church is an eschatological necessity" (1978: 321). Orthodoxy also recognizes the highest authority of the ecumenical councils because they have this living charism of apostolicity.

A Church Local and Universal

Orthodoxy's conciliar principle is intrinsic to its Eucharistic ecclesiology; in other words, every local church is in accord with the other local churches and they are drawn together by love and harmony (a "consilience into unity" as the Council of Chalcedon described the Christ-mystery) above and beyond their legal unity afforded by means of the canons. Every local church bears the fullness (*pleroma*) of the Church of God precisely because it is the undivided Church of God, not a mere part of it. This fullness is a gift of God to every local church and all stand in agreement with each other, forming a living interdependence of churches. This interdependence is interpreted within Orthodox ecclesiology as fundamentally a matter of connectedness of witness and testimony, rather than of canonical submission. It is a dialectic of unity in diversity which is very descriptive of Orthodox ecclesiology, and very important to it. Orthodox ecclesiology does not exclude the notion of a primacy of authority, but it interprets this in precise ways, and does not associate it with a power of supremacy in the church, which it regards as incompatible with the nature of the church as communion in Christ.

The church has been placed in the world by its Lord and master on a pilgrimage. It does not belong to the world (Jn. 17.16–18), but its task is to illumine it as it progresses towards its own glorious communion with the Lord of Ages. It lives in tension with the world, which cannot understand it unless God enlightens it to do so, and it has to resist the spirit of the world. But at the same time it does not reject the world; just as its Master did not reject the world but loved it and gave his life for it (Jn. 3.16), and sees that its destiny as eschatological mystery is to catch the very world into the New Creation which the church inaugurates as its ultimate goal. The church, "the inaugurated *Eschaton*," already belongs to the New Creation (Gal. 6.15), but as to its final glory, that remains unseen in this earthly time.

SEE ALSO: Apostolic Succession; Baptism; Communion of Saints; Deification; Ecumenism, Orthodoxy and Eucharist; Evangelism

References and Suggested Readings

Afanasiev, N. (1992) "The Church Which Presides in Love," in J. Meyendorff (ed.) *The Primacy of Peter: Essays in Ecclesiology and the Early Church*. Crestwood, NY: St. Vladimir's Seminary Press.

Behr, J. (2006) *The Mystery of Christ, Life in Death*. Crestwood, NY: St. Vladimir's Seminary Press.

Cabasilas, N. (1974) *The Life in Christ*, trans. C. J. de Catanzaro. Crestwood, NY: St. Vladimir's Seminary Press.

Clément, O. (1995) *The Roots of Christian Mysticism*. New York: New City Press.

Cyril of Jerusalem (1989) *Catechetical Lecture 18*, chs. 23–24, in *Nicene and Post-Nicene Fathers of the Christian Church*, vol. 7. Edinburgh: T&T Clark.

Florovsky, G. (1972) "The Church: Her Nature and Task," in *Bible, Church, Tradition: An Eastern Orthodox View, Collected Works*, vol. 1. Belmont, MA: Nordland.

Hopko, T. (ed.) (1990) *Liturgy and Tradition: Theological Reflections of Alexander Schmemann*. Crestwood, NY: St. Vladimir's Seminary Press.

Khrapovitsky, A. (1911) *Works, Vol. 2: The Moral Idea of the Dogma of the Church*. St. Petersburg.

Lossky, V. (1991) *The Mystical Theology of the Eastern Church*. Cambridge: James Clark.

Meyendorff, J. (1978) "Unity of the Church – Unity of Mankind," in C. G. Patelos (ed.) *The Orthodox Church in the Ecumenical Movement: Documents and Statements*. Geneva: World Council of Churches.

Ware, T. (Bishop Kallistos) (1993) *The Orthodox Church*: New Edition. New York: Penguin.

Zizioulas, J. D. (1985) *Being As Communion: Studies in Personhood and the Church*. Crestwood, NY: St. Vladimir's Seminary Press.

Communion of Saints

MARIA GWYN MCDOWELL

For Orthodoxy this signifies the ongoing participation (*methexis*, or *koinonia* – communion) in God by all of God's holy elect: those still living on earth, those passed to the Lord, and the holy angels who also form part of the heavenly church. The letters to the churches of Corinth and Ephesians are addressed to the "saints" (Eph. 1.1; 2 Cor. 1.11) surrounded by a "great cloud of witnesses" (Heb. 12.1). Aside from Scripture, the earliest attestations to a cult of the saints is the early cult of martyrs. Ignatius of Antioch asserts that true discipleship lies in the witness, the *martyria*, of a confessing death. The 3rd-century *Life of Polycarp* testifies to 2nd-century Eucharistic meals at the graveside of martyrs, and encourages the honoring of the saints by following their example. Origen of Alexandria in the 3rd century emphasizes the singularly united life of the whole body of Christ, in which those in heaven continue in the struggle of faith through their sustaining love and intercession for the living. When St. John Chrysostom preached in the late 4th century, the cult of the saints was well established. In his sermons martyrdom is a powerful act of love; martyrs "speak" their faith through deeds and speak freely to God, their human lives encouraging imitation (Chrysostom 2006: 29–33). The martyr and saint has thus become an exemplar of virtue, a spiritual model.

Chrysostom highlights the transition from martyrdom to asceticism as persecution gave way to peace and to an increasingly institutionalized Christianity. In part inspired by Athanasius' *Life of Antony*, asceticism through bodily virginity, separation from the world, and a life of prayer was increasingly idealized. Ironically, often the greatest advocates of asceticism were active members of urban and ecclesial life. St. Basil the Great's social programs inaugurated their own attendant form of monasticism, in which serving others was considered integral to an ascetic life. Contemporary studies of holy men and women emphasize their role as agents of change who ignored social divisions in order to serve the needs of all, rich and poor alike (Hackel 1983).

By the 8th century, St. John of Damascus speaks of venerating saints as friends of Christ and temples of the Holy Spirit. This concept of holiness as the presence of God is crucial. Holiness is thus not reserved for exemplary individuals only, but is the common promise of Christ's people, and part of the standard graced way of life for all disciples. In the divine liturgy the giving of Eucharistic Communion is preceded by the celebrant saying "Holy things for the holy," referring to both the gifts being offered and the people receiving them. The people's response, "One is holy, one is Lord, Jesus Christ," underscores the singular divine source of the church's holiness. An individual's holiness is the synergy between personal freedom and the grace of God which results in both repentance and virtue.

The participation of believers in the holiness of Christ leads to three important points. First, saints are not those whose lives are perfect, but whose lives at some point and in some manner exemplify the virtues and holiness of God. Second, just as God cannot be contained in a single description, neither can the image of God in the saints. Saints are those in whom the image and likeness of God are embodied in a uniquely distinctive manner. Third, unity with Christ in holiness crosses boundaries of time and "matter." As living members of Christ, our spiritual forebears continue to be present. Just as God deified matter in the incarnation, even the bodies of saints participate in holiness, something that is underscored in the Orthodox Church's *cultus* of holy relics.

The church does recognize particular persons as exemplary. These men and women are "glorified" saints, and their prayers are requested in public worship. The process of glorification has no fixed process nor firm regulation. Nektarios, Patriarch of Jerusalem (d. 1680), established three conditions for glorification: indisputable orthodoxy of faith; a holy life and confession of faith with an openness to martyrdom; and manifestations of divine grace via miracles, posthumous healings, spiritual assistance, or bodily incorruptibility. In practice not all of these signs need be present together. Sainthood among the Orthodox is often the result of a popular devotion. The recognition by the church is a response to the evident grace of God. Today, glorification involves a formal service in which the saint is no longer prayed *for*; instead, God is thanked for the holy person and his or her intercessions are requested: they are prayed *to*.

Participation in the holiness of God has given rise to an astonishing diversity of Orthodox saints. In an age of persecutions, the Great Martyrs exemplify steadfast faith in the face of suffering and death. The desert fathers and mothers and stylite saints manifest personal holiness and offer intercession on behalf of urban neighbors. Military saints, once glorified for their (frequent) refusal to fight, become defenders against non-Christian attackers. Unmercenary saints-physicians offer free medical assistance and spiritual healing. The liturgy lists among the saints patriarchs, prophets, martyrs, wonderworkers, theologians, fathers, mothers and teachers of the church, monastics, ascetics, spiritual guides, physicians, and healers.

This diversity is conditioned by social context. Susan Ashbrook Harvey observes that the early church is noted for its diversity of holy lives in which female saints always exemplify a public role. But as the criteria for sainthood increasingly involves ecclesial leadership, not only did the number of female saints decline in later centuries, but their lives, while no less holy, were increasingly conducted in private (Harvey 1998: 104). Fr. Michael Plekon (2009) notes the dangers of an exaggerated reverence which can obscure complex lives. The controversy surrounding Mother Maria Skobtsova (newly glorified) and Fr. Alexander Men highlights the tension often lost in idealized hagiographies between participation in the holiness of God and an Orthodox "life in progress" revolving around the struggle of repentance and transformation. Yet it is this coexistence of imperfection and holiness which inspires and comforts believers as they are accompanied in the life of faith by their spiritual forebears.

SEE ALSO: Deification; Elder (Starets); *Menaion*; New Martyrs; Newly Revealed Saints; Passion Bearers; Relics; St. Nicholas the Wonderworker; Soteriology

References and Suggested Readings

Chrysostom, J. (2006) *The Cult of the Saints: Select Homilies and Letters*, trans. W. Mayer and B. Neil. Crestwood, NY: St. Vladimir's Seminary Press.

Hackel, S. (1983) *The Byzantine Saint*. San Bernardino: Borgo Press.

Harvey, S. A. (1998) "Holy Women, Silent Lives," *St. Vladimir's Theological Quarterly* 3–4: 101–4.

Plekon, M. (2009) *Hidden Holiness*. Notre Dame: University of Notre Dame Press.

Confession

TENNY THOMAS

The term "confession" has several meanings. Confession of faith was an integral part of the baptismal ceremony (Cyril of Jerusalem, *Catechetical Orations* 2.4) and is represented today in the creeds still used in

Plate 12 The Orthodox confession service. Photo © Sergey Lavrentev/istockphoto.

the liturgies. When infant baptism became more common, it was still required that someone should speak the confession on behalf of the child (Hippolytus, *Apostolic Tradition* 21). The close association of confession and witness made it a term that after the 3rd century came to be closely associated with the most particular witness (*martyrium*) that the Christian was expected to give when arrested and questioned by hostile magistrates. Those who survived trial and imprisonment and returned to the community enjoyed great positions of honor. They were referred to as "confessors." Until the early 4th century, those who confessed the faith under persecution were considered as "ordained by God." Confession is also an ancient term that denotes the tomb of a Latin martyr. Not least, the popular sense of the word refers to an acknowledgment of sin by an individual, made either privately or publicly. Confession (Greek, *Exomologesis*) is one of the major sacraments of the Orthodox Church. Its various elements include (1) individual private prayer, spoken or unspoken; (2) spoken confession by individuals discreetly before a priest; followed by (3) individual or group absolution.

Tertullian is one of the first, in the late 2nd century, to speak of the idea of public confession (*On Penance* 9). A system of public confession was put in place by the ancient church after the many lapses occurring during the era of the persecutions. This system (reflected in the early canons of the church which are very severe regarding penitents) was relaxed by the late 4th century (fading away in most churches) and was replaced by a more individual system of "penitence" and confession of the sins of the heart (whereas the ancient system dealt with public and scandalous sins), a development probably originating from the monastic practice of opening the heart out to the elder of a monastic community, and which extended outwards to the laity as a spiritual praxis.

The forms of absolution in use in the Orthodox Church today are slightly different in Slavic and Greek usage; so too does the frequency vary with which confession is approached – it being a much more normal part of Slavic church life than Greek.

SEE ALSO: Elder (Starets); Excommunication; Repentance

References and Suggested Readings

Cullman, O. (1949) *The Earliest Christian Confessions*. London: Lutterworth.

Ferguson, E. (1987) *Early Christians Speak*. Abilene: Christian University Press.

Fitzgerald, A. (1988) *Conversion through Penance in the Italian Churches of the Fourth and Fifth Centuries*. Studies in Bible and Early Christianity 15. Lewiston: Edwin Mellen Press.

McGuckin, J. (2004) "Confession – Confessor," in *The Westminster Handbook to Patristic Theology*. London: Westminster/John Knox Press.

Palmer, P. F. (1959) *Sacraments and Forgiveness*. Westminster, MD: Newman Press.

Watkins, O. D. (1920) *A History of Penance*, 2 vols. London: Longmans Green.

Constantinople, Patriarchate of

JOHN A. MCGUCKIN

The patriarch of Constantinople is today rooted in the ancient former capital city of the Roman Empire (not Rome, but after the 4th-century Christian ascent to power, "New Rome" or Constantine's City, *Konstantinopolis*). The city retained the ancient name of Constantinople until the early decades of the 20th century when Ataturk, signaling new beginnings after the fall of the Ottoman sultans whose capital it had also been, changed the name to Istanbul (originally another Greek Christian shorthand for "To the City" – *eis tin polin*) and at the same time moved the capital of Turkey to Ankara. After the rise of Turkish nationalism, and the disastrous Greco-Turkish War of the early decades of the 20th century (reflected, for example, in Kazantzakis' novel *Christ Recrucified*), Constantinople, which had always been a major hub of world affairs, and a massively cosmopolitan city, changed into becoming a monochromatic backwater. The many religious communities that had remained there even after its fall to Islam in the 15th century dwindled, until today, demographically, Orthodox church life in that once great metropolis is a sad shadow of what it once was.

From the foundation of the city as a Christian hub of the Eastern Empire by Constantine in the early 4th century, the city was the center of a great and burgeoning Christian empire: the Christian style and culture of Byzantium made its presence felt all over the world, from the Saxons of England, to the Slavs of the cold North, to the southern plateaux of Ethiopia. The Great Imperial Church (once the cathedral church of the patriarchate, too) was Hagia Sophia. After the conquest of the city by Islamic forces in 1453, the last emperor was killed and Byzantine dynastic rule was ended, and the patriarchate took over (under the sultans) political and religious supervision of all the Christians of the large Ottoman dominion. Under Mehmet II and his successors, many churches in Constantinople were seized as mosques. It had lost the Great Church of Hagia Sophia at the time of the conquest, but was also later ousted from the large headquarters of St. Mary Pammakaristos. After many vicissitudes and sufferings, the patriarchate came in

1603 to be established in its present location in the very modest Church of St. George at the Phanar in Istanbul.

Today, the patriarch of Constantinople has a primacy of honor within Eastern Orthodoxy. There is enduring historical controversy among the scholars (as was the case in ancient church history, too) over the precise meaning of the 28th canon of the Council of Chalcedon (451) which gave the (relatively recent) see of Constantinople a primacy of jurisdictional sway. Did the canon of Chalcedon intend to make New Rome first after Old Rome, that is, "second" in rank and precedence among the five patriarchates then existing, which was more or less the import of the third canon of Constantinople 1 (381), or did it mean to make it into the new first see of Christendom, the "next" of that "first rank," that is, New Rome succeeding to the privileges of the first see (Old Rome) which itself had enjoyed its erstwhile primacy by virtue of being the capital of the empire, but now had to yield that privilege to the current and real capital of the empire? The Chalcedonian canon reads:

> Following in all things the decisions of the holy Fathers, and acknowledging the canon, which has been just read, of the One Hundred and Fifty Bishops beloved-of-God (who assembled in the imperial city of Constantinople, which is New Rome, in the time of the Emperor Theodosius of happy memory), we also do enact and decree the same things concerning the privileges of the most holy Church of Constantinople, which is New Rome. For the Fathers rightly granted privileges to the throne of old Rome, because it was the royal city. And the One Hundred and Fifty most religious Bishops, actuated by the same consideration, gave equal privileges to the most holy throne of New Rome, justly judging that the city which is honoured with the Sovereignty and the Senate, and enjoys equal privileges with the old imperial Rome, should in ecclesiastical matters also be magnified as she is, and rank next after her; so that, in the Pontic, the Asian, and the Thracian dioceses, the metropolitans only and such bishops also of the Dioceses aforesaid as are among the barbarians, should be ordained by the aforesaid most holy throne of the most holy Church of Constantinople; every Metropolitan of the aforesaid dioceses, together with the bishops of his province, ordaining his own provincial bishops, as has been declared by the divine canons; but that, as has been above said, the metropolitans of the aforesaid Dioceses should be ordained by the archbishop of Constantinople, after the proper elections have been held according to custom and have been reported to him. (Canon 28, Council of Chalcedon, 45)

The wording and intention of the Chalcedonian canon remain the subject of historical exegesis, as it is not simply the case that Constantinople is made "second in rank after Rome" as most western church writers have presumed. The range of privileges granted to it as court of appeal, especially in canon nine of the same Council of Chalcedon, far exceeded those which Old Rome had commanded up to that time. The issue of Canon 28 would be a constant friction in Orthodox–Latin Church relations afterwards, until the Great Schism of the 11th century made it, practically speaking, irrelevant. It continues to have controversial status as to its exact sense of application in contemporary church law: not merely with regard to ecumenical relations between Orthodoxy and Roman Catholicism, but also internally (especially in a lively tension between the patriarchates of Constantinople and Moscow) as to the extent of Canon 28's applicability in terms of executive "superintendence" in world Orthodoxy.

The patriarch, known as His All-Holiness the Archbishop of Constantinople, the New Rome, and Oecumenical Patriarch, is still resident in Istanbul. This capital of "New Rome" was founded by Constantine the Great in the early 4th century to be the military and political center of the Roman Empire. From this time onwards (and it remained the case until the 9th century) the fortunes of the older western capital at Rome went into serious decline. Even late into the 4th century, however, Constantinople's ecclesiastical significance was very modest, reflecting its origins (as the colonial port of Byzantium) as a subordinate part of the diocese of Thrace (now Bulgaria). Byzantium had been a thoroughly insignificant city before Constantine's refoundation, and the new capital took some time to establish itself as a powerful magnet of ecclesiastical affairs, just as it did to establish itself as the veritable center of all political power in the Roman world. The rise to preeminence was rapid enough when it did happen, of course. And by the late 4th and early 5th centuries the bishops of Constantinople had become in effect archbishops by gathering together a whole ecclesiastical territory that looked to them for supervision and guidance. The institution of the home synod was encouraged by the archbishop of Constantinople. Because so many bishops came to the capital so regularly, to pursue political and other business there, they were invited to share in the deliberations of the local church. The home synod still functions in a more limited way as the governing body of patriarchal affairs. It is now made up of the ecclesiastical eparchies which are still immediately subject to the patriarch (Derkos, Chalcedon, Prinkipo, and Imbros), along with other titular archbishops who, as senior hierarchs, govern the diaspora churches as exarchs on behalf of the patriarch.

This ever-increasing and effective functioning as an international clearing house in the heart of the capital set Constantinople on a path of collision with the more ancient patriarchates, particularly Rome, Alexandria, and Antioch. Their grumbling and friction marks the pages of almost every ecclesiastical argument of Antiquity. Rome, by the universal agreement of all until the time of the Council of Chalcedon, was regarded as the primary court of appeal for the Christian world. Even though the city had lost much of its effective political power after the 4th century, it was still afforded the "right" to be considered as last ecclesiastical court of appeal. This right was effectively undercut in practice for the simple reason that travel in Antiquity was immensely difficult, so only the most critical of any issues from the Eastern, Greek-speaking churches would ever be heard as an appeal in Rome anyway. To complicate matters, language difficulties also stood in the way, and this too was reflected in the ancient canons of the church. For most practical affairs, then, the see of Alexandria at first held the precedence in the Eastern Church, mirroring what Rome did in practical terms for all the Western Churches, where it was the sole patriarchal and apostolic see. The rise to political preeminence of Constantinople changed this system of ecclesiastical governance. Constantinople's expansion not only "put out" Alexandria, it also began to overshadow the patriarchate of Antioch and the Syrian hierarchs, whose territory it was very close to. There were moments of tension between Constantinople and Antioch, also reflected in the decisions of the early councils, but many of the most important of the early Constantinopolitan archbishops were drawn from the ambit of the Syrians and Cappadocians who adjoined that region.

The Second Ecumenical Council of Constantinople in 381 and the Council of Chalcedon in 451 (again at Constantinople's eastern suburb – indeed, almost all the great councils after Nicea were held here), gave the precedence of Constantinople greater clarity and force. It has always been seen as a matter of "normalcy" among the Orthodox that a city's ecclesiastical importance should reflect its role in the structure of the civic governance. This principle was enshrined in the canons of the Council of Nicea I in 325. By the later 5th century the ecclesiastical position of the imperial capital was unarguably central in church affairs just as it was in political affairs, and from this time on the patriarchate of Constantinople was established as the real center of precedence among the Eastern Churches. The Roman patriarchate continued to resist the implication that a see's precedence should be tied to its geopolitical importance. Nevertheless, the canonical position of the patriarchate of Constantinople was universally accepted in the East, and Rome itself came to admit it (at least in relation to other Eastern Churches), long before the time of the Great Schism of the Middle Ages. After the rise of Arab power in the 7th century, the once great Christian communities of Antioch and Alexandria fell into disastrous decline, which further elevated the prestige and importance of Constantinople as a Christian nucleus. At many times in history the patriarchs of those sees were actually resident in Constantinople, and their senior clergy were supplied from out of the Phanariot ranks (those Greeks who lived in the Constantinopolitan patriarchate's administrative zone, the Phanar).

The decree of the sultan set the patriarch of Constantinople as the political superior of the other patriarchs for the first time ever. This immense temptation to follow the path to political domination over the other churches was largely resisted. The potential of the patriarchate under Islamic power to lord it over the other sees was also undermined by a certain degree of corruption of the Phanar which closeness to the seat of the sultanate brought with it; for in the late 15th and throughout the 16th and 17th centuries the patriarchate was massively unsettled by the extent of bribery the sultans encouraged for elevation to that sacred office. After the first cabal of Greek merchants from Trebizond offered to the sultan a bribe of 1,000 florins to depose the incumbent Patriarch Mark II (1466–7) and replace him with a candidate of their own choice, the sultan's eyes were opened to the possibilities. By 1572 the standard "investiture fee" for the patriarch was the substantial "gift" of 2,000 florins, and an annual payment of 4,000 more, gathered from taxation of the Christian "Rum" people who were placed under the patriarch's supreme charge throughout the Ottoman Empire. There were always more than enough Christian factions lining up to pay the highest premium to ensure the election of their candidate after that point. Accordingly, the tenure of the patriarchs under Turkish rule was usually very short. Sometimes the same candidate acceded to the office, was deposed, and reelected to it five or six times (each time paying the necessary fees). Between the 16th century and the early part of the 20th century, 159 patriarchs held office. Of this number, the Turks drove out of office 105. Several were forced to abdicate and six were judicially assassinated. The cadre of Greeks who sailed this stormy sea, trying to keep the prestige of the patriarchate intact and effective (sometimes using it for unworthy ambitions), tended to live in what was then the wealthy suburb called the Phanar; and were thus known as Phanariots. Many of the higher offices of the church were subsequently put into their hands when a new patriarch acceded, and this in turn led to the Phanariot Greek clergy becoming a kind of colonial superior race directing churches in distant lands, using the mandate of the sultan and the decree of the patriarch to justify it. They in turn, as local archbishops, levied taxes on their new people. As a result, the Turkish "yoke" cast a long pall over Orthodox relations with the patriarchate. The British historian Kidd acerbically described the situation in the following terms:

> Thus the Patriarchate, degraded by simony and made the sport of intrigue by its own people, has come to be regarded by many of the Orthodox as an agent of the Turkish government, and identified with its oppression. But the Patriarchate has also come to be identified by such of the Orthodox as are non-Greek, with the cause of Hellenic nationalism.... A widespread hostility has

thus pursued the Phanariot clergy among the non-Greek Orthodox; and the revolts which the Phanar puts down to Phyletism (Inappropriate nationalism) have issued in the enforced recognition of national churches, as a refuge from Phanariot oppression. (Kidd 1927: 305)

His view, not a last word on the subject by any means, for it glosses over the heroic reality of how Constantinople "kept things going" in these dark times, nevertheless explains why some of the newer national Orthodox churches sprang into being after the collapse of the power of the sultanate in the 19th century; although this too does not give the whole picture – how in most instances this "return to independence" was a return to more venerable ecclesiastical situations that had predated the Turkish yoke. Hostile critics of the Orthodox scene have sometimes been too ready to cry "collaboration" and "simoniacal conformism" when they have seen Orthodoxy under the foot of either Turkish or Soviet oppressions. But they have generally done so from the comfort and safety of their armchairs and the financial security of their own ecclesiastical establishment. The blood that has been spilled in the Orthodox Church over the last three centuries is incomparably greater than the amount of the blood of the martyrs that was shed in the first three centuries of what we now call the period of the Great Persecutions. Today, the main entrance gate to the Phanar buildings is kept closed, in honored memory of the Patriarch Gregory who was the incumbent in the time of the 19th-century Greek Revolution, and who was dragged from the altar of the Church of St. George, still wearing his liturgical vestments, to be hanged from the gate. The patriarchate can boast of its martyrs.

The end of political coherence within the sprawling Ottoman Empire, which was becoming more and more obvious at the end of the 19th century, certainly witnessed the breaking up of the immediate jurisdictional sphere of Constantinople. Russia had already detached from its orbit in the 15th century following the controversy concomitant on the Council of Florence. It declared itself a new patriarchate in 1589. Greece (while remaining in the closest of all ties of affection and loyalty to the patriarchate) declared its independence from the Phanar organizationally in 1850, Bulgaria in 1870, Serbia in 1879, and Romania in 1885. Georgia and Ukraine did the same in regard to the Moscow patriarchate, which had formerly supervised them, in 1919, but these would be brought back under control through the enforced Sovietization of their nations later, and would again seek independence when those powers of political control were once more loosened from the Russian center. In the 10th century, however, when it was in its glory, Constantinople had supervisory rank over no fewer than 624 dioceses. In its heyday its ecclesiastical territory of influence embraced all the Balkans, all Thrace, all of Russia from the White Sea to the Caucasus, and the whole of Asia Minor.

Today, five and a half centuries after the fall of the city to the power of Islam, it is in a state of very sad decline "on the ground," though it remains a brightly shining beacon and example to Orthodox the world over by virtue of its spiritual fidelity and the enduring ecclesiastical role of the patriarch as *Primus inter pares*, "first among equals." Many of the patriarchs of Constantinople, throughout its long history, have been Christian leaders of the highest calibre, and the historical record of the Throne is, overall, a vastly prestigious one. It continues this office in straitened circumstances, under difficult political and religious constraints. Today, there are hardly any resident Greeks left of the thousands of Greeks, Armenians, and other Christian nationals who once made Istanbul a truly universal and cosmopolitan center of world affairs; and to that extent the city's Christian life enters a state of unreality: a massive concern to preserve the monuments and relics of an important past.

Since the bitter Greco-Turkish War of 1922 the massive exchange of populations that took place meant that Asia Minor was more or less denuded of its Greek inhabitants – then numbering 1.5 million souls – for the first time in recorded history. Turkish law only permits the residence of Greeks in Istanbul itself, but after 1922 the situation became more and more impossible for most Christian families to feel secure, and so the mass exodus began. Current Turkish law forbids monks or nuns, priests or bishops, to wear clerical dress in public (with the single exception of the patriarch), and there is much popular hostility to the idea of a Greek Christian leader living in the heart of this Islamic city. On September 6, 1955 a large anti-Greek riot, sparked by the Cyprus problem, led to the burning or sacking of 60 out of the 80 Orthodox churches remaining in Istanbul, and most of the surviving Christian community lost heart at that point. Damage to Christian property was then estimated at more than £50 million. The Turkish government subsequently paid £4 million in compensation. With deportations and voluntary emigration following, the resident Greek population continued over the remainder of the second half of the 20th century to dwindle to demographic insignificance.

Those entering the Phanar today are swept with electronic search devices to discourage hidden weapons or the leaving of bombs in church (incidents which are, alas, not imaginary). The Orthodox theological school of Halki, on one of the adjoining islands of the city, founded in 1844, was once a center of the advancement of the clergy. In the middle of the century it had begun to acquire an international reputation among the Orthodox Churches as a center of learning. In 1971 the Turkish government forcibly suppressed the admission of new students, on the grounds of preventing "propaganda and anti-Turkish sentiment" (a reference to the Cyprus crisis) and despite many efforts since to reopen it, its enforced closure remains a stain on that government's record of religious toleration. The modern postwar patriarchs Athenagoras, Dimitrios, and Bartholomew have brought great dignity and honor to their office, enduring these difficulties, and by their personal gifts restoring an internationally luminous reputation to their throne, far beyond the formal extent of Orthodox circles. Relations with the Turkish secular powers have tended to improve, and the mooted prospect of Turkey's entrance into the European Union has also acted as a spur to better relations between the Phanar and its political overlords. The Treaty of Lausanne (1923) formally governs relations between the Phanar and the Turkish state. It currently requires the patriarch always to be a Turkish citizen. It also restricts his role to "only spiritual" matters, preventing him from being involved in politics. The state's forced closure of the patriarchate's seminary at Halki is seen widely by the world outside Turkey as an attempt to suffocate the patriarchate by not allowing the training of new clergy, who are Turkish citizens and who could be of the calibre to assume the office in the future.

The present territorial extent of Constantinople's ecclesiastical jurisdiction comprises Turkey, the ancient parts of Thrace that are not in present-day Bulgaria, Crete, some Greek islands in the Aegean (Rhodes, Leros, Kos, and Karpathos), the monasteries of Mount Athos, all Greeks of the diaspora (large numbers in Europe, America, and Oceania), a jurisdictional oversight over the church of Finland (since 1923), and some parts of the Russian diaspora communities who have sought the Phanar's guidance for historical reasons related to the Russian Revolution. The total number of faithful directly belonging to the jurisdiction of the patriarchate is today in the region of 7 million. The vast majority of them are in the diaspora. The category of the diaspora at first initiated as a mission to Greeks who came to the West has now been extended, in some places over many generations, to cover the very large Greek Christian communities of America and Australia, and also the smaller Exarchate of Great Britain and Ireland, which can less and less be considered as missionary territories any longer. Much more than half the lay members of the patriarchate, for example, now reside in North America, and many of the Greek Orthodox there are so thoroughly Americanized that some of them have forgotten their ancestral language. The Phanar continues to exercise jurisdictional oversight over several Slavonic rite dioceses in "exile," Russian, Ukrainian, Polish, and Albanian, which put themselves under the patriarchal protection in the difficult times following the large flight westwards from communist oppression in the early part of the 20th century. The question of the continuing need for "exile" is a current point of inter-Orthodox tension.

The patriarchate today continues a policy, evident among its leaders from the beginning of the 20th century, of encouraging the senior hierarchs of world Orthodoxy to meet regularly and intercommunicate on wide levels. It has sponsored Orthodoxy's international dialogues with other non-Orthodox Churches, and despite frequent shrill cries from some of the most traditionalist Orthodox critics of its behavior, it has done so with enormous wisdom, charity, and reserve; never rushing into statements or deeds that it would have to regret or later withdraw. Its model in ecumenical communication has been to establish a "dialogue of love." The present Patriarch Bartholomew I is an internationally renowned voice for preservation of the world's ecosystem, and a strong and respected moral teacher of international stature on issues of compassion and justice.

SEE ALSO: Bulgaria, Patriarchal Orthodox Church of; Cyril Lukaris, Patriarch of Constantinople (1572–1638); Ecumenical Councils; Ecumenism, Orthodoxy and; Greece, Orthodox Church of; Iconoclasm; Jeremias II, Patriarch (1572–1595); Ottoman Yoke; Russia, Patriarchal Orthodox Church of; St. John Chrysostom (349–407); Scholarios, George (Gennadios) (ca. 1403–1472); Serbia, Patriarchal Orthodox Church of; Stethatos, Niketas (ca. 1005–1085)

References and Suggested Readings

Imber, C. (1990) *The Ottoman Empire 1300–1481*. Istanbul: Is Press.

Kidd, B. J. (1927) *History of the Church to AD 461*. London: Faith Press.

Mainstone, R. J. (1988) *Hagia Sophia*. London: Thames and Hudson.

Nicol, D. M. (1993) *The Last Centuries of Byzantium: 1261–1451*. Cambridge: Cambridge University Press.

Runciman, S. (1968) *The Great Church in Captivity*. Cambridge: Cambridge University Press.

Sherrard, P. (1965) *Constantinople: Iconography of a Sacred City*. Oxford: Oxford University Press.

Contemporary Orthodox Theology

ARISTOTLE PAPANIKOLAOU

The fall of Constantinople in 1453 silenced a long and vibrant intellectual tradition within Orthodox Christianity. It would take nearly 400 years before a revival occurred in 19th-century Russia, which then saw the emergence of an intellectual tradition that was rooted in the Orthodox theological and liturgical tradition, but that also sought to engage modern philosophical currents streaming into Russia, especially German idealism. From this particular trajectory emerged what is referred to as the Russian school. The best-known and most influential scholar of the Russian school is Vladimir Sergeevich Solovyov (1853–1900), considered to be the father of Russian Sophiology. Two ideas were central to Solovyov's thought: the humanity of God (*bogochelovechestvo*) and *Sophia*.

Solovyov's concept of the humanity of God is related to the Orthodox dogmatic principle of the divine–human union in Christ. Solovyov, however, was far from a dogmatician. His philosophy attempts to express the Orthodox principle of the divine–human union in Christ in critical engagement with the categories of German idealism. The humanity of God forms the basis for Solovyov's attempt to conceptualize a God who is both transcendent of and immanent to creation. Solovyov expresses this particular understanding of the God–world relation with the concept of Sophia, and by so doing gives birth to the Sophiological tradition of the Russian school. God is Sophia, which means that God eternally relates to creation, and creation itself (that is, created Sophia) is a movement of reconciliation towards divine Sophia. More than any other contemporary Orthodox theologian, Solovyov attempted to develop the implications of divine–human communion for a political theology and for a theology of culture.

Although the thought of the Russian school bears the stamp of Solovyov's Sophiology up until the 1917 Revolution, it was Sergei Nikolaevich Bulgakov (1871–1944) who advanced the most sophisticated development of Solovyov's thought. Bulgakov was more conversant than Solovyov with the eastern patristic tradition, and his Sophiology is expressed explicitly in the idiom of the traditional theological dogmas and categories of the Orthodox tradition. The most developed form of Bulgakov's Sophiology appears in his dogmatic trilogy *On Divine Humanity* (*O bogochelovechestve*, 1933–45), the first English translation of which would only appear nearly sixty years later.

Unlike Solovyov, Bulgakov's Sophiology is more explicitly trinitarian and appropriates traditional trinitarian language. The Trinity is the Father's self-revelation in the Son, who is the objective content of the Father's self-revelation. According to Bulgakov, the self-revelation of the Father is not complete until the content that is revealed in the Son is actualized as life by the Holy Spirit. Sophia is identified with the

homoousion of the Trinity, but particularly as the *ousia* hypostatized as the self-revelation of God. As such, it is more than simply what the persons possess in common, but the very trinitarian being of God. As the very being of God, Sophia must necessarily refer to God's relation to the world, and not simply to the intra-trinitarian relations, because, for Bulgakov, the self-revelation of God in the *Logos* and the Holy Spirit is the revelation of all that God is, and included in "all that God is" is God's relation to creation and humanity.

For Bulgakov, the relations between the trinitarian persons are best understood in terms of *kenosis*, as a movement of self-giving and self-receiving that has the capacity to overflow and reflect itself in the creation of the world. Anticipating later liberation theology, Bulgakov argues that the crucifixion of Christ reveals the *kenosis* of each of the persons of the Trinity, which includes the co-suffering of the Father with the Son. Always participating in the divine Sophia, the world as created Sophia is moving toward the unity of all in God's life, which is given in and made possible by the *kenosis* of the Son and completed by the Holy Spirit.

Sophiology did not survive in the Orthodox world in any influential form past Bulgakov. Its demise was partly due to the explicit refutation of Sophiology by Orthodox thinkers in the Russian diaspora whose own understanding of Orthodox theology would come to be known as the Neopatristic school. Although this school has roots in the translations of the eastern patristic texts made in Russia, it is most associated with Georges Florovsky (1893–1979) and Vladimir Nikolaevich Lossky (1903–58). Florovsky framed the debate with Russian Sophiology in terms of the relation between theology and philosophy. He coined the phrase "Neopatristic synthesis," asserting that theology must be rooted in the language and categories of the eastern patristic texts.

For Lossky, however, the debate with Sophiology was not primarily about the relation between theology and philosophy; it was about conceptualizing the transcendent and immanent God. Both Bulgakov and Lossky share a similar starting point in theology: the principle of divine–human communion, that is, *theosis*. They both agree that divine–human communion is not simply the goal of the Christian life but the very presupposition, the first principle, in all theological thought. Their debate over the relation between theology and philosophy is really a disagreement over the implications of the affirmation of divine-human communion.

For Lossky, much like Bulgakov, the divine-human union in Christ is the starting point for theological thinking about God. Insofar as this union is one between two opposites, between what is God and what is not God, it is beyond the grasp of human reason, whose capacity for understanding is restricted to created reality. While human reason functions on the basis of the law of non-contradiction, the incarnation demands that theology be antinomic, that is, it must affirm the non-opposition of opposites. Theology's function is to give expression to the divine-human communion in Christ, which reveals the antinomic God, the God who is radically immanent in Christ and whose very immanence reveals God's radical transcendence. Its purpose is not to attempt to resolve the antinomy through reason but to stretch language so as to speak of the divine-human communion in Christ in such a way that it might guide a person toward true knowledge of God, which is mystical union with God beyond reason. Theology is apophatic, by which Lossky means two things: that language is inadequate to represent the God beyond all representation, and that true knowledge of God consists in experience of God and not in propositions rooted in human logic.

The affirmation of the God who is beyond being, and yet radically immanent to creation, is the basis for the essence-energies distinction. The essence of God refers to God's transcendence, while the energies refer to God's immanence and the means for communion with God. True knowledge of God consists in participation in the energies of God, which are uncreated. The crystallization of the essence-energies distinction can be traced back to the medieval hesychast St. Gregory Palamas. Lossky, together with Florovsky and John Meyendorff (1926–92), represented the essence-energies distinction as uniquely characteristic of, and central to, Orthodox theology. Its centrality has since been affirmed by virtually every 20th-century Orthodox theologian, including the Romanian Dumitru Stăniloae (1903–93), the most famous outside the Russian and Greek orbits, and it is the reason why Orthodox theology today is often referred to as Neo-Palamite. The distinction was also used in polemics against neo-scholastic understandings of created grace.

In addition to the essence-energies distinction, an additional antinomy is foundational for theology: God as Trinity. The goal of theology is not to explain how God is Trinity but to express the antinomy. The patristic categories of *ousia* and *hypostasis* are given in the tradition in order to express what is common and incommunicable in God as Trinity. The trinitarian categories, however, also provide the foundation for an understanding of personhood that is defined as irreducible uniqueness to and freedom from nature. Lossky was also a vehement opponent of the *filioque*, which he interpreted as the natural result of the rationalization of the doctrine of the Trinity.

Beginning in the 1960s, the work of Lossky and Florovsky had a significant influence on a group of young theologians in Greece, most notably Nikos Nissiotis (1925–86), Christos Yannaras (b. 1935), and John Zizioulas (b. 1931). Elements of Lossky's theology, such as apophaticism, the essence-energies distinction, and the theology of personhood, are evident in Yannaras's major work of 1970, *Person and Eros*. The most influential of these theologians is John Zizioulas, who synthesized the Eucharistic theology of Nicholas Afanasiev (1893–1966) and Alexander Schmemann (1921–83) with the theology of personhood of Lossky, via Yannaras.

Zizioulas, like Bulgakov and Lossky, affirms the principle of divine-human communion as the starting point of all theology, but unlike Lossky's emphasis on the ascetic, mystical ascent to God, Zizioulas argues that the experience of God is communal in the event of the Eucharist. According to Zizioulas, early Christians experienced the Eucharist as the constitution of the community by the Holy Spirit as the eschatological body of Christ. This experience of Christ in the Eucharist is the basis for the patristic affirmation of the divinity of Christ and the Spirit and, hence, of the affirmation of God as Trinity.

Zizioulas's emphasis on the experience of God in the *hypostasis*, or person, of Christ has at least two implications. First, it is a noticeable break with the virtual consensus in Orthodox theology on the use of the essence-energies distinction for expressing

Orthodox understandings of salvation as the experience of the divine life. Second, it is the foundation for what Zizioulas calls an "ontological revolution," insofar as it reveals God's life as that which itself is constituted in freedom and not necessity. If the Eucharist is the experience of God, and if such an experience is for created reality the freedom from the tragic necessity of death inherent to created existence, then God exists as this freedom from necessity, even the necessity of God's nature, since God gives what God is. The freedom of God from the necessity of God's nature is the meaning of the patristic assertion of the monarchy of the Father; the Father "causes" the Son and the Spirit and, in so doing, constitutes God's life as Trinity through a movement of freedom and love. With the doctrine of the Trinity, for the first time, otherness, relation, uniqueness, freedom, and communion become ontologically ultimate.

This understanding of divine-human communion in the life of the Trinity through the hypostasis of Christ also grounds Zizioulas's theology of personhood. *Person* is an ecstatic being, that is, free from the limitations of created nature; it also a hypostatic being, that is, unique and irreducible to nature. This freedom and irreducibility is possible only in relation to God the Father through Christ by the Holy Spirit, because it is only in the eternal relations of love that one is constituted as a unique and free being, that is, a person. Zizioulas maintains the building blocks of Lossky's theology of person, but with a new emphasis on relationality and in a decidedly non-apophatic approach. Zizioulas's theology of personhood is the organizing principle for this theology, and it is evident in his theology of ministry, his ecclesiology, and his theology of the environment.

At least three central issues face Orthodox theology in the immediate future. One is the centrality of the essence-energies distinction for expressing the transcendence and immanence of God, as well as the compatibility of this distinction as the language of divine-human communion with the language of the Trinity. A second issue is the question of the patristic interpretation of *hypostasis* and whether the contemporary Orthodox theology of personhood, which is arguably one of the most distinctive contributions of modern Orthodox theology, is a logical development of patristic thought, or not. Finally, the revival of Russian Sophiology, especially that of Bulgakov, and its impact on the engagement of Orthodox theology with non-theological currents of thought must be further studied. The Russian school was actively engaged in social issues, and its influence is evident in the work of Mother Maria Skobtsova (1891–1944), who died in a German concentration camp because of her work in protecting Jewish victims of the Nazis; also in the work of Elisabeth Behr-Sigel (1907–2005), who wrote extensively on gender issues and on women's ordination. Issues of engagement in social action have been noticeably absent, however, in the Neopatristic school. The challenge for Orthodox theology is to retrieve what is best in the Russian and Neopatristic schools in order to produce a theology that is simultaneously mystical and political.

SEE ALSO: Berdiaev, Nikolai A. (1874–1948); Bulgakov, Sergius (Sergei) (1871–1944); Deification; Eucharist; *Filioque*; Florensky, Pavel Alexandrovich (1882–1937); Florovsky, Georges V. (1893–1979); Holy Spirit; Holy Trinity; Humanity; Incarnation (of the Logos); Khomiakov, Aleksey S. (1804–1860); Logos Theology; Lossky, Vladimir (1903–1958); St. Gregory Palamas (1296–1359); Solovyov, Vladimir (1853–1900); Sophrony, Archimandrite (1896–1993); Stăniloae, Dumitru (1903–1993)

References and Suggested Readings

Giannaras, C. and Yannaras, C. (1991) *Elements of Faith: An Introduction to Orthodox Theology*. Edinburgh: T&T Clark.

Lossky, V. (1997) *The Mystical Theology of the Eastern Church*. Crestwood, NY: St. Valdimir's Seminary Press.

Papanikolaou, A. (2006) *Being with God: Trinity, Apophaticism, and Divine-Human Communion*. Notre Dame: University of Notre Dame Press.

Valliere, P. (2000) *Modern Russian Theology: Bukharev, Soloviev, Bulgakov. Orthodox Theology in a New Key*. Grand Rapids, MI: Eerdmans.

Williams, R. (2005) "Eastern Orthodox Theology," in D. F. Ford (ed.) *The Modern Theologians*, 3rd edn. Oxford: Blackwell, pp. 572–88.

Zizioulas, J. (1997) *Being as Communion: Studies in Personhood and the Church*. Crestwood, NY: St. Valdimir's Seminary Press.

Coptic Orthodoxy

JUSTIN M. LASSER

The enchanting land of the Nile produced one of the most mystically penetrating expressions of Orthodoxy in the ancient world, making the Egyptian Church's intellectual and spiritual life internationally renowned, and profoundly influential in the formative era of ancient Christian thought. For many centuries this church had the eyes of world Orthodoxy fixed upon it, in emulation. It was a land where multiple currents of thought and practice lived tolerantly side by side; over time, however, the Orthodox were forced to live out most of their history as an endangered minority in their own land. The survival of the Coptic Orthodox Church to this day, now flourishing in a lively diaspora in America and Australasia, as well as enjoying a rebirth in its ancient monastic sites, and in the modern cities such as Cairo and Alexandria, is a testament to its martyr's fidelity and to its irrepressible spiritual vitality.

The term "Coptic Orthodoxy" has often been used by historians to describe the multicultural Christianity of Egypt from the vantage point of the city of Alexandria, a perspective which tends to approach Coptic Christianity as basically a form of Greek Christianity expressed on Egyptian soil. The word *Copt* derives from a corruption of the Greek term for "Egyptian" (*Aigyptos*) signifying (pejoratively at first) a native of the hinterland outside the Greek-speaking littoral cities. The word carried with it in early Byzantine times a freight of disapproval, and this aura of prejudice lasted long into the modern age, with theological historians regularly presuming (without having looked at the evidence) that Coptic Christianity had to be uneducated, peasant, and therefore unsophisticated. It was a colonial blindness among Eurocentric commentators that accounts for the late emergence of the real significance of Coptic theology in the textbooks. This scholarly confusion of earlier times, eliding the life of the Greek Alexandrian Church with the conditions of Christian Egypt in the interior, failed to distinguish sufficiently between native Egyptians (Copts) and their colonial, almost foreign, neighbors to the north in the Romanized cities and in places of power throughout the Egyptian

chora (countryside), as well as failing to engage thoroughly with the literature of the Coptic speaking Church, especially as it developed after the Council of Chalcedon. After the 8th century the distinction between Greeks and Copts became less important, given the new circumstances that faced the church in the form of the deep isolation that the overwhelming advent of Islam brought. In the long period of Islamic domination the fortunes of the minority Greek Orthodox were sustained by the favor of the sultans, whose hierarchy was acknowledged as ethnarchs under the terms of the sultan's ascription of dominion to the patriarch of Constantinople. The Greek patriarch of Alexandria, therefore, became a virtual part of

Plate 13 Coptic fresco of Christ in glory from the Monastery of St. Antony by the Red Sea: the oldest continually inhabited monastery in the world. Photo by John McGuckin.

the administration of the Phanar until modern times. The Coptic clergy, heirs of those who had renounced links with Constantinople in the aftermath of the christological controversies of the 5th century, had a closer link with the people of the countryside and the towns, adopting Arabic as their normal mode of discourse, but rooting themselves in the Coptic tongue for liturgical purposes. The use of the ancient Coptic served to underline their distinctive traditions, their sense of ethnic antiquity, and their differentiation from the Byzantine Orthodox world.

The life and development of the patriarchate of Alexandria has its own entry in this encyclopedia, and therefore our present essay will address the expressions of Coptic Orthodoxy beyond the city's environs. Even in Antiquity Alexandria was known by the native Egyptians as the "great city *near* Egypt," a characterization of Alexandria as a foreign city, which is telling. The advent of Christianity in the land of the Pharaohs came at a time when Egypt was deeply segregated, ruled by imperial masters, with native Egyptians in the status of near-powerless aliens in their own land.

Traditionally, Egypt was for a time the home of Jesus, Joseph, and the Theotokos. Heeding the call of the Angel of the Lord, the holy family, according to Matthew, fled Herod's persecution into the land of Egypt (Mt. 2.13–15). The Coptic Church has subsequently identified numerous holy sites in Egypt related to this story, and (as pilgrimage and cultic centers) they have long played a powerful role in the sustaining of indigenous Coptic identity. Beyond the gospel accounts, Alexandria is also remembered among the Copts as the see of St. Mark. Tradition recounts Mark to have been a disciple of St. Peter in Rome, and after St. Peter's martyrdom St. Mark left for Alexandria in order to proclaim the good news, as articulated in his gospel written in Rome under the auspices of St. Peter (see the *Acts of Mark*). This tradition, though it is now deeply engrained in the Coptic soul, is historically a relatively late one.

The numerous intriguing questions about Christian origins in Egypt (stimulated immensely after the finding in the late 19th century of many new and apocryphal early Christian writings, and perhaps culminating in the discovery of the Nag Hammadi texts) have called out to many 20th-century scholars to investigate the history of Coptic Christianity more fully. Bauer (1971), Roberts (1979), and Pearson and Goehring (1986) have all in different ways looked at a diversity of strands in early Christian Egypt, and pointed to the powerfully formative influence of Gnostic and Jewish communities, especially in the crucible of late Antique Alexandria. The Jews in Alexandria gave the church its ancient Scriptures in the form of the Septuagint, a Greek translation of the Hebrew Bible. This text also acted as the catalyst by which Jewish Scriptures entered into the Hellenistic philosophical world. Connections between the Jewish communities of Jerusalem and Alexandria were quite possibly regular (if even only for the pilgrimage route) from the earliest Christian times. In the earliest centuries many Christians in Alexandria seem to have worshipped using both Jewish and Christian calendars without any perceived contradiction. In time, however, the Jewish revolt against Emperor Trajan (115–17) strained relations between Jews and Christians. It is at this time, perhaps, that the Jewish and Christian communities in Egypt more distinctly separated off from one another (Pearson 2007: 99). However, the break was hardly final or thoroughly pervasive, as there is considerable evidence of continued contact between Christians and Jews. Philo of Alexandria and the exegetical methods of his school had a dominant effect on Christian theologians. From the time of Origen of Alexandria in the 3rd century, to St. Cyril in the 5th, Christian leaders started to complain of the many ways in which Jewish life in the city influenced their faithful. Cyril in particular wanted to stop the Christians observing Jewish festivals, a practice that must still have been common in his day.

The character and ethos of the native Christian Egyptians are most clearly displayed in their editing and redacting of earlier Christian and pre-Christian texts. It is this activity that reveals their interests and concerns. Coptic Christianity did not emerge in a vacuum but in the multicultural and philosophical center of the Roman world. One of the earliest Christian manuscripts was uncovered at the Upper Egyptian site of Oxyrhynchus in 1897 and 1903. Three separate copies of a sayings-gospel were discovered and it was later determined that these sayings derived from the *Gospel of Thomas*, which also exists in a complete Coptic version recovered in Upper Egypt at Nag Hammadi near the Pachomian monastery at Chenoboskion. The *Gospel of Thomas* is a collection of 114 sayings with clear evidence of later redactional activity. The nature of these redactions is what concerns us in regard to early Coptic monasticism and theological interests. The most obvious redactions include the phrase "one alone" and the term *monachōs* ("single-one"). Given the early 2nd-century dating of the Greek fragments this may be the first-ever use of the term "monk" in specifically Christian history. Of course, exactly what the early Christians meant by these terms in the *Gospel of Thomas* is debated, but what is indisputable is that here we have a deeply serious and mystical Christian theology that is refined and highly subtle.

What did it mean for early Egyptians to "become *one* and *alone*" and to "become *monachōs*"? This early usage of the term suggests that St. Anthony, traditionally remembered as the founder of eremitic monasticism, was preceded by nearly a century. Recent studies have challenged the traditional picture of the "first" emergence of monasticism in Egypt. Especially important in this vein is the work of Goehring (1996) and Pearson (2007). What Goehring discovered, to replace an older and more simplistic view that monasticism simply "began" with Anthony and Pachomius, was the earlier phenomenon of what he calls "village monasticism in Upper Egypt." And, it may be assumed, the phenomenon was active also in the more suburban settings of Alexandria. Anthony, we recall from his Athanasian *Vita*, delivered his sister into a "house of virgins" in the city before leaving for the desert. And city-ascetics such as Syncletica are also said to have predated him. Moreover, the fact that the *Gospel of Thomas* provides the earliest evidences of the term *monachōs* suggests very early links between Syrian Christianity and Egyptian Christianity, as St. Thomas was traditionally the apostle to Syria. The same connection is also evinced in the writings of St. Macarius (author of the highly influential *Great Letter* and the *Spiritual Homilies*), now generally assumed to be of Syrian provenance, not the Macarius of Egypt to whom the writings were later ascribed. This lively pseudepigraphical "trade" in writings that often raised eyebrows in Christian Antiquity demonstrates signs of how asceticism moved fluidly between these two significant and foundational sites of Egypt and Syria, and

also gives testimony to a rapid transmission of ideas that were not always valued first and foremost in terms of how the local episcopate would validate them, rather in terms of how local ascetics and sages found them useful in their inner lives. Egypt was therefore much closer to Syria in this specifically Christian proto-monastic philosophy than has been traditionally thought.

Egypt introduced a third form of monasticism besides the anchoritic (eremitic) and coenobitic (communal) archetypes. This third form, probably the earliest, comprised "solitaries" living *within* the villages and participating in liturgical and communal functions, while still remaining "alone ones." This too resonates with what is seen in the Syrian *Book of Steps*, which exhibits evidence of a class of Christians (the "Perfect") that lived on the outskirts of villages and which the "Upright" Christians supported. The work of E. A. Judge (1977) on an early 4th-century papyrus from Karanis highlights a petition from a certain Isodorus to a local official concerning an offense at the hands of two thieves. What is significant in this text is Isodorus' recounting that he had been saved by two people, the deacon Antoninus and the *monk* Isaac. This "monk" may be an instance of the "third form of monasticism" – the village monk. St. Jerome offers further evidence of this type of monasticism when he complained that "there are monks ('solitaries') living in small household communities, who exercise too much independence of clerical authority" (Pearson 2007: 108). Further evidence of this Coptic "village monasticism" is suggested by recent studies pertaining to the origins of Pachomian monasticism (Goehring 1996). According to the *Life of Pachomius* in the Bohairic Coptic version which has been interpreted by Joest (1994), St. Pachomius was imprisoned in Thebes, Egypt, after refusing to serve in the military around 312. In such times prisoners had to depend on the goodness of others to provide them food and clothing while in prison. The *Life* narrates that the Coptic Christians so impressed Pachomius with their hospitality and care for prisoners that he was so convinced of this "new" and true religion and its compassionate God that he prayed that night and committed his life completely to this same God. When he was finally released from prison, Pachomius sought out the nearby Christians in the town of Chenoboskion and was received into the church there.

In time Pachomius became a disciple of a local anchoritic monk named Palamon. This Palamon was not a monk living in a monastery or living the life of a hermit, but a monk of the third way living amid the town's environs and, presumably, partaking in church life in the village. The great Pachomius one day stumbled upon a deserted village about 10 miles south of Chenoboskion called Tabennisi. This village was to become resettled as the first Pachomian (meaning chiefly "coenobitic") monastery. However, Pearson has challenged the extent to which this town was actually deserted. "While the Pachomian accounts suggest a completely vacant village akin to the ghost towns of the old American west, it is possible that the label indicates nothing more than that a sufficient degree of vacancy and open space existed within the villages to enable Pachomius to establish ascetic communities there" (Goehring 1996: 275). In short, we ought not to take too drastic a division between monastery and settlement as we have hitherto. Though St. Anthony is remembered as the *first* eremitic monk, and Pachomius the *first* coenobitic monk, the evidence suggests they were not so novel. However, the Coptic Church remembers them "iconically." They present the *reality* of forsaking the world for quiet contemplation – with St. Anthony, being alone; with St. Pachomius, together–alone: that is, degrees of the same charism. The early evidence suggests that the Copts practiced a very early and unique form of village monasticism. The "interior desert," therefore, was much closer to the village and city than had been earlier assumed. St. Anthony and St. Pachomius were, then, the icons of a practice that was already well established in the land of the Nile – the "solitary" movement that once operated in near historical anonymity was given a name: monasticism. This would change the Christian world forever: forging a link between urban Christianity with its hierarchical and liturgical focus, and village life, in which the monastics would serve as a powerful bridge, eventually taking over the episcopate entirely.

Beyond the historical circumstances of the village monastic movement in Coptic Egypt, the texts they produced and copied present most surprising representations of their theological and philosophical char-

acter. What a community reads often mirrors what they practice, or at least their interests. The historian of the early Coptic Church must be wary of reading Alexandrine theological policy into the countryside of Upper and Lower Egypt. There are numerous instances of animosity between the monks in the *chora* and the clergy in the "great city near Egypt." It is not without significance that one of the most important and famous manuscript finds was discovered buried in a jar near Chenoboskion and the first Pachomian monastery near the modern town of Nag Hammadi. This eclectic collection of texts bound in 14 codices is certainly indicative of the wide-ranging character of nearby Coptic Christians. Whether or not the Nag Hammadi codices derive from the library of the Pachomian monks is still debated. Though, given the practice of monastic copying and the fragments contained in the cartonnage of the codices, a monastic origin is plausible, if not probable. If this is the case, the student of early Coptic Christianity must recognize that the Nag Hammadi texts were used by Copts, which means they considered them spiritually relevant, at least, if not enlightening. The fact that the divine names (such as the *Holy Spirit*, *Christ*, etc.) throughout the texts are written in reverent manner suggests a serious Christian interest in them.

The Nag Hammadi codices are often termed the "Gnostic Scriptures," but this is a misleading description. The Nag Hammadi find contains pieces of Plato's *Republic*, early Christian wisdom literature such as the *Teachings of Silvanus*, instances of Christian "Platonism" in texts such as *Marsanes*, sayings and dialogue gospels such as the *Dialogue of the Savior* and the aforementioned *Gospel of Thomas*, and gnostic treatises such as the *Apocryphon of John*. The immense importance of the Nag Hammadi find lies in its rare snapshot of the widely disparate currents already existing within early Coptic Christianity before later attempts to impose a more episcopally approved standard of teaching (especially after the Arian crisis was resolved) and economic adversity conspired to iron out the wrinkles of earlier experimental diversity. It is also important to recognize the eclecticism of the Pachomians. They were able to read excerpts from Plato, Valentinus, the Apocryphon of John, and letters of Athanasius and reflect on them all intelligently and maturely: a far cry from the parody of "peasant Copt" that earlier scholarship imagined. This ability to draw insight from a variety of disparate sources is something inherent in the early Coptic spirit. These texts were the product of Coptic Christian copying. Their significance for interpreting early Coptic Christianity cannot be overstated.

If the earliest literature from Alexandria and Coptic Egypt thus reflects the diversity of the region, it can also serve to remind us of the influence the already established Jewish presence in Egypt must have had on the nascent church. Both in terms of influence and reaction, Judaism shaped the form of Coptic Christianity. Two early Egyptian Christian documents from the 2nd century reflect this diversity and struggle for self-definition: the *Epistle of Barnabas* and the *Gospel of the Hebrews* (both can be partly reconstructed from patristic quotations; cf. Cameron 1982). The *Epistle of Barnabas* refutes some who "believed that the covenant of God was both theirs [presumably the Jews] and ours" (perhaps Jewish Christians). The *Gospel of the Hebrews*, on the other hand, reflects a form of Christianity that strongly preserved Jewish identity markers and Semitic theology. Thus the *Epistle of Barnabas* may reflect the gentile interests of the Greek districts of Alexandria, while the *Gospel of the Hebrews* rises from the Jewish quarter. Another text, known as the *Gospel of the Egyptians*, represents the early trajectories of the native Coptic district at Rakotis. In fact, two texts from this period claim to be the *Gospel of the Egyptians*; the first as collated from patristic quotations and the other which was found as part of the Nag Hammadi codices. The first, the patristic version, expresses a deeply ascetic form of Coptic Christianity, one that believed Jesus Christ came to "undo the works of womanhood." In this sense, it was believed that birth extended the suffering of this world, bringing more and more people into a fallen cosmos. It also adhered to an exegetical tradition which interpreted the "fall" of humanity in the Garden to be the result of the separation of the sexes, rather than the eating of the forbidden fruit (this hermeneutic was not uncommon, as traces of it lasted into both Origen and Clement of Alexandria). In the Nag Hammadi codices the *Gospel of the Egyptians* (also called the *Holy Book of the Great Invisible Spirit*) exists in two forms and represents an amalgamation of pre-Christian Egyptian religious thought with the new Christian message. This very important text introduces much of the vocabulary for early Coptic Christianity which would define Orthodoxy in the years that followed. Like other texts in Nag Hammadi, the *Gospel of the Egyptians* represents one of the earliest forms of Christian apophaticism. It describes the Father as one "whose name cannot be uttered" and he is called the "Father of the Silence." A very similar text entitled *Eugnostos the Blessed*, later Christianized in dialogue form as *The Sophia of Jesus Christ*, also from Nag Hammadi, echoes the *Gospel of the Egyptians* in its use of the term *auto-genēs* or "self-begotten" (derived from Plato's *Timaeus*), terms that would be at the center of 4th-century theological controversy as the Alexandrian priest Arius introduced them to the wider Christian world in what would become the defining argument that made for the elaboration of Nicene Orthodoxy.

The emergence of Coptic Christianity unintentionally preserves snapshots of an important transition period in Egyptian religious history. Very early Coptic materials from Nag Hammadi and Greek fragments from Oxyrhynchus show a deep interest among the Coptic Christians in the names of God, and the power the divine names contain. This has been approached in recent times in terms of a fine line between Coptic healing and popular Christian "magic" (cf. Meyer 1999); but the belief that the divine titles convey healing power is a very ancient one, and the emphasis on healing ritual is a deep characteristic of the ancient Coptic church. It can be seen running on to the still lively interest in healing scrolls as used in the Ethiopian Orthodox tradition. These divine mysterious names are preserved in a great number of Coptic prayer scrolls which exhibit a unique feature: the use of "secret" divine names in association with the names of more familiar Orthodox intercessors such as the Archangel Gabriel or the Evangelists. The eclectic spirit again seems to define much of early Coptic Christianity. These early Coptic healing scrolls were undoubtedly the product of local Christian writers and healers, not the master theologians of Alexandria or the larger desert communities, but they nevertheless reflect the daily life of the village Copts. They depict women praying for healing and children praying for their dying mothers, among many other concerns. The Coptic prayer scroll fragments are one of the most important windows into early Coptic Orthodoxy, as they capture the concerns of the common person, the real life of an ancient Christian village.

Emerging Coptic Christianity exhibits a strong proclivity to personify and hypostatize abstract concepts and attributes. Orthodoxy, after the Gnostic era, became uncomfortable with such moves, but the phenomenon was part of the particular character of earliest Coptic Christianity. Egyptian Christianity was heavily involved in the Gnostic movement. It was at the great city of Alexandria that international gnostic theologians such as Basilides, Valentinus, and Heracleon were the first to introduce Christianity to the wider Hellenistic intellectual world, as well as inventing the genre of literary scriptural commentary (albeit of a highly symbolic and allegorized form). The anti-Gnostic Christian response is first found in the important intellectual Pantaenus. According to Clement of Alexandria (*Stromata* 1.11), it seems that Pantaenus was from Sicily and according to Eusebius (*History of the Church* 5.10) he was a convert Stoic philosopher. Pantaenus was one of the first intellectuals to embrace and develop the seeds of Christian Logos theology that had been prepared by the gospel of John, and by the early writers such as Justin and Theophilus. According to Clement, Pantaenus was also an excellent exegete of the Scriptures. It was in Alexandria that Pantaenus founded the first Christian theological "school." For the first five centuries the schools of Alexandria and Rome stood out as the greatest centers of Christian thought in the world. Very little is known about the accomplishments and character of Pantaenus, but his student Clement was a worthy testament. Clement of Alexandria himself served as head of the "school": at first this was more a matter of private rhetoricians taking learned Christian students for higher studies, and only later did it devolve into what can be more accurately seen as an episcopally directed catechetical school. Clement established a most important precedent in Orthodox theology: the use of philosophy in the formation and discovery of theological truths. Prior to Clement many Christians, such as the North African Tertullian and the Syrian Tatian, believed that Christian truth was incompatible with (Greek) philosophy; however, Clement believed that philosophy was given to the Greeks by God. Thus philosophy was considered revelatory and was not to contradict scriptural truth. The pinnacle of the mystical life in Christ was, according to Clement, manifested in a "true gnosis."

Though Clement forever altered the landscape of Christian intellectual engagement, he was still a Greek. It was his student Origen of Alexandria (ca. 185–253) who manifests a truly marvelous synthesis between native Egyptian theological styles, Greek philosophical interests, and biblical prescripts. Origen (whose name means "son of Horus") was not a full citizen of the Roman Empire, as he was the son of a mixed marriage. He was the first truly significant international intellectual Christianity had yet produced. His writings (whether adopted or rejected) served to set the agenda for much of Christianity's theological path after him. Origen's more speculative theological writings share aspects of both Neo-Platonic and native Egyptian cosmological speculation. Like many of the Coptic sources before him, Origen shows, despite all the complex and esoteric elements in his cosmology, a constant interest in the interior, spiritual life of the individual. His work, appearing as philosophy, is thus more properly understood as the first exemplar of Christian mysticism, as a way of understanding the soul's mystical union with the incarnate Logos. He became, therefore, the guiding light of the later patristic mystical tradition, and as such was the midwife of ancient patterns of Coptic thought to the international Orthodox world. The mid-3rd and early 4th centuries mark the consolidation of ecclesiastical oversight and unity in Egypt, especially under the Alexandrian Bishop Demetrius (ca. 189–233). Many Egyptian Christian leaders, including Bishop Dionysius (247–64), fled Alexandria during persecutions. The persecution under Diocletian (303) was the greatest test of the resolve of the Egyptian Christians and inaugurated an "age of martyrs." The persecution also wrought internal divisions within the church. While Bishop Peter the Martyr (ca. 300–11) was in exile, Bishop Melitius of Lycopolis began to ordain clergy in his absence, creating a parallel hierarchy, later termed the "Melitian Schism."

During the barrage of persecutions many of the Alexandrian clergy fled into the Egyptian countryside, which led to increased contact and unity. By the early 4th century the Alexandrine episcopate had extended its authority over nearly a hundred bishops throughout Lower and Upper Egypt, as well as neighboring Libya, Nubia, and Cyrenaica. It is also in this period that more Greek Christian texts were being translated into the native Egyptian Coptic language (a form of ancient Egyptian language written in primarily Greek characters).

The 4th century marks the flourishing of Coptic monasticism. Following the models of St. Anthony and St. Pachomius, Copts and Greeks set off to the desert in search of God. St. Macarius the Great (ca. 300–90), a disciple of St. Anthony, attracted many followers and developed a vast network of monks in the Fayyum, at Scetis and Nitria (today, Wadi Natrun). The monks of Scetis were the principal fonts of the *Sayings of the Desert Fathers*, one of the most precious gems of Coptic Orthodoxy.

The monastic movement in Egypt was primarily a lay phenomenon. While most of the monks supported the Alexandrine clergy during the Arian controversy, they remained suspicious of the powerbrokers in Alexandria. In the 5th century the Great Shenoute of Atripe founded the large White Monastery which offered a more unified and disciplined form of Coptic monasticism. Abba Shenoute also represents a response to the plight of the native Copts under the yoke of oppressive landlords. His monastery became not only a refuge for the poor, but a symbol of Coptic unity. Shenoute was also a stalwart supporter of Bishop Cyril of Alexandria in his controversy with Nestorius at the Council of Ephesus (431).

The Coptic monks, however, also expressed their own theologies which were, at times, at odds with Alexandria. Many of the monks of Upper Egypt were vigorous supporters of "Origenist" theology, while others were literal exegetes of the Scriptures (what the Origenist ascetics denounced as "fundamentalists"). Again we note that Egyptian monasticism had remained significantly diverse, capable of coexisting with multiple strands, even with tensions that frequently broke out (and would need an international attempt at resolution in the condemnation of Origen and Evagrius in the time of Justinian). At times, certain monasteries were set up in opposition to each other (take, for example, the pro-Chalcedonian monastery at Canopus and the anti-Chalcedonian monastery at Enaton).

The 5th and 6th centuries were the most important time for the consolidation of a unified Coptic Orthodoxy. Though much of the 5th century was characterized by deepening internal fractures caused by the post-Chalcedonian controversies and the emergence of rival hierarchies, the very struggles served to produce a self-conscious "national" Coptic Church that, whether Chalcedonian or anti-Chalcedonian, distinguished itself from the other great patriarchal centers of Christianity. The influence and power of the Egyptian Christians reached their pinnacle in the victory of Cyril of Alexandria at the Council of Ephesus (431). However, St. Cyril's victory also marks the beginning of the slow demise of Egyptian patriarchal power and influence. Egypt's constant slippage away from the ambit of the Byzantine and Roman ecclesiastical worlds coincided with the advent of Islam as overlord. The glory days of Egyptian Christianity were fast coming to an end, and centuries of difficult survival were to be its future lot.

After the Council of Ephesus the divisions within the Christian world were progressively entrenched, rarely alleviated. In a post-Ephesine effort to heal the fractures of christological division, St. Cyril and John of Antioch reached a compromise in the form of the "Formula of Reunion" of 433. This compromise, brokered by the court of Constantinople, did not long hold. With St. Cyril's death in 444 the possibility of reunion died along with him. Cyril's successor Dioscorus of Alexandria undermined the effort by attacking the Formula of Reunion and advocating for the Christology of Eutyches of Constantinople, which asserted that there were no longer two natures (human and divine) after the union (the incarnation), but only one. Eutyches was soon after condemned by Patriarch Flavian of Constantinople. Prior to the rise of Dioscorus of Alexandria, Rome had been a staunch ally of the patriarchate of Alexandria. However, in 449 a second council at Ephesus was convened, which resulted in the rehabilitation of Eutyches, but also included a direct challenge to the theology of the other patriarchal centers. With the death of Emperor Theodosius in 450, another council was convened in 451, this time at Chalcedon. In an age when the philosophy of language and the use of words decided policy and the fates of empires, this council sealed the fate of the Coptic Christians. Dioscorus was deposed and the Tome of Leo was proclaimed consistent with the theology of St. Cyril. The Council of Chalcedon (451) affirmed the Orthodox position proclaiming that there exist two natures after the union, indissolubly and unconfusedly bonded, in the single person of the Lord. Ironically, the Rome that once stood with Alexandria now became the main opponent of Alexandrine Christology. Furthermore, the fact that Nestorius himself (now in exile in Upper Egypt) believed that the Council of Chalcedon rehabilitated his original theology scandalized the Egyptians and convinced them that Chalcedon was ill-conceived and therefore not an authentic ecumenical council. From this time onwards Coptic Christianity formally took a different path from the other Orthodox centers, a division which remains unhealed to the present day. According to the *History of the Patriarchs*, when Dioscorus was deposed, the pro-Chalcedonian Proterius was consecrated bishop of Alexandria. However, the native Egyptian populace rejected this imperial interference, assassinated Proterius, and consecrated Bishop Timothy Aleurus ("The Cat") in his place in 457. For many years afterwards, pro-and anti-Chalcedonian hierarchs vied for supremacy in the city of Alexandria; the internal division of the Christian community ever weakening it, and causing large sections of the Egyptian population to resent the interference of the Byzantine court. During this period the western part of the empire was in near-collapse, which left open the prospect of the fall of the whole of western Christendom. These conditions strengthened the hand of the bishop of Rome as the official powerbroker in the West and encouraged Constantinople to make important concessions to "Old" Rome in an effort to keep them in the fold. However, this led to the alienation and isolation of the other patriarchal centers in the East.

Proterius' pro-Chalcedonian successor, another Timothy, called Salofaciolos ("Wobble Cap"), was installed under the auspices of Emperor Leo, who exiled Timothy Aleurus. When Emperor Basiliscus ascended the throne, Timothy the Cat returned from exile and brought the relics of Dioscorus with him. This event also marks an important step in isolating Coptic Orthodoxy from the Chalcedonian Orthodox communion, for when Timothy effectively canonized Dioscorus, the teaching of the earlier archbishop was effectively elevated into becoming a standard of the complete rejection of Chalcedon, and more – a rejection of the principles of compromise that even Cyril himself was willing to entertain. To this day the canonization of Dioscorus (and the concomitant view that his thought is the authentic Cyrilline heritage) remains one of the principal disagreements between anti-Chalcedonian and Chalcedonian Orthodox communions.

When Emperor Zeno expelled Basiliscus the fortunes of the Copts seemed to change. Timothy the Cat's successor, the theologian Peter Mongos ("The Stammerer"), communed with Akakios, the patriarch of Constantinople. In 482 the Emperor-theologian Zeno entered the fray by publishing his *Henoticon*, which was ultimately an effort to circumvent the Council of Chalcedon, acting as if the council never occurred. Zeno simply affirmed the "Twelve Anathemas" of St. Cyril as a standard of Christology, condemned the theologies of Nestorius and Eutyches, and sidelined the Council of Chalcedon and other "councils." The importance of the *Henoticon*, however, exists not in what is contained within, but what is noticeably absent – that is, any discussion of the "natures" of Christ. Zeno's ecumenism lay not in what was said, but what it tried to smooth over. His was an ecumenism of agreeing not to discuss whatever it was which divided. This move by Emperor Zeno was of strategic significance; it incorporated Rome by not condemning (or even addressing Leo's Tome), it brought the Copts back in by affirming their great theologian-saint, and dismissed the council (Chalcedon) that had caused such dissention in the empire and church. However, the Roman Church was outraged by Zeno's attempts, which they perceived as unprincipled compromise. In 484 Pope Felix convened a council that condemned Constantinople's Patriarch Akakios on account of his support for this policy of degrading Chalcedon (and Leo), resulting in what was later termed the "Acacian Schism."

It seemed for a time that the impact of Chalcedon was waning and the empire was yearning to forget both Dioscorus' council in 449 and the appearance of Leo's Tome at Chalcedon. However, the ascension of Justinian in the early 6th century marked an end to this consensual amnesia. Justinian revived the imperial ambitions to recapture the whole Mediterranean as Roman territory. This meant drawing Egypt back close to the Byzantine bosom. He realized that in order to accomplish this he needed the support of the bishop of Rome, who was still the main powerbroker in the western regions. Though Justinian tried with all his might to unify the Chalcedonians and anti-Chalcedonians, his attempts ultimately failed and alienated many communities in the East while failing to impress on the West the extent to which the inclusion of Leo's Tome in the Chalcedonian "picture" was deeply problematical. Justinian's efforts were also very complicated, as is evinced in the activities of his wife Empress Theodora, who supported the Monophysite clergy just as much as he tried to hinder them. This intra-family dispute helped institutionalize the various theological principles throughout the empire, especially under the efforts of Jacob Baradaeus, whom Theodora greatly patronized. Coptic Christians began to be called "Jacobites" by the Chalcedonian party because of the immense efforts of Jacob Baradaeus in ordaining and establishing a separate anti-Chalcedonian hierarchy. After this period it is customary to designate the pro-Chalcedonians as "Melkites" (from their imperial allegiance; the word deriving from the term "royal") and the anti-Chalcedonian majority, the "Copts."

While the 6th century marked the isolation of the Coptic Church from the larger Orthodox world, it also deepened a greater sense of Coptic "national" unity and cohesive identity. The strained relations between Egypt and Constantinople made the Copts ready to accept the divorce that occurred after the Arab invasion of the peninsula. In some instances the Copts received improved treatment under the Arabs; they were granted religious freedom, their taxes were greatly reduced (even if they had to pay the *dhimmi* which separated them as "protected" religious people under Sharia), and they were given many important posts within the government (a state of affairs that lasted politically until the 20th century). Over time, however, it was inevitable that Coptic Christian culture should be deeply suppressed, and the Copts often were subjected to bitter oppressions, losing their living language (it survived only as liturgically ossified) and most of their cultural institutions along with it.

The centuries that followed produced many martyrs and confessors for the faith. The Copts had to learn to survive the Fatimid and Ayyubid rulers and the cruel Mameluk rule in the 13th to 16th centuries. The rule of the sultans led to a comparative time of peace, as the patriarch of Constantinople was given overall leadership of all Christians in the Islamic world, and thus the Copts could have a voice, albeit one they would not have chosen for themselves. Well into the middle of the 20th century Coptic intellectuals ran many departments of the government and made Alexandria into a truly international city. The year 1952 marked an important change of tide in the affairs of Coptic Orthodoxy. The Egyptian Revolution in that year under Colonel Nasser, who broke with the British postwar administration, inspired a "return to Islam" which left the minority Copts out of the representational process. The remaining economic and political influence of the Copts began to erode. A period of the Copts being closed out of higher education and professional employment followed, and led to a massive exodus of Coptic Christians from Egypt. The spreading of the Copts all over the world, and their assumption there of significant professional roles, in turn led to an increasing renaissance in Coptic culture, which fed back to the motherland and caused a major revival in the fortunes of the Coptic Church in Egypt in the latter part of the 20th century and today. Additionally, increased contact with Chalcedonian Orthodox and Roman Catholics has led to vigorous dialogues and realistic prospects of reunification, based on the serious yet honest and open analysis of the original causes of the rupture of union.

To this day Egypt is still home to surviving Chalcedonian Orthodox Christians. The majority of these Orthodox pledge allegiance to the Greek Orthodox patriarchate of Alexandria. After the collapse of the sultanate in the aftermath of World War I, and then the collapse of the support of the Russian Orthodox tsars, the political and economic condition of the Alexandrian Chalcedonian Orthodox community dwindled significantly. In Nasser's period of Arabization, the very large community of Greeks in Alexandria (the city of Kavafy and Durrell) took flight in great numbers. The great spiritual center of Chalcedonian Orthodox Christianity in Egypt is located at the foot of Mount Sinai in the Monastery of St. Catherine. It is certainly an irony of history that once more in modern times the great division between Greek in the city and Copt in the country seems to have emerged. The modern dialogue between the Coptic and the Chalcedonian Orthodox has largely been stimulated and sponsored by the outlying communities, international pressures being exerted on the local Christians. The time is now at hand when the next real steps in that dialogue of love need to be taken to a new level by the local churches themselves, leaving aside centuries of distrust and resentments (on both sides) and learning to respect and trust one another again. The theological dialogues have abundantly shown that the present Coptic confessions of their "Miaphysite" faith in Christ are reconcilable with the early theology of St. Cyril, in turn reconcilable with the doctrine (properly understood) of the Council of Chalcedon in 451. What remains for a real movement towards union, however, is more than theological analysis, rather a movement towards the restoration of fraternal affection. A common realization is perhaps called for, that in the present circumstances of such massive challenges facing the very continuance of a Christian presence in the land of Egypt, the Coptic and Orthodox communities, who truly have so very much in common, cannot any longer pretend that a continued parallel existence is a good idea or a sustainable goal.

SEE ALSO: Africa, Orthodoxy in; Alexandria, Patriarchate of; Apostolic Succession; Council of Chalcedon (451); Council of Ephesus (431); Council of Nicea I (325); Gnosticism; Heresy

References and Suggested Readings

Barnard, L. W. (1964) "St. Mark and Alexandria," *Harvard Theological Review* 57: 145–50.

Bauer, W. (1971) *Orthodoxy and Heresy in Earliest Christianity,* trans. R. Kraft et al. Philadelphia: Fortress Press.

Bell, D. N. (ed. and trans.) (1983) *The Life of Shenoute: By Besa.* Kalamazoo: Cistercian Publications.

Bleeker, C. J. (1967) "The Egyptian Background of Gnosticism," in U. Bianchi (ed.) *Le Origini dello Gnosticismo.* Leiden: E. J. Brill, pp. 229–36.

Burmester, O. H. E. (1973) *The Egyptian or Coptic Church: A Detailed Description of Her Liturgical Services and Rites and Ceremonies Observed in the Administration of Her Sacraments.* Cairo: Centro Francescano di Studi Orientali Christiani.

Cameron, R. (ed.) (1982) *The Other Gospels: Non-canonical Gospel Texts.* Philadelphia: Westminster Press.

Carter, B. L. (1986) *The Copts in Egyptian Politics.* London: Croom Helm.

Chitty, D. J. (1999) *The Desert A City: An Introduction to the Study of Egyptian and Palestinian Monasticism under the Christian Empire.* Crestwood, NY: St. Vladimir's Seminary Press.

Clarke, S. (1918) *Christian Antiquities in the Nile Valley.* Oxford: Clarendon Press.

Goehring, J. E. (1996) "Withdrawing from the Desert: Pachomius and Development of Village Monasticism in Upper Egypt," *Harvard Theological Review* 89: 267–85.

Joest, C. (1994) "Ein Versuch zur Chronologie Pachoms und Theodoros," *Zeitschrift für die neutestamentliche Wissenschaft* 85: 132–4.

Judge, E. A. (1977) "The Earliest Use of Monachos for 'Monk' (P. Coll. Youtie 77) and the Origins of Monasticism," *Jahrbuch flit Antike und Christentum* 20: 72–89.

McGuckin, J. A. (2001) *St. Cyril of Alexandria: The Christological Controversy, Its History, Theology and Texts.* Crestwood, NY: St. Vladimir's Seminary Press.

Meyer, M. W. (1999) *Ancient Christian Magic: Coptic Texts of Ritual Power.* Princeton: Princeton University Press.

Orlandi, T. (1986) "Coptic Literature," in B. Pearson and J. Goehring (eds.) *The Roots of Egyptian Christianity.* Philadelphia: Fortress Press, pp. 53–8.

Parrott, D. M. (1987) "Gnosticism and Egyptian Religion," *Novum Testamentum* vol. 29, Fasc. 1, pp. 73–93.

Pearson, B. A. (2007) "Earliest Christianity in Egypt," in J. E. Goehring and J. A. Timbie (eds.) *The World of Early Egyptian Christianity: Language, Literature, and Social Context.* Washington, DC: Catholic University of America Press, pp. 97–112.

Pearson, B. A. and Goehring, J. E. (eds.) (1986) *The Roots of Egyptian Christianity.* Philadelphia: Fortress Press.

Roberts, C. (1979) *Manuscript, Society, and Belief in Early Christian Egypt.* Oxford: Oxford University Press.

Robinson, J. M. (ed.) (1990) *The Nag Hammadi Library,* revd. edn. San Francisco: Harper San Francisco.

Council of Chalcedon (451)

STAMENKA E. ANTONOVA

After the death of Emperor Theodosius II, his sister Augusta Pulcheria married General Marcian, and the two emperors summoned the ecumenical council of

Chalcedon (a suburb of Constantinople on the Asia Minor shore) in 450, to meet in 451. It was occasioned by a crisis that had flared up in Christology, resulting from the varied reception that the Council of Ephesus (431) had received since its promulgation. Large parts of the Syrian churches remained unhappy, and Rome wished to have a review of matters related to the pugnacious affirmation of Ephesus 431 that had taken place at Ephesus in 449 under the presidency of Dioscorus of Alexandria. Chalcedon was meant in part as a trial of Dioscorus for his behavior there. The other (related) immediate cause of the council was the controversial teaching of the highly placed Constantinopolitan Archimandrite Eutyches, who began to preach in 448 that Christ had two natures before the incarnation but only one nature (Monophysis) after the incarnation. He did this so as to assert the profound unity of the two natures and the integral oneness of the person of Christ. He thought he was following in the footsteps of Cyril of Alexandria, though his thought significantly deformed Cyril's theology. Archbishop Flavian of Constantinople condemned his teachings in 448 and, consequently, Eutyches turned for help to the Emperor Theodosius II and to Pope Leo I. Hearing that Dioscorus of Alexandria supported Eutyches, they were convinced that the issue merited a much wider discussion at a new council. In 449, therefore, a synod was called in Ephesus, which led to the highly controversial deposition of Archbishop Flavian, and the acceptance of Eutyches' Monophysitic teaching. Both Flavian and Theodoret of Cyr appealed to Pope Leo I about the legality of the council, which subsequently gained the epithet of the *Latrocinium* (Synod of Thieves). Chalcedon was in large measure meant to reopen this case and bring healing to a bitter controversy since Flavian had died, seen by many as a direct result of his mistreatment. While he was alive Emperor Theodosius would not countenance a "revision" of what he saw as the united policy of Ephesus 431 and 449, but his accidental death (he fell from his horse) in 450 allowed Pulcheria to move.

Pope Leo I presented the Roman views to the Chalcedonian meeting of largely Greek bishops (they had been refused a reading in 449) in a theological treatise known as *Leo's Tome*, which was composed of traditional christological statements drawn from Tertullian and Augustine. The council fathers declared the rightfulness of asserting two natures (*physeis*), one divine and one human, inhabited by the single divine person (*hypostasis*) of Jesus Christ, the selfsame who was Word of God; with both natures indivisibly but unconfusedly united. This christological formula rested on Greek philosophical concepts and carefully tried to balance all the controversial issues. It was resisted by many in the East who wished to make Cyril of Alexandria's thought the standard term of reference, though Rome and Syrian voices demanded that a clearer sense of the "two natures after the union" must be proclaimed. Even so, the safeguard of the unity of the single divine person was heavily emphasized. The Chalcedonian settlement also taught the doctrine of the "Exchange of Properties" (*antidosis idiomatum*), namely that it was theologically legitimate (because of the singleness of subject in the Lord) to refer the deeds and *propria* of each nature to the same person: thus the Word of God could be said to weep at the tomb of Lazarus, and the human flesh of Christ could be worshipped as Life and Life-giving. Nevertheless, many churches in Egypt and Syria rejected the Chalcedonian statement of faith because of the reference to "Two Natures after the Union," seeing it as a denial of the unity of the One Christ. They have remained to this day as the Non-Chalcedonian Oriental Orthodox.

The council condemned Eutyches for his teachings and deposed Dioscorus of Alexandria, rehabilitating the memory of Flavian. The Egyptian hierarchs at Chalcedon then left in a bloc, and the resulting divisions caused one of the greatest and longest rifts in church unity in the East. The anti-Chalcedonian movement (the Monophysite/Miaphysite schism) spread from Egypt to Syria and beyond, leading to extensive religious and political opposition between the Byzantine and the eastern provinces of the empire. The dissatisfaction in Syria and Egypt with the Chalcedonian Greek Church and the Byzantine emperors perhaps facilitated the Islamic conquest of these Christian territories in the 7th century, thus hindering further the possibility for reconciliation. The Chalcedonian fathers also added canons to the council, reforming many aspects of the church, and elevating the ecclesial status of Constantinople, establishing the chief sees of the empire as a pentarchy of patriarchates. Rome, for many years, accepted the teaching of the council but refused to endorse the ecclesiastical canons. It did so later; though the relative interpretation of the statutes regarding the relative precedence of the churches remained controversial for centuries between Rome and Constantinople, and eventually was at the center of the Great Schism of East and West.

SEE ALSO: Christ; Constantinople, Patriarchate of; Ecumenical Councils; Monophysitism (including Miaphysitism)

References and Suggested Readings

Gray, P. T. R. (1979) *The Defense of Chalcedon in the East (451–553).* Leiden: E. J. Brill.

Grillmeier, A. and Bacht, H. (1973) *Das Konzil von Chalkedon: Geschichte und Gegenwart,* 3 vols., 4th edn. Wuerzburch: Echter.

Samuel, V. C. (1977) *The Council of Chalcedon Re-examined.* Serampore, India: Serampore College.

Sellers, R. V. (1953) *The Council of Chalcedon: A Historical and Doctrinal Survey.* London: SPCK.

Tanner, N. P. and Albergio, G. (eds.) *Decrees of the Ecumenical Councils.* London: Sheed and Ward.

Council of Constantinople I (381)

TARMO TOOM

The Council of Constantinople met "for the purpose of confirming the decrees of Nicaea" (Sozomen, *Historia Ecclesiastica* 7.7) in the light of recent controversies with Apollinarians, Heteroousians, and Pneumatomachians, and of confessing the orthodox doctrine of the Trinity. The original text of the Niceno-Constantinopolitan Creed, the Ekthesis, is not extant. Neither is the copy of the council's decisions (Tomos). The Ekthesis is known through the documents of the second session of the Council of Chalcedon (451), where it was called "the faith of the 150 fathers."

In the Constantinopolitan Ekthesis the Son was confessed in the words of the Nicene Creed, and only a few expressions, along with the Nicene anathemata,

were dropped. The credal section on the incarnation of the Son was expanded and an anti-Marcellian phrase – "His kingdom will have no end" – was added (but see Marcellus Fragment 106). Most significantly, the Ekthesis elaborated on the role and status of the Holy Spirit. The Spirit is said to be "co-worshipped" (*symproskynoumenon*) and "co-glorified" (*syndoxazomenon*) with the Father and Son. The creed further identified the Spirit as "the one proceeding from the Father" (*to ek tou patros ekporeuomenon*). The phrase "and [from] the Son" (*filioque*) is not found in the authentic text of the Niceno-Constantinopolitan Creed. The Council of Constantinople also attempted to bolster the religious unity of the empire and therefore, despite the protests of St. Gregory of Nazianzus who wanted this outcome, the Spirit was diplomatically never called *homoousios* or explicitly "God" (*theos*). The affirmation of the Spirit's divinity is carried instead by implication in the terms "co-worshipped" and "co-glorified" with God. Accordingly, the Definition of Faith of the Council of Chalcedon (451) said about the Ekthesis of 381 that "Its teaching about the Father and the Son and the Holy Spirit is complete."

Though it did not bring all trinitarian controversies to an end, the Council of Constantinople nevertheless established the pro-Nicene theology as the imperially endorsed orthodoxy of the empire (Theodosius, *Codex Theodosianus* 16.5.6). After its promulgation all Christians were expected to follow the bishops "who affirm the concept of the Trinity by the assertion of three persons and the unity of the Divinity" (Cod. Th. 16.1.3).

The Niceno-Constantinopolitan Creed has become an international ecumenical symbol of Christian faith (see the World Council of Churches' *Faith and Order*, 1927), despite the fact that no representatives of the Western Church were present at Constantinople, and the Western provinces took some time to accept its ecumenicity.

The council issued seven canons and a letter (*Epistula Constantinopolitani concilii*, 382) to the pope and the Western bishops. Canon 1 condemned various heresies. Canon 3 acknowledged the honorary primacy of the See of Constantinople, of the "New Rome," as second only to Rome. Other canons, some of them from 382, dealt with particular theological and disciplinary issues.

SEE ALSO: Cappadocian Fathers; Council of Nicea I (325); Ecumenical Councils; Holy Spirit; Holy Trinity

References and Suggested Readings

Centre Orthodoxe du Patriarcat Oecuménique (1982) *La Signification et l'actualité du IIe Concile Œcumenique pour le monde chrétien d'aujourd'hui.* Chambésy, Switzerland: Centre Orthodoxe du Patriarcat Oecuménique.

L'Huillier, P. (1996) *The Church of the Ancient Councils.* Crestwood, NY: St. Vladimir's Seminary Press.

Need, S. W. (2008) *Truly Human and Truly Divine.* Peabody, MA: Hendrickson.

Staats, R. (1996) *Das Glaubensbekenntnis von Nizäa-Konstantinopel: Historische und theologische Grundlagen.* Darmstadt: Wissenschaftliche Buchgesellschaft.

Tanner, N. P. and Alberigo, G. (1990) *Decrees of the Ecumenical Councils.* Washington, DC: Georgetown University Press.

Council of Constantinople II (553)

JULIA KONSTANTINOVSKY

The Second Council of Constantinople, also known as the Fifth Ecumenical Council (553), was the culmination of Justinian's (527–65) ecclesiastical policy in his struggle to heal imperial Christian divisions. The council's concern was twofold: the condemnation, firstly, of the so-called "Three Chapters" and, secondly, of Origenism.

The appellation "Three Chapters" refers to three 4th-and early 5th-century theologians: Theodore of Mopsuestia, Theodoret of Cyrrhus, and Ibas of Edessa, widely believed to be adherents of Nestorius' "two-sons" and "two-natures" Christology, sharing with Nestorius an aversion to the title *Theotokos* applied to the Virgin Mary. In condemning these figures, Justinian sought to reconcile dissident parties with the Chalcedonian definition (451), whereby Christ was "one person in two natures." Chalcedon's monophysite opponents claimed to follow only St. Cyril of Alexandria's theological formula of "one incarnate nature of God the Logos." To achieve the unification of the imperial Chalcedonian church with the anti-Chalcedonian ecclesiastical bodies of

Syria and Egypt, Justinian procured the anathemas of the person and writings of Theodore, the writings of Theodoret, and one letter by Ibas. Justinian's intention was to demonstrate to the non-Chalcedonians that Chalcedon's "in-two-natures" Christology was no avowal of Nestorius, but that it was to be apprehended in the light of Cyril's "one-incarnate-nature" formula and as proclaiming the single hypostatic synonymity of Christ and the divine *Logos.* Yet, because these condemnations were of persons long dead and since Chalcedon had deemed Theodoret orthodox and the letter of Ibas beyond reproof, they were perceived as controversial and caused hostilities in the West. Moreover, in the East, they failed in their purpose of reconciling Chalcedon's opponents with its supporters.

The condemnations of Origenism combated the following ideas allegedly traceable to Origen of Alexandria and further developed by Evagrios Pontike: that bodiless minds were fashioned first, while bodies for them were made second and as a consequence of their delinquency (the double creation); that numerically and ontologically the human Christ was not the divine *Logos*, but was created and united with the *Logos* in a moral union (a type of adoptionism); that the end of things will be just like the primordial beginning and that all will inevitably be saved, including the Devil (the *apokatastasis* belief). Far from being a counterbalance to the condemnation of the Three Chapters, the condemnation of Origenism can be seen as its amplification, since it too targets a specific kind of adoptionist Christology. Anti-Origenist anathemas have likewise been seen as an attack upon pagan Neoplatonism. Notwithstanding, Origenist ideas showed vitality among more independently minded monastics of Palestine. Books of Origen and Evagrios, although proscribed, continued to be popular. In the East the Fifth Ecumenical Council promoted a Cyrilline theopaschite understanding of the incarnation and the development of the cult of the Virgin Mary as the Theotokos.

SEE ALSO: Council of Chalcedon (451); Monophysitism (including Miaphysitism); Nestorianism; Pontike, Evagrios (ca. 345–399); St. Cyril of Alexandria (ca. 378–444); Theotokos, the Blessed Virgin

References and Suggested Readings

Grillmeier, A. (1995) *Christ in Christian Tradition*. Louisville: Westminster John Knox Press.

Hussey, J. M. (1986) *The Orthodox Church in the Byzantine Empire*. Oxford: Oxford University Press.

Kelly, J. N. D. (1977) *Early Christian Doctrines*. London: A. & C. Black.

Shepard, J. (ed.) (2008) *The Cambridge History of the Byzantine Empire, c. 500–1492*. Cambridge: Cambridge University Press.

Council of Constantinople III (680–681)

STAMENKA E. ANTONOVA

Emperor Constantine III (668–85) recognized the problem that the heavily Monophysite territories of the empire had been lost to the Muslims, and feared the future threat that the Arabs posed for the empire. Accordingly, he decided to convene a great council in order to conciliate the pope and gain support from the West by reaffirming commonality of faith. The main objective was to reopen the issue of Christology and the relative significance of Chalcedon 451, for which a new settlement had been favored by Emperor Justinian and his pro-Monophysite Empress Theodora at the Council of Constantinople II in 553, in an effort to pacify the Monophysite churches and to win back the eastern provinces (without much success). After that time the emperors pursued a variety of strategies, including Monoenergism and Monotheletism, the notion that Christ had but one operative and divine will since he, as a morally perfect human being, could never conceivably go against the divine will. This was meant to be a christological compromise with the Monophysite party, a "moving away" from Chalcedon without actually saying so openly, and it had roused the opposition of the West, as well as many of the leading Orthodox fathers of the day, including St. Maximos the Confessor. Although Emperor Constans II (641–68) and Sergius II, Patriarch of Constantinople, supported the Chalcedonian party, they nevertheless saw Monotheletism as a possible way to conciliate the Monophysites.

Pope Martin I, however, opposed this christological formula vehemently, and as a result he was arrested in 653 and died in exile. The harsh treatment of the pope by the emperor had strained Byzantine relations with the West, a fact that now prompted Emperor Constantine III to act for conciliation in the face of the empire's Islamic invaders, whom many took to be a scourge from God.

At the Council of Constantinople which the emperor convened, the conciliar fathers asserted the doctrine that Christ was at one and the same time both fully human and fully divine, complete man and God. They emphasized the importance of his full humanity and the importance of never diminishing this aspect of the person of Christ in favor of a sense of the great power of divinity that "absorbed" or "occluded" the human nature. The definition regarding the will of Christ pointed to two faculties, two wills, pertaining to Christ's two natures, whose goals were not directed against each other, since the human will was in all things subject to the divine will. As such, the council was a clear reaffirmation of the enduring significance of Chalcedon 451. In addition to the main focus of the council on the christological question of the will of Jesus, important rules and canons were later added with a view to reforming the discipline of the church. It is classed as the Sixth Ecumenical Council of the church.

SEE ALSO: Council of Chalcedon (451); Council of Constantinople II (553); Ecumenical Councils; Monophysitism (including Miaphy-sitism); St. Maximos the Confessor (580–662)

References and Suggested Readings

Davis, L. D. (1987) *The First Seven Ecumenical Councils: Their History and Theology*. Wilmington: M. Glazier.

Frend, W. C. H. (1979) *The Rise of the Monophysite Movement*, 2nd edn. Cambridge: Cambridge University Press.

Meyendorff, J. (1975) *Christ in Eastern Christian Thought*, revd. edn. Crestwood, NY: St. Vladimir's Seminary Press.

Norris, R. A. (1980) *The Christological Controversy*. Philadelphia: Fortress Press.

Schroeder, H. J. (1937) *Disciplinary Decrees of the General Councils: Texts, Translation and Co006Dmentary*. St. Louis: Herder.

Tanner, N. P. and Albergio, G. (eds.) (1990) *Decrees of the Ecumenical Councils*. London: Sheed and Ward.

Wigram, W. A. (1978) *The Separation of the Monophysites*. New York: AMS Press.

Council of Ephesus (431)

STAMENKA E. ANTONOVA

Nestorius, an Antiochene monk, who was appointed as the archbishop of Constantinople in 428 by Emperor Theodosius, desired to eradicate what he saw as heresy in the capital city, especially the popular belief held there (as well as in Alexandria) that the Virgin Mary was *Theotokos*, or Mother of God. Nestorius claimed that the Virgin Mary ought to be called only *Christotokos*, the Mother of Christ, and any other title given to her designated a false understanding of Christology, betraying (as he thought) a confusion of the divine and human properties in Jesus. Initially, Nestorius preferred to designate the Virgin Mary as *Anthropotokos*, Mother of the Man, but eventually chose to refer to her as *Christotokos*, Mother of Christ, as he sought to bring about unity in his divided church. The title *Christotokos*, however, was vehemently opposed not only by monks who came to Constantinople to protest, but also by the laity of the imperial capital, led at the time by Bishop Proclus. The teaching of Nestorius implied to his opponents, such as Cyril of Alexandria, that he was separating the one person of Christ into two: a human Jesus and a divine *Logos*. St. Cyril of Alexandria garnered the support of Pope Celestine and began a campaign against Nestorius. Cyril penned several letters to Nestorius in order to explain and to persuade him of the orthodoxy of the *Theotokos* title, but he was criticized in return on account of these letters. Cyril sent on several of Nestorius' sermons to Rome, where they were presented to John Cassian and occasioned the writing of his treatise *On the Incarnation of God*, a work that essentially rejected Nestorius' teachings and confirmed Rome in its support of Alexandria. In order to vindicate himself, Nestorius asked Emperor Theodosius II to call a council, which convened at Ephesus in 431. Cyril of Alexandria, who was also appointed as the representative of Pope Celestine I, assumed the presidency and stirred the local populace against Nestorius, convincing the bishops to condemn his teaching as deeply heretical. When the episcopal delegates from Antioch, who arrived too late to attend the opening of the council but who were sympathetic to Nestorius, heard about the outcome, they too convened their own council and condemned Cyril. The Roman church legates, who arrived even later, took the side of Cyril and supported the decisions of the first council. As a result of this predicament, Emperor Theodosius II decided to intervene and hold discussions at Constantinople, putting both Cyril and Nestorius under house arrest at Ephesus, and holding all the bishops there through the long summer. Eventually, he too took the side of Cyril of Alexandria. For several years afterwards, Antioch and Alexandria remained out of communion, but a reconciliation was brokered in 433 with the Formula of Union (in Cyril's *Letters* as "Let the Heavens Rejoice"), according to which they agreed that Christ was one person (*hypostasis*) with two natures (*physeis*), one human and one divine. Nestorius' deposition was confirmed and he was sent back to Antioch (eventually to be condemned to exile, as he would not cease protesting the justness of his cause). The Council of Ephesus was recognized as of ecumenical status at Chalcedon in 451, and set the terms of the fundamental Christology of the church, determining the agendas of the next three ecumenical councils to come. It was the last of the ecumenical councils to be adopted by the Oriental Orthodox Churches.

SEE ALSO: Christ; Ecumenical Councils; Episcopacy; St. Cyril of Alexandria (ca. 378–444); Theotokos, the Blessed Virgin

References and Suggested Readings

Aprem, M. (1978) *The Council of Ephesus of 431*. Trichur, Kerala: Mar Narsai Press.

McGuckin, J. A. (2004) *St. Cyril of Alexandria and the Christological Controversy*. Crestwood, NY: St. Vladimir's Seminary Press.

Margull, H. H. (ed.) (1966) *The Councils of the Church, History and Analysis*. Philadelphia: Fortress, Press.

Tanner, N. P. and Albergio, G. (eds.) (1990) *Decrees of the Ecumenical Councils*. London: Sheed and Ward.

Council of Nicea I (325)

TARMO TOOM

The Council of Nicea, which "defines and glorifies the great mystery of Orthodoxy" (kontakion of the feast), is retrospectively considered the first ecumenical council (Eusebius, *Vita Const.* 3.6.1). The Nicene Creed became the basis for the Niceno-Constantinopolitan Creed, which is popularly known as the "Nicene Creed."

Emperor Constantine needed to secure the religious unity of the Christians in his empire. Among several things that threatened it were the ecclesiological controversies, especially the Melitian schism, the liturgical controversy over the right date of Easter, and the increasingly internationalized theological controversy between Alexander of Alexandria and Arius. Accordingly, more than 200 bishops were summoned to the Council of Nicea (now Iznik: site of his imperial palace). A few came from North Africa and the Western Churches, while most were from the Greek-speaking Eastern Churches.

The Acta of the council, if ever written, are not extant. Eusebius, highlighting the role of the emperor, provided his description of the council in the *De vita Constantini*, and several years later St. Athanasius offered his version of events in his *De decretis*.

Although it is common now to think about the Council of Nicea as primarily a doctrinal gathering (and one has to thank Athanasius writing out of his apologetic context for popularizing such a perception), it was originally largely an administrative meeting which addressed ecclesiological-liturgical questions. This can be borne out by looking at the substance of its twenty reformatory Canons.

In its Creed, the Council of Nicea affirmed the eternal generation of the only-begotten Son (*monogenēs*) from the Father's "essence" (*ousia*). Father and Son were said to be "consubstantial" (*homoousios*). However, what this term exactly meant and implied was left to be hammered out during the 4th-century trinitarian controversies (Hilary of Poitiers, Syn. 67–9; Trin. 4.4). Basil of Caesarea remarked at the time, "The term *homoousion* [is] ill received in certain quarters" (Ep. 52.1). The main problem proved to be that it could be interpreted in several senses, not least in a modalist meaning.

Moreover, despite rising to almost archetypal status, the Creed of Nicea is by no means a complete summation of the Christian faith. While trinitarian in structure, it says almost nothing about the Holy Spirit and does not even mention the church and Virgin Mary. Instead, it is case specific, rising out of a particular apologetic, focusing on the full divinity of the Son and issuing anathemas against Arius. The original Nicene Creed, which was later called at the Council of Ephesus in 431 "Pious and sufficiently helpful for the whole world," was written for bishop-theologians and was probably never actually used in the celebration of baptisms. It had to wait for its decisive modification, reaffirmation, and (in a sense) completion by the Council of Constantinople in 381.

SEE ALSO: Arianism; Christ; Council of Constantinople I (381); Council of Ephesus (431); Ecumenical Councils; Fatherhood of God; Holy Trinity; St. Constantine the Emperor (271–337)

References and Suggested Readings

Ayres, L. (2004) *Nicaea and Its Legacy*. Oxford: Oxford University Press.

Coakley, S. (ed.) (2007) "Disputed Questions in Patristic Trinitarianism," *Harvard Theological Review* 100/2: 125–75.

Edwards, M. (2006) "The First Council of Nicaea," in M. Mitchell and F. M. Young (eds.) *The Cambridge History of Christianity*, vol. 1. Cambridge: Cambridge University Press, pp. 552–67.

L'Huillier, P. (1996) *The Church of the Ancient Councils*. Crestwood, NY: St. Vladimir's Seminary Press.

Need, S. W. (2008) *Truly Human and Truly Divine*. Peabody, MA: Hendrickson.

Tanner, N. P. and Alberigo, G. (1990) *Decrees of the Ecumenical Councils*. Washington, DC: Georgetown University Press.

Council of Nicea II (787)

STAMENKA E. ANTONOVA

After the doubly successful defense of Constantinople against the Arabs by General Leo the Isaurian in 717 and 718, he claimed for himself the title of emperor, reigning as Leo III. The new emperor (possibly because of his Syrian background) had a particularly strong dislike for the widespread veneration of icons in the East, as he considered it to be a form of idolatry which was forbidden by Scripture. Leo was determined to cleanse the Eastern Churches of this cultic practice and in 730 he embarked on a policy of iconoclasm for the destruction of sacred images by publishing an edict against the cult of icons and ordering their removal from the churches and from public places. Consequently, Leo's agents destroyed thousands of images, beginning with the Great Image of Christ on the Chalke Gate into the palace, and including many other great works of art; for the soldiers were generally indifferent to the sentiments of the people and to their expressions of piety and worship.

From the beginning, a rift was set up between *Iconoclasts* (emperor and soldiery) and *Iconodules* (monastics and aristocratic women, and laity). When the iconodules attempted to protest these radical measures, many were brutally arrested, abused and exiled. Upon Leo's death in 740, he was succeeded by his son Constantine V (740–75), who continued stringent policies against iconodules and executed 16 iconodule martyrs in 766. During the reign of Leo III and Constantine V, their policy of iconoclasm created a deep rift between Rome and Constantinople, especially as the pope gave protection to the iconodule cause. Constantine V was succeeded by Leo IV (775–80), who abolished the radical measures of persecutions against iconodules, although he himself was not interested in the restoration of the cult of icons. After the death of Leo IV in 780, his wife Empress Irene became the regent of their son Constantine VI and the co-emperor, since the heir of the deceased emperor was too young to assume power independently. It was she who worked to reverse the imperial iconodule policy. In 786 she summoned a council in Hagia Sophia to restore the icons, but it was disrupted by rebellious guards from the capital. She quietly reassigned them outside the city and in the following year, 787, achieved a great triumph for the iconophile party by holding the planned council at Nicea, which legitimated the use of images, clarifying the terminology appropriate to worship. The council affirmed that adoration (*latreia*) was due to God alone, but that reverence to saints and holy things (*douleia, proskynesis*) contributed to the proper worship of God and was not in conflict with it. The teachings of the iconodule theologians, especially

Sts. John of Damascus, Germanus of Constantinople, and Theodore the Studite, were elevated as Orthodox standards. Veneration of icons was affirmed as central to Orthodox faith.

The Second Council of Nicea was soon seen as an ecumenical council (though the West was dubious about it for a while, having received a defective copy of the statement of faith) and it has remained as the seventh and last of the ecumenical councils in Orthodox estimation. Empress Irene and her son were present for the proceedings, as were two papal legates and over three hundred bishops. Behind the theological debate on the appropriateness of the use and veneration of icons was a deeper metaphysical dialogue centered on the concepts of reality and image, on sacramentality and right representation. These complex ideas were deeply rooted in ancient philosophy. The Council of Nicea exposed iconoclasm as a form of Platonism, or a belief system that denigrated the central fact of the incarnation, preferring abstract symbolism, and a tendency of thought that resisted the idea that matter could be a valid medium of grace and divine revelation.

Despite the political effects of the iconoclastic problem on the East and the West and the eventual agreement between the two on the validity of the cult of icons, the attachment to the principle of the quasi-sacramental character of the holy icons was to a certain degree a special *proprium* of the Orthodox world, an attitude to worship that partly separated it from the Latin Church, and much more so from the later Reformed Churches that arose out of western Catholicism.

SEE ALSO: Ecumenical Councils; Iconoclasm; Iconography, Styles of; St. John of Damascus (ca. 675–ca. 750); St. Theodore the Studite (759–826)

References and Suggested Readings

Giakalis, A. (1994) *Images of the Divine: The Theology of Icons at the Seventh Ecumenical Council.* Leiden: E. J. Brill.

Lossky, V. and Ouspensky, L. (1982) *The Mean-ing of Icons,* trans. G. E. H. Palmer and E. Kadloubovsky. Crestwood, NY: St. Vladi-mir's Seminary Press.

McGuckin, J. A. (1993) "The Theology of Images and the Legitimation of Power in Eighth Century Byzantium," *St. Vladimir's Theological Quarterly* 37, 1: 39–58.

Sahas, D. (1986) *Icon and Logos: Sources in Eight-Century Iconoclasm.* Toronto: University of Toronto Press.

Tanner, N. P. and Albergio, G. (eds.) (1990) *Decrees of the Ecumenical Councils.* London: Sheed and Ward.

Wolmuth, J. (ed.) (1989) *Streit um das Bild: Das II Konzil von Nizaea (787) in okumenische Perspektive.* Bonn: Bouvier.

Cross

JOHN A. MCGUCKIN

Orthodox theology approaches the cross of Christ most characteristically as a trophy of divine glory. It is the cipher above all others that sums up and encapsulates the love and mercy of the Lord for his adopted race. It is the "sign of salvation," the icon of hope. In many Orthodox painted crosses the title bar does not read "Jesus of Nazareth King of the Jews" (INRI in Latin, INBI in Greek, ІНЦІ in Slavonic), but is made to read "The Lord of Glory," and often on Orthodox devotional crosses one reads marked there the generic superscription *Philanthropos Theos*: "The God Who Loves Mankind."

At first, early Christian theology demonstrated mainly a horrified sense of awe that the powers of wickedness could treat the Lord in such a violent way (Acts 2.22–35). But the tone was decidedly that God's glorification of his servant Jesus far outweighed the dishonor that the dark spiritual powers tried to inflict. The Apostle Peter, in his speech to the people of Jerusalem, sums it up in the words: "God has made this Jesus whom you crucified, both Lord and Christ" (Acts 2.36). There is a regular contrasted pairing of the ideas of humiliation (in the cross) and exalted glorification of Jesus by God (because of the faithfulness to the point of crucifixion) such as can be seen in the ancient hymn which the Apostle Paul quotes (Phil. 2.6–11), as well as in the schemes of Ascent (*Anabasis*) and Descent (*Katabasis*) that structure St. John's theology of crucifixion and glorification in his profound gospel (cf. Jn. 3.13–15). St. Paul took a decisive step when he made the cross not merely a scandal to be explained away but a mystery of faith and God's love that ought to be celebrated as pivotal (Gal. 6.14). The cross in Christian use was already, and rapidly, shifting away from a thing of shame to being the great sign of the new covenant of reconciliation (Eph. 2.16; Col.

1.20; Heb. 12.2). In the early apologists and apostolic fathers the cross is rarely mentioned (though see Ignatius of Antioch, *Letters to the Ephesians* 9.1; 18.1; *To the Trallians* 11.2; *To the Philadelphians* 8.2). But popular devotion to it as a confident symbol of Christian victory over the powers of this world was steadily growing, as can be seen in the appearance in art and inscription from the 2nd century onwards of the cross-shaped monogram *Fos – Zoe* ("Light and Life in the Cross": one must imagine the words written at right angles to one another, *Fos* down vertically, *Zoe* horizontally, making a cross, with the middle letter of both being shared in common).

The cross is depicted in later Orthodox iconography in distinctive ways. The usual iconic (painted) cross of the Lord shows the Savior in the moment of death and in profound serenity. There is nothing in the Orthodox tradition that presents the vivid torments of the crucifixion such as can be seen in post-Quattrocentro art of the West. This is deliberately done, for doctrinal reasons, to present the cross to the faithful as the "Victory" over sin and death. Moreover, the Lord's corpus is drawn in a highly sinuous way in many of the representations, so as to evoke the Johannine phrase: "As Moses lifted up the serpent in the wilderness, so must the Son of Man be lifted up" (Jn. 3.14). The iconic form of the serpent on a beam of wood, of course, is a profound resonance between Mosaic traditions of God's salvation of his people in the wilderness (see Num. 21.9) when anyone who looked upon this icon "lived," and Hellenistic understandings of the healing power of deity (for Hellenes, the motif was the cipher of Aesculapios, god of healing, and even today is a widely recognized sign of the medical profession). Christ crucified is thus presented by the Evangelist John as the healing and life-giving antidote to sin for all the world. Those who look upon the victory of the cross, see the trophy (*trophaion*) of the Life-Giver. In Byzantine processional crosses the corpus was frequently omitted, and floral motifs abounded. This may have been partly influenced by Iconoclastic themes (while the icons were destroyed, the Iconoclasts encouraged the prevalent use of the motif of the cross without corpus), but it also had resonances with the floral trophy of Victory. Many fresco versions of the cross are thus still decorated with floral motifs. Blessing crosses in the Orthodox Church (used in almost every

Plate 14   Orthodox pilgrim in Jerusalem venerating the icon of the cross held by a monk. Darren Whiteside/Reuters/
Corbis.

service by the priest and bishop to deliver blessings in
the name of the crucified and Risen One) often have
the corpus of the Lord on them, with the feet always
nailed separately and distinctly (not as crossed over in
the Latin tradition). The foot cross beam is a distinctive
mark of the Orthodox Cross, thus making three cross
beams (the titular notice board at the head of the cross,
the main cross beam in the middle on which are the
arms of the Lord, and the pedal cross beam). The latter
is often drawn at a slant, and symbolically interpreted
as tipped weighing scales: Christ as the "weigher of
souls" and his cross as the balance beam that brings
Justice to the world. In many representations of the
cross (icons, frescoes, processional and hand crosses)
one finds the added motifs of the sun and moon at the
top (recalling the eclipse on Golgotha: Mt. 27.45) and
a skull at the bottom of the main beam (signifying the

pious tale that the hill of crucifixion was called the
"place of the Skull" because it was the reputed burial
place of Adam). The theological point of this symbolism is, of course, that the death of the Second Adam
restores the ontological collapse of the First Adam: and
indeed the icon of the resurrection (the Harrowing of
Hades) demonstrates that point graphically in the
manner in which the Lord, in death, goes straight to
Hades to lift Adam and Eve by hand out of the grave.
The most remarkable instance of this iconography can
be seen in the funerary chapel at the Savior in Chora
Church at Constantinople (Kariye Jamii).

The cross features highly and predominantly in
Orthodox liturgy and spiritual life. It is the most
common and popular form of prayer. Orthodox people "cross themselves" many times, both in private
prayers and in public at the liturgy: not only at the

recitation of every doxology, but at every significant moment in the course of their prayers. The divine liturgy is regularly interspersed with the priest or bishop emerging from the Royal Doors to offer blessings to the people with a hand cross, or with their own hands, making the sign of the cross over them. The sign of the cross is made in the Orthodox Church by the faithful with the first two fingers closed with the thumb (to signify the double nature of Christ, and the Trinity of Divine Persons) and touching the forehead while saying "In the Name of the Father," touching the waist saying "And of the Son," touching the right shoulder while saying "And of the Holy Spirit," and then the left shoulder saying "Amen." The Orthodox Church celebrates St. Helena (mother of Emperor Constantine) together with her son for instigating the mission that searched for and found the cross of Christ in 4th-century Jerusalem. The feast of the Exaltation of the Cross (September 14) was merged with the earlier feast of the Finding of the Cross (the "Invention" of the Cross) after the 7th-century recapture of the relic taken from Jerusalem by the Persians. Since the time of St. Constantine the Great the relics of the wood of the True Cross have been highly prized above all other church relics; first in the churches of Constantinople, Jerusalem, and Rome, which treasured them, and from them outwards to the whole world. The old mockery that all the relics of the True Cross put together would be enough to build a wooden ship was disproved in the 19th century by De Fleury, who mathematically estimated that all surviving fragments amount to less than one third of a typical Roman cross. Relics of the cross, wherever they are held in churches, are usually a central feature of the service of the veneration of the cross on Great Friday.

SEE ALSO: Iconoclasm; St. Constantine the Emperor (ca. 271–337); Soteriology

References and Suggested Readings

de Fleury, R. (1870) *Mémoire sur les instruments de la passion*. Paris.

de Jerphanion, G. (1930) *La Représentation de la croix et du crucifix aux origines de l'art chrétien*. Paris.

Drijvers, J. W. (1991) *Helena Augusta: The Mother of Constantine the Great and the Legend of Her Finding of the True Cross*. Leiden: E. J. Brill.

Frolow, A. (1961) "La Relique de la vraie croix: recherches sur la développement d'une culte," *Archives de L'Orient* 7.

Cyprus, Autocephalous Orthodox Church of

SERGEY TROSTYANSKIY

The Church of Cyprus has its origin in apostolic times. The Book of Acts tells us that Cyprus was evangelized by St. Barnabas, who was a Cypriot from the city of Salamis. St. Barnabas is considered to be Cyprus' first bishop. In 57 CE he was martyred by stoning for preaching Christ in a Cypriot synagogue. His body was hidden by disciples, and local traditions tell of the manifestation of his relics four centuries later.

By the 4th century Christianity had made considerable headway on the island. Because of its geographical location, close to the city of Antioch, Cyprus was at first ecclesiastically administered from that patriarchate, up until the late 4th century when the Cypriots, defending the Nicene faith, made an attempt to disassociate themselves from the Arian leadership in Antioch and gain autocephaly. The patriarchs of Antioch, in turn, attempted for some time to regain their jurisdictional control over Cyprus. The ecclesiastical dispute was discussed by the Council of Ephesus in 431. The Cypriot Church used that occasion to petition formally for its independence from Antioch. The Antiochene Patriarch John objected, arguing that since the Arian crisis was no longer a common threat for Orthodoxy, the jurisdictional control of the patriarchate of Antioch over Cyprus should be reestablished. The synodical fathers, conscious of John's refusal to join the Ephesine assembly, took the side of the Church of Cyprus, approved its autocephalous status, and ordered the archbishops of Cyprus to be elected and consecrated henceforward by the synod of Cypriot bishops. In 488, however, the Monophysite patriarch of Antioch, Peter the Fuller, made another attempt to reclaim Antiochian jurisdiction over Cyprus, arguing that Cyprus had originally been evangelized by the Antiochians. Even though they had scriptural attestation for the mission of St. Barnabas, it was said that the Cypriot Orthodox then had difficulties in making their case stand, until the miraculous rediscovery of the tomb of St. Barnabas resolved the controversy, by providing an essential witness to the church's apostolic foundation. As a result of the manifestation of the relics of the apostle, a synod of the Constantinopolitan patriarchate confirmed the autocephaly of the Church of Cyprus and the Emperor Zeno granted special privileges to archbishops of Cyprus (to wear special vesture and to use imperial purple ink). Since that time the venerable autocephaly of the Cypriot Church has been accepted by the entire Orthodox world.

Orthodoxy in Cyprus flourished for several centuries afterwards but, starting from the 7th century, the island experienced multiple invasions of Islamic Arabs. Towards the end of the 7th century Emperor Justinian II had to evacuate the Orthodox population of the island to the mainland of Asia Minor. Following this, Cyprus was devastated and Orthodox life diminished significantly. The local church leaders at that time assumed the responsibilities of ethnarchs, leaders of the local population both on a political as well as an ecclesiastical level. The 10th century eventually saw the liberation of Christian Cyprus as a consequence of the successful military campaign against the Arabs by the Byzantine Emperor Nicephorus II Phocas. Orthodoxy was soon revitalized and many churches and monasteries were founded on the island.

The end of the 12th century saw the conquest of Cyprus by the Crusaders. The new French rulers of the island attempted to impose Latin ecclesiastical control over the Church of Cyprus. A Latin archbishop was appointed as head of the local bishops, and all monasteries were made subject to Latin bishops. Venetian rule over Cyprus that followed from the conquest of the island by Venice in 1489 continued the Latinization process. Nevertheless, despite all attempts made by the Latin rulers to change the religious ritual and allegiances of the Cypriots, they strongly defended their Orthodox identity and protected the Orthodox faith. The Turkish occupation of the island in the second half of the 16th century completely removed the Latin Church colonial dominion from Cyprus and gave the Orthodox the necessary breathing space to restore their hierarchy. However,

the Church of Cyprus could not flourish much under the Turkish occupation. Church hierarchs once again assumed the role of ethnarchs, providing civil and spiritual guidance for the Christian population of the island. The Greek Revolution of 1821 against the Ottomans resulted in severe persecution of the Cypriot bishops and priests who were suspected of being supportive to the revolutionaries. Many of them were murdered.

The beginning of British rule over the island in 1878 seemed promising for the Cypriots, as they hoped that their dream of union with Greece – cherished for centuries – was about to come true. However, the British authorities did not really wish to encourage the "Great Idea." As a result, losing patience with British colonial rule, the Church of Cyprus, supported by the population of the island, organized the liberation movement which began in 1955. Archbishop Makarios III, Ethnarch of Cyprus, assumed leadership of the movement and finally became the first head of an independent Cyprus in 1960. The clash between the Greek and Turkish communities of Cyprus reached its peak in 1974, when invasion by the armed forces of Turkey immensely disturbed the ecclesiastical life of the church. The northern territories, occupied by Turks, suffered enormous losses, as many monasteries and churches were then destroyed or heavily damaged. To this day the situation has not been politically resolved. The Church of Cyprus has consistently denounced the division of the island and struggled for its reunification. In 2003 the Turkish administration of Northern Cyprus relaxed some of the restrictions of access and allowed Greek Cypriots to visit the monastic sites and churches in the North.

As of today the Church of Cyprus has 10 bishops, over 600 priests, 6 dioceses, 628 parishes, and about 650,000 members. The archbishop of Cyprus is known as His Beatitude. He himself is the archbishop of Constantia (Famagusta) and is resident at Nicosia. He has five suffragan eparchs. Together, they comprise the holy synod. The church has ten active monasteries, some dating back to Byzantine times. Among these monasteries the Kykko monastery in the Troodos Mountains is an important pilgrimage center of the Orthodox world. The monastery of St. Neophytos outside Paphos is another major Byzantine site. There are also a total of 67 other monasteries which are either currently unused or presently in ruins. The main seminary is that of the Apostle Barnabas in Nicosia. The church is renowned for sending out an abundant number of priests to serve in missionary capacities in other Orthodox communities overseas. There are also numerous Cypriots in the diaspora, especially England. The Greek Cypriot Orthodox of Great Britain, however, belong to the oversight of the patriarch of Constantinople in the archdiocese of Thyateira, even though so many of the parishes there are composed entirely of Cypriot Orthodox, with clergy who are also chiefly Cypriot. For a small island, Cyprus' contribution to the Orthodox world has been both remarkable and rich.

SEE ALSO: Antioch, Patriarchate of

References and Suggested Readings

Englezakis, B. (1995) *Studies on the History of the Church of Cyprus, 4th–20th Centuries*. Aldershot: Variorum.

McGuckin, J. (2008) *The Orthodox Church: An Introduction to Its History, Doctrine, and Spiritual Culture*. Oxford: Blackwell.

Mayes, S. (1981) *Makarios: A Biography*. New York: St. Martin's Press.

Cyril Lukaris, Patriarch of Constantinople (1572–1638)

A. EDWARD SIECIENSKI

The so-called "Calvinist Patriarch" of Constantinople, Cyril Lukaris was among the most brilliant and influential Greek ecclesiastics of the 17th century. Born in Crete in 1572, he was educated by the great scholar Maximos Margunios, bishop of Kythira (1549–1602). He completed his studies in Venice and later enrolled as a student at the University of Padua. Ordained as a deacon in 1593, in 1596 Lukaris participated in the Constantinopolitan Synod that condemned the Union of Brest, traveling to Poland-Lithuania to communicate the synod's decision to King Sigismund. From 1597 to 1602 he taught at Vilna and Lvov, where he was confronted with the success of Jesuit mission-

aries among the Orthodox. Lukaris's experiences during these years convinced him of two things – that the Orthodox clergy needed to be better educated and that an Orthodox-Protestant alliance was the only possible recourse against Roman hegemony. In 1602 he succeeded his uncle Meletios as patriarch of Alexandria and in 1612 served as *locum tenens* of the ecumenical patriarchate. In 1620 he was elected patriarch of Constantinople, a post he would hold five times between 1620 and 1638 (1620–3, 1623–33, 1633–4, 1634–5, 1637–8). As patriarch, Lukaris actively worked to establish better relations with both the Calvinists and the Anglicans, even presenting King Charles I of England with an early Greek manuscript of the Bible (*Codex Alexandrinus*). In 1629, influenced in large part by the theology of Antoine Leger, he affixed his name to a *Confessio Fidei* (which he also may have authored), an attempt to harmonize traditional Orthodox thought with Calvinist theology. This confession was later condemned at several Constantinopolitan Synods (1638, 1642), the Synod of Jassy (1642), and the Synod of Jerusalem (1672), in particular for its teachings on predestination, Eucharist, free will, and justification by faith. The other patriarchs, while reluctant to call Lukaris's personal orthodoxy into question (unsure whether he authored it), pressed him to disavow the *Confessio*; something he never did.

His enemies, including Cyril Kontaris (later Patriarch Cyril II) and the Jesuits, frequently conspired together against him, allegedly offering the sultan money in exchange for Lukaris's life. In 1638 he was accused of inciting the Cossacks against the Turks and executed by agents of Sultan Murad IV. His body was thrown into the Bosphorus, where it was washed ashore and secretly buried by his supporters. Only later, under Patriarch Parthenius, was he granted an honorable burial. Even today there remains debate as to Lukaris's legacy – some seeing him as a staunch defender of Orthodoxy against the machinations of Rome, and others dismissing him as a crypto-Protestant whose teachings were rightly rejected by the church.

SEE ALSO: Anglicanism, Orthodoxy and; Eastern Catholic Churches; Ecumenism, Orthodoxy and; Iasi (Jassy), Synod of (1642)

References and Suggested Readings

Calian, C. (1992) "Patriarch Lucaris's Calvinistic Confession," in *Theology Without Boundaries: Encounters of Eastern Orthodoxy and Western Tradition*. Louisville: Westminister/ John Knox Press.

Hadjiantoniou, G. (1961) *Protestant Patriarch: The Life of Cyril Lucaris*. Richmond: John Knox Press.

Schlier, R. (1927) *Der Patriarch Kyrill Lukaris von Constantinopel*. Marburg.

Czech Lands and Slovakia, Orthodox Church of

JOHN A. MCGUCKIN

Orthodoxy was present in Moravia – the medieval forerunner of Czechoslovakia – from the time of the mission of Sts. Cyril and Methodios in the 9th and 10th centuries, but the majority religion of the region had always been Roman Catholic. The stirrings of the Reformation secessions were severely controlled by the Habsburgs in the early 17th century when they gained power over Bohemia and Moravia. Czechoslovakia was constituted as an independent nation in the years following World War I, part of the extensive process of the breaking up of the Austro-Hungarian Empire. The Orthodox churches of recent times were founded in Prague in the mid-19th century, and since then have come under, at various times, the patronage of the patriarchates of Serbia, Constantinople, and Moscow.

In 1918 the vast majority of the population was Roman Catholic. During World War I, Orthodoxy had been suppressed in the country, and it was also to endure some element of persecution again during World War II. When the Czechoslovakian Orthodox Church was reconstituted in the aftermath of the first war, approximately 40,000 declared themselves and a bishop (Gorazd Pavlik) was appointed for them by the Serbian patriarch. Bishop Pavlik succeeded in rallying together most of the Orthodox faithful under the jurisdictional care of the Serbian patriarch, but in 1942 he and several of his clergy were assassinated by the Nazi invaders. By 1946 the political mantle of the Soviets had fallen over the country, and the patriarch of Moscow acted independently to assume jurisdictional charge of the Czechoslovakian Orthodox. This was one of the reasons the phanar for some time looked askance at the canonical status of the churches of Czechoslovakia and Poland. The concept, and reality, of a separate Czechoslovakian Orthodox Church had been significantly shrunk by the Soviet annexation of much of its former territory in Podcarpatska Rus, but was soon after swollen in 1950 by the supposedly free return to Orthodoxy of the Byzantine-rite Catholics of the diocese of Preshov in Slovakia. These reunited congregations demonstrated their truer sentiment in 1968 when large numbers elected to return to the Roman Catholic eastern-rite communion. In 1951 the patriarchate of Moscow declared the Orthodox Church of Czechoslovakia to be henceforward autocephalous under the guidance of the metropolitan of Prague. Constantinople at first did not accept this status and declared it to be an autonomous church under the jurisdiction of Constantinople. It was not until 1998 that Constantinople recognized the autocephaly. The country separated politically once more into its chief constituent parts, namely the Czech lands and Slovakia, after the collapse of communism in the last decade of the 20th century. Even with this political severing, however, the Orthodox remained united across the national divide. There is a smaller Orthodox presence in Slovakia with 10 parishes and 23,000 faithful; while the Czech Republic has 100 parishes and 51,000 faithful who use the Slavonic rite. The total number of Orthodox in the region amounts to not much more than 74,000 faithful.

SEE ALSO: Sts. Constantine (Cyril) (ca. 826–869) and Methodios (815–885)

References and Suggested Readings

Barrett, D., Kurian, G., and Johnson, C. (eds.) (2001) *World Christian Encyclopedia*, vol. 1, 2nd edn. New York: Oxford University Press.

D

Deacon

JOHN CHRYSSAVGIS

The diaconate is the first order of priestly ministry. The Orthodox Church has traditionally held that the ordained ministry includes "three divinely established degrees" of bishop, presbyter, and deacon. In recent centuries, however, the diaconate has enjoyed a more transitional role, with candidates to the priesthood ordained after only a brief period serving as deacons. In some Orthodox churches there has been a recent effort to rejuvenate the diaconate.

The historical sources of the diaconate are difficult to trace. In the early centuries the usage of the term "deacon" was very fluid and its application quite varied. Nonetheless, the diaconate developed organically out of the church's response to increasing pastoral needs. The classic biblical foundation is Acts 6.1–6, which also reveals the broader social dimensions of diaconal ministry. This passage refers to the appointment of "the Seven," although the word "deacon" never actually appears.

In the second and third centuries the functions and influence of deacons grew dramatically. Their increased responsibility and prominence are described in various documents of the early church. The first post-apostolic writer explicitly referring to the role of deacons within the threefold ministry is St. Ignatius of Antioch, who referred to deacons as "fellow servants"

and "special friends." However, later tensions, already evident in the *Apostolic Tradition* and the *Didascalia Apostolorum*, between bishops and deacons on the one hand and presbyters on the other, continued to develop in the 4th century. Thus, the Council of Arles (314) explicitly forbids deacons "to make a [Eucharistic] offering," an indication that such offerings were occurring. Nevertheless, deacons participated in this council, even signing for absent bishops. Canon 18 of the First Ecumenical Council (325) concerned itself exclusively with deacons, itself an indication of their importance and an affirmation of their role as episcopal assistants.

Following the Golden Age of the early councils, the diaconate became increasingly limited to a liturgical role. Later church councils dealt with the ministry and manner of deacons, reflecting their ongoing and widespread influence, but conciliar decisions in the form of canons assumed a more legalistic, almost prescriptive tone with regard to maturity, marriage, and demeanor (for instance, the Council of Trullo, 691), as well as marital, spousal, and familial relations (for instance, the Seventh Ecumenical Council, 787). Nonetheless, in the 4th and 5th centuries, deacons remained important. According to the *Apostolic Constitutions*, deacons normally represented bishops at synods in their absence. They initiated and even presided over the settlement of disputes among Christians. Indeed, the *Apostolic Constitutions* include

The Concise Encyclopedia of Orthodox Christianity, First Edition. Edited by John Anthony McGuckin.
© 2014 John Wiley & Sons, Ltd. Published 2014 by John Wiley & Sons, Ltd.

some 85 canons about ecclesiastical order, a surprising number of which (almost one third, and all of them prohibitive!) concern deacons. This indicates that deacons were still prominent in the East, although their function was being more narrowly defined and increasingly confined

Formerly attached to the bishop, the deacon was in later centuries attached to the presbyter or the parish, resulting in a reduction of the diaconate to a decorative, even superfluous, aspect of the ministry. Still, in the early 7th century, under the Emperor Heraclius, the number of deacons at St. Sophia Church in Constantinople was limited to 150, dwindling to 60 by the late 12th century. From the 11th century, deacons were even members of the

Plate 15　Deacon wearing vestments of his order with the diagonally placed stole and carrying the bishop's blessing candle (Dikeri). Sandro Vannini/Corbis.

Endemousa Synod, wielding considerable influence within the ecumenical patriarchate, which to this day preserves a central administrative and pastoral role for its deacons. The late Ecumenical Patriarch Athenagoras, while still deacon, served as secretary general of the Holy Synod of the Church of Greece (1919–22).

Much that is said about the role and function of male deacons is applicable also to female deacons. Indeed, in scriptural and patristic literature, the Greek word *diakonos* can denote either a male or a female deacon. Moreover, in manuscripts containing the sacrament of ordination (especially the *Codex Barberini* and the Constantinopolitan *Euchologion*), the rite for male deacons bears striking resemblance to the service for female deacons. In the past, women deacons served in dynamic ministries as educators, evangelists, spiritual mothers, and social workers; questions regarding their liturgical role remain. However, contemporary perception and practice with regard to the female diaconate will not advance smoothly unless the church understands the role and function of deacons in general.

To this day, the Orthodox Church regards the diaconate as an essential part of the ordained ministry, without which the pastoral ministry would be incomplete. Thus, a comprehensive vision of the sacramental ministry recognizes the central role of the bishop as bond of visible unity; it respects the critical role of the presbyter in celebrating the presence of Christ in the local community; and it realizes the complementary role of the deacon in completing this circle of unity within the local community.

The diaconate further provides occasion for appreciating the diversity of gifts among the laity as the "royal priesthood." By means of ordination to the diaconate, such gifts may be embraced and ministerial dignity can be conferred upon certain members of the laity, whose skills would be incorporated and integrated within the community. As a result, such persons would be empowered through the imposition of the hands and by the grace of the Spirit, their various charismata and professional contributions recognized and intimately bound with the altar. They would support – and not substitute – the priestly ministry of the church.

While the diaconate clearly changed in scope and function over the centuries, it has always remained in essence true to its origin, at once distinguishing and combining the liturgical *diakonia* and what the Council of Neo-Caesarea (ca. 314) called "the pattern of philanthropy." In general, however, it was the liturgical function of the deacon that gradually assumed greater prominence, becoming both elaborate and impressive. This change – or decline – in the diaconate is already evident in the 14th century when Nicholas Cabasilas, the formidable liturgical commentator of Byzantium, is reticent about the function of deacons in his formative books on the sacraments of eucharist and baptism. Thus, while the diaconate survived in the Eastern Church, it did so in a limited and specific form.

SEE ALSO: Deaconess; Episcopacy; Ordination

References and Suggested Readings

Chryssavgis, J. (2009) *Remembering and Reclaiming Diakonia: The Diaconate Yesterday and Today*. Brookline, MA: Holy Cross Press.

Fitzgerald, K. (1998) *Women Deacons in the Orthodox Church*. Brookline, MA: Holy Cross Press.

Deaconess

MARIA GWYN MCDOWELL

An ordained female member of the priestly order, at the level of diaconate. The office reached its zenith in the early Byzantine period, though it has never been altogether abandoned.

Phoebe, commemorated as "equal to the apostles," is referred to by Paul as a deacon (*diakonos*, Rom. 16.1) and is the prototype of the later office of the deaconess. The church also commemorates as deacons Tabitha (or Dorcas, Acts 9.36), Lydia (Acts 16.14), Mary, Persis, Tryphosa and Tryphena, Priscilla and Junia (Rom. 16.3–15), the daughters of Philip (Acts 21.9), Euodia and Syntyche (Phil. 4.2–3), all of whom were fellow-workers with Paul and laborers in the gospel; 1 Timothy 3.8–11 presents the requirements for diaconal service. An array of early theologians such as Clement of Alexandria (*Stromateis* 3, 6, 53.3–4), Origen (*Commentary on Romans* 10.17), John Chrysostom (*Homily 11 on 1 Timothy*), Theodoret of Cyrrhus and Theodore of Mopsuestia,

all interpret 1 Timothy 3.11 as referring to female deacons. The 4th–7th centuries are rich in archeological, epigraphical, and literary references in which *diakonos* with a feminine article and *diakonissa* are used interchangeably.

There is no evidence of significantly different functions between male and female deacons in the earliest church, a time when the diaconate itself was rapidly evolving. By the 3rd century the liturgical function of ordained women mirrored the culturally normative public/private segregation of roles and functions. Early deaconesses assisted in the baptism and anointing of adult (naked) women, and engaged in catechetical, pastoral, social, and evangelistic work among women. Like the male deacon, they were liaison officers for the bishop, specifically with a ministry to the women among whom it would have been inappropriate for a man to venture. The rise of infant baptism reduced their baptismal role but they continued to supervise the liturgical roles of women, to lead them in liturgical prayer, to chant in the church, participate in liturgical processions, and like the other priestly orders, the deaconesses all received the Eucharist at the altar with their fellow clergy. The deaconess did not lead worship in the same manner as male deacons reciting the Ektenies. However, in absence of male clergy, monastic deaconesses read the gospel and scriptures among women, and evidently poured water and wine into the chalice (Madigan and Osiek 2005: 6–7).

The requirements and regulations governing deaconesses were far stricter than for men, a double standard accounted for by ancient cultural biases regarding women's abilities and their supposedly over-sexualized nature (Karras 2004: 294). Regulations were modified and not always strictly observed. Deaconesses were mostly, though not entirely, celibate (Justinian, *Novellae* 6.6), and were permitted ordination at 60 years of age, a requirement later reduced to 40 or younger.

There is no clear reason for the order's decline, and no canon forbids its existence. Late-Byzantine speculations reflect stereotypical misogyny. The 12th-century canonist Theodore Balsamon declares Canon 15 of Nicea outdated based on his own experience that a deaconess is merely a titular honor for monastic women. The 14th-century canonist Matthew Blastares acknowledges an earlier role in baptism, noting "others say that they were allowed to approach the holy altar and perform nearly all the functions done by male deacons" (*Alphabetical Collection* 11; Madigan and Osiek 2005: 138). Both medieval canonists attribute the order's decline to menstruation, but expand their reasoning by commenting on women's general impurity, weakness and inability to teach publicly. This reasoning coincides with the developing theological typology of the Eucharist as a Temple sacrifice requiring cultic purity, and ignores the ancient canonical denunciation of any reimposition in the church of Levitical notions of purity. The order has never lapsed in the Armenian, Coptic, and Ethiopian Churches.

Ordination prayers for female deacons, the earliest ones appearing in the *Didascalia*, remain in the Euchologion today, and are consistently placed in conjunction with prayers for the male deacon. The 19th and 20th centuries saw a debate elevating a distinction between the terms *cheirotonia*, an "ordination," and *cheirothesia*, a "blessing" (i.e., if the female diaconate was a *cheirothesia* it would be a minor order different from the male diaconate). In fact these terms were historically used interchangeably until only recently (Fitzgerald 1998: 111–33). More importantly, like ordination to other major orders, female ordination occurs at the altar during the divine liturgy (Karras 2004: 298). The prayers for male and female deacons are distinct but structurally similar, with an epiclesis, reference to God's call, and an identical litany. Textual differences lie in a reference, calling on the example of Phoebe rather than Stephen, and other female predecessors, and the mention of purity language which may reflect late-antique beliefs regarding women's sexuality. Variance in rubrics reflects different liturgical functions as well as Byzantine ideas of gender propriety (Karras 2004: 302–8). The deaconess's participation in the Eucharist with fellow clergy is a clear demonstration that this office was considered in the Byzantine era a major order of the clergy.

Revitalizing the order has been repeatedly proposed among the Orthodox churches during the 19th and 20th centuries, most frequently in Russia, spearheaded by female royalty (Fitzgerald 1998: 149–51). In 1911 in Greece, Bishop Nektarios ordained a nun to the diaconate, an act poorly received by some. Continued ambivalence towards its restoration is evident in St. Nektarios' later public downplay of an act which bore all the marks of an ordination, and in the 2004 ordinations to the female diaconate in the Church of Greece. The press releases announcing the decision to restore the office of female diaconate there used ambiguous terminology, perhaps intentionally, simultaneously acknowledging the historical facticity of deaconesses while denying any priestly role for them. The current state of impasse remains despite many international conferences, sponsored by various patriarchates and regional churches, which have repeatedly called for the restoration of the order as one of the three recognized priestly orders of the church. These conferences were held at Agapia, Romania (1976), Rhodes, Greece (1988), Crete, Greece (1990), Damascus, Syria (1996), Istanbul, Turkey (1997), and Volos, Greece (2008).

Many Orthodox today believe that the restoration of the female diaconate should be implemented in a way that appropriately addresses contemporary cultural expectations and needs, just as the ancient order did. The restored office would be as similar to and different from the early church practice as was the Byzantine practice in its time. Its full restoration would make a positive statement about how Orthodoxy respects the dignity and ministry of women, and genuinely recognizes their ongoing contribution. The restoration of the order would revitalize the pastoral ministry of the diaconate itself; a role that has frequently been reduced to the liturgical margins or used as a mere stepping stone on the way to presbyterate. It would also accord to women the privileges and responsibilities of a clerical office that many fulfill in all but name.

SEE ALSO: Deacon; Episcopacy; Ordination; Women in Orthodoxy

References and Suggested Readings

Fitzgerald, K. K. (1998) *Women Deacons in the Orthodox Church: Called to Holiness and Ministry*. Brookline, MA: Holy Cross Orthodox Press.

Karras, V. A. (2004) "Female Deacons in the Byzantine Church," *Church History* 73: 272–316.

Madigan, K. and Osiek, C. (2005) *Ordained Women in the Early Church: A Documentary History*. Baltimore: Johns Hopkins University Press.

Death (and Funeral)

PERRY T. HAMALIS

While death undeniably shapes Eastern Orthodoxy's worldview, Orthodox Christians understand and respond to this phenomenon in a way that is complex, affirming both sharply negative and positive assessments of human death. On the one hand, death is not from God (Wis. 1.13), human beings were created in order that they should live, not die (Ezek. 33.11), death enters the world through humanity's sin (Rom. 5.12), and the New Jerusalem is characterized by the absence of death (Rev. 21.4). Reflecting these beliefs, death is described variously by Orthodox voices as "the enemy," "a painful metaphysical catastrophe," "a deep tragedy," and "a failure of human destiny" (Florovsky 1976). It is "foreign," "unnatural," and "perverted" (Schmemann 2003). Death grounds an existential condition that is

"profoundly abnormal," "monstrous," and "distorted" (Ware 2000), as anyone who has lost a loved one can attest (Hamalis 2008). It follows that, for the Orthodox, God's saving action through Christ's crucifixion and resurrection is, first and foremost, victory over death. On Easter and throughout the paschal season the Orthodox proclaim joyously and repeatedly, "Christ is risen from the dead! And death by his death is trampled. And to those in the tombs he is granting life."

Yet Orthodoxy also sees in death both God's mercy and the means through which the faithful participate in Christ's victorious resurrection. Death reveals God's mercy insofar as it limits the fallen condition of creation and prevents human beings' earthly sufferings from becoming a condition of everlasting torment. Furthermore, death is the mystery through which resurrection in Christ can be experienced (Rom. 6.3–11). Recalling the paschal hymn mentioned above, for the Orthodox it is "by his death" that Christ's victory

Plate 16   Russian Orthodox funeral. Interstock/Superstock.

was achieved, and it is both by dying with Christ through baptism and by ascetically dying to the passions that the faithful are themselves resurrected (Col. 2–3). In these ways, death is also a blessing – even a sacrament – within Orthodoxy's worldview (Bobrinskoy 1984; Vassiliades 1993; Behr 2006). Without mitigating death's catastrophic nature, then, Orthodoxy complements its negative assessment of death with a positive one.

While the sources within Orthodox tradition do not provide a univocal comprehensive teaching on the nature of human death, several widely shared claims can be discerned. Orthodox thinkers universally reject a "physicalist" understanding of death: the view that human existence wholly ceases with the death of the body. In contrast to a physicalist understanding, Orthodox thinkers generally affirm the following four claims: (1) the human being is a unified reality with both physical and non-physical (spiritual) dimensions; (2) non-metaphorical death pertains to both the physical and the spiritual dimensions; (3) in a real and personal sense, a human being's spiritual dimension exists after physical death; and (4) spiritual death, which is a condition possible before and after physical death, does not imply annihilation but rather a state of radical separation, rupture, or alienation from God (Florovsky 1976; Vassiliades 1993; Hamalis 2008).

The above claims are supported by the church's liturgical practice of praying both for and to the dead (Fedwick 1976; Ware 2000). For recently deceased members of the church, a funeral service is held. Typically, the casket remains open as a countercultural acknowledgment of death's reality, a way of honoring the body, and an opportunity for mourners to offer a face-to-face farewell and be provoked toward repentance. Death's antinomic nature as both a terrible tragedy and a marvelous mystery is reflected in the Orthodox funeral prayers. One hymn, attributed to St. John of Damascus, states:

> I weep and I wail when I think upon death, and behold our beauty, fashioned after the image of God, lying in the tomb disfigured, dishonored, bereft of form. O marvel! What is this mystery which doth befall us? Why have we been given over unto corruption, and why have we been wedded unto death? Of a truth, as it is written, by the command of God, who giveth the departed rest. (Hapgood 1956: 386)

Memorial services are also held for departed Orthodox, most frequently forty days and one year after death, as well as during occasional "Saturday of Souls" liturgies. A clear indication of Orthodoxy's understanding of death lies in the practice of venerating saints. The saints, commemorated liturgically on the day of their death, are not merely remembered for their exemplary lives but rather are engaged personally – as alive in Christ – through believers' requests for intercessory prayers.

Regarding after-life existence and eschatology, Orthodox thinkers are reticent and quick to acknowledge such realities as mysteries (Florovsky 1976; Vassiliades 1993). Nonetheless, two generally taught claims are, first, that immediately following physical death, a human being's spirit or soul experiences a foretaste of heaven or hell and, second, that the dead will receive resurrected bodies of glory and experience a final judgment at Christ's second coming.

SEE ALSO: Baptism; Communion of Saints; Eschatology; Judgment; Kollyva; Original Sin; Psychosabbaton; Resurrection

References and Suggested Readings

Behr, J. (2006) *The Mystery of Christ: Life in Death*. Crestwood, NY: St. Vladimir's Seminary Press.

Bobrinskoy, B. (1984) "Old Age and Death: Tragedy or Blessing?" *St. Vladimir's Theological Quarterly* 28: 237–44.

Fedwick, P. J. (1976) "Death and Dying in Byzan-tine Liturgical Traditions," *Eastern Christian Review* 8: 152–61.

Florovsky, G. (1976) *Creation and Redemption: Collected Works*, vol. 3. Belmont, MA: Nordland.

Hamalis, P. T. (2008) "The Meaning and Place of Death in an Orthodox Ethical Framework," in A. Papanikolaou and E. Prodromou (eds.) *Thinking Through Faith: New Perspectives from Orthodox Christian Scholars*. Crestwood, NY: St. Vladimir's Seminary Press, pp. 183–217.

Hapgood, I. F. (1956) *Service Book of the Holy Orthodox-Catholic Apostolic Church*, 3rd edn. New York: Syrian Antiochian Orthodox Archdiocese.

Schmemann, A. (2003) *O Death Where Is Thy Sting?* trans. A. Vinogradov. Crestwood, NY: St. Vladimir's Seminary Press.

Vassiliades, N. P. (1993) *The Mystery of Death*, trans. P. Chamberas. Athens: Orthodox Brotherhood of Theologians "The Savior."

Ware, T. (2000) *The Inner Kingdom: Collected Works*, vol. 1. Crestwood, NY: St. Vladimir's Seminary Press.

Deification

STEPHEN THOMAS

"Deification" and sometimes "divinization" are English translations of expressions used by the church fathers to describe the manner in which God saves his elect by mercifully initiating them into his communion and his presence. The most-used Greek term, *theōsis*, acts as a master-concept in Greek theology, by which the truth of doctrinal statements is assessed. The fathers used *theosis* to bring out the high condition to which human beings are exalted by grace, even to the sharing of God's life. *Theosis* means that, "In Christ," we can live at the same level of existence as the divine Trinity, to some extent even in this life, and, without possibility of falling away, in the next. Closely connected with *theosis* is the pervasive use of Genesis 1.26 – "Then God said, 'Let us make man in our image, after our likeness'" – as a description of human anthropology. A distinction is often made in Orthodox theology between the *image*, which is the human potential to be as Christ, the perfect image of God (so that we are made "in the image of the image"), and the *likeness*, which is the actualization of this in the possession of God-like qualities, that is, human perfection. But spiritual teachers often refer to *theosis* without using the term, preferring simpler expressions such as "grace" and "life." In biblical terms, the nearest expression to *theosis* is "glory" (Greek *doxa*, Hebrew *kavod*). While the divine glory is communicable, the divine nature (Hebrew *panim*, God's "face") cannot be seen or known: in the expression of St. John the Theologian and Evangelist, "No one has even seen God; the only Son, who is in the bosom of the Father, he has made him known" (Jn 1.18). The revelation of God is, however, still a matter of present experience in this life before a fuller and perfect vision of God after death, through the knowledge of God's glory, divine grace, which brings likeness to God.

The patristic expressions "theosis," "theopoiesis," and "being made gods by grace" point to the consequences of our adoption as children of God which Scripture teaches (1 Cor. 8.15–17; 1 Jn. 3.1–3): Christ's faithful are promoted, by grace, to the level of existence which the Son possesses though his divine nature (Rom. 5.2; 6.4, 22; 7.4; 8.1, 9–12). In an important text, which in Orthodox belief is the witnessing of the Apostle Peter, we become "partakers of the divine nature" (2 Pet. 1.4). We obtain eternal life, a state commencing here and now (1 Jn. 1.2). We have intimate communion with Christ in a manner hidden from the world; it is mystical knowledge (Col. 3.4; 1 Pet. 3.3–4). We possess "all truth," knowledge of the Trinity, knowing by experience the relationship of the Father to the Son, because the Holy Spirit takes everything belonging to the Father and shows us that it also belongs to the Son (Jn. 16.13–15). We are enriched with the gift of miraculous healing (Acts 3.6). As our standard of perfection we have God-like love, love of our enemies (Mt. 5.43–6). St. John's gospel, in the final discourses of Christ, in sublime language gives an account of how disciples can become "friends" of Christ (Jn. 16.14–15) and of God the Father through the comforting of the Holy Spirit (Jn. 14.16–17). Moreover, Christ promises to come to them, so that then "You will know that I am in my Father, and you in me, and I in you." The disciples are given a share in the divine glory (Jn. 17.22) and through this glory may be perfectly united to Christ (Jn. 17.22–23).

Jesus Christ blessed the idea of deification by using it himself. In his authoritative interpretation of Jewish Scripture, he demonstrated that it was an idea revealed to Israel: "Is it not written in your law, 'I said ye are gods?'" (Jn. 10.34; Ps. 82.6; Septuagint Ps. 81). In interpreting this psalm, Jesus taught the godhood of which the Israelites were capable. The psalm declares divine judgment to God's people, telling them what to do to be "gods": to treat with justice the weak, orphaned, and destitute, and to rescue the vulnerable from the power of the wicked. This is, in Christ's expression, to have the word of God come to one (Jn. 10.35). This word deifies man. Failure to receive and so obey God's word is to "die like men and fall like any prince" (Ps. 82.8).

In thus opening the scripture, Christ showed that human nature possesses two opposed possibilities: deification or death. The divine Word and Son of God took up this human nature, defeated death in it and divinized it. If we find perfection in Christ, identifying ourselves with him and living in faith and obedience to his commandments, then we come to share in Christ's divinized human nature and thereby share in the divine nature. Humankind is deified, not only by a participation in divine life which is experienced, felt, and lived, but also by service to others, just as God kenotically serves humankind, looking after us, bearing with us, and, ultimately, sharing our condition (Phil. 2).

The Bible taken as a whole narrates, in a history of salvation, the human potential for, and attainment of, deification. It is the history of God's grace as he puts forth his energies in various ways according to humanity's condition (Heb. 1.1–2). God created humankind in the image and likeness of God (Gen. 1.26); that is, as having deification as its potentiality, perfection, end, or ultimate purpose. But humankind, in Adam's person, was tricked by the serpent, that is, the Devil, who used the good and inborn desire "to be as gods" to induce him to disobey. In fact, the Devil subtly modified deification by adding the words "knowing good and evil" to the promise "You surely will not die" (Gen. 3.4–5). Disobedience led to alienation from God through shame, as humankind hid from God and no longer felt able to respond to God's call to walk with him (Gen. 3.9–10). To "walk with God" means in Hebrew to follow God's commandments. Humanity had been led to taste of the false wisdom of good mixed with evil ("knowing good *and* evil"), as one desires to know everything by tasting or experiencing it. Alternatively, the first human beings reached out for the fuller knowledge of what was good and evil before they were mature enough to receive it and were impatient to go beyond God's simple, protective command. Or, in yet another interpretation, humanity desired knowledge of everything, the expression "good and evil" meaning "everything." Whatever the interpretation, humankind could not have remained in Paradise to partake of immortality from the Tree of Life without suffering hell, that is, to be in a state of fear and shame forever. Out of compassion for

humanity, in view of the craftiness with which Adam had been tricked, God placed the race, male and female, into the world and gave human life a limit and set term (Gen. 3: 22–4). Death would not annihilate humankind but it would make us finite. From the moment humanity fell, moreover, according to the Orthodox tradition, God had the plan for humanity's restoration.

The above account of Genesis 3 gives the outline of the Orthodox interpretation of it, which takes a gentler and more merciful view than some others of "original sin." Humankind had been deceived. Being at an early stage of development, Adam was not fully responsible. He had contracted an illness, which all human beings came to share. Yet God is not a judge, but a healer (Mt. 9.12; Mk. 2.7). The therapeutic motif dominates in Orthodox language about salvation (Larchet 2000: 10). However, salvation, being an act of supreme generosity, is also deification; it takes humankind beyond the healing of our faults.

In earliest times only Enoch lived as God desired: "Enoch walked with God; and he was not, for God took him" (Gen. 5.24) He was truly "Man," as God first intended him (in Hebrew, *Enoch* means "Man"), Consequently, he, uniquely, did not suffer death, but was assumed into heaven. He was unique in living perfectly by following his conscience. Man needed more help to walk with God.

God chose Abraham and revealed himself to him and his descendants, the patriarchs, by *theophanies*, manifestations of God, some of which are quite strange, while others are very beautiful, for example Jacob's ladder, which is both about deification and a prophecy of Jesus Christ, who in his human nature descended from Abraham and the patriarchs (Gen. 28.12; Jn. 1.51). The descendants of Abraham became trapped and enslaved in a once-friendly and protective Egypt. God brought his people out through Moses, to whom he manifested himself in the theophany of the burning bush (Ex. 3.2). He revealed his holy name to Moses and gave him power to bring his people out of Egypt, revealing a Law for his people. As Origen saw, this drama, which had a historical reality, is also constantly being reenacted in the drama of human salvation, as humankind is exiled from God through enslavement to the Devil and to passion (Origen 1982: 230).

God showed to Moses his glory, the fiery light of the uncreated energy. The glory which the people saw only at a distance was experienced so fully and intimately by Moses, God's friend, that when he came out from the tent where God's presence rested, his face was transfigured. The glorified brilliant-white face of Moses had to be veiled for the sake of the people because they could not see it and live, since they were in an impure state (Ex. 34.30, 33–5). This was a prophecy of what was later possible for all through Christ: St. Paul refers to the glory or "splendor" (Greek, *doxa*) which is a matter of present experience in the "dispensation of the Spirit" and the "dispensation of righteousness" (2 Cor. 3.8–9) for the Christian. This glory makes the Christian "very bold" (2 Cor. 3.12). While Moses had to veil his face "because the people were afraid to come near him" (Ex. 34.30), "When a man turns to the Lord, there is freedom. And we all, with unveiled face, beholding the glory of the Lord, are being changed into his likeness from one degree of glory to another" (2 Cor. 3.17–18). The experience uniquely given to Moses in the Old Testament is offered to all Christians. In the passages examined above, Orthodoxy understands the "splendor" or "glory" to be a real light with a physical manifestation, rather than metaphors for inward experiences – even though the light is at the same time supernatural: St. Gregory Palamas cites St. Basil of Caesarea to this effect, making clear that the manifestation of divine light had a specific historical moment which was at the same time an eschatological moment – the apostles on Mount Tabor "Were privileged to see with their eyes a foretaste of his advent" (Palamas 1988: 252–3); that is, of his coming in glory at the end of the world.

Most closely associated with deification in Orthodox teaching is the transfiguration or metamorphosis: when Jesus was transfigured on the mountain, the dazzling light emanating from him was experienced by the three apostles, St. Peter, St. James, and St. John (Mt. 17.1–8; Mk. 9.2–8; Lk. 9.28–36). On the mountain (in Orthodox tradition, Mount Thabor), Christ was transfigured, shining with a supernatural brilliance (Mt. 17.1–8; Mk. 9.2–8; Lk. 9.28–36). He manifested God's glory, the uncreated light, to three chosen disciples. It continued to affect them throughout their lives, transforming them. St. Peter and St. John wrote in their

own words, in their epistles, of their experience of the glory, an experience which marks their writings. The persecutor Saul was transformed into St. Paul the apostle through a manifestation of this same uncreated light (Acts 9.3–7; 22.6–8; 26.13–18).

The liturgical poetry of the Feast of the Transfiguration bears witness to the historical circumstances of the event. The disciples, especially St. Peter, had been scandalized at the prospect of the Messiah, his master, submitting to death. Christ allowed the divinity to shine through the flesh in order that the disciples might be able to bear the crucifixion, by knowing Christ's divinity (Ware 1990: 477–88). It brings together the texts relating to the history of salvation, by which God revealed himself to the human race. In the biblical texts for Vespers, the events prefiguring and prophesying the transfiguration are read. They are the texts about Moses and Elijah in which their encounters with the divine glory are narrated (Ware 1990: 472–4; see Ex. 24.12–18; 33.11–23; 34.4–6, 8; I Kgs. 19).

However, the teaching of the feast is also about the possibility for every human being to experience the glory of God, his uncreated light, and to be transformed by it: "Let us be transformed this day into a better state and direct our minds to heavenly things, being shaped anew in piety according to the form of Christ" (Ware 1990: 468). This verse is drawn from Philippians: Christ was, by nature, "in the form of God" and by choice in "the form of a slave" (Phil. 2.5–7). Christ's voluntary humbling of himself enables humankind's exaltation: we may share in the "form of God." Divine grace takes the form of transforming light, which is both healing and exalting: "For in His mercy the Saviour of our souls has transfigured man/ And made him shine with light upon Mount Tabor" (Ware 1990: 468).

The transformation of the human condition is expressed in terms of an eschatological interpretation of the very psalm (psalm 82) to which Christ had referred: "To show plainly how, at Thy mysterious second coming, Thou wilt appear as the Most High God standing in the midst of gods, on Mount Thabor Thou hast shone in fashion past words upon the apostles and upon Moses and Elijah" (Ware 1990: 494).

While there is much in the theology of glory which is recognizable in other Christian traditions, there are a number of aspects of deification which are different in Orthodoxy from Western Christianity. Firstly, the experience of glory, the very idea of being *in glory*, is reserved in much Western Christian theology for the life after death; there being, in Catholic theology at least, a mystical way open to the few. In Orthodoxy the human person is being deified from the illumination of baptism throughout the course of his or her life, by participation in the sacraments or mysteries, especially the Eucharist, by prayer, and by following the commandments. Just as the prophets of the Old Testament knew Christ in a partial and hidden manner, while in the New Testament there is full knowledge, so Christians in this life experience a pledge and a foretaste of the uninterrupted brightness of the glory of the age to come. The saint is the paradigm of deification in this life, not a remote exception to normality.

The second difference concerns the salvific dimension of deification. Foreign to the Eastern Churches is a version of atonement theology in which Christ's suffering on the cross satisfies the offense of human sin to the divine majesty and justice. The Orthodox God is a God of mercy through and through, not a God whose justice predominates. Christ suffered not to pay a debt to justice; rather, Christ voluntarily suffered in order that the divine nature might encounter suffering and attain the victory over death. It is this victory which constitutes the ransom and redemption of which the New Testament speaks. Salvation consists of the deification of the human person, who is in Christ transformed into a being in whom death is conquered, and suffering no longer has a hold. The incarnation makes this deification possible. As St Athanasius said in his *De Incarnatione*: "He [the Divine *Logos*] assumed humanity that we might be divinized; He manifested Himself through the body in order that we might obtain knowledge of the invisible Father; and He endured insults from men in order that we might inherit incorruption" (Athanasius 1971: 268–9).

The third point of difference with western traditions is the doctrine of the uncreated energies of God and the metamorphosis of the human person through contact with these energies. "Energy" is the term used to describe the uncreated rays of goodness which the trinitarian God, in perfect agreement

between the persons, puts forth towards his creation in the great acts of God which constitute divine revelation. While on the one hand the nature or essence of God is unknown and beyond human comprehension, on the other hand the energies or operations of God interact with human freedom and raise the human person to knowledge of the uncreated. The energies mediate between the created and the uncreated. Orthodoxy understands grace as a deifying energy, salvation being the union of the divine energy and the human will or energy in *synergy*. Orthodoxy does not hesitate to describe grace as uncreated and has reservations about the Catholic scholastic formulation of grace as having a certain created modality in the soul.

SEE ALSO: Eschatology; Grace; St. Gregory Palamas (1296–1359)

References and Suggested Readings

Athanasius (1971) *Contra Gentes and De Incarnatione*, ed. and trans. R. W. Thomson. Oxford: Clarendon Press.

Gross, J. (2002) *The Divinization of the Christian according to the Greek Fathers*, trans. P. Onica. Anaheim: A&C Press.

Larchet, J.-C. (2000) *Thérapeutique des maladies spirituelles*. Paris: Cerf.

Origen (1982) *Homilies on Genesis and Exodus*, trans. R. E. Heine. Washington, DC: Catholic University of America Press.

Palamas, St. Gregory (1988) *The One Hundred and Fifty Chapters*, ed. and trans. R. E. Heine. Toronto: Pontifical Institute of Medieval Studies.

Russell, N. (2006) *The Doctrine of Deification in the Greek Patristic Tradition*. Oxford: Oxford University Press.

Thomas, S. (2007) *Deification in the Eastern Orthodox Tradition: A Biblical Perspective*. Piscataway, NJ: Gorgias Press.

Ware, K and Mother Mary (trans. and eds.) (1990) *The Festal Menaion*. South Canaan, PA: St. Tikhon's Seminary Press.

Deisis

KENNETH CARVELEY

The term means "intercession" and denotes the icon of Christ enthroned with the Theotokos to his right and John the Forerunner to his left. This iconographic scheme has a central place in the row of icon panels above the Royal Doors of the Iconostasis. The two intercessory figures are seen as supplicating Christ on behalf of humankind, possibly in the prospect of the Last Judgment, and may be related to intercessions within the liturgy. There are references to the Deisis (δέησις) in the 8th century. The most celebrated Deisis is in the gallery of Hagia Sophia, Constantinople (12th century). This trimorphon also appears in Byzantine carved ivories and other sculptural forms.

SEE ALSO: Divine Liturgy, Orthodox; Iconostasis; Icons

References and Suggested Readings

Buckton, D. (ed.) (1994) *Byzantium*. London: British Museum Press.
Lowden, J. (1997) *Early Christian and Byzantine Art*. London: Phaidon.
Matthews, T. (1998) *The Art of Byzantium*. London: Weidenfeld and Nicolson.
Walter, C. (1968) "Two Notes on the Deisis," *Revue des études Byzantines* 26: 311.

Desert Fathers and Mothers

M. C. STEENBERG

The desert fathers and mothers are those ascetics of the Christian deserts that flourished between the 3rd and (at the latest) 7th centuries. Due to the simple and straightforward nature of the spirituality enshrined in their *apophthegmata*, or "sayings," they are revered in wide circles for their memorable approach to living out the Christian virtues.

While the title "desert fathers/mothers" is often taken to refer solely to those ascetics who thrived in Egypt, in and around the territory of Nitria and Scetis, the extent of their "literary" geography is in fact much wider, encompassing Egypt, Syria, Palestine, and other desert regions to which monastics and ascetics fled in the early centuries. They are generally seen as beginning, at least symbolically, with St. Anthony the Great of Egypt, and span the culture of desert-dwellers through to the sacking of most Egyptian monastic communities by the Blemmyes tribes in the 6th century

and the Arabs in the 7th century. Many of their number were simple ascetics of little or no education who shunned public office and reputation; but their ranks also include important dogmatic and ecclesiastical teachers whose ascetical life was shaped by the influence of desert traditions (e.g., St. John Cassian, St. Athanasius the Great, St. John Chrysostom).

The heritage of the desert fathers and mothers is preserved in written form in various collections of "sayings" compiled in Greek and Latin from about the 6th century (though our earliest collection, the Latin *Sayings of the Elders* (*Verba Seniorum*), was translated in the mid-6th century from an older Greek collection, since lost). The best known is the *Alphabetical Collection*, which organizes its contents along an alphabetical index of personal names; thematic and systematic collections also exist.

The nature of the sayings in these collections reflects the ascetical life of the desert fathers and mothers themselves: they tend towards simplicity, stark literality, personal conviction, and rigorous struggle. Many of the sayings are single sentences, while the longer span a few paragraphs, often recounting a specific incident in the teaching life of a father (Abba) or mother (Amma), a significant word or a memorable encounter. Many of the sayings portray encounters between novices and elders, taking the form of questions and responses – often involving a turning of the original question on its head. So, for example, the notable example of the query on prayer and the spiritual life by Abba Lot, to which Abba Joseph "replies" by being visually transfigured before him (*Alphabetical Collection*, Joseph of Panephysis, Saying 7).

The desert fathers and mothers are remembered for a literal approach to living out the gospel life – an approach that saw Christ's "Go, sell all that thou hast … then come and follow me" (Mt. 19.21) as a literal injunction to be followed directly; they took the injunctions toward austerity and forceful struggle seriously and with full devotion. In the modern day they are considered a sourcebook for the spiritual life, whose legacy is – precisely due to its simplicity and purity – accessible to all.

SEE ALSO: Asceticism; Monasticism; St. Athanasius of Alexandria (ca. 293–373); St. John Cassian (ca. 360–ca.

Plate 17   Monastery of St. Antony in Egypt. Photo by John McGuckin.

435); St. John Chrysostom (349–407); St. John Klimakos (ca. 579– ca. 659); Sts. Barsanuphius and John (6th c.); Syrian Orthodox Churches

References and Suggested Readings

Gould, G. (1993) *The Desert Fathers on Monastic Community*. Oxford: Clarendon Press.

Ward, B. (ed.) (1984) *The Sayings of the Desert Fathers: The Alphabetical Collection*. Kalamazoo: Cistercian Publications.

Diakonikon

M. C. STEENBERG

The term Diakonikon normally refers to the south side of the altar apse in an Orthodox church, where vestments and books are kept, and where altar servers may prepare various items during the services. It often includes a small counter and sink, as well as a bench where deacons and servers may at times be seated (as they are not permitted to sit in the main altar).

Diakonikon can also refer to the deacon's service book (comparable to the priest's *Hieratikon*), which contains the fixed portions of the principal divine services with the priest's and people's parts abbreviated. Precise contents vary, but customarily include the deacon's parts at the divine liturgy, Matins, and Vespers, and other regular offices.

SEE ALSO: *Hieratikon*; Liturgical Books

References and Suggested Readings

Kraus, R. (1882) "Diaconicon," in *Real-Encyclopädie der christlicher Alterthümer*. Freiburg: Herder'sche, p. 358.

Divine Liturgy, Orthodox

JOHN A. MCGUCKIN

The divine liturgy of the Orthodox Church is its spiritual heart and soul. A closer and more revealing knowledge can be had of Orthodoxy by an observer from the study of the rituals and prayers than of any other external thing related to the church. The word "liturgy" (*leitourgia*) derives from the ancient Greek (pre-Christian) term for "public works" and grew in significance to mean a work conducted for the benefit of the state or community by a benefactor. It was with some of these residual associations that the term was then taken over by the writers of the Greek Septuagint Bible, and used by them to signify the Temple rituals of ancient Israel. It thus became, for the early Christians, the chief word to signify the divine "worship and sacrifice" of the church, a term which would distinguish it from the pagan sacrificial cults around them. The divine liturgy predominantly means the Eucharistic service of the Orthodox Church (often simply referred to as "the liturgy") and the other mysteries (what the western churches generally call the "sacramental" services). Orthodoxy's preferred term is *mysterion*. The latter word means "thing to be silent about" and was used by the apostles and fathers with deliberate analogous reference to the pre-Christian mysteries, or mystery religions, where the element of the *arcana* (refusing to divulge the contents of the initiation) became a very important identifying mark of the adherent. The mysteries are experiences of Christian initiation that are not easily explicable, and each one of them is deeply resonant with the grace of the Lord who has empowered them by his Holy Spirit, so as to use them as primary ways of manifesting his life-giving presence and energy within the earthly church until the Eschaton.

As Sergei Bulgakov once described it, the mysteries are the continuing signs that Pentecost is still occurring within the heart of Christ's church, and their youthful, unfailing freshness is a sure sign of the authenticity and truth of the church (Bulgakov 1988: 110–11). All the Christian mysteries are eschatological in essence. They stand, as does the earthly church itself, poised between the two ages: this age of conflicted loyalty to God, the expectation of the kingdom, and

the next Aeon where the Kingdom of God will be revealed as all in all. (Each of the greater mysteries – baptism, chrismation, Eucharist, confession [*metanoia* or *exomologesis*], ordination, marriage, and anointing of the sick – has a separate entry in this encyclopedia and can be further studied there.)

Sometimes the term "liturgy" is extended so as to designate the Services of the Hours. This is not an entirely accurate use of the term, and is certainly a misuse of the term "divine liturgy," but can be explained as a common usage whereby the Orthodox faithful denote all church prayer services. The latter ceremonies are the daily round of prayers, built out of the way monastic services developed the ancient Christian weekday prayer practices. Chief among the Hours are Vespers, Orthros (Matins), and the other prayer services of First, Third, Sixth, and Ninth Hours, along with Compline and Midnight Office. (These, too, have detailed entries under their respective headings in the encyclopedia.) This present article, therefore, will restrict itself to looking mainly at the ritual aspects of the Eucharistic liturgy.

The celebration of the Eucharist in the churches is the repeated entrance of the Orthodox into the one great act of Christ's self-sacrifice in his Passion. It is not the death and resurrection of the Lord happening time after time, for this mystery was once and for all and cannot ever be repeated (cf. St. John Chrysostom, *Homily 17* on Hebrews 3; Theodoret of Cyrus, *Interpretation of the 14 Epistles of St. Paul*, on Hebrews 8.4); rather, it is the recurring entrance of time-bound creatures into the "once-for-all-ness" of the supreme eschatological mystery of the Lord's redemption. The church experiences the Eucharist, therefore, as truly the sacrifice of the Lord's body and blood, his sacred and redeeming Passion, but it is a joyful experience; for this death and sacrifice are at one and the same moment the glorious resurrection, and the effusion of the light and energy of the resurrection on the worshipping church in the gift of the Spirit.

In the course of the divine liturgy all the elements of the Lord's saving ministry are recapitulated and reexperienced by his faithful and have been throughout the history of the church. The Eucharistic liturgy begins with prayers, moves on to the record of the earthly ministry through the reading of the Scriptures and the gospel, recalls the high-priestly prayer of the

Lord, and his Mystical Supper, witnesses the descent of the Spirit, and shares the Eucharistic gifts to the sound of hymns of the resurrection. All the prayerful oblation of the church runs to the Father, but only with and through the Spirit, and with and in the Word who became flesh for this very purpose, to bring all the world back to the knowledge of the One God. This is why the ancient prayers are so fundamentally trinitarian in all their structure and conception; something that is especially seen in the constantly reiterated trinitarian doxologies that punctuate every moment of the divine liturgy.

All the liturgy moves in a solemn unfurling that resists being split up into discrete divisions, for it is all a seamless union of parts. The Passion is thus made one with the resurrection and ascension. At the Epiclesis the Supper of the Lord is mystically perceived as one with the descent of the Holy Spirit also; for in the Lord's economy of salvation there is neither disruption of chronological time, nor separation of spatial dimension. This economy has the character of the Eschaton. The Person of the Savior is the church's gate to the glory of the Father, but only through the spiritual deification conferred on his Eucharistic community through the Holy Spirit. In fact, it is in the course of the liturgy that the church is most clearly revealed to be (and constituted as) the communion of praise that lives out of the doxology of its God, and finds within this glad thanksgiving (*Eucharistia*) the power of its communion of love with one another. As St. John of Damascus put it:

> We describe the Eucharist as participation [*metousia*] since through it we partake of the divinity of Jesus. We also call it Communion [*koinonia*], and it is an actual communion, because through it we have communion with Christ and share in his flesh and his divinity. Indeed, we also have communion, and are united, with one another through it. For since we partake of one bread, we all become one body of Christ and one blood, and members one of another, being of one body with the Christ. (*On the Orthodox Faith* 4.13)

Every moment of the liturgy tends towards a holistic in-gathering of the church into the seamless unity of Christ's own person (his divine and human condition theandrically united), as well as the deepening unity of the trinitarian oneness of *hypostases*, of which the church is also the living icon on earth.

The literary forms of the divine liturgies that were used in the ancient church were originally varied and diverse, but slowly came to a standardized set of fewer forms as the local churches more and more adopted the rituals and practices that were in use among the greater metropolitan churches, whose rites and ceremonies had become more universally known, and which generally excited admiration. So it was, for example, that ceremonies from the Church of the Anastasis in Jerusalem, and the various forms of ritual observed there, always had a very wide circulation among all the churches of the Christian world from an early time. The church of Rome used a vernacular Greek liturgy in its first four hundred years of life, only adopting a Latin-language liturgy in the time of Pope Damasus. Its practices, as the leading Christian city of the Latin-speaking world, then eventually displaced several other rival rites, such as the Gallican, Mozarabic, Ambrosian, or Sarum, to become a common and very widely diffused liturgical inheritance in the West. In the Eastern, Greek-speaking provinces of the early church, the ritual forms of the Antiochene, Syriac-speaking churches were very influential. The Byzantine rite is, at its heart, a form of the West Syrian liturgy, but by the later 4th century the new capital of the Christian Roman Empire at Constantinople had begun to serve as a central vortex, influencing all the other Greek Christian sees in its large ambit, and it spread out among them the Syro-Byzantine rite as a common syntax of international liturgy in the Eastern Christian world.

St. John Chrysostom, the archbishop of Constantinople at the very end of the 4th century, arranged slight changes to the prayers comprising the liturgy, and after his time the whole liturgical rite of Byzantium has been commonly attributed to him as its author. He thus became the symbolic father of all the liturgy which had existed (long) before his time, and would adapt after his time. The same is true for the other liturgies, of Saints Basil and Gregory. Both of these fathers of the church were responsible for liturgical developments and improvements in their own lifetimes, but became the symbolic authors of the whole liturgies that attached to them, even though these continued to adapt and change for centuries later, and had existed in substance long before them. The Divine

Liturgy of St. John Chrysostom shows many elements in it that date from the 6th century, and some later from the 9th. Both historically and theologically, there is a running and living line of tradition, from the institution of liturgy by Jesus among the apostles, to the present era of the Orthodox Church. Orthodoxy has rarely found its liturgy a controversial matter (excepting some divisive issues over the Old Believer schism in Russia), and its attitude to it has long been one of familiarity and loving protection. It has to be admitted, however, that the earlier centuries of the church were much more creative in terms of their different liturgical traditions. (For synoptic studies of the Orthodox Liturgy, see Oakley 1958; Wybrew 1989; Taft 1992.) If St. John Chrysostom was not the sole author of the liturgy that bears his name, the true story was one of more complex change and absorption of different liturgical "families" and customs that tended, as the centuries moved on, towards greater conformity of types in the East, rather than to greater diversity. The Byzantine liturgical rite did not assume its general (and more or less contemporary) shape until after the 9th century, but it has its roots in very ancient soil, with a direct continuity back to the Lord's own mystical supper, and his own command to "Do this in memory of me." The final shaping of the Byzantine liturgical rite was the result of several changes in the make up of the Eastern Christian world as it was facing the expanse of Islamic power. After Islam had cut off Palestine from ready communication with the other parts of the Roman Christian world, Mar Saba monastery, near Bethlehem, started to excel as an important center of monastic liturgical life and development. This, the so-called monastic ritual of the Eastern Church, laid out patterns of prayer services, monastic offices, and so on, that were heavily scriptural in form. The prayers of the desert ascetics were rooted in the Scriptures, and the recitation of the Psalter played a large part in them. Jerusalem liturgical traditions were also predominant, of course. The general character of these monastically designed services was significantly penitential in tone. The services were often long, meant in some cases to last the whole night through, and were very sober in style. The churches of the desert monks were usually small and poor buildings, designed for the use of single-sex communities of ascetics, devoted to the word of God in a common life of great simplicity and focus.

In the capital city, however, the liturgy was designed to revolve around the state buildings. It was a liturgical style that was built around many state processions, in which the emperor and patriarch played central parts with all their magnificent retinue of attendant clergy, and aristocrats. There were numerous stational liturgies (visits to significant city churches and holy shrines where relics were kept, each with their own local traditions). In the capital the very liturgical architecture played a significant part, too. Justinian's magnificent church of Hagia Sophia was a stage for awe-inspiring ceremonial, far removed from the tiny intimacy of the monastic chapels of the provinces. Professional choirs were brought together, employing some of the finest singers in the known world, and putting to work some of the most famous poets and hymn writers of the era, who composed extensive paraphrastic songs (*Kontakia, Troparia, Canons*), based on the scriptural narratives, but full of detail and rhetorical coloration. Accordingly, two types of ritual style grew up in the Eastern Church of the Byzantine era, known now as the Monastic and the Cathedral *Typika*. The liturgical process in general use, after the 9th century, was a form of synthesis of these two types. The different characters can now be seen juxtaposed in Orthodox liturgy, which is a rich weave of Syrian, Palestinian, Imperial Greek, and Monastic observances. It can be seen in the standard Liturgy of St. John Chrysostom: a splendid ceremonial sense of style, allied with a very sober use of a scriptural skeleton of supporting prayers, as it were, and profound patristic theological invocations shaped around the ancient liturgical kernel of the reading of the Word of God, followed by the celebration of "Thanksgiving" (Greek: *Eucharistia*) for God's wonderful creation, and redemption, as culminating in the Lord's gift of himself for his church.

The monastic style is predominant in the services of the Offices of the Hours, as might be expected. In the celebration of the mysteries, however, and in the public services of blessing, and the observance of the Feasts, especially Pascha, there is a sense of restrained magnificence and awesome ceremony. Today, even the humblest of Orthodox parish churches in the poorest of areas, glimmers with lights and incense, and the twinkle of golden vestments, and church vessels wrapped in precious cloths, and a sea of candles burning around the icons and altar. The fine synthesis of the sober monastic style of *Typikon* together with the ceremony inherent in the Cathedral rite gives the Orthodox liturgy a distinct flavor. At first it might appear to someone who is not familiar with it as perhaps unapproachable or even forbidding (especially if it is being celebrated in a language one does not know, such as Greek, Slavonic, or Romanian), but a closer familiarity, such as the Orthodox themselves develop over many years of attending church services, leads one to a deep level of "belonging" to the rhythms and nuances contained in this most rich of all languages. The ceremonies themselves are profoundly biblical in form and content, and the incessant use of scripture and intercession makes for a seamless weave between the activity of the clergy and the prayers and chanting of the people, something that is true even when a permanent choir is used to lead the people's prayers.

Today, there are four liturgies still serving as the common forms of Orthodox ritual. The first is the Divine Liturgy of St. John Chrysostom, which is the commonly used rite on Sundays and weekdays. The Liturgy of St. Basil the Great is also used ten times in the course of the church's year, mainly during the course of Great Lent. It is a more sober liturgy with much extended prayers. Most of the different elements of the service, however, are in those parts which the priest often says quietly behind the Iconostasis, and so most of the faithful would not normally recognize much difference between the two liturgies. In those places where the *Anaphora* is said aloud, however, there would be a significant difference observable in the great prayer of thanksgiving. The Liturgy of St. James, the brother of the Lord, was once the standard Eucharistic *Typikon* of the church of Jerusalem. Formerly, it was used only there and on the Greek island of Zante. Nowadays it has witnessed a revival among more of the Orthodox Churches. It is used once a year on St. James' feast day, October 23. The fourth is known as the Liturgy of the Pre-sanctified Gifts of St. Gregory the Dialogist. This is strictly speaking a liturgical service of Holy Communion, with several elements of Vesperal evening prayer, but without the consecration of the mysteries. The gifts that are received, therefore, are consecrated on the previous Sunday's Lenten liturgy of St. Basil, for use in the Presanctified liturgy of the weekdays following. The Presanctified liturgy is used on the Wednesdays and Fridays of Great Lent, and on the first three days of Great Week, leading up to Pascha.

The structure of the Orthodox liturgy follows the ancient pattern of the early Jewish-Christian communities, which used the forms of the synagogue meeting: reading and reflecting upon the Word of God and then giving God blessings (*Berakha*) for his salvific care for his chosen people. From the very beginning, this reading of the Word was conducted in the light of the great covenant-making they knew that God had contracted with them as the New People, in the mystery of the Lord's Passion, death, and resurrection. This is one of the reasons that the Passion account of the gospels was among the first long, through-written, narratives of the evangelical story. From earliest times also, the Passion story was read in the light of the New Passover of the Lord. Jesus' gift of the Eucharist to his church was the covenantal moment in which the scriptural types of Passover and Liberation reached their consummation. This is why, for example, the liturgy of the Word takes place on the road to Emmaus, when Jesus explains all the passages in Scripture that referred to his New Covenant, and why the veil is lifted from their eyes only as the Eucharist is given to them, and they realized his meaning retrospectively from the "burning" of their hearts (Lk. 24.25–32). To this day the liturgy of the Word, the service of Scripture readings and reflection (including the homily which ought to be a "breaking of the word of Scripture" to the people), takes place as the prelude, preparation for, and commentary on, the Eucharistic celebration which follows after it.

The liturgy thus falls into two major parts: Liturgy of the Word and Liturgy of the Eucharist (*Synaxis* and *Anaphora*), both of them being commentary upon the other. In the earliest times of the church the *Synaxis* was a separate service to the Eucharistic rite, but from the 4th century onwards they have been fused together. The climactic part of the *Synaxis* is always the chanting of the Holy Gospel by the deacon or priest. Similarly, the climax of the *Anaphora* is the consecration of the mysteries, as summed up in the *Epiclesis*. It is not possible, however, to single out the "single significant moment" when the whole structure of both the *Synaxis* and *Anaphora* is clearly designed to be an ongoing seamless doxology of consecration and thanksgiving. In later times this twofold simplicity of arrangement into these funda-mental parts was extended into five sections. Two preliminary, and preparatory, rituals were added to the beginning of the Liturgy of the Word, namely the *Proskomedie* (or *Prothesis*) rite and the *Enarxis* rite. And then a short ritual of thanksgiving and dismissal was added on to the end of the Eucharistic prayer. This gave the - Eucharistic service its complete, and present-day, form as follows in four major sections:

1 The *Proskomedie* (the Offering), which is the short service of preparation.

2 The *Synaxis* (the Gathering) which is composed of four episodes: (a) the *Enarxis* (opening rites) of the initial blessing, the first litanies and antiphons; (b) the Little Entrance with the gospel, the Introits and the singing of the Trisagion hymn (in ancient times this was actually the start of the divine lit-urgy in church); (c) the readings from sacred Scripture and the homily; and (d) the Great Litanies of Intercession ending with the Litany of the Catechumens.

3 The Holy Eucharist itself, which sectioned into nine separate movements of which the *Anaphora* is the core: (a) two Litanies of the Faithful; (b) the Great Entrance of the gifts; (c) the Litany of Supplication; (d) the Kiss of Peace (now normally exchanged only among the concelebrating clergy); (e) the Common recitation of the Nicene-Constantinopolitan Creed; (f) the *Anaphora* (the Great Eucharist Prayer, or Holy Oblation) extend-ing from the "Holy Holy Holy" to the consecra-tion *Epiclesis* and Great Commemoration of all the saints; (g) the Litany of Supplication and the Lord's Prayer; (h) the Elevation of the Mysteries ("holy things for the holy") and the Fraction (division) of the Lamb; and (i) the communion of the clergy and people.

4 The final section of the complete liturgy consists of the rites of *Apolysis* (Dismissal), comprising communion hymns and prayers of dismissal, thanksgiving, final blessing, and distribution of the *Antidoron* bread.

The Eucharistic liturgies of the Orthodox Church contain a wealth of the most profound prayers, hymns, and intercessions, and are universally regarded by believers as a major deposit of the highest level of theo-logical wisdom that the Orthodox Church possesses. They came to their literary maturity in a time of high patristic inspiration, and they bear a character of vener-able profundity, steeped in a rich conception of prayer as a trinitarian mystery which the entire church (heavenly and earthly) concelebrates together as a foretaste of the kingdom's arrival. The old rule of *Lex orandi lex credendi* ("the pattern of worship reveals the essence of the church's faith") is nowhere seen more aptly than here.

SEE ALSO: Anointing of the Sick; Baptism; Chrismation; Confession; Epiclesis; Eschatology; Eucharist; Incense; Liturgical Books; Marriage; Mystery (Sacrament); Ordination; Orthros (Matins); Vespers (Hesperinos)

References and Suggested Readings

Bulgakov, S. (1988) *The Orthodox Church.* Crestwood, NY: St. Vladimir's Seminary Press.

Florovsky, G. (1978) "The Elements of Liturgy," in C. G. Patelos (ed.) *The Orthodox Church in the Ecumenical Movement: Documents and Statements 1902–1975.* Geneva: World Council of Churches, pp. 172–82.

Janin, R. (1955) *Les Églises orientales et les rites orientaux.* Paris: Letouzey.

McGuckin, J. A. (2008) *The Orthodox Church: An Introduction to Its History, Theology and Spiritual Culture.* Oxford: Wiley-Blackwell.

Oakley, A. (1958) *The Orthodox Liturgy.* London: Mowbray.

Schmemann, A. (1966) *Introduction to Liturgical Theology.* London: Faith Press.

Taft, R. (1992) *The Byzantine Rite: A Short History.* Collegeville, MN: Liturgical Press.

Wybrew, H. (1989) *Orthodox Liturgy: The Development of the Eucharistic Liturgy in the Byzantine Rite.* London: SPCK.

Dormition

JOHN A. MCGUCKIN

The term refers to the "Falling Asleep" (death) of the Mother of God. Icons of the Dormition are traditionally placed over the western interior wall of Orthodox churches, so that they are the last thing believers see as they leave. A superlative example is the mosaic panel still surviving in the Savior in Chora Church in Constantinople. They are a didactic icon about the death of the elect believer. Christ, in glory, attends the bier of the Virgin and catches up her soul (depicted as a little child in swaddling clothes) while the attending apostles and ancient fathers (such as James of Jerusalem and Dionysius the Areopagite) surround her, grieving. After receiving her soul, Orthodox tradition states that three days later the Lord resurrected her body in anticipation of the End Day, and took it also into heaven. The Feast of the Dormition is one of the solemn festivals of the liturgical year, and observed in the Orthodox world on August 15 with a two-week fasting period preceding it.

References and Suggested Readings

Daley, B. E. (trans.) (1997) *On the Dormition of Mary: Early Patristic Homilies*. Crestwood, NY: St. Vladimir's Seminary Press.

Shoemaker, S. J. (2003) *Ancient Traditions of the Virgin Mary's Dormition and Assumption*. Oxford: Oxford University Press.

Dostoevsky, Fyodor Mikhailovich (1821–1881)

SAMUEL NEDELSKY

Russian writer, essayist, and philosopher famous for his exploration of the human psyche within the Christian context of sin, repentance, and rebirth. He was raised in a devoutly Orthodox home in Moscow, where he received formal religious instruction and made annual spring pilgrimages to the Trinity-Sergius Lavra. Following his arrest in 1849 for political conspiracy, he underwent a gradual spiritual regeneration following a "conversion experience" in the Omsk prison. In June 1878, following the death of his young son Alyosha, he visited the famous monastery of Optina Pustyn' with Vladimir Solovyov, where he had three meetings with Starets Amvrosii (Grenkov), who served as a model for Starets Zosima in *The Brothers Karamazov*.

SEE ALSO: Elder (Starets); Optina; Solovyov, Vladimir (1853–1900)

References and Suggested Readings

Cassedy, S. (2005) *Dostoevsky's Religion*. Stanford: Stanford University Press.

Frank, J. (1976–2002) *Dostoevsky*, 5 vols. Princeton: Princeton University Press.

Jones, M. (2005) *Dostoevsky and the Dynamics of Religious Experience*. London: Anthem Press.

Pattison, G. and Thompson, D. (2001) *Dostoevsky and the Christian Tradition*. Cambridge: Cambridge University Press.

Stanton, L. (1995) *The Optina Pustyn Monastery in the Russian Literary Imagination: Iconic Vision in Works by Dostoevsky, Gogol, Tolstoy, and Others*. New York: Peter Lang.

Doxastikon

DIMITRI CONOMOS

A troparion or sticheron that comes after the first half of the Lesser Doxology ("Glory be to the Father, and to the Son, and to the Holy Spirit"). In Greek services, from medieval times till today, it is a long verse set to a slow, elaborate chant, since it is intended to cover the time of processions in or around the church. The name *doxastikon* is derived from the Greek *doxa*, meaning "glory." It appears twice at Vespers, before the entrance of the clergy and at the end of the Aposticha, and at Matins at the end of Lauds.

E

Eastern Catholic Churches

A. EDWARD SIECIENSKI

Previously known as "Eastern Rite" or "Uniate" churches (terms that are now deemed either inadequate or derogatory), the Eastern Catholic Churches are the 22 autonomous churches of Alexandrian, Antiochian, Armenian, Assyrian, or Byzantine tradition that are in full communion with the bishop of Rome.

Historically, most (but not all) of the Eastern Catholic Churches came into being when hierarchs of local Assyrian, Eastern Orthodox, or Oriental Orthodox communities, often for very different reasons, sought to reestablish communion with the bishop of Rome. In a majority of these cases a percentage of the population refused to participate in the union, preferring instead to maintain communion with an eastern patriarch. For this reason almost all of the Eastern Catholic Churches have an Assyrian, Orthodox, or Oriental Orthodox counterpart, almost identical in their liturgies and religious practices, but separated by their respective views on communion with the see of Rome. An important exception are the Maronites, a community that existed in relative obscurity for centuries, only to be "rediscovered" by the crusaders in the 12th century. The Maronites have no counterpart among the other eastern churches, and claim never to have been out of communion with Rome.

Among the best known of these unions between an eastern church and Rome occurred at Brest-Litovsk in 1595. For various religious, cultural, and political reasons a large percentage of the Ukrainian Church, then living in the predominantly Catholic Kingdom of Poland-Lithuania, recognized the primacy of the pope and the orthodoxy of other western teachings (e.g., the *filioque*) in return for political protection and the right to retain their traditional liturgy and practices. The union was approved by King Sigismund III and promulgated by Pope Clement VIII in the constitution *Magnus Dominus*. In the following centuries several other churches entered into communion with Rome on this model, including (but not limited to) portions of the Syrian Church in 1662, most of the Antiochene Church under Patriarch Cyril VI in 1724, and the Armenian Catholic Church in 1742.

Although there were efforts by the popes to discourage the forced Latinization of the eastern churches (particularly Benedict XIV in *Etsi Pastoralis* [1742], *Demandatem* [1743], and *Allatae Sunt* [1755]), by the late 19th century many of them had increasingly become Latinized in both their beliefs and liturgical customs. However, following the release of Pope Leo XIII's apostolic constitution *Orientalium Dignitas* (1894) this trend began to subside. Particularly influential in the early battle against Latinization was the Eastern Catholic Metropolitan of Kiev-Halych, Andrew Sheptytsky (1865–1944). At the Second Vatican

The Concise Encyclopedia of Orthodox Christianity, First Edition. Edited by John Anthony McGuckin.
© 2014 John Wiley & Sons, Ltd. Published 2014 by John Wiley & Sons, Ltd.

Council, at the urging of Melkite Patriarch Maximos IV Sayegh (1878–1967), the rights and dignity of the Eastern Catholic Churches were clearly reaffirmed in *Orientalium Ecclesiarum* (1964). Since that time, almost all of the eastern churches have made efforts to rediscover their own liturgical and spiritual heritage and remove elements of Latinization where they have occurred. In 1990 a separate Code of Canon Law was issued for the Eastern Catholic Churches in the hope of aiding in this process.

Following World War II, under communist direction, a series of "reunion synods" were held (L'vov, 1946; Transcarpathia, 1947; Romania, 1948; Slovakia, 1950), at which several of the Eastern Catholic Churches were forcibly reincorporated into the local Orthodox churches. The Eastern Catholic church buildings in these territories were closed or given to the Orthodox, and dissenting clergy either sent to prison (e.g., Metropolitan Josyf Slipyj), killed, or forced to minister underground. However, following the political events of 1989, the Eastern Catholic Churches of Eastern Europe reemerged and disagreement (sometimes violent) over the ownership of seized church properties occurred, especially in the Ukraine and northern Romania. The Catholic and Orthodox hierarchies were forced to postpone their scheduled theological dialogue in order to address the issue of "Uniatism" and the possibility for a peaceful resolution to these tensions. In 1993 the Joint International Commission issued a document ("Uniatism, Method of Union of the Past, and the Present Search for Full Communion," better known as the "Balamand Statement") rejecting Uniatism as a valid method of church union, but maintaining, nevertheless, the Eastern Catholic Churches' right to exist.

The Eastern Catholic Churches include the Coptic Catholic Church; the Ethiopian Catholic Church; the Maronite Church; the Syrian Catholic Church; the Syro-Malankara Catholic Church; the Armenian Catholic Church; the Chaldean Catholic Church; the Syro-Malabar Church; the Albanian Greek Catholic Church; the Belarusian Greek Catholic Church; the Bulgarian Greek Catholic Church; the Byzantine Church of the Eparchy of Križevci; the Greek Byzantine Catholic Church; the Hungarian Greek Catholic Church; the Italo-Albanian Catholic Church; the Macedonian Greek Catholic Church; the Melkite Greek Catholic Church; the Romanian Greek-Catholic Church; the Russian Catholic Church; the Ruthenian Catholic Church; the Slovak Greek Catholic Church; and the Ukrainian Greek Catholic Church

SEE ALSO: Ecumenism, Orthodoxy and; *Filioque*; Lithuania, Orthodoxy in; Papacy; Romania, Patriarchal Orthodox Church of; Ukraine, Orthodoxy in the

References and Suggested Readings

Gudziak, B. (1998) *Crisis and Reform: The Kyivan Metropolitanate, the Patriarchate of Constantinople, and the Genesis of the Union of Brest*. Cambridge, MA: Harvard University Press.

Halecki, O. (1958) *From Florence to Brest (1439–1596)*. Rome: Sacrum Poloniae Millennium.

Keleher, S. (1993) *Passion and Resurrection: The Greek Catholic Church in Soviet Ukraine 1939–1989*. L'viv: Stauropegion.

Macha, J. (1974) *Ecclesiastical Unification: A Theoretical Framework Together with Case Studies from the History of Latin-Byzantine Relations*. *Orientalia Christiana Analecta* 198. Rome: Pontifical Oriental Institute.

Ecology

BRUCE FOLTZ

Etiologies of environmental crisis often indict Christianity for privileging divine transcendence at the expense of God's immanence in nature, leaving the world bereft of divine presence and vulnerable to human exploitation. And if human beings are created "in the image of God" (Gen. 1.27), they too would possess this transcendent, extra-worldly status, encouraging an "arrogant" and even "violent" attitude toward nature (White 1973). But this allegation, anticipated in the 19th century by Feuerbach and Nietzsche, overlooks deep divergences between Eastern and Western Christianity, long predating the Great Schism of 1054. For as British historian Steven Runciman has shown, there are from the beginning striking differences between East and West in cultural values, sociopolitical realities, and even differing theological capacities of the Greek and Latin languages (Runciman 2005: 8).

Moreover, the first and most influential scholar to blame Christianity for environmental crisis, historian Lynn White Jr., emphasized that his criticisms applied only to the Latin West, noting that "in the Greek East, nature was conceived primarily as a symbolic system through which God speaks to men…. This view of nature was essentially artistic rather than scientific" (White 1973: 88). Finally, it was within Western Christendom that the technologies generating environmental problems were fashioned and perfected. So it may be important to understand how the different views and sensibilities of the Christian East – more poetic than logical, more liturgical and sacramental than juridical, better characterized by the Byzantine dome bringing heaven down to earth than by the Gothic spires pointing away from earth toward heaven – support a different, and perhaps more salutary, understanding of creation than Western Christianity.

Byzantine Theology and Spirituality

Orthodoxy's understanding of the natural environment must be sought in relation to its spirituality, rather than through its theology taken as a self-sufficient enterprise. For as is often noted, the thought of the Eastern Church is so deeply rooted in ascetic practice and spiritual vision that it is best characterized as "mystical theology" (Lossky 1991). Only the theologian drawing upon first-hand experience of theological realities is recognized as authentic, in contrast to those merely demonstrating scholarly erudition or intellectual achievement. Hence the otherwise surprising statement of the contemporary Elder Aimilianos of Mount Athos that "through a life of prayer and participation in the mysteries of the Church, each one of us may become a theologian" (Aimilianos 2009). Nor does the Orthodox East recognize the distinction between "laity" and "religious" that came to prevail in Latin Christianity: the robust spirituality pursued by monastics does not follow from a division of labor, but rather serves as the exemplar to which all should aspire, in whatever degree may be possible. Most of its great theologians have been monastics, typically choosing to surround themselves with wilderness rather than cultured cloisters, and it was in the deserts of Egypt and the Sinai, of Palestine and Syria, and the wild highlands

of the Cappadocian Plateau, that the roots of Orthodox spirituality and its distinctive relation to the natural environment were established in the 4th and 5th centuries. It was, for example, in the rugged mountains of Egypt's Eastern Desert, near the Red Sea, that the celebrated exchange with St. Anthony the Great, the first great Christian monastic, gave us (long before Galileo, and for very different reasons) the powerful image of nature as a book: "A certain philosopher asked St. Anthony: 'Father, how can you be happy when you are deprived of the consolation of books?' Anthony replied. 'My book, O philosopher, is the nature of created things, and any time I want to read the words of God, the book is before me'" (Merton 1961: 62). Less well known is an exhortation cited in the *Philokalia*, where St. Anthony explains what it takes to "read the words of God" in nature: "let us purify our mind [*nous*], for I believe that when the *nous* is completely pure and is *in its natural state*, it sees more clearly … since the Lord reveals things to it" (Palmer et al. I: 194; italics added). For Orthodox spirituality and theology, then, *askesis* (spiritual discipline, "asceticism" in the broadest sense) and a life that sees and understands creation in a divine light are inseparable. As put by Evagrius, and others afterwards, the practice of the virtues and the purification (*katharsis*) of mind or consciousness (*nous*) prepares the soul for a certain illumination (*theoria*) by means of divine grace, i.e., allows us to see nature differently, more truly – permits the "contemplation of the divine in nature" (Palmer et al. I: 57, 61f.). "The soul's apprehension of the nature of things changes in accordance with its own inner state," states 11th-century Byzantine monk and mystic Niketas Stethatos, and only if our cognitive faculties once again operate naturally, i.e., "according to nature," will we grasp "the inner essence" of things "as they *are* according to nature"; only to the natural, ascetically purified soul will the "natural beauty [of things] exalt it to an understanding of their Maker" (Palmer et al. IV: 92; italics added).

Divine Essence and Divine Energies

Only subsequently, then, does theological reflection emerge to articulate and clarify this noetic seeing. And the most important intellectual resource in Eastern

Orthodoxy for understanding this kind of seeing (*theoria*) is the critical distinction between divine essence or substance (*ousia*) and divine energy or activity (*energeia*), since it elucidates how we can apprehend this divine light in nature at all. For does Scripture not enjoin that no one can see God and live? (Ex. 33.20; Jn. 1.18). The Byzantine East, however, understands this inaccessibility as referring to the divine Essence, what God is in himself, God as God understands himself, the very substance or beingness (*ousia*) of God; and more emphatically than the Christian West, it affirms that no creature (human or angelic) can comprehend or apprehend the divine essence, either in this life or the next. It remains radically transcendent, profoundly and eternally mysterious. But meanwhile, Orthodoxy also maintains that the divine energies or activities (*energeiai*) surround us everywhere at all times, permeating all creation, accessible in all things to those prepared to receive them. This distinction, then, revealed within its spiritual practice, long remaining unknown in the Latin West, and ultimately rejected by the Scholastics, has allowed the East to preserve divine transcendence more perfectly than the West, while encouraging the experience of radical immanence of God in nature, without risking pantheistic implications; for it is the divine energies (which being God, are nevertheless uncreated) that can be encountered, never the divine essence. The mystical experience of God in nature, then, the encounter with radical immanence that issues from a powerful sacramental sensibility, is not only tolerated in the Orthodox East, but regarded as salutary and even normative. To the purified heart, it is believed, created nature speaks everywhere of its Creator, not as an inferred conclusion, but as a living intuition.

Logoi of Creation and Contemplation of Nature (*Theoria Physike*)

The second concept vital to Orthodoxy's understanding of the natural world concerns the *logos* or inner principle unique to every created being, each mirroring in its own way the Eternal Logos through whom all things are created. These *logoi* are not forms or ideas (*eide*) in the Platonic sense, for both Plato and Aristotle understand such forms as universals, applicable to many things in general, but not to any one in particular. And Western European thought has consistently ratified the Platonic claim that what is intelligible in a particular being is just its form, i.e., something general or universal, with the corollary that whatever is unique and singular is unintelligible, apart from some additional universal concept that would render it comprehensible. This has led to an increasing divergence between poetic discourse, always inclining toward the local and particular – the universal as embodied in this time and place, in this particular individual being – and the conceptual discourses of the sciences, which seek knowledge only within universal laws, i.e., abstractions that bring to our lived experience of the world a reductionist predilection threatening to betray what it seeks to comprehend. In contrast, the Byzantine understanding maintains that every leaf and twig, every breeze that caresses the skin or bites the cheek, expresses something particular yet intelligible and eternal, a *logos* that manifests something unique and unrepeatable about the Eternal Logos who for Christian experience is Christ himself, the Son of the Father. *Logos* in Greek is something said, an audible "word" or "saying" or "meaning," and each *logos* embodies in one moment of creation something that God himself has willed to say, a singular iteration of the Word "by Whom all things were made," according to Nicea.

This concept of the *logoi* of creation is best developed in St. Maximos the Confessor, a 7th-century monk who completed an unsurpassed synthesis of Byzantine thought. Maximos maintained that the *logoi* correspond to what he calls *theoria physike* – the "natural contemplation," or purified and perspicacious "seeing," of the *logoi* embodied in nature. Thus, as the environmental movement in America was inaugurated by poets and writers and artists, and only later embraced by scientists, it is possible that figures such as Thoreau and Muir, both deeply religious, while critical of how Western Christianity regarded creation, expounded a spiritual perspective analogous to the Christian East, indigenous advocates of *theoria physike*. Nor should this "natural contemplation" be seen as something exotic or specialized, but as St. Athanasius argued in *Against the Hellenes*, simply as moving toward a restored reception of that original revelation through which the Creator has sought to remind us of himself, by means of the beauty of the *kosmos* (Athanasius 1999). The *logoi*, then, as Eastern Christians, and perhaps also certain environmental writers have suggested, are themselves what St. Anthony called "the word of God in nature," the intended objects of *theoria physike*, i.e., of our simple contemplation of the divine energies at work in the natural world around us.

Cosmic Redemption, the Iconicity of Creation, and the Priesthood of Humanity

Byzantine thought and spirituality speak to present-day realities of ecological disorder differently from the cybernetic model (which, parallel to modern political thought since Hobbes and Machiavelli, is based upon the concept of control; Greek: *kyberne*, "to steer") which the science of ecology generally employs in its ecosystemic ontology of nature. For the Orthodox, concern is with our lived relation to the cosmic dimensions of the Fall, maintaining the teaching of the ancient church that human sinfulness has disordered and distorted not only our own human reality, but also the *kosmos*, or "manifestly beautiful order" that silently surrounds it, an intuition acquiring new plausibility with the impending threat of global climate change. Thus, a tension between two seemingly contradictory understandings is discernable. On the one hand, the created world is God's first revelation, fashioned and ordered so that its beauty would recall us everywhere to its Creator, as St. Athanasius insisted. But at the same time, creation is disordered through the same human fall from divine grace that prevents us from apprehending what St. Isaac of Syria called "the glory of God hidden in creatures." Orthodoxy understands creation as a cosmic liturgy, as reflected in the poetry and iconography of the church celebrating earth and heaven alike as participants in God's great salvific deeds. Christ is both born and resurrected within the earth which "offers itself" to him, i.e., within caves; his baptism blesses and sanctifies not only the Jordan river, but simultaneously all of nature; at his triumphal entry into Jerusalem, the very stones of the earth strain to cry out in joy; at his death the heavens darken and the earth rends itself. On the other hand, nature for the most part does not (as the Byzantine icon is fashioned to do) open up for us a view to divine realities at all, but rather serves as a great, idolatrous mirror of our own desires, as St. Athanasius argued. Spiritual practice and ascetic purification, then, reconcile this dichotomy, not through a conceptual synthesis but as a task to be undertaken by each believer. This sacramental undertaking, in turn, is thought possible only because through his incarnation and resurrection Christ has already joined together heaven and earth, visible and invisible, reinstituting the cosmic priesthood to which humanity was originally ordained, and which it once exercised naïvely and prophetically, when Adam and Eve walked and spoke with God in the cool of the evening, enjoying the "primordial proximity to all existence, when we still nestled close to the life of nature" (Florensky 2002: 134). Nor has it been overlooked by contemporary Orthodox theologians that an "ecological asceticism," entailing not only spiritual purification but also simplified lifestyle, is needed if a sustainable environment is to be possible in the future (Zizioulas 1996).

It is increasingly recognized that Orthodox theology and spirituality may offer a deeper, more critical approach to environmental issues than analyses oriented primarily by the positive sciences, which even in their framing of the issues, exhibit a "naturalistic" bias, regarding humanity as just one animal species among others, inhabiting neither the *oikonomos* (shared world) nor the *kosmos* (ordered universe), but merely its own specific "ecological" niche, just as the common tick blindly inhabits its environment of mammalian blood, to use the favored example of German biologist Jakob von Uexküll, who coined the term "environment" (*Umwelt*). In the 20th century, Russian thinkers like Florensky and Bulgakov developed, somewhat controversially, the notion of Divine Sophia (based upon the Old Testament Wisdom Books, as well as Slavonic liturgical and iconographical practice) to further elucidate the experience of divine immanence within the created world. In contemporary Greek theology, Yannaras and Zizioulas have articulated an embodied understanding of "person" that radically embraces the creaturely, relational element of human existence, while the Romanian theologian Dumitru Stăniloae has emphasized (following Maximos) the deeply cosmic elements of Christian theology. The Ecumenical Patriarch Bartholomew I, through environmental writings and ecological initiatives, has earned worldwide acclaim and the designation of "Green Patriarch." Thus, if the current environmental crisis is less a problem for formal *ethics* than a crisis of lived *ethos*, then the solution may ultimately lie not in new conceptual schemata, nor even less in technological fixes, but in the lives of believers who, finding God in all things, manifest a certain comportment toward creation, a gentle and merciful attitude suggested in the West primarily by St. Francis, but in the East perennially embodied in holy men and women since the early desert fathers (St. Zosima of Palestine with his lion, St. Seraphim of Russia with his bear, St. Innocent of Alaska with his eagle, Elder Paisius of Greece with his snakes) that might save not only the created order, but ourselves as well. In the resonant words of St. Isaac of Syria:

An elder was once asked, "What is a compassionate heart?" He replied: "It is a heart on fire for the whole of creation, for humanity, for the birds, for the animals, for demons and for all that exists. At the recollection and at the sight of them such a person's eyes overflow with tears owing to the vehemence of the compassion which grips his heart. … This is why he constantly offers up prayers full of tears, even for the irrational animals and for the enemies of truth, even for those who harm him. … He even prays for the reptiles as a result of the great compassion which is poured out beyond measure – after the likeness of God – in his heart." (Isaac of Syria 1989: 29)

SEE ALSO: Deification; Ethics; St. Gregory Palamas (1296–1359); St. Maximos the Confessor (580–662); Soteriology

References and Suggested Readings

Aimilianos of Simonopetra (2009) *The Way of the Spirit: Reflections on Life in God*, trans. M. Simonopetrites. Athens: Indiktos.

Athanasius (1999) *Against the Heathen*, trans. A. Robertson, in P. Schaff and H. Wace (eds.) *Nicene and Post-Nicene Fathers, Vol. 4: Athanasius: Select Works and Letters*, 2nd series. Peabody, MA: Hendrickson, pp. 4–30.

Chryssavgis, J. (1999) *Beyond the Shattered Image*. Minneapolis: Light and Life.

Chryssavgis, J. (2000) "The World of the Icon and Creation: An Orthodox Perspective on Ecology and Pneumatology," in D. Hessel and R. Ruether (eds.) *Christianity and Ecology*. Cambridge, MA: Harvard University Press.

Chryssavgis, J. (ed.) (2009) *Cosmic Grace, Humble Prayer: The Ecological Vision of the Green Patriarch Bartholomew I*. Grand Rapids, MI: Eerdmans.

Clément, O. (1993) "The Glory of God Hidden in His Creatures," in *The Roots of Christian Mysticism*. Hyde Park, NY: New City Press, pp. 213–29.

Florensky, P. (1997) *The Pillar and Ground of the Truth: An Essay in Orthodox Theodicy in Twelve Letters*, trans. B. Jakim. Princeton: Princeton University Press.

Florensky, P. (2002) *Beyond Vision: Essays on the Perception of Art*, ed. N. Misler. London: Reaktion Books.

Foltz, B. V. (2001) "Nature Godly and Beautiful: The Iconic Earth," *Research in Phenomenology* 31, 1: 113–55.

Foltz, B. V. (2006) "The Resurrection of Nature: Environmental Metaphysics in Sergei Bulgakov's *Philosophy of Economy*," *Philosophy and Theology* 18, 1: 121–41.

Isaac of Syria (1989) *Daily Readings with St. Isaac of Syria*, trans. S. Brock, ed. A. M. Allchin. Springfield, IL: Templegate.

Keselopoulos, A. G. (2001) *Man and the Environment: A Study of St. Symeon the New Theologian*. Crestwood, NY: St. Vladimir's Seminary Press.

Lossky, V. (1991) *The Mystical Theology of the Eastern Church*. Crestwood, NY: St. Vladimir's Seminary Press.

Merton, T. (ed.) (1961) *The Wisdom of the Desert: Sayings from the Desert Fathers of the Fourth Century*. New York: New Directions.

Palmer, G. E. H., Sherrard, P., and Ware, K. (trans.) (1979–95) *The Philokalia*, compiled by St. Nikodimos of the Holy Mountain and St. Makarios of Corinth, vols. 1–4. London: Faber and Faber.

Runciman, S. (2005) *The Eastern Schism: A Study of the Papacy and the Eastern Churches During the XIth and XIIth Centuries*. Eugene, OR: Wipf and Stock.

Sherrard, P. (1992) *Human Image, World Image: The Death and Resurrection of Sacred Cosmology*. Ipswich: Golgonooza Press.

Stăniloae, D. (2000) *The Experience of God: Orthodox Dogmatic Theology, Vol. 2: The World: Creation and Deification*, trans. I. Ionita and R. Barringer. Brookline, MA: Holy Cross Orthodox Press.

Theokritoff, E. (2009) *Living in God's Creation: Orthodox Perspectives on Ecology*. Yonkers, NY: St. Vladimir's Seminary Press.

Thunberg, L. (1995) *Microcosm and Mediator: The Theological Anthropology of Maximus the Confessor*. Chicago: Open Court.

Vasileios, Archimandrite (1996) *Ecology and Monasticism*, trans. C. Kokenes. Montreal: Alexander Press.

White, L., Jr. (1973) "The Historical Roots of Our Ecologic Crisis," in *The Dynamo and Virgin Reconsidered: Essays in the Dynamism of Western Culture*. Cambridge, MA: MIT Press.

Yannaras, C. (2007) *Person and Eros*, trans. N. Russell. Brookline, MA: Holy Cross Orthodox Press.

Zizioulas, J. (1989–90) "Preserving God's Creation: Three Lectures on Theology and Ecology," *King's Theological Review* 12: 1–5, 41–5; 13: 1–5.

Zizioulas, J. (1996) "Ecological Asceticism: A Cultural Revolution," United Nations Environment Program, *Our Planet* 7, 6.

Ecumenical Councils

MATTHEW J. PEREIRA

The ecumenical councils were a development of the ancient Christian practice of holding synods of bishops in a given region to settle larger-scale disputes and to establish patterns of discipline. Roman emperors and empresses convoked the seven ecumenical councils (325–787) that brought together the leading bishops from across the imperial world for the purpose of articulating major doctrinal and canonical outcomes, which in principle were intended to promote universal agreement. Without a doubt, the conciliar decisions had significant ecclesiological and political ramifications, but the outcomes often inflamed division rather than advanced unity. The apostolic council of Jerusalem (Acts 15), along with Roman senatorial procedures (from the 5th century onwards), provided the basic foundation and structure for the ecumenical councils. The emperor had the duty of convoking the meetings, and afterwards applying their decisions as Christian law insofar as they pertained to social life. But they had no role in the theological deliberations, which fell to the bishops themselves, acting as heirs of the apostles.

In chronological order, the seven ecumenical councils which are recognized by Orthodoxy as the supreme doctrinal authorities of the church's tradition after the scriptures are: Council of Nicea I (325); Council of Constantinople I (381); Council of Ephesus (431); Council of Chalcedon (451); Council of Constantinople II (553); Council of Constantinople III (680), and Council of Nicea II (787). The Quinisext council (between the fifth and sixth, and containing disciplinary decisions, held in 692 at Constantinople and also known as the Council in Troullo) is also added to the list but not reckoned as a separate event.

Constantine the Great summoned the first ecumenical council to convene at Nicea (325). Arianism, which served as theological shorthand for the denial of the full divinity of Jesus Christ, was the primary theological issue of Nicea. Hosius of Cordoba, who served as Constantine's adviser, introduced the term: "Of one substance with the Father (*homoousios*)" into the broader christological description of the Son of God's status that was based upon scriptural affirmations (i.e., Light of Light, True God of True God, begotten, and so on). The *homoousion* remained controversial throughout the 4th-century Arian crisis, but its acceptance by the universal church as the quintessential standard of Orthodoxy gave Nicea a highly elevated symbolic status in retrospect, and provided a pattern of how subsequent "ecumenical" (worldwide) councils could be envisaged. Beyond Christology, the twenty canons of Nicea also provided precedence for future councils, by offering important disciplinary decisions for the organization of Christian affairs. St. Athanasius of Alexandria reports that 318 bishops attended Nicea; though modern scholarly estimates range between 220 and 250, with only eight western participants. Both Eusebius of Caesarea (*Life of Constantine* 3.6) and Athanasius (*Letter to the Africans* 1) declared Nicea an "ecumenical" council. In his defense of Nicea (*De Synodis*), Athanasius advances criteria for determining the ecumenical status of a council, which thereafter influenced future assessments.

Following a series of Arian emperors, the Nicene Theodosius I ascended to supreme power and summoned the second ecumenical council at Constantinople (381). The Council of Constantinople, which reaffirmed Nicene Orthodoxy, addressed the Melitian schism and the Macedonians (also known as the Pneumatomachians) who resisted the ascription of deity to the Holy Spirit. After the president of the council (Melitius of Antioch) suddenly died,

St. Gregory of Nazianzus was appointed his successor. The creed of Constantinople, later known as the Nicene Creed, enlarged the doctrine of the Holy Spirit by asserting, "We believe in the Holy Spirit, the Lord and Giver of Life, who proceeds from the Father. Together with the Father and Son he is worshipped and glorified." While not naming the Holy Spirit *homoousion* with the Father and Son, the theology of the council affirmed St. Basil of Caesarea's solutions, on the deity of Son and Spirit, thus establishing the Orthodox doctrine of the Holy Trinity of three co-equal persons. Despite being limited to the eastern half of the Roman Empire, Constantinople I was declared to have ecumenical status at the Council of Chalcedon (in 451).

Emperor Theodosius II convoked the third ecumenical council at Ephesus (431). The christological debate between Nestorius, archbishop of Constantinople since 428, and St. Cyril of Alexandria, who presided as president of the council, was the central theological issue at Ephesus. Nestorius emphasized the two disparate christological operations (i.e., the human and divine) within Jesus Christ. Cyril's Christology unified the actions of Jesus Christ in one divine person. Ultimately, Nestorius was condemned while Cyril's Christology was received as a faithful articulation of the mystery of the unity of Jesus Christ, and the view of redemption as deification of the human race through the divine incarnation of the Logos.

The Empress Pulcheria and Emperor Marcian convoked the fourth ecumenical council at Chalcedon (451). The Council of Chalcedon was intended to reconcile ecclesial relations, which had worsened since the Council of Ephesus (431). The outcome of Chalcedon was a theological compromise that blended Cyrilline unification of the two natures (*henosis*) and the two-nature Christology of Leo's Tome. The Chalcedonian definition affirmed:

Following the holy Fathers, we unanimously teach and confess one and the same Son, our Lord Jesus Christ: the same perfect in divinity and perfect in humanity, the same truly God and truly man, composed of rational soul and body; consubstantial with the Father as to his divinity and consubstantial with us as to his humanity; "like us in all things but sin." He was begotten from the Father before all ages as to his divinity and in these last days, for us and for our salvation, was born as to his humanity of the virgin Mary, the Mother of God.

We confess that one and the same Christ, Lord, and only-begotten Son, is to be acknowledged in two natures without confusion, change, division, or separation. The distinction between natures never being abolished by their union, but rather the character proper to each of the two natures being preserved as they ran together in one prosopon and one hypostasis.

The Emperor Justinian summoned the fifth ecumenical council to meet at Hagia Sophia, Constantinople (553). A total of 165 eastern bishops attended Constantinople II, which was intended to reconcile the Eastern Churches after the polarizing effects of Chalcedon (the Monophysite schism). Emperor Justinian sought to reunite the Eastern Churches through reaffirming Cyrilline Christology and the councils of Ephesus (431, 449). Further, in order to appear universal, Justinian compelled the reluctant Pope Vigilius to condemn the *Three Chapters* (writings of notable Antiochene thinkers who opposed Cyrilline theology). Also of note, the 15 anathemas of Constantinople II addressed the issue of Origenism.

The sixth ecumenical council, Constantinople III (680–1), was the third to be held at the capital city. Emperor Constantine IV convoked it under the presidency of Patriarchs George of Constantinople and Macarius of Antioch. Constantine IV presided over the first 11 of 18 sessions. Over 164 bishops participated in the council. In hopes of advancing reconciliation in the Eastern Churches, Constantinople III continued addressing the christological issues by condemning Monothelitism and Monoenergism. Consequently, Patriarch Macarius was expelled for insisting that two wills in Christ signified a return to Nestorianism. The theology of St. Maximos the Confessor was elevated at this council.

Empress Irene summoned the seventh ecumenical council to convene, first at Constantinople, then after political troubles, at Nicea. The iconoclastic controversy was the central issue of Nicea II (787). The debate over icons was an extension of the ongoing christological debates inasmuch as the Iconodules argued the veneration of a material image was a manifestation of the incarnation, whereby the flesh (materiality) was seen to have become divinely and sacramentally graced. Icons became a critical demonstration of the principle of the incarnation of the Godhead and the deification of humanity.

There were other notable councils (e.g., Sardica, 343; Ariminum, 359) that almost achieved ecumenical status, only to eventually lose that distinction (Socrates, *H.E.* 2.20, 37). The Latin Church replaced the Council of Constantinople (880), which was initially deemed ecumenical, with the earlier Council of Constantinople (870). After the schism between East and West (1054), there were two reconciliation councils (Lyons, 1274; Florence, 1439), but they were never afforded ecumenical status in the East, showing that "receptionism" is an important aspect of how a council is recognized as ecumenical in stature: how it is seen to manifest the universal mind of the church by its reception and defense over time. The Orthodox world restricted the number to seven, although Roman Catholicism continued to declare ecumenical councils into the 20th century.

SEE ALSO: Cappadocian Fathers; Christ; Council of Chalcedon (451); Council of Constantinople I (381); Council of Constantinople II (553); Council of Constantinople III (680–681); Council of Ephesus (431); Council of Nicea I (325); Council of Nicea II (787); Holy Spirit; Holy Trinity; Icons; St. Athanasius of Alexandria (ca. 293–373); St. Cyril of Alexandria (ca. 378–444)

References and Suggested Readings

Ayres, L. (2004) *Nicea and Its Legacy: An Approach to Fourth Century Trinitarian Theology*. Oxford: Oxford University Press.

Davis, L. D. (1983) *The First Seven Ecumenical Councils*. Wilmington, DE: Michael Glazier.

Davis, L. D. (1987) *The First Seven Ecumenical Councils: Their History and Theology*. Wilmington, DE: Michael Glazier.

Florovsky, G. (1967) "The Authority of the Ancient Councils and the Tradition of the Fathers," in G. Muller and W. Zeller (eds.) *Glaube, Geist, Geschichte*. Leiden: E. J. Brill.

Hanson, R. P. C. (1988) *The Search for the Christian Doctrine of God: The Arian Controversy 318–381*. Edinburgh: T&T Clark.

Hefele, C. J. and Leclercq, H. (1907–52) *Histoire des conciles*, 11 vols. Paris: Letouzey et Ané.

McGuckin, J. A. (2001) *Saint Gregory of Nazianzus: An Intellectual Biography*. Crestwood, NY: St. Vladimir's Seminary Press.

McGuckin, J. A. (2004) *Saint Cyril of Alexandria: The Christological Controversy, Its History, Theology and Texts*. Crestwood, NY: St. Vladimir's Seminary Press.

Ecumenism, Orthodoxy and

TAMARA GRDZELIDZE

The general view among Orthodox participants in the ecumenical movement is that their contribution has been highly significant. At present, twenty-one Orthodox Churches are full members of the World Council of Churches (WCC) and officially take part in the international ecumenical movement. The Churches of Georgia and Bulgaria are exceptions. Of this number, fifteen are Eastern Orthodox and six belong to the family of Non-Chalcedonian Orthodox Churches. From the early 20th century the Eastern Orthodox have been aware of the issue of the unity of the church to which the encyclical of Ecumenical Patriarch Joachim III in 1902 alerted them (Patelos 1978). His letter was written as a response to the international congratulations he received on the occasion of his enthronement as ecumenical patriarch. It speaks of his desire for union with all who share faith in Christ and talks of it as the subject of his constant prayer and supplication. The letter also sets out frankly how the differing doctrinal positions of the western churches create a problem on the way towards any hope of restored unity. Thus, from the very beginning of the Orthodox participation in the ecumenical movement, the prevailing theme has been a desire for unity in spite of the challenges that obvious and well-known ecclesiological differences between the churches bring to the fore. In facing up to this challenge of "difference" it soon becomes obvious how the Orthodox ecumenist needs discernment to tell apart legitimate differences of church practice (*Diaphora*) from differences which are "divisive" (*Diairesis*).

Even more significant and overtly ecumenical in tone was the encyclical of Ecumenical Patriarch Germanos, issued in 1920, which was addressed "To the Churches of Christ Everywhere" and which announced its theme in the epigraph taken from the First Letter of Peter: "Love one another earnestly from the heart" (1 Pet. 1.22) (Limouris 1994). This encyclical is considered foundational to the ecumenical movement in general, setting forth the very notion of creating a "league" or fellowship of churches. It speaks about the "blessed union" of the churches that awaits the faithful and urges all the different traditions to engage in joint study of the central issues surrounding the concept of reunion. The letter suggests that, as a first step towards union, the fostering of contacts between the churches is a most important thing. When the first such contacts were initiated, two prerequisites were asked to be kept in mind: first, "the removal and abolition of all the mutual mistrust and bitterness"; and secondly, that "love should be rekindled and strengthened among the churches." Germanos then went on to list some eleven fundamental points as a working proposal and agenda for future collaboration among the churches: a list which indeed became the basis of the programmatic work of the WCC at the time of its creation in 1948. Then, only three Orthodox churches participated: the ecumenical patriarchate itself, the Church of Cyprus, and the Church of Greece; though the Romanian Orthodox Episcopate in the USA sent representatives. The spirit of Germanos' influential agenda was the mutual enrichment of divided Christians through the sharing of experience, the common study of existing problems, and the charitable recognition of one another at various levels. In its final paragraph the encyclical referred to the fellowship it envisaged growing between the churches by using the Greek word *Koinonia*, which has since become a landmark, a focal idea, in the history of the worldwide ecumenical movement. It was on this encyclical that W. A. Visser't Hooft, the first general secretary of the WCC, commented: "With its 1920 encyclical, Constantinople rang the bell of our assembling."

One of the important messages reiterated throughout the history of the Orthodox participation in the ecumenical movement has been the Orthodox statement delivered at the First World Conference of Faith and Order in Lausanne in 1927. The Faith and Order Commission started as a movement of churches within the WCC to combat church division and seek unity according to the expressed will of Christ: "That all may be one" (Jn. 17.21). It grew into being a commission of nominees from different churches, currently totalling 120 representatives, who assemble regularly to reflect on divisive and non-divisive issues which keep the churches away from full communion. At the 1927 meeting in Lausanne, the Orthodox laid down the principle that reunion could take place "only on the basis of the common faith and confession of the undivided church," acknowledged as the reality of the first eight centuries of the Christian era. Real union, therefore, was seen only as *communio in sacris*, a sharing in the sacred mysteries, and this could happen only on the basis of full agreement in faith. The Orthodox delegates, having made this significant policy statement, then expressed their readiness to continue the search for unity by acknowledging "a partial reunion" currently happening among other churches in anticipation of the "general union" to which they looked forward in hope. By this means, establishing limits and terms to the notion of the ecumenical quest, the Orthodox were able more comfortably to situate themselves in the syntax of their own traditional ecclesiology, and were enabled to address the others as one rather than many. Although fully conscious of the challenge of being divided from the others by dogmatic differences, the Orthodox declared their readiness to continue devotedly to seek the rapprochement of the churches, with those who shared and confessed faith in the Lord Jesus Christ. As Fr. Georges Florovsky (the noted Orthodox theologian who was involved with the ecumenical movement from its earliest days) expressed it in 1949, the Orthodox understood their mandate to participate in ecumenical movement "as a direct obligation which stems from the very essence of Orthodox consciousness" (Florovsky 1989).

Other landmarks of the Orthodox contribution to world ecumenism occurred at the New Delhi (1961) and Nairobi (1975) Assemblies of the WCC. If the meeting at Toronto had claimed that "the WCC is composed of churches which acknowledge Jesus Christ as God the Savior," the New Delhi meeting went further, on the urging of the Orthodox members present, to define the "Christian" basis of the WCC as rather being rooted in the matrix of the trinitarian confession of God, a fundamental approach of all Orthodox theology, and the core of its distinctive ecclesiology. The first address given by an Orthodox theologian at a plenary WCC Assembly was by Nikos Nissiotis at the New Delhi Assembly. He spoke about the highest level of authority given by "the unbroken continuity of the life of the historical church" (Patelos 1978: 278). Unity was there presented by Nissiotis not as an option but rather as the source of life, the origin and the goal of the creation in Christ, as manifested by the church. "Unity among men in the church," he said, "Is the result, the reflection, of the event of the Father's union with Christ by his Spirit realized in the historical church on the day of Pentecost" (Patelos 1978: 232). This introduction, by the Orthodox, of the centrality of pneumatology and the idea of conciliarity into ecumenical conversations changed the worldwide ecumenical scene forever. A good example of this was seen at the WCC Assembly in Uppsala (1968), which focused on the catholicity of the church. Continuing discussions on conciliarity and catholicity happened at the Nairobi Assembly (1975) and resulted in the stressing of the notion of the unity of the church as "a conciliar fellowship of local churches which are themselves truly united" (Paton 1976).

The recognition of Orthodox participation was reflected in the direction the Faith and Order Commission chose to give to its study program, focusing it on the ecumenical councils of the early church (Faith and Order Paper 59, on Chalcedon's significance) and on the patristic heritage (Faith and Order Paper No. 50, focused on the work of St. Basil the Great, *On the Holy Spirit*). A common approach to the writings of the church fathers was again addressed by the Faith and Order Commission in 2009, following a consultation in Cambridge (2008) after a hiatus of forty years. At the First World Conference of Faith and Order the Orthodox expressed their regret in not being able to accept the basic principles of the two published WCC reports on the nature of the church and the faith of the church because both these documents set off from the consideration that the Scriptures were the only source of revelation, and did not recognize the Nicene-Constantinopolitan Creed as the common symbol of Christian faith; nor did they refer to the threefold priestly ministry instituted by Christ. In the following years, sometimes because of Orthodox initiatives and sometimes not, the Faith and Order Commission dealt with both issues, conducting a study on the apostolic faith (Faith and Order Paper 153, on the Nicene-Constantinopolitan Creed; after which point the WCC members agreed to use in common the text without the *filioque* addition) and a convergence document on the church ("Baptism, Eucharist, Ministry": Faith and Order Paper 111). Having criticized the "secular categories used in the shaping of ecumenical thinking," Fr. John Meyendorff (then a chairman of the Faith and Order Commission) proposed in his book *Unity of the Church – Unity of Mankind* that the WCC should henceforth approach the issue of ecclesial unity without excluding the unity of humankind, by means of the church's Eucharistic theology, as understood in eschatological perspective.

The Orthodox wisdom on the mission of the church was unfolded in the consultation in Etchmiadzin (1975) before the Nairobi Assembly in a document entitled "Confessing Christ through the Liturgical Life of the Church Today." The liturgical life of the church continues on when the liturgical celebration is over; its mission is based on the transforming power of the liturgy. Later, these formulations were further developed into the now famous concept of the "Liturgy after the Liturgy" (Bria 1996). In the same spirit of the liturgical understanding of the world and history, the Orthodox offered the ecumenical movement its theological reflection on Diakonia in the church in a study entitled *Orthodox Visions of Ecumenism*, composed after the consultation meeting in Crete in 1978. Moreover, the presence of the Orthodox in the WCC has also been marked by the way that its traditions of spirituality have clearly penetrated non-Orthodox circles, whether through reflection on the meaning of icons (Limouris 1990) or the cult of the saints (Grdzelidze and Dotti 2009).

Participation in the ecumenical movement has undoubtedly opened up a new set of perspectives for the Orthodox churches interacting with one another in this international and studious environment, and there have been pan-Orthodox meetings and inter-Orthodox consultations held on several occasions within the framework of the WCC. At these meetings the Orthodox churches have discussed various ecclesiastical issues, together giving a united witness to the world. It was in this context that the first attempts were made to clarify the christological ambiguity existing between the Eastern and Oriental Orthodox churches (Chaillot and Belopopsky 1998). Also, the issue of the role of women in the Eastern church first was addressed by the Orthodox under the aegis of WCC sponsorship. To this end there were several important Orthodox meetings: Agapia (1976), Rhodes (1988), Crete (1990), Damascus (1996), Istanbul (1997), and Volos (2008) (see Soumakis 2009). The ecumenical movement has thus allowed for an enriching exchange for the Orthodox with the Protestant churches. While the Orthodox offered to the West their unique tradition and spirituality, they in turn were stimulated to get to know better both western theology and the churches of the Reformation tradition.

A great deal of Orthodox theology in the 20th century has thus been written in the context of lively encounter with the non-Orthodox, which is especially true of the Orthodox theologians of the diaspora and also beyond (Lossky, Krivocheine, Florovsky, Schmemann, Meyendorff, Nissiotis, and others). There was a question of some urgency at first in terms of the self-defense and self-explanation of the Orthodox to the wider world (Western Europe and North America) which knew very little or nothing about the Orthodox Church. Ecumenical Orthodox theologians of our time, whether from traditional Orthodox countries or not (Zizioulas, Clapsis, Limouris, Vassiliadis, Alfeyev, and Bouteneff, for example), address theological issues in their ecumenical setting, proclaiming the teaching of the Orthodox Church but also sharing the riches of their tradition with the rest of Christendom. Where else but in the ecumenical movement could Orthodox address such issues as world violence? From one such dialogue emerged this Orthodox reflection: "Orthodoxy provides a non-violent alternative to Western Christianity's atonement theology (based on Christ as sacrificial scapegoat) with an incarnational soteriology in which Christ shares our mortal human nature, restoring it through His death on the Cross and His resurrection.... There is no just war theology in the Orthodox Tradition" (Clapsis 2007). In such a context Orthodox emphasize their eschatological vision of reality (the church as a foretaste of the kingdom) and offer critique of the present condition from the viewpoint of God's intent for the whole of creation.

Orthodox hierarchs, clergy, or lay theologians known to the world through their ecumenical endeavor, use their authority for the benefit of the Orthodox Church, and one of the best examples of this can be seen in the revival of the Church of Albania under the spiritual leadership of Archbishop Anastasios Giannoulatos (Forest 2002). Orthodox actors in the ecumenical movement bring back to their own churches the deep experience gained through encountering Christians from all over the world. There are numerous examples of Orthodox churches having learned faster and acquired strength through ecumenical commitment so that they have become impressively articulate in bilateral and multilateral conversations.

Ecclesiological challenges remain, of course. The main source of the division between the churches, ecclesiology, has been treated at different points in the ecumenical movement, but it has not been solved to any great extent – at least, as much as would be of significance to allow all the Orthodox to pray with the others, not to mention the level of unity required for the sharing of communion. The first "concession" of the WCC to Orthodox ecclesiology was the so-called "Toronto Statement" (1950) on "The Church, the Churches, and the World Council of Churches." Here, the Orthodox concern was to avoid identifying the WCC as a church in itself, a super-church, membership of which implied any specific doctrine concerning the nature of global church unity. Some commentators called the series of negations in this statement a "provisional neutrality" which should be a starting point meant to be dissolved with the passing of the years (Newbigin 1951). The Toronto Statement, in fact, allowed the Orthodox to carry on participating in the ecumenical movement without feeling compromised. Some consider the very fact of the Orthodox continuing participation, in spite of the huge ecclesiological challenges involved, as a contribution in itself. The most recent ecumenical claim (2002) on two basic ecclesiological self-understandings is that some churches (such as the Orthodox) "*identify* themselves with the one, holy, catholic and apostolic church" and others "see themselves as *parts* of the one, holy, catholic and apostolic church" (WCC 2003). Such positions define whether churches are able, in the first instance, to recognize one another as churches.

Although the Orthodox have constantly referred to the necessity for all to return to the bosom of the mother church of the first centuries, an acceptable formulation of such a demand must be a joint rediscovery of our common roots. "Return" to the ancient church will not be easy for many non-Orthodox churches that are living bodies and have been exposed to history throughout numerous vicissitudes. Nor does much contemporary western biblical scholarship accept the idea that there was "an ideal, homogenous church" in ancient times. Therefore, all churches are at various stages on a journey of rediscovery of their common heritage, which may bring the churches closer than has been possible at present.

The reception of the WCC statement on *Baptism, Eucharist and Ministry* was a step forward in the process of growing together, but did not imply "ecclesiological or practical recognition of the ministry and sacraments of non-Orthodox churches" (Limouris and Vaporis 1985). On the way to creating a common statement on the nature and mission of the church, the ecclesiological challenges raised by the Orthodox became even more apparent. Although, once again, it was because of their participation in the dialogue that the sacramental dimension of the church became a central topic of multilateral discussions and found its way in the convergence document on the nature of the church (Faith and Order Paper 198). The basic standpoint for the Orthodox in all ecclesiological discussions is the primacy of Eucharistic ecclesiology: *Koinonia* does not know division. Church unity exists only in Christ and is actualized in the Eucharist. How far can Orthodox Eucharistic ecclesiology embrace other ecclesiologies? Can Orthodox pneumatology allow full sharing of gifts with other churches? Or, as the Final Report of the WCC Special Commission has recently asked the question: "Is there space for other churches in Orthodox ecclesiology? How would this space and its limits be described?"

The ecclesiological challenge has proved to be the major obstacle for some Orthodox envisaging legitimate participation of the church in the global ecumenical movement. This comes to a crisis often over the issue of common prayer. All actors in the ecumenical movement are aware of the difficulties related to common worship. There are theological, canonical, traditional, historical, and ethical reasons behind the

question, but in general two sets of problems can be identified. Firstly, there is a canonical problem for the Orthodox who have an authoritative canonical statement to the effect "Do not pray with heretics" (*Apostolic Constitutions* 45; *Laodicea* 33–4) which some have interpreted as meaning that Orthodox today ought not to worship or even pray with Christians of other communions. Secondly, there is the ethical problem related to the nature of ecumenical prayer. The Orthodox do not have a single approach to the matter of praying ecumenically (with the exception of "intercommunion" or "Eucharistic hospitality," which in the ecumenical context is excluded by the Orthodox entirely). Regarding common prayer, those Orthodox who are willing to participate actively in the ecumenical movement accept the practice of offering prayers along with fellow Christians as an important one. However, this is not a standard behavior, as many Orthodox simply refuse to allow this as viable. At the level of the churches, at present, there are some Orthodox churches which find it immensely difficult to hold a common prayer service with non-Orthodox, and others which are more open to common prayer; though even among the latter there are voices among the clergy, monastics, and laity who refuse to participate in the common prayer their church organizes. In other words, there is no one established rule or attitude shared by all the Orthodox at present. The key to such a resistance on the part of some Orthodox lies in their ecclesiology and the role of the Eucharist in Orthodox theology which claims that true spiritual unity can be expressed only through the shared body and blood of Christ.

The very character of ecumenical prayer, its eclectic nature, often raises many questions. There is also a sensitivity issue, especially when using symbols and symbolic actions in prayer. Cultural misunderstanding is liable to cause problems as much as genuine theological differences. The stark difference of ethos involved in a typical ecumenical worship service is apparent to any Orthodox who attend. Sometimes the Orthodox envisage various "threats" implied by ecumenical prayer, such as proselytism or westernization or an imposed uniformity in worship. The report of subcommittee III of the Special Commission on Orthodox Participation in the WCC (Crete, August 2000, printed for internal use only) says: "Orthodox participants have found certain elements within the worship life of the WCC to be incompatible with apostolic tradition. These include (a) the use of inclusive language in referring to God, (b) the leadership of services by ordained women, (c) the introduction of syncretistic elements." The WCC has tried to tackle the issue, by means of this Special Commission, which consists of a party of sixty high-church officials and theologians. Although it started as a committee to meet precise Orthodox concerns, it finally played a remarkable role in renewing some policies of the WCC and thus met the concerns of a wider constituency and embraced a broader realm of issues than initially had been envisaged, such as ecclesiology, common prayer, social-ethical issues, decision-making processes, and membership. The accumulating dissatisfaction of the Orthodox participants in relation to the content and style of the WCC was strengthened by widespread political changes in Eastern Europe after the fall of communism. This era saw the formal separation of Orthodox churches from state control, and a renewed protest against some of the Orthodox churches' earlier involvement in the ecumenical movement under the aegis of the communist regimes. This latest crisis began in the late 1990s. In 1998 representatives of the Eastern Orthodox churches gathered in Thessaloniki and proposed to set up a "mixed commission" which was paralleled by the creation, in the same year, of the WCC's own Special Commission. The Orthodox expressed concern about their unequal footing with the Protestant communities, for the number of the Orthodox churches remained the same over the years while the Protestant churches proliferated, a demography which affected decision-making in governing bodies. Another Orthodox concern was voiced also as to the way in which the whole ethos of the WCC was so predominantly Protestant. It was suggested that the voice of minorities should be better reflected in decision-making. The Special Commission recommended changing the decision-making procedures in the governing bodies of the WCC from majority vote to one of consensus.

Orthodox concern over common prayer was taken up seriously at this time and a recommendation was put forward that "a clear distinction is proposed between 'confessional' and 'interconfessional' common prayer at WCC gatherings. Confessional common prayer is the prayer of a confession, a communion, or a denomination within a confession. 'Interconfessional common prayer' is usually prepared for specific ecumenical events." This distinction was meant to free the traditions to express themselves either in their own integrity or in combination, all the while being true to the fact that Christians do not yet experience full unity together, and that the ecumenical bodies in which they participate are not themselves churches.

All in all, Orthodox concerns related to their participation in the ecumenical movement, and in its headquarters at the WCC, predominantly stem from their unique ecclesiology, which in turn defines their attitude towards matters of worship and ethics. However, considering the past giants of the ecumenical movement such as Fr. Georges Florovsky or Prof. Nikos Nissiotis, the qualified eagerness of the Orthodox to stay in the movement and make their witness to the world together with other fellow Christians seems a continuing imperative to the Orthodox worldwide (Nissiotis 1978). The work of the Special Commission has given ground to the Orthodox for developing their participation in fresh and constructive ways.

SEE ALSO: Church (Orthodox Ecclesiology); Contemporary Orthodox Theology

References and Suggested Readings

Bria, I. (1996) *The Liturgy after the Liturgy: Mission and Witness from an Orthodox Perspective*. Geneva: World Council of Churches.

Chaillot, C. and Belopopsky, A. (1998) *Towards Unity: The Theological Dialogue between the Orthodox Church and the Oriental Orthodox Churches*. Geneva: World Council of Churches.

Clapsis, E. (ed.) (2007) *Violence and Christian Spirituality: An Ecumenical Conversation*. Geneva: World Council of Churches.

Florovsky, G. (1989) *The Orthodox Contribution to the Ecumenical Movement, in Collected Works, Vol. 13*. Vaduz: Büchervertriebsanstalt, p. 160.

Forest, J. (2002) *The Resurrection of the Church in Albania: Voices of Orthodox Christians*. Geneva: World Council of Churches.

Grdzelidze, T. and Dotti, G. (2009) *A Cloud of Witnesses: Opportunities for Ecumenical Commemoration.* Geneva: World Council of Churches.

Limouris, G. (1990) *Icons: Windows on Eternity: Theology and Spirituality in Colour.* Geneva: World Council of Churches.

Limouris, G. (1994) *Orthodox Visions of Ecumenism: Statements, Messages and Reports on the Ecumenical Movement, 1902–1992.* Geneva: World Council of Churches.

Limouris, G. and Vaporis, N. M. (1985) *Orthodox Perspectives on Baptism, Eucharist and Ministry.* Faith and Order Paper 128. Boston: Holy Cross Press.

Newbigin, L. (1951) "Comments on 'The Church, the Churches, and the World Council of Churches'," *Ecumenical Review* 3, 3: 153–4.

Nissiotis, N. (1978) *Called to Unity: The Significance of the Invocation of the Spirit for Church Unity.* Faith and Order Paper 82. Geneva: World Council of Churches.

Patelos, C. G. (ed.) (1978) *The Orthodox Church in the Ecumenical Movement: Documents and Statements.* Geneva: World Council of Churches.

Paton, D. M. (ed.) (1976) *What Unity Requires: Breaking Barriers, Nairobi 1975.* Geneva: World Council of Churches; London: SPCK; Grand Rapids, MI: Eerdmans.

Soumakis, F. (2009) "World Council of Churches: The Long Road from Agapia to Volos," in J. Lasser (ed.) *Sophia: Studies in Orthodox Theology* Vol. 1. New York: Sophia Institute, pp. 30–43.

World Council of Churches (2003) "Final Report of the Special Commission on Orthodox Participation in the WCC," *Ecumenical Review* 55.

Education

SAMUEL NEDELSKY

Education has played a central role in conveying the tradition of the Orthodox Church throughout its history, from the catechizing activities of the first generations of Christian teachers to the theological seminaries and parish schools of the present day. Jesus Christ himself was the Teacher (*didaskalos*) of his disciples, who in turn became the first generation of Christian teachers (*didaskaloi*), instructing catechumens and the newly baptized in the principles of faith.

The 2nd century saw the formation of centers of catechetical and theological education gathered around learned private teachers. The most famous such "school" was that of Alexandria, home to both Clement and Origen, two of the first Christian theorists of education. Clement laid out his program of study in his trilogy on education: *Protrepikos pros Hellenas* (Hortatory Discourse to the Greeks), *Pedagogos* (The Tutor), and *Stromateis* (Miscellanies). Origen later founded a Christian *schola* in Caesarea in the mid-3rd century; his curriculum began with grammatical studies, progressed through the natural sciences and rhetoric, and culminated in theology (*Letter of Thanksgiving of Theodore*).

The early church inherited the Greco-Roman system of education (*paideia*) for the young, heavily based on Homer and other poets, omitting only reference to the pagan cults and the "immoral stories" of the old gods. Emperor Julian's edict of 362, which briefly banned Christians from teaching the pagan classics, prompted a number of prominent 4th-century theologians to reconsider the relationship between Hellenic *paideia* and Christian education, such as the two Apollinarii of Laodicea (father and son) and Gregory of Nazianzus, who each began a process of preparing refined Christian texts for use in schools. Basil of Caesarea, in his "Address to Young Men on the Right Use of Greek Literature," treated the study of Greek learning as preparatory training for Christians, advising young men to take whatever was beneficial from the pagan Greeks and pass over the rest, an approach that was widely adapted thereafter and became known as "despoiling the Egyptians" (from the Exodus story detail where the liberated Israelites took gold and silver from their Egyptian captors).

In the Byzantine Empire boys and girls received religious instruction primarily from their parents (although clergy or "grammarians" sometimes performed this task) through listening to and reading Scripture and church prayers and often by learning the Psalter by heart. Secular education for boys normally involved three stages: (a) preliminary education in orthography (reading and writing); (b) secondary education in grammar, based largely on the study of Homer; and (c) higher learning, which involved studying rhetoric and philosophy along strictly classical lines. While all classical literature tended to be interpreted theologically, theology itself had no defined place as a separate discipline. Monastery schools existed, but generally admitted only aspiring monastics, and instruction was limited to the study of Scripture.

The Byzantine Empire had no organized theological schools, nor was theology taught as a subject in schools of higher learning. Theology was viewed as the highest form of knowledge, but not as a "science" to be studied among others at school. The Patriarchal Academy in Constantinople, which is first heard of in the 7th century and best known from the 12th, trained primarily ecclesiastical administrators and canonists, although the gospels were taught by the academy's rector. The primary locus of theological education was the liturgy, in which people of all classes could participate.

Education among Greeks suffered as a result of the fall of Constantinople. Young Greeks frequently traveled to Western Europe, especially to Venice, to pursue higher studies, although the Patriarchal Academy continued to operate.

The first Orthodox theological school employing the methods of western academia was the Kiev-Moghila Academy, which evolved out of the Kiev Brotherhood School (1615–32) and the Kiev-Moghila Collegium (1632–58); it obtained the status of an academy in 1658, and in 1819 was renamed the Kiev Theological Academy. A similar institution, the Slavic Greek Latin Academy, was organized in Moscow in 1685–7; in 1814 it was relocated to the Trinity-Sergius Lavra and renamed the Moscow Theological Academy. These institutions were initially directly based on contemporary Jesuit models and offered instruction in Latin. The system of theological education begun under Peter the Great and continuing until the Revolution of 1917 included three levels: elementary (spiritual schools), undergraduate (seminaries), and graduate (theological academies). By the end of the 19th century there were 158 elementary ecclesiastical schools, fifty-eight seminaries, and four theological academies (in Kiev, Moscow, St. Petersburg, and Kazan).

The University of Athens was founded by royal decree in 1837 with faculties of theology, law, medicine, and philosophy. The theological faculty was outside direct supervision by the Greek Church and based chiefly on the Protestant German model. In 1844 the patriarchate of Constantinople founded the Theological School at Halki; in 1853 the patriarchate of Jerusalem founded the Theological School of the Holy Cross in Jerusalem. A second state theological faculty in Greece was founded at the University of Thessalonica in 1925, although it did not become operational until 1941–2.

The most significant Orthodox theological institution in Western Europe is the St. Sergius Orthodox Theological Institute in Paris, founded by Russian émigrés in 1925. After World War II a group of professors from the St. Sergius Institute joined the faculty of St. Vladimir's Seminary, which had been founded in New York in 1938. Other prominent seminaries in North America include the Holy Cross Greek Orthodox School of Theology, Brookline, Boston, founded in 1937, and St. Tikhon's Seminary. Orthodox seminaries and theological faculties now exist throughout the world. Many, such as the Bucharest or Iasi Theological Academies, or Moscow Theological Academy, are now enjoying dramatic recoveries after decades of state oppression.

Today, it is the local parish school that serves as the primary vehicle for the formation of both religious and ethnic identity in the young.

SEE ALSO: Cappadocian Fathers; Catechumens; Constantinople, Patriarchate of; Moghila, Peter (1596–1646); Ottoman Yoke; Russia, Patriarchal Orthodox Church of

References and Suggested Readings

Alfeyev, H. (1998) "Problems of Orthodox Theological Education in Russia." *Sourozh* 71: 4–28.

Alfeyev, H. (2003) "Theological Education in the Christian East, First to Sixth Centuries," in J. Behr, A. Louth, and D. Conomos (eds.) *Abba: The Tradition of Orthodoxy in the West*. Crestwood, NY: St. Vladimir's Seminary Press, pp. 43–64.

Browning, R. (1962, 1963) "The Patriarchal School at Constantinople in the Twelfth Century," *Byzantion* 32: 167–202; 33: 11–40.

Buckler. G. (1948) "Byzantine Education," in N. Baynes and H. Moss (eds.) *Byzantium: An Introduction to Eastern Roman Civilization*. Oxford: Oxford University Press, pp. 200–20.

Hussey, J. M. (1937) *Church and Learning in the Byzantine Empire, 867–1185*. Oxford: Blackwell.

Eiletarion

JOHN A. MCGUCKIN

Greek term for "wrapper." It primarily signifies a liturgical scroll that unravels vertically and which featured in ancient liturgical celebrations (before the use of the codex became widespread) but which was kept on, for archaizing reasons, in the liturgical practices of several churches in later times. Today, the practice still survives in some churches on Mount Athos. The Holy Mountain's archives also contain several examples of liturgical eiletaria. The eiletarion also features as the unrolled scroll of the gospel carried by the Christ Emmanuel (child) or by the apostles in their iconic images, and by some other saints.

Eileton

JOHN A. MCGUCKIN

Greek term meaning "wrapped" or "folded." In reference to ancient manuscripts it can mean a folded papyrus or simple type of book made up from folded leaves. In common use among the Orthodox it signifies the plain cloth wrapping, linen or silk, that was kept under the gospel book on the holy table and solemnly unfolded in the divine liturgy after the dismissal of the catechumens and during the Litany of the Faithful, so as to be ready to receive the chalice and diskos. The latter are placed upon it after the completion of the Great Entrance when the gifts are brought in procession to the holy table. To this extent it was the equivalent of the Western Church's corporal. Later liturgical practice replaced the Eileton with an Antimension cloth which bore the printed symbols and images of the Passion (in its latest phase the icon of the deposition of Christ from the cross), but the Antimension itself increasingly came to be wrapped in a protective cloth (both cloths with a threefold horizontal fold and a threefold vertical fold), so that now the Eileton is fundamentally the outer covering of the Antimension, and both are unfolded at the same time, and folded up after the communion when they are replaced underneath the gospel.

SEE ALSO: Anaphora; Antimension; Divine Liturgy, Orthodox

References and Suggested Readings

Taft, R. (1978) *The Great Entrance. Orientalia Christiana Analecta*, vol. 200. Rome: Pontifical Institute of Oriental Studies.

Ekphonesis

JOHN A. MCGUCKIN

From the Greek word for "sounding out" or "speaking out." It signifies those parts of the prayers of the divine liturgy and other Orthodox services where the bishop or priest, having said much of the prayer quietly (*mystikos*, or *sotto voce* – often while the deacon or choir recites other prayers simultaneously) concludes with the doxology sung out loud so that all the congregation can hear and assent with an "Amen." In many liturgical books the "mystical" sections of the prayer that are said inaudibly are printed in italic, and the final section, or the doxology, is the Ekphonesis.

Elder (Starets)

MARIA GWYN MCDOWELL

A man or woman (Slavonic: *Starets*, *Starissa*), often (though not exclusively) monastic, gifted with spiritual discernment (*diakrisis*) who is able to offer wisdom to members of a monastic community or the wider church as they pursue the Orthodox Christian life. Most probably a practice originating in the desert monasticism of the early church, elders were individuals specially recognized as teachers and advisers, spiritual mothers and fathers, as a result of their ascetic lives, their evident practice of virtue, and possession of the spiritual gift of discernment. Informed by the traditions of teaching and care existing in late-ancient philosophical schools, the goal of disciple-elder relationships within ascetic and other Christian communities was the growth of the soul. The collections of "sayings" (*Apophthegmata*) from desert fathers and mothers are a written record of responses to specific questions regarding how to live a Christian (and often ascetic) life. One of the best examples of this is the material preserved in the traditions associated with Sts. Barsanuphius and John, though the famous text of the *Ladder* by St. John Klimakos also

Plate 18   Father Pavlos, the spiritual Elder (Starets) of the Sinai monastic community. Photo by Dwight Grimm.

demonstrates the principle, and the writings of St. Symeon the New Theologian give high priority to the relation of elder and disciple (Turner 1990). The responsibility of the elder to the disciple is to pray, rightly discern individual needs, offer encouragement and discipline, and when necessary apply *oikonomia* ("economy" or "condescension"), the adjustment of rules in the light of what discipline will best help a particular person return to proper conduct. While in practice an elder is often a monastic, neither monasticism nor ordination is a requirement. The consistent practice of confession with an elder often confuses the question of ordination as it became a primary sacrament long after its inception as an essential practice of the spiritual life. The elder's authority is granted through the recognition of wisdom by the larger community, and may or may not have any official correspondence. Consulting with a trusted elder continues to be encouraged among the Orthodox, often designated by the more modern phrase "spiritual direction," but with a much more specific and deeper sense of spiritual bonding under the eyes of God than this phrase often conveys.

SEE ALSO: Desert Fathers and Mothers; St. John Klimakos (ca. 579–ca. 659); St. Paisy Velichovsky

(1722–1794); St. Seraphim of Sarov (1759–1833); St. Silouan of Athos (1866–1938); Sts. Barsanuphius and John (6th c.); Sophrony, Archimandrite (1896–1993)

References and Suggested Readings

Demacopoulos, G. D. (2007) *Five Models of Spiritual Direction in the Early Church*. Notre Dame: University of Notre Dame Press.

Hadot, P. (2002) *Exercices spirituels et philosophie antique*. Paris, Albin Michel.

Swan, L. (2001) *The Forgotten Desert Mothers: Sayings, Lives, and Stories of Early Christian Women*. New York: Paulist Press.

Turner, H. J. M. (1990) *St. Symeon the New Theologian and Spiritual Fatherhood*. Leiden: E. J. Brill.

Ward, B. (2003) *The Desert Fathers: Sayings of the Early Christian Monks*. New York: Penguin.

Eleousa (*Umilenie*)

VERA SHEVZOV

Translated as "tenderness," "compassion," "mercy," and "loving-kindness," Eleousa (Slavonic: *Umilenie*) is the name of a well-known iconographic type of the Mother of God, characterized by an affectionate cheek-to-cheek embrace of Mary and the Christ child. Generally considered to have originated in Byzantium after the iconoclastic period, the image combines the themes of maternal love and the Passion of Christ. Prophetically anticipating the fate that awaits her Son, the Mother of God's loving expression carries a hint of deep sadness. One of the best-known images of this type is that of the 12th-century Vladimir icon of the Mother of God, housed in the Tretyakov Gallery in Moscow.

SEE ALSO: Hodegitria; Icons; Panagia; Platytera; Protecting Veil; Theotokos, the Blessed Virgin

References and Suggested Readings

Bergman, R. P. (1990) "The Earliest Eleousa: A Coptic Ivory in the Walters Art Gallery," *Journal of the Walters Art Gallery* 48: 37–56.

Plate 19   Icon of the Virgin Mary, Mother of God of Tenderness (Eleousa). Photo by John McGuckin.

Ouspensky, L. and Lossky, V. (1982) *The Meaning of Icons*, trans. G. E. H. Palmer and E. Kadloubovsky. Crestwood, NY: St. Vladimir's Seminary Press.
Vassilaki, M. (ed.) (2000) *Mother of God: Representation of the Virgin in Byzantine Art*. Milan: Skira Editore.

Environmental Ethics *see* Ecology

Eothina

JOHN A. MCGUCKIN

The Eothina (a Greek word for "dawn") are 11 gospels of the resurrection that constitute a weekly revolving liturgical cycle. One of these 11 gospels is recited at the completion of successive Sunday services of Orthros (in ancient times as the sun rose). After its completion, the 11-week cycle always repeats from the beginning except during the period between Pascha and Pentecost, where the sequencing tends to some disruption. In addition to the Orthros gospel reading, other hymns of the service change their content based on the Eothina cycle, namely the *Exaposteilarion* and the Glory following the Praises (also known as the *Doxastikon*). Both of these hymns refer to the Orthros gospel. A church cantor needs to know which Tone of the day any given Sunday represents (given in the liturgical calendar in the sequence 1–8) and also which Eothina number it is (given in a sequence 1–11). The chanting of the Great Doxology at the end of Orthros follows a Tone number not determined by the general Tone assigned for that Sunday, but by reference to the Eothinon cycle.

SEE ALSO: Liturgical Books; Orthros (Matins); *Paraklitike*

Ephymnion *see* Kontakion

Epiclesis

TODD E. FRENCH

The Epiclesis is the invocation of the Holy Spirit in the Eucharistic Anaphora so as to descend and sanctify the people of God, and especially the holy gifts which have been offered. The Epiclesis (Greek for "calling upon") is solemnly recited by the presiding bishop or priest after the words of institution, and is seen as a defining moment when the gifts are sanctified and become the body and blood of the Lord. Although several commentators resist the splitting up of the whole liturgical action of the divine liturgy into moments of consecration (as in line with the Catholic belief that the words of institution form the precise moment of eucharistic consecration), it is nevertheless widely understood in Orthodoxy that the Epiclesis is that most sacred moment when the words of Christ over the holy gifts are spiritually effected by the descent of the Holy Spirit. The faithful bow down low at this solemn moment in the liturgy.

The first attestation of the Epiclesis is found in the *Apostolic Tradition* of St. Hippolytus from the 3rd century.

Within this text is a call for the Holy Spirit to descend and strengthen the church through the sacrifice. There are also 4th-century versions of the Epiclesis in the liturgy of St. James, the *Euchologion of Serapion* of Der Balyzeh, and the writings of St. Cyril of Jerusalem. The theology that serves as a foundation for this prayer demonstrates the patristic teaching that God the Father's revelation and work comes through the Son and is completed by the Holy Spirit. The church's call to the Spirit to sanctify and strengthen the community of believers (as well as consecrating the gifts) relates the church and the Holy Eucharist to the day of Pentecost and shows the eschatological nature of the church's trinitarian prayer. The Epiclesis in the Liturgy of St. John Chrysostom marks a shift from the Holy Spirit "showing" the gifts to be the body of Christ towards "making" the gifts into the body of Christ. The earlier form in the Epiclesis of St. Basil is still used on those days on which his liturgy is appointed to be served, notably the Sundays of Great Lent.

SEE ALSO: Divine Liturgy, Orthodox; Eucharist; Holy Spirit; St. John Chrysostom (349–407)

References and Suggested Readings

Atchley, C. F. (1935) *On the Epiclesis of the Eucharistic Liturgy and in the Consecration of the Font*. Oxford: Oxford University Press.

Solovey, M. M. (1970) *The Byzantine Divine Liturgy: History and Commentary*, trans. D. E. Wysochansky. Washington, DC: Catholic University of America Press.

Stuckwisch, R. D. (1997) "The Basilian Anaphoras," in P. F. Bradshaw (ed.) *Essays on Early Eastern Eucharistic Prayers*. Collegeville, MN: Liturgical Press, pp. 109–30.

Taft, R. F. (1997) "St. John Chrysostom and the Byzantine Anaphora that Bears His Name," in P. F. Bradshaw (ed.) *Essays on Early Eastern Eucharistic Prayers*. Collegeville, MN: Liturgical Press, pp. 195–226.

Episcopacy

PHILIP ZYMARIS

The episcopacy is the highest rank of holy orders (priesthood) in the Orthodox ecclesiastical hierarchy, based on the tradition of the New Testament

and Canon Law. The earliest historical reference to the episcopacy is to be found in the New Testament. Although the distinction between *presbyteros* (elder) and *episkopos* (overseer-bishop) was initially vague (cf. Phil. 1.1; Acts 20.28), the latter crystallized to denote the specific ministry of the president of the Eucharistic assembly. In this capacity the bishop presides as icon of Christ and successor of the apostles (see Ignatios of Antioch, *To the Smyrneans* 8.1–2).

The acceptance of Christianity by the Roman Empire led to changes in the administrative structure of the episcopacy. Whereas in New Testament times St. Paul simply refers to one bishop in each city (Zizioulas 2001: 47f.), the administrative structure of

Plate 20   Ukrainian bishop giving the blessing at the divine liturgy with the Dikeri and Trikeri candlesticks, standing in front of the iconostasis. Photo © Joyfull/Shutterstock.

the church later coincided with the civil organization of the empire. This allowed the development of the metropolitan system of church government where bishops of a group of provinces would refer administratively to the bishop of the main city (*meter-polis*, "mother city," hence the *metropolitan*) of the wider region. The metropolitan would preside over a synod composed of bishops from the provinces under his ecclesiastical authority. According to the 34th Apostolic Canon the "many," i.e., the bishops of a region, could do nothing without the "first," i.e., the metropolitan, and the metropolitan could do nothing without the many. At every level of episcopal activity this became the basis for the teaching on canonical primacy in the Orthodox Church; namely, the first who acts as coordinator for the many but who is not an overlord above the others. The later development in the West of the papal primacy as a jurisdictional superiority was a significant departure from this notion.

The subsequent appearance of the pentarchy developed along these same lines. Eventually, a group of main cities (*metropoleis*) would belong administratively to an even more significant city. The metropolitans of the significant five cities of Rome, Constantinople, Alexandria, Antioch, and Jerusalem were eventually given the title of patriarch. These patriarchs would preside over a synod made up of the metropolitans from the provinces under the civil authority of the aforementioned five cities. These patriarchates were also organized according to the tenets of primacy. The pope of Rome originally fulfilled this role of "first among equals." The patriarch of Constantinople presently fulfills this role for the Orthodox subsequent to the schism of 1054, although there is not full agreement on this issue in contemporary Orthodox practice. This is because new patriarchates have been founded since then, as well as other autocephalous churches headed by metropolitans or archbishops. In theory all these churches relate to each other according to the aforementioned tenets of primacy. In general, metropolitans were considered to rank higher in the episcopal lists than archbishops, but this is not always the case in contemporary practice.

As the focal point of unity for the local church, the bishops collectively express the consciousness of their local churches and promulgate the canon law of the church in the context of the synods of the church. This conciliar role of the episcopacy serves as a tangible link between the local churches and the one "Church in the World" (Zizioulas 2001: 125f.).

This link between the local and universal church inherent in the episcopacy is also evident in the service of ordination to the episcopate. In this service the connection of the ordained to a specific city is emphasized, yet canonical practice also links this local church to all other local churches. Thus, according to the Council of Nicea (325), episcopal ordinations require the participation of at least three other bishops (Canon 4).

In contemporary practice the connection with a specific community implicit in the ordination service is sometimes overshadowed by administrative concerns. Thus, a bishop may be "titular," i.e., attached at ordination to a city no longer in existence. Such bishops are distinguished from bishops who pastor a living community, but they are also distinguished from so-called *en energeia* (acting) bishops, i.e., bishops who possess an existing see but are unable to serve there due to historical circumstances. Most of the metropolitans serving at the ecumenical patriarchate today fall into this category because the cities they preside over no longer have Christian populations to pastor. For this reason the ecumenical patriarchate is governed by the so-called resident (*endemousa*) synod, which is composed of metropolitans possessing titles of various cities but residing in Constantinople.

The New Testament and the canonical tradition of the church offer clear prescriptions regarding the character of candidates for the episcopacy. They are to be of upright character (Canon 10 of Sardica), experienced in the faith (Canon 2 of the First Council) and of a minimum age of 35. They are also to be proven as good managers of the affairs of their families (Tit. 1.6–9; 1 Tim 3.1–13; 3rd Canon of Sixth Council), a prescript that became symbolically exegeted after the 4th century when celibacy was later required of bishop-candidates. Absolute monogamy was also required of all candidates. However, in Byzantine practice, by the 7th century most episcopal candidates were already taken only from the celibate (but not necessarily monastic) clergy (Kotsonis 1964: 784).

In contemporary practice the primarily Eucharistic, pastoral roles of the episcopacy have been slightly overshadowed by increased administrative duties. This is in part due to the precedent set during the Ottoman era in the East. During this period, together with their ecclesiastical duties bishops were compelled to assume administrative roles for the sake of their people according to the Ottoman *millet* system.

SEE ALSO: Chorepiscopos; Deacon; Eucharist; Ordination; Priesthood; Vestments

References and Suggested Readings

Clapsis, E. (1985) "The Sacramentality of Ordination and Apostolic Succession: An Orthodox Ecumenical View," *Greek Orthodox Theological Review* 30, 4: 421–32.

Kotsonis, I. (1964) "Episkopos," in *Threskeutike kai ethike egkyklopaideia*, vol. 5. Athens: A. Martinos, pp. 782–78.

Zizioulas, J. (1980) "Episkopé and Episkopos in the Early Church: A Brief Survey of the Evidence," in *Episkopé and episcopate in ecumenical perspective*. Faith and order Paper 102. Geneva: World Council of Churches, pp. 30–42.

Zizioulas, J. (1985) "The Bishop in the Theological Doctrine of the Orthodox Church," in R. Potz (ed.) *Kanon* 7: 23–35.

Zizioulas, J. (2001) *Eucharist, Bishop, Church*, trans. E. Theokritoff. Brookline, MA: Holy Cross Orthodox Press.

Epitrachelion

PHILIP ZYMARIS

A Byzantine vestment equivalent to the western stole, which is a symbol of priestly office. It consists of a narrow cloth worn (scarf-like) over neck (hence its name: *epitrachelion*, "upon the neck") and linked over the chest. It is worn by both bishops and presbyters and is a required vestment for all priestly functions.

SEE ALSO: Phelonion; Sticharion

References and Suggested Readings

Day, P. (1993) "Epitrachelion," in *The Liturgical Dictionary of Eastern Christianity*. Collegeville: Liturgical Press, p. 90.

Plate 21   Priest blessing Paschal foods. RIA Novosti/AKG.

Phountoulis, I. (2002) "Paradose kai exelixe leitourgikon hieron amphion," in *Ta hiera amphia kai he exoterike eribole tou orthodoxou klerou*. Athens: Church of Greece Publications, pp. 63–78.

Eschatology

WENDY PAULA NICHOLSON

Eschatology (from the Greek, "doctrine of the last things") is concerned with mysteries which will be revealed at the Judgment. However, in the Orthodox faith, eschatology is a reality *now* as well as in times to come. The uncreated energies of God transform the created order at any point in time, fulfilling the promise of the kingdom even before the end of our age.

It is, above all, in the church and its sacraments, particularly in the divine liturgy, that this fulfillment is realized, when uncreated grace breaks through the limits of our fallen temporal existence, offering healing and a foretaste of Eternity. As Vladimir Lossky put it: "Eschatology becomes present at the moment when man becomes capable of cooperating in the divine plan" (Lossky 1989: 224). The extent to which this cooperation is reached in the created realm is believed to determine the experience of entry into the uncreated realm of God after death: what will become an individual's judgment of paradise or hell.

Orthodoxy practices a notable level of caution in interpreting the biblical apocalyptic narratives. It is generally accepted that apocalyptic literature uses coded expressions equal to the mystery of the age to come, something beyond our experience. The practice of *Nipsis* (watchfulness) and the "remembrance of death" are ways in which the majority of the faithful will more profitably heed Christ's instruction: "Watch therefore, for you do not know on what day your Lord is coming" (Mt. 24.42)

After the time of St. Augustine (5th century), the church came to regard "chiliasm" or "millenarianism" (the idea that before the Last Judgment Christ will return for a thousand year earthly reign), as an error in the interpretation of Revelation 20.4. Augustine rejects the idea as "carnal" and interprets the thousand year reign as the current age of the church, over which Christ already reigns with the saints (Augustine 1993: 426–31). There is scant evidence that chiliasm has ever been condemned by an ecumenical council (*pace* Pomazansky 1983: 344) and the idea is present in the writings of early Latin fathers, as well as in St. Justin Martyr, St. Irenaeus, and St. Hippolytus. However, by reducing the kingdom to a finite duration analogous to an earthly regime, chiliasm runs counter to the Orthodox belief and experience that we are already invited to enjoy uninterrupted and unending participation in God's uncreated grace.

The extreme opposite of chiliasm, Origen's doctrine of universal *Apokatastasis* (restoration) was condemned by the Second Ecumenical Council of Constantinople in 553 (Schaff and Wace 1983: 318–20). In rejecting biblical literalism, Origen taught that all souls, even the Devil, would eventually return to an original preembodied state contemplating the divine *Nous*

(mind). He thus reduced creation and redemption to a *protology* which Orthodoxy definitively rejected.

SEE ALSO: Council of Constantinople II (553); Deification; Divine Liturgy, Orthodox; Grace; Judgment

References and Suggested Readings

Augustine, St. (1993) *The City of God*. Library of Nicene and Post Nicene Fathers, Vol. 2. Grand Rapids, MI: Eerdmans.

Hierotheos, Metropolitan of Nafpaktos (2000) *Life after Death*, trans. E. Williams. Levadia-Hellas, Greece: Birth of the Theotokos Monastery.

Lossky, V. (1989) *Orthodox Theology*. Crestwood, NY: St. Vladimir's Seminary Press.

Pomazansky, Protopresbyter Michael (1983) *Dogmatic Theology*, trans. S. Rose. Platina, CA: St. Herman of Alaska Brotherhood.

Schaff, P. and Wace, H. (eds.) (1983) *The Seven Ecumenical Councils*. Grand Rapids, MI: Eerd-mans.

Estonia, Orthodox Church in

TARMO TOOM

Orthodox faith has been confessed by Estonians for a millennium. The first written sources about Orthodoxy in Estonia come from the 11th century. In 1030 Russians conquered Tartu (Jurjev) and built some churches there. Several bishops of Jurjev are mentioned in 11th- and 12th-century Russian documents. In 1210 Russian missionaries were baptizing local people in southern Estonia. The derivation of some Estonian theological keywords from Russian is a telling factor. This may indicate that the Estonians' initial knowledge of Christianity came through Byzantine-Russian missions. The Estonian word *rist* ("cross"), for example, comes from the Russian *krest*, *ristima* ("to baptize") derives from *krestit*, *raamat* ("book, Bible") from *gramota*, and *papp* ("priest") from *pop*.

In the Middle Ages, long after the Northern Crusades and the arrival of Teutonic knights and Catholic priests, the larger Estonian cities belonged to the Hanseatic (Commercial) League. At that time Orthodox churches were built mostly for the use of Russian merchants from Pskov and Novgorod. In 1438 a high church official who visited Tartu wrote in his diary that there were two Orthodox churches "but very few Christians" in that city. Some thirty years later, Germans expelled the Orthodox from Tartu and killed a priest named Isidor.

In the 1550s Russia conquered the eastern part of Estonia and established the diocese of Jurjev-Viljandi. Yet, by the end of the 16th century, Orthodox faith was found mostly among those Russians who had remained in Estonia after the defeat of the Russian armies by Swedes and Poles. By the very end of the Swedish period (1710), there was only one Orthodox place of worship left standing: St. Nicholas' Church in Tallinn.

When Estonia was subjected to Russia during the Great Northern War (1710–21), the Orthodox Church received its full privileges and consequently the Protestant churches of the Swedish garrisons were turned into Orthodox temples. Yet, as the German barons and the larger cities remained relatively independent, the preeminence of Lutheranism was never seriously threatened.

In the middle of the 19th century some 47,000 Estonian Lutheran peasants converted to Russian Orthodoxy after hearing a rumor that by doing so they might get some land. This phenomenon is known as *usuvahetus* ("the change of faith"). It led to the establishment of an independent diocese of Livonia with a vicariate in Riga. (The first ethnically Estonian bishop, Platon, was ordained in 1918 and killed by Bolsheviks in 1919.) However, large numbers soon reconverted, primarily because the adoption of Orthodoxy did not bring about the expected betterment of their socioeconomic situation. In 1864 an ambassador, Vladimir Bobrinski, reported to Tsar Alexander II that Orthodoxy had remained alien to the Estonian people and that only about one tenth of the Estonian Orthodox were really true to their faith. Many allegedly converted Estonian Orthodox had continued to participate secretly in the Lutheran Eucharistic services. Russification attempts during the last decades of the 19th century did not have a lasting effect, except perhaps as seen in the building of the Alexander Nevsky Cathedral, which still stands in the midst of the gothic churches of Old Tallinn.

The collapse of tsarist Russia in 1917, the establishment of the Republic of Estonia (1918), the War of Liberation (1918–20), and the signing of the Tartu Peace Treaty (1920) created a situation in which Tikhon, the incumbent patriarch of Russia, acknowledged the autonomy of the Estonian Orthodox Church in 1920 (Resolution No. 1780), but postponed the discussion of its autocephaly. After Patriarch Tikhon's arrest by the Soviet government, contacts between him and the autonomous Estonian Orthodox Church were severed. Consequently, the autonomous Estonian Orthodox Church, which wanted to assert its ecclesiastical independence, decided to seek a fuller and final canonical recognition from the patriarch of Constantinople. In 1923 Patriarch Meletios IV proclaimed the autonomy of the Estonian Apostolic Orthodox Church (EAOC), with three dioceses, under his patriarchal jurisdiction and spiritual protection (Tomos 3348). (In 1923 the same status was given to the Finnish Orthodox Church.) However, despite this, some of the Orthodox Russians in Estonia attempted to remain in continuing communion with the patriarch of Moscow (an example being the controversy over Petseri [Pechery] Monastery, 1930–2).

The first Soviet occupation of Estonia in 1940–1 brought about the abrupt reunification of the Estonian Orthodox believers with the Russian Orthodox Church. Over half of the serving priests resigned in protest over this. Soon, however, the German occupation of Estonia in 1941 allowed the EAOC briefly to reclaim its relations with the patriarch of Constantinople, with the exception of the diocese of Narva, which consisted mostly of ethnic Russians. As a result, the Orthodox Church in Estonia found itself in schism. In 1944 Metropolitan Alexander of EAOC, together with 23 priests and some 8,000 faithful, was forced to go into exile.

In 1945, a year after Estonia was territorially annexed by the Soviet Union, the patriarch of Moscow terminated the legal activity of EAOC, yet acknowledged the Orthodox Church in Estonia as an eparchy of the Russian Orthodox Church. Congregations and priests were reaccepted after they officially repented of being "schismatics." In addition, the Stalinist repopulation policies caused an influx of ethnic Russians whose religious background, if any, was Orthodox. The very fact that the Russian Orthodox Church was used as an extension of the occupying Soviet power alienated many Estonians from the church, despite the fact that almost three quarters of the Orthodox churches were closed in Estonia by the 1960s, and regardless of the fact that the Russian Orthodox Church itself suffered from harassment and atheistic propaganda as much as any other.

Estonia regained its political independence in 1991. All structures and organizations quickly claimed their sovereignty. So it was that in 1996 the canonical autonomy of the EAOC was reactivated by Patriarch Bartholomew I on the basis of its continued existence in exile (Sweden). This caused much animosity and initiated a breakdown of the communion between the Constantinopolitan and Russian Orthodox Churches. Both sides met in Zürich later in the same year and agreed to tolerate, at least temporarily, the existence of two Orthodox Churches in the same territory (54 parishes of the EAOC and 29 parishes of the patriarchate of Moscow).

Unfortunately, tensions and mutual defiance between these two Estonian Orthodox Churches have continued to this day. In 2008 the Russian Orthodox Church suspended its membership of the Conference of European Churches over the dispute about the non-admittance of that part of the Estonian Orthodox Church which had decided to remain linked to the patriarchate of Moscow. In the same year the Russian Orthodox Church terminated its ecumenical dialogue with the Anglicans because the EAOC was participating as a recognized member church in this dialogue. The Moscow patriarchate continues to make two major claims that are unacceptable to the EAOC. The first is that the EAOC was established in 1996 (thus negating the Tomos of 1923); and the second is that Estonia remains as a canonical territory of the Russian Orthodox Church – widely taken to be a negation of Estonia as a sovereign state, deserving autocephaly in due season.

As of 2007 there were approximately 18,000 members in the EAOC: 1 metropolitan, 27 priests, and 10 deacons. It has its own seminary and a journal, *Usk ja elu* (Faith and Life). In 2009 it opened its first new convent in Saaremaa. The Estonian Orthodox Church under the jurisdiction of the patriarch of Moscow has about 170,000 members, 1 metropolitan, 44 priests, and 16 deacons. It publishes a newspaper, *Mir Pravoslavia* (Orthodox World), in Russian. From 1961 to 1990 this church was headed by Metropolitan Alexius Ridiger, who was elected as Alexius II, the Patriarch of Moscow and All Russia, in 1990. Its largest monastery is Pühtitsa Dormition Convent with approximately 170 nuns in residence.

Old Believers also settled in Estonia, near Lake Peipus, by the end of the 17th century. In the 18th century they had their own monastery in Räpina, which was destroyed by tsarist forces. Although all the churches belonging to the Old Believers were closed down in 1840, they regained their right to exist in the Republic of Estonia in 1920. Currently, there are about 15,000 Old Believers with three priests in Estonia. The Armenian Apostolic Church, with about 2,000 members, was founded in Estonia in 1993. There is also a small communty of Ruthenians.

SEE ALSO: Constantinople, Patriarchate of; Finland, Autonomous Orthodox Church of; Russia, Patriarchal Orthodox Church of

References and Suggested Readings

Au, I. and Ringvee, R. (eds.) (2007) *Usulised ühendused Eestis*. Tallinn: Allika.

Burgess, M. (2005) *The Eastern Orthodox Churches: Concise Histories with Chronological Checklists of their Primates*. Jefferson, NC: McFarland.

Istina (2004) "Le plaidoyer de l'Église orthodoxe d'Estonie pour la défense de son autonomie face au patriarcat de Moscou," *Istina* 49/1: 3–105.

Papathomas, G. D. and Palli, M. (eds.) (2002) *The Autonomous Orthodox Church of Estonia/L'Église autonome orthodoxe d'Estonie*. Athens: Éditions Épektasis.

Patriarch Aleksius II (1999) *Pravoslavie v Estonii*. Moscow: Pravoslavnaja entsiklopedija.

Sôtšov, A. (2004) *Eesti õigeusu piiskopkond Stalini ajal aastail 1945–1953*. Tartu: Tartu Ülikooli Kirjastus.

Sôtšov, A. (2008) *Eesti Õigeusu piiskopkond nõukogude religioonipoliitika mõjuväljas 1954–1964*. Tartu: Tartu Ülikooli Kirjastus.

Vööbus, A. (1969) *Studies in the History of the Estonian People*, vol. 1. Stockholm: ETSE.

Webster, A. F. C. (1996) "Split Decision: The Orthodox Clash over Estonia," *Christian Century* 113/19: 614–23.

Ethics

PERRY T. HAMALIS

The term "ethics" commonly carries three meanings, all of which apply within the context of Orthodox Christianity. First, stemming from the Greek word *ethos*, the term refers to a community's or person's implicit beliefs about how to live, about right and wrong, or about what it means to flourish, as manifested through behavior. Second, "ethics" refers to a particular person's or community's explicit teachings about how human beings ought to live. The second meaning differs from the first insofar as it shifts from implicit ethos to normative and axiological claims made explicit and recommended to others. Third, "ethics" refers to a discipline of scholarly inquiry and application. It encompasses the assessment of ethical visions held or taught by persons, communities, and institutions, including the examination of moral capacities (e.g., freedom, reason, conscience, will, etc.), authoritative sources (e.g., tradition, scripture, reason, experience, etc.), methods for interpreting and applying ethical claims to specific issues and circumstances, and bases for grounding and defending ethical and moral visions.

Within Orthodox theology the first meaning of ethics reflects the fact that Orthodoxy is more a form of existence than a form of discourse, more a lived way than a spoken word. At Orthodoxy's core is the simple belief that to be a Christian is to be a follower of Christ (Jn. 12.24) and a member of the church (cf. 1 Cor. 12 and Rom. 12). To be a Christian is to strive for holiness and perfection as modeled by God (cf. Lev. 11.44 and Matt. 5.48) and to participate fully in the sacramental life, worship, and ascetical practices of the ecclesial community. According to this first meaning, Orthodox ethics pertains to the normative ethos of the church as a whole and, especially, the ethos of the saints as followers of Christ and exemplars of Orthodox Christian life.

According to its second meaning, Orthodox ethics encompasses the church's normative teachings on how human beings ought to live as expressed in the Holy Scriptures, the canon law tradition, and in the writings of saints and authoritative teachers. One can speak, for example, of the ethics of the *Didache* or of St. John Klimakos when referring to a text's or author's claims about human nature, the purpose of human life, and how Christians ought to live in light of the reality and revelation of God. Nearly all sermons, ascetical treatises, and works on the spiritual life by Orthodox authors are articulating an ethical vision or expressing normative and axiological teachings that both reflect and shape the ethos of Orthodox Christians as a whole.

Applying the third meaning of ethics to the context of Orthodox Christianity has been somewhat controversial during the past century. Orthodox ethics, as a discrete discipline of academic study and scholarship, began developing in 18th-century Russia, influenced in part by similar trends among Western Christians. A parallel discipline of Orthodox ethics developed in Greece and Constantinople beginning in the late 19th century (Harakas 1983: 8–15). Critics of this trend argue that, historically, the Orthodox Church never separated out ethics as its own discipline (that is, as discrete from theology) and that doing so subjects Orthodox thought to concepts, categories, and methods that grew not out of Orthodoxy's own tradition and spirit but rather out of the foreign mindset of western scholasticism (Yannaras 1984). Other critics also contend that the academic discipline of ethics seeks to articulate, defend, and apply universal normative principles or moral laws in a way that eclipses the uniqueness of human persons and depersonalizes the church's teachings on the Christian life (Zizioulas 2006). Contemporary defenders of Orthodox ethics acknowledge the merits of such critiques, but argue that an authentically Orthodox discipline of ethics is both possible and necessary: possible, by approaching ethical questions and dilemmas with the fullness of Orthodoxy's resources, with an openness to insights from natural and social science, and with an ecclesial mindset; and necessary because of the tremendous difficulties Orthodox Christians face today as their personal and family lives intersect with contemporary issues in bioethics, ecology, economic justice, sexual ethics, war, and other social challenges (Harakas 1983, 1992; Guroian 1987; Mantzarides 1995).

Drawing from the church's scriptural, credal, dogmatic, liturgical, ascetical, hagiographical, canonical, and iconographic sources, Orthodox ethicists today generally agree that the church's overarching ethical vision has as its aim the deification (Greek, *theosis*) of human persons through the grace of the Holy Trinity and the development of the virtues. This vision entails a movement from the fallen human condition to the perfected human condition, from the reality of death and sin to the reality of resurrection and divine-human communion (Harakas 1983; Yannaras 1984; Guroian 1987; Mantzarides 1995; Woodill 1998; Hamalis 2008). Orthodox ethicists also generally agree on their own calling to acquire the mind of the church and the virtue of discernment so that they may apply the tradition's overarching vision appropriately to the wide spectrum of personal and communal issues facing the faithful and the world today.

SEE ALSO: Asceticism; Bioethics, Orthodoxy and; Deification; Ecology; Humanity; Original Sin; Repentance; Sexual Ethics; War; Wealth

References and Suggested Readings

Guroian, V. (1987) *Incarnate Love: Essays in Orthodox Ethics*. Notre Dame: University of Notre Dame Press.

Hamalis, P. T. (2008) "The Meaning and Place of Death in an Orthodox Ethical Framework," in A. Papanikolaou and E. Prodromou (eds.) *Thinking Through Faith: New Perspectives from Orthodox Christian Scholars*. Crestwood, NY: St. Vladimir's Seminary Press, pp. 183–217.

Harakas, S. (1983) *Toward Transfigured Life: The Theoria of Eastern Orthodox Ethics*. Minneapolis: Light and Life.

Harakas, S. (1992) *Living the Faith: The Praxis of Eastern Orthodox Ethics*. Minneapolis: Light and Life.

Mantzarides, G. (1995) *Christianike Ethike* [in Greek], 4th edn. Thessaloniki: Pournara.

Woodill, J. (1998) *The Fellowship of Life: Virtue Ethics and Orthodox Christianity*. Washington, DC: Georgetown University Press.

Yannaras, C. (1984) *The Freedom of Morality*, trans. Elizabeth Briere. Crestwood, NY: St. Vladimir's Seminary Press.

Zizioulas, J. D. (2006) *Communion and Otherness: Further Studies in Personhood and the Church*, ed. P. McPartlan. Edinburgh: T&T Clark.

Eucharist

M. C. STEENBERG

The Eucharist is the mystery (sacrament) of Holy Communion, in which Christian faithful partake of the body and blood of Jesus Christ through gifts of bread and wine sanctified and consecrated during the celebration of the divine liturgy. The Eucharist is considered by Orthodox to be the chief of the church's mysteries, effecting the true communion of God and humankind and serving as the highest point of union, toward which all the sacraments aim. Its name, which comes from the Greek for "thanksgiving" (*eucharistia*), has been in use to refer to the sacrament since the 2nd century.

The Eucharist and Incarnation

The Eucharist is fundamentally an incarnational mystery: it is grounded in the Son's taking of human flesh and becoming a person of true human nature. As the Son united to himself the nature of man in his human birth, so the faithful Christian receives into himself or herself the true person of the Son in the Eucharistic gifts, sanctified to the Father by the Holy Spirit. From the early centuries, the fathers of the church have drawn attention to the interaction between Christ's human and divine natures, between the Son's eternal divinity and full humanity, in expounding the significance and power of the Eucharist. St. Gregory of Nyssa, speaking of Christ's eating of bread in his human life, wrote:

> [Christ's] Body too was maintained by bread; which Body also by the indwelling of God the Word was transmuted to the dignity of Godhead. Rightly, then, do we believe that now also the bread which is consecrated by the Word of God is changed into the Body of God the Word.... So the bread, as the Apostle says, is "sanctified by the Word of God and prayer" (1 Timothy 4.5). It is at once transformed into His body by means of the Word, as the Word itself said, "This is my body." (*Great Catechism* 37)

In a similar vein, St. Irenaeus of Lyons drew a direct correlation between the reality of the Eucharist and the reality of the incarnation:

> For blood can only come from veins and flesh, and whatsoever else makes up the substance of man, such as the Word of God was actually made. By His own Blood he redeemed us, as also His Apostle declares, "In whom we have redemption through His blood, even the remission of sins" (Colossians 1.14).... He has acknowledged the cup, which is a part of the creation, as His own Blood, from which He bedews our blood; and the bread,

also a part of the creation, He has established as His own Body, from which He gives increase to our bodies. (*Against Heresies* 5.2.2)

The Mystical Supper

St. Gregory's emphasis on Christ's words "This is my body" exemplifies Orthodox attention to the source of the Eucharistic mystery in the Son's "last supper" with his apostles, which is known in Orthodoxy as the "Mystical Supper" (see Mt. 26.17–29; Mk. 14.12–25; Lk. 22.7–23). The statements "This is my body … this is my blood" are taken in the literal sense of providing for the direct communion of the disciples with Christ's physical nature, as summed up in St. Leo the Great's brief apothegm, "What was visible in our Savior has entered into the sacraments" (*in sacramenta transivit*; Homily 74.2). That is, in the Eucharist the incarnate reality of the Son – true God and true man – is made available to communicants. This is summed up in the traditional pre-communion prayer at the altar, also said by the priest as a direction to the people immediately prior to receiving the holy gifts: "I believe that this is, in truth, thy very Body and thy most precious Blood."

The Eucharist, then, is, understood by Orthodox as a sacramental participation in that mystical supper of the Lord recounted in the gospels. The traditional placing of an icon of this event over the Royal Doors of the iconostasis, beyond which lies the holy table on which the gifts are consecrated and through which they are brought to the people, emphasizes this connection to the gospel event. The temple itself becomes the "upper room" of that ancient meal, in which the Lord is made immediately present. As St. Cyril of Alexandria once said, "This a mystery beyond understanding: we close the doors of the church, but then Christ joins us, and appears to all of us, invisibly and visibly at the same time … allowing and presenting His sacred body to be touched."

The Real Presence

While questions over the nature of the Eucharistic presence (that is, whether the bread and wine are understood truly to become Christ's body and blood, or whether they are representative memorials only) have been pivotal in much of Western Christian history, in Orthodoxy the matter has rarely been of substantial issue. Church fathers and other ecclesiastical writers such as Clement of Alexandria often reflect on the symbolic and metaphorical aspects of the Eucharistic gifts:

> Elsewhere the Lord, in the Gospel according to John, brought this out by symbols, when He said: "Eat ye my flesh, and drink my blood" (John 6.34), describing distinctly by metaphor the drinkable properties of faith and the promise, by means of which the church, like a human being consisting of many members, is refreshed and grows. (*Paedagogus* 1.6)

However, this is rarely separated from commentary on the Eucharist as the true communion in Christ's genuine flesh and blood. St. Cyril of Alexandria (*Against Nestorius*; *Commentary on John*) raised the Eucharist up as a primary instance of the reality of the incarnation of the divine Logos, and the method by which reception of the Word in communion "deified" the believer. For their part, the liturgical texts of the divine liturgies are explicit on the true nature of the body and blood present at communion; and the renunciations traditionally recited at the reception of converts into the church at the service of chrismation include sections which make it an explicit and cardinal dimension of taking on the Orthodox faith (Hapgood 1975: 454–8), as well as positive affirmations that set it at the heart of the church's confession: "Dost thou believe and confess that in the Divine Liturgy, under the mystical forms of the holy bread and wine, the faithful partake of the Body and Blood of our Lord Jesus Christ, unto the remission of sins and life eternal? This I do believe and confess" (Hapgood 1975: 459).

Given the Orthodox insistence that the Eucharist offers to the faithful Christ's true body and blood, its position is sometimes compared to the Roman Catholic doctrine of transubstantiation (that the bread and wine are substantively transformed into body and blood; and more specifically, that the substance of the elements is transformed, while the accidents – those things discernable to the senses, such as taste and appearance – remain unchanged), contrasted with the

Lutheran conception of consubstantiation (that Christ's body and blood are "with" the bread and wine in sacramental experience). While it may rightly be said that the Orthodox view accords more strongly with a transubstantionist position, the traditional Orthodox response has been to insist that both views are external to the church's normal mode of expression, and that transubstantiation in particular suffers from proposing too scientific a means of explaining the Eucharistic mystery (its specific definition being rather late, likely dating to the 12th century, and building upon a renewed attention in the West to Aristotelian categories of substances and accidents). Nonetheless, the Greek term *metousiosis*, which is comparable to the Latin *transubstantiatio*, does appear in Orthodox liturgical and theological texts – though not as often as other vocabulary (e.g., *metastoicheiosis*, "a change of elements").

A Liturgical Mystery

The Eucharist stands at the heart of the divine liturgy, and in Orthodox understanding the liturgy is the sole venue of Eucharistic consecration. While the holy gifts sanctified during the liturgy may be taken to the sick or housebound and administered there with care by a priest, the liturgy nonetheless remains the one supreme venue of Eucharistic sacramentality.

This is an important point, for while the Eucharist may be the chief Orthodox mystery, it is not an element that can be detached from the full liturgical life of the church. Participation in Christ's body and blood is understood as part of a life of ascetical worship that culminates in the liturgical act, and in which the whole "mystical life" (that is, the life of the sacraments) has a part.

In typical Orthodox practice this means that the Eucharist, celebrated in the context of the liturgy, forms the central event of the weekly cycle of liturgical worship. It is preceded by Vespers and Matins, which may (as in the Russian/Slavic practice) be served together the night before as the All-Night Vigil, or (as in the Greek) separately on Saturday evening and Sunday morning. While distinct in office and form, these services are not separate from the overarching liturgical act that leads to the Eucharistic chalice, and provide both the ascetical and theological focus for the celebration of the liturgy. These services constitute an experiential recollection of the whole of creation (particularly symbolized in the first half of Vespers), through the coming of Christ in the incarnation (poignantly the focal point of the Evloghitaria of Matins), and ultimately to the joining of the faithful to this incarnation in the Eucharistic mystery of the liturgy itself.

Similarly, the liturgical context of the Eucharist means that it is intrinsically joined to the other liturgical mysteries of the church. Baptism and chrismation are understood as fundamental prerequisites for participating in the Eucharist, as the foundations of entry into the Christian body which has its center and head in the presence of the Lord – the very Eucharistic reality. The sacrament of confession, too, is traditionally tied to the reception of communion as a means of preparing the heart to receive its King worthily, not harboring hatred against a brother nor retaining iniquities without repentance. Differing local traditions within the church foster this practice differently: some encourage (or require) confession prior to every reception of the Eucharist, while others may not insist as strongly upon a one-to-one correlation of the two sacraments. But in all cases, regularity of confession and its importance in terms of preparing for communion are foundational to Orthodox practice. Nonetheless, Orthodox saints have been keen to emphasize that the need for confession and repentance prior to communion does not make one "worthy' to partake of the Eucharistic mystery. In the words of St. John Cassian:

> We must not avoid the Lord's Communion because we consider ourselves sinful, but should more and more eagerly hasten to it for the healing of our soul and purifying of our spirit, and seek there rather a remedy for our wounds with humility of mind and faith, as considering ourselves unworthy to receive so great grace. Otherwise we cannot worthily receive the Communion even once a year, as some do, who live in monasteries and hold the dignity and holiness and value of the heavenly sacraments in such high regard as to think that none but saints and spotless persons should venture to receive them, instead of thinking rather that they would make us saints and pure by taking them. (*Third Conference of Abbot Theonas: On Sinlessness*, 21)

Receiving the Eucharist

As intimated above, customary practice in the Orthodox Church is for the faithful to participate fully in the liturgical life and cycles of the church, including attendance at Vespers and Matins (or the combined Vigil) previous to the divine liturgy, when it is intended that one will receive communion. In many Slavic traditions, confessions are heard on the eve of reception (normally at or after the Vigil service). Specified pre-communion prayers are normally read at home or in the church directly before communing. In some traditions these are combined with the recitation of other special prayers (canons and Akathists) to form a longer prayer-rule of preparation for the Eucharist.

It is expected that all the Orthodox who are to commune will observe a strict fast prior to receiving the holy gifts. This means complete abstention from all food and drink from midnight beforehand, or at least the moment of rising from sleep on the morning a liturgy will be served – though in some places a stricter practice of fasting from the Vigil earlier the evening before may be followed.

The holy gifts are received by all the faithful in both kinds (that is, all partake of both the body and blood), though there is a distinction in the form of reception between clergy and laity. The former commune in the altar, at the holy table, partaking of the elements individually: the body is received in the hand, and the blood in a threefold partaking of the chalice. The laity receive both kinds together outside the Royal Doors, presented to them on a spoon by the priest.

Following the receipt of the holy gifts, the faithful receive *zapivka*: a "break-fast" (literally, a breaking of the pre-communion fast) of bread and wine mixed with warm water, both as a source of refreshment after the fast which has culminated in the Eucharist, as well as a practical means of ensuring that all of the gifts have been consumed and do not remain in the mouth.

Post-communion prayers are normally said immediately following the divine liturgy, either in the church by a reader, or at home by an individual or family.

The frequency of participation in communion is a point of variance among different Orthodox traditions. While the practice of only communing a few times a year (for example, on Pascha and Nativity), which had become widespread in the 19th and early 20th centuries, is now regarded as regrettable by most, there is no consensus on what a regular pattern for reception ought to be in the Orthodox life. In some local practices the Eucharist is received nearly every week, and nearly every liturgy, while in other practices it is received less frequently, though still regularly. While ultimately a person's frequency of communion is a matter for discernment with the aid of his or her spiritual father, it remains the case that there is some disagreement among local Orthodox churches as to what the norms should be in this regard.

The Purpose of the Eucharist

In liturgical form, rite, theology, and praxis, therefore, the Eucharist is at the center of Orthodox worshipping life. What, then, is the purpose of this sacrament that holds so central a position in the church? The Eucharist is offered, first and foremost, "for the remission of sins," as Christ himself says (see Mt. 26.28). By serving as the abiding memorial of the Lord's incarnation, offered "for the life of the world," the Christian liturgical memory makes ever present the self-offering of the one who "takes away the sins of the world" (Jn. 1.29). The Eucharist, then, serves as the perfection and fulfillment of confession: the sinner, who has offered up his transgressions and received absolution, is united in flesh and blood to the Son who is the true Redeemer of the fallen creature.

Secondly, and in a directly connected way, the Eucharist serves as the height of human persons' union with, and communion in, his or her Maker. In the remission of sins, the fallen person is drawn into renewed communion with the Lord, which leads to their deeper union in the Lord's person. In this way, the Eucharist is inextricably connected to the Orthodox understanding of deification, whereby the human creature participates in God's glory, the divine energies, being transfigured thereby into "god by participation." To put it in the words of St. John of Damascus:

> Participation is spoken of, for through [the Eucharist] we partake of the divinity of Jesus. Communion, too, is spoken of, and it is an actual communion, because

through it we have communion with Christ and share in His flesh and His divinity: yea, we have communion and are united with one another through it. For since we partake of one bread, we all become one body of Christ and one blood, and members one of another, being of one body with Christ. (*Exact Exposition of the Orthodox Faith* 4.13)

The Eucharist, therefore, is the mystery of the Son's incarnation – his gift in coming to humankind – made wholly accessible to the human creature, drawing the latter up into that sacred and central reality of the Christian faith. The incarnation, which once took place in Bethlehem and united the Creator to his creation, is rendered present, and the faithful are drawn into its full reality,

for we do not receive these things as common bread or common drink; but as Jesus Christ our Saviour, having been made flesh by a word of God, had both flesh and blood for our salvation, so we have learned that the food, made a Eucharist by a word of prayer that comes from Him, from which our blood and flesh are nourished, by change are the flesh and blood of the incarnate Jesus. (St. Justin Martyr, *First Apology* 66)

This flesh and blood, which draw the person into the incarnation of the Son, at one and the same time draw him or her into the full life of the Trinity, for the power of the Spirit effects the offering by which the Son draws creation to his Father. It is this that allows the Christian faithful, having partaken of the sacred mysteries, to pronounce together at the end of the divine liturgy: "We have seen the true light; we have received the heavenly Spirit; we have found the true faith, worshipping the undivided Trinity; for the Trinity has saved us."

SEE ALSO: Christ; Confession; Deification; Divine Liturgy, Orthodox; Iconostasis; Mystery (Sacrament); St. Cyril of Alexandria (ca. 378–444)

References and Suggested Readings

Gebremedhin, E. (1977) *Life-Giving Blessing: An Inquiry into the Eucharistic Doctrine of Cyril of Alexandria*. Uppsala: Almqvist and Wiksell.

Goguel, M. (1910) *L'Eucharistie des origines à justine martyr*. Paris: Editions du Cerf.

Hapgood, I. (ed.) (1975) *Service Book of the Holy Orthodox-Catholic Apostolic Church*. Englewood, NJ: Antiochian Orthodox Christian Archdiocese.

Sheerin, D. J. (ed.) (1986) *The Eucharist: Message of the Fathers of the Church*, Vol. 7. Wilmington: M. Glazier.

Wainwright, G. (1978) *Eucharist and Eschatology*. London: Epworth Press.

Eucharologion

JOHN A. MCGUCKIN

The Greek term (Slavonic: *Molitvoslov*) for "Book of Prayers." Today, it denotes one of the main liturgical books of the Orthodox Church, giving directions for the ordering of many of the chief services. It contains ritual instructions for Vespers and Matins (Orthros), as well as rubrics and texts for the Divine Liturgy of St. John Chrysostom, along with the variations found in the Liturgy of St. Basil, and the ordering of the Vespers and Communion ritual of the Presanctified Liturgy of St. Gregory the Dialogist. The book is a collection of, and commentary on, many other services and blessing rituals and gives texts as well as rubrical instructions necessary to the priest and bishop. Its range includes the three major ordination rites, the office of monastic tonsure, the ritual of exorcism, the rites of the minor orders, the initiatory rites for monastics and the establishment of monastic superiors, and the ordering of the funeral service and the sacraments of baptism, confession, anointing, and marriage, along with many other various blessings and prayers. Since the *Eucharologion* is intended primarily for the clergy it does not contain the detailed responses of the choir, which has its own service books called respectively *Triodion*, *Pentekostarion*, *Oktoechos*, and *Menaion*. A very important witness to the state of the Orthodox liturgical ritual is the Barberini *Eucharologion* (Ms. Gr. 336) from the late 8th or early 9th century. The *Eucharologion* today comes in various editions (depending on the extent of its contents). The standard is called the *Great Eucharologion*, but there is also found a *Small Eucharologion* (Slavonic: *Trebnik* or "Book of Needs"); the Priest's Service Book (Greek: *Hieratikon*; Slavonic: *Sluzhebnik*). The services properly pertaining to the episcopate are also collated in the *Archihieratikon* (Slavonic: *Chinovnik*).

SEE ALSO: Divine Liturgy, Orthodox; Liturgical Books

References and Suggested Readings

Duchesne, L. (1903) *Christian Worship: Its Origin and Evolution*. London: SPCK.

Evangelism

CHAD HATFIELD

Evangelism in the Eastern Orthodox Christian context is commonly associated with the dominical foundation of the Great Commission as found at the conclusion of Matthew's gospel: "Go therefore and make disciples of all the nations, baptizing them in the name of the Father and of the Son and of the Holy Spirit, teaching them to observe all things that I have commanded you" (Mt. 28.19–20). It is also generally understood that the context of this command puts the emphasis on the power of God and not the strength of humankind to evangelize. To evangelize is to be an *evangelistes*, the deliverer of *evangelion*, or the Good News of salvation. In the synoptic gospels there is also a very close relationship between the verbs *evangelizein* and *kerussein*, the gospel term for proclaiming the word, or teaching, of God (*kerygma*).

The post-Pentecost sharing of this Good News, in many languages as Acts records, was the beginning of the fulfillment of the Great Commission. At first the evangelistic efforts of the disciples were centered on the Jews, but in a short period of time Antioch would become a great center for more global Christian evangelism, with the word spreading to gentile communities through the preaching of Peter and Paul. In fact, it was in Antioch where the disciples were first called "Christians" (Acts 11.26).

Christian history records the rapid spread of the Christian message in the Roman Empire, despite both persecution and the radical nature of the gospel. The hagiographies of the early saints also give a clear picture of the witness of the many martyrs. Tertullian's dictum that "the seed of the Church is the blood of the martyrs"

is for the Orthodox still a most powerful evangelistic testimony, for the stories and legends associated with a multitude of saints continue to be a voice of witness. The popular Orthodox devotion to saints such as the Forty Martyrs of Sebaste, Perpetua and her companions, the archdeacon Lawrence, and many others is woven deep into the fabric of the Orthodox Christian proclamation of the truth of the gospel, and for this reason the best examples of Eastern Orthodox evangelism are found in the lives of saints rather than through para-ecclesiastical organizations or societies. Among the best known of the evangelizing saints are the two brothers Cyril (ca. 826–69) and Methodios (815–85), apostles to the Slavs. Sons of aristocratic parents from Thessalonica, they used their education in philosophy and diplomacy to great advantage when they responded to the request of Prince Rastislav for missionaries to come and teach his people in their native language. It was Cyril who, in preparation for this new work, invented the Glagolitic alphabet, which is the basis for what is today called "Old Church Slavonic." The Eastern Orthodox model of using the vernacular tongue to evangelize was firmly established by these two missionaries who translated the Bible and patristic and liturgical texts into the language understood by the people. This crucial principle is regrettably still not fully supported or practiced as Eastern Orthodoxy expands beyond the borders of traditionally Orthodox Christian countries.

Another of the most significant mileposts in Eastern Orthodox evangelism is dated 988 with the baptism of the Rus. Inspired by his Christian grandmother, Prince Vladimir sent emissaries to explore various religions. They reported that when they were in Constantinople at the Divine Liturgy in Hagia Sophia they "knew not whether they were in heaven or earth" (*Russian Chronicle*). It has remained a testimony to the power of the liturgy and the beauty of church services to move the hearts and minds of the hearers. Even though catechism may have been poorly done or many (as in the case of the Rus) were compelled to be baptized by those in authority, a true evangelism of the Russian peoples began which would have an immense flowering and effect. It was this blessed foundation that sustained persecuted Christians during the bitter seventy-year reign of godless communism and which began to publicly flower again in 1988 with the millennium celebrations of the baptism of Kievan Rus.

Other mileposts in Eastern Orthodox evangelism include the work of St. Stephen of Perm (1340–96) among the Zyrian people of Siberia. Notable were his convictions that Russian culture and Slavic language were not a crucial part of authentic Orthodox evangelism. He was also another great proponent of the power of liturgy and the beauty of church culture for evangelizing non-Christians.

The Russian missions to Siberia, Korea, Japan, and Alaska beginning in the late 1700s and continuing through the 1917–18 Russian Revolution reflect in each region the Eastern Orthodox commitment to avoid religious syncretism and yet not confuse Orthodoxy with ethnic culture. St. Herman of Alaska (1756–1837) is considered a model of evangelism by ascetical example. Innocent of Alaska (1797–1878) is also another example of a great missionary who contextualized Orthodoxy while respecting the local customs of the people to whom he ministered and advocated the use of the vernacular.

Interest in Eastern Orthodoxy, beginning in the 1980s, by other Christians living in western countries intensified with the collapse of the communist yoke in the former Soviet Union and Eastern Europe. In 1987 some 2,000 former Evangelical Christians were received into the Antiochian Archdiocese of North America. Since then many more thousands of converts have reenergized the Orthodox presence in many parts of the world.

Use of contemporary media such as the Internet, podcasts, radio, and magazines by Orthodox preachers, writers, and broadcasters has grown at a rapid rate during the last decades. However, even with these new tools for evangelism, the saying of Seraphim of Sarov still holds true as the standard for how Eastern Orthodoxy understands evangelism. His advice was: "Acquire the Holy Spirit and thousands around you will be saved."

SEE ALSO: Sts. Constantine (Cyril) (ca. 826–869) and Methodios (815–885)

References and Suggested Readings

Oleksa, M. (1998) *Orthodox Alaska: A Theology of Mission.* Crestwood, NY: St. Vladimir's Seminary Press.

Veronis, L. (1994) *Missionaries, Monks and Martyrs: Making Disciples of All Nations.* Minneapolis: Light and Life Publications.

Evlogitaria
DIMITRI CONOMOS

Troparia sung on Sundays and Great Feasts, following the reading from the Psalter. The word *evlogitarion* comes from the Greek word for "blessed" and is so named for the refrain "Blessed are You, O Lord; teach me Your statutes" (Ps. 118.12 *LXX*) which punctuates these hymns devoted to the resurrection of Christ. (For Saturdays commemorating the dead and for funerals there is a second series of evlogitaria.) The evlogitaria are exclamations of joy in the risen Christ.

SEE ALSO: Troparion

Exaposteilarion
DIMITRI CONOMOS

A troparion occurring after the ninth ode of the Canon in Matins, and frequently developing the theme of Christ as light of the world. It is termed *exaposteilarion* because it "sends forth or gives the dismissal" at the end of the Canon and before the Praises. The exaposteilaria are without preceding verses and on Sundays they are always linked with the gospel of the resurrection, used earlier in the service. Those chanted during the weekdays of Great Lent are called *photagogika* ("hymns of light"). There is one for each of the eight modes and each one refers to the "sending forth" of divine illumination.

SEE ALSO: Canon (Liturgical); Orthros (Matins); Troparion

Exarch
ANDREI PSAREV

The Council of Sardica (347) used this term interchangeably with *metropolitan* to describe senior bishops. By the time of the Council of Chalcedon (451), exarchs, or archbishops, of the capital cities were independent and exercised jurisdictional power beyond the borders of their own civil provinces. When in the 6th century the five major sees evolved into patriarchates, heads of the dependent dioceses continued to be called exarchs. Since the Byzantine period the term has chiefly denoted patriarchal representatives of various ranks, including lay persons. In modern times exarch is most commonly used as a title of the most senior hierarch of an autonomous church entity.

SEE ALSO: Church (Orthodox Ecclesiology); Pentarchy

References and Suggested Readings

Kazhdan, A. P. et al. (1991) "Exarch." In the *Oxford Dictionary of Byzantium*. Oxford: Oxford University Press.

L'Huillier, P. (2000) *The Church of the Ancient Councils*. Crestwood, NY: St. Vladimir's Seminary Pess.

Rodopoulos, P. (2007) *An Overview of Orthodox Canon Law*. Rollinsford, NH: Orthodox Research Institute.

Excommunication

ANDREI PSAREV

Excommunication is a formal exclusion from church fellowship until repentance has been attained (cf. 1 Tim. 1.20). According to the gospel, the church may excommunicate a transgressor if all attempts at persuasion have failed (Mt. 18.17). Excommunication may be public (called *anathema*; cf. 1 Cor. 16.22) or private (called *aforismos*; cf. 1 Cor. 5.20).

Private excommunication may be prescribed by a priest for scandalous personal sins. Nowadays privately excommunicated Christians are allowed to participate in worship, but not to partake of the Eucharist. Excommunication in the Orthodox understanding is not tantamount to damnation. It is meant as a therapeutic remedy intended to hasten an errant Christian's realization that he or she has deviated, to make necessary life-changes and to appreciate the church membership that their actions have

deprived them of. Bishops are required to take care that excommunicants shall not be lost to the church (*Apostolic Constitutions* 3.12). Canon 4 of the seventh ecumenical council forbade a bishop to impose excommunication while under the influence of passion (anger).

The Apostolic Canons (3rd–early 4th centuries) identify the sins that must necessarily be punished by excommunication, although without specifying duration. The Ancyra Council (314) specified for excommunicants various degrees of participation in communal worship (Canon 25). The duration of excommunication depends on the depth of the repentance shown (Canon 5).

An anathematized person, whether alive or dead, is not eligible for public Orthodox commemoration. The names of excommunicated bishops are removed from the lists for commemoration. Excommunication is considered a means of exerting moral pressure on errant bishops. An Orthodox Christian cannot take part in the worship of a community that has been excommunicated since it would be a demonstration of disloyalty toward the church hierarchy (Council of Antioch, Canon 2). In order to protect the flock from heterodoxy, Orthodox bishops have usually prescribed rigor toward heretics, but leniency in relation to offenders against ethical or church discipline.

Anathema is proclaimed for grave dogmatic and disciplinary crimes only by a bishop in the context of a council after a determination of the guilt of a person or a group, and when all attempts to elicit repentance have failed. The anathemas against those heretics condemned by the seven ecumenical councils are solemnly repeated throughout the Orthodox Church on the first Sunday of Great Lent. The Council of the Russian Church of 1666–7 also anathematized schismatic Old Believers. However, in 1971 this anathema was found inappropriate and was revoked.

Rules regarding Orthodox clergy are more strict than those pertaining to the laity. Excommunication for a priest may be temporary (suspension) or permanent (deposition). Normally, the excommunication of a clergyman or a layman can be reversed only by the bishop or priest who originally imposed the sanction. But the ritual of confession (Greek rite) also contains provision for a confessor to lift "the ban of a priest." In cases of unfair excommunication a clergyman may appeal to the synod of bishops (Antioch, Canon 20).

Byzantine aristocrats, even emperors, could be excommunicated. In the times of the Byzantine and Russian empires, excommunicants were also deprived of civil rights. Excommunication could thus be used for political purposes. In Muscovy St. Sergius of Radonezh (d. 1392) ordered that all churches in Nizhnii Novgorod be closed for civil insubordination. In 1943 Metropolitan Sergii Stragorodskii anathematized Russian clergy who collaborated with the Nazis.

SEE ALSO: Canon Law; Confession; Metanie (Metanoia); Repentance

References and Suggested Readings

Kiparisov, V. (1897) *O tserkovnoi distsipline*. Sergiev Posad.

McGuckin, J. A. (2004) "Excommunication" and "Penance," in J. A. McGuckin (ed.) *The West-minster Handbook to Patristic Theology*. Louis-ville: Westminster/John Knox Press.

Maksimovich, K. (2001) "Anafema," in *Pravoslavnaia Entsiklopedia*, vol. 2. Moscow: Pravoslavnaia Entsiklopedia.

Exorcism

JOHN A. MCGUCKIN

Exorcism (*exorkizo*) in biblical idiom meant to "swear" ("to adjure") in a solemn manner (Gen. 24.3; Mt. 26.63). It is in this way that it is associated in the New Testament accounts with the act of expelling demons (*ekballo*, "to cast out") and hostile spiritual influences from people, a deed which is associated throughout the gospel with Jesus (Mk. 1.23–27; 3.20–27; 16.17; see also Origen, *Against Celsus* 6.44) and is closely related to his healing ministry (Mk. 1.29–34; 1.40–2.12; 3.1–6; 5.21–43; 6.30–44, 53–56; 7.24–37; 8.22–26; 10.46–52), where both exorcisms and healings are seen as part of the proclamation of the nearness of the kingdom (Mt. 12.24f), which casts out evil and oppression from among human society.

Jesus himself gave his disciples authority (*exousia*) to cast out (*exballein*) unclean spirits (Mt. 10.1, 8; Lk. 10.17–20).

Exorcism became a term prominent in early Christianity from the 2nd century onwards (cf. Justin, *Dialogue With Trypho* 76.6; 85.2) to refer to the casting out of devils. In ancient exorcism rituals the command (*adjuration*) to the demon was a central part of the casting-out process, something that was common to Hellenist (cf. Philostratus, *Life of Apollonius*), Judaic (Acts 13.6; 19.14; Josephus, *Antiquities* 8.46–9), and early Christian practice. In Orthodox Christian practice the ritual of exorcism continued throughout history to the present day, but no longer commanded the prominent place that it seemed to have in the primitive church's mission among the pagans. The ritual survived prominently in the baptismal initiatory exorcisms (Hippolytus, *Apostolic Tradition* 20–1) which involved anointing with oil, the laying on of hands, making the sign of the cross over the candidate, reading the Scriptures, and "blowing in the face" (*exsufflation*). The Pseudo Clementine treatise *On Virginity* (1.12) preserves one of the first explicit accounts of exorcism. On Virginity also mentions the laying on of hands, and anointing with blessed oil, as part of the ritual.

Up until the 3rd century the exorcists were a regular part of the church's clergy. Pope Cornelius explicitly lists them as such (Eusebius. *Church History* 6.43.11); but after that point the ministry fell into relative abeyance, taken over by the higher clergy, and surviving (apart from the baptismal rites) in the monastic penitential practices which attributed temptation to demonic activity (dealt with by the expulsion of demonic influence by means of confession), and in aspects of the healing services that make a regular correspondence of sickness with "hidden sin." The formal ritual of exorcism was always occasionally invoked for special needs. In exorcisms today (among the Orthodox it is not seen in the "extraordinary" and "alarmist" categories that later western and modern secular imaginations attribute to them) the clergy approach the ritual as a form of powerful blessing meant to liberate the person from oppression and/or sickness by using the sign of the cross, blessed oil, the invocation of the holy name, and the laying of the gospels on the head of the afflicted person. In the Orthodox service books the prayers of exorcism attributed to St. Basil the Great are predominantly in use, for common as well as particular cases of need.

SEE ALSO: Anointing of the Sick; Blessing Rituals, Cross; Healing

References and Suggested Readings

Litsas, F. (1984) *A Companion to the Greek Orthodox Church*. New York: Greek Orthodox Archdiocese.
McGuckin, J. A. (2004) "Exorcism," in *The Westminster Handbook to Patristic Theology*. Louisville: Westminster John Knox Press.
Prokurat, M. et. al. (eds.) (1996) *Historical Dictionary of the Orthodox Church*. Lanham, MD: Scarecrow Press.

F

Fasting

DIMITRI CONOMOS

Fasting, like prayer, demonstrates the essential duality that qualifies the Christian life. Both of these religious practices operate at two levels: the personal and the corporate, and together they are linked inseparably. At the personal level, fasting and prayer are actions enjoined by Christ to be carried out "in secret" (Mt. 6.6, 17–18). At the fully corporate level, the faithful are advised to pray together for certain things in common (Mt. 18.20). The analogy with fasting can be seen in the regulations for abstention prescribed by the Orthodox Church for the entire worshipping community. Whereas the fast in secret, normally known as the ascetic fast, has its own rule and rhythm, according to differing traditions and circumstances, and is essentially an abstinence (the avoidance of particular foods at certain periods of the year or on certain days of the week), the fast of the ekklesia is total (no food or liquid intake) and is in effect a preparation for the Eucharistic banquet, which is a type of the heavenly kingdom.

The divine injunction to fast is as ancient as humanity itself: "And the Lord God commanded the man, saying, 'Of every tree of the garden thou mayest freely eat: but of the tree of the knowledge of good and evil, thou shalt not eat of it: for in the day that thou eatest thereof thou shalt surely die'" (Gen. 2.16–17).

Original sin is thus revealed to us by the breaking of a fast by Adam in Eden. Succumbing to temptation and eating the forbidden fruit, he was expelled from Paradise and made subject to death. The New Adam of the gospels, on the other hand, begins his mission with fasting (Mt. 4.1–11). In overcoming the temptation to eat, Christ destroyed death and opened once more the gates of Paradise. From either perspective, the biblical view of fasting is of something vital (in the literal sense of "life-giving") and of decisive importance. The abstinence of the first Adam may be considered ascetical since its obvious purpose was to lead the moral head of the human race to recognize the necessary dependence of creature upon Creator. The total fast of Christ in the wilderness was undertaken as the immediate preparation for his public ministry: to lead humanity back to the Kingdom of God.

The notion of fasting (as opposed to the keeping of dietary laws) in preparation for a theophany is known both in Antiquity and in the Old Testament: Moses, on the mountain, fasted for forty days and forty nights (Ex. 24.18), while the Israelites below were instructed also to abstain from sexual activity (Ex. 19.15) and Daniel fasted as he awaited God's answer to his prayer (Dan. 9.3). There are many instances of fasting as an act of national penitence. After the disaster of the civil war with Benjamin, all Israel fasted (Judg. 20.26) and Samuel made the people fast because they had strayed

The Concise Encyclopedia of Orthodox Christianity, First Edition. Edited by John Anthony McGuckin.
© 2014 John Wiley & Sons, Ltd. Published 2014 by John Wiley & Sons, Ltd.

away to Baal (1 Sam. 7.6). Nehemiah also made the people fast and confess their sins (Neh. 9.1).

Some of these early characteristics of fasting recur in early Christianity, but in general the position adopted towards fasting was different and exceptional. Jesus had criticized the ritual formalism of the Pharisees because it assumed precedence over ethical action. However, he did not eliminate fasting, for he spent forty days in the desert praying and fasting and he suggested that both could be used as effective means against the devil, a view which is reminiscent of ancient practices. Yet, because of the prevailing view associating fasting with mourning, Jesus regarded fasting in his Messianic presence as meaningless (Mk. 2.18–20).

In the post-apostolic period, however, Christianity imposed its own rules with regard to fasting, which seem to have developed from Jewish ones. In the 2nd century the Pre-Pascha fast was established. The duration of this severe fast was analogous to the period of time that Christ spent in the tomb. However, it was not associated with mourning, but rather was viewed as a preparatory period for the celebration that lasted from Pascha to Pentecost and as an outward sign of the anticipation of spiritual fulfilment. During the course of the 4th century this fasting period was extended to forty days in commemoration of the forty years spent by the children of Israel in the wilderness (Ex. 16.35) and Jesus' forty-day fast in the wilderness, tempted by the devil (Mt. 4.1); from then onwards it was known as the Great Fast (Lent). Also, by the 3rd century, Wednesdays and Fridays were designated as fasting days for Christians. These days were chosen because they were days of mourning: Wednesday in remembrance of the betrayal of Jesus and Friday in remembrance of his death. To fast on Saturday, the day that the Lord rested from his work of Creation, and on Sunday, the day of Christ's resurrection, was prohibited since fasting and joy were regarded as antithetical.

Ascetic, or personal, abstinence is also understood as an act of restoration and reconciliation – not a measure of sacrifice as such, since the emphasis is not primarily a matter of giving up but of giving. Lenten Scripture readings and the hymns establish the priorities: persons come first, rules of fasting come afterwards. Abstinence is ineffective if it does not bring us closer to our fellow humans.

The collective fast of the church, the Body of Christ, presupposes a dimension that is essentially liturgical. It is an act of unification and time-reckoning. It unites the soul with the body, the one who fasts with the divine, and also all believers in the world in a shared action. Yesterday and tomorrow become ever-present in this time scale, for through liturgical fasting and feasting the faithful are given the opportunity to be actually present as contemporaries at the cardinal moments of salvation history. Liturgical life and everyday life are not viewed as separate compartments in the life of a Christian. Liturgy is life and all of life is liturgical, and this includes the fasting of the assembly.

SEE ALSO: Asceticism

References and Suggested Readings

Enisleidis, C. M. (1959) *O Thesmos tis Nistias* [The Institution of Fasting]. Athens.

Koutsas, S. (1996) *I Nistia tis Ekklisias* [The Church's Fasting]. Athens.

Schmemann, A. (1969) *Great Lent: Journey to Pascha*. Crestwood, NY: St. Vladimir's Seminary Press.

Fatherhood of God

JOHN A. MCGUCKIN

The Orthodox Church has a profound doctrine and understanding of the Fatherhood of God, but it is predominantly one that is approached through the mediating priesthood of the Divine Logos, since the Holy Word of God, as St. Irenaeus informs us, is the "visible of the Father's invisible" (*Adv. Haer.* 4.4.2; 4.6.5; Clement of Alexandria, *Stromata* 4.25). Orthodoxy understands, therefore, that who and what the Father is, is only given to the church through the revelation of the Divine Logos to the Creation, and thus the Father is approached by his world inextricably as the heart of the mystery of the Divine Trinity. For Orthodoxy (and in this it differs considerably from later western Christian traditions), the face of God manifested in the Creation is above all the face of the Logos of the Father. The epiphanies of God in the Old Testament, for example, are also taken, by and large, in the Orthodox tradition to be the manifestations of the Divine Word. The Word is the approachability of the Unapproachable and Utterly Transcendent God. He is the Revealer, and (with the Spirit) the Revealing of the Unseen Father. All apprehension of God, therefore, is understood in Orthodoxy to have been initiated by God himself. God is never truly an object of human discovery; always a self-revealing gift of his own graciousness.

The Father is, before ever the Creation was, the source of the outreach of the being of the Holy Trinity: the principle (*Arche*) of the Son and the Spirit, who share the Father's own single being; not as if they have a common participation in some generic "divine substance," but properly and precisely as the Son and Spirit receiving the Father's own very being as their own very being; a mystical doctrine which is the very heart of the ineffable Mystery of the Divine Trinity: that absolute oneness of God which is triune. This outreach of the divine Father demonstrates the quintessential character of the *God Who Is* as a communion, and who ever reaches out to the Creation too as source of life and communion. The Father who is Unapproachable to his Creation in his divine essence is at one and the same moment intimately near to it as its sustaining Father and Lord and has so structured the existence of all things that he can be made known to noetic vision therein. God's inner life, as an outreach that lies outside all created knowledge and is known only to the Trinity itself, is therefore imaged through the Son to the created order. This he patterns into being as that mode of existence which comes to life by the outreach of God beyond himself: God's beneficence to creation. Communion with God is life. For the noetic creation, communion with God is meant to be life eternal: the deification of humankind, and the angelic order's permeation by the bliss of the divine vision.

The Unapproachability of the Father, as far as humans are concerned, is a question of the divine nature that cannot be fully apprehended by limited creaturehood. St. Gregory Palamas expressed this gulf between the creature and the Uncreated One in the clearest terms: "Nothing whatsoever of all that is created has, or ever will have, the very slightest communion with the supreme nature, or nearness to it" (*The 150 Chapters. ch. 78*. PG 150. 1176).

Orthodox theology customarily describes this gulf between God and Creation (bridged by the condescension of the Divine Logos) in terms of the distinction between the essence (*ousia*) of God (utterly unknowable to all outside the persons of the Trinity) and the energies (*energeia*) of God. The latter describe the impact the divine nature and trinitarian persons have upon the cosmos: both in its making and in its regeneration. The nature is unapproachable, the energies reach out to all corners of the cosmos and penetrate all being; but as these energies are uncreated, they are nevertheless the true and direct presence of God at work in his creation. God is thus known accurately in both his immanent and transcendent dimensions. It follows then that the Father, as the most supremely distant being by virtue of his incomprehensible transcendence, is also the most intimately near reality. He is the paradox of the ground of our being, remaining uncontained yet containing us (Eph. 4.6). It is also the case, for the Orthodox, that only Jesus can make known this God to the world, as Father. For what is at stake is not simply the revelation of deity as a "fatherly being" (which many religious systems might presume to deduce), but precisely the coming to know God as "The Father" of Our Lord Jesus Christ; the Father who is the *Arche* of the Holy Trinity. As the Lord himself taught: "All things have been delivered to me by my Father; and no one knows the Son except the Father; just as no one knows the Father except the Son and any one to whom the Son chooses to reveal him" (Mt. 11.27). Without this voice of the Logos telling us that the Supreme God is our Father, theology would have remained locked in the sterility of ancient Greek thought about the "Uncaused Cause," or would have remained infantile, using only anthropomorphisms to speak of God.

The semantic terms of this revelation of the Word, regarding this known and yet unknown God, this stranger who is more familiar to us than ourselves, is at once the most sublime and the most homely, the most exalted and most humble: "Our Father." In these two words lie the complete mystery of the Lord's revelation to his church of the nature of God. It is a theological revelation which is an instruction in prayer, not metaphysics. "Hallowed be your name" is the only fitting response if the message has been received and understood. "Our Father": two words which are at once completely understandable by the most simple of minds (Mt. 11.25) and yet which remain transcendent in their depth and ramification. "May your Kingdom come; your will be done on earth as it is in heaven." Who can begin to imagine this fully, other than the Lord himself? When this eschatological mystery is complete, the revelation will correspond to "common sense." Until then it remains an insight reserved fully for the beloved of God only (who alone are able to enter into that relation of complete trust of the Father wherein life changes its aspect eschatologically), but "for all others on the outside it is given in riddles" (Mk. 4.11).

The Lord tells the church that like the love of a true father, God's care overflows in restlessly energetic actions for the benefit of his children: "If you then, who are evil, know how to give good gifts to your children, how much more will your Father who is in heaven give good things to those who ask him!" (Mt. 7.11; Lk. 11.11–13). God stands over the world like a father over a family. The very instinct in humans to care derives from the archetype of God's watchful care of his beloved: something the apostle repeats when he says: "For this reason I bow my knees before the Father, from whom every family in heaven and on earth is named" (Eph. 3.14–15). This simple truth was given to the church as a profound revelation of the character of the Father, by the Lord himself, in the agony of his suffering in the garden, when he said, "Abba, Father, all things are possible to you; remove this cup from me; yet not my will, but yours be done" (Mk. 14.36). It was not given to the church by the Lord in a careless way or a random moment of optimism, but as a pattern of truth from the heart of the economy of his suffering. In joy, or in sorrow, the Lord taught that all things come to the beloved of the Father, as from the hands of one who gives the gifts of love, for: "Are not two sparrows sold for a penny? Yet not one of them falls to the ground without your Father's will" (Mt. 10.29). This teaching is meant to give us courage: "For even the hairs of your head are all numbered. Do not be afraid, therefore; you are of more value than many sparrows" (Mt. 10.30–31). And it does: even though it was spoken with great challenge from the Lord to the disciples, as he invited them to walk with him to Jerusalem, where they

(rightfully) suspected he would come to his death, an event which would set them on the road to theirs.

The Lord, especially in his total abandonment to the Father's provident will throughout his ministry and in his Passion, modeled for disciples the illumined understanding of the nature of the Father's dealings with his elect: he challenged them to adopt his own perspectives of faith, that nothing comes by fate or chance, all comes from the invitation of the love of the Father; and it is manifested to them in love, and through love, for their perfection as children of God. If the disciples rise into this faith, accept it from the Lord's hands, so it becomes a luminous metaphysical reality for them. God is not merely revealed as their Father, but more than this: they themselves are now revealed as the children of God, in whom only the Love of God is manifested, and fate is overcome and cast aside, in favor of a God-graced destiny. What it is for those who are not the beloved children, is not said, and is obscure to theology; though God is all-merciful and infinitely generous.

Our God is the Father of Mercies (2 Cor. 1.3), the loving Father of the beloved: outside that relationship there is no knowledge of the true God; intimations of a self-made God, perhaps, which *de facto* prove to be false. Those who have glimpsed the light of this most simple of revelations of the inner structure of God's dealings with his cosmos understand in the same moment that they are lifted out of childish passivity to become "as gods" for others in their turn: "Be children of your Father who is in heaven," the Lord told his church, "For he makes his sun rise on the evil and on the good, and sends rain upon the just and the unjust alike" (Mt. 5.45). This is why the Lord's command (otherwise so impossible) can be fulfilled, to "Be as perfect as your heavenly Father is perfect" (Mt. 5.48), which is by loving without thought of cost, as the Father does. The summation of all ethics is this vital knowledge of how loving the Father is: "Be merciful, even as your Father is merciful" (Lk. 6.36), which preserves the pun in parallel to the Matthaean version (Mt. 5.8) by removing the initial *tau* from *teleos* (perfect) to make it *eleos* (merciful). Only the Father's love can make men and women rise to the stature of the beloved children of light (1 Thes. 5.5), for this is more than a mere philanthropy, it is a mystically graced lifestyle that begins to embrace all men and women in a power of love that exceeds the ordinary human capacity for affection, and takes on the character of the selfless "willing of the good of others" that marks God's character *vis-à-vis* his creation.

Only in this stature, as God's children of light, acting from the light of the Spirit and in the communion of the Son, can men and women understand the nature of God, as it is at its heart; "in spirit and in truth" (Jn. 4.24). For those who have become the children of God, in Christ and his transfiguring Spirit, all is changed. The world is utterly changed in that moment: essentially and metaphysically altered. The face of God is shown to be other than it could possibly have been understood to have been from the evidence of the world (so-called "natural theology"). Fate dies on the vine in that instant, and destiny flowers out in a binding together of creature and Creator, a fashioning of a new covenant that grows from the placing of the child's hand in that of the Father; following the example of the divine Son, who trusted his Father in all things, and made of the dark and bitter cross a source of light for the cosmos; challenging his disciples not to lose faith: "Let not your hearts be troubled; trust in God, trust also in me" (Jn. 14.1). This light falls upon a still troubled and darkened world where humans who resist the Fatherhood of God and the brotherhood of humanity continue to hold others in bitter forms of bondage. But even this fact reveals to the children of God paths to subvert the manifold forms of evil, for the enlightenment and liberation of the suffering. So it is that the "children of the day" fulfill the Lord's own urgent prayer: "Father, May your kingdom come! May your will be done on earth as it is in heaven."

The New Testament revelation of the Father is therefore at once a most simple one and an immensely complex one; one that is bound up in the Lord's own pilgrimage to his cross, and in the disciples' unfolding understanding of what the Lord himself meant by "Trust" (*Pistis*, faith) in God. It remains the case to this day, in the ongoing spiritual life of the church, that the Lord's faithful make their own progress into the active understanding of God's Fatherhood as they walk alongside their Lord, and learn total abandonment to the will of the Father for their good; the Father who knows what we need before we ask him (Mt. 6.8). The understanding of God as Father is a given revela-

tion. It is also an ongoing mystery of the Spirit which is only accessible to those who walk with the Lord, and thus share in his own Sonship. For it is through his Sonship that we have all become co-heirs (Rom. 8.17); in no other way is this possible.

The church fathers pondered this mystery of God the Father most deeply and left their characteristic marks on all subsequent Orthodox theology. For most of them, the two primary truths theology ought to confess about the Father are, firstly, the fact that it is he himself who directly wills and blesses the creation of all things as a good and light-filled act of beneficence, through the medium of his Son and Logos; and secondly, the manner in which the human mind falters in the face of describing God truly. The first thesis was designed to stand against all manner of Gnostics who believed that they could only defend the divine transcendence by denying a directly divine volition of creation. The second was comparable to the building of a fence of "reverent diffidence" around those affirmations that the feeble human mind could assert about the One who ultimately transcends. The latter amounts to the so-called "Apophatic" tradition of Orthodox thought, deriving its name from the Greek term meaning "to turn away from speech." It is most clearly exemplified in the theologian Dionysios the Areopagite (especially in his short but dense treatise *The Mystical Theology*), but it was a tradition within the church's theologians long before Dionysios. In the apophatic approach, the titles of God ("Lord" connoting his power, "Light" connoting his mercy, "Fire" connoting his restless energy, and so on) always describe the actions of God in the cosmos, rather than the nature of God in himself, which remains beyond the scope of human enquiry, except insofar as some of the revelations of the Logos have "imaged" it to the church in specific revelations. For Orthodoxy, "Father" is not a title, rather the Holy Name itself, which replaces the sacred Tetragrammaton of the Old Testament dispensation.

Most public prayer in the Orthodox Church tends to be addressed to Jesus or to the Trinity. The Father is often the focus, however, of perhaps the greatest and most solemn prayer of the church, namely the *Anaphora* or Great Eucharistic Prayer. This, too, of course, is set in a trinitarian context, if not explicitly so, then by the terms of the final doxology, but the

Great Eucharistic consecratory prayer often lifts its eyes and heart to the Father directly. We may fittingly end with a citation of the invocation of God as Father which begins the Eucharistic *Anaphora*, and which offers thanks for those particular characteristics of his fatherly love: his irrepressible condescension, his mercy, and his gift of life:

> It is fitting and right to hymn you, to bless you, to praise you, to give you thanks, and worship you in every place of your dominion; for you are God, ineffable, incomprehensible, invisible, inconceivable, ever-existing, eternally the same, You and your only-begotten Son, and your Holy Spirit. You brought us out from non-existence into being, and when we had fallen, you raised us up again, and left nothing undone until you had brought us up to heaven, and granted us the Kingdom that is to come. For all these things we give thanks to you, and to your only-begotten Son, and to your Holy Spirit; for all the benefits that we have received, both known and unknown, manifest and hidden. We thank you also for this liturgy which you have been pleased to accept from our hands, even though there stand around you thousands of archangels and tens of thousands of angels, the Cherubim and the Seraphim, six-winged and many-eyed, soaring aloft upon their wings, singing the triumphant hymn, shouting, proclaiming and saying: Holy, Holy, Holy, Lord of Hosts. Heaven and earth are full of your glory. Hosannah in the highest. Blessed is he who comes in the name of the Lord. Hosannah in the highest. (*Liturgy of St. John Chrysostom*)

SEE ALSO: Christ; Contemporary Orthodox Theology; Deification; Holy Spirit; Holy Trinity; Incarnation (of the Logos); Logos Theology; Perichoresis; St. Dionysius the Areopagite; St. Gregory Palamas (1296–1359).

References and Suggested Readings

Bentley-Hart, D. (2003) *The Beauty of the Infinite: The Aesthetics of Christian Faith*. Grand Rapids, MI: Eerdmans.

McGuckin, J. A. (1994) "Perceiving Light from Light in Light: The Trinitarian Theology of St. Gregory The Theologian," *Greek Orthodox Theological Review* 39: 1–2, 7–32.

McGuckin, J. A. (2008) *The Orthodox Church: An Introduction to Its History, Theology and Spiritual Culture*. Oxford: Wiley-Blackwell.

Russell, N. (2004) *The Doctrine of Deification in the Greek Patristic Tradition*. Oxford: Oxford University Press.

Stăniloae, D. (1998) *The Experience of God: Orthodox Dogmatic Theology Vol. 1: Revelation and the Knowledge of the Triune God*. Brookline, MA: Holy Cross Orthodox Press.

Feasts

JOHN A. MCGUCKIN

Feasts or festivals are a regular occurrence in the liturgical calendar of the Orthodox Church. There are three main types of feast: firstly, the Dominical Festivals, which reflect significant events from the Lord's ministry (such as the Nativity, the Presentation of Jesus in the Temple, the Baptism of Jesus, the Transfiguration, the Entry to Jerusalem, or Great Week Passion services); secondly, the festivals relating to the Theotokos (such as the Entrance of the Theotokos into the Temple; the Dormition, or the Protecting Veil); and third, the many feasts of the saints.

There is not one day of the year that does not have some form of special commemoration attached to it, or which does not feature the memorial day for one or many of the saints listed together. Mondays celebrate the Holy Angels; Tuesdays St. John the Forerunner; Wednesdays and Fridays the Holy Cross; Thursdays the Apostles; Saturdays All the Saints. Just as it is true that the Orthodox liturgy and prayer services are generally characterized by a distinct ascetical element (a certain sobriety of tone), it is equally the case that at a feast day or festival the church also knows how to rejoice. Often in the Orthodox world a special feastday is accompanied by many civic aspects of rejoicing. St. John's day, in summer-time, for example, is accompanied by many celebrations in Greece, and jumping through fires. In Greece the transfiguration (August 6) is marked by the bringing in of the grape harvest, and the blessing of fruit in the church (in Russia, apples replaced grapes). Many local saint's days (held around the churches dedicated to them) will witness a yearly fair at the festival, too. One cycle of festivals rotates entirely around the Paschal Mystery: Lent precedes it, Great Week synopsizes it, and Pentecost concludes it. Another cycle is static in the

Plate 22 Russian bishop blessing the Kollyva memorial dishes at the liturgical commemoration of the dead. Olivier Martel/Corbis.

year: each year on January 6, for example, occurs the feast of the Baptism of the Lord, known as Theophany; each year on August 15 there occurs the Dormition of the Theotokos; each year on June 29 there occurs the feast of the Apostles Peter and Paul, and so on.

The theological character of the festival reflects the joy of the Paschal event: the hope of the believers that one day they also will be able to share the joys of heaven with the communion of elect saints who have already "entered into the joy of the Master" (Mt. 25.21). The feast of feasts, therefore, is Pascha itself, the liturgical memorial (*anamnesis*) of the resurrection of the Lord; and indeed every Eucharist of the Orthodox Church is a new Pascha made present; for all sacramental mysteries derive their force and grace from the paschal grace of Christ. The dividing up of the year with a series of festivals is a liturgical way of reflecting

on how the Pascha is appropriated among his church today. The cycle of dominical feasts presents for joyful reflection one aspect of the saving ministry; so too the reflection on the life of the Virgin presents to the church an icon of the redeemed believer, the earthly woman who was lifted up to be "more honorable than the Cherubim" because of the grace of her Son. The lives and deeds of the saints (of so many different stations in life) are celebrated as icons for emulation and as testaments (*martyria*) of the power of Christ's grace still operating in the world.

The feasts themselves have special liturgical texts associated with them. Those for the major feasts can be found in the *Festal Menaion*; and each saint (as well as each type of saint – such as martyr, hierarch, Unmercenary healer, and so on) have particular Troparia and Kontakia associated with them, as found in the *General Menaion*. If a festival of a saint is being

Plate 23   Vasily Grigorevich Perov (1834–1882), *Easter Procession in the Country*. Tretjakov Gallery/AKG.

specially marked the church may gather for special Vespers and Orthros (Matins) followed by divine liturgy. The major Dominical and Marian festivals will always be marked in the monasteries, and usually have a special divine liturgy in the parishes.

SEE ALSO: Canonization; Dormition; Great Week; *Menaion*; Orthros (Matins); Theotokos, the Blessed Virgin; Vespers (Hesperinos)

References and Suggested Readings

Brotherhood of St. Seraphim (1994) *The General Menaion*. Wallasey, UK: Anargyroi Press.

Farmer, D. H. (1978) *The Oxford Dictionary of Saints*. Oxford: Clarendon Press.

Ware, K. and Mother Mary (eds.) (1969) *The Festal Menaion*. London: Faber and Faber.

Filioque

MARCUS PLESTED

The single most vexed theological issue dividing Greek East and Latin West, referring to the addition of the word *filioque* ("and from the Son") to the Creed of Nicea-Constantinople (381) to denote the Latin Church's doctrine of the eternal procession of the Holy Spirit from the Father and the Son. This doctrine of double procession is rooted in Latin patristic sources, above all St. Augustine, for whom it served to affirm the divine unity. Hints of *filioque* language can also be found in certain early Syriac sources (Brock 1985). Creedal usage employing the *filioque* is first attested at the Council of Toledo (589), underscoring there the divinity of the Son against continuing Arianism in Visigothic Spain. The double procession spread to become the received doctrine of much of the Latin Christian world, as witnessed by the Council of Hatfield (680). East–west polemic enters the equation only with the Carolingians. Frankish monks in Jerusalem had encountered Greek objections to the addition and this prompted the canonization of the addition and the doctrine at the Council of Aachen (809). While a desire to combat resurgent christological adoptionism was certainly in the background here (Gemeinhardt 2002), there is no doubt but that the council served Charlemagne's broader policy of confrontation with the Eastern Roman Empire. Rome would have none of it: Pope Leo III unequivocally condemned the addition of the phrase to the ancient creed, while recognizing the legitimacy of the doctrine it represented. He caused the uninterpolated creed to be inscribed on silver plates and displayed in St. Peter's. Rome adopted the addition only in the early 11th century. Competition in the Bulgarian mission field in the 9th century stirred further polemic, with St. Photius condemning both the addition and the doctrine it conveyed, proposing instead an uncompromising monopatrism (the Spirit's eternal procession from the Father *alone*). Other eastern theologians, such as St. Maximus the Confessor and St. John of Damascus, have affirmed the underlying harmony of the trinitarian doctrine of east and west through some sort of doctrine evoking a *per filium* formula ("through the Son," *dia tou uiou*). Patriarch Gregory of Cyprus nuanced this approach with his understanding of the eternal "shining forth" of the Spirit through the Son. This is a position embraced by St. Gregory Palamas, who allowed for *filioque* language within the immanent Godhead while firmly rejecting the doctrine in respect of the divine origination. The reunion council of Ferrara-Florence (1438–9) saw a partial concession to Orthodox sensibilities in equating the Latin *filioque* with the Greek *dia tou uiou* and the affirmation of procession "As if from one principle." Ottoman-era Orthodox theologians tended to veer between an uncompromising rejection of the *filioque* (Eustratios Argenti) and the pursuit of underlying harmony (Maximos Margounios). In the modern period, Orthodox theologians have been wholly united in rejecting the addition but have often found grounds for rapprochement in the matter of the doctrine or language of the *filioque*. When detached from the creed and the related question of papal authority

there seems no insurmountable reason for this legitimate patristic *theologoumenon* to continue to bedevil relations between Orthodoxy and the western confessions.

SEE ALSO: Fatherhood of God; Holy Spirit; Holy Trinity

References and Suggested Readings

Brock, S. (1985) "The Christology of the Church of the East," in G. Dragas (ed.) *Aksum-Thyateira*. London: Thyateira House, pp. 125–42.

Gemeinhardt, P. (2002) *Die Filioque-Kontroverse zwischen Ost-und Westkirche im Frühmittelalter*. Berlin: de Gruyter.

Finland, Autonomous Orthodox Church of

SERGEY TROSTYANSKIY

Finland has a long and dramatic church history. Orthodoxy's presence in Finland can be traced back to the late 11th century, as contemporary archeological explorations suggest. The 12th century, in turn, was marked by very significant activities of merchants and monks from Novgorod in Karelia (a region which is now divided between Russia and Finland). The missionary activities of Russian and Byzantine monks played a key role in the introduction of the Orthodox faith to the Finnish people. The greatest and most glorious signs of Orthodox presence in Finland are traditionally associated with its monastic communities. The Valamo (in Russian, Valaam) monastery, which was founded in the 12th century, stands out as among the most important of all. Among the other monastic communities, the Konevitsa (Russian, Konevets) monastery, established in the 14th century, and the monastery at Petsamo (Russian, Pechenga), set up in the 16th century beside the Arctic Ocean, are also distinguished as the great centers of Orthodox spirituality.

The Orthodox presence in Finland up until the 20th century was primarily localized in the region of Karelia, a territory that was subjected to a number of regional wars (between Novgorod and Sweden, and later between Russia and Sweden). Thus, Karelia, as the spiritual heartland of Orthodoxy in the North, tended always to be caught up in political turmoil and suffered enormously during its history. Even in the 12th century the Valamo monastery experienced several Swedish invasions. In the 16th and 17th centuries the struggle over Finland between Russia and Sweden brought more instability, and the destruction of the monasteries followed, causing the majority of the Orthodox population to flee to Russia as the western parts of Karelia were occupied by Sweden. Those who remained on these territories were generally forced to convert to Lutheranism.

In the 18th century, Tsar Peter the Great took control once more of some parts of Karelia, including the most significant sites around Lake Ladoga. Since then, Orthodoxy was restored and the Valamo and Konevitsa monasteries were rebuilt. This period was characterized by many spiritual and material restorations of the Orthodox faith in Finland. At the beginning of the 19th century, when Finland had become a Grand Duchy of the Russian Empire, the Orthodox population there once again increased significantly as many merchants, soldiers, and others moved to Finland from Russia to settle the new territories. Many churches and chapels were built at that time to accommodate settlers. In 1892 an independent diocese of Finland was established in order to serve the multi-ethnic Orthodox population, which included Finns, Karelians, Skolt Saame, and Russians.

The early part of the 20th century marked a new turn in the history of Orthodoxy in Finland. Among the consequences of the Russian Revolution of 1917 was the creation of an independent Finland. An edict of 1918 by the Finnish government granted the Orthodox Church the status of the second national church of the country, with all attendant rights and privileges. This edict was very favorable for the church as it provided a secure status for the Orthodox minorities of Finland. The political turbulence in Russia after the 1917 Revolution, on the other hand, created extremely unfavorable conditions for the Russian Orthodox Church, which was severely persecuted by the Bolsheviks; many Russian clergy and laity were murdered, and many exiled. By the early 1920s it became almost impossible for the Russian synod to oversee the diocese of Finland. Therefore, in 1921, the Russian Patriarch Tikhon granted autonomy to the Finnish Church. However, in the light of multiple difficulties in maintaining the relationship with the mother church due to the political instability in Russia, the Finnish Orthodox Church elected to change its jurisdictional position, and in 1923 became an autonomous archbishopric of the patriarchate of Constantinople.

World War II began another epoch in the history of Orthodoxy in Finland. At this time the eastern part of Finland was occupied by forces of the Soviet Union, which brought about the large-scale exile of the Orthodox population of Karelia to other parts of Finland. At that time the Finnish Church lost its most significant properties, including its major monastic sites. The monks were forced to flee and relocate with what little they could carry. The monastic sites were devastated for many years afterwards, until the early 1990s, when the Russian government gave them back to the church. The Finnish government, on the other hand, provided significant financial support for the Orthodox refugees, to assist them in building new churches and monasteries on their free territories.

The Valamo monastery has had a long and glorious history. It was established in the 12th century by the Byzantine monk St. Sergius and his Finnish disciple St. German, on the border between the lands of Novgorod and Sweden. In the next few centuries it became one of the greatest centers of Eastern monasticism. From the beginning of the 15th century it was known as the "Great Lavra" and its spiritual outreach became immense. At that time the monastery had twelve sketes on the shore of Lake Ladoga. In the following century, however, the monastery suffered significant damage by the Swedes who, in 1578, attacked and in the process killed eighteen elders and sixteen novices. In the following years the monastery was burned. Restorative help came from the Russian tsars, who rebuilt the monastery's cloister. However, in the 16th century Karelia was taken over by Sweden once again, and Valamo was burned and became deserted.

When Peter the Great reincorporated Western Karelia into the Russian Empire, he also rebuilt the monastery, but the end of the 18th century brought more trouble to Valamo, as Catherine the Great deprived Russian monasteries of their holdings. A major revival of the monastic life there was initiated by the followers and disciples of St. Paisy Velichkovsky. In the late 18th century Hieromonk Nazary, an elder from the Sarov Hermitage, introduced the Sarov Rule in Valamo, which revivified the spiritual tradition of the place. As higumen he also designed and constructed the five-domed stone Cathedral of the Transfiguration. In 1794 Higumen Nazary blessed eight monks from Valamo and Konevitsa to go to establish an Orthodox mission in Alaska. St. Herman, the first Orthodox saint of America, was one of those monks.

At the beginning of the 19th century Tsar Alexander I visited the Valamo monastery and granted it a first-class status. Towards the middle of the 19th century, under the spiritual guidance of Higumen Damaskin, Valamo became one of the major pilgrimage sites for Russian intellectuals. The 20th century, however, did not prove a fruitful time for the monastery. In 1918, after the Russian Revolution, the buildings became the property of the Finnish Orthodox Church, which in the next few years became independent of Russian influence. The newly established church sought visible symbolic reforms. It adapted the Gregorian calendar for its liturgical purposes, but this change was rejected by a large part of the monastic community. The repression of the dissident monks soon followed, and as a result several of them fled to the Soviet Union, and others to Serbia. The exiled monks brought with them the tradition of Valamo to various parts of the world, including Western Europe, North America, and Africa.

During the Winter War of 1940 (which took place between the Soviet Union and Finland) the monastery was bombed by the Soviets, but miraculously escaped major damage. It became the property of the Soviet Union and was turned into a Navy school. The monks from the Valamo monastery were forced to relocate to Heinavesi, where the New Valamo monastery was established in 1940. Since then that site has become a major pilgrimage destination of the Finnish Church. Over the next few decades the buildings of Old Valamo monastery were used for various secular purposes. The new owners failed to maintain them properly and the monastery was almost destroyed. The desolation ended in 1989 when the Council of Ministers of Karelia returned the monastery to church ownership. Over the last decade the monastery has been given very sig-

nificant attention by the Russian government. The monastery now appears to be regaining its spiritual and material wealth and is gradually becoming a significant Orthodox monastic center.

As of today, the Finnish Orthodox Church is one of the autonomous Orthodox churches under the jurisdictional authority of the patriarchate of Constantinople. Its members exceed 60,000. It has three dioceses (Karelia, Helsinki, and Oulu), twenty-four parishes, a monastery, and a convent. The Department of Orthodox Theology at the University of Joensuu offers courses for the education of Orthodox priests and teachers. There is also a seminary at Joensuu and the Valamo Lay Academy, which both play a significant role in providing training for clergy and laity. Even though the Orthodox population of Finland is small in terms of numbers, its spiritual outreach is very significant. When one approaches Helsinki by ferry, the Uspenski (Annunciation) Cathedral, one of the major features of the city's skyline, gives a glimpse of the rich Orthodox heritage of the country.

SEE ALSO: Russia, Patriarchal Orthodox Church of; St. Paisy Velichovsky (1722–1794); St. Tikhon (Belavin) (1865–1925)

References and Suggested Readings

Purmonen, V. (1984) *Orthodoxy in Finland: Past and Present.* Kuopio, Finland: Orthodox Clergy Association.
Sinnemaki, M. (1973) *Church in Finland.* Helsinki: Otava.
Sviato-Troitskaia, L. (2000) *Valaam Khristovoi Rusi.* Moscow: Khrizostom.

Florence, Council of (1438–1439)

DIMITRI CONOMOS

After roughly three-and-a-half centuries of schism, the churches of the East and West met in the Council of Florence between 1438 and 1439 to discuss unity. Meeting first at Ferrara, a transfer to Florence was soon effected because of plague and because the city fathers there were willing to defray the costs. On the

Plate 24   Emperor John VIII Palaeologos depicted as one of the Magi by Benozzo Gozzoli (1420–1497). Florence, Palazzo Medici-Riccardi. © 2010. Photo Scala, Florence. Courtesy of the Ministero Beni e Att.

Latin side there was a genuine desire to end the schism, but they also desired to extend the jurisdiction of the papacy over all Christendom. The Greeks also had the genuine Christian desire for church union, but also what made them accept the West as a venue was the fact that Constantinople, with a population of less than 50,000 inhabitants, was then in terminal decline. The Turks had conquered most of its ancient empire; surrounding it on all sides, they were now only awaiting the opportunity to deliver the *coup de grâce*. The Byzantine Empire was in most urgent need of help to be able to defend itself. Hope for that lay

only in the West. The one institution there that might channel effective aid was the papacy, which had launched and directed so many Crusades of European Christianity. The Byzantine emperor believed that the pope was able to speak for all Latins and raise immediate military help against the Ottomans. The best way of winning papal support would be the union of the churches. So the Greeks came to Florence in 1439 to discuss unity with the Latins.

Indeed, it was not only the Greek Church that came but also the Oriental Church, for the Council of Florence was, to all appearances, the most ecumenical of councils. Emperor John VIII Palaeologos attended, as did Joseph, Patriarch of Constantinople, accompanied by twenty Greek metropolitans, as well as bishops from Russia, Georgia, and Moldo-Wallachia. Moreover, five of the Greeks were procurators of the oriental patriarchates, nominated as delegates by those patriarchates themselves. Delegates from Ethiopia were sent by Emperor Zara Yacqob at the pope's request.

A decree of union, signed on July 6, 1439, was the result, for agreement had been reached by the delegates on the main doctrinal points that were held to divide the two churches: Purgatory, papal primacy, the use of leavened or unleavened bread in the Eucharist and, more especially, the *filioque*, both in regard to its legitimacy as an addition to the creed apart from an ecumenical council and in terms of its orthodoxy as a doctrine. Only Markos Eugenikos, metropolitan of Ephesus, who was later canonized by the Orthodox Church, refused to sign. He proved to represent the prevailing mentality of the Orthodox populations in the East. Patriarch Joseph died two days after the agreement, and the Orthodox hierarchs did not then elect another leader but took the position that the Florentine decision needed ratification by an eastern synod. Thus, the Union of Florence, though celebrated throughout Western Europe (bells were rung in all the churches of England), proved no more of a reality in the East than its predecessor at Lyons (1274). Emperor John VIII and his successor, the last Emperor Constantine XI, both remained loyal to the Union, but they were powerless to enforce it on their subjects and did not even dare to proclaim it publicly in Constantinople until 1452, after which many Orthodox refused to attend services at Hagia Sophia. The Grand Duke Lucas Notaras remarked on this occasion: "I would rather see the Moslem turban in the midst of the city than the Latin mitre."

SEE ALSO: *Filioque*; St. Mark of Ephesus (1392–1445)

References and Suggested Readings

Alberigo, G. (ed.) (1991) *The Council of Ferrar-Florence*. Louvain: Presses Universitaires de Louvain.

Conomos, D. (2003) "Music as Religious Propa-ganda: Venetian Polyphony and a Byzantine Response to the Council of Florence," in J. Behr, A. Louth, and D. Conomos (eds.) *"Abba": The Tradition of Orthodoxy in the West*. New York: St. Vladimir's Seminary Press, pp. 111–34.

Geanakoplos, D. J. (1955) "The Council of Florence (1438–9) and the Problem of Union between the Byzantine and Latin Churches," *Church History* 24: 324–46. Reprinted in D. J. Geanakoplos (1989), *Constantinople and the West*. Madison: University of Wisconsin Press, pp. 224–54.

Gill, J. (1959) *The Council of Florence*. Cambridge: Cambridge University Press.

Siecinski, E. (2010) *The Filioque: History of a Doctrinal Controversy*. Oxford: Oxford University Press.

Florensky, Pavel Alexandrovich (1882–1937)

BRUCE FOLTZ

Pavel Alexandrovich Florensky was a mathematician, physicist, engineer, and inventor, as well as a distinguished linguist, art historian, theologian, and philosopher, who is often compared to Leonardo and Leibniz, as one of Europe's great polymaths. Of Russian and Armenian ancestry, his youth in the Caucasus Mountains gave him an enduring, mystical affinity for nature. He graduated with highest honors from Moscow University in 1904, with an extraordinary thesis that earned him the offer of an immediate position in the mathematics faculty. Instead, Florensky entered the Moscow Theological Academy, where he was later appointed senior lecturer in philosophy. Ordained an Orthodox priest in 1911, he insisted on wearing cassock and cross while conducting his university duties, even through the Stalinist purges. He was exiled to the labor camps in Siberia in 1933, and ultimately to the infamous Solovetsky gulag on the White Sea, where he nevertheless conducted original scientific research on Arctic flora, while ministering to his fellow prisoners. He was murdered by the KGB in 1937, a loss lamented in Solzhenitsyn's *Gulag Archipelago*.

Florensky's major work, *The Pillar and Ground of Truth* (Russian original, 1914; English translation, 1997), brings to the tradition of Byzantine philosophy and theology the rich resources of Russian mystical spirituality and a thorough grasp of western philosophy.

Plate 25   Mikhail Vasilievich Nesterov (1862–1942), *The Philosophers*. Painting of Pavel Florensky and Sergius Bulgakov. State Museum, St. Petersburg, Russia/Bridgeman Art Library.

The book is dialectical and synthetic, traversing dichotomies in ways that may seem paradoxical to the conceptual landscape of Western Europe. And it is indeed one of its primary claims that the truth that matters most must appear antinomial to discursive thought – that it is something paradoxical, best encountered in "discontinuities." In a series of twelve letters, each beginning like a haiku poem with reflections infusing seasonal and affective ambience with metaphysical insight, he proceeds from the principle of identity (A = A) to an affirmation of radical otherness (A + [−A]), maintaining that "the act of knowing is not just gnoseological but also an ontological act," and that "knowing is a real going of the knower out of himself." Genuine knowledge thus entails a union of love between the knower and the known, which Florensky understands in trinitarian terms: from the side of the knower, it is truth; from the side of the known, it is love; and from the extrinsic perspective of a third party, it is beauty. Florensky maintains that the only escape from the torment of doubt, and from a skepticism that cannot ground even itself, is to be caught up in the love of a trinitarian God whose unity

of "one essence" (*homoousion*), affirmed in the Nicene Creed, consists in the love that radically unites what is both same and other: Father, Son, and Holy Spirit. *Pillar and Ground* is also known for its elucidation of the Divine Sophia, or Holy Wisdom, understood aesthetically as a numinous depth of nature and principle of cosmic ordering, while stopping short of theological claims that would become controversial in the case of his friend and colleague, Fr. Sergei Bulgakov. It is a masterpiece of extraordinary intellectual achievement, rare poetic beauty, and compelling spiritual power.

Many of his later essays have been published posthumously (in Russian) as *From the Watersheds of Thinking* (1990). In his aesthetics, Florensky was associated with the Russian Symbolists, and some of his more important essays on the theory and history of art have been translated into English.

SEE ALSO: Bulgakov, Sergius (Sergei) (1871–1944); Russia, Patriarchal Orthodox Church of

References and Suggested Readings

Bychkov, V. (1993) *The Aesthetic Face of Being: Art in the Theology of Pavel Florensky*, trans. R. Pevear and L. Volokhonsky. Crestwood, NY: St. Vladimir's Seminary Press.

Florenskij, P. (1995) "Christianity and Culture," in R. Bird (ed.) *Culture and Christian Unity: Essays by Pavel Florenskij and Lev Lopatin*. New Haven: The Variable Press.

Florenskij, P. (1995) *The Trinity: St. Sergius Lavra and Russia*, trans. R. Bird. New Haven: The Variable Press.

Florensky, P. (1986) "Mysteries and Rites," trans. R. Pevear and L. Volokhonsky. *St. Vladimir's Theological Quarterly* 30, 4.

Florensky, P. (1993) "The Point," *Geografitty* 1, 1: 28–39.

Florensky, P. (1996) *Iconostasis*, trans. D. Sheehan and O. Andrejev. Crestwood, NY: St. Vladimir's Seminary Press.

Florensky, P. (1997) *The Pillar and Ground of the Truth: An Essay in Orthodox Theodicy in Twelve Letters*, trans. B. Jakim. Princeton: Princeton University Press.

Florensky, P. (2002) *Beyond Vision: Essays on the Perception of Art*, ed. N. Miller, trans. W. Salmond London: Reaktion Books.

Florensky, St. P. (1999) *Salt of the Earth: An Encounter with a Holy Russian Elder*, trans. R. Betts. Platina, CA: St. Herman of Alaska Brotherhood.

McGuckin, J. A. (2009) "Fr. Pavel Florensky (1882–1937) on Iconic Dreaming," in J. Gattrall and D. Greenfield (eds.) *Alter Icons: The Russian Icon and Modernity*. University Park: Pennsylvania State University Press, pp. 207–23.

Slesinski, R. (1984) *Pavel Florensky: A Metaphysic of Love*. Crestwood, NY: St. Vladimir's Seminary Press.

Florovsky, Georges V. (1893–1979)

PASCHALIS GKORTSILAS

Georges V. Florovsky has been called "the most profound Orthodox theologian of the twentieth century" (Blane 1993: 9). Florovsky was a historian of Russian thought and a scholar of patristics as well as an ecumenist. His overall thought has not been as systematically studied as the other Russian religious thinkers of the 20th century, such as Berdiaev, Bulgakov, or Florensky.

The son of a Russian clerical family, Florovsky studied history and philosophy at the University of Odessa. His first academic appointment was at his *alma mater*, but the 1917 Revolution compelled Florovsky and his family to abandon the country. After an initial move to Sofia, Florovsky eventually settled in Prague, where he taught at the Russian Law Faculty for four years. His first theological appointment was as Professor of Patristics at the newly founded St. Sergius Institute of Orthodox Theology in Paris. Patristics was to be Florovsky's true academic vocation and a major force in the shaping of his theological thought. Florovsky taught at St. Sergius until the outbreak of World War II and most of his books, such as his two volumes on the church fathers (four volumes in the English translation) and the *Ways of Russian Theology*, along with some of his most important essays, come from this period. During the mid-1930s Florovsky also became increasingly involved with the ecumenical movement, especially through the Anglican-Orthodox Fellowship of St. Alban and St. Sergius. A lifelong member of Faith and Order, Florovsky was a founding member of the World Council of Churches since its First Assembly in Amsterdam in 1948. He was a pivotal figure in the involvement of the Orthodox Church in the ecumenical movement.

Florovsky's next academic appointment was as Professor of Dogmatic Theology and Patristics at St. Vladimir's Orthodox Theological Seminary in New York. In 1949 Florovsky was appointed as Dean of St. Vladimir's while simultaneously teaching courses at Columbia University and Union Theological Seminary as adjunct professor. In 1956 Florovsky was appointed Professor of Eastern Church History at Harvard University, a post he held until 1964. From 1964 to 1972 he was Visiting Professor in the Departments of Slavic Studies and Religion at Princeton University. His academic career was concluded at Princeton Theological Seminary, where he held the post of Visiting Lecturer in Church History until his death.

Florovsky's contributions to Orthodox theology are a reflection of his character as a scholar that overcame the temptation of over-specialization. Thus, his first and primary achievement was his call for a neo-patristic synthesis, meaning "a deeper search of the existential meaning of patristic theology and a synthesis that requires rare creative abilities and a synthetic charisma" (Zizioulas 1997: 15). The key for all Christian theology, according to Florovsky, is the person of Christ, and his insistence on that matter is probably an outcome of his opposition to the Sophiology of Florensky and Bulgakov.

SEE ALSO: Bulgakov, Sergius (Sergei) (1871–1944); Contemporary Orthodox Theology; Ecumenism, Orthodoxy and; Florensky, Pavel Alexandrovich (1882–1937); Sophiology

References and Suggested Readings

Blane, A. (ed.) (1993) *Georges Florovsky: Russian Intellectual and Orthodox Churchman*. Crestwood, NY: St. Vladimir's Seminary Press.

Florovsky, G. (1972–9) *The Collected Works*, vols. 1–5 of 14 vols. Belmont, MA: Nordland.

Florovsky, G. (1987–9) *The Collected Works*, vols. 6–14. Vaduz, Liech: Buchervertriebsanstalt.

Gudziak, B. (2000–1) "Towards an Analysis of the Neo-Patristic Synthesis of Georges Florovsky," *Logos* 41–2: 197–238.

Klimoff, A. (2005) "Georges Florovsky and the Sophiological Controversy," *St. Vladimir's Theological Quarterly* 49: 67–100.

Kunkel, C. (1991) *Totus Christus: die Theologie Georges V. Florovskys*. Göttingen: Vandenhoeck and Ruprecht.

Nichols, A. (1999) "George Florovsky and the Idea of Tradition," in *Light from the East: Authors and Themes in Orthodox Theology*. London: Sheed and Ward, pp. 129–224.

Shaw, L. (1990) *An Introduction to the Study of Georges Florovsky*. Unpublished PhD thesis, University of Cambridge.

Zizioulas, J. (1997) "Fr. Georges Florovsky: The Ecumenical Teacher (in Greek)," *Synaxi* 64: 13–26.

Fools, Holy

JUSTIN M. LASSER

The term "holy fool" (Gk. *Salos*; Slav. *Iurodivye*) describes a distinctive and unusual phenomenon within Orthodox spirituality: the hagiographical account of saintly protagonists who, to all the world, look as if they are mad, so great is their departure from "normal" social standards. This revelatory stupidity of the Christian protagonist carries with it an impressive prehistory in both Israelite and Classical Hellenic society. The Hebrew prophets took it upon themselves of old to lambast the wealthy and powerful for ignoring justice while merely "honoring God with their lips" and priding themselves over pious subtleties. Accordingly, the prophets were often socially marginalized. It was a similar passion to point to the neglect of justice and expose the prevalence of false piety that drove the holy fool.

Like the Hebrew prophet, the Greco-Roman Cynic philosophical school had also established a robust critical apparatus within ancient Greek society. The greatest virtue, and weapon, of the Cynic philosopher was wit. Indeed, both the Holy Fool and his Cynic sage predecessor shared a rhetorical style of luring the unwary into their dialectical nets by teasing remarks, stinging barbs, and highly symbolic puzzling behavior. The founder of the Cynic school was Diogenes of Sinope, who could be seen walking the streets of Athens in broad daylight with a lighted lamp. If an unsuspecting observer asked him what he was doing he would receive the reply: "I am looking for an honest man!" before he, pointedly, moved off again on his disappointed search. The term "Cynic" derives

Plate 26 The Cathedral of St. Basil, Red Square, Moscow, dedicated to the Fool for Christ Basil of Mangazeia (d. 1552). Photo © ImageDesign/Shutterstock.

from the Greek word for dog, an epithet earned by the custom of the Cynic sages of barking at their allegedly civilized compatriots while themselves living a "natural" dog-like life of begging and grazing for scraps on which to subsist. The Cynic sages were notorious for the lengths to which they pushed this symbolism of the "return to nature" and were known to defecate in public and walk around naked, the latter being a trait which is repeated by several Christian holy fools and desert ascetics. St. Gregory Nazianzen, like most of the fathers of the church, studied the famous sayings of Diogenes, whose rhetorical wit was used in the schools to teach the arts of persuasion. Most masters of ancient rhetoric were trained in the *chreia* (sayings) technique (see Hock and O'Neil 2002), which are demonstrated in the Cynic apophthegms designed as "performance philosophy." These books of *Chreia* were the standard manuals of rhetoric in the time of the fathers, and they were used liberally. It is not surprising, therefore, that we can detect many resemblances between Cynic definitions of the performance of "the sage" and the life of the Christian "Sophist" as it later appeared in the hagiographies concerning holy fools. They belong, essentially, to the world of late Antiquity, though Christian hagiographical texts would propel the practice through the Middle Ages and even beyond in the Orthodox world. The parallels between Jesus' and the Cynic's use of sharp wit to make a telling point are instructive.

One of the earliest references to the holy fool is the story of the "Mad Nun of Tabennisi" as recorded in the Egyptian desert literature. A holy bishop visiting a convent is able to recognize that the allegedly mad and much despised nun who cleans in the kitchens is actually the leading spiritual sage of the community. After his revelation the community is suitably chastened, but the nun disappears to live unnoticed elsewhere. The first major literary account of a holy fool is found in the *Life of St. Symeon the Holy Fool* (d. 590), written by Leontius of Cyprus. Here we find classical motifs reminiscent of the Cynics, woven with deliberate parallels of the life of Jesus as imaged in the life of his disciple. Like Jesus, St. Symeon moved to the Judean desert with his companion John, where they lived an ascetic life of prayer. After many years, however, St. Symeon chose to leave his rigorous seclusion and return to the great city of Emesa. His companion is scandalized, but Symeon presents the choice as a divine mandate for the preaching of salvation to others, and as being a stage higher in the spiritual life than radical seclusion. He returns to the city dragging a "stinking dead dog" behind him, and begins a series of exploits that turn the life of the town upside down. He "liberates" bread for the poor from his employers; he raids the bath-house when it is women's day and is beaten by the female guards for forcing his way in among them (to demonstrate his passing beyond sexual temptation); he eats in a revolting way and passes wind ostentatiously. Most famously of all he waits in the church and at any sign of pious behavior he throws nuts at people. The odd actions annoy and stimulate the people to reflect. Symeon is presented as a fool in the eyes of the world, who is wise in the sight of God, for he has turned away to "mock the world" and remind his co-religionists that it is passing away. His voluntary debasement is a mark of witness undertaken for their benefit. We note the common element in the life of the fool, which is the embracing of suffering in imitation of the suffering Christ. The common theme of all lives of holy fools is that God sees where human superficiality cannot. The fool's antics serve to call for repentance, humility, and renewed sincerity in a tired church. Their deep interior life of holiness serves as a powerful force of intercession for their compatriots, which is usually only realized in retrospect – for they remain hidden and unappreciated while they are alive.

After Symeon came a series of holy fools. The *Life of Andrew the Scythian* (9th century) made a transition between the old Byzantine models (looking back to a classical past) and the newer Slavic Orthodox world which took to the idea enthusiastically. The holy fool was a vivid aspect of both ancient and modern Russian society and provided an important counterbalance to absolutist tendencies in both church and state. The beautiful Cathedral of St. Basil in Red Square, Moscow, is dedicated to the Fool for Christ Basil of Mangazeia (d. 1552), a saint who would bark at the cruelties of Tsar Ivan the Terrible, walk naked in winter, and shoplift for the benefit of the poor. Later Russian fools for Christ include St. Isidor of Rostov (d. 1474), St. Xenia of St. Petersburg (d. 1796), Feofil of Kiev (d. 1853), Terentii (d. 1886), Pelagia (d. 1884), and Pasha of Sarov (d. 1915). Comparatively there were very few renowned *Saloi* in the modern Greek tradition. Panagis Basias (d. 1888) is a rare exception (Gorainov 1993). In Tolstoy's *Boyhood and Youth* there is a beautiful recollection of a holy fool, whose peasant simplicity and dedication to prayer touches the heart of the young protagonist who had set out to laugh at him. More recently, Eastern Europe's long winter under Soviet persecution has provided many more examples of "holy fools" in the eyes of the wider society: saints who danced to their deaths, to silent obscurity and harsh imprisonment, or sank under officially imposed impoverishment because of their single-mindedness in following God. As in the icon of the Protecting Veil of the Theotokos, it was the holy fool alone who could see the heavenly life all around with clear eyes and courageous heart.

SEE ALSO: Charity; Monasticism; Protecting Veil; Repentance; Wealth

References and Suggested Readings

Gorainov, I. (1993) *Oi Dia Christon Saloi*. Athens: Tinos.

Hock, R. F. and O'Neil, E. N. (eds.) (2002) *The Chreia and Ancient Rhetoric: Classroom Exercises*. Atlanta: Society of Biblical Literature.

Ivanov, S. A. (2006) *Holy Fools in Byzantium and Beyond*, trans. S. Franklin. Oxford: Oxford University Press.

Krueger, D. (1996) *Symeon the Holy Fool: Leontius' Life and the Late Antique City*. Berkeley: University of California Press.

Saward, J. (1980) *Perfect Fools*. Oxford: Oxford University Press.

G

Georgia, Patriarchal Orthodox Church of

TAMARA GRDZELIDZE

The Church of Georgia has historically existed on territory situated between modern Turkey in the West, Armenia and Azerbaijan in the Southeast, and small Caucasian ethnic groups of the Russian Federation in the North. It is a church of a small nation and its land has long known hardship, yet also benefits from fellow Christians across its borders. Neighboring Byzantium once guaranteed its security, though not unconditionally nor unfailingly. Georgia was Byzantium's old ally in consolidating Christian forces against Islam in the East, and at certain moments of history it served beneficially in Georgian ecclesiastical and political matters. Georgia's relations with the Church of Armenia became problematic in the light of the theological tension in the aftermath of the Council of Chalcedon (451), and in spite of a significant attempt to find a compromise solution at the Council of Dvin (506) a lasting ecclesiastical division resulted after 609. Georgia's immediate neighbor, the Christian state of Russia, actively began seeking influence over the Caucasus after the fall of Constantinople (1453) and spread out powerfully, resulting in the gradual annexation of the Georgian kingdoms after 1801, and in the abolition of the longstanding autocephaly of the Church of Georgia in 1811. In 1921 Georgia was made one of the republics of the Soviet Union and the Orthodox Church of Georgia exercised a form of quasi-independence *vis-à-vis* other Orthodox churches, as well as within the ecumenical movement, but it was also seriously challenged and threatened by the Soviet ideology and anti-church repressions. It has been exercising its independence once more since 1991.

Language and Alphabet

The 5th-century Georgian language (*Kartuli*) preserved in the oldest manuscripts is not entirely alien to contemporary Georgians. Together with Megrelian, Svan, and Laz, it forms part of the Kartvelian group of southern Caucasian languages. The Georgian language has been one of the most important factors in the self-understanding and definition of Christians who spoke Georgian/Kartuli. In the 10th century, George the Canonist, author of *The Life of St. Gregory of Khandzta*, expressed it graphically: "The lands where church services are proclaimed in the Georgian (Kartuli) language constitute [the state of] Georgia (Kartli)." He thus stated the link between territorial integrity and the development of national identity, which has always defined the Georgian Church's sense of itself. In the surviving manuscripts scholars recognize three stages of development of the original script: Asomtavruli, Nuskhuri (from the 9th century),

The Concise Encyclopedia of Orthodox Christianity, First Edition. Edited by John Anthony McGuckin.
© 2014 John Wiley & Sons, Ltd. Published 2014 by John Wiley & Sons, Ltd.

and Mkhedruli (used today but originating from as early as the 12th century). The most commonly accepted theory of the development of the language is to connect the creation of the Asomtavruli script with the process of the first Christianization of Georgia under Byzantine influence.

Kartli/Iberia and Egrisi/Colkheti

When Christianity began to spread throughout Georgia, different principalities and regions accepted it in different degrees and under different circumstances. The leading role in the Christianization process was assigned to Kartli (or Iberia, as it was referred to in the Greek sources) in the east of the country. West Georgia, or Egrisi (otherwise named Colkheti or Lazika – the ancient goal of the Greek Argonauts who came to take the Golden Fleece), also received the gospel in the 4th century. Bishop Stratophilos of Bichvinta/Pitiunt (in Abkhazeti) was present at the Council of Nicea (325). Until the 9th century, western Georgia was under the jurisdiction of the patriarchate of Constantinople and deeply influenced by Byzantium. Some of the mountainous parts of Georgia received Christianity considerably later than the valley settlements between the Caucasian gorges. Written sources relating the conversion of Georgia are preserved in collections from the 10th century onwards.

St. Andrew's Visitation

In the 11th-century *Kartlis Tskhovreba* (Life of Kartli) it is said that:

> The holy Apostle Andrew set off and reached Atskhuri, earlier called Sosangeti, which lies opposite Sakrisi. He stopped to rest at a place that was a sanctuary of idols, and is now called the Old Church. The icon of the Holy Virgin lay in the fortress and great radiance could be seen there…. A great many people filled the valley of Sakrisi…. There was a sanctuary of idols in the town where their evil gods were worshipped…. But the great icon of the All Holy Virgin of Atskveri lay at a little church. (Licheli 1998)

This source refers to the arrival of the apostle Andrew in Samtskhe, southeastern Georgia, bringing with him the holy icon of the Mother of God. The archeological investigations carried out in the area between 1988 and 1991 gave support to the tradition witnessed in the text that in Samtskhe, at a very early time, the first Christian center was established on Georgian territory. The traditions of Georgia that focus on the preaching there of the Apostle Andrew also mention the preaching of the apostles Simon the Canaanite, Bartholomew, and Matthias.

The Life of St. Nino

St. Nino, known as the illuminator of Georgia, is one among a handful of women in the Orthodox tradition who are given the title of "Equal to the Apostles." Her mother Susanna served in the house of an Armenian woman, Miapar, in Jerusalem and married Zabulon, a famous Cappadocian general. When Nino turned 12 years old, the parents divorced, selling all their belongings and returning to settle in Jerusalem. Nino first served an Armenian woman in Dvin, then an Armenian of royal descent, and fled together with 50 other women to Armenia. Surviving the persecution of the Armenian King Trdat, Nino, following divine inspiration, turned towards Georgia and accepted the mission of evangelizing the people. After reaching Mtskheta, the capital of Iberia, Nino discovered that the local population worshipped the idols Armazi, Gatsi, and Gaim. Her *Vita* says that by the grace of her prayers Nino caused a great storm that destroyed the idols. She settled in the royal garden of King Mirian (today, this is the site of the Svetitskhoveli cathedral in Mtskheta), then moved near the bramble bush (today, the site of the Samtavro monastery), made a cross from the vine branches and preached the faith of Christ and performed miracles, one of which was the healing of Queen Nana. By this means Nana was turned to the faith of Christ and spoke about it to her husband, who remained an idol-worshipper until converted by a wonder: one day, while out hunting, the king was startled by a total eclipse of the sun. He prayed to the god of Nino and the light returned, and by this means he was convinced and accepted Christian faith. By this admission to the royal court,

Christianity thereafter became the official religion of Iberia and the first church was constructed within the royal gardens.

Emperor Constantine the Great (ca. 337) sent priests to baptize the royal family, the nobility, and the common people, and to establish political alliances. Three crosses were erected: on the hill where today the monastery of the Holy Cross (5th–6th centuries) is situated; on the mountain of Tkhoti, where King Mirian was converted; and in the town of Ujarma. The Iberian population of the lowlands took to the new religion quickly, though the mountain dwellers resisted for a longer time.

Conversion of Kartli (*Moqcevai Kartlisai*) and Life of Kartli (*Kartlis Tskhovreba*)

Although known from written sources of the 10th to 13th centuries (the *Conversion of Kartli* and the *Life of Kartli*), the three earliest layers of the Life of St. Nino probably derive from the 4th–5th centuries, from the end of the 5th century, and from the 7th century, respectively. At the cusp of the 4th and 5th centuries there existed a version of the Life of St. Nino which was known in Palestine. This version is reflected in the church history of Rufinus, who says: "At the time of Athanasius and Frumentius' mission to India, the Georgians who dwell in the region of Pontus accepted the word of God.... The cause of this was a woman captive who lived among them." Rufinus had lived for 24 years both in Egypt and Jerusalem, where he may well have come in contact with Iberians. Rufinus' version of the *Conversion of Kartli* was later copied by the Greek historians Socrates, Sozomen, and Theodoret. Recent scholarship has also traced links between Rufinus' Greek version and Gelasius of Caesarea. The versions of the Life of St. Nino as recorded in the sources of the 10th to 13th centuries show some distinctive if incompatible facts about her life; the common elements of the different versions include the healing activity of St. Nino, the vision of King Mirian, and the miracle of the pillar.

The texts of the *Conversion of Kartli* and a version of the *Life of St. Nino* by Leonti Mroveli contained in the

Life of Kartli both connect the establishment of Christianity in Kartli with the Jewish communities already resident there. When Christianity was established as a state religion in Kartli, it was introduced in its Hellenistic form, but significant Judeo-Christian traditions remain in the written sources (see Mgaloblishvili and Gagoshidze 1998) and speak eloquently of Semitic origins as also significant for the Georgian Church. In the 4th century Kartli was a constant ally of Byzantium in its ongoing struggle with Persia for influence in the Caucasus. The Truce of Nisibis made with the Persians in 298 had enabled Emperor Diocletian to benefit from forty years of peace in the eastern regions, including Armenia and Iberia. It was precisely during this period that Iberia declared Christianity an official state religion (326/330). According to her Life, Nino approached Kartli from the mountains of the southern province of Javakheti and stopped at Lake Paravani. Following the River Mtkvari, she is said to have arrived at Urbnisi, where she stayed a month with local Jewish inhabitants. It is also recorded that the very first Christian converts in Georgia were Jews: Abiatar, his daughter Sidonia, and her friends, who first recorded Nino's missionary activities. In this missionary environment Nino would probably have used Aramaic, the language of the local Jews, and from this basis may have learned some Georgian. The Prayer of St. Nino, some scholars think, reflects church practice prior to the Council of Ephesus (431). Also, the symbolism of the Feast of the Holy Cross as celebrated in Mtskheta reflects the liturgical rites of the ancient Jerusalem festival. Although the first bishops, priests, and deacons were sent as a mission to Iberia by Constantine the Great, the *Life of Nino* shows much affinity with the Church of Jerusalem. Georgian church tradition recounts that Elioz, a Jewish merchant from Mtskheta, brought with him from Jerusalem the robe of Christ, which was buried with his sister. The first church in Mtskheta, Svetitskhoveli, was built over her grave. In Kartli the first missionaries were linked to the Church of Palestine, and again reminiscences remain in the text of the *Vita*. All the significant points of the earthly life of Christ were subsequently to be used in topographically naming the area of Mtskheta: Bethlehem, Thabor, Bithynia, Gethsemane, and Golgotha. Liturgical linkages between Georgia and the Jerusalem Church seemed to be very strong until later times, when new associations with Byzantium in western and south-eastern parts of Georgia became remarkably close and overlaid them.

Georgian–Armenian Church Conflict

The confessional conflict between the two churches followed the adherence of the Church of Georgia to the Council of Chalcedon and the rejection of the latter by the Church of Armenia. At the council of Dvin in 506 the Georgians, Armenians, and Albanians accepted the Henoticon of Zeno (476–91), which attempted to set aside the divisive terms of the Chalcedonian council; but in 609, at the time of Catholicos Kirion I (ca. 614), the Georgians rejected their adherence to the non-Chalcedonian Christology (which they had formerly accepted under the pressure of political exigency, since they were under threat from the Persians, and King Vakhtang Gorgasali (ca. 502/3) tried all means at his disposal to show loyalty to the Byzantine emperor), accordingly accepting the Henoticon in 482. The churches in Armenia and Georgia became estranged after the 7th century. Territorial proximity between the two nations added extra tension to the confessional conflict, and after this era a level of intolerance, sometimes amounting to open hostility, can be traced in Georgian sources dealing with their neighbors. A number of tractates against the anti-Chalcedonian Christology began to appear in Georgian, some of them compilations of extracts from writings of the church fathers, while others are original works. The celebrated treatise *On the Division between Iberia and Armenia* was composed in the 9th century by Arsenios of Sapara. Confessional disputes between the two churches took place at the Council of Grtila in 1046 and again at the time of King David IV (1089–1125), with a number of Armenian and Georgian hierarchs involved in what were heated discussions. Such public disputes occurred again in the 18th century when the Armenian non-Chalcedonian influence reemerged. This confessional, inter-Christian struggle against the church of the adjacent country was undoubtedly

a factor that weakened the political life of Georgia throughout the Byzantine era.

Monasticism

The earliest origins of monastic life in Georgia are traditionally connected with the Syrian ascetic fathers who fled their own land in the face of a purge of non-Chalcedonians (540–2) and settled in Georgia. Before that time there are isolated mentions of Georgians living in monasteries outside the country. In Kartli the Syrians found confessional tolerance. Monastic foundations of the Syrian ascetics have survived to the present time and are scattered throughout East Georgia. The *Lives of the Syrian Fathers* have been preserved in shorter and longer versions, notably by Ioane of Zedazeni, Shio of Mgvime, Abibos of Nekresi, David of Gareja, Anthony of Martkopi, Ise of Tsilkani, and Joseph of Alaverdi. The earliest surviving ascetical literature in Georgian dates from the 7th century: notably the treatise *On Repentance and Humility* by the monk Martyrios. Between the 9th and 11th centuries monasticism in Georgia enjoyed its golden age.

St. Gregory of Khandzta

There are few figures in the life of the Church of Georgia whose activities can match those of Gregory of Khandzta. His life and work had a huge influence over the political and cultural development of the nation. Gregory revived monasticism in southeastern Georgia, especially in Tao-Klarjeti. Born in the 8th century into the family of one of the rulers of Kartli, Gregory was ordained priest at an early age and was prepared for episcopacy. However, he preferred the life of a hermit monk and fled from Iberia, going to Klarjeti with three disciples. The first place they founded was the monastery of Opiza, and after two years Gregory built a new monastery at Khandzta. During the difficult times of the Arab invasion of Iberia by Caliph Alf-Mamun (813–33), the Georgian ruler Ashot Bagrationi (ca. 830) moved his court to Klarjeti. Ashot was to be supported by the Byzantines and was given the high title of *Kouropalates*. The proximity of the royal court contributed greatly to the monastic revival in this region. Most of the existing monasteries were built during the reign of the son of Ashot, Bagrat (826–78). Shatberdi, Opiza, Daba, Bana, Parekhi, Doliskana, Jmerki, Berta, Tskarostavi, Baretelta, Mere, and Khandtza itself all became centers of spiritual revival at the time when Tbilisi, the capital of Iberia, lay under Arab siege. Today, a number of these churches lie within the territory of modern Turkey. Known as the "Georgian Sinai," they comprised an organizational matrix supervised by Gregory of Khandzta. From the 830s onwards he was named archimandrite of the twelve deserts. As his *Vita* poetically describes it: "By the rivers of his wisdom all the deserts of Klarjeti were irrigated." In the monasteries under his supervision Gregory introduced a Typikon based on those of St. Sabas in Palestine and the Studion at Constantinople. It was because of Gregory's efforts that after the 9th century the holy chrism was prepared in Georgia instead of importing it from Antioch (a sign of mature autocephaly of the Christians there). It was from their base in Tao-Klarjeti that the Georgian royal family of Bagrationis made strides towards the unification of the different Georgian lands. The nobility in Tao-Klarjeti fully supported the Georgian community on Mount Athos and funded the establishment of the Georgian monastery of Iviron (Greek for "Of the Iberians"). The 10th-century text of the *Life of St. Gregory of Khandzta* was rediscovered only in 1911 and remarkably amplified the history of the Church of Georgia in the 9th century.

Georgians outside of Georgia

Christian Georgians are known to have been present in Palestine from the 5th century. The oldest inscription in Georgian is actually found in mosaics at Jerusalem (433). The will of St. Sabas (ca. 532), founder of the Lavra in Palestine, states: "The Iberians and the Syrians cannot celebrate the liturgy in their own languages but should only read the Hours, the Typika, the Epistle and the Gospel in those tongues." Between the 8th and 10th centuries Iberian monks were actively involved in the life of St. Sabas monastery; as a result a special handwriting called *Sabatsmiduri* was created. Later, they were also present in the

Lavra of St. Chariton, the so-called "Palailavra." In the 6th to 7th centuries Georgians possessed the monastery of St. Theodore the Tyro in Bethlehem. Their monastery of the Holy Cross was built in the 11th century by Prochorios in Jerusalem itself. After the 9th century Georgian ascetics were also present on Mount Sinai; once again their literary activities resulted in a special handwriting, named *Sinaite*. Georgian monks were present on the Black Mountain in Antioch at the time of St. Symeon the Stylite (ca. 596) living in his monastery. In the 11th century there were purely Georgian monasteries on the Black Mountain (Romana, Kalipos, one in the desert, and at least two sketes of George the Recluse and his disciple Theodore) where George the Hagiorite stayed after resigning as the higoumen of Iviron, and where he gathered together a number of talented Georgian monks who left behind them a large collection of translations and other original writings. The most distinguished among this band were Ephrem the Younger and Arsenios of Ikalto. After the 13th century there are no more references to a Georgian presence on the Black Mountain. Two Georgian monasteries founded in Byzantine territory can be connected with Hilarion the Iberian: one on Mount Olympus in Bithynia (Asia Minor) where Hilarion arrived in 864, the other in Romana. In 1083 Gregory Bakuriansidze built the monastery now located in modern-day Bachkovo in Bulgaria.

Iviron on Mount Athos

The "Monastery of the Iberians," as it was then called, Iviron as it is now known, has long been a powerful symbol of the Georgian Church and culture. Although it remained in the full possession of Georgians only until the 1340s, Iviron both initiated and epitomized many precious things in Georgian history, not least the translation into Georgian and the correction (according to the Byzantine model) of liturgical and other spiritual texts. Through the exercise of Byzantine imperial patronage over the Holy Mountain, the Iberian ascetics and aristocrats maintained active links with the imperial capital. John the Iberian (ca. 1002) was with St. Athanasius, the founder of the Great Lavra (ca. 1000), at the time that the solitary monks on the peninsula started to accept large coenobitic settlements among them. Athanasius was a welcome patron to a small Georgian community and provided whatever they needed to live first in Kellia and then to establish their own monastery. The main patron for the building of Iviron was Tornike, a retired general from the family of the Chordvaneli in Tao, who was seeking peace for his soul and thus joined the Georgian monks on Mount Athos. Shortly after initiating his attempt to become an ascetic he was summoned back by his Georgian prince, David Kouropalates (ca. 1000/1), to lead an army in support of the young emperors Basil (ca. 1025) and Constantine (ca. 1028) in their fight against the revolt of Bardas Skleros. After consultation with Prince David and St. Athanasius of the Great Lavra, a new settlement for the Georgian community was inaugurated. The most remarkable higoumeni of Iviron were Euthymios (ca. 1028) the son of John the Iberian, and George (ca. 1066). Both contributed enormously to the enrichment of the Georgian Church and its spiritual writings. The world-renowned, and miraculous, icon of the Mother of God called *Portaitissa* ("Door-keeper") is one of the best-known treasures of Iviron. Today, it is a Greek monastery, but the library still preserves a number of ancient Georgian manuscripts.

Liturgical Traditions

Liturgical texts were translated into Georgian from as early as the 5th century. The major influence on liturgical practice in the Church of Georgia, at least until the 10th century, was Palestinian, the rite of the Church of Jerusalem. At Iviron, the Georgian community in the midst of the Athonite Greeks, the Typikon of the great cathedral of Hagia Sophia in Constantinople (known as the *Synaxarion*) was translated twice in the 11th century: a shorter version by Euthymios the Hagiorite and later a complete edition by George the Hagiorite. The Typikon of Iviron monastery also shows liturgical traces of the ritual practice of the Stoudion monastery in Constantinople. In the 12th century at the time of David IV, the Palestinian monastic Typikon of Mar Sabas was introduced and became widely used in Georgia. Gradually,

the Typikon of Mar Sabas was enriched by elements introduced from the Athonite Typikon and the synthesis remained as common practice until the mid 18th century, when it was corrected after the model of the Slav Typikon by Catholicos Anthony, during his stay in Russia. There are also Georgian Typika surviving from the ancient founders (Ktetors) such as Gregory of Khandzta (9th century) in the monastery of Tao-Klarjeti, Euthymios the Athonite (11th century) at Iviron, from Gregory Bakurianisdze (11th century) in the Petritsoni monastery in Bachkovo, Bulgaria, and the Typikon of the Vahani Caves (13th century) in south Georgia. Until the 10th century, Georgian lectionaries had a particular style of arranging their readings of Holy Scripture. The style is illustrated in the 7th-century Typikon from Jerusalem. Since the Church of Georgia generally followed Jerusalemite practice until after the 10th century, the most widely used liturgy was that of the Holy Apostle James, which was gradually replaced by the liturgies of St. Basil the Great and St. John Chrysostom. St James' Liturgy has been preserved in four Georgian versions (9th–11th centuries), all of them based on the Greek text composed between the sixth and seventh ecumenical councils. Euthymios the Hagiorite commented:

> The Liturgy of St. James is indeed the true one which was first used in Greece and also in our churches. When St. Basil and blessed John Chrysostom composed liturgies, people chose them because they were short and thus forgot St. James. Now all celebrate the Liturgy of St. Chrysostom, and the Liturgy of St. Basil during the Great Lent, but all those who wish to celebrate the liturgies of St. James and St. Peter are completely right to do so.

In the 11th century, therefore, the great Athonite authority still found it acceptable for the Georgians to celebrate the distinctive liturgies of St. James and St. Peter.

Georgian Literature and Arts

The Church of Georgia is proud of its numerous witnesses who have been canonized by the church across the centuries. The Lives of many of them were composed for following generations to learn about their faith in Christ. The oldest original hagiography is considered to be the *Martyrdom of St. Shushaniki* (Susanna). In 466 Varsqen, the ruler of Kartli/Iberia, visited the Persian Shah Peroz and was received into Zoroastrianism, renouncing his Christian faith. On his return home he found that his wife Shushaniki, daughter of the renowned Armenian General Vardan Mamikonian, had abandoned the palace in order to make her protest. Many representatives of Kartli society respected her stand, but they could not prevent her martyrdom. The Georgians ever afterwards accepted Shushaniki, an Armenian-born woman, as their own national witness. The church canonized her and her martyrdom was described by Jacob, a local priest and her spiritual guide in Tsurtavi. Shushaniki as a saint is shared with the Armenian Apostolic Church.

Also from the earliest literary period, the 6th century, there survives the *Martyrdom of St. Eustathios*, as described by an eyewitness of the events recorded in the text. At the end of the 8th century the *Martyrdom of Abo of Tbilisi* was written. He was an Arab by birth who came to Kartli, received Christianity, and openly confessed his faith at a time when Tbilisi was under Islamic rule. He was martyred in 786, and his martyrdom was described by Ioane Sabanisdze, one of his close friends.

From the first millennium there also survive the *Life of St. Gobroni*, the *Life of St. Serapion of Zarzma*, and the *Life of St. Gregory of Khandzta*. The 11th century witnessed the composition of the Lives of famous Georgian Athonites, notably John the Iberian, Euthymios, and George the Hagiorite. The longer versions of the Lives of the Syrian fathers were also composed in this same period. The second major period of Georgian hagiography occurred in the 18th century. At this time the Lives of the Georgian king martyrs Archil and Luarsab, and the *Martyrdom of Queen Ketevan*, were composed.

Georgian Christian Philosophy: Ioane Petritsi

Ioane Petritsi is the only Georgian philosopher in the authentic sense of that term whose works have been preserved from medieval times. While never questioning his Christian faith, he declared himself to be a follower of Aristotle; meaning that he strove to follow an empirical process for searching out new ideas. He was educated either at the philosophical academy founded by Emperor Constantine Monomachos in the brief period between 1045 and 1084, or by the immediate followers of this school, which roughly places his life somewhere between the second half of the 11th century and the early 13th century. Three authentic works survive under his name: a Georgian translation of the 4th-century text of Nemesius of Emesa, *On the Nature of Human Being*; an introduction to his translation of the Psalter; and a translation of, and commentaries on, the *Elements of Theology* by the 5th-century Neo-Platonist philosopher Proclus. Petritsi attempted to simplify the hierarchy of Proclus and cut through the disputes of the inner circles of Neo-Platonism, so as to present a homogenized overview that by and large adheres to Proclus more than Plotinus. Believing in the truth of Christ but also believing in the truths of Neo-Platonism, Petritsi tried to synthesize Christian faith and philosophical speculation. His approach is bold and creative. He was persecuted in his day, but still managed to leave behind students of his philosophical theology.

Georgian Christian Art

A number of churches in Georgia are considered among the finest examples of Christian architecture in the world, notably Bolnisi Sioni (5th century), Holy Cross in Mtskheta (6th–7th centuries), Tsromi and Bana (7th century), Gurjaani and Vachnadziani All Saints (8th–9th centuries), Oshki, Khakhuli, Kumurdo, and Mokvi (10th century), and the cathedrals of Bagrati in Kutaisi, Svetitskhoveli in Mtskheta, and Alaverdi in Kakheti (11th century). The earliest surviving Christian buildings are 4th-century martyr shrines in Bodbe and Nekresi, which set out elements that would be reproduced in the most of the 5th–6th century churches in Georgia, as well as in those of Armenia, Mesopotamia, and the High Plateau of Asia Minor. This was a style that remained alien to Constantinople. The so-called *Antiokia* (Antioch) Church in Mtskheta is a simple vaulted, single-nave structure with two wide openings on the south side, and was built around 420. It provides the earliest example of horseshoe-shaped arches made of smoothly hewn stone blocks. Bolnisi Cathedral, a basilica of considerable size, with five pairs of piers and a projecting apse, was built between 478 and 493. From the second half of the 6th century the domed church structure became the most common type of church building. The Svetitskhoveli Cathedral has ancient roots in Georgian church life, and is today dedicated to the twelve apostles. It is the descendant of the church that was built over Nino's first place of residence in the royal gardens of King Mirian, and was eventually replaced by a large domed church in the 11th century. Its title of "life-giving pillar" refers to the tradition that one of its wooden pillars was made out of the wood of a cedar that once grew over the shrine of the robe of Christ. Other aspects of Christian art were also developed from early times in Georgia: iconography, monumental painting, magnificent manuscript illuminations, the art of enameling, stone-carving, and polyphonic church singing.

The Autocephaly of the Georgian Church

Christianity in Iberia was first formally organized as part of the jurisdictional remit of the great church of Antioch and of All the East. The Antiochian bishop Eustathius consecrated the first bishop in Iberia and until the 480s all Georgian bishops were consecrated in Antioch and sent to Iberia. Ecclesiastical reforms were carried out by King Vakhtang Gorgasali in the 5th century, who petitioned Byzantine Emperor Zeno (476–91) and Patriarch of Constantinople Akakios (471–89) to appoint a Greek priest, Peter, as *catholicos* in Iberia. The patriarch of Antioch, through the mediation of the patriarch of Constantinople, consecrated the first catholicos of Kartli together with a body of 13 bishops. The catholicos resided in Mtskheta. By this means, the Church of Georgia was granted partial independence, comparable to what is now called autonomous status (though this term was introduced to make a distinction from autocephaly only after the 19th century). The number of eparchies increased and a local synod was established with the

catholicos as its head. According to the Antiochene canonist and patriarch Theodore Balsamon (1140–95), "When the Lord Peter was the Holy Patriarch of the great and godly city of Antioch, the Synod decided to make the Church of Iberia autocephalous." The patriarch he refers to must be Peter the Fuller (ca. 488). Even so, the church in Iberia did not gain complete independence from the mother church of Antioch. Until the 740s the Antiochian patriarch was commemorated at the liturgy and a locally elected catholicos of Mtskheta had to be confirmed by the synod of the Church of Antioch. Annual payment of 1,000 drahkanis was made to the Church of Antioch even after the 8th century and the holy chrism was imported from Antioch until the 9th century.

This situation of continuing canonical dependence was altered after the 11th century, when the catholicos of Mtskheta spread out his jurisdiction over western Georgia. Since then, the head of the Autocephalous Church of Georgia has been the catholicos-patriarch of all Georgia, and the church has been fully independent in its domestic and foreign affairs, with the exception of the period between 1811 and 1917. Melchisedek I (1010–33) was the first catholicos-patriarch of all Georgia. In 1811, following the annexation (in 1801) of the Kartl-Kakheti and Imereti kingdoms by the Russian Empire, the autocephaly of the Orthodox Church of Georgia was abolished little by little by political pressure until it became merely an exarchate of the Russian Orthodox Church. In 1811, after the Russian annexations, the autocephaly of the Church of Georgia was dissolved, and it was made subject to the holy synod of the Russian Orthodox Church – in violation of the eighth canon of the third ecumenical council. The administrative system of the church in the Russian Empire differed fundamentally from that of the church in Georgia. Following the reforms of Emperor Peter I (1689–1725), the patriarchal office was abolished in 1721 and collegial management was introduced through a governmental synod which, after 1722, was led by a layman called the over-procurator. In 1784 Empress Catherine II subordinated the church to the state apparatus on an even larger scale than before. Under her rule all church and monastic property was confiscated. As a result the state inherited thousands of peasants and vast estates. Similar changes were planned to be implemented in Georgia.

By contrast, the Georgian Church resembled a large-scale feudal organization. It was regulated by the catholicos-patriarch, or occasionally by a member of the royal dynasty of the Bagrationis who had unlimited rights. The Orthodox Church of Georgia owned large arable lands and pastures, forests, mills, fishing areas, candle factories, and other property, which gave it a significant independence. Besides, the secular authorities almost never interfered in the management of the church; it was the catholicos-patriarch who controlled all affairs at his own discretion. In the 1900s, when Georgian clergy and historians renewed the struggle to restore Georgia's autocephaly, the matter was raised in St. Petersburg before the Russian Church and the secular authorities. Certain Russian hierarchs at that time attempted to prove that up until 1811 the Orthodox Church of Georgia was subordinate to the Antiochian patriarchate and had never been autocephalous. Within the Russian Church, however, there existed an alternative opinion on its history. Professor I. Berdnikov, the noted canon lawyer, wrote: "Whatever the civil government be – whether secular or Christian – it has no right to interfere with Church affairs. Above all it must not pass any laws or make other governmental decisions on any aspect of Church life including its administration." In March 1917, in the aftermath of the Russian October Revolution, the Georgian hierarchs convoked an assembly in which secular persons participated along with the clergy. The assembly declared the autocephaly restored. However, the Russian Orthodox Church did not recognize the autocephaly of the Church of Georgia until 1943; the ecumenical patriarchate not until 1990. On January 23, 1990 the synod of the Church of Constantinople made a decision to recognize the autocephaly of the Georgian church and to rank its head as the catholicos-patriarch of all Georgia. The issue of Georgian autocephaly has now been resolved among the Orthodox, but the issue of diptychs still remains unclear. According to 13th-century Georgian documents, and the diptychs used at the Council of Florence-Ferrara in 1438, the see of Mtskheta was ranked in sixth place of historical honor among the Orthodox churches. After the recognition of its autocephaly by the Russian Orthodox Church, the Church of Georgia was reinstated in the sixth rank of honor among the churches, although this has not been recognized universally in the Orthodox family today.

Present Circumstances

In 1921, when Bolshevik Soviet rule was applied in Georgia, the church had 2,455 parishes. Soon they were systematically silenced and suppressed until the church was in a terrible condition. Christian practice has dramatically increased since 1977, when Ilya II became catholicos-patriarch of Georgia. He encouraged a revival of daily devotion by writing a popular prayer book, and he instituted reforms to enable the Georgian Orthodox Church to regain its role in social life and recapture its prestige in society. These reforms, which began with a confrontation with Soviet ideology, led to a revival of monastic life. In 1977 there were four Georgian monasteries with a complement of 20 monks and nuns; in 1988 that rose to seven monasteries and 55 monks and nuns; and in 2003, 65 monasteries with 250 monks and nuns. A great number of churches were reopened. In 1977 there were 25 parishes with 50 clergy; in 1988, 200 parishes with 180 clergy; and in 2003, 550 parishes with 1,100 clergy. Today, the church owns its own newspapers, journals, a publishing house and radio station, a TV channel, and a university. The Constitution of Georgia written in 1995 reaffirmed freedom of religion (including rights for Roman Catholics, Baptists, Muslims, and Jews), yet specifically mentions "the special role of the Orthodox Church in the history of Georgia." In a 2002 agreement between the church and the state, the Church of Georgia received the status of *primus inter pares*. The church is now governed according to the Statutes of Governance (1995) of the Orthodox Autocephalous Church of Georgia.

Since the middle of the 1980s the church has canonized a number of martyrs from the 19th and 20th centuries, such as Ilya the Righteous (Chavchavadze), a writer and public figure assassinated in 1907, who contributed to many spheres of Georgian life, especially to the national-liberation movement and the restoration of the autocephaly of the Georgian church. Among the new martyrs of Georgia are the 19th-century hierarchs Gabriel (Kikodze, 1896) and Alexander (Okropiridze, 1907). The primates of the church who restored autocephaly (March 1917) for only a few years before the Russian Red Army took over the country (1921) also rank as martyrs: the catholicos-patriarchs Kirion (Sadzaglishvili, 1921), Leonide (Okropirisdze, 1921), and Ambrosi (Khelaia, 1927). Many priests were canonized who had witnessed to their faith even at the cost of death; notable among them was Archimandrite Grigol (Peradze, 1942). The primate of the Georgian Orthodox Church today is Ilya II (Shiolashvili) catholicos-patriarch of all Georgia, archbishop of Mtskheta and Tbilisi. The holy synod of the church consists of 16 metropolitans, 10 archbishops, 10 bishops, and 37 dioceses. The overall population of Georgia is approximately 4.6 million, of whom 83.9 percent are Orthodox, 3.9 percent Armenian-Georgian, 0.8 percent Roman Catholic, 0.3 percent Baptist, 0.25 percent other forms of Protestant, 9.9 percent Muslim, 0.25 percent Jews, and 0.7 percent self-describing as non-religious.

SEE ALSO: Armenian Christianity; Russia, Patriarchal Orthodox Church of

References and Suggested Readings

Gigineishvili, L. (2007) *The Platonic Theology of Ioane Petritsi*. Piscataway, NJ: Gorgias Press.

Kekelidze, K. (1960) *History of Georgian Literature*, vol. 1. Tbilisi: Sabchota Sakartvelo.

Lerner, C. (trans.) (2004) *The Wellspring of Georgian Historiography: The Early Medieval Historical Chronicle, The Conversion of Kartli and the Life of St. Nino*. London: Bennet and Bloom.

Licheli, V. (1998) "St. Andrew in Samtskhe – Archaeological Proof?" in T. Mgaloblishvili (ed.) *Ancient Christianity in the Caucasus, Iberica Caucasia*, vol. 1. Richmond, UK: Curzon.

Mgaloblishvili, T. and Gagoshidze, I. (1998) "The Jewish Diaspora and Early Christianity in Georgia," in T. Mgaloblishvili (ed.) *Ancient Christianity in the Caucasus, Iberica Caucasia*, vol. 1. Richmond, UK: Curzon.

Glykophilousa

NIKI J. TSIRONIS

The term refers to the specific iconographic type of the Virgin Theotokos, where Mary is shown holding the Christ child tenderly in her arms. Literally, in Greek the term means "the one kissing sweetly" and corresponds to the more notable aspect of tenderness expressed in this specific iconic pattern, although one sometimes finds little direct relevance between iconographic type and the epithet employed as an inscription. The Glykophilousa typology expresses developments related to the growing cult of the Virgin during and after the Iconoclastic period, when the figure of Mary was employed by writers defending the Iconophile cause on the basis of incarnational theology.

SEE ALSO: Icons; Theotokos, the Blessed Virgin

Gnosticism

JUSTIN M. LASSER

The term *gnosticism* derives from the Greek *gnosis*, which can be translated as "knowledge" or "wisdom." *Gnosis* commanded a variety of uses and applications in pre-Christian Hellenistic schools. The concept of *gnosis*, however, was never the possession of any one school; nor did there ever exist a particular group that condemned *gnosis per se*; rather, each group of teachers in the ancient world sought to lay claim to the "true" *gnosis* in their own unique way. The knowledge expressed by *gnosis* is not some form of secret knowledge as is often assumed, but a certain enlightened perspective. The Orthodox claimed their own form of *gnosis*, as expressed by figures such as Clement of Alexandria and Irenaeus of Lyons, whereas competing theologians, such as Valentinus and Heracleon, claimed their own. The early Orthodox heresiologists were concerned with protecting their faithful from what they considered dangerous corruptions of Christian theology. These early heresiologists wrote treatises detailing and exposing the theological systems of the "gnosis false so-called," as Irenaeus and other fathers called it (Irenaeus, *Adversus Haereses*; Tertullian, *On the Prescription of the Heretics*; Hippolytus, *Refutation of all Heresies*). The modern term *Gnosticism*, and the presupposition that it was a single school of thought, is largely the creation of 19th-century scholarship often falsely extrapolating data it has synthesized from the heresiologists' hostile accounts. These presuppositions have been extensively challenged by contemporary scholarship.

For centuries scholars interested in the gnostics had to rely on the works of ancient writers who opposed the movement. This changed in 1945, however, with the discovery of the Nag Hammadi codices in Upper Egypt near what was once the first Pachomian monastery at Chenoboskion. These codices challenged many of the presentations of the early heresiologists. The Nag Hammadi collection contains a great variety of texts which cannot be described as gnostic in any meaningful sense (fragments of Plato's *Republic*, the *Sentences of Sextus*, and so on). This discovery revealed that the Nag Hammadi library was not necessarily a "gnostic collection" in the first place, also that the gnostics were hardly a coherent or theologically consistent group. The Nag Hammadi codices produced two main currents of modern research in the study of the gnostics: the first seeks to harmonize the diverse Nag Hammadi texts into a coherent theological system, and the second seeks to attend to the uniqueness of each single treatise within the corpus of finds. Scholars working within the second trajectory have questioned the basic relevance of the term *gnosticism* altogether. From the close study of the Nag Hammadi texts it would seem that Irenaeus, in his time, was critiquing primarily one particular gnostic group, those associated with the teacher Valentinus. Apart from Valentinus, about whom there is much confusion as to what he taught, there really exist only two groups of gnostics that can be discussed with any precision: the Manicheans and the Mandaeans, the latter of which still survives in modern Iraq.

The primary difference between early gnostic and Orthodox theology seems to concern the status of the material world. For the Orthodox, the material world is good (Gen. 1.31) and created directly by God, but for the gnostics the material world was generally the result of a cosmic accident, and produced at several removes from the True and beneficent God. This belief in the accidental character of materiality needs to be distinguished from the belief that the material world was evil; the latter being the position of Marcion and Mani, not necessarily held by all the gnostics. The Valentinian theology concluded from the evil and suffering that existed in the world that something drastic had gone wrong in its production.

In this theology Valentinus was attempting to "protect" God from the responsibility of cosmic disasters by radically demarcating the Unknown and Transcendent True God from the material world. The gnostic systems were generally more comfortable with personifying the various attributes of God (hypostatization) than the early Orthodox fathers were, though Orthodox theology is itself familiar with this form of personification in relation to its biblically found examples, such as the designation of the Wisdom of God as Sophia. Sophia also played a seminal role in many of the gnostic systems as the expression of the Wisdom of God as a distinct hypostasis (see St. Irenaeus, *Adversus Haereses* I, 2). Despite their hostile reaction to the gnostic teachers, the gnostic thinkers did provide the church with a significant part of the technical vocabulary that it would borrow and use itself in new ways to articulate the mysteries of the Divine Trinity.

The Orthodox anxiety about gnosticism in general faded away by the late 3rd century as the prolixity of philosophically speculative schools in Late Antiquity itself declined in the light of the massive economic collapse and the incessant civil wars that racked the 3rd-century empire. By the time of the new empire of Constantine, in the Golden Age of the fathers of the church, the Orthodox theologians were able to look back on Irenaeus as a definitive "response" to the problems of the Pseudo-Gnosis, even though he was no longer much read by that stage. It was Clement and Origen, however, who in many ways can be seen as bringing the best of the gnostic insights into the mainstream, and censuring what they saw as their greatest threats to Orthodoxy. Irenaeus had abstracted from his localized anti-gnostic reactions certain broader principles that he recommended and which would become constitutive of all later Orthodoxy. Three of them can be listed in particular. The first was the apostolic succession of an ordered line of bishops. By this he meant bishops in a delineated tradition, a conservative line of teachers that the larger churches recognized and could list, a practice Eusebius underlines in his *Church History*, and thus which excluded speculative innovators from arising to proclaim "new" doctrine. The bishops were now afforded the sole right to speak for authentic Orthodox doctrine. Irenaeus thus put the episcopal principle of church authority on a significant new footing, which it would never lose in later Orthodox history. The second of the large anti-gnostic reactions was the underscoring of the need for a limit to what scriptures would be regarded as holy, and which would thus be read in the gatherings for worship. Irenaeus greatly advanced, therefore, the church's passage to a closed canon of scripture, which Athanasius, Gregory the Theologian, and Amphilokios helped to finalize with precision in the late 4th century. Irenaeus, aided in this greatly by Origen and the later Alexandrian fathers, made the focus of all Orthodox theology the earthly and directly personal incarnation of the Logos. This christocentricity gave Orthodox thought thereafter a very concrete and historical rootedness, less speculative and more grounded in the sayings tradition of the four gospels. Despite Origen's popularizing of symbolic exegesis (in his deliberate attempt to bring Valentinian patterns of scripture commentary into the mainstream Orthodox world) the Orthodox largely rejected the Gnostic preference for highly symbolistic and cosmological readings of the scriptures in preference for moral interpretations; and in affirming the substantive unity of Old and New Testaments, the Orthodox drew a strong line of connection between God as Maker and Sustainer, and the creation in which he was profoundly and continuingly involved. The first stanza of the Nicene Creed reflects this position starkly and boldly. The third principle was what Irenaeus called the priority of the *regula fidei*, or the manner in which established liturgical practice (especially the simple baptismal creed) ought to be held up against doctrinal speculation as a rule or canon of judgment. All of these things became constitutive of mainline Orthodox belief.

So, while the Orthodox rejection of many Gnostic propositions helped them to affirm a more positive and direct link between God and the world, and taught them to erect as defensive shields the organizing principles of canonical scripture, episcopal authority, and the primacy of liturgy, nevertheless the story of the interaction is not all one way, and not entirely a question of wholesale rejection. The wide ranging insights of the gnostic movements taught the Orthodox Church much about the importance of establishing principles of exegesis. It also led many in the intellectual ascetic movement to treasure mystical insights concerning the vastly cosmic nature of the battle of good and evil, and the divine presence in the soul. Its encounter with gnosticism, in short, took Orthodox theology out of its somewhat narrow perimeters of the 2nd century, towards a much larger perspective of thought appropriate to its new role, after the 4th century, as the mainstream of Christian religious reflection.

SEE ALSO: Apostolic Succession; Ecology; Episcopacy; Fatherhood of God; Heresy; Sophiology

References and Suggested Readings

Edwards, M. J. (2009) *Catholicity and Heresy in the Early Church*. Farnham, UK: Ashgate Press.

King, K. L. (2003) *What is Gnosticism?* Cambridge, MA: Harvard University Press.

Lawson, J. (1948) *The Biblical Theology of St. Irenaeus*. London: SPCK.

Robinson, J. M. (ed.) (1990) *The Nag Hammadi Library*, revd. edn. San Francisco: Harper.

Rudolph, K. (1987) *Gnosis: The Nature and History of Gnosticism*. San Francisco: Harper.

Steenburg, M. C. (2008) *Irenaeus on Creation: The Cosmic Christ and the Saga of Redemption*. Leiden: Brill.

Gospel

THEODORE G. STYLIANOPOULOS

"Gospel" (from the Anglo-Saxon "god-spell") or "evangel" (from the Greek *euangelion*) defines the central message of Christianity: the "good news" of God's gift of salvation (John 3.16). The essence of the gospel is God's gracious liberation of humanity from the powers of sin and death, and its restoration and communion with God in Christ and the Spirit. The centrality of Christ and his saving work, prophesied in the Old Testament and revealed in the New, means that the gospel message is proclaimed not only in the scriptures, but also, properly speaking, in all aspects of the church's life which are intrinsically evangelical – her identity, worship, sacraments, mission, creed, theology, and practice. Although the term "gospel" (*euangelion*) occurs most frequently in Paul, the primary sources of the gospel are the four canonical gospels – Matthew, Mark, Luke, and John – each of which as a book is also called "gospel." The same term also designates in the Orthodox Church the separately printed gospel lectionary (the annual cycle of selected readings from the four gospels, distinct from the parallel lectionary called Apostle – *apostolos*). The term "gospel" is also customarily applied to the specific lesson from the gospel lectionary recited in worship and often to the sermon itself.

The first allusion to the gospel, traditionally called "first gospel" (*proto-euangelion*), is found in Genesis 3.15 announcing God's promise that Eve's offspring, the Messiah, will crush the serpent's head while the serpent will strike the Messiah's heel. A focal and explicit reference to the good news is Isaiah 7.15 concerning Emmanuel, "God-with-us," born of a virgin (*parthenos*, *LXX*), fulfilled in the virginal conception and birth of Jesus by Mary (Matt. 1.23). The Old Testament generally looks forward to a great future era when God's good news will be proclaimed (*euangelizesthai*, Isa. 61.1 and Ps. 95.1–3, *LXX*), a day when God would decisively defeat evil and establish his rule over all the nations, ushering in an age of universal justice and peace. However, it is the New Testament that provides the theological angle from which innumerable references to Old Testament texts are freely and variously cited as messianic, that is, texts that prefigure the good news of God's promised salvation, fulfilled in the ministry of Jesus and the life of the early church, including the preaching of the gospel itself (Rom. 10.8/Deut. 30.14, *LXX*).

Mark announces that the whole narrative of Jesus' ministry is gospel (*euangelion*, Mark 1.1). Luke chooses the verb *euangelizesthai* for the good news of the Savior's birth (Luke 1.10–11). In Matthew and Mark, and also Luke but without the same terminology, Jesus begins his public ministry with the announcement that the dawn of the awaited age of salvation is fulfilled in him (Matt. 4.17; Mark 1.14–15; Luke 4.16–21). John presents Christ as the incarnation of the eternal Logos or Word of God who mediates the very presence and power of God as grace, glory, truth, light, bread, life, and love (John 1.1–18; 3.16; 8.12; 17.24–26). The witness of the four gospels confirms that the entire ministry of Jesus is good news for humanity, which is the very reason why these documents themselves were eventually named gospels. Their titles "Gospel according to Matthew," "Gospel according to Mark," and so forth, derive from the 2nd century, and signify both the essential unity of the gospel message and the freedom of the evangelists to narrate Jesus' ministry from their own perspective.

The heart of the gospel, distinguishable by content, blessings, and demands, is Christ and his saving work. The content is the person of Christ himself in whom God's rule or kingdom is inaugurated. Jesus not only announced but also enacted the good news of the dawn of God's rule, bestowing blessings in forgiving sinners, healing the sick, eating with the outcast, instructing the ways of God's righteousness, anticipating his death and resurrection as the cosmic defeat of evil, and gathering around him followers who formed the nucleus of the church. Jesus' gospel, proclaimed as the "word of God," included radical demands most notably recorded in the Sermon on the Mount (Matt. 5–7). Jesus challenged his followers to take up their cross, pray for persecutors, freely forgive others, tend to the needy, and love enemies, to be worthy of him and not risk being cast out of the kingdom (Matt. 7.21–23; 16.24–26; 25.11–12, 46).

St. Paul is the foremost preacher of the gospel that he calls the gospel of God or gospel of Christ. For Paul, the content of the gospel is Jesus Christ as Son of God and universal Lord in whom the awaited future age has been decisively established through his death and resurrection (Rom. 1.1–4; 8.31–34; 1 Cor. 15.1–4). Received by faith, the gospel is actualized in baptism and lived out as spiritual worship of God (Rom. 1.16–17; 6.1–11; 12.12). The results or benefits of the gospel are expressed through a rich terminology: salvation, justification, redemption, expiation, reconciliation, adoption, sanctification, transformation, new creation, and the fruit of the Spirit such as love, peace, and joy. (Rom. 3.21–26; 5.1–11; 1 Cor. 1.30; 2 Cor. 3.18; 5.17; Gal. 5.22–23). But the gospel, both as announcement and summons, also called "word of God" and "heralding" (*kerygma*), entails serious demands: to put to death sinful deeds or risk losing Christ and the kingdom (Rom. 6.12–23; 8.12–13; 1 Cor. 6.9–10; Gal. 5.19–21, 24).

Finally, the gospel includes the good news of the birth of the church which is the body of Christ and the temple of the Holy Spirit (1 Cor. 3.16; 12.27). Church and gospel belong together. The gospel is the gospel of God, bearing God's power, and grounded in God's saving acts in Christ and the Spirit. But the church also is the "Church of God" (1 Cor. 1.2), an intrinsic part of God's saving work and thus constitutive of God's revelation. Without the church there is no gospel to be preached. But without the gospel, there is no church worthy of God's loving will and grand plan to save the world.

SEE ALSO: Bible; Christ; Church (Orthodox Ecclesiology); Cross; Evangelism; Resurrection; Soteriology

References and Suggested Readings

Breck, J. (1986) *The Power of the Word in the Worshiping Church*. Crestwood, NY: St. Vladimir's Seminary Press.

Dunn, J. D. G. (1998) *The Theology of Paul the Apostle*. Grand Rapids, MI: Eerdmans.

Hengel, M. (2000) *The Four Gospels and the One Gospel of Jesus Christ: An Investigation of the Collection and Origin of the Canonical Gospels*. Harrisburg, PA: Trinity Press.

Kesich, V. (1992) *The Gospel Image of Christ*. Crestwood, NY: St. Vladimir's Seminary Press.

Stylianopoulos, T. G. (2002) *The Way of Christ: Gospel, Spiritual Life and Renewal in Orthodoxy*. Brookline, MA: Holy Cross Orthodox Press.

Trakatellis, D. (1987) *Authority and Passion: Christological Aspects of the Gospel According to Mark*. Brookline, MA: Holy Cross Orthodox Press.

Wright, N. T. (2005) *Paul in Fresh Perspective*. Minneapolis: Fortress Press.

Grace

STEPHEN THOMAS

An important local council held on Mount Athos in 1341 defined grace as "God's deifying gift … uncreated … eternally existent, proceeding from the eternally existing God" (Ware et al. 1995: 419). Grace is aligned with the rays of the Divine Trinity, the *energies*, put forth by the Persons. These are the uncreated operations of God (Stăniloae 1994: 125–39; Lossky 1998: 67–90) which transform those they encounter by divine light. Christ's transfiguration on the mountain was not only a manifestation of his divinity but a demonstration of what is possible for the believer who pursues the contemplative life in *hesychasm*, or stillness. The 1341 council was concerned about what "hesychasts" might experience without delusion. Against Barlaam the Calabrian, St. Gregory Palamas's

teaching was affirmed: even in this life, one may experience the uncreated light of God, at least for a time.

However, even in heaven, the blessed never know the divine essence, so that the Latin doctrine of beatific vision is foreign to Orthodoxy (Aquinas 2002: 118, 185). What we have instead in heaven is the uninterrupted experience of the energies which were experienced only occasionally and for a time in the earthly life: in heaven, grace is complete, the divine light shining uninterruptedly, so that the blessed cannot fall back or lapse. Conversely, those who have rejected God also experience the same light of grace, but as fire. Grace is enlightening or caustic, depending upon the state of the recipient.

Orthodox writers oppose "uncreated grace" to the erroneous doctrine of "created grace" of scholastic theology and the Latin West. Roman Catholics may be surprised to learn that they believe in created grace, since they generally regard it as supernatural. However, there are nuances which give substance to the Orthodox generalizations. Aquinas' approach is an intellectual one. He tries to explain by efficient causality the manner by which grace comes into existence in the soul, so that something in the soul is, in a sense, made: grace is *a certain something supernatural* coming from God (Aquinas 1997 [ST I–II.110]).

Grace is offered universally, even to the Devil (Grégoire de Nysse 2000: 262, n.2), but is not irresistible. Divine predestination expresses the foresight and desire of God but does not determine the outcome absolutely. Free will and agreement, the energy of the created being, is necessary for salvation, which comes through *synergy*, the union of divine grace and human will. It is a position which marks off Orthodoxy from the classic formulations about predestination of Reformed Christianity.

SEE ALSO: Hesychasm; Judgment; St. Gregory Palamas (1296–1359)

References and Suggested Readings

Aquinas, St. Thomas (1997) *Basic Writings of Saint Thomas Aquinas, Volume 2*, ed A. C. Pegis. Indianapolis: Hackett.

Aquinas, St. Thomas (2002) *Aquinas's Shorter Summa. St. Thomas's Own Concise Version of His Summa Theologica*. Manchester, NH: Sophia Institute Press.

Grégoire de Nysse (2000) *Discours catéchétique*, ed. R. Winling. Sources Chrétiennes 453. Paris: Cerf.

Lossky, V. (1998) *The Mystical Theology of the Eastern Church*. Crestwood, NY: St. Vladimir's Seminary Press.

Stăniloae, D. (1994) *The Experience of God*. Brookline, MA: Holy Cross Orthodox Press.

Ware, K., Palmer, G. E. H., and Sherrard, P. (eds. and trans.) (1995) *The Philokalia, Volume* 4. London: Faber and Faber.

Great Week

SOTIRIOS A. VLAVIANOS

Great Week (or Holy Week) is the most important part of the liturgical year for the Eastern Churches. It belongs to the moveable liturgical cycle and follows the Holy and Great Lenten period, beginning with Palm Sunday and ending on Great Saturday evening before the Divine Liturgy of the Resurrection (Pascha). It includes prolonged services, which are rich in liturgical material and symbolism. Every day a special event is commemorated: Joseph the all-beautiful and the cursing of the barren fig-tree (Great Monday), the wise and foolish virgins of the parable (Great Tuesday), the anointing of Jesus by the sinful woman (Great Wednesday), the Last Supper and the institution of the Eucharist (Great Thursday), the crucifixion (Great Friday), and the burial and the appearance of the resurrected Christ to the myrrh-bearing women (Great Saturday). A strict fast is observed throughout Great Week and xerophagy (eating dry or uncooked food, such as fruit and nuts) is practiced during the last three days. Many Orthodox, especially monastics, would not eat at all on Great Friday, others only after the afternoon service.

SEE ALSO: Fasting; *Pentekostarion*; Resurrection; *Triodion*

References and Suggested Readings

Calivas, A. (1992) *Great Week and Pascha in the Greek Orthodox Church*. Brookline, MA: Holy Cross Orthodox Press.

Schmemann, A. (1961) *Holy Week: A Liturgical Explanation for the Days of Holy Week*. Crestwood, NY: St. Vladimir's Seminary Press.

Webrew, H. (1997) *Orthodox Lent Holy Week and Easter: Liturgical Texts and Commentary*. Crestwood, NY: St. Vladimir's Seminary Press.

Greece, Orthodox Church of

JAMES C. SKEDROS

The Church of Greece is an autocephalous Orthodox Church headed by an archbishop (of Athens) and a holy synod, with jurisdiction over the majority of Orthodox Christians living in the modern state of Greece.

Christianity in the Greek peninsula dates back to apostolic times and has its origin in the missionary activity of Apostle Paul. The very names of his New Testament epistles attest to the earliest of the churches, such as those at Corinth, Thessalonica, or Philippi. He preached at the Areopagus in Athens. Intermittent historical references and limited archeological finds attest to the presence of Greek-speaking Christian communities on mainland Greece during the first three centuries of the universal church's life. From the 4th through the early 8th centuries, Greece and its islands (Illyricum) were under the ecclesiastical authority of Rome, with the metropolitan of Thessaloniki serving as papal vicar for the region. From ca. 730 onwards, Greece came within the ecclesial orbit of the patriarchate of Constantinople and its cultural, linguistic, and liturgical identity became firmly rooted in the Eastern Christian tradition. During the medieval and Ottoman periods, the institutional organization of Christianity in Greece remained under the auspices of Constantinople.

Autocephaly and the Young Greek Nation, 1821–1852

The history of the Orthodox Church of Greece, as distinct from the patriarchate of Constantinople, begins with the establishment of the Kingdom of Greece shortly after the declaration of Greek independence from Ottoman rule in 1821. The first constitution of revolutionary Greece (1822) identified "Hellenes" as "those who believe in Christ." Important leaders of revolutionary Greece, among them

Adamantios Koraes and Theokletos Pharmakides, argued that an independent Greek nation must also have an independent church free from the control of the patriarch of Constantinople, who lived at that time under Ottoman suzerainty. In 1833 the Greek state unilaterally declared the Church of Greece autocephalous. However, spiritual, historical, and ecclesiastical ties with Constantinople ran deep, and the patriarchate, though not without limitations and challenges, was the most important institution for worldwide Greek religious and ethnic identity. A break with Constantinople would be, for many, a break from Orthodox Christian roots extending back fifteen hundred years. National consciousness and Greek identity were not limited to the territorial boundaries of independent Greece (Attica, the Peloponnese, and the Cycladic and Sporadic Islands). The church, with its epicenter at Constantinople, was the one Hellenic institution of the medieval and Ottoman worlds that continued to function. The Ottomans, for their part, understood this only too well, and in retaliation for the Greek revolt, in April of 1821 Patriarch Gregory V was executed by hanging outside the main gate of the patriarchate in Constantinople.

Early post-revolutionary Greek governments were supportive of the church, although many Greek political leaders who had been educated in the West were critical of the backwardness of the church and the relative isolation of its leadership, even though a number of clergy and bishops had died in the struggle for independence. Western powers appointed Otto, a Bavarian prince and a Roman Catholic, to be the first to head the new Kingdom of Greece, and to oversee the creation of a constitutional monarchy to rule over it. Otto brought with him Bavarian officials, in particular George von Maurer, a German Protestant, respected lawyer, professor, and bureaucrat. Von Maurer and Pharmakides were instrumental in drawing up the Ecclesiastical Charter of 1833 which served as a blueprint for the organization of the Church of Greece and its relationship to the state. The charter declared the Church of Greece autocephalous, with the head of the church being Jesus Christ. At the time of its publication, the patriarchate of Constantinople rejected outright this unilateral declaration of autocephaly. According to the charter, the Church of Greece was to be governed by a permanent synod,

"The Holy Synod of the Kingdom of Greece," consisting of a president and two to four additional members. All members, including the president, were appointed by the government and served for terms of one year. The synod served under the remit of the authority of the ministry of ecclesiastical affairs. Additionally, a government official assigned to the synod had the right to submit petitions to it, and no decision or action of the synod could take place without the presence of this governmental procurator. This constitution greatly curtailed the authority of individual Greek bishops. The king was constitutionally "the highest ecclesiastical authority" but transferred this authority to the permanent holy synod.

One of the first acts of the newly created synod was the consolidation of monastic communities and the expropriation of monastic properties by the state. Any monastery that had fewer than six monks was closed; all female monasteries were closed with the exception of three, one each for the Peloponnese, the islands, and mainland Greece. Donations to monasteries were prohibited and property belonging to the closed monasteries was confiscated in order to pay for a (non-existent) state educational system. Very little of the assets taken were ever used for this purpose, most of them disappearing through corruption and theft. Of the 563 monastic settlements in the newly independent state of Greece (of which 18 were female monasteries), no fewer than 412 were dissolved. The monasteries that remained lost any autonomy they once had; their finances were now directly controlled by regional governmental officials to whom taxes on landed property were paid.

The State Constitution of 1844, the first issued under the monarchy, acknowledged that the Church of Greece was "united by an indissoluble bond to the Great Church of Constantinople," but remained "autonomous and exercises independently of any church its rights of sovereignty." In addition, the constitution stated that all future monarchs after Otto must be Orthodox Christians. Not all Greeks favored the autocephalous status of the Church of Greece. Many identified with the larger Greek Orthodox world, the majority of which still resided outside of the territories of independent Greece. A popular resistance movement argued against independence from Constantinople and the imposition of a non-Orthodox monarch. Opposition was fueled by itinerant lay and monastic preachers, among whom was the popular monk Christophoros Papoulakos. After lengthy and tension-ridden negotiations, on June 29, 1850 the patriarchate of Constantinople formally granted autocephaly to the Church of Greece. A series of Greek legislative decisions in 1852 affirmed the recognition of autocephaly by Constantinople though keeping the essential organization of the church the same; one important change was to put in place the archbishop of Athens as the *ex officio* president of the permanent five-member synod. In addition, the 1852 Ecclesiastical Charter acknowledged the state's right to confirm the appointment of bishops and priests and to administer church property. The Church of Greece during this early period lacked enlightened leadership and was profoundly beholden to the state.

From Autocephaly to the end of the 19th Century

During the second half of the 19th century the Church of Greece faced four major challenges: the activity and influence of foreign missionaries, the expansion of the borders of independent Greece, the lack of education of both clergy and laity, and the ongoing problem of simony. Within the first few years following the declaration of Greek independence, western missionaries were active in Greece. Early on, they established schools for Greek children. In Athens, the well-known Anglican missionary John Hill established an all-girls school. Schools were also established on the islands of Aigina and Syros. Protestant religious materials were translated into Modern Greek, many of which were adopted as required textbooks for state schools. A Modern Greek translation of the Bible by Neophytos Vamvas, a Greek Orthodox cleric and professor at the University of Athens, was first published in 1850 and was adopted as a primary text for schools. There was strong opposition to the imposition of a translation of the Bible into demotic Greek, primarily out of a fear that such a move reflected the westernization or Protestantization of the church. The institution of the Sunday school was also introduced by western missionaries.

Irredentist desires of the fledgling Greek state were realized twice during the latter half of the 19th century. As a demonstration of support to the Greek state for their acceptance of the newly imposed King George I, England ceded the Ionian Islands to Greece in 1864. In 1881 the Greek nation added additional territories in Thessaly and parts of Epirus which were formerly under Ottoman control. The added territories were tangible expressions of the dominant foreign policy of the Greek nation, namely, the expansion of free Greece to include all Greek Orthodox peoples in historically Greek lands, the vast majority of which were presently in Ottoman hands. Known as the *Megali Idea* ("Great Idea"), this vision of incorporating unredeemed Greeks was connected, for some, with the hope of recreating the Byzantine Empire.

The involvement of the government in the election and appointment of bishops to metropolitan sees remained commonplace. For the election of new hierarchs, the holy synod would produce a list of three candidates from which the king, in consultation with the government, would choose the new metropolitan or bishop. One particularly damaging episode occurred in 1874 and resulted in the downfall of the Greek prime minister. That year, bureaucrats of the ministry of ecclesiastical affairs received bribes for the election of candidates to four Greek metropolitan sees. The plot became public and parliament created a special court to try the governmental officials for bribery and the bishops for simony. The court fined the bishops double the money they had paid as bribes. This affair reaffirmed the distrust of the laity towards the official church.

The education of clergy was one of the acute challenges of the Greek Church after the early days of independence. The University of Athens was founded in 1837 with four faculties: theology, medicine, law, and philosophy. The faculty of theology functioned independent of church authority. Though imperative to counter the presence and efforts of western missionaries, the Theological School, as it was popularly known, was based on western models of theological education and had a limited impact on the majority of Orthodox Christians, focusing mainly on the training of theologians and scholars. From its founding until 1904, no class ever graduated more than three students. In 1844 the Rizarios ecclesiastical school was established in Athens for the education of priests. By 1864, four additional schools for the education of future clergy were established at Chalkida, Tripoli, Syros, and Kerkyra. These schools were essentially secondary schools offering predominantly practical (liturgical) training for future clergy.

From 1900 to 1940

During the first quarter of the 20th century Greece continued its policy of territorial expansion. In 1905 Crete proclaimed union with Greece. The Balkan Wars of 1912 and 1913 resulted in additional gains. Greece added nearly 70 percent to its land area through the acquisition of southern Macedonia, Ioannina, Thrace, and some northern Aegean islands, and its population nearly doubled in this period to 4.8 million. These "New Lands," as they were called, had been historically under the jurisdiction of the ecumenical patriarchate. World War I brought with it immense political turmoil. The "National Schism" of 1915 between the supporters of the popular and charismatic Prime Minister Eleftherios Venizelos and the "royalists" who supported the monarchy affected the church as well. In 1918 the pro-Venizelist Metropolitan Meletios Metaxakis became archbishop of Athens, only to be replaced in November of 1920 after the fall of the Venizelist government and the return of the king. Metaxakis was an important and controversial figure. He supported ecumenical dialogue, inaugurating official discussions with the Church of England and personally arguing for a Greek Orthodox acknowledgment of Anglican ordinations.

The defeat of the Axis Powers in 1918 dismantled the Ottoman Empire. In May 1919 Greek forces landed in Smyrna and occupied the area. Two years later, Greece went on the offensive in mainland Turkey, only to be eventually defeated, with Turkey occupying Smyrna. The military disaster of 1922 in Asia Minor, and the subsequent Treaty of Lausanne of 1923, led to the relocation of some 1.1 million Greek Orthodox Christians from Smyrna and its surrounding areas to independent Greece, and 380,000 Muslims residing in Greece were transferred to Turkey. This exchange of populations created immense economic, political, and social challenges for the church.

With the arrival of the Asia Minor refugees, the church's role in the formation of a national Greek identity intensified. This is reflected in the change of the title of the archbishop of Athens who, according to the Ecclesiastical Charter of 1923, was now to be called "Archbishop of Athens and all Greece." Additionally, the five-member synod was abolished and the highest governing authority of the church became its complete hierarchy, which was required to gather synodically every three years. For administrative purposes, and in order to keep in check the authority of the archbishop, a permanent holy synod of the Church of Greece consisting of eight members plus the archbishop was established. For the next fifty years the archbishop of Athens became more visibly involved in Greek national affairs.

The ecclesiastical jurisdiction of the New Lands was settled with the Patriarchal and Synodical Act of 1928. Accordingly, the ecumenical patriarchate, which held jurisdiction over these areas, granted the metropolitans of these regions the freedom to participate fully in the life of the Church of Greece, to sit on the permanent holy synod, and to participate in the institutional organizations of the church. However, Constantinople retained the right to approve all elections of metropolitans in the New Lands. The metropolises on the island of Crete obtained more freedom than their counterparts in the New Lands, with the Church of Crete, whose metropolitans were not members of the holy synod of the Church of Greece, recognized as semi-autonomous church leaders under Constantinople.

Changes in the organizational structure of the Greek Church were met with additional moves that had significant impact on the faithful. In 1919 the government of Venizelos adopted the use of the Gregorian calendar (New Calendar) for civil purposes. Within the Orthodox world, discussions regarding the replacement of the Julian calendar, which lagged 13 days behind the Gregorian calendar used by Western Christians, had been going on since 1902. In April 1923 the Church of Greece, following the lead of the ecumenical patriarchate, accepted the New Calendar and, one year later, on March 10, 1924, the Church of Greece's ecclesiastical calendar was suddenly advanced to become March 23. The calendar change met with some resistance, and unfortunately the state resorted to the use of force to ensure the adoption of the new calendar among some communities. In 1935 three Greek metropolitans came together and ordained new metropolitans for the Old Calendarist movement in Greece, giving the movement an identifiable hierarchy. The movement has since fragmented, though it still claims the loyalty of many.

World War II, Civil War, and Dictatorship

World War II and the Greek Civil War (1943–9) unleashed a period of personal and national suffering unmatched in the history of the Greek nation. With the Axis occupation of Greece complete by April 1941, the archbishop of Athens, Chrysanthos, refused to participate in the swearing in of a provisional government under German control and was replaced by the hierarch Damaskinos. Although not liked by all (Churchill once called him "a pestilent priest, a remnant from the Middle Ages") Damaskinos worked hard to alleviate the incomparable suffering of the Greek people. He created the National Organization of Christian Solidarity to provide social welfare to his needy faithful, many of whom were dying of starvation. He protected Jewish families in Athens from the Nazis. He became the most visible of Greek citizens as he interacted with the various Greek political factions, the occupying forces, and the British. At the end of the war, he was appointed regent (December 1944– September 1946). He was criticized for his ambition, but he provided needed leadership and bravery at a time of crisis. In one of his last moves he placed the Greek clergy on the public payroll as a means of improving their economic condition.

As early as 1943, Greece became embroiled in an internal struggle between leftists and rightists seeking political influence and power. The struggle turned into a bitter civil war after the defeat of the Germans in 1944. The church leadership sided with the British and Americans against the leftist and communist groups and eventually purged the church of clergy who had supported the leftist groups. Along with the Axis occupation, the Civil War caused the widespread destruction of churches and monastic property. The decades of the fifties and sixties saw the rebuilding of many of these ecclesiastical edifices, along with a large-scale urbanization occurring throughout the country.

Indicative of church–state relations during this period was the permanent synod's congratulatory dispatch to the leaders of the April 1967 military coup which sent the king into exile and inaugurated a seven-year military dictatorship. During the first year of the dictatorship, a new archbishop was appointed, Ieronymos, who according to different perspectives, either led the church admirably during a difficult time, or sold out to the radical right. Nevertheless, Ieronymos governed with the intention of improving the status of the church, its clergy, and its institutions. A student uprising in November 1973 led to a change in the leadership of the dictatorship and to the eventual ousting of Archbishop Ieronymos. The following July, the Regime of the Colonels collapsed and the abolition of the monarchy, through a plebiscite, was declared in December 1974.

The lack of education of the clergy continued to be a problem for the church (Rinvolucri 1966: 13–30). Attempts to provide theological education for clergy were begun under Archbishop Chrysostomos (1923– 38) with the creation of *ierodidaskaleia* (schools for priests) and the so-called *Frontistiria* or Higher Schools for students who had graduated from high school. In Northern Greece a new school of theology was opened at the University of Thessalonike in 1942.

From 1974 to the Present

For more than two decades following the collapse of the dictatorship, the Church of Greece was led by Archbishop Seraphim, who replaced Ieronymos in January 1974. A former member of the largest noncommunist Greek resistance group during the Axis occupation of Greece, Seraphim oversaw a period of relative peace for the Church of Greece and the rapid democratization and secularization of the state. A new state constitution was passed in 1975 in which Article 3 states: "The prevailing religion in Greece is that of the Eastern Orthodox Church of Christ. The Orthodox Church of Greece, acknowledging our

Lord Jesus Christ as its head, is inseparably united in doctrine with the Great Church of Christ in Constantinople." Additionally, the constitution did away with the requirement that the head of state, the president, be a member of the Orthodox faith, and asserted that freedom of religious consciousness is the inviolable right of every citizen. Two years later a new Ecclesiastical Charter for the Church of Greece acknowledged the right of the church to regulate its own internal affairs without state interference. This right was challenged in 1987 when the government of Andreas Papandreou attempted to expropriate lands from monastic holdings for use by poor villagers. A compromise was reached in which Archbishop Seraphim approved the transfer of some limited land but rejected the nationalization of church property.

Upon the death of Archbishop Seraphim in April 1998, the holy synod of Greece elected Christodoulos, who at the age of 58 became the youngest archbishop to serve the Church of Greece. Christodoulos' appointment marked a significant shift in the accommodationism that had dominated church-state relations in Greece for most of its history. It was the first election of an archbishop of Athens conducted without the intervention of the government. Christodoulos successfully utilized a populist approach in leading the church and employed the Greek media (appearing frequently on television and radio) to get his message across. He particularly focused his attention on Greek youth. As he attempted to bring the church into dialogue with modernity and with a pluralistic and secular European Union (of which Greece became a full member in 1981), he maintained a traditional view regarding the close affinity between Orthodox Christianity and the Greek nation, between national identity and Orthodoxy. For 15 months Christodoulos led an unsuccessful public campaign against the government's proposal to remove religious affiliation from identity cards. In one particularly massive rally, the archbishop himself held the original banner of the 1821 revolution.

The Christodoulos era was marked by another struggle, this time with the patriarchate of Constantinople. In July 2003 Christodoulos proceeded to elect new metropolitans for the vacant see of Thessaloniki and two neighboring metropolises without the involvement of Constantinople. This action was in violation of the 1928 Patriarchal Tome which stated that episcopal vacancies in the New Lands were to be filled with the approval of the phanar. The controversy came to a head in April 2004 when the resident synod of the patriarchate broke off communion with Christodoulos. The Greek state, through the ministry of education and religious affairs, worked behind the scenes and shortly afterwards resolved the crisis with a compromise which included an apology from Christodoulos to the patriarchal synod and an agreement that the Church of Greece would abide by the Tome of 1928. Christodoulos died in January 2008, eight months after being diagnosed with cancer. He was succeeded by Ieronymos II.

Lay Piety, the Brotherhoods, and Monastic Revival

The religious needs of the majority of Orthodox Christians in Greece, from the time of independence to the present, have been met through the basic liturgical and extra-liturgical functions carried out by the clergy. With the exception of the last twenty years, most clergy have been poorly educated and not prepared to meet the challenges of a rapidly changing world. Within this spiritual and catechetical vacuum emerged the phenomenon of lay brotherhoods: para-ecclesial associations of men (and later women) dedicated to living a celibate Christian lifestyle for the purpose of their own salvation and to educate the Greek Orthodox faithful in the salvific message of Christianity. The earliest figure of this movement was Apostolos Makrakis (1831–1905). Born in Greece, he studied at Constantinople and later in Paris, where he read European philosophy from Descartes to Hegel. In 1866 he returned to Athens and began preaching each evening in Omonia Square. One of his early followers was Archimandrite Eusebios Matthopoulos (1849–1929), the future founder of Zoe. The simony scandal of 1874 prompted Makrakis and his followers to denounce the leadership of the Church of Greece. In September 1876 Makrakis founded the Logos School, the first para-ecclesial group in Greece. A man of brilliance, he was a prolific author and produced commentaries on all the books of the Bible. Towards the end of his life his political positions became enmeshed with eschatological and millenarian views.

The most important para-ecclesial organization was the Zoe Brotherhood of Theologians. Founded in 1907 by Matthopoulos, Zoe became a centralized organization of dedicated members whose immense influence impacted the ecclesiastical, social, political, and spiritual life of Greece for the next fifty years. At age 14, Matthopoulos became a novice at the monastery of Mega Spelaion. He eventually moved to Athens, studied philosophy at the university, and was ordained a priest and appointed confessor to a small monastery. He had been given permission to preach as well. In 1907 he organized a small group of young theologians, students, and other lay individuals establishing a community he called Zoe ("Life"). The organization was a civil association governed by the laws of the state, not the church. Matthopoulos required members to adopt the three virtues of chastity, poverty, and obedience, yet not within a traditional monastic context. The chief purpose of the society was missionary work among the people of Greece through preaching, catechesis, and exemplary lifestyles.

By 1911 the brotherhood began publishing a periodical in which sermons and teachings on the Bible, especially the gospels and letters of Paul, were a constant presence. By 1959 the periodical had 170,000 subscribers. The brotherhood, most especially through the writings and influence of Matthopoulos, developed a strong pietistic attitude towards the Christian lifestyle. The movement did not renounce the sacramental life of the Orthodox Church, but placed special emphasis on scriptural reading and catechetical instruction (Bible study). Under the leadership of Seraphim Papakostas, Matthopoulos' successor, Zoe greatly expanded its influence through the establishment of catechetical schools for children patterned after English and French Sunday schools. These schools followed a nine-year curriculum. By 1936 Zoe had 300 catechetical schools, and by 1959 the number had increased to 2,216 with some 147,000 pupils. The leadership and its publications became associated with the struggle against communism in the second half of the 1940s, while satellite associations for students, workers, women, and others flourished. At the core of the brotherhood were the 175 dedicated and disciplined members who oversaw the movement's organization and publications.

Disagreement over succession and the particular direction of the movement led to a major split in April 1960, led by professor of theology Panayiotis Trembelas, with 60 members leaving the brotherhood to form a new organization called the "Sotir ["Savior"] Brotherhood of Theologians." The breakup led to litigation over property, and further volatile disagreements made the brotherhoods the objects of ridicule in the press. Membership in Zoe suffered, and the revival of interest in historical Orthodoxy and the fathers, along with a renewed understanding of the role of Eucharistic celebration, made the ecclesial life of the church more attractive, and the piety and moralism of the brotherhood movements less appealing.

Responding to the success of Zoe, in 1947 the church established its own missionary agency, Apostolike Diakonia ("Apostolic Ministry"), a self-governing legal entity under the supervision of the holy synod. This organization responded with its own publications and catechetical schools. Although never able to match the organization and commitment of the Zoe movement, Apostolike Diakonia, along with Zoe and Sotir, provided a network of educational and spiritual opportunities for the Greek Orthodox faithful. Their publications and bookstores were an important source for the dissemination of Orthodox theological, biblical, and catechetical literature. Today, Apostolike Diakonia has expanded its educational efforts through a variety of electronic media.

Closely connected to the spiritual aspirations of the lay brotherhood movements was the issue of a Modern Greek translation of the Bible. As noted above, a translation was published in 1850 but was quickly rejected by the church. On September 9, 1901 the Athenian newspaper Acropolis began publishing in its broadsheets a translation of the New Testament. The patriarch of Constantinople, the archbishop of Athens, and the Theological School of the University of Athens all protested against the translations. On November 5 a group of university students marched to the offices of the newspaper and after looting them proceeded to do the same at other newspaper headquarters. Three days later, on November 8, the protests had grown to include other laity, and fighting broke out with police, leading to eight dead and some seventy wounded.

Known as the *Evangeliaka* or "Gospel riots," the incident typically reflects the conservative and traditional character of the Church of Greece. So too does its rejection of the demotic movement, the attempt to replace the archaizing and artificial *katharevousa* with the popular spoken Greek idiom; a struggle which was not resolved until the adoption of demotic as the official language of instruction in the Greek educational system in 1975. It was not until 1985 that the first complete edition of the New Testament in demotic appeared.

By the early 1960s the monastic tradition in Greece was in an alarming state of decline. This was due to several factors: the dissolution of the monasteries in the 1830s; the pietistic and catechetical emphasis of the lay brotherhoods in the first half of the 20th century; the general mistrust of the laity towards the official church; and the strict divide between theology and monastic asceticism which permeated the theological schools. However, beginning in the second half of the 1960s, a handful of young theologians entered the monastic life on Mount Athos under the guidance of Elder Paisos (d. 1994). Thus began a most remarkable renaissance of monasticism on the Holy Mountain which extended also throughout Greece. This rebirth of traditional Athonite asceticism coincided with a rediscovery of Greek patristic theological and biblical thought. Though not a monk, and predating this revival, Photios Kontoglou (1897–1965), author and iconographer, contributed to this monastic revival by reawakening an appreciation of the Byzantine aesthetic tradition.

For most of its history, nearly all citizens of modern Greece have affiliated with the Greek Orthodox Church. Today, however, with immigration and secularization, only 85 percent of the Greek population identify (and often only culturally so) with the Orthodox Church. Nevertheless, the church is the most significant institution of Greek national identity and as such it remains a conservative entity enmeshed in its Helleno-Orthodox roots. Most civil holidays in Greece are religious ones: Independence Day is connected to the Feast of the Annunciation (March 25) and August 15, the most important summer holiday, celebrates the Koimesis of the Theotokos. In 1953 the Church of Greece moved the commemoration of the feast of the Protection of the Mother of God from October 1 to October 28, *Ohi* Day ("No! Day"), a civil holiday commemorating the Greek government's rejection of the 1939 Italian ultimatum demanding the entry of Axis troops.

The Church of Greece is currently organized into 80 metropolises with a reported 8,515 priests actively serving (as of 2006), not including Crete and the Dodecanese Islands which are under the jurisdiction of the ecumenical patriarchate. The Church of Greece remains governed by two synods both presided over by the archbishop of Athens. The special synod consists of 12 metropolitans elected once a year and also serves as a permanent synod dealing with ongoing business, while the entire assembly of Greek metropolitans gathers once every three years. Salaries for the clergy (all ranks) and administrative positions within the church are paid by the state. Religious instruction is mandatory for Greek Orthodox students attending public primary and secondary schools.

The most significant challenges facing the Church of Greece are a diminishing ethno-historical consciousness and the trajectory towards total secularization. From the second half of the 20th century, the Church of Greece has also had a significant impact on Orthodox communities in East Africa (in collaboration with the patriarchate of Alexandria) and Asia through missionary and social work.

SEE ALSO: Constantinople, Patriarchate of; Elder (Starets); Mount Athos; Ottoman Yoke; St. Silouan of Athos (1866–1938)

References and Suggested Readings

Rinvolucri, M. (1966) *Anatomy of a Church: Greek Orthodoxy Today*. New York: Fordham University Press.

Tomkinson, J. L. (2004) *Between Heaven and Earth: The Greek Church*. Athens: Anagnosis.

Yiannaras, H. (1992) *Orthodoxia kai Dysi sti Neoteri Ellada*. Athens: Domi.

Gregory of Cyprus *see* Lyons, Council of (1274)

H

Hades

NIKI J. TSIRONIS

Hades is the figure in Greek mythology that dominates the underworld, but is also the generic way in which the underworld itself was known in Antiquity. In the course of history he has undergone significant changes and eventually he was adopted by Christianity along with other personages deriving from ancient Greek mythology. Originally, in Greek mythology, Hades was one of the three sons of Cronus and Rhea (the other two being Zeus and Poseidon, who took command of the upper world). Hades was assisted in his work – which was to reign over the kingdom of the dead – by Thanatos (death), Hypnos (sleep), the ferryman Charon, and the hound Cerberus, who guarded the dead, not allowing them to return to life. The transition to the use of Hades to signify the after-life place of the dead occurred first in the Septuagint (especially the Psalms and the Book of Isaiah) and was followed by the Gospel of St. Luke, Revelation, and Acts). Christ, for example, refers to Hades in Matthew 16.17–19: "And I tell you, that you are Peter, and on this rock I will build my church, and the gates of Hades will not overcome it," where it also bears the meaning of the forces of evil, insofar as the realm of the dead is the home of Satan. In both the New Testament and in the writings of the fathers, Hades predominantly signifies death, especially as the result of the fall from divine life and grace because of sin. Christ's death brought him to the realm of Hades from which he liberated man. The hymns of Romanos (*On the Death of Christ*) are a clear example of the use of this symbolism, where both Death and Satan become sick and fearful as the cross of Jesus breaks through the roof of Hades. In Eastern Christian iconography Hades is never portrayed in human form, but he is referred to indirectly in the title of the iconography depicting Christ's descent into Hell (*he eis Hades kathodos*), and his symbols are usually represented at the foot of the cross (keys to Hades, chains, and a skull appearing through a bottomless hole). Christ's resurrection signifies the defeat of death ("trampling death by death" as the Paschal Troparion puts it) and numerous patristic homilies dedicated to the crucifixion allude to the fight between Christ and Hades and the latter's grief upon his loss of the formerly enslaved human race.

SEE ALSO: Death (and Funeral); Deification; Soteriology

Hagiography

MONICA M. WHITE

Hagiography is a diverse body of devotional literature connected with the cults of saints. Although its content

The Concise Encyclopedia of Orthodox Christianity, First Edition. Edited by John Anthony McGuckin.
© 2014 John Wiley & Sons, Ltd. Published 2014 by John Wiley & Sons, Ltd.

is usually biographical, hagiography can take almost any form–prose or poetry, extended stories or brief calendar entries, dialogues or first-person narratives – and is a vital aspect of the veneration of saints. It is therefore a widespread genre in all of the eastern churches, and something which continues to be produced today.

The earliest hagiography probably appeared as part of Christians' commemorations of the deceased, at which eulogies might be read out and later incorporated into narratives (Van Ommeslaeghe 1981: 158–60). The most widespread type of early hagiography was the *Acts of Martyrs*, which were based (or purportedly based) on transcripts of trials and embellished with details about the saint's conversion, arrest, imprisonment, and martyrdom (Musurillo 1972).

This emphasis on struggle and combat continued to influence hagiography after the end of the persecutions, as pagan tormentors were replaced with demons and temptations. Yet hagiography also changed as new types of saints emerged. Monastic hagiography, for example, usually includes descriptions of the saint's ascetic training (often with a spiritual father), attainment of full powers, and posthumous miracles (Louth 2004).

There was little standardization or systematic collection of hagiography until the middle Byzantine period. During the 10th century the imperial official Symeon Metaphrastes led a project to rewrite important hagiographic texts and compile them into a *Menologion* (Høgel 2002). Similar efforts during the same period resulted in the appearance of the *Synaxarion of Constantinople*, a collection of abridged versions of saints' lives (Delehaye 1902) that had a profound influence on liturgical calendars. Both of these works became standard throughout Byzantium and beyond, although they were also widely adapted to incorporate local saints.

Hagiography is primarily concerned with describing ideals of Christian behavior and spiritual attainment rather than historical fact. The hagiography of some of the most famous saints is sometimes so fabulous that it cannot even be taken as evidence for their existence, much less for details of the society in which they lived. Even less obviously embellished texts can present interpretative difficulties, yet scholars in many fields have used hagiographic texts as major sources for the study of the early Eastern Christian world. Some of the most important work has been carried

out by the Bollandists, a Jesuit society devoted to the critical study of hagiography (Van Ommeslaeghe 1981). In the Orthodox Church today hagiographies are widely read as a devotional exercise in monastic communities and in the homes of the faithful.

SEE ALSO: Calendar; Canonization; Feasts; Liturgical Books; Miracles

References and Suggested Readings

Delehaye, H. (ed.) (1902) *Synaxarium Ecclesiae Constantinopolitanae.* Brussels: Typis Regis.

Delehaye, H. (1998) *The Legends of the Saints: An Introduction to Hagiography*, trans. D. Attwater. Dublin: Four Courts Press.

Høgel, C. (2002) *Symeon Metaphrastes: Rewriting and Canonization.* Copenhagen: Museum Tusculanum Press.

Louth, A. (2004) "Hagiography," in F. Young, L. Ayres, and A. Louth (eds.) *The Cambridge History of Early Christian Literature.* Cambridge: Cambridge University Press, pp. 358–61.

Musurillo, H. (1972) *The Acts of the Christian Martyrs.* Oxford: Oxford University Press.

Van Ommeslaeghe, F. (1981) "The *Acta Sanctorum* and Bollandist Methodology," in S. Hackel (ed.) *The Byzantine Saint.* London: Fellowship of St. Alban and St. Sergius, pp. 155–63.

Healing

ANDREI I. HOLODNY

In Orthodox Christian perspective, healing of both specific infirmities as well as the fallen nature of humankind is accomplished through the incarnation, suffering, and resurrection of Christ. Prior to the Second Coming and the bodily resurrection of the saints, the church, as the Body of Christ (Col. 1.24) cares for the spiritual and physical wellbeing of her members through the holy sacraments and the merciful caring for the sick.

Patristic teaching suggests that Adam was originally created by God not only holy, passionless, and sinless, but also physically without blemish or illness. Adam's sin, therefore, had spiritual as well as physical consequences. Following the fall of humanity, death, corruption, and decay became characteristic not only of Adam, but also of all of his progeny. Hence, the purpose of the promised Redeemer was to heal both humanity's spiritual nature as well as its physical nature: both the specific ills which affect every person individually as well as what afflicts humanity as a whole, understanding that the former is a consequence of the latter.

In the Old Testament, God's mercy and the foreshadowing of the coming Redeemer are emphasized by healings and even resurrections of the dead – for example, the resurrection of the widow's son by Elijah (1 Kgs. 17.8–23) and the reviving of the dead child by Elisha (2 Kgs. 4.8–27). God's promise of the restoration of humanity extends also to the healing of the infirmities of old age – the paradigmatic example of this is the elderly Abraham and Sarah's conception of a child, Isaac (Gen. 15.1–6; 18.10–15; 21.1–8). The ultimate restoration of humanity, including our physical wellbeing, is foretold by many Old Testament prophets – for example, Isaiah:

> Strengthen the feeble hands, steady the knees that give way… Then will the eyes of the blind be opened and the ears of the deaf unstopped. Then will the lame leap like a deer, and the mute tongue shout for joy… They will enter Zion with singing; everlasting joy will crown their heads. Gladness and joy will overtake them, and sorrow and sighing will flee away. (Is. 35.3, 5–6, 10)

The physical and spiritual restoration of humankind to health is vividly described in the prophecy of Ezekiel in the valley of the dry bones (Ezek. 37.1–28). Liturgically, the Orthodox Church places the readings of the most important of these Old Testament miracles and prophesies during services of the latter part of the Week of Christ's Passion. Fifteen Old Testament texts are proclaimed during the divine liturgy on Holy Saturday directly prior to the triumphant singing of "Arise Oh Lord" (during which the dark vestments of Great Lent are exchanged for the white of Easter) and the first reading of the epistle and gospel which is the first to announce the paschal resurrection of Christ (Rom. 6.3–11 and Mt. 38.1–20).

For Orthodox theology, the true healing of our nature, which was distorted as a consequence of Adam's sin, can only be achieved through Jesus Christ:

"For the wages of sin is death, but the gift of God is eternal life in Christ Jesus our Lord" (Rom. 6.23). This complete healing of the fallen nature of humankind – that is, the elimination of disease, decay, and death – is in contrast to the examples from the Old Testament, where healings and even resurrections were on an individual, symbolic basis, rather than applying to all of humanity: "For since death came through a man, the resurrection of the dead comes also through a man. For as in Adam all die, so in Christ all will be made alive" (1 Cor. 15.21–22). The apostle sums up this cosmically all-embracing doctrine:

> Therefore, just as sin entered the world through one man, and death through sin, and in this way death came to all men, because all sinned. … For if the many died by the trespass of the one man, how much more did God's grace and the gift that came by the grace of the one man, Jesus Christ, overflow to the many! (Rom. 5.12, 16)

The New Testament (especially in the synoptic gospels) is replete with examples of Jesus Christ healing the sick: "And people brought to him all who were ill with various diseases, those suffering severe pain, the demon-possessed, those having seizures, and the paralyzed, and he healed them" (Mt. 4.23–24; see also Mk. 6.56; Lk. 4.40). All of the gospel accounts of these numerous healings possess a deeper allegorical and theological meaning aside from the actual remedying of the physical infirmity itself. Overcoming physical sightlessness is often used as a metaphor for Christ's overcoming spiritual blindness. For example, the healing of the blind man which actually required two separate actions by Christ is described as analogous to the apostles' gradually coming to understand who Christ truly is (Mk. 8.21–30). The evangelical accounts of Christ performing resurrections demonstrate his complete command over the forces of the universe, including death and decay. This is emphasized especially in the story of the resurrection of Lazarus, where the Lord raises his friend from the grave even though he has been dead for four days and has already begun to decay (Jn. 11.1–46).

In order to understand the taking on by Christ of all of humankind's sins and iniquities and the healing of our nature through his death and resurrection, it is essential to appreciate his true incarnation. Since

Christ was both true God and true man, he was able to facilitate the healing and resurrection of the whole race on his own person. Following his resurrection, Christ continued to possess a true, physical, human body. He ate and drank (Jn. 21.13) and the apostles (including Doubting Thomas) were able to touch him (Jn. 20.24–29). However, after the resurrection, the body of Christ was no longer subject to illness or death. The restoration of health in the Old Testament, the New Testament, and during the history of the church is often accomplished through what can be termed miracles of grace. In the Orthodox understanding of the order of things, however, sickness and death are an anomaly in the human situation, and it is this which is remarkable and unusual, rather than the return of a person to health. In this sense, therefore, a "miracle" (called in Orthodox tradition a *thauma*, or sign of wonder) given as a sign of God's mercy is actually a restoration of things to their natural order and a premonition of how life will be after the resurrection from the dead.

The healing of our physical infirmities plays a central role in the sacramental life of the Orthodox Church. The sacrament of the anointing of the sick is usually administered to those who are grievously ill and is wholly dedicated to the purpose of healing the person both spiritually (and especially) physically. All of the other sacraments are dedicated to this same purpose to varying degrees. For example, the Eucharist is administered "for the healing of soul and body," as is repeated in the prayer recited by the priest before each person's communion.

Orthodox tradition addresses even the ordinary concerns of Christians, as seen in its prescription for everyday life – fasting is an example of this, and is closely related to bodily issues. Clearly, the main goal of fasting is spiritual. Fasting is supposed to focus one's attention on eternal and essential concerns and move one away from the mundane; however, by its very nature, fasting has profound physical and health dimensions. It is interesting to note that the fast prescribed by the church is completely in concert with contemporary recommendations by health professionals regarding diets intended to counteract the epidemic of obesity that is manifested in the western world: a general decrease in caloric intake, less meat and more fish, less fatty foods, more fruits and vegetables.

Healing of the infirmed plays a central role in the life of the church today, following Christ's example and directive: "They will place their hands on sick people, and they will get well" (Mk. 16.18), as well as the parable of the merciful Samaritan (Lk. 10.33–35). Christ's directive was taken up by the apostles immediately after Pentecost: "Then Peter said, 'Silver and gold I have not, but what I have I give to you. In the name of Jesus Christ of Nazareth, walk'" (Acts 3.6). During Late Antiquity and the Middle Ages, monasteries played a central role in the establishment of healthcare facilities (including psychiatric ones) in Orthodox countries. These efforts were suppressed to a large degree by loss of political independence in the Balkans and Greece and by the secularizing reforms of Peter the Great in Russia. Even so, the tradition of the healing of the sick was continued by many Orthodox saints who were also physicians, for example the Evangelist Luke, Sts. Cosmas and Damian, and the martyr Panteleimon, and several others known as the "Holy Unmercenaries."

Orthodox theology avers that both the immaterial and material parts of the human person have to strive for salvation and that we will be resurrected not only spiritually but also in the body. Salvation of the entire person is emphasized by the entire tradition of Orthodox asceticism, especially among the hesychasts with their strong emphasis on how the body needs to participate in prayer. Notwithstanding the promise of eternal life, Orthodox Christians are often faced with the problem and meaning of suffering in their present lives. Orthodox Christians tormented either by life's circumstances, or by oppressors, are reminded that Christ himself suffered on the cross, and given the example of the myriad of martyrs. An excellent compilation of the thoughts of the ancient fathers, for the guidance of the Orthodox of his time, was compiled by Bishop Ignatius Brianchaninov. This book served as a spiritual guide to the martyrs of the imperial family during the Russian Revolution.

Orthodox theology avers that the saints will be resurrected bodily following the example of Christ. Like his own glorious body, the bodies of the saints will also no longer be subject to the forces of decay: "The dead will be raised imperishable, and we will be changed. For the perishable must clothe itself with the imperishable, and the mortal with immortality"

(1 Cor. 15.52–3). A similar promise of complete healing is given in the Book of Revelation, as accomplished after the Second Coming:

> Now the dwelling of God is with men, and he will live with them. They will be his people, and God himself will be with them and be their God. He will wipe every tear from their eyes. There will be no more death or mourning or crying or pain, for the old order of things has passed away. He who was seated on the throne said, "I am making everything new!" (Revelation 21.3–5)

The healing power of Christ continually abides in his church throughout its earthly pilgrimage, as a consolation and foretaste of his mercy. It will be the final glory of all his saints at the end.

SEE ALSO: Anointing of the Sick; Charity; Death (and Funeral); Deification; Fasting; Gospel; Incarnation (of the Logos); Old Testament; Original Sin; Paradise; Resurrection; St. Ignatius Brianchaninov (1807–1867)

References and Suggested Readings

Athanasius, St. (2002) *On the Incarnation.* Crestwood, NY: St. Vladimir's Seminary Press.

Brianchaninov, I. (1986) *O terpenii skorbei po ucheniu sviatikh otsev.* Montreal: Job of Pochaev Brotherhood Press.

Horden, P. (2008) *Hospitals and Healing from Antiquity to the Later Middle Ages.* Aldershot: Ashgate Press.

Larchet, J.-C. (2002) *The Theology of Illness.* Crestwood, NY: St. Vladimir's Seminary Press.

Philaret, Metropolitan of Minsk (ed.) (2002) *Materials of the Theological Conference of the Russian Orthodox Church: "The Teachings of the Church on Man."* Moscow: Synodal Theological Commission.

Symeon the New Theologian, St. (1994) *The First Created Man,* trans. S. Rose. Platina, CA: St. Herman of Alaska Brotherhood Press.

Heirmologion

DIMITRI CONOMOS

A music book for church singers containing only the *heirmoi* (Gk. "links") or model verses for the odes in a Canon. It is not a liturgical book; the singers are meant to learn the melodies of the original *heirmoi* by heart in order to apply them to the texts of the *heirmoi* based on their meter and melody. The *heirmologion* is, in other words, an auxiliary book, of no value to the singers unless they have access at the same time to a collection of Canon texts. Early *heirmologia*, dating from the 10th century, transmit a simple, syllabic, musical style.

SEE ALSO: Canon (Liturgical); Liturgical Books

Heresy

JUSTIN M. LASSER

The term "heresy" derives from the Greek term *hairesis,* which, in classical usage, typically meant "a diversity of opinion." This usage was common within pre-Christian Hellenistic schools but acquired a new usage in the Christian era. In the Hellenistic schools a thesis or question would be offered and students or disciples would offer their opinions on the matter. In the case of a resulting diversity of opinion the matter would remain unresolved in a state of *hairesis.* In the classical schools the matter would be followed by extended debate and varying conclusions. In this usage "heresy" was the beginning of fruitful debate. On occasion these "heresies" would consolidate into cohesive "schools of thought." These schools of thought are exhibited most clearly in the various ancient philosophical schools (i.e., the Epicureans, the Platonists, the Stoics, etc.). Though the schools had many disagreements they rarely "condemned" each other – they merely maintained different opinions.

This classical usage of the term "heresy" was expanded in the Christian era. Whereas theologians such as Origen and Clement of Alexandria tended to view heresies as diverse schools of thought, other theologians, such as Irenaeus of Lyons and Justin Martyr, actively sought to characterize these diverse opinions or novelties as "corruptions" of the simple truth of the Christian faith handed down by the apostles. This move by the early heresiologists was not made out of vain intentions, but rested upon the belief that the Christian truth they were taught was not created but revealed and discovered. In this sense, Christian truth was not viewed as the result of theological speculation but as the recording and preserving of revealed truth. The simplicity and communicability of Christian truth was most important to the apologists such as St. Irenaeus and St. Justin, and became a paradigm for influential theologians such as St. Athanasius. It was a view that was first laid down in the Catholic epistles of the New Testament (see the letters of John, for example) which defined "those that had come out from among us" (heretical dissidents) as never having really belonged in the first place.

The term "Orthodoxy" derives from the Greek word for "straight" (*ortho*) and the word for "belief" (*doxa*) – "straight belief." In Orthodox opinion, its faith is not just one school among others, but *the* school which represents authentic Christianity. With this conviction the early heresiologists and later theologians viewed various opinions that challenged the core of Orthodox truth as cancerous corruptions. In the early periods of the church these heresies were often challenged in the public forum with few repercussions. However, when the church acquired imperial support the subsequent decisions on certain issues were endowed with the power of the state, and all the force of legal proscription. In such instances the antagonists were often exiled and deposed – with the suffering (sometimes fatal) that accompanied such penalties in Antiquity. Orthodoxy's own great confessors and theologians, however, occasionally experienced this uncomfortable label of "heresy." One recalls the state punishments imposed on St. John Chrysostom and St. Maximus the Confessor, and in the Iconoclast controversy, for example, the Orthodox faithful felt the full wrath of an oppressive state which regarded itself as endowed with divine authority to establish the canons of Orthodoxy. Orthodoxy's survival, however, demonstrates that its preservation of the truth does not depend on coercive state power, but on the testimonies of the faithful, and the living sense of what Orthodoxy means coherently, as a living system of truth.

Certain primary mechanisms were employed as means to ensure and preserve Orthodox belief – chief among these were the succession of bishops as purveyors of Christian truth, the creeds, and conciliar decisions. The first, apostolic succession, was established in response to the popularity and frequency of

the *didaskaloi* (ecclesiastically independent teachers) in the 2nd and 3rd centuries. Initially, Christianity depended on the work of these teachers (or apostles), but after various churches were established the relations between local overseers (bishops) and itinerant prophets (teachers) became strained. This is most clearly exhibited in the Apostle Paul's controversy with "rival" teachers (Galatians 1.9), as well as the controversy alluded to in the *Didache* (*Teaching of the Twelve Apostles*). The Apostle Paul's example also emphasizes the important function the creeds play in ensuring Orthodoxy when he demands that they hold true to what they were first taught. In the *Didache* the church expresses a more nuanced approach to the issue raised by traveling apostles and prophets: "Whosoever, therefore, comes and teaches you all these things that have been said before, receive him" (*Didache* 11). In this case, the local church is only to receive those that reinforce the message they had already been taught. If the visiting apostle preached anything foreign they were not to listen to him or her. Not only were the local churches to listen to the itinerant preacher, they were also to support him. "But he shall not remain more than one day; or two days, if there's a need. But if he remains three days, he is a false prophet. And when the apostle goes away, let him take nothing but bread until he lodges. If he asks for money, he is a false prophet" (*Didache* 11). These instructions reveal what was an emerging controversy between itinerant preachers and established local authorities. The controversy, it seems, was initially resolved by limiting the time the prophet was allowed to stay. This served to stem any potential challenges to the local bishops' authority and charisma.

St. Irenaeus articulated a systematic basis for local Christian authority by resting it with the bishops as "successors to the apostles." This was in direct contradistinction to the "gnostic" teachers that believed that the charisma and authority of the church rested with the *didaskaloi* who could prove their inspiration by the quality of their personal words. The ancient and more recent history of the Orthodox Church reveals that the occasional tension between teacher and bishop has never been completely resolved. Origen, for example, encountered much ecclesiastical resistance but remained convinced of the importance of the *didaskaloi* in communicating Christian truth and expressing it in a manner that was sensible to the contemporaneous generation. After the 4th century the episcopacy was more and more drawn from the ranks of the rhetorically educated; and in the golden age of patristic literature (and long after) almost all the major theologians of the church have been its bishops.

The most visible means of preserving Orthodoxy and defining what is heresy has been the synodical and conciliar system of the church. The local and ecumenical councils resolved the various and major differences of opinion according to consensual decisions guided by the Holy Spirit. In this manner the church operates according to the structure expressed by St. Irenaeus: from Christ to the apostles and from the apostles to the bishops. Thus in Orthodox belief the ecumenical councils are a convening of the "apostles," not just bishops, and in this state the Holy Spirit is set to guide the church in the Spirit of Truth. It is for such reasons that at a council a majority view on matters of doctrine is never acceptable: the gathered bishops are expected to be able to articulate as with one mind and one heart what is the faith of the church, that faith into which they were baptized: to confess it, not to have to seek for it in the face of bewildering "new heresies." As such the council always demanded total uniformity of confession from its constitutive members, and expected the obedience of the faithful to its decrees as resulting from the laity's own charism of "recognizing the truth." It is for such reasons that a council is only recognized as ecumenical once it has gained the assent of the Orthodox faithful in general – the *consensus fidelium* being a very important part of what is meant by Orthodoxy and the very antithesis of what it means by heresy.

SEE ALSO: Apostolic Succession; Gnosticism

References and Suggested Readings

Behr, J. (2001) *The Formation of Christian Theology, Vol. 1: The Way to Nicaea.* Crestwood, NY: St. Vladimir's Seminary Press.

Irenaeus of Lyons (1997) *On the Apostolic Preaching.* Crestwood, NY: St. Vladimir's Seminary Press.

McGuckin, J. A. (1998) "Eschaton and Kerygma: The Future of the Past in the Present Kairos: The Concept of Living Tradition in Orthodox Theology," *St. Vladimir's Theological Quarterly* 42, 3–4: 225–71.

Osborn, E. F. (2001) *Irenaeus of Lyons.* Cambridge: Cambridge University Press.

Simon, M. (1979) "From Greek Haeresis to Christian Heresy," in *Early Christian Literature and the Classical Intellectual Tradition.* Paris: Beauchesne, pp. 101–16.

Hesychasm

METROPOLITAN KALLISTOS OF DIOKLEIA

The terms "hesychasm" and "hesychast" are derived from the Greek word *hesychia*, meaning "quietness," "silence," or "inner stillness." From the beginning of Christian monasticism, *hesychia* has been regarded as a primary characteristic of the monk: in the words of Neilos of Ankyra (d. ca. 430), "It is impossible for muddy water to grow clear if it is constantly stirred up; and it is impossible to become a monk without *hesychia*" (*Exhortation to Monks*, PG 79: 1236B). The essence of hesychasm is summed up in the command given by God to the desert father Arsenios (d. 449): "Arsenios, flee, keep silent, be still [*hesychaze*], for these are the roots of stillness" (*Apophthegmata*, alphabetical collection, Arsenios 2). The term "hesychasm" has sometimes been rendered as "quietism," but this is potentially misleading, since the Quietist movement in the 17th-century West is significantly different from the hesychast tradition in the East.

In early sources (4th–6th centuries), *hesychia* sometimes indicates the solitary life; a hesychast is a hermit or recluse, as contrasted with a monk dwelling in a cenobium or organized community. More commonly, however, especially in later sources, *hesychia* is given an interiorized and spiritual sense, and denotes silence of the heart. It usually signifies the quest for union with God through "apophatic" or "non-iconic" prayer, that is to say, prayer that is free from images and discursive thinking. From the 5th century onwards, one of the chief means for attaining such hesychast prayer has been the Invocation of the Holy Name or Jesus Prayer. By the 14th century, if not before, the Jesus Prayer was often accompanied by a psychosomatic technique, involving in particular control of the breathing.

Plate 27   Monastic cells of the monks at the Sinaya Monastery, Romania, once a dependency of Mount Sinai. Photo by John McGuckin.

Origins

A decisive role in the emergence of hesychasm was played by Evagrios Pontike (346–99). Taking up a scheme devised by Origen (ca. 185–ca. 254), Evagrios divided the spiritual life into three stages or levels:

> *Praxis* or *praktikē*, the "active life," i.e., the struggle to eliminate evil thoughts (*logismoi*) and to acquire the virtues. This begins with repentance (*metanoia*) and leads eventually to "dispassion" or freedom from the passions (*apatheia*), which in its turn is closely linked to love (*agapē*).

1   *Physikē*, "natural contemplation" or the contemplation of God in nature. This includes contemplation of the angelic orders.

2   *Theologia*: the contemplation of God in himself, on a level above creation.

Prayer, for Evagrios, is above all an activity of the intellect (*nous*). In its highest expression, prayer is "pure" or image-free: "When you are praying," writes Evagrios, "do not shape within yourself any image of the Deity, and do not let your intellect be stamped with the impress of any form; but approach the Immaterial in an immaterial manner. ... Prayer is a putting-away of thoughts" (*On Prayer* 66 [67], 70 [71]). Pure prayer is often accompanied by a vision of light. This exists at two levels. First, the hesychast may behold "the light of the intellect"; this is evidently a created light, an experience of the self as totally luminous. Then, at a more exalted level, he or she may behold the "light of the Holy Trinity," that is to say, a light that is divine and uncreated.

A somewhat different approach to prayer is to be found in the Macarian Homilies (? late 4th century).

Plate 28   A hermitage in the complex of buildings at the Romanian women's monastery at Varatec. Several thousand nuns live and pray at this site. Photo by John McGuckin.

Great emphasis is placed by the Homilies upon direct experience of the Holy Spirit. The Homilies do not differentiate clearly between advancing stages in prayer, nor do they speak of the need to lay aside images and thoughts. They treat prayer as an activity not primarily of the intellect (*nous*), but of the heart (*kardia*). Yet the contrast between Evagrios and the Macarian Homilies should not be exaggerated. *Nous* in Evagrios does not mean the reasoning brain (*dianoia*), but the faculty whereby we apprehend truth intuitively, through an act of inner vision, a sudden flash of insight. On the other hand, *kardia* in the Homilies does not signify only or primarily the emotions and feelings, but it denotes the moral and spiritual center of the total human person; the *nous* is regarded as dwelling within the heart, and in the Homilies there is no head/heart contrast. In common with Evagrios, the Macarian Homilies speak of

a vision of light, which is clearly understood as uncreated and divine.

Both Evagrios and the Macarian Homilies belonged in this way to the tradition of "light mysticism," as also did Gregory of Nazianzos (ca. 329–ca. 389). None of them assigned a significant place to the symbol of divine darkness. The Jewish writer Philo (ca. 20 BCE–ca. CE 50), however, and after him the Christian author Clement of Alexandria (ca. 150–ca. 215), both made use of the notion of mystical darkness. Drawing on them, Gregory of Nyssa (ca. 330–ca. 395) assigned a central place to divine darkness in his treatise *The Life of Moses*. Here he distinguished three stages in the spiritual journey, which differ markedly from those in the triadic scheme in Evagrios:

1   Moses, who is treated as a paradigm of mystical theology, was first granted a vision of light in the

burning bush (Ex. 3). For Gregory, this is not an ordinary physical radiance, but a light that is divine.

2 After this came a vision of mingled light and darkness (Ex. 13.21, the pillar of cloud and fire).

3 Moses then met God in the "thick darkness" of Sinai (Ex. 20.21), signifying the divine incomprehensibility. On the basis of this encounter with God in darkness, Gregory propounded a series of paradoxes: the true vision of God is non-vision; the true contemplation of God consists in the realization that he cannot be contemplated; the true knowledge of God is unknowing. But Gregory also spoke of the darkness of Sinai as "luminous," for the darkness is not a symbol of separation but of union with God in love.

In this way, Gregory reversed the usual sequence: the spiritual journey is not from darkness to light but from light to darkness. After the ascent of Sinai, there is a fourth and further stage, when Moses was hidden in the crevice of a rock, and saw not God's face but his back (Ex. 33.20–23). Gregory interpreted this to mean that the spiritual journey involves perpetual progress, an unending "reaching forward" or *epektasis* (Phil. 3.13–14). Even in heaven the saints never cease the advance from "glory to glory" (2 Cor. 3.18). The essence of perfection consists in the fact that one never becomes perfect; every endpoint is but a new beginning. Yet to follow God is to be united with him, and to seek him endlessly is precisely to find him.

Diadochos of Photikē (mid-5th century) took up the teaching of Evagrios on "pure" prayer, and he offered a practical method whereby this image-free prayer may be attained: through the invocation "Lord Jesus," that is to say, through what later became known as the Jesus Prayer. In common with Evagrios, Diadochos believed that inner prayer leads to a vision of light: first, an experience of the light of the *nous*, and then an experience of divine light. But this vision of light is *aneideos*, without form or shape; it is an experience of pure luminosity.

The unknown author of the writings attributed to Dionysius the Areopagite (ca. 500) followed Clement and Gregory of Nyssa in interpreting the mystical ascent as an entry into the darkness of Sinai. At that same time, he (or she) insisted upon a "coincidence of opposites"; at the divine level there is a convergence between the symbols of light and darkness. Just as Gregory of Nyssa described the darkness as luminous, so Dionysius wrote: "The divine darkness *is* the Light to which no one can approach" (*Letter* 5; cf. 1 Tim. 6.16). Dionysius proposed a threefold scheme of the spiritual life: purification, illumination, union. While this Dionysian scheme was widely adopted in the Latin West, it is the somewhat different Evagrian scheme that prevailed on the whole in the Greek East, most notably in Maximos the Confessor (ca. 580–662). Some writers, such as Niketas Stethatos (11th century), combined the two schemes together.

Middle Byzantine Period

John Klimakos (ca. 570–ca. 649), abbot of Sinai, in Step 27 of his *Ladder of Divine Ascent*, provided a classic definition of what it is to be a hesychast: "The hesychast is one who strives to confine his incorporeal self within the house of the body, paradoxical though this may sound." Thus hesychasm is an entry within oneself, a discovery of the indwelling Christ within the secret sanctuary of the heart. Hesychasm, Klimakos continued, involves *nepsis*, "wakefulness" or "vigilance": the hesychast is one who says, "I sleep, but my heart is awake" (Song of Songs 5.2). Hesychia is in this way a continual awareness of God's presence: as Klimakos put it, "*Hesychia* is worshipping God unceasingly and waiting upon him." This continual awareness is maintained through the Jesus Prayer: "Let the remembrance of Jesus be present with your every breath. Then indeed you will appreciate the value of *hesychia*." The hesychast seeks union with God on a level free of mental images and discursive thinking. Adapting the words of Evagrios, Klimakos wrote: "*Hesychia* is a putting-away of thoughts." From all this it is evident that, for Klimakos, *hesychia* meant not primarily the life of a hermit but a way of inner prayer.

Symeon the New Theologian (949–1022) revived the emphasis placed by the Macarian Homilies upon conscious experience:

Do not say, It is impossible to receive the Holy Spirit.
Do not say, It is possible to be saved without him.
Do not say, then, that one can possess him without knowing it
(*Hymn* 27.125–7)

The conscious experience of the Spirit takes the form of a vision of the light of Christ (for Christ and the Spirit are inseparable). Symeon affirmed clearly and definitely that this light is not physical and created, but non-material and divine: "Your Light, my God, is you yourself" (*Hymn* 45.6). The divine light has a transforming effect upon the one who beholds it, so that he himself becomes light. Although Symeon has left accounts of how Christ spoke to him out of the light, it seems that he did not actually see the face of Christ in the light. As with Diadochos, the vision is one of pure luminosity, without shape or form (although in one vision Symeon saw his spiritual father standing close to the light).

Hesychast Controversy

In the last years of the 13th century an Athonite monk, Nikiphoros the Hesychast, wrote a short but influential treatise *On Watchfulness and the Guarding of the Heart*. Here he spoke of "returning" or "entering" into oneself and "seeking the treasure within the heart." To facilitate this, he suggested that the recitation of the Jesus Prayer should be accompanied by a psychosomatic technique, involving the descent of the intellect, along with the breath, into the heart.

A similar technique was recommended by another Athonite monk in the following generation, Gregory of Sinai (d. 1346). Gregory set the Jesus Prayer in a sacramental context, seeing it as a means whereby we rediscover the grace received in baptism: prayer, he said, is nothing else than "the making manifest of baptism" (*On Commandments and Doctrines* 113). Using Eucharistic symbolism, he also described how the hesychast through prayer enters "the inner sanctuary," where he "celebrates the triadic liturgy," "offering up the Lamb of God upon the altar of the soul and partaking of him in communion" (*On Commandments and Doctrines* 43, 112).

In 1337–8 the Athonite tradition of hesychast prayer was attacked by a learned Greek from Southern Italy, Barlaam the Calabrian (ca. 1290–1348). It has been suggested that he was influenced by western Nominalism, but this is unlikely; he was basically a Neoplatonist. He argued that the light seen by the monks in prayer was not divine but created, an illusion conjured up by their own fantasy; and he criticized the physical technique as superstitious and grossly materialistic.

The defense of the hesychasts was undertaken by Gregory Palamas (1296–1359), a monk of Athos who became at the end of his life archbishop of Thessaloniki. According to Palamas, the vision that the monks beheld was not created and physical, but was identical with the divine and uncreated light that shone from Christ at his transfiguration on Tabor. Distinguishing, however, between the essence and the energies of God, he maintained that this divine light is not a vision of God's essence, which transcends all participation and remains for ever unknowable, but it is a manifestation of his eternal energies. These energies, however, so far from being a created intermediary between God and humankind, are nothing less than God himself in action: "Each power and energy is God himself" (*Letter to Gabras*); "God is wholly present in each of his energies" (*Triads* 3.2.7). This teaching of Palamas concerning the divine light was endorsed by three councils of Constantinople (1341, 1347, 1351), which, although they were not ecumenical, have come to be accepted by the Orthodox Church as a whole.

Palamas also defended the physical technique used with the Jesus Prayer. He did not consider it an essential part of the prayer, but saw it as an optional aid, suited chiefly for beginners; yet in his view it is theologically defensible. Since the human person is an integral unity of soul and body, the latter should play its part in the work of prayer. Here Palamas upheld a holistic view of the human person. Christ, through his incarnation, "has made the flesh an inexhaustible source of sanctification" (*Homily* 16); and so "the body is deified along with the soul" (*Triads* 1.3.37, quoting Maximos the Confessor).

An excellent summary of hesychast teaching was provided, towards the end of the 14th century, by the Constantinopolitan monks Kallistos and Ignatios Xanthopoulos in their treatise *On the Life of Stillness and Solitude*. In common with Gregory of Sinai, they established a close link between the sacraments and the inner prayer of the hesychast. The aim of the spiritual life is the ever-increasing "manifestation" of baptism (§4); the reception of holy communion by the hesychast should be "continual" and if possible daily (§§91–2).

In this way, for writers such as Gregory of Sinai and the Xanthopouloi, the recitation of the Jesus Prayer deepens and enriches the sacramental life, but does not by any means replace it. It is important to recognize that throughout the history of hesychasm, from the 4th century onwards, those who wrote about inner contemplation and the Jesus Prayer took it for granted that anyone pursuing the spiritual way would be an active member of the ecclesial community, regularly participating in the sacraments of confession and holy communion. If hesychast writers do not always speak of this explicitly, it is because they assume it as axiomatic.

Another basic presupposition in hesychast teaching is the need for spiritual direction. The hesychast should, if possible, be under the personal guidance of an experienced elder (Greek *geron*; Russian *starets*). This was emphasized, at the first beginnings of monasticism, by Antony of Egypt (251–356): "If possible, for every step that a monk takes, for every drop of water that he drinks in his cell, he should entrust the decision to the elders, to avoid making some mistake in what he does" (*Apophthegmata*, alphabetical collection, Antony 38). "Above all else," Kallistos and Ignatios Xanthopoulos insisted, "search diligently for an unerring guide and teacher" (§14).

Hesychast Renaissance

The hesychast tradition of prayer, as taught by Symeon the New Theologian, Gregory of Sinai, and Gregory Palamas, was reaffirmed in the 18th century by the movement of the Greek Kollyvades, especially through the publication in 1782 of the vast collection of ascetic and mystical texts entitled the *Philokalia*. Edited by Makarios of Corinth (1731–1805) and Nikodemos of the Holy Mountain (1749–1809), this constitutes a veritable encyclopedia of hesychasm.

In Russia, the first detailed account of Hesychast teachings was provided by Nil Sorskii (ca. 1433–1508), who during a stay on Athos had gained a first-hand knowledge of the practice of the Jesus Prayer, and who was particularly influenced by Gregory of Sinai. The Slavonic translation of the *Philokalia*, made by Paisy Velichkovsky (1722–94) and published in 1793, proved widely influential in 19th-century Russia, and was used by Seraphim of Sarov (1759–

1833) and by the elders of the Optino hermitage. Hesychast teaching was likewise disseminated by Ignatius Brianchaninov (1807–67) and Theophan the Recluse (1815–94); the latter prepared a greatly expanded Russian translation of the *Philokalia*.

During the 20th century hesychasm underwent a further renewal, both in Greece and in the western world. It remains today very much a living tradition. In the second half of the century, particularly through the research of John Meyendorff (1926–92), the theology of Gregory Palamas came to be far better understood. At the same time, hesychast writings reached western readers through translations of the *Philokalia*. In the past hesychasm was chiefly propagated in certain Orthodox monastic centers, but today it has come to be practiced by many lay Christians, not only Orthodox but non-Orthodox. The spread of hesychasm among the laity is something that its 14th-century protagonists would have applauded. Gregory of Sinai sent his disciples out from the Holy Mountain to the city of Thessaloniki, to act as guides to lay people; and Gregory Palamas, in a dispute with a certain monk Job, insisted that Paul's words, "Pray without ceasing" (1 Thes. 5.17), are addressed not just to monastics but to every Christian without exception. Hesychasm is in principle a universal way.

SEE ALSO: Contemporary Orthodox Theology; Elder (Starets); Jesus Prayer; Kollyvadic Fathers; Optina; *Philokalia*; *Pilgrim, Way of the*; Pontike, Evagrios (ca. 345–399); St. Gregory Palamas (1296–1359); St. Ignatius Brianchaninov (1807–1867); St. Nikodemos the Hagiorite (1749–1809); St. Paisy Velichovsky (1722–1794); St. Seraphim of Sarov (1759–1833); St. Symeon the New Theologian (949–1022); St. Theophan (Govorov) the Recluse (1815–1894)

References and Suggested Readings

Adnès, P. (1968) "Hésychasme," in *Dictionnaire de spiritualité* 7: cols. 381–99. Paris: Cerf.

Alfeyev, H. (2000) *St. Symeon the New Theologian and Orthodox Tradition*. Oxford: Oxford University Press.

Hausherr, I. (1956) "L'hésychasme, Étude de spiritualité," *Orientalia Christiana Periodica* 22: 5–40, 247–85; reprinted in I. Hausherr (1966) *Hésychasme et prière*, Orientalia

Christiana Analecta 176. Rome: Pont. Institutum Orientalium Studiorum, pp. 163–237.

Horujy, S. S. (2004) *Hesychasm: An Annotated Bibliography.* Moscow: Russian Orthodox Church.

Lossky, V. (1957) *The Mystical Theology of the Eastern Church.* London: James Clarke.

Lossky, V. (1963) *The Vision of God.* London: Faith Press.

Louth, A. (1981) *The Origins of the Christian Mystical Tradition.* Oxford: Clarendon Press.

McGuckin, J. A. (2001) *Standing in God's Holy Fire: The Spiritual Tradition of Byzantium.* London: Darton, Longman and Todd.

Meyendorff, J. (1964) *A Study of Gregory Palamas.* London: Faith Press.

Meyendorff, J. (1974) *St. Gregory Palamas and Orthodox Spirituality.* Crestwood, NY: St. Vladimir's Seminary Press.

Meyendorff, J. (1983) "Is 'Hesychasm' the Right Word? Remarks on Religious Ideology in the Fourteenth Century," in C. Mango and O. Pritsak (eds.) *Okeanos: Essays presented to I. Ševčenko on his Sixtieth Birthday.* Harvard Ukrainian Studies 7. Cambridge, MA: Harvard University Press, pp. 447–57.

Ware, K. (2000) *The Inner Kingdom.* Crestwood, NY: St. Vladimir's Seminary Press, pp. 89–110.

Hexapsalmoi

JOHN A. MCGUCKIN

The Greek word for the "Six Psalms." It denotes the preliminary prayers which the reader intones at the commencement of Matins (Orthros). The Six Psalms comprise Psalms 3, 37, 61, 87, 102, and 142 in the Septuagint numbering. They are penitential in tone and are regarded as a very important part of the Matins service, which in ancient times always began in darkness and moved through sunrise (when the gospel was sung). The Six Psalms begin the vigil aspect of Matins and in many places the church candles are extinguished and people stand very quietly for the penitential prayers. Halfway through the Six Psalms, the officiating priest leaves the altar and comes before the Iconostasis silently to say the Morning Prayers of Matins, as intercessions for the people. It is a pious belief among some Orthodox that at the Last Judgment the guardian angel shall recite these psalms before the throne on behalf of the soul. This is why many stand with specially close attention, thinking of the Judgment of God when they are read in church.

Hieratikon

JOHN A. MCGUCKIN

Greek for "Priest's [Book]" (Slavonic, *Sluzhebnik*), referring to the collection of liturgical services (for which reason it is sometimes also referred to as the *Liturgikon*) edited to be of use particularly to the officiating priest (omitting the choir parts). It contains the priest's prayers for Vespers, Matins, and the three main liturgies of St. Chrysostom, St. Basil, and the Presanctified of St. Gregory. Various editions of the *Hieratikon* also usually contain other materials, such as the calendar of the saints (*Menaion*), dismissal texts for various days, special *Prokeimena* or psalm verses for various feasts, and rubrics (instructions on liturgical form).

SEE ALSO: Divine Liturgy, Orthodox; *Euchologion*; Liturgical Books

Hodegitria

JOHN A. MCGUCKIN

Greek term meaning "She who shows the way." In Antiquity this meant a guide, but in Christian usage it alludes to the role of the Virgin as parallel to that of John the Forerunner, showing to humankind the "Way, the Truth, and the Life" by witnessing to Jesus. In Byzantine icons of the Deisis, the Virgin and St. John are always closely associated as the supreme eschatological intercessors, because they were the two preeminent witnesses of Christ's First Coming. The term especially refers to a classical and early type of iconography of the Virgin Mary, where she is usually shown in a three-quarter frontal view, holding the Christ-child on her left arm and pointing to him with her right: showing to the observer him who is "The Way" (Jn. 14.6). The shrine of the Icon of the Panagia Hodegitria in Constantinople (attributed to St. Luke) was one of the most venerated holy places of the ancient city.

References and Suggested Readings

Vassilaki, M. (ed.) (2005) *Images of the Mother of God: Perceptions of the Theotokos in Byzantium.* Aldershot: Ashgate Press.

Plate 29 Fresco of the Virgin Mary from the Monastery Church of St. Antony, Egypt. Photo by John McGuckin.

Holy Spirit

SERGEY TROSTYANSKIY

The subject of the Holy Spirit is one of the deepest mysteries in the church. He is the Sanctifier who never becomes incarnate and whose personal being always stays mysteriously hidden, though universally extensive. From the beginning to the present day the Holy Spirit has never been a subject to comprehend, or an easy subject to speak about. Sergius Bulgakov suggested that this will not change until that time beyond time when the glorified church in Heaven, at the last day, will be able to look upon the true icon of the Holy Spirit, in the form of the glorious communion of elect saints, the completion of the sanctifying operations of the Divine Spirit in the cosmos; as then

it will have a more graphic understanding of his hypostatic reality. In the meantime, the church knows him through his fundamental energy of sanctifying believers, molding them into conformity with the redeeming Christ.

This mysterious character is equally present in the history of the expression of the church's theological tradition. Orthodox pneumatology passed through a number of stages in its development. The basic insights of the New Testament authors presented the Spirit as a personal being. They concurred with the Old Testament view that the Spirit raised up judges, prophets, and seers, friends of God who led the people correctly in worship and belief, speaking as of God himself (Judg. 3.10, 6.34; Neh. 9.30; Is. 11.2). The Old Testament also associates the gift of the Spirit with creativity (Gen. 1.2), with the finding and making of beauty (especially human craft and skill: Ex. 35.31). However, the proper terminology capable of expressing the Spirit as a personal subsistence (*hypostasis*) of the trinitarian God was yet to be developed. The profound teachings on the Spirit as presented by Jesus in the final discourses in the Gospel of John have always been the church's goal and inspiration for all pneumatological thought. The early patristic authors, in their turn, attempted to comprehend the Spirit in terms of his operations and relations to the Father and the Son. These attempts were not without certain historical and semantic confusions, witnessed among the early 2nd-century writers such as Theophilus of Antioch, and other early fathers concerned with understanding God's work of creation and revelation.

The Monarchian crisis of the 3rd century highlighted a new stage in the development of Christian pneumatology. In response to the Monarchians (most notably, Sabellius and Paul of Samosata) who argued for an idea of the unity of God in which the varied "names" of Father, Son, and Spirit were simply variant aspects of the selfsame single being (a monad with different non-hypostatized external aspects), the early Logos school of patristic theologians, especially Tertullian, Hippolytus, and Origen, provided an explicit account of the Father, the Son, and the Spirit as three distinct personal realizations of one divine substance. At this time a distinct terminology was introduced. Origen expressed it clearly in his celebrated formula "one *ousia* [Substance] and three *hypostases* [Persons]." Tertullian presented it as a relation of one Nature (*natura*) to three Persons (*personae*). For a while there was confusion between the western and eastern churches over the terminologies used in Latin and Greek (*hypostasis* among the Greeks being used for differentiation, while its semantic parallel, the Latin word *substantia*, connoted the unity of divine being for westerners). But by the 4th century clarity returned as they realized that the two approaches were saying the same thing by different semantic routes.

The Arian controversy of the 4th century marked a critical stage in the development of pneumatological language in the church. Arius and his later radical followers, Eunomius and Aetius, elevated as a chief theological axiom the philosophical assumptions that cause is always greater than its effect, and that a name has an essential connection with what it designates. These presuppositions forced the Arians to insist that the Father was greater than the Son as the cause of the Son's being, and that the Son was greater than the Spirit as the cause of the Spirit's mission. The radical Arians (*Heterousians*) argued that such names as Unbegotten, the Only Begotten, and the Sanctifier were essential properties that designated different substances. Thus, the Spirit, for these Arians, had to be *Heteroousion*, of a different substance to God, and thus not God.

It was the great Nicene fathers, Athanasius of Alexandria and the Cappadocians (Basil the Great, Gregory the Theologian, and Gregory of Nyssa), who took up the cause to refute such views of the Spirit's role in the Divine Trinity, and in the course of their efforts to establish Nicene Orthodoxy, greatly elaborated the church's theological vocabulary about the Holy Spirit. The Nicene fathers argued against the Heterousian Arians that the Father's causality was the very bond of the Trinity, not its dissolution; his gift of his own being as the common *ousia* of the Divine Triad establishing a perfect equality of nature among the three *hypostases*, and thereby demonstrating the full divinity of the Son and Spirit alongside the Father. They demonstrated that the divine attributes as described in human terms could refer legitimately to the operations of God in the world, but could never clearly express the inner life of God which is always a sublimely ineffable and transcendent mystery. St. Athanasius argued in his *Letters to Serapion* that the

Spirit's sanctifying functions in the church were consummated in the manner in which he deified believers through baptism. This making of the elect into sons and daughters of God, he argued, could not have been effected by one who was not himself divine. St. Basil argued strongly in the treatise *On the Holy Spirit* that the church's ancient doxology demonstrated the Spirit's divine status, and that his primary role in the church and the world was the sanctification and deification of believers. He describes the soul's acquisition of the Holy Spirit beautifully as comparable to a glass lit up by the sun so as to become all light itself. St. Gregory the Theologian argued in his *Theological Orations* (27–31, especially *Oration* 31) that the Holy Spirit must be confessed as *Homoousion* in strict logic, and although the wider church was content to accept his teaching in the course of history, the fathers of the Council of Constantinople in 381 were content to follow St. Basil, and add to the older Nicene Creed simply these extension terms to elaborate the Orthodox core of belief in the Holy Spirit: "And [we believe] in the Holy Spirit, the Lord and Giver of Life who proceeds from the Father, who with the Father and Son is together worshipped and glorified, who spoke through the prophets." The operations of sanctification and inspiration are especially seen as charisms of the Spirit of God, who is also confessed as "Lord of Life," especially that divine life (*zoe* more than *bios*) which he communicates to the faithful to conform them into the mystery of Christ.

Orthodox theology is far more than a semantic history, however, and it is especially in the church's doxological and ascetical traditions that we find extensive evidence of how the church has celebrated and experienced the Holy Spirit of God: as comforter, sanctifier, illuminator, and initiator. The roles of the Spirit in the process of the progressive cleansing and deification of the Christian are especially prevalent in the Orthodox baptismal liturgy and prayers. In the celebration of the Holy Eucharist (and equally in the ordination prayers and prayers of blessing), the most sacred moment of the consecration is attributed to the descent and operation of the Holy Spirit (*Epiclesis*). The lyrical prayer to the Holy Spirit in the words of the Byzantine mystic Niketas Stethatos (*Kephalaia Gnostica* 46) sums up well the church's passionate desire for the Spirit:

The Spirit is light, life, and peace. If you are illumined by that Spirit your life will be established in peaceful serenity; a spring will gush out from within you, being the wisdom of the Logos, and the mystical knowledge of existent being. On that day you will come to have the mind of Christ, and know the mysteries of the Kingdom of God, and you will enter the depths of the deity.

SEE ALSO: Baptism; Cappadocian Fathers; Council of Constantinople I (381); Epiclesis; Holy Trinity; Logos Theology

References and Suggested Readings

Basil the Great (1980) *On the Holy Spirit*. Crestwood, NY: St. Vladimir's Seminary Press.

McGuckin, J. A. (2001) *St. Gregory of Nazianzus: An Intellectual Biography*. Crestwood, NY: St. Vladimir's Seminary Press.

McGuckin, J. A. (2008) *The Orthodox Church: An Introduction to Its History, Doctrine and Spiritual Culture*. Oxford: Wiley-Blackwell.

Holy Trinity

ARISTOTLE PAPANIKOLAOU

The Trinity is what Christians eventually came to refer to as the New Testament witnesses to a faith in Jesus as the Son of God, who as a result of his unique relation to the Father, reveals the Father and offers the eschatological gift of salvation by the power of the Holy Spirit. The New Testament itself does not give any definitive or creed-like statements about God as Trinity. What the earliest followers and interpreters of Jesus do is to continue to speak about Jesus and interpret his life, sayings, and deeds, together with the salvation he offers, in terms of Jesus' relationship to the Father and the Spirit.

Although there existed a variety of interpretations of Jesus in the earliest formulations of Christianity, two positions became predominant. The first consists of understanding Jesus as a divine mediator, but not generally seen as divine in the same degree as God the Father (often known as Pre-Nicene subordinationism); the second affirms Jesus as of equal divinity with the Father. It is important for the understanding of the doctrine of the Trinity to notice that these two positions share many common assumptions: (1) that Jesus is the Messiah and, as such, the one who fulfills the promise of salvation; (2) that this salvation consists in the bringing of creation into some form of renewed contact with the divine; and (3) as mediator of this contact between divinity and creation, Jesus is revealed as the divine Son of God. The core of the debates of the identity of Christ in the 2nd and 3rd centuries gravitated around the question of the degree and nature of divinity ascribed to Jesus by the church.

These two parallel trajectories would ultimately culminate – and critically so – in the famous controversies of the 4th century between St. Athanasius of Alexandria and the Nicene theologians, and the so-called "Arians." Athanasius would stand in continuity with Sts. Ignatius of Antioch and Irenaeus of Lyon in emphasizing salvation as humanity's freedom from death and corruption, and that this freedom requires a conceptualizing of the God–world relation in terms of a communion between the created and the uncreated. The unequivocal declaration of the co-equal divinity of the Son with the Father occurs first in Athanasius, who argues that there is no freedom from death and corruption, and hence no eternal life, without a communion of the created with the full divinity as revealed in the person and work of Christ.

What the debate between Athanasius and the Arians makes fundamentally clear is Athanasius' prioritization of a grammar of divine–human communion in discourse about God's relation to the world. The Arians did not deny the necessity of creation's communion with the divine; nor did they deny that such a communion required mediation; but their particular understanding of divine simplicity forced them to reduce the mediator to something in between the uncreated and created, with the net effect being both the negation of their own notion of divine simplicity and the denial of real communion with the fullness of the divine life. St. Athanasius was not attempting to reject the notion of divine simplicity, but rather attempting to radicalize it so that it allowed for communion between two ontologically distinct realities: the uncreated and the created. Such a radicalization requires conceptualizing God in terms of distinctions that do not negate the unity of God's eternal being. For his theology, in God's being, there is Father and Son, with the Son being of co-equal divinity with the Father, and who mediates the created to the uncreated by being united to human-ity, incarnated as Jesus. For Athanasius, anything less than this affirmation negates the possibility of divine–human communion and thus the possibility of crea-tion's overcoming of death and corruption, i.e., annihilation. It would thus be wrong to see the 4th-century debates as simply about the divinity of the Son. The debates are also about understanding God, whose simplicity is such that God's being is freedom to be in communion with creation through the death and resurrection of the incarnate Son.

After Athanasius, the three Christian thinkers most credited with further elaborating the Christian doc-trine of the Trinity are those who have usually been called the Cappadocian fathers: Basil of Caesarea, Gregory the Theologian, and Gregory of Nyssa. These Christian thinkers were responsible for two important contributions to the doctrine of the Trinity: the clear

Plate 30 Contemporary icon of the Divine Trinity (after Rublev). By Eileen McGuckin. The Icon Studio: www.sgtt.org.

affirmation of the divinity of the Holy Spirit and the further clarification of trinitarian language. In *On the Holy Spirit*, St. Basil defends the divinity of the Holy Spirit on the basis of the Spirit's activity in bringing creation into communion with the uncreated. On the basis of the patristic axiom that only God can effect communion between the uncreated and created, if the completion of this communion is left to the Holy Spirit, then the Holy Spirit is evidently of co-equal divinity with the Father and the Son. In *Oration 31*, St. Gregory the Theologian went further than his friend Basil in explicitly declaring that the Holy Spirit is God, consubstantial with Father and Son. If, then, we understand that the full doctrine of the Trinity is no less than the affirmation of the co-equal divinity of the Father, Son, and the Holy Spirit, without negating monotheism, then the unequivocal and explicit decla-ration of this affirmation comes in the 4th century. It would be wrong, however, to see this doctrine as a late Hellenized form of Christianity, since the patristic formulation simply gives expression to the God who offers communion with God's life in Jesus Christ by the Holy Spirit, and in so doing, is in direct continuity with the New Testament apostolic witness of the eschatological salvation offered in the person of Jesus.

The questions and challenges to Christian procla-mations of Jesus as fully divine necessitated the use and creation of categories beyond the earliest apos-tolic witnesses of Jesus. In order to express the unity and distinctions within the trinitarian Godhead, Basil of Caesarea and Gregory of Nyssa employed the use of the distinction between *ousia* (essence, nature) and *hypostasis* (person, proprium). Although these catego-ries are derived from Greek philosophy, they were given new meaning within the context of the trini-tarian controversies. *Ousia* refers to the divine essence, that which as uncreated is ontologically distinct from creation and is possessed by Father, Son, and Holy Spirit; *hypostasis* refers to that which is distinct in the Godhead, i.e., that the Father is neither Son nor Holy Spirit, that the Son is neither Father nor Holy Spirit, and that the Holy Spirit is neither Father nor Son. Metropolitan John Zizioulas (b. 1931) has recently claimed that the use of these terms by the Cappadocian fathers did more than simply indicate sameness and distinction in God, but inaugurated an ontological revolution. His claim has sparked a wide debate in contemporary Orthodox theology over the proper interpretation of the Cappadocians and over the implications of the doctrine of the Trinity.

During the patristic and medieval period there emerged a controversy between Latin and Greek Christendom around the so-called *filioque* clause, which refers to the affirmation of the procession of the Holy Spirit "From the Father *and from the Son*." This theological speculation is attributed to Augustine of Hippo, but he was never condemned in Greek Christendom for this particular theological claim. The controversy began when the phrase "and from the Son" was inserted into the Latin version of the Nicene-Constantinopolitan Creed, and was increasingly prayed with this insertion during the Latin Mass. Its insertion into the creed in Latin Christendom was then used to amplify the differences between Latin and Greek Christendoms, which gradually became alienated the one from the other for a variety of reasons, not least of which were political and cultural. The inclusion of the *filioque* in the creed eventually led to a response by Byzantine intellectuals, most notably by Photius in his *Mystagogy*. The problem with the *filioque* is not the theological speculation *per se* of the Holy Spirit's relation to the Father and the Son; there is ample evidence of this kind of speculation in the Christian thinkers of Greek Christendom. The real issue is its inclusion into the creed, which raises such speculation to the level of a dogmatic truth, which then becomes an occasion for exacerbating and hardening divisions between Christian communions. The fact that the *filioque per se* should not be a cause for divisions among Christians was reiterated in a recent statement (October 2007) produced by the North American Orthodox-Catholic Theological Consultation.

After the fall of Constantinople in 1453 there is little evidence of any extensive theological thinking on the doctrine of the Trinity. The first signs of a revival of trinitarian theology occur in 19th-century Russia. From the 19th century forward, three basic trajectories emerge within contemporary Orthodox theology of the Trinity: the Sophiology of Sergius Bulgakov; the apophaticism of Vladimir Lossky; and the relational ontology of John Zizioulas. Each in his own way attempted to interpret further the patristic understanding of the doctrine of the Trinity.

In 19th-century Russia, trinitarian speculation reemerges with the Sophiology of Vladimir Solovyov (1853–1900), which received its most sophisticated theological development in Sergius Bulgakov's (1871–1944) trilogy, *On Divine Humanity*. At its core, Bulgakov's Sophiology is a trinitarian theology. The key to understanding Bulgakov's trinitarian theology is to, literally, decipher what he means by *Sophia*, which has been the chief stumbling block to fully appreciating Bulgakov's work. The question that must be posed to Bulgakov is the following: why is the concept of Sophia necessary for trinitarian theology?

In the end, Sophia is identified with *homoousios* in Bulgakov's system. Sophia is, quite simply, the *ousia* of God hypostatized in the tri-hypostatic self-revelation of God; but, as such, it is no longer simply *ousia*. Bracketing the self-revelation of the Father in the Son and the Spirit, Bulgakov argues that the Father remains undisclosed. It is only in the self-revelation of God in the Son and the Holy Spirit that all that God is finds expression by being revealed, and only in this self-revelation that all that God is, actually is. There is thus an identification in Bulgakov between the self-revelation of God to Godself and the fullness of God's existence. In this fullness of God's existence, *ousia* is no longer an apophatic concept indicative of impenetrable mystery and transcendence of the Absolute; *ousia* is Sophia. Sophia, for Bulgakov, then, is God's being as the self-revelation of the Father in the Son and the Holy Spirit.

As the very being of God, Sophia must necessarily refer to God's relation to the world, and not simply to the intra-trinitarian relations. If the self-revelation of God in the *Logos* and the Holy Spirit is the revelation of all that God is, then God's relation to creation and humanity is to be included in all that God is. Bulgakov is not here arguing for the eternity of a creation that is restricted by time and space. If, however, all theology is grounded in the premise that God has revealed Godself as creator and redeemer, it becomes impossible for Bulgakov to conceive the thinking of the divine that does not include God existing as eternally relating to creation in some way. Therefore, God's self-revelation as the revelation of all that God is, is also God's being as love, and, to this extent, being as the freedom to create and redeem what is not God; in short, as eternally relating to creation. Replying to those who argued that he was making creation constitutive of the being of God, Bulgakov explicitly denied the charge. For Bulgakov, it is impossible to conceive of God's being as not already existing as an eternal relation to creation, even if that means that God is not compelled to realize this creation in time and space.

Together with Georges Florovsky (1893–1979), Vladimir Lossky (1903–58) was responsible for inaugurating the movement most influential within contemporary Orthodox theology known as the "neo-patristic synthesis." For Lossky, the doctrine of the Trinity is a revealed fact and the goal of theology is to find the proper language to express the antinomic belief of God's unity-in-distinction. The revelation of the divine–human communion in the incarnation, for Lossky, demands that theology be apophatic, which is not simply defining God in terms of what God is not. Apophaticism, according to Lossky, is the rejection of the rationalization of theology; that is, the understanding of knowledge of God in terms of rational propositions rather than a mystical union that transcends reason. If the ultimate goal is for the Christian to progress toward union with the divine, then the purpose of dogma is not to arrive at propositions of faith to which one must give assent, but rather to express the antinomy of divine–human communion so as to guide the Christian toward this *telos* (goal). The distinction between *ousia* and *hypostasis* functions, therefore, is simply to indicate the antinomy, without attempting to give a definitive understanding of the doctrine of the Trinity.

Another crucial antinomy for Lossky is that between the essence and energies of God. The essence of God refers to the impenetrable mystery of God, while the energies refer to that aspect of God in which creation participates and is deified. It is not necessarily clear in Lossky how the antinomy of essence-energies coheres with the trinitarian antinomy of *ousia-hypostasis*, other than the trinitarian persons conveying the energies of God. In other words, if God relates to creation through God's energies, it is not clear in Lossky how God's being as Trinity is the same as God's freedom to be in communion with creation. A tension also exists in Lossky between his apophatic approach to the Trinity and his more Kataphatic statements about personhood as being

freedom from the necessity of death and the corruption inherent in created nature, and as that term which indicates irreducibility and uniqueness.

John Zizioulas is responsible for the most influential and the most controversial contemporary Orthodox trinitarian theology. The controversy centers on his theology of personhood, which he links directly to the distinction between *ousia* and *hypostasis* given by the Cappadocian fathers. It would be a mistake, however, to place Zizioulas in the camp of theologians who espouse a "Social Trinity": his theological understanding of personhood is not simply a derivation from a community of three eternal, self-conscious persons. The basis for his theology of personhood is the divine–human communion experienced in the Eucharist.

This personal understanding of divine– human communion in Christ informs Zizioulas' trinitarian theology, especially his understanding of the monarchy of the Father. According to Zizioulas, the source of God's trinitarian being is God the Father. The net result is that being is critically identified with personhood and not with essence, as it was in Greek philosophy. The emphasis on the monarchy of the Father, the distinction between *hypostasis* and *ousia*, the identification of *hypostasis* and *prosopon*, and the distinction between the uncreated and the created (all of which are informed by the experience of divine-human communion in the Eucharist), are nothing short of an "ontological revolution" in philosophy and Christian theology, as Zizioulas sees it. The emphasis on the monarchy of the Father is especially important for Zizioulas, since only if God is free from the necessity of nature can God be free to be in communion with creation. If God is confined to the necessity of nature, then God cannot give what God does not have, and thus created existence is destined to the death and corruption inherent in created nature.

The Christian doctrine of the Trinity, for Zizioulas, is a revolution in ontology insofar as it gives expression to the being of God who in freedom and love is in communion with the ontological other – creation; but the ontological implications of such a communion are such that for the first time in philosophy and theology primacy has been given to the concepts that were thought by the ancient Greeks not to have ontological content: ideas such as person, relation, uniqueness, irreducibility, and freedom (the "accidentals" of Greek thought).

Zizioulas' interpretation of the Cappadocians has come under fire from several patristic scholars for reading into the fathers a theology that is simply not there. That notwithstanding, it could be argued that Zizioulas' understanding of personhood as a relational event of freedom and uniqueness is that which is logically implied in the high patristic doctrine of the Trinity, especially if this doctrine is governed by the Christian grammar of divine–human communion. What is clear, around this period, is that the goal was to avoid anti-Nicene interpretations, because something less than full communion with the One God would be given, and not simply because there was concern to safeguard an already given faith in a God who is three and one. *Hypostasis* is appropriated so as to indicate distinctions within God that would allow for communion with the "true" God in the person of the Son; the language of *ousia* simply cannot do that work. Within the context of the grammar of the doctrine itself, *hypostasis* is that category which emerges as an attempt to make sense of the God who, in love and freedom, is incarnate in Jesus Christ. Thus, the reworking of *hypostasis* and *prosopon* emerges against the background of a grammar of divine–human communion. What was being settled in these patristic controversies, therefore, was not simply language that would identify what is common or particular in God, but the very language of divine–human communion itself.

Each of these contemporary Orthodox trajectories share in common an understanding of the doctrine of the Trinity as the Christian expression of God's being as free to be in communion with what is not God. The disagreement lies in the implications of this consensus of divine-human communion for trinitarian theology. In the future, Orthodox trinitarian theology faces at least two issues. First, the perennial question of patristic hermeneutics: is the question of God as Trinity a settled one; or (if one agrees that the settling of the question of God is an impossibility for faith), what might constitute authentic amplification of the classic patristic theology? Second, Orthodox thought is in serious need of a theology that integrates two not so manifestly compatible strands of thought: apophaticism, together with its essence-energies distinction, and the classically formulated doctrine of the Trinity.

SEE ALSO: Berdiaev, Nikolai A. (1874–1948); Bulgakov, Sergius (Sergei) (1871–1944); Cappadocian Fathers; Christ; Deification; Eucharist; Fatherhood of God; *Filioque*; Florovsky, Georges V. (1893–1979); Holy Spirit; Incarnation (of the Logos); Lossky, Vladimir (1903–1958); Patristics; Solovyov, Vladimir (1853–1900); Sophiology; Soteriology

References and Suggested Readings

Bobrinskoy, B. (2001) *The Mystery of the Trinity*. Crestwood, NY: St. Vladimir's Seminary Press.

Bulgakov, S. (1933) *L'Orthodoxie*. Paris: Alcan.

Hanson, R. P. C. (1988) *The Search for the Christian Doctrine of God*. Edinburgh: T&T Clark.

Lonergan, B. (1976) *The Way to Nicaea*. London: Darton, Longman, and Todd.

McGuckin, J. A. (2001) *St. Gregory of Nazianzus: An Intellectual Biography*. Crestwood, NY: St. Vladimir's Seminary Press.

Papanikolaou, A. (2006) *Being with God: Trinity, Apophaticism, and Divine-Human Communion*. Notre Dame: Notre Dame University Press.

Zizioulas, J. (1985) *Being as Communion: Studies in Personhood and the Church*. Crestwood, NY: St. Vladimir's Seminary Press.

Horologion

TODD E. FRENCH

From the Greek meaning "Book of Hours" (Slavonic, *Chasoslov*), the *Horologion* is the primary book of divine services as designed for use by the reader and chanter. In distinction to the *Euchologion*, which is the priestly service book, the abbreviated versions of the *Horologion* often omit the words of the priest's part. Taking its rise from the regular hours of monastic prayer and the specific interest the ascetics had in organizing the reading and singing of the entire collection of psalms, the liturgical hours organize the weekly recitation of the psalms by sections known as *kathismata*. The book of the *Horologion* contains the rite of the Vespers service moving through the Prayer at the Supper Table, Compline, Great Compline, Midnight Office, Matins (Orthros), the services of first, third, sixth, and ninth hours, as well as the text of various Canons and Akathists, hymns of the day (Apolytikia and Kontakia) and the service of Preparation for and Thanksgiving after Communion. Commonly published in its most popular form as the *Great Horologion*, the book may also contain the feast dates of the saints (a small *Menaion*), as well as giving short biographies of the more significant ones. Given its popularity as a primary source for individual prayer among Orthodox laity as well as in churches, it has also recently found translation into digital formats and is currently accessible through the Internet, a testament to its broader appreciation.

SEE ALSO: *Akathistos*; Apolytikion; *Euchologion*; Kathisma; Kontakion; Liturgical Books

References and Suggested Readings

Orthodox Eastern Church (1997) *The Great Horologion*, trans. Holy Transfiguration Monastery. Boston: Holy Transfiguration Monastery

Raya, J. and Jose De Vinck, B. (1969) *Byzantine Daily Worship*. Allendale, NJ: Alleluia Press.

Humanity

M. C. STEENBERG

"Humanity" derives from the Latin *humanitas*, referring to the whole of the human race. In theological terms, it may refer both to the collective species of the human creature, or to the nature of man. Hence, in Orthodox theological writings, "humanity" describes both the created essence of man (thus being largely synonymous with "human nature"), or the race of those creatures who bear this nature.

Theological Fundamentals

Christianity is, at its heart, a story of humanity. It takes its beginning from the apostolic encounter with the Son of God met and known in his humanity, and through that encounter reveals the economy of the salvation of humanity as a whole. The starting point for an Orthodox understanding of humanity, then, is not in a narrative or scientific definition of abstract origins of species, but in the concrete humanity encountered in the incarnate Jesus Christ. It is his person that reveals to us the authentic contours of human nature, as well as its potential for restoration and perfection in union with God.

Too often, attempts to articulate a Christian definition of humanity begin with wholly protological discussions (that is, those that deal with origins, with creation). However, the christological revelation of human nature demands that the initial point of reference is not the first man (Adam), but the perfected man: the New Adam, Jesus. So it is that the fundamental affirmations the church makes about humanity come from the example of the incarnate Lord. These affirmations begin with the experience of Christ's humanity as created and material: that he was born in the flesh and so existed in his earthly sojourn. Human nature, as beheld in this human Christ, is affirmed as a material nature, made by God of the stuff of the cosmos – that very act and reality thereby affirming the sanctity of the material in the most transcendent order possible. Humanity cannot be understood as a spiritual nature residing in a secondary material shell, or as existing in some state of corporeal purgatory: to be human is fundamentally to be material, and the existence of Christ in his material human nature enshrines the Orthodox confession that this physicality is not a defect in human nature, but a holy dimension of humankind's created state.

This material aspect to human nature does not mean, however, that humanity is solely corporeal. The incarnate Christ revealed a humanity in which the physical body was wholly united to an immaterial soul, and the lengthy theological disputes over the relationship between this human soul and the eternal existence of the *Logos* (as, for example, in the Apollinarian disputes of the 4th century and the Monothelite disputes of the 7th) emphasize how central this confession was, and is, to the Orthodox vision of the Son. In terms of the Son's incarnational witness to human nature, it affirms that humanity is fundamentally a commingling of material and immaterial, in which the sacredness of both elements of its composition is affirmed by their perfect union and concord.

Further, the incarnate Christ, who is confessed to exist as perfect God as well as perfect man, conveys a third dimension to the nature of humanity: in addition to being material as well as immaterial (of body and of soul), the human creature is fashioned to attain and exist in union with God himself. Beholding the true union of divine and human in the incarnation, humanity is able to see that its nature is wholly capable of union with God, and that its created condition does not bar it from such union. In this way, Christ's incarnation shows the doctrine of deification to be a fundamental precept of an Orthodox understanding of humanity. Such deifying communion with the Father is the natural potential of every human creature, as fashioned first in Adam and met in perfection in the Son.

From the Incarnation to Creation

Mention of Adam draws our attention to creation. Taking its beginning from the revelation of the incarnate Christ, Orthodoxy articulates the origins of humanity from this incarnational perspective. The chief scriptural confessions of humanity's creation, used in conveying the story of human origins, come in Genesis 1–3 and John 1. It is the gospel's accounting of creation by the Word, "through whom all things were made" (Jn. 1.3), and in whom was the life of man (cf. Jn. 1.4), that the fully christological perspective of Genesis has its orientation. When the opening book of the Scriptures relates that "In the beginning God created' (Gen. 1.1), and later that the Lord "formed man of the dust of the ground and breathed into his nostrils the breath of life" (Gen. 2.7), the church is able to confess that this Creator God is none other than the eternal Son, that the breath is that of the Spirit. Similarly, the church is able to see the confession that man is created "in our image, according to our likeness" (Gen. 1.26, 28) as a wholly trinitarian proclamation, in which humanity's fashioning after the image of the Son is identified – he who is "the Image of the invisible God, the firstborn over all creation" (Col. 1.15).

This incarnational vision opens up a number of key realities in the scriptural accountings of humanity's first formation. First of all, the fact that it is fashioned directly by the "hands" of God (the Son and Spirit) sets it apart from all else in the created order.

While God fashions all that exists, only humanity is taken up from the dust, rather than being called into creation by a command alone. This unique intimacy in the manner of humanity's formation identifies in the creation story a reality already seen in the incarnation of the Son; namely, that humanity is fashioned for a particular and precious union with its Maker (that very union seen perfected in the harmony of divine and human natures in the Son). Similarly, the fact that God "breathed into [man's] nostrils the breath of life" shows forth the spiritual dimension of that incarnational communion, by which humanity's life becomes fulfilled in the indwelling of the Holy Spirit. Thus the creation story is seen to reveal the very dimension of human existence of which St. Paul would speak in writing to the church at Corinth: "Do you not know that your body is the temple of the Holy Spirit who is in you, whom you have from God …?" (1 Cor. 6.19).

Secondly, the scriptural creation accounts emphasize the dual reality of human nature to which Christ's incarnation bears witness; namely, the material and immaterial realities in man. While Genesis relates a human formation in which the handiwork of God is truly a "dust creature" (indeed, the Hebrew *Adam* is built on the same word root as *Adama*, "dust"), thus intrinsically material and corporeal, this creature is nonetheless only a "living being" (Gen. 2.7) when the physical body is infused with the breath of God. The creation sagas therefore show forth humanity as a composite creature, in which these two aspects of materiality and immateriality are intrinsic to the living, God-fashioned, creature.

There is some variation among the fathers of the church as to whether this composite reality of humanity is best expressed as being "bi-partite" (that is, a composite of two elements: body and soul) or "tri-partite" (of three: body, soul, and spirit); and they, like the Scriptures on which they are normally commentating, at times alternate between the two descriptions (e.g., Mt. 10.28; 1 Thes. 5.23). In fact, the variation between the two serves to emphasize the very points revealed through the incarnation: that man is of material as well as immaterial dimensions (body and soul), and fashioned for union with the Father's Spirit. Expressing humanity as a creature of body, soul, and spirit points to the union in the one Spirit – the Holy

Spirit. This was perhaps expressed most clearly in the writings of St. Irenaeus of Lyons:

> As the body animated by the soul is certainly not itself the soul, but has fellowship with the soul as long as God desires, so also the soul herself is not life, but partakes in the life bestowed on her by God. Wherefore also the prophetic word declares of the first made man, "He became a living soul," teaching us that by participation in life the soul became alive. Thus the soul and the life which it possesses must be understood as separate existences. (*Against Heresies* 2.34.4)

St. Irenaeus, like other fathers, draws attention to the fact that that condition of communion in God's Spirit is intrinsic to the created state of the human creature, while at the same time the Spirit is never a creaturely part of man, but rather the fruit of his union with God.

Created into the Image of God

Mention has already been made of the scriptural affirmation that humanity is created in the "image and likeness of God" (Gen. 1.26, 28). Just what constitutes the "image" after which humanity is fashioned finds different expression among various fathers of the church. For some, it is the possession of an immaterial soul; for others, the freedom and dominion of the human creature which reflects God's own; for some, the fashioning into the form of the incarnate Son; for others, the creative potential in humanity that reflects the nature of the Creator. What is common to all of these differing expressions is the notion that humanity created "after God's image" implies a direct connection between the Creator and the creature, realized across the various dimensions of human nature. One encounters, in the human creature, a vision of God in whose image the creature is fashioned, and whose contours it thus bears forth into the cosmos. In this way, humanity serves as an "icon" of God in creation.

What is important to the scriptural testimony of the divine image is the differentiation maintained between Christ who is the "Image proper" and humanity which is created *after* or *according to* this true Image which is Christ. Being created "after the image of God" is thus a participatory reality, not a static dimension of human existence. At times, in the patristic teachings, the phrase "image and likeness" is taken as a single unit; at others, a distinction is drawn between image and likeness, with the latter being the actual approximation of the human creature to God into whose image the creature has been fashioned. In this latter distinction, "image" is generally taken to describe the unchanging nature of humanity as created by God, while "likeness" refers to the actual living out and realization of this image.

The One Race of One Blood

As all humanity is fashioned by God and fully exists in communion with him, humanity is itself created for unity. Characteristic of the church fathers is the reading of humanity's interconnection through St. Paul's analogy of the one body with many members (Rom. 1.4). Rather than as autonomous beings in social or fraternal association, the patristic writings tend to treat of humanity as a single organic entity – "one race" of "one blood" – which experiences both its advantages and disadvantages in the contact of this unity. The theological implication of this vision is that sin and redemption operate both at the personal level in the human economy, but also at the level of humanity as a whole.

Once again, this vision takes its centering in Christ. Writing on the taking up of human nature by the Son, St. Athanasius the Great would emphasize that in so doing he "joined himself to all by a like nature, and naturally clothed all with incorruption" (*On the Incarnation of the Word* 9), just as St. Gregory the Theologian would later famously remark, in the context of a christological debate, that Christ took to himself the entirety of human nature, "since what is not assumed is not healed" (*Epistle* 101). While these are important texts in the context of christological discussion, with regard to the church's vision of humanity they are equally central. Each shows forth, through an emphasis on the true and full humanity of the Lord in the incarnation, the manner in which the human race is seen "summed up" in human nature itself – that Christ, by becoming fully human, affects and transforms the lives of *every* human. So it is that by taking on human nature he unites to himself the whole ailing race; so it is that in assuming humanity to himself, he saves humanity therapeutically as a whole.

So it is, too, that Christ shows forth a "re-heading" of the one body of which St. Paul spoke, and in so doing reveals the intrinsically interconnected nature of the race. At the same time, this witness to humanity's redemption through the race's union with God discloses the manner in which sin has affected it, historically as well as in present and ongoing experience. Just as "when one member of the body suffers, the whole suffers with it" (1 Cor. 12.26), the engagement in sin by any member of the "one blood" has detrimental effects on the whole. Thus, while Orthodoxy has always resisted the idea that human nature is somehow altered or made deficient through sin itself, humanity perceived as a single body has always provided it with an effective way of understanding how sin in one place or era affects the lives of men and women in another; of how sin itself can become the context of the whole race's existence.

This same witness of humanity's interconnection as one race lies behind the missionary imperative of Orthodox ascesis. While ascesis is important at a personal level, as the struggle to overcome sin and the passions in one's life, it is important too as a ministry to the whole of the human race – a race which is wounded when anyone sins, and which is healed when anyone is redeemed. This is the theology of the human person that lies behind one of the most famous of the apophthegmata of St. Seraphim of Sarov: "acquire the Spirit of peace within you, and a thousand around you will be saved." The interconnected nature of humanity means that each human person has at his or her disposal a share in the stature of all humankind. A sin committed may wound the race, and yet a life transformed through struggle and the grace of God may serve to heal it in its wholeness; and this is why the ascetical struggle to which each Christian person is called is understood in the church to be a missionary work for the redemption of all humankind.

Summary

Humanity, therefore, is understood in Orthodoxy as that reality experienced in the incarnate Jesus Christ; there wholly united to divinity. That union shows forth the authentic contours of the human creature which God had once fashioned from the dust, and which at every birth he fashions anew. This being composed of body and soul, of materiality and the immaterial, is fashioned for a life of communion in the Spirit; enabled to this through its crafting and recrafting by the Son. By virtue of its one blood as well as its union in the one God, humanity is a single body in which each person is a member, of precious value to, and of singular influence upon, the entire whole. This vision of humanity reveals both the full scope of the tragedy of sin, but also the nature of man's redemption in Christ, who takes humanity to himself in its wholeness and thereby draws it fully into the eternal life of God.

SEE ALSO: Christ; Deification; Soteriology

References and Suggested Readings

Lossky, V. (1997) *In the Image and Likeness of God.* Crestwood, NY: St. Vladimir's Seminary Press.
McGuckin, J. A. (2008) *The Orthodox Church: An Introduction to Its History, Doctrine, and Spiritual Culture.* Oxford: Wiley-Blackwell.

Hymnography

DIMITRI CONOMOS

It may be argued that Byzantine hymnody originates from the establishment of the first Christian community: that of Christ and his disciples. Evidence of early Christian hymns can be extracted from the New Testament. Matthew and Mark, describing the Last Supper, report that when Jesus and his followers had finished the meal, *and when they had sung a hymn,* they went out to the Mount of Olives (Mt. 6.30; Mk. 14.26). This "hymn" may well have been the traditional Passover Hallel (Ps. 112–117). In Colossians 3.16 St. Paul admonishes the new Christian assemblies, saying: "Let the word of Christ dwell in you richly in all wisdom; teaching and admonishing one another *in psalms and hymns and spiritual songs,* singing with grace in you heart to the Lord." Biblical scholarship has now identified a considerable amount of hymnodic material embedded in the text of the New Testament, as for example in Romans 11.33–36, Ephesians 1.3–14, and Revelation 1.5–8.

Subsequent evidence for this tradition may be traced in the writings of the early fathers whose prose texts, using hymnodic techniques, actually follow a practice of Greek literature older than the Christian Scriptures. Poetic homilies prove to be extremely valuable, for they represent the transition from pagan to Christian Greek hymns in prose, and they greatly influence the formation and consolidation of the expressive apparatus of hymnody whose elements of style include simple, lively language, elevated character and manner, striking imagery, deft figures of speech, and so forth. Important examples are the 2nd-century Easter Homily (*Peri Pascha*) of Melito of Sardis and the *Partheneion* of Methodios, 4th-century bishop of Olympus. Other early Christian hymns, still used in Orthodox services, are the well-known *Phos Hilarion*, the *Doxology*, *Only-begotten Son*, and the *Trisagion*.

The acquisition of more detailed information about the development of hymnody in the early Christian centuries is frustrated by a lack of secure evidence. Some early monastic resistance to the chanting of hymns in worship was based on the belief that the practice was detrimental to the soul. Equally decisive was the prohibition of the church, following the legalization of Christianity (312), relating to the employment of hymns in worship because of the fear of non-conformist doctrines. The church was, at this time, on its guard against pagan and heretical hymns, *psalmoi idiotikoi* ("personal chants"), as the 4th-century Council of Laodicea calls them. Not only was a canon of Scripture identified, but also the performance of hymns, as were found exclusively in church-approved books, was given to ordained clerks. This conservatively motivated exclusion of non-scriptural hymnody, however, proved to be both a shortsighted

Plate 31 An Orthodox church cantor. Almost all public church services are sung in Orthodox ritual. Photo by John McGuckin.

measure and an extremely dangerous one, because, by restricting the scope of prospective hymnodists, it left the faithful exposed to the charms of an escalating and alluring heretical hymnody. Finally, the Orthodox learned to combat their enemies by using the latter's own weapons; that is, they composed Orthodox hymns which were built on the same metrical and musical patterns as those of the heterodox. Sozomenos, the church historian, is very clear about this when he speaks of how Ephrem the Syrian wrote his own hymns to weaken the sinister influence of the hymns of the Gnostic poets on the souls of his countrymen. Ironically, the growth of Christian hymnody was promoted by the success that the Gnostic and heretical hymns enjoyed, which attracted many Christians to the services in which they were chanted.

Byzantine hymnody written in the new rhythmic (as opposed to the archaic quantitative) verse may be broadly classified into three genres. The earliest is the *troparion*, which makes its appearance in the 3rd century. A generic term, troparion designates any stanza of religious poetry. It is also a collective term for several species of hymn in the Byzantine liturgy. The second is the *kontakion*, a long and elaborate metrical sermon whose history begins in the 6th century. And finally there is the hymn cycle known as the *canon*, known from the 7th century. Each species continued to be composed and to evolve for many centuries side by side with other forms of religious poetry that gradually developed.

After the 5th century, there are indications that Old Testament psalms and canticles, used as lections in the offices of the burgeoning monastic communities, were assumed in urban worship though in an innovative hymnodic form: newly composed stanzas (later known as *stichera*), offering poetic commentaries (literary tropes) with unchanging pendant refrains, were inserted between the biblical verses and executed in responsorial fashion by congregational choirs.

Although no music for the early hymns survives, it is generally held that, like their Gregorian counterparts, the Byzantine melodies were unpretentious, generally composed on the rule of one tone to each syllable of the text, to render them suitable for congregational singing. They were familiar to everyone (the melodies were usually transmitted by oral tradition) and consequently did not need to be written down.

The earliest notated chants reflect the characteristics of a widespread oral tradition. Their simple tunes use a restricted stock of musical phrases indicative of each mode; they often divide into sections, each consisting of a pair of lines with the same music, and end with a separate refrain-like line known as the *akroteleution*. Although the music appears to be rather plain, these verses could be performed in different ways: congregation alone; soloist alone; soloist followed by congregation; congregation singing the *akroteleution* responsorially; or with melodic elaboration.

The hymns can be grouped according to their subject matter, liturgical position, melodic type, scriptural context, or geographic origin. An *anastasimon* makes reference to the resurrection and is normally appointed on Sundays; a *theotokion* honors the Blessed Virgin (and a *stavrotheotokion* relates to Mary at the foot of the cross); a *triadikon* is addressed to the Holy Trinity; a *doxastikon* is sung with the Lesser Doxology; the *eisodikon* is an introit, while an *apolytikion* is the dismissal hymn of Vespers; the *exaposteilarion* develops the theme of Christ as Light of the world and occurs towards the end of Matins; and *anatolika* hymns originate "from the East."

SEE ALSO: *Akathistos*; Apolytkion; Cherubikon; Ekphonesis; Eothina; Evlogitaria; Exaposteilarion; *Heirmologion*; Idiomelon; Ode; Troparion

References and Suggested Readings

Beck, H.-G. (1959) *Kirche und theologische Literatur im byzantinischen Reich*. Munich.

Conomos, D. (1985) *Byzantine Hymnography and Byzantine Chant*. Brookline, MA: Holy Cross Orthodox Press.

Follieri, E. (1960–6) *Initia hymnorum ecclesiae graecae*. Rome: Vatican City.

McGuckin, J. A. (2009) "Poetry and Hymnography (2). The Greek Christian World," in S. Ashbrook Harvey and D. Hunter (eds.) *The Oxford Handbook of Early Christian Studies*. Oxford: Oxford University Press.

Mitsakis, K. (1986) *Byzantine Hymnographia 1: Apo tin epoche tis Kainis Diathikis eos tin Eikonomachia*. Athens.

Szövérffy, J. (1978–9) *A Guide to Hymnography: A Classified Bibliography of Texts and Studies*. Brookline, MA: Holy Cross Orthodox Press.

Hypakoe

JOHN A. MCGUCKIN

From the Greek term for "hearing" or "responding." In Orthodox usage it denotes a short liturgical hymn formerly sung at Orthros, now generally recited, its content determined by which of the Tones of the *Oktoechos* apply for that day, as eight standard Hypakoe are in the service books. A great feast may have its own proper Hypakoe. It was in origin perhaps a responsorial hymn. Tradition ascribes the composition of the first Hypakoe to Emperor Leo the Wise (d. 912). The hymn celebrates the wonderment of the myrrhbearers, or otherwise refers to the resurrection event as cause of praise. Its location in the service varies according to the level of feast being celebrated. On Sundays it comes after the Resurrectional Evlogitaria. At Pascha it comes after Ode Three of the Canon, and again in the liturgy after the Little Entrance.

SEE ALSO: Liturgical Books; Orthros (Matins); *Paraklitike*

I

Iasi (Jassy), Synod of (1642)

DAN SANDU

The Synod of Iasi (also referred to as the Council of Jassy) was convened by Prince Vasile Lupu of Moldavia and was held from September 15 to October 27, 1642. The purpose of the synod was to counter certain Catholic and Protestant doctrinal errors which had infiltrated Orthodox theology and to offer a comprehensive Orthodox statement on the truth of faith. At the time, the *Confession of Faith*, attributed to the Ecumenical Patriarch Cyril Lukaris, was circulating in Europe. It deviated sharply from the Orthodox faith.

Peter Moghila (1596–1646), the metropolitan of Kiev, wrote *Expositio fidei* (*Statement of Faith*, known also as the *Orthodox Confession*), a description of Christian Orthodoxy in a question and answer format. This treatise had already been approved by a synod held in Kiev, yet two doctrinal issues it mentioned, considered to be of Western Catholic origin, had not been agreed upon, namely the existence of Purgatory and the moment of the transformation of the gifts of bread and wine into the Lord's body and blood. Accordingly, Moghila's *Expositio fidei* was reviewed and amended at the Synod of Iasi by Orthodox scholars of theology and the synod of bishops. It became the most authoritative

statement on Orthodox doctrine for centuries afterwards. After its revision by the synod the text was translated into Greek by the theologian Meletios Syrigos.

The *Expositio* was approved by the ecumenical patriarchate at the synod held on March 11, 1643 and subsequently by the other historical patriarchal sees: Alexandria, Antioch, and Jerusalem. In 1696 Patriarch Hadrian of Moscow described the *Expositio fidei* as "inspired by God."

The Synod of Iasi did not stand out in terms of the number of participants or the attendant ceremonies; nevertheless it was a highly effective meeting attended by prominent theologians, bishops, and heads of Orthodox theological schools and monasteries. It was the most significant international event in the Orthodox world of the 17th century because of its approval of the *Statement of Faith*, which became fundamental for establishing the Orthodox world's attitude to Reformation thought. The major contribution of the synod was the restoration of unity in the Orthodox Church through the promulgation of an authoritative statement agreed upon by all the major sees.

SEE ALSO: Cyril Lukaris, Patriarch of Constantinople (1572–1638); Moghila, Peter (1596–1646); Romania, Patriarchal Orthodox Church of

The Concise Encyclopedia of Orthodox Christianity, First Edition. Edited by John Anthony McGuckin.
© 2014 John Wiley & Sons, Ltd. Published 2014 by John Wiley & Sons, Ltd.

References and Suggested Readings

Eliade, M. (1987) *The Encyclopedia of Religion*, Vol. 11. New York: Macmillan.

Plamadeala, A. (1981) *Eveniment mondial la Iași: Sinodul din 1642* (International Event at Jassy: The Synod of 1642), in *Dascăli de cuget și simțire românească* (Teachers of Romanian Feeling and Thought). Bucharest: Enciclopedica.

Plamadeala, A. (2002) *Sinodul de la Iași și Petru Movilă: 1642–2002)*. Iași: *Trinitas*.

Ware, K. (1997) *The Orthodox Church*. London: Penguin Putnam.

Iconoclasm

M. C. STEENBERG

Iconoclasm (literally, "icon-smashing") refers to a period in church history, usually considered as spanning 730 to 842, in which the legitimacy of the veneration of icons was questioned in parts of the Byzantine Empire. Generally considered as beginning with Emperor Leo III, policies of removing icons from Orthodox churches were followed by the destruction of the icons themselves. The origin of the name lies in this pattern of destroying the sacred images, whether by smashing, burning, or the whitewashing of churches.

Those in opposition to the destruction of the icons (*iconodules*, "those who venerate icons") successfully defended their use on theological and traditional grounds at the Seventh Ecumenical Council in Constantinople (787), given impetus by the support of the Empress Irene. A resurgence of iconoclastic fervor took place under Leo V, who from 813 instituted a second period of iconoclastic imperial policy, albeit less severe in tone than the first. The definitive restoration of the icons did not take place until the first Sunday of Great Lent, 842, when, under the leadership of regent Theodora, a synod was held in Constantinople that culminated with a procession from the Blachernae to Hagia Sophia, restoring the icons to the Great Church and establishing a feast in honor of the event (commemorated ever after as the Triumph of Orthodoxy).

These periods of iconoclasm were formative in the Orthodox articulation of its theology of worship, during which time such figures as St. John of Damascus compiled tracts (e.g., his three treatises against those who defame the images) demonstrating the coherence of iconographic representation in a worshipping theology grounded in the incarnation.

SEE ALSO: Council of Nicea II (787); Iconography, Styles of; Icons; Pantocrator Icon; St. John of Damascus (ca. 675–ca. 750)

References and Suggested Readings

Bryer, A. M. and Herrin, J. (1977) *Iconoclasm*. Papers given at the 9th Spring Symposium of Byzantine Studies, Birmingham University, 1975. Birmingham: Birmingham University Press.

Cormack, R. (1985) *Writing in Gold: Byzantine Society and its Icons*. London: George Philip.

Hussey, J. M. (1986) *The Orthodox Church in the Byzantine Empire*. Oxford: Oxford University Press.

Louth, A. (trans.) (2003) *St. John of Damascus: Three Treatises on the Divine Images*. Crestwood, NY: St. Vladimir's Seminary Press.

McGuckin, J. A. (1993) "The Theology of Images and the Legitimation of Power in Eighth Century Byzantium," *St. Vladimir's Theological Quarterly* 37, 1: 39–58.

Ouspensky, L. (1992) *Theology of the Icon*, 2 vols. Crestwood, NY: St. Vladimir's Seminary Press.

Roth, C. P. (trans.) (1981) *St. Theodore the Studite: On the Holy Icons*. Crestwood, NY: St. Vladimir's Seminary Press.

Iconography, Styles of

PHILIP ZYMARIS

Christian art, while initially linked to the artistic style of Antiquity, baptized the existing forms with a new religious content. The methods worked out to accomplish this led to the evolution of different styles of iconography. These styles evolved over three major productive periods of Byzantine history. These three periods may be defined as the Early Byzantine (4th–8th centuries), the Middle Byzantine (867–1204), and the Late Byzantine (1204–1453). These periods of Byzantine art also laid the foundation for all the various schools of Orthodox iconography that continued to develop after the fall of the Byzantine Empire.

Plate 32   Nun painting an icon. RIA Novosti/Topfoto.

Early Byzantine Period

The acceptance of Christianity as the official faith of the Byzantine Empire freed Christian art from its previous attachment to symbolic representations common in the catacombs and sarcophagi of Late Antiquity. The grand building programs of Constantine (4th century) and later of Justinian (6th century) fostered the development of an explicitly Christian iconographical style. Art of this early period represented two main tendencies: a Hellenistic and an oriental style. The former, based on Hellenistic naturalism, was dominant in the centers of Greek culture such as Constantinople. In this style classical forms were imbued with a Christian spirituality as can be seen in the renowned Pantocrator icon (6th century) at St. Catherine's Monastery, Sinai. A typical example of the oriental or ascetic style, originating in the eastern reaches of the empire and Egypt, can be seen in the icon of Christ and St. Menas (in the Louvre collection). Typical of this style are bright colors, strongly marked outlines, and isocephaly of rigid, frontal, and symmetrical figures – features that are common to the art of Syria and Egypt.

Middle Byzantine Period

The defeat of iconoclasm and the ascendancy of the Macedonian dynasty in the second half of the 9th century was a turning point for Byzantine art. During this period a renewed interest in classical models is evident. Yet, at the same time, the desire to point to the spiritual dimension beyond, and the transformed life of the kingdom, leads to a departure from classical three-dimensional depictions and an emphasized tendency towards reverse perspective that becomes a hallmark of Byzantine iconography. This is evident in even the earliest mosaics of Hagia Sophia that are typical of this early Macedonian Renaissance style. It continues in the second phase of the Macedonian period (first half of the 11th century) where classical and Justinianic models were employed with renewed interest. The exquisite mosaics of the Monastery of Daphne (near Athens, ca. 1080) and Hosios Loukas (Phokida, ca. 1030) are products of this period. This style is marked by seemingly immobile, austere, static figures with heavy, powerful proportions, symmetrical features, and proportionately large eyes. The Comnenan dynasty (second half of the 11th–12th centuries) brought with it different emphases in iconography. The ascetic forms of the preceding period tended to be abandoned in favor of more classical models characterized by a subtle spirituality, elegance, peace, and harmony (Zachaeus 2007: 53). This period also saw the genesis of the *Menologion* type of icon, that is, a calendrical icon of many figures, depicting the feasts and saints celebrated on a given month. The end of this period (early 12th century) saw once again a revisiting of the ascetical ideals of the early 11th century coupled with a return to classical balance conveying subtle spirituality. The most representative icon of this era is the so-called Vladimirskaya Icon (Tretyakov, Moscow). The second half the 12th century then developed three main styles: a *classical* style evident in icons such as the St. Demetrios mosaic (Xenophon Monastery, Athos); a *dynamic* style marked by efforts to express inner fervor as well as external physical expression, as seen in the Descent into Hell (St. Catherine's, Mt. Sinai); and a so-called "post-Comnenan mannerism" seen in the restless contours, aristocratic features, and elegant gestures in the annunciation (St. Catherine's, Mt. Sinai).

Late Byzantine Period

In 1261 Michael VIII Palaeologos regained control of Constantinople from the Crusaders who had taken the city in 1204. This marked the beginning of a final golden age in imperial Byzantine art despite the rapid dwindling of the empire. The early part of this era represented a new monumentalism featuring larger, simpler images expressing a radiant inner beauty reminiscent once again of the first half of the 11th century. The Hagiographical icon (the depiction of a saint framed by smaller scenes from his life as recorded in the Synaxarion) also appeared during this period. The dawn of the 14th century marked the beginning of the Palaeologue Renaissance. Significant for this period are the frescoes at the Monastery of Christ at Chora (Kariye Djami) and the works of the Athonite artist Manouel Panselinos. Typical of this style are supple movement of figure and classical beauty, noble "Greek faces" with high bulging foreheads, deep-set eyes and a three-quarter turn of the head. The first half of the 15th century marked the final chapter in imperial Byzantine art. Despite the constant shrinking of the empire, artistic life was not extinguished during this period. Local schools of iconography such as the Serbian and Bulgarian (Rice 1963: 187f.) continued to develop. With the fall of Constantinople in 1453 many artists fled the former territories of the empire and some migrated to Crete where the significant Cretan school of iconography developed (Zachaeus 2007: 95f.). The continuation of the Byzantine art tradition after the fall of the empire is evident especially in the great Russian schools of iconography (Moscow, Tver, Rostov, and Novgorod) (Zachaeus 2007: 119ff.) and in great artists such as St. Andrei Rublev.

Plate 33 Part of the newly restored gallery of priceless icons preserved at St. Catherine's Monastery, Mount Sinai, Egypt. Photo by John McGuckin.

SEE ALSO: Architecture, Orthodox Church; Council of Nicea II (787); Icons; St. Andrei Rublev (ca. 1360–1430)

References and Suggested Readings

Gervase, M. (1963) *Byzantine Aesthetics*. New York: Harper and Row.

Kalokyris, C. (1971) *The Essence of Orthodox Iconography*, trans. P. Chamberas. Brookline, MA: Holy Cross School of Theology.

Rice, D. (1963) *Art of the Byzantine Era*. New York: Oxford University Press.

Schug-Wille, C. E. (1969) *Art of the Byzantine World*, trans. M. Hatt. New York: Harry N. Abrams.

Zachaeus (Wood), Archimandrite (ed.) (2007) *A History of Icon Painting*, trans. K. Cooke. Moscow: Grand-Holding Publishers.

Iconostasis

MARIA GWYN MCDOWELL

An icon screen demarcating the nave from the sanctuary. It originates from the π-shaped Byzantine templon, a low rail (easily seen over) eventually interspersed by columns topped by an architrave which served to marshal worshippers crowding around the altar. The earliest known examples are the archeological findings at Hagios Ioannes Studios (463) and descriptions of Hagia Sophia. As liturgical movement concentrated in the altar (ca. 9th century), icons were extended along the architrave though the partition remained transparent up until approximately the 13th century.

The vertical ascent and solidification of the iconostasis began in 14th-century Russia, perhaps influenced by contemporary theological conflicts. The

Plate 34   An icon-screen of an Orthodox church (iconostasis). Photo by John McGuckin.

resulting many-tiered edifice that closes off the altar area subsequently became widespread. The first "local" tier of icons on the full Iconostasis includes the Royal Doors (usually the Annunciation) surmounted by the Mystical Supper or the Hospitality of Abraham. To the left (as one faces the screen) is the icon of the Theotokos, then the church's patron saint, and the north (exit) door portraying either St. Michael or a deacon-saint, and then another patronal saint. On the right is the icon of Christ (usually the Pantocrator), then John the Forerunner, the south (entrance) door with Gabriel or a deacon-saint, and then another patron saint. Ascending tiers of icons usually include a Deisis, the Twelve Great Feast icons, and rows of prophets and patriarchs.

SEE ALSO: Ambo; Iconography, Styles of; Icons

References and Suggested Readings

Arida, R. M. (2008) "Another Look at the Solid Iconostasis in the Russian Orthodox Church," *St. Vladimir's Seminary Quarterly* 52: 339–66.
Florenskii, P. A., Sheehan, D., and Andrejev, O. (1996) *Iconostasis*. Crestwood, NY: St Vladimir's Seminary Press.
Ouspensky, L. (1964) "The Problem of the Iconostasis," *St Vladimir's Seminary Quarterly* 8: 186–218.

Icons

THEODOR DAMIAN

The theology of the image of God represents one of the principal Orthodox Christian doctrines that has enjoyed a great level of attention and development over the centuries. This theology, closely linked to the whole problem of Christology, has generated and has become a criterion, first, of the legitimization of the tradition of the icon in the early church and second, in the Orthodox tradition after the great schism, until the present day.

In Orthodoxy the icon is understood as a sign of the divine presence in the world and as a reminder of our essential relationship with God. The icons were used in the worship of the early church. They expressed an incarnational focus of thinking and were considered complementary to the gospel, as both

things spoke of the same saving events. In the early church not everybody was in favor of the use of icons liturgically; however, both groups lived together without serious conflict. There were some church fathers who spoke against the use of icons and several others who approved them in this early period.

A special confirmation of their existence and acceptance was given at the Quinisext Council (692) held in Constantinople under Emperor Justinian II whose Canon 82 states: "The Christian images are legitimate. They are accepted by the Church and even considered useful, because by the fact of representing Christ they remind all of his salvific work." The synod even decided to forbid the representation of Christ in symbols (such as the Lamb that had become popular in western art to "stand in for" the Savior) so as to encourage the iconography of his human face and figure.

Plate 35 Russian Orthodox icon of the Virgin Mary, Theotokos, or Mother of God. Photo by John McGuckin.

The history of the veneration of icons witnessed periods of great troubles and misunderstandings. The chief controversy over the legitimacy of images, especially as that broke out in the two periods of Byzantine Iconoclasm, was based on a literal interpretation of the second commandment of the Decalogue which forbids the creation of idolatrous images and bans their worship. The controversy also arose because of Eastern influences on Byzantine Christianity from Judaism and Islam, as well as because of the iconoclasts' desire to "reform and purify" the content of worship.

Whatever the political and social contexts surrounding Iconoclasm, the major theological aspect of this controversy was related to the identity of Christ. Who is he? This was, and remains, the central theme of the dispute between iconoclasts and iconodules. Orthodoxy's vindication of the use of icons in worship stressed that they legitimately represented the divine Lord, precisely because he had been truly incarnated as God who was also truly man. Materiality was thus a genuine sacrament of the divine presence. The fight against icons involved people of all categories of life up to the highest level. The most influential iconoclasts, however, were the emperors of the Isaurian dynasty and their soldiers, who made their views felt dynamically because of their social power. When they engaged in the controversy, the iconoclastic rulers tried to convert to their side the representatives of the church; when they did not succeed, the emperors simply replaced them with conformers who shared, or at least did not openly oppose, their views. The persecution involved fines, flogging, exile, mutilation and torture, and sometimes even death.

Byzantine iconoclasm occurred in two major phases. The first started with Emperor Leo III the Isaurian (717–41) and in particular with the repressive edict of 726, followed later by another in 730 when the icons were denounced as idols. It continued under Emperor Constantine V Copronymos (741–75), the son of Leo III, and lasted until 775 when Constantine died. In his zeal against the icons Constantine convoked the iconoclastic Synod of Hieria in 754, where the icons were condemned in christological terms. Since Christ was possessed of a divine and a human nature, it was argued, icons cannot depict him authentically, since the wood and paint can only represent a symbol of his material nature. Icons were thus classed alongside the anti-Chalcedonian Christology as either "Monophysitic" or "Nestorian" (confusing or dividing the two natures of Christ). It would be left to the works of Sts. John of Damascus and Theodore Studite, as well as Patriarch Germanos of Constantinople, to make an answer to these charges and to develop the church's theology of the icon extensively.

Between 775 and 780 Emperor Leo IV the Khazar reigned, the son of Constantine V, who was neither an iconodule (one who venerates icons), nor an iconoclast (one who fights those who venerate icons). There was a respite between the two phases (780–813) when the Empress Irene (mother of Constantine VI Porphyrogennetos, who was aged 10 when he became emperor in 780) convened a synod in Nicea in 787 (Council of Nicea II) in order to restore the veneration of icons in the churches. This synod, the seventh and last of the ecumenical councils of the church, was presided over by Patriarch Tarasius. It confirmed that the use of icons was already an ecclesiastical tradition, and decided that church traditions ought to be preserved reverently, and without innovations; whether these longstanding traditions were written or oral. The painting of icons was declared such a foundational tradition which is in conformity with the gospel. Icon and gospel were indeed complementary to each other.

The synod of 787 also made clear the critically important distinction between the veneration of icons (*proskynesis*) and adoration (*latreia*). The first (veneration) is given by Christians to holy persons and things (including images of Christ, his Mother, and his saints); the latter (adoration) is due, in spirit and truth, to God alone. The distinction introduced an important semantic sophistication into the church's understanding of prayer, reverence, and the sacramentality of icons. It was based on the teaching of St. Basil the Great, echoed by St. John of Damascus, which stated that whoever venerates an image in fact venerates only the person there depicted, since the reverence shown to the icon passes immediately as honor given to its archetype.

The second phase of the iconoclastic crisis started with Emperor Leo V the Armenian (813–20) and lasted until the death of Emperor Theophilus in 842. Leo V also convened a synod in Constantinople in order to condemn the statements of the synod of Nicea of 787 and to restore the teaching of the iconoclastic synod of Hieria. Between 820 and 829 Emperor Michael II, while still prohibiting icons (though this time only in the city of Constantinople), did not advance his policy of hostility to the point of persecution. His successor, Emperor Theophilus (829–42), admitted that icons could be useful decorations in the church, but commanded that they were not to be "worshipped." When Theophilus died in 842 his wife Theodora became regent for her son Michael. Being a fervent iconodule, she appointed Methodius as patriarch and in 843 convened a local synod in Constantinople where icons were restored and definitely established in the church as being essential to its worship, and as important theological symbols of true Orthodoxy. On this occasion the synod decided that the first Sunday of Great Lent should be instituted as the "Sunday of Orthodoxy," in perpetual memory of the triumph of the icons against their persecutors.

St. John of Damascus (ca. 675–ca. 750) was the first great defender of icons. He developed his *apologia* in a more general manner, yet in a literary style and with a logic that greatly appealed to the public. Together with Patriarch Germanos he offered strong resistance to the iconoclastic pressure. His apologetic model was followed by Patriarch Nicephorus (758–828). The defense of icons was subsequently undertaken by St. Theodore the Studite (759–826), who was more specific in the theological development of his arguments, especially basing them on, and elaborating them in relation to, the mystery of the hypostatic union of the two natures in Christ. To questions related to the identity of Christ the defenders of icon veneration responded clearly: in the womb of the Holy Virgin, the second person of the Holy Trinity, the divine Logos, became human being; such that Jesus was true God and true man. The icon is thus an authentic depiction of Christ and graced as a holy thing in a way comparable to the manner in which his real humanity was the authentic bearer of the full divine presence.

In reference to the iconoclasts' invocation of the second commandment of the Decalogue, which forbade the worship of idols, the defenders of icons explained that figurative representations had indeed been forbidden by God in the Old Testament for the sake of protecting the Jews from falling into idolatry, but that all depictions were not so forbidden (the specifics relating the carving of the ark [Ex. 25.18–22] for example, or the figures of Cherubim on the Temple Veil, or the graphic symbol of the serpent in the desert [Num. 21.8–9]). In fact, all the texts from the Old Testament that the iconoclasts mistakenly interpreted as banning all graphic representations in worship should rather be seen to refer to the interdiction of false idols, through which the divine transcendence was interpreted wrongly by simpler minds before the time of the incarnation. Idolatry foolishly maintains that the infinity of God can be contained within and by the idol. When the problem of the idols was no longer present, however, as in the case of the instructions for Temple worship in the Old Testament, or in the case of the illumined church celebrating the incarnation of the Lord, then the divine attitude toward iconographic representations has to be seen as completely different. God not only does not stop them, but on the contrary, he commands and commends them. The Orthodox Church thus considered the Old Testament-based interdiction of the image as being a provisional, pedagogical measure. The difference between icon and idol becomes evident since the idol pertains to polytheism while the icon pertains to the divine economy which has overthrown idolatry from (Christian) society. The Old Testament interdiction of images was disputed by the iconodules through the comparison that they made between the two testaments; using the parallel between law and grace as it is found in the Pauline theology. They invoked the text of St. Paul (Gal. 3.23) from which one sees the inferiority of the law compared to the time of faith (grace); thus, as the Old Testament could not be compared in authority to the New, the character of this commandment (circumstantial, contextual, and transitory) needed also to be seen in the light of the new principles of monotheistic worship established in and by the incarnation. The iconodules also invoked the assertion of St. Paul (Heb. 10.1) regarding the law as being a shadow, and the Christians as living in the era of grace, not of law. If the law still held literal validity in all respects, they argued, Christians would also need to keep its other imperatives, such as the Sabbath or circumcision. But this would clearly be to deny the radical new element of the religion of the incarnation, which the icon celebrates.

According to St. John of Damascus, if, in the Old Testament, the direct revelation of God was manifested only through the word, then now, in the New Testament, it has been manifested through word and image alike, because the divine unseen has become the seen, and what was non-representable has now been truly represented. Thus, in the icon, the depiction of this mystery is made possible. The basis of the true representative character of the icon consists in the decision of God himself to assume a visible human face in the incarnation of his Son. Christ, being the divine image *par excellence*, thus represents the fulfillment of all images from the Old Testament, and fulfils them all. In short, the incarnation of the divine Logos makes the icon an effective instrument of final revelation and thus of the divine grace of that saving revelation. This is the point of departure of all Orthodox teaching on the icon.

This doctrine about the capacity of the uncircumscribable God to be "circumscribed" (the semantic term is closely related to the word for drawing, or image making) in the incarnation of his Son (and this understood as a basis for the making of icons) was formulated at the Third Ecumenical Council at Ephesus in 431, where Mary was declared to be not merely *Anthropotokos* (Mother of a man), and not even *Christotokos* (Mother of the Christ), but precisely and wondrously, *Theotokos* (the very Mother of God). Because of this mystical hypostatic union of God and his flesh, the church can legitimately use the paradoxical language of the capacity of the uncircumscribable God to be circumscribed, and can legitimately apply the sign of the icon in its worship. The incarnation, however, represents in itself an abiding paradox, and this quality passes on into the icon, as well.

In turning to the incarnation as the basis for the possibility of the icon, the iconodules affirmed as the teaching of the Orthodox Church that what appears as presented by the icon is not the nature of the Son of God, but his hypostasis as incarnated. The iconoclasts had raised the question: "What do we actually see represented in the icon? The humanity or the divinity of Christ?" Theodore the Studite, speaking for the iconodules in general, answered with an apologia based upon the theology of similarity and dissimilarity between image and prototype. The icon or image is dissimilar to the prototype as far as nature is concerned, but it is, at the same time, similar to the prototype as far

as the hypostasis and name are concerned. Thus, in the case of the icon, it is not just one of the two natures of Christ that is represented, but both of them, hypostatically joined as in the single incarnate Lord. Following from this, the iconodule theologians made it clear that in Orthodox theology the icon is a real "incarnation" of the image of Christ (or of the saints) and is a fundamental witness to Christian anthropology. If one were to reject the icon on theological grounds, therefore, it would be tantamount to rejecting fundamental truths of the real incarnation of Christ.

The incarnation as foundation of the theology of the icon gives it a dynamic, rather than a static or merely representational role in the life of the church. The use of icons in the church of the first centuries illustrates the conviction that, from Christ onward, the icon is not only permissible, but also constitutes a fundamental way of transmitting and maintaining alive, in the conscience of Christians, the mystery that in the incarnation of the Son the full revelation of God was given within time and space. By means of the iconoclastic controversy, and its attendant persecutions, the Orthodox Church was enabled to consolidate its theological perspectives on the incarnation and to strengthen its unity and ecumenicity.

In Orthodox tradition the icon cannot be separated from its ecclesiastical liturgical context. In this liturgical dimension the icon shows with precision the transformative character of the work of the Holy Spirit in the church. An icon expresses the artistic and spiritual struggle, indeed the suffering, of the iconographer, offered for the benefit of fellow believers. It also shows at one and the same moment the spiritual struggle (for the world) of the one it depicts (whether Christ, the Virgin, or a saint) and the glorious fulfillment of that struggle. In the context of the heart of the Christian experience, in the Eucharistic liturgy, the icon of Christ (or of the saint) promotes the opening up of the inner icon of the one who prays, to its penetration by the sanctifying grace of the Holy Spirit. Icons, therefore, never belong to an individual. Regardless of where they are (ecclesiastic or domestic), they actually always belong to the church as a whole. They express the church, introduce us to it and to the communion of the saints, to that total communion of those who have already left this earthly life, as well as the communion of those who still live here yet are on the way to the kingdom. The icons affirm all of the church's belonging to God.

For St. John of Damascus, icons are a sacrament, not by virtue of divine manifestation, but through the energy of a divinely graced presence. Considering their whole place and liturgical role, their presence and participation in the church's invocation (*epiclesis*), and because of what they represent, icons unquestionably receive the grace of the Holy Spirit. Also, because the veneration of the icon does not pass to the material object but always to that sacred figure depicted on it, then in just the same manner, a spiritual blessing returns from the icon. For the grace of the Holy Spirit who lived in that holy person remains also in his or her enduring spiritual existence. Thus, because the icon is a means of communion in the church between that sacred figure and us, it derives its sanctifying power from the grace of that holy person who is always ready for communion. St. John of Damascus teaches that since during their lives the saints have been full of the Holy Spirit, after their deaths the grace of the Holy Spirit continues to live in their souls, and in their bodies in the grave, as well as in their forms on the icons; a presence not manifested in virtue of essence, but in terms of grace and energy.

The icon must also be considered as a doxological expression of the divine liturgy. It is a theology in images. The icons of the Orthodox Church graphically help believers to have a deeper understanding of the liturgical texts, and serve as aids for their reading so that it might become contemplative. This notion emphasizes for us the theological and didactic role of icons in the spiritual understanding of the divine liturgy. In terms of what they represent, icons are an open Bible or even a theological treatise. Throughout Christian history they have spoken with power and beauty and grace. Sometimes they teach in a simple way about events from church life or from the history of salvation. Sometimes they are full of profound depths and hint at unseen mysteries. Through the details of their representations they stimulate meditation and reflection. Through their colors they enchant the eye and keep the believer's heart close to them. But especially, through the way that they are reverently made in the church, through the transparency that they manifest, they serve to open the spirit toward a profound longing for God.

In the sentiment of St. Basil the Great and St. John of Damascus, what the word is for the power of hearing, the icon is for the power of seeing. Since the prototype of the icon is Christ himself, the icon is an energized intermediary, a way that helps us follow the Lord so that through him and in him we may stand in communion with God.

SEE ALSO: Council of Nicea II (787); Ecumenical Councils; Heresy; Iconography, Styles of; Logos Theology; Monasticism; Patristics; Quinisext Council (Council in Trullo) (692); St. John of Damascus (ca. 675–ca. 750); St. Theodore the Studite (759–826)

References and Suggested Readings

Damian, T. (2002) *Theological and Spiritual Dimensions of Icons According to St. Theodore of Studion.* Lewiston: Edwin Mellen Press.

Damian, T. (2003) *Implicatiile Spirituale ale Teologiei Icoanei.* Cluj: Eikon.

John of Damascus (1989) *Exposition of the Orthodox Faith*, in P. Schaff and H. Wace (eds.) *The Nicene and Post-Nicene Fathers* second series, vol. 9. Grand Rapids, MI: Eerdmans.

McGuckin, J. A. (1993) "The Theology of Images and the Legitimation of Power in Eighth Century Byzantium," *St. Vladimir's Theological Quarterly* 37, 1: 39–58.

Meyendorff, J. (1979) *Byzantine Theology, Historical Trends and Doctrinal Issues.* New York: Fordham University Press.

Nyssen, W. (1975) *Das Zeugnis des Bildes im frühen Byzanz.* Bucharest: Institului Biblic si de Misiune Ortodoxa.

Ouspensky, L. and Lossky, V. (1989) *The Meaning of Icons.* Crestwood, NY: St. Vladimir's Seminary Press.

Stăniloae, D. (1987) *Chipul Nemuritor al lui Dumnezeu.* Craiova: Mitropoliei Olteniei.

Theodore Studites, St. (1903) *Opera Omnia*, in J. P. Migne (ed.) *Patrologia Graeca*, vol. 99. Paris: Garnier.

Ugolnik, A. (1989) *The Illuminating Icon.* Grand Rapids, MI: Eerdmans.

Idiomelon

DIMITRI CONOMOS

The monostrophic stanzas (*troparia*) of the Byzantine rite (*apolytikia, stichera, kathismata*, etc.) may be set to music by the poet-composers in two different ways.

A troparion that is endowed with a metrical pattern and a melody that are unique and original to itself is known as an *idiomelon*. However, if a liturgical poet fashions a new sacred verse which possesses the same meter and music as those of a preexisting hymn (that is, if it is a contrafactum), then the ensuing troparion is called a *prosomion*. An idiomelon that serves as a model for such prosomoia receives the special name, *automelon*.

SEE ALSO: Apolytikion; Hymnography; Music (Sacred); Sticheron; Troparion

Imiaslavie

SAMUEL NEDELSKY

Imiaslavie (lit. "glorification of the name") was a doctrine, popular among Russian monks on Mount Athos in the first two decades of the 20th century, maintaining that the name of God is itself divine; it resulted in a major controversy culminating in the expulsion of over 800 Russian monks in 1913. Adherents referred to this teaching as *imiaslavie* ("name-glorifying") and called themselves *imiaslavtsy* ("name-glorifiers"); opponents referred to this doctrine as the *imenobozhnicheskaia eres'* ("the nameworshipping heresy") and to its adherents as *imenobozhniki* ("name-worshippers"). The controversy arose in reaction to the book *Na Gorakh Kavkaza* (*In the Mountains of the Caucasus*) by Schemamonk Ilarion, first published in 1907 with ecclesiastical sanction. Although primarily concerned with the practice of the Jesus Prayer, it came under criticism for passages appearing to identify the name of Jesus with Christ himself. The key phrase under dispute (one not used by Ilarion) became "the Name of God is God Himself" (*Imia Bozhie est' Sam Bog*). By 1911–12 Russian Athonites were divided into opposing camps. On January 12, 1913, following a disputed election to the abbacy, the *imiaslavtsy* forcibly drove their opponents out of St. Andrew's Skete. Several official condemnations of both the actions and teachings of the *imiaslavtsy* were subsequently published: an epistle of Patriarch Germanos of Constantinople on February 15, 1913; a written judgment by the faculty of the theological school at Halki on March 30, 1913; and an epistle by the Synod of the Russian Church on May 15, 1913. In 1913 Bulatovich's pro-*imiaslavie*

work *Apologiia very vo Imia Bozhiia i vo Imia Iisus* (*Apology of Faith in the Name of God and in the Name Jesus*) was published with an unsigned foreword by Pavel Florensky. When efforts to convince the *imiaslavtsy* to renounce their teaching failed, the Russian Navy forcibly removed over 800 monks from Athos in the summer of 1913. This marked the end of the movement, although some *imiaslavtsy* remained active in the Caucasus through the 1920s. The theological issues raised in this controversy were on the agenda for discussion at the 1917–18 All-Russian Council, which was interrupted before turning its attention to this question.

SEE ALSO: Florensky, Pavel Alexandrovich (1882–1937); Jesus Prayer; Monasticism; Mount Athos

References and Suggested Readings

Alfeev, I. (2007) *Spory ob imeni Bozhiem. Archivnye dokumenty 1912–1938 godov*. St. Petersburg: Izdat. Olega Abyshko.

Dykstra, T. (1988) "Heresy on Mount Athos: Conflict Over the Name of God Among Russian Monks and Hierarchs, 1912–1914." Unpublished MDiv thesis. Crestwood, NY: St. Vladimir's Orthodox Theological Seminary.

Graham, L. and Kanton, J.-M. (2009) *Naming Infinity: A True Story of Religious Mysticism and Mathematical Creativity*. Cambridge, MA: Belknap Press of Harvard University Press.

Hamburg, G. (2003) "The Origins of 'Heresy' on Mount Athos: Ilarion's *Na Gorakh Kavkaza* (1907)," *Religion in Eastern Europe* 23, 2.

Kenworthy, S. (2003) "Church, State, and Society in Late Imperial Russia: Nikon (Rozhdestvenskii) and Imiaslavie." Paper presented to the Midwest Historians' Workshop, Miami University.

Nedelsky, S. (forthcoming) "Archbishop Antonii (Khrapovitskii), Imiaslavie, and Hesychasm," in V. Tsurikov (ed.) *Archbishop Antonii (Khrapovitskii)*. Jordanville, NY: Holy Trinity Seminary Press.

Incarnation (of the Logos)

JOHN A. MCGUCKIN

The term denotes the concept of the eternal Word of God (the divine *Logos*) "becoming flesh" within history for the salvation of the human race. It derives from the Latin *in carne* and hence "incarnation," or enfleshment. In Orthodoxy the preferred term is significantly different, deriving from the Greek of St. Athanasius of Alexandria (as set out in his masterful 4th-century treatise *Peri Enanthropeseos tou Theou Logou*): the "En-Manment" or "Inhomination" of the Logos (*Enanthropesis*). In Orthodox understanding, incarnation does not simply refer to the act itself (such as the conception of Jesus in the womb of the Virgin, or the event of Christmas); it stands more generically for the whole nexus of events of the life, teachings, sufferings, and glorification of the Lord, considered as the earthly, embodied activity of the Word of God. As such the theological concept of incarnation is a profoundly soteriological term: it always has reference to the dynamic effects of God's involvement in the cosmos. It is also an obviously Christocentric way of approaching the concept of salvation.

As was always true in Christian history, when one approaches a theology of salvation through the medium of the incarnation of the Logos, one soon finds the argument turns into the profoundly related areas of the trinitarian doctrine of God and transfigured anthropology. If we strictly applied the concept of incarnation as it derives from the Latin "in the flesh," it would be a translation of the Greek "made flesh" (*sarkothenta*). This was one element (mainly 3rd and 4th century) of the overall scheme of patristic incarnational theology. It was latterly defended by Apollinaris of Laodicea, so as to lay a heavy stress on the divinity of Jesus, and the subordination of his human reality to his divine will. But many at the time (especially St. Gregory the Theologian in his *Letter 101*) felt that this was a serious undermining of the truly human reality of Christ's incarnation; one that rendered it mythological, wherein the Word had merely visited humankind, not become a man himself.

After the 4th-century refutation of Apollinaris, this schema was extensively rejected from the writings of the fathers, though it can be discerned in many patterns of proto-Christian writings, especially of the heterodox type. To envisage that the Word of God enters the "flesh" of Jesus of Nazareth is often called in modern textbooks a *Logos-Sarx* Christology. It implies something of a fundamental contrast between categories of "divinity" and "flesh" (standing in for "God and creature"). This *Logos-Sarx* theology was witnessed in early christological schemes, most radically in the Gnostic Docetics who could not accept any fundamental connection between the Logos and a "fleshly" reality which they saw as profane. More sophisticated *Logos-Sarx* thinking can be seen vividly in Apollinaris of Laodicea, who thought that the intellectual power of the Logos of God "stood in" for the human powers of reason in Jesus. When the Logos entered flesh, therefore, it had no need of a human mind or soul, itself providing for those basic functions. Apollinaris thought that this was a useful way of insisting on the single personality of the Divine Word in the figure of the Incarnate Christ, but his opponents such as the Cappadocian fathers soon answered that it was a highly defective Christology since it rendered the humanity of Christ mindless and soulless (cf. Gregory of Nazianzus, *Epistle 101 to Cledonius*).

From the beginning, Christian acceptance of the scheme of incarnation was widespread, with several variants in early times. Most writers before the 3rd century do not think about it in great detail, concerned only when extremes appeared, such as the denying of the full reality of either the human or divine character of the Christ. After the 3rd century the particular issues of incarnationalism become more and more specified, and turn mainly on the issue of the problem of a coherent subjectivity: in what way could a divine being (the Logos) be a human being? The Greek fathers generally used a broader range of terms than incarnation and thus the simple and singular application of the English word commonly falsifies their varied senses. They generally speak of the "En-hominization" of the Word of God (*enanthropesis*), a broader and more inclusive notion (the Greek term "Man" in this instance being seen as the genus, as well as being a biblicism directly evoking "The Man" or New Adam). The mainstream christological tradition (and it is something that applies to the Greeks and Latins alike) was adamant that the humanity was not merely an empty suit that the Word "put on" (even though this Pauline image of putting on clothes was heavily used), but a genuine human life which the Word of God used as his primary medium of living on earth. Origen had tried to insist on the authenticity of both the Logos and the earthly Jesus, in the face of several alternatives (such as the Gnostics, who argued for an apparitional Christ, or the Adoptionists, who argued that the Spirit of God possessed a man temporarily), by his own complex theory of the Word dwelling in the Great Preexistent Soul Jesus who had become human within history. The scheme never quite managed to work, for it never saw Jesus as synonymous with the Word-Incarnate.

Later theologians such as Athanasius (*On the Incarnation of the Word of God*) set out a fuller elaboration of the Word as the single psychic subject of the Christ. His work was taken to a pitch by St. Cyril of Alexandria (*That The Christ is One*), who argued against Nestorius that a single subjectivity in the Incarnate Lord meant that flesh and spirit, God and Man, previously alien and disparate categories, had finally been reconciled in the Mystery of the Christ. This mystery of communion which belonged to Christ naturally was passed on to the church as a grace. Thus the incarnation of the Word became the paradigm for the deification of the race. Humanity's previous inevitable subjection to corruption and death (*ptharsia, thanatos*) had now given way to the potential for immortalization and divine communion (*metousia theou, theopoiesis*). Cyril argued that nowhere was this more vividly seen than in the deifying grace of the Eucharist and the sacraments, which ensured the immortality of the Christian.

The Alexandrian incarnation (Enhominization) theology became standard in the Orthodox Church through its adoption and promulgation by the 4th- and 5th-century ecumenical councils.

SEE ALSO: Christ; Council of Chalcedon (451); Council of Ephesus (431); Deification; Ecumenical Councils; Eucharist; Holy Trinity; Humanity; Logos Theology; St. Athanasius of Alexandria (ca. 293–373); St. Cyril of Alexandria (ca. 378–444); Sophiology; Soteriology

References and Suggested Readings

Fairburn, D. (2003) *Grace and Christology in the Early Church.* New York: Oxford University Press.

Gavrilyuk, P. (2005) *The Suffering of the Impassible God: The Dialectics of Patristic Thought.* New York: Oxford University Press.

Grillmeier, A. (1975) *Christ in Christian Tradition*, Vol. 1. London: Mowbray.

McGuckin, J. A. (2001) *St. Cyril of Alexandria: On the Unity of Christ (That the Christ Is One).* New York: St. Vladimir's Seminary Press.

McGuckin, J. A. (2004) *St. Cyril of Alexandria and the Christological Controversy: Its History, Theology and Texts.* New York: St. Vladimir's Seminary Press.

Norris, R. A. (1980) *The Christological Controversy.* Philadelphia: Fortress Press.

Incense

JEFFREY B. PETTIS

The word *incense* comes from the Latin *incendere*, "to burn." According to Exodus 37.29 incense (Hebrew, *qtrt;* Greek, *thymiama*) consists of sweet spices made by an apothecary or skilled perfumer. In ancient Judaism the main ingredient for incense was frankincense or *olibanum*, a whitish resin from southern Arabia (see Pliny, *Natural History* xii.14; Jer. 11.20; Isa. 60.6). Other ingredients might include a combination of gum resins including stacte, onycha, and galbanum (Ex. 30.34–35). Although burning incense was seen as a domestic luxury in ancient Israel, and sold by specialist perfume merchants (Song of Songs 3.6; 4.6, 14), incense had a particular liturgical use in the Temple as an offering to atone for the people's sins and propitiate the wrath of God (Num. 26.46–48; cf. Lev. 16.12–13; cf. Ps. 141). In this sense it was distinguished as being sacred and "holy for the Lord" (Ex. 30.37). Incense was burned in portable censers in the Tent of Meeting (Lev. 10.1; 16.12) and later the altar before the Holy of Holies in the Temple was used (Ex. 40.26; 1 Kings 7.48). Only the High Priest burned incense, in the morning and in the evening (Ex. 30.7–8). The scripture recounts the improper making and use of incense (referred to as "strange fire") as exacting the divine wrath (Num. 10.1–2).

In the New Testament references to incense are predominantly connected with prayer and the concept of prayer arising like incense (see Psalm 141.2, which is used in the Orthodox Vesperal service at the time of the incensing of the church). Zechariah enters the Temple of the Lord "praying in the sixth hour of the incense offering [*thumiamatos*]" (Luke 1.9–10). The use of incense in the funeral procession of St. Peter of Alexandria in 311 represents one of the earliest attestations in Christian liturgical practice. Earlier Greek Christian writers tended to frown upon it because of its associations with the veneration of the pagan gods (Tertullian, *Apologeticus* 42; cf. 30; Athenagoras, *Supplication for the Christians* 42). Its use in the West is attested only after the 9th century. In the Eastern Church the incensing of the altar, church, people, etc. is recorded in the 5th entury by Dionysius the Pseudo-Areopagite. He explains how it symbolizes prayer and occurs as an invariable accompaniment to Orthodox services. The priestly prayer of blessing which precedes every burning of incense in church reads: "Incense we offer to Thee, O Christ our God, do Thou receive it on Thy heavenly throne, and send down on us in return the grace of Thy all-holy Spirit." The prayer of incensing in the Presanctified liturgy also expresses the similar thought from Psalm 141: "Let my prayer be directed to Thee as Incense before Thy presence."

All the divine liturgies of the Orthodox Church are now accompanied by several formal incensings of the altar, the holy gifts, the gospel book, the icons, and the people. When the deacon or priest conducts the incensings of the church they recite Psalm 50, the penitential psalm, thus demonstrating a symbolic connection with all the biblical strands: an ascentive offering of prayer, a petition for the aversion of the wrath of God, and the offering of honor to various forms of the *Imago Dei*. Orthodox censers are used with chains that (in Greek practice) have 12 bells attached (symbolizing the 12 apostles) whose joyful sounds represent the transmission of the Good News. In Lent a hand-held silent form of censer is used (*katzio*). Orthodox laity never use the censer in church, its employment being reserved to the ordained: the bishops, priests, or deacons. At home, however, a hand-held censer is often used by the laity in the censing of domestic icons.

SEE ALSO: Divine Liturgy, Orthodox

References and Suggested Readings

Cross, F. L. (ed.) (1957) *The Oxford Dictionary of the Christian Church*. Oxford: Oxford University Press.

Jackson, S. M. (1953) *Schaff-Herzog Encyclopedia of Religious Knowledge*. Grand Rapids, MI: Baker Book House.
Litsas, F. (1984) *A Companion to the Greek Orthodox Church*. New York: Greek Orthodox Archdiocese.

Islam, Orthodoxy and

TIMOTHY J. BECKER

Orthodoxy has existed alongside Islam since the time of Muhammad. From the 7th century to the 21st, from Arabia and Anatolia to America, the two faiths have played decisive roles in each other's histories. From the outset, Christians were influential. Arab Christians introduced the Arabic writing used in the Qur'an and it was interactions with Ethiopian and Arab Christians in south Arabia that shaped Muhammad's conception of what Christianity was.

When Islam emerged from Arabia in 632 CE it encountered an Orthodox Byzantine Empire extending east to Armenia and south to Egypt. Within a decade, Islamic armies had gained control of the major centers of the Middle East, including such major Christian centers of learning as Damascus, Jerusalem, Antioch, Caesarea, Edessa, Ctesiphon, Dwin, and Alexandria. Much of the conquest came through negotiated terms of peace rather than physical destruction, as the cities lacked necessary defenses. The Byzantine army, unprepared for the organized Arab Muslim force, had retreated to Asia Minor. What remained was the long pilgrimage under Islamic rule of the Orthodox patriarchates of Alexandria, Jerusalem, and Antioch, and that of the Coptic Orthodox, Syrian Orthodox, Armenian Orthodox, and Assyrian Church of the East.

Life for Christians under Islam was a mixed reality. As fellow monotheists and "People of the Book" (*ahl al-kitāb*) with the Jews, they were spared the harsher persecution experienced by groups like the Zoroastrians and polytheists. However, Christians remained a subjugated people with restrictions placed on them. Though officially recognized as a "protected minority" (*dhimmī*) and governed by their own leaders, "protected" implied inferior and Christians had to wear distinctive clothing, refrain from public religious practice, and avoid proselytizing Muslims. Their property was subject to seizure and they were obliged to quarter Islamic soldiers. Moreover, Christians could not build new churches and were forced to pay a special head tax (*al-jizyah*), which was imposed in addition to land and property taxes.

Even so, Christians remained influential, possessing a cultural heritage developed in their schools and monasteries. This equipped them to play important social roles in medicine, law, philosophy, and particularly administration. Perhaps most influential was the Syriac Christian translation project of ancient Greek texts into Arabic, which proved critical to the development of Islamic culture and the rise of Muslim philosophy and science, seen foremost in the 'Abbasid period (750–1258).

In time, many of the subjugated eastern Christians found a place within Islamic society, but their place involved both polemics and dialogue. Figures such as St. John of Damascus (Manṣūr ibn Sarjūn) (d. 749/764) and Patriarch Timothy I of Baghdad (727/8–823) represent differing approaches, the former more bracing and the latter more eirenic in terms of their respective assessments of Islam. St. John, it is worth remembering, was writing to Christian monks, while Timothy I was carrying on a public debate with the caliph. The former defines Islam as the latest Christian "heresy"; the latter is more ready to affirm the God-given attributes of an Islamic faith that has led so many to monotheism.

In the Islamic dominated territories there also developed a particular inter-Christian culture. Confessional disputes remained between Assyrians, Oriental Orthodox, and Orthodox, and yet, in certain ways, Islam set these disputes into a new relief, facilitating Christian cooperation. Examples include the prolific scholars 'Abd Allāh ibn aṭ-Ṭayyīb (d. 1043), whose works on the Trinity and on Christology were widely used across confessional lines, and al-Mu'taman ibn al-'Assāl (fl. 1230–60), who wrote that the various Christian communions all substantially professed the same faith in Christ.

Encounters with Islam also shaped how Christians presented their faith. Islam's nearly complete rejection of Christian belief, seen foremost in its dismissal of the Trinity, the concept of divine incarnation, and the reality of Jesus' crucifixion, led Christian writers to defend and demonstrate Christian belief and practice more comprehensively than at any time since

the 4th century. Early examples include John of Damascus' *The Fount of Knowledge* and Theodore bar Kônî's (fl. ca. 792) *Scholion*.

For Byzantium, various Islamic empires now started to replace the fallen Persian Empire as its resident rivals in the East. However, Byzantium faced a greater disadvantage, having lost Egypt, Palestine, and Syria. These losses were commonly seen to bolster Muslim claims to divine favor and contributed to an Orthodox penitential sense of judgment. A result of this may be seen in the rise of iconoclasm in the 8th and 9th centuries, where Islam's aniconic nature and military strength may well have been decisive factors in the Byzantine imperial reaction against icons.

Two further events were defining moments in Byzantium's relationship with Islam. The Turkish victory at Manzikert in 1071 was the culmination of decades of jihad and raids into Anatolia and led to further Islamic penetration of the Byzantine heartland. Not only did this weaken the empire fatally, it also was an instigation of the Crusades, which, arguably, did greater damage to Byzantium than Islam ever did. It was a severely crippled Byzantine Empire that finally was abandoned to fall to the Ottomans in 1453.

Unlike the mixed assessment of Christians living under Islamic rule, the Byzantine attitude on its side was decidedly polemical and overarchingly hostile. The prevailing belief was threefold: Muhammad was a false prophet, the Qur'an is a false scripture, and Islam is a false religion. And yet the Byzantines were not just distant rivals. A number of Byzantium's most important figures had close ties with Muslims. It was Maximus the Confessor's spiritual father, Patriarch Sophronius of Jerusalem, who negotiated terms of peace for the city during the Muslim conquest. St. John of Damascus served in the administration of the Umayyad Caliph for many years. And St. Gregory Palamas spent a period of time in Turkish captivity, during which he intelligently debated issues regarding Islam, Christianity, and the religious significance of ascendant Turkish military power.

While Ottoman rule was largely a change in administration for those Christians who had lived under Islamic dominance for centuries, it was a radical and dramatic shift for Byzantium. The great cathedral of Hagia Sophia was made into a mosque along with numerous other churches, and the capital city, Constantinople, was redesigned and renamed Istanbul. Moreover, the patriarch of Constantinople's role changed to that of a politician, ruler of the Orthodox *millet* (nation). Although life under the Ottomans fluctuated between times of tolerance and active persecution, two notable hardships were lodged in the memories of the Orthodox: the periodic practice of taking one boy from each Christian home and converting him to Islam (*devshirme*) and the recurring enslavement of Christian children resulting from Turkish slave-raiding under acquiescent Ottoman rule.

The 15th century marked the end of the Byzantine Empire; it also saw the rise of the Russians and the decline of the Assyrians. The Russian Orthodox Church emerged from centuries of Islamic Mongol rule and sought to fill the place of Byzantium as the Third Rome and ostensible protector of Eastern Orthodox Christendom. For the Assyrian Church, however, it was the beginning of its long decline, having been left reeling in the aftermath of the Turko-Mongol ruler, Timur the Great (Tamerlane) (d. 1405).

Under the Ottomans, there were originally three *millet* groups, Greek, Jewish, and Armenian. By the 19th century the Christian numbers had proliferated, contributing to the rise in 19th and 20th-century Balkan nationalisms. This new situation helped place Eastern Christians in often precarious environments, amid Islamic divisions, political turmoil, ethnic strife, and global migration. Examples can be seen in the bitter experiences of modern Christians in Armenia, Palestine, the Balkans, and Iraq.

SEE ALSO: Africa, Orthodoxy in; Alexandria, Patriarchate of; Antioch, Patriarchate of; Armenian Christianity; Assyrian Apostolic Church of the East; Constantinople, Patriarchate of; Coptic Orthodoxy; Jerusalem, Patriarchate of; Syrian Orthodox Churches; World Religions, Orthodoxy and

References and Suggested Readings

Badr, H. (ed.) (2005) *Christianity: A History in the Middle East*. Beirut: Middle East Council of Churches/Studies and Research Program.

Braude, B. and Lewis, B. (eds.) (1982) *Christians and Jews in the Ottoman Empire: The Functioning of a Plural Society*, 2 vols. New York: Holmes and Meier.

Griffith, S. H. (2008) *The Church in the Shadow of the Mosque: Christians and Muslims in the World of Islam*. Princeton: Princeton University Press.

Grypeou, E., Swanson, M. N., and Thomas, D. (eds.) (2006) *The Encounter of Eastern Christianity with Early Islam*. Leiden: Brill.

Khoury, A. (1982) *Apologétique byzantine contre l'islam; VIIIe–XIIIe siècles*. Altenberge, Germany: Verlag für christlich-islamisches Schrifttum.

Runciman, S. (1968) *The Great Church in Captivity: A Study of the Patriarchate of Constantinople from the Eve of the Turkish Conquest to the Greek War of Independence*. Cambridge: Cambridge University Press.

Vryonis, S., Jr. (1971) *The Decline of Medieval Hellenism in Asia Minor and the Process of Islamization from the Eleventh through the Fifteenth Century*. Berkeley: University of California Press.

Ison *see* Music (Sacred)

J

Japan, Autonomous Orthodox Church of

SCOTT M. KENWORTHY

Orthodoxy in Japan began with the Russian Orthodox mission in 1861. Its great success was largely due to the efforts of one man, St. Nikolai Kasatkin (1836–1912). Today, the Japanese Orthodox Church has autonomous status under the Moscow patriarchate and claims some 10,000 active members. At its peak before the Russian Revolution there were 40,000 Japanese Orthodox Christians. Serge Bolshakoff termed it the most spectacular achievement of Russian missionary activity.

Russia first established relations with Japan in the 1850s and founded a consulate in Hakodate on the island of Hokkaido. Ivan Kasatkin, a student at the St. Petersburg Theological Academy, volunteered for the position of chaplain of the consulate because of an interest in mission and in Asia. He was the son of a deacon from the Smolensk region of Russia; he finished at the Smolensk seminary before entering the St. Petersburg Theological Academy for advanced studies. Before departing for Japan he was tonsured a monk with the name Nikolai and was ordained to the priesthood. He arrived in Hakodate in 1861. Innokentii (Popov-Veniaminov), the great missionary to Alaska, encouraged Nikolai to immerse himself in Japanese language and culture, which Nikolai did for most of the 1860s. In the 1860s the Japanese government opposed Christian missionary activity, but Nikolai still managed to gain Japanese converts. His first convert was the Samurai Sawabe, baptized in 1868 (with two other men) with the name Paul. The early converts in turn acted as missionaries among their families and communities, and the number of converts in different regions of the country quickly rose. The Russian Holy Synod formally established the mission in 1871, which resulted in more clergy and funds for the mission. A new priest in Hakodate allowed Nikolai to move to Tokyo to devote himself completely to missionary activity in 1872. This move coincided with the removal of the anti-Christian edict (in 1873) and opened the door for much more active missionary effort. In Tokyo Nikolai gave Russian language classes during the day and catechetical lectures in the evening, which attracted a steady stream of converts.

For the next forty years until his death, Nikolai would inspire a dramatic expansion of the mission. He was consecrated bishop in 1880 and archbishop in 1906. In 1891 he consecrated the great Cathedral of the Holy Resurrection, commonly referred to as *Nikolai-do*. At the time of his death in 1912, there were over 33,000 Japanese Orthodox Christians in 266 parishes served by 35 Japanese priests, 22 deacons, and 106 catechists. By 1900 there was a bimonthly official periodical as well as two monthly journals, all

The Concise Encyclopedia of Orthodox Christianity, First Edition. Edited by John Anthony McGuckin.
© 2014 John Wiley & Sons, Ltd. Published 2014 by John Wiley & Sons, Ltd.

in Japanese. Nikolai also kept an extensive diary, which was recently published in its entirety in Russia in five massive volumes.

Nikolai's mission was so successful because of his vision to form a truly indigenous national church. He had great respect for the language and tradition of the Japanese, and he labored to translate the Bible, liturgy, and other Christian literature into Japanese from the beginning so as to develop native-language Orthodoxy. Indeed, the liturgy was served only in Japanese after Nikolai moved to Tokyo. The number of Russian missionaries was deliberately small so that native converts would assume leadership positions. A particularly important role was played by lay catechists who were supported for full-time church work by the Russian Church and who, in turn, became active missionaries. Moreover, in 1875 two of the first converts (including Paul Sawabe) were ordained as the first Japanese priests.

Nikolai also developed Orthodox education. He established a school for catechists and a seminary to train native clergy in Tokyo. A school for girls was established in Tokyo and another in Kyoto, while one for boys and girls existed in Hokaido. There were also many church schools to teach catechism and instruct the children. Nikolai laid great emphasis on education for converts both before and after baptism (especially reading the New Testament) and for their children. A further reason for the success of the mission was Nikolai's insistence on a great deal of functional autonomy for the Japanese Church. The church was administered by a synod that included lay delegates from every congregation and met every two years. Moreover, Nikolai successfully separated the mission from Russian political interests. This was particularly important during the Russo-Japanese war in 1904–5. During the war Nikolai decided to remain in Japan but refrained from public services in the cathedral because he personally could not pray for Japanese victory over the Russians. At the same time he encouraged the Japanese converts to remain patriotic citizens of their country. His position won the respect of the Japanese government, which protected the Orthodox Church and granted it unusual freedom to minister to 73,000 Russian prisoners of war.

The Russian Revolution of 1917 had a devastating impact on the Japanese Church. Financial support ceased, which meant that the educational institutions were forced to close. Moreover, the church could no longer support the catechists – who had served as the primary agents of the mission – as it had done before. A massive earthquake in 1923 destroyed numerous church buildings in Tokyo, including the great cathedral, which was reconstructed with great sacrifice by 1930. Nikolai's successor, Metropolitan Sergii (Tikhomirov), remained loyal to the Moscow patriarchate through the 1920s and 1930s despite the difficulties of the Russian Church under the Soviets. Rising nationalism in Japan in the 1930s also created new difficulties. The government required that all leaders of Christian churches should be ethnic Japanese, which forced Metropolitan Sergii from his position.

A national Council of the Japanese Church declared itself independent of the Moscow patriarchate in 1940, but could not reach consensus on a candidate for bishop. A year later another council elected Archpriest John Ono to be the first Japanese bishop. Ono was a respected married parish priest in Tokyo. In order to become a bishop, he and his wife (the daughter of one of the first converts) separated and both simultaneously took monastic vows, in accordance with tradition. He was consecrated in Harbin, Manchuria, by Metropolitan Meletii (of the Russian Church in Exile) with the name Nikolai.

In the postwar period the Japanese Church was divided as to the question of affiliation. Bishop Nikolai Ono worked to restore relations with the Moscow patriarchate, a move which was opposed by the American occupying forces as well as many within the church. A council of 1946 requested that they come under the jurisdiction of the American metropolia, which sent bishops to head the church (Benjamin, 1947–53; Irenei, 1953–60, Nikon, 1960–2, and Vladimir, 1962–72). The Japanese Church received autonomous status from the Moscow patriarchate at the same time the metropolia received autocephaly (as the Orthodox Church in America), although this status has not been recognized by the ecumenical patriarch. As an autonomous church, the election of its primate (metropolitan) must be confirmed by the Moscow patriarchate, but it can elect its own bishops without such confirmation. In 1972 Bishop

Theodosius (Nagashima) was installed as the first native Japanese metropolitan, and he served as head of the church until his death in 1999. In 2000 a local council elected Daniel (Nushiro) as metropolitan; Russian Patriarch Aleksii II traveled to Japan to enthrone him.

Today, the Church of Japan consists of three dioceses: the archdiocese of Tokyo, the western diocese based in Kyoto, and the eastern diocese based in Sendai. In 2007, sixty-seven parishes were served by the metropolitan and one other bishop, twenty-two priests, and twelve deacons. Almost all of the clergy are Japanese who were trained at the seminary in Tokyo.

Nikolai Kasatkin, who is acknowledged even by non-Orthodox as one of the greatest modern missionaries, was canonized by the Orthodox Church of Japan and the Russian Orthodox Church in 1970 as "equal to the apostles."

SEE ALSO: Evangelism; Russia, Patriarchal Orthodox Church of; United States of America, Orthodoxy in the

References and Suggested Readings

Bartholomew, J. (1987) "The Missionary Activity of St. Nicholas of Japan," MDiv thesis, St. Vladimir's Orthodox Theological Seminary.

Besstremiannaia, G. E. (2006) *Iaponskaia Pravoslavnaia tserkov': Istoriia i sovremennost'.* Sergiev Posad: Sviato-Troitskaia Sergieva Lavra.

Bolshakoff, S. (1943) *The Foreign Missions of the Russian Orthodox Church.* London: SPCK.

Drummond, R. H. (1971) *A History of Christianity in Japan.* Grand Rapids, MI: Eerdmans.

Naganawa, M. (1995) "The Japanese Orthodox Church in the Meiji Era," in J. T. Rimer (ed.) *A Hidden Fire: Russian and Japanese Cultural Encounters, 1868–1926.* Stanford: Stanford University Press; Washington, DC: Woodrow Wilson Center Press, pp. 158–69.

Nakamura, K. (ed.) (2004) *Dnevniki Sviatogo Nikolaia Iaponskogo,* 5 vols. St. Petersburg: Hyperion.

Remortel, M. V. and Chang, P. (eds.) (2003) *St. Nikolai Kasatkin and the Orthodox Mission in Japan.* Point Reyes Station, CA: Divine Ascent Press.

Roberson, R. (2008) *The Eastern Christian Churches: A Brief Survey,* 7th edn. Rome: Orientalia Christiana.

Sablina, E. (2006) *150 let Pravoslaviia v Iaponii: Istoriia Iaponskoi Pravoslavnoi Tserkvi i ee osnovatel' Sviatitel' Nikolai.* Moscow: AIRO-XXI; St. Petersburg: Dmitrii Bulanin.

Ushimaru, P.Y. (1980) "Japanese Orthodoxy and the Culture of the Meiji Period," *St. Vladimir's Seminary Quarterly* 24: 115–27.

Jeremias II, Patriarch (1572–1595)

JOHN A. MCGUCKIN

Jeremias was a patriarch of Constantinople from 1572 to 1595, at a time when the higher offices of the Orthodox Church were being regularly "auctioned off" by the sultans. This "Babylonian captivity" caused much instability in the governance affairs of the church. His period of tenure, being exceptionally long for that period, allowed him to emerge as a significant and learned leader. During his tenure, Jeremias was approached by Lutheran theologians from Tübingen university who wished to gain his favorable opinion to assist them in their struggle with Counter-Reformation theologians over issues of justification theology. The exchange is symbolic in a sense, as it was the first time that the Reformation came into the official purview of Eastern Orthodoxy. The written three *Answers* of Jeremias to the Lutherans became part of the collection known as *Symbolical Books* which were extensively used by the Orthodox from the early modern era to the 19th century as highly authoritative statements of worldwide Orthodox dogma. Jeremias had clearly studied the Augsburg Confession (1530) and decided that there were too many significant differences between Orthodoxy and Lutheranism in matters concerning holy tradition, sacraments, and justification theory for him to give any straightforward endorsement of the Reformation theology as such. Jeremias was also patriarch at the time (1582) when Pope Gregory XIII promulgated the change to the civil and ecclesiastical calendar (from Julian to Gregorian), a move that he protested against strongly. His visit to Russia (1588–9) to seek funds from the tsar for the assistance of the Orthodox people in the Ottoman Empire was the occasion when he formally agreed to the elevation of the metropolia of Moscow to the rank of patriarchate.

SEE ALSO: Constantinople, Patriarchate of; Cyril Lukaris, Patriarch of Constantinople (1572–1638); Iasi (Jassy), Synod of (1642); Russia, Patriarchal Orthodox Church of

References and Suggested Readings

Mastrantonis, G. (1982) *Augsburg and Constantinople.* Brookline, MA: Holy Cross Press.

Runciman, S. (1968) *The Great Church in Captivity.* Cambridge: Cambridge University Press.

Jerusalem, Patriarchate of

JOHN A. MCGUCKIN

The ancient see of Jerusalem ranks fourth in the precedence of honor of the autocephalous Orthodox churches today. At the time of the Council of Chalcedon in 451 it was raised to the status of a patriarchate, although in ancient times it was the Romano-Palestinian see of Caesarea Maritima which held the jurisdictional position of superiority over all churches in Palestine (then including Israel and Jordan) and Arabia. After the era of Constantine, however, Caesarea Maritima (once a leading Christian university city, and home of Origen the exegete, Pamphilus the philosopher martyr, and Eusebius the historian) fell into terminal decline, and Jerusalem emerged as a significant see with (by the 4th century onwards) a vibrant and powerful monastic movement surrounding it in the Judean desert. Mar Saba is a striking reminder of that history, but there are also numerous ancient sites still preserved, such as St. George the Chozebite off the Jericho-Jerusalem road, or the Monastery of the Forty Days (of Christ's temptation) at Jericho itself. Stories from this era are known throughout the Orthodox world today in the form of the paranetic tale of St. Mary the Harlot, whose feast is celebrated every Lent in Orthodox services as a model of repentance.

Even in Antiquity Jerusalem was never a large church with a significant sphere of political influence, but it always had a different kind of symbolic influence, and importance, for the universal Christian imagination, chiefly as the site of the holy places where the Lord taught, suffered, and rose again. In its most important patristic phase it was the center of an internationally influential liturgical revival, which followed after Constantine's building of the Church of the Resurrection (*Anastasis*) which in the West is more commonly called by its medieval name: the Church of the Holy Sepulchre. The story of St. Helena's discovery of the true cross in Jerusalem was added to by several other major discoveries (by aristocrats, founders, and archbishops) of the relics of New Testament saints such as John the Forerunner or Stephen the Protomartyr; these were stories of visions and findings that electrified not only Jerusalem itself but Christian cities from Constantinople to Rome and Syria, and which led to a massive movement of the building of pilgrimage churches in the Holy Land (many of which are still being excavated – the finding of an octagonal site being the give-away evidence of it as a Byzantine place of pilgrimage). From the late 4th to the 6th centuries, Roman Palestine, with Jerusalem at its center, was renowned throughout the Christian world as a thriving church based around such pilgrim traffic. Its liturgical traditions thus spread because of this to influence many of the rites celebrated in Orthodoxy today. The influence can especially be seen in festivals such as the blessing of the waters on Theophany (formerly a pilgrimage rite peculiar to Jerusalem, when the clergy and people would make the journey from the holy city to the Jordan river) and the ritual of the Exaltation of the Cross (September 14), which was based around the acts of veneration celebrated in the courtyard of the Anastasis church buildings where a great cross was raised containing relics of the Lord's own cross. The current festival commemorates the loss of these relics from Jerusalem to Persian raiders and their eventual reclamation by the Byzantine emperor. Jerusalem also seems to have adopted the common Orthodox liturgical practice of having the multinational congregation respond to complex prayer-petitions with a simple responsorial "Lord have mercy," easily learned, in Greek, as *Kyrie Eleison.* The beautiful Liturgy of St. James is still in use in the Orthodox Church today, though rarely witnessed in the course of a year. It remains as the standard liturgical rite of Jerusalem.

Pilgrimage continued throughout ancient times. The Jerusalem Church's moment of glory really came

Plate 36 Pilgrim carrying Orthodox cross. Hanan Isachar/Corbis.

treaty. So it was that, until the massive disruptions of the first three Crusades, the church centered round Jerusalem continued as a fairly lively nexus of pilgrim sites, sustained by the city clergy with high ceremonial liturgies funded by visitors and aristocratic patrons, along with numerous monasteries in the desert regions of Judea and modern Jordan, reaching down to Gaza and Sinai. The fame of these Judean monasteries rivaled that of the earlier settlements of Christian Egypt, which by this stage had themselves fallen into a degree of obscurity following barbarian devastations of the ancient desert settlements. In the 5th century the instability of the churches wracked by the christological controversy following in the aftermath of the Council of Chalcedon (451) was acutely felt in Jerusalem and the surrounding regions. Accounts from this time, such as the *Lives of the Fathers* by Cyril of Scythopolis (which narrates the hagiographies of some of the Judean hermits), show significant tensions within the same houses between pro- and anti-Origenist monks; and between pro- and anti-Chalcedonian spiritual leaders. St. Saba and his fraught battles to secure control of the Judean monasteries witnesses to the same tensions. It was a time when one bishop, preaching a christological message that was unacceptable to his monastic hearers, was surrounded in church, his wooden raised pulpit wrenched from the walls with him still in it, and bishop and furniture alike taken outside and thrown into a ditch. Such theological and cultural tensions clearly weakened Christian life in the city during this time.

The 7th century, however, was definitely to throw a curtain over any further expansion of the patriarchate, as it soon found itself thereafter in the unenviable position of a city that was not only sacred to the Jews and the Christians alike, but had now also become a holy site for the new politically ascendant religion of Islam. Even so, with a few exceptions, the Christian holy places were allowed to operate in reduced numbers for most of the time. Islam attributed to Jerusalem a role as the site of Mohammed's ascent from the earth, and commissioned Byzantine craftsmen to build the exquisite shrine of the Dome of the Rock over the place where it declared Abraham's sacrifice had taken place.

In hard times, Mar Saba, the great fortified monastery near Bethlehem, emerged as a strong center of

at the time of the Council of Chalcedon, when Bishop Juvenal managed to secure from the conciliar fathers the admission of its right to be regarded as the primary see of Palestine (by virtue of its ancient status and contemporary importance) and they also gave to it the status and title of a patriarchate (though without extending its territorial jurisdiction). After the 7th-century Islamic occupation of the holy city a long decline set in concerning its Christian vitality, but the pilgrimage movement still continued, even if abated. The Byzantine emperors often secured the agreement of the Islamic caliphs to allow Christians passage, and there were many times when the Byzantine emperors regained control of the land routes. Even when the emperors lost the upper hand in negotiations, they still could easily negotiate pilgrim access by means of

Orthodox literary activity. St. John of Damascus worked from this base in the 8th century, and it also attracted numerous other theologians and scholars, several of whom in the 9th century translated the writings of some of the early Syriac fathers into Greek, a development that would lead to the hesychastic revival in medieval Byzantium. This time also witnessed to Mar Saba's role as a major clearing house for international Orthodox liturgy. It was largely due to the influence of this monastic community that the so-called "City" or "Cathedral Rite of Byzantium" (high ceremonial, choral singing, and processions) was fused with the monastic ritual (heavy use of the psalter, simplified chant, and extended prayers for the liturgy of hours) so as to become the shape of Orthodox liturgical practice ever afterwards.

The high Middle Ages when the western armies intervened militaristically, known to us now as the Crusades, were obviously times that reflected major tensions between the Christians and their Islamic masters, and were a very mixed blessing for the Jerusalem Church. Crusader intervention followed soon after the partial demolition of the shrine of the tomb of the Lord by "Mad" Caliph Hakim in the early 11th century, but Crusader presence in the city was intermittent, and ultimately not long lasting. When the western armies did control the city, they had a tendency to prefer a new set of church leaders who followed the western rites, a practice they also followed at Constantinople after the infamous Fourth Crusade, when they ousted the Orthodox patriarch and substituted a Latin one. The Al Aksa mosque built on the platform in Jerusalem where the Temple once stood (actually on the site of the southern portico of Herod's Temple complex) incorporates the Latin Crusader church of the Templars. The excited romance of the discovery of Jerusalem can be traced in the legends of the medieval West from this time, with tales such as the Holy Grail gaining lively currency.

Pilgrimage has always been one of the *raisons d'être* for the patriarchate of Jerusalem, therefore, and continues to be so. But in saying this it is extremely important not to overlook the profound significance of the increasingly dwindling local population of about 35,000 Arab Christians who have been suffering politically for so long, in a veritable silent martyrdom. Modern demographic changes in Israel today, in a context of rising Islamic Arab nationalism, has left little room in anyone's political map for the Arab Christians, and they have been leaving Israel in massive numbers since the middle of the 20th century. The Jerusalem patriarchate had the closest links, especially after its occlusion by Islamic power, with the patriarchate of Constantinople, and phanariot higher clergy were regularly used to staff its offices under the Ottomans. It also has historical and very close links with the Church of Sinai.

In 1672 an important synod (often called the Synod of Jerusalem, although it took place in the Bethlehem Nativity Church) took place under the direction of the patriarch, and made some first moves in Orthodoxy to classify theological positions affirmed by Protestantism and Catholicism, and where Orthodoxy stood in relation to both. The council confirmed the canonicity of the Deuterocanonical literature, thus rejecting the Reformation world's adoption of the shorter Hebrew canon. It also affirmed the real presence of Christ in the Eucharist, but countered trends in Roman Catholic Augustinianism with an insistence on the integral role that good deeds play in the process by which God justifies the believer (Robertson 1899).

The Church of the Anastasis, with the patriarch at its center, continues to be governed by the monastic Brotherhood of the Holy Cross, which still makes up a powerful and focused Greek clerical community in Jerusalem. The monks are known as *Hagiotaphites* ("brothers of the holy tomb") and the patriarch is *ex officio* the head of all the Brotherhood's affairs. His title is "His Beatitude the Patriarch of the Holy City of Jerusalem and of All the Promised Land." All bishops of the local synod (two eparchies at Akka (Ptolemais) and Nazareth, and several other titular archbishops such as Mt. Tabor, Jordan, and Kerak) whose complement does not exceed eighteen, must be members of the Brotherhood. The senior hierarchs are all predominantly occupied with the administration of one of the chief shrines of the Holy Land.

The local faithful are almost entirely Arabs (the resident Greek Christians number in the low hundreds today) with predominantly Arabic parish priests.

The latter are mostly married, and the celibates among them historically have rarely been admitted to the higher offices of the church, presumably so that the synod of the Jerusalem patriarchate will never lose its operative Greek majority. Since 1958 there has been a new constitution for the administration of the patriarchate, replacing the one composed in Ottoman times and revised by the British administration following World War I. This was partly influenced by the Hashemite Kingdom of Jordan, and it gave the Christian Arabs more voice. Since then (from 1960 onwards) there has been a growing admission that there should always be a small number of Arab bishops in the local synod. There are currently about 156,000 Orthodox faithful belonging to the jurisdiction of the Jerusalem patriarchate, living in the Roman Palestinian territories, now Israel, the West Bank, Gaza territory, and Jordan.

Throughout the 20th century there have been regular occasions of disruption and unrest in the patriarchate's affairs. Relations with the Israeli government have sometimes caused difficulties, with the patriarch at times caught between state political interests, those of the Brotherhood, and those of the Arab Christian faithful. Recent land deals involving the patriarchate and Israeli authorities caused great stresses in the church and involved a major (and bitterly contested) turnover of the leadership.

SEE ALSO: Constantinople, Patriarchate of; Cross; Islam, Orthodoxy and; Sinai, Autocephalous Church of

References and Suggested Readings

Hunt, E. D. (1982) *Holy Land Pilgrimages in the Later Roman Empire, AD 312–460*. Oxford: Oxford University Press.

McGuckin, J. A. (2004) "Jerusalem," in *The Westminster Handbook to Patristic Theology*. Louisville: Westminster John Knox Press.

Melling, D. (2001) "Jerusalem," in K. Parry et al. (ed.) *The Blackwell Dictionary of Eastern Christianity*. Oxford: Blackwell.

Robertson, J. N. (1899) *The Acts and Decrees of the Synod of Jerusalem*. London: T. Baker.

Wilken, R. L. (1992) *The Land Called Holy: Palestine in Christian History and Thought*. New Haven: Yale University Press.

Jesus Prayer

METROPOLITAN KALLISTOS OF DIOKLEIA

A short invocation, designed for frequent repetition, addressed to Christ and using his human name "Jesus" (Mt. 1.21). Most commonly the Jesus Prayer is said in the form "Lord Jesus Christ, Son of God, have mercy on me" (see the prayer of the blind man Bartimaeus in Mk. 10.47; Lk. 18.38). But there are many variants. Particularly in the Russian tradition, the words "the sinner" are often added as the end (see the prayer of the publican in Lk. 18.13). It is possible to say in the plural "have mercy on us." The prayer may be abbreviated: "Lord Jesus, have mercy," "My Jesus," or even "Jesus" on its own (but this is rare in Orthodoxy, although frequent in the medieval West). What is constant among all the variants is the employment of the name "Jesus." There are basically two ways in which the Jesus Prayer is said: either it is recited on its own, in conditions of outward quiet, as part of our appointed prayer time; or else it is used in a free way, in unoccupied moments as we go about our daily tasks (when performing simple manual labor, walking from place to place, and so on).

Fundamental to the tradition of the Jesus Prayer is a sense of profound reverence for the holy name "Jesus." This is felt to act in a semi-sacramental way as a source of grace and strength. There is, it is believed, an integral connection between the name and the person named; to call on the Son of God by name is to render him directly and dynamically present. In this way the distant origin of the Jesus Prayer is to be found in the veneration of the name of God in the Old and New Testaments. Especially influential is Philippians 2.10: "At the name of Jesus every knee should bend" (cf. Jn. 16.23–24; Acts 4.10–12). The same reverence for the name is found in early Christian texts such as the 2nd-century *Shepherd of Hermas*: "The Name of the Son of God is great and boundless, and it upholds the whole world" (*Similitudes* 9.14.5).

The more immediate source of the Jesus Prayer is the practice of "monologic prayer" (i.e., prayer of a single word or phrase) found among the monks of 4th-century Egypt. Seeking to fulfill Paul's injunction to "Pray without ceasing" (1 Thes. 5.17), while performing manual labor they repeated short phrases or sentences, often from Scripture (e.g., Ps. 50/51.1).

Plate 37   One of the nuns in the Varatec monastic community in Romania: a veritable monastic village of many buildings, and several thousand nuns. Photo by John McGuckin.

Augustine of Hippo (354–420) described these prayers as "suddenly shot forth" into heaven like arrows (*Letter* 130.20). In the *Apophthegmata* or *Sayings of the Desert Fathers* there was a variety of such "arrow prayers"; the name "Jesus" sometimes occurs in them, but enjoys no special prominence.

It is in the writings of Diadochos, bishop of Photikē in Northern Greece (mid-5th century), that the Jesus Prayer first emerged as a distinctive spiritual way. Whereas the 4th-century desert fathers used many different "monologic" formulae, Diadochos recommended adherence to a single, unvarying phrase: "Give to your intellect [*nous*] nothing but the prayer *Lord Jesus*" (*Century* 59). He did not say whether other words

are to follow this opening invocation. Diadochos adopted from Evagrios of Pontos (346–99) the teaching that inner prayer should take an "apophatic" or "non-iconic" form, being free from images, intellectual concepts, and discursive thinking. While Evagrios himself did not suggest any practical method whereby such prayer can be achieved, Diadochos saw this as precisely the function of the Jesus Prayer. The human mind has an intrinsic need for activity, and this can be satisfied by giving it as a task the constant recitation of the words "Lord Jesus": "Let the intellect continually concentrate on these words within its inner shrine with such intensity that it is not turned aside to any mental images" (*Century* 59). Thus the Jesus Prayer, as an image-free manner of praying, is not a form of imaginative meditation on specific incidents in the life of Christ, but a means whereby, in the words of Diadochos, we block "all the outlets" of the *nous*. As we recite the prayer, we are to have a vivid sense of the immediate presence of Christ, but this is to be unaccompanied, so far as possible, by images or intellectual concepts.

In this way, the Jesus Prayer is a prayer in words; but because the words are few and simple, and because the same words are repeated over and over again – because, moreover, the mind of the one who prays is to be stripped of images and thoughts – it is a prayer that leads us through words into silence, initiating us into *hesychia* or inner stillness of the heart.

The use of the Jesus Prayer seems at first to have been somewhat restricted. It is mentioned by Sinaite authors in the 7th to 9th centuries, such as John Klimakos and Hesychios of Batos. But there are no references to it in Maximos the Confessor (ca. 580–662) or in the authentic works of Symeon the New Theologian (959–1022), although texts relating to it occur in the 11th-century anthology *Evergetinos*. It comes to greater prominence in the late 13th and 14th centuries, through Athonite writers such as Nikiphoros the Hesychast, Gregory of Sinai, and Gregory Palamas, and through the Constantinopolitan monks Kallistos and Ignatios Xanthopoulos. In these authors there are two important developments:

1   The recitation of the Jesus Prayer is seen as leading to a vision of divine light, which is regarded as identical with the light that shone from Christ at his transfiguration upon Mount Tabor.

2   A psychosomatic technique is recommended when reciting the prayer, which may in fact be more ancient than the 14th century (there are possible allusions in Coptic sources of the 7th–8th centuries). The technique involves three elements: (a) a specific bodily posture (sitting on a low stool, with head and shoulders bowed); (b) regulation of the rhythm of the breathing; (c) inner concentration upon the place of the heart.

There are parallels to all this in Yoga and among the Sufis. But this bodily method is no more than an optional accessory and does not constitute the essence of the Jesus Prayer.

Another external aid is the use of a prayer rope (Greek: *komvoschoinion*; Russian: *tchotki*), usually made of knotted cord or wool, although it can be of beads or leather. This is not mentioned in the 14th-century Greek sources, but it can be seen in icons of saints from the 16th and 17th centuries.

The leading figures in the 18th-century hesychast renaissance, such as Nikodimos of the Holy Mountain, greatly valued the Jesus Prayer, and there are many references to it in the *Philokalia*. From the Kievan period (11th–12th centuries) onwards, it was known and used in Russia. Since the 1920s it has also become familiar in the West, especially through translations of the anonymous 19th-century Russian work *The Pilgrim's Tale* (also called *The Way of the Pilgrim*). Indeed, it may confidently be claimed that the Jesus Prayer is more widely practiced today than ever in the past, alike by monastics and lay people, both Orthodox and non-Orthodox.

SEE ALSO: Desert Fathers and Mothers; *Imiaslavie*; St. Maximos the Confessor (580–662); *Philokalia*; *Pilgrim, Way of the*; Pontike, Evagrios (ca. 345–399); St. Gregory Palamas (1296–1359); St. John Klimakos (ca. 579–ca. 659).

References and Suggested Readings

Adnès, P. (1974) "Prière de Jésus," in *Dictionnaire de spiritualité* vol. 8, cols 1126–50. Paris.

Alfeyev, H. (2007) *Le Nom grand et glorieux: la veneration du nom de dieu et la prière de jesus dans la tradition orthodoxe.* Paris: Cerf.

Brianchaninov, I. (2006) *On the Prayer of Jesus*, revd. edn. Boston: New Seeds.

Hausherr, I. (1978) *The Name of Jesus*. Cistercian Studies Series 44. Kalamazoo: Cistercian Publications.

Mainardi, A. (ed.) (2005) La Preghiera di Gesù nella spiritualità russa del XIX secolo. Magnano: Edizioni Qiqajon/ Communità di Bose.

Monk of the Eastern Church [Lev Gillet] (1987) *The Jesus Prayer*. Crestwood, NY: St. Vladimir's Seminary Press.

Ware, K. (1986) *The Power of the Name: The Jesus Prayer in Orthodox Spirituality*. Fairacres Publication 43. Oxford: SLG Press.

Ware, K. (2003) "The Beginnings of the Jesus Prayer," in B. Ward and R. Waller (eds.) *Joy of Heaven: Springs of Christian Spirituality*. London: SPCK, pp. 1–29.

John Bekkos *see* Lyons, Council of (1274)

Judaism, Orthodoxy and

EUGEN J. PENTIUC

Early Jewish–Christian Interaction with Scripture

In the last decades of the first century CE nascent Jewish Christianity was gradually outnumbered by the ever-growing Gentile element. From the outset, early Christianity and evolving Judaism experienced a long and intricate process of the "parting of the ways," although there are an increasing number of scholars today who question this construct's absolute nature, pointing to many continued interactions between the two communities of faith for many centuries.

Christians have always been aware of their links with the Jewish people and interacted with them, not least through the sharing of Scripture and moral and prophetic attitudes. The Old Testament, the first part of the Christian Bible, is essentially the Jewish Scripture. The very title "Old Testament" given by Christians to the Hebrew Scripture is a phrase coined by the Apostle Paul with regard to the writings attributed to Moses (2 Cor. 3.14–15) and popularized by Origen of Alexandria in the 3rd century. The title "New Testament," referring to the new collection put together by the early church, is taken from the Book of Jeremiah announcing that God will make a "new covenant" with Israel (Jer. 31.31).

What was the relationship between Jesus and Judaism and its Scripture? Any attempt to define this relationship should keep in mind two factors. On the one hand, Jesus places his sayings on the same level of authority as Moses' teachings (Jn. 5.47), stating that he came to fulfill the whole entirety of the law (Mt. 5.17). On the other hand, Jesus relativizes several important Old Testament injunctions, among which were the Sabbath observance (Mt. 12.8, 12) and ritual purity laws (Mt. 15.11). This makes one think of the relation of the Old and New Testaments as being a relationship balanced between conformity and disruption: a unity under tension. The Lord Jesus stands at one and the same moment within Judaism and beyond it. Although St. Paul never removed the Jews – the heirs of biblical Israel considered as the people of God – from the salvific framework of his theology of redemption (Rom. 9–11), he certainly moved them away from the center, at which axis point he located submission to Jesus, Lord of the New Covenant.

Anti-Judaic Sentiments and Attitudes in Christian History

There are two foundational attitudes that have tended historically to fuel a certain level of anti-Jewish sentiment and negative attitude towards Judaism among the Christians from the 4th century onwards. The first of these was the position of theological supersessionism attested in some of the New Testament and patristic writings, especially those using the typological imagery of the movement from Old to New as being the passage from shadow to reality. The second was the spreading out of an early Christian interpretation (based upon a certain exegesis of Mt. 27.25) that the entire nation of Israel was responsible for the death of Christ.

Anti-Judaism in Byzantium took both literary and popular forms. With some few exceptions, such as Clement of Alexandria (ca. 150–ca. 215), the major patristic writers evidence a considerable degree of anti-Jewish biases. Scholars have noted that the tension that existed between the communities, as evidenced in the

production of this type of literature, may also witness to the degree of "interrelation" that must have been happening – and which alarmed the clerical leaders and literary elite, eliciting their literary products of *apologia*. Many treatises *Adversus Judaeos* (*Against the Jews*) from the early church theologians continued this attitude and hardened it in later ages, especially when the familiarity between church and synagogue (that can be presumed as a feature of daily life in the cities of the Roman Empire in Late Antiquity) became more and more a thing of memory. Among the writers of this genre can be noted Melito of Sardis, who in *Peri Pascha* (mid-2nd century) suggests that because the Jews did not recognize God in the person of Jesus, then God "Unchose" them. Justin Martyr in his *Dialogue with Trypho* (second half of the 2nd century) also argued in turn that the common Jewish people were misled by their teachers who misinterpreted the prophetic texts of the Old Testament, and for this reason the Gentile Christians irreversibly "replaced" Israel. Origen in *Against Celsus* insisted on the fact that the Kingdom of God was given to Christians by virtue of being taken from the Jews, who nevertheless remained God's chosen people until the time that they shall be returned to obedience to Christ, an event which will occur at the final *Apokatastasis*, humanity's eschatological return to God.

After 380, when Christianity became the official religion of the Byzantine Empire, the image of the Jews among the church gradually deteriorated, and their political position deteriorated as well. In his *Eight Homilies Against the Jews* (386–7), John Chrysostom with fiery rhetoric accused the Jews of the greatest crimes. Since they killed the Lord, Chrysostom argued, the demons dwell in them and in their synagogues. Since they are guilty of deicide, he said, then God hates them, and their synagogues are "assemblies of animals." Such rhetoric has, sadly, often been used to inflame anti-Semitism in Christian history; the more eirenic and respectful view of the Apostle Paul and other fathers of the church being forgotten in favor of this alone. In this case, and perhaps other examples of violent anti-Jewish rhetoric (e.g., Ambrose of Milan, indignant in the case of the burning of the synagogue of Callinicum, where the local bishop was commanded by the emperor to make restitution to the local Jewish community, and Ambrose rebuked him for supporting the "enemies of

Christ"; or Cyril of Alexandria, who reacted to the burning of the Alexander church by rioting Jewish factions in his city), local political tensions between two lively communities can perhaps explain the abrasiveness of the language (Greco-Roman rhetoric always needing to be contextualized). But it left a record that tended to become absolutized. Byzantine state legislation, while offering limited protection to Jewish members of the empire, also put a heavy burden on them, so much so that many scholars left for the more welcoming environment of Babylon.

In 438 Theodosius II promulgated the revised code of laws that reflected many Jewish-orientated prescripts: Jews were forbidden to retaliate against converts from their number to Christianity; Jews were no longer allowed to own Christian slaves; and they were not allowed to hold posts in the imperial administration. Justinian went further: in 553 Novella 146 banned the publication of rabbinic interpretations and demanded the use of languages other than Hebrew in the imperial synagogues; Jews were strongly "urged" to go beyond the historical (plain literal) meaning of the biblical text, and the Mishnah was prohibited from being read in the synagogues because it was not part of the sacred books.

New Perspectives after the 20th-Century Shoah

The pattern of Jewish–Christian interactions thus goes back a long time, but it took the shock of the Nazi war crimes of the 1930s and 1940s and the traumatic event of the Shoah for a true and sustainable new consciousness of Jewish–Christian relations to arise. It grew up along with the sense that embittered relations of the past need not constitute an enduring pattern for the future. A first step towards reconciliation and dialogue was made in 1947 when Christians and Jews met at Seelisberg (Switzerland), calling on Christian churches to revise their attitude and preaching about Judaism and its people. Yet another turning point occurred in 1965 when Pope John XXIII issued the encyclical *Nostra Aetate*, insisting that "Jews should not continue being presented as rejected by God." In Orthodox Christianity the patriarchs of Constantinople and

Moscow have both issued statements condemning anti-Semitism. Leaders of the Orthodox Churches today have often taken initiatives to foster respectful relations and respectful dialogue with Jewish leaders. However, within world Orthodoxy, there has as yet been no sustained effort to review commonly available educational and theological materials which are so heavily indebted to patristic writings, or to explain them situationally, something that occurred as a necessary step to renewing relations in recent Roman Catholicism and Protestantism.

There are only a few direct contacts between Jews and Orthodox Christians outside the framework of the World Council of Churches. In March 1977 a dialogue between Jewish and Greek Orthodox leaders was held at Lucerne University. In October 1979 another dialogue took place in Bucharest between Jewish leaders and Orthodox theologians from Romania, Bulgaria, Cyprus, Greece, France, Switzerland, and the United States. It is certainly a time for learning and reflecting. In the sentiment of Professor Rabbi Jacob Neusner, after both Golgotha and Shoah, Christians and Jews should return to Sinai, to Moses' cleft in the rock, and there listen to God's revelatory silence.

SEE ALSO: Bible; Christ; Church (Orthodox Ecclesiology); Old Testamen

References and Suggested Readings

Berdiaev, N. (1952) *Christianity and Anti-Semitism*, trans. A. Spears and V. Kanter. Aldington: Kent Publishing.

Cohen, J. (ed.) (1991) *Essential Papers on Judaism and Christianity in Conflict: From Late Antiquity to the Reformation*. New York: New York University Press.

Justin Martyr (1930) *Dialogue with Trypho*, trans. A. L. Williams. London: SPCK.

Melito of Sardis (2001) *On Pascha: With the Fragments of Melito and Other Material Related to the Quartodecimans*. Crestwood, NY: St. Vladimir's Seminary Press.

Pentiuc, E. J. (2011) *The Old Testament in Eastern Orthodox Tradition*. Oxford: Oxford University Press.

Shepardson, C. (2008) *Anti-Judaism and Christian Orthodoxy: Ephrem's Hymns in Fourth-Century Syria*. Washington, DC: Catholic University of America Press.

Siegel, S. (1976) "Judaism and Eastern Orthodoxy: Theological Reflections," *Journal of Ecumenical Studies* 13: 579–85.

Judgment

WENDY PAULA NICHOLSON

Orthodoxy teaches two judgments: "particular" and "general" or "Last Judgment." Particular judgment occurs immediately after death (Lk. 16.19–31; 23.43) The newly departed experience either a foretaste of the eternal blessedness promised to the righteous at the Last Judgment, or a foretaste of punishment if there has been incomplete or no repentance of sin before death. The Last Judgment will occur at the second, glorious coming of Christ, when he will resurrect the dead. The effect of this judgment will be eternal.

Plate 38 The western outside wall of the 16th-century church at Voronets, Romania, depicting the Doomsday. The golden gate depicts the entrance to Paradise guarded by an Archangel. Photo by John McGuckin.

The subject of judgment is not limited to these two critical moments, but is pervasive in Orthodox thought, finding its strongest expression in the ascetical writings. There are two notable features, which appear, at first, contradictory. The first is the insistence that God's judgments are designed for healing and regeneration, not for retribution: He takes "no pleasure in the death of the wicked, but that the wicked turn back from his way and live" (Ezek. 33.11, cf. St. Basil the Great 1987: 338). The second is the call frequently to bring to mind death and judgment. Liturgically and iconographically, judgment is remembered in vivid scriptural images of hell-fire, punishment, and eternal torment (Ware 1984: 150–67).

The first feature, merciful judgment, corresponds to healing and deification at the heart of Orthodox soteriology, as opposed to the idea of Christ's appeasement of the wrath of God, which came to dominate western theology and was built largely upon the Augustinian doctrine of Original Sin. According to Augustine of Hippo, the human being, from conception, is so corrupted that he has no freedom with respect to God or his salvation (St. Augustine 1993a: 247). In Orthodoxy, conversely, "it is not God who punishes, but a person who punishes himself because he does not accept God's gift" (Hierotheos 2000: 252). Christ is hardly envisioned as *passing* judgment upon the sinner. Judgment is generally regarded as occurring in the actual encounter of the unrepentant sinner with Christ, and is thus always an essential element of the divine-human relationship. Every word of God will be experienced as judgment by those living in opposition to the "Truth and the Life" (Jn. 14.6). It is in this sense that Christ, the incarnate Word, is the one entrusted by the Father with all judgment (Jn. 12.46–50).

God's judgment upon the fallen Adam is believed to have issued conditions under which human beings can realize their sickness, turn, and be healed. The idea of future retribution is rejected as unworthy of God in the *Homilies* of St. Isaac the Syrian:

> It is not the way of the Compassionate Maker to create rational beings in order to deliver them over mercilessly to unending affliction in punishment for things of which

He knew even before they were fashioned, aware how they would turn out ... and whom nonetheless He created. (Isaac of Nineveh 1995: 165)

"Fire" in the biblical judgment narratives is, in Orthodox theology, nothing other than the uncreated Light of God. To those who choose to share in this divine energy, it is an experience of love and overflowing blessedness, but it is a dark and caustic bitterness to those who are not akin to it, on account of their conformity and blind attachment to the world (Syméon, n.d.: 45). The Orthodox believe that before the Last Judgment the soul can be purified of this attachment. This is a painful process only as long as the soul continues to cling to what cannot exist in the Kingdom of God:

> The divine judgement ... does not primarily bring about the punishment of sinners ... it operates only by separating good from evil and pulling the soul towards the fellowship of blessedness. It is the tearing apart of what has grown together which brings pain to the one who is being pulled. (St. Gregory Nyssa 1993: 84)

This is in contrast to the Latin doctrine of purgatory or punishment by a temporal fire created by God, which the Orthodox reject as error. Punishment by material fire after the particular judgment is clearly present in St. Augustine (St. Augustine 1993b: 461–4). The doctrine had been refuted by St. Mark of Ephesus at the Council of (Ferrara) Florence (1438–45), but a modified form of it was approved at the Synod of Jerusalem (1672) in the Confession of Dositheus. The extent to which this is the same as the western concept of purgatory is debatable, and it is generally interpreted as having been a dogmatic expression unduly influenced by western scholasticism.

The irrevocable nature of the Last Judgment in Orthodoxy maintains God's beneficence versus mercilessness. God will not destroy human freedom even in eternity, and will allow those who turn against him to do so eternally. For this reason, Origen's *apokatastasis*, the final restoration by which even the Devil has to be redeemed, was anathematized by the Second Council of Constantinople in 553.

The second feature of judgment in Orthodoxy, remembrance of death and the "dread judgment seat," is primarily an ascetic practice, attesting to the infinite blessedness of fellowship with the Holy Trinity tasted by the saints before death, compared with the desolation of its absence. In recent times this is found in the writings of St. Silouan of Athos (d. 1938), where its philanthropic power is manifest. St. Silouan describes how knowledge of God by the Holy Spirit inspires one to pity and pray with tears "more especially for those who do not know God, or who resist Him and therefore are bound for the fire of torment" (Sophrony 1991: 352). Our judgment of others is therefore irreconcilable with the Holy Spirit, who imparts God's universal love to the humble so that they may participate in the salvation of souls. By voluntarily accepting judgment upon oneself alone, following Christ's humble descent even to hell, one is also joined with him in his victory over death. The teaching "keep thy mind in hell, and despair not" (Sophrony 1991: 298, 430f.), which Christ imparted to St. Silouan, is, for the ascetic, a way of maintaining humility.

SEE ALSO: Eschatology; Grace; St. Isaac the Syrian (7th c.); St. Mark of Ephesus (1392–1445); St. Silouan of Athos (1866–1938); Soteriology

References and Suggested Readings

Augustine, St. (1993a) *Enchiridion*. Library of Nicene and Post Nicene Fathers Vol. 3. Grand Rapids, MI: Eerdmans.

Augustine, St. (1993b) *City of God*. Library of Nicene and Post Nicene Fathers Vol. 2. Grand Rapids, MI: Eerdmans.

Basil the Great, St. (1987) Pre-communion Prayer. *Prayer Book for Orthodox Christians*. Boston: Holy Transfiguration Monastery.

Gregory of Nyssa, St. (1993) *On the Soul and Resurrection*. Crestwood, NY: St. Vladimir's Seminary Press.

Hierotheos Metropolitan of Nafpaktos (2000) *Life after Death*, trans. E. Williams. Levadia-Hellas, Greece: Birth of the Theotokos Monastery.

Isaac of Nineveh (1995) *The Second Part*, trans. S. Brock. Louvain: Peeters.

Sophrony, Archimandrite (Sakharov) (1991) *Saint Silouan the Athonite*, trans. R. Edmonds. Maldon, UK: Stavropegic Monastery of St. John the Baptist.

Syméon, Archimandrite (n.d.) "L'enfer, chemin vers Royaume," in *Buisson ardent*. Paris: Le Sel de la Terre.

Ware, Archimandrite Kallistos and Mother Mary (trans.) (1984) *The Lenten Triodion: Texts for The Sunday of Last Judgement*. London: Faber and Faber.

K

Kalymauchion

JOHN A. MCGUCKIN

The headgear of clergy in the Orthodox Church. In Greece the priests and deacons wear a stiff cylindrical hat with a small top brim (colloquially a "stovepipe").

In Romania the kalymauchion is soft and cylindrical with no brim and is shorter than the Greek version. In Russia the priests and deacons wear a taller, stiff felt version which has a slight tapering outwards, and can come in various colors denoting the rank of the wearer. Monks, whether clergy or not, wear the small

Plate 39   Orthodox monk wearing the kamilavki (hat) sounding the monastic tantalon (bell for service) with the semandron (wooden hammer beam) in the corner. Marc Dozier/Hemis/Corbis.

The Concise Encyclopedia of Orthodox Christianity, First Edition. Edited by John Anthony McGuckin.
© 2014 John Wiley & Sons, Ltd. Published 2014 by John Wiley & Sons, Ltd.

cylindrical hat (also known as the *skoupho*). For church services or when in choir dress they also wear the stiff skoupho with a veil (*koukoulion*, cowl or hood) attached to the back and sides. In Greek tradition the veil is detachable (in Russian practice it is fixed permanently, the whole being known as the *klobuk*). Russian nuns also wear the klobuk, but most other Orthodox nuns wear a head covering in the form of a tightly wrapped black scarf, with Romanian nuns also wearing the skoupho with this.

Katavasia

DIMITRI CONOMOS

The concluding stanza of an ode, so called because originally the two choirs of singers at this point came down (Gk. *katavaino*, "go down") from their stalls and joined in the middle of the church (a custom maintained by some monasteries in Lent). On Sundays and feasts there is a katavasia at the end of every ode, but on ordinary weekdays at the end of the third, sixth, eighth, and ninth odes only. Festal katavasiai are sung in anticipation of a great feast and often continue to its afterfeast. For example, the katavasiai for Christmas begin on November 21.

SEE ALSO: Ode

Kathisma

DIMITRI CONOMOS

Kathisma (Gk. "seat") is the name given to the monastic division of the Psalter into twenty sessions (*kathismata*), each one being further subdivided into three stations (Gk. *staseis*). The term also signifies a set of troparia which is chanted after each kathisma from the Psalter at Matins. The twenty kathismata are distributed between Vespers and Matins, so that all 150 psalms are read during the course of a single week. Normally there is one kathisma recited at Vespers and either two or three at Matins. During Great Lent kathismata are read during the Little Hours also, so that the entire Psalter is completed twice in a week.

SEE ALSO: Troparion

Kathismata *see* Idiomelon; Kathisma

Kazakhstan, Orthodoxy in

SERGEY TROSTYANSKIY

Having been a subject of missionary activities from as early as the 4th century, Central Asia has a long history of Christianity. The territories of Turkestan (a region of Central Asia inhabited by Uzbeks, Kazakhs, Kyrgyz, and others) lay at the very heart of the Great Silk Road, the network of trade routes connecting Asia with the Mediterranean world. Starting from the 4th century the Silk Road channeled the missionary activities of the Syrian Christians (largely Nestorians, or Chaldaeans) who first introduced Christianity to these territories. From the 4th until the 6th centuries, therefore, it may be assumed that the population of Central Asia in general and of Kazakhstan in particular knew a Christian presence. This situation changed dramatically in the 6th century as Sufi Muslim missionaries started to make inroads there and established Islam as a dominant religious tradition.

Another more recent turning point in the religious history of Kazakhstan grew out of the external threats posed by the nomadic tribes of Kalmykia in the 18th century. The Kazakhs at that time asked for protection from the Russian government and received it. As a result, by the mid-19th century Kazakhstan was completely integrated into the Russian Empire. Many Russians came to Kazakhstan attracted by the new opportunities. Moreover, Russian military settlements were established all across Turkestan. Among the new settlers the vast majority were Orthodox, and brought with them a desire to establish churches and schools. In addition, the Orthodox Missionary Society, established in 1870, was active in Kazakhstan from the second half of the 19th century onwards. Russian missionaries converted many Kazakhs to Orthodoxy. Eventually, in 1871, the Turkestan eparchy of the Russian Orthodox Church was established. Thus, at the end of the 19th century, Orthodoxy found its canonical place in Kazakhstan and became the second major religious movement witnessed there after Islam.

Before the 1917 Revolution, Orthodoxy in Kazakhstan flourished under the protection of the tsars. However, the events after 1917, with the oppression of the church in Russia, meant also a significant diminishing of ecclesiastical life in Kazakhstan. After World War II, however, Orthodoxy in Kazakhstan was revitalized by the establishment of the new Kazakh eparchy and the ruling eparch, Archbishop Nikolai.

In 1991, after the dissolution of the Soviets, Kazakhstan became an independent country and declared religious freedom. Since then Orthodox life in Kazakhstan has been flourishing. Many Orthodox churches and religious institutions were restored. Orthodox education regained a formal place in Kazakh social life (it had formerly been declared illegal under the Soviet system). As a consequence, a significant segment of the population that had once self-identified as atheist or non-religious was brought back to the church. In 2003 the Russian synod established the metropolitan district in Kazakhstan which includes the Astana, Urlask, and Shymkent eparchies.

As of today, Orthodoxy in Kazakhstan is represented primarily by the parishes of the Russian Orthodox Church and by Communities of Old Believers (opponents of the 17th-century ecclesiastical reforms of the Russian Patriarch Nikon). Approximately one-third of the population of Kazakhstan identify themselves as Orthodox Christians, including Kazakh, Russian, Ukrainian, Belarusian, and other ethnic groups, with a total of just under 6 million believers. Orthodoxy remains the second largest religious movement in Kazakhstan after Islam. The Kazakh metropolitan district of the Russian Orthodox Church lists 281 active religious associations, including churches, monasteries, convents, a spiritual academy, a theological missionary college, and numerous Sunday schools.

SEE ALSO: Islam, Orthodoxy and; Old Believers; Russia, Patriarchal Orthodox Church of

References and Suggested Readings

Sadvokasova. Z. T. (2007) *Religioznaya Ekspansia Tsarisma v Kazaxstane*. Almaty: Kazak Universiteti.

Trofimov, Y. F. (1996) *Religia v Kazaxstane*. Almaty: Odilet Press.

Khomiakov, Aleksey S. (1804–1860)

KONSTANTIN GAVRILKIN

Aleksey S. Khomiakov, a Muscovite landowner with broad intellectual interests, is mostly known as one of the founders of the Slavophile movement with its belief that Russia's identity was shaped by its Eastern Orthodox tradition, and that her authentic political, social, economic, and cultural life had been seriously disrupted and corrupted by the westernizing policies of Peter the Great and his heirs. He studied a variety of subjects – theology, philosophy, history, art, literature, science, medicine, engineering, and agriculture – but left no systematic study of any kind, as the eight-volume collection of his works attests, consisting as it does of essays, correspondence, drafts of unfinished works, and various notes. His religious views were shaped by a strict Orthodox upbringing and an intense lifelong study of church history and the fathers of the church.

Khomiakov's reputation as an Orthodox theologian rests on a number of ideas, especially ecclesiological, articulated in *The Church is One* and a few polemical essays, articles, and correspondence with Roman Catholic and Protestant theologians. He believed that the church was a "spiritual organism," the unity in grace of free rational beings, embodied historically in the Orthodox Church, with its ethos of "unity in plurality," which was well expressed in the term "catholicity" (Rus. *sobornost'*). This vision of Orthodoxy is deliberately and polemically contrasted by Khomiakov with the depiction of the Roman Catholic Church as a schismatic patriarchate which substitutes the spiritual unity in freedom, characteristic of the early church, with a compulsory "monarchic" rule, in short an ethos of "unity without freedom." This deviation, in turn, generates a Protestant revolt, which he sees as continuing to fragment Western Christianity with an ever-increasing loss of the sense and concept of the church as "unity in love and freedom" and a turn towards ecclesial identity as "freedom without unity" (Khomiakov 1997).

Khomiakov's critics, while recognizing the importance of his attempt to renew discussion on the nature of the church, pointed out that his ecclesiological polemic with Western Christianity was self-serving rather than open to dialogue. On the one hand, an idealized Eastern Orthodoxy was compared to the historic shortcomings of Catholicism and Protestantism, presented as embodiments of opposite qualities (Solovyov 1901: 170–1). On the other hand, while in the writings addressed to the Russian public Khomiakov recognized the oppression of the Russian Church by the state and the absence of *sobornost'* and freedom in her life, when he spoke "before the West," as Berdiaev says, "he pretended that everything was fine in the East" (1971: 85).

Khomiakov's theological texts, first printed in Berlin in 1868, were allowed to be published by the censors in Russia only in 1879 with a disclaimer, mandatory for subsequent reprints, that "the vagueness and imprecision of some expressions were due to the author's lack of proper theological education" (Khomiakov 1907). His ideas had a very limited impact on Russian academic theology: in their essence, they repeated a century-long Orthodox ecclesiology, while in style and form of argumentation Khomiakov's "freshness" (to use Berdiaev's term) appealed mostly to lay intellectuals dissatisfied with the very dry academic literature on ecclesiology then prevalent.

SEE ALSO: Russia, Patriarchal Orthodox Church of

References and Suggested Readings

Berdiaev, N. (1971) *Aleksei Stepanovich Khomiakov*. Westmead, UK: Gregg.

Khomiakov, A. S. (1907) *Polnoe sobranie sochinenii, Vol. 2: Sochineniia bogoslovskie*, 5th edn. Moscow: Kushnerev.

Khomiakov, A. S. (1997) "French Writings," in B. Jakim and R. Bird (eds.) *On Spiritual Unity: A Slavophile Reader. Aleksei Khomiakov. Ivan Kireevsky. With Essays by Yury Samarin, Nikolai Berdiaev, and Pavel Florensky*. Nudson, NY: Lindisfarne Books, pp. 55–139.

Solovyov, V. S. (1901) "Slavianofil'stvo i ego vyrozhdenie," *Sobranie sochinenii* 5: 161–223. St. Petersburg: Obshchestvennaia pol'za.

Tsurikov, V. (ed.) (2004) *A. S. Khomiakov: Poet, Philosopher, Theologian*. Jordanville, NY: Holy Trinity Seminary Press.

Klobuk *see* Kalymauchion

Kollyva

JOHN A. MCGUCKIN

Kollyva is the sweet boiled wheat used in the church services of the commemoration of the dead (*Mnemosyna*). The use of wheat is reminiscent of the gospel: "Unless a grain of wheat falls into the earth and dies it remains alone, but if it dies it bears much fruit" (Jn. 12.24–25). After the liturgy is concluded, the commemoration ritual blesses the wheat that is brought by the family of the deceased and often decorated with refined sugar and other devices, while the family hold lighted candles, and prayers and litanies are offered for the deceased, ending with the hymn "Memory Eternal." Those attending the service are given, on leaving the church, packets of kollyva to eat or to take home, a remembrance of the ancient Christian custom of the funeral feast.

SEE ALSO: Kollyvadic Fathers

Kollyvadic Fathers

CYRIL HOVORUN

These were monastics who participated in the Kollyvadic Movement beginning on Mount Athos in the mid-18th century, which advocated faithfulness to traditional liturgical and monastic traditions. Its active phase lasted until the beginning of the 19th century. Some of the kollyvades were mere zealots for certain liturgical forms – such as the restriction of the blessing of wheat as a commemoration of the dead (*Kollyva*) – to Saturdays only. The sobriquet "kollyvades" derived from this as an ironic criticism of them. Others in the movement sought after the deeper revival of hesychastic and coenobitic monasticism at large. Among the latter were St. Makarios of Corinth (the compiler of the *Philokalia*) and his co-worker St. Nikodemos the Hagiorite (who wrote widely on Eucharistic, monastic, hagiographical, pastoral, and canonical issues). Another leading Kollyvadist was St. Athanasios of Paros, a significant polemicist against

Latin Christianity and western secularism. Several Kollyvadists advocated more frequent reception of the Holy Eucharist.

SEE ALSO: *Philokalia*

Kontakion

DIMITRI CONOMOS

The first and dominant form of Byzantine hymnody. A long metrical homily cultivated in the 5th century or early 6th, it consists of a preface (*prooimion* or *koukoulion*) which introduces the subject and its refrain (*ephymnion*), followed by a series of metrically identical stanzas or strophes (*oikoi*) that are linked by an acrostic that may render the alphabet, the author's name, or the feast commemorated. The *prooimion* is in a different meter from the stanzas, whose length can be anything from four to eighteen lines. Kontakia were performed paraliturgically between the offices of an all-night urban (or cathedral) vigil (*pannychis*).

SEE ALSO: St. Romanos the Melodist (6th c.)

References and Suggested Readings

Carpenter, M. (ed.) (1970–3) *Kontakia of Romanos*, 2 vols. Columbia: University of Missouri Press

Lash, E. (trans.) (1995) *St. Romanos "On the Life of Christ": Kontakia*. San Francisco: Harper Collins.

Koukoulion *see* Kalymauchion; Kontakion

L

Lamb *see* Lance; Proskomedie
(Prothesis)

Lampadarios *see* Music (Sacred)

Lance

THOMAS KITSON

Blade (also known as "Spear") with which the priest cuts the Lamb (the actual square of bread that will be consecrated in the Eucharist) from the loaves of offering (the *prosphora*) according to the preliminary ritual of the Proskomedie. It is a flat iron knife in the form of a spearhead, sharpened along both edges, and with a wooden (or other) handle. The priest lightly pierces the Lamb that will be offered during the liturgy to recall the lance used to pierce Christ's side. Like the cross, the lance symbolizes the powers of cruelty and death that seek to overcome the divine in this world, but providentially carve out and manifest what God has chosen for his kingdom. Thus, its symbolic significance transcends its practical use.

SEE ALSO: Proskomedie (Prothesis)

Latvia, Orthodoxy in

JOHN A. MCGUCKIN

The Latvian and Estonian territories were first missionized by the Church of Pskov from neighboring Russia, and by the 13th century there were several Orthodox churches established. These were given a serious setback as the 13th century progressed, however, and with it vigorous military campaigns of the Teutonic Knights in the Baltic lands, who forcibly replaced Orthodox Church culture with Latin. Orthodoxy recovered somewhat with the annexation of Latvia to the Russian Empire in the 18th century, but the modern story of Orthodoxy really begins again in the 19th century with the appointment in 1842 of the energetic missionary bishop of Riga, Filaret Gumilevskii (d. 1866). Orthodoxy, however, was predominantly seen as a "Russian" Church. Within five years of his arrival, Filaret had energized an Orthodox native language translation program and supervised the building of twenty permanent and forty temporary churches. Six years after the initiation of his ministry, the German aristocratic establishment in Latvia took fright at this, and in 1848 secured from the Russian Holy Synod Filaret's transfer out of the country. His successor as Orthodox bishop of Riga, Platon Gorodetskii

The Concise Encyclopedia of Orthodox Christianity, First Edition. Edited by John Anthony McGuckin.
© 2014 John Wiley & Sons, Ltd. Published 2014 by John Wiley & Sons, Ltd.

(d. 1891), was quiet for only a few years, however, before continuing a vigorous missionary campaign of his own. It has been estimated that between 1845 and 1850 as many as 100,000 Latvians may have converted to the Orthodox faith. The Orthodox were popular in that they used Latvian language in their church services, while the Lutheran majority were seen as "German" to Orthodoxy's character as "Russian."

After the Russian Revolution the Latvian Orthodox suspended relations with the Russian Orthodox Synod because of its perceived submission to the Bolsheviks. In 1920 Bishop Janis Pommers (1876–1934), a native Latvian, was released from captivity by the Soviets and assumed the leadership of Orthodoxy in Latvia, negotiating with the political authorities in 1926 to recognize the Orthodox Christians' right to assemble, and their political distinction from the "Russians" which had been a source of great tension in the country, causing the destruction of many Orthodox churches in the years between the Russian Revolution and 1925. In that year the bishop was himself elected to the Latvian parliament. Bishop Pommers was assassinated by the Soviet secret service in 1934, and in 1936 the Latvian Orthodox petitioned to be released from Moscow's ecclesiastical jurisdiction and placed under the omophorion of the patriarch of Constantinople. When the Soviet armies invaded Latvia in 1940 the Latvian Orthodox hierarchy was brought once more under enforced obedience to the Moscow patriarchate, and the incumbent Metropolitan Augustin Peterson (1873–1955) was ejected and Bishop Sergey Voskresenskii was installed. He too was shortly afterwards murdered, in the events surrounding the German invasion of the country. The Nazi authorities refused to allow the "Russian" Orthodox to reestablish themselves in Latvia in any form, but Metropolitan Augustin Peterson led a diaspora community into exile, and from postwar Germany, beginning in 1946, the Latvian Church Abroad was organized by him, under the aegis of an exarchate of the patriarchate of Constantinople. After the fall of the Soviet system, a Latvian Orthodox Church structure was initiated once more. After 1990 the senior hierarch was Metropolitan Alexander Kudryashov. The church relates most closely to the patriarchate of Moscow, with some local autonomy.

There are estimates of approximately one third of a million Latvian Orthodox today, predominantly of ethnic Russian origin.

SEE ALSO: Lithuania, Orthodoxy in; Russia, Patriarchal Orthodox Church of

References and Suggested Readings

Cherney, A. (1985) *The Latvian Orthodox Church*. Welshpool, UK: Stylite Publishing.

Lithuania, Orthodoxy in

JOHN A. MCGUCKIN

The history of Lithuanian Orthodoxy (a country first mentioned in 1009 in the German *Annals of Quedlinburg* recounting Catholic missionary efforts) is closely related to that of its southern neighbor Belarus, along with the latter's neighboring countries of Russia, Ukraine, Latvia, and Poland. The religious history mirrors the fluid boundaries of these territories in the course of the last millennium. Lithuania, in the form of the Yatavag tribe, had Orthodox Christianity present (as a tiny minority) from the time of the 10th-century Kievan evangelization initiated by the Byzantines. Numbers of the Lithuanian Imuds also became Orthodox from the 15th century onwards. Belarus missionaries influenced some of the Lithuanian nobility, but the Christianization process did not progress very far, the Lithuanian state seeing Christianity chiefly in the form of the Teutonic Knights who wished to convert and annex it. The Lithuanian court culturally turned towards the East at first, using a form of Slavonic in its official records, but westward contacts and inclinations became increasingly strong. Lithuania conquered Ukraine by the beginning of the 14th century, a time when the metropolitanate of Kiev was being devastated by Mongol invasions, its hierarch eventually moving to Moscow and assuming the title of Metropolitan of Kiev and All the Rus. In 1316 the rulers of Lithuania gained from the patriarch of Constantinople the establishment of a separate metropolitanate for Lithuania, at Novahradak. Orthodox Lithuanians commemorate as their particular patron saints three Orthodox leaders martyred by pagans in

Vilnius in 1347, namely Sts. Antony, John, and Eustathy. Soon afterwards, in 1385, there occurred the union of Lithuania and Poland by terms of royal marriage: a time when the Lithuanian prince Jaigalo adopted Roman Catholicism. After the Union of Lyublin in 1569, Lithuania was progressively absorbed into Poland's slipstream and increasingly Latinized. The westernization of Lithuania was symbolically manifested at the Union of Brest-Litovsk in 1596, which created the "Unia." Immense pressure was, after this point, placed on the Orthodox Church's daily life. By the 19th century the Russian Church became Lithuanian Orthodoxy's dominant patron, abolishing in 1839 the terms and existence of the Unia, a deed which proved to be a dubious liberation for Orthodoxy in the country, since it was locally seen as an attempted suppression of Lithuania's political existence as other than a Russian satellite.

The modern history of the nation (modern Lithuania is only a small portion of the ancient lands) has been one of many political and ecclesiastical vicissitudes. In 1923, when Poland again annexed Lithuania, the leading Orthodox hierarch, the Russian bishop of Vilnius, Eleutherius Bogoiavlenskii (1868–1940), was deported from the country. Between the two world wars he headed the Autonomous Lithuanian Orthodox Church from exile, and briefly assumed headship of the Latvian and Estonian Orthodox Churches, too. The Russian Empire and the Polish state dominated the territories from the eastern and western sectors, respectively. The Orthodox Church in Poland, covering most of the lands that had once been part of the autonomous metropolias of Kiev and Lithuanian Navahradak, was granted autocephaly by the patriarch of Constantinople in 1924 in order to extricate it from Russian domination. The tension of due canonical order between the two patriarchates (and independently proclaimed Belorussian Orthodox church bodies) continues to the present in Baltic church affairs, and especially in the wide diaspora. In 1939 Poland itself disappeared between the parturition enforced by Germany and Russia. Soviet rule proved no kinder to Orthodoxy in Lithuania than anywhere else in the communist empire. In 1942 under German occupation Orthodox hierarchs in Lithuania voted for the establishment of the Belorussian Autocephalous Orthodox Church, which was quickly destroyed by the returning Soviets, and its leaders were either killed

or fled from the country to the West, where they organized synods in resistance. The Orthodox in Lithuania today are a very small minority of 114,000 faithful out of the national Christian population of 3,250,000, the majority of whom are Roman Catholics. The historical problems of the past have left abiding canonical divisions that require healing.

SEE ALSO: Eastern Catholic Churches; Latvia, Orthodoxy in; Russia, Patriarchal Orthodox Church of; Ukraine, Orthodoxy in the

References and Suggested Readings

Barrett, D., Kurian, G., and Johnson, T. (eds.) (2001) *World Christian Encyclopedia*, vol. 1, 2nd edn. Oxford: Oxford University Press.

Brady, D. (1999) "Lithuanian Orthodox Church," in K. Parry et al. (eds.) *The Blackwell Dictionary of Eastern Christianity*. Oxford: Blackwell, p. 295.

Mankouski, P. (n.d.) *One Thousand Years of Christianity in Byelorussia*. Brooklyn, NY: St. Cyril's Byelorussian Autocephalous Orthodox Cathedral.

Urban, W. (1987) "The Conversion of Lithuania: 1387," *Lituanus: Lithuanian Quarterly Journal of Arts and Sciences* 33, 4.

Liturgical Books

JOHN A. MCGUCKIN

The priest and cantor need a veritable library of books in order to complete all the ceremonies, prayer services, rituals, and blessings of the Orthodox Church, so rich is its liturgical tradition, and so varied the range of ceremonies it has established and adapted over the ages of its existence.

There are several small but significant variations of style and form among the different language families of Orthodoxy, especially in relation to liturgical customs prevalent among the Greeks and the Slavs, which grew up in the course of the last millennium. English-language translations of Orthodox liturgical texts tend to fall between the three ritual forms most common today in the United States of America: that of the Antiochene patriarchate; the ritual of the Russian Church as adapted for use by the Orthodox Church in America (OCA); and the English language publications of the Greek Orthodox archdiocese, which are generally straightforward translations of the ceremonies of the Great Church of Constantinople. Many of the most important liturgical books have separate entries in this encyclopedia. Chief among them are the *Euchologion* (altar book for the liturgy and sacraments); the *Hieratikon* (priest's parts for the services); and the *Horologion* (book of texts and rubrics for the celebration of the services of the Hours). Among the Russians the collection of special services and blessings that might be celebrated outside of the church is known as the *Trebnik* (Book of Needs) and there are English versions of it in one volume or several volumes (covering a greater array of services). The Antiochene patriarchate has issued a *Liturgikon* in English that covers aspects of the *Euchologion* and the *Trebnik*. The special texts and prayers for the liturgical services are also to be found in the literature that follows the monthly calendar of saints, and takes its name from this as the (twelve-volume) *Menaion*. The book known as the *Triodion* contains the liturgical texts proper to Lent, and the *Pentekostarion* has those proper to the Paschal season up to Pentecost. The third book in this series, containing the normal range of texts for Sundays of the year, takes its name from the eight "Tones" that are used to attribute proper texts to various parts of the weekly services, namely the *Oktoechos*.

SEE ALSO: Blessing Rituals; Canon (Liturgical); *Euchologion*; *Hieratikon*; *Horologion*; *Menaion*; Music (Sacred); Psaltes (Cantor); *Triodion*

References and Suggested Readings

McGuckin, J. A. (2008) *The Orthodox Church: An Introduction to Its History, Theology and Spiritual Culture*. Oxford: Wiley-Blackwell.

Logos Theology

JUSTIN M. LASSER

The meaning of the Greek term *Logos* is intimately related to what it means to be human and what it means to contemplate a significant and meaningful world. *Logos* carries a plethora of uses, but takes its origin from the notion of speech and language. The early Greeks intuited that speech was closely, if not inalienably, connected to thought. In this sense speech became something more – it symbolized thought itself. As language moved beyond ostensive definition it acquired the capacity to name things that existed outside empirically demonstrative categories (such as "The Good"). It is uncertain how this potential within language was realized but, in reference to later *Logos* theology, mathematics had a seminal role to play. With the advent of ethereal mathematical entities (such as the Pythagorean theorem), two very important uses of the term *Logos* emerged in the philosophical vocabulary: first, as connoting the method of logical discourse or rationale of proof and, second, to evoke the apparent existence of pure forms existing beyond the present world.

The theologian philosophers among the ancient Greeks (especially Plato and his school, but also Pythagoras and the Stoics) intended to intuit these ethereal entities. In this manner the earliest *Logos* theology, if it could be called such, assumed that forms and principles were discovered, not invented. Furthermore, these forms that existed beyond this world also informed the form of the material world. However, the division of the material from the formal created a chasm between the perfect heavenly realm and the material world below. Plato in his *Timaeus* resolved this issue by introducing the notion of a *demiourgos* or "demi-god" that formed the world according to the perfect formal principles (the *logoi*) but managed to do so imperfectly. In this vein the duty of the philosopher was to contemplate the world in order to intuit the more perfect *logoi* or principles of the perfect (or Ideal Platonic) realm. Among the later Christians this aspect of *Logos* theology survived to become a major aspect of the ascetical mystical tradition, especially visible in Evagrios Pontike, Maximos the Confessor, and the later Byzantine ascetics. Evagrius used *Logos* theology in the service of his theology of prayer (*Kephalaia Gnostica*), in which he instructed his disciples to begin by contemplating the natural *logoi* and to progress toward the contemplation of the supreme *Logos*.

Initially, *Logos* speculation among the Greek philosophers was concerned with the *logoi* (or principles) of creation, but in time the interest moved beyond the individual *logoi* and gravitated toward the overarching or supreme *Logos*, the parts being subsumed into the larger governing principle. In this manner the *Logos* operated as creator of categories or sets – or, as Origen was later to phrase it, "the Essence of essences" or the "Infinity of infinities."

Early Christian thinkers were inheritors of the ancient proclivity to personify certain governing principles and this can be seen in their development of the Hellenistic *Logos* theory as a way of expressing a biblical cosmology. They had already witnessed the manner in which Philo had combined *Logos* theology with the biblical *Sophia* tradition (the so-called Wisdom literature). They understood the *Logos* as the divine agency acting beside God the Father as the force of creation (the rational principle of all that is, and the head of all that derives from that – revelation and salvation especially). Clement and Origen of Alexandria did much to popularize this association of biblical and sophistic thought, and other leading patristic contributors to the *Logos* school were Justin Martyr, Tertullian, and Hippolytus. At first they were criticized by opponents as having elevated "two godheads" in the church's monotheistic faith, and early attempts to resolve this accusation led to a stress on the subordination of the *Logos*/Son to the Father's monarchy. But if this was seen as a defect of early *Logos* theology, the alternative proposals of the 2nd-century Monarchians (Sabellius and the Theodoti) proved even more unsatisfying, in their apparent confusion of the Father and the Son. The association of *Logos* and *Sophia* among the 3rd-century *Logos* theologians helped to precipitate the Arian controversy in the 4th century, which was concerned with the nature and operations of the *Logos*/Christ. In Proverbs 8.27–31 Wisdom/Sophia proclaims very beautifully: "When God set the heavens in place, I was there … I was by God's side, a master craftswoman, delighting God day by day, ever at play at God's side, at play everywhere in God's domain." The status of the *Logos* in creation was made unclear in this proclamation, for Prov. 8.22 was remarked to have stated: "The Lord created me at the beginning of his work, the first of his acts of old," which was taken by a range of Arian theologians to denote the ontological subordination of the *Logos*/Son to the Father, and his creaturely status. Anti-Arian theologians such as Athanasius were able to raise up a host of alternative biblical proof texts such as the preface of the Gospel of John: "In the beginning was the *Logos*, and the *Logos*

was with God, and the *Logos* was God." In so far as the Arian controversy was precisely concerned with the question of the *Logos*' origins (was the *Logos* created or eternally existent?), the Orthodox answer to this question, as eventually articulated in the Nicene Creed, affirmed that the *Logos* was "eternally begotten of the Father," "true God from True God," and consubstantial with him. According to one of the greatest *Logos* theologians, Origen of Alexandria, the *Logos* was the governing principle of creation and *was* God precisely because the *Logos* essentially existed *towards* God (*Commentary on John*, 2.10), that is in terms of his relationship with the Father, as manifesting Son of that incomprehensible Father. In this manner the *Logos* is omnipresent as architect and accessible as Lord *within* the world. Beyond the world the *Logos* exists as one of the three *hypostases* within the trinitarian Godhead. Humanity intuits the *Logos* as revealed in the world (the economy of the Son, made apprehensible by the sanctifying power of the Spirit), but the inner, essential, relations within the Trinity remain absolutely beyond the power of human theological speculation (a point brilliantly sustained in Gregory of Nazianzen's *Orations* 27 and 28). In Orthodox theology, therefore, the *Logos* specifically denotes the second person of the Trinity, the eternal Lord who was incarnated on earth as the Christ, and it is the language of *Logos* theology that thus made the articulation of trinitarian theology possible. After the resolution effected by the Council of Nicea, *Logos* theology became the church's stable and primary means of expressing Christology, and it underpins all the major ecumenical statements. It's high point is generally taken to be as manifested in the work of the great fathers Athanasius, the Cappadocians, Cyril of Alexandria, and Maximos the Confessor.

Modern Orthodoxy has standardized and fixed its hypostatic language about God, reserving it to trinitarian theology. It is uncertain about the value, even the permissibility of other forms of theological "personification" (hypostatization). It is comfortable with the biblically supported personification of Sophia, and the patristic biblico-philosophical tradition of *Logos*, but remains uncomfortable with the personification of other attributes of God (such as *pistis* faith), which play a very important role in early Gnostic texts, and which was also a tendency in the ethos that led the Byzantines at Constantinople to dedicate their greatest churches to abstract principles such as Holy Wisdom and Holy Peace. However, it is precisely this proclivity to hypostasize abstract concepts (take infinity as an example) that led Orthodox mathematicians in early 20th-century Russia to provide possible answers to the most perplexing age-old mathematical and cosmological problems. It is in this sense that *Logos* theology is hardly a closed chapter in Orthodoxy's past but, rather, remains a catalyst for continuing Orthodox contributions to modern philosophy. The works of such as Pavel Florensky, Sergius Bulgakov, Vladimir Solovyov, Nikolai Berdiaev, and Nikolai Luzin demonstrate that *Logos* theology is still alive and well in wider Orthodox intellectual circles.

SEE ALSO: Apophaticism; Berdiaev, Nikolai A. (1874–1948); Bulgakov, Sergius (Sergei) (1871–1944); Cappadocian Fathers; Council of Nicea I (325); Florensky, Pavel Alexandrovich (1882–1937); Gnosticism; Holy Trinity; Pontike, Evagrios (ca. 345–399); St. Athanasius of Alexandria (ca. 293–373); St. Cyril of Alexandria (ca. 378–444); St. Maximos the Confessor (580–662); Solovyov, Vladimir (1853–1900); Sophiology

References and Suggested Readings

Evagrius of Ponticus (1990) "The Kephalaia Gnostica," trans. D. Bundy, in V. L. Wimbush (ed.) *Ascetic Behavior in Greco-Roman Antiquity: A Sourcebook*. Minneapolis: Fortress Press, pp. 175–86.

Florensky, P. (1997) *The Pillar and Ground of Truth*, trans. B. Jakim. Princeton: Princeton University Press.

Graham, L. and Kantor, J.-M. (2009) *Naming Infinity: A True Story of Religious Mysticism and Mathematical Creativity*. Cambridge, MA: Belknap Press of Harvard University Press.

Wolfson, H. A. (1970) *The Philosophy of the Church Fathers*. Cambridge, MA: Harvard University Press.

Lossky, Vladimir (1903–1958)

PAUL GAVRILYUK

Together with Georges Florovsky, Vladimir Lossky is one of the main architects of the turn to the Greek fathers in recent Russian Orthodox theology. Born into the family of a well-known philosopher-intuitivist, Nicholas Lossky, Vladimir spent his childhood and began his university education in St. Petersburg, Russia. Expelled from the Soviet Union in 1922, the Lossky family first settled in Prague (1922–4) and then moved to Paris, where Vladimir Lossky was to spend the rest of his life. In Paris Lossky continued his education at the Sorbonne (1924–7), studying the history of western medieval philosophy under the supervision of Étienne Gilson. During this period Lossky developed what would become a lifelong interest in the mystical theology of Meister Eckhart, eventually resulting in a doctoral thesis posthumously published in French under the title *Théologie negative et connaissance de Dieu chez Maître Eckhart* (1960). In 1928 Lossky became a member of the Brotherhood of St. Photius, a group which promoted the Orthodox Christian witness in Europe.

In the 1930s Lossky became involved in the debate over Sergius Bulgakov's Sophiology. As an intellectual of a younger generation, Lossky viewed the heritage of religious idealism, especially Vladimir Soloviev and the writers of the Silver Age, with suspicion. To the end of his life, Lossky would remain one of the most outspoken critics of Bulgakov's system. In his essay *The Sophia Debate* (1935, original in Russian), Lossky faulted Bulgakov for converting Christian theism into a pantheistic system, for breaking down the fundamental ontological distinction between Creator and creation, for confusing nature and person in God, and for a "Gnostic" lack of apophatic reserve when speaking about the immanent Trinity. The condemnation of Bulgakov's system issued by the Russian Orthodox Church was based to a large degree upon Lossky's summary report.

Lossky's brief involvement with the French resistance movement is reflected in his autobiographic essay *Sept jours sur les routes de France* (1940). After the war Lossky taught, among other places, in the newly founded Institute of St. Dionysius the Areopagite. His *Mystical Theology of the Eastern Church* (appearing first in French, 1944) is regarded as a classic exposition of Orthodox apophaticism. Using the work of Pseudo-Dionysius the Areopagite as his starting point, Lossky argues that apophatic theology is more than a corrective to Kataphatic theology, that negative theology is rather a contemplative practice intended to purify the human mind from the idolatry of concepts with the purpose of bringing the human knower into union with God. The book also defends the Palamite essence-energies distinction in God against its Roman Catholic critics.

Lossky continued to pursue the question of the knowability of God and related epistemological problems in his lectures at the Sorbonne (posthumously published as *The Vision of God*, French original in 1962) and other essays (which became part of two collections: *In the Image and Likeness of God*, French original in 1967, and *Orthodox Theology: An Introduction*, English translation in 1978). Lossky was convinced that the dogma of *filioque* was the root cause of the division between the East and the West. Lossky's over-arching "personalism" (the claim that persons are ineffable, unobjectifiable agents, irreducible to common nature) has received continuing attention in the works of Rowan Williams, John Zizioulas, Aristotle Papanikolaou, and others.

SEE ALSO: Apophaticism; Bulgakov, Sergius (Sergei) (1871–1944); Florovsky, Georges V. (1893–1979); St. Dionysius the Areopagite; Sophiology

References and Suggested Readings

Clément, O. (1959) "Vladimir Lossky, un théologien de la personne et du St. Esprit," *Messager de L'Exarchat du Patriarche russe en europe occidentale*, 30, 1: 137–206.
Lossky, V. (1997a) *In the Image and Likeness of God*. Crestwood, NY: St. Vladimir's Seminary Press.
Lossky, V. (1997b) *The Mystical Theology of the Eastern Church*. Crestwood, NY: St. Vladimir's Seminary Press.
Lossky, V. (1997c) *The Vision of God*. Crestwood, NY: St. Vladimir's Seminary Press.
Lossky, V. (2001) *Orthodox Theology: An Introduction*. Crestwood, NY: St. Vladimir's Seminary Press.

Love

JOHN A. MCGUCKIN

In Orthodox theology love is understood as the ineffable energy that is at the heart of God's very being, the power that causes God to make the entire cosmos in the first place, the motive behind the divine investment in its redemption, and the rationale for God's continuing care to call forward all humanity into deepening communion, in love, with the God of Love. Human love for God mirrors the love God first has for creation. It is life-giving. Jesus elevates it as the human heart's response to the good news of salvation (Mk. 12.29–31). The Apostle John expresses the way humanity can experience the unapproachable love of God most eloquently when he says: "Whoever does not love does not know God; because God is love. And the love of God was made manifest among us especially in this, that God sent his only Son into the world, so that we might live through him." Shortly after this he adds memorably: "God is love, and whoever abides in love abides in God, and God abides in them" (1 Jn. 4.8–9, 16). The medieval English author of the *Cloud of Unknowing* got it right when, paraphrasing St. Dionysius the Areopagite, he said of God: "By love he may be gotten and holden, but by thought, never." True love overflows philanthropically: the lovers of God will also be the lovers of their fellows, as the Lord commanded them (Jn. 13.14; 15.12, 17).

SEE ALSO: Christ; Fatherhood of God; Soteriology

References and Suggested Readings

Prat, F. (1953) "Charité," in *Dictionnaire de spiritualité*, Vol. 2. Paris: Beauchesne, cols. 508–691.
Raven, C. E. (1931) *Jesus and the Gospel of Love*. Robertson Lectures for 1931. New York: Henry Holt.

Lyons, Council of (1274)

A. EDWARD SIECIENSKI

The Council of Lyons, like the later Council of Florence (1438–9), was an unsuccessful "reunion council" that attempted to end the schism between Rome and Constantinople. Shortly after recapturing Constantinople in 1261, Emperor Michael VIII Palaeologus (1259–82) proposed the idea of a reunion council to Pope Urban IV (1261–4), although preparations did not begin in earnest until after the election of Pope Gregory X (1271–6). Michael's reasons were chiefly political, since union with the Latin Church had little support among the Byzantines. Among those who refused to participate in the council was Patriarch Joseph I (1267–75, 1282–3), who led the growing anti-unionist movement.

The council opened on May 1, 1274 despite the absence of the Byzantine delegation (consisting of George Akropolites, former Patriarch Germanos III, and Bishop Theophanes of Nicea), who did not arrive until June 24. The council's teachings (e.g., on the *filioque*) restated the historic Latin position, which the Greeks were simply expected to accept. On July 6 the emperor's own confession of faith was read out and the schism formally proclaimed at an end. The Byzantines left shortly after, although the union was not formally proclaimed in Constantinople until January 16, 1275. The emperor and Patriarch John XI Bekkos (1275–82), who had been influenced by the theology of Nikephorus Blemmydes (1197–1272), tried unsuccessfully to enforce the union, but Michael died in 1282 and his son, Andronicus II (1282–1328), immediately repudiated his father's policies. Under Patriarch Gregory II of Cyprus (1283–9), the Synod of Blachernae (1285) met and officially denounced the teachings of Lyons on behalf of the Eastern Church.

SEE ALSO: Ecumenism, Orthodoxy and; *Filioque*; Florence, Council of (1438–1439)

References and Suggested Readings

Franchi, A. (ed.) (1965) *Il Concilio II di Lione (1274)*. Studi e Testi Francescani 33. Rome: Edizioni Francescane.

Papadakis, A. (1996) *Crisis in Byzantium: The Filioque Controversy in the Patriarchate of Gregory II of Cyprus 1283–1289*. Crestwood, NY: St. Vladimir's Seminary Press.

Roberg, B. (1990) *Das Zweite Konkil von Lyon (1274)*. Paderborn: Ferdinand Schoningh.

M

Malankara Orthodox Syrian Church

TENNY THOMAS

The Malankara Orthodox Syrian Church, also known as the Indian Orthodox Church, is one of the oldest churches in India. The church is believed to have been founded by the Apostle St. Thomas in 52 CE. In ancient times, and up to the Islamic invasions of the 7th century, there were strong Christian and Jewish communities on the Malabar coast, and traders from Persia were active there. Today, the Malankara Church is an autocephalous community and a member of the family of Oriental Orthodox Churches.

Sources for the history of Christianity in India during the early centuries are very limited. Some confusion is also caused because many of the references to "India" in ancient Christian writings refer primarily to Ethiopia. St. Ephrem the Syrian states that the relics of the Apostle Thomas in Edessa had been brought there from India where he first evangelized and was martyred. St. John Chrysostom attests that the tomb of St. Thomas in India is as much venerated, in his day, as that of St. Peter in Rome. The Portuguese writer Antonio de Gouvea wrote down, in around 1600, the Indian version of the Thomas tradition which gives details of St. Thomas's journey through the Persian Empire and his taking ship from Arabia to India. He landed in Kodungallur, which was a large port and seat of the great King Kelaputra. From there, he traveled south as far as Quilon and established seven churches, afterwards heading for Mylapore and thence to China. On his return to Mylapore Thomas is said to have been martyred around 72 CE.

By the 7th century, specific references to the Indian Christian Church began to appear in Persian records. The metropolitans of India and China are first mentioned in some of the consecration records of patriarchs of the East. In the 8th century the primate of the Indian Church was referred to as "The Metropolitan and the Gate of All India," a title that shows Islamic resonances. Vatican Codex 22, written in Cranganore in 1301, gives the title as "The Metropolitan of the Throne of St. Thomas and of the whole Church of the Christians in India." The minority status of the Christians in India led to many influences from the wider community on church practices, parts of the Hindu caste system being one example that led to a highly refined system in the church of degrees of relationship, and an anxiety at times about the origins of new potential converts.

The coming of the Portuguese marked a distinct change in the history of Christianity in India. When the Portuguese penetrated into the interiors of Kerala and came across the churches of the St. Thomas Christians, they realized that these indigenous faithful did not recognize ecclesiastical allegiance to Rome, and were very different from them in terms of church traditions. After learning more about their theology

The Concise Encyclopedia of Orthodox Christianity, First Edition. Edited by John Anthony McGuckin.
© 2014 John Wiley & Sons, Ltd. Published 2014 by John Wiley & Sons, Ltd.

they found that the Indian Christians were East Syrian in origin and thus "Nestorian," according to their reckoning. The Portuguese missionaries were eager to bring the Indian Church into communion with Rome. In 1599 at the Synod of Diamper the assembly of representatives from the churches was compelled to give up its connection with the Oriental Orthodox Churches and brought under the authority of Rome. Until 1653 three Jesuit bishops effectively ruled over the church in India, executing the decrees of the Diamper Synod and thus forcing the church to become Eastern Rite Catholic.

The majority of Thomas Christians soon reacted antagonistically to this situation, though a large minority remained in communion with Rome. They took a collective oath at the Coonen Cross in Mattancherry in 1653, resolving to preserve the faith and autonomy of their church and to elect its head themselves. The leaders of the Indian Church assembled at Edapally, where four councilors (Parambil Chandy, Kadavil Chandy, Vengoor Gheevarghese, and Anjilimoottil Itty Thoman) were appointed senior agents for church administration. This was followed by a general meeting at Allangad on May 22, 1653 where Archdeacon Thomas was elevated as a bishop with the title "Mar Thoma" by the laying on of hands by twelve senior priests of the Church of St. Thomas. After the Dutch captured Cochin, ending Portuguese rule in 1663, at the request of the Thomas Christians the Syrian Orthodox bishop, Mar Gregorios of Jerusalem, came to India in 1664 to confirm the episcopal consecration of Mar Thoma I as the head of the Orthodox Church in India. Thus began the formal relationship of the Malankara Church in India with the Syrian Orthodox Church which continues to the present.

By 1795 the British established themselves in South India and Kerala came under their jurisdiction. During the time of the British Resident, Colonel Munroe, Pulikottill Ittoop Ramban expressed his interest in founding a seminary for the training of the church's clergy. The Resident supported him and the seminary was founded in 1815. At the request of the Resident, Joseph Ramban was appointed bishop in 1816 with the name Mar Dionysius II and as metropolitan of Malankara. Cooperation between the Malankara Church and the Anglican Christian Missionary Society continued from 1816 until 1836,

when the connection was severed at the Synod of Mavelikkara. This incident led to several divisions in the community and a reformation in the liturgy and practices of the church as a whole, leading to the formation of what became known as the Anglican Syrian Church in 1840, and the Mar Thoma Syrian Church in 1889, dividing from what was then commonly known as the "Orthodox Jacobite" (Non-Chalcedonian Orthodox). This split in the church organization caused the leaders of the Malankara Church to appeal for help from the Syrian Orthodox patriarch. In 1875 Patriarch Peter III came to Kerala and held a synod of representatives of the churches at Mulanthuruthy in 1876. Following the Synod of Mulanthuruthy litigations in court ensued between the Mar Thomas and the Malankara Church for legitimate control of church property. It came to an end in 1889 with a judgment in favor of the Malankara Church by the highest court of Kerala, the Royal Court of Appeal.

Patriarch Peter III tried to establish the full canonical jurisdiction of the Syrian Church over the Malankaran. When this was resisted he ordered the suspension of the Malankara Metropolitan Pulikottil Joseph Mar Dionysius. Peter III's successor, Mar Gregorios Abdullah, was determined to follow up the matter, and thus came to Kerala in 1909 demanding that Mar Dionysius VI pledge complete obedience to the Syrian patriarch. Mar Dionysius refused on the grounds that the church in India had always been autonomous and he was thereby excommunicated by Mar Abdullah. Mar Dionysius refused to comply, given that there was a division at the time over the rightful incumbent to the Syrian patriarchal office (Mar Abdel-Messih claimed legitimacy and supported Mar Dionysius, also transferring on his authority the Catholicate of Persia to India), and so he continued on as metropolitan. This action resulted in a further division within the Malankara Church from 1912 onwards, with one group, who are now called the Malankara Orthodox Syrian Church, siding with Metropolitan Mar Dionysius, and the other group affirming their loyalty to the Syrian Orthodox patriarchate in the line of the officially instituted Mar Abdallah, and who are called Malankara Syrian Orthodox. Both Orthodox Churches share the same faith, and together constitute about 2 million members, seeing themselves as the continuators of the original St. Thomas communities.

Today, the catholicos is the supreme head of the Orthodox Church in India, and he also holds the office of metropolitan of the Malankara Orthodox Syrian Church. The metropolitan is elected by the Malankara Association, a larger association representing clergy and laity, and this election is formally approved by the episcopal synod. The catholicos presides over the Holy Episcopal Synod, which is the supreme authority for the church in all matters concerning faith, order, and discipline. The church follows the West Syrian liturgical tradition, is part of the family of the other Oriental Orthodox Churches, and fosters ecumenical relationships with the Eastern Orthodox, Roman Catholic, and Protestant Churches.

SEE ALSO: Antioch, Patriarchate of; Syrian Orthodox Churches

References and Suggested Readings

Brown, L. W. (1956) *The Indian Christians of St. Thomas.* Cambridge: Cambridge University Press.

Cheriyan, C. V. (2003) *Orthodox Christianity in India: A History of the Malankara Orthodox Church AD 52–2002.* Kottayam: Academic Publishers.

Firth, C. B. (1961) *An Introduction to Indian Church History.* Madras: Christian Literature Society.

Gregorios, M. P. (1982) *The Orthodox Church in India: An Overview.* Kottayam: Sophia Publications.

Jonas, T. (1958) *The Synod of Diamper.* Rome: Orientalia Christiana Analecta 152.

Keay, F. E. (1951) *A History of the Syrian Church in India,* 2nd edn. Kanpur: SPCK.

Mundalan, A. M. (1984) *History of Christianity in India, Vol. 1: From the Beginning up to the Middle of the Sixteenth Century (to 1542).* Bangalore: Church History Association of India.

Neill, S. C. (1984) *A History of Christianity in India, Vol. 1: The Beginning to AD 1707.* Cambridge: Cambridge University Press.

Podipara, P. J. (1970) *The Thomas Christians.* London: Darton, Longman and Todd.

Pothan, S. G. (1968) *The Syrian Christians in Kerala,* 4th edn. Madras: K. M. Cherian.

Van der Ploeg, J. P. M. (1983) *The Christians of St. Thomas in South India and Their Syriac Manuscripts.* Bangalore: Dharmaram Publications.

Mandorla

KENNETH CARVELEY

Mandorla (Italian for "almond"; or *Vesica Piscis* – lit. "fish bladder shape") is the elliptical or round aureole, or extended nimbus, which in Christian art indicates the holiness, spiritual power, or divine glory, drawn around the iconographic figure of Christ or the Theotokos. It may be derived from imperial motifs in Roman art, but is also found in oriental religious symbolism, and appears in iconography from the 6th century onwards. In the form of the Ascension icon, Christ enters the cloud of heaven; in the Transfiguration icon he emanates rays of divine light; and in the Dormition icon he takes the soul of the Virgin into the Mandorla that surrounds him.

SEE ALSO: Dormition; Iconography, Styles of; Iconostasis; Icons

References and Suggested Readings

Didron, M. (1851) *Christian Iconography.* London: Henry G Bohn.

Schiller, G. (1971) *Iconography of Christian Art,* Vol. 1. London: Lund Humphries.

Maronites

CYRIL HOVORUN

A Christian community shaped in Syria in the 5th century, around the monastery of St. Maron (Bêth Maron). Originally Chalcedonian, in the 7th century they adopted Monothelitism as part of the official Orthodoxy currently being promoted by the Byzantine Emperor Heraclius, retaining a formal profession of two natures and one will in Christ even after the condemnation of Monothelitism at the Seventh Ecumenical Council in 787. The Maronite Church, having been separated from the Latin, Byzantine, and non-Chalcedonian communions for centuries, accepted union with Rome in the 12th century. Presently, it is one of the Eastern Catholic churches *sui iuris,* headed by its own patriarch.

Nowadays Maronites constitute the majority of the Christian population of the Lebanon, and are spread across the Middle East, with an extensive international diaspora.

References and Suggested Readings

Mahfouz, J. (1987) *Short History of the Maronite Church*. Beirut.

Moosa, M. (1986) *The Maronites in History*. Syracuse, NY: Syracuse University Press.

Marriage

DAN SANDU

Marriage is the Holy Mystery celebrated in the Orthodox Church which blesses the bond of mutual love between a man and a woman, for the purposes of sharing their love more fully, the creation of children, and the common attainment of salvation. The union between man and woman originates in Paradise, where God created and placed Adam and Eve (Gen. 1.27) so that human nature could be "very good" (Gen. 1.31). It was reemphasized and blessed by the Lord Jesus who participated in the wedding at Cana and taught more deeply about the relationship between a man and woman. Marriage signifies the admission of the couple into the Christian community as husband and wife, following their request to have their union blessed in the church. It involves a free, individual intent, based on a shared vocation of love and sacrifice, and thus becomes a redeeming event.

The union of a man and a woman is founded on two theological components: our ontological need for interpersonal relationship and our social need for shared and responsible love offered by a free, intelligent person. Through marriage, man and woman become "one flesh" (Eph. 5.31) and belong to each other eternally ("into the Kingdom"). Orthodox marriage is not seen as being only "Until death doth you part."

Holy Scripture does not prescribe any specifics regarding the celebration of marriage. It does use the wedding feast in Cana (Jn. 2.1–11) to show where the Lord performed the first miracle of his earthly economy, symbolically turning water into wine. The symbol of the wedding feast is also used habitually in the parables to describe the joy of the Kingdom of God, and the symbol of the bridal chamber is used many times in Orthodox tradition to depict the soul's union with Christ its Lord. In Eastern Christiantiy, marriage is compared to the bond between Christ and his church, like a groom and bride existing in a state of sacrifice and faithfulness to each other (Eph. 5.21–33). We have no definite information about how marriage was celebrated in early Christian centuries, but the practice of having Christian marriages blessed by the bishop or priest during the liturgy was established by the 4th century. Crowning was an ancient rite throughout the Roman Empire, which Orthodoxy Christianized.

The legal obligation for the Orthodox to conduct marriage in a church ceremony occurred during the reign of Emperor Leo VI the Wise (895). After that time marriage in the Christian East was always celebrated in church, although later Bolshevik and secular legislation has sometimes tried to reassert the separation of the civil (legal) union and the church (religious) marriage which Christian Byzantium made one. The Orthodox marriage liturgy includes several important moments: the community's prayer for the union of bride and groom, the blessing by the priest, the office of the crowning of the couple (Greek ritual with floral crowns, Slavic ritual with metal), the declaration of the wedding formula, the drinking from a common cup, and the promise of fidelity by the placing of hands on, and the kissing of, the Holy Gospel and the Cross. The Orthodox wedding ceremony is preceded by the office of betrothal involving the exchange of rings. In Byzantine times this was a separate ritual; now they are performed on the same day as the wedding.

To receive the mystery of marriage in the Orthodox church, at least one of the partners must be Orthodox. The couple must freely express their consent to marry, be of marriageable age and not have blood relationships (or spiritual kinship as established by the sacrament of baptism), and the service must observe the correct ritual. Orthodox practice requires the presence of another married couple who

Plate 40   Orthodox wedding ritual. Ed Kashi/Corbis.

will act as spiritual parents (godparents or sponsors) and who pledge to guide the newlyweds in their family life.

The Orthodox marriage ceremony, as essentially a celebratory one, cannot be held on fast days (Wednesdays or Fridays, on September 14 and August 29, during Great Lent, including Cheesefare Week, the pre-Christmas Lent, or the summer Apostles' Fast and Dormition Fast). Nor can marriages be celebrated on the Royal Feasts, during the (post-paschal) Bright Week or in the period running from Christmas to Theophany.

The holy mystery of marriage is intended to guide family members on the endless pathway to growth and salvation in Christ, and therefore emphasis is laid on the indissolubility of marriage (Mt. 19.3–12) and the practical exercise of Christian life together. Faith is a fundamental context for Orthodox married life, as it fosters mutual respect and fidelity and encourages spouses to recognize one another as "images of God." A wholesome family is built, by God's grace, on the joint efforts of the spouses and on sacrifices justified by faith and love. Mutual sacrifice plays a significant role in the Orthodox theology of marriage, for it is the existential space where each person receives the freedom to be generous and forego the self out of a constant desire to enhance the happiness of the other. This is why marriage is a school of unconditional generosity, for love involves self-sacrifice, since there can be no true love without giving.

In Ephesians 5.21–33 the apostle emphasizes the essential and mutually subordinating roles of love in marriage: both parties are to be subject to one another out of reverence for Christ; the husband must love his wife "as Christ loved the church" (laying down his life), while the woman should reverence her husband as she does Christ (live in harmony and accord). This mystery of Christian marital love is everlasting because it flows out from Christ and makes the person eternal (deified by grace) through their partaking in the communion of the chosen one. Shared sexuality, or conjugal relations, are a very important aspect following the marital union. The body's sexual identity is not seen in Orthodoxy as theologically irrelevant, but natural needs are satisfied and lifted up into the mystery of love in graced conjugal relations, fulfilling sexuality's destiny in a context that reserves its expression to the married couple, and celebrates it in a full mutual knowledge of the consequences (caring love, protecting the welfare of the spouse, the creation and upbringing of beloved children). Christian marriage eradicates the tyranny of attempts to take advantage of another by reducing them to objects of pleasure. Orthodoxy no longer asserts earlier (Byzantine era) marital restrictions of the conjugal life, but instead asserts the essential principle that the spouses should mutually agree on all decisions, in the light of their spiritual advancement, and in harmony with St. Paul's recommendation in 1 Corinthians 7.5.

Divorce is actively discouraged because all the work of God in the church is aimed at unity. Divorce is anti-trinitarian, damaging the notions of motherhood, fatherhood, and communion. Divorce distorts love and may cause children to be unable to love freely. Nevertheless, the church does not preclude divorce (for the good of the separated parties) when all attempts to salvage the marriage have failed. Consequently, the Orthodox Church accepts a second or third marriage as a dispensation (1 Cor. 7.9), after the first marriage has ended because of the death of one of the spouses, or was dissolved on grounds accepted by the church, or when it has been nullified by certain preexisting impediments. A divorce and permission to remarry can only be pronounced by the local bishop.

SEE ALSO: Chastity; Sexual Ethics

References and Suggested Readings

Archidiocese of Antiochia (2001) *A Pastoral Guide to the Holy Mysteries*. Cambridge: Acquila.

Evdokimov, P. (1985) *The Sacrament of Love: The Nuptial Mystery in the Light of the Orthodox Tradition*. Crestwood, NY: St. Vladimir's Seminary Press.

Maximus the Greek (1470–1555)

SERGEY TROSTYANSKIY

Maximus the Greek (Michael Trivolis) was an Orthodox writer, translator, and exegete. Born to a noble Greek family, he moved to Italy where he received a classical education. In Florence he heard Savonarola's sermons and was deeply affected by them. He also had encounters with some great Renaissance humanists. In 1502 he became a Dominican monk but resigned from the monastery soon afterwards. In 1505 he moved to Mount Athos where he became a monk in the monastery of Vatopedi. In 1516 he was sent by the ecclesiastical authorities to Moscow to work on translations of patristic commentaries on the Psalter. He also worked on revisions of Slavonic texts of the Bible and other liturgical books. Later in his life he became involved in the controversy racking the Russian Church over the legitimacy of ecclesiastical (and especially monastic) possessions, in the party of those who opposed the holding of monastic estates (non-possessors). Acting as an agent of the patriarch of Constantinople, he argued against the proposed autocephaly of the Russian Church, and as a consequence he was arrested and tried in 1524. He was sentenced, excommunicated, and forbidden to write. Soon after his death he was canonized as a saint and martyr. His legacy in Russia exalts him as a symbol of the learned monk, upholder of the patristic tradition, reformist defender of Christian simplicity, and a symbol of the emergence of the Russian Church from its Byzantine infancy.

References and Suggested Readings

Geanakoplos, D. J. (1988) "The Post-Byzantine Athonite Monk Maximos 'the Greek': Reformer of Orthodoxy in Sixteenth-Century Muscovy," *Greek Orthodox Theological Review* 33, 4: 445–68.

Obolensky, D. (1988) *Six Byzantine Portraits*. Oxford: Clarendon Press.

Meatfare *see* Cheesefare (Sunday of)

Megalomartyr Saints

JOHN A. MCGUCKIN

Megalomartyr is a term that derives from the Greek for "Great Martyrs" (*megalomartyroi*) and designates a special category of Orthodox saints (also widely venerated in the Western Catholic calendar because their festivals were established so early in Christian history) and refers chiefly to the leading martyr saints of the Age of the Persecutions, before the 4th-century Edict of Milan, when the Emperor St. Constantine I gave peace to the church. It encompasses a range of men and women saints, several soldiers among them, who were not only held up as having given an exemplary witness (suffering great tortures with noble courage), but who also enjoyed a lively and widespread cult in the ancient church ("great," that is, in terms of their renown). Among the most popular of the male Megalomartyrs were the soldier saints George, Dimitrios, Theodore the General, and Theodore the Recruit, as well as Sts. Phanourios and Procopios. Among the most revered women great martyrs were Catherine of Alexandria, Barbara, Euphemia, Paraskeva, and Irene. Some of their number, such as Panteleimon, Orestes, Diodore, and Tryphon, are also called Unmercenary Healers (Greek: *Anargyroi*) as well as Megalomartyrs. Several of them are commemorated specifically by name in the preparatory (*Prothesis*) ritual of the divine liturgy, when particles of bread are set aside to commemorate them among the "Nine Ranks of Saints," and their prayers are asked for as the church gathers for the synaxis.

SEE ALSO: Military Saints; New Martyrs; Proskomedie (Prothesis); Unmercenary Saints

References and Suggested Readings

Farmer, D. H. (1978) *The Oxford Dictionary of Saints*. Oxford: Clarendon Press.

Melismas *see* Music (Sacred)

Men, Alexander (1935–1990)

KONSTANTIN GAVRILKIN

Bible scholar, theologian, religious writer, and evangelist, Alexander Men was born to a Jewish family, but in 1935 his mother decided to become Orthodox Christian and he was baptized together with her in the Russian Catacomb Church. In his teens, Alexander had a spiritual experience that prompted him to write a book about Jesus: the first draft was finished when he was 15, and *The Son of Man*, published in 1969, was its final version. Around the same time, Alexander discovered the writings of the Russian philosopher Vladimir Solovyov, who shaped his understanding of history and Christianity. In fact, Solovyov's idea to write a Christian interpretation of the history of world religions was later turned by Alexander Men into the six-volume series *History of Religion: In Search of the Way, the Truth, and the Life*, published in Russian between 1970 and 1983.

When, in 1958, he was expelled from college for his religious beliefs, he was ordained a deacon and in 1960 a priest. He served in a number of parishes in the Moscow region; for the last twenty years of his life as a pastor of the Annunciation Church in Novaia Derevnia. In the 1960s Fr. Alexander became a supporter of human rights activists, some of whom joined the Orthodox Church because of his influence. He also continued to write on the Bible, the history of salvation, and the Orthodox Church, publishing his books in the West under various pseudonyms (E. Svetlov, A. Bogolyubov, and A. Pavlov) with the help of the Catholic publishing house in Brussels, La Vie avec Dieu, which was instrumental in supplying Christians in the Soviet Union with Russian religious literature. In the 1970s and 1980s Fr. Alexander became a recognized spiritual leader of many Soviet intellectuals who were baptized and joined the Orthodox Church despite KGB harassment and political persecution.

During the Gorbachev years, Fr. Alexander took full advantage of new avenues for evangelization and ministry: he and his followers founded the Russian

Bible Society and the Open Orthodox University in 1990, created a network of Sunday schools, and initiated charitable ministries at various hospitals. An eloquent speaker with broad knowledge of world culture, Fr. Alexander used all available opportunities for public lectures and preaching, including national television, and his name became synonymous with the spiritual awakening of the period. At the same time, he spoke openly of the dangers emerging in post-communist Russian society: the rise of fascism, xenophobia, and anti-Semitism, and the emergence of an unrealistic nostalgia for the Romanov Empire and its state-supported church. He was murdered near his home on September 9, 1990. The case has never been solved. Both during his life and after his death, Fr. Alexander had been attacked repeatedly by Russian Orthodox nationalists, fundamentalists, and anti-Semites, and there have been continuous attempts on their part to marginalize and compromise his legacy. Since 1991 his books on the Bible, Jesus Christ, Christianity, and the Orthodox Church have finally been published in Russia under his own name.

SEE ALSO: Russia, Patriarchal Orthodox Church of; Solovyov, Vladimir (1853–1900)

References and Suggested Readings

Hamant, Y. (1995) *Alexander Men: A Witness for Contemporary Russia (a Man for Our Times)*. Torrance, CA: Oakwood Publications.
Men, A. (1998) *Son of Man: The Story of Christ and Christianity*. Crestwood, NY: St. Vladimir's Seminary Press.
Roberts, E. and Shukman, A. (eds.) (1996) *Christianity for the Twenty-first Century: Life and Work of Alexander Men*. London: SCM Press.

Menaion

JOHN A. MCGUCKIN

The *Menaion* (plural *Menaia*, since there are usually twelve volumes) derives from the Greek word for "month" and refers to the books of special liturgical texts associated with, and assigned as propers to, the feastdays of the various saints (or holy days related to the life of Jesus and the Virgin Theotokos) who are commemorated on each day of the twelve months of the year. Often, several saints may be commemorated together on the same day. A church cantor, therefore, will use the proper texts contained in the *Menaia* for every service. The *General Menaion* is a collection of generic services for various "types" of saints (prophets, apostles, angels, hierarchs, and so on). The *Menaia* texts for the greater feastdays of the church year were assembled and given a modern English version in 1969. They demonstrate how much theology is contained in these prayers, hymns, and antiphons, and show how the liturgy gives a truer sense of the character of Orthodoxy than can often be found in any other way – which illustrates the patristic adage *Lex orandi, lex credendi*; or "the way the church prays is demonstrative of what it believes."

SEE ALSO: Calendar; Feasts; Liturgical Books

References and Suggested Readings

Brotherhood of St. Seraphim (1994) *The General Menaion*. Wallasey, UK: Anargyroi Press.
Ware, K. and Mother Mary (eds.) (1969) *The Festal Menaion*. London: Faber and Faber.

Mesonyktikon

JOHN A. MCGUCKIN

Greek term meaning "Middle of the Night." It signifies the Midnight Office of monastic prayers that takes place in sequence after Compline. In ancient times it was a service of all-night vigil composed of psalms and long meditations. The monks used to spend the greater part of the night praying, with sleeping time being reserved for the heat of the day. In contemporary Orthodox usage the service is a shorter one, reminiscent of elements of Compline (Apodeipnon), recited immediately before Matins (Orthros). It begins with the Trisagion Prayers and Psalm 50, and then on Sundays and Feast days continues with a Canon to the Trinity (by Metrophanes of Smyrna) and the *Triadika Megalynaria* (solemn Trinitarian Praises). The service ends with a Litany, a Short Dismissal, and a final Litany of Intercession. On weekdays Psalm 118 (the *Amomos*) is added after Psalm 50, and there are also recitations of patristic prayers from St. Mardarios and St. Basil the Great. The theme predominating is that of "keeping watch" (the appointed troparion is "Behold the Bridegroom is Coming!") and the commemoration of the faithful departed.

Metanie (Metanoia)

MARIA GWYN MCDOWELL

A reverent physical movement indicating repentance (Greek: *metanoia*), made by making the sign of the cross with the right hand and either bowing at the waist and knees until the hand on its downward final stroke touches the ground (small metanie), or lowering the whole body onto the knees and bowing down fully until the forehead touches the ground (great metanie). Metanies are prescribed at specific liturgical times, particularly during the Lenten prayer of Ephrem the Syrian, but are proscribed from Pascha through Pentecost. They are a part of personal prayer and are an integral element of monastic training. Metanies are distinct from the still kneeling position, and also from the bowing of clergy to one another known as the *schema*.

SEE ALSO: Feasts; Prayer; Repentance

Meteora

NIKI J. TSIRONIS

Standing out from the great plain of Thessaly in northern Greece is a group of phenomenal rocks in which Christian ascetics found refuge after the 11th century. From the 14th century onwards, more than twenty monasteries were built, perched upon the rock outcrops, and large monastic communities flourished in them, so that the place was once called the second Mount Athos. Today, only six monasteries host communities, while another fifteen are uninhabited. In the Meteora monasteries, distinguished artists executed extraordinary iconographic programs (such as Theophanes' paintings which decorate the narthex

of the Monastery of St. Nicholas Anapausas). The Great Meteoron house possesses a large number of invaluable manuscripts.

SEE ALSO: Monasticism

Meyendorff, John (1926–1992)
see Contemporary Orthodox Theology

Military Saints

MONICA M. WHITE

Military saints were venerated as the protectors of armies in the medieval Orthodox world. Although this category was large, five of them – Theodore Teron (The Recruit), Demetrios, Prokopios, Merkourios, and George – had particularly vigorous cults (Delehaye 1909).

All were martyrs of the pre-Constantinian persecutions, although only three are described as soldiers in early hagiographic works. Theodore Teron, Merkourios, and George had similar stories, despite having lived at different times and in different places: they came to the attention of an emperor after distinguishing themselves in battle, but were killed when they refused to offer sacrifices with him. Prokopios and Demetrios, by contrast, are described as clerics: Prokopios worked for the church in Skythopolis, while Demetrios preached the gospel in Thessalonika (Walter 2003).

Despite his lack of experience in the army, Demetrios' military cult blossomed after he was credited with saving his city from destruction during the invasions of the early 7th century (Lemerle 1979 I: 141). Prokopios, for reasons which are less clear, experienced a similar transformation by the 8th century.

Further changes were in store for all of the saints during the middle Byzantine period, when members of the military elite began looking for divine patrons for their wars against the Arabs. The saints' lives and posthumous heroism made them attractive candidates, and efforts were made to establish their veneration in the capital. Their hagiography was rewritten to give more emphasis to their military prowess, and at this time Theodore Teron acquired a higher-ranking "twin," Theodore Stratelates. The new saint resembled his namesake in every respect except that he was a general rather than a recruit, illustrating the concern with prestige and station among the saints' adherents in the court (Delehaye 1909: 41).

Another innovation was the saints' invocation and depiction as a group, a practice which contrasted with their largely independent cults in late Antiquity. From the mid-10th century onward they began to appear together in a variety of artistic media, and this form of veneration was exported throughout the Byzantine Commonwealth. They were received with particular enthusiasm by the Orthodox Slavs, and their cults continued to grow and evolve beyond the empire's borders. They were also beloved by the Komnenoi emperors and continued to be widely depicted and invoked in Byzantium until the Ottoman conquest (Kazhdan and Epstein 1985: 116).

SEE ALSO: Hagiography; Megalomartyr Saints; War

References and Suggested Readings

Delehaye, H. (ed.) (1909) *Les Légendes grecques des saints militaires*. Paris: Librairie Alphonse Picard et fils.

Kazhdan, A. and Epstein, A. (1985) *Change in Byzantine Culture in the Eleventh and Twelfth Centuries*. Berkeley: University of California Press.

Lemerle, P. (1979) *Les Plus anciens recueils des miracles de saint Démétrius*. Paris: Centre National de la Recherche Scientifique.

Oikonomides, N. (1995) "The Concept of 'Holy War' and Two Tenth-century Byzantine Ivories," in T. Miller and J. Nesbitt (eds.) *Peace and War in Byzantium*. Washington, DC: Catholic University of America Press, pp. 62–86.

Walter, C. (2003) *The Warrior Saints in Byzantine Art and Tradition*. Aldershot: Ashgate Press.

White, M. (forthcoming) *Military Saints in Byzantium and Rus, 900–1200*. Cambridge: Cambridge University Press.

Miracles

VERA SHEVZOV

Orthodox thinkers from Late Antiquity to modern times have understood miracles as actions or events that manifest or point to the presence of God. Orthodox Christians have associated miracles not only with individual experiences, but also with experiences of entire communities and even nations. Miracles are associated with healings, historical events, visions, dreams, and foresight, and with such phenomena as inexplicable displays of myrrh or tears on icons. Throughout history, Orthodox pastors and spiritual guides have drawn on accounts of miracles for pedagogical purposes. Such accounts provided lessons concerning vices and virtues along with lessons concerning "right faith." In addition to the realm of lived Orthodoxy, where accounts of miracles have often resulted in the special veneration of certain icons and the veneration of saints and their relics, miracles have also figured in the Orthodox theological and philosophical considerations of history, science and nature, and anthropology. Reports of miracles have also periodically begged the question of authority in the church (who in the church is it that finds and declares them miraculous?). Although miracles may be integral to its worldview, Orthodox Christianity nevertheless is deeply nuanced in its approach to them.

In part, the Orthodox understanding of miracles is rooted in the complex view of miracles reflected in the New Testament. On the one hand, patristic authors such as Origen of Alexandria (d. 254) and St. John Chrysostom (d. 407) maintained that Jesus' miracles played a significant role in the establishment of the Christian faith. Signs, acts of power, and works testified to the power of God manifested in and through Christ. Accordingly, Orthodox writers maintained, miracles accompanied his words in order to confirm his identity for those who were unable to recognize his power and authority through his words alone. In this sense, miracles were a form of divine condescension. Following the death of Jesus, in this view, the apostles performed numerous miracles in Jesus' name as a way further to cultivate the Christian faith. As Origen wrote in his mid-3rd century treatise *Against Celsus* 1.46, had it not been for miracles, people would not have been persuaded to accept the new teachings. On the other hand, patristic authors also pointed to the more negative aspects of miracles in the gospel texts. Particularly objectionable was the pursuit of, and demand for, miracles as a condition for faith (Mt. 16.4; Jn. 6.30–31) or as a curious spectacle (Lk. 23.8). Even the Devil tempted Jesus to perform a miracle (Mt. 4.1–11; Lk. 4.1–13). Finally, according to Jesus' testimony, not every "wondrous sign" was from God (Mt. 24.24–25; Acts 8.9–13); they could even be detrimental to believers by distracting or turning them from the path to salvation.

Because of their recognition of the possibility of miracles (especially in light of the core teachings on the incarnation and resurrection), both patristic and modern Orthodox writers have affirmed the reality of miracles. They have considered miracles as attestations to divine providence and as affirmations of God's active presence in the world. The faithful often consider them as wondrous signs (*thaumata*) meant to be discerned and read. "Wonders" of faith in this sense are not necessarily the great contradictions of natural laws that are so often the focus of western theological reflection on miracles, but are often small, personal, signs: understood as a message from God, and which, accordingly, cause wonderment (*thauma*) in the heart; a term which in the New Testament accompanies moments of divine epiphany and grace. Modern Orthodox writers, especially beginning in the 19th century, sought to defend the credibility and reasonableness of miracles in light of modernity's challenges. While maintaining a critical approach that recognized the possible interplay of superstition, they nonetheless distinguished between superstitious attitudes and the phenomenon of miracles. In so doing, as a rule they argued against the modern understanding of the "causal closure principle." Instead, they argued for a reality that existed beyond nature and for an understanding of the world that was more permeable to that reality. The priest theologian Sergius Bulgakov, for instance, encouraged viewing the world as a dynamic organism rather than a static mechanism. Miracles in such a view do not *per se* violate the natural order; but neither are they to be considered as "random" actions or events.

Despite its modern apology for miracles, Orthodox Christianity nevertheless does not emphasize miracles as in any way essential to the Christian life. Salvation does not depend on them; they are not foregone signs of sanctity. According to patristic and modern Orthodox authors, the virtuous life consists not in the working of miracles, but in "the beauty of one's life" (St. John Cassian, *Conferences* 2.7, 9). As St. John Chrysostom pointed out, Christ did not direct his dis-

ciples to "perform miracles," but to feed his sheep (*Homilies on St. Matthew* 46). Similarly, St. John Cassian maintained that discipleship involves primarily love and not signs and miracles. Patristic and modern Orthodox writers also maintain that Christ's teachings are paramount to the Christian life, while a preoccupation with miracles is a sign of a lower state of spiritual life. The Orthodox monastic tradition in particular discourages and even warns against engaging the miraculous, seeing it as a potential source of pride, delusion, and downfall.

Because of the potential spiritual pitfalls associated with miracles, Orthodox pastors and spiritual guides have traditionally called for spiritual sobriety in the approach to miracles. Miracles, they maintain, demand discernment and the cultivation of what St. Ignatius Brianchaninov, the well-known 19th-century bishop and spiritual guide, termed "spiritual reason" in order to "test the spirits" and distinguish between "true" and "false" miracles. Such discernment, according to the Orthodox tradition, is profoundly more beneficial on the path toward salvation than miracles.

Historically, there has been no systematic institutional effort across the Orthodox churches to regulate and officially ratify miracles, comparable to the way this is done in modern Roman Catholic practice. Many of Orthodoxy's best-known miracle-working icons, for instance, were never officially ratified as such but became specially revered on the basis of a "tradition of faith." Nevertheless, periodically, certain efforts were made to regulate and add institutional weight to the discernment of "true" and "false" miracles on the local ecclesiastical level. In 18th- and 19th-century Russia, for instance, guided by the *Spiritual Regulations* of Peter the Great, the Russian Holy Synod was charged with investigating reported miracles and ascertaining their veracity – a process which often caused tensions among the faithful. More recently, in 1999, faced with a wave of reported miracles, the Orthodox Church in Russia established a commission, composed predominantly of scientists, whose task is to document, investigate, and analyze such reports. The commission's current co-chairman is Pavel Florensky, a geologist, academician, and grandson of the Orthodox priest, theologian, and martyr, Fr. Pavel Florensky.

SEE ALSO: Florensky, Pavel Alexandrovich (1882–1937); Hagiography; Icons; Myrobletes Saints; Relics; Russia, Patriarchal Orthodox Church of; St. Ignatius Brianchaninov (1807–1867)

References and Suggested Readings

Bulgakov, S. (1932) *O chudesakh evangel'skikh*. Paris: YMCA Press.

den Boeft, J. (2004) "Miracles Recalling the Apostolic Age," in A. Hilhorst (ed.) *Apostolic Age in Patristic Thought*. Boston: Brill, pp. 51–62.

Glagolev, S. (1893) "Chudo i nauka," *Bogoslovskii vestnik* (June): 477–514.

Ward, B. (1999) "Monks and Miracle," in J. C. Cavadini (ed.) *Miracles in Jewish and Christian Antiquity*. Notre Dame: University of Notre Dame Press, pp. 127–37.

Mission *see* Evangelism

Moghila, Peter (1596–1646)

KONSTANTIN GAVRILKIN

Plate 41   St. Peter Moghila. RIA Novosti/Topfoto.

One of the highly significant figures in the post-Byzantine history of Eastern Orthodoxy, Peter Moghila was raised and educated in the Polish-Lithuanian Commonwealth in the decades after practically all Orthodox bishops in the region submitted to the Union with Rome in 1596 (Dmitriev et al. 1996). He first studied at the school of the L'vov Orthodox Brotherhood, which defended Orthodoxy with a group of similar brotherhoods under the leadership of a few Orthodox magnates. He then went to the Polish Academy in Zamość with its university curriculum, and later continued his education in France and Holland. After a short secular career, he dedicated his life to the Orthodox Church. An important role in his formation was played by Iov Boretskii, his former teacher in L'vov, who in 1620–31 served as metropolitan of Kiev and exarch of Constantinople under the ecumenical patriarchate.

Moghila joined the Kiev Caves Lavra in 1625 and by 1627 became its abbot. In 1632 he founded the Collegium in Kiev, later known as the Kiev-Moghila Academy, with the curriculum based on the Jesuit model and Latin as primary language of the eleven-year-long course of study. Moghila believed that the Orthodox Church in Galicia, with its poorly educated clergy and mostly peasant membership, could survive and succeed only through integrating into Polish culture and modeling its education after European universities. The school would remain the leading center of Orthodox higher education in Europe until the early 19th century; many of its graduates later moved to Russia and became the core of its intellectual elite, both secular and ecclesiastic.

In 1632 Moghila was able to secure the legalisation of the Orthodox Church, outlawed by the Polish state since 1596. In 1633 he was installed as metropolitan of Kiev and Galicia under the jurisdiction of Constantinople. Active in restoring the order and wellbeing of many Orthodox churches and monasteries, editing and printing various liturgical and theological books, and developing theological education, Peter Moghila also wrote the famous *Orthodox Confession* (1640), later translated into several languages, which was adopted by contemporary Orthodox churches as a standard introduction to the Orthodox faith. He and his followers have been accused sometimes of bringing the Orthodox Church into the "western captivity" by adopting the Roman Catholic standards of theological polemic and education (such was Florovsky's opinion). Today, however, many recognize him as the outstanding leader and defender of the Orthodox Church of his day, and, as such, he was canonized by the Romanian, Polish, and Ukrainian Orthodox Churches.

SEE ALSO: Iasi (Jassy), Synod of (1642)

References and Suggested Readings

Charipova, L.V. (2006) *Latin Books and the Eastern Orthodox Clerical Elite in Kiev, 1632–1780.* Manchester: Manchester University Press.

Dmitriev, M. N., Floria, V. N., and Iakovenko, S. G. (1996) *Brestskaia uniia 1596g. i obshchestvennopoliticheskaia bor'ba na Ukraine i v Belorussii v kontse XVI-nachale XVII v.* Moscow: Indrik.

Golubev, S. (1883–98) *Kievskii mitropolit Petr Mogila i ego spodvizhniki (Opyt tserkovnoistoricheskogo issledovaniiia),* 2 vols. Kiev: G. T. Korchak-Novitskogo (vol. 1); S. V. Kul'zhenko (vol. 2).

Popivchak, R. P. (1975) *Peter Mohila, Metropolitan of Kiev (1633–47): Translation and Evaluation of his "Orthodox Confession Of Faith" (1640).* Washington, DC: Catholic University of America.

Pritsak, O. and Sevcenko, I. (eds.) (1985) "The Kiev Mohyla Academy (Commemorating the 350th Anniversary of Its Founding, 1632–1982)," *Harvard Ukrainian Studies* 8, 1/2.

Moldova, Orthodoxy in

SCOTT M. KENWORTHY

The Orthodox Church in the post-Soviet Republic of Moldova is divided between two parallel jurisdictions belonging to the Russian Orthodox Church (Moscow patriarchate) and the Romanian Orthodox Church. According to a 1989 census, 98.5 percent of Moldova's 4.3 million citizens are nominal Orthodox Christians, though ethnically divided between Romanians (65 percent), Ukrainians (14 percent), Russians (13 percent), Gagauz, and Bulgarians.

The territory of the Republic of Moldova historically formed the eastern part of the medieval principality of Moldavia which had its own metropolitanate under the jurisdiction of the patriarch of Constantinople. In 1812 the Russian Empire took control over the eastern part of Moldavia between the Prut and Dnestr rivers, which came to be known as Bessarabia. In 1813 the Russian Orthodox Church established the diocese of Chisinau. The Russian state and church carried out a policy of Russification that included the imposition of Church Slavonic instead of Romanian as the liturgical language.

With the collapse of the Russian Empire, Bessarabia voted in favor of unification with Romania in 1918. The diocese was then incorporated into the Romanian Orthodox Church in 1919. The diocese was raised to the status of a metropolitanate in 1928. The Romanian church and state conducted a counter-campaign of Romanianization in the interwar period, forcing Bessarabians to accept the Latin alphabet, the Gregorian calendar, and Romanian language for education and liturgy. In 1939 the Soviet Union occupied Bessarabia and formed the Moldovan Soviet Socialist Republic, and the Russian Orthodox Church established an archdiocese of Chisinau and Moldova. Soviet authorities restricted religious life in Moldova as elsewhere in the Soviet Union.

The Republic of Moldova declared its independence from the Soviet Union in August 1991. The Moscow patriarchate continues to claim jurisdiction over the church in Moldova (with over 1,000 parishes), to which it granted autonomy and appointed an ethnic Romanian hierarchy, headed by Metropolitan Vladimir Cantarean. In 1992 the Romanian Orthodox Church established a jurisdiction known as the Bessarabian metropolitanate (with some 120 parishes). The Bessarabian metropolitanate justifies its existence not on territorial grounds, but by arguing that different ethnic groups have the right to separate (if parallel) church structures. Under pressure from Russia and the Russian Church, the Moldovan government refused to recognize or register the Bessarabian metropolitanate (with important implications for property ownership) until it was forced to do so by the European Court of Human Rights in 2002. Although there have been ongoing talks between the Russian and Romanian churches, no solution has yet been reached to the problem of parallel jurisdictions in Moldova.

SEE ALSO: Romania, Patriarchal Orthodox Church of; Russia, Patriarchal Orthodox Church of

References and Suggested Readings

Bespalko, V. (2002) "Bessarabskaia mitropoliia," in *Pravoslavnaia entsiklopediia*, Vol. 4. Moscow: Pravoslavnaia entsiklopediia, pp. 724–5.

King, C. (1999) *The Moldovans: Romania, Russia, and the Politics of Culture*. Stanford: Hoover Institution Press.

Păcurariu, M. (1993) *Bessarabia: Aspecte din istoria bisericii si a neamului Românesc*. Iasi: Trinitas.

Turcescu, L. and Stan, L. (2003) "Church–State Conflict in Moldova: The Bessarabian Metropolitanate," *Communist and Post-Communist Studies* 36: 443–65.

Monasticism

TENNY THOMAS

The term "monasticism" refers to a form of life involving separation from the world for the purpose of ascetical dedication to prayer, with a view to achieve perfect obedience to the gospel life. In the Eastern Christian tradition, monasticism is understood as full discipleship of Jesus Christ and traced back to the New Testament example of St. John the Baptist, to Jesus' own virginal celibacy, and to the many calls for renunciation (e.g., Mt. 10.37; Mk. 10.21). It is often called the "barometer of the spiritual life of the church." So great has the influence of and appreciation for this way of life been, that its existence and status have been equated with those of the church as a whole: as flourishes the monastic life, so flourishes the church.

Plate 42 Romanian nun carrying basket of Paschal painted eggs. Bogdan Cristel/Reuters/Corbis.

Plate 43   Romanian monastery of Simbata de Sus: a key monastery in the history of the national revival of Romania, and recently rebuilt after its destruction by Habsburg cannons. Photo by John McGuckin.

Monasticism is not just a part of the greater scope of Eastern Christian life; it is the very center and heart of the church. The monastics (both men and women) choose to follow with singular devotion and obedience the call of Christ. They are thus the models in which the church sees one of her most radiant icons: a communion of souls wholly living the life in Christ. Monasticism refers to that ascetic movement characterized by *anachoresis*, or withdrawal from the Christian community and the rest of society. Monasticism does not have a monopoly on asceticism, as this is a characteristic of all Christians following the gospel prescripts; thus all monasticism is ascetic, while all asceticism is not necessarily monastic. What distinguishes monasticism from the broader category of Christian asceticism is monasticism's emphasis on withdrawal, on solitude. The Greek word for "monk," *monachos*, meant, in its origins, "a solitary."

Two classic forms of monasticism emerged from early times: the anchoritic, or solitary life or the hermit, and the coenobitic (the Greek *koinos bios* means "common life"), that is, a life within a structured (and often secluded) community. Monastic life required from the outset stark renunciations: of family, property, marriage, and career. Early monks typically joined together ascetical disciplines (fasting, vigils, poverty, and lifelong celibacy) with a life of manual labor.

Egypt has often been called the birthplace of Christian monasticism, though this is only a partial truth. Scholars now recognize that other early Christian regions – especially Syria, Palestine, and Asia Minor – had their own ascetical traditions, as old as Egypt's. Christian monasticism put down visible roots in the early 4th century, though there were individuals and communities living austere, solitary, and ascetic lives long before this time. Nonetheless, it was in this era that St. Antony of Egypt lived and had his story recorded by Athanasius, bishop of Alexandria, in the classic text, the *Life of St. Antony of Egypt*. This book recorded the saint's departure into the solitary deserts of Egypt to live a life wholly devoted to God, modeled on a daily routine of prayer and manual labor born of the scriptural call to follow the Lord. What Antony did for the solitary (*eremitic*) life so did Pachomius for the communal (*coenobitic*) monastic way. They were two symbolic founders: manifestations of a life that soon spread throughout the Christian world. Within the lifetimes of these two founders, thousands of men and women began fleeing the cities for the solitude of the desert, and the recognizable conception of the Christian monastic life was born.

Types of Monasticism

Monasticism can thus be broadly distinguished in its two major prototypes: the *anchoritic* (the word means "withdrawn" apart), which is also known as the *eremitic* (the word means "in the desert") and the *coenobitic* (based on common life around a common table and shared church service).

Anchorites

First, there is the unmitigated life of withdrawal and seclusion: the *eremitic* life. This is found especially in Lower Egypt, as well as in Palestine and Syria, after the 5th century. The great founding father of this form of monasticism is St. Antony. At about 20 years of age (ca. 269), he heard Christ's words, "Go, sell all you have and give to the poor and come and follow me" (Mt. 19.21), as they were read aloud in the church. The text struck his heart. He thus freed himself of the burden of his possessions, although not without first securing a stable existence for his sister, for whose care he was responsible at the time. He is said to have entrusted her to a Christian community of virgins (a *Parthenon*), showing that community life for Christian women already existed in Alexandria in his day. He then followed Christ into the desert. His withdrawal was a gradual one: he moved further and further away from

human society until, by circa 285, he had reached the deep desert by the Red Sea, the outer mountain at Pispir, where he struggled day and night to liberate his true self from the delusions of the passions and the demons. Around 305, having attracted a number of followers who were inspired by his discipline and holiness, he came out of his seclusion to advise others in their own struggles.

Each practitioner of the life of the hermit typically lives alone or with one or two attendant disciples nearby, in a rigorous ascetic lifestyle, practicing sexual abstinence, fasting, and engaging in mortifications of various kinds, praying constantly, and engaging in light work, with a view to ward off all external influences and demonic passions, so as to achieve perfect penitence and discipleship.

Coenobites

In many ways, the anchoritic life is the most powerful form of monasticism, yet, precisely for this reason, can be the most dangerous, with great spiritual risks involved. An alternative form of monasticism, possessing great inherent safeguards against delusion, is the communal life under the guidance of elders, especially the chief monastic leader of a household known as the higumen or abbot. In this style of monasticism a group of monks lives together, under a common rule and sharing a common house, table and church, mutually supporting and encouraging one another. There are two great founding fathers of this form of monastic life in the Orthodox world: St. Pachomius of Egypt (286–346) and St. Basil the Great (ca. 330–79). They have the status that St. Benedict has for western monks.

The coenobitic monastery often took the form of a walled compound in which the community followed a uniform lifestyle built around common meals, set hours of prayer, and prescribed dress. This more tightly organized form replaced the looser colony of hermits gathered in a valley, meeting only for Sunday prayers (Lavriotic monasticism), and an abbot with strong central authority replaced the more informal and charismatic authority of the early spiritual leaders. Light work was replaced by obligatory group work, with a set allocation of tasks (called "obediences") according to the needs of the whole community.

Individuals no longer handled the minimum resources they needed themselves, for property belonged now to the monastery, a common form of life which allowed individual members to renounce all their possessions, and yet still be secure. Instead of an individual pursuit of the highest possible ascetic achievement, unconditional obedience became the norm. *Koinonia* (fellowship) became a key concept for this style of monastic life. Coenobitic monasticism became common primarily in Egypt and Asia Minor. It was especially popular in Upper Egypt, a part of the country less remote than St. Antony's area by the Red Sea. Pachomius' communities were found around Tabennisi in the Thebaid, near the Nile. Pachomius himself attracted a number of followers. At his death he was ruling higumen over nine monasteries for men and two for women.

Shenoute of Atripe (334–450) was abbot of the famous White Monastery at Sohag in Upper Egypt. He governed his coenobitic monastery with somewhat harsher rules than those of Pachomius. He was heavily involved in the wider community of Upper Egypt and struck out violently against the remnants of Egyptian pagan culture, using his monks as a missionary force. His participation in the Council of Ephesus (431) underscores the growing monastic influence in the church at large. As an author, Shenoute marks the highest development of Coptic literature. But because he wrote at a time when Coptic Christianity was becoming increasingly isolated from most of wider Christianity, his works were never translated into Greek, and as a result his history and significance have been largely forgotten outside of Egypt. Today, he is increasingly being recognized as one of the preeminent figures in Coptic Christianity. Shenoute was the first monastic leader to require a written profession from his monastics.

Egyptian monasticism spread to all areas of Christianity through personal acquaintance and literary testimonies such as Palladius' *Historia Lausiaca*, Athanasius' *Vita Antonii*, and other compendium texts such as *The Lives of the Desert Fathers*, the *Apophthegmata Patrum*, and the *Rule of Pachomius*. In Egypt a variation, something halfway between eremitical and common life monasticism, also appeared. The great centers of this semi-eremitic life were Nitria and Scetis, colonies just south of Alexandria; which by the end of the 4th century had produced many outstanding monks – Ammon the founder of Nitria, saints Macarius of Egypt and Macarius of Alexandria, Evagrius of Pontus, and Arsenius the Great. Nitria was the nearer of the two to Alexandria and formed a natural gateway to Scetis. It was a meeting place between the world and the desert where visitors, like John Cassian, could make first contact with the traditions of the desert. Here, a more Greek-influenced type of monasticism evolved around an educated minority, of whom Evagrius Ponticus is an outstanding example. This lifestyle would grow to influence the Lavriotism we find in Palestine. Not all early monasticism, however, was an offshoot of Egypt's traditions, and other parts of the early Eastern Christian world show significant variations on a common theme of ascetical endeavor.

Asia Minor

The beginning of monasticism in Asia Minor was the movement initiated by Eustathius (ca. 300–after 377), bishop of Sebaste in Pontus. He was a teacher for St. Macrina and for St. Basil the Great in his early life. The extreme program of this group called for complete rejection of marriage and property and was (probably) condemned at the Council of Gangra in Paphlagonia around 341 for causing dissension among the churches. St. Basil moderated Eustathius' rigorism, and combining Egyptian and Syrian influences he set up monasteries in Pontus and Caesarea. He strongly encouraged this form of coenobitic monasticism as being more suitable for most people than the eremitical lifestyle. Basil also closely associated his monks with the daily life of the Church. When he was elected as archbishop of Cappadocian Caesarea it was an important symbol of how episcopacy and monasticism were growing closely intimate. Basil feared that the detachment involved in the eremitic life could perhaps lead to a neglect of the evangelical call to charity and philanthropy, and so his monasteries were also concerned directly with issues of social justice. Basil added to the existing mystical and inner concerns of monasticism, a strong stress on external acts of charity and philanthropy. He also insisted on monastic obedience as a check on the excess, the competitiveness, and the ostentation of histrionic individuals who were bringing the monastic movement into disrepute. St. Basil was also careful to insist that monks remain mindful of the normal liturgical life of the church and that they remain connected with, and obedient to, the local bishop.

With the organizations and rules that he composed, St. Basil laid the foundations for monasticism throughout the Orthodox Church. Basil preferred to hold up only the coenobitic form, for he believed that true Christian living was possible only in a community. The bedrock of this style of monasticism was perfect obedience to the leader who is the spiritual father or mother, the teacher and physician of the soul of the brothers or sisters. As a therapeutic tool St. Basil developed the practice of the confession of sin (the opening of the thoughts of the heart) to the elder. For monastic life he prescribed a fixed rhythm of prayer, Bible reading, common worship, and work. Pursuing his ideal, Basil established a monastery in his own city of Caesarea and allotted to it social tasks on behalf of both church and society (including a lepers' hospital, a school, and a center for the relief of the poor).

Constantinople

Towards the end of the 4th century, monasticism came into Constantinople, the imperial capital, and new foundations followed constantly in the city until the fall of the empire in 1453. A new type of city monasticism was born here. Many monks worked in the imperial service. Many looked to St. Gregory the Theologian's conception of the monk as "quiet in the midst of the city." Most important was the Studios Monastery, with its reforming of coenobitic life along the lines of a highly liturgical community schedule, and a family of monks bonded in strong obedience to a single higumen. The example of the Studios community, especially under its dynamic leader St. Theodore the Studite (d. 816), became the basis for foundations all over the Orthodox world. Not least among them was the Studite inspired foundation in 961 of the first monastery at Mount Athos, later known as the Great Lavra, which marked the beginning of the rise of Athos as a center of Orthodox monasticism. Athos combined all forms of monasti-cism: coenobitic, eremitical, and small communities (Sketes) of loosely organized semi-hermits. The great spiritual movement known as Hesychasm, which flourished on Athos in the 13th and 14th centuries, gave spiritual expression to the upsurge and renewal of the anchorite ideal in Orthodox monastic life.

Palestine

The eremitic monasticism of Egypt had a direct influence on Byzantine Palestine, where notables such as saints Silvanus, Hilarion of Gaza, Sabas, and Epiphanius of Salamis all built monasteries. This became the site for the semi-eremitic form of monasticism, where the monks did not live in complete separation, like the hermits; nor in complete community, like coenobitic monks. Rather, there existed a number of independent groups of monks, each of which varied greatly in size, but which would all come together for a Saturday vigil in common, the dawn divine liturgy, and a shared meal, on Sunday. This style often involved a small colony of monks living very secluded lifestyles during the week, perhaps all associated along the same desert valley. Their respective separate dwelling places were linked by a small path (*Lavra*, or lane) along which they would have some communication, and by which they would all gather for the Saturday vigil services; returning to their hermitages on Sunday evenings. Lavriotic monasticism thus developed, even when the original separate dwellings came to be enclosed in one surrounding wall. Some of the greatest Russian and Greek monasteries today are known as Lavras.

This semi-eremitic model could also be found in Jerusalem, which became a great monastic center later in the 5th century. In the Judean wilderness, and especially around the desert of Gaza, there were great spiritual fathers of the Egyptian tradition. Indeed, in the 5th and 6th centuries, leadership in the monastic movement shifted to Palestine through the influence of such figures as St. Euthymius the Great (d. 473) and his disciple St. Sabas (d. 532). Judea especially became the home of the Lavra. This style of monasticism preserved a greater level of solitude than was common in a coenobium. Another difference between the semi-eremitic and the coenobitic models was that the arrangement often functioned as a preparatory phase for the anchoritic life, and seemed tacitly to presume that the anchoritic life was the superior.

Russia and the Balkans

With the coming of Christianity, monasticism also entered the Slavic Balkans and Russia. The coenobitic cave monastery at Kiev came into being in about 1050 under the influence of Athos. The Mongol hoard destroyed most Russian monasteries in the 13th century. The flight of many monks and the restoration in the 14th century led to new monastic regions in the wilder parts of northern Russia and the area around Moscow. Here we find coenobitic, eremitic, and mixed forms alongside one another. Among the great Russian monastic founders and heroes are St. Sergius of Radonezh (Sergei Posad near Moscow); St. Daniel the Hermit (Danilovsky Monastery at Moscow); St. Joseph of Volokolamsk (d. 1515) who strongly represented the coenobitic form; and St. Nil Sorskii (d. 1508) who defended the eremitic life. Secularization in the 18th century reduced the number of Russian monasteries considerably. The 19th century, however, brought a new upsurge. St. Seraphim of Sarov and the Optina monastic elders represent a flowering of the monastic life comparable to the ancients. The 1917 Revolution left only a few monasteries intact, which were put under strict state control.

The communist collapse opened the door to the revival of monastic life throughout Russia and the former Soviet zones. Monasticism in Romania spread out extensively from the 15th century onwards, and disseminated Hesychastic spirituality throughout the country. St. Paisy Velichovsky in the 18th century brought the patristic traditions of prayer to the Slavic world from his printing house at Neamt in Romania: the birthplace of the Russian *Philokalia*. His movement did so much to revive and renovate Orthodox monasticism from the 19th century to the present despite all outward reversals.

Syria

In order to understand the history of monasticism in Syria, we must consider two distinct phases in Syrian monasticism. The first we may call "proto-monasticism,"

which is the period prior to the 5th century, and differs considerably from Egyptian monastic traditions. The second phase is one that receives the most attention from modern historians, no doubt because it is also the time in which all the remarkable accounts of stunning acts of self-mortification are to be found. This second phase reflects a fundamental shift of the Syrian Church towards the Egyptian model, which had gained an irresistible prestige and momentum throughout the Eastern Christian world. Syria tends to press the model to an extreme, however.

There is very little direct information concerning the first, and quite different, phase of Syrian monasticism. The primary sources for this period are the early (4th century) Syrian fathers Aphrahat and Ephrem. To understand the distinctive characteristics of Syrian proto-monasticism, two phrases need to be understood: *ihidaya* (literally, "solitary," "monk") and *Bnay Qyama* (literally, "sons of the covenant"). Aphrahat especially uses these phrases almost interchangeably, but they do seem to convey different nuances. The ways in which they are used, primarily by Aphrahat, give us an important glimpse into the character of Syrian proto-monasticism.

The *ihidaya* refers to single persons who were committed to serving God. The *ihidaye* occupied a special status in the church. But while they could occasionally be found among the clerical orders (particularly the lower ones), this was rare. They were primarily laypersons, whether male or female. The term *ihidaye*, more specifically, seems to have been used with three major senses in mind, and accordingly tells us three main things about the monastic movement: the first sense is that of *monachos*, conveying the sense of unmarried or celibate person; the second is that of *monozonos* or *monotropos*, conveying the idea of single-mindedness, that is the ascetic as a dedicated seeker after prayer; and third we find the term *monogenes*, conveying the idea of the ascetic's union with the *Monogenes* (the Only-begotten Son), the *Ihidaya par excellence*.

The other important term that helps us understand native Syrian monasticism is the phrase *Bnay Qyama*. The word *Qyama* refers primarily to the idea of "covenant," though it also connotes "station" and possibly "resurrection"; it was even used by Aphrahat to denote the whole church. Accordingly, the *Bnay Qyama* (Sons of the Covenant) refers to a group of celibates who took upon themselves a special "station" in the life of the community. They assumed this station by individual covenant, or solemn pledge, at their baptism, at which time they assumed the obligation of celibacy and became *ihidaye* (solitary ascetics). They also accepted to follow Christ's lifestyle in a uniquely uncompromising way, and in so doing they were deliberately trying to manifest the form of life that would be lived in the "age to come," the life to which all the baptized are finally called. Through their celibacy and uncompromising pursuit of holiness, they stood among their community as anticipatory images of the resurrection to come.

It is difficult to say very much more about this movement. We can surmise that it was carried out neither in a strictly eremitic, nor in a coenobitic form, although there may have been a proto-rule that the *Bnay Qyama* followed. They seem to have existed as communities close to the churches and were an integral part of Syrian church life. But by the 5th century this ascetic tradition, whatever its characteristics, quickly became displaced by the Egyptian variety of monasticism. However, the Syrians did not simply import Egyptian monasticism; they incorporated it into their region in a creative way that reflected their own idiosyncrasies. We find that these idiosyncrasies were expressed in a range of behavior that might strike the modern reader as deeply disturbing, even inhuman. In Syria and Mesopotamia asceticism occasionally took bizarre forms. The majority of the monks were simple Syriac-speaking people, ignorant of Greek. Violent forms of asceticism were common. A heavy iron chain as a belt was a frequently practiced austerity. A few adopted the life of animals and fed on grass, living in the open air without shade from the sun and with the minimum of clothing, and justifying their method of defying society by claiming to be "fools for Christ's sake." Some Syrian ascetics manifested special feats of penance, such as going without sleep for long periods, being walled up, or spending a lifetime on exposed pillars (Stylites), among whom St. Simeon the Stylite (ca. 390–459) was the most famous. Syrian monasticism should therefore not be seen simply as a more extreme form of monasticism stemming from either a greater degree of dualism or intellectual simplicity, but rather as a form of monasticism stemming from a different theological emphasis.

From its beginning, therefore, Christianity involved a substantive call to self-denial, to a life shadowed by the cross; a life in the light of eschatological imperatives. The monks with their austerities were martyrs in an age when the martyrdom of blood no longer existed; they formed the counterbalance to an established and protected church. Monasticism, a formal life of internally imposed self-renunciation, emerged in response to the diminishing presence of externally imposed deprivations. It has had an incalculable effect on the development and on the sustenance of Christianity, offering to the church most of its greatest leaders throughout history.

SEE ALSO: Elder (Starets); Greece, Orthodox Church of; Hesychasm; Mount Athos; Non-Possessors (Nil Sorskii); Pontike, Evagrios (ca. 345–399); Possessors (Joseph of Volotsk); Romania, Patriarchal Orthodox Church of; Russia, Patriarchal Orthodox Church of; St. Dorotheos of Gaza (6th c.); St. Isaac the Syrian (7th c.); St. Macarius (4th c.); St. Paisy Velichovsky (1722–1794); St. Sergius of Radonezh (1314–1392); Stylite Saints

References and Suggested Readings

Alfeyev, H. (2001) *The Spiritual World of Isaac the Syrian.* Cistercian Studies 175. Kalamazoo: Cistercian Publications.

Athanasius (1980) *The Life of Antony*, trans. R. C. Gregg. Classics of Western Spirituality. New York: Paulist Press.

Binns, J. (1994) *Ascetics and Ambassadors of Christ: The Monasteries of Palestine, 314–631.* Oxford Early Christian Studies. New York: Oxford University Press.

Brock, S. (1987) *Syriac Fathers on Prayer and the Spiritual Life.* Cistercian Studies 101. Kalamazoo: Cistercian Publications.

Brown, P. (1988) *The Body and Society: Men, Women, and Sexual Renunciation in Early Christianity.* New York: Columbia University Press.

Chitty, D. (1997) *The Desert A City.* Crestwood, NY: St. Vladimir's Seminary Press.

Cotelier, J. B. (ed.) (1647) *Apophthegmata Patrum.* Alphabetical Collection. PG 65.

Dunn, M. (2000) *The Emergence of Monasticism: From the Desert Fathers to the Early Middle Ages*. Oxford: Blackwell.

Goehring, J. E. (1999) *Ascetics, Society, and the Desert: Studies in Early Egyptian Monasticism*. Harrisburg: Trinity Press International.

Harmless, W. (2004) *Desert Christians: An Introduction to the Literature of Early Monasticism*. New York: Oxford University Press.

Johnston, W. W. (ed.) (2000) *Encyclopedia of Monasticism*, 2 vols. Chicago: Fitzroy Dearborn.

Krawiec, R. (2002) *Shenoute and the Women of the White Monastery: Egyptian Monasticism in Late Antiquity*. New York: Oxford University Press.

Patrich, J. (1995) *Sabas, Leader of Palestinian Monasticism: A Comparative Study in Eastern Monasticism, Fourth to Seventh Centuries*. Washington, DC: Dumbarton Oaks.

Pseudo-Macarius (1992) *The Fifty Spiritual Homilies and the Great Letter*, trans. George A. Maloney. Classics of Western Spirituality. New York: Paulist Press.

Rousseau, P. (1999) *Pachomius: The Making of a Community in Fourth Century Egypt*. Transformation of the Classical Heritage, 6 revd. edn. Berkeley: University of California Press.

Rubenson, S. (1995) *The Letters of St. Antony: Monasticism and the Making of a Saint*. Minneapolis: Fortress Press.

Vivian, T. (ed) (2004) *Four Desert Fathers: Pambo, Evagrius, Macarius of Egypt and Macarius of Alexandria*. Popular Patristics Series. Crestwood, NY: St. Vladimir's Seminary Press.

Voobus, A. ((1958) *History of Asceticism in the Syrian Orient*, 3 vols. Louvain: Secrétariat du Corpus SCO.

Ward, B. (trans.) (1980) *The Sayings of the Desert Fathers: The Alphabetical Collection*. Cistercian Studies 59. Kalamazoo: Cistercian Publications.

Monophysitism (including Miaphysitism)

JOHN A. MCGUCKIN

In Byzantine and Latin Church usage the term *Monophysitism* (from the Greek: "Holding to One Nature") historically designated those who rejected the Christology of the Council of Chalcedon (451), with its insistence on two perfect natures (human and divine) harmonized without confusion or separation in the single (divine) person of the Christ. As the Chalcedonian theology was Di-Physite (two-nature) so, by implication, the rival party were increasingly called Monophysites.

Many Chalcedonians, past and present, have erroneously gone on from the basis of this pejorative and rather simplistic summation of their opponents' beliefs (including most of what today is termed the Oriental Orthodox or Non-Chalcedonian Orthodox churches) to presuppose that such an "imputed" single nature of the Christ must, of necessity, be a hybrid or mingled nature of God-manhood. The implications of this, forcefully expressed in many earlier European patristic studies, are that Dyo-physite thought represents christological clarity, where the one divine person of the incarnated *Logos* presides directly over two distinct natures; whereas Monophysitism represents muddy thinking where deep piety (affirming Christ's unquestioned divine status) underestimated the full authentic range of the incarnate Lord's human experiences. Some of the opponents of Chalcedon undoubtedly did follow a line of thought that paid less than sufficient attention to Christ's human actuality. Following in varying degrees in the steps of Apollinaris of Laodicea, they sometimes believed that to affirm human limitation was a disservice to the divine Christ. Thinkers such as Julian of Halicarnassus and Eutyches of Constantinople represented this kind of confused piety. There were other opponents of the Chalcedonian Christology, however, such as Philoxenus of Mabbug, Timothy Aeluros ("the Cat"), and Severus of Antioch, whose sophisticated theology cannot be reduced to this level.

The major argument, if hostile apologetics can be cleared away, turns around two closely related issues: first that St. Cyril of Alexandria (who had become a towering authority on Christology in the East) had used certain terms simultaneously in two senses. Chalcedon, for the sake of clarity, wished to move towards one agreed technical vocabulary and had vetoed some of his early expressions. His followers (not least the majority of the Egyptian Church) refused to accept such a veto. In his early writings, ten times St. Cyril had spoken of the seamless union of divine and human activity in a single Christ under the party slogan: "One *Physis* of the Word of God incarnate" (*Mia Physis*). It was a phrase coined by Apollinaris, which mistakenly in his archives had been attributed to St. Athanasius, and which he thus felt had the authentic stamp of patristic orthodoxy about it. Here Cyril applied *physis* in the antique sense of "one concrete reality," which was more or less a synonym for the central idea of his (and later, Chalcedon's) Christology that there was only "One *hypostasis*" in Christ. Unfortunately, even by his day the word *physis* was coming to be taken as a synonym for *ousia*, or nature understood not as a concrete reality (a subjective presence), but more as a set of (natural) properties or attributes (such as "human nature" and "divine nature"). Thus, to describe Christ as one single *physis*-nature, in this latter and modern sense, was generally taken by non-Cyrillians (such as the majority of Syrian theologians in the 5th century) to be advocating for a new form of hybrid nature (divino-human synthesis) in Christ; which would *de facto* be a mythical construct, and impute changeability to the deity. They thus regarded St. Cyril (actually a brilliant thinker) as either a pious ignoramus (Nestorius underestimated him this way) or a deliberate resuscitator of Apollinarianism (Theodoret of Cyr regarded him in this way). For his part, St. Cyril felt such graphic language of *physis* unity was necessary, for he was worried that those parties who ostensibly wished to defend the authenticity of human experience in Christ, and the differentiated spheres of human and divine actions in his life (the two natures emphasized by the Syrians under the term of "Two Sons"), had actually strayed into such a polarization that the incarnation had become artificial; a disunion rather than a union of God and man; and often loosely described by the Syrians as "Association" rather than "Union."

Cyril's followers, alienated after the Council of Chalcedon by the condemnation and deposition of Dioscorus, his successor at Alexandria, were more and more labeled as Monophysites, and accused of teaching the doctrine of a confused hybrid of natures (Eutychianism). They themselves saw their defense of the "Union of Natures" (a union logically meaning a "making into one," not an association of two disparates) as something far removed from Eutychianism (which may rightly be termed Monophysitism), and rather as a last stand for the belief in the deification of the human race that came from the dynamic of the incarnation of God. They identified their own position as advocating a truth about two perfect natures in Christ (Godhead and Manhood) that had mystically been rendered as "one concrete reality" without the destruction of either. This "rendering as one," in their

estimation, did not necessarily imply that it thus became a single *thing*, more a single *factor*: namely, "the one divine Christ with his flesh." Such a position is better described as Miaphysitism, in acknowledgment of its indebtedness to that formula made current by St. Cyril: "One *physis* [concrete reality] of God the Word made flesh." This position of St. Cyril was the one he had adopted before his agreement with the Syrians in the *Formula of Reunion* of 433. Thus to propagate it after the mid-5th century was a deliberate strategy on the part of anti-Chalcedonian theologians to "turn back the clock" and veto the objections the Roman and Syrian churches had expressed to taking Cyril's christological *corpus* as a superior guide to ecclesial dogma than the conciliar formulations of Chalcedon in 451 and Constantinople in 553.

If they were generally classed as Monophysites, the radical anti-Chalcedonian Cyrillians in turn regarded the Chalcedonians as no better than defenders of Nestorianism. In this they were quite wrong; just as their opponents were wrong to caricature them as Eutychians, but widespread semantic confusions, and a certain lack of desire to give the opponent a fair hearing, made the controversy run on bitterly for many centuries. After the Islamic seizure of Syria and Egypt in the 7th century, the possibilities of reconciliation of the anti-Chalcedonian Easterners (more and more commonly called Monophysites or Jacobites) with the Byzantine and Roman traditions became increasingly slight. The best of the so-called Monophysite theologians actually represent the *Mia Physis* formula of St. Cyril, which is theologically compatible with Chalcedonian Orthodoxy, if rightly understood as not synthesizing the natures into a *tertium quid* which is a hybrid, and if the *physis* is understood (as Cyril meant it) to signify "concrete reality" and not nature*ousia* (as Eutyches seemed to have meant it). The anti-Chalcedonians, however, consistently rejected any Two-Nature language as both a betrayal of Cyril (hence of Ephesus 431) and of the belief that the incarnation was a dynamic of unity. As such they were increasingly prosecuted by the imperial government, and sadly failed to see Chalcedon itself, and even more so, Constantinople II (553), as a serious attempt to meet them half way in a shared expression of an agreed insight. It is one of the great tragedies of the patristic era that so many attempts to reconcile the Chalcedonian dissidents failed, when clearly the central issues (integrity of humanity and divinity in the Christ, who is but a single divine person, and who has dynamically brought the human and divine realities into a profound personal unity in himself as a paradigm for the salvation of all humanity) were things agreed on both sides. Political and ethnic factors played a considerable part in this. In the late 20th century, tentative efforts between the Orthodox and Non-Chalcedonian Churches to reopen the christological debate with clarity and coolness of exchange have revealed once more how much of the alienation was a result of unnecessary confusion over terms, but they have also shown the enduring problems still existing between churches who approach the conciliar record (that is, which councils have ecumenical status) so differently that the saints of one church can be anathematized as the heretics of the other.

SEE ALSO: Alexandria, Patriarchate of; Antioch, Patriarchate of; Assyrian Apostolic Church of the East; Christ; Council of Chalcedon (451); Council of Constantinople II (553); Council of Ephesus (431); Deification; Ecumenical Councils; Nestorianism; Oriental Orthodox; St. Cyril of Alexandria (ca. 378–444); Syrian Orthodox Churches

References and Suggested Readings

Frend, W. H. C. (1972) *The Rise of the Monophysite Movement.* Cambridge: Cambridge University Press.
Grillmeier, A. and Hainthaler, T. (1996) *Christ in Christian Tradition,* Vol. 2, part 4. London: Mowbray.
Luce, A. A. (1920) *Monophysitism Past and Present: A Study in Christology.* London: SPCK.
Meyendorff, J. (1975) *Christ in Eastern Christian Thought.* New York: Fordham University Press.

Monothelitism

EDWARD EPSEN

The teaching that the person of Christ has "one will" or voluntative activity was promulgated by Patriarch Sergius in his statement entitled *Psephos* (633), and officially endorsed by Emperor Heraclius in his *Ekthesis* (638) in an effort (given the increasingly fragile state of Byzantine imperial unity) to appease the monophysites of Armenia, Syria, and Egypt without abandoning the Council of Chalcedon (451). With origins lying in the writings of Theodore of Pharas and Cyrus of Phasis, the appeal of Monothelitism owed to its apparent consistency with the Chalcedonian confession of "two natures … in one person." Nevertheless, while having two natures, might not the oneness of Christ's person be manifested in a single voluntative activity? St. Maximos the Confessor argued that this approach confused the agreement of two wills with their identity, and confused the activity of willing with the condition willed. Drawing on the example of the prayer in Gethsamene, Maximos articulated the orthodox *dythelite* (two wills) position eventually upheld by the Sixth Ecumenical Council (Constantinople III, 681) that the Savior, in accordance with his two natures, willed as human that his own divine will (which he shares with the Father) should be fulfilled.

SEE ALSO: Council of Constantinople III (680–681); St. Maximos the Confessor (580–662)

References and Suggested Readings

Lethel, F.-M. (1979) *Theologie de l'agonie du christ.* Theologie historique 52. Paris: Beauchesne.
Maximos the Confessor (1865) *Opuscula* 3, 6, & 7 in J. P. Migne (ed.) *Opuscula theologica et polemica. Patrologia Graeca,* Vol. 91, pp. 10–286. Paris.

Mother Maria Skobtsova (1891–1945) *see* Contemporary Orthodox Theology

Mount Athos

DIMITRI CONOMOS

Located in northern Greece, the peninsula of Athos has for more than 1,000 years been the principal center of male monasticism for all Orthodox Churches. Since Byzantine times it has offered its diverse landscape to religious habitations for Albanians, Bulgarians, Georgians, Greeks, Moldavians, Russians,

Serbs, and Wallachians. Exceptionally, a Benedictine monastery operated there from the 10th to the 14th centuries.

Athos is dedicated to and protected by the Virgin Mary. Of the twenty ruling monasteries existing today (many more are known from earlier times), seventeen are Greek, one Serbian, one Russian, and one Bulgarian. Each monastery sends an elected representative for twelve months to Karyes, the capital of the peninsula, where, in the building of the Holy Community, administrative decisions of pan-Athonite concern are made. Otherwise each monastery is a self-governing, independent entity within the monastic federation.

Aside from Athos's monasteries there are other smaller settlements, each of which functions as a dependency of one of the twenty main houses. First are the *sketes*. Typically, a skete is a compound containing three to six cottages – each of which may have from around two to ten monks – clustered around a church, known as the *Kyriakon* (a monastery church is called the *Katholikon*). Every cottage has its own chapel: services are conducted by its inhabitants on weekdays. On Saturday evening and Sunday morning, however, the entire population of the skete worship together in the Kyriakon. Because the number of monasteries has been fixed by charter at twenty, the term "skete" has been given to a number of large edifices, such as the Skete of St. Andrew (formerly Russian, now Greek) which is under Vatopedi Monastery, and that of Prodromou (Romanian) which is under the Great Lavra. In all respects these large foundations look and function like monasteries.

After the sketes come the isolated cells (*kellia*) – small domiciles with integrated chapels that house one or two monks. Then the smaller huts (*kalyves* or *kathismata*), and finally the solitary, somewhat inaccessible hermitages (*hesychasteria*) and caves (*spelaia*) for those who have received a blessing to live the ascetic life entirely in seclusion. The parent monasteries care for these dependencies by providing, whenever necessary, food and clothing. In most cases, however, these dwellers are self-sufficient: some cultivate vegetable patches and orchards; others engage in handicraft (wood and metalwork) or icon painting.

Prayer life in the monastery follows the sequence of services for the year as arranged in the church hymnals. Katholikon worship is mostly from sunset to sunrise (with breaks for a meal and time in one's cell) – an arrangement that leaves all of daylight for monastic work and other duties (*diakonimata*). This system of monastic life is known as *cenobitic* and requires that all monks pray, work, and eat in common. The dependencies, however, are *idiorhythmic*: there is more flexibility in how a day is divided up. Weekday worship here concentrates on the steady repetition of the Jesus Prayer instead of the canonical hours. On Sundays and feasts the appointed liturgical services are celebrated in the normal way.

References and Suggested Readings

Sherrard, P. (1960) *Athos, the Mountain of Silence*. Oxford: Oxford University Press.

Sherrard, P. (1982) *Athos: The Holy Mountain*. London: Sidgwick and Jackson.

Speake, G. (2002) *Mount Athos: Renewal in Paradise*. New Haven: Yale University Press.

Music (Sacred)

DIMITRI CONOMOS

The liturgical rites celebrated in Orthodox churches originate principally in three *loci*: the worship of the primitive Christian church; the desert and urban monastic prayer of the East; and the elaborate imperial services in the great Byzantine city cathedrals. Choral music constituted a component (of varying importance) at each major stage in the development of Eastern Christian ceremony.

The Byzantine musical tradition of monophonic plainchant prevailed for over 1,000 years in all Eastern churches irrespective of liturgical language or jurisdiction. For a long period, moreover, a clear distinction was made between musical renditions of psalmody (singing the Davidic Psalter) and of hymnody (settings of non-scriptural religious verse, usually by named poets). Both genres appear in notation (*neumes*) after the 9th century, at which time they exhibit a predilection for anonymous musical settings, of no fixed rhythm, built out of little, age-old twists and turns of melody (conventional melodic formulas) that were active in the communal memory and had been used for generations, long before the invention of musical *neumes*. Each "new" tune, therefore, was rarely unique and innovative. Rather, it was a modification of some preexisting fragments produced by nameless musical craftsmen who were content to work within the traditional melodic parameters of what had been transmitted vocally.

This ultra-conservative approach to composition is abundantly found in medieval hymn texts whose verses are musically amplified by single-stranded tunes, unfettered by contrapuntal voices or accompanying instruments. Their rhythm is free and unregulated: there are no divisions that fashion predictable metrical units. Musical style is directly influenced by liturgical requirements and by the solemnity of the occasion. Simple, syllabic chants (one note per syllable) were assigned to the faithful worshippers while trained choirs (usually two, located to the right and left of the sanctuary screen) and soloists (choir directors, the *Protopsaltes* and *Lampadarios*) were accorded more elaborate settings. Whatever the style, the chants are systematically assigned to the eight ecclesiastical modes (or tones) which, from about the 8th century, provided the compositional framework for eastern musical practices. Research has demonstrated that, for all practical purposes, this *Oktoechos*, as the system is known, was the same for Latins, Greeks, and Slavs in the Middle Ages. Each modal setting is characterized by the deployment of a restricted set of melodic formulas, peculiar to the mode, that constitute the substance of the chant. Although these formulas are arranged in many different combinations and patterns, most of the phrases of any given chant are nevertheless reducible to one or another of this small number of melodic fragments. This procedure may, more or less, be compared with that employed by the unnamed icon painters and mosaicists, who constantly recreated the same narrow repertory of pictorial subjects while adding relatively modest personalizing touches each time.

The emergence of a written notation in the 8th and 9th centuries had a direct and negative impact on the ancient tradition of congregational singing. The *neumes* could only be read and interpreted by trained musicians and they, in turn, demanded complex settings whose profiles conformed to their virtuosic tastes. Notation became a means of artistic experiment, since it gave composers a way to try out new musical ideas, letting them ponder their novelties and circulate them for others to examine and compare.

Thus, by the 13th century in the Greek-speaking orbit, and around 300 years later in the Slav world, there is a notable shift from the restrained early practices and styles of the early church to the emergence of uninhibited, highly ornate stylizations. The latter, championed on the Holy Mountain and in Constantinople by St. John Koukouzeles (ca. 1300) and other Paleologan composers, is characterized by a marked expansion both of music and of text. Traditional chants were lengthened in three ways: by giving many notes (*melismas*) to the individual syllables of the hymn texts; by interpolating new words and phrases in preexisting texts (*tropes*), thereby providing opportunities for composers to add more original music; and by inserting long passages of nonsense syllables set to music into preexisting chants – vocalizations such as *te-re-re*, *to-ro-ro*, *ti-ri-ri*, and so on. These are usually known as *teretismata* (comparable to the Russian *anenayki* of later times), and for the past 600 years they have come to occupy a key musical position in monastic vigil services, especially on the Holy Mountain.

With the Latin occupation of Byzantium's chief religious and cultural centers (1204–61) and the fall of Constantinople to the Turks in 1453, church musicians in late medieval times were, depending on their location, exposed to the art of polyphony of the Latin Church and/or the suave, alluring sounds of Ottoman court music. Both species became integrated – in one way or another – in Orthodox Church music at large. In Greece, imitations of western styles infiltrated Crete and the Ionian islands, while on Mount Athos polyphonic music (especially before 1917) was heard in the ubiquitous Russian monastic settlements. As for the Anatolian tradition, among the Orthodox under Islamic rule (today's Greece, Bulgaria, Serbia, Albania, Romania, and the Middle East), the serpentine exoticism of Arabo-Persian melody – undergirded by a drone (*ison*) – infiltrated chant performance practice and its ethos. It is this latter tradition which, more or less, prevails today, not only in these countries but also in the lands to which their populations have migrated.

In the 20th century the proliferation of diverse musical styles within the monophonic and polyphonic genres has, through printed anthologies and electrical recordings, affected radically the sacred music heard in the worldwide Orthodox Church. During the Soviet period, Russian *obikhod*-style choral polyphony all but eradicated the received chant traditions of Georgia, Armenia, and Carpatho-Russia, but currently there is a trend to revive the Znamenny, Iberian, and Ruthenian chant repertories. In much the same way, new polyphonic compositions by Orthodox composers, especially in America, England, Finland, and Estonia, have received wide acceptance. New settings of the Psalms from Mount Athos, the music of which has taken an independent stylistic path, have recently earned popularity in monasteries and many parishes throughout the Orthodox world.

SEE ALSO: Kathisma; Kontakion; Ode; *Oktoechos*; Troparion

References and Suggested Readings

Conomos, D. (1984) *Byzantine Hymnography and Byzantine Chant*. New York: Harper Collins.
Strunk, O. (1977) *Essays on Music in the Byzantine World*. New York: W. W. Norton.
Wellesz, E. (1961) *A History of Byzantine Music and Hymnography*. Oxford: Oxford University Press.

Myrobletes Saints

JOHN A. MCGUCKIN

The term *Myrobletes* derives from the Greek for "emitting myrrh." It describes a category of saint (and sometimes designates an icon, too – such as that of Christ, or the Virgin, or one of the saints) whose relics emit a sweetly and gently fragranced oil after their death. These relics (often but not solely the skull) are frequently kept separately in the catacombs (many examples are preserved in the Kiev Pechersky Lavra, for example, or at Mount Athos) and can be recognized as such by the dark brown character of the bone. The perfumed oil is not always emitted, but is so on a regular basis, and often across many generations. If a perfume only is emitted (such as on the occasion of the opening of a grave of a saint) it is technically called *Euodia*. The perfume from the phenomenon of myrobletes relics is quite unmistakeable when experienced, and is widely taken in the Orthodox Church as a sign of the great sanctity of the saint in question, and their bestowal of blessing on those who have come to venerate them in pilgrimage. Shrines of the Myrobletes saints are frequent sites of Orthodox pilgrimage, where pilgrims gather to seek the saint's intercession and cures, for themselves or for family members. An icon can become a Myrobletes if it starts to emit perfume, oil, or tears. This phenomenon is often a temporary one. It is widely understood in Orthodoxy to mean that the sacred figure whom the icon depicts is giving a special blessing, or drawing attention to some notable thing transpiring, or delivering a warning to the faithful. The most notable of myrrh-gushing icons is perhaps the (Myroblitissa) icon of the Dormition of the Mother of God in the Malevi convent in Arcadia. Throughout the history of the Orthodox Church such things have been extensively recorded, understood as *thaumata*' (or signs to cause "wonderment" and spiritual reflection), and are still a regular feature of Orthodox life. The most famous of the Myrobletes saints is perhaps St. Dimitrios of Thessalonike, the Great Martyr. St. Charbal (Makhlouf), the 19th-century Maronite saint, is perhaps the most famous of the 20th-century Myrobletes, whose perfumed *myron* accounted for numerous cures all over the world, making his shrine in Lebanon one of the great pilgrimage sites of the Middle East in recent times.

SEE ALSO: Anointing of the Sick; Healing; Icons; Unmercenary Saints

References and Suggested Readings

Thurston, H. (1952) *The Physical Phenomena of Mysticism*. Chicago: Regnery.

Mystery (Sacrament)

MARIA GWYN MCDOWELL

The Greek term *mysterion*, equivalent to the Latin usage of sacraments, refers in Orthodox theology to Christ himself, to specific rites, and to any action or material thing which is an outward sign of the energy of divine grace.

Early Christian terminology absorbed and changed the language of the pagan mystery religions, just as it did Greek philosophy. Gregory the Theologian describes baptism, for example, as a "fulfillment" of the Mysteries (*Orations on the Lights*). Scriptural language references Wisdom as the mystery of the knowledge of God (Wis. 8.4), and gives mystery the less technical meaning of a "secret" (Mt. 13.11; Mk. 4.11–12). Significant for subsequent theological development is the Pauline equation of Christ as the *mysterion* who dwells within believers (Col. 1.27). This serves as the basis of a developing Orthodox theology of mystery and sacrament inextricably tied to the incarnation, an ongoing Pentecost, and the concept of salvation as deification. Foundational to this is the idea of sacrament or mystery as that which manifests Christ through the Holy Spirit, indwelling the believer and enabling his or her participation by grace in the life of Christ.

On the one hand, the one true mystery is Christ himself. On the other hand, all actions and material things which signify the presence of Christ in the world are sacramental. Through the incarnation, the most mundane of material things – water, bread, wine, oil – become vehicles of the Spirit, underscoring the impact of the incarnation as redeeming all matter. The use of mundane materials incorporates a participant's body and soul into Christ, an outward and visible act signifying an inward and divine grace; such as the external washing of the body and the soul's cleansing from sin.

While contemporary Orthodoxy does not distinguish between sacraments and sacramentals as does the Roman Catholic Church, under its influence it has in later times adopted the convention of seven sacraments: Baptism, Chrismation, Eucharist, Confession, Marriage, Ordination, Unction. These seven are customary since the 15th century, reinforced by the Synod of Jerusalem (1672). However, this list is neither dogmatic nor entirely consistent. Through the 4th century, only baptism, Chrismation, and Eucharist were spoken of as sacraments in the patristic mystagogic liturgy. St. John of Damascus appears to recognize only two great mysteries (baptism and Eucharist), while Dionysius the Areopagite adds to that list ordination, monastic tonsure, and burial. At various times, blessing the waters at Theophany, consecrating a church, naming a child, and memorial services have been included among the Orthodox "Mysteries" as well. Regardless of the number, baptism and Eucharist are consistently regarded as preeminent. No sacrament other than baptism is a prerequisite for the Eucharist, a point the liturgist Alexander Schmemann repeatedly emphasizes in highlighting the Eucharist as the primary ecclesial act of cooperating with the Holy Spirit which fully manifests the being of the church.

SEE ALSO: Anointing of the Sick; Baptism; Chrismation; Confession; Eschatology; Eucharist; Healing; Marriage; Ordination

References and Suggested Readings

McGuckin, J. A. (2008) *The Orthodox Church: An Introduction to Its History, Theology and Spiritual Culture*. Oxford: Wiley-Blackwell.

N

Name (Name Day)

JOHN A. MCGUCKIN

Orthodox tradition from early times suggested to the faithful that their names ought to be taken from the lists of the great saints of the church, rather from the generally prevailing customs of the period that took names honoring the (pagan) gods or great heroes of the ancient world. Just as in most Orthodox countries (the Mediterranean Basin demonstrates it still) the names of the days of the week were wrested from the pagan cults (Sun day, Moon day, Wodin's day, Thor's day, and so on) so as to be "renamed" (Kyriake, or Lord's day instead of Sunday), so too on a personal level the clergy encouraged the faithful to reflect their religious commitments with different personal names. In the 3rd century the martyr Leontios of Alexandria and his son (soon to become) the great Christian theologian Origen, bear names that are indistinguishable from their pagan compatriots. Origen, named so presumably by his Christian father, bore a name derived from the Egyptian cult of Horus. In the later 4th century the Christian bishop and father of St. Gregory the Theologian (his own name reflected a Syrian title for the angels: "watchers") named his daughter Gorgonia (after the mythical monster!). Basil the Great was similarly designated from a common nickname ("royal one") also seen in the naming of Augustine ("little prince") by his parents in the 5th century. At the end of the 4th century and into the 5th, however, a predominance of "Christian names" starts to show. Some were generic titles that had a common resonance with Christian and pagan culture alike, such as Athanasius ("immortal one"), but others were more explicitly Christian and biblically derived, such as Peter, or Timothy. By the end of the 6th century both those sets of earlier classical names that did not have biblical origins (Basil, Augustine, Macrina, Emmelia, Hilary, and the like) and those that did (Mary, Elizabeth, John, Peter, and so on) had accumulated "saints" to go with them, biblical or not. By the medieval period, in both the eastern and western churches the daily liturgical calendar of saints that were commemorated had grown apace; and Christian families were offered a very large choice of patronal names that had reference to the saints or the angels. By this stage it was common to suggest the dedication of a new Christian child to the saint on whose day it had been born (though this never completely superseded family choices according to ancestral traditions). Eight days after the birth, the child was named in a ceremony of prayers, so that it had a name already at its subsequent baptism. Nowadays at the reception of adult converts to Orthodoxy a new name is often suggested at the baptism or chrismation service (especially if the original one is not particularly "Christian") and the convert is known by that for the purposes of receiving communion and other mysteries, at least.

The Concise Encyclopedia of Orthodox Christianity, First Edition. Edited by John Anthony McGuckin.
© 2014 John Wiley & Sons, Ltd. Published 2014 by John Wiley & Sons, Ltd.

Monastics also receive a new name, a new "dedication" at the time of their profession; a custom that is repeated sometimes if they are elevated to the episcopate. The fathers interpreted this process as being a displacement of "birth-days" so as to be able to celebrate the saint's day, which became known in Orthodox life as the celebration of the Name Day. The symbolism suggests that birth into the world, as such, is not a matter of rejoicing, for it is birth into mortality and suffering; whereas birth into the communion of the saints is a true occasion for joy. It is a widespread custom today among the Orthodox to send greetings and congratulations, and to meet for festive parties, on the occasion of a friend's Name Day. And most Orthodox will usually have about the house the icon of their "patronal" saint.

SEE ALSO: Baptism; Chrismation

Nativity of the Lord

DAN SANDU

The Nativity of the Lord is the liturgical feast commemorating the coming in flesh (incarnation) of the Second Person of the Holy Trinity: God made man, Jesus Christ, the Son of God among us. It is popularly known as Christmas. Jesus was born in Bethlehem of the Holy Virgin Mary, through the descent of the Holy Spirit, without the contribution of a human father. The Orthodox doctrine affirms the virginal conception and birth of the Lord and venerates Mary as the Ever-Virgin (*Aei-Parthenos*). Jesus was born during the reign of the Roman Emperor Caesar Augustus, in the year 754 *ab Urbe condita*, when a census was taking place in the Roman Empire.

The event has a universal dimension, as it is accomplished for and through the whole creation. The icon of nativity depicts hosts of angels singing joyous hymns, shepherds who come to worship the light in the cave and a star guiding the three wise men who traveled from the Far East to glorify the Holy Infant and offer precious gifts. The icon is inspired by the liturgy and reflects the biblical account, yet also includes elements handed down by tradition.

Nativity is celebrated on a fixed date (December 25) in the Orthodox Churches (those following the old calendar still celebrate it on that date, although they reckon it as falling 13 days later). It is one of the most important feasts in the calendar after the Great Feasts of Pascha and Pentecost. The dates of other fixed feasts (Annunciation, for example) are established in relation to it.

The Nativity of the Lord is to be understood as a spiritual symbol too, because Jesus must be born in the soul of each human being, a mystery which will determine an ontological change in those who accept Christ as Lord and Savior. His birth is the premise of all his redeeming work, through which human persons can attain godlikeness (Greek *theosis* or deification).

SEE ALSO: Deification; Incarnation (of the Logos); Nativity of the Theotokos; Theotokos, the Blessed Virgin

References and Suggested Readings

McKinion, S. A. (2000) *Words, Imagery, and the Mystery of Christ*. Leiden: Brill.
McGuckin, J. A. (2004) *St. Cyril of Alexandria: The Christological Controversy*. Crestwood, NY: St. Vladimir's Seminary Press.
Macleod, D. (ed.) (1998) *The Person of Christ*. Westmont, IL: InterVarsity Press.
O'Collins, G. (2002) *Incarnation*. London: Continuum.

Nativity of the Theotokos

JEFFREY B. PETTIS

The Orthodox ecclesiastical year is marked by the Twelve Great Feasts which commemorate the saving events of the life of Jesus Christ. Most of these are fixed calendar days. The Nativity of the Theotokos is the first of the Twelve Great Feasts. In this way the birthday of the Blessed Virgin Mary is celebrated as being that event in human history which makes possible all of the other Great Feasts of the year. The Nativity of the Theotokos is attested in two sermons by the theologian and hymn writer St. Andrew of Crete (ca. 660–740). In Byzantine and Latin liturgical tradition it is celebrated on September 8, the reason for the selection of this date being uncertain (the feast falls on May 1 for some Oriental Orthodox traditions). The liturgical title of the feast always associates the birth of Mary with her role as *Theotokos*, "Birthgiver of God," to show the theological significance of the event as the turning point of salvation history in the coming in the flesh of the Divine Word, the Son of God, through Mary the Virgin. The liturgical troparion of the Nativity of the Theotokos proclaims: "Your birth, O Virgin Mother of God, announces the joy of the whole world, for from you has come forth and shines out the Sun of Justice, Christ our God." The icon of the nativity of the Mother of God shows Anna the mother of Mary sitting upright in an inclined bed, as Joachim her husband looks down upon her from inside the window of his house. In the bottom right of the icon a midwife reposes with the infant Mary resting in her lap.

SEE ALSO: Nativity of the Lord; Theotokos, the Blessed Virgin

Nestorianism

TENNY THOMAS

The doctrine that emerged from the christological controversies of the 5th century, ascribed to Nestorius of Constantinople, that there were two separate persons in Christ, one human and one divine: the man Jesus and the divine Logos. Nestorianism grew out of the Christology developed at the school of Antioch by Diodore of Tarsus (d. before 394) and Theodore of Mopsuestia (ca. 350–428). Nestorius himself, arguably, did not actually teach a two separate person Christology as much as he was "heard" to teach one by the Alexandrian theologians. He himself was under the impression that he was representing the traditional Christology of Syria as exemplified in Diodore's and Theodore's Christologies, which stressed the need to preserve the distinct integrity of the two natures (divine and human) in Christ. One of the critical issues of the era was the lack of a distinct terminology for "Person," which was to be worked out in this dispute for the benefit of the wider church, introducing technical terms into the Christian theological vocabulary such as *persona*, *prosopon*, *hypostasis*, and *physis*.

Diodore and Theodore followed a tradition of historical exegesis very different from the allegorical tradition of the School of Alexandria. Diodore presented Christ as subsisting in two natures, human and divine. The images of temple and priest were central to this school's Christology. In the womb of Mary, the Logos had fashioned a temple for himself, in which he dwelt. This temple, the man Jesus, was the subject reference of Christ's human experiences of suffering. The full divinity of the Logos, he thought, was thus protected from any hint of diminishment. This idea was first developed by the Syrians against the heresies of Arius and Apollinaris. In refuting the christological monism that was Apollinarism, Diodore leaned heavily towards an opposing emphasis that at the time of the incarnation and after it, the divine and human natures of Jesus Christ were distinctly separate to such an extent that there was never an admixture or a union possible. This was meant to stress that the natures, created and uncreated, could not be confused, but it tended to underplay the sense in which the two natures dynamically interacted in the Lord's incarnation, and left unsaid in what medium they interacted.

Diodore prepared the way for the work of his student Theodore, who taught that there were two clearly defined natures of Christ: the assumed Man, perfect and complete in his humanity, and the Logos, the Son, true God of true God and consubstantial, complete, and perfect in his divinity. These two natures (*physeis*) were united by God in grace in one person (*prosopon*). The unity did not produce a "mixture" of the two natures but an equality in which each was left whole and intact. The older Syrian scheme of using the "Assumed Man" to refer to the human nature, here starts to be mixed with a newer attempt to conceive of the "person as a medium of interaction." This scheme has been known in shorthand as "Two Sons" Christology. Physis in the older sense meant not necessarily a nature (human or divine) as such, but also a concrete representation of something. The terminology was thus set on a course that was to cause much confusion as it negotiated the new theological waters of distinction of natures and singleness of personhood.

Theodore, horrified by the concept of "confusion" and "mixture that destroyed integrity," taught that the human and divine natures of Christ were so separate that there was only correspondence (*synapheia*) between them, but not union. In developing his ideas he wrote that the Man Jesus was born of the Virgin Mary completely naturally and with all faults of men, and that God the Word (Logos), having foreknown the Man's triumph over sin, chose to redeem the human race through him by becoming united with him through grace (*kata charin*) from the time of his conception. Because of his triumph over sin, the Man Jesus was made worthy of being called Son of God at the time of the theophany. Then, after his complete triumph over sin during his Passion, he was united even more closely with the Divine Logos, becoming God's medium for the salvation of humankind. Theodore also stressed the theological significance of history as a progressive enactment of God's purpose and thereby justified theologically the Antiochene exegetical methods.

Based on these ideas, Theodore was one of the first to be opposed to the use of theological language that strictly applies to God, being affirmed as a description of things that apply to the human life of Jesus Christ. Thus, he was passionately opposed to the terms "God was crucified," "God suffered," or "God was born," because, he believed, only the Man Jesus was born and God dwelt in the Man Jesus. God could not die, only the human could die, and so on. For this reason, Theodore called Jesus the *Theophoros* (Bearer of God). Syrian thought after him referred commonly to the idea of "Two Sons," the divine Son of God and the human Son of Man. The idea of Jesus as High Priest was also used as a way of connoting how the human realities were "lifted up" so as to become redemptively significant.

The early 5th century it seemed to many Alexandrian thinkers, especially St. Cyril of Alexandria, that this was not so much a legitimate traditional way of Syrian theologians speaking about the diversity of the natures, as rather a novel form of teaching that a simple man, Jesus (Son of Man or Son of God understood merely honorifically) was associated in the work of salvation along with the Logos (Son of God). If there are two Sons, Cyril thought, there must be two subject centers in Christ: and who then is the human son? Cyril castigated the theological language of two persons in Christ as a betrayal of the fundamental belief in the union of Godhead and humanity in the single Christ: a union which was not a confusion of

natures, but a dynamic coming together in the crucible of one single divine person (the Logos) who was the personal subject of both natures, and who, in that single personhood, united them both in a mystically dynamic synthesis. For Cyril, therefore, the Eternal Word was actually Jesus of Nazareth. Jesus' body was thus the body of God; and therefore statements like "the Sufferings of God" were not only admissible but expressed exactly what the incarnation achieved, the union (*henosis*) of God and humanity in the single person of the God-Man.

Nestorius first came to Cyril's attention because he was vehemently opposed to a term used in Alexandrian theology: *Theotokos* (Mary as the Birth-Giver of God). In contrast, Nestorius argued, Mary is not *Theotokos* because she gave birth only to the Man Jesus. Once again, and in less than careful language, he probably meant to say Mary gave birth only to Jesus' humanity, not his divinity (which has no earthly origination), but his language sounded to many ears as if Mary simply gave birth to an ordinary man, who was thereafter, somehow, "assumed" by a divine force (the old psilanthropist heresy of Paul of Samosata). Nestorius and Cyril engaged in a fierce controversy in the years leading up to the Council of Ephesus in 431 (the Third Ecumenical Council) and at that council Nestorius was condemned as a heretic who taught that two persons coexisted in Christ, and he was deposed amid a great scandal that involved all the great sees of Christendom, and which would run on in the agendas of the next three international synods (Ephesus 449, Chalcedon 451, Constantinople 553). In 435 Emperor Theodosius II ordered his writings to be burned (only a few survived). In his post-conciliar writings Nestorius condemned the heresy that had been attributed to him – the extreme view that the human Jesus and divine Christ were two different persons. For Nestorius himself, salvation required both the human and divine natures of Christ to be complete, to guarantee the integrity of the incarnation and to protect the divine Logos from what he most feared (and paradoxically what Cyril wanted to affirm by means of the theory of hypostatic union), namely the blasphemous assertion that God could suffer pain or weakness. Nestorius' Christology asserted that both natures were discrete and continued in the incarnation. "Two natures after the incarnation" was elevated in Syria as a refutation of "Union" language. He asserted sometimes that the natures were separate centers of operation (*prosopa*), a word that could hold this meaning, but also suggested "person" understood as a psychic subject (which caused the confusion). At other times, however, he went further (especially in his post-Ephesine book the *Tome of Heracleides* – first translated erroneously as the *Bazaar*), that a correlation or conjunction between the divine and human was effected in the "Prosopon of Union," which he designated by "common terms" and titles such as Christ, or Lord. In short, for Nestorius, purely human activities (eating, drinking) were to be designated by human titles (Jesus, Son of Man, and so on) and divine acts were to be attributed to the Logos, or Son of God, and "mixed activities" could be attributed to a "Prosopon of Union" (Christ, or Lord). The seeking after a more satisfactory concept of the christological term of association/union is marked in this late writing of the *Tome of Heracleides*. It was only discovered in the early 20th century in Syriac, and has caused much scholarly revision of what Nestorius actually held and taught as opposed to what he was heard as saying and teaching at the time.

Diodore and Theodore were considered "orthodox" during their lifetimes, indeed as normative for much of Syrian theological thought, but both of them came under posthumous suspicion during the christological controversies of the 5th century as the two who had sown the seeds for Nestorian heresy. The writings of both were also to be subsequently condemned, by virtue of their association with Nestorius. The condemnation of Nestorius in 431 was the beginning of a sustained attack on the early Syrian Christology across the next two centuries in the ecumenical synodical process. The great controversies that then resulted led to major disruptions in the life of the Eastern Churches that have still not been resolved. The strongly pro-Cyrilline Christology of Ephesus 431, Ephesus 449, and Constantinople 553 is held in some tension by the doctrine of the "two unconfused natures" of Chalcedon 451, where the diphysite language of Rome and Syria was affirmed alongside the union language of Cyril (thus "Two natures after the Union"). It is for this reason, perhaps, that Chalcedon proved to be so divisive in the later history of so many Eastern Churches.

SEE ALSO: Assyrian Apostolic Church of the East; Council of Ephesus (431); St. Cyril of Alexandria (ca. 378–444); Syrian Orthodox Churches; Theotokos, the Blessed Virgin

References and Suggested Readings

Abramowski, L. and Goodman, A. E. (1972) *A Nestorian Collection of Christological Texts*. Cambridge: Cambridge University Press.

Bethune-Baker, J. F. (1908) *Nestorius and His Teaching*. Cambridge: Cambridge University Press.

Brock, S. P. (1992) *Studies in Syriac Christianity: History, Literature and Theology*. Aldershot: Variorum.

Clayton, P. B. (2007) *The Christology of Theodoret of Cyrus: Antiochene Christology from the Council of Ephesus (431) to the Council of Chalcedon (451)*. Oxford Early Christian Studies. Oxford: Oxford University Press.

Driver, G. R. and Hodgson, L. (eds.) (1925) *Nestorius: The Bazaar of Heraclides*. Eugene: Wipf and Stock.

Greer, R. A. (1966) "The Antiochene Christology of Diodore of Tarsus," *Journal of Theological Studies* 17, 2: 327–41.

McGuckin, J. A. (2004a) "Nestorianism," in *The Westminster Handbook to Patristics Theology*. London: Westminster/John Knox Press.

McGuckin, J. A. (2004b) *St. Cyril of Alexandria: The Christological Controversy: Its History, Theology and Texts*. Crestwood, NY: St. Vladimir's Seminary Press.

McLeod, F. G. (1999) *The Image of God in the Antiochene Tradition*. Washington, DC: Catholic University of America Press.

McLeod, F. G. (2005) *The Roles of Christ's Humanity in Salvation: Insights from Theodore of Mopsuestia*. Washington, DC: Catholic University of America Press.

McLeod, F. G. (ed.) (2008) *Theodore of Mopsuestia*. Early Church Fathers. New York: Routledge.

Norris, R. A. (1963) *Manhood and Christ: A Study in the Christology of Theodore of Mopsuestia*. Oxford: Clarendon Press.

Neumes *see* Music (Sacred)

New Martyrs

THOMAS KITSON

Orthodoxy calls those who died witnessing to their faith in the eras following Constantine's Edict of Milan (313) the "New Martyrs." The title was first used for the victims of heretical rulers during the Byzantine Iconoclastic controversies that preceded the Triumph of Orthodoxy in 843. While there was no systematic persecution during the Ottoman period, Christians were often punished for activities that directly threatened the Islamic faith. New Martyrs of the Turkish Yoke (commemorated on the third Sunday after Pentecost) suffered for openly preaching Christianity, for converting others (or reverting to the faith after adopting Islam), and for causing disturbances by promoting Christian revival (which, beginning with the 19th-century liberation movements, often carried ethnic and national overtones). There were numbers of New Martyrs in China and Japan also. The actively atheist Soviet government encouraged varying degrees of organized church persecution after the 1917 Russian Revolution, involving many thousands of martyrs. In 1981 the Russian Orthodox Church Outside of Russia recognized many Soviet victims, hierarchs, clergy, monks, and laity (including Tsar Nicholas II and his family) as New Martyrs and commemorates them on January 25, the date of Metropolitan Vladimir of Kiev's martyrdom in 1918. In recent years the Moscow patriarchate has also systematically extended the lists of the New Martyrs of Russia. Many other New Martyrs suffered under the Nazis (including Mother Maria Skobtsova) and their allies (the Serbian New Martyrs are commemorated on June 15), as well as subsequently under the violently repressive communist regimes in Romania, Bulgaria, Albania, and other parts of the Soviet Eastern bloc.

SEE ALSO: Albania, Orthodox Church of; Bulgaria, Patriarchal Orthodox Church of; Contemporary Orthodox Theology; Romania, Patriarchal Orthodox Church of; Russia, Patriarchal Orthodox Church of; St. Elizaveta Feodorovna (1864–1918); Serbia, Patriarchal Orthodox Church of

References and Suggested Readings

Cavarnos, C. (1992) *The Significance of the New Martyrs*. Etna, CA: Center for Traditionalist Orthodox Studies.

Papadopoulos, L. J. and Lizardos, G. (1985) *New Martyrs of the Turkish Yoke*. Seattle: St. Nektarios Press.

Polsky, M. (1979) *The New Martyrs of Russia*. Munich: St. Job of Pochaev Press.

Newly Revealed Saints

JOHN A. MCGUCKIN

The title of "Newly revealed" (*Neophaneis*) refers to those saints of the Orthodox Church whose relics have been discovered in relatively recent times, often after years of being lost or forgotten, and whose cult has accordingly revived. From the earliest times the concept of the "revelation of a saint" following a significant and wondrous event (*thauma*) or a dream in which the saint appears to an individual have been a commonly known part of the cult of saints in the Eastern Church. So it was that in the 5th century St. Cyril of Alexandria discovered the relics of Sts. Cyrus and John, Empress Eudoxia discovered the relics of St. Stephen the Protomartyr in Jerusalem, and the priest Nicholas Calligraphos discovered the relics of Sts. Andronikos and Junia at Constantinople. The cult of St. Phanourios of Rhodes developed in 1500 after an icon was discovered in a hidden chapel; and in 1798 a child's visions led to the discovery of the relics of the Megara martyrs, whose cult became especially popular after the Greek War of Independence. The relics of St. Patapios and companions were discovered in a cave church at Geraneia in 1904 and became a focus of much pilgrimage. The New Martyr Ephraim (martyred in the 15th century) was found after a series of visions by a Greek nun in 1950 at Nea Makri. Unknown saints' relics have also been discovered in the monasteries, such as St. Eudokimos found at Vatopedi in 1841, St. Basil of Akarnania found in 1923, and the relics found after a monk's grave started one day to emit a fountain of water at Neamt in Romania, after the fall of the communist regime there (St. Paisy Velichovsky's monastery).

SEE ALSO: Megalomartyr Saints; Military Saints; Myrobletes Saints; Unmercenary Saints

References and Suggested Readings

Anon. (1983) *Hagios Ephraim*. Nea Makri: n.p.

Gerasimos of Mikrayiannitis (1990) *Hosios Patapios*. Loutraki: n.p.

Mourtzoukou, D. (1984) *Ton en Megarois Athlesanton Neophanon Martyron*. Megara: n.p.

Nikephoros Blemmydes (1197–1272) *see* Lyons, Council of (1274)

Niptic Books (*Paterika*)

JOHN A. MCGUCKIN

This extensive corpus of monastic literature, in several different "sets" and collations, gains its collective title from the Greek word *nipsis* meaning "sobriety," a concept that was elevated to prominence in Orthodox thought after the 4th-century fathers applied the word and its cognate *sophrosyne* ("wise temperance") to be central terms of monastic spirituality, signifying the sober vigilance the ascetic ought to cultivate in the life of attentiveness to God. The Niptic fathers are thus the large assembly of Orthodox ascetical authors who wrote about the spiritual life. Over the course of the centuries many various editors collated the different ascetical writers into compendia and florilegia for ready access by monks to important formative literature. The collections are also known as *Paterika*, a word signifying "books of the (monastic) fathers." The single form, *Paterikon*, often simply means a monastery's special collation of primary monastic literature designed for exercises of spiritual reading and guidance. The Niptic books and *Paterika*, therefore, do not exhaust the monastic writings of the Eastern Church, which far exceed them in the amount of literature extant, but they do represent some of the most important collections of those texts which were felt to be standard and exemplary.

The first instances of Niptic books collected into *Paterika* were popularized in the 4th century as the monastic movement took shape. First at this early stage was the *Apophthegmata Patrum*, the sayings and deeds of the desert fathers, which were collated at Scete and other monastic centers, and from there passed on to have a wide readership in Byzantium. Latin translations were also made at a very early date. The 4th-century Byzantine writer Palladius, in his *Lausiac History* (stories of the monks sponsored by the Constantinopolitan aristocrat Lausos) produced an early exemplar that caused a literary sensation in its day (not only among ascetical readers) in the imperial capital, which was added to with the *History of the Monks in Egypt*, known often as the *Egyptian Paterikon*. The genre was very popular in classical Byzantine times. Cyril of Scythopolis produced a version outlining the deeds and miracles of the Palestinian monks in the 5th century and the *Evergetinon*, originating at the large Constantinopolitan monastery of Theotokos Evergetes, amounted to a large multi-volume *Paterikon* collection that had a massive distribution and subsequently formed generations of Orthodox in the "tales and deeds of the saints." To this day many Orthodox, not connected otherwise with the monastic movement, can recount stories and legends derived from this literature, which have become part of the folk memories of the different Orthodox countries. The *Philokalia* is another example of *Paterikon*, assembled in the 18th century from a wide body of patristic and later medieval monastic writings, and is perhaps the one most widely known today; but there were several others before it that had an influence on early Russian monasticism, and which continued to be produced in the later history of the Russian Church, such as the *Kiev Caves Paterikon* (13th century) associated with St. Mark of Pechersky Lavra, the *Skete Paterikon* (which is an old Slavonic version of the Egyptian desert literature), the *Valaam Paterikon*, the 16th-century *Volokolamsk Paterikon*, and others, including Romanian and Serbian *Paterika* collections.

SEE ALSO: Asceticism; Desert Fathers and Mothers; Elder (Starets); Monasticism; *Philokalia*; St. Paisy Velichovsky (1722–1794)

References and Suggested Readings

Harmless, W. (2004) *Desert Christians: An Introduction to the Literature of Early Monasticism*. Oxford: Oxford University Press.

Nissiotis, Nikos (1925–1986) *see* Contemporary Orthodox Theology; Ecumenism

Non-Possessors (Nil Sorskii)

KONSTANTIN GAVRILKIN

Monks from a number of Russian northern monasteries, associated with Nil Sorskii (1433–1508), who based his monastic rule on early Christian writers and advocated a moderate ascetic life in small communities, centered on contemplative prayer, discernment, and studying Scripture, with a focus on inner transformation of mind and heart. Nil criticized "external" asceticism and extensive decoration of churches, and argued that monastic landownership, despite its application for social welfare, corrupted the church. At the Moscow church council of 1503 he and his followers questioned the legitimacy of monastic estates, covering one third of Muscovy's territory at the time, and argued for their transfer to the poor. Eventually, they were defeated by their opponents the Possessors, led by Joseph of Volotsk.

SEE ALSO: Hesychasm; Monasticism; Possessors (Joseph of Volotsk); Russia, Patriarchal Orthodox Church of

References and Suggested Readings

Nil Sorskii (2008) *The Authentic Writings*, ed. And trans. D. Goldfrank. Kalamazoo: Cistercian Publications

Pliguzov, A. I. (2002) *Polemika v russkoi tserkvi pervoi treti XVI stoletiia*. Moscow: Indrik.

O

Ode

DIMITRI CONOMOS

A liturgical composition, originally attached to the nine biblical canticles sung at Matins and related to these by means of corresponding poetic allusion or textual quotation. Each ode consists of an initial model troparion, the *heirmos*, followed by three, four, or more troparia that are exact metrical reproductions of the *heirmos*, thereby allowing the same music to fit all troparia texts equally well. The nine *heirmoi*, however, are metrically dissimilar but united musically by the same mode and textually by references to the general theme of the occasion as well as sometimes by an acrostic.

SEE ALSO: *Heirmologion*; Music (Sacred); Orthros (Matins); Troparion

Oktoechos

DIMITRI CONOMOS

The collection of eight modes forming the compositional framework of Christian chant. Each mode comprises a restricted set of flexible melody types peculiar to it. Byzantine theorists refer to them as Modes I–IV Authentic and I–IV Plagal. While the origins of the *Oktoechos* are obscure, by the 8th century the system had become established within the

Greek liturgical orbit. St. John of Damascus (675–ca. 749) contributed significantly to the formation of the *Paraklitike* (*Oktoikh* in Russian), a liturgical book which allocates proper chants for the Office to the eight modes over a recurring cycle of eight weeks.

SEE ALSO: Liturgical Books; Music (Sacred); *Paraklitike*

References and Suggested Readings

Jeffery, P. (2001) "The Earliest Oktōēchoi: The Role of Jerusalem and Palestine in the Beginning of Modal Ordering," in P. Jeffery (ed.) *The Study of Medieval Chant, Paths and Bridges, East and West, In Honour of Kenneth Levy.* Woodbridge, UK: Boydell, pp. 147–210.

Old Believers

IRINA PAERT

Old Believers (*starovery*), also known as *staroobriadtsy* ("old ritualists"), is a generic term for the religious dissidents who split from the Russian Orthodox Church in and after the second half of the 17th century. Church reforms carried out in the 1660s under the leadership of Patriarch Nikon created a formal reason for the dissent. The changes introduced by the reformers in accordance with

The Concise Encyclopedia of Orthodox Christianity, First Edition. Edited by John Anthony McGuckin.
© 2014 John Wiley & Sons, Ltd. Published 2014 by John Wiley & Sons, Ltd.

the contemporary Greek practice (concerning primarily language and ritual forms) alienated a large number of Russian Orthodox who adhered to the traditional Russian ritual practice, including baptism by immersion, the sign of the cross made by two fingers (rather than three), the spelling of the name of Jesus with one "I" (Isus) rather than two, double rather than triple Alleluias, the clockwise (rather than anticlockwise) order of liturgical processions in church, the use of seven rather than five prosphoras for the Eucharist, to name just a few. Moreover, the violent state-advocated methods that characterized the reformist behavior stimulated intense apocalyptic sentiment. Mass self-immolations took place among dissenters and continued until religious toleration was declared in the 1760s. The important centers of Old Believers in Tsarist Russia were in the northern Trans-Volga regions, the border between Russia and the Polish Commonwealth, the Baltic provinces, Bessarabia, Moscow, the Urals, and Siberia.

According to official data, 190,944 men and women registered as Old Believers under Tsar Peter I. However, the numerical strength of the Old Believers could not be determined precisely as many of them also formally belonged to the Orthodox Church. In 1912 there were 1,807,056 Old Believers, which made less than 2.5 percent of the population in the Russian Empire. Their geographical distribution was very uneven: while some regions had a high proportion, others had a more or less homogenous Orthodox population. However, the strength of the Old Believers lay not in their numbers but rather in their literacy, their economic power, and strong communal identity. With the exception of the period of enlightened toleration between 1763 and 1814, the Imperial government did not recognize the legal rights of the Old Believers and tried to assimilate them into the Orthodox population. It was only in 1905 that they received equal legal rights with the members of the Orthodox Church. In the Soviet Union the number of Old Believers dropped because of repression, with groups emigrating to China in the 1920s–1930s, and then to Australia and America. Apart from Russia, Old Believer communities can be found in Byelorussia, Ukraine, Latvia, Lithuania, Estonia,

Poland, Romania, Bulgaria, Italy, Brazil, USA, and Canada. Following the breakdown of the Soviet Union, there has been a revival of Old Believer religious life, but its impact remains quite limited.

The main division is between the priestly (*popovtsy*) and priestless (*bespopovtsy*). The *popovtsy* Old Believers differed from the mainstream Orthodox Church only on the issues of ritual, while *bespopovtsy* justified lay ministry and had fewer sacraments than the Orthodox Church (notably, the Eucharist is absent). The Old Believers who did not wish to part with holy orders and the Eucharistic communion continued to recruit priests from the Russian Orthodox Church, who thus received the popular name "fugitive priests" (*beglopopovtsy*). Following the conversion in 1846 of the retired Bosnian bishop Amvrosii (Pappa-Georgopoli) to Old Belief, the *beglopopovtsy* founded a hierarchy independent from the Russian Orthodox Church with the center in Belaia Krinitsa (then in the Austro-Hungarian Empire). In post-Soviet Russia, this section of Old Belief declared its independence from the Belokrinitskaia Old Believer church in Romania and has its center in the Rogozhskoe cemetery in Moscow. It consists of eleven dioceses and is headed by Metropolitan Kornilii. The *beglopopovtsy* reemerged in the 1920s when two Russian Orthodox bishops converted to Old Belief and founded the Russian Old Orthodox Church with its headquarters in Novozybkovo (Briansk Oblast). At the moderate end of the movement, there has been a union effected between Old Believers and the Orthodox Church, called *Edinoverie* (United Faith), which was officially approved in 1801. The priestless Old Believers have more internal divisions than the priestly section, splitting over the issue of the Antichrist (whether this can be understood as a spiritual force or a distinct person) and over the role of sacraments. Marriage, in particular, became a subject of fierce debates among the priestless: while some advocated celibacy as the only way of salvation on the basis of radical eschatological views, others practised marriage assisted by a non-ordained minister. Most radical offshoots (*spasovtsy*, *stranniki*) preached a total break with the world (refusing to hold passports, sabotaging state campaigns, and rejecting military service). As a rule, the priestless Old Believers require their new members to be re-baptized on the grounds that their previous baptism was invalid. They also maintain strict taboos regarding food and hygiene, often keeping separate dishes for use by outsiders. Ritual prohibitions typical for all sections of the Old Believers include shaving beards (for men) and smoking tobacco.

Old Believers preserved the medieval Orthodox rite and liturgy, including the monophonic (*znamennyi*) chant that has a Byzantine origin, traditional iconography, and a fascinating book culture. Old Believers were instrumental in the revival of interest for traditional Russian icon painting both in Russia and abroad during the first half of the 20th century. Generally, the Old Believer culture is regarded as a reflection of the way of life typical for Russia before the westernization introduced by Peter the Great. Like many religious dissenters in other cultures, Old Believers were active merchants and differed from the average Russian peasants by their well-organized and sustainable agricultural economy. Among them, both the priestly and priestless, the role of the laity was, and remained, very developed. Laymen interpreted the scripture and participated in interconfessional debates. Women as a rule had a high status among the Old Believers both in everyday and in religious life. It was not unusual for women to carry out the roles of ministers among the priestless Old Believers.

SEE ALSO: Russia, Patriarchal Orthodox Church of

References and Suggested Readings

Crummey, R. (1970) *The Old Believers and the World of Antichrist: The Vyg Community and the Russian State 1694–1855*. Madison: University of Wisconsin Press.

Iukhimenko, E. I. (2002) *Vygovskaia staroobriadcheskaia pustyn'. Dukhovnaia zhizn' i literatura*, vols. 1–2. Moscow.

Michels, G. (1999) *At War with the Church: Religious Dissent in Seventeenth-Century Russia*. Stanford: Stanford University Press.

Paert, I. (2003) *Old Believers, Religious Dissent and Gender in Russia, 1760–1850*. Manchester: Manchester University Press.

Robson, R. (1996) *Old Believers in Modern Russia*. DeKalb: Northern Illinois University Press.

Rogers, D. (2009) *The Old Faith and the Russian Land: A Historical Ethnography of Ethics in the Urals*. Ithaca: Cornell University Press.

Old Testament

EUGEN J. PENTIUC

Two Testaments, One Bible

The Jewish Bible, also known as Tanakh or Hebrew Scriptures, is for the Orthodox Church the first part of the Christian Bible or Holy Scripture. It is called by Christians the Old Testament in a precise theological balance to the affirmation of the New Testament. These terms were first signaled by Origen of Alexandria in the 3rd century and were developed into a theory of interpretation using Hellenistic hermeneutics where typology was used to read the Old Testament in the light of the New (Kannengiesser 2006). The early church's struggle with Marcion of Pontus over the Old Testament's place and role besides the emerging Christian scriptures occupied most of the 2nd century. Marcion (d. 160) rejected the Old Testament as having any authority for Christians. He argued that the God of the Jews was totally different from, and inferior to, the Christian God. His radical view, one that was often echoed by Gnostic teachers, accelerated the broader Christian embrace of the Hebrew Scriptures as a whole, and most scholars agree that the defeat of Marcion greatly helped to fix the church's canon of received scriptures. Another early danger, supersessionism, discernible in the indictment of the Parable of the Wicked Tenants (Mt. 21.33–46) and supported by Paul's teaching that the coming of Christ put an end to the custodian role of the Law (Gal. 3.24–5; Rom. 10.4; cf. Heb. 8.13), led to a premature devaluation of the Old Testament among some Christian commentators. The idea that the church and its new Scripture (New Testament) superseded the old Israel and its Hebrew Scripture is attested in many early Christian writings. Even so, the church as a whole has been able to keep the two Testaments in a dialectical unity, in the main avoiding factual reductionism and supersessionism as dangers. The centrality of the Christ event in Christian tradition, not least as a key hermeneutical principle, helped in reaching this objective.

The Received Text

Although there is no clear conciliar statement on this topic, the Septuagint (*LXX*) remains the quasi-official form of the Old Testament for Eastern Orthodox Christianity. The popularity of this Greek text comes from its use by the New Testament writers and the Greek fathers. Accordingly, the Eastern Orthodox Church tends to rely on the Septuagint for its Old Testament teachings, and still uses it, at least in its Greek-language services. In recent times the wealth of Qumran findings and modern studies on the Dead Sea Scrolls has suggested the volatility of issues concerning the textual transmission of scripture in both Hebrew and Greek. Given this ethos of scholarly discovery, modern biblical scholars within the Eastern Orthodox tradition are now having to take a closer look at the long-neglected Hebrew text in conjunction with their traditional approach to the Greek *LXX*. Since the Eastern Orthodox tradition relies on the concept of the *phronema* or "mind" of the fathers in establishing a sense of interpretation of texts, rather than appealing to a fossilized patristic corpus of authorities (see Stylianopoulos 2006), it follows that Orthodox biblical scholars in this generation also have the noble duty of redeeming those Semitic nuances that may have been missed by those fathers who worked exclusively with the Greek text (see Pentiuc 2005).

Canon

According to the Roman Catholic Church following the Council of Trent (1545–6), the Old Testament contains forty-six canonical books (thirty-nine of the Jewish Bible and the seven "deuterocanonicals" of the Septuagint). Protestants, today, accept the same thirty-nine canonical books as the Jews. While accepting all thirty-nine books of the Jewish canon, the Orthodox have a peculiar view in relation to the Septuagintal additions. These are not considered "canonical" or "deuterocanonical" – to use the Roman Catholic terminology – but neither are they listed as "apocrypha" according to the Protestant terminology. On the contrary, since the time of St. Athanasius' 39th *Festal Letter* (367) they have been designated as the Anaginoskomena, the books that are "readable" (for the purposes of piety). This intricate and more relaxed view on canonicity aligns Eastern Orthodoxy closely with the position of prerabbinic Judaism, while it also recalls the situation of the historical era when the emerging church first used these Septuagintal additions as important proof-text material for their preaching of the Messiahship of Jesus.

Inspiration

The Eastern Orthodox view on the inspiration of the Old Testament text is perfectly exemplified in the writings of St. John Chrysostom, who applies the Greek word *synkatabasis* ("condescension") (see Chrysostom's *Homilies on Genesis*, PG 53.29A; 34B; 44A). This key term seeks to define God's ability and willingness to adjust himself to the *astheneia* or "weakness" (defectibility) of the human author, so that the scripture might be eventually acknowledged and praised for its *akribeia* (exactness, precision) being essentially God's word. A modern recast of such a balanced view might creatively employ two biblical paradigms. The first we can suggest as humanity's creation by God's breathing into the dust which thereby became a "living breath" (Gen. 2.7), and this understood as an analogy of how the human expressions of scripture are continuously infused by God's Spirit and thereby turned into a "living breath" of God for the church. The second paradigm, the incarnation of the preexistent Logos again accomplished through God's Spirit (Lk. 1.35), can point to the comprehension of the scripture as a progressive enfleshing of God's eternal word. These two paradigms keep both communicative directions (from God' side to humanity and from humanity's to God) in a creative tension, as is revealed in this elaborate New Testament introductory formula: "What had been spoken by the Lord through the prophet" (Mt. 1.22; 2.15).

Byzantine Modes of Interpretation

There have been many various ways that the Eastern Orthodox have sought through history to assimilate, in a conscious manner, the Old Testament as scripture.

Classic among them are the Byzantine modes of reception and interpretation which can be briefly summarized as follows. In the first place stand the patristic works (commentaries, biblical interpretations found in various writings, and *catenae* or florilegia of verse comments preserved in Greek, Syriac, and Coptic). What makes the patristic expositions of scripture valuable even in a postmodern world dominated by a hermeneutic of suspicion is the church fathers' persistent search for the *skopos*, the "goal" of the biblical text, its moral sense allied with a desire to apply an immediate pastoral application for it. Patristic exegesis with its overarching christological orientation and its typological searching moves from plain historical meanings (the literal sense) through allegorical reading, to search out higher moral and mystical senses. In the second place, Orthodoxy approaches the Old Testament through the major route of liturgy (hymnody, lectionaries, and liturgical symbolism as reflected in various Byzantine "rubrics"). The Old Testament texts and themes found so extensively in the Byzantine hymns show a very high degree of exegetical freedom within a dynamic liturgical setting. In the third place, Orthodoxy approaches and interprets the Old Testament through iconography (frescoes, icons, the arts of illumination), a process which sheds additional and sometimes invaluable light on the way the Byzantines read and understood the Old Testament in relation to the New. For example, the iconographic positioning of the ancient biblical episodes and figures in an Eastern Orthodox church can reflect the way in which specific Old Testament symbols were interpreted within the wider context of Byzantine tradition. The ascetical and spiritual tradition of Orthodoxy (Burton-Christie 1993) also determines how the Old Testament is seen within the church (monastic rules, canons, ascetical texts). Both cenobitic and individual forms of monastic spirituality are thoroughly regulated by specific scriptural readings, helping the ascetic and lay believer embark on what the fathers call the path of *theosis* or "deification." Lastly, it goes without saying that the dogmatic tradition of Orthodoxy is profoundly influenced by the Old Testament. Conciliar resolutions (creeds and decisions of local and ecumenical councils) crafted during the Byzantine period are based primarily on canonical scriptural texts, and the Byzantine modes of reception and interpretation of the Old Testament feature deeply within them (see Pentiuc 2011).

SEE ALSO: Bible; Canon (Liturgical); Christ; Church (Orthodox Ecclesiology); Judaism, Orthodoxy and

References and Suggested Readings

Breck, J. (2001) *Scripture in Tradition: The Bible and Its Interpretation in the Orthodox Church.* Crestwood, NY: St. Vladimir's Seminary Press.

Burton-Christie, D. (1993) *The Word in the Desert: Scripture and the Quest for Holiness in Early Christian Monasticism.* Oxford: Oxford University Press.

Hall, C. A. (1998) *Reading Scripture with the Church Fathers.* Downers Grove, IL: InterVarsity Press.

Heine, R. E. (2007) *Reading the Old Testament with the Ancient Church: Exploring the Formation of Early Christian Thought.* Grand Rapids, MI: Baker.

Kannengiesser, C. (2006) *Handbook of Patristic Exegesis.* Boston: Brill.

Magdalino, P. et al. (eds.) (2009) "The Old Testament in Byzantium," in *Dumbarton Oaks Byzantine Symposia and Colloquia.* Washington, DC: Dumbarton Oaks Research Library and Collection.

Oikonomos, E. (1992) "The Significance of the Deuterocanonical Writings in the Orthodox Church," in S. Meurer (ed.) *The Apocrypha in Ecumenical Perspective.* UBS Monograph Series 6. Reading, UK: United Bible Societies, pp. 16–32.

Pentiuc, E. J. (2005) *Jesus the Messiah in the Hebrew Bible.* New York: Paulist Press.

Pentiuc, E. J. (2011) *The Old Testament in Eastern Orthodox Tradition.* Oxford: Oxford University Press.

Stylianopoulos, T. G. (ed.) (2006) *Sacred Text and Interpretation: Perspectives in Orthodox Biblical Studies. Papers in Honor of Professor Savas Agourides.* Brookline, MA: Holy Cross Orthodox Press.

Sundberg, A. C. (1964) "The Old Testament in the Early Church," *Harvard Theological Review* 20: 205–26.

Optina

THOMAS KITSON

The Optina Hermitage (near Kaluga) promoted hesychast spirituality in 19th-century Russia, inspired by Sts. Paisy Velichkovsky and Seraphim of Sarov. Metropolitan

Plate 44   Liturgical procession at Optina Hermitage. RIA Novosti/Topfoto.

Plate 45   Optina Hermitage recently restored. RIA Novosti/Topfoto.

Filaret Drozdov supported Abbot Moses' ambitious publishing program there of Russian translations from patristic works. The monastery's reputation, however, rested, until its closure in 1923, on its many renowned elders (*startsy*) – especially Sts. Leonid, Macarius, and Ambrose – whose teachings on humility and obedience attracted several secular intellectuals, including Turgenev, Gogol, Dostoevsky, Leontyev, and others. The elders also filled a deeply felt spiritual need for the crowds of pilgrims who traveled to Optina to confess and receive their blessing. The Optina saints are commemorated on October 10.

SEE ALSO: Elder (Starets); Hesychasm; *Philokalia*; St. Filaret (Philaret) Drozdov (1782–1867); St. Paisy Velichovsky (1722–1794); St. Seraphim of Sarov (1759–1833)

References and Suggested Readings

Dunlop, J. (1972) *Staretz Amvrosy*. London: Mowbray.
Meletios of Nikopolis (1987) *Starets Varsanouphios*, 2 vols. Preveza: n.p.
Sederholm, C. (1990) *Elder Leonid of Optina*. Platina, CA: St. Herman of Alaska Press.
Sederholm, C. (1994) *Elder Antony of Optina*. Platina, CA: St. Herman of Alaska Press.

Ordination

JEFFREY B. PETTIS

The Orthodox Church looks upon ordination (derived from the Latin term for registering clerics in the official lists of the church), which it designates using the biblical term as the "laying on of hands" (*cheirotonia*), as the sacramental continuation of the setting apart of leaders for the Christian community. Ordination is the regular transmission through the ages of the church of the charism of priesthood, as derived from the apostolic succession the church protects within itself. The Book of Numbers 27.15–23 speaks of the setting apart of Joshua by the Lord to be a leader and shepherd of the congregation. Joshua is one who is "in the Spirit" (18), and Moses places him before the priest and the congregation, lays hands on him, and gives him a charge according to divine command (22–3; cf. Deut. 34.9). In the gospels Jesus himself sets apart for ministry the twelve apostles (Mt. 10.1–5; Mk. 3.13–19; Lk. 6.12–16). He also commissions the Seventy to do the work of evangelizing (Lk. 10.1). In Acts 14.23 the Apostle Paul lays hands (*cheirotonēsantes*) on designated church elders (*presbyterous*). The laying on of hands is the transmission of the sacred gift of the Spirit, confirming the gift given in Chrismation, for the special role of sanctifying, teaching, healing, and witnessing that constitutes the priestly service in the church. The Apostle Paul also refers to the bishop (*episkopos*) who tends the church of God like a shepherd (Acts 20.28; cf. Ignatius, *Eph.* 1.3; 2.1f.; 3.2; 4.1; 5.1f.). The *Didache* refers to the electing of bishops and deacons "who are worthy of the Lord, gentle men who are not fond of money, who are true (*alētheis*) and approved" (*Didache* 15). The earliest evidence for the church's formal service of ordination is found in the *Apostolic Tradition of Hippolytus* (ca. 215):

> He who is ordained as a bishop, being chosen by all the people, must be irreproachable. When his name is announced and approved, the people will gather on the Lord's day with the council of elders and the bishops who are present. With the assent of all, the bishops will place their hands upon him, with the council of elders standing by, quietly. Everyone will keep silent, praying in their hearts for the descent of the Spirit. After this, one of the bishops present, at the request of all, shall lay his hand upon him who is being ordained bishop, and shall pray. (*Apostolic Tradition* 2.1–5)

The Orthodox Church recognizes the transmission of the priesthood in three degrees, designated "major orders." These are bishop, presbyter, and deacon. The minor orders today include the subdeacon and readers (formerly there was a larger range of offices), who receive not the laying on of hands for admission into the priesthood but a lesser blessing (*cheirothesia*) to perform their special ministry. At an ordination a candidate is brought to the Iconostasis by fellow members of his rank (deacons by deacons, presbyters by deacons and presbyters) for "passing on" into the hands of ordained clergy of the rank to which he is being inducted. All priestly ordinations take place at the Eucharist, and only one ordination to any given rank can be celebrated at a single liturgy. The ordination of a bishop precedes the scripture reading and the

Eucharistic Anaphora, in this way recognizing him as the expounder of the faith and celebrant of the mysteries. The candidate confesses his Orthodoxy and recites the creed, declares his fidelity to the canons and the ecumenical councils, vows to preserve the peace of the church and always to teach the people faithfully. Following the Trisagion chant the candidate is brought before the holy table and the book of the gospels is opened and placed upon his head. The presiding bishop offers a prayer and makes three crosses in the name of the Holy Trinity over the head of the initiate. The other bishops lay their hands upon his head while the consecratory prayers are said. Once ordained, he receives the *Sakkos* and other episcopal vestments. The presiding bishop places upon him the episcopal encolpion, the jeweled icon of Christ or the Mother of God which he will always wear upon his breast, the monastic mantle, the Komboskini rosary, and the pastoral staff.

The ordination of a presbyter directly follows the Eucharistic Great Entrance and thus again takes place before the Anaphora to show the presbyter's central office as celebrant of the mysteries. During the ordination the candidate is taken from the deacons by presbyters and led around the altar three times as he kisses the four corners, and reverences the ordaining bishop. He kneels at the altar bending both knees and places his head upon the holy table as the bishop lays hands on his head, to recite the consecratory prayer. He is then invested before the people with the priest's epitrachelion, zone (liturgical belt), and phelonion. He is also given the service book to guide his future ministry.

The ordination of deacons, whose chief service is to read the Holy Gospel and assist at the divine liturgy and the distribution of the Holy Gifts, comes after the consecration of the gifts and prior to Holy Communion, to symbolize that his is the office of assistance (not consecration). As the choir sings the deacon is led three times around the altar, the four corners of which he kisses, reverencing the bishop. Following his ordination, which takes place with a different prayer of consecration while he kneels at the altar on one knee, he receives the liturgical fan (rhipidion) as a symbol of his office.

Ordination to minor orders is performed by a bishop or monastic higumen who has received the blessing to do this, outside the sanctuary and at any communal worship service apart from the Eucharist. In the Orthodox Church all ordinations symbolically follow the consent given by the congregation and the clergy who say *Axios* when the candidate is presented by the bishop ("He is worthy to be ordained"). Because the nature of ordination is indelible, it can occur to the same rank only once and may never be repeated.

SEE ALSO: Anagnostes (Reader); Deacon; Deaconess; Episcopacy; Epitrachelion; Phelonion; Priesthood; Rhipidion (Fan)

References and Suggested Readings

Langford-James, R. (ed.) (1975) *A Dictionary of the Eastern Orthodox Church*. New York: Burt Franklin.

Litsas, F. (1984) *A Companion to the Greek Orthodox Church*. New York: Greek Orthodox Archdiocese.

Parry, K. et al. (eds.) (1999) *The Blackwell Dictionary of Eastern Christianity*. Oxford: Blackwell.

Oriental Orthodox

PETER C. BOUTENEFF

Oriental Orthodox is the name by which several "non-Chalcedonian Churches" have come to be collectively known. This category has tended to include the Syrian Orthodox Patriarchate of Antioch and All the East, the Coptic Orthodox Patriarchate of Alexandria, the Ethiopian Orthodox Tewahedo Church, the Eritrean Orthodox Tewahedo Church, the Armenian Apostolic Church, and the Malankara Orthodox Syrian Church.

Each of these churches has traditionally rejected the authority of what the Eastern Orthodox Church considers its Fourth Ecumenical Council, held in Chalcedon in the year 451. They recognize only three ecumenical councils: Nicea (325), Constantinople (381), and Ephesus (431). Although historical and political factors cannot be ignored, neither can the role of the *Tome* of Pope Leo I and its theologically controversial language. The chief theological rationale for their rejection of Chalcedon rests in the council's statement that Jesus Christ was known "in two natures." This statement was interpreted by the non-Chalcedonians as leading inexorably to a Nestorian

Plate 46 A Coptic monk in the Monastery of St. Antony, Egypt. Photo by John McGuckin.

Plate 47 Pope Shenouda, leader of the world's Coptic Orthodox faithful. Photo by John McGuckin.

understanding of Christ, i.e., seeing Christ as constituted by two personal subjects ("two Sons"), one divine and one human.

The non-Chalcedonian Orthodox see Chalcedon's "in two natures" language as a betrayal of the formula identified with St. Cyril of Alexandria: "One incarnate nature of God the Word" (*mia physis tou theou logou sesarkomene*), alternately rendered "One nature of the divine Word incarnate" (*mia physis tou theou logou sesarkomenou*). Their preference for one-nature formulations has long earned them the collective title of "Monophysites." However, since (as twentieth-century dialogues have affirmed) the non-Chalcedonians insist upon Christ's consubstantiality (*homoousion*) with both God the Father according to his divinity, and with us according to his humanity, that title has increasingly

been seen as misleading. Monophysitism, it is argued, best describes the radical (and bilaterally condemned) position of Eutyches the Presbyter, who rejected Christ's consubstantiality with humanity, and thus the non-Chalcedonians are sometimes called either "Henophysites" – the Greek *Hen* denoting a union rather than a radical monad – or "Miaphysites" – following the wording of the Cyrilline formula, again allowing for a union of divinity and humanity in one nature without separation, without confusion, and without change.

The title "Oriental Orthodox" arose in the context of the bilateral dialogues with the Eastern Orthodox Church, whose identity as a family or communion of autocephalous churches had been long established. The dialogues therefore played a vital role in establishing a rubric that would assemble the non-Chalcedonian churches and identify them as a coherent body. Calling these churches "Oriental" was not meant to elicit the stereotypic *Orientalism* of which Edward Said has written, but rather deliberately to evince a title that was essentially indistinguishable from "Eastern." The name "Orthodox," which did not figure previously into the self-appellations of all the churches (e.g., the Armenian Apostolic Church), was also meant to identify a parity of legitimacy and fidelity to world Orthodoxy through the ages.

These modern dialogues between the Oriental and Eastern Orthodox churches began unofficially, as a direct result of the multilateral ecumenical encounters through the World Council of Churches. Four unofficial meetings held from 1964 to 1971 were followed by a series of official dialogues constituted by church-appointed delegates from 1985 to 1993. These covered theological as well as pastoral issues, which in turn have been applied in local pastoral agreements, notably in the Middle East and in Egypt. While their theological conclusions were at points unequivocal – "both families have always loyally maintained the same authentic Orthodox Christological faith, and the unbroken continuity of the apostolic tradition" (Chambésy, 1990) – the dialogue statements have yet to be fully received or acted upon among the Eastern and Oriental churches in the wider sense.

SEE ALSO: Africa, Orthodoxy in; Armenian Christianity; Council of Chalcedon (451); Council of Constantinople I (381); Council of Ephesus (431); Council of Nicea I (325); Ecumenism, Orthodoxy and; Malankara Orthodox Syrian Church; Monophysitism (including Miaphysitism); Syrian Orthodox Churches

References and Suggested Readings

Gregorios, P. (ed.) (1981) *Does Chalcedon Divide or Unite? Towards Convergence in Orthodox Christology.* Geneva: World Council of Churches.
Ware, T. (1993) *The Orthodox Church.* London: Penguin.

Original Sin

M. C. STEENBERG

The term "original sin" is normally taken to indicate a specific view on the origin of sin and its effects in the world, as read through the perspective of the Genesis account of Adam and Eve in Eden (Gen. 2–3ff.). Specifically, it reads this text as suggesting a state of original perfection in which humanity was created and from which it "fell" through transgression. This fall affected the nature of humanity, such that it was to some degree imbued with sin, thereafter inherited by future generations. This condition of in-built sin (described in certain Latin authors as *concupiscence*, a process of being bound up in errant desire) is in moderate writers of the early Latin Church taken to indicate a general propensity or inclination toward error, while in more extreme exponents it has been developed into doctrines (particularly in post-Reformation western theology) of "total depravity" or an inheritance of the guilt of Adam's transgression.

The doctrine of original sin originates largely from St. Augustine and certain other writers of the patristic Latin West, such as Tertullian. From the outset it has been questioned by exponents of Orthodox theology. While the emphasis on the universal scope of sin is certainly consonant with Orthodox thought, notions of a perfect "pristine condition" and a fall from grace have often been seen as at variance with Orthodox anthropology – or at least as a reading of Genesis that puts excessive emphasis on a transformation of human nature that results from its first transgression. Orthodox writers have tended to emphasize the developmental nature of humanity's creation *into* perfection, rather than *as already perfected* before declining; and have resisted strongly the conceptions of inherited guilt that are often central to western expositions of original sin. As a result, there is a preference among some Orthodox writers in the modern era to use the phrases "ancestral sin" or "primal sin" as a means of distinguishing a non-"Augustinian" reading of the Genesis account of transgression from the understanding of original sin now dominant in the West. A precise definition of original sin is, however, difficult to pin down historically, and presentations of "Augustinian" doctrine in this regard are often generalized and imprecise, leading at times to a popular "East versus West" rhetoric on the point that has little concrete basis in the actual writings of the early church.

Nonetheless, what has become the popular definition of original sin (i.e., a perfect original state, a fall, a transformation of nature) does establish a point of contrast with traditional Orthodox anthropology and conception of sin, which is more dynamic, open-ended, developmental, and therapeutic. It thus forms an issue of ongoing disputation between Eastern and Western Christianity at large.

SEE ALSO: Humanity; Repentance; Soteriology

References and Suggested Readings

Williams, N. P. (1927) *The Ideas of the Fall and of Original Sin: Bampton Lectures for 1924*. New York: Longmans, Green.

Orthros (Matins)

JEFFREY B. PETTIS

The Greek word *orthros* translates as "dawn" or "early morning." In early Christian usage it referred to early morning prayer, or (as in monastic usage) dawn prayers after the night vigil (see Basil of Caesarea, *regulae fusius tractatae* 37.3, 5 [PG.31.1013A,1016B]). After the 4th century the word came to designate the early morning service of psalms and canticles (a parallel to the western monastic services of Matins and Lauds) as one of the regular hours of Byzantine monastic prayer, in the sequence of Vespers, Compline, Midnight Office, Orthros, First, Third, Sixth, and Ninth Hours. In Greek practice Orthros is conducted by itself, or as the immediate prelude to the divine liturgy. In parishes it occurs chiefly on Sundays before the liturgy. In Russian practice it is often combined with preceding Sunday Vespers (on Saturday evening) as the Vigil Service. Orthros begins with the Trisagion prayers and the reading of the Six Psalms (Hexapsalmoi), and includes litanies alternating with hymns (especially in the form of canons) and recitations of appointed sections (kathismata) of the Psalter. In parish practice the psalm readings are much abbreviated. The service culminates with the reading of a resurrection gospel. If not followed by the liturgy, Orthros ends with the small doxology; if the liturgy follows the great doxology is used.

SEE ALSO: Canon (Liturgical); Eothina; Hexapsalmoi; Kathisma; Kontakion; Ode

References and Suggested Readings

Litsas, F. (1984) *A Companion to the Greek Orthodox Church*. New York: Greek Orthodox Archdiocese.
Patrinacos, N. E. (1984) *A Dictionary of Greek Ortho-doxy*. Pleasantville, NY: Hellenic Heritage Publications.
Taft, R. (2004) *The Liturgy of the Hours in East and West*. Collegeville, MN: Liturgical Press.

Ottoman Yoke

EVANGELOS KATAFYLIS

The Ottoman Yoke signifies the political and religious subordination of the Greek Christians to Islam after the fall of Constantinople in 1453 and the abolition of the Byzantine Empire. The Yoke is seen as having started to lift after the revolutionary declaration of Greek independence from the Turks in 1821. Though many parts of the Orthodox world (such as Egypt and Anatolia) never regained any form of political independence, other conquered Orthodox nations (especially in the Balkans) followed the Greek example soon after. After the fall of Constantinople the Orthodox Church was the only institution that continued the religious legacy of Byzantium, preserving and organizing Christianity throughout the sultan's extensive dominions. The conqueror, Sultan Mehmet II, recognized the Greek patriarch as the legal head of the Orthodox Christian community (*ethnarch*), and designated him supreme religious leader of all his Orthodox subjects (*dhimmi*) among whom he included non-Chalcedonian and non-Greek Orthodox too; allowing them freedom of worship under Ottoman protection provided the taxes of a subject nation were paid. Mehmet first appointed Gennadios Scholarios to take over the patriarchal office, giving to him and his successors full jurisdiction over the education of all the Orthodox Christians across the Ottoman Empire. The Orthodox Church was, at that time, the only organized institution which could represent Christians in their dealings with the Ottoman administration (*Porte Sublime*), and apart from the church, the Orthodox Christian population had no centrally surviving institutions.

Between the 15th and 16th centuries the Ottoman sultans succeeded in making Constantinople the center of their empire. It became a vibrant city, retaining Greek as the diplomatic language of the empire. When the empire became less tolerant of its Greek subjects, they were often forced to adopt a new way of life, for the sake of their survival. Accordingly, this period saw the progressive Islamicization of the Christians, the phenomenon of crypto-Christianism, the recruitment of underage Christian children (*devşirme*) for the sultan's personal guard, the prohibition of the erection of churches (and often of their repair), the seizure and destruction of what church property remained after the conquest, the obstruction of Christian worship, the compulsory enlistment in the navy for Greeks, the growth of piracy and lawlessness against Christian merchants who were regarded as an easy target, and an oppressive poll tax (*haraç*) which was given to the patriarchate to enforce, thereby earning him unpopularity. This system of the patriarch acting as empire-wide ethnarch led to the rise of the so-called Phanariots, members of prominent Greek families in Constantinople who, from the second half of the 16th century until the 18th century, offered their services as *dragomans* (translators, or agents) to the Ottoman government, and thereby often commandeered leading political and ecclesiastic posts in all the Christian territories across Ottoman dominions.

The regime under which Christian subjects were living after the conquest was a harsh one, punctuated by many examples of captivities and persecutions, one that has been globally designated by the dramatic word *Yoke*, a term meaning "Slavery." Living under such conditions, many Greek Christians of the Turkish mainland emigrated to safer places in southern Italy, around the Danube, to Russia, Venice, or the Venetian colonies in Greece. Despite the migration, the spirit of Greek Orthodox culture continued to exist, with many eminent scholars of this time active on mainland Greece. The Greek Orthodox College, established in

1454 by Gennadios Scholarios, played an important role in continuing Orthodox Christian culture under the Yoke. In Crete and on Mount Athos, Greek letters and iconic painting also flourished. The migrations were a demographic shift which significantly contributed to a wide dissemination of Greek culture and language in Orthodox lands, resulting in the establishment of schools and the publication of many books.

From the beginning of the 18th century the decline of Ottoman power in the face of European advances became increasingly evident. It led to a widespread sense among the Orthodox of the Ottoman domains that certain instances of independence could be achieved: something that became realized with the 1821 declaration of Greek independence. This led to rapid economic and cultural developments among the Greek and other newly independent Orthodox nations in the 19th century and beyond.

SEE ALSO: Constantinople, Patriarchate of; Mount Athos; Romania, Patriarchal Orthodox Church of; Scholarios, George (Gennadios) (ca. 1403–1472)

References and Suggested Readings

Chasiotes, I. (2001) Μεταξύ Οθωμανικήςκυριαρχίας και Ευρωπαϊκής πρόσκλησης: Οελληνικός κόσμος στα χρόνια της Τουρκοκρατίας [Between Ottoman Domination and European Challenge: The Greek World in the Years of the Ottoman Yoke]. Thessaloniki: University Studio Press.

Metallenos, G. (1998) Τουρκοκρατία: Οι Έλληνες στην Οθωμανική Αυτοκρατορία [Ottoman Yoke: The Greeks in Ottoman Empire]. Athens: Akritas.

Vakalopoulos, A. (2001) Ιστορία του νέου Ελληνισμού [History of Modern Greece]. Thessaloniki: Hyrodotos.

Zakythinos, D. (1957) Τουρκοκρατία: εισαγωγή εις την νεωτέραν ιστορίαν του ελληνισμού [Ottoman Yoke: Introduction to Modern History of Hellenism]. Athens.

P

Panagia

JEFFREY B. PETTIS

The word *Panagia* is the Greek term (feminine form) for "She who is all holy." In common Orthodox usage today, Panagia is the most common title of honor for the Virgin Mary, the Mother of God. The word Panagia may also refer to the medallion icon of the Virgin that a bishop wears on his breast (*enkolpion*), or to the ritual blessing of a loaf bearing a stamped icon of the Virgin, usually held on feast days in monasteries.

References and Suggested Readings

Langford-James, R. (ed.) (1975) *A Dictionary of the Eastern Orthodox Church*. New York: Burt Franklin.
Litsas, F. (1984) *A Companion to the Greek Orthodox Church*. New York: Greek Orthodox Archdiocese.
Zernov, N. (1961) *Eastern Christianity: A Study of the Origin and Development of the Eastern Orthodox Church*. New York: Putnam's Sons.

Panikhida *see* Death (and Funeral); Kollyva

Pannychis *see* Kontakion

Pantocrator Icon

MARIA GWYN MCDOWELL

The broad range of Pantocrator ("Ruler" or "Preserver of all") icons of the Lord in majestic judgment and blessing serve as "a flexible spiritual aid for the devout viewer" (Onasch and Schnieper 1995: 129). Initially appearing on coins and in manuscripts, then domes and apses, Pantocrator icons proliferated during the high Middle Ages. A bearded Christ, hair neatly parted, sits on a throne (often absent), right hand raised in blessing, left hand holding the gospel, expression varying from severe to compassionate. The background may include a mandorla, angelic figures, and gospel symbols. Famous examples include the earliest known 6th-century Sinai encaustic and the 11th-century Daphni mosaic.

SEE ALSO: Deisis; Icons

References and Suggested Readings

Onasch, K. and Schnieper, A. (1995) *Icons: Fascination and Reality*. New York: Riverside Books.
Ouspensky, L. and Lossky, V. (1982) *The Meaning of Icons*. Crestwood, NY: St. Vladimir's Seminary Press.

The Concise Encyclopedia of Orthodox Christianity, First Edition. Edited by John Anthony McGuckin.
© 2014 John Wiley & Sons, Ltd. Published 2014 by John Wiley & Sons, Ltd.

Plate 48 Coptic fresco of Christ in glory from the Monastery of St. Antony by the Red Sea. Photo by John McGuckin.

Papacy

AUGUSTINE CASIDAY

A statement of the Eastern Orthodox ideal of the papal office, and its role in relation to the churches, can be supplied from St. Ignatius of Antioch's salutation in his letter *To the Romans*, where he speaks of how the pope presides over the Church of Rome: "which presides in love." Similarly, the problems experienced by Orthodox Christians with respect to the papacy can also be summed up from Ignatius' further description of the Church of Rome as functioning to "maintain the law of Christ." Under the concept of "maintaining the law of Christ" can be accommodated many of the Eastern Christian world's experiences of the papacy that have been disagreeable, ranging from doctrinal assertions to political interventions, with the result that Orthodox perspectives on the papacy and especially its ecclesiological theory of primacy, above all in the second millennium of Christianity, have frequently been negative. Attention to several key episodes and particular claims will substantiate and nuance this general view.

Ignatius' high regard was reinforced by Rome's ancient reputation for orthodoxy, unrivalled by any other major see in the early Christian world. Situated a convenient distance from an interfering emperor, the pope of Rome almost always spoke conservatively for the good of the churches, and with a degree of impartiality, even if that came occasionally at a steep price. During the 7th-century Monothelite controversy, Pope Martin I paid with his life for opposing imperial policy. During the same crisis, St. Maximos the Confessor exclaimed at his trial: "I love the Romans because we share the same faith, whereas I love the Greeks because we share the same language." But already by Maximos' day a far-reaching difference between Greek and Latin theology was emerging as a contested issue, namely, the broad-based western affirmation that the Holy Spirit proceeds from the Father "and from the Son" or, in Latin, *filioque* (Louth 2007: 84–6). Initially outside of Rome, and eventually in Rome itself, that clause was incorporated into the Nicene-Constantinopolitan Creed. Such a modification raised important questions about what kind of authority the pope claimed to alter the creed set out by an ecumenical council. It also created a symbolic issue of high theological significance over which Orthodox and Latin Christians would argue fiercely.

With the increasing social and political prominence of the Roman Church in post-Byzantine Italy, the parameters of papal leadership expanded and frequently clashed against the secular powers of the Franks, the Byzantines, the Lombards, and others (see Noble 1984). Religious clashes occurred, as we have noted, increasingly over the matter of the *filioque*. Was the pope's authority limited to final jurisdiction for appeals (as was the general eastern opinion in the first millennium) or did he enjoy the prerogative to intervene spontaneously whenever and wherever he considered such intervention justified (as became an increasingly affirmed Latin theory based on the idea of the pope as the extraordinary vicar of St. Peter)? What of the matter of jurisdictions extending as a result of sometimes competitive missionary activity (see Louth 2007: 167–92)? It was by no means unheard of for papal power to be exercised against the interests of the Christian East. Conflicting interests naturally led to confrontations, such as can be seen in Pope Nicholas I's interventions during the patriarchate of Photios (Chadwick 2003: 95–192). Nicholas eventually answered an appeal by Photios' deposed predecessor, but surely was also interested in the Christianization of Bulgaria, poised to come under either Roman or Constantinopolitan influence. For decades after this period, problems were rife between the Constantinopolitan patriarchate and the papacy, and matters only worsened as time went on. As Chadwick describes it: "In the century following the patriarchate of Photios, relations between Constantinople and Rome or the West generally fluctuated in close correspondence with political factors, and political concerns became a more potent factor than religious or theological matters" (2003: 193).

In 1054 another rupture opened in the tense existing communion between Rome and Constantinople, caused by diverging practices in liturgy and church discipline, and exacerbated by irreconcilable expectations about the exercise of authority in such cases (Chadwick 2003: 206–18; Louth 2007: 305–18). Although the mutual excommunications delivered in July 1054 were of doubtful importance, or even legality, in retrospect they more and more came to signify the formal separation of the Western Catholic Church from the Eastern Orthodox Churches. The events of 1054 certainly reveal "underlying issues of authority that were not to go away" (Louth 2007: 318).

That a confluence of competing political, doctrinal, and canonical interests contributed substantially to the estrangement of the Christian West from the Orthodox world is by no means solely a modern perception. The 12th-century historian Anna Comnena bundled ecclesiastical privileges together with political ascendancy in her claim for Constantinopolitan primacy: "The truth is that when power was transferred from Rome to our country and the Queen of Cities, not to mention the senate and the whole administration, the

senior ranking archbishopric was also transferred here" (*Alexiad* 1.13). Her assessment suggests that 11th-century Rome was commonly seen by the Byzantines to lack ecclesiastical and political preeminence; and its claims for primacy as refuted in a reading of the Chalcedonian canons about jurisdictional precedence that interpreted Rome as having been subordinated to Constantinople. Such is Anna's brisk response to the Gregorian reforms of an ascendant papacy.

Relations between the sees of Rome and Constantinople continued to deteriorate during the course of the Crusades. Anna Comnena saw in them, from their inception, a sinister western plot to subvert Constantinople (*Alexiad* 10.5), an eventuality which indeed transpired in 1204. As the figurehead for the Christian West, the papacy's reputation in the East was enormously damaged by the fall of Constantinople to Latin Crusaders, and by the papacy's subsequent activities, installing parallel Latin patriarchates in the conquered territories.

The popes hosted several attempts at reconciliation between the churches, such as the Second Council of Lyons (1274) and the Council of Ferrara-Florence (1438–9). Sometimes the initiative in reconciliation came from the East, as with the Union of Brest (1596), or it may have been a personal initiative, such as the contributions by Leo Allatius (1648) or Vladimir Solovyov. But these attempts were all overshadowed by widespread Orthodox distaste for the "Unia," or Eastern-Rite Christian churches that accepted Papal obedience. The papacy's invitation to the leading Orthodox hierarchs to attend Vatican Council I in the mid-19th century drew from them only a formal rebuke of his jurisdictional pretensions. Much tension still exists in terms of the papacy's installation and continuing administration of a parallel Latin hierarchy in Orthodox lands (such as Russia).

In recent times, however, some Orthodox theologians have been revisiting the question of the papacy in a more pacific light (see Meyendorff 1992). The mutual excommunications of 1054 were rescinded on December 7, 1965 in a dramatic mutual gesture of reconciliation between Pope Paul VI and Patriarch Athenagoras of Constantinople (Abbot and Gallagher 1966: 725–7); and subsequent Constantinopolitan patriarchs have continued what has been called the "Dialogue of Love." It suggests that further developments of

Orthodox reflection on the role and position of the papacy will be forthcoming.

SEE ALSO: Church (Orthodox Ecclesiology); Eastern Catholic Churches; Episcopacy; *Filioque*; Rome, Ancient Patriarchate of; St. Maximos the Confessor (580–662); St. Photios the Great (ca. 810–893); Sts. Constantine (Cyril) (ca. 826–869) and Methodios (815–885); Solovyov, Vladimir (1853–1900)

References and Suggested Readings

Abbot, W. and Gallagher, J. (ed. and trans.) (1966) *The Documents of Vatican II*. New York: Corpus Press.

Allatius, L. (1648) *De ecclesiae occidentalis atque orientalis perpetua consensione*. Cologne: Kalcovius.

Allen, P. and Neil, B. (ed. and trans.) (2004) *Maximus the Confessor and His Companions: Documents from Exile*. Oxford: Oxford University Press.

Chadwick, H. (2003) *East and West: The Making of a Rift in the Church*. Oxford: Oxford University Press.

Comnena, A. (1969) *The Alexiad*, trans. E. R. A. Sewter. London: Penguin.

Louth, A. (2007) *Greek East and Latin West: The Church AD 681–1071*. Crestwood, NY: St. Vladimir's Seminary Press.

Meyendorff, J. (ed.) (1992) *The Primacy of Peter*, 2nd edn. Crestwood, NY: St. Vladimir's Seminary Press.

Noble, T. (1984) *The Republic of St. Peter: The Birth of the Papal States, 680–825*. Philadelphia: University of Pennsylvania Press.

Paradise

PETER C. BOUTENEFF

The Greek *Paradeisos* (cf. the Persian *Pardez*, meaning "enclosure") in the Septuagint refers to any enclosed garden (cf. Num. 24.6; Neh. 2.8; Eccl. 2.5; Jer. 29.5), but remains particularly associated with the Garden in Eden (Gen. 2–3, 13.10; also Is. 51.3; Ezek. 28.13). In Second Temple Jewish literature (e.g., 1 Enoch 60.8, 23, 61.12; Apoc. Abraham 21.3, 6; 3 Baruch 4.10) as well as in the New Testament (Lk. 23.43; Rev. 2.7), Paradise comes to refer also to the destination of the righteous, whether it is an earthly or heavenly *topos*. St. Paul's mystical experience which associates Paradise with the Third Heaven (2 Cor. 12.2–3) has deeply influenced the Greek patristic literature, and is frequently cited.

Paradise as the Garden of Human Origins

Paradise as the earthly garden in Eden, into which the first-created humans were placed, and which Genesis 2 locates on Earth (in what is modern-day Iraq), is treated variously in the Greek fathers. Theophilus of Antioch, almost unique among the early writers for the absence of a typological (christological) exegesis of the Paradise narrative, is concomitantly almost unique in attempting to pinpoint the chronological dating of the events narrated in Genesis 1–3 (as did Eusebius of Caesarea, in his *Chronicle*, no longer extant). Conversely, and possibly following Philo (cf. *Laws of Allegory* 1.43), Origen practically mocks anyone who would interpret Paradise as an actual place with physical trees and chewable fruit (*On First Principles* 4.3.1). Precisely this notion, however, featured strongly in Ephrem's *Hymns on Paradise* (Brock 1990). Gregory of Nazianzus is open and provisional in his interpretation: God placed the human person in Paradise, "Whatever this Paradise actually was," and introduced him to trees which Gregory supposes might represent contemplation (*theoria*) (*Oration* 38.12).

Contemporary Orthodox theologians tend to follow the fathers in paying scant attention to the question of the physical historicity of the Paradise of Genesis 2–3, focusing rather on its existential significance or more often on its christological sense. Those who address the question of historicity answer it variously. Fr. Seraphim Rose insists on a literal reading of Genesis 1–3, rejecting any evolutionary theory and believing the universe to be less than ten thousand years old. Archbishop Lazar Puhalo associates the insistence upon the physical historicity of Genesis 1–3 with a weak faith in God, who quite evidently creates through an evolutionary means over the course of billions of years. A range of positions exists spanning these extremes, alternately accommodating or rejecting evolutionary theories and the scientific dating of the universe at 13.7 billion years. But again, most focus on the existential character of the narrative (Orthodox hymnography and patristic texts usually place "us" in the Garden, and lament "our" sin therein), or the christological (Adam being a type for Christ [Rom. 5.14], and the entire narrative describing what Christ comes to restore).

Paradise as Destination

Some of the Greek fathers saw Paradise, albeit in various ways, as the resting place of the (righteous) dead. Some periodically distinguished Paradise from Heaven, the former being a kind of interim space before arrival in Heaven (cf. Origen, *First Principles* 2.11.6). Reckoning Paradise as the destination of the righteous relied on several factors that presented the age to come as a return to origins. One was the dynamic of typology, which related the events, personae, and even the "space" of Eden to the passion and resurrection of Christ. Christ is the New Adam, Mary the New Eve, the tree of the cross is the new tree of life, and the heavenly Paradise, and/or the church, is the new Eden. This manner of understanding the Scriptures came to a particularly full theological expression in St. Irenaeus's concept of recapitulation (*Adversus Haereses*).

Of related significance is the understanding of the age to come as a restoration (*apokatastasis*) (cf. Acts 3.21). "The end is always like the beginning," says Origen (*First Principles* 1.6.2). Although steeped in a classical Greek mindset which espoused a broadly cyclic understanding of time and destiny, he is here speaking of a restoration – through subjection to Christ in the Holy Spirit – to a single end which is like the single beginning. In so doing he articulates a consistent trajectory of thought in the Greek fathers. This is not properly understood as a return to a place or state that was ever historically realized, but rather as the realization of the divine will, the fulfillment of the original (or better, eternal) divine intention and principle (*logos*) for humanity, *unrealized* by Adam and Eve in the Garden of Eden. Frequently, then, the effective identity of end and beginning is expressed through this common *topos* of Paradise.

On this score, while the primeval Paradise was seen as an ideal place and condition, its human denizens (the biblical Adam and Eve) are not generally portrayed as icons of a fully realized state of human personhood. Maximus the Confessor asserts that humans fell "together with their coming into being" (*To Thalassius* 61). Irenaeus, Gregory of Nazianzus, and Ephrem the Syrian understood Adam and Eve to be "works in progress," innocent like children and, if anything, terribly weak. They partook of a fruit that was always intended for human consumption, but not for persons in their yet-underdeveloped state. The Eucharistic Anaphora of Basil the Great says that the human creature was placed in Paradise with "the *promise* of immortality." Adam and Eve represent an unrealized potential, while the icon of perfected, immortal humanity is the New Adam, Jesus Christ, through whom humans may now attain to the Paradise always intended for them, as a life in free and full communion with God – a place of ineffable, inexhaustible, and ever-surprising sweetness, beauty, and joy.

SEE ALSO: Ecology; Original Sin; Soteriology

References and Suggested Readings

Bouteneff, P. C. (2008) *Beginnings: Ancient Christian Readings of the Biblical Creation Narratives*. Grand Rapids, MI: Baker Academic.

Brock, S. (trans.) (1990) *St. Ephrem the Syrian: Hymns on Paradise*. Crestwood, NY: St. Vladimir's Seminary Press.

Rose, S. (2000) *Genesis, Creation, and Early Man: The Orthodox Christian Vision*. Platina, CA: St. Herman of Alaska Brotherhood.

Paraklesis

DIMITRI CONOMOS

A service of supplication and intercession. Loosely based on the structure of Matins, this unique service combines litanical prayer, a gospel reading, psalmody, and hymnody. It may be celebrated in church with a priest or at home as a service of the laity. Its function is to call upon Christ or one of his saints for succor, blessing, and mediation. The most popular (and presumably the model for subsequent imitations) are the Great and Small Parakleses to the Mother of God.

Either one is chanted (often in alternation) each day during the fast of the Dormition (August 1–14).

Paraklitike

JEFFREY B. PETTIS

The *Paraklitike* is the Byzantine liturgical book containing the variable hymns of divine service. The texts are arranged according to the eight tones of Byzantine church music, each having its own hymns and antiphons. Accordingly, the *Paraklitike* is also known as the *Oktoechos* (Greek, "book of eight tones"). The texts are inclusive for All Saints Day (Sunday after Pentecost) to the 4th Sunday before the Great Lent. St. Joseph the Hymnographer (9th century), a prolific composer of liturgical canons, gave the final form to the *Paraklitike*. St. John of Damascus (ca. 665–749) is also traditionally thought to have contributed to its composition.

SEE ALSO: *Anastasimatarion*; Hymnography; Liturgical Books; Music (Sacred); *Oktoechos*; St. John of Damascus (ca. 675–ca. 750)

Parousia

MATTHEW J. PEREIRA

The Greek term *parousia*, within the context of the New Testament, denotes the "presence" or "arrival" of Jesus Christ at the Eschaton (Matt. 24.3; 1 Cor. 15.23). Early Christian expectations of apocalyptic salvation were foreshadowed in Palestinian literature, as can be seen by reference to the Old Testament pseudepigrapha and the Qumran texts (Russell 1964). The early church's sense of the delay of the glorious return of Christ in judgment (Jn. 21.21–23) provided Christians the opportunity to rearticulate the Parousia in a manner that reflected their own theological concerns, which were shaped within specific social and ecclesial settings (Aune 1975). Beyond exclusively focusing on the "last days," patristic theologians extensively interpreted the Parousia as a present spiritual reality, part of the resurrection mystery, which pointed towards a future hope.

In the early church the Parousia denoted a wide range of spiritual realities, such as the nearness of the gospel, the day of resurrection, Christ's healing ministry, judgment, and accommodation to humanity. In his *Letter to the Philadelphians* Ignatius of Antioch (ca. 35–ca. 98/117) proclaimed that the gospel possesses the transcendent "appearance" of our Lord Jesus Christ, his passion and resurrection (*Phil.* 9.2). Justin Martyr (ca. 100–165) interprets the Parousia as Christ's power, whereby the Lord resurrects the dead and heals the sick upon his arrival. In his *Dialogue with Trypho* Justin Martyr also interpreted the deluge as a Christ-event; Noah and his family totaled eight people and thus allegorically represented the eighth day, which is when Christ "appeared" (had his Parousia) and rose from the dead (*Dial.* 88.2). Further, in his *First Apology*, Justin parallels the prophecy of Isaiah with Christ's healing presence; it is at the Lord's "coming" that the "lame shall leap … the lepers be cleansed, and the dead shall rise" (*I Apol.* 48.2). In the *Stromateis* Clement of Alexandria (ca. 150–215) argues that the "advent" of the Savior will divide the believers from the disobedient (*Strom.* 1.18). The Lord's arrival clearly reveals the spiritual state of each person, and thus ensures there will be only just judgment. Further, Clement teaches God has no natural relation with humanity, yet the Lord "accommodated" himself to our weakness (*Strom.* 2.16). In brief, Christian theologians in the first three centuries interpreted the Parousia as a fundamental christological event associated with Christ's resurrection power, healing, judgment, and nearness to redeemed humanity.

Origen of Alexandria (d. 253/254) enlarged the doctrine of the Parousia through emphasizing the possibility, for the spiritually advanced, to experience God in the present moment. While known for his speculative tendencies, Origen's pastoral concerns informed his theology of the Parousia (Etcheverría 1969; Daley 2003: 48). Origen predominantly understood the Apocalypse of John through the lens of Christ, rather than focusing on the "last days" (Daley 2003: 49). There is another "second coming," according to Origen, where the Lord becomes present to the souls who are being perfected. Overall, Origen interprets the "last times" in a manner that primarily is meant to illuminate Christian spiritual growth. The consummation of the world, according to Origen, involves the present process of spiritual growth realized within each soul (*De Principiis* 3.6.6). The Kingdom of God is already present in virtuous Christians, while not fully realized (*Comm. on Matt.* 12.14; *Or.* 25.2). The Parousia is presently experienced; however, the coming of Christ also remains a future hope only fully realized when "God becomes all in all" (*Comm. on Jn.* 20.7.47). God's presence, according to Origen, is experienced through contemplation. The heavenly banquet is analogous with contemplation of God, which is delimited by our human capacity (*De Princ.* 2.11.7). Further, Origen insists our knowledge of God will never be complete; rather, the sojourner is always spiritually advancing through entering deeper into the presence of God (*Hom. 17 on Numbers*).

With the ascendancy of Constantine as emperor (ca. 272–337) the church entered into an era of relative security. In this new situation a more church-centered eschatology became common; for example, Eusebius of Caesarea declared the first fruits of future rewards bring assurance to the faithful in their present state (*Vita Const.* 1.33; Thielman 1987). The first two ecumenical councils emphasized Christology and the doctrine of God; consequently, there was perhaps less of a lively theological interest in a future-looking eschatology throughout the 4th century. The Cappadocian fathers primarily understood the Parousia as a spiritual grace related to the process of divinization (Gross 1938). St. Basil of Caesarea (ca. 330–79) mediates between spiritual interpretations and a theology of apocalyptic judgment when reflecting upon the Lord's second coming. But of particular note is the way in which St. Basil associates the coming of Christ with judgment when addressing monastic communities (e.g., *Ep.* 46.5). St. Gregory of Nazianzus (ca. 329/330–90) interpreted the Lord's presence as both a judgment and a grace (Mossay 1964). In his oration "On Holy Baptism" Gregory speaks of Christ's cleansing fire and then adds the caveat, "I know also a fire that is not cleansing, but avenging" (*Or.* 40.36). This fire, which represents Christ's judgment, is for the wicked that are in need of chastisement. Consequently, for Gregory, the fire, that is the presence of Christ, can be either blessing or bane. St. Gregory of Nyssa (ca. 335–94) developed Origen's doctrine of perpetual spiritual growth

through his interpretation of the beatitude as *epektasis* (constant spiritual progress). In his *Life of Moses* Gregory asserts Christians are "never to reach satiety in one's desire," for they are inflamed with the desire to see more of God (*Life of Moses* 2.239).

The Parousia, therefore, had multiple and significant meanings throughout the Eastern Church, but ultimately each definition expressed some aspect of Christ's redemptive and lordly presence. The Parousia, for some theologians, was predominantly an eschatological event, whereas others emphasized the presence and coming of Christ in their present spiritual lives. Ultimately, Christians' ongoing experience of Christ is the basis for their future hope (e.g., St. John Chrysostom, *Homily on Philemon* 3.3; Daley 2003: 223). The Parousia, more than anything else, expresses the mystery of Jesus Christ, who is with humanity in the present situation and yet will come back again in his gloriously revealed resurrectional power (St. Cyril of Alexandria, *Commentary on 1 Cor.* 15).

SEE ALSO: Cappadocian Fathers; Eschatology; St. Constantine the Emperor (ca. 271–337); St. Cyril of Alexandria (ca. 378–444); St. John Chrysostom (349–407)

References and Suggested Readings

Aune, D. E. (1975) "The Significance of the Delay of the Parousia for Early Christianity," In G. F. Hawthorne (ed.) *Current Issues in Biblical and Patristic Interpretation*. Grand Rapids, MI: Eerdmans, pp. 87–109.

Daley, B. E. (2003) *The Hope of the Early Church: A Handbook of Patristic Eschatology*. Peabody, MA: Hendrickson.

Etcheverría, R. T. (1969) "Epidhimia y Parousia en Origenes," *Scriptorium victoriense* 16: 313–37.

Florovsky, G. (1956) "Eschatology in the Patristic Age," *Greek Orthodox Theological Review* 2: 27–40.

Gross, J. (1938) *La divinisation du Chrétien d'après les pères grecs*. Paris: J. Gabalda.

Mossay, J. (1964) "Perspectives eschatologiques de Saint Grégoire de Nazianze," *QLP* 45: 320–39.

Russell, D. S. (1964) *The Method and Message of Jewish Apocalyptic, 200 BC–AD 100*. Philadelphia: Westminster Press.

Thielman, F. S. (1987) "Another Look at the Eschatology of Eusebius of Caesarea," *Vigiliae Christianae* 41: 226–37.

Pascha *see* Calendar; Feasts

Passion Bearers

JOHN A. MCGUCKIN

Passion Bearers are saints in the Orthodox Church who underwent cruelty and oppression in a spirit of meekness and non-resistance to evil, regarded as tantamount to the status of martyrdom, especially as that witnesses to the church the heroic gentleness of Christ. The most famous of the Passion Bearers are the 11th-century Rus princes Boris and Gleb, sons of Prince Vladimir, who offered no resistance to their brother Sviatopolk who murdered them to attain political eminence. Other Passion Bearers include the Serbian St. John Vladimir (d. 1015) and (as many consider) the more modern examples of the Romanov royal family, whose spiritual fortitude in their final days won wide admiration, and others such as Grand Duchess St. Elizaveta Feodorovna, killed by the Bolsheviks, and Mother Maria Skobotsova, who witnessed heroically in a Nazi death camp.

References and Suggested Readings

Demshuk, V. (1978) *Russian Sainthood and Canonization.* Minneapolis: Light and Life.

Lenhoff, G. (1989) *The Martyred Princes Boris and Gleb: A Socio-Cultural Study of the Cult and the Texts.* Columbus: Ohio University Press.

Paterikon *see* Niptic Books (Paterika)

Patristics

JOHN A. MCGUCKIN

A relatively modern term deriving from the Latin *Patres*, or "Fathers." It was also known as patrology up to the mid-20th century, though this latter designation has now been restricted mainly to signify reference manuals dealing with the works of the fathers of the church. The fathers were the bishops, outstanding theologians, and leading monastic elders of the early church, who left behind them authoritative bodies of spiritual, biblical, liturgical, and dogmatic writings. The age of the fathers is generally seen as extending from after the apostolic era (beginning of the 2nd century) to the 8th and 9th centuries, whose great luminaries then included St. John of Damascus and St. Photios the Great. John is, in many ways, a certain sign of the closing of the patristic age, with his works gathering together as a kind of encyclopedia of the earlier authoritative materials to form a synthesis of patristic theology for the later church's reference. In terms of Latin patristics, the traditional cut-off point has been significantly extended beyond this time, even up to the medieval western theologian Bernard of Clairvaux, who is sometimes called, in the Catholic Church, the "last of the fathers." Even so, there is not a hard and fast historical line, as Orthodoxy understands it, for some of the late Byzantine writers such as St. Symeon the New Theologian of the 11th century, or St. Gregory Palamas (1296–1359), for example, certainly enjoy a high "patristic status" in contemporary Orthodoxy. The word generally means, in Orthodox circles, those definitive and highly authoritative theologians of the church in its classical ages who represent purity of doctrine allied with great holiness of life; a life that manifests the indwelling of the Holy Spirit in their acts and their consciousness, such that they are not merely good speculative thinkers, or interesting religious writers, as such, but rather substantial guides to the will of God, and Spirit-bearers (*pneumatophoroi*) whose doctrine and advice can be trusted as conveying the authentic Orthodox tradition of faith and piety. This does not mean that every single thing any one of the fathers ever wrote is given "canonical" status. Orthodoxy admits that the general rule of human authorship applies even among the saints, for as the adage tells, "even Homer nods," but it does mean that collectively, and by the consensus of the fathers among themselves, and by the manner in which they stand in a stream of defense of the ecumenical faith of the church, they together comprise a library of immense prestige and authority. They are thus collectively strong and concrete evidence for the central tradition of the Orthodox Church. This is why the church affords them a very high theological authority, not as great as the Scriptures or the ecumenical councils, but certainly alongside the latter; for it was from their writings that the doctrine of the great councils generally emerged.

The concept of "patristic witnesses" can be seen in the earliest writings of the church. Notable figures such as Ignatius, Polycarp, or Clement of Rome clearly enjoyed a significant status even in their own times as elders in the faith. But the formal growth of the idea that the "fathers" were a collective defense against heterodoxy was mainly a product of the anti-Arian writers of the 4th century, which came to be adopted passionately by the Greek and Latin churches of the 5th century and afterwards. One of the early and classical examples of this specifically happening is the hagiography of Antony the Great written by Athanasius of Alexandria (*Life of Antony*), which depicts him as one of the great fathers who personally represents a standard of truth, holiness, and orthodoxy. Another is the hagiography of Athanasius by St. Gregory the Theologian (of Nazianzus: *Oration* 21; see also *Oration* 33.5), which lauds Athanasius as a father and pillar of orthodoxy for his defense of Nicea (see also St. Basil the Great's *Epistle* 140.2). By the 5th century, the concept of "authoritative fathers" was being appealed to specifically and systematically to establish pedigree lines of doctrine; most notably by St. Cyril of Alexandria, who began to assemble florilegia of the "sayings of the orthodox fathers" in his conflict with Nestorius, thus beginning a style of theologizing that soon became a standard way of doing Orthodox theology ever after. The idea of bringing the evidence of the fathers together soon came into the synodical process of the ecumenical councils, which more and more, after the 5th century, saw themselves as the defenders and propagators of the "theology of the fathers" (see Canon 7 of the Council of Ephesus, 431; and the Acts of the Council of Chalcedon, 451; *Definition of the Faith* 2; 4). Patristics in this sense clearly corresponds to a certain vision of theology as the "defense and maintenance of Orthodoxy." This remains its essential meaning in the Orthodox Church today. Orthodoxy has generally accepted the great fathers of the Latin church as its own (Sts. Ambrose, Gregory the Great, Leo, and so on), though it has significantly distanced itself from many of the

ideas of other influential early Latin thinkers (Arnobius, Tertullian), including St. Augustine, who so dominated the West's sense of patristic teaching, but hardly impressed himself upon the East.

In modern academic use "patristics" means something more general, less specific, than this idea of the "guides of Orthodoxy," and simply designates the study of Christian antiquity, leading to the often paradoxical position that much of modern academic patristic study is devoted to the heterodox writers of the ancient world: a thing which Orthodoxy would strictly exclude from the category of "patristics," though in so doing it has perhaps tended to narrow down the field in some unfortunate ways, leaving out some of the great contributors to Christian theology who were not bishops, or monastics, such as the numerous women saints from ancient times (who were literarily "invisible" in the main) or heterodox theologians of great merit (of significance, that is, beyond the specific "mistakes" of certain of their stances) such as Origen or Mar Theodore Mopsuestia (both of whom were major and lofty biblical interpreters of high spirituality but were the subjects of conciliar condemnations for specific doctrinal errors that caused their larger body of writings to be marginalized or lost). The massive 19th-century collections and editions of J. P. Migne (*Patrologia series graeca* and *series latina*) comprising hundreds of volumes of ancient and medieval Greek and Latin texts is a virtual canon of patristic literature (understood in the wider sense of a library of all the early theologians). Patristic theology today generally remains an important and valid branch of the theological disciplines, perhaps given a greater stress in Orthodox and Roman Catholic academies than Protestant, and one that enjoyed a veritable renaissance in the 20th century as many excellent critical editions of primary texts, and sophisticated historical analyses, enlivened the field.

SEE ALSO: Cappadocian Fathers; Christ; Ecumenical Councils; Fatherhood of God; Holy Spirit; Incarnation (of the Logos); Logos Theology; Philosophy; St. Athanasius of Alexandria (c. 293–373); St. Cyril of Alexandria (ca. 378–444); St. Gregory Palamas (1296–1359); St. John Chrysostom (349–407); St. John of Damascus (ca. 675–ca. 750); St. Maximos the Confessor (580–662)

References and Suggested Readings

Bardenhewer, O. (1908) *Patrology*. St. Louis: Herder.
McGuckin, J. A. (2004) *The Westminster Handbook to Patristic Theology*. Louisville: Westminster John Knox Press.
Prestige, G. L. (1940) *Fathers and Heretics*. London: SPCK.
Quasten, J. (1975) *Patrology*, vols. 1–3. Utrecht: Spectrum.

Pentarchy

GEORGE E. DEMACOPOULOS

Pentarchy refers to the ancient division of the Christian world into five autonomous and autocephalous jurisdictions, each under the leadership of a patriarch. Canon 28 of the Council of Chalcedon ranked the five sees in order of preeminence as Rome, Constantinople, Alexandria, Antioch, and Jerusalem. Both the principle and ranking were confirmed by Justinian's *Novella* 123, which asserted that each patriarch would serve as a court of last appeal for internal church legislative and disciplinary matters. Neither the borders that separate their jurisdictions nor the number of autocephalous churches remained static in the Byzantine period, but the original five have retained a measure of preeminence in the later expansion of the concept of Orthodox patriarchies.

SEE ALSO: Alexandria, Patriarchate of; Antioch, Patriarchate of; Constantinople, Patriarchate of; Council of Chalcedon (451); Jerusalem, Patriarchate of; Rome, Ancient Patriarchate of

Pentecost, Feast of

MARIA GWYN MCDOWELL

A great feast of the church observed fifty days after Pascha, celebrating the descent of the Holy Spirit, the full revelation of the trinitarian mystery, and the commencement of the church's mission in the world. On the Jewish pilgrimage feast of Pentecost commemorating the presentation of the law to Moses, the Holy Spirit descended upon the followers of Jesus gathered in Jerusalem, inspiring the preaching of the gospel in languages comprehensible to all present (Acts 2). A fulfillment prophecy (Joel 2.28–9) liturgically com-

memorated by the singing of Galatians 3.27, joyfully acknowledges the ongoing participation of the baptized, regardless of social status, in Christ through the Holy Spirit. At Vespers on this day solemn prayers of intercession are made.

SEE ALSO: Deification; Evangelism; Holy Spirit

Pentekostarion

SOTIRIOS A. VLAVIANOS

The *Pentekostarion* (meaning "the book of the fifty days"), alternatively known as the "Flowery Triodion" (still known as such in the Slavonic tradition), is the continuation of the *Lenten Triodion* book of liturgical texts. It contains the chanting and reading materials used in the services of the fifty-day season of Pentecost. The Pentecost season begins with Orthros (Matins) on Easter Sunday and lasts up until the Sunday of All Saints, following Pentecost Sunday. It has its roots in the *Triodion*, but by the 14th century it had evolved into a new book with its new name. Its initial version comprised short canons (*triodia*) that were gradually eliminated after the 14th century. The chanted material related to the saints (*Synaxaria*) of the Sundays and Feastdays, as composed by Nikiforos Kallistos Xanthopoulos, was also eventually incorporated into the *Pentekostarion* as it now stands. It is a book rich in theological content and spiritual teaching.

SEE ALSO: Canon (Liturgical); Feasts; Great Week; *Horologion*; Liturgical Books; *Menaion*; *Paraklitike*; Pentecost, Feast of; Resurrection; *Triodion*

References and Suggested Readings

Schmemann, A. (2003) *Introduction to Liturgical Theology*. Crestwood, NY: St. Vladimir's Seminary Press.
Taft, R. F. (1992) *The Byzantine Rite: A Short History*. Collegeville, MN: Liturgical Press.
Taft, R. F. (1997) *Beyond East and West: Problems in Liturgical Understanding*, 2nd edn. Rome: Pontifical Oriental Institute.

Penthos see Repentance

Perichoresis

THEODOR DAMIAN

The term *Perichoresis* indicates the mode of existence of the persons of the Holy Trinity characterized by interpenetration, co-inhabitation, mutual fellowship, surrounding, or indwelling. In Greek, *perichoreo* means to "make room," to "go or revolve around."

The basis of the doctrine of Perichoresis lies in Christ's declaration about the co-inhabitation between him and the Father ("I and the Father are one," Jn. 10.30; "I am in the Father and the Father is in Me," Jn. 14.11) which indicates a relation of consubstantiality (*homoousion*) of the trinitarian persons. Even so, the first application of the notion in patristic times was not in the context of trinitarian theology, but in Christology, and it was used in order to emphasize the unity of the one divine person and the distinctiveness of the two natures in Christ.

The idea appeared often in early patristic theological works (Justin the Martyr, Origen, Athanasius, Basil the Great) and though the term itself was also explicitly used in Sts. Gregory the Theologian and Maximos the Confessor, it was St. John of Damascus, in his work *Exposition of the Orthodox Faith*, who was really the church father to develop the term and concept most fully, especially where Perichoresis is used to describe the type of intratrinitarian relationships. It was from the trinitarian context that St. John extrapolated the concept back to Christology; the perichoretical relations in the Trinity being used by him as a paradigm for the coexistence of the two natures in Christ.

The term Perichoresis essentially indicates that at the heart of God's life is supreme personal relationship; and that relation is one of total intimacy. According to St. John of Damascus, the persons of the Trinity live together in union in a relationship without coalescence or commingling; they cleave to each other and have their being in each other. When applied to the two natures of Christ, Perichoresis indicates their co-inhabitation and interpenetration, or mutual permeation, yet without any loss on the part of any of the two natures of its specific properties, and without any confusion or mixture. The *ekthesis* (credal definition) of the Council of Chalcedon expresses the idea succinctly. Trinitarian perichoresis also grew in the Orthodox tradition to become a paradigm for the spiritual union and interrelation of members of the Christian Church based on Christ's intentions as expressed in John 17.21: "That they all may be one; as You, Father are in Me, and I in You, that they also may be one in Us."

SEE ALSO: Church (Orthodox Ecclesiology); Council of Chalcedon (451); Holy Trinity; Patristics; St. John of Damascus (ca. 675–ca. 750)

References and Suggested Readings

Crisp, O. D. (2005) "Problems with Perichoresis," *Tyndale Bulletin* 56, 1: 119–40.

John of Damascus (1989) *Exposition of the Orthodox Faith*, in P. Schaff and H. Wace (eds.) *The Nicene and Post-Nicene Fathers*, Vol. 9. Grand Rapids, MI: Eerdmans.

Lossky, V. (1968) *The Mystical Theology of the Eastern Church*. Cambridge: James Clarke.

Prestige, L. (1928) "Perichoreo and Perichoresis in the Fathers," *Journal of Theological Studies* 24: 242–52.

Stăniloae, D. (1996) *Teologia Dogmatica Ortodoxa*. Bucharest: Editura Institutului Biblic si de Misiune al BOR.

Phelonion

PHILIP ZYMARIS

A Byzantine vestment equivalent to the western chausible. It has its origins in a poncho-like garment referred to by St. Paul (2 Tim. 4.13). It was once worn by bishops but was later replaced by the *sakkos*. Presently, priests wear them at all sacramental services.

SEE ALSO: Epitrachelion; Sticharion; Vestments

References and Suggested Readings

Day, P. (1993) "Phelonion," in *The Liturgical Dictionary of Eastern Christianity*. Collegeville: Liturgical Press, p. 233.

Phountoulis, I. (2002) "Paradose kai exelixe leitourgikon hieron amphion," in *Ta hiera amphia kai he exoterike eribole tou orthodoxou klerou*. Athens: Church of Greece Publications, pp. 63–78.

Plate 49 Orthodox priest wearing the phelonion vestment and the pectoral cross (stavrophore). PhotoEdit/Alamy.

Philokalia

ANDREW LOUTH

Philokalia is the Greek term for an anthology. Nowadays, *the Philokalia* virtually invariably refers to a collection of Byzantine ascetical and mystical texts published in Venice in 1782 by St. Macarius of Corinth and St. Nikodemos of the Holy Mountain, although there is another famous *Philokalia*, of extracts from Origen, mostly on the problem of free will and the interpretation of the Scriptures, composed 358–9 by St. Basil the Great and St. Gregory of Nazianzus. The 18th-century *Philokalia* is a collection of texts from the 4th to the 14th centuries, culminating in works drawn from St. Gregory Palamas and his circle, both

predecessors and followers, representing "hesychasm," the monastic movement centered on the recitation of the Jesus Prayer which claimed that it was possible to behold the uncreated light of the Godhead in prayer. This claim was reconciled with the apophatic doctrine of God's unknowability by the distinction drawn by Gregory, based on earlier Greek patristic writings, between God's essence, which is indeed unknowable, and his uncreated (and therefore divine) "energies" or activities (*energeiai* in Greek) through which God makes himself known personally in the created world.

The texts in the *Philokalia* present a historical sequence of Byzantine ascetical texts, presented as the historical tradition leading up to Palamite hesychasm, but there is very little in them about the Jesus Prayer, and even less about the essence-energies distinction (the historical arrangement is probably due to St. Nikodemos, who had imbibed from the West a sense of history). Pride of place is given to St. Maximos the Confessor, Peter of Damascus, and St. Gregory Palamas himself, but many other important Byzantine ascetical writers are present, including Evagrios (both under his own name and that of Neilos), Mark the Monk, Diadochos of Photiki, John of Karpathos, Niketas Stethatos, and St. Gregory of Sinai. There are some, at first sight, surprising omissions: notably St. John of Sinai, author of the *Ladder of Divine Ascent*, and St. Symeon the New Theologian, who is represented by a few, unrepresentative, and even spurious, writings. St. John of Sinai is probably omitted because he was already well known in the Byzantine monastic tradition, his *Ladder* being read in the course of each Lent. The poor showing of St. Symeon is more mystifying, given that St. Nikodemos himself produced the first collected edition of his works.

Very little is known for sure about the origin of *Philokalia* and how the texts were selected. It belongs to a reform movement that sought to return to original monastic traditions of Athonite monks known as the "Kollyvades." However, in 1793, very shortly after the publication of the *Philokalia*, a Slavonic translation, called the *Dobrotolyubie* (a calque of *philokalia*), by the Ukrainian monk, St. Paisy Velichkovsky, was published in Iaşi in Moldavia (modern Romania). St. Paisy's selection is smaller than the Greek version (and, in particular, omits the more intellectually demanding writers such as Maximos the Confessor and even

Gregory Palamas), but draws on the same collection of material. His translation, which took some years, cannot be a selection from the printed Greek text, and must therefore be thought of as drawing from an already known – and presumably traditional – collection of ascetical texts, already current on the Holy Mountain. In 1822 a second edition of the *Dobrotolyubie* came out, supplemented by various other texts from the Greek *Philokalia*. Between 1877 and 1905 there appeared in Russia a further translation in five volumes, translated (into Russian) by St. Theophan the Recluse. This version restores Maximos and Palamas, omitted by St. Paisy, and considerably expands the list of philokalic fathers, including John of Sinai (in extracts), as well as the ascetics of Gaza, Barsanuphios, John, and Dorotheos, and St. Isaac the Syrian (in his lifetime a Nestorian bishop), as well as a more substantial group of texts by St. Symeon the New Theologian, and further texts from the original Greek *Philokalia*.

The immediate influence of the *Philokalia*, or rather *Dobrotlyubie*, was most immediately felt in Russia, where it was read by St. Seraphim of Sarov and the monks of Optina Pustyn', the monastery south of Moscow that became a center for the Slavophiles and other members of the Russian intelligentsia. It led to a revival of monasticism in Russia, in which stress was laid on the practice of private prayer, especially the Jesus Prayer, and the institution of spiritual fatherhood (*starchestvo*), echoes of which can be heard in Dostoevsky's *Brothers Karamazov*. It also inspired a revival of interest in the fathers, among whom the philokalic fathers formed a core. A work with a complex history, known in English as *The Way of the Pilgrim*, popularized the Jesus Prayer and (in its most common form) the institution of *starchestvo*, both in Russia and then through translations in the 20th century throughout the world. The Jesus Prayer, from being the preserve of primarily Athonite monks, came to gain a popularity that now reaches well beyond the bounds of Orthodoxy.

In the 20th century there were translations into many European languages, mostly selections from the Greek *Philokalia*. In the English-speaking world the first translations were from the Russian of St. Theophan's *Dobrotolyubie*, though there is a projected (not yet completed) translation of the whole Greek text of the original. Rather different is the Romanian translation, the work of the great Romanian theologian, Fr. Dumitru Stăniloae. This version is much longer than the Greek original, and often includes a more comprehensive selection of the works of the fathers included, as well as supplementing the selection found in the Greek version by other philokalic fathers, frequently following the example of St. Theophan. It also includes a commentary, recognizing that a reader of a printed book now cannot be sure of the guidance of a spiritual father, a thing taken for granted by the original compilers.

SEE ALSO: Elder (Starets); Hesychasm; Jesus Prayer; *Pilgrim, Way of the*; St. Gregory Palamas (1296–1359); St. Isaac the Syrian (7th c.); St. Maximos the Confessor (580–662); St. Nikodemos the Hagiorite (1749–1809); St. Paisy Velichovsky (1722–1794); St. Seraphim of Sarov (1759–1833); St. Symeon the New Theologian (949–1022); St. Theophan (Govorov) the Recluse (1815–1894); Sts. Barsanuphius and John (6th c.); Stăniloae, Dumitru (1903–1993)

References and Suggested Readings

Kadloubovsky, E. and Palmer, G. E. H. (1973) *Writings from the Philokalia on Prayer of the Heart*. London: Faber and Faber.

Palmer, G. E. H., Sherrard, P., and Ware, K. (1979) *The Philokalia*, Vols. 1– 4. London: Faber and Faber.

Smith, A. (2006) *The Philokalia: The Eastern Christian Spiritual Texts – Selections Annotated and Explained*. Woodstock, VT: Skylight Paths.

Philosophy

MARCUS PLESTED

Philosophy has long been integral to Eastern Orthodox theology, but the relationship has never been unproblematic. Distinct philosophical concerns can be traced in the earliest of the fathers, such as Justin Martyr, Theophilus of Antioch, or Clement and Origen of Alexandria, the latter being the first Christian philosopher of international stature. St. Basil the Great (and Augustine after him) regarded the church's use of philosophy as comparable to the manner in which the Jews escaping their servitude "despoiled the Egyptians"; and St. Gregory the Theologian used the memorable image of the Christian use of Greek philosophy as that of a gardener who carefully clips his roses of their thorns. Rooted in the patristic sense of the indispensability of a discerning use of human wisdom coupled with an understanding of Christianity as the true philosophy, Byzantine fathers such as St. Maximos the Confessor and St. John of Damascus make extensive use of philosophical categories and constructs. Maximos' theory of the divine *logoi*, the underlying principles of all things grounded in the *Logos*, clearly owes something to the Platonic understanding of Ideas but has been radically transformed in its christocentric focus and insistence upon the ontological gap between creature and Creator.

Between Maximos and John a general shift may be detected from a predominantly Platonic to a predominantly Aristotelian mode of discourse, without supposition of any incompatibility between the two. This Aristotelian preponderance was to obtain through the Byzantine and into the Ottoman era. Indeed, ongoing interest in Plato could often provoke controversy. The brilliant 11th-century writer Michael Psellos was appointed "Consul of Philosophers" by Constantine IX Monomachos at the newly established school of philosophy of the University of Constantinople. Psellos placed special emphasis on Plato and the Neoplatonic tradition, but was forced to clarify his position as to the ancillary status of philosophy in response to hostile criticism. His disciple and successor, John Italos, did not escape so lightly. John was indicted for heresy on a number of counts: for using reason to probe divine realities and for adhering to certain Platonic concepts, notably the reality of the realm of Ideas. Elements of his condemnation live on in the anathemas of the *Synodikon of Orthodoxy*.

St. Gregory Palamas is a useful example of the extreme care with which philosophy was employed in the later Byzantine era. Praised for his mastery of Aristotle in his youth, Palamas went on to draw on that expertise in his critique of Barlaam's theological agnosticism, asserting the propriety of apodictic argumentation in the articulation of divine revelation. Palamas excoriates philosophy when removed from its proper subservient status, but allows it when rightly ordered in the service of theology. The natural wisdom implanted in us can be cultivated through application and learning, including the standard curriculum of "outer learning." This outer learning has a role to play in the proclamation and defense of spiritual truths manifest in Scripture and witnessed in the lives of the saints. But it is always relative and potentially dangerous when misused. Indeed, it is this misuse of our God-given endowments that St. Paul targets in his blistering critique in 1 Corinthians and not, Gregory is careful to point out, natural human wisdom *per se*.

Such strictly ordered use of philosophical argumentation remained normative down to the last days of the Byzantine Empire, as witnessed, for example, in the anti-Latin syllogisms of St. Mark of Ephesus or the thoroughgoing Aristotelianism of George (later Gennadios) Scholarios, who was Mark's successor as leader of the anti-unionist party. Scholarios' philosophical sensibilities fostered his warm embrace of Aquinas and his polemic against his enthusiastic Neoplatonist contemporary, the crypto-Pagan George Gemistos Plethon. Plethon's espousal of Plato greatly impacted the West but gained little purchase in the Greek world in which Aristotelianism retained its dominance, aided by figures such as Theophilos Korydaleus and Maximos Margounios. An indication of this ongoing preponderance is evident in the condemnation in 1723 of Methodios Anthrakites by the church authorities in Constantinople. Methodios was branded a modernist for rejecting alike the salutary philosophy of Aristotle and the divinely inspired teachings of the fathers, favoring instead the new philosophy of Descartes.

Enlightenment ideas developed significant currency in the Greek thought-world, attacked by philosopher-theologians such as Vincent Damodos but more sympathetically, if by no means uncritically, received by figures such as Eugenios Bulgaris. Bulgaris taught and translated Wolff, Leibniz, and Locke. In 1753 he was appointed head of the new patriarchal academy on Mount Athos. But while in many respects a deeply traditional and anti-Latin theologian, Bulgaris' cautious openness to modern philosophy earned him no little hostility on the part of the monks of the Holy Mountain and the academy was eventually forced to close. The ruins can still be seen today, close to the monastery of Vatopedi. Thereafter, Enlightenment ideas are associated with Greek nationalists and secularists such as Adamantios Koraes, but were generally eschewed by prominent churchmen such as St. Athanasius of Paros and St. Nikodemos the Hagiorite – forefather, with St. Macarius of Corinth, of a remarkable Hesychast renaissance.

In the Slavic world, a broadly scholastic mode of theologizing prevailed on the level of official church teaching and instruction. Resistance to this tendency took shape not only in the Hesychast revival spearheaded by St. Paisy Velichkovsky, but also with recourse to German Idealism. This latter dimension is particularly evident in the Russian "Slavophile" school. Kireevsky, for one, was delighted to find in the church fathers all the essential insights of Schelling. In 1860 Alexander Bukharev published a compelling case for explicit engagement with contemporary philosophy, arguing from the fact of the incarnation that such philosophy must contain, at the least, signs of redemption and glimpses of truth. German Idealism was to remain a vital force in Russian religious thought, notably within the powerful but perplexing phenomenon of Sophiology. Indeed, it served many key thinkers, such as Sergius (Sergei) Bulgakov and Nikolai Berdiaev, as a bridge from Marxism into Orthodoxy.

In the post-World War II period, Orthodox theology has often entered into a creative dialogue with contemporary philosophical concerns. The presentation of Orthodox theology by Vladimir Lossky and John Meyendorff certainly taps into and addresses French personalism and existentialism, as does Metropolitan John Zizioulas' deeply influential exploration of personhood. Christos Yannaras makes intriguing use of Heidegger in his exploration of the opposition between Orthodoxy and the West. So-called postmodernist philosophies have yet, however, to provoke any very substantial Orthodox response. In a nutshell, while philosophy has rarely, if ever, been determinative of Orthodox thought, let alone of Orthodox practice, it has always been very much close at hand, and used to a considerable extent.

SEE ALSO: Berdiaev, Nikolai A. (1874–1948); Bulgakov, Sergius (Sergei) (1871–1944); Contemporary Orthodox Theology; Gnosticism; Hesychasm; Logos Theology; Lossky, Vladimir (1903–1958); Patristics; St. Gregory Palamas (1296–1359); St. John of Damascus (ca. 675–ca. 750); St. Mark of Ephesus (1392–1445); St. Maximos the Confessor (580–662); St. Nikodemos the Hagiorite (1749–1809); St. Paisy Velichovsky (1722–1794); Scholarios, George (Gennadios) (ca. 1403–1472)

References and Suggested Readings

Hussey, J. M. (1937) *Church and Learning in the Byzantine Empire*. Oxford: Oxford University Press.
Tatakis, B. (1959) *La Philosophie byzantine*. Paris: PUF.

Photogogika *see* Exaposteilarion

Pilgrim, Way of the
KONSTANTIN GAVRILKIN

An anonymous Russian book first published in 1881, containing an account of the narrator's spiritual journey through life while studying the *Philokalia* and practicing the Jesus Prayer. The text in its current version is the result of the editorial work of Bishop Theophan (Feofan) the Recluse, who also gave it the Russian title *Otkrovennye rasskazy strannika* (1884). For the authorship of the original text, see Basin (1996). The book was designed to popularize the radical development of the interior life in the spiritual tradition of St. Paisy Velichovsky and the Optina Elders, by showing that it could be adopted even by simple laity (the protagonist is a wandering peasant). The English translation received a wider notice in the West after its appearance in Salinger's novel *Franny and Zoey*.

SEE ALSO: Jesus Prayer; Optina; *Philokalia*; St. Paisy Velichovsky (1722–1794); St. Theophan (Govorov) the Recluse (1815–1894)

References and Suggested Readings

Basin, I. V. (1996) "Avtorstvo 'Otkrovennykh rasskazov strannika dukhovnomu ottsu svoemu'," in *Arkhim. Mikhail Kozlov, Zapiski i pis'ma*, ed. I. V. Basin. Moscow: Bogoroditse-Rozhdestvenskii Bobrenev monastyr', pp. 123–56.
Pentkovsky A. (ed.) (1999). *The Pilgrim's Tale*, trans. A. Smith. New York: Paulist Press.

Plate 50 The medieval pilgrim's entrance gate to the Monastery of the Holy Trinity at Sergiev Posad, near Moscow. Photo by John McGuckin.

Platytera

JOHN A. MCGUCKIN

The word comes from the Greek, meaning "She Who is More Wide" (or more "spacious") and refers to a type of the iconography of the Blessed Virgin where she is depicted, frequently in the eastern apse of the churches, with arms held out wide in prayer (Orans) and often horizontally distorted to emphasize the verbal symbol. On the Virgin's breast is the figure of Christ Emmanuel (sometimes in a roundel – *clypeus*, an iconographic symbol of the Logos conceived in his mother, but not yet born; which is an iconic type often called, in the Russian church, the "Virgin of the Sign" after Isaiah 7.14, or in the

Byzantine tradition *Blachernitissa*, after the palace chapel of that name in Constantinople). The Platytera icon is a Marian Christological symbol taken from the hymn "In You Rejoices All Creation" of the Liturgy of St. Basil, which speaks of the paradox of the incarnation, wherein the Logos who is greater than, and cannot be contained by, the heavens (as their Maker), is nevertheless perfectly fitted to the narrow constraints of the Virgin's womb. Accordingly, the Mother of God is shown to be "Wider than the Heavens," for she could contain the divine Lord whom the vast heavens could not.

References and Suggested Readings

Ryden, L. (1976) "The Vision of the Virgin at Blachernae and the Feast of the Pokrov," *Analecta Bollandiana* 94: 63–82.

Pneumatology *see* Holy Spirit

Pokrov see Protecting Veil

Poland, Orthodox Church of

JOHN A. MCGUCKIN

The Polish Orthodox Church takes its origins from two chief periods of establishment; the first in the 10th century, and the second revival after the political union of Lithuania and Poland in the 14th century. Its history and development have been closely bound up with the ebb and flow of the religious affiliations of the rulers of the area, the proximity and great influence of Russia, and the ascendancy of Catholicism. When the nation of Poland was politically dismembered in 1722, its Orthodox population was absorbed by the Russian church. When the country was reconstituted as a sovereign independent state after the cessation of World War I in 1918, her new borders contained about 4 million Orthodox faithful, mainly Ukrainians and Belo-Russians who inhabited the eastern part of the country. They had all belonged up to that time to the jurisdiction of the patriarch of Moscow. The Moscow patriarch of that time, St. Tikhon, was willing to grant autonomous status to the Polish church, but the new government, eager for all signs of national independence, was pressing the Polish hierarchy to declare their complete independence from Russian control by making a declaration of autocephaly. The senior Polish hierarch Archbishop George Yoroshevsky was attempting to resolve the tensions, and pressing towards a more limited autonomous status in 1923, when he was assassinated by a mentally deranged Russian monk who believed the hierarch was leading the Church into schism. The degree of scandal this murder caused occasioned the Polish government to appeal directly to the patriarch of Constantinople for the award of autocephalous status, and this was granted *sui jure* by Constantinople in a *Tomos* of 1924. The Moscow patriarchate did not recognize this situation until the country was subjugated under Russia's political control once more in 1945 and then, in 1948, the Moscow Patriarch Alexei wrote to the Phanar announcing that the Russian Orthodox Church had itself conferred autocephaly upon the Polish Orthodox. The Catholic majority in Poland tended to regard the Orthodox now among them as former Greek rite Catholics (Uniates) who had been pressured to enter the Orthodox Church in the 19th century. Catholic missionary attempts in the prewar years over-zealously tried to persuade the Orthodox to come back into union; a process that involved many cases of law suits to claim back churches and buildings, allied with the forcible closures of Orthodox institutions. The heavy-handedness shown in this period extensively soured relations between the Orthodox and the Catholics for generations afterwards. Prior to 1918 the Orthodox had 10 bishops in their synod, 5 dioceses, 15 monasteries, and about 2,000 parishes with 4 million faithful. By 1960 the Orthodox totalled only 4,500 faithful. Today, there are eight dioceses (one providing military chaplains, another supervising Polish Orthodox parishes abroad) with 400 parishes with just over 1 million faithful. The senior hierarch of the Polish Orthodox is now known as the Metropolitan of Warsaw and All Poland. The church retains very close ecclesiastical links with the Moscow patriarchate.

SEE ALSO: Lithuania, Orthodoxy in; Russia, Patriarchal Orthodox Church of

References and Suggested Readings

Kloczowski, J. (2000) *A History of Polish Christianity*. New York: Cambridge University Press.

McGuckin, J. A. (2008) *The Orthodox Church: An Introduction to Its History, Theology and Spiritual Culture*. Oxford: Wiley-Blackwell.

Ramet, P. (1988) *Eastern Christianity and Politics in the 20th Century*. Durham, NC: Duke University Press.

Reddaway, W. F. et al. (ed.) (1950) *The Cambridge History of Poland*, 2 vols. Cambridge: Cambridge University Press.

Rowell, S. C. (1994) *Lithuania Ascending: A Pagan Empire within East Central Europe*. Cambridge: Cambridge University Press.

Pontike, Evagrios (ca. 345–399)

JULIA KONSTANTINOVSKY

The celebrated guide of semi-eremitic monks of the North Egyptian desert of Nitria; likewise a prolific biblical exegete and author of numerous ascetical and mystical treatises on the soul's ascent to God.

Born in Ibora on the Black Sea, Evagrios enjoyed a close connection with the Cappadocian fathers: a pupil of Gregory of Nazianzus, he was ordained reader by Basil. Later (380–1), he accompanied Gregory of Nazianzus to Constantinople as Gregory's theological assistant in the time he composed the Five Theological Orations. There he enjoyed acclaim for his success in disputes against Eunomians. Around 383, when Nektarios was patriarch, he fled Constantinople on account of its spiritual perils and in search of a life of stillness (*hesychia*). At the monastery on the Mount of Olives (near Jerusalem) he was tonsured a monk by Rufinus and Melania, then traveled via Alexandria to settle in the Nitrian desert as a solitary. Having spent several years under the spiritual direction of St. Macarius of Egypt and standing within the tradition of the desert fathers, Evagrios himself became a spiritual guide of great renown. His *Praktikos*, *Gnostikos*, *Chapters On Prayer*, *Antirrhetikos*,

On Evil Thoughts, and Commentary on the Psalms were celebrated throughout late Antiquity and the Middle Ages. Styled as collections of mellifluous pithy maxims (apophthegmata), these expound the mind's journey of purification from obstreperous thoughts, the acquisition of virtues, and ascent to divine knowledge: the praxis-contemplation-theology trilogy. Via Cassian, Evagrios's ideas spread in the West at an early stage, while remaining ascetical classics in the Greek-speaking East. The late 5th century saw his writings translated into Syriac. He likewise authored other, more esoteric treatises (Gnostic Chapters, Letter to Melania) containing speculations about creation, Christ, and salvation, some of which were developed directly from Origen's works. There he argued that bodies and matter were fashioned subsequently to the creation of souls, as remedy for the souls' disobedience; Christ is not the divine Logos but is created; in the End of Things, all shall be saved (the Devil included, while bodies and material beings shall be destroyed). For these latter views, which first aroused the suspicions of Theophilus of Alexandria and Jerome (early 5th century), Evagrios was condemned as heterodox at the Fifth, Sixth, and Seventh Ecumenical Councils. Many of his Greek originals were destroyed, to remain only in Syriac translations. Other works survive under the names of persons of untainted reputation: notably, St. Nilus (Chapters on Prayer, in the Philokalia). Evagrios also appears in the Philokalia as Abba Evagrios the Monk (On Eight Thoughts). In later times Sts. John Climacus, Maximus the Confessor, and Symeon the New Theologian were deeply influenced by Evagrios's spiritual teachings; and in the later part of the 20th century he once again emerged as a spiritual master as his works found English translations.

References and Suggested Readings

Casiday, A. (2006) Evagrios Ponticus. Abingdon: Routledge.

Dysinger, L. (2002) Psalmody and Prayer in the Writings of Evagrios Ponticus. Oxford: Oxford University Press.

Evagrios (1972) The Praktikos and Chapters on Prayer, trans. J. E. Bamberger. Kalamazoo: Cistercian Publications.

Evagrios Ponticus (2003) Ad Monachos, trans. J. Driskoll. New York: Oxford University Press.

Konstantinovsky, J. (2009) Evagrios Ponticus: The Making of a Gnostic. Burlington, VT: Ashgate Press.

Palmer, G. E. H., Sherrard, P., and Ware, K. (eds. and trans.) (1979) The Philokalia: The Complete Text, 5 vols. London: Faber and Faber.

Sinkewicz, R. E. (trans.) (2003) Evagrios of Pontus: The Greek Ascetic Corpus. Oxford: Oxford University Press.

Possessors (Joseph of Volotsk)

KONSTANTIN GAVRILKIN

A loose translation of the Russian word stiazhateli (from the verb stiazhat', "to acquire," "to gain"), a disparaging nickname given by the followers of Nil Sorskii to Joseph of Volotsk (1439–1515) and his associates, who defended strict ascetic life in big monastic communities, argued for the church's and monasteries' rights of landownership for administering social welfare, and justified the use of secular power in defense of Orthodoxy, including persecution of heretics. Joseph is the author of the first Russian dogmatic treatise "Enlightener" (Prosvetitel'), written in response to the so-called heresy of the Judaizers (late 15th century).

SEE ALSO: Non-Possessors (Nil Sorskii); Russia, Patriarchal Orthodox Church of

References and Suggested Readings

Goldfrank, D. (ed.) (2000) Monastic Rule of Iosif Volotsky, rev. edn. Kalamazoo: Cistercian Publications.

Volotskii, I. (1993) Prosvetitel', ili, Oblichenie eresi zhidovstvuiushchikh. Moscow: Valaamskii monastyr'.

Zimin, A. A. and Lur'e, I. S. (eds.) (1959) Poslaniia Iosifa Volotskogo. Leningrad: Izd-vo Akademii nau.

Prayer

THEODORE G. STYLIANOPOULOS

Prayer by means of words, thoughts, gestures, gifts, and rites is a universal religious phenomenon through which human beings have expressed their dependence on, or need of, assistance from a higher power. The Christian meaning of prayer is deeply rooted in the biblical understanding of God, his saving work and will. In Orthodox Christianity, prayer, both private and corporate, is absolutely central, as is manifest in Orthodox worship, piety, and spirituality. Energized by the Holy Spirit, prayer is the soul of the church and the breath of life for the striving believer.

The Old Testament is a treasure house of prayers of praise, glorification, and thanksgiving as well as of petition, confession, repentance, intercession, lament, and complaint to God. Such prayers are expressed through words, songs, and gestures such as standing, outstretched hands, kneeling, and prostration. Magnificent examples of prayers include the Song of Moses (Exod. 15.1–18), Solomon's prayer at the dedication of the Temple (1 Kings 8.22–53), the Prayer of Hannah in the dedication of Samuel (1 Sam. 2.1–10), the priestly benediction (Num. 6.24–26), and the prayers of Ezra (Neh. 9.6–37) and Daniel (Dan. 9.3–19) for the restoration of God's people. The Book of Psalms, the hymn book of Israel and later that of the church, is the primary Old Testament example of the rich variety of prayers already mentioned. Here also we find the astonishing dynamic of the human–divine relationship ranging from exultation and thanksgiving to bitter lament and despair, yet hanging on by faith in the God of steadfast love and mercy. St. Athanasius' *Letter to Marcellinus*, an extraordinary essay on the Psalms that classifies and explains their usage, likens the Book of Psalms to a garden offering many beautiful flowers and a mirror of the soul reflecting the whole range of human feelings and experiences with God.

The New Testament presupposes the stream of Jewish worship and prayer. The Gospel of Luke records exquisite prayers by the Virgin Mary (Lk. 1.46–55), the priest Zechariah (Lk. 1.68–79), and the elder Simeon (Lk. 2.29–32). Jesus himself, circumcised on the eighth day and presented at the Temple on the fortieth, grew up in the tradition of Jewish prayer and piety with frequent appearances at the Temple and the synagogue. He not only gave instructions on prayer but also practiced heartfelt prayer, seeking solitude in the hills where he could pray all night, not least before making important decisions (Mk. 1.35; Lk. 6.12). The personal depth of Jesus' prayers to God the Father breaks forth in dramatic moments of joyful confession (Mt. 11.25), the giving of the Lord's Prayer (Mt. 6.5–13), the high priestly prayer to the Father (Jn. 17), and the agony at Gethsemane (Mk. 14.33–5), all of which exemplify the intimate relationship with God as a personal and loving Father which Jesus lived and taught. While the early church inherited much of the Jewish tradition of prayer, it gradually moved away from the Temple worship and cultic practices such as animal sacrifices, circumcision, and kosher foods, regarded as no longer compatible with the gospel. Instead, the church focused on its own rites of baptism, the Mystical Supper or Eucharist, and other rites that gradually developed into a whole tradition of worship continuously elaborated in content and structure. St. Paul, large sections of whose letters read like prayers, is a primary figure of the Christian renewal of prayer and worship in trinitarian forms based on the view that each baptized Christian is a living sacrifice to God (Rom. 6.4, 13; 12.1) and the church is the body of Christ and the temple of the Holy Spirit (1 Cor. 3.16–17; 12.12–27). Stirring echoes of early Christian prayers and aspects of worship, replete with Old Testament language, frequently occur in the Book of Revelation, where the eschatological drama of salvation itself is recounted from the perspective of the worship of God (Rev. 4.4–11; 5.8–14; 7.9–12; 11.15–18; 12.10–12; 15.3–4; 19.1–8).

The biblical foundations of prayer – the accessibility of a personal and moral God worthy of all honor and praise, the reciprocity of the divine-human relationship in freedom and faith, and the active saving purpose of God to rescue from evil and sanctify all things in Christ and the Spirit – shine through the development of an immensely rich tradition of Orthodox worship, piety, and spirituality. In Orthodox worship, next to the main sacraments of baptism and Eucharist, numerous other sacraments and rites sustain the community's engagement with the mystery of God and invoke God's blessings on key events or moments of life, such as birth, marriage, the need for forgiveness and healing, ministry, and death itself. Orthodox piety seeks the sanctification of every conceivable human activity through prayers for the blessing of schools, programs, homes, buildings, fields, agricultural products, animals, and (in modern times) automobiles.

Orthodox spirituality, flourishing in monastic traditions but not to be separated from church worship and practice, celebrates prayer as a highly intentional and focused activity in pursuit of Christian perfection through inner cleansing and sublime experiences of God. Origen, Gregory of Nyssa, Isaac the Syrian, Maximos the Confessor, Symeon the New Theologian, Gregory Palamas, the many authors included in the *Philokalia*, and modern saints and authors such as Theophan the Recluse and Silouan of Athos, are primary bearers of this Orthodox mystical tradition which has had significant impact on contemporary clergy and laity. The focus of this life of prayer is the recitation of the Jesus Prayer that, along with other ascetic disciplines, and above all reliance on God's grace, guide the Christian to deeper levels of prayer in the process of *theosis* (deification), including purification, illumination, and glorification. The striking metaphors – "heaven in the heart," "light of the mind," "food for the soul," "secret work of the heart," "spiritual breathing," "inner worship," "standing before God" – richly suggest the meaning and value of concentrated personal prayer. Prayer's ultimate purpose is the transformation of daily life into a sacrament of the presence, power, and holiness of God.

SEE ALSO: Baptism; Blessing Rituals; Deification; Eucharist; Jesus Prayer; Mystery (Sacrament)

References and Suggested Readings

Balentine, S. E. (1993) *Prayer in the Hebrew Bible*. Minneapolis: Fortress Press.

Bloom, A. (1970) *Beginning to Pray*. New York: Paulist Press.

Chariton, Higoumen. (1966) *The Art of Prayer: An Orthodox Anthology*. London: Faber and Faber.

Clément, O. (1996) *The Roots of Christian Mysticism*. Hyde Park, NY: New City Press.

Cullmann, O. (1995) *Prayer in the New Testament*. Minneapolis: Fortress Press.

McGuckin, J. A. (1999) "The Prayer of the Heart in Patristic and Early Byzantine Tradition," in P. Allen, W. Mayer, and L. Cross (ed.) *Prayer and Spirituality in the Early Church*, vol. 2. Banyo: Australian Catholic University, Centre for Early Christian Studies, pp. 69–108.

Miller, P. D. (1994) *They Cried to the Lord: The Form and Theology of Biblical Prayer*. Minneapolis: Augsburg Fortress.

Palmer, G. E. H. et al. (eds.) (1979–95) *The Philokalia: The Complete Text*, vols. 1–4. London: Faber and Faber.

Payne, R. (1979) *The Classics of Western Spirituality: Origen on Martyrdom, Prayer, et al*. New York: Paulist Press.

Payne, R. (ed.) (1980) *The Classics of Western Spirituality: Athanasius, the Life of St. Anthony and the Letter to Marcellinus*. New York: Paulist Press.

Prayer of the Heart *see* Jesus Prayer; St. Isaac the Syrian (7th c.); St. Paisy Velichovsky (1722–1794)

Priesthood

GEORGE E. DEMACOPOULOS

The term "priesthood" (*hierosynes*) in Orthodox thought simultaneously refers to the clerical orders in general and the specific clerical rank of the priest or presbyter (*presbyteros*). The concept of Christian priesthood originated during the 1st and early 2nd centuries through a conceptual bridging of the Eucharistic meal and the ancient Hebraic practice (shared by many Greco-Roman cults) in which a specific group of leaders was responsible for making a sacrificial offering to God on behalf of the community. In Christian theology, of course, the Eucharistic meal is understood to be a bloodless sacrifice through which Christ himself, in the form of the High Priest (Heb. 2.17, 3.1, 4.14), offers the sacrifice of himself in order to reconcile to God those who consume the meal. In the celebration of the divine liturgy, the priest stands in the place of Christ, leading the community in the presentation of the bread and wine as the sacrifice. As a consequence, the celebrant is sometimes understood to represent Christ within the community of believers. With time, the function of the priesthood expanded greatly beyond its initial Eucharistic role to incorporate other sacramental, pastoral, and administrative responsibilities.

In the New Testament the terms for presbyter (literally, "elder") and bishop (*episkopos*, literally, "overseer") seem to be interchangeable (e.g., Titus 1.5–7). By the late 1st or early 2nd century, however, the bishop emerged as the clear leader of the local community. Presbyters played a subordinate role as teachers, administrators, and as a council of advisers, but were clearly seen to outrank the order of deacons. As Christianity expanded and local communities grew larger than a single (cathedral) city church could contain, both urban and rural bishops began to invest individual priests with the authority to celebrate the Eucharistic meal in outlying parishes and perform baptisms in their stead. In this early period the priest was only permitted to serve this function within those parishes directly under his bishop's jurisdiction and he was not permitted to serve private chapels (see Trullo, Canons 31, 59). Moreover, a priest was not permitted to move to another diocese without approval. Similarly, teaching authority remained technically within the bishop's domain, but parish priests increasingly assumed primary catechetical and doctrinal instruction for most Christian communities.

The New Testament does not offer specific instructions regarding the selection of presbyters. Both 1 Timothy and Titus list a number of regulations concerning the appointment of bishops and deacons and we might reasonably assume that the earliest selection of presbyters followed similar criteria. In the Byzantine period, canon law increasingly incorporated Old Testament proscriptions to block certain persons (e.g., the deaf, the blind, the deformed, proscriptions that were often subjected to allegorical interpretation) from the priesthood. Canon law also set a minimum age for ordination at 30 (by comparison, a deacon was required to be 25 and a bishop 35). And while ordination to the deaconate and the priesthood was certainly possible for married men (unlike bishops, who after the 4th century were drawn from the celibate clergy), most patristic descriptions of the ideal priest are laden with ascetic credentials.

Theological reflection on the priesthood began in earnest with Gregory the Theologian's (330–90) *Apology for Flight* (Oration 2), which was the first Christian treatise to explore in detail the criteria for ordination and the pastoral responsibilities for leadership. Written ostensibly at the time of his ordination to the deaconate, Gregory moves frequently between generic terms for Christian leadership and that of the bishop specifically. He argues that all Christian leaders should possess an advanced education and extensive ascetic experience. Gregory further suggests that the ideal leader must learn to strike a balance between private ascetic retreat, in order to experience the contemplative life, and active service in the form of ministering to others. His model of an "active contemplative" became the prevailing model for the priesthood in the Byzantine period and remains so for the Orthodox Church to this day. Not surprisingly, John Chrysostom's (349–407) rhetorical masterpiece, *On the Priesthood*,

which borrows extensively from Gregory's *Apology*, cautioned that the balance between service and personal contemplation was often elusive. Like Gregory, Chrysostom typically employs the generic term *hierosynes*, rather than *presbyteros* or *episcopos*, in his description of the pastoral leader. While it did little to alter Gregory's theology of the priesthood, *On the Priesthood* enjoyed one of the largest readerships of any Greek text in the Middle Ages and did much to advance the idea of clerical importance. It suggests, for example, that the priest is more important than the angels because he, unlike they, baptizes and celebrates the divine liturgy.

The most sophisticated treatise of pastoral literature in the Orthodox tradition is the Treatise on Pastoral Care (*Liber regulae pastoralis*) by Pope Gregory the Great (540–604), which was the only Latin treatise of the Middle Ages to be translated into Greek and disseminated by imperial order during the author's lifetime. Like Chrysostom, Pope Gregory borrowed directly from Gregory the Theologian's concept of the active contemplative. He also greatly expanded the earlier Gregory's list of spiritual characteristics, which required individualized spiritual remedies. Indeed, the *Liber pastoralis* describes 72 spiritual personality traits set in pairs of opposites, for which he offers a corresponding regimen for spiritual therapy. The pastoral solutions, especially, demonstrate Gregory's extensive familiarity with the patterns of spiritual direction then operative in the ascetic community and represent a direct bridging of the monastic and lay patterns of spiritual direction.

In the modern Orthodox world the most thorough treatment of the priesthood came indirectly through the work of Fr. Nicholas Afanasiev (1893–1966), a prominent Russian theologian and member of the St. Sergius faculty in Paris. Afanasiev's Eucharistic ecclesiology radically challenged contemporary bifurcations between lay and cleric, priest and bishop, and local church versus institutional church. Afanasiev viewed the local Eucharistic community as a complete embodiment of the entire Christian community and held that the clergy and laity were ontologically equal. Relying on the biblical concept of a priesthood of all believers (cf. 1 Pet. 2.9) and the interchangeability of presbyter and bishop in the pastoral epistles, Afanasiev took aim at what he perceived to be an Orthodox form of clericalism that had initially developed in the Byzantine period, but also later seeped into the Orthodox tradition from Roman Catholic sources. The ritual for Orthodox priestly ordination states: "The divine grace which always heals that which is infirm and completes that which is wanting elevates through the laying on of hands, the Reverend Deacon -N- to be a priest." The secret prayers of the bishop accompanying the laying on of hands speak also about the "great grace of the Holy Spirit" which is to be conferred, the advancement to the degree of priesthood, the standing at the altar, the ministry of the word, the proclamation of the gospel, the offering of gifts, and the renewing of the people through baptismal regeneration.

SEE ALSO: Baptism; Contemporary Orthodox Theology; Deacon; Eucharist; St. John Chrysostom (349–407)

References and Suggested Readings

Afanasiev, N. (2007) *The Church of the Holy Spirit*, trans. V. Permiakov. Notre Dame: University of Notre Dame Press.

Brown, R. E. (1970) *Priest and Bishop: Biblical Reflections*. New York: Paulist Press.

Chryssavgis, J. (1992) "Ministry in the Orthodox Church," *Sourozh* 50: 27–30.

Gregory the Great, St. (2008) *Book of Pastoral Rule*, trans. G. Demacopoulos. Crestwood, NY: St. Vladimir's Seminary Press.

Gregory of Nazianzus, St. (1994) *Apology for his Flight (Oration 2)*. Nicene, Post-Nicene Fathers series, second series, vol. 7, trans. C. Browne. Peabody, MA: Hendrickson Publishers.

John Chrysostom, St. (1984) *On the Priesthood*, trans. G. Neville. Crestwood, NY: St. Vladimir's Seminary Press.

Norris, R. A. (1984) "The Beginnings of Christian Priesthood," *Anglican Theological Review*, Supplement Series 9: 18–32.

Proimion *see* Kontakion

Prokeimenon

JOHN A. MCGUCKIN

The Prokeimenon (the Greek word means "what precedes," that is, a prelude, or introduction) is a liturgical refrain taken from a verse of a psalm which is interspersed (usually by means of the cantor alternating in chant with the reader) with a selection of other verses, or half-verses, from that psalm. It serves to introduce the scriptural reading (the "Apostle") at the divine liturgy. Prokeimena also occur at the Vespers and Orthros services before the Old Testament readings (and even when these may not have scriptural readings appointed for the day). The current system of Prokeimena is a survival from earlier times in the liturgy when the entire psalm would have been read as part of the cycle of biblical readings in church. In current Greek practice the reading of the verses is relatively simple. In Slavic use it is a more extended antiphonal refrain.

Proskomedie (Prothesis)

JOHN A. MCGUCKIN

The ritual preparatory to the celebration of the divine liturgy, which is substantially the preparation of the *prosphora* or loaves of offering. Greek usage involves the cutting out, from a single large loaf, of a cube of bread marked on its surface with the cross-shaped ICXC NIKA cipher ("Jesus Christ Conquers") which has been baked into it. Slavic use generally employs five smaller prosphora, the first being used for the Eucharistic Lamb (*Amnos*) and the others for various commemorations. The priest who celebrates the Proskomedie (it is always celebrated by one priest alone) will leave some of the final elements unfinished if it is an episcopal service, since the presiding bishop will complete the prayers just before the Great Entrance. After the central cube of bread has been cut out, with attendant prayers, using a ceremonial knife (or *lance*), other particles of bread are also removed to symbolize the Blessed Theotokos, and the nine orders of saints (including angels, prophets, apostles, hierarchs ascetics, and martyrs), which conclude with the saint who composed the liturgy being celebrated (St. John Chrysostom, Basil, or James). These are laid on either side of the Lamb on the *diskos*. Particles are then removed to commemorate the ruling bishop, "the emperor" (civil authorities), the founders of the church, and those living and dead whom the priest wishes to remember. Wine is mixed with a little water in the chalice and the ritual concludes with the incensing of the veils that are laid over the sacred vessels in readiness for the Eucharist to begin. The faithful also provide other lists of names, and offerings of prosphora breads, to commemorate their own family lists (*diptychs*) for the living as well as the dead. The particles are placed into the chalice after communion with an intercessory prayer: "for all those commemorated here." In earlier times the Proskomedie was celebrated in a separate building (as at Hagia Sophia, Constantinople), but in most Orthodox churches today the northern side of the altar area is used, where a small altar of preparation (*prothesis*) can be found, usually adorned with iconic symbolism recalling the nativity.

SEE ALSO: Amnos; Eucharist; Lance

Prosomoia *see* Idiomelon

Prosphora *see* Lance; Proskomedie (Prothesis)

Protecting Veil

VERA SHEVZOV

The Protecting Veil (Greek *skepê*, *maphorion*; Russian, *Pokrov*), celebrated on October 1, is one of the most beloved Marian feasts on the Orthodox calendar in Slavonic Orthodox lands. The inspiration for the feast was a 10th-century vision in the Church of the Virgin of Blachernae, Constantinople, by the Blessed Andrew, the Fool for Christ, as recorded by the presbyter Nicephoros. According to the tradition, the Mother of God spread her protective veil, which "radiated the glory of God," over all those present in church. The celebration of the Protecting Veil thus recognizes the *Theotokos* as the universal heavenly protectress of all Christians. While there is scant evidence of any liturgical commemoration of this feast in Byzantium, it became immensely popular in Russia; whether developing from origins at Constantinople, Kiev, or Northern Russia remaining a point of controversy. By the end of the 19th century the feast was usually dated to the 12th century and was credited to the Grand Prince Andrei Bogoliubskii, who took St. Andrew as

Plate 51 Icon of the Protecting Veil depicting the Holy Fool Andrew. Photo Temple Gallery, London.

his patron saint. Liturgically, it parallels the feast of the Deposition of the Precious Robe of the Theotokos at Blachernae for July 2. The festal icon shows the central figure of the Mother of God spreading her protective veil, Blessed Andrew pointing her out to his disciple Epiphanius, St. John the Forerunner (who in Andrew's vision accompanied Mary into the Blachernae church), and St. Romanos the Melodist (whose commemoration also occurs on October 1).

SEE ALSO: Fools, Holy; Theotokos, the Blessed Virgin

References and Suggested Readings

Lyden, L. (1976) "The Vision of the Virgin at Blachernae and the Feast of the Pokrov," *Analecta Bollandiana* 94: 63–82.

Presbyter Nicephorus (1976) "Life of Andrew, the Fool for Christ," in J. P. Migne (ed.) *Patrologiae Graecae*, Vol. 111. Turnhout, Belgium: Brepols, cols. 620–887.

Prothesis *see* Proskomedie

Protodeacon

MARIA GWYN MCDOWELL

A rank of the diaconate, historically the protodeacon is a title of honor given to chief deacons who are not monastics. In contemporary practice the protodeacon is the senior deacon attached to a cathedral or principal church. The protodeacon is elevated, not ordained, to the new rank. The protodeacon can claim precedence when serving with other deacons. If more than one protodeacon serve together, precedence is given according to the dates of their elevation.

SEE ALSO: Archdeacon; Deacon; Deaconess; Ordination

Protopsaltes *see* Music (Sacred)

Psaltes (Cantor)

DIMITRI CONOMOS

One of the minor clerical orders in those Orthodox Churches that employ monophonic chants. The chief cantor, the protopsaltes, initiates choral performances by intoning a conventional formula or, more frequently, by singing one or two starting notes to establish the pitch. The earliest testimonies to a solo cantor are from Constantinople (second half of the 4th century) where, in the responsorial execution of scriptural verse – especially psalmody – the cantor sang refrains which were repeated by the congregation. In Byzantium there were two choirs, each with its own leader: the protopsaltes for the right choir and the lampadarios for the left.

Plate 52   Bishop in the Monastery of St. John on Patmos, Greece, talking to two monks. ILM Image Group/Alamy.

Psilanthropism

JOHN A. MCGUCKIN

From the Greek meaning "Merely a Man." It signifies the heretical doctrine that Jesus was a human being who was highly graced by God, as a Prophet, or Spirit-bearer (*pneumatophoros*), or even the greatest of all the saints; but was not, in the proper sense of the term, "divine." The heresy has appeared in numerous forms throughout church history, associated first with the Judeo-Christian Ebionite sect, and the 2nd-century "Modalists" who approached Christology in terms of a holy servant of God, Jesus, being caught up in the energy and work of the Spirit, and "manifested" as the Son of God in this sense, though not being divine in anything other than an exemplarist sense, a matter of honorific association of words. Paul of Samosata made this view notorious, and was one of the first public dissident bishops to be censured by a formal council of the church. In patristic times, however, the position was most closely associated with the person and teachings of Photinos, bishop of Sirmium (d. ca. 376), who was deposed for his christological views at the Council of Sirmium in 351 (Socrates, *Church History* 2.18, 29–30; Sozomen, *Church History* 4.6; Epiphanius, *Heresies* 71), and once more symbolically censured at the Council of Constantinople in 381, and yet again by the imperial decree of Theodosius II in 428. The heresy is thus also known in the Orthodox Church as "Photinianism."

Origen had partly clarified the Modalist problem, but also confused the matter for the 4th-century theologians, by his earlier and peculiar Christology that Jesus had to be distinguished from the Divine Logos, as being the bearer of the Logos, not synonymous with him. Origen, however, cannot rightly be classed as a Psilanthropist because his understanding of the "Preexistent Soul Jesus" belongs more to a category of Angelic Christology fused with a theology of the Incarnation of the Divine Logos. The Christology of Arius is more confused still, but it is clear enough that though he leaned away from seeing Jesus as the Divine Logos he nevertheless did not see him as "merely a man." Many of the ancient Orthodox polemicists were less careful in their analysis, and often fathered Psilanthropism onto their heterodox opponents in the course of the centuries when it seemed that they were advocating less than the full Nicene Christology (manifested in the Nicene Creed, St. Athanasius, St. Gregory the Theologian, and St. Cyril of Alexandria, for example): namely, that Jesus was synonymous with the Eternal and Divine Logos himself, as incarnated within history. For polemical reasons, therefore, several heterodox theologians of Antiquity such as Theodore Mopsuestia and Nestorius were erroneously accused of Psilanthropism. The heresy has been seen as a fundamental one, attacking the central and basic faith of the Orthodox Church that in the person of Christ Jesus we were "not saved by an angel, or a servant, but by God himself." Psilanthropism has been on the Christian horizons for a very long time, and its reappearance as widespread phenomenon in many parts of the modern world is nothing new, although the extent to which forms of Psilanthropism are now sustained among many western academic theologians (such as parts of the "Jesus of History" Movement, or aspects of the Liberation Christology movement) is unusual.

SEE ALSO: Christ; Council of Nicea I (325); Incarnation (of the Logos); Logos Theology; St. Athanasius of Alexandria (ca. 293–373); St. Cyril of Alexandria (ca. 378–444)

References and Suggested Readings

Bardy, G. (1935) "Photine," in *Dictionnaire de théologie catholique*, vol. 12, pt. 2. Paris: Letouzey et Ané.

Hanson, R. P. C. (1988) *The Search for the Christian Doctrine of God*. Edinburgh: T&T Clark.

McGuckin, J. A. (2000) "Quest for the Historical Jesus," in A. Hastings (ed.) *The Oxford Companion to Christian Thought*. Oxford: Oxford University Press. pp. 587–9.

Petavius, D. (1636) *De Photino Haeretico eiusque Damnatione*. Paris.

Simonetti, M. (1965) "Studi sull'Arianesimo," *Verba Seniorum* 5: 135–59.

Psychosabbaton

JEFFREY B. PETTIS

The Greek word *psychosabbaton* ("soul Sabbath") refers to the Saturdays in the Orthodox liturgical year set aside for a special remembering of the departed.

On these "Sabbata" days special hymns are added to the divine service to commemorate the dead. The designation of the day of Saturday stems from its symbolic association with Christ's own entombment on that day. The designated days include the Saturday of Meatfare week, or the second Saturday before Great Lent; the Saturday before the Sunday of the Last Judgment; the second, third, and fourth Saturdays of Great Lent; the Saturday before Pentecost; and the Saturday prior to the Feast of St. Demetrius the Great Martyr. The divine service on these days has special hymns selected for the commemoration of the dead. Usually the memorial observance of the Panikhida follows the divine liturgy on Saturday morning, but it may also occur after Vespers on the preceding Friday evening (vigil of Saturday). Prayers are offered for the repose of those who have departed and for the comfort of the living. The service has a penitential emphasis, in that it calls believers to humility before the reality of the brevity of mortal human life. The service may include the use of the ancient tradition of Kollyva, a liturgical meal blessed and taken in memory of the dead. A service celebrated on behalf of an individual on these days will usually take place at the grave site, but memorial services for all the faithful who have departed occur in the church, as do services for those whose graves may be located at a far distance. In some cases the Saturday liturgy takes place in the cemetery chapel. The Orthodox Church additionally recognizes and prays for the dead on the holiday called "The Day of Rejoicing" which falls after St. Thomas Sunday in the post-Pascha Bright week.

SEE ALSO: Death (and Funeral); Kollyva

References and Suggested Readings

Krueger, D. (ed.) (2006) *Byzantine Christianity*. Minneapolis: Fortress Press.

Langford-James, R. (ed.) (1975) *A Dictionary of the Eastern Orthodox Church*. New York: Burt Franklin.

Q

Quinisext Council (Council in Trullo) (692)

M. C. STEENBERG

The Quinisext Council (Latin, *quinisextum*, "fifth-sixth": so named as it was seen to complete the work of the fifth and sixth ecumenical councils) was convened in 692 by Emperor Justinian II and held in Constantinople's Trullo ("domed") palace, where the sixth council had convened in 681 (hence its alternate name, the Council in Trullo, or Troullo). Its purpose was to issue legislative canons, which neither the fifth nor sixth councils had done. These include injunctions against fasting on Saturdays, celebrating full liturgies on weekdays in Great Lent, and so on. Many of the canons address differences in Eastern and Western Church practice, and this, together with the lack of western representation at the council, ensured its disputed place in the ecumenical conciliar lists of the Western Churches, while in the Byzantine world it was widely assigned the same ecumenical status of its conciliar predecessors.

SEE ALSO: Canon Law; Ecumenical Councils

References and Suggested Readings

Davis, L. D. (1987) *The First Seven Ecumenical Councils: Their History and Theology*. Wilmington: Michael Glazier.

Meyendorff, J. (1989) *Imperial Unity and Christian Divisions: The Church 450–680AD*. Crestwood, NY: St. Vladimir's Seminary Press.

The Concise Encyclopedia of Orthodox Christianity, First Edition. Edited by John Anthony McGuckin.
© 2014 John Wiley & Sons, Ltd. Published 2014 by John Wiley & Sons, Ltd.

R

Relics

MONICA M. WHITE

Relics – objects connected with a holy person or event – are venerated in all Eastern Churches. Primary relics are from the body of a holy person (usually bones, but also hair, blood, etc.), while secondary relics are objects from an event in sacred history or with which a holy person has come into contact, most famously the True Cross. Relics can play an important role in the cult of a saint. The discovery of incorrupt relics has often been taken as a sign of sanctity, particularly in Kievan Rus, although this has never been an official requirement for sainthood (Lenhoff 1993). Relics can also help spread a saint's cult by being broken up and distributed, or by exuding oil which can be collected by pilgrims.

The healing power of relics is attested in the Old Testament. In 2 Kings 13.21 a dead man was revived when his body touched that of Elisha. Although the New Testament makes no reference to human remains effecting cures, it does describe miracles accomplished through secondary relics, such as the woman with a haemorrhage who was healed by touching the hem of Christ's garment in Mark 5.25–9 (see also Acts 19.12).

These stories shaped Christian beliefs about relics, encouraging the idea that the body of a holy person had a power which could be transferred to objects with which it came in contact, both before and after death. The practice of keeping relics in homes and churches may have originated in Egypt, where it was not unusual for pagans and Christians alike to store the mummies of relatives in their homes. Christians may have begun distributing pieces of such mummies, particularly if they had belonged to martyrs or holy men, in the belief that they had healing properties (Wortley 2006: 12–14, 18–27).

Attempts by the authorities to discourage the distribution of relics (contrary to early Roman Law) were largely ineffectual, and their veneration quickly became widespread in the churches. As their popularity grew, so did the trade in them and the distribution of false relics. Athanasius of Alexandria and the Theodosian Code attacked these practices, apparently to no avail (Wortley 2006: 24–6).

In addition to curing individuals, relics took on broader political and ecclesiastical functions. Gregory the Illuminator, for example, brought relics with him to use in his work in Armenia. Despite his desire for his own body to remain concealed after his death, his relics were eventually discovered, and possession of them became a source of authority for heads of the Armenian Church from the 12th century onward (Kouymjian 2005: 221–5).

Constantinople soon after its foundation amassed a spectacular collection of relics from across the Christian world. They do not seem to have been banned during Iconoclasm, possibly because biblical

The Concise Encyclopedia of Orthodox Christianity, First Edition. Edited by John Anthony McGuckin.
© 2014 John Wiley & Sons, Ltd. Published 2014 by John Wiley & Sons, Ltd.

Plate 53 Exhuming relics of the saints at Optina Hermitage. RIA Novosti/AKG.

precedents existed for their veneration (Wortley 2003: 169–73). Particularly prized were the city's Marian relics, which included her milk, spindle, girdle, and robe. The robe, in particular, was believed to have saved the city from destruction on a number of occasions (Wortley 2005).

Relics were well represented in Byzantine iconography, and by the 10th century a complete graphic "life cycle" had been developed for them. This included the Invention or discovery of a relic, its Translation to a new city or church, the Adventus or formal greeting of the relic when it arrived, its Deposition in its new resting place, and its Veneration (Walter 1982).

Although relics were numerous, they came from a relatively restricted group of saints. In his survey of relics in the Greek Orthodox church, Otto Meinardus (1970/71) found evidence for 3,602 relics of 476 saints, out of the approximately 3,800 saints who were liturgically recognized by the late Ottoman period.

Furthermore, five saints (Charalampos, Panteleimon, Tryphon, Paraskeva, and George) accounted for nearly a quarter of all relics.

Because relics were coveted, theft was common. The relics of many famous saints were taken to the West in the medieval period, and Constantinople lost most of its relics when the city was sacked in 1204 (Geary 1990). The Vatican has, however, returned a number of relics to various Eastern Churches since the mid-1960s as part of efforts to improve ecumenical relations (Meinardus 1970: 348–50).

Relics attracted international attention when the Russian government sponsored the exhumation of Tsar Nicholas II and his family, who were murdered by Bolsheviks and buried outside the city of Ekaterinburg in 1918. Although DNA tests made a strong case that the remains were those of the Romanovs, Patriarch Aleskii II refused to accept the findings and did not send a representative to the reburial ceremony on

Plate 54   A reliquary containing the remains of several saints. Relics are commonly found in Orthodox ritual and the saints are widely venerated by the faithful as vessels of the Holy Spirit, still active after their deaths. Photo by John McGuckin.

July 17, 1998. Nevertheless, the Russian Orthodox Church canonized the family, along with other new martyrs of the Soviet period, at a bishop's council in August 2000 (King and Wilson 2003: 381–503).

SEE ALSO: Ecumenism, Orthodoxy and; Healing; Iconography, Styles of; Myrobletes Saints; New Martyrs; Old Testament

References and Suggested Readings

Geary, P. (1990) *Furta Sacra: thefts of Relics in the Central Middle Ages*. Princeton: Princeton University Press.

King, G. and Wilson, P. (2003) *The Fate of the Romanovs*. Hoboken, NJ: John Wiley.

Kouymjian, D. (2005) "The Right Hand of St. Gregory and Other Armenian Arm Relics," in P. Borgeaud and Y. Volokhine (eds.) *Les Objets de la mémoire: pour une*

approche comparatiste des reliques et de leur culte. Bern: Peter Lang, pp. 221–46.

Lenhoff, G. (1993) "The Notion of 'Uncorrupted Relics' in Early Russian Culture," in B. Gasparov and O. Raevsky-Hughes (eds.) *Christianity and the Eastern Slavs*, vol. 1. Berkeley: University of California Press, pp. 252–75.

Meinardus, O. (1970) "An Examination of the Traditions Pertaining to the Relics of St. Mark," *Orientalia Christiana Periodica* 36: 348–76.

Meinardus, O. (1970/71) "A Study of the Relics of Saints of the Greek Orthodox Church," *Oriens Christianus* 54/55: 130–278.

Walter, C. (1982) *Art and Ritual of the Byzantine Church*. London: Variorum.

Wortley, J. (2003) "Icons and Relics: A Comparison," *Greek, Roman and Byzantine Studies* 43: 161–74.

Wortley, J. (2005) "The Marian Relics at Constantinople," *Greek, Roman and Byzantine Studies* 45: 171–87.

Wortley, J. (2006) "The Origins of Christian Veneration of Body-Parts," *Revue de l'histoire des religions* 223: 5–28.

Repentance

ANDREI PSAREV

In Orthodox thought repentance is the blessed mourning of a person and longing for God (*penthos*) following after a sense of having moved away from him. It is a conversion to God and, as a result, is what scripture describes as radical change of mind or heart (*metanoia*, see Mk. 1.15). Christ came to save sinners having called them to repentance and belief in his gospel (Mt. 9.13). The parable of the prodigal son (Lk. 15.11) outlines the stages of how Orthodox understand the process of repentance: contrition, aversion from sin, repudiation of evil, confession, reconciliation with God and one's neighbor.

The words from the apostle about the impossibility of repentance for those who, by sinning, crucify Christ again (Heb. 6.4–6) reflect a dilemma of the early church; for in the 3rd and 4th centuries the Novatianists and Donatists permanently excluded from Eucharistic communion those who were guilty of serious sins. The greater church would not accept this rigorist approach, having prescribed in its canons various terms of abstinence from the Eucharist on account of grave sins; but no transgressor was ever to be deprived of the Eucharist at the time of their death (Nicea 1. Canon 13). There are no sins that may prevent a person from entering into the dedicated life of repentance which is monasticism (Quinisext Council. Canon 43). Repentance has been called in Orthodoxy the "second baptism."

Canon 12 of St. Gregory the Wonderworker (3rd century) defines how the church classifed penitents. In early times certain classes of sinners were debarred from full Eucharistic membership and had to stand apart from the community, in the narthex or outside the church building, sometimes for many years. St. Basil the Great (4th century) was not just occupied with the impact of sin on an individual, but also with the spiritual health of the entire congregation (St. Basil. Canon 88). In the same way as sin injures the body of the whole ecclesiastical community, through the healing of each member the entire church body acquires reconciliation with God (1 Cor. 12.26).

Although public ceremonies of repentance were already common in the time of St. Basil the Great, private repentance, appropriate for particular sins, was also in use (St. Basil. Canon 34). The successor of St. Gregory of Nazianzus, Nectarius of Constantinople, was the first major hierarch known to formally abolish the ecclesiastical office of public repentance in Constantinople in the late 4th century. By the 9th century, after the triumph of the monks over the iconoclasts, the practice of private monastic confession became standard. Nevertheless, the correspondence of Archbishop Demetrios Chomatenos demonstrates that the arranging of public penance was occasionally known even in 13th-century Byzantium. Current Orthodox practice is that a Christian repents secretly of personal sins, while a more public acknowledgment of repentance may be appropriate in case of widely known offenses. It is Christ himself who receives the believer's repentance. The priest, acting as confessor, is only a witness, a spiritual therapist who gives advice, or who may prescribe a penitential remedy (*epitimion*). The church annually assigns the time of Great Lent as an occasion for repentance. During this forty-day period Christians are called to turn from self-love towards deeper love of God and one's neighbor. Various ascetic and pious deeds – fasting, almsgiving, extended prayer with tears – may go along with the Orthodox practice of repentance.

According to the desert fathers, St. Gregory Palamas, and other church teachers, repentance signifies the beginning of the process of rebirth. Through this process a person becomes a participant in divine nature (2 Pet. 1.4). Repentance is not simply a matter of rejecting sin and leading a life of virtue, but rather a transformation that helps the person to discover in the soul's depths the very likeness of God.

SEE ALSO: Asceticism; Canon Law; Confession; Metanie (Metanoia)

Rferences and Suggested Readings

Antonopoulos Nektarios, Archimandrite (2000) *Return*. Athens: Akritas Publications.

Chrysostomos, Archbishop of Etna (1997) *Repentance*. Etna, CA: Center for Traditionalist Orthodox Studies.

Chryssavgis, J. (1990) *Repentance and Confession*. Brookline, MA: Holy Cross Orthodox Press.

Erickson, J. H. (1991) "Penitential Discipline in the Orthodox Canonical Tradition," in *Challenge of Our Past*. Crestwood, NY: St. Vladimir's Seminary Press.

Melling, D. J. (2001) "Metanoia," in *The Blackwell Dictionary of Eastern Christianity*. Oxford: Blackwell.

Resurrection

THEODORE G. STYLIANOPOULOS

Belief in resurrection, and specifically resurrection from the dead, is a distinct biblical teaching that derives from Judaism and finds its full significance in the person and life of Jesus of Nazareth, historically proclaimed to have died, been buried, and risen from the dead. Much more so than in Judaism, resurrection is absolutely central to Christianity (1 Cor. 15.12–19), especially Eastern Christianity, because the death and resurrection of Jesus Christ constitute the foundational saving events, and the core of the gospel, which lie behind the birth and character of the church, the New Testament, and Christian theology and spirituality. While resurrection is chiefly tied to the resurrection of Jesus and to the hope of the resurrection of the dead at his glorious return, the term also carries diverse metaphorical meanings such as the historical restoration of a people, life after death, immortality of the soul, and even an experience of spiritual renewal in this present life. In ancient paganism the theme of resurrection was connected not to a historical person or historical event, but rather to mythological deities such as Isis and Osiris whose cult celebrated the annual rebirth of nature and the power of fertility, a phenomenon that scholarship has widely judged to be entirely different from the Christian understanding in origin, scope, and meaning.

In the Old Testament the focus was on this present order of life, the main arena of God's blessings and chastisements. Existence after death was viewed as virtual non-existence, called Hades, a "land of forgetfulness," a place of shades (Ps. 88.10–12; 87.11–13 *LXX*), having no contact with the living and cut off from God himself (Ps. 6.5; 6.6 *LXX*). Exceptionally, some righteous persons such as Enoch (Gen. 5.24) and Elijah (2 Kings 2.11) escaped death not by resurrection but by direct transfer to heaven. In other rare cases, Elijah and Elisha revived dead children to ordinary life as apparent acts of healing (1 Kings 17.21–22;

2 Kings 4.34–5). Texts such as Hosea 6.1–3 and Ezekiel 37.1–14 look to the resurgence and restoration of Israel in space and time, although also easily seen by Christian interpreters as prophecies of the final resurrection of the dead. A singular text such as Isaiah 26.19 that foresees a resurrection of the dead is as rare as it is peripheral to classic Old Testament teaching. Regular belief in a future resurrection of the dead, especially of the righteous as reward for their persecution and martyrdom, developed among Jews after 200 BCE and is attested notably in Daniel 12.1–3 and 2 Maccabees 7.9, 22–9. By the time of Jesus, among other divergent views of the afterlife, this doctrine was firmly established among the Pharisees (in contrast to the Sadducees, Mk. 12.18) and subsequently became a key teaching of mainstream Christianity.

In the New Testament the accounts of Jesus' resurrection, based on apostolic memories and oral traditions, vary widely in detail. However, the fact and centrality of the resurrection constitute the bedrock of the Christian faith, attested by more than five hundred eyewitnesses (1 Cor. 15.5–8). The gospels indicate that Jesus anticipated his death as blood covenant renewal and viewed his resurrection as God's vindication of his ministry (e.g., Mk. 8.27–31; 14.22–5, 36, 61–2; cf. Acts 3.13–15). Matthew, Luke, and John link Jesus' resurrection with the gift of the Spirit and the inauguration of the early Christian mission (Mt. 28.16–20; Lk. 24.44–9; Jn. 20.19–23; cf. Acts 2.32–3). The Gospel of John magnificently integrates the life, death, resurrection, and enthronement of the Son of God as the mutual glorification between the Father and the Son, marking the decisive victory over the power of death and the gift of abundant life through the Spirit, available to believers in the present as well as the future (Jn. 1.14; 5.24–9; 7.37–9; 12.30–1; 14.15–24; 17.1–5). In this similar rich vein, the Apostle Paul provides the most detailed theological explication of the death and resurrection of the incarnate Son (Gal. 4.4–6; Rom. 1.1–4) and Lord of glory (1 Cor. 2.8; 15.1–4). For Paul, the death and resurrection of Jesus the Christ mark the cosmic shift from the old age of sin, corruption, and death to the new era of grace, life, incorruption, and transformed bodily immortality (Rom. 3.21–6; 5.12–21; 8.18–39; 1 Cor. 15.50–7). In Paul, as in John, God's powers of salvation are at work both now and in the future in those who are united with Christ through

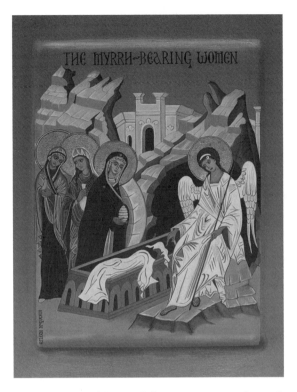

Plate 55 Icon of the myrrh-bearing women at the tomb. By Eileen McGuckin. The Icon Studio: www.sgtt.org.

faith and baptism, and who enact the pattern of Jesus' death and resurrection by crucifying their sinful passions and offering themselves as living sacrifice to God (Rom. 6.1–23; 8.9–13; 10.9–13; 12.1–2; 2 Cor. 4.7–18; Gal. 3.16–24).

The New Testament includes mention of the resurrection of Lazarus and of several others who are returned to ordinary life and presumed that they will die again (Jn. 11.43–4; Mk. 5.41–2; Mt. 27.52–3). But Jesus' resurrection, and the expected future resurrection of the dead at the consummation, is of an entirely different order, involving God's decisive process of salvation and a radical transformation of soul and body in which "the corruptible must put on the incorruptible and the mortal must put on the immortal," and death will be swallowed up by life (1 Cor. 15.53–5). Thus the significance of Jesus' death and resurrection is summed up not only in resolving the problem of sin and guilt, but also in overcoming the tragic reality of decay and death through the new creation, the epoch

of the Holy Spirit, moving toward the glorification of creation itself. Here lie the elements of the sharpest differences in theology between on the one hand medieval Western Christianity with its emphasis on the cross and penal theories of substitutionary satisfaction of the divine justice, and on the other hand the tradition of Orthodoxy with its emphasis on the resurrection and therapeutic views of salvation as rescue, healing, and liberation from humanity's true enemies – the powers of sin, corruption, death, and the devil.

SEE ALSO: Christ; Cross; Deification; Parousia; Soteriology

References and Suggested Readings

Athanasius, St. (1976) *On the Incarnation.* Crestwood, NY: St. Vladimir's Seminary Press.

Aulen, G. (1965) *Christus Victor: An Historical Study of the Three Main Types of the Idea of the Atonement.* London: SPCK.

Florovsky, G. (1976) *Creation and Redemption, Vol. 3: The Collected Works of Georges Florovsky.* Belmont, MA: Nordland Publishing.

Kirk, J. R. D. (2008) *Unlocking Romans: Resurrection and the Justification of God.* Grand Rapids, MI: Eerdmans.

Levenson, J. D. (2006) *Resurrection and the Restoration of Israel: The Ultimate Victory of God.* New Haven: Yale University Press.

Martin-Achard, R. and Nickelsburg, G. W. E. (1992) "Resurrection," in *The Anchor Bible Dictionary,* vol. 5, ed. D. N. Freedman. New York: Doubleday, pp. 680–91.

Pelikan, J. (1971) *The Christian Tradition, Vol. 1: The Emergence of the Catholic Tradition.* Chicago: University of Chicago Press.

Pelikan, J. (1974) *The Christian Tradition, Vol. 2: The Spirit of Eastern Christendom.* Chicago: University of Chicago Press.

Wright, N. T. (2003) *On the Incarnation of the Son of God.* Minneapolis: Fortress Press.

Rhipidion (Fan)

KENNETH CARVELEY

A round, sometimes "six-winged" disc placed on the end of a pole which was originally used as a liturgical fan to keep the Eucharistic elements free from flying insects. Symbolically, these represent the cherubim or angelic overshadowing and may reflect images from the mercy seat or Ark of the Covenant. Deacons are presented with these on their ordination for use during the anaphora, waving them over the elements until the elevation. Some rhipidia have bells attached. In the medieval West, these fans were known as *flabella*. Rhipidia are sometimes carried in procession at the Great Entrance of the Liturgy and are usually kept near the holy table.

References and Suggested Readings

Schuilz, H. J. (1986) *The Byzantine Liturgy*. New York: Pueblo.

Romania, Patriarchal Orthodox Church of

THEODOR DAMIAN

According to the census of 2002, 18,817,975 people out of the 21,680,974 inhabitants of Romania are Orthodox Christians; that is, 86.8 percent. In terms of population the Church of Romania is second in size only to Russia, and the most numerous Orthodox Church of any state of the European Union.

The Romanian Orthodox Church is an institution of apostolic origin. The Christian faith was known south of the Danube river, in the regions inhabited by Illyrians, Thraco-Dacians, and Greeks (today's Serbia, Bulgaria, and Greece), as far back as the second half of the 1st century, through the preaching of St. Paul and his disciples. More specifically, Christianity was spread through the preaching of the Apostle Andrew in what is today the Romanian province of Dobrogea, which, after the administrative reform of Diocletian, was called Scythia Minor. In local traditions St. Andrew is called the "Apostle of the wolves," which is historically significant in a context where the ethnic symbol of the Dacians was the wolf's head. In the northern part of the Danube river, in Dacia, which in 106 became a Roman province after being conquered by Trajan, the new faith arrived in the 1st, 2nd, and 3rd centuries, brought by merchants, colonists, and the

soldiers of the Roman army who were settled in the newly occupied territory. After the retreat of the Roman legions to the south of the Danube (271) and later, after the promulgation of the Edict of Milan (313), through which Emperor Constantine the Great granted liberty for Christians, the new religion expanded. Significant Christian archeological evidence discovered in the northern territories, as well as all the words of Latin origin in the Romanian language which define fundamental notions of the Christian faith, stand as proof of this expansion. During the 4th century there also existed, on the eastern borders of the Danube, several diocesan seats such as Singidunum, Viminacium, Bononia, Ratiaria, Oescus, Novae, Appiaria, Abritus, and Durostorum, whose bishops took care of the spiritual needs of the faithful north of the Danube, too. There was a metropolitan seat at Tomis in Scythia Minor (today, Constanta) with as many as fourteen dioceses, active in the 4th century and led by diligent bishops (Bretanion, Gerontius, Teotim I, Timotei, Ioan, Alexandru, Teotim II, Paternus, and Valentinian). According to the historian Eusebius of Caesarea, a Scythian bishop was present at the First Ecumenical Council at Nicea (325) and other bishops who followed him took part in the works of the subsequent councils, as well as in the christological disputes of the time. There are also indications of the existence of diocesan seats in other towns. Well-known theologians from Scythia Minor are St. John Cassian and St. Dionysius Exiguus.

During the time of the persecution of Christians, many priests and faithful of the Danubian lands suffered martyrdom for Christ, such as Bishop Ephrem, killed in 304 in Tomis; the Daco-Roman priest Montanus and his wife Maxima, who were drowned, also in 304; and martyrs Zoticos, Attalos, Kamasis, and Filippos (whose relics were discovered in 1971 in a paleo-Christian basilica in Niculitel, Dobrogea). We also know of St. Sava called the Goth, St. Niceta the Roman, and several others. Relics of martyrs who died in the Decian persecutions (249–51) have also been recently discovered by archeologists.

The second and fourth ecumenical councils put the territories north of the Danube under the jurisdiction of the patriarchate of Constantinople. Later, the faithful in the Dacian lands of present-day

Plate 56 The monastic cells (living quarters) of Rohia Monastery in Northern Romania. The monastery flourished even under communist oppression under the leadership of its higumen bishop, Justinian Chira. Photo by John McGuckin.

Romania, north of the Danube, were placed under the ecclesiastical jurisdiction of the archbishopric Justiniana Prima, founded by Emperor Justinian (535). The city of Sucidava, where probably a diocesan seat existed (the ruins of a basilica from the 4th to 5th centuries were discovered there), had an important role in the introduction of Christianity north of the Danube.

All these diocesan seats disappeared about the year 600, during the great Avaro-Slavic migration. During the 7th to 10th centuries the Slavs settled on the territories of present-day Serbia, Bulgaria, and their sur-

roundings, and exerted a strong influence on Dacian Christianity to the point where even the Slavic language penetrated into Daco-Romanian worship, even if this language was not generally understood by the community. Thus, the Romanian people were the only people of Latin origin confessing the Orthodox faith to use the Slavic (Slavonic) language in worship until about the end of the 17th century. Starting in the early 16th century, Slavonic was slowly replaced by Romanian once more. The last liturgy in Slavonic was published in Wallachia in 1736 and in 1863 Romanian became the only official language of the church.

Information about the Christian life of the Daco-Romanians after 600 is scant. However, there are archeological vestiges of the 7th to 10th centuries that certify its continuity on the ancient territory of Romania: ruins of churches at Niculitel and Dinogetia, in the north of Dobrogea, the small rock churches at Basarabi near Constanta, the church ruins at Dabaca (Cluj district) and at Morisena-Cenad (Timis district). In the 13th century the Romanians had bishops of their own, as can be seen from a letter of Pope Gregory IX of 1234, as well as from other records.

After the founding of the two Romanian principalities of Wallachia or Muntenia (ca. 1330) and Moldavia (ca. 1359), metropolitan sees were established in the capitals of both countries. Since Dacia, south of the Danube river, was known as Greater Wallachia, in 1359 the ecumenical patriarchate acknowledged the metropolitanate of Ungro-Wallachia for Dacia north of the Danube, having its seat in Curtea de Arges, and Bishop Iachint of Vicina became its first metropolitan. At the beginning of the 16th century two other diocesan sees were founded, subject to the metropolitanate, at Ramnic and Buzau, which have continued to the present day.

In 1401 the ecumenical patriarchate acknowledged a second Romanian metropolitanate, that of Moldavia, with its seat at Suceava. At the beginning of the 15th century, two suffragan dioceses were founded at Roman and at Radauti, and later in 1598 another one at Husi. In Transylvania, under the rule of the Hungarian Catholic kings, three Romanian diocesan seats were created even though the Romanians were not officially recognized as a nation by the political authorities of the time. At the end of the 15th century

St. Stephen the Great, prince of Moldavia, founded a diocesan see at Vad in the district of Cluj. The Romanian Orthodox metropolitanate of Transylvania did not have a permanent residence. Hence the metropolitan resided at Hunedoara, at Feleac in the vicinity of Cluj (at the end of the 15th century), at Geoagiu and at Lancram, near Alba Iulia (in the middle of the 16th century), and then at Alba Iulia. This metropolitanate was suppressed by the Habsburgs in 1701.

With the help of the princes of Wallachia and Moldavia, the Romanian Orthodox Church started to flourish. Many of its hierarchs became eminent scholars, such as the metropolitans Macarie, Teofil, Stefan, Antim Ivireanul, Neofit Cretanul, and Grigorie Dascalul of Ungro-Wallachia and Anastasie Crimca, Varlaam, Dosoftei, Iacob Putneanul, and Veniamin Costachi of Moldavia. The first manuscript translations into the Romanian language were liturgical books (the Codex of Voronet, the Psalter of Scheia, and the Hurmuzaki Psalter). Book printing began in Wallachia in 1507 by the monk Macarie and was continued by Dimitrie Liubavici and the monk Lavrentie. They printed liturgical texts in the Slavonic language. In Transylvania in the 16th century the printing of books in the Romanian language was started by Filip the Moldavian at Sibiu and the deacon Coresi at Brasov.

Monasticism, always an important dimension of the Romanian Orthodox Church, began steady development from the 14th century when great monasteries began to be built, many of them existing to this day: Vodita, Tismana, Cozia, Cotmeana, Snagov, Dealu, Bistrita, and later Arges, Arnota, Caldarusani, Cernica, Hurezi in Wallachia; Neamt, Bistrita, Moldovita, Humor, and later still Putna, Voronet, Sucevita, Secu, Dragomirna in Moldavia; St. Michael at Peri in Maramures, Ramet, Prislop, and Sambata in Transylvania, Hodos-Bodrog and Partos in Banat, and also many others. The monasteries played not only an important religious role in the spiritual life of the faithful, but also a cultural one. In these monasteries diptychs and chronicles were written, liturgical manuscripts or teaching books in the Slavonic or Romanian languages were copied in beautiful calligraphy, and sacerdotal vestments and other liturgical objects were produced. It was in these monasteries that the first Romanian schools were founded: elementary and secondary first, later also encompassing higher education, such as the academies at St. Nicolae in Brasov-Schei, at Putna, at the Three Hierarchs in Jassy, St. Sava's Academy in Bucharest, and others.

The Romanian Orthodox Church contributed not only to the improvement and development of the moral, social, and cultural life of its people; it also supported other Orthodox Churches, by printing liturgical books in Greek, Slavonic, Arabian, and Georgian, and by other kinds of help offered to them. The princes of the Romanian principalities were generous founders and protectors of the monasteries at Mount Athos and Sinai, as well as benefactors of the patriarchates of Constantinople, Alexandria, Antioch, Jerusalem, and Georgia, and of other churches in many countries. The Romanian Church contributed to the strengthening and preservation of world Orthodoxy through the well-known work *The Orthodox Confession of Faith* written by the Metropolitan Peter Moghila of Kiev, a Moldavian by birth. This work was approved by a synod held in Jassy in 1642, at which representatives of the Greek, Russian, and Romanian Orthodox Churches were present.

Unlike the Church of Wallachia and Moldavia, the Church of Transylvania passed through numerous difficulties because of the proselytizing campaigns undertaken by the Roman Catholic Church (14th–15th centuries), the Calvinists (17th century), and again the Roman Catholics (18th century). The first two were not successful, but the third one, in 1698–1701, had a more lasting effect. Transylvania was then ruled by the Habsburgs. As a result of intrigues at the imperial court in Vienna and by the Jesuits of Transylvania, a small part of the Romanian Orthodox clergy and faithful embraced the "Union with Rome" (the *Unia*). This diocese resulting from the *Unia* was placed under the jurisdiction of the Roman Catholic archbishopric of Esztergom, which later moved to Fagaras and then to Blaj, where in 1853 it was raised to the level of a metropolitanate. The Orthodox Romanians remained without bishops until 1761, when the court in Vienna, compelled by the revolt led by monk Sofronie, appointed for them a Serbian Orthodox bishop. The Orthodox Romanians were granted the right to elect a Romanian bishop only in 1810. The most important Orthodox hierarch of this period was Andrei Saguna, bishop and (from 1864) metropolitan, who succeeded in reestablishing the ancient Orthodox metropolitanate of Transylvania and in restoring its former development. This situation lasted until 1948, when the clergy and faithful belonging to the *Unia*, under pressure from the communist regime, again merged with the old Romanian Orthodox Church.

In 1859, after the union of Wallachia and Moldavia into a single state called Romania, the issues of ecclesiastical unity and autocephaly were once more raised. In 1864 Prince Alexandru Ioan Cuza proclaimed the autocephaly of the Romanian Orthodox Church. In 1865 the metropolitan of Bucharest became "Metropolitan Primate." In 1872 the Holy Synod was created and in 1885 the Ecumenical Patriarch Joachim IV acknowledged its autocephaly. In 1925 the Romanian Orthodox Church became a patriarchate with the first patriarch as Miron Cristea (1925–39).

In parallel with these developments, in the 19th and early 20th centuries, as always during its history, the Romanian Orthodox Church was fully involved in the major events of the Romanian people. Thus in the 1848 revolutions in the three Romanian principalities of Moldavia, Wallachia, and Transylvania, hierarchs, priests, and monks militated energetically for the realization of the national ideals of liberty and unity. Some of the notables from this time were Bishop Andrei Saguna, the priests Ioan Popasu and Simion Balint of Rosia Montana (Transylvania), Metropolitan Meletie of Jassy (Moldavia), Bishop Filotei of Buzau, the priests Radu Sapca of Celei, Oprea and George (Wallachia), and many others.

In 1859, when the Union of Romanian Principalities (Moldavia and Wallachia) took place, the church expressed itself through numerous representatives from the ranks of the clergy. Actively involved were Metropolitan Sofronie Miclescu, Bishop Melchisedec Stefanescu of Roman, Hierarch Filaret Scriban and his brother archimandrite Neofit (Moldavia); Metropolitan Nifon, Bishop Filotei of Buzau, Bishop Calinic of Ramnic, and others, who delivered sermons, wrote letters, booklets, and articles in newspapers, addressed the authorities, and mobilized the faithful in favor of the political union. Some of them were co-presidents and members in the Ad-Hoc Council and the Electoral Assembly that elected Prince Alexandru Ioan Cuza as single ruler over both principalities, thus achieving the long fought-for dream of national unity.

In 1877 the church was actively involved in the war of independence from the Ottoman Empire. Many priests, monks, and even nuns enrolled in the army at different levels; others organized committees of support and collections of goods needed for the troops. Archimandrite Ignatie Serian and Ghenadie Merisescu, protosincel Sava Dumitrescu, and hieromonk Veniamin Alexandrescu are just a few. In World War I (1916–18) hundreds of priests went to serve; some were killed on the front lines, others taken prisoner, deported or exiled. Another great event in the nation's history was the Great Union of 1918, when the Romanian principality of Transylvania was united with Romania (Moldavia and Wallachia). Among many clergy and hierarchs who took active part in this event were the priest Vasile Lucaciu of Sisesti, Bishops Ioan Papp of Arad and Dimitrie Radu of Oradea (who were co-presidents of the Great National Assembly of Alba Iulia where the Union was declared), and Metropolitan Miron Cristea (the future patriarch), who was the head of the delegation of the Romanians from Transylvania that presented to the authorities in Bucharest the document of the Union (December 1, 1918).

In 1925 the new patriarch Miron Cristea set among his priorities the construction of a new cathedral in Bucharest that he called the Cathedral for the Nation's Salvation. He also wrote and published several books on folklore and iconography, and collections of sermons; he supported the participation of Romanian theologians in international ecumenical congresses and meetings and initiated such events in Romania, too. He was followed by Patriarch Nicodim Munteanu (1939–48). Patriarch Nicodim excelled by translating and editing over one hundred theological works from Russian into Romanian. He wrote several original books and also was one of the translators of the Bible into Romanian. From 1948 to 1977 the Romanian Orthodox Church was led by Patriarch Justinian Marina. Under his leadership, although shadowed under the communist regime with all its restrictions and pressures, important events occurred in the life of the church, such as the organization and creation of new legislation in the church, the reintegration of the

Eastern rite Catholic churches of Transylvania, the reorganization of theological education, the canonization of several Romanian saints, the reorganization of monastic life, the restoration of many ancient monuments of religious art, and the erection of new churches in villages and towns throughout the country. In his time the Romanian Orthodox Church reentered the World Council of Churches (New Delhi, 1961) and participated in all its Pan-Christian and Pan-Orthodox meetings, maintaining fraternal relations with the other Orthodox Churches, as well as with other Christian denominations.

The fourth patriarch of the Romanian Orthodox Church was Justin Moisescu, who carried out his responsibilities from June 19, 1977 until his death on July 31, 1986. It was through his special care that the church attained a notable level of development in the administrative, theological, and cultural fields, as well as in foreign ecclesiastic relations. On November 16, 1986 the leadership of the Romanian patriarchate was entrusted to His Beatitude Teoctist Arapasu. He was elected for this ministry, having served for four decades as a high prelate at the head of some of the most important dioceses of the Romanian Orthodox Church: in Bucharest as an assistant bishop to the patriarch; at Arad as diocesan bishop; at Craiova as a metropolitan; at the Jassy seat as metropolitan. He was also *locum tenens* for the metropolitan of Sibiu during the vacancy there.

On September 30, 2007 the sixth patriarch of the Romanian Orthodox Church was enthroned: His Beatitude Patriarch Daniel (metropolitan of Moldavia and Bucovina from 1990 to 2007). Under his leadership the new bylaws for the organization and functioning of the Romanian Orthodox Church were finalized. He created a new media system for the church, laid the cornerstone of the new patriarchal cathedral in Bucharest while consolidating the structures of the current one, established over a dozen social, cultural, charitable, and educational programs, created new dioceses in the country, and canonized several new Romanian saints.

As of September 1, 2008 the Romanian patriarchate was made up of six metropolitan sees in the country and three metropolitan sees abroad (there are about 12 million Romanians living outside Romania), with forty-one eparchies: the Metropolitan See of Muntenia

and Dobrogea at Bucharest, the Metropolitan See of Moldavia and Bucovina at Jassy, the Metropolitan See of Transylvania at Sibiu, the Metropolitan See of Cluj, Alba, Crisana and Maramures at Cluj, the Metropolitan See of Oltenia at Craiova, the Metropolitan See of Banat at Timisoara, the Metropolitan See of Bessarabia at Chisinau (Republic of Moldova), the Metropolitan See for Germany, Central and North Europe at Nurnberg, Germany, and the Metropolitan See for Western Europe at Paris. There is also the Romanian Orthodox archdiocese in the Americas based at Chicago. Other dioceses are in Hungary, at Gyula, in Serbia and Montenegro (Dacia Felix) at Varset, and the Romanian Orthodox diocese for Australia and New Zealand at Melbourne.

Of all Romanians living abroad today there are also many who belong to other ecclesiastical jurisdictions, such as the over eighty Romanian parishes in the United States and Canada that belong to the Orthodox Church of America (OCA) or the Romanians around the current borders of Romania who belong to the jurisdictions of their respective countries (Serbia, Bulgaria, Ukraine). There are other Romanian monasteries and churches in different places, such as Prodromou and Lacu sketes on Mount Athos, establishments in Jerusalem and Jericho, and parishes in Cyprus, Istanbul, South Africa, and other places.

The Republic of Moldova was in its entire history a Dacian and then Romanian territory. It was annexed by the Russian Empire in 1812, until 1918, when it was reunited with Romania. In 1944 it was reannexed by the Soviet Union and became a Soviet republic. In 1991 it became an independent state. At this time, the Romanian patriarchate created the metropolitanate of Bessarabia for the spiritual needs of all Romanians who (except during the time of the Russian Soviet occupation) had always belonged to the Romanian Orthodox Church and who now wanted to rejoin it. However, the government in Moldova did not allow the metropolitanate to function in Moldova officially. It was only in 2001 that the European Court ruled that the metropolitanate of Bessarabia was officially part of the Romanian patriarchate and allowed it to function there.

In the six metropolitanates in the country there is currently a total of 13,612 parishes and branches with 15,083 churches. There are also 637 monasteries and sketes with over 8,000 monks and nuns. At the central administrative level the Romanian Orthodox Church is structured as follows: Central deliberative bodies: the Holy Synod, the Standing Synod, and the National Church Assembly; central executive bodies: the Patriarch, the National Church Council, the Standing Committee of the National Church Council; Central administrative bodies: the Office of the Holy Synod and the patriarchal administration.

The highest authority of the Romanian Orthodox Church in all fields of activity is the Holy Synod, made up of the patriarch, as president, all the metropolitans, archbishops, eparchial bishops, vicar bishops, and all other serving bishops. Four synodal committees are appointed for preparing the sessions of the Holy Synod: the Pastoral, Monastic and Social Committee; the Theological, Liturgical and Didactic Committee; the Canonical, Juridical and Disciplinary Committee; the Committee for External Communities, for the Inter-Orthodox, Inter-Christian and Inter-Religious Relations. Between the sessions of the Holy Synod the Standing Synod is the central deliberative body which takes decisions for the life of the church. It is constituted by the patriarch, as president, the metropolitans and three other hierarchs appointed by the Holy Synod every year (an archbishop and two bishops). The central deliberative body of the Romanian Orthodox Church for all administrative, social, cultural, economic, and patrimonial issues is the National Church Assembly, made up of three representatives of each diocese (one clergy and two lay people), appointed by the respective diocesan assemblies for four years. The members of the Holy Synod take part in the meetings of the National Church Assembly with deliberative vote. The patriarch is the head of the hierarchs of the Romanian Orthodox Church and the president of its central deliberative and executive bodies. The full title of the current patriarch of the Romanian Orthodox Church is His Beatitude Daniel, Archbishop of Bucharest, Metropolitan of Wallachia and Dobrogea, *Locum tenens* of the Throne of Caesarea of Cappadocia and Patriarch of the Romanian Orthodox Church (or Patriarch of Romania).

The central executive body of the Holy Synod and of the National Church Assembly is the National Church Council, made up of twelve members of the National Church Assembly (one clergy and one lay person representing every metropolitan see of the country, appointed for four years). The members of the Holy Synod can participate with deliberative vote in the meetings of the National Church Council. The assistant bishops to the patriarch are lawful members of the National Church Council, with deliberative vote; the patriarchal administrative vicar, patriarchal counselors, and the general ecclesiastical inspector are standing members with consulting vote.

The Standing Committee of the National Church Council functions between the meetings of the National Church Council, as central executive body, made up of the patriarch, as president, vicar bishops to the patriarch, patriarchal administrative vicar, patriarchal counselors, and the ecclesiastical general inspector. The patriarch is assisted in the exercise of his duties as president of the central deliberative and executive bodies, as well as primate of the Romanian Orthodox Church, by the Office of the Holy Synod and by the patriarchal administration, with the following departments: theological-educational, social-charitable, economic-financial, cultural, patrimony, church and interreligious relations, external communities, communications and public relations, church monuments and constructions, patriarchal stavropegias and social centers, body for inspection and audit. At the local level, the component units of the Romanian Orthodox Church are the parish, monastery, protopresbyterate (deanery), vicariate, eparchy (archdiocese and diocese), and the metropolitanate.

During the communist regime, while it managed to survive and even have certain accomplishments, the church was severely restricted in its potential, mission, and activities. In the initial phases of communist rule in particular, the faithful were direct witnesses of the persecution, arrest, torture, and killing of thousands of Orthodox priests. One recent study documents that approximately 4,000 Orthodox priests were sent to communist prisons, sometimes two or three times, while others were killed. From the upper ranks of the hierarchy, seventeen bishops were demoted and fifteen were exiled. Many had to endure long years of detention (Caravia et al. 1999).

In a book published by the Romanian Academy, where the authors present a small, but representative selection of 180 informative notes, reports, referrals and accounts, addresses of various informers, militia and security agents, and administrative functionaries from the communist system at the local or national level, over 1,800 references are made to Orthodox bishops, priests, deacons, theology professors, theology students, monks, chanters, and believers who were opposing the regime and who were conducting so-called "anti-democratic" activities, speaking against the communist government or writing articles of anti-communist propaganda in the ecclesiastical press (Paiusan and Ciuceanu 2001). Though derided by communist propaganda it was because of Patriarch Justinian Marina's extraordinary skill and practical wisdom that while suffering this level of persecution the church could still not only hold on, but also develop and grow. In many other countries under communist rule such growth was not possible.

The church was forced to renounce its social philanthropic activities arising from its vocation of mercy; it had to strictly limit itself to the liturgical-sacramental dimension of its existence. The formation of priests and theologians was restricted to five theological seminaries at the high-school level (one at each of the five existing metropolitan sees) and two schools of theology at the university level. The patriarchate and each metropolitan see had its own theological journal published a few times a year, besides a pastoral guide published once a year. The communist government exerted strict control over their content. In the metropolitanate of Transylvania there was also a bi-weekly newspaper, *Telegraful Roman*, which was and still remains the only publication in the entire country to appear without interruption since its foundation in 1853.

After the fall of the communist regime in 1989 the Romanian Orthodox Church, which, according to repeated surveys, continues to enjoy the highest trust among Romanians, had a chance to develop at all levels. The church canonized thirty-six Romanian saints and extended the honoring at the national level of another forty-two local saints, so that the total number of Romanian saints, including those previously canonized, rose to ninety-seven. Some of these are Daniel the Hermit (Sihastrul), Evangelicus of Tomis, Gherman of Dobrogea, John Cassian, Gheorghe of Cernica, Nicodim of Tismana, Oprea Nicolae, Paisy Velichovsky of Neamt, Sofronie of Cioara, Visarion Sarai, and Voivode Stephen the Great.

One of the most important aspects of the church since 1989 has been its engagement in social work. At the central and regional levels, departments, programs, and branches were created that cover a vast and diverse area of social work. To enhance the efficiency of its philanthropic activity the church signed several protocols with the government and in 2007 it established the Philanthropic Federation of the Romanian Patriarchate. There are now in the Romanian patriarchate over forty offices of coordination of social work and assistance, with over 200 employees qualified in social work as well as theology. The number of social assistance establishments founded and administered by the patriarchate is over 350 and includes shelters for children (109) and for the elderly (51), soup kitchens and bakeries (106), clinics and pharmacies (37), counseling centers (33), centers for victims of human trafficking (2), and centers for assistance for families in difficulty (19).

These institutions are developing programs for the help of children who come from poor families, for the prevention of school drop-out, for orphan children, for those in correctional facilities, and for the help of the Roma population. There are also programs for religious assistance in hospitals, in nursing homes, and in homeless shelters, where well over 300 churches and chapels exist with over 300 priests; programs of religious assistance in prisons (over fifty churches and chapels with as many working priests), and programs of religious assistance in the military units (over eighty churches and chapels with about eighty military priests). The church trains its own workers in such fields. For this reason it introduced in theological schools at the university level sections, programs, and curricula of social assistance. Another expression of the social engagement of the church is evident in the constitution of local committees of bioethics in Cluj, Jassy, and Bucharest, and a National Committee on Bioethics with the special task to study and evaluate the specific issues raised by bioethics, such as abortion, contraception, genetic manipulation, *in vitro* procreation, and organ transplants. These committees are creating the documentation based on which the church will express its official position.

After 1989, religious education has been expanded at all levels. Religion has been reintroduced as a compulsory discipline in high schools, a subject taught by over

10,000 teachers. The number of Orthodox theological seminaries at high-school level has risen from five to thirty-nine (with over 700 teachers and over 6,000 students annually); there are now schools of religious chanters and post-high-school departments with double specialization in theology and social work; fifteen schools of theology at university level with eight specializations and approximately 450 professors teaching over 11,000 students (7,000 male and 4,000 female). There are master's programs at eleven of the fifteen schools of theology and doctoral programs at the theological schools in Bucharest, Sibiu, Cluj, and Oradea. The church offers scholarships for students from the Republic of Moldova and from other Romanian areas around the current borders of the country.

The Romanian Orthodox Church has a long and significant tradition of theological education. Among the best-known theologians, past and present, are Dumitru Stăniloae (dogmatic theology); Petru Rezus (fundamental theology); Ioan Zagrean (moral theology); Bartolomeu Anania, Vasile Tarnavschi (biblical studies); Mircea Pacuraru (historical studies); Ioan G. Coman (patristics); Liviu Stan (canon law); Ene Braniste (liturgics); Atanasie Negoita (Oriental studies); Ioan Bria (ecumenical studies). At the present time the most widely known Romanian theologian in Romania and abroad is Dumitru Stăniloae (1903–93). He taught at the theological schools of higher education in Sibiu and Bucharest, but also spent five years in communist prisons (1958–63). He published many books of dogmatic and moral theology, and translated works from the church fathers in a series called *Philokalia* that appeared in twelve volumes. His works have been translated and published in French, English, German, Greek, and Serbian. He is considered one of the most important theologians and Christian thinkers in the world today.

One of the most important achievements of the church after 1989 has been the unprecedented use of mass-media technology. In a world dominated by communication, the church remains faithful to the traditional means of conveying the right teaching of faith, but is open to modern technology in its missionary work. Thus the Basilica press center of the Romanian patriarchate was set up in Bucharest shortly after the inauguration of Patriarch Daniel Ciobotea in the fall of 2007. The new institution is seated in the patriarchal palace and made up of five branches: the Trinitas radio station, the Trinitas TV station, a group of three publications (*Lumina* – "The Light," a daily newspaper; *Lumina de Duminica* – "Sunday Light," a weekly publication; *Vestitorul Ortodoxiei* – "Herald of Orthodoxy," a monthly magazine), the Basilica news agency, and a press and public relations office. There is also a multitude of other magazines and publishing houses for religious books, from those belonging to major church dioceses, to those belonging to deaneries and even parishes. The radio stations and programs that were created at the diocesan centers are part of this revival, too, as well as numerous workshops where religious objects for liturgical use and daily spiritual needs are manufactured.

During its entire existence the Romanian Orthodox Church has brought its direct and effective contribution to the most important events that marked the history of the nation and to the development of Romanian culture, while maintaining the aspirations of the Romanian people for national liberty and social justice and helping strengthen the consciousness of national unity. The Romanian Orthodox Church is thus one of the most vigorous branches of world Orthodoxy. It is capable of a significant contribution for furthering the cause of Orthodoxy, to help improve ecumenical and brotherly relations among all Christian churches and denominations, and to promote peace and good understanding among peoples.

SEE ALSO: Canonization; Contemporary Orthodox Theology; Education; Newly Revealed Saints; *Philokalia*; St. John Cassian (ca. 360–ca. 435); St. Paisy Velichovsky (1722–1794); Stăniloae, Dumitru (1903–1993)

References and Suggested Readings

Caravia, P., Constantinescu, V., and Stanescu, F. (1999) *The Imprisoned Church: Romania 1944–1989.* Bucharest: Romanian Academy, National Institute for the Study of Totalitarianism.

Damian, T. (2005) "The Romanian Orthodox Church Between Deja-vu and Pas encore," *La voie de la Lumiere,* year 11, Nos. 129–30, Montreal.

Daniel, Patriarch of the Romanian Orthodox Church (2009) "Situatia Bisericii Ortodoxe Romane si Legaturile ei Ecumenice in Contextul Noii Europe (1989–2009)," *Meridianul Romanesc*, year 36, No. 13, Santa Clarita, CA.

Danila, N. (2001) *Daco-Romania Christiana: Florilegium Studiorum*. Bucharest: Danubius.

Diaconescu, M. (1999) *Istoria literaturii daco-romane*. Bucharest: Alcor Edimpex.

Metes, St. (1935) *Istoria Bisericii si a vietii religioase a romanilor din Transilvania*. Sibiu: Diecezana.

Pacurariu, M. (2002) *Dictionarul Teologilor Romani*. Bucharest: Editura Enciclopedica.

Pacurariu, M. (2006) *Istoria Bisericii Ortodoxe Romane*. Bucharest: IBMBOR.

Paiusan, C. and Ciuceanu, R. (2001) *The Romanian Orthodox Church under the Communist Regime, Vol. 1: 1945–1958*. Bucharest: Romanian Academy, National Institute for the Study of Totalitarianism.

Romanian Patriarchate (2009) *The Romanian Patriarchate: Mission, Organization, Activities*. Bucharest: Basilica.

Vicovean, I. (2002) *Istoria Bisericii Ortodoxe Romane*, Vols. 1 and 2. Jassy: Trinitas.

Rome, Ancient Patriarchate of

BRENDA LLEWELLYN IHSSEN

By the 5th century a system of pentarchy existed among the apostolic sees of Rome, Constantinople, Alexandria, Antioch, and Jerusalem. Though the patriarchates of Rome and Constantinople would eventually enter into periods of dispute and eventually schism, the ancient patriarchate of Rome was, in the first millennium of Christianity, held in high regard as a significantly important see due to multiple factors: the city of Rome was an early recipient of the Christian message; Rome was an apostolic foundation; it was a city where the foremost of the apostles, Peter and Paul, visited; it was where they were martyred; and it is where their bodies remain to this day. Rome was also a city noted for edifying resistance to Roman oppression on the part of many Christians, for the development of poor-relief programs, for strong resistance to internal schism and heresy, for lively theological discussion, and as an early model of noteworthy leadership for the international church. All of these factors would be significant in the initial development of the ancient patriarchate of Rome and contributed to the development of papal theory.

Roman Christianity and Apostolic Foundation in the First Centuries

As the capital, Rome was a city of primary importance in a largely urban empire that was in the process of transforming itself in the 1st century. With a population of roughly half a million inhabitants, and with both people and philosophies arriving frequently, Rome was a natural goal. Evidence suggests that Christianity arrived in the city shortly after the death of Jesus, likely arriving in the 40s due in part to the migration of Jews as merchants, immigrants, or prisoners from Syria and Palestine to the Trastevere, the Jewish quarter of Rome. The constant flow of individuals, ideas, and influence between Rome and Jerusalem attests to the close relationship that the two cities shared prior to the rise of Christianity, a relationship that aided in the development of an immigrant Christianity when it arrived (Vinzent 2007).

Once in Rome, Christianity appears to have organized into various small cells and house churches of predominantly Jewish and then Greek-speaking gentiles in a fairly rapid and reasonably stable way, to the degree that it soon was a mission force. The author of Acts claims that the followers of Jesus present at Pentecost from Rome were both "Jews and proselytes" (Acts 2.10). Further, the Apostle Paul's Letter to the Romans, containing as it does fairly complex theology not suitable for a novice community, suggests that the recipients had by that time begun to move beyond basic organizational issues to address significant issues for the future of the Christian movement, specifically the potentially tense relationship between gentile converts and Jewish Christians, or even other competing Christian cells and philosophical schools of which, in a city of émigrés, there must have been several (Vinzent 2007; Hall 2007a). Evidence for the presence of Christianity in Rome as early as the 40s can also be found in additional passages in Acts (18.2–3), and exterior to the New Testament in the work of historian Suetonius, who wrote of Emperor Claudius'

(41–54) expulsion of "Jews from Rome because of their constant disturbances impelled by Chrestus" (Suetonius, *The Lives of the Caesars II*, 25) – which suggests interference in worship-related activities on the part of Jewish Christians (Brown and Meier 1983).

Each of the ancient patriarchates of Rome, Constantinople, Alexandria, Antioch, and Jerusalem is traditionally held to have been founded by the most prominent among the apostles. Early sources, representing traditional stories more than hard historical data, maintain that Peter and Paul both traveled to Rome, where they established Christian communities. The New Testament evidence speaks only of Paul being in Rome (Acts 18). St. Clement of Rome (ca. 96) wrote in his *Epistle to the Corinthians* on behalf of the Roman Church only that Peter "went to the glorious place which was his due," and Paul, more specifically, "reached the limits of the West" (*I. Clement* 5). Ignatius of Antioch (35–107), when making his plea to the Christians in Rome to refrain from interfering in his forthcoming martyrdom, wrote that he (Ignatius) does "not order you as did Peter and Paul" (*Ignatius to the Romans* 4), a statement which suggests relationship but not necessarily proximity. More specifically, Irenaeus of Lyons (135–200), writing on the importance of the succession of bishops in his treatise *Against Heresies*, says that this "tradition derived from the apostles, of the very great, very ancient, and universally known Church founded and organized at Rome by the two most glorious apostles, Peter and Paul" (*Against Heresies* 3.3.2). While Irenaeus' claim of apostolic foundation has been interpreted as evidence of Peter's personal activity in Rome, what is more evident, however, is the importance that will consistently be placed on the tradition of apostolic foundation itself, as well as the meaning that the tradition will hold in successive centuries for the subsequent Roman theory of primacy. It is worth noting that while these ancient writers do not leave the historian with incontestable evidence about any extensive activity of Peter's in Rome, they do leave the historian with evidence about Christian attitudes and structures in ancient Rome. Though there was likely at first no united single community, it was from earliest times to some degree organized, it already had a developing sense of its own history, and though archeology, epigraphy, and historical records indicate that Christianity

flourished in the poorer districts, there were, even by the beginning of the 2nd century, Christians in Rome who enjoyed influence among the political powers and elite members of society.

The Challange of Pagan Rome and the Roman Response

In addition to this early tradition that holds Peter and Paul as central to the foundation of Christianity in Rome, the ancient patriarchate of Rome was further enhanced by the various ways in which Christians responded to the surrounding community that threatened their religious identity. Christian intellectuals rose to the challenge of pagan apologists, whose opposition afforded them the opportunity to defend with eloquence a vigorous new faith against cults that promoted morally repulsive gods and goddesses. This apologetic process helped to shape both the public and internal self-identity of Roman (and other) Christians in relation to the Greco-Roman world. The anonymous 2nd-century (allegedly Roman) author of the *Epistle to Diognetus* argued the superiority of Christianity over paganism, idolatry, and Judaism's ritual rigidity, and defended the manner by which Christians live as citizens of one world but detached from it as citizens of another, presenting an eloquent explanation of God's plan for salvation in light of previous human understandings of God (Hall 2007b).

For those who lacked opportunity or intellectual ability, martyrdom also provided Christians the occasion to refute by use of the body what the scholarly did using their rhetorical skill (a few, such as Justin Martyr, had the opportunity for both forms of witness). Concerned and angered by what were regarded as the "sins" of an unauthorized religion, various pogroms took place to cleanse Rome and appease the authorities who were anxious to put down what they believed to be a dissident and seditious cult, or a repugnant sect of Judaism, too much like a conspiracy to be tolerated. Chief among the martyrs were Peter and Paul, but included among the many that perished in these first persecutions at Rome were notable figures such as Ignatius of Antioch (107), Justin Martyr (165), and Hippolytus (236). While hard historical evidence with respect to Christian foundations at the direct hands of

Peter and Paul is inconclusive, it is generally admitted that both apostles died in Rome during the purge of Emperor Nero, who was anxious to divert suspicion for a fire that destroyed ten of the fourteen districts of Rome in 64. Senator and historian Tacitus later wrote that Nero, the first of several emperors to inflict persecutions on this new sect, attempted to suppress rumors for his own responsibility for the fire by rounding up "the notoriously depraved group who were popularly called Christians" (*Annals* 15.44). Later described by Eusebius as the "first heralded as a conspicuous fighter against God" (*Hist. Eccl.* 2.25), Nero had Christians torn to pieces by dogs or burned alive, occasioning the pity of the Roman population who were witnesses to this cruel torture (Jeffers 1991). While Tacitus says nothing of the famous apostles perishing in this purge, Eusebius writes that during Nero's reign the apostles were murdered: "It is recorded that in his reign Paul was beheaded in Rome itself, and that Peter likewise was crucified, and the record is confirmed by the fact that the cemeteries there are still called by the names of Peter and Paul" (*Hist. Eccl.* 2.25). Eusebius includes in his *Ecclesiastical History* the valuable words of a churchman named Gaius who, in the late 2nd or early 3rd century wrote concerning their burial places that "I can point out the monuments of the victorious apostles. If you will go as far as the Vatican or the Ostian Way, you will find the monuments of those who founded this church" (*Hist. Eccl.* 2.25). In this passage we identify not only early public veneration of the space where the apostles were believed to be, but also clear indication that they are understood as the founders of Christianity in Rome. Further confirmation is offered by Eusebius in a letter written by Bishop Dionysius of Corinth to the Romans, who likens the two communities of Rome and Corinth as spiritually bound by apostolic foundation. However, what Rome has, that Corinth does not, is the site of the martyrdom of the apostles: "For both of them sowed in our Corinth and taught us jointly. In Italy too they taught jointly in the same city, and were martyred at the same time" (*Hist. Eccl.* 2.25).

Located today under an elaborate baldachin constructed by Bernini in 1633, the original cult center of a trophy (the "Red wall" shrine) identified as that of St. Peter's on Vatican Hill was originally quite inconspicuous among adjoining mausolea of adherents of multiple cults. Similar to Peter, Paul's body was buried in an ancient simple tomb over which a trophy was erected, and both apostles were venerated together in an equally unremarkable cult center located underneath *catacombo* San Sebastiano on the Via Appia, where the veneration of their relics (or at least a portion of them) was translated temporarily in 258 to protect them during the persecutions of Emperor Valerian (253–60) (Holloway 2004). The persecutions of Christians by the state were consistently interpreted apocalyptically and historically as manifestations of the secular world unleashing its venom and rage against the spiritual elect, who were honored and even envied for the opportunity to publicly portray their devotion to Christ through the offering of their bodies in imitation of the Passion. Those who survived the attempt on their lives (the *confessors*) emerged as respected leaders of various communities of Christians, wearing the evidence of their faith in sometimes quite visible ways in their flesh, and drawing support strong enough to enable them to challenge the decisions of local bishops (Hall 2007b). Christian Rome especially benefited by the prestige that the martyrs provided by their resolute resistance to the civil authorities and, for the future organization of the church, the martyrdoms of Peter, Paul, and other leading Christians challenged the rising and developing episcopacy to love the church like a devoted spouse to the degree that they too needed to be willing to suffer martyrdom on her behalf. Finally, the point here must be emphasized: while the three most important cities in the empire – Rome, Jerusalem, and Antioch (though we might include also Corinth and others) – could claim association and relationship with Peter, only one city, Rome, could claim that they possessed the body.

The Organization of Christianity in the Ancient Patriarchate of Rome

Modern scholarly debate continues around the time frame of the development of the organization of city-wide Roman Christian leadership, and modern scholars generally believe that that the lineaments of a city-wide monarchical bishopric were retrojected with some hindsight (Hall 2007a). While Christianity came early to Rome, a single city-wide organization did not, and the very earliest Christian communities combined elements of philosophical school, extended household, oriental cult, and social club, and yet refrained from being truly any single one of those options. Recent studies suggest that only after the mid-3rd-century opposition to Pope Cornelius led by the intellectually gifted presbyter (later anti-pope) Novatian, does the issue of Roman Christian leadership emerge in terms of a series of recognizable central authority figures: *papae*. Before that time the various and sometimes quite disparate communities were held together in their commitment to being a household of God, a commitment that was reflected in the practice of sharing portions of the Eucharist bread among them (Vinzent 2007).

The earliest patristic literature maintains that the position of a monarchical bishop existed in Rome from the time of Peter himself, which reflects the strong desire of this patristic generation to set the monarchical episcopate on a firmer footing. Clement of Rome, a notable leader at the end of the 1st century, reproves the Corinthian church in his *Epistle* for community instability that culminated in the expulsion of their leadership. Clement advocates the recognition and support of the apostolic foundation and succession of the episcopate, which he asserts is a stabilizing factor for the normative Christian community:

> The Apostles received the Gospel for us from the Lord Jesus Christ, Jesus the Christ was sent from God. The Christ therefore is from God and the Apostles from the Christ. In both ways, then, they were in accordance with the appointed order of God's will. ... They preached from district to district, and from city to city, and they appointed their first converts, testing them by the Spirit, to be bishops and deacons of the future believers. ... Our Apostles also knew through our Lord Jesus Christ that there would be strife for the title of bishop. For this cause, therefore, since they had received perfect fore-knowledge, they appointed those who have already been mentioned, and afterwards added the codicil that if they should fall asleep, other approved men should succeed to their ministry. (*I Clement* 42, 44)

Ignatius of Antioch, also writing at an embryonic time in the Roman church's developing episcopacy, also consistently raised in each of his letters to Christian communities the motif of the *single* bishop. Those who are subject to him, Ignatius says, are the ones subject to Jesus Christ himself: "See that you all follow the bishop, as Jesus Christ follows the Father. ... Let no one do any of the things appertaining to the Church without the bishop" (*Smyrn.* 8; *Trall.* 3.1).

As is the case in the development of any group dynamic, circumstances forged internal doctrinal debates that began to present difficulties first within the communities and then eventually among them. The 2nd-century *Shepherd of Hermas*, a text considered at one time for inclusion in the New Testament canon, speaks to the elasticity of many elements of the early Roman church, such as how to address the problem of sin committed after baptism. Eventually it was maintained that unity needed to be established and brought under the control of a central figure whose authority was neither ambiguous nor indistinguishable from presbyters. Such leadership would provide a necessary stability in the face of the more charismatic leadership provided by the prophet, martyr, confessor, and teacher. Writing during a time prior to publicly fixed creed or canon, and in opposition to those who maintained a secret oral knowledge apart from the gospels, Irenaeus of Lyons insisted that the true gospel was preserved through faithfulness to an apostolic succession and apostolic tradition that emerged and was witnessed in the churches of apostolic foundation. These were the pillars upon which the voice of authority should rest. Hinting at what will later be used to defend the specific issue of Roman primacy, Irenaeus claimed that the truth could be maintained solely in the churches tied to the apostles, and, more specifically, the church in Rome:

> Tradition derived from the apostles, of the very great, the very ancient, and universally known Church founded and organized at Rome by the two most glorious apostles, Peter and Paul; is also the faith preached to men, which comes down to our time by means of the succession of bishops. For it is a matter of necessity that every Church should agree with this Church, on account of its preeminent authority, that is, the faithful everywhere, inasmuch as the apostolic tradition has been preserved continuously by those who exist everywhere. (*Adv. Haer.* 3.3.3)

Irenaeus' late 2nd-century thesis rests in the security of an apostolic foundation and succession that is difficult to correlate exactly with the historical condition of Christian social origins in Rome at that time, a reality in which communities largely managed their own local affairs. Nevertheless, Irenaeus himself was said to have journeyed to speak to the "Bishop" of Rome, Victor, on his mission to advocate for the Quartodecimans, and he clearly appeals to the concept of the monarchical bishop as an "apostolic" notion, to serve as a future norm for wider Christian organization. He also calls for Christians to reject innovations present in communities struggling with teachers of Gnostic Christology, and advises them to look to the faithful presentation of the gospel as it has been preserved in the church of Rome.

In addition to heresy (or internal debate) as an instigation for greater, overarching unity centered on a single apostolic bishop, threats of schism or external challenges to authority must also have prompted the move towards a more cohesive organization. Conflicts such as those waged by Cyprian of Carthage during the course of the mid-3rd-century persecution by Emperor Decius (and threats to do likewise by Emperor Gallus) needed the defense of a strong universal episcopate acting as a singular judge and authority over both individuals and communities (Hall 2007b). Facing division within the church over the restoration of the lapsed in the wake of persecution, the distribution of the sacraments at the hands of heretical clergy, and direct challenges to the authority of the bishop by confessors and their supporters, Cyprian made it his life's work to establish, if not a sole authority, at least a monarchical authority within each location. Distinct from his claim in *De unitate ecclesiae* that Christ "set up one throne and by his authority appointed one source and principle of unity" (*Unit. Eccl.* 4) (a statement intended not to press for Roman primacy as would be later alleged, but directed against those who resist their bishop), a synod held in Carthage concluded that while Peter was a special symbol of authority, his preeminence did not extend to other bishops, but was a "charism" that was passed to every bishop who was "apostolic" (Cyprian, *Ep.* 69.17); namely the corporate body of bishops in the international Christian community (Hall 2007b).

Like martyrs resisting civil authorities, Roman leaders who resisted doctrinal innovations were regarded as particularly meritorious and therefore worthy of respect and honor. In time, Rome would be regarded as a model of moderation and conventionality, holding firm in the face of theological positions that would eventually be labeled heretical. Organization did not, however, simply emerge in defense of circumstances, but also through the need to respond to human despair in the city. Determined to meet slander head-on with public good works that could stand as evidence to their faithful citizenship for those who might have reason to judge them harshly, and following Jewish models of charity, Roman Christians established the practice of providing for the needy within the city. Following the biblical model set by Paul and his collection for the saints in Jerusalem (Rom. 15.25–26), contributions were gathered once a week by those in a position to give. Justin Martyr notes a variety of social services to which the Christians attended:

> Those who prosper, and who so wish, contribute, each one as much as he chooses to. What is collected is deposited with the president, and he takes care of orphans and widows, and those who are in want on account of sickness or any other cause, and those who are in bonds, and the strangers who are sojourners among [us], and, briefly, he is the protector of all those in need. (*1 Apol.* 67.5–6)

And while texts such as the *Shepherd of Hermas'* careful castigation of the wealthy attest to the existence of predictable problems of avarice, nevertheless Clement of Rome writes of those in Rome who "have even given themselves into bondage that they might ransom others" (*1 Clem.* 55.2). Hippolytus notes the gifts for the sick, the widows, and the "bread for the poor" (*Apostolic Tradition* 24), and Bishop Cornelius' account of the synod of Rome attests to the "more than fifteen hundred widows and distressed persons" (*Hist. Eccl.* 6.43.11) who were supported by the church. By the end of the 3rd century giving and social programs were so central to the Christian mission at Rome that the need to coordinate charitable activities led, in part, to the need for a greater, city-wide organization. By the 5th century, in the absence of effective civil attention to such matters, the church in Rome was responsible for the care of widows, orphans and minors, prisoners, and public health and sanitation; further, it provided more than social services, for Rome was the logical launching point from which Christianity traveled to many parts of the Roman Empire, including parts of Africa, Spain, and Gaul, all of which looked in time to Rome as a leader and organizer of international Christianity (Dvornik 1966; Hall 2007a; Vinzent 2007; Winter 1994).

When Constantine arrived in Rome in 312, the Christian community there had certainly evolved beyond the early Jewish–Christian house churches gathered in the Trastevere. In less than 300 years it had been influenced in its organization and identity by the different types of people who embraced Christianity, by the traditions of Peter and Paul, by the resistance of Christians to the violent and public persecutions of the civil government, by the theological positions set up against pagan intellectuals, by Christian social practices, mission programs, resistance to internal heretical strains and schism, and by the rise of the Roman bishops, who were willing to care for, teach, preach to, die for, advise, and sometimes discipline Christian communities both in Rome itself and in various parts of the empire. These factors naturally contributed to the unwillingness of Rome to play any lesser role than that of a primary leader of international affairs in the church, as Christianity entered a new global era.

The Ancient Patriarchate of Rome in the Era of Constantine

The first to favor Christianity so extensively, the Emperor Constantine (ca. 271–337) was apparently anxious (for diverse reasons) to incorporate the benefits of Christianity into the fabric of the Roman Empire. Social-scientific studies of Christianity estimate that at the time of Constantine's defeat of Emperor Maxentius in 312 there were approximately 9 million Christians, comprising roughly 15 percent of the population (Stark 2006). Neither large enough to pose too great a threat nor small enough to be safely ignored, Christians had become a part of the religious map of empire alongside Judaism, state cults, and eastern mystery cults. After promulgation of the emancipatory Edict of Milan with co-emperor Licinius, Constantine, the emperor in the western portion of the empire, demonstrated a steady interest in the doctrine and organization of Christianity, and his imperial generosity greatly enhanced Christianity in Rome. His

wife's palace on the Lateran was donated in 313; he made grants of land to various churches and restitutions, as well as donations to the church of more than 400 pounds of gold per year. He promoted the building in 322 of a monumental church in honor of St. Peter on the Vatican Hill (its cut pillars are still visible in the crypt of St. Peter's). Clergy also rose in privilege and status both financially and jurisdictionally, becoming, in point of fact, a substructure of the civil administration (Cameron 2007; Holloway 2004). Within a short period of time ecclesiastical courts assumed responsibility for ruling in Christian municipal cases. So intimate was Constantine's involvement with church affairs that in 314, after an appeal by North African bishops, he appointed arbitrators headed by Miltiades, the bishop of Rome, to investigate the disturbance in the African church caused by Donatism and tensions among clergy in Carthage. It is noteworthy, however, that although the bishop of Rome headed this first inter-province council in the West, the Emperor did not take his pronouncement on the matter as final, for he called a second council the following year, which the current Pope Sylvester did not attend, though legates did. Pope Sylvester's legates also attended the first Ecumenical Council of Nicea, held in 325, where they were the first among all the bishops present to sign their names to the acts of the synod in agreement with the Nicene faith (Kelly 1996).

The transfer of the capital city of the empire from Rome to Constantinople in 324 altered the relationship between Rome and the other major eastern ecclesiastical centers in Antioch, and Alexandria. But while the site of the imperial residence and center of power had shifted, the "apostolic" status of Rome had not, and probably this challenge to its centrality contributed to the development by the Roman bishops of the *theologoumenon* of papal primacy, a doctrine that increasingly emerged in the latter half of the first millennium.

Claims for Papal Primacy in Post-Constantinian Rome

The doctrine of papal primacy is dependent on acceptance of the three claims that Peter was the "prince" among the apostles, that he was the first "bishop" in Rome, and that he transferred to the leading authorities in the Roman Christian community only the authority which he received from Christ. The passage upon which this latter claim is dependent is Matthew 16.18–19. After Peter answers Jesus' question about his identity correctly with the confession that Jesus is "the Messiah, the son of the living God" (Mt. 16.16), Jesus' response to this admission of faith is "And I tell you, you are Peter, and on this rock I will build my church, and the gates of Hades will not prevail against it. I will give you the keys of the kingdom of heaven, and whatever you bind on earth will be bound in heaven, and whatever you loose on earth will be loosed in heaven" (Anastos 2001). Later inscribed in Greek around the base of the dome of St. Peter's in Rome, this passage was employed by Pope Callistus I in the early 3rd century as justification for a single papal (*papae*) decision on penance (*De Pudicitia* 1.6; 21.9), his understanding of which was vigorously contested by his opponent Hippolytus (Kelly 1996).

The church in the eastern provinces never contested Peter's signal symbolic importance for the city of Rome, but the problem that emerged in the relationship between the various sees was the question of the (honorific) primacy of the ancient patriarchate of Rome as distinct from ecclesiastical jurisdiction over the others. For the eastern churches, the organizing element of church jurisdiction was not so much an apostolic origin but rather how church government could be accommodated to the political regulation of the empire. This principle of conforming to civic administrative boundaries was sanctioned in Canon 4 of the First Ecumenical Council of Nicea (325), as well as in Canons 2 and 3 of the First Ecumenical Council of Constantinople (381), and it was upheld in the Synod of Antioch, and referenced by Pope Boniface (PL 20.773), who forbade metropolitans to exercise authority in other than their own provinces; as well as by Pope Innocent I (PL 20.548) (Anastos 2001).

The question of accommodation versus primacy deserves a longer treatment than can be offered here, but there are a few things worth noting. First, accommodation, which is also understood as an apostolic institution, was merely a natural outgrowth of the new social circumstances of a Christianized empire.

Economic, social, judicial, and political life is naturally focused in any diocese on a central or capital city, and accordingly the bishop of that city would have to be a man of particular strength and character in order to meet the needs of the populace. It is understandable that over time the primary bishops of central cities in the empire would see themselves as more important than bishops in smaller, more backward towns, thus the origin of the concept of metropolitan archbishops. This applies all the more to the case of Rome because Rome was *the* central city of the empire, and not only was it "apostolic" in multiple ways, but it was the primary residence of the emperor. When the latter ceased to be the case, especially when Constantine shifted the capital to Constantinople, Rome remained apostolic but was no longer primary. Second, even though the Eastern Churches made attempts to advance a literary tradition lauding the apostolic foundation of Constantinople (mainly originating after the construction of the Church of the Holy Apostles as a shrine for the relics of St. Andrew), nevertheless the roots of this principle were never deep (Anastos 2001). What mattered more to the Eastern Churches than a historically provable apostolic foundation of any see was the more compelling belief that all sees were apostolic by virtue of correct "apostolic" doctrine, maintained by the succession of legitimate teaching bishops.

Second-millennium focus on the conflicts between the sees of Constantinople and Rome has overshadowed the many years of concord that existed between these two preeminent patriarchates. Nevertheless, differences in language and culture added to the mix of things that brought about increasing liturgical and theological discord between the two sees. Because the political position of accommodation to civic borders in the eastern portions of the empire was of greater importance than the Roman *theologoumenon* of special apostolic status, the fathers of the Council of Constantinople (381) were happy enough to establish Canon 3 in their deliberations, which gave the bishop of Constantinople second rank in the ecclesiastical hierarchy because it was the "New Rome." While this preserved the honorific rights of Old Rome, it was seen as a natural result of the shift of the imperial residence to Constantinople, and an important safeguard against the aspirations of Alexandria (Anastos 2001;

Dvornik 1966). The whole process of the rise of Constantinople to ecclesiastical eminence was bitterly resisted by Rome at first. Soon after the Council of Chalcedon (451), Pope Leo I declared its Canon 28 (which had just ratified Canon 3 of the Council of Constantinople) to be invalid (Kelly 1996). Canons that were anti-Roman in character from the Constantinopolitan Council in Trullo (692) did not do much to ease relations between the sees, nor did Emperor Leo III and Pope Gregory II's late 8th-century dispute over images and taxes during the period of the first Iconoclastic Controversy (Noble 2009); nor Charlemagne's coronation on Christmas Day in 800 by Pope Leo III as *Imperator Romanorum*; nor the formal condemnation of Patriarch Photios in 863 by Pope Leo III (Anastos 2001). By the time of Photios' patriarchate, both Constantinople and the patriarchate of Rome functioned as largely independent sees, and the eventual fracture of the pentarchy was in process, accelerated by disputes over ecclesiastical jurisdiction in "new" Christian territories. Photios was one of the first patriarchs of Constantinople to entertain serious doubts over the continuing orthodoxy of Rome, not simply on matters of wider doctrine (the *filioque* issue), but also on the basis of the papal claims to special primacy as manifesting a form of ecclesiology not in harmony with the wider sentiment of the Eastern Churches. Growing fractures and theological differences were to come to a head as the tide of Islam pressured the Eastern Churches more and more, and Rome's papal monarchy rose to political precedence. The Crusades (especially the Fourth) left a lasting damage in relations; more so perhaps than the notional date of schism between the two patriarchates of 1054.

The Importance of the Ancient Patriarchate of Rome for Orthodoxy Today

In October 2008 Pope Benedict XVI, the current leader of the world's more than 1 billion Roman Catholics, received as his guest in Vatican City the Ecumenical Patriarch Bartholomew I, and prayed with him in the Sistine Chapel. The two, who met together four times since the election of Pope Benedict, seemed eager for a continuing ecumenical dialogue in a world fractured by religious strife. The ecumenical patriarch described the service in the famous Sistine Chapel as a "joyous experience of unity, perhaps not perfect, but true and deep." While the place of the papal primacy among Christian hierarchs continues to be a strongly divisive and inflammatory aspect of the larger divisions between Eastern Orthodoxy and Roman Catholicism, nevertheless, both pope and patriarch are to be lauded for their willingness to work together for unity on wider church issues that can legitimately be undertaken in a spirit of Christian openness. If their joint works can contribute towards the healing of a planet that groans under the weight of significant social, ecological, and political challenges, it will be a blessing not only for Christianity, but even for the world at large.

SEE ALSO: Alexandria, Patriarchate of; Antioch, Patriarchate of; Constantinople, Patriarchate of; Iconoclasm; Jerusalem, Patriarchate of; Pentarchy; St. Constantine the Emperor (ca. 271–337); St. Photios the Great (ca. 810–ca. 893)

References and Suggested Readings

Anastos, M.V. (2001) "Constantinople and Rome: A Survey of the Relations between the Byzantine and the Roman Churches," in S.Vryonis, Jr. and N. Goodhue (eds.) *Aspects of the Mind of Byzantium: Political Theory, Theology and Ecclesiastical Relations with the See of Rome*, vol. 8. Aldershot: Ashgate/Variorum, pp. 1–119.

Brown, R. E. and Meier, J. P. (1983) *Antioch and Rome: New Testament Cradles of Catholic Christianity*. Mahwah, NJ: Paulist Press.

Cameron, A. (2007) "Constantine and the 'Peace of the Church'," in M. M. Mitchell and F. M. Young (eds.) *The Cambridge History of Christianity: Origins to Constantine*. Cambridge: Cambridge University Press, pp. 538–51.

Dvornik, F. (1966) *Byzantium and the Roman Primacy*. New York: Fordham University Press.

Hall, S. G. (2007a) "Institutions in the pre-Constantinian *Ecclesia*," in M. M. Mitchell and F. M. Young (eds.) *The Cambridge History of Christianity: Origins to Constantine*. Cambridge: Cambridge University Press, pp. 414–33.

Hall, S. G. (2007b) "Ecclesiology in the Wake of Persecutions," in M. M. Mitchell and F. M. Young (eds.) *The Cambridge History of Christianity: Origins to Constantine*. Cambridge: Cambridge University Press, pp. 470–83.

Holloway, R. R. (2004) *Constantine and Rome*. New Haven: Yale University Press.

Jeffers, J. S. (1991) *Conflict at Rome: Social Order and Hierarchy in Early Christianity*. Minneapolis: Fortress Press.

Kelly, J. N. D. (1996) *The Oxford Dictionary of Popes*. Oxford: Oxford University Press.

Meeks, W. A. (1993) *The Origins of Christian Morality: The First Two Centuries*. New Haven: Yale University Press.

Meyendorff, J. (1996) *Rome Constantinople Moscow: Historical and Theological Studies*. Crestwood, NY: St. Vladimir's Seminary Press.

Noble, T. F. X. (2009) *Images, Iconoclasm, and the Carolingians*. Pittsburgh: University of Pennsylvania Press.

Stark, R. (2006) *Cities of God: The Real Story of How Christianity Became an Urban Movement and Conquered Rome*. San Francisco: Harper One.

Vinzent, M. (2007) "Rome," in M. M. Mitchell and F. M. Young (eds.) *The Cambridge History of Christianity: Origins to Constantine*. Cambridge: Cambridge University Press, pp. 397–412.

Winter, B. W. (1994) *Seek the Welfare of the City: Christians as Benefactors and Citizens*. Grand Rapids, MI: Eerdmans.

Royal Doors

DAN SANDU

The two, often elaborate, doors in the center of the iconostasis in Eastern Orthodox churches. They are called royal because Christ the Emperor mystically passes through them, and because the Byzantine emperor entered through these doors together with the patriarch or a bishop prior to the start of the Holy Eucharist. They are a sign of the unity of the two Testaments which are the pathway to the Kingdom of God, the Holy of Holies represented in the church by the Sanctuary.

On the royal doors there is a diptych icon of the annunciation, which symbolizes the fact that this event

Plate 57 The seminarians' chapel of Sergiev Posad Academy, near Moscow. Founded by St. Sergius of Radonezh, the monastery with its attached theological school is a center of Russian church life. Photo by John McGuckin.

opened the gates of Heaven to humanity. The four corners of the double doors feature medallions of Sts. Matthew, Mark, Luke, and John, the authors of the gospel of Christ. Behind the doors there is often a velvet or cotton veil or curtain, which is opened and closed by being moved upward or to the side at specific moments during liturgical services. The royal doors are not used for regular access to the altar, and are only opened during the celebration of the mysteries, which offer redeeming grace and access to the heavenly kingdom. Only bishops and priests ever pass through them at designated moments in the liturgy. The doors are kept closed strictly outside religious ceremonies.

During the morning services the royal doors are kept closed until the Great Doxology as a reminder of man's banishment from heaven for failing to observe God's commandment. At the intoning of the Great Doxology – the hymn of praise based on the glorification by the angelic hosts of the nativity of Christ – the doors are opened to reflect the reopening of heaven following the coming of the Son of God into the world as a man and to proclaim the blessing for the start of the Holy Eucharist.

SEE ALSO: Diakonikon; Divine Liturgy, Orthodox; Iconostasis

References and Suggested Readings

Braniște, E. (2002) Liturgica Generală (General Liturgics). Galați: Editura Episcopiei Dunării de Jos.

Florensky, P. (1996) Ikonostasis. Crestwood, NY: St. Vladimir's Seminary Press.

Taft, R. F. (2004) A History of the Liturgy of Saint John Chrysostom, Vol. 2: The Great Entrance. Rome: Pontifical Oriental Institute.

Russia, Patriarchal Orthodox Church of

KONSTANTIN GAVRILKIN

The Russian Orthodox Church (hereafter, ROC), also known as the Moscow patriarchate, is ranked fifth in the listing of the autocephalous Orthodox Churches (after Constantinople, Alexandria, Antioch, and Jerusalem). The largest multinational church in the world, it has jurisdiction over most of the Orthodox parishes in Russia, Ukraine, Belarus, and other territories of the former Soviet Union (except for Georgia, which has its own autocephalous church), as well as a number of parishes in various regions of the world, organized in dioceses or under the direct authority of the patriarch of Moscow. There are also a number of ecclesiastical entities that emerged after the breakdown of the ROC caused by the Bolshevik Revolution of 1917 and incessant persecution of the church by the Soviet government (Tsypin 2006). Some were part of the massive Russian diaspora, others emerged from the Catacomb movement (Beglov 2008).

An outline of the history of the ROC helps to understand the difficulties encountered when dealing with the complex phenomenon of Russian Orthodoxy.

Kievan Rus Late 9th–Early 13th Centuries

In 988, Vladimir, the Grand Prince of Kiev (980–1015), ordered the inhabitants of the capital to be baptized in the Dnieper river, following his own baptism in Chersonesus earlier that year. There were, however, Christians in Kiev already by the mid-10th century, and their numbers grew after the conversion of Vladimir's grandmother Olga, who ruled in Kiev from 945 to 963 and was baptized in Constantinople in 954 (Golubinskii 1901). The missionary work of Sts. Cyril and Methodius, and especially their disciples in Bulgaria, who translated the basic corpus of Christian texts, including the liturgy, into Slavonic in the late 9th and early 10th centuries, were factors that eased the Christianization of the region. The mission was sponsored by the patriarchate of Constantinople, which exercised control over the ecclesiastical life of Ancient Rus and appointed all the Metropolitans "of Kiev and All Rus" until the mid-15th century (on the profound Byzantine legacy in Ancient Rus, see Thomson 1999).

Under Vladimir and his dynasty, Kiev and then such cities as Novgorod, Pskov, Vladimir, Rostov, and Suzdal' gradually emerged as important regional cent-

Plate 58   The Danilovsky Monastery, Moscow. Home of the Russian Orthodox Patriarchate. Photo by John McGuckin.

Plate 59   Patriarch Kiril, head of the Russian Orthodox Church. Photo by John McGuckin.

ers of Christian culture and spirituality. Kiev's Monastery of the Caves (later known as Kievo-Pecherskaia Lavra), founded in 1051 by St. Antonii Pecherskii, played a key role in shaping Russian monastic traditions and creating an original Christian literature, with its monks becoming the first Russian chroniclers, hagiographers, and spiritual writers.

The Mongol invasion of 1220–40 left most of the Kievan Rus in ruins. Afterwards came a short period of control by the principality of Vladimir-Suzdal', but in 1238 its capital, Vladimir, was itself destroyed, and in 1240 Kiev suffered a similar fate. After that point there followed dynastic and political reorganizations, and the northeastern lands became increasingly dominated by Moscow (Fennell 1983). Having recognized the long-lasting changes in the Russian

political landscape, Maksim the Metropolitan of Kiev (1283–1305) abandoned the impoverished old capital and moved to Vladimir in 1299. His successor, Metropolitan Peter (1308–26), moved his court to Moscow permanently.

Rise of Moscow: 14th–Mid-15th Centuries

The presence of the metropolitan's court in Moscow increased the authority and ambition of the local Muscovy princes to unify the land under their sole rule. The metropolitans, in turn, used the new situation to secure the stability of the ROC and inspire unity among the divided Russian principalities. Most

Plate 60 The Monastery of the Holy Trinity, Sergiev Posad, one of the homes of the Moscow Patriarch. Photo by John McGuckin.

of them, such as Theognostus (1328–53) and Photius (1408–31), were Greeks from Constantinople who were able to use diplomatic skill, wisdom, and personal courage in dealing with the rival Russian rulers on the one hand, and the Golden Horde on the other (Meyendorff 1981). Some were locals, like Metropolitan Aleksii (1354–78), who prior to his election was for many years an assistant to Metropolitan Theognostus and, at the latter's advice, was appointed his successor, ruling with authority and insight and striving to unite the Russian lands in their fight against Tatar oppression. His contemporary, St. Sergius of Radonezh (d. 1392), inspired a massive monastic movement that covered Russian territories with hundreds of monasteries, spreading

the influence of hesychasm and ecclesiastical culture and further colonizing the land. The building of monasteries was accompanied by a broader cultural revival, one of the most remarkable examples of which was St. Andrei Rublev (d. 1430) and his school of iconography.

During the reign of Vasilii II (1425–62), the ROC underwent a dramatic change that redefined its identity. In the 1430s, Byzantine Emperor John VIII Palaeologus negotiated with Rome regarding the reunification of the Western and Eastern Churches in order to save Constantinople from the looming takeover by the Ottoman Turks. His chief negotiator at the Council of Basle in 1434 was Bishop Isidor, who in 1437 was sent by the emperor to Moscow as Metropolitan of Kiev and All Russia in order to bring Muscovy into the union with Rome for the goal of the rescue of Constantinople. At the Council of Florence in 1439, Isidor was one of the chief Greek spokesmen for the reunion, and, upon signing the agreement, he was made by Pope Eugene IV the papal legate to All Russia and Lithuania and, later, Cardinal-Priest. When Isidor arrived in Moscow in the spring of 1441 as cardinal and papal legate he announced the union with Rome as official Orthodox Church policy. Vasilii II and the council of the Russian bishops rejected Isidor's authority: he was deposed and imprisoned, but allowed to escape in the autumn of 1441. At the end of 1448, a few weeks after the death of the Byzantine "unionist" Emperor John VIII, the council of the Russian bishops finally decided to act independently, and elected Jonah, Bishop of Riazan (who had been the local candidate to the metropolitan's office since 1431), who thus became the first head of the ROC not affirmed by Constantinople. The Church of Constantinople itself eventually rejected the union with Rome (1472), but its synod refused to recognize the ROC's claim to independence until the late 16th century.

In 1458 the uniate patriarch of Constantinople, Gregory III Mamma, who was living in Rome under papal protection, appointed the Bulgarian Gregory II as Metropolitan of Kiev, Galicia, and All Rus. Recognized by the Polish King Casimir IV, and with a unionizing policy in mind, Gregory's legitimacy was rejected by Moscow, and its choice of metropolitan

Jonah was reasserted. The *de facto* existence of two Russian metropolias was finally resolved by all involved parties in 1460. And in 1461, after the death of Metropolitan Jonah, the Russian bishops elected Archbishop Theodosius of Rostov with the title "Metropolitan of Moscow and all Rus."

Independence: 1448–1589

The fall of Constantinople in 1453 made Muscovy the only free Orthodox country. Its leaders turned the tragedy of Constantinople into Moscow's triumph, claiming that their country providentially became the sole successor of the fallen Byzantine Empire. Ivan III (1462–1505) assumed firm control over most of the Russian lands through marriage, purchase, or war, tripling the size of the state. In 1478–88 he also crushed the Republic of Novgorod, which immediately became the source of a significant and lengthy ecclesiastical and political crisis, caused by the so-called "heresy of Judaizers" (Klier 1997), instigated (to believe Joseph of Volotsk, its chief prosecutor and author of *Prosvetitel'* [The Enlightener], a polemical treatise against the "Judaizers") by a certain learned Jew, Skhariia (Zacharia), who in 1470 came to Novgorod from Kiev. Under his influence, some Orthodox clergy secretly embraced a "Judaic faith" (circumcision and other customs and rituals) and secretly rejected Christian teaching on the Trinity and divinity of Jesus, icon veneration, monasticism, and church sacraments. Two of them, the priests Denis and Aleksei, were eventually brought by the Grand Prince Ivan III to Moscow to serve in the capital's cathedrals, where they managed to attract a significant group of followers in high places: the list of suspects included the Metropolitan of Moscow Zosima (1490–4), members of Ivan III's family, and his high officials. The Judaizers capitalized on the absence of the full Bible in Slavonic and a rudimentary knowledge of theology among the locals. To neutralize their influence, Archbishop Gennadii of Novgorod organized a circle of translators, both Orthodox and Catholic, to collect existing biblical texts and translate the missing ones, and by 1499 he assembled the first full Slavonic Bible. Historians argue that Gennadius' reliance on the expertise of a certain Dominican monk, Veniamin, could explain the favora-

ble view of the Spanish Inquisition that he and Joseph of Volotsk seemed to display in their arguments and actions against the Judaizers, who were subjected to execution, imprisonment, and exile.

Simultaneously, Russian ecclesiastics were involved in the dispute regarding the nature of monastic life in relation to land ownership. Joseph of Volotsk and his party, heavily dependent on state protectionism, defended the vast monastic estates, covering one-third of the country at the time, as the basis of monasteries' wellbeing and intense involvement in social welfare. Their opponents, led by Nil Sorskii, defended contemplative monasticism and warned of the corruption of the church by power, both economic and political. The two parties also sharply disagreed in their attitude to heretics in general and to the Judaizers in particular. Joseph of Volotsk praised the Inquisition and justified violence against the heretics (including their public burning at the stake), while Nil Sorskii argued for tolerance and the arts of non-violent persuasion. The Josephites, as they were called, won the support of the Grand Prince and dominated the ecclesiastical life of Muscovy in the 16th century, for most of which Muscovy was ruled by two people: Vasilii III (1506–33) and his son, Ivan IV (1533–84). Crowned tsar in 1547, Ivan IV greatly expanded the state by war and conquest, and completed Muscovy's transition to autocracy by destroying regional elites and replacing them with his own appointees.

As long as it elevated and strengthened their authority, both subscribed to the ideology of Joseph of Volotsk, who, like his followers, was hopeful that a symphony of church and state in Muscovy was in sight. The whole 16th century, however, provides examples of how Russian rulers constantly kept their metropolitans in check: the latter always ran a risk of being deposed, imprisoned, and exiled (like Varlaam, 1511–21, or Ioasaf, 1539–42, or Dionisii, 1572–81), or even killed (like Philip, 1566–8), regardless of the significance of the issues involved.

Metropolitan Makarii (1542–63), himself a Josephite, became the most important figure in his century's Russian ecclesiastical, as well as cultural, life. While archbishop of Novgorod (1526–42), he initiated a complex program of collecting and organizing all available translations of ecclesiastical texts, as well as Russian original literature (compiled in the *Velikie Minei-Chet'i*). His further significance as the metropolitan was demonstrated graphically, one might argue, by the fact that Ivan IV's turn to uncontrollable violence (the so-called *Oprichnina*) took place after the metropolitan's death in December 1563. Makarii presided over a number of local councils – in 1547, 1549, 1551, and 1553–4 – some (the so-called *zemskie sobory*) with the ecclesiastical and secular authorities gathering together for the purpose of resolving both religious and secular issues. Among other actions, the councils canonized many Russian saints, certified legal codes (both secular and ecclesiastical), organized the life of monasteries and their estates, and codified liturgical rites and the calendar. Makarii also supervised an extensive building of new monasteries and churches throughout Muscovy.

Autocephalous Patriarchate: 1589–1720

During the reign of Tsar Feodor 1 (1584–98), when the government was controlled by his brother-in-law, Boris Godunov (himself a tsar in 1598–1605), Russian authorities on a number of occasions attempted to engage the patriarchs of Constantinople, Alexandria, Antioch, and Jerusalem in negotiations regarding the establishment of the office of patriarch of Moscow and, *de jure*, recognition of the ROC's autocephaly. Only in 1589, however, when Patriarch of Constantinople Jeremiah II came to Moscow for help and alms after several years of harassment by the Turkish sultan, did the tide turn. Jeremiah had little choice but to agree to enthrone Job, metropolitan of Moscow since 1586, as the first Russian patriarch. The synods of Constantinople in 1590 and 1593 (in the latter case, with all Eastern patriarchs in attendance) confirmed Job's enthronement, accorded the ROC the fifth place in the diptych of the Orthodox Churches, and accepted the Muscovites' designation of their destiny, the only Orthodox country in the world, as now being the "Third Rome," the successor of Constantinople (i.e., the "Second," or New Rome, as the Greeks called their capital).

The 17th century became for the ROC a time of change and crisis. Several factors played a role in compromising what, after the establishment of the Russian patriarchate in 1589, looked like a bright and promising future. First were the developments in the neighboring Polish-Lithuanian Commonwealth, where the metropolia of Kiev broke down under pressure from the Polish government and Catholic propaganda, led by the Jesuit Order. By the 1590s many of the previously Orthodox nobles converted to Catholicism, practically all the Orthodox bishops favored the union with Rome, and only a few self-organized Orthodox brotherhoods, with the support of the monasteries and a few landowners, engaged in active self-defense through education and the printing of Orthodox literature, encouraged to that end by the patriarch of Constantinople. The declaration of the Union with Rome, signed by the Kievan hierarchy at the Synod at Brzezno (Brest), allowed the Polish authorities to deny the weakened Orthodox community in the Commonwealth their own legal hierarchy. Only in the early 1630s did the Polish King Ladislas IV (1632–48) agree to the consecration of Peter Moghila as Orthodox metropolitan of Kiev (1633–46) in the jurisdiction of Constantinople. Moghila believed that, in order to survive in Poland, the Orthodox needed education first and foremost, modeled after the European universities. He turned around the Kiev Orthodox Academy by introducing an eleven-year course of study and set it on the path to becoming an intellectual center of Eastern Orthodoxy for years to come. One of the immediate results of the Russo-Polish War of 1654–67 and Russia's annexation of the Left-Bank Ukraine was the migration of Ukrainian learned ecclesiastics, associated with the Kiev Academy, to Moscow at the invitation of Tsar Alexis Mikhailovich Romanov (1645–76) and his successors. Shortly after, they began to play prominent roles in ecclesiastical affairs, theology, and education (Saunders 1985). But their dominance and undermining of local (and "older," as their defenders claimed) traditions of religious and cultural practice began to generate strong resistance and opposition in Muscovy, erupting in the later 17th century in relation to the reforms of Patriarch Nikon (1652–66).

Another important factor was the increased authority of the Moscow patriarch, especially in the Time of Troubles (1603–13) and its aftermath. First, both Job (d. 1607) and Hermogen (1606–12) rejected two pretenders to the Moscow throne who relied on Polish troops and managed, albeit for a short time, to usurp the throne. Both ecclesiastics, together with Filaret, father of Tsar Michael Romanov (1613–45) and who would be a future patriarch himself (1619–33), became symbols of national resistance against the imposters and the Polish occupation. After the election of his son as the tsar in 1613, Filaret became the administrator of state affairs, accumulating in his hands that extensive personal authority which was later claimed for himself and his office by Patriarch Nikon, enthroned by Tsar Aleksei Mihailovich (1645–76).

By the mid-17th century the ROC was in need of reform. Liturgical abuses of various kinds, low moral standards, use of conflicting editions of liturgical texts, translated from varying sources both by Ruthenian and Muscovite printers, and the absence of the recognized experts in Greek and Latin to verify translations, created a conflictual situation requiring radical intervention. As soon as he was installed as patriarch, Nikon claimed absolute authority and power over the reform project, making changes in liturgical books according to the new Greek editions. The opponents of changes argued, however, that the traditional Russian practice originated from the earlier Greek sources and that the new editions all came from the Catholic countries and could not be relied on. Unwilling to take Nikon's side without negotiations, Tsar Aleksii eventually grew weary of the patriarch's overbearing personality, his constant demands of obedience, and refusals to collaborate. In 1666 Nikon was deposed and imprisoned in Ferapontov Monastery. Simultaneously, at the councils of 1666–7, the new rites were approved and the old ones condemned, together with the previous councils that endorsed them (the famous council of 1551, led by Metropolitan Makarii of Moscow). The opponents of the new practices were subjected to various forms of punishment after their refusal to accept the reforms. The leaders of what became known as the "Old Belief" (*staraia vera*, or *staryi obriad*) were executed, imprisoned, or exiled, while thousands escaped abroad or to Siberia; the persecution of the Old Believers continued until the 1905 Edict on Religious Tolerance.

Synodal Period: 1721–1917

Peter I, who was in conflict with Patriarch Adrian (1690–1700) for most of the 1690s, did not allow for the election of his successor. Instead, in 1700 he estab-

lished a commission for drafting new legislation limiting the privileges of the church and introducing taxation of dioceses. The reform, however, was delayed until 1721, when a manifesto on the establishment of the Spiritual Collegium (later, the Holy Governing Synod) was published, abolishing the office of the patriarch. In 1722 Peter I introduced the office of Chief Procurator of the Holy Synod (*oberprokuror*), who was directly appointed by the emperor from the ranks of career bureaucrats to supervise the daily operations of the holy synod. Until 1917 all resolutions of the synod of the ROC were published with the logo: "By decree of His Imperial Majesty." Soon after, he also secured the agreement of the Eastern patriarchs to treat the synod as the legitimate successor of the Russian patriarch in all ecclesiastical affairs of the ROC.

The state's encroachment on the ROC reached its peak after the ascension to power of Catherine II (1762–96), who in 1764 initiated a full secularization of ecclesiastical lands (they were confiscated with the attached serfs, almost a million of them) and sharply reduced the number and size of monasteries by dividing them into several categories: *shtatnye* (supported by the state) and *zashtatnye* (self-supporting), with each category subdivided into three classes according to the permitted number of monastics. The reform had a devastating effect on ecclesiastical life in general and monasticism in particular. Its opponents were subjected to a brutal persecution which made most of the bishops unwilling to voice their objections publicly, especially after what happened to the metropolitan of Rostov, Arsenii Matsisevich (d. 1772), who was deposed and imprisoned for the rest of his life.

Peter's reforms, and their later augmentations, created a centralized administrative system with effective control over all dioceses of the ROC (previously covering an enormous territory, they were gradually reduced in size, as were the number of parishes). On the parish level, the state's attempt to increase parishes' size by reducing their number in order to improve the clergy's material support, proved difficult. The liturgical burden of the priests increased considerably and left them with little time for educational and catechetical activities. Another government objective – the raising of the level of clerical education – was addressed only from the early 19th century onwards, when reforms in church education raised educational standards and significantly increased the number of seminary graduates among the clergy. This in turn, however, led to a new set of problems related to the hereditary structure of Orthodox clergy, a dynastic clerical tradition solidified by the legislation of the 18th century (Freeze 1977). Church schools, where only sons of the clergy could study, produced too many seminary graduates with a limited number of parishes to go to. Also, their appointment had little to do with professional or moral qualifications. Rather, it was based on the candidate's willingness to marry a priest's daughter and inherit the parish in due time (almost always, only after the death of the incumbent family-related priest). Even then, parish economy provided no adequate material support for priests, trained in superfluous subjects according to a Latin curriculum that laid emphasis on classical languages, as well as on agronomy, mathematics, medicine, and physics. In addition, priests depended on peasants' voluntary payments for services or on the small produce the priest's family could grow on the tiny land allotment belonging to the church, leaving little time for pastoral service.

Efforts by the government of Tsar Nicholas I (1825–54) to solve such problems proved insufficient (Freeze 1983: 3–187). A new attempt at reform of the ROC was made during the reign of Alexander II (1855–81), who had inherited the Russian Empire in a state of deep crisis, something that was abundantly revealed to him during the disastrous Crimean War (1853–6). The government was forced to reexamine the whole foundations of the Russian social and economic order, based on the labors of millions of enslaved serfs. Then the policy of *glasnost'* (openness) was deployed to engage the educated elite, alienated by Nicholas I, in debating the problems faced by the country. Major changes, initiated by the government, included the emancipation of the serfs (1861), establishment of representative local government (1861–4), and creation of an independent judicial system (1864), as well as the reforms of education (1863–4), municipal government (1870), the military (1874), and, finally, the ROC. While the reforms set the country on the path of rapid industrialization, they created new problems, caused by the inadequate legislation relating to the more than 20 million former serfs who were declared free without the legal right to the land they had formerly toiled. Millions moved to the sprawling cities and joined the quickly growing Russian proletariat, feeding the social unrest and the stormy revolutionary movement. This, in turn, gave rise to nationalism, xenophobia, and stubborn opposition to the reforms among the upper classes, thus further polarizing and destabilizing the country. On March 1, 1881, the very day when Alexander II approved a proposal for further and more substantial liberalization of the state policies on all levels – from the political structure of the empire to peasant land ownership – he was killed by a terrorist bomb, and the country was pulled back in the opposite direction by his son, Alexander III (1881–94), and his grandson, Nicholas II (1895–1917).

In the period of the Great Reforms, Russian ecclesiastics (bishops, priests, seminary professors, and synodal officials), as well as state bureaucrats and intellectuals, representing both liberal and conservative wings, got an opportunity openly to debate the situation of the church. The majority argued for the relaxation of state control over the church or even for the latter's full independence. The government, however, needed to make the church a more effective pastoral, educational, and ideological institution, providing Russian society with social and political unity and stability, which seemed to it to require more effective state control over the church.

These contradictory objectives defined the trajectory and dynamic of the reforms attempted in the 1860s and 1870s (Freeze 1983: 191–347). Parish councils were established in 1864 with the expectation that they would focus on improving the material conditions of clergy and schools. The new seminary statute (1867) opened church schools to students of all social groups (estates), while allowing seminarians also to enter the universities. The ban on hereditary transfers of parishes (1867) was followed by a reorganization of the parishes in general (1869): cutting down their number, increasing the average size, and limiting clerical positions within them, aiming to improve the material conditions of the priest. A set of additional measures freed clerical children from previous limitations imposed by law: they were now free to pursue career and marriage outside of the clerical estate (1869–71). Parallel positive developments included the revival of preaching, mission, charity, and conciliar practices (such as the institution of diocesan councils).

A slow implementation of the reforms made their results visible only in the late 1870s to 1880s. Although the priesthood became a vocation and the identity of the Russian clergy was greatly strengthened in the public eye, the reforms disrupted the functions of many of the institutions they aimed to improve. Parish councils spent most of their allotted money on decorations, rather than on priests and schools. The best students were leaving seminaries to pursue secular careers through university education. Academic standards in seminaries declined and they experienced acute reductions in enrollment, and the resulting lack of candidates for ordination began to affect dioceses. If priests wanted their sons to study at seminaries, they now had to pay for them (prior to the reform, it was free). Closure of many parishes was accompanied by a widespread bitterness of affected parishioners who were neither consulted nor provided with means of traveling to now-remote parishes. It was not surprising that the parish clergy, who suffered the most by losing privileges of free seminary education, and who now faced a shortage of parish appointments, were among the largest group who saw the reforms as a disaster for the ROC. There were, however, positive developments in the life of the ROC as well. Many bishops and priests now came to service in the ROC from nonpriestly backgrounds, and one could find among them charismatic figures of both peasant and aristocratic origin. Revival of monastic spirituality led to the repopulation of many previously deteriorated monasteries. Russian missionaries labored in various regions of the multiethnic and multireligious Russian Empire, as well as abroad (such as in Japan and the United States). Numerous charities were administered by the ROC on behalf of the poor and destitute families, mostly in the industrialized urban areas. The remarkable advancement in critical religious and theological studies in the late 19th and early 20th centuries, especially in the areas of church history, patristics, and comparative religion (albeit for missionary purposes), was another positive result of the educational reform of the 1860s. The Russian religious renaissance of the early 20th century would not have been possible without the groundwork provided by the graduates of the

reform theological schools who served as professors in many Russian universities.

The appointment of K. P. Pobedonostsev, one of the major promoters of counter-reforms under Alexander III, as chief procurator of the synod (1880–1905), reversed the changes of the reform period. The new statute of theological schools (1884) simplified the curriculum with a focus on "spiritual formation" rather than scholarly training, cancelled elections of rectors and deans, and gave overall control over the schools to diocesan bishops instead of faculty. Seminarians were no longer allowed to leave for universities. Seminaries were changing into caste training institutions once again, with rigid disciplinary regimes, places that were intolerant of critical thinking. In the late 1890s and 1900s riots and clashes between administrations and seminarians took place in a number of seminaries; in some schools, fewer and fewer students sought ordination, such as in the seminary of Blagoveshchensk, where no priest could be found among any of its graduates between 1903 and 1913 (Smolich 1996).

These and similar changes in other areas, suffocating creativity and initiative, as introduced by Pobedonostsev's policies, became another proof of the detrimental effects of state control over the church. A growing number of ecclesiastics, both liberal and conservative, began to raise voices in support of restoration of the office of Russian patriarch and called for a return to the principle of the administration of the ROC on the basis of canon law, rather than on the confusing, restrictive, and often arbitrary policies of the state. The whole synodal period became subject to critical reevaluation in the reign of Nicholas II, especially after the country's defeat in the war with Japan, and the political crisis of the revolution of 1905. The unrest was aggravated by the inconsistent policies of the imperial government, oscillating between reform and reaction. In the polarized empire, nationalist and monarchist groups sought the support of the church in their struggle against liberalism and socialism, while representatives of the liberal wing within society and the ROC were increasingly critical of the state policies and doubtful that the autocratic monarchy of the Romanovs was capable of leading the country out of its political and economic crises, especially as they had been exacerbated by World War I.

The empire's collapse in 1917 gave the ROC a chance finally to convene the All-Russian Church Council of August 1917–August 1918, which restored the office of the patriarch and proposed significant changes in the administration of the church on all levels. However, immediately after the Bolshevik Revolution in October 1917 the ROC came under increasing attack from the Soviet government, which immediately declared a separation of church and state only to unleash systematic propaganda against the church with openly repressive policies in the aftermath of the Civil War of 1918–22. Within twenty years, the country with more than 50,000 churches would see most of them destroyed or converted for different use (with only a few hundred deliberately kept open for propaganda purposes). Under the increasingly violent hostility of the Soviets most of the ROC's 200,000 clergy and monastics were killed or imprisoned, and around 1,000 monasteries closed (except for those in the territories that became independent).

Soviet Period: 1917–1988

The collapse of the Russian Empire and the Bolshevik Revolution disturbed the unity of the ROC. The Civil War, with quickly shifting frontlines and local governments and dislocation of hundreds of thousands, made it impossible for Patriarch Tikhon and the synod of the ROC to maintain normal communications with various dioceses in regions affected by unrest and bloodshed, or taken over by foreign armies, or even belonging to a separate state. In a few years a number of Orthodox entities in now independent and sovereign countries (Poland, the Baltics, Bessarabia, Ukraine, Georgia, the Far East) declared their independence from the administration of the ROC, which had no capacity to control the situation or assist them, or else they joined the patriarchate of Constantinople. Already in 1920, Patriarch Tikhon decided to give the former dioceses of the ROC freedom to choose their own course of action: he issued a decree allowing diocesan bishops, who had no more contact with the administration of the ROC, to pursue the best solution to their immediate problems by uniting with the bishops of neighboring territories.

Some of the bishops, clergy, and the faithful began to reorganize already in the course of the Civil War but later, forced to escape, continued to maintain their temporary jurisdictional affiliations. The largest group of the Orthodox, represented by a group of exiled Russian bishops, took the next step when in 1920, in Constantinople, creating the Synod of the Russian Church in Diaspora (later, the Russian Orthodox Church outside Russia, or ROCOR), including also the Russian dioceses in Finland, China, Japan, and Manchuria. Led by Metropolitan of Kiev Antonii Khrapovitsky, in 1921 they moved to Yugoslavia. In 1936 a group led by Metropolitan Evlogy joined the patriarchate of Constantinople and has remained in its jurisdiction to this day. During and after World War II, a substantial number of Russian émigrés moved farther west into Europe, or to the Americas and Australia. Another part of the ROC, the American metropolia, maintained its operational independence from both the Moscow patriarchate and the ROCOR, until it was granted formal independence by the Moscow patriarchate in 1970, becoming the Orthodox Church in America (its autocephalous status has not been recognized by Constantinople and several other churches). After the collapse of the Soviet Union in 1991, it took more than fifteen years to see the ROCOR and the Moscow patriarchate sign the Act of Reunion in 2007, with ROCOR retaining its operational autonomy according to the agreement.

The main body of the ROC, led by Patriarch Tikhon, was subjected to brutal persecution. Within a few years of 1917, all theological schools were closed, printing of religious literature was prohibited, and most of the active and noteworthy clergy and monastics who had survived murder, torture, and execution were imprisoned in concentration camps. A short-lived attempt of the Renovationist movement, or the so-called "Living Church" (*obnovlentsy*), supported by the Soviet government so as to gain the trust of the Russian Orthodox and, simultaneously, pose as the "new," progressive church that embraced the Soviet ideology, ended in disgrace, soon exposed as a puppet organization controlled by the Soviet secret police.

With the beginning of World War II and the German occupation of a substantial part of the Soviet Union, thousands of churches were reopened in the occupied territories, reigniting anti-Soviet sentiments among the local population. To counteract the success of the Nazis in the region and encourage local support for the retreating Soviet troops, Soviet dictator Joseph Stalin met with a few Russian bishops in September 1943 and agreed to give the ROC some freedom in exchange for their visible public support of the regime. A few days later, the church council was convened and Sergey Stragorodskii (1867–1944), metropolitan of Moscow, who in 1927 had issued a "Declaration of loyalty to the Soviet government" (further antagonizing the Russian Orthodox outside the Soviet Union), was elected patriarch, only to die in 1944. In 1945 Alexey (Simanskii), metropolitan of Leningrad (formerly St. Petersburg), was elected patriarch (1945–70). Although thousands of churches were reopened, many bishops and priests released from prisons and camps, and a few theological schools and monasteries reestablished in the postwar years, the Soviet leader Nikita Khrushchev (1953–65) subjected the ROC to another wave of persecution that lasted, with different degrees of intensity, until the *perestroika* initiated under the leadership of Mikhail Gorbachev (1985–91).

Current Period

The beginning of the latest period of Russian Church renaissance could be linked either to the celebration of the millennium of the Baptism of Rus or to the collapse of the Soviet Union in 1991, when liberalization of Soviet policies towards the ROC gradually led to the latter's full independence. The year 1990 marked the election of Aleksii II as Patriarch of Moscow and All Russia (1990–2008), and he it was who oversaw the revival of the ROC after decades of violent and systemic repression, with the restoration of thousands of churches and monasteries, and the reopening of numerous dioceses and theological schools. Among other things, the ROC initiated the ongoing canonization of thousands of Russian Orthodox clergy and laity who had been persecuted and killed during the Soviet period, on the basis of the archival documents dispersed throughout the country.

Since the 1990s the ROC has had to deal with intra-Orthodox jurisdictional conflicts with the ecumenical patriarchate (over Estonia and Ukraine) and the Romanian Orthodox Church (over Moldavia); some of them are still unresolved. There are also, internally, a few minority groups (often vaguely) linked to the Catacomb movement of the Soviet period, claiming the status of the "true Orthodox Church" and accusing the ROC of being a "grace-less" political institution that has betrayed "true Orthodoxy." The ROC has also been deeply affected by the tides of widespread xenophobia, nationalism, fundamentalism, anti-Semitism, and even fascism that have washed over Russian society in the traumatic post-communist years. Since the collapse of the Soviet regime, the ROC has been also increasingly criticized in the Russian democratic press for being more interested in state protectionism, rather than in its own moral integrity and issues of spiritual freedom, criticized for restoring and guarding its privileged status, rather than addressing systemic social and economic problems, causing child abuse, alcoholism, prostitution, and drug use of catastrophic proportions. The church started to make its stance clearer in significant policy documents addressing moral and social problems, especially in the so-called "Social Contract Document" issued by the synod in recent times. In addition, as in other multiethnic and multireligious countries, the ROC has also been confronted with the increasingly difficult problem of finding a proper way for conducting missionary work without being accused of proselytizing among other religious minorities. It has objected loudly to proselytism from Catholic and Protestant "missionaries," which it sees as taking advantage of its long years of martyrdom, and often of being wholly ignorant of its enduring deep Christian roots in Russian culture and life.

The present leader (as of 2009) of the ROC is Patriarch Kiril. In terms of its institutional structure, the ROC is administered on the basis of the Church Statute of 2000 and includes the direct administration of all Orthodox parishes in Russia (or jurisdictional guidance for the autonomous churches, including the Autonomous Church of Japan; the self-ruling Churches of Latvia, Estonia, Moldova, and Ukraine; the Belorussian Exarchate). The ROC has 160 dioceses, including all regions of Russia; 24 synodal departments; 788 monasteries, 30,142 parishes; and numerous educational institutions of various types and levels such as universities, institutes, academies, and seminaries.

SEE ALSO: Berdiaev, Nikolai A. (1874–1948); Constantinople, Patriarchate of; Khomiakov, Aleksey S. (1804–1860); Men, Alexander (1935–1990); Moghila, Peter (1596–1646); Non-Possessors (Nil Sorskii); Possessors (Joseph Volotsk); St. Andrei Rublev (ca. 1360–1430); St. Elizaveta Feodorovna (1864–1918); St. Filaret (Philaret) Drozdov (1782–1867); St. Ignatius Brianchaninov (1807–1867); St. Seraphim of Sarov (1759–1833); St. Sergius of Radonezh (1314–1392); St. Theophan (Govorov) the Recluse (1815–1894); St. Tikhon (Belavin) (1865–1925); Solovyov, Vladimir (1853–1900); Ukraine, Orthodoxy in the; United States of America, Orthodoxy in the

References and Suggested Readings

Aleksii, Patriarch of Moscow (ed.) (2000) *Pravoslavnaia entsiklopediia: Russkaia Pravoslavnaia Tserkov'*. Moscow: Pravoslavnaia Etsiklopediia.

Beglov, A. L. (2008) *V poiskakh "bezgreshnykh katakomb." Tserkovnoe podpol'e v SSSR*. Moscow: Izdatel'stvo Moskovskoi Patriarkhii.

Fennell, J. (1983) *The Crisis of Medieval Russia, 1200–1304*. London: Longman.

Franklin, S. (2002) *Writing, Society and Culture in Early Rus, c. 950–1300*. Cambridge: Cambridge University Press.

Franklin, S. and Shepard, J. (1996) *The Emergence of Rus, 750–1200*. London: Longman.

Freeze, G. L. (1977) *The Russian Levites: Parish Clergy in the Eighteenth Century*. Cambridge, MA: Harvard University Press.

Freeze, G. L. (1983) *The Parish Clergy in Nineteenth-Century Russia: Crisis, Reform and Counter Reform*. Princeton: Princeton University Press.

Golubinskii, E. E. (1901) *Istoriia Russkoi Tserkvi. Tom 1. Period pervyi, Kievskii ili domongol'skii*, 2nd edn. Moscow: Universitetskaia tip.

Klier, J. D. (1997) "Judaizing Without Jews? Moscow–Novgorod, 1470–1504," in G. D. Lenhoff and A. M. Kleimola (eds.) *Culture and Identity in Muscovy, 1359–1584*. Moscow: ITZ-Garant, pp. 336–49.

Kosik, V. I. (2008) *Russkoe tserkovnoe zarubezh'e: xx vek v biografiiakh dukhovenstva ot Ameriki do Iaponii*. Moscow: PSTGU.

Meyendorff, J. (1981) *Byzantium and the Rise of Russia: A Study of Byzantino-Russian Relations in the Fourteenth Century*. Cambridge: Cambridge University Press.

Pliguzov, A. (1992) "Archbishop Gennadii and the Heresy of the 'Judaizers'," *Harvard Ukrainian Studies* 16: 269–88.

Plokhy, S. (2006) *The Origins of the Slavic Nations: Premodern Identities in Russia, Ukraine, and Belarus*. Cambridge: Cambridge University Press.

Saunders, D. (1985) *The Ukrainian Impact on Russian Culture, 1750–1850*. Edmonton: CIUS Press.

Smolich, I. K. (1996) *Istoriia Russkoi Tserkvi*, Vol. 1. Moscow: Izd-vo Spaso-Preobrazhenskogo Valaamskogo monastyria.

Thomson, F. J. (1999) *The Reception of Byzantine Culture in Medieval Russia*. Brookfield, VT: Ashgate Press.

Tsypin, V. (2006) *Istoriia Russkoi Pravoslavnoi Tserkvi: Sinodal'nyi i noveishii periody*, 2nd edn. Moscow: Izd-vo Sretenskogo monastyria.

S

St. Andrei Rublev (ca. 1360–1430)

KONSTANTIN GAVRILKIN

Little is known of the life of Russia's greatest icon painter. The indirect evidence suggests that he was born around the 1360s and settled in the Trinity Monastery (later, the Troitse-Sergieva Lavra) near Moscow shortly after the death of its founder, St. Sergius of Radonezh (1392), presumably already as a monk. Rublev is first mentioned in the *Chronicle of the Trinity Monastery* under the year 1405, when he is said to have worked on the frescoes and icons of the Annunciation Cathedral of the Moscow Kremlin together with Theophanes the Greek, a prominent Byzantine master who is believed to have been associated with the hesychast movement and who trained Andrei in icon painting. In this and other sources associated with the same monastery, Andrei is mentioned in later years as a man of holy life and master of remarkable talent who decorated churches in Moscow, Vladimir, and other places. The last place Rublev was known to be working was at the Moscow Andronikov Monastery, where he died around 1430. In the Soviet period this monastery was closed but has since reopened as the Andrei Rublev Museum of Early Russian Art, with a collection representing Russian works from the 15th to 17th centuries.

Although the authority of Andrei Rublev as model icon painter was recognized by the Stoglav Council of 1551, which declared that iconographers should follow the ancient standards of Greek icon painters, Andrei Rublev, and other famous masters (Lazarev 1966: 75–8), the decline of Russian iconography after the late 16th century led to a gradual loss of that knowledge and skill associated with Rublev and his school. By the 19th century virtually only the Old Believers who treasured the liturgical and spiritual traditions of the Muscovite Rus remembered his name without, however, being able to identify his works. With the beginning of the scholarly study of early Russian iconography at the beginning of the 20th century, the only starting point for the recovery of Rublev's legacy was the Icon of the Holy Trinity in the Trinity Cathedral of the Troitse-Sergieva Lavra, which, according to all the sources, was painted by Andrei Rublev alone. Cleaned in 1904, the icon provided iconologists with the stylistic and technical clues for further research. After a century-long study of his frescoes and icons, St. Andrei Rublev is recognized today as a great master of composition, light, and color, who was able to express through his works the peace and beauty of the world transformed by grace, the vision of the human being transformed by the Spirit into the true image and likeness of God. He

The Concise Encyclopedia of Orthodox Christianity, First Edition. Edited by John Anthony McGuckin.
© 2014 John Wiley & Sons, Ltd. Published 2014 by John Wiley & Sons, Ltd.

was officially canonized as a saint by the Russian Church in 1988.

SEE ALSO: Iconography, Styles of; Iconostasis; Icons; Russia, Patriarchal Orthodox Church of

References and Suggested Readings

Alpatov, M. A. (1972) *Andrei Rublev*. Moscow: Iskusstvo.

Bunge, G. (2007) *The Rublev Trinity*. Crestwood, NY: St. Vladimir's Seminary Press.

Lazarev, V. N. (1966) *Andrei Rublev i ego shkola*. Moscow: Iskusstvo.

Lazarev, V. N. and Vzdornov, G. I. (eds.) (1997) *The Russian Icon: From Its Origins to the Sixteenth Century*. Collegeville, MN: Liturgical Press.

Shchennikova, L. A. (2007) *Tvoreniia prepodobnogo Andreiia Publeva i ikonopistsev velikokniazheskoi Moskvy*. Moscow: Indrik.

Vzdornov, G. I. (ed.) (1989) *"Troitsa" Andreia Rubleva*. Moscow: Iskusstvo.

St. Antony of Egypt (the Great) (ca. 251–356)

JOHN A. MCGUCKIN

St. Antony has a symbolic stature in the Orthodox world as the "first monk" of Christian tradition, There were, of course, ascetics and hermits before him, historically speaking, and even his *Vita* mentions that he placed his sister in the care of the city communities of virgin ascetics before he went off to the desert as an ascetic himself. But Antony was one of the most dramatic teachers of the early Egyptian desert, who adopted a life of profound seclusion (the "eremitical" life) when this was still very rare in Christianity (the city communities of ascetics being preferred as a *modus operandi* or settlements just on the outskirts of villages which allowed limited communication). The *Life of Saint Antony* written by the great Egyptian hierarch and theologian St. Athanasius of Alexandria very shortly after Antony's death, became one of the most popular Christian texts of Antiquity and was responsible for making Antony paradigmatic for much of subsequent monastic theory. Athanasius' *Vita* sparked an interest in hagiography that would grow to immense proportions in later ages, and it set the terms of much that would follow in imitation. It is one of the earliest of all canonization narratives, and depicts the monastic life as a Christian parallel to the ancient Sophists.

The outline of Antony's career was that by the age of 20 he had inherited his father's wealth and became head of an Alexandrian merchant household. He experienced a dramatic conversion while hearing the gospel text read out in church: "Sell all that you have and come follow me." Taking it to heart, he dispossessed himself for the benefit of the poor, broke his familial ties, and left Alexandria for a life of ascetical seclusion in the semi-desert around the Nile, near Fayyum, which itself later became a great monastic center. He began his first exercises in the ascetical life near *fellahin* settlements and with some limited guidance from other desert dwellers (and from this period come the stories of his famous "wrestling with demons" in deserted

Plate 61 Icon of St. Antony of Egypt, father of monks. Photo by John McGuckin.

Plate 62   The tiny cave where St. Antony of Egypt spent forty years in solitary prayer. Now it is a shrine many hundreds of feet above the monastery dedicated to his name by the Red Sea in Egypt. Photo by John McGuckin.

leys and meet for Sunday vigil worship, under the spiritual authority of an elder (*geron*); and finally the eremitical life proper, where a monk would live in more or less complete seclusion.

Antony has several short letters attributed to him, which are generally regarded as genuine. His reputation as a leading "philosopher" is probably more a rhetorical *topos* of Athanasius'. The writings focus on the need to acquire freedom in the inner life, so that the vision of God could be sought with a focused heart. His reputation as a holy man, counselor, exorcist, and thaumaturg, even in his own lifetime, was such that the bishop of Alexandria, St. Athanasius, called on his assistance and used the power of his reputation to combat the Arian movement. Antony's final monastic settlement, Deir Mar Antonios, passed through numerous iterations, but today still functions as a living monastic settlement. It is located at the foot of the mountain in the face of which his tiny cave is still preserved as a shrine, in which he spent more than forty years of prayer.

SEE ALSO: Coptic Orthodoxy; Monasticism

References and Suggested Readings

Gregg, R. C. (1980) *Athanasius: The Life of Antony*. New York: Paulist Press.

Rubenson, S. (1990) *The Letters of Saint Antony: Origenist Theology, Monastic Tradition, and the Making of a Saint*. Bibliotheca Historico-Ecclesiastica Lundensis, 24. Lund: Lund University Press.

tombs), but by 285 he moved deeper into the Egyptian desert seeking a more solitary lifestyle, at a place called Outer Mountain (*Pispir*). Here he organized a colony of disciples under a loose form of early communal "rule" (called "coenobitic" monasticism, from the Greek term for shared lifestyle). In 305 he moved even further into the wilderness to a place called Inner Mountain (*Deir Mar Antonios*) by the Red Sea. Here he presided over a much looser association of senior and experienced monks living as hermits. So it is that he traditionally came to be associated with the foundation of the three basic types of Christian monastic structure: communes (*koinobia*) under the direction of a senior monk (*abba* or *higumen*); *lavras*, where scattered groups of individual hermits would inhabit neighboring val-

St. Athanasius of Alexandria (ca. 293–373)

TARMO TOOM

St. Athanasius, who is called "a pillar of orthodoxy" (festal troparion) by the Orthodox Church, is best remembered for his defense of Nicene theology and his role in promoting monastic ideals. In the writings of his friends, Athanasius is depicted as a "very dear brother" (Hilary, *Adversus Valentem et Ursacium* 1.3.1), but by his opponents, he was called a "villain" (ibid., 1.2.21).

Athanasius was born in Alexandria and served as a deacon and secretary of Bishop Alexander of

Alexandria, whom he accompanied to the Council of Nicea in 325. In 328, after a disputed election, Athanasius was consecrated as the twentieth patriarch of Alexandria, and had to face immediately the assaults of Melitian and Arian opponents, and experience the wrath of unfriendly emperors, whose christological policy he opposed. At the Synod of Tyre in 335 Athanasius was accused of sacrilege, bribery, rape, and murder. Although none of these accusations stuck, Athanasius had to spend some fifteen years of his 46-year episcopacy in exile, where he established useful contacts with western theologians and Egyptian monks. After ordaining his successor Peter, "who followed him in all things" (*Historia Acephala* 13.19), Athanasius died in 373. Soon his corpus would gain a very highly authoritative status.

Athanasius' works are preserved in Greek, Coptic, and Syriac. A twofold apology *Against the Pagans* and *On the Incarnation* contends that the incarnation of the Son of God restored the damaged relationship between the Creator and the creation. "He was made human [both body and soul (Tom. 7)] so that we might be made God" (*On the Incarnation* 54). Among Athanasius' many anti-Arian works are *Orations against the Arians*, *Apology against the Arians*, *Defense of the Nicene Definition*, and the *History of the Arians*. For Athanasius, who was applauded as the first true trinitarian theologian by St. Gregory of Nazianzus (*Oration* 21.33), the Son is consubstantial and co-eternal with the Father. Even his enemies called him the "mighty champion of the consubstantialist doctrine" (Philostorgius, *Ecclesiastical History* 3.17). Athanasius also wrote many personal letters and, annually, the paschal *Festal Letters*. His *Letters to Serapion* defended the full divinity of the Holy Spirit, and his *Letter to Epictetus* presents an anti-Apollinarian Christology. All of these works were to gain a high authority in the next generation and to determine ecumenical conciliar Christology. His ascetical writings include the *Life of Anthony*, which presents the desert saint as an ideal Christian, the four *Letters to Virgins*, and the *Letter to Marcellinus* on biblical interpretation. Some fragments of his *Catenae* (isolated comments) on various biblical books are also extant. St. Athanasius' feast day is January 18, and he is also celebrated with St. Cyril of Alexandria.

SEE ALSO: Alexandria, Patriarchate of; Coptic Orthodoxy; Council of Nicea I (325); Deification; Desert Fathers and Mothers; Holy Spirit; Holy Trinity

References and Suggested Readings

Anatolios, K. (1998) *Athanasius: The Coherence of His Thought.* London: Routledge.

Barnes, T. D. (1993) *Athanasius and Constantius: Theology and Politics in the Constantinian Empire.* Cambridge, MA: Harvard University Press.

Dragas, G. D. (2005) "Saint Athanasius: Original Research and New Perspectives," in G. D. Dragas and D. R. Lamoureux (eds.) *Patristic Theological Library* vol. 1. Rollinsford: Orthodox Research Institute.

Martin, A. (1996) *Athanase d'Alexandrie et l'église d'Egypte au IVe siècle (328–373).* Rome: École Française de Rome.

Tetz, M. (1995) *Athanasiana: zu leben und lehre des Athanasius,* ed. W. Geerlings and D. Wyrwa. Berlin: De Gruyter.

Weinandy, T. G. (2007) *Athanasius: A Theological Introduction.* Aldershot: Ashgate Press.

St. Augustine of Hippo (354–430)

JOHN A. MCGUCKIN

St. Augustine, known commonly in the Orthodox Church as "the Blessed Augustine," is perhaps the single most important Christian writer of the ancient Christian West. He came from Thagaste, near Madauros, in Roman North Africa. His father Patricius was a pagan (until his deathbed), and his mother, Monnica, a Catholic Christian who enrolled her infant son as a catechumen. Augustine's talent was noticed early, and a wealthy patron, Romanianus, sponsored his education. He studied rhetoric at Carthage, where at the age of 19 he was powerfully attracted to the vocation of rhetor-philosopher by reading Cicero's (lost) treatise *Hortensius*. His mother pressured him to enrol for baptism but Augustine had already set up house with a concubine (whom he never names) to whom he was deeply attached, and he was not willing to threaten that relationship, or to submit himself to the doctrines of the Catholics, which he had come to regard as simplistic. He attached himself to the Manichean movement (as a "Hearer") and belonged to them for the next ten years until 387.

Augustine's career took him from Carthage, to Rome, and eventually Milan, where he occupied the position of Rhetoric Professor, won for him by Manichean patrons. In Milan he became increasingly disillusioned with the Manicheans, and a series of crises shook his security; beginning with increasing asthmatic troubles (fatal for an ancient orator) and his agreement with his mother's plan to dismiss his partner of fifteen years' standing (the mother of his son Adeodatus) so that he could make a rich marriage to advance his career. His heartless agreement to her dismissal was soon followed by heartbreak at her loss, and his rapid employment of a sexual surrogate caused him to regard his philosophical aspirations with a depressed skepticism; but his increasing contact with one of the leading rhetorical and philosophical circles in the city (the group of theologians associated with the priest Simplicianus and Bishop Ambrose) opened up new vistas for him. He was greatly impressed by Ambrose, and began to consider the possibility of a similar career as ascetic philosopher. He describes his psychosexual and spiritual struggle in a famous autobiography (the *Confessions*) which he wrote many years later, and here he depicts the turning point of his life as occurring dramatically in a quiet Milanese garden when he abandoned his destiny to Christ and subsequently petitioned for admission to the church. For a while he stayed with Christian friends who formed a scholarly college around him. Soon, however, he returned to Rome, where Monnica died, and then he made his way back to Africa, in 388, where he intended to live with his companions (more cheaply) at Thagaste. One day in 391, while making a visit to the seaport of Hippo Regius, he was seized by local Christians and forcibly ordained priest by Bishop Valerius, so that he could help the old bishop in the church administration. He and his companions accepted the forced initiation into church administration, and by 395 Augustine was consecrated as Valerius' episcopal assistant and, soon afterwards, his successor. Local bishops in Africa regarded his promotion as canonically dubious, and even his baptism as somewhat irregular – for the news of his early life (both his sexual liaisons and his membership of the heretical Manichees) was common gossip in a church much

troubled by the rigorist dissidents the Donatists. To defend himself Augustine composed treatises against the Manichees after his priestly ordination, and after his consecration as bishop wrote the *Confessions*, an exercise in how self-scrutiny can be a salvific reading of the story of God's providence in creation and in a human life. It was a brilliant answer to his episcopal colleagues who had criticized him for slipping through the rigorous baptismal "scrutinies" of the African church.

As bishop, Augustine made profound moves to resolve the schism of the Donatists, which led to his enunciation of important principles that would form the basic substructure of western Catholic ideas of sacramentality and ecclesial legitimacy. His works greatly developed the Latin Church's understanding of itself as both a heavenly and earthly body (like Christ himself – whose body it was – a complete and perfect synthesis of flesh and divine spirit). Opposed at first to applying secular pressure on dissidents, he reluctantly came to a position by 411 that allowed for the partial legitimacy of such a policy. His immediate context was the lively Donatist threat of violence against him, but his authority seemed to have been placed behind the idea of religious compulsion when necessary, and it was an authority much evoked to justify forms of ecclesiastical oppression in later centuries. The publication of his *Confessions* had caused some outrage in Rome, where a moralist preacher, Pelagius, was appalled by Augustine's apparently fatalist resignation of his salvation to God's grace. Pelagius called for a more robust personal commitment and moral effort, and so began a controversy that was to mark all of Augustine's later life, and cause him to elaborate a profound and careful doctrine of Grace that would become determinative for Western Catholicism. Augustine regarded humanity as having nothing on which it could base its salvation: all was a free gift of God. Humanity left to itself could only slip into the slavery of sin and corruption. His ideas were set out as a theology of praise for God's merciful providence, but in some, more negative, readings of his legacy, the pessimistic tone predominated in an unbalanced way, and Augustine in a real sense has to be seen as the author of a tendency in Latin theology to focus on the notions of Original Sin, and the corruption of the material world, along with an ever-present tendency of the whole race to depravity. Most Orthodox theological writers never laid such stress on this pessimism, and never adopted as elements of the faith (unlike subsequent Western Catholicism) what they regarded as peculiarities of Augustine's local church (*theologoumena*). After the sack of Rome in 410, Augustine began a work of large-scale apologetic to answer those who laid the blame for the decadence of the Western Empire at the door of the Christians. Between 412 and 427 he produced a monumental work called the *City of God*, where he elaborated the first extensively considered ethical and political view of what Christianity conceived of as a civilized order, in distinction to pre-Christian ideas. He stresses the earthly city's (human society's) radical dissociation from the true City of God (the eschatological realization of the kingdom), but makes a case for how the earthly city is informed and guided by heavenly ideals. Slavery is a prime symptom of the inherent corruption of the world's affairs. In the midst of endemic violence and disorder the church has the destiny to represent mercy and reconciliation, guiding society to a perfection it might never attain, but to which it is inexorably summoned.

To stand with the *Confessions* and *City of God*, in his triad of "world classics," we should add Augustine's monumental work of theology *On the Trinity*, composed between 399 and 419. In this he constructs a major anti-Arian apologetic around the Nicene faith in Christology and pneumatology. He demonstrates from a wide variety of triadic cosmic patterns the reasonableness of the trinitarian doctrine of three divine persons subsisting in one single divine nature. Much use is made of triadic patterns of human psychology (the soul as the image of God), and he emphasized once again his deeply sensed connection between self-scrutiny and theological method (something common to Augustine and the Platonic tradition). His vast corpus of writings became, of course, his own form of ascetical exercise. The great extent of his work made him function as an encyclopedic theological authority for the next millennium in the West. But he had only a very minor influence on the Eastern Church, though translations were made of him into Greek in the medieval period, and he had a small circle of interested Greek readers. His spiritual writings gave a great impetus to monasticism as the organizing structure of the Latin Church (something which Pope St. Gregory the Great later picked up and developed).

He particularly stressed the element of true faith leading to a deep desire of the heart for God, an affective spiritual tradition that made him an attractive and highly approachable Christian writer – aspects that still appear from engagement with his work.

Only a few treatises can be singled out for special mention, such as *De Doctrina Christiana* which laid out his biblical hermeneutical philosophy, or *De Bono Conjugali* which argued (somewhat reluctantly) for the intrinsic holiness of sexuality in marriage (against St. Jerome's deeply hostile opinions). *De Peccatorum Meritis et Remissione* and *De Natura et Gratia* both demonstrate why he thought Pelagianism so destructive of Christian religious experience. The *Enchiridion* is a summatic handbook of theology, composed for reference. His greatest exegetical works are perhaps his Tractatus CXXIV in *Joannis Evangelium* and *De Genesi ad Litteram* (commentaries respectively on John's Gospel and the Book of Genesis). The commentary on the Psalms (*Enarrationes in Psalmos*) demonstrates his deep love for them as prayers. There is hardly a sermon, however, that is not an exposition of scripture, or a serious theological reflection, in the manner he approaches it. Augustine's friend and monastic companion Possidius wrote a biography soon after his death, and made an invaluable list of all his writings, most of which are still extant.

Augustine died as the Vandals were besieging his city on August 28, 430. One of his last instructions was to have his favorite psalms written in large letters around his walls so that he could read them as he died. Soon after his death, Prosper of Aquitaine began a process to lobby for Augustinianism as the standard theological system of the Latin West; a movement that slowly gathered momentum, culminating in Pope Gregory the Great's enthusiastic endorsement of Augustine as preeminent Latin theologian in the late 6th century.

SEE ALSO: Grace; Holy Trinity; Original Sin

References and Suggested Readings

Brown, P. (1967) *Augustine of Hippo: A Biography*. Berkeley: University of California Press.

Chadwick, H. (1986) *Augustine*. Oxford: Oxford University Press.

Fitzgerald, A. D. (ed.) (1999) *Augustine Through the Ages: An Encyclopedia*. Grand Rapids, MI: Eerdmans.

Schaff, P. (trans.) (1887–92) *Works of St. Augustine*, 8 vols. Grand Rapids, MI: Eerdmans.

Smith, W. T. (1980) *Augustine: His Life and Thought*. Atlanta: John Knox Press.

van der Meer, F. (1961) *Augustine the Bishop*. London: Faber and Faber.

St. Basil of Caesarea (Basil the Great) (330–379)

JOHN A. MCGUCKIN

Known even in his lifetime as the "Great Basil" (a title ascribed to him by his friend St. Gregory of Nazianzus), Basil was the most dynamic and politically active of the Cappadocian fathers, and if not the most intellectually original of them, certainly one of the leading intelligences of the early church. He was the son of a rhetorician, from a wealthy Christian family. He studied in Cappadocia (where he first met Gregory of Nazianzus), then in Constantinople, and finally for six years at Athens, where his friendship with Gregory was deepened into a lifelong alliance (one that witnessed some strain towards its end, on Gregory's part, though the final funeral oration Gregory delivered for Basil is one of the most famous of all Christian orations).

In 355 Basil returned to Cappadocia, expressing disillusionment with the academic life, and taught rhetoric for a restless year before he made his way (probably in the company of the radical ascetic Eustathius of Sebaste) to tour the ascetical communities of Syria, Mesopotamia, Palestine, and Egypt. He described this encounter with Christian asceticism as like waking up after a long sleep, and from that time onwards his religious life was given precedence over all other things. Basil was baptized on his return to Cappadocia and embraced the ascetical life under the influence of Eustathius and his own sister, Macrina, who had already adapted their country estate at Annesi in Pontus as a monastic retreat. Here he invited Gregory Nazianzen, though the latter found the style of monasticism not to his taste, preferring a more scholarly seclusion on his own estates. Gregory and Basil collaborated in producing the *Philocalia* (a first

edition of selected passages on the subject of exegesis from Origen) as well as writings about the monastic life. This early work of writing manuals for the ascetics gathered around them (especially Basil's treatise *Asceticon*, though some see it as a work of Eustathius) had a historic impact in the form of the "Monastic Rules" which gave Basil the title of "Father of Eastern Monks"). The *Moralia* came first in 358, which was a largely traditional collection of ascetical maxims (each one attached to their suitable biblical proof text) and this work was followed by the *Asceticon* (ca. 363) (which is what most modern scholars refer to as the "Rule" of Basil, though it too is more in the form of generic maxim than detailed prescription).

Ordained a reader in 360 and then priest for the church at Cappadocian Caesarea in 362, Basil was actively involved in the resistance of the radical Arian party (the Heterousians or Anhomoians) led by Aetius and Eunomius. At first attached to the Homoiousian party which was dominant in Cappadocia, Basil increasingly aligned himself with the defense of the Nicene Creed (and the Homoousian party) as it had been orchestrated and aligned by the eminent figures of Athanasius in Egypt, and by Meletios of Antioch and Eusebius of Samosata in the provinces of the Orient. His attachment to Meletios was the reason Basil never quite gained Athanasius' complete trust. He fell out with his bishop, Eusebius, who seems to have been jealous of his younger assistant's capabilities, and to avoid rancor he retired to his estates until, in 364, the threat of an installation at Caesarea of an Arian bishop of the entourage of Emperor Valens brought him back to the service of the Caesarean church, and to the aid of his anxious bishop. Gregory Nazianzen mediated that return, and the threat from Valens was deflected. It won him friends and much popular acclaim, but also many enemies among the Caesarean clergy and the leading members of the local Curia.

In 368 he administered the church's relief effort for a great famine in the region and won the support of the people. Gregory of Nazianzen (Oration 14) preached the need for a large hospital facility attached to the Caesarean church, and the effort was successful: the creation of philanthropic institutions staffed by monastics becoming a great innovation introduced by Basil, that would have a long subsequent history in the church. In 370 he was elected bishop of his city, despite the opposition of the town officials and many neighboring bishops. Shortly afterwards, the great civil diocese of Cappadocia was divided in two, and to offset the influence of the new ecclesiastical metropolitan, Anthimos of Tyana, Basil desperately tried to fill small towns in his remaining district with episcopal appointments drawn from his circle of friends. It elevated Gregory of Nyssa and Gregory of Nazianzus to episcopal status, but also caused rifts among his immediate circle, who felt his machinations were chiefly squabbles about revenues dressed up as theological conflicts (Basil was anxious to retain Caesarea as a significant metropolitan see staffed by Nicene believers).

As he moved more and more, as he grew older, to become the public face of the Nicene party, he stood in alliance with Meletius of Antioch, one of the few remaining first-generation Nicene stalwarts. This alliance (which brought him into conflict with Athanasius and Pope Damasus) he saw as fundamental for the Nicene cause in the East, and he was faithful to it, even though it alienated his old friend and mentor, Eustathius of Sebaste, who then went on to espouse the Pneumatomachian doctrine, denying the deity of the Holy Spirit. The public breach with Eustathius was marked by Basil's publication of a highly influential work, *On the Holy Spirit* (Books 1–3), where Basil affirms the deity of the Son and Spirit, and it paved the way for the full Neo-Nicene confession of the Trinity which Gregory of Nazianzus would elaborate at the Council of Constantinople in 381.

Basil died, worn out with his labors, in 379. His letters are major sources of information about the life of the church in the 4th century. His Hexaemeron, or interpretation of the creation through the Genesis account, is a masterpiece of early Christian scriptural theology, and shows him as a moderate Origenist, with a fine feel for the moral power of scripture. His treatise Against Eunomius was a major force revitalizing the Nicene resistance, and he did much in his time to persuade the Homoiousians that their position was in substance reconcilable with that of the Homoousians, something that historically speaking was a key element for the long-term success of the Nicene cause. His work in his church as teacher and public defender of his town, as well as his learned canonical writings (setting wise rules of governance that the Eastern Church formally endorsed as universal authorities at the Quinisext Council of 692), made Basil a model for future eastern bishops, and in Byzantine times he was designated along with Gregory Nazianzen and John Chrysostom as one of the "Three Holy Hierarchs," the most important bishop theologians of the ancient period. His reputation as one of the most important early monastic theorists also gave him a reputation among the eastern ascetics akin to the greatest of the monastic theorists, Antony, and Theodore the Studite.

SEE ALSO: Cappadocian Fathers; Monasticism; St. Gregory of Nazianzus (Gregory the Theologian) (329–390)

References and Suggested Readings

Clarke, W. K. L. (1913) *St. Basil the Great: A Study in Monasticism*. Cambridge: Cambridge University Press.

Holman, S. R. (2001) *The Hungry Are Dying: Beggars and Bishops in Roman Cappadocia*. Oxford: Oxford University Press.

Jackson, B. (1989) *St. Basil: Letters and Select Works*. Grand Rapids, MI: Eerdmans.

Rousseau, P. (1994) *Basil of Caesarea*. Berkeley: University of California Press.

St. Constantine the Emperor (ca. 271–337)

JULIA KONSTANTINOVSKY

Constantine I was an enigmatic figure yet a unique saint in the Orthodox Church: the first Christian emperor (discounting the possible candidacy of Philip the Arab), Constantine abolished the persecution of Christians, making Christianity a favored state religion. His status as the benefactor of the church and Christ's emissary on earth is reflected in his titles in Orthodoxy as "the Great" and "Equal-to-the-Apostles."

Flavius Valerius Constantinus was born to the military officer Constantius and St. Helena, in Naissus (Nish in Serbia), on February 27 between 271 and 273. His youth corresponded to the time his father was a junior Caesar in the First Tetrarchy. Classically and militarily educated while held as Diocletian's hostage at the Nicomedian court, Constantine fought (in the 290s) under Diocletian and Galerius in Asia, witnessing the outbreak of the Great Persecution of Christians (303–13), though playing no role therein. Eusebius styles Constantine an early sympathizer of Christianity, while the pagan sources (notably *Pan.Lat.* 6.21.4–5) and coin evidence suggest his enduring links with the Apollinine *Sol Invictus* cult.

On his accession, which began the civil war, Constantine spent several years eliminating all of his political rivals. Assuming the purple in July 306 on the death of his father Constantius in York, Constantine defeated Maximian Daia Augustus (his father-in-law) in 310. In 312 he presided over a miraculous victory over Maxentius (Maximian's son) in the famous battle of the Milvian Bridge at Rome. Lactantius maintains (*De Mortibus Persecutorum* 44.5–6) that shortly before the battle Constantine had an epiphanic dream instructing him to inscribe "the heavenly sign of God" (the Chi-Rho shaped mark of Christ, *labarum*) upon his soldiers' shields. The ensuing victory convinced the emperor of Christ's divine power and his particular gift of favor to his dominion. By 323 he had become the empire's sole ruler.

After 312 Constantine manifested himself as a Christian and protector of the church by stopping the persecution of Christians (Edict of Milan, 313), initiating extensive construction of Christian buildings (notably Rome's Lateran Basilica, Bethlehem, and other buildings later in Rome and Palestine), ordering that the property of North African Christians confiscated in the persecutions should be restored, and addressing the North African Donatist problem. In 325 he was requested by Alexander Bishop of Alexandria to help resolve a bitter dispute (the Arian controversy) about the status of the Second Person of the Trinity. Constantine's response was to organize the first general church council at his palace in Nicea in 325. The resulting conciliar creed anathematized Arius, famously proclaiming the Son to be "consubstantial" (*homoousion*) with the Father, a mainstay of the Orthodox and many other Christian traditions. So overwhelming was the participant bishops' banquet at the emperor's palace that Eusebius (an eyewitness) strikingly likened it to the eschatological gathering of saints in Christ's kingdom, and compared Constantine to Christ. Constantine died on May 22, 337, having received baptism at the hands of bishop Eusebius of Nicomedia while on a military expedition.

Despite committing acts hardly compatible with Christian precepts (having his wife Fausta and son Crispus executed, 325), Constantine's impact on imperial Christianity was profound. By 337, Christianity had become the official state religion; public pagan sacrifices had become outlawed; Christian clergy had joined the state elite; Palestine had been reclaimed for Christianity; Constantinople, the new Christian capital named after Constantine, had replaced the old pagan Byzantium. The Orthodox Church commemorates him on May 21, together with his mother Helena.

SEE ALSO: Council of Nicea I (325); St. Athanasius of Alexandria (ca. 293–373)

References and Suggested Readings

Edwards, M. J. (ed.) (2003) *Constantine and Christendom: The Oration to the Saints*. Liverpool: Liverpool University Press.

Eusebius of Caesarea (1989) *Historia Ecclesiastica*, trans. G. A. Williamson. London: Penguin.

Eusebius of Caesarea (1999) *The Life of Constantine*, trans. A. Cameron and S. Hall. Oxford: Oxford University Press.

Lactantius (1886) *Of the Manner in Which the Persecutors Died (De Mortibus Persecutorum)*, trans. W. Fletcher, in A. Roberts, J. Donaldson, and A. Cleveland Coxe (eds.) *Ante-Nicene Fathers*, vol. 7. Buffalo: Christian Literature Publishing.

Lenski, N. (ed.) (2006) *The Age of Constantine*. Cambridge: Cambridge University Press.

St. Cyril of Alexandria (ca. 378–444)

JOHN A. MCGUCKIN

Although he himself saw his role as a continuator of St. Athanasius, and though the ecumenical conciliar tradition later wove in much of the Cappadocian fathers and Latin patristic thought into his conceptions,

St. Cyril is undoubtedly the single most important theologian of the Orthodox tradition who wrote on the person of Christ (Christology). He was the major figure, both intellectually and politically, in the great crisis of doctrine in the international church of the 5th century, and presided over the Third Ecumenical Council of Ephesus (431), where the teaching of Nestorius was condemned, and his own teaching, that affirmed the single subjectivity of the Divine Logos personally present in Jesus, the incarnate Lord, was adopted. Cyril's teaching went on to determine the agenda of three following ecumenical councils up to the 7th century.

Cyril was a native of Egypt, and when his uncle Theophilus became the archbishop of Alexandria in 385, he brought the young man to Alexandria for advanced studies. In 403, when he was 25 years old, Cyril was ordained lector, and in the same year attended Theophilus at the notorious Synod of the Oak, which deposed John Chrysostom. At his uncle's death in 412, after a tumultuous election, Cyril was consecrated archbishop. His early years were marked by several major conflicts between the Christians and both the pagan and Jewish factions of the city. At the same time, he was using the monastic movement to advance the Christian evangelization of a country where the old religions still held considerable sway. After 428 Cyril was increasingly drawn into conflict with the new archbishop of Constantinople, Nestorius, who conceived of two centers of operation simultaneously present in the life of Christ: one human and one divine, with one sometimes predominating over the other. Cyril denounced this as heretical, insisting that Jesus was wholly and completely divine, thus only one single person, and that person God. For Cyril, everything that Jesus did, whether it was a human act such as sleeping, or a powerful act such as raising the dead, was equally a work of the single divine Lord, now embodied within history. The divine power present in the humanity was also an archetype of how God had intended to "divinize" the human condition in the act of incarnation. Thus Christ is the pattern of the world's salvation. The process of deification is best exemplified in the reception of the Eucharist, the "life-giving blessing" of the divine flesh that immortalizes the believer. It was a dynamic

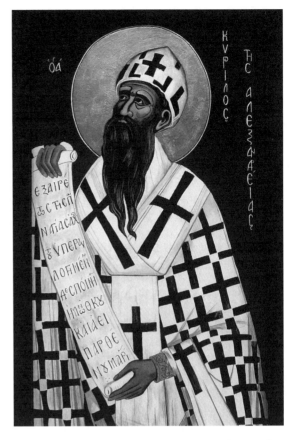

Plate 63 Contemporary icon of St. Cyril of Alexandria. By Eileen McGuckin. The Icon Studio: www.sgtt.org.

Christology which eventually came to represent the classical statement of the Christian East, but not without major resistance on the way, especially from theologians in Rome and Syria. The Council of Ephesus, where Cyril was judge and jury simultaneously, caused great bitterness in its aftermath, and the emperor's negotiators had to work for several years to restore church communion, especially between Alexandria and Antioch. Eventually, in 433, a compromise was agreed on (the Formula of Reunion) where important points of the Antiochene position (Christ had two authentic natures – both human and divine) could be reconciled with Cyril's insistence that Christ was a single reality, one divine person, but the precise ramifications of that agreement still needed much clarifying debate, and in default of this it was inevitable that the whole argument would soon break out again. It did so with great force in the following generation. St. Cyril died on June 27, 444, a little short of his seventieth year. He is known in the church as the "Seal [sphragis] of the Fathers."

SEE ALSO: Christ; Deification; Eucharist; Nestorianism; Soteriology

References and Suggested Readings

McGuckin, J. A. (1994) *St. Cyril of Alexandria and the Christological Controversy: Its History, Theology and Texts.* Leiden: E. J. Brill.
Russell, N. (2000) *Cyril of Alexandria.* London: Routledge.

St. Dionysius the Areopagite

PETER C. BOUTENEFF

Acts 17.34 mentions one Dionysius the Areopagite among St. Paul's converts. Eusebius (*Church History* 3.4) identifies this figure as the first bishop of Athens. Later on the name came to be identified with St. Denys, first bishop of Paris. Yet the most enduring legacy associated with Dionysius the Areopagite is a corpus of four larger works and ten letters, these latter also constituting something like a self-contained treatise. These writings, appearing for the first time in the 6th century under this authorship, place themselves (pseudepigraphically) in the apostolic context: they are addressed to personalities such as John the Evangelist and speak of witnessing the darkening of the sun at Christ's crucifixion. Their provenance went virtually unquestioned until the late Middle Ages. Owing both to their content and their alleged sub-apostolic origins, they were deeply influential on subsequent Christian authors, notably Maximos the Confessor, John Scotus Eriugena, John of Damascus, Thomas Aquinas, Gregory Palamas, and the anonymous author of *The Cloud of Unknowing*, the very title of which is taken from Dionysius' *Mystical Theology*. Anachronisms in liturgical practice and in theologico-philosophical terminology have since conspired to make it impossible to date this corpus before the end of the 5th century or later.

Certain liturgical details have suggested a Syrian monastic identity to an otherwise unidentified author. Orthodox theologians have tended to react ambivalently to the increasingly evident impossibility of identifying the 1st-century bishop with the written corpus, almost as if they ignore its significance. The Dionysian writings lose none of their credibility owing to the "problem" of authorship; they rise or fall in Orthodox esteem on the basis of their content alone. The feast day of St. Dionysius the Areopagite, October 3, officially commemorates one sole person, and the hymnography conflates the martyred bishop with the author-mystic.

Other controversies surround the content of the corpus itself: its message is expressed in the language of Middle-Platonism, and Jesus Christ is scarcely mentioned by name. A sympathetic appraisal, arguably regnant in contemporary Orthodox scholarship (Golitzin 1994; Louth 2002), avers that the treatises were written as a missionary outreach to educated Platonists. The pseudonym itself, it is argued, was chosen to identify the works as the product of the "conversion" of Greek philosophy to the gospel of Christ. Others (Meyendorff 1975) have contested that the corpus effectively amounts to a Platonic treatise with merely a Christian veneer.

By the 20th century Dionysius' main influence on Orthodox theologians lay in his apophaticism. Vladimir Lossky, the title of whose flagship monograph *The Mystical Theology of the Eastern Church* testifies to his commitment to the Dionysian heritage, constructed his entire theological outlook on the basis of apophaticism as construed by Dionysius (and Eckhart), contrary to what he saw as a Thomist "essentialism." Christos Yannaras also steeped himself in Dionysius as a part of his broader engagement with Martin Heidegger, similarly taking God's radical and essential non-knowability as the starting point of any contemporary Orthodox theological reflection. Yannaras further explored implications of the apophatic semiotics of Dionysius' *The Divine Names*, which had also been taken up by Jean-Luc Marion and Jacques Derrida.

SEE ALSO: Angels; Apophaticism; St. Gregory Palamas (1296–1359); St. Maximos the Confessor (580–662)

References and Suggested Readings

Golitzin, A. (1994) "Et Introibo ad altare dei: The Mystagogy of Dionysius Areopagita," *Analecta Vlatadon* 59. Thessaloniki: George Dedousis.

Lossky, V. (1976). *The Mystical Theology of the Eastern Church*. Crestwood, NY: St. Vladimir's Seminary Press.

Louth, A. (2002) *Denys the Areopagite*. London: Continuum.

Meyendorff, J. (1975) "Pseudo-Dionysius," in *Christ in Eastern Christian Thought*. Crestwood, NY: St. Vladimir's Seminary Press, pp. 91–111.

Yannaras, C. (2007) *On the Absence and Unknowability of God: Heidegger and the Areopagite*. London: T&T Clark.

St. Dorotheos of Gaza (6th c.)

THOMAS KITSON

We know Dorotheos primarily from his own *Discourses* and from his correspondence with the "Old Men" of Gaza, Sts. Barsanuphius and John. He was born wealthy in early 6th-century Antioch and probably studied rhetoric at Gaza before entering the Monastery of Abbot Seridos at Tawatha, not far from the city. Seridos charged him with supervising the monastery's guest house and then, because he had medical knowledge, its infirmary, which was a donation of Dorotheos' brother. Dorotheos handled John's correspondence for nine years preceding the recluse's death in 543, when Barsanuphius decided to forego all human contact. Little is known of Dorotheos' subsequent life and whether or not he succeeded Seridos as abbot. He may have sought a more solitary contemplative life by moving from Tawatha's coenobium to the Lavra. John Moschos mentioned Dorotheos briefly in his *Spiritual Meadow*.

Dorotheos' *Discourses* may have been compiled before the 7th century, soon after his death. The earliest extant manuscripts of his work are in Arabic and Georgian (9th century), while the first Greek manuscript, including the Studite preface, dates to the 10th century. Dorotheos' main sources are scripture, especially the gospels and Psalms, and the *Apophthegmata* of the desert fathers, which he imbibed from Barsanuphius and John. He also cites liberally from the Cappadocian fathers, from Evagrios Pontike, and, it seems, from an early Greek translation of St. John Cassian's *Conferences*. Thus, he crucially combines the experience of the Egyptian desert with Syrian practices and the sophisticated theology of the Cappadocians to shape the ascetic life. Dorotheos exhorts listeners to cut off the will through humility and obedience, frequently citing Christ's injunction: "Learn of me, for I am meek and humble of heart, and you shall find rest for your souls" (Mt. 11.29). These themes ground the *Life of Dositheos*, Dorotheos' young disciple. They are also exemplified by Dorotheos' plain-spoken use of anecdotes from his own life, his willingness to risk losing the respect of his listeners by giving sometimes unseemly evidence against himself.

The christological and Origenist controversies that raged in Palestine during the 6th century colored the *Discourses'* initial reception. St. Theodore the Studite attested to their orthodoxy in the late 8th century, although it is possible that St. John Klimakos had already written the *Ladder of Divine Ascent* with them in mind. Dorotheos' influence spread with the Studite monastic reforms, especially to Mount Athos, and his works were read in refectories throughout the Greek East, along with those of St. Ephrem and the desert *Apophthegmata*. St. Nil Sorskii partially translated Dorotheos into Church Slavonic in the 15th century. Since Dorotheos' writings also indicate early traditions of the Jesus Prayer, they were incorporated into St. Paisy Velichovsky's hesychast renewal movement. St. Theophan the Recluse accordingly appended Dorotheos' works, which had been translated and published separately by the Optina Hermitage in the 1850s, to the 19th-century Russian translation of the *Philokalia*.

SEE ALSO: Cappadocian Fathers; Desert Fathers and Mothers; Hesychasm; Jesus Prayer; Optina; *Philokalia*; Non-Possessors (Nil Sorskii); Pontike, Evagrios (ca. 345–399); St. John Klimakos (ca. 579–ca. 659); St. Paisy Velichovsky (1722–1794); St. Theophan (Govorov) the Recluse (1815–1894); Sts. Barsanuphius and John (6th c.)

References and Suggested Readings

Chryssavgis, J. (trans.) (2003) *Barsanuphius and John, Letters from the Desert: A Selection of Questions and Responses*. Crestwood, NY: St. Vladimir's Seminary Press.

Wheeler, E. (trans.) (1977) *Dorotheos of Gaza: Discourses and Sayings*. Kalamazoo: Cistercian Publications.

St. Elizaveta Feodorovna (1864–1918)

KONSTANTIN GAVRILKIN

Born as Princess Elizabeth Alexandra Luise Alice of Hesse, she was the older sister of Alexandra of Hesse, the future wife of Tsar Nicholas II (1872–1918). In 1884 Elizabeth became Orthodox and married Grand Duke Sergei (1857–1905), the fifth son of Emperor Alexander II (d. 1881). She assumed the name of Grand Duchess Elizaveta Feodorovna of Russia and quite soon became actively involved in various charities, especially for women and children from poor and destitute families, creating for them jobs, hospitals, schools, and affordable housing. In 1891 the couple moved to Moscow, where her husband was to serve as governor general. In 1905 the terrorist Ivan Kaliaev assassinated Grand Duke Sergei by throwing a bomb at his carriage.

Widowed, Elizaveta decided to stay in Moscow and dedicate her life to poor and sick women and children through personally supervised charities in a

GRAND DUCHESS ELIZABETH FEODOROVNA

Plate 64   Portrait of St. Elizaveta Feodorovna as Princess "Ella" before her widowhood and monastic profession. Topham Picturepoint/Topfoto

convent she founded in 1907. The Marfo-Mariinskaia Obitel' Miloserdiia (Mercy Convent of Saints Martha and Mary) was established on the territory of the estate near the Kremlin, purchased with the funds raised from the sale of the Duchess's personal items and jewelry. It was rebuilt to include a hospital, pharmacy, and soup kitchen for the poor, a library, and school for girls and women, and was officially opened in 1909. In 1910 Grand Duchess Elizaveta became a nun herself. According to the statute of the convent, approved by the holy synod in 1911 (and revised in 1914), she was to remain the head of the convent for life. During World War I, Elizaveta helped with creating moveable hospitals, medical emergency teams, and commissions for accommodating the wounded who returned from the war zone and for helping the families of military personnel. Her convent was reorganized to accommodate a military hospital where 150 nuns worked under her direct supervision.

In addition, after the death of her husband who had chaired the Imperial Orthodox Palestine Society since its establishment in 1882, Elizaveta assumed his post and held it until her resignation after the February Revolution of 1917. The society supported Orthodox institutions in the Holy Land (churches, monasteries, hospitals, and schools), pilgrimages, and scientific studies of the region.

She refused to leave Russia after the Bolshevik coup in October 1917. Arrested in the spring of 1918 with the nun Barbara, her assistant, she was sent to Siberia, where other members of the Romanov family had also been imprisoned. In July 1918 she and others were thrown alive into a mine shaft a few miles from Alapaevsk. Their bodies were recovered in the fall of the same year by the White Army, which advanced to the region in October 1918. Eventually, the bodies of Elizaveta Feodorovna and the nun Barbara were taken to Jerusalem and buried in the Church of St. Mary Magdalene, according to the will of the Grand Duchess expressed in 1888 during her visit to Jerusalem. In 1992 the Moscow patriarchate canonized her and Barbara as new martyrs of Russia.

SEE ALSO: New Martyrs; Russia, Patriarchal Orthodox Church of; Women in Orthodoxy

References and Suggested Readings

Mager, H. (1998) *Elizabeth, Grand Duchess of Russia*. New York: Carroll and Graf.

Miller, L. (1991) *Grand Duchess Elizabeth of Russia*. Redding, CA: Nikodemos Orthodox Publication Society.

Tsitriniak, A. and Khemlin, M. (2009) *Velikaia kniaginia Elizaveta Fedorovna*. Moscow: Tsentr knigi VGBIL im. M. I. Rudomino.

Warwick, C. (2006) *Ella: Princess, Saint and Martyr*. Hoboken, NJ: John Wiley & Sons, Inc.

St. Ephrem the Syrian (ca. 306–373/379)

KENNETH CARVELEY

Ephrem was born to Christian parents in Nisibis. Legend describes his father as a heathen priest. During his youth he was influenced by Bishop Jacob (d. 338; present at Nicea 325, possibly with Ephrem) who appointed him as a church teacher. During the episcopate of Bishop Vologeses, the Persian Shapur II besieged the city and Ephrem migrated with the people to the Christian city of Edessa in 363, where he is said to have worked in the bath house. Teaching in the *schola* he defended the Orthodox Nicene teaching (the Edessene Orthodox group then called "Palutians," so named after Bishop Palut), and countered Arianism, Marcionism, the Bardesainians, and other Gnostic heresies. A prolific Syriac hymn writer, Ephrem wrote poetic homilies, biblical commentaries, and graceful hymns affirming Orthodox Christology, meant to counter the metrical hymns of Bardesanes' son Harmodios. He was possibly employed as liturgical chant writer for a community of Syriac women ascetics. His chief writings include *Carmina Nisibena*, *Hymns On Faith*, *Hymns on Paradise*, *On Virginity*, *Against Heresies*, and an (attributed) panegyric on St. Basil of Caesarea. His hymns, many of which mirror Hebraic parallel form, constitute part of the Syriac Church's liturgy, particularly for major feasts; a very popular prayer of repentance of St. Ephrem ("Lord and Master of my Life") is preserved in the regular Orthodox Lenten cycle of prayers. Sayings attributed to him appear in the *Apophthegmata Patrum*, and he had a distinctive influence over the traditions of Syro-Byzantine hymnody and liturgical chant. Scholars are still in the process, however, of disentangling the real Ephrem (the Syrian sage) from the so-called Greco-Byzantine Ephrem, with whom he was confounded at an early date. He supported the people of Edessa indefatigably during persecution by the Arian Emperor Valens (370–2) and in times of severe famine. Later Edessene hagiographic tradition developed his life and legend extensively.

SEE ALSO: Council of Nicea I (325); Gnosticism; Hymnography; Virgins

References and Suggested Readings

Brock, S. (1992) *The Luminous Eye: The Spiritual World Vision of St. Ephrem*. Kalamazoo: Cistercian Publications.

Brock, S. (1999) "St. Ephrem in the Eyes of Later Syriac Liturgical Tradition," *Hugoye Journal of Syriac Studies* 2, 1.

McVey, K. E. (trans.) (1989) *Ephrem the Syrian: Hymns*. New York: Paulist Press.

Mayer, R. T. (trans.) (1964) *Palladius: The Lausiac History*. New York: Newman Press.

Schaff, P. and Wace, H. (eds.) (1976) *Gregory the Great, Ephraim Syrus*. Aphrahat Select Library of Nicene and Post-Nicene Fathers, 2nd Series, vol. 13, part 2. Grand Rapids, MI: Eerdmans.

St. Feofan *see* Theophan the Greek (ca. 1340–1410)

St. Filaret (Philaret) Drozdov (1782–1867)

KONSTANTIN GAVRILKIN

Vasilii M. Drozdov was born into a clerical family in Kolomna and studied at the seminary in St. Sergius Lavra, where he also taught after graduation and was tonsured a monk with the name Filaret. Brilliant erudition, colorful preaching, and a gift for languages were decisive in his appointment in 1812 to the post of rector of St. Petersburg Theological Academy, where he had been teaching since 1810, and in 1817 he was elevated to the rank of bishop of Revel and vicar of St. Petersburg. During his rectorship (1812–19), Filaret completely revised the curriculum of all the Russian ecclesiastical schools, introduced the study of European scholarly literature, and practically created biblical studies as an academic discipline in Russia. Because of his organizational skills and effective leadership, he was also gradually introduced to a number of state and ecclesiastical committees, including the holy synod in 1819. Very shortly, however, because of intrigues and the growing influence of conservatives over Tsar Alexander I, he was removed from the capital though, after short terms at Tver' and then Iaroslavl', he was appointed archbishop of Moscow in 1821, becoming metropolitan in 1826.

From 1814 to 1826 Filaret was active in the Bible Society, believing that translation of the Scriptures into modern Russian (they were then available only in Church Slavonic) would revive the Russian Church. However, after printing a few books (the Psalms in 1822 and the New Testament in 1823) the society was closed down at the beginning of Nicholas I's reign (1825–55) amid accusations that its leadership, including Filaret, were "freemasons" seeking to destroy the Orthodox Church. Filaret remained at odds with Nicholaevan bureaucrats, and after the early 1840s would not attend meetings of the synod until the beginning of Alexander II's reign in 1855. Nevertheless, it was during the rule of Nicholas I that Filaret acquired the reputation of being a great hierarch. Despite his withdrawal from the synod, he was consulted on every important question, and his opinions, decisions, and reviews of various ecclesiastical and secular subjects were regularly published. Even though he was academically brilliant, Filaret did not have the opportunity to develop truly scholarly work after he left St. Petersburg, although he continued to follow European scholarship throughout his life. Administrative and pastoral duties, together with frequent liturgical services and constant preaching, consumed his time. His ascetical lifestyle, pastoral wisdom, administrative efficiency, remarkable knowledge of the patristic tradition and of canon law, and, most of all, his unrivaled preaching, made him the most influential bishop of the Russian Orthodox Church in the 19th century, overshadowing every other Russian ecclesiastic from the 19th century onward. He was canonized in 1994.

SEE ALSO: Russia, Patriarchal Orthodox Church of

References and Suggested Readings

Filaret, Mitropolit of Moscow (1873–85). *Sochineniia: slova i rechi*, 5 vols. Moscow: A. I. Mamontov.

Filaret, Mitropolit of Moscow (1877–84) *Pis'ma k namestniku Sviato-Troitskoi Sergievy lavry arkhimandritu Antoniiu, 1831–1867*, 4 vols. Moscow: A. I. Mamontov.

Filaret, Mitropolit of Moscow (1885–8) *Sobranie mnenii i otzyvov po uchebnym i tserkovnym voprosam*, 6 vols., ed. Savva, Archbishop of Tver'. Moscow: Synod. Tip.

Filaret, Mitropolit of Moscow (1903–16) *Polnoe sobranie rezoliutsii*, 5 vols. Moscow: Dushepoleznoe chtenie.

Tsurikov, V. (ed.) (2003) *Philaret, Metropolitan of Moscow (1782–1867): Perspectives on the Man, His Works, and His Time*. Jordanville, NY: Variable Press.

St. Gregory the Great, Pope (ca. 540–604)

JOHN A. MCGUCKIN

Gregorius Magnus was one of the most important of the Late Antique bishops of Rome. He was a masterful political administrator and a significant theologian who, if not innovative in his writing, served to arrange and codify much that was important in the Latin theological tradition, and pass it on in a condensed form that would assume immense weight for the dawning medieval West. His work codifying and simplifying much of St. Augustine's complicated thought made it possible for Augustinianism to be passed on in a popular form, so as to become the most significant single strand of the later Latin tradition.

Gregory belonged to an aristocratic Christian family in Rome at a time when the fortunes of both Italy and the ancient city were in decline because of Justinian's wars of re-conquest, and later (from 586 onwards) because of raids from Lombardian brigands from the North. His father was a Christian senator, and in 573 Gregory himself became the prefect of Rome (the highest civic office possible). Soon afterwards he announced his retirement from public life and dedicated his extensive properties in Rome and Sicily to the cause of Christian asceticism, in the form of the retired life of the Sophist. His large villa on the Caelian hill, near the Colosseum, became his monastery of St. Andrew (still functioning), where he lived a life of scholarship and prayer with companions. As a dedicated ascetic, however, he fell under ecclesiastical obedience, and soon Pope Pelagius II ordered him to resume public service for the church. Accordingly, he was ordained deacon and sent as papal ambassador (*apocrisarius*) to Constantinople, where he lived from 579 to 586, engaging in dispute with the Patriarch Eutyches. In this period Gregory began one of his greatest works, the *Magna Moralia in Job*, designed as an ascetical commentary on the text of Job, for the use of his monastic companions. It assumed the status of a paradigmatic patristic book of exegesis for the later West, constantly seeking a moral end to scriptural reading.

After resuming his duties back in Italy as papal secretary at Rome, Gregory administered the church during the time of plague in the year 590, and on Pope Pelagius' death in that same year, he was himself elected pope (much against his inclination) as Gregory I. He rallied the city with extensive penitential processions to ask for God's mercy. Later tales spoke of a vision of an angel putting away his sword over Hadrian's mausoleum (now Castel San Angelo) where today the statue of the same is a familiar Roman landmark. Gregory began a highly efficient administration in Rome, a symbolic end to a long decline of the Roman church and city that began with Constantine's removal of the capital eastwards to Constantinople. He profoundly monasticized the Roman church administration, despite protests of the ordinary clergy, so beginning a long tradition along these lines that would mark western Catholicism ever afterwards. His successful leadership over Rome and its province led to his papacy becoming a symbol of how the papal office could develop in the future.

Gregory, realizing the futility of the local Byzantine imperial administration at Ravenna, independently negotiated peace with the Lombard invaders. Many later reforms (such as the liturgical changes that came to be called Gregorian chant) were retrospectively fathered on him. His writings on theological matters were chiefly pastoral, biblical, and hagiographical. His extensive biblical exegesis and theological comments were a moderated and simplified form of St. Augustine,

and Gregory did more than any other (except perhaps the Latin theologian Prosper of Aquitaine) to elevate Augustine's influence over the whole western church, giving a theological preeminence to the doctrine of grace, and adding his own views on the need for a cleansing post-death purification of souls, a view that eventually grew into the distinctive Roman doctrine of Purgatory. His *Pastoral Rule* (written largely for his own guidance soon after he assumed the papacy) was designed as a manual of instruction for a bishop. It became a standard text in western church schools. In line with the central premise of the current educational system of his day, he elevates rhetoric as the chief tool of the leader. But he also adds that the bishop is above all else a pastor of souls, as well as the leader and expositor of the divine word of scripture. Gregory's exegetical works standardized the subsequent western view of biblical exegesis as the three stages of housebuilding, where the foundations were the exposition of the literal and historical sense of the text; followed by the roof and walls of the allegorical sense which interprets higher Christian mysteries present within the old narratives; and finally the beautiful decorations that perfect and finish off a building, in the form of moral counsels designed to elevate the lives of the hearers. His insistence that a preacher should pay attention to all three aspects of a text proved determinative for the later western Middle Ages. His *Dialogues* were also immensely popular. In these four books Gregory recounts the lives of Italian ascetic saints. The miraculous element abounds in them, marking an important stage in the development of the cult of the saint at a time when, both in Byzantium and the West, the fundamental idea on how to access the divine presence and favor was undergoing radical reconstruction, and local democratization. In the second book of *Dialogues* Gregory popularized St. Benedict, the hermit of Nursia, thus providing an enormous impetus to the spread of Benedictinism as the central exemplar for Latin monasticism. His spiritual writings had a similarly determinative effect on the Latin Middle Ages insofar as he emphasized the monastic life as the "perfect" way of contemplation, far excelling the lay married state.

In the Orthodox tradition Gregory is mainly known for the liturgy attributed to him of the Presanctified Gifts, now celebrated in the course of

Great Lent. This ritual is basically a communion service attached to a penitential form of Vespers, and served to allow the communion of the faithful on Wednesdays and Fridays in the course of the Great Fast, when the divine liturgy was not celebrated. The holy gifts are consecrated (presanctified) at the liturgy of the preceding Sunday. In the Orthodox tradition Gregory is known (from the title of his hagiographic work) as Pope St. Gregory the Dialogist.

SEE ALSO: Papacy; Vespers (Hesperinos)

References and Suggested Readings

Dudden, F. H. (1905) *Gregory the Great*, 2 vols. London: Longmans, Green.

Evans, G. (1986) *The Thought of Gregory the Great*. Cambridge: Cambridge University Press.

Markus, R. A. (1983) *From Augustine to Gregory the Great*. London: Variorum.

Richards, J. (1980) *Consul of God: The Life and Times of Gregory the Great*. London: Routledge and Kegan Paul.

Straw, C. (1988) *Gregory the Great: Perfection in Imperfection*. Berkeley: University of California Press.

St. Gregory of Nazianzus (Gregory the Theologian) (329–390)

JOHN A. MCGUCKIN

Gregory was the son of a wealthy landowning bishop in Nazianzus, Cappadocia (also named Gregory). His father was the second bishop of the town, following after someone who was described as a "rustic," and after his consecration he built a splendid marble shrine to replace the old wooden church that had previously existed. In many ways Bishop Gregory the Elder and his more famous son demonstrate the "ascent" of the church in the Constantinian era. The younger Gregory received the finest local schooling, taught partly by his uncle, the rhetorician Amphilokios, and then (with his brother Caesarios) was sent to Alexandria, and finally to Athens, where he spent ten years perfecting his rhetorical style and literary education. Gregory the Theologian thus emerged as the finest Christian rhetorician of his day, and certainly the most learned bishop of the entire early church.

His sea journey to Athens in 348 was interrupted by a violent storm and, fearing for his life, Gregory seems to have promised himself to God's service, a vow he fulfilled by accepting baptism at Athens and beginning his lifelong commitment to the ascetical life. It was a dedication he saw as entirely consonant with the commitment to celibacy required of the serious philosopher. Gregory did much to advance the theory of early Christian asceticism, but always with the stress on seclusion in the service of scholarly reflection. He regularly described Christianity as "Our Philosophy." At Athens he shared lodgings with his close friend Basil of Caesarea, with whose later Christian career he was closely associated. Returning to Cappadocia, in 358, Gregory's plans to live in scholarly retirement on his family estate were rudely interrupted by his father, who forcibly ordained him to the priesthood in 361. Gregory fled in protest to Basil's monastic estates at Annesi, where he edited the *Philocalia of Origen*, a collation of texts from the great Alexandrian theologian of the 3rd century, whose reputation was increasingly being attacked. The purpose of the edition was to focus on the exegetical brilliance of the Alexandrian scholar, and deflect attention from the metaphysical speculative elements that had tarnished his ecclesiastical reputation. Throughout all his later life Gregory represents a very profound, but also very skilfully moderated, form of Origenian thought.

As a priest, Gregory was no longer free to devote himself to the life of scholarly detachment that he had imagined for himself, and soon returned to assist in the administration of his local church alongside his father, whose increasing age and illness placed large demands on his son. His letters from this time give us the only window we possess on the life and conditions of St. Basil and St. Macrina's monastic foundation on the family estates. In 363 Gregory led the literary attack against Julian the Apostate's imperial policy of barring Christian professors from educational posts (*Invectives Against Julian*). In 364 he negotiated Basil's reconciliation with his estranged bishop, and eventually in 370 assisted him to attain the archiepiscopal throne at Caesarea. Thereafter began their long alienation. Basil (in his many fights) accused him of pusillanimity, and Gregory regarded Basil as having become too high and mighty. In 372 Basil and Gregory's father conspired, against his will, to appoint him as bishop of Sasima, and accordingly Gregory found himself placed as a suffragan bishop of Basil's in a rather miserable frontier town, at the center of a lively row with the neighboring metropolitan over church revenues. When he realized that he was supposed to galvanize street armies and thrash the followers of the rival metropolitan, he simply refused to occupy the see, leaving caustic (although funny) descriptions about it. He resumed duties of assisting his father as suffragan bishop of Nazianzus instead (quite oblivious to canons regulating episcopal successions), and began his series of episcopal homilies, all of which were taken down by scribes and edited at the end of his life for publication as a basic dossier of "sermons on every occasion" for a Christian bishop. In this guise they enjoyed an immense influence throughout the Byzantine centuries. His collected writings have been compared with the works of Demosthenes. In their purity and refinement of doctrine they have been rarely equalled. In the consummate power of their rhetoric, never.

From the outset Gregory stood for the Nicene cause of the *Homoousion* (the consubstantiality of the Son with the Father), and advanced it to the classic Neo-Nicene position of demanding that the *Homoousion* of the Holy Spirit (with the Father, and thus with the Son) should also be recognized. He thereby became one of the church's primary theological articulators of the classical doctrine of the Co-equal Trinity. He constantly pressured Basil to make his own position clear and led him, eventually, to break with his erstwhile mentor Eustathius of Sebaste and instead to declare openly for the deity of the Spirit of God, which he did in his famous classic *On the Holy Spirit*. On his father's death in 374 Gregory retired to monastic seclusion, but was summoned, after Valens' death gave new hope for a Nicene revival, by the hierarchs of the Council of Antioch (379) to assume the task of missionary apologist at Constantinople, where he had high-ranking family in residence. He began, in 379, a series of lectures in Constantinople on the Nicene faith (the *Five Theological Orations*), and was recognized by the leading Nicene theologians, Meletius of Antioch,

Eusebius of Samosata, and Peter of Alexandria (though not by Pope Damasus), as the true Nicene bishop of the city. When Theodosius took the capital in 380 his appointment was confirmed when the incumbent Arian bishop Demophilos was exiled. In 381 the Council of Constantinople was held in the city to establish the Nicene faith as standard in the eastern empire, and when its president, Meletius, died, Gregory was immediately elected in his place. His mild and reasoned leadership, and also probably his prosecution of the doctrine of the Homoousion of the Spirit, soon brought the council into crisis, for Theodosius was anxious that the party of 30 Pneumatomachian bishops (who admitted the inferior deity of, but denied the title "God" to, the Spirit) should be reconciled and Gregory was anxious that they should not. After they left the conciliar deliberations, refusing to admit any change to the pneumatological clauses of the creed, there were then calls for Gregory to initiate penal moves against dissidents. His response was that they ought to be forgiven as the gospel demanded, and that a mild treatment would be more likely to result in their return than any prosecution. This eirenic attitude lost him many friends at a time when scores were ready to be settled with Arians who had long been using state pressure against the Nicenes. Unable to convince the majority of the wisdom of his approach, Gregory bowed to increasing calls for his resignation, and decided to retire. He came back to his estates at Nazianzus and composed a large body of apologetic and theological poetry which gives crucial information on the controversies of the time. In his final years he focused chiefly on poetry (some of it very good) and prepared his orations for publication.

In the Byzantine era Gregory was the most studied of all the early Christian writers. His theological works against Apollinaris (especially *Letter 101 to Cledonius*) were cited as authorities at the Council of Chalcedon (451), where he was posthumously awarded the title "Gregory the Theologian." His writing on the Trinity was never rivaled in patristic times, and he is the chief architect of the church's understanding of how the divine unity coexists in three co-equal hypostases, as the essential dynamic of the salvation of the world.

SEE ALSO: Cappadocian Fathers; Council of Constantinople I (381); St. Basil of Caesarea (Basil the Great) (330–379)

References and Suggested Readings

McGuckin, J. A. (2001) *St. Gregory of Nazianzus: An Intellectual Biography*. Crestwood, NY: St. Vladimir's Seminary Press.

Norris, F. W. (1991) *Faith Gives Fullness to Reason: The Five Theological Orations of Gregory of Nazianzus – Text and Commentary*. Leiden: E. J. Brill.

Ruether, R. (1969) *Gregory of Nazianzus: Rhetor and Philosopher*. Oxford: Oxford University Press.

Winslow, D. F. (1979) *The Dynamics of Salvation: A Study in Gregory of Nazianzus*. Philadelphia: Philadelphia Patristic Foundation.

St. Gregory Palamas (1296–1359)

STEPHEN THOMAS

St. Gregory Palamas was born in 1296 in Constantinople into an aristocratic family, receiving a thorough education in Greek philosophy and rhetoric. His adoption of monasticism involved his whole family. Having tried this life on Mount Athos both as a solitary hermit and in a monastic community, he preferred to live with a small group of monks under the tutelage of a spiritual father. The writings of Barlaam the Calabrian led him to respond polemically, defending the hesychasts (those monks who practised inner stillness) against a philosophy so apophatic that it denied the possibility of experience of God. The whole of Palamas's theology addresses this question: if we cannot grasp God with the intellect, is he absolutely unknowable? Palamas argued that, just as the prophets of ancient Israel partially knew Christ as a foretaste of things to come, so do the hesychasts experience the glory of the Age to come in this life; it is a partially realized eschatology (Ware et al. 1995: 418). Palamas used a distinction between essence and energies to explain how God is knowable through divine revelation and can be experienced in the life of prayer: we know the uncreated energies of God, while his essence remains unknown. But while

Palamas was competent in philosophy, especially that of Aristotle, and knew about the developments in the sciences of his time, he was not interested in an intellectual synthesis: having reviewed these, Palamas exclaims: "Where can we learn anything certain and free from deceit about God, about the world as a whole, about ourselves? Is it not from the teaching of the Spirit?" (Sinkiewicz 1988: 102–3; Ware et al. 1995: 354).

This is for from the medieval interest in human science burgeoning in the West during his time. Barlaam's teaching was universally rejected by the Orthodox Church, and he ended his days as a bishop, teaching Greek to Petrarch in Italy. A new challenge arose in Akyndinos, a former pupil of Palamas, who argued from a very static and formal view of tradition that the experiences of the hesychasts were not Orthodox. Against Akyndinos, Palamas eventually prevailed. He was appointed bishop of Thessalonica by the emperor, an appointment which saw him produce a series of pastoral sermons which encapsulate his teaching in a more popular way. He died in 1359 and was soon canonized (1368). His memory is celebrated in the liturgy on the second Sunday of Lent; no theologian is praised more highly as "a true follower and companion of thy namesake Gregory the Theologian" (Ware 1984: 318). Palamas was a theologian of "the glory of God," the light of Mount Tabor which shone upon three chosen apostles at the transfiguration of Jesus Christ (Mt. 17.1–8; Mk. 9.2–8; Lk. 9.28–36), these expressions being the biblical ones which correspond to the patristic formulations "divine or uncreated energy" and "uncreated light." This glory God chose to share with the human race. It is God's deifying grace transfiguring human life. That it is a matter of experience even in this earthly existence is the main feature of Palamas's understanding of Orthodoxy.

SEE ALSO: Deification; Grace; Hesychasm

References and Suggested Readings

Gendle, N. (trans.) (1983) *Gregory Palamas: The Triads*. London: SPCK.

Meyendorff, J. (1974) *St. Gregory Palamas and Orthodox Spirituality*. Crestwood, NY: St. Vladimir's Seminary Press.

Meyendorff, J. (1974) *A Study of Gregory Palamas*. Crestwood, NY: St. Vladimir's Seminary Press.

Sinkiewicz, R. W. (ed.) (1988) *Saint Gregory Palamas: The One Hundred and Fifty Chapters*. Toronto: Pontifical Institute of Medieval Studies.

Ware, K. and Mother Mary (eds. and trans.) (1984) *The Lenten Triodion*. London: Faber and Faber.

Ware, K, Palmer, G. E. H., and Sherrard, P. (eds. and trans.) (1995) *The Philokalia Volume IV*. London: Faber and Faber.

St. Herman of Alaska *see* Finland, Autonomous Orthodox Church of; United States of America, Orthodoxy in the

St. Ignatius Brianchaninov (1807–1867)

KONSTANTIN GAVRILKIN

Born to an aristocratic family, in 1822 Dmitrii A. Brianchaninov was sent by his father to St. Petersburg to enroll in the Imperial School of Military Engineers, despite his expressed desire to become a monk. While at school, Brianchaninov enjoyed the patronage of Tsar Nicholas I, as a student with exceptional intellectual and artistic gifts. During this time he also took part in the capital's literary circles, and this exposure to what became known as the Golden Age of Russian poetry played an important role in shaping the style of his religious writings, which have been praised for their literary quality and poetic eloquence. Although he graduated first in his class, Dmitrii immediately attempted to leave the military service for a monastic vocation, but Nicholas I refused his initial resignation in 1826. Only the next year, when Brianchaninov fell gravely ill and then repeated his request, did the emperor grant him release from military service.

In 1831 he was tonsured a monk with the name Ignatius, was ordained deacon, then priest, and for a short time he served as superior of a monastery in the Vologda diocese, only to resign a year later because of poor health. In 1833 Nicholas I made an imperial order to discover what had happened to his former protégé. Brianchaninov was then brought back to the capital and appointed higumen of the Troitse-Sergiev

Monastery near Moscow. In the twenty-four years he spent there, the monastery was rebuilt, its liturgical life became exemplary, and Ignatius its superior became one of the prominent spiritual guides and writers of all Russia. In 1857 he was consecrated bishop of the Caucasus and Black Sea, although his tenure there lasted only four years: he had to resign in 1861 after falling seriously ill; and he spent the last years of his life at Nikolo-Babaevskii Monastery in the Kostroma diocese, where he died in 1867. He was canonized by the Russian Orthodox Church in 1988. His life and spiritual heritage can be properly understood in the context of the monastic revival associated with St. Paisy Velichkovsky, hesychasm, and the tradition of spiritual direction, of which the monastery Optina Pustyn' is the best-known example. He left a substantial body of writings, and it could be argued that many of his works are the finest prose ever written by a Russian ecclesiastic. The eight-volume Russian edition of his *Complete Works*, published in 2007 to celebrate the bicentennial of his birth, contains reflections on scripture and various theological subjects, writings on prayer and ascetic life, a Paterikon, poetic meditations, sermons, materials related to his episcopal administration, his reactions on contemporary political, ecclesiastical, and cultural life, and an extensive correspondence with state officials, clergy, monastics, and others. For a full bibliography of publications by and on Ignatii Brianchaninov (valid up to 2001), see Brianchaninov (2001–7, vol. 4: 644–776).

SEE ALSO: Hesychasm; *Philokalia*; Russia, Patriarchal Orthodox Church of; St. Paisy Velichovsky (1722–1794)

References and Suggested Readings

Brianchaninov, I. (1997) *The Arena: An Offering to Contemporary Monasticism*, trans. Fr. Lazarus. Joardanville: Holy Trinity Monastery.

Brianchaninov, I. (2001–7) *Polnoe sobranie tvorenii*, 8 vols., ed. A. N. Strizhev. Moscow: Palomnik.

Brianchaninov, I. (2006) *On the Prayer of Jesus*, trans. Fr. Lazarus. Boston: The New Seeds.

Sokolov, L. A. (1915) *Episkop Ignatii Brianchaninov: Ego zhizn', lichnost' I moral'no-asketicheskie vozzreniia*, 2 vols. Kiev: I-yi Kievskoi arteli pechatnago dela.

St. Innocent of Alaska *see* United States of America, Orthodoxy in the

St. Isaac the Syrian (7th c.)

JOHN A. MCGUCKIN

Also known as St. Isaac of Niniveh, one of the great ascetical and mystical writers of the Eastern Church. Isaac was a monk of the Chaldaean Church (or Assyrian Church of the East) from Beit Quatraye, possibly Qatar on the Persian Gulf. He was appointed bishop of Niniveh sometime before 680, but after a few months in the position resigned his charge and returned to the solitary life of an ascetic. In later life he became blind from his scholarly labors. His spiritual authority and the beauty of his writings on prayer and mystical experience made his works cherished by both the rival Monophysite and Nestorian factions of the Persian Church of his time. In the 9th century his texts on ascetical prayer were translated from the Syriac into Greek and Arabic versions, and came to Byzantium shortly after, where they had a large impact on the developing hesychastic spiritual theology. Isaac lays great stress on the sensibility of the grace of God in the heart, and is one of the most mature and gentle authors on the spiritual life from Christian antiquity. His writings were treasured on Mount Athos and highly regarded by St. Paisy Velichovsky in the time of the Philokalic revival (18th century) of Greek and Slavonic monastic spirituality. In recent years lost works have been rediscovered, and by virtue of new English translations he is once again becoming known as one of the great masters of early eastern Christian spirituality.

SEE ALSO: Assyrian Apostolic Church of the East; Hesychasm; Jesus Prayer; Monasticism; Monophysitism (including Miaphysitism); Nestorianism; *Philokalia*; St. Macarius (4th c.); St. Paisy Velichovsky (1722–1794)

References and Suggested Readings

Alfeyev, H. (2000) *The Spiritual World of Isaac the Syrian*. Cistercian Studies Series 175. Kalamazoo: Cistercian Publications.

Brock, S. (1995) Isaac of Niniveh (Isaac the Syrian): The Second Part. Chapters 4–41. Corpus Scriptorum Christianorum Orientalium 554–5; Scriptores Syri. 224–5. Louvain: Peters.

Miller, D. (trans.) (1984) *The Ascetical Homilies of St. Isaac The Syrian*. Boston: Holy Transfiguration Monastery.

Wensinck, A. J. (1923) *A Mystic Treatise by Isaac of Niniveh Translated from Bedjan's Syriac Text*. Amsterdam: Koninklijke Akademie van Wetenschappen.

St. John Cassian (ca. 360–ca. 435)

TARMO TOOM

St. John Cassian was a monastic writer, theologian, and renowned churchman. Little is known about his birth and upbringing. Tradition suggests a Scythian origin and the Romanian Orthodox Church accordingly looks to him as a patron. Around 380, Cassian traveled to Bethlehem and then on to Egypt. In Scetis and Kellia Cassian learned the monastic wisdom from Abba Moses and Evagrios of Pontike (whose name Cassian never mentions for diplomatic reasons). The first Origenist crisis compelled him to move to Constantinople, where he was ordained to the diaconate by St. John Chrysostom. Here he became notable as an ecclesiastical diplomat. At Rome he sought help for John Chrysostom, and there Pope Leo asked him, as a bilingual westerner, to review and refute Nestorius's teachings (*On the Incarnation of the Lord* – written beween 429 and 430). Cassian was eventually ordained a priest and energetically promoted Egyptian monastic traditions in Gaul.

Although his conception of radical monastic asceticism was not generally or unqualifiedly accepted, Cassian nevertheless had a profound influence on western monasticism. St. Benedict recommended Cassian's *Conferences* and *Institutes* for the reading at Compline (Rule of Benedict 73) and Cassiodorus insisted that Cassian should be read "diligently" and "frequently" (Inst. 1.29) by all monks. Cassian is the only western father whose sayings have been included in the *Apophthegmata* and the collection of the *Philokalia* (1:72–108).

Gennadius (in *De Viris Illustribus* 62) gives a list of Cassian's works, noting that Cassian wrote "from personal experience." His two chief writings are the *Institutes* and the *Conferences*. The first is about the external aspects of monastic life and the eight evil thoughts, and the longer treatise of *Conferences* is about internal aspects, such as temptation, discernment, and chastity. *Conferences* 9–10, which include wonderful insights on unceasing and fiery prayer (see Ps. 70.1), were originally intended as the climax of the treatise. Purity of heart (Mt. 5.8) was Cassian's perceived goal (*scopos*) for all monastic striving, and the reign of God was its end (*finis*) (Conf. 1.4.1–3).

In the West, Cassian's admittance that "the slightest glimmer of good will" might be attributed to human effort was widely regarded as unacceptable in the light of the ascendant Augustinianism of the day (Conf. 13.7.1; cf. Prosper of Aquitaine, *Contra Collatorem*; Cassiodorus, *Institutiones* 1.29; *Decretum Gelasianum* V.7). Writing on this to the monks of Lerins, Cassian immediately added the qualification that even this good will arising from human effort was "stirred" by God (cf. Inst. 12.18; Conf. 13.9.5, 16.1). But it was enough to damage his later reputation. Cassian's emphasis on grace, as he speaks about free will, does not really allow one to accuse him of an alleged semi-Pelagianism (Inst. 12.14; Conf. 3.10, 15). He insisted that everyone was "in need of the Lord's help in whatever pertains to salvation" (Inst. 12.17). For him, sinlessness was an eschatological reality (Conf. 23). His liturgical feast day is February 29 (28).

SEE ALSO: Asceticism; Monasticism; *Philokalia*; Pontike, Evagrios (ca. 345–399); Prayer

References and Suggested Readings

Casiday, A. M. (2007) *Tradition and Theology in St. John Cassian*. Oxford: Oxford University Press.

Chadwick, O. (2008) *John Cassian*. Cambridge: Cambridge University Press.

Driver, S. D. (2003) *John Cassian and the Reading of Egyptian Monastic Culture*. London: Routledge.

Goodrich, R. J. (2007) *Contextualizing Cassian*. Oxford: Oxford University Press.

Merton, T. (2005) *Cassian and the Fathers*, ed. P. F. O'Connell. Kalamazoo: Cistercian Publications.

Stewart, C. (1998) *Cassian the Monk*. Oxford: Oxford University Press.

St. John Chrysostom (349–407)

TENNY THOMAS

St. John was born at Antioch in Syria of noble parents: his father was a successful civil servant in the bureau of the commander of military operations in the diocese of Oriens, the *magister militum per Orientem*. His father died soon after his birth and his mother Anthusa brought him up. He began his education under the renowned pagan rhetorician Libanius. He went on to study theology under the Syrian theologian Diodore of Tarsus and was baptized in 368, after which he spent the next three years as an aide to Bishop Meletius of Antioch. In 371 he was ordained reader and spent time in strict asceticism, though he was forced to abandon the monastic life because of the breakdown of his health. In 381 Flavian, the newly appointed archbishop of Antioch, ordained John deacon, and then priest in 386. Both as priest at Antioch and as archbishop of Constantinople he won the greatest renown as a preacher; hence his epithet *Chrysostomos* ("golden mouthed"), given to him posthumously.

His writings are most notable as expositions of pastoral teaching. His many biblical commentaries became a general model for ancient Christian preaching in the East; they wove together a straightforward narrative style with rhetorical flair and vivid moral instruction. The most valuable part of his works is perhaps his *Homilies* on various books of the Bible. He particularly emphasized almsgiving and was most concerned with the spiritual and temporal needs of the poor. He often spoke out against abuse of severe disparities of wealth and poverty in the cities of the empire, and the main themes of his discourses were eminently social, explaining the proper manner of a Christian's conduct in life.

In 387 after a riot in Antioch had destroyed statues of the emperor, threatening to bring down military punishment on the city, John delivered a series of passionate appeals for clemency (*Homilies on the Statues*), and his reputation was established. Against his wish, he was made archbishop of Constantinople in 398, and immediately set about the work of reforming the city, where the decadent standards of the court had been encouraged among the clergy by the worldly and princely style of his predecessor. His outspokenness and asceticism alienated many of the court and clergy, and especially the Empress Eudoxia. Theophilos of Alexandria saw his opportunity to assert dominance over the capital when Chrysostom gave shelter to the Tall Brothers, monks whom Theophilos had censured and exiled from Egypt because of their Origenism. At the Synod of The Oak, held with imperial approval at Chalcedon in 403, Theophilos tried and deposed John for canonical irregularities. The emperor deposed him, though shortly afterwards recalled him from exile. As soon as he was back in the city he renewed his reform program with even greater zeal, earning the undying enmity of the empress. He was exiled again, on the specious grounds that he had resumed his see after a synodical condemnation without canonical rehabilitation. At first John was sent to Antioch, but later his punishment was increased by an enforced winter march to Pityus, situated on the eastern shores of the Black Sea. John died in exile on September 14, 407, at Comana in Asia Minor. The Orthodox Church commemorates his feast day on November 13, and again in the company of Sts. Basil and Gregory the Theologian as one of the Three Holy Hierarchs.

References and Suggested Readings

Baur, C. (1959) *John Chrysostom and His Time.* Westminster, MD: Newman Press

Hartney, A. M. (2004) *John Chrysostom and the Transformation of the City.* London: Duckworth.

Kelly, J. N. D. (1995) *Golden Mouth: The Story of John Chrysostom – Ascetic, Preacher, Bishop.* London: Duckworth.

Maxwell, J. (2006) *Christianization and Communication in Late Antiquity: John Chrysostom and His Congregation in Antioch.* Cambridge: Cambridge University Press.

Mayer, W. and Allen, P. (2000) *John Chrysostom.* London: Routledge.

St. John of Damascus (ca. 675–ca. 750)

ANDREW LOUTH

Monk and theologian. Born probably in Damascus, John belonged to a family that had played a prominent role in the fiscal administration of Syria throughout the political changes of the 7th century, and he himself served under the caliph in Damascus. Probably early in the 8th century he left the service of the caliph and became a monk in or near Jerusalem (according to a late tradition at the Monastery of Mar Sava in the Judean Desert).

He was a prolific writer, most of his works being written while he was a monk. In his day, he had, as the chronicler Theophanes bears witness, a great reputation as a preacher, though only about a dozen of his homilies survive. He was also an important composer of liturgical poetry, much of which is still sung in the churches of the Byzantine tradition, and was one of the first to develop the genre of the canon, which forms the heart of the dawn office (Orthros). His prose works are mostly polemical or expository, defending and setting forth the theological tradition of the ecumenical councils against those groups who rejected it and had found relative religious freedom under the Muslim yoke. He is the first Christian theologian to write about Islam from direct knowledge. He also achieved renown in his own lifetime for his opposition to the Byzantine iconoclasm introduced by Emperor Leo V.

John saw himself as a defender of conciliar orthodoxy, as it had developed up to St Maximos the Confessor, and he epitomized the Greek patristic tradition in an important trio of works based on the genre of a century, primarily a vehicle for monastic meditation. These included a handbook of logic (*Dialectica*), which expounded a basically Aristotelian logic and the technical language of Greek theology; a century on heresies – the eighty chapters of an epitome of Epiphanios' *Panarion*, supplemented by twenty chapters of John's own composition, the last of which was on Islam; and a century summarizing the essential points of the Christian faith (*On the Orthodox Faith*, or *Expositio Fidei*) on the doctrines of God and the Trinity, creation (including a great deal of astronomical, geographical, physiological, and psychological learning), Christology, and various points concerned with Christian worship, the sacraments, icons, and the last things. *On the Orthodox Faith* was translated into many languages, including Latin, in which form it provided valuable access to Greek patristic theology for the Scholastics and later western theologians up to Schleiermacher. Perhaps his most creative theology is to be found in the three treatises John composed against iconoclasm, which contain a classical defense of icons in Christian worship, based principally on the doctrine of the incarnation, but which give imagery a central epistemological role in Christian theology. The same use of imagery lies at the heart of his liturgical poetry. His treatises against the iconoclasts were translated into Slavonic in the early modern period and provided an Orthodox defense of religious painting against Calvinist Protestantism.

SEE ALSO: Canon (Liturgical); Hymnography; Iconoclasm; Orthros (Matins)

References and Suggested Readings

Anderson, D. (trans.) (1980) *St. John of Damascus: On the Divine Images.* Crestwood, NY: St. Vladimir's Seminary Press.

Chase, F. H. (trans.) (1958) *St. John of Damascus: The Fount of Knowledge.* Fathers of the Church 37. New York: Fathers of the Church.

Louth, A. (2002) *St. John Damascene: Tradition and Originality in Byzantine Theology.* Oxford: Oxford University Press.

Nasrallah, J. (1950) *St. Jean de Damas: son époque, sa vie, son oeuvre.* Paris.

O'Rourke-Boyle, M. (1970) "Christ the Eikon in the Apologies for Holy Images of John of Damascus," *Greek Orthodox Theological Review* 15: 175–86.

Sahas, D. J. (1972) *John of Damascus on Islam: The "Heresy of the Ishmaelites."* Leiden: Brill.

Salmond, S. (trans.) (1978) "St. John of Damascus: On the Orthodox Faith," in *The Nicene and Post-Nicene Fathers* vol. 9. Grand Rapids, MI: Eerdmans.

St. John Klimakos (ca. 579–ca. 659)

JOHN CHRYSSAVGIS

The ascetic author *par excellence*, John Klimakos (meaning John "Of the Ladder") lived on Mt. Sinai as a hermit and, later, abbot in the great monastery of St. Katherine there. The precise dates of his life are difficult to determine, but he is probably a contemporary of Maximos the Confessor (580–662). It seems reasonable to place his dates between ca. 579 and ca. 659.

It is not known where John was born but he arrived at Sinai when he was only 16. When already quite advanced in age he accepted to write the *Ladder* at the request of another John, Abbot of Raithou. Originally entitled *Spiritual Tablets*, as many manuscripts indicate, it was the title *Ladder* which ultimately prevailed and which gives the book its unique flavor and feature. The *Ladder* consists of thirty steps (sections), including a range of virtues to acquire and vices to avoid. As a supplement to this John also authored a short treatise entitled *To the Shepherd*, describing the spiritual task of the abbot and likewise addressed to John of Raithou. Each step opens with a series of brief definitions, followed by a detailed exposition of the theme with illustrative anecdotes, and a terminal summary with inspiration.

John is deeply influenced by the early desert tradition of Egypt as well as the Gaza monastics, such as Barsanuphius and John. In some ways, he lays the foundations for the "school" of Sinaite spirituality commonly attributed to Hesychios and Philotheos. His extensive influence is witnessed in the writings of St. Symeon the New Theologian (especially in his teaching on tears) and the 14th-century hesychasts, such as St. Gregory Palamas (especially in his teaching on silence and prayer).

With the exception of the scriptures and the liturgical books, no other writing in Eastern Christendom has been studied, copied, and translated to the same extent as John's *Ladder of Divine Ascent*. It has shaped not only Eastern Orthodoxy, and especially its monastic tradition, but also the entire Christian world. Even today, the *Ladder* is appointed to be read aloud in churches or in the refectory, as well as privately in the cells of Orthodox monasteries, each year during Lent, a practice that may date back to the time of the author's life. There is no equivalent of the *Ladder* in the West, but its popularity may be compared with that of the *Imitation of Christ*, though the two books differ greatly in character.

Some of the key doctrines of the *Ladder* include the notion of spiritual direction (the separate treatise *To the Shepherd* is sometimes known as the "31st step"), the remarkable concept of joyful-sorrow (perhaps John's most original and most influential contribution), the emphasis on "divine eros" or "holy passion" (to describe the soul's mystical yearning for God), and certain key phrases that proved crucial passages in the development of the Jesus Prayer (John speaks of using a "single-phrase" or the "name of Jesus"). St. John Klimakos is liturgically commemorated on March 30 and on the fourth Sunday of Lent.

SEE ALSO: Jesus Prayer; St. Gregory Palamas (1296–1359); St. Maximos the Confessor (580–662); St. Symeon the New Theologian (949–1022); Sts. Barsanuphius and John (6th c.)

References and Suggested Readings

Chryssavgis, J. (2004) *John Climacus: From the Egyptian Desert to the Sinaite Mountain*. London: Ashgate Press.

Ware, K. (1982) "Introduction to John Climacus: The Ladder of Divine Ascent," in *Classics of Western Spirituality*. New York: Paulist Press.

St. Macarius (4th c.)

MARCUS PLESTED

This anonymous author (also known as Macarius-Symeon or pseudo-Macarius) stands as a principal source of Orthodox mystical and ascetic theology. He flourished in Syro-Mesopotamia between ca. 370 and ca. 390. His writings were variously ascribed to a Macarius (of both Egypt and Alexandria) or, later, Symeon – hence the many names of this elusive theologian.

The direct experience of God forms the cornerstone of the Macarian vision. He speaks with astonishing precision and poetry of the operation of the Spirit. Bestriding Greek and Syriac thought-worlds, Macarius was able to combine the philosophical reflection of the Greek fathers with the vivid symbolism of the Syriac tradition. His writings call every Christian to directly experience the triune God, an experience described as the vision of uncreated light, a formulation of great import for later Orthodox teaching.

The tone of Macarius' call to perfection is compelling and encouraging. The writings use an exuberant abundance of imagery and metaphor to convey the progressive deification of the Christian, setting out a dizzying vision of the mutual indwelling of man and God. Macarius is a key witness to the patristic doctrine of deification, insisting on the perfect union of man and God without ever compromising their ontological discontinuity and hypostatic distinctness.

His is a heart-centered anthropology. The heart is the point at which soul and body meet and the dwelling-place of the intellect. It is the deep self, the battleground between good and evil. In and through the struggle of the heart Christ restores man to the primal state of Adam and grants him in addition the grace of the Holy Spirit. Through cooperation (*synergeia*) with divine grace the perfect grace of baptism is manifested and revealed.

His legacy began to take shape with Gregory of Nyssa's reworking of the Macarian Great Letter (*Epistola Magna*) as his own *De Instituto Christiano*. Works of Macarius rapidly appeared under an array of illustrious names and in numerous translations. Many of the authors of the *Philokalia* stand in the Macarian tradition, most obviously Sts. Mark the Monk, Diadochus of Photice, Maximos the Confessor, and Gregory Palamas. Macarius himself is also included in that seminal publication and went on to play a major role in the Hesychast revival of late-imperial Russia.

Much was made in the early 20th century of the apparent connection with the condemned propositions of the Messalian heresy, an ascetic tendency that allegedly held prayer, and not the sacraments, to be the only sure vehicle of grace. Recent researches have established Macarius as a reformer of the nascent Messalian tendency, not an adherent. The way is now clear for further explorations of the impact and importance of this most blessed of spiritual masters.

SEE ALSO: Jesus Prayer; St. Isaac the Syrian (7th c.)

References and Suggested Readings

Dörries, H. (1978) *Die Theologie des Makarios-Symeon*. Göttingen: Vandenhoeck and Ruprecht.

Plested, M. (2004) *The Macarian Legacy: The Place of Macarius-Symeon in the Eastern Christian Tradition*. Oxford: Oxford University Press.

Stewart, C. (1991) *"Working the Earth of the Heart": The Messalian Controversy in History, Texts and Language to AD 431*. Oxford: Clarendon Press.

St. Mark of Ephesus (1392–1445)

A. EDWARD SIECIENSKI

Mark Eugenicus was metropolitan of Ephesus and leader of the anti-unionist party during and after the Council of Florence (1438–9). He claimed that the Western teachings on purgatory and the *filioque* were heretical, and were supported by the Latins only on the basis of corrupted and spurious texts. He alone among the Greek delegates refused to sign the *Tomos* of union, returning east to lead the campaign against it until his death in 1445.

SEE ALSO: Ecumenism, Orthodoxy and; *Filioque*; Florence, Council of (1438–1439)

References and Suggested Readings

Constas, N. (2002) "Mark Eugenicus," in C. Conticello and V. Conticello (eds.) *La Théologie byzantine et sa tradition*, vol. 2. Turnhout: Brepols, pp. 411–75.

St. Maximos the Confessor (580–662)

ANDREW LOUTH

Monk and theologian. Born in Constantinople (though an alternative nearly contemporary Syriac life makes him a native of Palestine), in 610 Maximos became the head of the imperial chancery under Emperor Herakleios. Soon, he withdrew from public life and became a monk, first at Chrysopolis, opposite Constantinople, and later at Kyzikos, on the Erdek peninsula. When the Persians laid siege to Constantinople in 626, he fled with other monks to North Africa. As a monk he retained his contacts with the court, as his correspondence demonstrates, and quickly became a renowned theologian. His early works – up to the early 630s – are addressed primarily to monks, and are concerned with the ascetic life and the interpretation of Scripture and the fathers. One besetting problem in the monastic circles known to Maximos was Origenism,

which had provided a metaphysical context for understanding monastic asceticism. In these early works, Maximos corrects Origenist errors and provides an alternative metaphysical understanding of the goal and purpose of asceticism. Drawing on the Cappadocian fathers and the Alexandrine tradition of Athanasius and Cyril, combining this with the ascetic wisdom of Evagrios Pontikos and the Egyptian desert, and also with Dionysius the Areopagite's cosmic, liturgical vision, Maximos set out a theology cosmic in scope, with intensely practical ascetic implications, that focused on the church's liturgy, where the drama of salvation drew in the participation of humankind.

The Persian occupation of the eastern provinces of the empire in the 610s and 620s exposed the weakness of the empire caused by christological divisions, and led to attempts to reconcile those who accepted the Christology of Chalcedon (451) and those, called by their opponents "Monophysites," who rejected it. In 633, during Maximos' African sojourn, a dramatic reconciliation was achieved in Egypt, on the basis on the doctrine that Christ had a single "divine-human" (theandric) activity, the doctrine known as "Monoenergism." This was opposed by Sophronios, Maximos' abbot in North Africa, soon to be patriarch of Jerusalem. Next, a refinement of Monoenergism known as "Monothelitism," the doctrine that Christ had a single (divine) will, became the favored imperial christological compromise, and from the end of the 630s Maximos took on Sophronios' mantle and became the principal theological opponent of Monothelitism, arguing that it compromised Christ's perfect human nature. He sought to solve the problems raised by Christ's having two wills by distinguishing between the natural will (Christ having both a divine and human natural will) and the gnomic will (*gnômē*: Greek for "opinion") involved in deliberating over moral decisions, that was absent in Christ. His attack on Monothelitism eventually took him to Rome, where the christological heresies were condemned at the Lateran Synod of 649. By this time it was Islam that threatened the empire; Maximos and Martin's actions were regarded as seditious. The architects of the synod – Pope Martin and Maximos – were arrested, condemned, and exiled: Martin to the Crimea, where he died in 655, and Maximos to Lazica, in Georgia, where he died in 662.

SEE ALSO: Council of Constantinople III (680–681); Monophysitism (including Miaphysitism); Monothelitism

References and Suggested Readings

erthold, G. (trans.) (1985) *St. Maximus the Confessor.* Classics of Western Spirituality. New York: St. Paul Press.

Louth, A. (1996) *Maximus the Confessor.* London: Routledge.

Thunberg, L. (1965) *Microcosm and Mediator: The Theological Anthropology of Maximus the Confessor.* Lund: C. W. K. Gleerup.

St. Nicholas Cabasilas (ca. 1322–ca. 1391)

A. EDWARD SIECIENSKI

Byzantine theologian and spiritual writer known chiefly for his books *The Commentary on the Divine Liturgy* and *The Life in Christ.* Born Nicholas Chamaetos in 1322, he was the nephew of Nilus Cabasilas (1298–1363), whose surname he used throughout his life. Nilus had succeeded Gregory Palamas as archbishop of Thessalonica and was the author of several important anti-Latin tracts later used at the Council of Florence (1438–9). Although born in Thessalonica, Nicholas was educated at Constantinople and entered the imperial service, later becoming an official and friend of John VI Cantacuzenos (1347–54). During the civil war between John VI and John V Palaeologus (1341–91), Cabasilas sided with Cantacuzenos, who entrusted him with several important diplomatic missions and (briefly) considered him as candidate for patriarch following the deposition of Callistus I. When in 1354 John VI Cantacuzenos was deposed, Nicholas retired from public life and concentrated his energies on theological matters. He was once thought to have succeeded his uncle Nilus as archbishop of Thessalonica; however, it is more likely that he entered monastic life, serving as a priest at the Manganon monastery near Constantinople.

Cabasilas's hospitable open-mindedness has led some to believe that he was influenced by the so-called "Latin-minded" theologians surrounding his contemporary, Demetrius Cydones (1324–98). However,

among Cabasilas's works are a firm defense of hesychasm against Nicephorus Gregoras (ca. 1295–1360) and a new edition of his uncle's book against the Latins on the procession of the Holy Spirit. He also wrote several homilies and hagiographical works, many of which manifest a particular concern for social justice and the need to redress economic and institutional inequities.

Cabasilas's two most famous works are his *Life in Christ* and *Commentary on the Divine Liturgy. The Life in Christ* emphasized the synergy of divine and human activity in the process of salvation, the role of individual and public prayer, and the union with Christ made possible by the mysteries of baptism, chrismation, and Eucharist. Although thoroughly Eastern in its outlook, the influence of Latin theology can be seen in Cabasilas's explanation of the atonement, which closely follows Anselm of Canterbury's satisfaction theory. His *Commentary on the Divine Liturgy* (a work that found admirers in the West and was even quoted favorably by the Council of Trent) spoke of the transformative and mystical aspects of the liturgy, especially as it related to the eternal, heavenly liturgy. It became, alongside the earlier work of Patriarch Germanus of Constantinople (715–30), the most significant commentary on the Byzantine liturgy in the Eastern tradition.

SEE ALSO: Divine Liturgy, Orthodox; Mystery (Sacrament)

References and Suggested Readings

Cabasilas, N. (1960) *A Commentary on the Divine Liturgy,* trans. J. M. Hussey and P. A. McNulty. London: SPCK.

Cabasilas, N. (1974) *The Life in Christ,* trans. C. de Catanzaro. Crestwood, NY: St. Press.

St. Nicholas the Wonderworker

MARIA GWYN MCDOWELL

A "super-saint" (Onasch 1963: 205) in whom the "Church sees ... a personification of a shepherd, of its defender and intercessor" (Ouspensky and Lossky 1982: 120), the received story of St. Nicholas the Wonderworker is a conflation of the 4th-century Nicholas of Myra and the historical 6th-century Nicholas of Sion (d. 564).

Nicholas of Sion's cult was well established by the end of the 6th century, aided by his Life written soon after his death by a disciple (Ševčenko and Ševčenko 1985: 11). To this abbot of the Monastery of Holy Sion and later bishop of Pinara belong the popular birth miracles, felling of the cypress tree, miracles at sea, and many healings (ibid.: 13). Exemplifying a "down-to-earth piety" (ibid.: 15), the Life is modeled after the New Testament and Psalms. Its historical credence is partly due to its detail, which likely reflects first-hand knowledge of itemized monastery records; for example, the amount of oxen Nicholas ordered slaughtered to feed the populace after the bubonic plague of 541–2. The Life also refers to the earlier St. Nicholas who had a coastal shrine in or near Myra. This earlier saint's small 6th-century cult engulfed that of Nicholas of Sion by the 10th century – the distinction between the two saints blurred by the extensive borrowing of Byzantine hagiographers from the later Life on behalf of St. Nicholas of Myra.

The earliest known account of Nicholas of Myra is likely the *Vita per Michaelem* from the 10th century, though isolated stories appear earlier. Eustratios of Constantinople (late 6th century) cites the story of the falsely accused generals, while the terminology of the *On the Tax* indicates a 9th- or 10th-century composition. Icons of the saint often feature two medallions of Christ and the Virgin, alluding to St. Nicholas' presence at the Council of Nicea in 325. Angered, Nicholas is said to have slapped Arius, resulting in the suspension of his episcopal office and the removal of its attributes – the Gospel Book and Omophorion. In the icons, Christ and the Virgin Mary return these items to Nicholas, reflecting their appearance in dreams to the emperor's advisers advocating his reinstatement. This event, as well as his appearances to Constantine I (d. 337) in a vision on behalf of the three generals and a dream in which Nicholas receives a chrysobull exempting the city of Myra from taxation, place his activity in the early 4th century. However, there is no historical evidence of such a bishop nor any official written record of his presence at the council.

Plate 65   Icon of St. Nicholas, 10th century (tempera and gold leaf on panel), from the Monastery of St. Catherine, Mount Sinai, Egypt. Ancient Art and Architecture Collection/The Bridgeman Art Library.

Issues of historicity aside, by the time of iconographic portraiture the two saints had merged into Nicholas the Wonderworker whose miracles during and after his life produced an extraordinary cycle of icons. Maguire attributes his immense popularity, second only to the Theotokos by the 12th century, to his being "somewhat of a generalist" (Maguire 1996: 169). The many, often mundane miracles depicted in spare iconographic detail allow for a wide range of intercessory prayers by the patron saint of mariners, scholars and students, merchants, marriageable women, bankers, thieves, and pugilists.

SEE ALSO: Communion of Saints; Iconography, Styles of

References and Suggested Readings

Maguire, H. (1996) *The Icons of Their Bodies: Saints and Their Images in Byzantium*. Princeton: Princeton University Press.

Onasch, K. (1963) *Icons*. London: Faber and Faber.

Ouspensky, L. and Lossky, V. (1982) *The Meaning of Icons*. Crestwood, NY: St. Vladimir's Seminary Press.

Ševčenko, I. and Ševčenko, N. P. (1985) *The Life of St Nicholas of Sion*. Brookline, MA: Hellenic College Press.

Ševčenko, N. P. (1983) *The Life of Saint Nicholas in Byzantine Art*. Turin: Bottega d'Erasmo.

St. Nikodemos the Hagiorite (1749–1809)

CYRIL HOVORUN

Leading spiritual writer and Kollyvadic Father. He was born Nikolaos Kallivourtsis on the island of Naxos in 1749, and died a leading monastic theologian, canonist, and hymnographer on Mount Athos in 1809. He spent much of his life as a hermit, and in his writings advocated frequent participation in the Holy Eucharist. Nikodemos composed numerous books on ascetical and pastoral theology, canon law, hagiography, and exegesis of the Holy Scripture and liturgical texts. He adapted the writings of St. Symeon the New Theologian and St. Gregory Palamas for modern Greek readers, and was the author of more than fifty liturgical hymns. He had profound knowledge of Latin spiritual traditions and made Greek adaptations of Ignatian and Theatine spiritual texts such as the *Exercises* and the *Spiritual Combat*. He is chiefly known today as the co-editor of one of the major collections of Eastern Christian spirituality, the *Philokalia*, as well as codificator and commentator on the Eastern Canon Law (the *Pedalion*, or Rudder).

SEE ALSO: Kollyvadic Fathers; *Philokalia*; St. Gregory Palamas (1296–1359); St. Symeon the New Theologian (949–1022)

References and Suggested Readings

Chamberas, R. (trans.) (1989) *Nikodemos of the Holy Mountain: A Handbook of Spiritual Counsel*. New York: Paulist Press.

St. Paisy Velichovsky (1722–1794)

JOHN A. MCGUCKIN

Also known as St. Paisy of Neamt, from the Romanian monastery where he did most of his publishing work. He was a very important disseminator of the spiritual tradition of the *Philokalia* to the Slavic Orthodox lands. Along with the original Greek editors of the *Philokalia* – St. Nikodemos the Hagiorite and St. Macarius of Corinth – he is one of the major early modern Philokalic fathers. His intense labors for the rediscovery of the classical hesychastic tradition bore fruit in many revivals across the Orthodox world, lasting to the present. He was a native of the Ukraine, son of the dean of Poltava Cathedral. Orphaned at an early age and brought up by his elder brother, the priest John, the child learned to read from the holy books (scripture and the *Menaion*) and developed a great love for the works of the Fathers. He entered the Kiev Mohyla Academy (1735–9) but was attracted to the ascetic life, and in 1740 entered the monastery of Lubetch, moving soon after to St. Nicholas' monastery where he was tonsured in 1741. It was a time when many Orthodox monasteries were being forcibly closed. He himself took refuge with Hieromonk Michael in 1743, who brought him to the Romanian Skete of St. Nicholas at Traisteni. After two years there, following Athonite observance, he left to study under the hermit Onuphrios in Wallachia, and in 1746 finally made his way to Mount Athos, where he entered the Great Lavra before moving to settle at St. Panteleimon's. In 1750 he was admitted to the Lesser Schema and began accepting disciples. His first followers were Romanians, and shortly after he accepted Russian monks, making his foundation a dual-language community. In 1758 he was ordained priest and became a highly regarded spiritual father on Athos. His community grew rapidly and he first realized the need to provide serious spiritual seekers with a library of patristic advice. He commissioned several monks to translate patristic mystical texts into Slavonic. This labor was carried with his community when it relocated to Romania in 1764, at Dragomirna, and would be constitutive of the mission of the Paisian houses. In 1775 the Austrian forces captured Bukovina, and Paisy was forced to relocate once

Plate 66   Domes of the Kiev Pechersky Lavra. Photo © Sergey Kamshylin/Shutterstock.

more. In 1779 he was given charge of the monastery of Neamt. His community here soon numbered more than 700. After the publication of the Greek *Philokalia* in 1782, Paisy made a version in Slavonic (*Dobrotoloubié*) which from its appearance in 1793 electrified the Russian monastic world. In 1790 he was given the Great Schema and made archimandrite, and died at Neamt on November 15, 1794, aged 72. Mount Athos and the Romanian Church were the first to venerate him as a saint, and this was followed by the Russian Synod in 1988. Paisy's main labors were the dissemination of Philokalic texts, but he also presided over a radical reorganization of the monastic Typikon or structure of the daily life in Athonite-style monasteries. His purpose (causing controversy at the time) was to bring back into cenobitic houses a greater flexibility which would allow monastics greater possibilities for solitude and prayer. The later Russian hesychastic tradition owes much to him, including such figures such as St. Seraphim of Sarov, the Optina Elders, Bishop Ignatius Brianchaninov, and St. Theophan the Recluse.

SEE ALSO: Hesychasm; *Philokalia*

References and Suggested Readings

Chetverikov, S. (1933) *Paisius: Starets of Neamt Monastery in Moldavia. His Life, Teaching, and His Influence on the Orthodox Church* (Romanian text). Neamt, Romania: Neamt Monastery.

Joanta, S. (1992) *Romania: Its Hesychastic Tradition and Culture*. Wildwood. CA: St. Xenia Skete, pp. 128–57.

Tachiaos, A. E. N. (1986) *The Revival of Byzantine Mysticism among Slavs and Romanians in the 18th Century: Texts Relating to the Life and Activity of Paisy Velichovsky* (Greek and Slavonic texts). Thessalonica.

Zaharia, C. (1985) "Paissij Velichovskij et le role oecumenique de l'Église Orthodoxe Roumaine," *Irenikon* 58: 3–27.

St. Photios the Great (ca. 810–ca. 893)

BRENDA LLEWELLYN IHSSEN

St. Photios was an intellectual, a member of Byzantine aristocracy, and a teacher, theologian, and bibliophile. He remains one of the most highly venerated patriarchs of Constantinople, a position he held from 858 to 867 and again from 877 to 886.

Photios was born to aristocratic Christian parents and was related to both the imperial family and the ecumenical patriarch. Devoted at a young age to scholarship, at the completion of his education he became a teacher of philosophy and dialects, and was eventually appointed to the position of Protoasecretis in the Byzantine bureaucracy. Though a layman, Photios was elevated to the ecumenical patriarchate when Patriarch Ignatios was forced to resign by Caesar Bardas, uncle of Emperor Michael III. Though widely admired as an intellectual and administrator, Photios himself was surprised at the high clerical appointment he had not sought, not least because of his lay status.

Pope Nicholas I, who along with the other three patriarchs received the customary letter declaring Photios' dedication to Orthodoxy, had previously been contacted by supporters of Ignatios, and sent delegates to a synod in 861 to investigate the resignation of Ignatios and the elevation of Photios. Further complicating the situation was the dispute over the territories of Sicily, Calabria, and Illyricum, which had been removed from Roman jurisdiction and transferred to Constantinople during the first phase of iconoclasm. The question of the jurisdiction of the newly formed Bulgarian Church was aso a lively issue at this time. While the papal legates found Photios' election legal, Nicholas subsequently declared that he had deposed Photios and reinstated Ignatios; pronouncements which the East at first ignored. Photios' denunciation in 867 of Nicholas' claims for papal primacy, and his critique of the Latin innovation of the *filioque*, manifested to Christianity the first clear sign of significant theological differentiation and large-scale division between the churches of the East and of the West.

At the death of Emperor Michael III in 867, Emperor Basil I sought reconciliation with Rome. Ignatios was elevated to the patriarchate for a second term, while Photios was deposed and subsequently condemned and anathematized at the Fourth Council of Constantinople (869–70). This synod is not recognized as having ecumenical status by the Orthodox Church. After Ignatios died, Photios was again reinstated as patriarch until his forced resignation in 886, after which he devoted the remainder of his life to his academic pursuits.

Details of the schism with Rome tend to overshadow Photios' additional accomplishments, including his support of vigorous missionary activity to the Bulgars, Georgians, Moravians, and Khazars; achievements which were not divorced from his advancement of Hellenic culture, his noble leadership in the city during the siege of the Rhos (Rus) and their subsequent baptism, and his development of a refined prospectus on the relationship between church and state. Furthermore, Photios' scholarly contributions are remarkable in both quantity and diversity of subject matter. He wrote extensively not just on theology and philosophy, but also on scientific matters, on history, mathematics, astronomy, music, poetry, and law. One of his most important theological contributions is *The Mystagogy of the Holy Spirit*, a sweeping indictment of the major theological distinction between Orthodox and Latin Christianity, the *filioque*. He is one of the first, and the most significant, to set out the critical issues involved.

SEE ALSO: *Filioque*

References and Suggested Readings

Dvornik, F. (1948) *The Photian Schism, History and Legend*. Cambridge: Cambridge University Press.

Farrell, J. P. (trans.) (1987) *Patriarch St. Photius, The Mystagogy of the Holy Spirit*. Brookline, MA: Holy Cross Orthodox Press.

Hergenröther, J. (1867–9) *Photios, Patriarch von Constantinopel*, 3 vols. Regensburg.

Kallos, J. (1992) *Saint Photios: Patriarch of Constantinople*. Brookline, MA: Holy Cross Orthodox Press.

Photios (1959) *Homiliai*, ed. V. Laourdas. Thessaloniki: Hetaireias Makedonikon Spoudon.

Treadgold, W. (2002) "Photius Before His Patriarchate," *Journal of Ecclesiastical History* 53, 1: 1–17.

White, D. S. (1980) "Patriarch Photios – A Christian Humanist," *Greek Orthodox Theological Review* 25, 2: 195–205.

White, D. S. (1982) *Patriarch Photios of Constantinople*. Brookline, MA: Holy Cross Orthodox Press.

White, D. S. (2000) "The Dual Doctrine of the Relations of Church and State in Ninth Century Byzantium," *Greek Orthodox Theological Review* 45, 1–4: 443–52.

St. Romanos the Melodist (6th c.)

DIMITRI CONOMOS

The greatest of all Byzantine poets. Little is known about his life, but it is likely that he was born in the city of Emesa, Syria, and that he was of Jewish origin. As a young man he served as deacon at the Church of the Resurrection in Beirut, before coming to Constantinople during the reign of Anastasius I (491–518), where he was attached to the Church of the Virgin in the Kyros quarter of the city. At an unknown time after his death (late 6th century) he was canonized as a saint of the Orthodox Church (his feast day is October 1).

Eighty-five kontakia attributed to Romanos have survived, thirty-four of which are on the person of Christ; the rest deal with other figures of the New and Old Testaments. Around sixty out of the eighty-five (those with his name as part of the acrostic) are considered to be genuine. A great number appear to be spurious (probably all those on martyrs and saints), for it has been proved that the acrostics were frequently falsified to include the poet's name. The grand christological kontakia bear vivid dramatization; monologues are used to reveal the inner mind of his agents and dialogues to explain the motives of their actions. Opinions would no doubt differ as to which are the best, but *On the Nativity*, *On the Presentation in the Temple*, *On Mary at the Cross*, and *On the Resurrection VI* would be a reasonable shortlist. Romanos did not avoid contemporary topics, however, and the hymn *On the Earthquake and Fire* depicts the Nika Riots

(532) and praises "the new Solomon," Justinian I, for the restoration of Hagia Sophia.

Romanos' language is the Atticizing "literary *koine*" or Hellenistic Greek, which does not escape the influence of the simple spoken language or that of the Scriptures, with their many Jewish-Greek elements. His style is marked by simplicity, dignity, and emotional directness, the sentences moving in short and uninvolved phrases well adapted to the intricate meters of which he is a master. In one kontakion only, *On Judas*, does he make use of rhyme, following the example of the *Akathistos*. His dialogues are embellished by rhetorical devices such as parallelism, oxymoron, and word play. Clarity of style, striking imagery, arresting similes, bold comparisons, sharp metaphors, irony, and a dexterous use of discourse characterize his writing and add dramatic tension.

The full texts of Romanos' hymns first appear, without musical notation, in manuscripts of the 11th century. The music of the hymns of Romanos is unfortunately lost, but the dramatic character of their content suggests that they were chanted in a kind of recitative, resembling oratorio. Originally, the poems would have been recited in full during the services, and since the texts are very long, the musical texts were probably syllabic. This theory is partly based on the assumption that Romanos' metrical system is stable and conforms to the principles of *homotonia* (identical stress patterns in corresponding verses) and *isosyllabia* (identical number of syllables in corresponding verses).

SEE ALSO: Kontakion; Music (Sacred)

References and Suggested Readings

Brock, S. (1989) "From Ephrem to Romanos," *Studia Patristica* 20: 139–51.

Carpenter, M. (ed.) (1970–3) *Kontakia of Romanos*, 2 vols. Columbia: Missouri University Press.

Grosdidier de Matons, J. (ed.) (1964–81) *Romanos le Mélode: Hymnes*, 5 vols. Paris: Cerf.

Grosdidier de Matons, J. (ed.) (1977) *Romanos le Mélode et les origines de la poésie religieuse à Byzance*. Paris: Beauchesne.

Lash, E. (trans.) (1995) *St Romanos "On the Life of Christ": Kontakia*. San Francisco: Harper Collins.

St. Seraphim of Sarov (1759–1833)

KONSTANTIN GAVRILKIN

St. Seraphim belongs to that tradition of monastic spirituality which was brought to Ancient Rus from Mount Athos in the early 11th century and revived in the late 18th to 19th centuries by Paisy Velichovsky and his followers, among whom one should note St. Ignatius Brianchaninov, St. Feofan (Theophan) the Recluse, and the Optina elders.

Prokhor Moshnin (Seraphim's name prior to his monastic tonsure) was born into a pious merchant family in Kursk. In 1776 he visited the Kiev Caves Monastery, where the elder Dosifei advised him to practice the Jesus Prayer continuously and to enter the Sarov monastery (in Nizhnii Novgorod province). He arrived there in 1778, took monastic vows in 1786, and received the name Seraphim. From his disciples and early biographers, who relied both on his personal testimony and eyewitness accounts, we know that he had multiple mystical experiences, including revelations of Christ and many visitations by the Virgin Mary who guided him throughout his 55-year monastic life and healed him on a number of occasions from severe illnesses and injuries. Between 1794 and 1810 Seraphim lived a reclusive life in the forest outside the monastery, spending his time in the practice of the Jesus Prayer, reading Scripture and patristic literature, and engaging in manual labor. One day he was savagely beaten by robbers who left him crippled for the rest of his life; when the attackers were later arrested, he persuaded the authorities to let them go. He returned to the monastery in 1810, but remained in seclusion until 1825, when, at the command of the Virgin Mary, he began to receive people seeking his guidance and healing, and became one of the most renowned *startsi* of Russia.

Seraphim's extraordinary asceticism and mystical life were witnessed by several of the inhabitants of the Sarov monastery and by visitors whose lives were dramatically changed by their encounter with the saint. In his later years some of the nuns of the Diveyevo Convent of the Holy Trinity, which was under his personal supervision, also witnessed his spiritual gifts and power of prayer. The most famous description of the latter is found in the recollections of N. A. Motovilov (1809–79), a lay disciple who was particularly close to Seraphim and left autobiographical notes, a fragment from which was published in 1903 (Nilus 1903), the year St. Seraphim was canonized at the initiative of Nicholas II. It contained Seraphim's conversation with Motovilov on the meaning of Christian life, defined by the saint as the "Acquisition of the Holy Spirit" (hence the known title of the fragment). During Seraphim's explanation of what it meant "To be in the Spirit," both he and Motovilov went through a number of mystical experiences of illumination similar to those described by St. Symeon the New Theologian and mystical writers of other periods, giving the most striking demonstration of what the concept of theosis means within the Eastern Orthodox tradition.

Plate 67   St. Seraphim of Sarov. RIA Novosti/Topfoto.

SEE ALSO: Jesus Prayer; Monasticism; Russia, Patriarchal Orthodox Church of; St. Paisy Velichovsky (1722–1794); St. Theophan (Govorov) the Recluse (1815–1894)

References and Suggested Readings

Arkhimandrit Sergii (1851) *Skazanie o zhizni i podvigakh blazhennyia pamiati ottsa Serafima, Sarovskoi pustyni ieromonakha i zatvornikas prisovokupleniem dukhovnykh ego nastavlenii*, 3rd edn. Moscow: A. Semena.

Nilus, S. (1903) *Dukh Bozhii, iavno pochivshii na ottse Serafime Sarovskom v besede ego "O tseli khtistianskoi zhizni."* Moscow: Universitetskaia tipografiia.

Veniamin (Fedchenkov) (1996) *Vsemirnyi svetil'nik prepodobnyi Serafim Sarovskii.* Moscow: Palomnik.

Zander, V. (1997) *St. Seraphim of Sarov.* Crestwood, NY: St. Vladimir's Seminary Press.

St. Sergius of Radonezh (1314–1392)

KONSTANTIN GAVRILKIN

Founder of the Trinity Monastery, now known as Troitse-Sergieva Lavra (Sergiev Posad, north of Moscow), St. Sergius of Radonezh is considered the most influential saint of the Russian Orthodox Church. Together with his great contemporary Alexii, Metropolitan of Moscow in 1354–78, he is credited with the spiritual revival of Ancient Rus at the time of the Mongol invasion and, ultimately, with liberation from that oppression. Sergii, known before monasticism as Bartholomew, was born to a noble family near Rostov, but in the late 1320s the impoverished family moved to the Moscow region and settled in the town of Radonezh (10 miles from

Plate 68   Icon of St. Sergius of Radonezh, founder of the Sergiev Posad monastery, and one of the most important saints of Russian Church history. Photo by John McGuckin.

Sergiev Posad). His parents eventually became monastics in a local monastery, and after their death the youth Bartholomew himself began an ascetic life, joined by his widowed brother Stefan. In 1335, on a site occupied by today's Cathedral of the Holy Trinity, he built a wooden church with the same name. When his brother left for a Moscow monastery, he invited another monk, Igumen Mitrofan, to join him as a replacement companion. Mitrofan tonsured Bartholomew with the name Sergius. Within a few years, other ascetics, attracted by Sergius' strict ascetic life, discipline of prayer, humility, and wisdom, came to join him, and in 1345 they officially established the Holy Trinity Monastery. Although Sergius demanded that all monks sustain the monastery by their manual labor, with time the community grew and among those who joined it were people of different ranks and means – from peasants to princes – who often donated their wealth to the monastery. Patriarch of Constantinople Philotheus (1300–79) advised Sergius to introduce the coenobitic rule. With the blessing of Metropolitan Alexii of Moscow, he followed the advice; within a few decades his disciples founded many monasteries of the same style in various Russian principalities. In his late years, Alexii of Moscow urged Sergius to became his successor, but the latter would not abandon his monastery for the metropolitan throne. Sergius is credited with playing a peacemaking role in the disputes among Russian princes whose dynastic quarrels divided and weakened Rus at the time of the Mongol oppression, and encouraging their union with the Moscow principality and its ruler Dmitrii Ioannovich (1350–89), who in 1380 led the united Russian forces to victory against the Golden Horde in the Battle of Kulikovo.

Epifanius the Wise (d. ca. 1420), the disciple of the saint, wrote the first biography (*Zhitie*) of Sergius, which was later revised by the famous hagiographer Pachomius the Serb. Prior to the mid-16th century the Russian Church did not have a formal process of canonization, but according to the available sources Sergius of Radonezh was venerated as saint already in the 15th century for his spiritual wisdom, his asceticism, and the power of his healing prayer.

SEE ALSO: Monasticism; Russia, Patriarchal Orthodox Church of

References and Suggested Readings

Golubinskii, E. E. (1892) *Prepodobnyi Sergii Radonezhskii i sozdannaia im Troitskaia Lavra*. Sergievskii Posad: A. I. Snegireva.

Kloss, B. M. (1998) *Izbrannye trudy. T. 1: Zhitie Sergiia Radonezhskogo*. Moscow: Iazyki russkoi kul'tury.

Kovalevsky, P. (1976) *Saint Sergius and Russian Spirituality*, trans. W. Elias Jones. Crestwood, NY: St. Vladimir's Seminary Press.

Tsurikov, V. (ed.) (2004) *The Trinity: Sergius Lavra in Russian History and Culture*. Jordanville, NY: Holy Trinity Seminary Press.

St. Silouan of Athos (1866–1938)

JULIA KONSTANTINOVSKY

St. Silouan of Athos, also known as Silvanus, was born Simeon Ivanovich Antonov of Russian peasant origin, and became a schema-monk of the St. Panteleimon monastery on Mount Athos. He was a revered mystic and spiritual director (*starets*) of monastics and laypeople alike. St. Silouan was the spiritual father of Archimandrite Sophrony (Sakharov), who, on Starets Silouan's request, edited and published his handwritten notes on the spiritual life and salvation. Archimandrite Sophrony likewise prepared an introduction to St. Silouan's writings, expounding the teachings from the perspective of the Orthodox ascetic tradition (*Saint Silouan the Athonite*, first published in Paris, 1948). Largely because of the testimony of this spiritual biography, which elucidates the inner progress of Silouan's life, St. Silouan was canonized as a holy Orthodox ascetic (*hosios, prepodobny*) in 1987 by the ecumenical patriarchate of Constantinople. The Orthodox Church commemorates him on September 24, the day of his repose. Through his prayer, life, and writings, St. Silouan delivered a potent message about the boundlessness of God's love, forgiveness, and healing, which has been widely received as strikingly modern, pertinent to the contemporary social predicament. Silouan, therefore, became acknowledged as "the saint for the present day." Although possessed of little secular learning and never ordained as a priest, through years of monastic training St. Silouan became a spiritual giant, achieving a full measure of "passionlessness" (*apatheia*). While standing firmly within the continuity of the patristic tradition, he also possesses striking originality. His contribution to Orthodox theology and soteriology encompasses the chief following ideas: unbounded love; prayer for the whole world; the prioritization of the love of "enemies"; stress on the power of repentance; and Christ-like humility.

St. Silouan's teaching on the love of all humanity and the love of "enemies" is the guiding tenet of his thought, proceeding from his understanding of the fundamental requirement of Christian charity towards all people in general, good or bad. To him, this was the essence of the human being's likeness to God and perfect discipleship of Christ. St. Silouan, strikingly, asserts that if one fails to love one's enemies, one's salvation is not assured. Having received in his youth a mystical vision of the merciful Christ, Silouan viewed the attainment of "the humility of Christ" as the highest degree of Christian perfection, that which in patristic tradition was frequently termed "deification." However, having had this vision of the glory of the humble Lord, Silouan likewise experientially knew that the greatest misfortune a human being can suffer is to lose touch with Christ through wrongful actions and even mere evil thoughts (*pomysly*), pride being the deepest root of sin. He thus saw pride as the origin of all evil and suffering in the world, what he called "the seed of death and despair." For this reason Silouan concentrated all his powers upon striving relentlessly, through the gospel commandments, to overcome pride in himself and to obtain "Christ-like humility." St. Silouan stands as the icon of Christ's saint: the one who presents to the world the Lord's own depths of humility and love to all humankind.

SEE ALSO: Asceticism; Elder (Starets); Monasticism; Sophrony, Archimandrite (1896–1993)

References and Suggested Readings

Larchet, J. C. (2001) *Saint Silouane de l'Athos*. Paris: Editions du Cerf.

Sophrony, Archimandrite (Sakharov) (1985) *We Shall See Him as He Is*. Maldon, UK: Monastery of St. John.

Sophrony, Archimandrite (Sakharov) (1999) *Saint Silouan the Athonite*. Crestwood, NY: St. Vladimir's Seminary Press.

St. Symeon the New Theologian (949–1022)

JOHN A. MCGUCKIN

St. Symeon is a major mystic, a precursor of the hesychasts, emphasizing the themes of illumination by the Spirit, the role of the spiritual father, the importance of the gift of tears, and the necessity of personal experience of God. He was a controversial figure in his time. His *Discourses* re-present much of the classical Studite monastic teaching but with a deeply personal charismatic spirit. Symeon's aristocratic father brought him to Constantinople in 960, and his uncle (killed in the Phocas riots of 963) advanced his career until the young man assumed senatorial rank. In 969 he first encountered the monk Symeon Eulabes who became a father-confessor. In the time of the Tzimisces revolt, he was sheltered by Symeon Eulabes, who ever after appeared to him as a mediator of Christ's salvation. He tells how, once when he was overwhelmed by a consciousness of his sinfulness, he saw during his evening prayer a brilliantly shining light, and behind that an even greater radiance. He interpreted the vision as his spiritual father interceding for him with Christ.

In 976 another palace coup brought Basil II to power and marked the end of Symeon's political life. He took refuge with his confessor and once again experienced a vision of the light of Christ, which became for him a definitive moment of conversion. He entered the monastic state. In a short time (979) he became the higumen of the St. Mamas monastery in Constantinople and refurbished it. The traditional morning *Catecheses* to the monks have survived as a central body of his work. Some time between 995 and 998 the growing opposition to his discipline broke out as a revolt by a section of his community. Patriarch Sisinnios II (995–8) heard charges against him and found in his favor; but Patriarch Sergios II (999–1019) opened new legal proceedings against him (instigated by the court). In 1003 an attempt was made to entangle him in a public theological dispute (it produced as his response the *Theological Chapters*). His answer took the form of an excoriation of the synod's chief theologian and confidant to the Emperor, Stephen of Alexina, for attempting to theologize without first having experienced the divine light. In 1005 he was subjected to house arrest and exile followed in 1009.

Symeon regarded the *casus belli* as his claim that the present generation had the same charismatic right to live in the freedom of the ancient saints. In exile he bought the oratory of St. Marina at Chrysopolis and wrote some of his most famous works, including the *Hymns of Divine Love*, a classic of mysticism. He died aged 73 in 1022. His relics were not admitted back into the capital until 1054, when Niketas Stethatos composed a *Vita* for the occasion. Symeon was revered as a great master of the inner life by the Hagiorites. In recent decades he has attracted much scholarly attention. His teaching is important both for the light it throws on a dark period of Byzantine affairs, but more so for the spiritual themes it treats with such vigor. He is a major advocate of the power of repentance: a force that is not simply for "beginners" in the ascetical life, but which makes the human soul into the "friend of Christ." His descriptions of visions of the divine light inspired generations after him, as did his devotion to the Eucharist. The practice of the Jesus Prayer, however, does not make much of an appearance. Symeon is also important for the doctrine of Spiritual Fatherhood which had a marked impact on Orthodox spiritual praxis in the time of the 18th-century Philokalic revival.

SEE ALSO: Hesychasm; Jesus Prayer; *Philokalia*; Stethatos, Niketas (ca. 1005–1085)

References and Suggested Readings

de Catanzaro, C. J. (trans.) (1980) *Symeon the New Theologian: The Discourses* [Catecheses]. New York: Paulist Press.

Golitzin, A. (1995–7) *St. Symeon the New Theologian* [trans. of "The Ethical Discourses"], 3 vols. New York: St. Vladimir's Seminary Press.

Hausherr, I. (1928) "Un grand mystique byzantin: Vie de S. Syméon le Nouveau Théologien [par Nicétas Stéthatos]," *Orientalia Christiana* 12, 45.

Holl, K. (1898) *Enthusiasmus und Bussgewalt beim griechischen Mönchtum, eine Studie zu Symeon dem Neuen Theologen.* Leipzig.

Krivocheine, B. (1987) *In the Light of Christ.* New York: St. Vladimir's Seminary Press.

McGuckin, J. A. (1996a) "St. Symeon the New Theologian and Byzantine Monasticism," in A. Bryer (ed.) *Mount Athos and Byzantine Monasticism.* London: Variorum Press, pp. 17–35.

McGuckin, J. A. (1996b) "St. Symeon the New Theologian (d. 1022): Byzantine Theological Renewal in Search of a Precedent." In R. N. Swanson (ed.) *The Church Retrospective: Studies in Church History*, vol. 33. Oxford: Boydell Press.

McGuckin, J. A. (1996c) "The Notion of Luminous Vision in 11th C Byzantium: Interpreting the Biblical and Theological Paradigms of St. Symeon the New Theologian." In *Acts of the Belfast Byzantine Colloquium – Portaferry 1995* (The Evergetis Project). Belfast: Queen's University Press.

McGuckin, P. (1994) *Symeon the New Theologian: Chapters and Discourses.* Kalamazoo: Cistercian Publications.

Maloney, G. (1975) *The Hymns of Divine Love.* New Jersey: Dimension Press.

Maloney, G. (1975) *The Mystic of Fire and Light.* Denville, NJ: Denville Books.

Palmer, G., Sherrard, P., and Ware, K. (1995) *Philokalia*, vol. 4. London: Faber and Faber, pp. 11–75.

Turner, H. J. M. (1990) *St. Symeon the New Theologian and Spiritual Fatherhood.* Leiden: E. J. Brill.

St. Theodore the Studite (759–826)

JOHN A. MCGUCKIN

Theodore was the aristocratic abbot (higumen) first of the Sakkudion Monastery (founded with his uncle Platon on family estates in Bithynia) and then, in 798, of the large and important Stoudium Monastery at Constantinople (by the patronage of Empress Irene). His monastic reforms (refining and systematizing the ascetic corpus of St. Basil the Great) led to his Studite Typikon becoming a "standard" model for the majority of Eastern Orthodox monasteries in the Byzantine era. He encouraged the many hundreds of monks of his cenobitic establishment to engage in literary, as well as liturgical, activities; and scholars have surmized that it was in the scriptoria of the Stoudium that the minuscule script was invented. He was a vigorous defender of the rights of the monastics against both the imperial and patriarchal throne when he felt canonical limits had been transgressed; and was particularly noted as a strong advocate of the Iconodule cause in the second phase of the Iconoclastic crisis, beginning in 814. After the Triumph of Orthodoxy, in 843, his memory was elevated along with that of St. John of Damascus as among the chief of the Iconodule saints, and his treatise *On the Holy Images* has been an influential text.

SEE ALSO: Iconoclasm; Icons; Monasticism

References and Suggested Readings

Roth, C. P. (trans.) (1981) *St. Theodore the Studite: On the Holy Icons.* Crestwood, NY: St. Vladimir's Seminary Press.

St. Theophan (Govorov) the Recluse (1815–1894)

KONSTANTIN GAVRILKIN

Born into the family of a rural priest, after the seminary Georgii V. Govorov continued his studies at Kiev Theological Academy, where, under the influence of the Kievan Cave Monastery, he decided to become a monk. Prior to his graduation in 1841, he was tonsured (with the name Theophan) and ordained deacon and priest shortly afterwards. For a few years he served as instructor and administrator at a number of ecclesiastical schools, but in 1847 he resigned from St. Petersburg Theological Academy in order to join the Russian Mission in Jerusalem, where he studied Greek, Hebrew, Arabic, and French. He also traveled throughout the Middle East and visited many holy places in Syria, Egypt, and Palestine. In 1854, because of the Crimean War, the Mission was closed, and upon his return to Russia he was appointed again to St. Petersburg Academy, and then, five months later, to the Olonetskaia Seminary (Petrozavodsk). Less than a

year later he was sent to the Russian Embassy Church in Constantinople. In the summer of 1857 he was made dean of St. Petersburg Theological Academy, only to be consecrated bishop of Tambov in 1859 and moved again in 1863 to the see of Vladimir. In 1866, tired of his endless transfers and busy administrative life, he petitioned the synod to allow him to resign and live as a "simple monk" in a monastery of his choice in order to dedicate his life to the study of Scripture, prayer, and writing. The synod (after launching an inquiry into his "unusual" request) accepted his resignation, and Theophan moved to Vyshenskaia Pustyn' (Tambov province).

For six years he followed the monastery's regular life, but in 1872 withdrew from direct contact with all people, both inside and outside the monastery, except for the abbot, his father-confessor, and the *keleinik*, a monk assigned to assist him. His life in seclusion followed a classic monastic model: prayer, study, manual labor. For the first ten years he served liturgy on Saturdays and Sundays, and for the last twelve he did so every day. He sent out between twenty and forty letters a day in response to people seeking his spiritual advice. His ever-expanding library contained several encyclopedias in various languages, Migne's *Patrologia*, Russian editions of the fathers of the church, books of the liturgical cycle, many theological journals, commentaries on Scripture, and such like. He wrote continuously, authoring more than fifty books by the end of his life: commentaries on Scripture, manuals on Christian life and prayer in particular, meditations on various subjects, theological treatises, and collections of letters of spiritual direction. In addition, he translated two volumes of Symeon the New Theologian, the *Unseen Warfare* in the version of Nicodemus the Hagiorite, as well as texts of the major ascetic writers, included in his five-volume *Philokalia*, which was supplemented by a volume including the monastic rules of Pachomius, Basil of Caesarea, John Cassian, and Benedict of Nursia. In the last years of his life, Theophan suffered from a number of ailments, including blindness in one eye. He died on the Feast of Theophany, January 6, 1894. Having become one of the most popular and influential spiritual writers of the Russian Orthodox Church in the 19th and 20th centuries, he was canonized in 1988.

SEE ALSO: Monasticism; Russia, Patriarchal Orthodox Church of

References and Suggested Readings

Amis, R. (ed.) (1991) *The Heart of Salvation: The Life and Teachings of Russia's Saint Theophan the Recluse*, trans. E. Williams. Newbury, MA: Robertsbridge.

Theophan the Recluse (1997) *The Path to Salvation: A Manual of Spiritual Transformation*, trans. S. Rose. Platina, CA: St. Herman of Alaska Brotherhood.

St. Tikhon (Belavin) (1865–1925)

KONSTANTIN GAVRILKIN

Vasilii I. Belavin was born into a priestly family in the Pskov diocese. He studied at the Pskov Seminary and St Petersburg Theological Academy, became a monk with the name Tikhon in 1891, and was ordained to the diaconate and priesthood shortly after. After a few years at the Kholm Seminary, where he became the dean, he was consecrated bishop of Lublin, vicar of the Kholm-Warsaw diocese, in 1897, but a year later was sent to the United States as bishop of the Aleutians and Alaska, and he remained there until 1907. In his nine years in America, Tikhon reorganized and expanded the diocese, initiated a number of missions, and encouraged the use of the English language (instructing that Anglican prayer books should be used until translations of Orthodox texts could be published). He provided pastoral care for diverse ethnic groups of Orthodox immigrants from the Old World, since the Russian Church was the only autocephalous church with a proper administrative presence and resources in the United States at the time (the situation dramatically changed after the collapse of the Russian Empire in 1917, when its material support of the church also evaporated). By 1907 the now archdiocese of the Aleutians and North America had two vicar bishops (in Alaska and Brooklyn) and St. Tikhon's Monastery in Pennsylvania was under construction, together with new churches in various regions.

In 1907 Tikhon was summoned back to Russia and appointed first to Yaroslavl', then to Vilnius (1913), and

Plate 69   Portrait of St. Tikhon (Belavin). Topfoto.

finally to Moscow (June 1917). When the Council of the Russian Orthodox Church was convened in Moscow in August 1917 for the first time since the 17th century, Tikhon was elected its chairman and elevated to the rank of metropolitan. The council continued its work despite the Bolshevik *coup d'état* in October and the beginning of the new regime's persecution of the church, which intensified after the outbreak of the Civil War in 1918. Among the council's primary goals was reestablishment of canonical order in the administration of the church and, first of all, the restoration of the office of patriarch, which had been abolished by Peter the Great in the early 18th century. After a few rounds of voting, Tikhon was elected out of the three leading candidates by the drawing of lots.

Tikhon led the Russian Church in the period of persecution by the hostile regime, when virtually all of its infrastructure was destroyed and internal divisions weakened its unity. In addition, the Bolshevik government used various provocations to undermine

Tikhon's authority and legitimacy, and his condemnation of the violent repression of the church was widely publicized as anti-Soviet ideology. Eventually, in order to protect thousands of people from certain death, the patriarch appealed to the clergy to abstain from direct involvement in the political struggle, but this measure did not change the Bolsheviks' attitude to the church or alleviate mass repressions of the Orthodox clergy and laity. Between 1922 and 1925 Tikhon was practically under house arrest in the Donskoi Monastery in Moscow, where he died in 1925. He was canonized in October 1989. His shrine is today in the Donskoi monastery church.

SEE ALSO: New Martyrs; Russia, Patriarchal Orthodox Church of; United States of America, Orthodoxy in the

References and Suggested Readings

Gubonin. M. (ed.) (2007) *Sovremenniki o Patriarkhe Tikhone*, 2 vols. Moscow: PSTGU.

Lobanov, V.V. (2008) *Patriarkh Tikhon i sovetskaia vlast' (1917–1925 gg.)*. Moscow: Panorama.

Swan, J. (1964) *The Biography of Patriarch Tikhon*. Jordanville, NY: Holy Trinity Russian Orthodox Monastery.

St. Tikhon of Zadonsk (1724–1783)

JOHN A. MCGUCKIN

Russian bishop and spiritual theologian of the baroque era. He was born Timothy Sokolov, son of a village church lector, who died when he was a child, leaving the family impoverished. He entered the Novgorod seminary (with a very pro-western curriculum) where his extreme poverty evoked ridicule from other students, but eventually became a professor, and rector of the Tver seminary. His lectures on dogmatics were later published and focus on the doctrine of the redemption in western terms of atonement. In 1758 he was tonsured as a monk and priested, and in 1760 he became head of the Otroch monastery. In 1761 he was consecrated as assistant bishop in Novgorod, and two years after that was appointed bishop of Voronezh. He was active in restoring the diocesan seminary and trying to institute schemes to raise the standard of the diocesan clergy. But in 1767 he suddenly, and without explanation, sought permission to retire into an obscure monastery, settling at Zadonsk, where he stayed until he died in 1783, aged 59.

All his life he found it difficult to engage with people. He suffered from irritability, and what his first biographer, Bishop Eugene Bolkhovitinov, described as a "melancholy nervous illness" and which we today would probably call serious bi-polar disorder. One of his monastic assistants, after his death, spoke about his nervous hypochondria. His forced involvement in the state-mandated deposition of Metropolitan Arseniy Matsievich in Moscow in 1763 deeply disturbed him. Tikhon always preferred to avoid social engagement, making an exception (which he had to force against his inclination) to visit the imprisoned, and minister to the peasants, whom he helped from his state pension while living in great personal simplicity.

Tikhon was canonized in 1861. His spiritual work, mostly composed in solitude in Zadonsk, is typical of much that was happening in 18th-century Russia, and shows familiarity with western pietistic and evangelical trends. His *Spiritual Treasure* is an Orthodox adaptation of *Occasional Meditations* by the 17th-century Anglican theologian Joseph Hall, bishop of Norwich. Johann Arndt's treatise *True Christianity* also was a strong influence on him, though in his own book, of the same title, Tikhon moderated Protestant pietism with deep currents from Russian Kenoticism that were familiar to him. Fedotov, in his study of Russian spiritual masters, says that his "personality is much more interesting than his writings. He is the first 'modern' among the Russian saints, with his interior conflicts, his painful groping for his spiritual way – the constant shift of light and shadow, of ecstasy and depression" (Fedotov 1950: 183–4). At Zadonsk, Tikhon devoted every night to prayer, sleeping only at sunrise. When he was overcome with depression he would ceaselessly chant: "Lord have mercy on me. Lord forgive. Giver of life have mercy on me." And when he was happy he would replace the invocation with "Praise the Lord in heaven." Late in life he received ecstatic visions of Christ, the

Theotokos, and the joy of heaven. In his writing profound devotion and love for Christ crucified are manifested. His path to sanctity was one that was navigated through many psychological fragilities; a fact that makes him unusual in the annals of Orthodox spiritual writing of the modern period. Dostoevsky saw in Tikhon a model of spirituality that he reflects in several of his writings.

SEE ALSO: Russia, Patriarchal Orthodox Church of

References and Suggested Readings

Bolshakoff, S. (1980) *Russian Mystics*. Kalamazoo: Cistercian Publications, pp. 61–78.
Fedotov, G. P. (ed.) (1981) *A Treasury of Russian Spirituality*, 3rd edn. London: Sheed and Ward, pp. 182–241.
Spidlik, T. (1991) "Tikhon de Zadonske," in *Dictionnaire de spiritualité*, Vol. 15. Paris: Beauchesne, cols. 960–4.

Sts. Barsanuphius and John (6th c.)

JOHN CHRYSSAVGIS

In the early 6th century Barsanuphius, an Egyptian monk, entered the hilly region of Thavatha in Southern Palestine (near Gaza) as a recluse, acquiring a remarkable reputation for discernment and compassion. Abba Seridos, who attended to Barsanuphius as his scribe, was later appointed abbot of a monastery created to organize the increasing number of monks that gradually gathered around the elder. The community included workshops, two guest-houses, a hospital, and a large church where women, too, could receive instruction. Seridos acted as mediator for those wishing to submit questions in writing. Since Seridos did not know Coptic, he would write in Greek. Some time between 525 and 527, another hermit, John, came to live beside Barsanuphius, who became known as the "Great Old Man"; John was called the "Other Old Man." The two shared the same way of life and supported one another's ministry. John's attendant and scribe was Dorotheus of Gaza (later an important spiritual writer in his own right).

John's letters were more "institutional," responding to practical matters; those of Barsanuphius were more "inspirational," responding to spiritual problems. Their authority is uniquely refreshing. At a time when monastic life in the West was becoming increasingly more regulated, Palestinian monasticism preserved flexibility and fluidity. The letters are not a monastic "rule"; they are very personal in style and content.

While scholarship sometimes emphasizes the more "extraordinary" characteristics of the desert elders, Barsanuphius and John are less spectacular. Sensational miracles and exceptional charisms are hardly the most striking feature of their spirituality; they defy the romanticized hagiographical picture of the Late Antique holy man. They do not provide wisdom on request; nor do they attempt to solve all problems presented before them. Their purpose is to inspire and to exhort.

In all, there are approximately 850 letters. Almost 400 of these letters (the longer ones) belong to Barsanuphius, while almost 450 letters belong to John. Whereas early monastic literature has concentrated on monastic development, the correspondence of Barsanuphius and John redresses a balance in this regard, focusing much attention on the concerns of lay persons. The letters involve more or less all of the main actors of the period, with the exception of women. They include monks from the monastery of Abba Seridos and simple laypersons from the surrounding community, through to high-ranking political officials and ecclesiastical leaders; bishops ask about ordinations; lay people inquire about illness and healing, legal and economic matters, marriage and death, property rights and popular superstitions. The ascetic teaching of the letters includes such concepts as gratitude in all circumstances and constant joy, as well as two terms that they coin, namely "not reckoning oneself as anything" and avoiding "the pretense to rights."

Beyond scriptural references, relatively few proper names are recorded in the letters, which continue the tradition of the *Apophthegmata Patrum*. Through Dorotheus of Gaza, Theodore the Studite also accepts the authority of their teachings, whose extensive influence is evident in John Klimakos and, through John, in Symeon the New Theologian and the 14th-century Hesychasts. Barsanuphius and John are liturgically commemorated on February 6.

References and Suggested Readings

Chryssavgis, J. (2003) *Letters from the Desert: A Selection of the Spiritual Correspondence of Barsanuphius and John.* Crestwood, NY: St. Vladimir's Seminary Press.

Hevelone-Harper, J. L. (2005) *Disciples of the Desert: Monks, Laity, and Spiritual Authority in Sixth-Century Gaza.* Baltimore: Johns Hopkins University Press.

Sts. Constantine (Cyril) (ca. 826–869) and Methodios (815–885)

BRENDA LLEWELLYN IHSSEN

Brothers Constantine-Cyril and Methodios were born, raised, and educated in Thessaloniki, an area populated by Slavs for several centuries before them. Their heritage is uncertain, but their home was probably bilingual, Greek and Slavic. Constantine studied at Constantinople under the guidance of future patriarch Photios, and was elevated to chartophylax, a position he resigned in favor of a monastic vocation. Constantine was appointed professor of philosophy at the imperial university, his brother Methodios was appointed archon of an unnamed Slavic territory, a position he also renounced in favor of monasticism. The brothers were united again for a diplomatic and religious mission in the Crimea, where their talents with languages and apologetics were tested in conversation with Jewish and Islamic-influenced Khazars, as well as the Rus.

Facing territorial pressure from Germans and Bulgars, Moravian Prince Rastislav requested that Byzantine Emperor Michael III (842–67) send a bishop and teacher to provide ecclesiastical instruction in Slavonic for building national unity and consciousness, and intellectual and religious culture among various tribes in the territory known to historians as "Greater Moravia." A secondary goal was a diplomatic alliance with Byzantium, which would be able to provide political protection for Moravia from menacing neighbors. The brothers, with language and diplomatic skills recently tested on their mission in the Crimea, were suited for the appointment. Prior to the departure and under Cyril's supervision, a team translated sacred texts from Greek into Slavonic using a rough Slavic alphabet that possibly existed in a rudimentary form prior to Rastislav's request. As developed and finally attributed to Constantine, Glagolitic is a creative and original alphabet that is a testament to his talents as a philologist.

Though the embassy was received favorably in Moravia, German Catholic clergy bitterly opposed their work on the grounds that the gospel ought to be preached only in three languages: Hebrew, Greek, or Latin (trilingualism). This argument would be dismissed by Pope Hadrian II, who greeted the brothers when they arrived to appeal in Rome in 867 with native Slavic clergy to be ordained, and offering the relics of St. Clement (currently at rest in the Basilica di San Clemente). While in Rome the brothers learned of Emperor Michael III's death and the deposition of Patriarch Photios; Constantine, who was ill, recognized that he would likely die in Rome, and subsequently took solemn monastic vows, electing the name "Cyril." Since transfer to Constantinople was impractical, Cyril's body was also buried in the Basilica di San Clemente at Methodios' request.

Methodios was consecrated as archbishop and returned to Moravia, where he faced mounting opposition from Frankish clergy. After successfully defending his Orthodoxy in Constantinople he returned to Moravia and labored to complete a full translation of the Bible into the vernacular before he died in 884.

The brothers are central figures in the history of Slavic Orthodoxy. In addition to the alphabet and the transmission of sacred texts, they were responsible for transmitting the wider context of meaning for what was translated. Subsequently, the Slavic world inherited the harvest of their labors in the form of a literary, spiritual, theological, and artistic tradition which is marked to this day in the unique character of the Slavic Orthodox people.

SEE ALSO: St. Photios the Great (ca. 810–ca. 893)

References and Suggested Readings

Dvornik, F. (1970) *Byzantine Missions Among the Slavs: SS. Constantine-Cyril and Methodius.* Piscataway, NJ: Rutgers University Press.

Soulis, G. C. (1965) "The Legacy of Cyril and Methodius to the Southern Slavs," *Dumbarton Oaks Papers 19*.

Tachiaos, A. N. (2001) *Cyril and Methodius of Thessalonica: The Acculturation of the Slavs*. Crestwood, NY: St. Vladimir's Seminary Press.

Vlasto, A. P. (1970) *The Entry of the Slavs into Christendom: An Introduction to the Medieval History of the Slavs*. Cambridge: Cambridge University Press.

Schmemann, Alexander (1921–1983) *see* Contemporary Orthodox Theology

Scholarios, George (Gennadios) (ca. 1403–1472)

A. EDWARD SIECIENSKI

George Scholarios was a great admirer of Thomas Aquinas and an advocate of union with Rome at the Council of Florence (1438–9). However, following the death of his friend and teacher Mark of Ephesus in 1445, Scholarios became a staunch anti-unionist and then first patriarch of Constantinople (as Gennadios II) following the fall of the city in 1453.

SEE ALSO: Ecumenism, Orthodoxy and; Florence, Council of (1438–1439); *Filioque*; St. Mark of Ephesus (1392–1445)

References and Suggested Readings

Petit, L. and Jugie, M. (eds.) (1928–36) *Oeuvres complètes de Georges (Gennadios) Scholarios*, 8 vols. Paris: Maison de la bonne presse.

Tinnefeld, F. (2002) "George Gennadios Scholarius," in C. Conticello and V. Conticello (eds.) *La Théologie byzantine et sa tradition*, vol. 2. Turnhout: Brepols, pp. 477–549.

Semandron

DIMITRI CONOMOS

A struck instrument used on Mount Athos and in many other Orthodox monasteries. Its rhythmic percussions call worshippers to a service or to a meal. On important occasions its resonating claps lead an outside litanical procession. Semandra are made of wood or metal. If wooden, it is either a long plank, grasped by the player's left hand and struck by the right with a wooden mallet, or a larger and heavier timber block suspended by chains and struck by one or two mallets. The metallic semandron is not portable, but often horseshoe shaped and struck by a metal mallet.

Serbia, Patriarchal Orthodox Church of

GORDON N. BARDOS

In the ecclesiastical hierarchy of the Orthodox Church, the autocephalous Patriarchal Church of Serbia ranks sixth in terms of primacy (behind the patriarchates of Constantinople, Alexandria, Antioch, Jerusalem, and Russia). Since the Middle Ages, the Serbian Church has been spread territorially across many parts of the Balkan peninsula, from southern Dalmatia on the Adriatic coast, to parts of present-day Albania, Bosnia and Herzegovina, Kosovo and Metohija, Macedonia, and Serbia.

Today, as a result of centuries of migrations and emigrations, the Orthodox Church of Serbia consists of approximately thirty dioceses worldwide, governed by a standing holy synod of bishops representing the highest executive and judicial body within the church. The holy synod of bishops is composed of the patriarch (*ex officio*) and four bishops who are elected bi-annually by the holy assembly of bishops of the Serbian Orthodox Church. The holy assembly of bishops, in turn, is a body which represents all of the metropolitans and bishops in the church.

Throughout its history, the Serbian Orthodox Church has portrayed itself, and has been widely perceived by the Serbian public, as being the most consistent, strongest, and sometimes the sole, defender of the Serbian people. This has on occasion led to charges that the Serbian Orthodox Church is overly nationalistic, yet it is a phenomenon common to most of the religious organizations in Southeastern Europe. Because of a variety of historical and cultural circumstances, religion and ethnicity have become strongly intertwined in the Balkans; in this sense, the relationship between the Serbian Orthodox Church and the Serbian people follows the general Balkan rule, rather than being an exception.

Conversion of the Serbs to Christianity

Along with other Slavic tribes, the Serbs migrated to the Balkan Peninsula in the 7th century. In the 10th century, followers of Sts. Cyril and Methodios converted the pagan Serb tribes to Christianity. In the late 12th century a powerful Serb state emerged during the rule of Stefan Nemanja (1109–99), centered on the mountainous regions straddling the borders of modern-day Kosovo and Metohija. Serbs commonly refer to Kosovo as "Kosovo and Metohij." The word *Metohija* is derived from the Greek meaning "land of the monasteries." It specifically refers to the many monasteries spread throughout northern and western Kosovo, Serbia, and Montenegro. Under Nemanja and his heirs, the Serbian state grew and expanded territorially until the mid-14th century, largely at the Byzantine Empire's expense. The history of medieval Serbia and, by extension, the medieval Serbian Church, is intimately connected with the Nemanjić dynasty, so much so that most of the rulers from the Nemanjić dynasty were canonized as saints by the Serbian Church. The most important and venerated figure in Serbian history is Stefan Nemanja's son, Ratsko (1175–1235), who left his father's court for Mount Athos, became a monk, and adopted the monastic name of Sava. After his death he was canonized by the Serbian Church, thereafter becoming known as St. Sava the Enlightener.

St. Sava played a crucial role in forming the Serbs' religious and national identities. Given the Balkan Peninsula's geographical location between East and West, for several centuries it remained unclear whether the Serbs as a people would ultimately fall under the fold of the Western Church, with all of the political and cultural implications that entailed, or accept Orthodox Christianity, and thereby draw their spiritual and cultural inspiration from Constantinople and the Byzantine world. St. Sava was a determined proponent of the latter. A few years after moving to Mount Athos, Sava was joined there by his father, Stefan Nemanja, who also became a monk and adopted the monastic name of Simeon. Together, Simeon and Sava founded one of the most important religious and cultural centers of the Serbian people, the Monastery of Hilandar on Mount Athos. Hilandar's (and, by extension, Mount Athos') influence on Serbia's subsequent development would be of tremendous importance, as many of Sava's Serb contemporaries and successors would spend their spiritually and intellectually formative years there.

Simeon and Sava returned to Serbia in approximately 1196–7 to develop spiritual and religious life in the Serbian lands. Coinciding with the Latin conquest of Constantinople in 1204, the subsequent weakness of the Byzantine Empire at this time allowed Sava to build a strong, indigenous church organization. In 1219, during the Byzantine court's exile in Nicea, Sava convinced the patriarch of Constantinople, Manuel I, to grant the Serbian Church autocephaly. In granting his assent, Patriarch Manuel also consecrated Sava the first archbishop of the autocephalous Serbian Church.

Upon his return to Serbia, Sava reorganized Orthodoxy in the Serbian lands, consecrating new bishops, creating new dioceses, and founding new monasteries to serve as episcopal seats. Many of the monasteries built during the Nemanjić period, such as Studenica, Gračanica, Visoki Dečani, the Peć Patriarchate, Sopoćani, and Žića, are considered to be the most important cultural, spiritual, and historical landmarks of the Serbian people. Sava was also careful at this time to give the newly autocephalous church a distinctively Serbian national character; thus, for instance, he ordered that the abbots of the leading monasteries be Serb rather than Greek, and also that inscriptions on church buildings or frescoes be in Slavonic rather than Greek. St. Sava the Enlightener's legacy would prove to be profound. Largely thanks to his efforts and personality, both the Serbian state and the Serbs as a people became firmly anchored in the Orthodox world, and would in subsequent centuries come to represent the westernmost frontier of Orthodoxy.

A century after Sava's death, during the reign of Serbia's most powerful medieval ruler, Stefan Dušan Nemanjić (the "Mighty"), the Serbian state expanded to the point of becoming an empire that included most of the southern Balkans, and Dušan's ambitions had grown to include capturing Constantinople itself. Towards this end, he had the Serbian archbishopric elevated to the status of a patriarchate (without, however, the blessings of the ecumenical patriarch in Constantinople), which was given the name of the patriarchate of Peć. In 1346 in Skopje, the newly installed Serbian patriarch, Joanikije II, crowned Dušan "Emperor and Autocrat of the Serbs and Greeks." Dušan also had the new patriarchate assume jurisdictional authority over several traditionally Greek metropolitan sees throughout the southern Balkans, further alienating and deepening the hostilities between him and his Byzantine rivals. In 1353 Ecumenical Patriarch Kallistos excommunicated Dušan, Joanikije, and the Serbian Church as a whole.

Dušan's empire, however, was short-lived. Upon his death in 1355, his successors began to compete for different parts of his realm, while the simultaneous Ottoman advance into southeastern Serbia proved unstoppable. Some degree of reconciliation between the Serbian Church and the ecumenical patriarchate was achieved under Dušan's eventual successor, Prince (popularly called Tsar) Lazar Hrebljanović, although the precise details of this reconciliation remain unclear. The Serbian state gradually collapsed between the Battle of the Maritsa in 1371, the famous Kosovo battle of 1389, and the final fall of the last Serbian capital, Smederevo, in 1459. The patriarchate of Peć itself became vacant with the death of Patriarch Arsenije II in 1463.

Cultural Heritage of Serbian Orthodoxy

Although the medieval Serbian state drew most of its spiritual and cultural inspiration from the Byzantine Empire and the Orthodox East, Serbia's geographical location ensured that it would also be significantly affected by intellectual and artistic influences from the West. In the late 9th and early 10th centuries the Serbs had already adopted a modified version of the Glagolithic script devised by Sts. Cyril and Methodios. The new version, known as Cyrillic, was created by St. Clement of Ohrid. Many of the earliest written works produced in Serbia in the medieval period were based on translations of various Greek (or in some cases, Bulgar) biblical, patristic, and liturgical texts.

In later centuries, influences from the Latin West and Old Muscovy became more apparent. Monasteries built during the 12th and 13th centuries, such as Studenica (founded in 1190), represent a particularly Serbian blend of both Byzantine and Romanesque architectural styles which became known as the Raška School, described as a style linking "Latin rationalism with Greek mysticism" (Peić 1994: 29). Thus, Serbian monasteries during this period were frequently built by Adriatic stonemasons, while the frescoes inside the churches were drawn by Greek painters. The frescoes of this period, most especially in monasteries such as Studenica and Sopoćani, are frequently described as "monumental," in the sense that themes such as the crucifixion are often 8–10 feet tall.

In the 14th century, partly under the influence of the Palaeologue Revival in Constantinople, Serbian art and architecture evolved into a more purely Byzantine/Orthodox form. Monasteries such as Gračanica (built 1313) were constructed using the standard Greek cross floor plan, with anywhere from one to five domes. The years before and after the famous Battle of Kosovo in 1389 saw a final flourishing of Serbian art exhibiting many indigenous qualities in which Roman and Byzantine influences were less obvious. This new style came to be known as the Morava School. Examples of the Morava School include Ravanica (built 1375), Kalenić (ca. 1407), and Manasija (also known as Resava, ca. 1407).

As throughout medieval Europe, monasteries in the Serbian lands served both as spiritual centers and as centers of great learning and artistic creativity. Thus, Serbian monasteries were frequently multipurpose enterprises, incorporating icon studios, woodworking shops, scriptoria for producing and reproducing Bibles, liturgical texts, and biographies of the saints, and medical centers.

Serbian Church Under Ottoman and Habsburg Rule

The demise of the medieval Serbian state in the 14th and 15th centuries, and the imposition of Ottoman rule in the Balkans, significantly changed the position and role of the Orthodox Church in Serbian society. The Ottoman *millet* system was a form of indirect rule and corporate self-government by ethno-confessional groups first established in 1454 by Sultan Mehmet II after the fall of Constantinople. The *millet* system has been described by Sugar (1977: 44) as "basically a minority home-rule policy based on religious affiliation," whose roots can be found in Ottoman rule in Sassanid Iran, and even in some of Justinian's edicts concerning Jews in the Byzantine Empire. Sugar notes that under the *millet* system:

> Besides full ecclesiastical powers and jurisdiction, the patriarch acquired legal powers in those cases, such as marriage, divorce, and inheritance, that were regulated by canon law.... certain police powers that even included a patriarchal jail in Istanbul. Naturally, the church was also permitted to collect the usual ecclesiastical dues, but it was also made responsible and was often consulted in the assessing and collecting of taxes due the state. Finally, ecclesiastical courts had the right to hear and decide cases in which all litigants were Christians, provided they voluntarily submitted their cases to church courts rather than to the kadi. (Sugar 1977: 46)

In the Serbian case, somewhat paradoxically, the practical result of the *millet* system was that the church became a more powerful institution among the Serbian people under the Ottomans than it had been while the Serbs had their own native rulers, with the Serbian people's ecclesiastical leaders henceforth becoming their secular leaders as well.

Historical records of this period in Serbian Church history are scarce. Soon after the fall of Smederevo, in 1463 the Ottoman state abolished the patriarchate of Peć and ecclesiastical authority over the Serbs was turned over to the archbishop of Ohrid. Some one hundred years later, however, the rise to power of a Bosnian Serb boy, Mehmet Paşa Sokollu (in Serbian, Mehmet Paša Sokolović, 1506–79) to the position of grand vizier of the empire would lead to the reestablishment of the patriarchate of Peć in 1557, when Sokollu installed his relative Makarije Sokolović as Orthodox Serbian patriarch. Territorially, the reestablished patriarchate of Peć stretched from southern Hungary in the north to Macedonia in the south, and from the Dalmatian coast (as far north as Šibenik) to parts of western Bulgaria in the east.

The existence of the Peć patriarchate provided the Serbs with a symbolic reminder of their lost medieval state, and was consequently a natural focal point for Serb insurrections against the Ottoman Empire. During this period, monasteries frequently served as natural places for insurrections to be planned and proclaimed. In April 1594, to discourage further Serb revolts, Turkish troops removed the relics of St. Sava from Mileševo Monastery and burned the remains on the site of Vračar, one of Belgrade's most prominent hills. The Serbian Orthodox Church since the 19th century had plans to build a monumental memorial temple to St. Sava on the site. Construction began after World War I, but completion was delayed by World War II and then by the communist government. In the late 1980s work resumed in earnest, and today construction on the Temple of Saint Sava (*Hram Svetog Save*) has been completed. It is one of the largest Orthodox Churches in the world.

The Ottoman conquest of Southeastern Europe had another important effect on the Serbian Orthodox Church, inasmuch as large numbers of Serbs fleeing Ottoman rule spread the Serbian Church territorially and jurisdictionally to many parts of the Habsburg Empire as well. From the 15th century onwards, large-scale migrations pushed the Serbs from their historic religious and cultural homelands in Kosovo, Montenegro, and the Sandzak, northwards to the Krajina in central and western Croatia, and the Vojvodina region north of Belgrade, bounded by the Danube and Tisa rivers.

One of the most important of the Serb revolts under Turkish rule occurred in 1690, when Patriarch Arsenije (Crnojević), seeing a strategic opportunity arise after the Habsburgs went to war with the Ottoman Empire, decided to support the Austrians in a bid to liberate the Serbs from Ottoman rule. The Ottomans, however, ultimately proved successful in the conflict, as a result of which Arsenije led a legendary "Great Migration" of several tens of thousands of Serbs from present-day Kosovo and Metohija northwards into Habsburg territory.

As a result of centuries of Ottoman persecution and out-migrations, by the 18th century the Serbian Church under Turkish rule had become a very weak institution. In 1766 the patriarchate of Peć was again abolished, whereupon the Serbian Church in the Ottoman Empire again fell under the jurisdiction of the ecumenical patriarch, beginning a period of attempted Hellenization of the Serbian Church led by Greek Phanariot bishops. Ultimately, however, these efforts made little headway because of the social and cultural distance between the Greek hierarchy and lower-ranking Serb clerics and laity.

In the Habsburg Empire during this same period, the Serbs populated what became known as the "Military Frontier" (*vojna krajina*) of the Habsburg territories, where they enjoyed special forms of self-government in return for serving as full-time soldiers protecting the imperial borders. Importantly, the Habsburgs adopted many features of the *millet* system, insofar as the Serbs' spiritual and ecclesiastical authorities again became intermediaries between the Habsburg monarch and their own people in secular matters. The Serbian Church organization in the Habsburg monarchy was centered on the metropolitan of (Sremski) Karlovac, which in 1710 the patriarch of Peć, Kalinik I, recognized as autonomous. In 1848, during the general uprisings against absolutism in the Habsburg monarchy, a Serb revolt against Magyar rule proclaimed the metropolitan of Karlovci, Josif Rajačić, as "patriarch." His successors continued to use that title until 1913, although the metropolitans of Karlovci are not generally considered to be successors to the patriarchs of Peć.

The Serbian Church in Montenegro developed along somewhat different lines. Given Montenegro's forbidding geography, after the Battle of Kosovo in 1389 Serbian religious and even political life was able to continue in somewhat freer circumstances, and with considerable autonomy. Although in the 18th century Montenegro was essentially composed of a collection of extended mountain clans formed into "tribes," a rudimentary form of state, led by the metropolitan of Montenegro, continued the Serbian state traditions from the Nemanjić period and drew its legitimacy and inspiration from them. By the 18th century, Montenegro had evolved into a form of theocracy in which secular power was passed down from the metropolitan (who, by tradition, came from the Petrović-Njeguši clan) to his nephew. By tradition, the Montenegrin prince-bishops went to Moscow for their consecration. The greatest of these religious-secular rulers, Bishop Petar II Petrović Njegoš, became one of the greatest poets of the South Slavs. By the mid-19th century, however, Montenegro's

hereditary theocracy died out, and a more formal secular government was formed.

Liberation and Reunification

As the Ottoman Empire began a slow but steady decline in the latter part of the 17th century, the Balkan Christian peoples again began to contemplate their liberation from Turkish rule. In 1804 the Serbs began the first Balkan Christian revolt under the leadership of Djordje "Karadjordje" Petrović. Although Karadjordje's insurrection was defeated after a few years, in 1815, the Serbs launched a second, ultimately more successful insurrection under the leadership of Miloš Obrenović. By 1830 the sultan was forced to recognize Serbian autonomy, and with it religious autonomy; henceforth, the Serbs would be allowed to elect their own metropolitans and bishops, who were only required to go to Constantinople for their consecration by the ecumenical patriarch.

At the Congress of Berlin in 1875 the Serbian principality was recognized as an independent state, and consequently, in 1879, the ecumenical patriarch granted the church in Serbia proper full autocephaly. Nevertheless, the various branches of the Serbian Church still found themselves disunited during this period. The Serbs in Bosnia and Herzegovina were still under the spiritual authority of the ecumenical patriarch in Constantinople, while the Serbian Church organizations in Austria-Hungary and Montenegro had *de facto* (although not canonical) autocephaly.

The full reunification of the Serbian Orthodox Church only became possible after World War I, with the collapse of the Austro-Hungarian and Ottoman Empires, and the creation of the Kingdom of Serbs, Croats and Slovenes (renamed the Kingdom of Yugoslavia in 1929). In 1919 the ecumenical patriarch recognized the will of the Serbian Orthodox jurisdictions within the new kingdom to unite in one church organization, and in 1920 the modern patriarchate of Serbia was proclaimed. The first modern Serbian patriarch, Dimitrije, assumed the title "Archbishop of Peć, Metropolitan of Belgrade-Karlovci, and Serbian Patriarch."

World War II

The Axis invasion and dismemberment of Yugoslavia in April 1941 led to one of the most difficult periods in the history of the Serbian Orthodox Church. Under Nazi sponsorship, a political puppet *Nezavisna Država Hrvatska* ("Independent State of Croatia," hereafter, NDH) was created which incorporated most of present-day Croatia, Bosnia and Herzegovina, and parts of Vojvodina. An extreme fascist group, the Ustaša, were brought to power in the NDH, and initiated what proved to be one of World War II's most horrific reigns of terror. Tens of thousands of Serbs, Jews, Roma, and anti-fascist Croats were liquidated in the NDH during World War II, with the Serbian Church becoming a special target of the Ustaša. The Ustaša-led NDH was a criminal regime of almost incomprehensible brutality, mainly targeted against the Orthodox population of Croatia and Bosnia and Herzegovina. The Roman Catholic bishop of Mostar, Monsignor Alojzije Mišić, communicated some of these crimes against the Serb population of Herzegovina to the archbishop of Zagreb, Alojzije Stepinac, in a letter in August 1941:

> Men are captured like animals. They are slaughtered, murdered; living men are thrown off cliffs…. From Mostar and Čapljina a train took six carloads of mothers, young girls, and children ten years of age to the station of Šurmanci. There they were made to get off the train, were led up to the mountains, and the mothers together with the children were thrown alive off steep precipices. In the parish of Klepci 700 schismatics from the surrounding villages were murdered. Must I continue this enumeration? In the town of Mostar itself, they have been bound by the hundreds, taken in wagons outside the town, and there shot down like animals. (Tomasevich 2001: 57)

Together with the general Serb Orthodox population of the NDH, Serb hierarchs and clerics were also especially targeted by the Ustaša regime. The ferocity of the Ustaša attack on the Serbian Orthodox Church can be seen in the following figures: in April 1941 the Serbian Orthodox Church had eight bishops and 577 priests in the territories which comprised the NDH. By the end of 1941, three bishops and 154 priests had been killed outright, while three bishops and some

340 priests were expelled from the NDH or fled of their own accord. It is estimated that only approximately eighty-five Serbian Orthodox priests remained on NDH territory by the end of 1941. Nor did the Ustaša spare the physical and material infrastructure of the church. For instance, in the Orthodox diocese of Plaški-Karlovac alone, of the 189 Orthodox churches in that bishopric, the Ustaša destroyed eighty-eight and badly damaged a further sixty-seven.

Serbia itself was divided and occupied by Nazi Germany and its fascist allies, Hungary and Bulgaria. To further weaken popular resistance to Nazi rule, the Nazis deported the Serbian Patriarch Gavrilo (Dožić) and interned him in the Dachau concentration camp during the war, along with Bishop Nikolai (Velimirović), generally considered the most important Serbian theologian of the 20th century.

The Serbian Orthodox Church in Bulgarian-occupied southeast Serbia, Kosovo, and Macedonia was also persecuted. The Bulgarian occupying forces in these regions expelled Orthodox clerics considered to be Serbs, including the metropolitan of Skopje, Josif. In the parts of Kosovo and Macedonia annexed to the Nazi-sponsored "Greater Albania," the church administration was incorporated into the expanded Albanian Orthodox Church. Many of these changes were reversed after the war, however, as with the victory of Tito's communist movement, Yugoslavia was reestablished in its prewar borders, and some attempt was made to go back to the official *status quo ante* in these areas.

Nevertheless, the war and the communist takeover of Yugoslavia did have long-lasting repercussions for the Serbian Orthodox Church. In Bosnia and Herzegovina and Croatia, the Ustaša persecution of the Serbs and the Serbian Orthodox Church poisoned interethnic relations in ways that would become all too apparent two generations later. But World War II also had repercussions in places such as Macedonia. In October 1943, in the middle of World War II, a communist-sponsored organizing committee for church affairs in Macedonia was held which marked the first move by Macedonian clerics to break with the Serbian Orthodox Church. This meeting was followed by a National Church Assembly held in Skopje in March 1945, which, among other things, called for reestablishing the ancient archbishopric of Ohrid, making the Macedonian Church autocephalous, and insisted that only Macedonian nationals be allowed to serve as bishops and clerics in Macedonia.

Communist Rule

Due to its immense human and material losses during World War II, and the opposition many church hierarchs exhibited to the Nazi occupation, the Serbian Orthodox Church emerged from World War II with considerable prestige. Yugoslavia's postwar communist regime, led by Josip Broz Tito, however, came to power with the intent of severely limiting the role of religious organizations in the state. Toward this end, various proscriptions were placed on the activities of the Serbian Orthodox Church, as well as on other religious communities in the country. These included placing limits on the construction of new church buildings (or limiting the reconstruction of churches destroyed during the war). The most famous example of such legal and bureaucratic persecution and harassment was the placing of various obstacles in the way of completing the construction of the Temple of St. Sava in Belgrade.

The church's life in communist Yugoslavia was also affected by such things as a ban on religious education in schools and limitations on the ability of refugees to return to their prewar homes. This was particularly the case with respect to Kosovo and Metohija, where the communist government prevented tens of thousands of Serbs who had lived in Kosovo before 1941 from returning, effectively shifting the demographic balance in the province decisively in favor of the Albanian (Muslim) population.

Tito's communist government also attempted to weaken the Serbian Orthodox Church by promoting various schisms within it. In this it was somewhat successful. The most important example of such efforts was government pressure and support for the creation of the Macedonian Orthodox Church. In the general exhaustion and confusion of the immediate postwar years, relations between the Serbian Orthodox Church and the church in Macedonia were tenuous, but in 1957 Macedonian clerics recognized the Serbian patriarch as their head. The reconciliation was only nominal, however, and in July 1967 church

leaders in Macedonia formally broke with the Serbian patriarchate, declared their church autocephalous, and elected the archbishop of Ohrid and metropolitan of Macedonia as the leader of the "Macedonian Orthodox Church." Neither the Serbian patriarchate nor other Orthodox Churches around the world, however, recognized this as a move that was canonically valid.

In the 1960s the Serbian Orthodox Church was also afflicted by a schism in its overseas dioceses, primarily those in Western Europe and the United States, the basis of which could largely be found in postwar anti-communist émigré politics. Although only a minority of the Serbian churches abroad supported the clergy who accepted the break with the Serbian patriarchate, the schism nevertheless proved to be a long, costly, and painful problem for the church.

After Communism and the Yugoslav Wars

The fall of communism throughout Eastern Europe marked the beginning of the Serbian Orthodox Church's reemergence as a major social, cultural, and even political force in Serbia. Unfortunately, this was also the precise historical moment at which the former Yugoslavia began to collapse amid widespread interethnic violence. The Serbian Church found itself in an especially challenging situation, most especially because it had adherents and churches in all of Yugoslavia's republics and provinces.

The most difficult situation confronting the church was in Croatia and Bosnia and Herzegovina. As noted above, these two Yugoslav republics had together comprised most of the World War II "Independent State of Croatia," and the survivors of the NDH genocide against the Serbs were particularly alarmed that the political and security guarantees they enjoyed in Yugoslavia would be eliminated or reduced in the newly independent states, where Serbs would constitute a distinct minority *vis-à-vis* the Croats in Croatia and the Muslims in Bosnia and Herzegovina.

During the wars in Bosnia and Herzegovina, Croatia, and Kosovo, the Serbian Orthodox Church and its hierarchs had to walk a fine line between defending the legitimate interests of their flock while at the same time avoiding dangers of becoming an overtly nationalist organization that engaged in dealings with actual or perceived war criminals. Some members of the clergy managed to navigate successfully and honorably through those times; the behavior of others was more questionable. Undoubtedly, however, the most famous denunciation of the wars in Bosnia and Croatia, and of the nationalistic excesses that accompanied them, was made by Patriarch Pavle, who said during this period:

> If a "Greater Serbia" has to be maintained through crime, I would never accept that. Let Greater Serbia disappear, but to maintain it through crime, never. If it would be necessary and needed for Little Serbia to be maintained through crime, I would not accept that either. Let Little Serbia disappear as well, rather than having it exist through crime. And if we would have to maintain the last Serb, and I was that Serb, but to do it through crime, I do not accept that, let us cease to exist, but let us cease to exist as human beings, because then we will not cease to exist, we will as living beings go into the arms of the living God.

One of the most delicate balancing acts of all concerned the Serbian Orthodox Church's position *vis-à-vis* the regime of Slobodan Milošević, president of Serbia. As early as 1992, many Serbian Church officials, most prominently the bishop of Zahumlje-Hercegovina, Atanasije (Jevtić), had publicly called on Milošević to resign. Other members of the church hierarchy, however, were more sympathetic to Milošević and his regime (Bardos 1992). Nevertheless, most of the church opposed Milošević, and during the 1990s many opposition leaders in Serbia sought the church's support for their efforts.

Persecution in Kosovo and Metohija

Throughout the 20th century the Serbian Orthodox Church's position in Kosovo had been especially threatened. Albanian–Serb relations have been exceptionally hostile, with the two groups taking turns at being the oppressor and the oppressed as historical circumstances have varied. The rise in Albanian nationalism after Tito's death in 1980 marked the start of a new period of persecution for the Serbian Orthodox Church and Serbian Orthodox Christians in Kosovo. Throughout the 1980s, extremists engaged in various forms of harassment and intimidation against the Serbs in Kosovo, such as stealing livestock or engaging in various forms of verbal and physical harassment. In 1981 arsonists set part of the patriarchate of Peć on fire, and a few years later the bishop of Raška-Prizren, Pavle (later to become patriarch of the Serbian Church), was beaten on the streets so severely by youths that he had to spend several weeks in hospital.

Albanian–Serb tensions finally exploded into full-scale violence in 1998, and in March 1999 the North Atlantic Treaty Organization (NATO) initiated a three-month bombing campaign of the Federal Republic of Yugoslavia to wrest control of the province of Kosovo from Serbia. During the conflict, Serb government and paramilitary forces expelled tens of thousands of Albanians from the province and destroyed or damaged dozens of mosques. Under the terms of United Nations Security Council Resolution 1244, in June 1999 the conflict came to an end, and the UN, together with NATO, assumed responsibility for governing Kosovo.

During the UN–NATO occupation of Kosovo, some 200,000 Serb Orthodox Christians have been driven from Kosovo by ethnic extremists. Most of the remaining Serb Orthodox population in Kosovo lives in what are essentially ethnic ghettoes. During this time, over 130 Serbian Orthodox monasteries and churches have been destroyed, along with numerous cemeteries and other church properties. In just one outburst of anti-Serb pogroms in March 2004, extremists destroyed approximately thirty Orthodox churches, including priceless monuments of Byzantine culture in the Balkans, such as the Church of the Virgin Mother in Prizren. In February 2008, Albanian authorities in Kosovo unilaterally declared independence according to the terms of a plan drawn up by former Finnish president Marti Ahtisaari. The so-called "Ahtisaari Plan" provides for significant self-government of the Serb population in Kosovo and includes various protections for the Orthodox religious and cultural sites in Kosovo, but it remains to be seen whether and how these protections will be implemented in practice.

Future Challenges and Prospects

In November 2009 the highly respected and much beloved patriarch of Serbia, His Holiness Pavle, died after a long illness. In January 2010 the holy assembly of bishops of the Serbian Orthodox Church elected the bishop of Niš, Irinej, as Pavle's successor to the throne of the Orthodox Archbishopric of Peć, Metropolitan of Belgrade-Karlovci, and Serbian Patriarch.

Patriarch Irinej's early pronouncements suggest that the Serbian Church is ready to take some decisive steps on two issues of some debate within the church over the past several years. The first concerns promoting a rapprochement with the Roman Catholic Church. The late Pope John Paul II had been keenly interested in making a pilgrimage to Serbia, but many Serbian Church hierarchs opposed such a visit until the Vatican issued some form of acknowledgment or apology to the Serbian Orthodox Church for the role played by Catholic clerical officials in the genocide committed against the Serbs in the NDH during World War II. Upon assuming office, Patriarch Irinej suggested the possibility that John Paul II's successor, Pope Benedict XVI, might be invited to Serbia in 2013 to attend the commemoration of the 1,700th anniversary of Constantine the Great's proclamation of the Edict of Milan in Constantine's birthplace, the Serbian city of Niš. While it remains to be seen whether an official invitation to Pope Benedict will ultimately be issued, the fact that senior church officials are now suggesting such an invitation would be possible indicates that resistance to such a papal visit to Serbia is eroding.

Patriarch Irinej is also believed to be eager to resolve the long-running dispute with the Macedonian Orthodox Church. As bishop of Niš, Irinej had been personally involved in the near-successful negotiations in that city with Macedonian Church officials in 2002 to resolve the uncanonical status of the Macedonian Church and bring it back into communion with the Serbian Church and the rest of the Orthodox world. Patriarch Irinej's initial public statements suggest that the Serbian Church is ready to devote more effort to the problem of relations with the Macedonian Church than had

been possible during Patriarch Pavle's illness. The persistent persecution by Macedonian authorities of Archbishop Jovan of Ohrid, who has remained in canonical unity with the Serbian Church, nevertheless suggests that finding a compromise solution will remain difficult. Because of the Macedonian government's persistent attacks on him, Archbishop Jovan has been named a prisoner of conscience by Amnesty International.

Patriarch Irinej is also firmly committed to defending the Serbian Orthodox Church's existence and position on Kosovo and Metohija. In recent years, church hierarchs in Kosovo have been fiercely divided among themselves over how best to deal with both international officials in Kosovo and with the Albanian authorities there. More focused leadership on the part of the patriarch and the holy synod in Belgrade may help the church develop a more coherent policy on these issues.

The Serbian Orthodox Church also has to deal with a minor schism in Montenegro, where a so-called "Montenegrin Orthodox Church" has been proclaimed by a few defrocked clergy. The schismatic Montenegrin organization has no canonical standing and little popular acceptance. Even after Montenegro declared its independence in June 2006, for instance, the Serbian Orthodox Church in Montenegro, represented by the metropolitanate of Montenegro and the Littoral, continues to be one of the most widely respected institutions in Montenegro. Nevertheless, extremists within the schismatic organization regularly try to occupy churches and other properties belonging to the Serbian Church.

In many ways, the 20th century has proved to be one of the most turbulent and traumatic episodes in the history of the Serbian Orthodox Church. During the first decade of the 21st century the church entered somewhat calmer waters, but it still faces numerous challenges. It does so, however, with its reputation as the most trusted institution among the Serbian people largely intact.

SEE ALSO: Constantinople, Patriarchate of; Mount Athos; Russia, Patriarchal Orthodox Church of; Sts. Constantine (Cyril) (ca. 826–869) and Methodios (815–885)

References and Suggested Readings

Alexander, S. (1979) *Church and State in Yugoslavia since 1945*. Cambridge: Cambridge University Press.

Bardos, G. N. (1992) "The Serbian Church Against Milosevic," *RFE/RL Research Report* 1, 31 (July 31).

Mileusnić, S. (1996) *Duhovni genocide, 1991–95*. Belgrade: Muzej Srpske Pravoslavne Crkve.

Pavlovich, P. (1989) *The History of the Serbian Orthodox Church*. Toronto: Serbian Heritage Books.

Peić, S. (1994) *Medieval Serbian Culture*. London: Alpine Fine Arts Collection.

Perica, V. (2002) *Balkan Idols: Religion and Nationalism in Yugoslav States*. New York: Oxford University Press.

Slijepčević, D. (1962) *Istorija Srpske Pravoslavne Crkve*, vols. 1–3. Belgrade: Bigz.

Slijepčević, D. (1969) *Srpska Pravoslavna Crkva, 1219–1969*. Belgrade: Sveti Arhijerejski Sabor Srpske Pravoslavne Crkve.

Sugar, P. (1977) *Southeastern Europe under Ottoman Rule, 1354–1804*. Seattle: University of Washington Press.

Tomasevich, J. (2001) *War and Revolution in Yugoslavia: Occupation and Collaboration, 1941–45*. Stanford: Stanford University Press.

Velimirović, N. (1989) *The Life of St. Sava*. Crestwood, NY: St. Vladimir's Seminary Press.

Sexual Ethics

MARIA GWYN MCDOWELL

Human beings are sexual; human bodies are places where love, affection, and respect are often accompanied by physical desire; places, therefore, of both great joy and struggle. Orthodoxy recognizes the tension which often exists between love, desire, and respect. Questions of sexual ethics are dependent on an understanding of the human person as participating in an ongoing transformation into the likeness of God, one that includes joy and blessing as well as sin and repentance As unique, irreducible, and dynamic spiritual realities, personhood and relationship cannot be reduced to matters of "natural" or civil law. The pertinent questions for ethical decision-making are who am I/we becoming and how does a particular relationship, sexual behavior, or action enable me/us to be more like God; that is, to better love God and neighbor.

Modern Orthodox sexual ethics must honestly confront an ambiguous past history. While the written tradition has known outspoken defenders of the body and the value of sexual relations in the context of marriage, it has produced many detractors as well. Nor can we ignore the fact that while both men and women are ostensibly called to the same standards of virtue and sexual integrity, double standards existed and still exist which uncritically accepted preexisting cultural assumptions about women's weakness and supposedly greater struggle for virtue, which over-sexualized women and meted out harsher penalties for wrongdoing. This imbalance has not gone unnoticed by the tradition, but the misogyny pervasive in Late Antique and Byzantine cultures nonetheless affected the development and application of much Orthodox canon law, theology, and pastoral care. This is especially important to bear in mind as Orthodoxy now makes its home in western cultures and encounters feminist insights regarding the shared dignity of men and women, and new opportunities for articulating gender roles and responsibilities. Reenvisioning such roles must grapple with the difficulty engendered by phrases such as the "Manly-woman of God," something that was meant as a compliment in Late Antique discourse but which is completely lost on women today.

Discerning pastoral care is increasingly important in the Orthodox Church to modify rhetorically extreme views of sex and the body. It is increasingly important to move beyond a dominant monastic frame of discourse and acknowledge loving marital relationships as God-given and potentially deifying. Comparing the early with the late works of both Gregory of Nyssa and John Chrysostom evinces this shift from an initial idealization of virginity to a recognition of the life-giving potential of faithful, married intercourse. The early work of these fathers begins in the ascetic abstract ideal, but new-found pastoral involvements faced them with the grief and life-giving joy that marriage brought to their congregants. Consequently their attitudes shifted. It is paradigmatic of attitude changes Orthodoxy needs to articulate again.

Orthodox canon law regarding sexual behavior was developed mainly to address problematic behavior. It is not a manual of good practice, therefore, but an indication of appropriate boundaries. Further, given the contextual nature of the canons, their application in varying social contexts and relationships requires the careful exercise of discernment and compassionate application by all parties involved (the tradition of *oikonomia*).

Sexual expression is a way of one child of God relating to another, and the same criteria for Christian relationships (that is, the treating one another as "neighbor," granting love, dignity, respect, and joy to the other) govern sexual behavior. Pornography, prostitution, domestic abuse, and sexual exploitation of any kind deny and deface the image of God in another person. Sexual relations are best entered into, articulated, and sustained through relationships committed to all these elements. Orthodoxy always presumes a faithful marriage as the place of settlement where all this happens under a covenantal blessing.

Marriage is intended as a means to deification. Families are characterized as a "domestic church." Children are a blessing and parenthood is a respected and vital task. This ethos of respect underlies Orthodox critiques of social movements and systems which denigrate, or make difficult, motherhood or fatherhood. Traditionally, contraception has been forbidden by Orthodox teachers; not only because of the value of children and the issue of love's openness to life, but because in Antiquity contraceptives were largely synonymous with abortofacients. Non-abortofacient contraception, possible today, allows for discerning family planning. Couples who choose to plan or limit their families are unfortunately often still characterized as selfish by some Orthodox theologians; but even so *oikonomia* respects that many factors contribute to the decision and ability to bear or adopt children.

The church holds that life begins at conception. Modern science recently has greatly contributed to the understanding of the process of human life's development, but does not indicate when personhood is granted by God and the community to the child. Abortion has been consistently rejected by Orthodox tradition, and is frequently referred to as murder for which canon law prescribes a period of excommunication as penance. However, the church also recognizes that threats to the life of the mother, abject poverty, and the helplessness of women often complicate the ethical dimensions of what many portray as a simple issue. Orthodox pastoral practice is widely experienced on the individual level as being compassionate to parents who have been involved with abortions and repent of it. Further, modern Orthodoxy recognizes that social circumstances often aggravate beginning-of-life decisions, and advocates for the creation of conditions that protect parenthood, encourage adoption, and generally address dire circumstances of life, of which abortion is a symptom, not a cause.

The cultural androcentrism of Orthodoxy is particularly evident in some liturgical practices, especially those for miscarriage and the churching of infants. Traditionally, miscarriage has been attributed to a mother's sinfulness and forgiveness is requested on her behalf. Likewise the rite of the forty-day presentation of a newborn prays for the restoration of purity to the mother, strongly implying that the birth process renders her unclean and defiled. The longstanding dispute regarding women not receiving the Eucharist during *menses* reflects an ancient social context in which blood and purity held significantly different meanings to those they have today. Many priests now modify prayers to remove elements which impute sin or project shame or wrongdoing on women and parents involved in these moments, and some priests church male and female babies identically: either bringing both of them, or neither of them, into the altar area. The 20th century has seen increased conversation among the Orthodox regarding the whole issue of women's place in the church's ministries, and the related issues of how sexuality and gender stand in need of extensive reconsideration in the church today, in the light of how different philosophical and social conditions illuminate in new ways the ancient yet ever fresh and responsive Orthodox tradition of the appropriation of the gospel.

SEE ALSO: Bioethics, Orthodoxy and; Chastity; Deaconess; Deification; Ethics; Fasting; Humanity; Original Sin; Repentance; Women in Orthodoxy

References and Suggested Readings

Council of Russian Bishops (2000) *The Orthodox Church and Society: The Basis of the Social Concept of the Russian Orthodox Church*.

Guroian, V. (2002) *Incarnate love: Essays in Orthodox Ethics*. Notre Dame: University of Notre Dame Press.

Sin *see* Original Sin; Soteriology

Sinai, Autocephalous Church of

JOHN A. MCGUCKIN

One of the most venerable monasteries in the Orthodox world, St. Catherine's, is located in a powerfully dramatic setting at the foot of Mount Sinai in Egypt. The great mountain (Jebel Musa) that broodingly hangs over it is a sacred site to three world religions. The rocky area began to be occupied by hermit monks (it was and remains a true wilderness) who occupied caves in the region, and probably had a communal settlement there before the 4th century,

since parts of the present Justinianic site (dating from the 6th century and beyond) already incorporated Constantinian-era fortifications in the innermost buildings.

From ancient times, Sinai, and the monastic community which settled around it, was a major pilgrimage destination for Christians. It is first mentioned in Christian literary sources in the *Voyages of Egeria*, a travelogue written by a western lady (possibly a nun) from the late 4th century. Pilgrims were attracted there to see the site of the Burning Bush, the mountain top where the revelation of the covenant to Moses took place, and also because of the increasing reputation of the monastery's ascetics. Later in the monastery's history its dedication changed from the Transfiguration, and also the Virgin of the Burning Bush (an incarnational typology of the *Theotokos* in

Plate 70   The fortified monastery of St. Catherine at Sinai, built by Emperor Justinian in the 6th century to protect the monastic community who had been living there from the 3rd century. Photo by John McGuckin.

which she was compared to the bush that blazed containing the presence of God but could not be consumed by the flames) to that of St. Catherine the Great Martyr of Alexandria (patron of the "Catherine Wheel"), whose relics were laid in the monastery church and attracted large numbers of medieval pilgrims. The basilical church's apsidal end still contains the small Chapel of the Burning Bush, whose roots were originally here, but whose branches are now cultivated outside the eastern wall of the church so that pilgrims can take souvenir leaves. All entering this chapel still must remove their shoes, as Moses was once commanded by God.

By the late 7th century Sinai had produced (or influenced) some of the leading ascetical theorists of the Christian world, and was "in the mind" of world Orthodox leaders, who patronized it throughout its long history: from the Byzantine emperors, to the Romanian Voivodes, to the last tsar of Russia. The Sinai community first heard rumors of the Bolshevik Revolution of 1917 months afterward, when they were puzzled as to why the usual Romanov tributary caravan of supplies had not reached them from Cairo. One of its higumens was St. John Klimakos, who wrote his 7th-century text *The Ladder of Divine Ascent* for the instruction of the Sinai novices. It remains as one of the charter documents of Orthodox monastic spirituality. Anastasius of Sinai, Stephen, and Neilos are just a few of the other great saints the monastery produced.

By the late 5th century the desert monasteries of Egypt, including Sinai, were suffering increasing depredations from tribal raiders, as the Byzantine hold on the territories was increasingly relaxed. Mount Sinai itself was threatened on several occasions with complete extinction as a Christian settlement, but the

Plate 71   Once the only way into the Sinai monastery was to be wound up in a wicker basket on a rope, into the entrance high up in the wall. Photo by John McGuckin.

Emperor Justinian, with an eye to the venerability of the site, as well as its strategic advantage as a military post, deliberately fortified the buildings in a massive set of works in the 6th century, and stationed a garrison there, resettling several villages of Christians nearby for the service of the monks and the military garrison. Those who remain today as the tiny lay membership of this church often claim to be the descendants of those settlers, though the majority of the Bedouin (especially the Jelabiya tribe) are now Islamic. The architecture at St. Catherine's today is still largely from this period, with some medieval (the old refectory and the bell tower particularly) and modern additions (the rather awful library and monastic cell block in modern concrete). The refectory graffiti has the names of Crusader pilgrims, some of whom went on to scratch their names in other ancient pilgrim sites: the same culprit's handiwork being found scrawled on the walls of St. Antony's Church by the Red Sea, too. Today, St. Catherine's is unique among all Orthodox monasteries for having a small Fatimid mosque built within its grounds (now unused). The local Bedouin who serve the monastery themselves worship in their own mosque not far away from Jebel Musa.

The basilical church with world-renowned 6th-century apsidal mosaics of the transfiguration is one of the most venerable buildings in all the Orthodox world, largely untouched from the time of its first building. The monastery collection of manuscripts and icons is undoubtedly the most ancient and important in the Orthodox world, too. The library not only had some of the most important manuscripts of the New Testament; the *Codex Sinaiticus* for example (which was controversially removed from the site by Tischendorf, and which was probably one of the Pandects that Constantine the Great commissioned for the new churches of Palestine that he was building), but it is probably the most important single library in the world for the history of the binding of books. New manuscripts and icons are still coming to light, even in recent times, and in each instance it causes the textbooks to be rewritten. Sinai contains most of the known surviving pre-Iconoclastic icons that there are, and several of its old collection (including the Sinai Christ, the Sinai St. Peter, the Virgin attended by soldier saints, and the Ladder of Divine Ascent) are among the greatest iconic art pieces in

existence. Today, St. Catherine's is one of the last surviving monasteries of a once flourishing circle of Greek-speaking ascetic sites spread like a pearl necklace across the Middle East.

Sinai, therefore, is justifiably a world heritage center, a veritable jewel box of ancient and wonderful things in terms of art, manuscripts, and relics; but the monks who still live there point also, with a deep sense of satisfaction, to something they hold as even more precious than their treasures, namely their fidelity to the ascetical evangelical life after so many unbroken centuries of witness in the wilderness, which is one of the chief *raisons d'être* of Sinai as an Orthodox holy place apart from its geographical location. From the very beginning, the monks of Sinai kept up livelier relations with the Jerusalem patriarchate (of easier access) than with Alexandria, and eventually this was reflected in the structures of ecclesiastical organization, for Sinai became a monastery under the care of the Jerusalem church. At the height of its flourishing it had *Metochia*, or dependent monasteries and estates, in Egypt, Palestine, Syria, Crete, Cyprus, Romania, and Constantinople, which supported it financially and ensured its effective independence during the long years when (like the Athonite communities) it had to buy the patronage of its Islamic overlords at great expense.

All these important supports eventually eroded, but not before Sinai had more or less successfully asserted its importance and its claims for autonomous governance over and against the patriarchate of Jerusalem, which itself had fallen onto hard times. It's ecclesiastical independence (against the initial grumblings of Jerusalem) was affirmed by the patriarchate of Constantinople in 1575, and confirmed again in 1782. Today, the monks of the community (only a few dozen still resident there) elect one of their own number as the abbot and also as the prospective archbishop of Sinai. The patriarch of Jerusalem always has the right to perform the consecration (which fact, along with the peculiar smallness of the "Church of Sinai," limits its complete claim to autocephaly). After that point, however, the archbishop, with his synaxis, or monastic assembly and council, entirely governs the affairs of the monastery-church. The archbishopric also includes the churches of Pharan and Raithu (by the Red Sea shore) which are now only tiny outlying parish centers, but which were once monasteries of great repute in their own right. Sinai is thus the smallest independent church of the entire Orthodox world: a unique and special instance, poised between autocephalous and autonomous condition. The charnel house at Sinai contains the bones of its many saints and ascetics, piled up rank on rank. As a monastic of the community recently said while introducing visitors to it: "Although we have one of the world's most ancient libraries on site, this is the real library where a Christian must learn about life."

SEE ALSO: Iconography, Styles of; Monasticism

References and Suggested Readings

Galey, J. (2003) *Katherinenkloster auf dem Sinai*. Stuttgart: Belser.

Nelson, R. S. and Collins, K. M. (eds.) (2006) *Holy Image, Hallowed Ground: Icons from Sinai*. Los Angeles: J. P. Getty Museum.

Rossi, C. (2006) *The Treasures of the Monastery of Saint Catherine*. Vercelli, Italy: White Star Press.

Soskice, J. M. (2009) *The Sisters of Sinai: How Two Lady Adventurers Discovered the Hidden Gospels*. London: Chatto and Windus.

Walsh, C. (2007) *The Cult of St. Katherine of Alexandria in Early Medieval Europe*. Aldershot: Ashgate Press.

Weitzmann, K. (1973) *Illustrated Manuscripts at Saint Catherine's Monastery on Mount Sinai*. Collegeville, MN: St. John's University Press.

Weitzmann, K. (1976) *The Monastery of Saint Catherine at Mount Sinai: The Icons*. Princeton: Princeton University Press.

Skoupho *see* Kalymauchion

Solovyov, Vladimir (1853–1900)

KONSTANTIN GAVRILKIN

Russia's most significant religious thinker, Vladimir Solovyov experienced a crisis of faith in his youth but returned to Christianity through the study of philosophy. His teaching career was short: after graduation from Moscow University in 1874, he taught until late March 1881, until the occasion when, during a public lecture, he challenged the government of Alexander III to spare the lives of the terrorists who had assassinated his father, Alexander II, earlier that month. Shortly afterwards, he left university life and dedicated himself to writing.

His early texts focus on western rationalism, and only in the *Lectures on Godmanhood* (1878–81) did he turn to the problems of religion. There he presents the history of humanity as leading inexorably to the incarnation of Divine Logos in the person of Jesus of Nazareth (cf. Alexander Men's *History of Religion*, which was inspired by Solovyov). The next important work, the *Spiritual Foundations of Life* (1882–4), deals with Christology and the sacramental and spiritual life of the church, as well as the realization of salvation in human history. The union of divine and human natures in Christ, or his Godmanhood, given through the church to the world, is viewed by Solovyov not as an abstract principle, but as a living source of political, social, and cultural transformation of the world through a free choice of autonomous human beings. This vision would inform Solovyov's approach to all problems related to Christianity. The assassination of Alexander II, the wave of anti-Jewish pogroms of 1881–2, and the counter-reforms of Alexander III prompted Solovyov's turn to the question of religion and politics. Ancient Israel, Byzantium, Roman Catholicism, Poland, and Russia were interpreted by him as a series of failed theocracies (*The Great Debate and Christian Politics*, 1883; *Jewry and the Christian Question*, 1884; *History and the Future of Theocracy*, 1885–7). At the same time, while raising many of the problems of the later ecumenical dialogue, Solovyov saw relations between Russia and Roman Catholicism in the light of their mutual responsibility for the realization of Christian mission in history (Solovyov 1966–70, Vol. 11).

During the 1880s and 1890s Solovyov wrote extensively on Russian identity, Slavophilism, nationalism (Solovyov 1966–70, Vol. 5), the religious traditions in Judaism, Islam, and China (Solovyov 1966–70, Vol. 6.), Russian literature, and philosophy, especially in relation to the multi-volume *Brockhaus-Ephron Encyclopedic Dictionary*, then appearing, for which he wrote numerous entries as chief author responsible for the philosophy section. In the 1890s he also published his key works: *The Meaning of Love* (1892–4) and the massive *Justification of the Good* (1897), which was his *magnum opus* on ethics. His collection of poetry, including meditations on the encounters with what he called Sophia, the divine feminine (Solovyov 1966–70, Vol. 12), were published in the 1890s as well. Finally, in his last year of his life Solovyov wrote *Three Conversations on War, Progress, and the End of History*, an apocalyptic drama inspired by the philosopher's premonitions of the disasters facing the 20th century.

Although his writings played a key role in the Russian religious renaissance of the 20th century, Solovyov's legacy was viewed rather negatively within conservative ecclesiastical circles because of his sympathy for Roman Catholicism, his mysticism, and his sometimes sharp criticism of the Russian Church and of Slavophilism. While Sophiology has been sometimes attributed to him retrospectively, its significance in Solovyov's own corpus of texts is often overrated.

SEE ALSO: Russia, Patriarchal Orthodox Church of; Sophiology

References and Suggested Readings

Solovyov, S. M. (2001) *Vladimir Solovyov: His Life and Creative Evolution*, trans. A. Gibson. Fairfax, VA: Eastern Christian Publications.

Solovyov, V. S. (1966–70) *Sobranie sochinenii*, 13 vols. Brussels: Zhizn's Bogom.

Sutton, J. (1988) *The Religious Philosophy of Vladimir Solovyov: Towards a Reassessment*. Basingstoke: Macmillan.

Sophiology

JUSTIN M. LASSER

In Orthodox theology Sophia represents an evocation of the mystical apprehension of the divine mysteries in the life of the Godhead and the symphonic apparatus of the cosmos. The term derives from the Greek word for "wisdom" (*Sophia*). It is the Greek translation of the biblical Hebrew concept *Hokhma* (wisdom) in the Old Testament scriptures, which contain a rich and diverse tradition about "divine wisdom" (Deut. 34.9; 2 Sam.

14.20; 1 Kings 4.29; Job 12.13; Ps. 104.24; Prov. 3.19; Prov. 8.22–31; Sirach (Ecclesiasticus) 1.4, 7; 8.34). This tradition was taken up extensively, out of the biblical Wisdom literature, and also with reference to Greek philosophico-religious cosmology, and used by the Logos theologians of the early church to sketch out cosmological Christology. The concept of God's creative wisdom is deeply rooted in many ancient religious cosmologies (not least pre-biblical Egyptian). In their use of Wisdom Christology the fathers followed Greek and Hebrew sages before them in personifying the divine wisdom, hypostatically, under the feminine figure of Sophia. This tradition continued despite the overall preference of the patristic era for the (masculine) equivalent "Logos" (Word or Reason of God) which was used heavily in the conciliar christological tradition. The poetic play between creator and created, as evidenced in the Sophianic Wisdom literature (see Prov. 8.22), precipitated a fierce debate in the 4th-century Arian crisis. It is the ambiguity of Sophia's nature that lends her so easily to theological speculation. Sophiology, although subordinated after the 4th century to the terms of Logos theology, remained a significant part of the Orthodox mystical tradition, and was used to connote the eternal, creative, and preexistent Son of God, who entered into human history at the incarnation, and as "Wisdom of the divine" permeates the substructure of the entire cosmos which that Divine Wisdom personally shaped, and made, into a vehicle of revelation and grace. It is clear from this how pneumatology was closely related to Sophia. In the hands of later Orthodox thinkers (including Sts. Maximos the Confessor and Gregory Palamas) the study of Sophia became an issue of mystical initiation into the communion of the divine life of the Godhead, a way of considering Deification Christology with more of a cosmological stress, an approach that emphasized that true knowledge was not summed up solely in the domain of facts, or Kataphatic discourse, but rather pointed to the way that material realities open out beyond the world to signal the domain of mystical apprehension. In this sense Sophiology is inherently an esoteric venture. Sophiology, as it became increasingly known in later times, became one of the controversial centerpieces of early 20th-century Russian theology in the writings of Solovyov, Berdiaev, Florensky, and Bulgakov. It was Bulgakov who perhaps most made it a central pillar of his theological work, and most explicitly tried to demonstrate its central position in Orthodox dogmatics. It was certainly this aspect of his thought that occasioned most resistance from other Orthodox theologians of his time, not least Georges Florovsky and the Synod of the Russian Church in exile, fearing what they felt was its overly close association with similar esoteric trends in Rosicrucianism and other heterodox gnoseological approaches. Nevertheless, Orthodox understandings of Sophiology differ from gnoseology in this respect, that it stands for a summation of ways of "living in," more than ways of "knowing about," the Godhead. As Fr. Pavel Florensky wrote, Sophia is "not a fact, but an act" (Florensky 1997: 237).

Like her symbol, the great imperial church of Hagia Sophia in Constantinople, Holy Wisdom takes her place at the very center of Orthodox life. It is the Logos, yet it is also the outreach of the Logos to the world, in the intimacy of the human comprehension, as the scripture reveals. Sirach (Ecclesiasticus) 8.34 teaches that Sophia "is an initiate in the mysteries of God's knowledge. She makes choice of the works God is to do." Thus to learn wisdom (*Sophia*) is to be united to God. She exists as *the* choice of God, and yet she makes God's choices. Baruch 3.31–2 declares that "no one knows the way to her, no one can discover the path she treads. But the one who knows all knows her, for God has grasped her with God's own intellect." The Sophiological tradition in Orthodoxy, with various degrees of success, is the continuing contemplation of this ambiguity – the mystical path of the study of wisdom. Sophia is manifested as teacher, bride, lover, and Christ; both as within and without the human mind and soul. To acquire Sophia is not to acquire scientific knowledge but to begin to see the totality of knowledge from the right perspective.

SEE ALSO: Berdiaev, Nikolai A. (1874–1948); Bulgakov, Sergius (Sergei) (1871–1944); Florensky, Pavel Alexandrovich (1882–1937); Florovsky, Georges V. (1893–1979).

References and Suggested Readings

Bulgakov, S. (1993) *Sophia, the Wisdom of God: An Outline of Sophiology*. Library of Russian Philosophy. Great Barrington, MA: Lindisfarne Books.

Donskikh, O. A. (1995) "Cultural Roots of Russian Sophiology," *Sophia* 34, 2: 38–57.

Florensky, P. (1997) *The Pillar and Ground of Truth*, trans. B. Jakim. Princeton: Princeton University Press.

Sergeev, M. (2007) *Sophiology in Russian Orthodoxy: Solov'ev, Bulgakov, Losskii, Berdiaev*. Lewiston, NY: Edwin Mellen Press.

Sophrony, Archimandrite (1896–1993)

JULIA KONSTANTINOVSKY

Archimandrite Sophrony (Sergey Symeonovich Sakharov) was an outstanding Christian Orthodox ascetic, spiritual director, and theologian of the 20th century. Spiritual son of St. Silouan of Athos, Archimandrite Sophrony was the founder in 1959 of the Stavropegic Monastery of St. John the Baptist (Essex, UK) under the jurisdiction of the ecumenical patriarchate of Constantinople. He is the author of several major works on the spiritual and ascetical life in Christ and on Christian personhood, among them *Saint Silouan the Athonite*, *His Life is Mine*, *We Shall See Him As He Is*, and *On Prayer*. An accomplished artist, he also founded a unique school of iconography. Born in Moscow, he then lived most of his life in the West, a revered theologian and elder for the entire Christian world, Orthodox and non-Orthodox alike.

Fr. Sophrony was born into a bourgeois Russian Orthodox family and trained as an artist in the Academy of Arts and Moscow School of Painting, Sculpture, and Architecture. Arriving in Paris in 1922 to further his career, he underwent a profound conversion back to the Christian faith of his childhood, which compelled him to renounce his art and embrace a life of prayer. In 1924 he joined the Russian Saint-Panteleimon Monastery on Mount Athos, spending the next twenty years first as a coenobitic monastic and subsequently a hermit. Ordained to the priesthood in 1941, he acted as father confessor to numerous Athonite monks. After World War II he returned to France to write his highly acclaimed work on Starets Silouan. Enduring health problems prevented him from returning to Athos. Soon, an ascetic community, men and women, gathered around him in Paris. In 1956 it moved to Essex, England, where the present-day Monastery of St. John the Baptist was established.

Influenced by Lossky and Bulgakov, Fr. Sophrony's thought is nevertheless deeply original. Its fundamental principle is Christian personalism, whereby the Person/Hypostasis (*Lichnost'/Ipostas'*) is the *arche* of all being, Uncreated, as well as created. In his essence, the divine Absolute is personal: it is the Trinity of three divine hypostaseis indissolubly united by one common divine essence. This trinitarian principle is kenotic: the three hypostaseis inhere within one another through mutual self-emptying love. God's disclosure of himself as a Person to Moses (Ex. 3.10) is the beginning of all theology, its fulfillment consisting in Christ's self-revelation in his voluntary kenosis "for us men and for our salvation."

There is commensurability between the personal divine being, on the one hand, and the human person, on the other. Christ is the measure of man: just as he reveals and personifies the perfection of divinity and humanity, so equally man is able to comprise the fullness of the human and divine being (the latter by grace, not by nature). Archimandrite Sophrony saw this possibility as the foundation of the human freedom and of man's being in God's image (cf. Gen. 1.26). The following three principles sum up Archimandrite Sophrony's ecclesiology: there is no faith without doctrine; there is no Christianity outside the church; there is no Christianity without asceticism.

SEE ALSO: Elder (Starets); Monasticism; Mount Athos; St. Silouan of Athos (1866–1938)

References and Suggested Readings

Archim. Sophrony (1988) *We Shall See Him As He Is*. Maldon, UK: St. John's Monastery.

Archim. Sophrony (1997) *His Life is Mine*. Crestwood, NY: St. Vladimir's Seminary Press.

Archim. Sophrony (1998) *On Prayer*. Crestwood, NY: St. Vladimir's Seminary Press.

Archim. Sophrony (1999) *Saint Silouan the Athonite*. Crestwood, NY: St. Vladimir's Seminary Press.

Archim. Zacharias (Zacharou) (2003) *Christ, Our Way and Our Life: A Presentation of the Theology of Archimandrite Sophrony*. South Canaan, PA: St. Tikhon's Seminary Press.

Sakharov, N. V. (2002) *I Love Therefore I Am: The Theological Legacy of Archimandrite Sophrony*. Crestwood, NY: St. Vladimir's Seminary Press.

Soteriology

STEPHEN THOMAS

The ecumenical councils of the Orthodox Church do not give a soteriology or doctrine of salvation, but offer rather a rich and exhaustive Christology. Nevertheless, there is a profound soteriology underlying the Christology which the fathers used to support it. The main idea of salvation found in the eastern fathers, as well as western fathers such as Pope St. Leo the Great of Rome, concerns the victory over death which Christ won, and the victory over all the morbid limitations which humanity has acquired though sin, the alienation from God. Orthodox soteriology is extremely hopeful because it thinks of salvation as a victory over the malicious powers exercised by the demons (Heb. 11.35). It has two elements, which complement one another: salvation is, firstly, therapy, and, secondly, deification or divinization.

The victory motif dominates Orthodox liturgical texts, especially in the paschal liturgy. Continually repeated during the paschal season is the following poem: "Christ is risen from the dead, trampling down death by death, and on those in the graves, bestowing life" (*Pentekostarion* 1990: 27).

In Orthodox soteriology sin and death are personified as forces which belong to the sphere of the Devil and the demons, who, through divine respect to their freewill, are still active until the judgment. Christ's voluntary sacrifice on the cross brought the depths of suffering into intimate contact with the divine light, so that suffering could be transfigured and conquered. The victorious Christ descended to Hades, conquered the power of the Devil, and brought out the souls imprisoned there. While this idea is found in medieval Catholicism, in the form of the harrowing of hell, it is not as prominent as it is in the Orthodox services which accord to Holy Saturday an essential role in the process by which Christ saves humankind: "He quenched Death by being subdued by Death. He who came down into Hades despoiled Hades; And Hades was embittered when he tasted of Christ's flesh" (*Pentekostarion* 1990: 37).

Therapy, the dominant Orthodox expression of salvation theology (Larchet 2000), consists of the transformation of the human situation which has been damaged by sin, liberating it from its subordination to corruption, an ephemeral life of passion turned away from God which leads to death. Orthodoxy teaches that humanity was seduced by the Devil at an early stage in its development, and the whole human race contracted illness, which is both spiritual (sin, passion) and physical (illness and death), a malaise not caused or willed by God (Larchet 2002: 17). Particular sins issue from this sickness and are a form of madness or blindness rather than a deliberate revolt, provoking the divine compassion. The union of the divine and human natures in Christ heals the damaged human nature in its root. In these terms St. Athanasius explains why the divine Word and Son of God had to become human: only a divine nature could raise up the human nature (Athanasius 1971: 185). Equally, Christ had to have a human nature: St. Gregory of Nazianzus argues that Christ had to have a human intellect, in addition to the divine mind, because the mind especially was in need of salvation (Hardy 1995: 221). While the cross is the victory, the whole incarnation is saving, since every aspect of the human nature is healed by contact with the divinity, during the course of the Savior's earthly life. The sacraments, or mysteries, heal the various dimensions of human life, the Eucharist having a special place in divinizing the human person through reception of the holy gifts, Christ's deifying body and blood. However, salvation also means more than healing. Salvation is the process of the believer's deification, establishing the likeness to God intended for the original creation. The rays of God's goodness, being uncreated, draw humankind up into the uncreated dimension.

The various theories of the atonement in Catholic and Reformed Christianity, which present a rationale for Christ's death upon the cross, are foreign to Orthodoxy. In *Cur Deus Homo*, Anselm of Canterbury explained the relationship of incarnation to salvation very differently from St. Athanasius. Anselm uses the idea of the infinite offense to the honor of the deity, which Christ put right by his death upon the cross, a sacrifice earning an infinite treasury of merit upon which sinful Man could draw (Anselm 1998: 283).

Calvin thought in terms of the infinite majesty of God and the wrath provoked by human sin, which Christ suffered instead of us. But in Calvinism grace attained by the sacrifice is only received by those who are predestined to receive it; in this sense, the sacrifice is not for all. Orthodoxy, however, teaches that Christ offered "the life-giving and unslain sacrifice" (*Pentekostarion* 1990: 30) for all people. There was no debt required by God to appease his wrath or satisfy justice, and there is no transaction between Father and Son to effect human salvation. In Orthodox soteriology God goes far beyond justice; his mercy is paramount, (Alfeyev 2000: 292–7), still less is there predestination to hell (Isaac of Nineveh 1995: 165). Christ's sacrifice was that he "did not count equality with God a thing to be grasped but emptied himself taking the form of a servant, being born in the likeness of men" (Phil. 2.7). Christ obeyed the Father, becoming "obedient unto death, even death on a cross" (Phil. 2.8), in the sense that he united his will to that of the Father and assumed a human nature in order to heal and deify it: to save it from corruptibility and the sinking into nothingness, by offering Life.

SEE ALSO: Cross; Deification; Ecumenical Councils; Eucharist; Healing; Judgment; Mystery (Sacrament)

References and Suggested Readings

Alfeyev, H. (2000) *The Spiritual World of Isaac the Syrian*. Kalamazoo: Cistercian Publications.

Anselm (1998) *The Major Works*, ed. B. Davies and G. R. Evans. Oxford: Oxford University Press.

Athanasius (1971) *Contra Gentes and De Incarnatione*, ed. and trans. R. W. Thomson. Oxford: Clarendon Press.

Aulen, G. (2003) *Christus Victor*. Eugene, Ontario: Wipf and Stock.

Hardy, E. R. (1995) *The Christology of the Later Fathers*. Philadelphia: Westminster/John Knox Press.

Isaac of Nineveh (1995) *The Second Part*, trans. S. Brock. Louvain: Peeters.

Larchet, J.-C. (2000) *Thérapeutique des maladies spirituelles*. Paris: Cerf.

Larchet, J.-C. (2002) *Theology of Illness*, trans. J. and M. Breck. Crestwood, NY: St. Vladimir's Seminary Press.

Pentekostarion (1990) Boston: Holy Transfiguration Monastery.

Stăniloae, Dumitru (1903–1993)

ARISTOTLE PAPANIKOLAOU

Dumitru Stăniloae was born in Vladeni in the Romanian province of Transylvania. After studying in Romania, Athens, and Germany, Stăniloae began teaching in 1929 at the Theological Institute in Sibiu. Between 1946 and 1973 he taught at the Theological Institute in Bucharest, though between 1958 and 1962 he was incarcerated as a political prisoner at Aiud Prison. Early in his theological career, Stăniloae rejected the Orthodox dogmatic manuals, which he felt, together with his Russian émigré counterparts in Paris, Vladimir Lossky and Georges Florovsky, were under a "western captivity." In his initial theological studies he noticed that the spirituality of hesychasm and the thought of St. Gregory Palamas were offering a different theological vision than that presented in the manuals. His life work is a labor of attempting to articulate an Orthodox dogmatic theology that is existentially relevant and not simply a set of propositional truths. The fruit of this work began with the publication of his study on Palamas, *The Life and Teaching of Gregory Palamas* (1938), and culminated with his three-volume *Orthodox Dogmatic Theology* (1978). Stăniloae was also responsible for translating the *Philokalia* into Romanian (a larger edition by far than that of St. Nikodemos; nine volumes between 1946 and 1980). Up until his death, Stăniloae published numerous books and articles, achieved a national reputation as a public intellectual commenting on the political and cultural issues of Romania, and acquired an internationally recognized ecumenical stature, with his work continuing to exercise influence in both Orthodox and non-Orthodox circles alike. He is one of the best-known, respected, and influential Orthodox theologians of the 20th century.

Among the many theological insights contained within Stăniloae's corpus, two stand out as distinctive. First, Stăniloae insisted that trinitarian theology must articulate more explicitly the proper relation of the Son to the Spirit. Against what he saw as Lossky's separation of the work of the Son and the Spirit, Stăniloae argued that the Spirit proceeds from the Father and rests on the Son as the Father's love for the Son, and is reflected back from the Son to the Father as the Son's active love for the Father. Stăniloae rejects the *filioque* because it inevitably makes the Son a Father of the Spirit, rather than seeing the relation between the Son and the Spirit as a reciprocity that has its source in the Father, and one that allows for humans to share in the Son's filial relationship with the Father. The second distinctive aspect of Stăniloae's theology is his notion of creation as God's gift that initiates the possibility of an exchange of gifts between God and human beings, who function as priests of creation. This exchange of gifts is simultaneously a dialogue of love enabling a personal communion between God and creation. The fact that the world was created for the purpose of communion between the personal God and human persons is not simply a truth of revelation, but is indicated, for Stăniloae, in the iconic human experience of freedom and relationality.

SEE ALSO: *Filioque*; Holy Trinity; *Philokalia*; Romania, Patriarchal Orthodox Church of; St. Gregory Palamas (1296–1359)

References and Suggested Readings

Louth, A. (2002) "The Orthodox Dogmatic Theology of Dumitru Staniloae," *Modern Theology* 13, 2: 253–67.

Neamtu, M. (2006) "Between the Gospel and the Nation: Dumitru Stăniloae's Ethno-Theology," *Archaeus: Studies in History of Religions 10*, 3: 4.

Turcescu, L. (ed.) (2002) *Dumitru Stăniloae: Tradition and Modernity in Theology*. Palm Beach: Center for Romanian Studies.

Turcescu, L. (2005) "Dumitru Stăniloae," in J. Witte and F. Alexander (eds.) *The Teachings of Modern Christianity on Law, Politics, and Human Nature*, 2 vols. New York: Columbia University Press, vol. 1, pp. 685–711; vol. 2, pp. 537–58.

Starets *see* Elder (Starets)

Stavrophore

JOHN A. MCGUCKIN

Greek term signifying "cross-bearer." Its most frequent use is in reference to Orthodox monastics. In the entrance into monastic life there are several degrees. The first level, that of the Novice, can be left freely. The novice will wear the black cassock (*anterion*, *raso*) and headgear (*skouphos*) of the monk, but is not as yet tonsured and takes no vows. After tonsuring the novice is formally given the black habit (*raso*) consisting of the inner cassock with leather belt, the outer clerical robe with wide sleeves, and hat with black veil. He is now known as a Rassophore. If the monk perseveres and reaches a degree of maturity and asceticism deemed appropriate by his higumen (abbot) he may be initiated into a higher degree of monastic life known as the Little Schema. At this time the monastic makes formal vows of stability, poverty, chastity, and obedience, and may receive the more ample form of the outer cassock, along with the monastic mantle, and especially a symbolic garment known as the *paramandyas*. This is a square of black cloth worn on the back, embroidered in red with the instruments of the Passion, and connected by ties to a wooden cross worn over the heart. It symbolizes how the monk must bear the "yoke" of Christ. It is the act of putting on this cross which entitles the monk to be known as Stavrophore or Cross-bearer. The last and highest degree of monastic life is the Great Schema. The term *Stavrophore* can also refer to a priest who is awarded the right to wear a cross as a sign of special honor. In Russian tradition all priests wear the silver cross. A gold cross can be awarded as an honor. The gift of the "jeweled cross" is a significant award of honor to a priest from a bishop. In the non-Russian traditions, only those priests wear the cross who have received it as a special honor from the bishop or patriarch (equivalent to the jeweled cross). In the Greek custom their rank is designated as Oikonomos, in other churches they are known as Stavrophore.

SEE ALSO: Cross

Stethatos, Niketas (ca. 1005–1085)

JOHN A. MCGUCKIN

Niketas is an important but neglected Byzantine writer who composed treatises on mystical prayer, as well as being involved with the troubled relations between Patriarch Michael Caerularios and the papal legates leading up to the rupture of communion between Rome and Constantinople in 1054. Niketas entered the Stoudios monastery as a young man and eventually became its higumen (after 1076). In his youth he met St. Symeon the New Theologian (d. 1022). After the latter's death in exile, he became a dedicated follower, attributing the change to a vision he had of the saint (ca. 1035). He zealously defended Symeon's memory and teaching, publishing and editing his *Discourses* and *Hymns*, as well as composing a Life of the Saint, and arranging for the return of the saint's relics to the capital. In his own spiritual teachings (*Three Centuries of Practical and Gnostic Chapters*) Niketas largely follows Symeon in laying stress on the importance of the gift of tears, and on the role of the spiritual father. He also composed apologetic works against the Latins, the Armenians, and the Jews. In his minor works he often discusses the nature of the soul and the afterlife, and is thought to be part of the wider reaction to controversies initiated by Michael Psellos. Niketas' theology is very aware of the concept of hierarchy as mediated by Pseudo-Dionysius the Areopagite, and in this sense (emphasizing the parallels between heavenly and earthly hierarchy) he moderated Symeon's public hostility to the patriarchate and court. He is influenced by the spiritual tradition of Evagrios Pontike and St. Maximos the Confessor, mixing metaphors of divine union as brilliant illumination, with references to the Dionysian darkness of unknowing. He also has resonances from some of the teaching of Isaac the Syrian. Some think that he gained his nickname *Stethatos* ("big-heart" or "courageous one") because of his criticism in ca. 1040 of the relations between Emperor Constantine IX Monomachos and his mistress Skliraina.

SEE ALSO: Caerularios, Michael (d. 1059); Pontike, Evagrios (ca. 345–399); St. Maximos the Confessor (580–662); St. Symeon the New Theologian (949–1022)

References and Suggested Readings

Niketas (1928) "Vie de s. Syméon le Nouveau Théologien," ed. I Hausherr. *Orientalia Christiana* 12, 45.

Niketas (1961) *Opuscules et lettres*, ed. J. Darrouzes. *Sources Chrétiennes*, vol. 81. Paris.

Niketas (1995) *Centuries of Practical and Gnostic Chapters*, ed. G. Palmer, P. Sherrard, and K. Ware. London: Faber and Faber.

Solignac, A. (1982) "Niketas Stethatos," in *Dictionnaire de spiritualité*, vol. 11. Paris: Beauchesne, pp. 224–30.

Van Rossum, J. (1981) "Reflections on Byzantine Ecclesiology: Niketas Stethatos' *On the Hierarchy*," *St. Vladimir's Theological Quarterly* 25: 75–83.

Volker, W. (1974) "Nicetas Stethatos als mystischer Schriftsteller und sein Verhaltnis zu Symeon dem Neuen Theologen," in *Praxis und Theoria bei Symeon dem Neuen Theologen*. Wiesbaden, pp. 456–89.

Sticharion

VALENTINA IZMIRLIEVA

The sacramental vestment (Russian *Podrizhnik*) worn as an outer garment by deacons and sub-deacons and as the undergarment by bishops and priests. It is a long narrow robe that buttons down both sides and features an embroidered cross on the back. Its symbolic prototypes are Aaron's robe (ποδήρης, Ex. 25.7, 28.4) and Christ's "seamless tunic" (Jn. 19.23). It is usually white, symbolizing purity and the light of divine glory (Rev. 7.14). The priest's garment is covered by the *phelonion* and made of simple white fabric with narrow sleeves tied at the cuff. The wider-sleeved deacon's garb, usually made of brocade, bears decorative stripes that symbolize the power and grace bestowed through Christ's bonds.

SEE ALSO: Phelonion

Sticheron

DIMITRI CONOMOS

An appointed troparion inserted between, and providing poetic commentary on, psalm verses in the course of Byzantine Vespers and Matins. Stichera idiomela are sung to a unique melody; stichera automela function as melodic and metrical patterns for generating stichera with borrowed melodies (*contrafacta*) that are called *prosomoia*. In Byzantine manuscripts, sticheron melodies are generally syllabic; that is, they have one or two notes per syllable, although short melismas may occur on accented syllables or on words or phrases requiring special emphasis. Stichera for major feasts also may have more extensive ornamentation. Cadences are marked by recurring melodic formulae.

SEE ALSO: Idiomelon; Troparion

Stylite Saints

AUGUSTINE CASIDAY

Asceticism in the form of ascending a column (in Greek, *stylos*) and remaining there for extended periods as a "column-dweller" or *stylite* is a distinctive feature of Eastern Christianity. This way of life was pioneered in 5th-century Syria by Simeon the Stylite (ca. 389–459). From the 430s Simeon built his column and gradually extended it to a height of some 16 meters in order to escape the crowds who gathered around him, and to pray. But he did not sever his connections with the faithful. On the contrary, pilgrims came from afar to marvel at Simeon, seeking support and even adjudication of legal and political matters, no less than spiritual guidance from him (Theodoret, *Historia Religiosa* 26.26; Syriac, *Life of Simeon* 56, 60, 77; Brown 1971: 90–1). At least one pilgrim to Simeon's column actually followed his example: Daniel the Stylite (*Life of Daniel* 6, 21). In 460 Daniel (403–93) ascended his pillar near Constantinople, which allowed him to continue exercising influence albeit now within the imperial capital (Brown 1971: 92–3): "The Emperor Zeno is said to have taken his advice" (*Life of Daniel* 55).

Images and pilgrim tokens of the great stylites circulated within their own lifetimes as far away as Rome and Gaul. This probably explains how Walfroy of Carignan (d. 596 or 600) found out about Simeon Stylites. Unique among western ascetics, Walfroy set up a column near Trier, but he was sharply rebuked by bishops who compared him unfavorably to Simeon and then demolished the column to make sure he would not ascend it again (Gregory of Tours, *History of the Franks* 8.15). Walfroy's Byzantine contemporary, Simeon the Younger (521–96), was also precocious and more accepted. He took to a pillar when he was only seven. Some years later, he relocated to the Wondrous Mountain where a monastery formed nearby. Simeon left behind several writings, which may perhaps be compared to the case of the *Chronicle* of the wars between Byzantium and Persia which was purportedly written in 504 by Joshua the Stylite. These few men are the most eminent examples from a "golden age" of stylite asceticism.

From the Iconoclast controversies through the 9th century, the prominence of stylites began to wane. This is not to say that no stylites are found thereafter. We know of Luke the Stylite in the 10th century. Similarly, Lazarus of Mt. Galesios (ca. 972–1053) lived on a pillar near Ephesus where he was surrounded by three monasteries he had founded. And in the 12th century, Nikita the Stylite was a revered figure whose reputation spread from Pereyaslavl throughout the Slavic world. Reverence for stylites, however, was increasingly directed to historical figures of the past. So, for instance, in *The Travels of Macarius* 4.7.1, Paul of Aleppo reports on the Muscovites' special devotion to Simeon the Stylite on the first day of the year and describes its rites in some detail for the mid-17th century. A stylite monk lived on the top of one of the large columns in Hadrian's temple in Athens in the 19th century. Stylites became rare, then, but their memory has endured. Elevated between earth and sky, the stylites have for centuries directed the eyes – and sometimes the lives – of Orthodox Christians heavenward.

SEE ALSO: Asceticism; Iconoclasm; Monasticism

References and Suggested Readings

Brown, P. (1971) "The Rise and Function of the Holy Man in Late Antiquity," *Journal of Roman Studies* 61: 80–101.

Dawes, E. and Baynes, N. H. (1977) *Three Byzantine Saints*. Oxford: Mowbray.

Delehaye, H. (1923) *Les Saints stylites*. Brussels: Société des bollandistes.

Doran, R. (1992) *The Lives of Symeon Stylites*, CS 112. Kalamazoo: Cistercian Publications.

Schachner, L. A. (2009) "The Archaeology of the Stylite," in D. Gwynn and S. Bangert (eds.) *Religious Diversity in Late Antiquity*. Late Antique Archaeology 5.1. Leiden:. EJ. Brill.

Subdeacon *see* Ordination

Syrian Orthodox Churches

JUSTIN M. LASSER

Christianity in the lands of the Tigris and Euphrates and the Syrian Orient has both a rich and diverse history. The Syrian Christians represent some of the last remnants of the Aramaean civilizations that populated the region for millennia. The glories of these civilizations and cultures are not merely preserved by modern Syrian Christians, but lived out. Though their numbers in the original homelands have been steadily decreasing over the past centuries, their vitality has not. Most *Sūryāyē* (Aramaean and Assyrian) peoples trace their origins to a region occupying the northern limits of the Tigris and Euphrates rivers, now composed of southeastern Turkey, northern Iraq and Iran, Jordan, and Syria.

The Aramaean language that the *Sūryāyē* preserve in their hymns and holy books is a West-Semitic language, which is related to the Aramaic language of Jesus' world. The *Sūryāyē* also trace their Christian roots to the cultural world of Jesus and the earliest apostles. According to traditional accounts, St. Thomas "the Twin" served as the apostle to Syria and the accounts of his adventures are recounted in the Syriac *Acts of the Apostle Thomas*. The Osrhoene region (now southeastern Turkey) was a crucible for new ideas and cultural exchanges between the Hellenistic West and the Orient. Many literary works existed in both Syriac and Greek, which often stimulated intriguing syntheses, but also precipitated unfortunate linguistic and cultural misunderstandings (e.g., the Messalian, Nestorian, Gnostic, and Monophysite crises). From earliest times the two pearls of the Osrhoene region, the cities of Edessa and Nisibis, made great strides in translating the indigenous Syriac Christian experience and vocabulary into the Hellenistic and Byzantine West. Even the name of the Apostle to Syria, St. Thomas, illustrates this attempted cultural transmission. The name "Thomas" derives from the Aramaic word for "twin" (*tōma*). In the gospel attributed to St. Thomas, his name is presented as "Judas, Didymus Thomas," which uses both the Greek and

Aramaic locutions for "twin." This construction is intriguing in that it doubles "Judas'" name so that it reads, "Judas twin twin," emphasizing that the Apostle Judas Thomas was *twice* twin and an apostle to both the Greeks and the Aramaeans.

One of the earliest documents from Syria, the *Doctrine of Addai*, recounts the alleged correspondence between Jesus and King Abgar of Edessa. While the tradition is not historically demonstrable from any other sources, it does reveal important aspects of early Syrian Christianity. According to the tradition, King Abgar sent a letter to Jesus in Jerusalem asking him to come to the city of Edessa. Though Jesus turned down the request, he blessed King Abgar and promised to send one of his disciples to heal all of the infirmities of the king and his subjects. But before the king's entourage departed, Hannan, the king's "painter," tried to paint the likeness of Jesus and bring it to King Abgar. This tradition, as well as the variant version that recounts Jesus impressing his face upon a cloth (the *icon-painted-without-hands*), represents the central role that icons have played in Syrian Christianity from the beginning. After Christ's ascension, the tradition recounts how the Apostle Thomas sent Addai, one of the seventy, to Abgar to heal the sick in Edessa and to preach the gospel. The *Doctrine of Addai* represents one of the earliest attempts to weave together the diverse traditions associated with the advent of Christianity in Syria. It specifically merges the Thomas tradition with the Addai tradition, which may have developed in different locales and time periods. It is important to note that the Manichean "apostle" to Osrhoene was also an "Addai," which may suggest that the tradition in the *Doctrine of Addai* may be a later Orthodox response to the success of the Manichean missions in Syria in the 3rd century.

The traditions preserved in the *Doctrine of Addai* and in Eusebius' *Church History* describes how a certain Palūt was consecrated as the first bishop of Edessa (ca. 200) by Serapion, the bishop of Antioch. This story was also intended to establish the patriarchal jurisdiction of Antioch. However, these foundational stories must be tempered by the remembrance that the Orthodox in early Syria probably held a minority status. According to St. Ephrem, the greatest hymnographer in Syrian Christianity, the Orthodox were not first referred to as "the Christians" but rather as the "Palūtians" (*Contra Haereses* 22, 6, in Vööbus 1958: 4),

that is, "the Nicene party." Though a bishopric was established for the Orthodox in Osrhoene in the 2nd century, the church had to operate outside the Roman fold in a world where a wide diversity of Christian expressions was the norm. Within the 2nd-century crucible of the Syrian Orient there existed a variety of groups, including the Ebionites, "Jamesian" Christians, Jewish-Christians, Mandaeans, and the groups associated with the Pseudo-Clementine literature, in addition to many others.

The earliest chronological source for Syrian Orthodox Christianity exists in the *Chronicle of Arbēl*, which recounts the beginnings of Christianity in the environs of the great Syriac city of Hadiab in the villages of Arbēl. The tradition connects the work of Mar Addai with a certain Mar Peqida, whom Addai consecrated the first bishop of Hadiab (Vööbus 1958: 5). If the chronology can be trusted, it seems that Orthodoxy was established in the Arbēl region in the first quarter of the 2nd century, which suggests that Christianity had already made prior inroads into the Syrian Orient.

Beyond the traditional Orthodox foundational stories exists the tradition associated with the Apostle Thomas, which is, in all probability, the earliest Christian tradition in Syria. This tradition is recorded in the *Gospel of Thomas*, the *Book of Thomas the Athlete* (also the earliest Syrian ascetic text), and the *Acts of the Apostle Thomas*. The tradition represents a surprisingly coherent "school-of-thought" that spanned more than three centuries. One of the earliest specifically Syrian titles for Christ is represented in the Coptic *Acts of Peter and the Twelve Apostles*. This Syrian text describes how a certain *Lithargoēl*, playing the part of a pearl merchant, traveled the world offering pearls for free. In the story, the wealthy ignore this *Lithargoēl*, while the poor seek merely to catch a glimpse of the pearls. The pearl in question, of course, was a metaphor for the experience of the Kingdom of God, echoing Jesus' Parable of the Pearl Merchant (Mt. 13.45–6). The name *Lithargoēl* is Syriac for the "the light, gazelle-like stone," who in this story is the risen Christ offering the pearls of the kingdom. The pearl motif plays a central role within Syrian Christian spirituality, which is preserved in the *Acts of Thomas* as the *Hymn of the Pearl*. The later Syrian ascetical writers often depicted themselves as "pearl divers" seeking after the glories of the kingdom.

The temperament of the early Syrian Christians was often ascetically very severe. They are particularly known for their profound adherence to poverty and their strict exhortations toward virginity, self-flagellation, and constant prayer. One of the earliest groups was known as the *benai* and *benat qeiama*, Syriac for "the sons and daughters of the oath (or covenant)." These early Orthodox Christians swore an oath together, binding themselves in collective prayer, in a condemnation of wealth, in the struggle against the "world," and to a state where spiritual marriages would replace sexual marriages. It is important to note that this group was composed of both males and females without any identifiable leadership roles. Some scholars of Christian origins now believe that at one time (an "Encratite" position destined to give way before wider church practice) celibacy was required of early Syrian baptismal candidates, thus leaving a majority in the church in the condition of a long-term catechumenate. The origins of this movement are paralleled in the hermeneutical shifts reflected in the *Gospel of Thomas* and the *Book of Thomas the Athlete*. Later parallels are also manifested in the Syriac *Ketaba de Maskata* or *Book of Steps*. This uniquely Syrian late 4th-century text exhibits evidence of a gradually progressing moderation of the early Syrian severity. The *Book of Steps* details the responsibilities of two groups within Syrian Orthodoxy – "the Perfect" (*gmîrê*) and the "Upright" (*kênê*). The Upright were exhorted to live lives worthy of Christ while supporting the Perfect, who continued the practices of absolute poverty, virginity, and constant prayer. The great Aphrahat of Syria, author of the influential *Demonstrations*, was also a member of these *benai qeiama*.

Unlike the ascetics in the West, these "single ones" (Syriac: *ihidaya*) were both wanderers and active participants within village life. They often lived on the outskirts of villages and actively prayed for the communities that supported them. Their particularly severe form of asceticism is recounted in Theodoret of Cyr's *History of the Monks of Syria*. These ascetics would deprive themselves of sleep, mortify their bodies, chain themselves, bury themselves in caves, and walk naked during the winter, among a whole host of other practices. With their long fingernails, perched atop mountains, and with their long wild hair, these monks appeared to resemble eagles more than humans. In the eyes of many, these spiritual athletes had already taken flight into the world of the purely spiritual. This "perching" above the world in prayer and fasting was imitated by the early Syrian "stylites" (from the Greek *stylos*, "pillar"). These stylites would sit atop pillars acting as intercessors between the world below and the heavens above. According to tradition, the first to ascend a pillar was St. Simeon Stylites in the first quarter of the 5th century. This practice continued in Syria and the wider Orthodox world for centuries.

Any account of early Syrian Christianity would be incomplete without mentioning the towering character of Tatian (ca. 150). Traditionally a student of St. Justin Martyr, Tatian had renounced Hellenistic philosophy and embraced the Christian asceticism of his Syrian homeland. His greatest contribution was the *Diatesseron*, a Syriac harmony of the four gospels and other extra-canonical gospels. This harmony of the gospels remained one of the most important texts in Syriac history. St. Ephrem wrote a commentary on the *Diatesseron* and its influence beyond Syria is attested throughout the Mediterranean world and Northern Europe. Other important documents for early Syrian spirituality include the *Odes of Solomon*, the *Gospel of the Nazoreans*, the *Gospel of the Ebionites*, the *Psalms of Thomas*, and the works of Bardaisan of Edessa.

The remarkable richness of the Syrian Christian spiritual vocabulary was a cause for both controversy and inspiration. The cultural and linguistic divide widened as Byzantine control over the Osrhoene region decreased. The spiritual practices of the Syrians did not always translate easily into the Byzantine Orthodox world. These confusions were certainly manifested in the 4th century during what became known as the "Messalian controversy" (from the Syriac *messaltim*, "prayers"). Though the controversy was primarily the result of linguistic and cultural confusion, there were particular Syrian elements that caused a stir in Byzantine quarters. It seems the Syrian distinction between the "Perfect" and the "Upright" did not translate well into the established hierarchal church structures at Antioch or other Byzantine centers on the border with Syriac speaking lands. That the controversy was primarily linguistic is evinced by the extraordinary influence of the writings of St. Macarius. Most scholars agree that the writings of St. Macarius (*Fifty Spiritual Homilies* and the *Great Letter*) were actually written by a Syrian Orthodox Christian, which has led many to prefix Macarius' name with "pseudo," thereby dubbing him "Pseudo-Macarius." If so-called "Messalian" spirituality was unorthodox it would be difficult to make sense of Pseudo-Macarius' popularity among so many later mainline Orthodox mystics and saints, from the time of St. Gregory of Nyssa to St. Symeon the New Theologian. The primary linguistic misunderstanding derived from the Syrian proclivity to describe the spiritual struggle of the Christian in terms of the coexistent dwelling of both a demon (tendency to evil) and the Spirit of God (tendency to holiness) within the heart. Another important difference between Syrian and Greek spiritual traditions relates to the state of *apatheia*, or the advanced ascetic's release from the tyranny of the passions. This state, which many Greeks assumed was impossible – or at least delusional – was for the Syrians, the natural progression of the "Perfect." This association between perceived pride and Syrian spirituality eventually produced a unique spiritual experiment in the form of the "holy fool" as expressed, for example, in the *Life of St. Symeon the Holy Fool*. The holy fool combined the severity of Syrian spirituality with a guard against the "demon" of pride. The holy fool "mocked the world" and acted in such a way that would constantly cause him to be humiliated.

These linguistic, cultural, and theological differences eventually came to a head in the Council of Ephesus I (431). After Nestorius, bishop of Constantinople, was deposed, seen as a progressive silencing of the ancient Syrian church language in Christology, the Syrians were progressively cut off from the rest of the Byzantine world. Later, attempts at reunification were tried, but with little success. In time the Syrian Christians splintered into two main groups, now often pejoratively referred to as "Nestorian" and "Monophysite." The increased alienation of Syria made them particularly vulnerable to foreign attack. The isolated Syrians were finally completely cut off with the advent of Islam. Since the 7th century, Syrian Christians have existed as a persecuted church. Despite their tenuous status,

there continued a rich literary and spiritual tradition within the Christian Orient. St. Isaac of Nineveh represents one of the few Syrian voices that influenced the entire Christian world. The last flowering of Syrian spirituality is represented in the comedic and penetrating works of Barhebreus, bishop of Baghdad. He also epitomizes one of the most fruitful exchanges between the Islamic faith and Orthodox Christianity.

Today, the Syrian Christians are divided into a number of different churches. The Oriental Orthodox accept the first three ecumenical councils but reject the Council of Chalcedon. They are sometimes referred to as Monophysite or Jacobite Syrians. The Assyrian Church of the East represents the Oriental Christians of Syrian origin who affirm the paradigmatic standing of Nicea (325) and accept the dogmatic construct of the first two ecumenical councils, but reject the Council of Ephesus I, and advocate Christian positions dependent on the traditional saints of their church: Theodore Mopsuestia, Diodore of Tarsus, and Nestorius of Constantinople. The Assyrian Church of the East has also been referred to in earlier literature as the "Syrian Church," the "Persian Church," and the "Assyrian Orthodox Church." These are not to be confused with the "Oriental Orthodox" or the Chalcedonian/Byzantine Syrian Orthodox Christians. The Syrian Orthodox Christians, in the Byzantine sense (i.e., those that accept all seven ecumenical councils), are part of the Eastern Orthodox family of churches and belong either to the Greek Orthodox Patriarchate of Antioch and All the East or the Antiochian Orthodox Church. The Syrian Christians in communion with the Roman Catholic Church who are thus part of the family of Eastern Catholics comprise the Syriac Catholic Church, the Maronite Church, theMelkite Greek Catholic Church, the Chaldean Catholic Church, and the Syro-Malankara Catholic Church.

SEE ALSO: Antioch, Patriarchate of; Apostolic Succession; Assyrian Apostolic Church of the East; Council of Chalcedon (451); Council of Ephesus (431); Gnosticism; St. Ephrem the Syrian (ca. 306–373/379); St. Isaac the Syrian (7th c.); St. Macarius (4th c.)

References and Suggested Readings

Baker, A. (1965–6) "The 'Gospel of Thomas' and the Syriac 'Liber Graduum'," *New Testament Studies* 12: 49–55.

Brock, S. (1988) *Syriac Fathers on Prayer and the Spiritual Life*. Collegeville, MN: Cistercian Publications.

Brock, S. (1992) *The Luminous Eye: The Spiritual World Vision of Saint Ephrem*. Collegeville, MN: Cistercian Publications.

Brock, S. and Harvey, S. A. (1987) *Holy Women of the Syrian Orient*. Berkeley: University of California Press.

Klijn, A. F. J. (trans.) (1962) *The Acts of Thomas. Supplement to Novum Testamentum* 5. Leiden: E. J. Brill.

Quispel, G. (1964) "The Syrian Thomas and the Syrian Macarius," *Vigilae Christianae* 18: 226–35.

Stewart, C. (1991) *'Working the Earth of the Heart': The Messalian Controversy in History, Texts, and Language to AD 431*. Oxford: Clarendon Press.

Vööbus, A. (1958) *History of Asceticism in the Syrian Orient*. Louvain: Secretariat of the Corpus Scriptorum Christianorum Orientalium.

T

Teretismata *see* Music (Sacred)

Theophan the Greek (ca. 1340–1410)

THOMAS KITSON

Only two of the master icon painter Theophan's works in the Russian lands remain: the frescoes in Novgorod's Transfiguration Church (1379) and the deisis row of the iconostasis in the Annunciation Cathedral of Moscow's Kremlin (before 1405), where he worked with his student, St. Andrei Rublev. Nothing of his earlier life is certain, though he possibly came from Constantinople to Novgorod around 1370. He may have been influenced by the 14th-century hesychast controversies in Constantinople. His striking Novgorod frescoes emphasize ascetic labor with an ethereal, nearly monochromatic, reddish-brown palette, over which white, green, and blue brushstrokes create lightning-like effects. Rublev adopted but softened his highly individual treatment of faces and hands.

SEE ALSO: Hesychasm; Iconography, Styles of; Icons; Russia, Patriarchal Orthodox Church of; St. Andrei Rublev (ca. 1360–1430)

References and Suggested Readings

Hamilton, G. H. (1983) *The Art and Architecture of Russia.* London: Penguin.
Parry, K. (2001) "Theophan the Greek," in K. Parry et al. (eds.) *The Blackwell Dictionary of Eastern Christianity.* Oxford: Blackwell.

Theophany, Feast of

DAN SANDU

Theophany (Greek for "Manifestation of God") is the feast (January 6) celebrating the revelation of the Trinity at the river Jordan (Mt. 3.13–17). The troparia of the feast emphasize the divinity of Christ who was sent forth into the world by the Father through the Holy Spirit. The commemoration on January 6 derives from the 4th century, when eastern and western liturgical traditions were becoming united. Theophany marked three "revelatory" moments in the life of Jesus: the baptism in the Jordan, the adoration of the Magi, and the miracle at Cana. Solemn blessings of water occur in (and outside) churches on this day.

The Concise Encyclopedia of Orthodox Christianity, First Edition. Edited by John Anthony McGuckin.
© 2014 John Wiley & Sons, Ltd. Published 2014 by John Wiley & Sons, Ltd.

Plate 72   Ukrainian folk group celebrating the feast of the Theophany in the open-air Museum of Folk Architecture and Rural Life, Pyrogovo. Photo ©Viktor Mikheyev/Shutterstock.

References and Suggested Readings

Gillquist, P. E. (2001) *Becoming Orthodox: A Journey to the Ancient Christian Faith.* Ben Lomond. CA: Conciliar Press.

Theokritoff, E. (2009) "Theophany," in M. B. Cunningham and E. Theokritoff (eds.) *The Cambridge Companion to Orthodox Christian Theology.* New York: Cambridge University Press.

Tradigo, A. (2006) *Icons and Saints of the Eastern Orthodox Church.* New York: Oxford University Press.

Theophylact of Ohrid (ca. 1050–1108)

A. EDWARD SIECIENSKI

Byzantine theologian and ecclesiastic, Theophylact of Ohrid was born in Euboea, Greece, and became a student of Michael Psellos. He was appointed archbishop of Ohrid (in Bulgaria) in 1090, writing learned commentaries on both the Old and New Testaments. In his dealing with the West, Theophylact defended the traditional Eastern position on the *filioque* and the papacy, while simultaneously urging the Byzantines to charity with regard to other Latin divergent ecclesiastical practices.

SEE ALSO: Ecumenism, Orthodoxy and *Filioque*; Papacy

References and Suggested Readings

Mullett, M. (1997) *Theophylact of Ochrid: Reading the Letters of a Byzantine Archbishop.* Birmingham Byzantine and Ottoman Monographs 2. London: Variorum.

Obolensky, D. (1988) "Theophylact of Ohrid," in *Six Byzantine Portraits*. Oxford: Clarendon Press, pp. 34–82.

Theotokion

JOHN A. McGUCKIN

From the Greek meaning "Pertaining to the Mother of God." It denotes a short hymn (troparion or sticheron) in the Orthodox offices of prayers, which celebrates the role of the Virgin in the history of salvation and calls upon her help for the Church. A Theotokion occurs in each service and usually occupies a place at the end of a series of hymns. The Theotokion that occurs in Vespers after the "Lord I have Cried" hymn, and just before the Entrance, is called the Dogmatik since it contains a dense synopsis of the doctrines of Incarnation and Salvation. On Wednesdays and Fridays, and in prayer services focused on the Passion, the hymn is designated as Stavro-Theotokion (Cross-Hymn to the Virgin) and evokes the sorrow of the Virgin as she laments the sufferings and death of her Son.

SEE ALSO: Hymnography; Music (Sacred); Sticheron; Troparion

Theotokos, the Blessed Virgin

ANTONIA ATANASSOVA

The Blessed Virgin Mary has an indisputable place of honor in Orthodox Christianity. She is revered as "our all-holy immaculate, most blessed, and glorious Lady Theotokos and Ever-Virgin Mary," for through her the Word of God becomes incarnate. In Scripture her special status is foretold in the words of the angel Gabriel for whom she is "blessed among women" and "full of grace" (Lk. 1.26–38). Mary's motherhood serves in restoring the relationship between God and the human race, in fulfillment of Isaiah's prophecy of a virgin bearing a son who is "God with us" (Isa. 7.14). Her quiet acceptance of God's will: "Here am I, the servant of the Lord; let it be with me according to your word," her magnificent song of praise extolling God's care for the lowly (Lk. 1.46–55), and the blessing she receives from Elizabeth, the mother of John the Baptist, mark the incarnation as a pivotal moment of history, and Mary as the ideal follower of God. Throughout the course of her son's ministry, the Virgin plays a central role, from its inception at the wedding in Cana, where her intervention leads to the first sign of Jesus' exalted destiny, to its bitter fulfillment at the foot of the cross where Jesus commits her into the beloved disciple's care (Jn. 2.1–11; 19.25–7). In sum, the evangelists' account of Christ's life and mission recognizes the presence of his mother as no less than indispensable to the unfolding of the divine economy.

Scriptural references to Mary are further supplemented by a variety of beliefs widely held in Orthodoxy, many of which stem from devotional practices. In the popular apocryphon *The Protoevangelium of James*, Mary is described as a "creature of exceptional purity" set aside for a divine purpose from the moment of her conception. We meet her parents, Joachim and Anna, who surrender their only child in service to the Temple in Jerusalem and leave her there throughout her childhood, to converse with angels and weave a scarlet and purple veil for the Holy of Holies. Eventually, the Virgin leaves the Temple to be betrothed to Joseph and even in the context of her marriage remains perpetually virginal, since Jesus' brothers and sisters mentioned in Scripture are traditionally considered to be a part of a larger kinship group, not the offspring of Mary and Joseph. Orthodox traditions speak of Mary as receiving special revelation of Christ's resurrection at the first Pascha, and after Jesus' ascension tell of her being accompanied by John the Evangelist to Ephesus. Many devotional writings from the 6th century describe how she "falls asleep" in Jerusalem, surrounded by the apostles, and as her grave is opened to show her body to the latecomer, Thomas, it turns out to be empty. The liturgical hymns commemorating the greatest Marian feast, the day of her Dormition (August 15), sing of how Mary has joined the Lord in heaven, in body and soul. This glorious exaltation of the Virgin stands in Orthodoxy as a sign of eschatological hope and a foretaste of the reward reserved for the blessed at the end of time.

Historically speaking, the collage between scriptural record and traditions of piety provoked from

Plate 73 Mother of Tenderness. By Eileen McGuckin. The Icon Studio: www.sgtt.org.

early times the need for an explanation as to how and why the presence of the Virgin is essential to the Christian faith. Orthodox Marian theology developed in close correspondence with larger christological questions about the authenticity of Jesus' humanity, the manner of the incarnation, and the nature of the union of natures in Christ. It is a recurring motif and principle that the glorification of the Virgin Mary stems from her contribution to the incarnation, as explicitly stated in the Symbol of Faith accepted at the Council of Nicea (325). Far from being a mere footnote to the christological question, the recognition granted to Mary is a necessary corollary of the fact that, in her womb, the Word of God is made flesh "for our salvation."

The veneration of Mary as the one who gives birth to God (*Theotokos*) originated in Alexandria as early as the 3rd century, marking a rising tide of Marian piety that would soon encompass the Eastern Christian

Empire. The title did not gain universal acceptance immediately, and in 427 the Syrian archbishop of Constantinople, Nestorius, challenged it as reminiscent of paganism and logically untenable. He proposed that Mary be called *christotokos* (Christ-bearer), that is, mother only of the human nature of the incarnate Son. His opponent Cyril, archbishop of Alexandria, saw the rejection of the Theotokos title as a direct assault on the unity of the person of the Lord, on the creed of Nicea, and the legacy of the fathers. For Cyril, the title encapsulated the very meaning of salvation by underscoring the double generation of the Divine Logos: the "incomprehensible manner" of the Son's generation from the Father and the fact that "for our sake he economically underwent a self-emptying" (McGuckin 1994: 321, 324). In the Virgin's womb, Cyril argued, the union between God and humanity becomes a reality whose ultimate goal is the restoration and sanctification of all creation in God. Accordingly, to recognize and confess Mary as Theotokos is a safeguard against heretical perceptions of the christological union. At the Council of Ephesus in 431, Cyril's Marian theology was vindicated and the title Theotokos was confirmed as a fitting designation of Mary's special status in salvation history. It would also form an integral part of the theological definition of Christ's personhood promulgated at the Council of Chalcedon in 451.

To this principal Marian title of Theotokos, the Council of Constantinople added a second one of *Aei-Parthenos* or "Ever-Virgin" (553). Mary's perpetual virginity, before, during, and after Jesus' birth, is a fundamental tenet of Orthodox incarnational theology; it illustrates the divine identity of her son as well as her own cooperation in the history of salvation. Iconographically, its symbolism is conveyed by three stars embroidered on the Virgin's veil (*mapharion*). Its theological significance is well attested in early Christian literature and a parallel is often drawn between the two archetypal virgins, Mary and Eve. Unlike her biblical counterpart, Mary the Second Virgin proves herself to be obedient and faithful. Her virtue reverses the divine condemnation of Eve which has led the female race to lust after a husband and bear children in pain (cf. Gen. 2.16). In the words of Proclus, 5th-century archbishop of Constantinople, Mary's virginal womb is the bridal chamber uniting

God and creation where she gives birth without pain (Constas 2003: 263).

The Virgin Mary is the perfect prototype of a pure and holy life and the primary model for a life of asceticism and self-denial. Unsurprisingly, the first recorded Marian appearance in the church is in a vision ascribed to the ascetic Gregory Thaumaturgus (PG 46:1133D–1136B). Gregory of Nyssa, who relates the story of the apparition, praises Mary's chastity, her purity of body and soul, as a "frontier between life and death" reestablished by faithful Christians in the act of imitating Mary's piety. Textual evidence is complemented by formal cultic recognition of Mary as the champion of virginity as early as the 4th century, with the Jerusalem feast of the *Hypapante* celebrating Mary's purification and Jesus' presentation in the Temple. Another feast dedicated to the commemoration of Mary and the merits of virginity is recorded in Constantinople in the first half of the 5th century; most likely, it formed part of the Nativity liturgical cycle. During the 5th-century Theotokos controversy in Constantinople, this feast provided the occasion for Proclus' delivery of the first of several influential Marian homilies in the presence of Nestorius himself. Proclus praised Mary with the support of the monks and the ascetics who proved to be most vocal defenders of the Theotokos. In line with this tradition, the Virgin Mary is considered to be the primary benefactor and protectress of the autonomous monastic republic on Mount Athos, often described as "the garden of the Virgin." In the broader sense, the Theotokos is revered in Orthodoxy as the paragon of holiness to which the church, the bride of God, aspires as a whole. In this context Mary is a shining example of the rewards of a life of humility and obedience to God, the greatest of all the saints, and an eschatological intercessor at the throne of Christ.

The formal recognition of Mary in the doctrines of the church is complemented and (as in in the case of Ephesus 431) even pre-dated by a steady rise of her prominence in liturgical life and devotional practice. Early Marian veneration was especially notable in Constantinople, the capital city which, according to Byzantine legend, was dedicated to the Virgin by Constantine himself. The cult of Mary developed there under generous imperial patronage with the building of three major churches commemorating the Virgin: the Blachernae, the Hodegoi, and the Chalkoprateia. Priceless Marian relics and objects of pilgrimage were kept in those establishments, including the Virgin's belt and veil. Devotional objects related to Mary and Marian icons were exhibited on the city walls and carried not only in liturgical processions, but also in battle, by both Byzantine and Slav rulers, fortifying popular acclaim of the Virgin and highlighting her intercessory and protective powers (the Akathist designates her as *Promacheia* – "defending warrior"). The Virgin's glorification as the defender of the Christian empire and a military and civil leader *par excellence* is amply reflected in iconic depictions of Mary enthroned with the holy child in her lap and surrounded by angels and saints. In the Eastern Christian world victories on the battlefield and miraculous rescue were often ascribed to the Virgin. In Byzantium the Virgin protected her city from Slav, Persian, and Arab enemies; in Russia, miracle-working Marian icons were thought to have repeatedly saved Moscow, Kiev, and Novgorod from invasion. The Russian liturgical calendar records three occasions when the Virgin of Vladimir is said to have delivered Russia from the Tatars (Tradigo 2006: 28).

The fervor of Marian devotion reflects the fact that, by virtue of its intimate connection with the Savior, Mary is uniquely suited for the role of the most effective intercessor the church has on its behalf. The earliest extant prayer to the Theotokos (*sub tuum praesidium*) evokes the eagerness with which her protection was sought: "Under your mercy we take refuge, *Theotokos*, do not reject our supplications but deliver us from danger" (Limberis 1994: 104). In Eastern Christian art this entrusting of the prayers of the faithful to the Virgin would come to be depicted in the iconic composition of the Deisis, a grouping of Christ enthroned in glory with his mother to his right and John the Baptist to his left. As the iconostasis screen developed in Orthodox churches, the Deisis would come to be situated in its upper center, emphasizing the value and importance attributed to the Virgin's intercession. As a result of a Marian vision to St. Andrew the Fool in the church of the Blachernae, the Virgin's protective powers also acquired a separate liturgical feast, called the Feast of Protection or the Feast of the Protecting Veil (*Pokrov*, October 1/14), which remains highly popular in Russia.

Icon-centered liturgical iconography in the East uses Marian depictions in a variety of settings and always in a place of prominence. Traditionally, Mary's image is found above the sanctuary (Virgin *platytera*; "More Spacious than the Heavens"), where she presides over the consecration of the Eucharist as the Mother of the incarnate Word and a symbol of the church. The annunciation scene with Mary and the angel Gabriel bringing her the good news, flanks the royal doors leading to the altar area in Orthodox churches; the Deisis scene is situated above them. Mary is the central figure in icons related to her liturgical feasts: her nativity (September 8) and presentation in the Temple (November 21), the annunciation (March 2) and her Dormition (August 15), the post-Easter Feast of the Theotokos Life Giving Font, and the Protection of the Theotokos. An additional number of iconic types illustrate her instrumentality in the divine economy and the many roles she would come to play in response to the spiritual needs of the faithful. Marian typology is embedded in her depictions as a burning bush, an enclosed garden, and an unfading rose; other iconographic formulas have her nursing the holy child, contemplating the inevitability of his passion, or lamenting his death. The best known of those formulas is the canonical representation of the Virgin as *Hodegetria* ("The One Who Shows Us the Way"), in which Mary offers her child to the world as the way to salvation. A variation of the Hodegetria evolved into the image of the Virgin *Eleousa* ("Virgin of Mercy or Lovingkindness"), particularly widespread in the Balkans and in Russia. The Virgin of Vladimir is a famous example of the mixing of the *Eleousa* type and the Virgin of the Passion; the mutual embrace of mother and child in this icon reflects Mary's role as an intercessor as well as offering the assurance that Christ listens to his mother's prayers. The Virgin is also portrayed in the traditional posture of prayer (*Orans*), sending the supplications of the church to heaven, or enthroned with Jesus in her lap and accompanied by saints, apostles, emperors, or benefactors of the particular temple in which the icon resides. Of Russian origin is the popular representation of the Virgin as the Joy of All That Sorrow.

The wealth of Marian iconic types corresponds to the substantial liturgical hymnography dedicated to the Virgin. Each Orthodox service proclaims that "it is

meet and right" to praise the Virgin as "more honorable than the cherubim and more glorious beyond compare than the seraphim" because of her contribution to the history of salvation. Early examples of liturgical poetry are found in the hymns of Ephrem the Syrian (4th century) and the *kontakia* of Romanos the Melodist (6th century). These works rely on a deeply evocative language which is redolent with scriptural allusions and highlights Mary's distinctive status in relation to "all created women": she is the most joyous of all, for she has conceived God in flesh, and most "magnified," for she has given birth to him (McVey 1989: 77). In an array of breathtaking images, Ephrem delights in outlining the paradox of how Mary suckled the Word while he, the incarnate God, nourished the world with the restoring power of his life. Similarly, in his *kontakia* on the nativity and death of Christ, Romanos turns to Mary as a narrator and imagines her son's Passion through her eyes. The most impressive assembly of Marian praises is found in the Akathist, a (processional) hymn written after the Council of Ephesus and sung today on Fridays during Great Lent. The Akathist praises Mary redeemer of the ancient curse of Eve, as well as the "womb of the divine Incarnation." Particularly noteworthy is the insistence on presenting the Virgin as a "container of the uncontainable God." Mary is emphatically depicted as the God's indwelling and the new locus of salvation: she is an "ark gilded by the Spirit," an "immovable tower" of the Church, an "impregnable wall," a pillar, a tabernacle, a bridal chamber, a bridge, and a ladder. As the woman who unites God and humanity, the Akathist proclaims, the Virgin is the one who will always protect Christians, assure victory, and heal souls and bodies.

On the whole, the significance of the Virgin Mary in Eastern Christian culture and theology is clearly central. In consenting to do the will of God, Mary becomes the mother of the incarnate Word and makes salvation come true. She brings the human race back to the garden of life from which Adam and Eve were exiled and shines as the embodiment of eschatological hope. The veneration accorded to her is also an acknowledgment of the salvific power of Christ of which she is the first recipient. The church accordingly teaches that while the saints rightly receive honor (*douleia*), she alone of all creatures is appointed by God to receive "high honor" (*hyper-douleia*). As a popular hymn attributed to John Damascus aptly puts it, this is why "in you all creation rejoices, o full of grace."

SEE ALSO: Council of Chalcedon (451); Council of Ephesus (431); Eleousa (*Umilenie*); Iconography, Styles of; Iconostasis; Icons; Panagia; Platytera; Protecting Veil; St. Cyril of Alexandria (ca. 378–444); St. Ephrem the Syrian (ca. 306–373/379); St. Romanos the Melodist (6th c.)

References and Suggested Readings

Constas, N. (2003) *Proclus of Constantinople and the Cult of the Virgin in Late Antiquity*. Leiden: E. J. Brill.

Limberis, V. (1994) *Divine Heiress: The Virgin Mary and the Creation of Christian Constantinople*. New York: Routledge.

McGuckin, J. A. (1994) *St. Cyril of Alexandria: The Christological Controversy, Its History, Theology, and Texts*. Leiden: E. J. Brill.

McGuckin, J. A. (2008) *The Orthodox Church: An Introduction to Its History, Doctrine, and Spiritual Culture*. Oxford: Blackwell.

McVey, K. (ed. and trans.) (1989) *Ephrem the Syrian: Hymns*. New York: Paulist Press.

Tradigo, A. (2006) *Icons and Saints of the Eastern Orthodox Church*. Milan: Mondadori Electa.

Tradition

JOHN A. MCGUCKIN

"Tradition" is a central term for Orthodox theological life. The church understands the "Holy Tradition" (by no means signifying every ecclesiastical custom) to be the essence of the evangelical experience as it lives it out fully, and mediates it through each generation to the world. Orthodoxy is itself the embodiment of the essential Christian tradition in time and space. The Latin term *traditio* ("handing on") and its Greek counterpart *paradosis* both acquired technical meanings from the New Testament onwards (cf. 1 Cor. 11.23), signifying tradition as the central core of evangelical experience that was communicated from Jesus to the apostles and through them to the Christian world.

The concept of tradition was clarified and elevated by St. Irenaeus in the 2nd century as the ultimate safeguard against Gnostic "innovations," in an age when Christian self-identity was being publicly challenged by numerous speculative streams of redefinition. It was he who, in the *Adversus Haereses*, popularized the model of tradition as a conservatory force (not necessarily a conservative one) that guarded the transmission of the message of salvation, through a regularly constituted order (*taxis*) from Jesus, to the apostles, to the early episcopate, who maintained the apostolic succession of the *Kerygma*. Tradition, as St. Irenaeus understood it, was the vital force of evangelism, as much as (if not more than) it was the mechanism whereby the church was able to filter out what it felt was inauthentic in relation to its central self-identity, from generation to generation. Jesus himself was less than patient with those who could not differentiate between the "customs of men" and the perennial demands of the Word of God. His anger was directed at those who resisted the dynamic process of the saving Spirit, by opposing against it deliberately "deadening" appeals to past "traditions" (Mk. 7.13). In his argument with the Pharisees over the significance of traditions, the Lord was not opposing a developmental sense of theology to a "static" or "traditionalist" one; rather, he was opposing a concept of living tradition to a traditionalist attitude that opportunistically served to screen the elect community from the ever-present demands of God.

In the apostolic age, St. Paul operated with a double sense of tradition. At some times he is conscious of how carefully he must deliver to others "what I myself received" (1 Cor. 11.2, 23; 15.1–4), especially when it concerns traditions about the Lord, or liturgical process. At other times, in advancing the cause of the church's effective preaching of the message of salvation, he is more than conscious of how the Risen Lord has empowered him to "seize the moment" (*Kairos*), and how he himself authoritatively transmits his own contribution to the tradition, with the authority of no less than Christ, whom he serves apostolically. The first concept of tradition Paul sees as an unchanging verity. The second he sees as economically related to the saving *Kerygma*, and changing across the times as the servant of the efficient proclamation of the gospel in various conditions (1 Cor.

7.10–12, 25, 40). In his times of conflict with other apostolic missionaries of the Jerusalem Church, who resisted his boldly "innovative" apostolate to the Gentiles, Paul is ready to use this missionary sense of tradition not merely as a flexible kerygmatic tool – "To be all things to all" (1 Cor. 9.22) – but even in a fixed and canonical sense. He warns his disciples in several places to keep fast to the traditions he gave them, and to keep away from those who did not live accordingly (1 Thes. 2.15; 3.6). The generation after Paul, less confident than their teacher, represents a correspondingly more cautious attitude and speaks of that "deposit" of tradition that has to be preserved by the church with nothing added or taken away (1 Tim. 6.20). The sense of kerygmatic adaptability was being conditioned at this period, on the cusp of the 1st and 2nd centuries, by an imminent sense of the End Times approaching.

In the writings of Clement of Rome, later in that same generation, one witnesses the first attempt to make the tradition synonymous with that which the presbyters and bishops of the church both represent and protect. This first attempt to make the tradition align very closely with "authoritative preaching" on the part of church leaders was really the first formally elaborated patristic concept of tradition (more exactly, in this case, a doctrine of the episcopal inheritance of the charism of authority). It proved insufficiently flexible to meet the large range of challenges to church unity that the 2nd century threw out. In the following generation, witnessed both in Tertullian and Irenaeus, who were both much exercised with the problem of how to distinguish authentic tradition from heretical imposture, the broader principle of an appeal to the community's sense of basic truths was more noticeably elevated. For Irenaeus, the question of what was true tradition could be proven by appeal to the record of the main apostolic centers, the ancient and leading churches. He further developed his thought by suggesting that the apostolic churches possessed the "charism of truth" in a special way (*Adversus Haereses* 4.26.2). This was manifested above all in the manner in which they interpreted the Scriptures, soberly and with catholic consensus. In this context he developed his famous image of the interpretative "key" (*hypothesis*) which the church owned but which others do not possess. It was to grow into the fuller patristic concept

of the *Mens Ecclesiae*, the "Mind of the Church," what St. Athanasius was later to call the church's *dianoia* and its instinctive sense of the true intentionality (*skopos*) of both scripture and tradition; that is, the comprehensive overview given to the Spirit-illumined faithful, which was radically partialized and distorted by heretical dissidents. Irenaeus added further to the fundamental vocabulary of the theology of tradition when he developed the argument that the key to biblical interpretation was the "Canon of Truth" (*Adversus Haereses* 3.2.1), which in the Latin version of his works gave to the West (decisively so in the hands of Tertullian) the principle of the Rule of Faith: *Regula Fidei* or *Regula Veritatis*. This *Regula*, Irenaeus says, is the strongest refutation of heretical variability, for it is maintained in all the churches and goes back to the apostles. Apostolic succession, then, is not primarily a matter of succession of individual bishops one after another, but the succession of apostolic teaching from the time of the apostles to the present.

When the Arian controversy caused a crisis in the 4th-century church over the precise nature of fundamental truths (the divinity of Christ, the Trinity), the Orthodox fathers reacted instinctively by appealing to an older process of solving problems from the end of the 2nd century: that is, by holding regional synods where the church leaders would decisively address problems and offer solutions in a synodal consensus. At first, the "international" (ecumenical) synodical principle had a hopeful beginning, but soon the restless policy changes of the Imperial house and the party strife of bishops left the aspirations for public harmony in tatters. The 4th century saw the hope of an ecumenically led principle of synodical government heavily compromised as one synod countermanded and anathematized another.

The question of how to recognize the identifying marks of tradition rose again acutely at the end of the Arian period, over the issue of the deity of the Holy Spirit. Here, significant theologians such as Sts. Athanasius, Basil, and Gregory of Nazianzus all consciously theologized about the way in which tradition could make new statements about fundamental matters of faith that had not been explicitly witnessed hitherto. Gregory's *Oration 31* describes his own role in proclaiming the *homoousion* of the Holy Spirit (despite any lack of precedent) as a herald of God speaking in the time of a new "seismic shaking" of the world order. Similarly, Basil (typically, more cautiously) appeals to the range of "unwritten traditions" in the church's liturgical life (*On the Holy Spirit* 27) to justify the principle that the real inner life of the church (its core tradition) is something more extensive than its canonical or written traditions. This more or less stabilized the nexus of the ancient church's overall doctrine of tradition, apart from two last movements: one eastern and the other western. The christological crisis of the 5th century was so fast, furious, and subtle, that many of the same problems over discerning "true tradition" that had occupied Irenaeus rose again in this period. The 5th-century answer (as manifested in the Acts of the Councils from Ephesus in 431 to Nicea II in 787) was to assemble dossiers of patristic evidences. The very notion of "patristic theology" was born in this era. Fathers of the church were regarded as possessing significantly elevated authority, and when accumulated in a *florilegium*, collectively they made a powerful testimony for authentic tradition. After this period, most Latin and Greek theology was constructed on the basis of assembling *florilegia*.

In the West, Augustine's long fight with the Donatists had led him to elevate the principle of catholicity (a universal solidarity as opposed to a provincial regionalism) as a handy guide to authentic tradition. Catholicity was thus a necessary factor alongside antiquity (apostolic or scriptural status). This view of truth manifested by its geographical extension was always closely allied in the Western Churches with the principle of communion with the Roman see. It led inexorably to the famous formula of Vincent of Lerins, commenting on Augustine, who argued that "oral tradition" must always be subordinated to Scripture (*Commonitorium* 2.1–2) as being purely its exegesis. It was he who also defined the authentic Christian tradition as that which is held to be such "by everyone, always, and in all places." This gave rise in later Latin thought to the doctrine of the clear distinction of Scripture and tradition (as two sources of Christian *kerygma*). The Orthodox Churches never followed this latter path, seeing always Scripture itself as one of the primal (but not exclusive) manifestations of the core tradition of the gospel *kerygma*, of which the inner life of the church was certainly another; as were also the other principles of tradition-discernment

it had elevated across the centuries as a closely meshed interwoven web: namely the scriptural (canonic) principle, the apostolic principle, the episcopal, the synodical, the conciliar, the pneumatic, and the canonical principle (legislative decrees). All these things together, harmoniously commenting upon one another, their balance discerned by spiritual *Diakrisis*, manifested authentic tradition in each age of the church. The Orthodox Christian doctrine of tradition is thus an ancient and richly complex idea, which is no less than an investigation of the inner roots of Christian consciousness in history; and indeed more than this – for it is the tracing of the presence of the Divine Spirit in Christ's church across the ages.

SEE ALSO: Apostolic Succession; Bible; Ecumenical Councils; Episcopacy; Gnosticism; Heresy; Holy Spirit; Patristics

References and Suggested Readings

Bouyer, L. (1947) "The Fathers of the Church on Tradition and Scripture," *Eastern Churches Quarterly* 7 (special volume dedicated to scripture and tradition).

Florovsky, G. (1971) *Bible, Church and Tradition: An Eastern Orthodox View*, in *Collected Works* Vol. 1. Belmont, MA: Nordland.

McGuckin, J. A. (1998) "Eschaton and Kerygma: The Future of the Past in the Present Kairos: The Concept of Living Tradition in Orthodox Theology," *St. Vladimir's Theological Quarterly* 42, 3–4: 225–71.

Reynders, B. (1933) "Paradosis: Le progrès de l'idée de tradition jusqu'à S. Irenée," *Recherches de théologie ancienne et mediévale* 5: 155–91.

van den Eynde, D. (1933) *Les Normes de l'enseignement chrétien dans la littérature patristique des trois premiers siècles*. Paris: Gembloux-Paris.

van Leer, E. F. (1954) *Tradition and Scripture in the Early Church*. Assen, Netherlands.

Triodion

SOTIRIOS A. VLAVIANOS

The *Triodion* (Greek: Τριώδιον, "book of the three odes") is a liturgical book that contains service material from the Sunday of the Publican and the Pharisee (tenth Sunday before Easter) up until the night of Great Saturday. The name of this lengthy liturgical season (encompassing Great Lent) is both taken from and identified with this book. The title *Triodion* refers to short canons with only three odes which are sung at Orthros (Matins) on the weekdays of Great Lent. The book evolved around the 9th century and was largely the work of Studite monks from Constantinople. Currently, the texts found in the *Triodion* reflect the liturgical tradition of Jerusalem from various time periods: some early, some later. The *Triodion* used to be divided into two parts, the *Lenten Triodion* and the *Festal Triodion*. The *Festal Triodion* covered the liturgical cycle beginning on Easter up to the Sunday of All Saints. Eventually, the latter was incorporated into the *Pentekostarion* around the 14th century, when it then had its short canons (*triodia*) eliminated.

SEE ALSO: Canon (Liturgical); Great Week; Ode; *Oktoechos*; *Paraklitike*; *Pentekostarion*

References and Suggested Readings

Savas, S. J. (1983) *The Treasury of Orthodox Hymnology – Triodion: An Historical and Hymnographic Examination.* Minneapolis: Light and Life Publications.
Schmemann, A. (1974) *Great Lent: Journey to Pascha.* Crestwood, NY: St. Vladimir's Seminary Press.

Taft, R. F. (1985) *The Liturgy of the Hours in East and West: The Origins of the Divine Office and its Meaning for Today.* Collegeville, MN: Liturgical Press.

Troparion
DIMITRI CONOMOS

A short, monostrophic chant in rhythmic prose. The oldest stratum of hymnody for Vespers and Matins, the troparia constitute by far the largest body of sung texts in the Byzantine rite. The *kata stichon* hymns, of Syrian and Palestinian monastic origin, are important early examples. They exhibit the same number of syllables (usually eleven) and the same number of accents in every line. Although no music for primitive troparia survives, it is generally held that they were sung to unpretentious tunes, generally composed on the rule of one tone to each syllable, to render them suitable for congregational singing.

References and Suggested Readings

Conomos, D. (2008) "What is a Troparion?" *Sobornost* 30, 2: 59–80.
Trypanis, C. A. (1981) *Greek Poetry from Homer to Seferis.* London: Faber and Faber.

Tropes *see* Music (Sacred)

U

Ukraine, Orthodoxy in the

TODD E. FRENCH

The Ukraine is host to the rich history of the conversion of the Rus to Orthodoxy, which led to the further spreading of Christianity in Asia. Its capital city, Kiev, has served as the focal point of political maneuvering in the Slavic territories from the conversion of the Rus down through to modern times. It is worth noting that the history of this conversion, commonly associated with Vladimir in 988, overrides numerous alternative conversion stories. Ancient Christian legend tells that St. Andrew the "First-Called" embarked on a mission to convert the Scythians in 55 CE. Evidence only becomes clearer in the later medieval period, when one starts to find several clues to Christianity's influence on the Rus. Although the term "Rus" is used to describe the people of a diocese in Tmutorokan as early as the 860s, the Rus are historically associated with the Kievan centered kingdom. The distance between these two cities being roughly a thousand miles has raised questions about whether the two Rus settlements are both Slavic kingdoms or if the Black Sea Rus were the same as the Goths mentioned by St. John Chrysostom in the 4th century, as being an important community for missionary enterprise.

Few were more influential in the growth of Christianity in the Ukraine than St. Constantine (tonsured Cyril before his death) and his brother St. Methodios. They were chosen to lead a mission to the Slavic kingdom of Moravia in 864. Prior to their departure they devised an alphabet (Glagolitic) into which many texts were translated. Their successors, Clement and Naum of Ohrid, were instrumental in the development of the Cyrillic alphabet, named for their teacher.

Kiev, however, was a good distance from Tmutorokan and the story of the Kievan Rus conversion proper begins with two princes, Askold and Dir. A popular version of the story tells how after attempting to seize Constantinople, the princes saw their fleet destroyed through a miracle which they believed to have been called down by the Patriarch St. Photios and the emperor. This led to the baptism of the defeated (and impressed) leaders. A more textured account survives in Greek chronicles relating the defeat of Askold and Dir by Prince Oleg, who made Kiev his capital. Vladimir, one of four successor princes, was a pagan like his forebears but perhaps saw the need for a unifying religion that resonated with the population both within his kingdom and in neighboring lands, especially Byzantium. After dismissing the claims of Judaism and Islam, Vladimir settled on Christianity, but relied on ambassadors to the Latins and Greeks in order to decide on his preferred style. His emissaries returned explaining, famously, that they were not sure whether they were in heaven or on earth during a service at

Plate 74   The Kiev Mohyla Academy, founded by the great Ukrainian hierarch Peter Moghila for raising the standards of the education of clergy. It was the center of a great revival in Orthodoxy after the 18th century. Photo by John McGuckin.

St. Sophia's. The decision was made for Byzantine alliance and the Orthodox Church began to fuel Ukraine's religious history. In 988 Vladimir was baptized at Chersonesus. There were mass baptisms of the people in the river Dnieper following.

The conversion of Vladimir has been attributed to his Christian grandmother St. Olga and his political connections with the Byzantine ruler, Basil II (the "Bulgar Slayer"). Regardless of its origin, the spread of Christianity was initiated from the ruling classes down through Slavic society by a mix of incentive and coercion. The Byzantine church maintained important links with Vladimir's kingdom through missionaries and an appointment of a metropolitan archbishop in Kiev. Vladimir's son, Yaroslavl, consolidated his rule in 1036 and was able to build many churches. Among them was the renowned cathedral of St. Sophia (1044), built to rival its sister in Constantinople. Yaroslavl organized the

translation of important religious texts into the liturgical language of Church Slavonic. In 1051 he appointed the first non-Greek archbishop, Ilarion.

Ukrainian monasticism was first founded in the Kievan caves (Pechersky Lavra) in the 11th century. Built into the banks of the river Dnieper, the lavra's catacombs are a treasury of relics uniquely preserved through mummification and attesting to the rich history of saints this land has produced. The golden age of Kievan Rus began to deteriorate in the 12th century when princes began to challenge Kiev for autonomy in their territories. The result was a fractured kingdom with numerous claims to power. Disunity allowed for a national defeat when in 1237 Genghis Khan's grandson, Batu, invaded the northeastern Rus territories. By 1240, Kiev had fallen and its churches were burned by the Mongol invaders. Perhaps even more significant than the loss of the capital was the

Plate 75 St. Jonah's skete in midtown Kiev. The monastery was destroyed by the Soviets and the church turned into a warehouse. Today it has been refounded and the monastic life thrives there with a young community. Photo by John McGuckin.

shift of the metropolitan archbishop's seat from Kiev to the city of Vladimir in 1299 and then on to Moscow.

After Kiev fell, Danylo, the ruler of Galicia-Volhynia (1237–64), attempted to recapture the prominence of Kievan Rus by waging war against the Mongols. Although his efforts at first failed, he and his successors were finally able to wrest the kingdom back. After the archbishopric was moved and Kiev was destroyed through multiple wars, the Lithuanians, a pagan community living along the Baltic Sea, saw an opportunity in these lands. They invaded what is now Belarus and made their way to the Ukraine. Under Grand Prince Algirdas, the Lithuanians declared all of Rus to belong to the Lithuanians and in 1340 they made their move into the Ukraine. By 1362 they had taken Kiev and they definitively defeated the Mongols shortly after. Lithuanian power was rooted in their

amenability to Rus law (as constituted by Yaroslavl), culture, and language. Their rule was preferred over Mongol rule and thus the pagan Lithuanians gradually became the Orthodox-leaning Slavic state. This was once again to be challenged by the invasion of Polish Catholic interests in 1340, which promoted a westward leaning affiliation. Acquiring all of Galicia-Volhynia by 1366, the Poles ended the notion of Ukrainian self-rule in 1471 when they officially incorporated the Ukraine.

Meanwhile, Moscow imposed a decisive defeat on the Mongols in 1480 and emerged as the prominent power of the region. When the Ottoman Turks invaded Constantinople in 1453, Moscow was left as a "Third Rome" and the dominant sustainer of Orthodox belief. The church in Ukraine now found itself in a strange relationship with this new power.

In 1448 the hierarchy of the Orthodox Church were internally divided over the issue of the Imperial Byzantine policy of Union with Rome; and because of this Moscow was able to assert significant independence from Constantinople. This move promoted the development of the Russian Orthodox Church. Kiev lost its senior metropolitan status to Moscow in 1458, yet also needed Moscow's support in maintaining the vitality of an Orthodox Ukraine. The Union of Lublin in 1569 brought together the Lithuanian and Polish states, which housed nearly all of Ukrainian territory. This combined power rivaled Moscow for a time, but the Ukraine eventually found itself divided internally between powerful, landed nobility and peasant, Ruthenian, Orthodox who worked the lands.

In 1589 the Metropolitanate of Moscow became fully autocephalous and the Ukrainian Orthodox were further overshadowed as a dependent ecclesial domain. even so, along with the rise of Muscovite political control, there were regular calls in Ukraine for greater freedom from Moscow. This move toward independence partially came to fruition in an attempt to organize a Greek Catholic church. In the Polish-Lithuanian Union, Catholics stood to gain political privilege and preference over their Orthodox counterparts. In the interest of unity, the nobles proposed the conversion of the Ruthenian Orthodox quarter of their population by establishing a Greek-rite church (Unia) that maintained its Orthodox customs and liturgy but was subject to the Pope. Orthodox communities did not accede easily, however, and in 1578 Prince Konstantyn Ostrozky, a leading force for the Unia, established a printing press at Ostrih in Volhynia, which set out an educational agenda looking to the West. The press notably published the first Slavic Bible in 1581. He also founded a school which was turned over to the Jesuits in 1608 by his Greek-Catholic granddaughter, Anna.

Conflicts began to rage over properties and rights between the Greek Catholics and Orthodox, costing many clergy their lives. In 1632 the Polish government proposed a compromise in which the Orthodox hierarchy was recognized and properties were divided. Peter Mohyla (Moghila), the new archimandrite of Pechersky Lavra and eventual chief Orthodox hierarch of Kiev, utilized the peace after 1632 to print the

first Slavic Orthodox catechism. His Orthodox Academy at Kiev rivaled the educational work of Ostrozky.

In 1648 the uprising led by Khmelnytsky showed what a united Ukraine was capable of accomplishing. Revoking the Polish magnates' power, the Cossacks overthrew the political regime with a bloody revolution. Needing to call upon foreign assistance, Khmelnytsky first considered the Ottoman Porte, but ultimately secured the might of the Muscovites and their tsar, Aleksei Mikhailovich. The appeal was answered with a nod to the shared vision of state Orthodoxy. At the time of Khmelnytsky's death, 17 percent of the land formerly in Polish hands was designated as the property of the Orthodox Church. The metropolitanate of Kiev came more and more under the sway of the patriarch of Moscow after 1686.

Eventually, Russia, Prussia, and Austria divided Poland-Lithuania among themselves and by the late 18th century Russia was in control of 62 percent of the Ukrainian territories. There was a steady ongoing struggle between the tsars and indigenous Ukrainian notions of self-government. The period of Muscovite rule was marked with important moments for the Orthodox Church. During General Dmitri Bibikov's dominion (1837–52) the aim was to convert the 2 million remaining Greek Catholics to Orthodoxy through forced tactics such as deportation and executions.

When the tsarist regime collapsed in 1917 the Ukraine quickly responded with the formation of the Central Rada. A rival to Bolshevik power, it was ultimately put down by the Germans. The resulting Ukrainian Soviet government held some sovereignty until 1923. Orthodoxy in the Ukraine suffered significant setbacks during the communist era, but was never extinguished. When communism began to wane in its appeal, the Ukrainian Catholic Church began to move toward the restoration of its former properties to its 5 million remaining members. The Russian Orthodox Church in Ukraine responded to this by changing its name to the Ukrainian Orthodox Church in 1990, but it remained under the supervision of the Moscow patriarchate.

The Ukrainian Autocephalous Orthodox Church (UAOC) had been created in 1921 with Vasyl

Lypkivsky as its metropolitan. The UAOC grew quickly and was initially favored by the Soviets because of the (divisive) challenges it posed to Russian Orthodox unity. Once the movement took hold, however, it too became another threat the Soviets needed to suppress. Dismantled after the 1930s in the homeland, but enjoying a time of development in the diaspora countries of the West, the UAOC came back as a significant factor in Ukrainian church life after the fall of communism, and reaffirmed their distance from the Moscow patriarchate in 1990. They now are represented by 1,650 parishes. Under the persecution of Soviet rule, several Ukrainian diaspora parishes submitted to the leadership of the patriarch of Constantinople. In the US and Canada the UAOC communities have recently declared their independence from the Phanar.

When President Kravchuk came to power in Kiev in 1990, after the fall of the Soviet system, there was the hope that the diverging religious communities of the Ukraine might be united under one unified church. For this reason the new Kiev patriarchate of the Independent Ukrainian Orthodox Church was formulated. It was largely composed of those communities who wished to place distance between themselves and the Moscow patriarchate, which they characterized as a tool of oppression. The new political leadership of independent Ukraine fostered these ambitions for separate status. Wider world Orthodoxy, however, did not regard the Independent Ukrainian Orthodox Church as having legitimate canonical status, and it failed to take more than 14% of the Kievan Orthodox with it. Its first leader, patriarch Filaret of Kiev, was excommunicated by the Russian Orthodox Church in 1997. In response to continuing calls for Ukrainian autonomy, Moscow declared the canonical autonomous status of the Ukrainian Orthodox Church, which was no longer to be called simply the "Russian Church." It remained in the canonical system of the Moscow patriarchate: autonomous, not autocephalous.

This now made three Ukrainian churches claiming the title of the indigenous Ukrainian Orthodox Church. The largest is the autonomous communion of the Moscow patriarchate in Kiev. The second is the UAOC, and the third is the smaller community of the Independent Kievan Patriarchate. The Orthodox international communities recognize the first in favor of the third. The Ukrainian Orthodox Church (Moscow Patriarchate) represents 6,000 parishes mainly in the East and South. Their liturgical language remains Church Slavonic rather than the vernacular Ukrainian used by many communities in the diaspora UAOC. Representing over 27 million Orthodox parishioners, the Ukraine is today a major center of Orthodox energy and culture. This new vitality after communism, however, has found itself divided on account of its liminal position between Europe and Asia. Depending on Russia for 90 percent of its oil and 77 percent of its natural gas, the Ukraine has often found itself in a difficult relationship with Moscow power bases, both secular and ecclesiastical. Politically, the Ukraine often leans toward cooperation with Europe and the US, as can be seen in numerous treaties and disarmament proposals, but they continue to find themselves in a difficult geographical and political position with regard to Russia's interests. These colliding trajectories also affect church life and will for the foreseeable future.

SEE ALSO: Lithuania, Orthodoxy in; Sts. Constantine (Cyril) (ca. 826–869) and Methodios (815–885)

References and Suggested Readings

Kubicek, P. (2008) *The History of Ukraine*. Westport: Greenwood Press.

McGuckin, J. A. (2008) *The Orthodox Church*. Oxford: Blackwell.

Pospielovksy, D.V. (1998) *The Orthodox Church in the History of Russia*. Crestwood, NY: St. Vladimir's Seminary Press.

Prokurat, M., Golitzin, A., and Peterson, M. D. (1996) *Historical Dictionary of the Orthodox Church*. Lanham: Scarecrow Press.

Subtelny, O. (2000) *Ukraine: A History*. Toronto:.

Wlasowsky, I. (1974) Outline History of the Ukrainian Orthodox Church Toronto.

Uniate *see* Eastern Catholic Churches

United States of America, Orthodoxy in the

THOMAS FITZGERALD

The Alaskan Mission

The Alaskan territory became part of the United States in 1867 when it was sold by Imperial Russia. The Orthodox Church had a significant presence in the territory dating from 1794. In that year, eight monks and two novices from the Church of Russia established the first mission in Alaska. Led by Archimandrite Joseph Bolotov, the missionaries departed St. Petersburg on December 25, 1793 and arrived on Kodiak Island on September 24, 1794. They had traveled about a third of the circumference of the earth. Discovered and explored by Russian explorers from 1741 onwards, the Alaskan coastland and the numerous islands between North America and Siberia were claimed by Imperial Russia. A colony had been established in 1784 on Kodiak and became the center of trade.

While these early missionaries confronted numerous difficult challenges, their work in Alaska in the late 18th and early 19th centuries was remarkable. Spreading from its center on Kodiak to other populated regions, the Alaskan Mission was one of the largest and most significant missionary endeavors guided by the Church of Russia and supported by the imperial government. As a sign of its significance, the Church of Russia selected Fr. Joseph the head of the mission to serve as the first bishop in Alaska in 1796. After traveling to Siberia for his consecration, however, the new bishop died in a shipwreck before returning to Kodiak.

Two missionaries during this period have attracted particular attention. With little formal education, the monk Herman (1760–1837) came to exemplify the best qualities of the early missionaries in Russian Alaska. As one of the first missionaries, Herman, who was not ordained, instructed the natives both about Christianity and about agricultural techniques. He staunchly defended the rights of the natives in the face of exploitation by many Russian merchants and traders. By 1812, Herman moved to Spruce Island,

three miles from Kodiak, and established a chapel, an orphanage, and a hermitage. Not long after his death in 1837, the natives began to honor him as a saint. They collected stories about his service and recorded the miracles attributed to his intercession. His formal canonization took place in 1970.

Fr. John (Innocent) Veniaminov (1797–1879) and his family arrived on the island of Unalaska in 1824. As part of his missionary work, the young priest created an Aleut alphabet based upon Cyrillic characters. This was followed by a dictionary and grammar. These provided the basis for his translation of the Gospel of St. Matthew and portions of the liturgy. John also wrote a basic catechism entitled *Indication of the Pathway into the Kingdom*.

Like Herman, Fr. John was concerned with the needs and activities of the natives. He taught them agricultural techniques, carpentry, and metalworking. During ten years on Unalaska, Fr. John constructed a school, an orphanage, and a number of chapels. Moving to New Archangel (Sitka) in 1834, he continued his remarkable missionary work among the Tlingits, a tribe generally hostile to the Russian merchants. Fr. John also traveled to other missionary outposts. He visited Fort Rus in Spanish Northern California in 1836. He also visited a number of Roman Catholic missions and met with the missionaries.

Following the death of his wife, Fr. John became a monk and took the name Innocent. He subsequently was elected bishop of Kamchatka, the Kurill and Aleutian Islands. With his return to New Archangel (Sitka), a new period of missionary activity developed. Regarded as a great educator, he created schools offering a wide variety of subjects. In 1841 he opened a seminary at Sitka which included courses not only in religious but also in native languages, Latin, trigonometry, navigation, and medicine. He insisted that his priests learn native languages and customs. Innocent was elected metropolitan of Moscow in 1868 and established the Russian Orthodox Missionary Society before his death in 1879. He was canonized a saint in 1977 and given the title "Apostle to America."

Following the sale of Alaska to the United States, many Russian merchants and fur traders in Alaska subsequently returned to their homeland or traveled to San Francisco where there was a sizeable Russian colony. The formal interest of the Church of Russia in Alaska also diminished. Few competent clergy remained in Alaska to care for the faithful, which numbered about 12,000 gathered into about 43 communities. A new diocese encompassing Alaska and the Aleutian Islands was established in 1870, but the episcopal see was moved to San Francisco in 1872 and its affairs developed with less regular connection with the Russian synod.

The sale of Alaska also opened the territory to Protestant missionaries from the lower United States. Having little appreciation of the Orthodox Church, the Protestant missionaries proselytized among the native Orthodox, and showed little regard for their indigenous history and culture. Native languages and customs were discouraged. Assimilation was demanded. Despite this, the Orthodox Church continued to maintain a weakened presence in the Alaskan territory, and the mission continued to influence the subsequent development of Orthodoxy in the United States. The various Russian Orthodox jurisdictions which developed in the United States in the early 20th century claimed a direct continuity with the Alaskan Mission.

Early Orthodox Immigration and Church Development

The focus of Orthodox Christianity in the United States dramatically shifted to the east coast in the late 19th and early 20th centuries as a consequence of mass immigration. Thousands of Orthodox immigrants from Greece, Asia Minor, Carpatho-Russia, the Ukraine, and the Middle East came to the United States. Lesser numbers came from Serbia, Bulgaria, Romania, and Russia. Almost immediately, the immigrants set about establishing parishes, to construct church buildings, and to find a priest to serve their community. This was done often with little or no formal direction from church authorities either here or in the Old Country.

A number of the earliest parishes began as pan-Orthodox communities containing immigrants from various ethnic backgrounds. Among these parishes were those in New Orleans (1864), San Francisco (1868), and New York City (1870). There, a notable attempt to introduce Orthodox Christianity to the wider society in New York was made by Fr. Nicholas Bjerring (1831–84). Between 1879 and 1881 his journal, the *Oriental Church Magazine*, published essays on Orthodox teachings and liturgical texts in English.

As the number of Orthodox immigrants increased, these early parishes and most subsequent Orthodox parishes began to serve particular ethnic and linguistic groups. Since many immigrants intended to return to their homeland, the parishes became centers in which not only the faith was preserved but also the language and customs of the old country were carefully maintained. The church buildings were a place for worship. They also offered a secure place for fellowship and mutual support. There was a natural link between the family and the parish. There was also an intimate link between faith and the culture and language of the old world. Therefore, there was little contact among these parishes with other Orthodox groups and little sense of mission beyond the needs of a particular ethnic family. The large urban centers of the United States during the late 19th and early 20th centuries contained neighborhoods where the various immigrant groups could maintain their faith, culture, and language, somewhat insulated from the wider society. This was true not only for the various Orthodox immigrant groups. It was also true for certain Roman Catholic and Protestant immigrants.

The accomplishments of these early Orthodox immigrants were truly remarkable. By 1920 there were about 300 organized parishes composed primarily of Orthodox immigrants. As centers of religious and cultural life in a new country, set up and financed by the laity in the main, these parishes were usually built and maintained with very little formal direction from the hierarchical authorities.

Early Greek Orthodox Developments

The largest single group of Orthodox immigrants in this period were the Greeks. Although a community of Greek Orthodox workers came to New Smyrna, Florida in 1768, there is little evidence of organized Orthodox religious life. The great wave of Greek immigration occurred in the late 19th and early 20th centuries. By 1920 there were about 300,000 Greek immigrants in the United States organized into about 135 parishes. With few exceptions, these parishes in the early years sought to maintain some connection with dioceses of the Church of Greece or the ecumenical patriarchate of Constantinople. Many of the early Greek immigrants saw themselves as temporary residents in the United States and kept in close contact with families back home.

From the early decades of the 20th century the patriarchate of Constantinople affirmed its responsibility for all Orthodox living in America. This was done in accord with Canon 28 of the Council of Chalcedon in 451 and subsequent practical precedents. According to the commonly held Greek interpretation of the Chalcedonian canon, the ecumenical patriarchate had responsibility for all the Orthodox in territories beyond the canonical borders of other autocephalous churches. However, because of the acute political and financial difficulties which the patriarchate experienced throughout the late 19th and early 20th centuries, it was not in a position to assert its prerogatives or to exercise its ministry adequately in America. Orthodox church life in the United States continued to develop during this period with very little hierarchical supervision and not always in harmony with accepted church polity and canonical order.

Ecumenical Patriarch Meletios (Metaxakis) of Constantinople (1871–1935) envisioned a united Orthodox Church in the United States in his enthronement address in 1921. The patriarchate subsequently established the Greek Orthodox Archdiocese of North and South America as a canonical province. Prior to his election as ecumenical patriarch, Meletios, as archbishop of Athens, visited the United States in 1918 and 1921 and had begun to organize the Greek Orthodox parishes he found there. Nevertheless, the Greek Orthodox parishes in the Americas were deeply divided in the 1920s and 1930s because of political differences between royalist and republican sympathizers as these parties had arisen in Greece. Between 1931 and 1948, Archbishop Athenagoras Spirou (1886–1972), later patriarch of Constantinople, labored greatly to heal the divisions and to unify the Greek archdiocese. Faced with the specific pastoral needs of the Greek immigrants and with the acute divisions among them, however, little at that time could be done to broaden the patriarchate's embrace to include all Orthodox faithful in the Americas.

Early Russian Orthodox Developments

The late 19th century also witnessed the emigration of more than 150,000 Carpatho-Russians from the Austro-Hungarian Empire. In their homeland they had been Eastern Catholics, sometimes called "Greek Catholics." Their union with Rome dated from the 16th century. While permitted to maintain Eastern liturgical practices and a married priesthood, the Carpatho-Russians had accepted the ultimate authority of the pope. The basis for the "return" of many Carpatho-Russians to the Orthodox Church after they arrived in America was primarily the refusal of local Roman Catholic bishops and priests in the United States to honor the Eastern Catholic traditions, particularly the married priesthood. Beginning in 1891, Fr. Alexis Toth (1853–1909; now canonized as St. Alexis of Wilkes-Barre), a former Eastern Catholic priest, led about 65 parishes with about 20,000 Eastern Catholics into the Russian Orthodox archdiocese. By 1917 about 160 former Eastern Catholic parishes with about 100,000 faithful had become Orthodox. The Carpatho-Russian immigrants formed the foundation of a newly energized Russian Orthodox archdiocese.

Because of the increase of parishes in eastern America, the Russian Orthodox diocesan see was moved to New York in 1905 under Bishop Tikhon Belavin (1865–1925), later patriarch of Moscow, and canonized as St. Tikhon). The rapid increase of Russian Orthodox parishes comprising Carpatho-Russian immigrants radically changed the character of the Russian Orthodox Church in the United States. The Church of Russia in 1900 approved the request of Bishop Tikhon to change the diocese's title to the Diocese of the Aleutians and North America. Granted the title of Archbishop, he subsequently consecrated in 1904 a bishop for Alaska and Fr. Raphael Hawaweeny (1860–1915; now canonized as St. Raphael of Brooklyn) as bishop of Brooklyn to serve to oversee about six Syrian Orthodox parishes. Archbishop Tikhon subsequently presented a plan to the Church of Russia in 1905 which envisioned a unified church in America under the jurisdiction of the Moscow synod. About 200 parishes were part of the Russian Orthodox archdiocese. In addition to parishes of the Carpatho-Russian and Syrian immigrants, the Russian Orthodox archdiocese also included in the early 20th century parishes of Serbian Orthodox, Syrians, Romanians, Bulgarians, and Albanians.

Additional diocesan developments rapidly took place among the Russian Orthodox. Following the Bolshevik Revolution of 1917 in Russia, the administration of the Russian Orthodox archdiocese and its parishes was profoundly disrupted because of the effects of the political and religious developments in Soviet Russia, and because of the loss of imperial financial support for church affairs. There were at least four major Russian Orthodox jurisdictions in the United States by the year 1933. The largest was the Russian Orthodox Greek Catholic Church, frequently referred to as the "Metropolia," which declared itself temporarily independent from the Church of Russia in 1924. Its authority was challenged by a small number of clergy and laity associated with the Russian "Living Church" movement, especially between 1922 and 1943. A diocese of the Russian Orthodox Church Abroad was established in 1927 serving Russian immigrants with monarchist sympathies who refused to acknowledge the official leadership of the Church of Russia in the period after Patriarch Tikhon, who died in 1925. Repudiating both these jurisdictions, the beleaguered Church of Russia headed by Metropolitan Sergius as acting patriarchal *locum tenens* established an exarchate in the United States in 1933. Each of these rival jurisdictions claimed to be the historic continuation of the Alaskan Mission in the United States. Each also expressed very different attitudes toward the Church in Russia and the communist regime in the Soviet Union.

Other Diocesan Developments

In the wake of further immigration and unsupervised parish development, other autocephalous Orthodox Churches also acted to establish dioceses in the United States so as to serve their immigrant faithful. After preliminary local foundations in each case, new dioceses were subsequently established by the Church of Serbia in 1921, of Antioch in 1924, of Romania in 1930, of Albania in 1932, and of Bulgaria in 1938. The ecumenical patriarchate also established dioceses for Ukrainian parishes in 1937 and Carpatho-Russian parishes in 1938, and received Albanian parishes under its jurisdictional care in 1949.

The varied political allegiances of the immigrant communities often led to the creation of some separatist parishes and dioceses which were not part of the jurisdiction of any autocephalous Orthodox Church. With each wave of immigration, fresh political divisions in the homeland of the immigrants frequently manifested themselves in the church life of the Orthodox in the United States. Claiming to be united in faith, the Orthodox were actually fractured into numerous diocesan jurisdictions. Most had an "Old World" orientation and served a particular ethnic population. Some followed the "Revised Julian (New) Calendar" inaugurated in 1923 and others the "Old Calendar" (called the "Julian" because it was established by Julius Caesar in 45 BCE). Many parishes were marked at this time by a strong emphasis upon congregationalism which frequently challenged the leadership of the clergy. Attitudes of nationalism and parochialism pervaded much of church life. By 1933 there were no fewer than fifteen separate Orthodox jurisdictions comprising parishes serving particular ethnic communities and often reflecting political perspectives related to the old homeland. At that time, there were over 400 Orthodox parishes overall, serving about half a million believers.

A Time of Transition

Facing divisions both within and beyond their flocks, Archbishop Athenagoras and Metropolitan Antony Bashir (1898–1966) of the Syrian (Antiochian) Orthodox archdiocese recognized the need for greater cooperation. Metropolitan Antony advocated the greater use of English in liturgical services and envisioned a more united church in the United States. Together with Metropolitan Antony, Archbishop Athenagoras proposed a pan-Orthodox seminary in

1934 and a pan-Orthodox journal in 1941. Strife among the Russian jurisdictions prevented common action on these proposals. However, the Federated Orthodox Greek Catholic Primary Jurisdictions in America was established in 1943. This voluntary association brought together the primates of six Orthodox jurisdictions which were in communion with one of the patriarchates. During its early years the federation did much to achieve greater recognition of the Orthodox Church, especially by governmental agencies. Because it was not then in communion with the Moscow patriarchate, the Russian Orthodox metropolia, the largest of the Russian jurisdictions, was not a member of the federation. Its absence was a major weakness in the federation, which ceased to function by 1949.

The decades following World War II marked an important period of transition for the Orthodox in the United States. Demographics were changing. There was a notable decrease in immigration of Orthodox by the 1920s. Many parishes began to lose their predominantly immigrant character. At the same time, new parishes were being established in the suburbs beyond the center of immigrant life in the inner city. Born and educated in America, most parishioners became less and less in contact with the land of their grandparents and their political concerns. There was an increase in Orthodox marrying beyond their ethnic communities. There was also a gradual increase of marriages between Orthodox and Catholics or Protestants. Moreover, persons coming from other religious traditions were beginning to embrace the Orthodox Church and its teachings. This movement would increase as time went on.

The education of clergy and lay leaders acquired new significance. Following earlier attempts to establish pastoral schools, new theological schools came into existence. The Greek Orthodox archdiocese established the Holy Cross Greek Orthodox School of Theology near Boston in 1937. Likewise, the Russian Orthodox metropolia founded St. Tikhon's Seminary near Scranton, Pennsylvania, and St. Vladimir's Orthodox Theological School in Crestwood, New York in 1938. Since that time, these institutions have been responsible for educating most clergy and theologians in the United States. Their presses have also published a significant number of Orthodox theological books in English.

There was also an increase of pan-Orthodox endeavors. Orthodox from various jurisdictions began to recognize that they shared not only the same faith but also the same challenges and obligations within American society. A number of avenues of cooperation were established, especially in the areas of retreats, religious education, and campus ministry. New catechetical materials in the English language were published. There was growing use of English in the liturgy and other services as a result of translation efforts. Joint liturgical services began to become more common in larger cities, especially on the first Sunday of Great Lent, celebrated as the Sunday of Orthodoxy. Pan-Orthodox clergy associations and councils of churches also began to appear.

These developments were not without difficulties. New tensions developed in some jurisdictions related to these developments. Some felt that the role of the church as the preserver of a particular ethnic identity was being destroyed by the tendency toward greater cooperation. Indeed, additional divisions developed as new Orthodox immigrants arrived in the 1950s and 1960s, fleeing political changes in Eastern Europe. Opposing the communist governments there, rival dioceses developed among the Bulgarians in 1947, the Romanians in 1951, the Ukrainians in 1950 and 1954, and the Serbians in 1963. The larger jurisdictions, however, continued on a trajectory which recognized the growing American identity of its faithful.

The Standing Conference of Bishops

The establishment of the Standing Conference of Canonical Orthodox Bishops in America (SCOBA) in 1960 marked a significant move towards greater cooperation and unity among the Orthodox jurisdictions. Under the leadership of Archbishop Iakovos (1911–2005) of the Greek Orthodox archdiocese, SCOBA initially brought together the presiding bishops of eleven jurisdictions and developed a number of committees to deal with common challenges. Although SCOBA was not a formal synod, in canonical terms, many viewed it as the first step towards greater administrative and canonical unity. Each jurisdiction continued to maintain its own identity, yet SCOBA provided a significant means of cooperation. Unlike the earlier federation, SCOBA included the Russian Orthodox metropolia as well as the Moscow patriarchal exarchate. The Russian Orthodox Church Outside of Russia (the Synod Abroad) refused to cooperate at this time, citing its opposition to those who recognized the leadership of the Church of Russia.

SCOBA set about coordinating various national pan-Orthodox activities which had begun in earlier decades. These included programs related to religious education and campus ministry. An Education Commission and a Committee on Scouting were established in 1960. These were followed by a Campus Commission in 1965. The Orthodox Theological Society was established in 1965. With the development of the ecumenical movement, SCOBA became responsible for establishing formal bilateral theological dialogues with the Episcopal Church (1962), the Roman Catholic Church (1966), the Lutheran Church (1968), and the Reformed Churches (1968). A commission for dialogue with the Oriental Orthodox Churches was established in 2000.

In more recent years, SCOBA has formally sanctioned the establishment of a number of additional agencies. Among the most notable are the International Orthodox Christian Charities (1991), the Orthodox Christian Mission Center (1994), and the media outreach of the Orthodox Christian Network (2003). A Military Chaplaincy Commission supports chaplains for Orthodox Christians serving in the armed forces. In addition, seven other pan-Orthodox organizations have received SCOBA's endorsement. All the activities of SCOBA have provided rich opportunity for clergy and laity to join together in pan-Orthodox witness. These activities also served to deepen a desire for greater Orthodox unity.

The initial achievements of SCOBA occurred at a time when the Orthodox Churches on a global level were also engaged in a process of renewed conciliarity. Between 1964 and 1968, four pan-Orthodox conferences took place and began to address issues affecting all the autocephalous Orthodox Churches. These meetings led to the establishment of a conciliar process designed to prepare for the convocation of a Great and Holy Council. Among the topics which deserved attention by the churches was the so-called "Diaspora," the developing Church in America, Western Europe, and elsewhere.

In the light of these developments, the bishops of SCOBA in 1965 proposed to the autocephalous churches that it should be recognized as an episcopal synod having full authority to govern the life of the Church in America within the jurisdiction of the ecumenical patriarchate. A similar proposal was made in 1968 with the request that the American situation be placed on the agenda of the global pan-Orthodox conferences. While no action was taken by the ecumenical patriarchate or the other autocephalous churches, the appeals of SCOBA indicated that the situation in the United States could not be long ignored.

The conciliar process both in America and at the global level was, to an extent, disrupted in 1970 when the patriarchate of Moscow moved to grant autocephaly (self-governing status) to the Russian Orthodox metropolia. From then, the metropolia has been known as the Orthodox Church in America (OCA). This action regularized the formal relationship between the metropolia and the Church of Russia which had been lost in 1924, but the grant of autocephalous status to the OCA was not recognized by the ecumenical patriarchate or by most of the other autocephalous churches. This disputed status of the OCA immediately increased tensions among the jurisdictions in the United States. Eventually, it led to new discussions related to the presence of Orthodoxy in the United States and the meaning of autocephaly. Currently, while continuing not to recognize the autocephaly of the OCA, the ecumenical patriarchate determined to cooperate with it in the hope of encouraging a more comprehensive resolution of the overall canonical position of Orthodoxy in America.

Throughout the early 1970s the ecumenical patriarchate initiated a number of discussions on themes preparing for a Great and Holy Council. A list of ten topics for study was agreed upon by the representatives of the autocephalous churches in 1976. This list included the topics of the so-called "Diaspora" and the question of autocephaly. After dealing with a number of other topics, the theme of Diaspora was examined in meetings of the pre-conciliar committees in 1990, 1993, and 1995. In light of these discussions, a historic meeting of all Orthodox bishops in the United States was held in 1994. On the eve of a new millennium, the bishops issued a historic pastoral letter entitled *And the Word Became Flesh and Dwelt*

Among Us, which spoke about the responsibilities of the church and Orthodox Christians in contemporary society. Subsequent meetings of all the bishops were held in 2001 and 2006.

A number of significant developments occurred in several of the jurisdictions. Divisions among the two rival Syrian Orthodox (Antiochian) jurisdictions were healed in 1975, creating a unified Antiochian Orthodox Christian archdiocese. This provided a basis in 1987 for the reception of a number of convert clergy and 20 parishes of various evangelical Protestant traditions. The Serbian Orthodox dioceses healed their internal divisions in 1988. The two Romanian Orthodox jurisdictions began a dialogue aimed at reconciliation in 1992. The ecumenical patriarchate in 1996 restructured the Greek Orthodox archdiocese into an archdiocesan district and eight metropolises. In 1995 it also regularized the canonical status of a number of Ukrainian Orthodox bishops, clergy, and parishes. Likewise, the Antiochian Orthodox archdiocese in 2003 received a "self-rule" status from the Church of Antioch which also established nine dioceses. These new developments, as well as leadership changes and some financial difficulties in the OCA, led to some internal strife. The difficulties often served to highlight the need for greater unity among the Orthodox in America.

The SCOBA member jurisdictions as of 2010 are: the Albanian Orthodox diocese (Bishop Ilia), the American Carpatho Russian Orthodox diocese (Metropolitan Nicholas), the Antiochian Orthodox Christian archdiocese (Metropolitan Philip), the Bulgarian Eastern Orthodox Church (Metropolitan Joseph), the Greek Orthodox archdiocese (Archbishop Demetrios), the Orthodox Church in America (Metropolitan Jonah), the Romanian Orthodox archdiocese (Archbishop Nicolae), the Serbian Orthodox Church, the Ukrainian Orthodox Church (Metropolitan Constantine), and the Representation of the Moscow Patriarchate in America.

The New Episcopal Assembly

In October 2008, at a special synaxis of the heads of Orthodox Churches which he called at Constantinople, Patriarch Bartholomew (b. 1940) proposed that renewed attention be given to the so-called "Orthodox Diaspora." His proposal was unanimously accepted by hierarchs representing the other thirteen autocephalous churches. This historic gathering led directly to the Fourth Preconciliar Pan-Orthodox Conference, which met in Geneva on June 6–12, 2009. This meeting approved the creation of an Episcopal Assembly in North and Central America, as well as in eleven other regions. The new Assembly would bring together all the canonical Orthodox bishops from all jurisdictions in North and Central America to strengthen the unity of the church and to address together critical issues. At that time, there were over fifty canonical Orthodox bishops in this region.

During his visit to the United States in October 2009, Patriarch Bartholomew met with the presiding bishops of the SCOBA jurisdictions under the leadership of Archbishop Demetrios (b. 1928) of the Greek Orthodox archdiocese and exarch of the ecumenical patriarchate. Patriarch Bartholomew formally announced the decision of the synaxis in 2008 and the more recent decision of the fourth Preconciliar Pan Orthodox Conference. He urged the SCOBA bishops to begin the process of establishing the new Assembly. This body would build upon the significant work begun by SCOBA in 1960, and would be envisaged as succeeding and replacing SCOBA. Unlike SCOBA, however, the Assembly would now have the full recognition and support of the ecumenical patriarchate and the other autocephalous churches.

The new Assembly provides an important opportunity for the Orthodox Church to address the serious challenges and opportunities it has placed before it. The ongoing division of Orthodoxy in the United States into separate jurisdictions continues to weaken its mission and witness. Within most of the jurisdictions, the process of acculturation has not always been easy. As some of the jurisdictions move beyond their reliance upon ethnic loyalties, however, they are obliged to speak more clearly about the distinctive features of the Orthodox Christian faith within a religiously pluralistic society. They must express the Orthodox faith in terms which are understandable and develop ministries which respond to the spiritual need of persons living in this complex modern American society. The Orthodox in this context now need to distinguish between old world cultural practices, perspectives that are not essential to the faith, and those essential affirmations which are at the heart of the faith. Without diminishing the importance of worship, the Orthodox are challenged to enable greater participation in liturgical life, and relate this to all aspects of life. This will mean that a new spirit of mission must be cultivated and that a proper relationship between clergy and laity must be expressed at all levels of church life. In addition, the role of women and their contribution to the church will need to be appropriately recognized. With its profound affirmations about the loving triune God, the theocentric nature of the human person, and the deep divine blessing within the creation, Orthodox Christianity has much to offer American society and to contemporary Christianity in America. Even so, this offering can take place only if the Orthodox themselves take seriously their responsibility to this society and to all its people.

There are today about 3 million Orthodox Christians in the United States gathered in more than 1,500 parishes. The church has about twenty monasteries, three graduate schools of theology, a college and a number of other schools and charitable institutions. The Orthodox in the United States sponsor missions in Africa, Albania, and Asia. Likewise, the International Orthodox Christian Charities presently provide humanitarian assistance in over a dozen countries. Through their books and lectures, Orthodox theologians from the United States are influencing the church in many other parts the world. The Church in the United States is composed primarily of American members of a wide variety of racial, ethnic, and religious backgrounds who treasure the faith of Orthodox Christianity.

SEE ALSO: Constantinople, Patriarchate of; Greece, Orthodox Church of; Russia, Patriarchal Orthodox Church of; St. Tikhon (Belavin) (1865–1925)

References and Suggested Readings

Bogolepov, A. (2001) *Toward an American Orthodox Church: The Establishment of an Autocephalous Church.* Crestwood, NY: St. Vladimir's Seminary Press.

Bolshakov, S. (1943) *The Foreign Missions of the Russian Orthodox Church.* London.

Constantelos, D. J. (1967) *The Greek Orthodox Church: Faith, History, Practice.* New York: Seabury Press.

Litsas, F. K. (ed.) (1984) *A Companion to the Greek Orthodox Church.* New York: Greek Orthodox Archdiocese of North America.

McGuckin, J. A. (2008) *The Orthodox Church: An Introduction to Its History, Theology and Spiritual Culture.* Oxford: Wiley-Blackwell.

Ware, K. (1997) *The Orthodox Church.* London: Penguin.

Unmercenary Saints

SUSAN R. HOLMAN

"Unmercenary saints" were physicians, often martyrs of the late 3rd century, who healed without taking payment (known in Greek as *anargyroi*, "without money"). Ancient suppliants at their healing sanctuaries practiced incubation (sleeping at the shrine) and were sometimes healed through dream therapy; the saints treated or prescribed cures as the patient slept. This practice, similar to that of the pre-Christian healing sanctuaries of Asclepius, continued well into late Christian Antiquity.

The appendix to Dionysios of Fourna's 18th-century *Painter's Manual* lists forty-one *anargyroi*. The most popular, usually paired as siblings or co-workers, include Cosmas and Damian, Cyrus and John, Panteleimon and Hermolaos, Sampson and Diomedes, Photius and Antiketos, Thalleios and Tryphon, and sometimes the evangelist Luke. Of these, the two pairs best documented in contemporary scholarship are Cosmas and Damian and Cyrus and John.

The veneration of Cosmas and Damian was first mentioned by Theodoret of Cyrus in the late 4th century (PG 83.1373; PG 84.747). Their images are present in the life-size mosaic of calendrical saints in the rotunda Church of St. George in Thessalonica. Accounts of their miracles exist in six series totaling forty-eight stories; Ludwig Deubner's (1907: 52ff.) claim originating their cult in the pagan mythos of Castor and Pollux is now dismissed by most scholars. Festugière (1971: 87) notes that the early editor of Series 6 speaks of "the most ancient church situated at the famous monastery of the Cosmidion" at Constantinople, built ca. 439. The Emperor Justinian (527–65), finding the building in ramshackle condition, renovated and embellished it after being healed there. A monastery existed by 518. Both monastery and church were destroyed by the Avars, but in 1261 Michael VIII the Palaeologue spent the night at the site. Different dates for the saints' feast (September 27, July 1, and November 25) and several pairs with the same name attest to Cosmas and Damian's popularity in both East and West.

Sts. Cyrus (a physician) and John (a soldier martyred with him) were first venerated in the 4th century (McGuckin 1992); their shrine at Menouthis near Alexandria in Egypt and their miracles are attested by only one surviving text, by Sophronius of Jerusalem (d. 638). Sophronius notes that Cyril of Alexandria discovered them and translated their bones to Menouthis ca. 427/428 (celebrated on June 28). Scholars debate whether Cyril merely revived the shrine and cult or if it was founded after the destruction of the Isis sanctuary at Menouthis ca. 489. Sophronius' *Miracles of Saints Cyrus and John*, written after a healing at the sanctuary, emphasize Sophronius' opposition to the aphthartodocetic heresy and his defense of Chalcedonian orthodoxy. Neil (2006: 188) suggests that the text may have traveled to Rome when the saints' relics were transferred there in 634. Their festival is January 31.

Frescoes of several *anargyroi*, including Cosmas, Damian, Cyrus, and John, from both Greek and Syriac tradition were recently discovered at Deir al-Surien in Egypt (Innemée and Van Rompay 2002).

The Unmercenary Saints are evoked frequently throughout the healing services of the Orthodox Church, especially the healing ritual of the sacrament of anointing.

SEE ALSO: Healing; Relics; St. Cyril of Alexandria (ca. 378–444)

References and Suggested Readings

Deubner, L. (1907) *Kosmas und Damian: Texte und Einleitung.* Leipzig: Teubner.

Duffy, J. (1984) "Observations on Sophronius' Miracles of Cyrus and John," *Journal of Theological Studies* 35: 71–90.

Festugière, A.-J. (ed. and trans.) (1971) *Sainte Thècle, Saints Côme et Damien, Saints Cyr et Jean (extraits), Saint Georges.* Paris: Éditions A. et J. Picard.

Gascou, J. (2006) *Sophrone de Jérusalem: miracles des saints Cyr et Jean (BHG I, 477–479).* Paris: De Boccard.

Holman, S. R. (2008) "Rich and Poor in Sophronius of Jerusalem's Miracles of Saints Cyrus and John," in S. R. Holman (ed.) *Wealth and Poverty in Early Church and Society.* Grand Rapids, MI: Baker Academic, pp. 103–24.

Hronas, G. (1999) *The Holy Unmercenary Doctors: The Saints Anargyroi, Physicians and Healers of the Orthodox Church: Translated from the Greek Great Synaxaristes of the Orthodox Church.* Minneapolis: Light and Life Publishing.

Innemée, K. C. and Van Rompay, L. (2002) "Deir al-Surian (Egypt), New Discoveries of January 2000," *Hugoye, Journal of Syriac Studies* 3 (2); available online at www.syrcom.cua.edu/Hugoye/Vol3No2/HV3N2PR Innemee.html.

McGuckin, J. A. (1992) "The influence of the Isis cult on St. Cyril of Alexandria's Christology," *Studia Patristica* 24: 191–9.

Neil, B. (2006) "The Miracles of Saints Cyrus and John: The Greek Text and Its Translation," *Journal of the Australian Early Medieval Association* 2: 183–93.

Skrobucha, H. (1965) *The Patrons of the Doctors.* Pictorial Library of Eastern Church Art 7. Recklinghausen, Germany: Aurel Bongers.

V

Vespers (Hesperinos)

M. C. STEENBERG

Vespers (Greek, *Hesperinos*) is the divine service associated with the setting sun, and thus the beginning of the liturgical day in the Orthodox Church. It is made up of three broad parts: the great psalm of creation (Ps. 103 *LXX*) followed by the hymn "Lord, I have cried …" and its associated verses (*stichera*); the christological "Hymn of Light"; and the Aposticha and Song of Symeon ("Lord, Now Lettest Thou Thy Servant"). With these are interspersed various litanies and other prayers.

Theologically, Vespers signifies the calling out of creation for its Redeemer, who is encountered in the incarnate Jesus Christ: hence its focus on the created world (e.g., "There is the great and wide sea, wherein are creeping things innumerable," Ps. 103.25), expectation, and the encounter with Christ ("O Gladsome Light of God the Father's glory"; "Now Lettest Thou Thy Servant Depart in Peace," etc.). Liturgically, Vespers constitutes the shift from one day to the next (technically, this takes place at the prayer "Vouchsafe, O Lord"), building upon the biblical ordering of a "day" as starting with the night ("And there was evening and there was morning: one day," Gen. 1.5). Vespers can be served on its own, or (a common practice in the Russian parishes) as part of the monastic All-Night Vigil, where it is combined (abbreviatedly) with Matins (Orthros) and the First Hour.

Plate 76 An Orthodox bishop wearing the mantya robe and carrying the episcopal staff (rabydos) presides over the Vespers service. Pascal Deloche/Godong/Corbis.

The Concise Encyclopedia of Orthodox Christianity, First Edition. Edited by John Anthony McGuckin.
© 2014 John Wiley & Sons, Ltd. Published 2014 by John Wiley & Sons, Ltd.

SEE ALSO: Apodosis; Apolytikion; Aposticha; *Hieratikon, Horologion*; Kathisma; Orthros (Matins); Prokeimenon; Sticheron

References and Suggested Readings

Taft, R. (1985) *The Liturgy of the Hours in East and West*. Collegeville, MN: Liturgical Press.

Vestments

TENNY THOMAS

Sacred garments (*vestimenta* – Latin for "clothing") of the clergy worn for liturgical celebrations, and some also worn outside the church. The dress of Orthodox clergy is now held to symbolize the vestments of the Aaronic priesthood (see Exod. 28.2–43; 39.1–31), but it originated in the styles of ordinary costume of the Greco-Roman upper classes in the ancient Christian world. While a better form of dress was probably used at sacred functions during the earliest centuries, the development of specific clerical costume occurred between the 4th and 9th centuries, the church retaining antique dress in liturgy long after everyone else. Outside the celebration of liturgical service, Orthodox clergy usually wear a black under-cassock (*rason*) under a larger outer-cassock (*exorason*, like an enveloping overcoat with ample bell sleeves). The specifically liturgical vestments are different for each order of clergy. The deacon wears a *sticharion* (white robe) with separate brocade cuffs (*epimanikia*) and a diagonally worn *orarion* (stole) on top. The latter can also be worn (girded in a cross

Plate 77   A convent workshop in Romania. The monastics support themselves from their own labors. Photo by John McGuckin.

shape over the body) by subdeacons, and even by tonsured altar servers in the Greek tradition. The priest wears the *epimanikia*, the *sticharion*, and a stole falling vertically from the neck in the form of the *epitrachelion*. He belts the *sticharion* and *epitrachelion* with the *zone*, and on top of all else wears the sleeveless enveloping outer-garment known as the *phelonion*. Bishops and senior priests may also wear a *hypogonation* (a diamond-shaped stiff embroidery suspended on the right side, a remnant of what was once a purse). In the liturgy the bishop wears over all the priestly vestments (except the *phelonion*) the distinctive garment of the *sakkos*, a T-shaped brocade garment that once signified high rank in the imperial court. On the seams are sewn bells to remind the worshippers of the robes of the High Priest in the Temple (Exod. 28.33). On top of the *sakkos* he wears a distinctive episcopal stole called the *omophorion* (a wide cloth band draped about the shoulders). All priests of the Russian tradition also wear a silver (sometimes gold) cross over the *phelonion* or cassock. Greek and other Orthodox clergy only wear the pectoral cross (usually a jeweled or enameled cross) if they have been awarded this as a mark of special honor. The jeweled cross is also reserved for very senior priests in the Slavic Orthodox tradition. The bishop wears, in and out of church, a jeweled medallion or *panagia* over the chest of his cassock, normally featuring an icon of the Virgin Mary. Archbishops and metropolitans are denoted by a second *engolpion* (meaning "that which is worn on the breast") featuring Christ, or a jeweled pectoral cross alongside the *panagia*. In the liturgy the bishop also wears the mitre which is modeled on the ancient Byzantine imperial crown. In some Slavic traditions the mitre can be awarded as a sign of honor to an archpriest or higumen. The bishop's mitre is surmounted by a cross, while a mitred-archpriest's is not. A bishop will also carry a pastoral staff, usually T-shaped, symbolizing authority to govern. From early medieval times a code of vestment colors was developed to reflect the liturgical seasons: gold or white for normal Sundays, green for feasts of the Spirit, red for the Lord's festivals, purple for Holy Week, and white for Pascha.

SEE ALSO: Divine Liturgy, Orthodox; Episcopacy; Epitrachelion; Phelonion; Sticharion

References and Suggested Readings

Chrysostomos, A. (1981) *Byzantine Liturgical Dress*. Brookline, MA: Holy Cross Orthodox Press.

Cope, J. (1986) "Vestments," in J. G. Davies (ed.) *A New Dictionary of Liturgy and Worship*. London: SCM Canterbury Press.

McGuckin, J. A. (2004) "Vestments," in *The Westminster Handbook to Patristics Theology*. London: Westminster/John Knox Press.

Mayo, J. (1984) *A History of Ecclesiastical Dress*. New York: Holmes and Meier.

Pavan, V. (1992) "Liturgical Vestments," in A. Di Berardino (ed.) *Encyclopedia of the Early Church*, vol. 2. Cambridge: James Clarke.

Pocknee, C. E. (1960) *Liturgical Vesture: Its Origins and Development*. London: A. R. Mowbray.

Virgins

MARIA GWYN MCDOWELL

An order of the church primarily composed of women dedicated to God through renouncing marriage and committing to a life of holiness.

Basil the Great in the 4th century says that "She is named a virgin who has willingly consecrated herself to the Lord, and has renounced marriage and preferred the life of holiness" (*Ep.* 99; Elm 1996: 139). St. Basil is here defining and regulating a popular and varied group of early ascetics which existed from at least the early 3rd century and was in need of reform. The earliest textual witnesses to such women (and men) are of Syriac provenance ("Sons and Daughters of the Covenant"). Ignatius in his *Letter to the Smyrneans* refers to "widows who are called virgins." The well-established order of widows supplied a model for the newly developing order of virgins discussed in the *Apostolic Constitutions*, a 4th-century text based in part on the early 3rd-century *Didascalia*. Possibly, the orders were closely related; it is unclear whether the ambiguous term for widow assumed a deceased spouse or if a virgin was necessarily unmarried. Basil's sister Macrina, whose ascetic lifestyle and charitable service provide the basis for his regulations, insists on becoming a "virgin widow." Her "widowhood," however, is the result of the death of her fiancé, *not* her husband. The conflation between widows, virgins, and the deaconess makes it difficult to discern distinct functions, relationships, and the manner in which the rise of one may have precipitated or encouraged the demise of another.

As celibacy was increasingly esteemed in the patristic-era church, so too were the virgins. Seating arrangements in the liturgical assembly indicated rank,

Plate 78 Romanian nun of the community of Voronets engaged in making candles. Photo by John McGuckin.

and virgins eventually preceded widows. Vowed virginity allowed women to escape marriage and devote themselves to the service of God while remaining within social proprieties. A virgin might live with her family, in a community of women, in ascetic communities with men, even in popular but controversial "spiritual marriages." If wealthy, she might live in her own home. Virgins were present in urban centers and small towns. They had no apparent role in the ecclesial framework, though they engaged in charitable work (Macrina) and could wield considerable power (Empress Pulcheria). All followed very similar principles of self-control, fasting, and continence. By the 4th century the order was increasingly institutionalized, requiring a free confession at the age of reason, a period of trial to discern intention and suitability, and financial remuneration. Female monasteries resulted from the popularity of the order, but only became a viable option by the late 4th century, becoming the major social matrix of organized Christian virginal life thereafter.

As an eschatological sign, virginity indicates complete dedication to God as brides, as well as a rising above sexual passions. The ideal virgin in the Orthodox religious tradition is the holy Theotokos, whose faithfulness to God alone is the model for all Christians. The restoration of the order of virgins today (apart from female monasteries) seems difficult given radically different understandings of anthropology and social *mores*. What remains enduringly valuable about the virginal witness is the praxis of prayerful lives dedicated to God in charitable service to others in the midst of urban living rather than social separation.

SEE ALSO: Asceticism; Cappadocian Fathers; Chastity; Deaconess; Widows

References and Suggested Readings

Elm, S. (1996) *Virgins of God: The Making of Asceticism in Late Antiquity*. Oxford: Clarendon Press.

War

PERRY T. HAMALIS

"War" carries multiple meanings and describes phenomena from varied contexts within Eastern Orthodoxy. In addition to the common understanding of war as "organized violence carried out by political units against each other" (Bull 1977: 184), Orthodox sources discuss war as encompassing both the personal and communal, the physical and spiritual, the bloody and bloodless. St. John Chrysostom writes: "There are three very grievous kinds of war: The one is public, when our soldiers are attacked by foreign armies; the second is when, even in time of peace, we are at war with one another; and the third is when the individual is at war with himself, which is the worst of all" (*Hom. 7 on 1 Tim.*). In each of these contexts (interstate, interpersonal, and intrapersonal) the Orthodox Church has a threefold response: it proclaims the ideal of authentic peace, acknowledges the spiritual roots and implications of warfare, and affirms the sinfulness of physical violence even if such violence may be tragically necessary given humanity's fallen condition.

The ideal of authentic peace, while not unique to the Christian East, has been upheld as normative and is reflected clearly within the Orthodox tradition (cf. Harakas 1999; McGuckin 2006; Webster 1998). The Eastern Church's divine services, oriented toward the eschatological peace of God's kingdom, are replete with petitions for "peace from above" and "peace in the world," as well as with exhortations to pray "in peace." This focus reminds worshippers that the Lord being praised is the "Prince of Peace" (Isa. 9.6) who proclaimed a "gospel of peace" (Eph. 6.15), and that their identity as the church cannot be separated from their calling to be "peacemakers" and imitators of the non-violent Christ (cf. Mt. 5; Rom. 12; Heb. 12).

Notwithstanding their eirenic ideal, voices within Orthodoxy also express an acute sense of the depths of human corruption and resist naïve optimism about the possibility for peace on earth. For the Orthodox, the problem of violence and war within human social history goes all the way back to Cain's act of fratricide (Gen. 4), and stems from the passions that corrupt human beings' souls. Furthermore, the activity of war tends to exacerbate and institutionalize those same sinful proclivities that sparked conflict in the first place (cf. Harakas 1999). Thus, from an Orthodox perspective, the only truly effective response to the fundamentally spiritual roots of war begins with baptism and continues through a lifetime commitment to wage spiritual warfare against both human passions and the forces of evil in the world. Waging spiritual warfare in the intrapersonal context, then, is the necessary basis of a proper response to war in the interpersonal and interstate contexts. For the Orthodox,

The *Concise Encyclopedia of Orthodox Christianity*, First Edition. Edited by John Anthony McGuckin.
© 2014 John Wiley & Sons, Ltd. Published 2014 by John Wiley & Sons, Ltd.

such spiritual warfare is the only legitimate "holy war" (cf. Dennis 2001).

Like many ethical issues, the topic of war developed differently within Orthodoxy than it did within Western Christianity – both Roman Catholic and Protestant. Despite the reality of war in Byzantium, there was no single eastern father who wrote extensively and systematically on the subject of war in the way that, for example, St. Augustine, Gratian, Thomas Aquinas, or Erasmus of Rotterdam did in the West. Neither was there a controversy in the Orthodox Church like the one between the Reformers (e.g., Martin Luther and John Calvin) and the Radical Reformers (e.g., Thomas Münzter and Menno Simons) that engaged the questions of Christians' military service and use of the sword. Furthermore, the Orthodox Church never endorsed or practiced "crusades" (cf. Dennis 2001; McGuckin 2006). In fact, Orthodox Christians were the victims when, during the Fourth Crusade, Latin Christians turned their weapons against the citizens of Constantinople. In short, the different histories and theological styles of Western and Eastern Christianity led to different approaches to war ethics. The predominant categories used by Western Christian ethicists – "pacifism," "just war theory," "Christian realism," "just peacemaking," and "crusade" – do not exactly fit, therefore, within Orthodoxy. Strictly speaking, the Orthodox Church is not "pacifist" because, during the reign of the Emperor Constantine and, subsequently, in other predominantly Orthodox nations, military service by Christians became necessary (although canonically forbidden among clergy and monks). Important recent research, however, highlights the ways in which Orthodox Christian sensibilities shaped Byzantine military practices, reflecting a pro-peace bias (Miller and Nesbitt 1995). Similarly, "just war theory" is incompatible with both the spirit and substance of most Orthodox sources (Harakas 1999; McGuckin 2006). The Eastern Church, particularly in its canon law, acknowledges the tragic necessity of defensive wars in some circumstances, but resists efforts to justify wars according to formal criteria, which can easily be preempted by those in power, and affirms the need for repentance among all who are complicit in physical violence. Some debate within Orthodoxy has ensued recently over whether war is best described as a "necessary evil" or as a "lesser good" (Harakas 1999; Webster 2003), with the majority of Orthodox thinkers supporting the "necessary evil" position.

SEE ALSO: Ethics; Military Saints; Original Sin; St. Constantine the Emperor (ca. 271–337)

References and Suggested Readings

Bull, H. (1977) *The Anarchical Society*. New York: Columbia University Press.

Dennis, G. T. (2001) "Defenders of the Christian People: Holy War in Byzantium," in A. Laiou and R. P. Mottahedeh (eds.) *The Crusades from the Perspective of Byzantium and the Muslim World*. Washington, DC: Dumbarton Oaks, pp. 31–9.

Harakas, S. (1999) "The Teaching on Peace in the Fathers," in *Wholeness of Faith and Life: Orthodox Christian Ethics: Part One – Patristic Ethics*. Brookline, MA: Holy Cross Press, pp. 137–61.

McGuckin, J. A. (2006) "Non-violence and Peace Traditions in Early and Eastern Christianity," in K. Kuriakose (ed.) *Religion, Terrorism, and Globalization: Nonviolence: A New Agenda*. New York: Nova Science Publishers, pp. 189–202.

Miller, T. and Nesbitt, J. (eds.) (1995) *Peace and War in Byzantium: Essays in Honor of George T. Dennis, SJ*. Washington, DC: Catholic University Press.

Webster, A. F. C. (1998) *The Pacifist Option: The Moral Argument Against War in Eastern Orthodox Theology*. Lanham, MD: Rowman and Littlefield.

Webster, A. F. C. (2003) "Justifiable War as a 'Lesser Good' in Eastern Orthodox Moral Tradition," *St. Vladimir's Theological Quarterly* 47: 3–57.

Wealth

JUSTIN M. LASSER

From time immemorial Orthodox Christianity has struggled to harmonize the stringent ethical demands of the Lord (not least as they relate to personal economies) with the material realities of life in the world. Jesus' demands upon the wealthy are manifested paradigmatically in his encounter with a rich man (Lk. 18.18–25). The rich man wanted to know what he should do in order to inherit eternal life. He felt he had fulfilled all of the commandments but, Jesus told him, "There is still one thing lacking. Sell all that you own and distribute to the poor, and you will have treasure in heaven: then come follow me." But when the rich man heard this startling demand of Jesus he went away despondent. Jesus responded by saying, "How hard it is for those who have wealth to enter into the Kingdom of God! Indeed, it is easier for a camel to go through the eye of a needle than for a rich man to enter the Kingdom of God." Such is a stinging account of Christ's view of wealth.

The gospels at many instances denounce wealth, such as the occasion of Zaccheus' renouncing half his fortune, and paying back fourfold anyone he had cheated (Lk. 19.1–10). The severity of the gospel message concerning the necessary readiness to renounce wealth was sustained in the early apostolic era, as depicted in the Acts of the Apostles. In that time the followers of Christ held all things in common and "no one claimed private ownership" (Acts 4.32). Only Ananias and his wife Sapphira kept back some money privately from the sale of their property (Acts 5.1–11). St. Peter interprets such an action as the inspiration of Satan, and the death of Ananias and Sapphira soon after is lifted up as a mark of divine judgment against them.

In the post-apostolic period of the church this early attitude to wealth as a severe "problem" (a hard saying) is progressively relaxed. One can note four stages in a developing attitude to wealth in the wider church: first, the softening of these hard passages in patristic reflection (their "spiritual" exegesis); second, the abstraction of poverty and wealth from immediate economic realities and transmutation more into symbolic or "intentional" status; third, the institution of almsgiving as a redemptive force in wealth possession; and fourth, the use of public and private wealth, administered by both clergy and laity, in the service of the poor and in upbuilding the church's philanthropic institutions. It is important to note, however, that there have always existed specific Christian groups that did try to adhere to the radical ethical-economic demands of Christ without softening them, without realigning their apocalyptic bluntness in terms of the vicissitudes of "normal fiscal responsibility" in daily life. We can cite the instance of the early monks of Syria, the Ebionites, the Donatist Circumcellions, and the followers of Eustathius of Sebaste, as a few

examples. The later Russian Non-Possessors are examples of similar tendencies in the church.

The softening of Jesus' demands is readily apparent in Matthew's transformation of the Beatitudes text "Blessed are the poor" into the version "Blessed are the poor, *in spirit*." This minor variant opened the door to a variety of interpretations, to the effect that what was being called for was not literal poverty (or fiscal simplicity – living for the day) but a right attitude (of course, how attitude would manifest in right action was sometimes glossed over). Clement of Alexandria (2nd century) was one of the first theologians to respond reflectively to the issues of wealth and poverty for Christians in Greco-Roman society. In his treatise *Who is the Rich Man that can be Saved?* Clement asks: "What would there be left to share among people, if nobody had anything?" (*Quis. Div.* 13). Clement argued that the literal meaning of Christ's call for poverty could not have been what he meant. It would be senseless if God intended all to be poor. Clement was responding to a larger community that was antagonistic toward the wealthy. Being in the minority of the literate middle-class intelligentsia, Clement was evidently concerned with legitimizing the possession of wealth, and does so on the philosophical basis of advocating a "detachment" from the allure of riches, on the moral basis of adopting a simple (non-excessive) lifestyle, and on the biblical basis of symbolic (typological) rather than literal interpretation of the Scriptures. Origen of Alexandria would follow him in all three things, and establish this as the church's standard intellectual approach in later ages. Following the author of the *Shepherd of Hermas* Clement advocated the divine economy of "redemptive almsgiving." The terms of this economy are that the wealthy were to use their resources in the service of the poor, and would receive in return the intercessions of the poor who prayed for them. This approach, unfortunately, tended to justify the chasm that existed in antique society between rich and poor, by obscuring it. Clement sees it as a solution, an alternative economy: "What beautiful trade, what divine business! One *buys* incorruptibility with money, and by giving the perishable things of the world one receives an eternal abode in exchange" (*Quis. Div.* 32).

Clement stood at a transition point when for the first time, perhaps, a notable element of the church had excess wealth. For most of its existence, even now perhaps, the Orthodox Church has been chiefly composed of the poor (or relatively poor). The institution of redemptive almsgiving may partially succeed in reconciling the wealthy and intellectual elite with the overwhelming majority of the church's community of the poor, but the tendency of theologians to abstract and spiritualize the term of poverty has tended to lead not to the liberation of the poor but rather to specious justifications of their being (and remaining) poor. The best aspects of Orthodox thought on wealth and poverty have tended to stress the supreme generosity of God as common Father of men and women in the world, and to speak of the duty of philanthropy (especially to the suffering) as a necessary characteristic of a true disciple. The church has not always been so successful in elevating systematic ideas about wealth and its just distribution in society, preferring often an individual perspective.

The problem with constructing a workable modern Orthodox theory of wealth and poverty, built out of biblical or patristic sources and principles, is that the ancient authorities of the church always speak from a particular period in which they were located. In Antiquity there were vast disparities between a tiny minority of the wealthy and a mass of poor. In modern economies the terms of transaction have changed so vastly that new iterations are called for to clarify the perennial Christian principle of philanthropy (love for the neighbor as the mode of one's love for God) and how it can apply in modern society. In Orthodox theology, from ancient times, the bishop has always been the particular spokesman for, and defender of, the poor. A genuinely Orthodox response to the challenges posed on Christians by poverty, and by the possession of wealth or the desire to acquire it, can be offered in the lives of the saints, especially in those many who were the noted advocates of the poor. St. John Chrysostom has always been one to whom Orthodox turn for such an example. He expressed the problem, and the great Christian challenge it contains, in the following words : "If you cannot remember everything, instead of everything, I beg you, remember only this without fail, that not to share our own wealth with the poor is the same as theft from the poor and deprivation of their means of life.

It is not our own wealth that we are clinging on to, but theirs" (*Second Sermon on Lazarus* 55).

SEE ALSO: Charity; St. John Chrysostom (349–407)

References and Suggested Readings

Holman, S. R. (2001) *The Hungry are Dying: Beggars and Bishops in Roman Cappadocia*. Oxford: Oxford University Press.

Holman, S. R. (ed.) (2008) *Wealth and Poverty in Early Church and Society*. Grand Rapids, MI: Baker Academic.

John Chrysostom, St. (1984) *On Wealth and Poverty*, trans. C. P. Roth. Crestwood, NY: St. Vladimir's Seminary Press.

Western Europe, Orthodoxy in

JOHN A. MCGUCKIN

Orthodoxy in Western Europe remains a small, but significant, church minority and presence. Though there were earlier Orthodox visitors, the establishment of a permanent and noticeable Orthodox presence in Western Europe (chiefly France, Britain, and Germany) really came about as a result of two specific waves of Orthodox immigration in the early and the late 20th century. In both cases the Orthodox presence was in the form of "diaspora" communities. The diaspora consists of the Orthodox faithful of the patriarchal, autocephalous, or autonomous Orthodox Churches (often referred to as "the jurisdictions") who have moved elsewhere in the world and are, in their new countries, looked after by bishops appointed by the home synods of their originating churches. Only in America has there been any move to establish an indigenous Orthodox Church out of a diaspora community (the Orthodox Church of America). Throughout Western Europe the Orthodox institutional presence entirely relates back to missionary communities of the older churches. All Greeks (including Cypriots) living in the diaspora (a large number indeed) now fall under the jurisdictional care of the patriarchate of Constantinople, which has exarchates and missions in most western countries, given that the modern Greeks (like their ancient forebears) traveled far and wide. The Russian Orthodox also had a large diaspora population, especially after the great political upheavals caused by the Russian Revolution. Its diaspora institutions have also been profoundly complicated by those political troubles. The other larger churches that had a considerable number of faithful living abroad either set up pastoral missions for them, or knew that they could be pastorally cared for by the existing Greek and Russian ecclesiastical provisions.

In more recent times, following on the collapse of totalitarian communist regimes in Eastern Europe, and also on the lifting of border restrictions within the parameters of the European Union, there has been considerable mobility in Western Europe among younger Romanians and naturally an extension of the pastoral provision for Romanian Orthodox in Europe and America has followed. It has been organized by the Patriarchal Synod of Romania, with specific reference to the pastoral needs of the Romanians in the diaspora, with an archbishop in Western and Central Europe, respectively, and also one in America. All of them are members of the Patriarchal Synod.

"Diaspora church" in this sense means an outlying "mission" of the original church. Problems arise, of course, as to how long a church mission can be established in a land without becoming indigenized. It is invidious, to the Orthodox, to establish churches where the church has historically already been established under the protection of an ancient patriarchate (the West falling under the aegis of the Roman patriarchate). The overlaying of a separate ecclesial structure (indigenous dioceses and synods, for example) is regarded by the Orthodox as proselytism, not true missionary activity, and is taken as a sign of a profoundly defective ecclesiology when it is forced upon the Orthodox in their own countries by so-called Western Christian "missionaries" who are really proselytizers. This situation holds in reverse, even after the long-established secession of the Roman patriarchate from the Orthodox pentarchy of leading sees. Diaspora churches, therefore, which are in the traditional territories of the Roman patriarchate (which covers all Western Europe) are in a very different situation from those in the "New World" (Asia, Australasia, the Americas), a situation which was envisaged canonically by the fathers of Chalcedon in 451, who laid

responsibility for authentically "new" missions (to the "barbarians") with the patriarchate of Constantinople. The patriarchate of Constantinople regularly refers to the Chalcedonian canon in the sense that it ought to have supervision of all Orthodox communities all over the world who are outside the geographical territories of historically established Orthodox Churches. However, its radical interpretation of this conciliar decision is challenged by several other churches (especially Russia), and also by the facts of history, for it has never been as simple as this in "real life." The establishment of Orthodox mission churches has always followed the natural process of the establishment of trade with new countries, that immediately required the setting up of missions to care for the pastoral need of the traders from their different national churches. This particularly had reference to the Russians, who had an expanding empire of great proportions while the rest of the Orthodox world was politically in bondage under the Turkish yoke; but in more recent times it has also applied equally to a wide variety of ethnic Orthodox groups who moved to the West either for trade purposes or to escape persecution. Indigenous Orthodox hierarchies will not, then, be declared in the traditional regions of the Western (Catholic) Church but can, and perhaps ought to, be declared in the "new lands" that are neither part of Western Christianity nor Eastern Christianity. This whole, troubled, question of diasporas and jurisdictions is scheduled to be high on the agenda for the forthcoming Great Pan Orthodox Council which (it is hoped) may be convened before the new century grows old.

The Greek churches of the diaspora in Western Europe are the simplest to account for. All of them are under the immediate jurisdiction of the patriarchate of Constantinople. The largest grouping is the Greek Orthodox Archdiocese of Thyateira and Great Britain. There are a few communities in Ireland and Scotland which are part of the Thyateiran jurisdiction. Thyateira, named from an extinct see in Asia Minor and led by an archbishop with several assistant bishops, enjoys a large measure of autonomous government but is, canonically speaking, simply an extension of the Church of Constantinople in foreign parts. Its archbishop is a member of the Constantinopolitan Synod. It was founded earlier but grew in stature after a large wave of Cypriot immigration to England in the middle part of the 20th century, and the large majority of its clergy and people are of Cypriot ancestry, though today there are increasing problems as many of the children of the third generation are losing their grip on Greek language and customs. The church has attracted a small number of English converts, chiefly from Anglicanism (more have gone to the Russian parishes in England, which had a more developed sense of liturgical accommodation to English), and there are several parishes now that offer the divine liturgy with regular amounts of English in the service. A small minority (such as the mainly English community in Chester with an English priest) or the joint Russian-Greek parish in Oxford where Metropolitan Kallistos serves, offer the divine services more or less entirely in English.

The other largest Orthodox group comprising the Western European diaspora is the Russian Orthodox outside of Russia. This diverse and extended community of Orthodox faithful has been heavily disrupted both socially and ecclesiastically by the aftermath of the Bolshevik Revolution. Resulting from this time of persecution, and the considerable refugee problem resulting from it, the Russian Orthodox community abroad fragmented into several divisions. One of these groups is composed of those dioceses outside Russia that remained loyal to the allegiance of the Moscow patriarch. There are a number of such parishes, in Britain, France, and Germany. Well known is the British Russian Archdiocese of Sourozh, formerly led by the renowned Metropolitan Antony Bloom. Throughout his life he retained full relations with the Moscow patriarchate. After his death small parts of the Sourozh diocese preferred to place themselves under the jurisdiction of the Russian Archdiocese of Western Europe under the Omophorion of the patriarch of Constantinople.

The second division was composed of the group of churches organized after the Karlovtzy Synod (1921). St. Tikhon, the last patriarch of Russia before the communist yoke was imposed with a vengeance, disseminated an encyclical in 1920 that laid down emergency plans if communication between the Russians abroad and the patriarchate at home should become problematized. In 1921 the bishops of the Russian Orthodox Church outside the borders of Russia who were free to act, met at the invitation of the patriarch

of Serbia to discuss how to organize themselves in those difficult times. It was decided that the final authority over this "Russian Church Outside Russia" (ROCOR) would be vested in the holy synod of the free bishops, who should meet every year at Karlovtz (Sremsky Karlovtzy) in Yugoslavia. After World War II and the fall of Yugoslavia to communist control, it moved its headquarters to Munich, and after 1949 to buildings on the Upper East Side of New York City. Archbishop Antony Khrapovitsky, the former metropolitan of Kiev who had been exiled by the Bolsheviks, was elected as the synodical president. They had the allegiance and good will of many of the Russian exiles abroad, but by no means all of them, and not all were willing to recognize their authority when they constituted themselves, more and more, as an "alternative" to the Russian hierarchy in Russia. In 1921 a statement they issued declaring themselves for the restoration of the monarchy made their identification as "reactionaries" easy for Bolshevik propaganda at home, and caused much unease among the wider Russian Church, which did not universally have rosy memories of life under the tsars.

After the Bolshevik arrest (and suspected torture) of Tikhon (1922–3), he issued a statement expressing dissatisfaction with the way the Karlovtzy synod had arranged matters and appointed one of the leading Russian hierarchs, Metropolitan Evlogy (Georgievski) of Paris, to work out a new plan for the governance of the ROCOR. This, too, was adopted by the synod outside Russia, but received no official endorsement from Tikhon. Tikhon established Evlogy as his personal representative for Western Europe, and Bishop Platon (Rojdestvensky) for North America. At first the ROCOR synod was very anxious to keep Evlogy and Platon closely bound to its decisions, but the tension was soon to prove too much. After Tikhon's death in 1925 (thought by many to be another of Stalin's clandestine assassinations) the succession to the newly reestablished patriarchate was somewhat irregular, and Sergius of Moscow was widely seen in Western Europe as a communist puppet. In 1927 the ROCOR synod issued a condemnation of Evlogy and Platon. In the following year it flatly refused any ecclesiastical obedience to Patriarch Sergius following on his demand that all exiled Russian bishops should cease from political activities of any kind, and it was, in turn, condemned by the patriarch and the Russian synod. Evlogy was reconfirmed in his role as representative of the Russian Church in Western Europe by Sergius, but in 1930 he was relieved of his duties in a blatantly political move. From the death of Tikhon onwards the ROCOR synod was immensely suspicious of the Russian hierarchs, regarding them as tools of the state. In their turn they have been denounced and pilloried. In the decades following the fall of communism in Russia, however, there were strong moves for reconciliation. In autumn of 2006 the hierarchs declared their decision for the restoration of full canonical union with the patriarchate, though retaining the autonomous administration of their parishes and clergy. The reunion finally took place in 2007, and as a result the ROCOR parishes in America, France, Britain, and Germany were restored to full communion with the Moscow patriarchate. Some few ROCOR parishes, in Britain and America, refused to accept the union.

Metropolitan Evlogy of Paris continued to lead the major group of the Russian Orthodox diaspora in France. After 1926 he ceased to attend any meetings of the ROCOR synod. Separating from them, he had intended to keep lines of communication open with Patriarch Sergius in Moscow, but in 1927 he was denounced by the ROCOR synod for vacillation, and in 1930 he was personally disowned by Sergius for having had the audacity to pray in public for "persecuted Christians in Russia" when there was "no such thing." By 1931, therefore, Evlogy realized that his hope of keeping formal lines of connection open under such bizarre circumstances was not realistic, and he placed himself and his parishes under the jurisdictional care of the patriarch of Constantinople, despite the loud protests of both Moscow and the ROCOR synod. Evlogy was never happy with this arrangement, however, and at the end of his life was personally reconciled with the Moscow patriarchate, but the parishes of his jurisdiction had no desire to follow his example, seeing the communist powers in Russia gaining more and more of a stranglehold over their church and homeland. The ecclesiastical arrangement of Constantinopolitan supervision of the Russian parishes abroad was suspended in 1965 (one presumes after protests by Moscow), but even at that stage many Russian parishes in Western Europe harbored deep

suspicions of the intentions of the Moscow patriarchate, and refused to return to its allegiance, continuing their independent existence. In 1971 the patriarchate of Constantinople once more assumed a supervisory position. It was the French group of Russian Orthodox who had a massively important role in raising the consciousness of the Western Churches in regard to Orthodoxy after World War II. The White Russians in Paris were among the first to bring to the attention of most Europeans (especially French Catholics and British Anglicans) the beauties of the Orthodox liturgy, and the strengths of Orthodox theology. Many theologians were among the group of exiles: Bulgakov, Florovsky, Frank, Lossky, Zernov, and Evdokimov chief among them; and their works gained a large and sympathetic attention in Europe.

One of their number, Sergius Bulgakov, was instrumental in founding the Society of Sts. Alban and Sergius which did so much to open up friendly relations between the Anglican Church and the Russian Orthodox in exile. Bulgakov was a brilliant teacher and writer, a protégé of Evlogy of Paris, who appointed him as a professor in the Theological Institute of St. Sergius which he had founded in 1925, and which remains as the most prestigious Orthodox theological academy in Western Europe. Bulgakov's trial and condemnation for heretical teaching by the Karlovtzy Synod hierarchs was a *cause célèbre* at this period, and further complicated relations among the Russians in exile.

Today, the older disposition of Orthodoxy in Western Europe as a balance between Russians and Greeks is now triangulated as a result of the large, young, and relatively vigorous Romanian presence around the Mediterranean and in Germany. There are also smaller Orthodox communities of Bulgarians, Ukrainians, and Serbs in Germany, France, and Britain. Western European Orthodoxy has not seen any real rapprochement between the various ethnic jurisdictions, although a recent initiative in England has seen the establishment of a second theological institute (after St. Serge) based at Cambridge, and designed as a pan-Orthodox establishment to serve both clergy and laity (and function as an indigenous seminary course for Thyateiran ordinands). In France there is the well-known monastery of Bussy-en-Othe in Burgundy, and the largest in England is the Stavropegial foundation of St. John in Essex. In recent years a small Lavra of the Romanians has been established in England and a larger coenobitic hesychasterion in Nuremberg. The Orthodox presence in England owes a great deal to the generosity and warm hospitality of the Anglican Church, who welcomed and helped it considerably in its early stages of growth.

SEE ALSO: Bulgaria, Patriarchal Orthodox Church of; Constantinople, Patriarchate of; Cyprus, Autocephalous Orthodox Church of; Romania, Patriarchal Orthodox Church of; Russia, Patriarchal Orthodox Church of; Serbia, Patriarchal Orthodox Church of; Ukraine, Orthodoxy in the

References and Suggested Readings

McGuckin, J. A. (2008) *The Orthodox Church: An Introduction to Its History, Theology and Spiritual Culture*. Oxford: Wiley-Blackwell.

Widows

VALENTINA IZMIRLIEVA

Widows were the most prominent group of women in the first three centuries of the Christian church. The Greek term for widow, χῆρα (etymologically related to the preposition "without"), meant not merely a deceased man's wife, but any woman *without* a husband. Used as a cover term for celibate women living outside traditional matrimonial structures (whether widowed, separated, divorced, or unmarried) it became associated in the Christian context with *charisma*, following the Pauline treatment of celibacy as a spiritual gift (1 Cor. 7.7–17). Given the patristic understanding of virginity as a spiritual state that can be regained through continence, widows were often linked to virgins: Ignatius of Antioch hails "the virgins who are called widows" (*Smyrn.* 13.1), while Tertullian of Carthage commends the widows for "becoming virgins" (*Exhortation to Chastity* 1; *To His Wife*, 2.8). Thus, for the early Christian communities, widowhood came to represent an ideal lifestyle, a privileged opportunity for spiritual progress through chastity and service, offering a new social role for

independent women that granted them respectability outside the patriarchal constraints of their society.

In the biblical tradition, widows and their children (the orphans) symbolize all powerless people in society and fall directly under divine protection. Christian law, drawing on both its Jewish roots (Exod. 22.22; Ps. 68.5) and the personal example of Jesus (Mk. 12.38–44; Lk. 7.11–17), made widows the financial responsibility of the church (Acts 6.1–7). Not all widows in Late Antiquity, however, were in need of support. Upper-class widows could inherit substantial property under Roman law. Such financially independent women, who were often also highly educated, were among the most generous benefactors of the Christian communities and the ecclesiastical elite.

The early church generally encouraged widows of childbearing age to remarry (1 Tim. 5.11–14), even though St. Paul considered those who remain widows "more blessed" (μακαριωτέρα; 1 Cor. 7.39–40). Only menopausal widows (the age limit fluctuates between 60 in 1 Tim. 5.9 and 50 in the *Didascalia Apostolorum*) were entrusted with responsibilities toward their communities in exchange for subvention. To qualify for service, these "real" (ὄντως) widows had to have married only once, distinguished themselves by good deeds, and pledged a life of celibacy. They were appointed mostly for prayer, since the Lord never ignores the pleas of widows (Sirach 35.17–22) and a widow personifies the New Testament ideal of incessant prayer (Lk. 18.1–8). Yet both Tertullian and the *Didascalia Apostolorum* refer to more extensive communal duties (teaching, anointing the newly baptized, caring for the sick).

At the peak of their prominence in the 3rd century, widows personified active lay service in the church, rivaling the liturgical role of female deacons in later times, and offering a strong model of female Orthodox ministry. Vehement arguments against ordaining widows, especially in *Traditio Apostolica*, indicate that their exclusion from the clergy was hardly a matter of course. The "office" of widows stood for radical charismatic leadership and, as such, was not sufficiently under the control of the ecclesiastical hierarchy. It was eventually superseded by the clerical office of deaconesses.

SEE ALSO: Deaconess; Virgins

References and Suggested Readings

Eisen, U. (2000) *Women Officeholders in Early Christianity*. Collegeville, MN: Liturgical Press.

McNamara, J. (1979) "Wives and Widows in Early Christian Thought," *International Journal of Women's Studies* 2: 575–92.

Osiek, C. (1983) "The Widow as Altar: The Rise and Fall of a Symbol," *Second Century* 3: 159–69.

Stählin, G. (1985) "Hera," in G. Kittel (ed.) *Theological Dictionary of the New Testament*. Grand Rapids, MI: Eerdmans, pp. 440–65.

Thurston, B.B. (1989) *The Widows: A Women's Ministry in the Early Church*. Minneapolis: Fortress Press.

Women in Orthodoxy

NIKI J. TSIRONIS

The relatively marginal place of women in the contemporary Orthodox Church (as compared with the Western Christian denominations) might lead the casual observer to the assumption that this has always been the case in the tradition of Eastern Christianity. However, this would be far from the truth, as women have played an essential role in the spread of Christianity during the first centuries of our own era, as well as in the foundational development of the Orthodox world during the Byzantine era. Their role is testified in the written sources as well as in the material remains of the ancient and medieval periods. Women in Byzantium remained to a large extent anonymous and despite the flourishing of gender studies in recent years history cannot go back to retrieve all the anonymous women who so fundamentally and basically served society and the church. Speaking about women in Orthodoxy, we refer not only to the extraordinary amount of martyrs and saints, but also empresses and lay anonymous women who played an important part in the Orthodox tradition. This article will concentrate on the Byzantine period, as it was during that time that the presence of women marked the formation of the church.

In the context of the ancient Greco-Roman world, the role of women as taking precedence in religious rites and rituals (especially those of the home) was self-evident. This spirit seems to have been maintained in the early Christian centuries. In the gospels the place of women appears to have been crucial, as they were the first to hear the message of Christ and to witness his teaching, his mission, his sacrifice on the cross, and his resurrection. Mary Magdalene and the other Marys are only a few of the women who surrounded Christ during his earthly life. The Mother of God holds a unique place among women in the church ("our tainted nature's solitary boast") as she was the one through whom the Word of God was made incarnate. According to Orthodox tradition, Mary was not only present at the crucifixion but was also the first of all the disciples to witness his glorious resurrection. In the course of centuries the figure of Mary attained increasing importance and from the

Plate 79 A nun of the Romanian community of Voronets outside the famous "painted church." Photo by John McGuckin.

9th century onwards she became the symbol *par excellence* of the mystery of the incarnation. In this sense a female icon carries the great weight of the representation of Christ among the world.

The early Christian period is marked by the multitude of female martyrs who – even with their blood – helped the message of Christianity reach contemporary society. In the New Testament (Lk. 8.2–3) we encounter references to women as sponsoring patrons of the early missionary efforts of Christianity. Priscilla and Aquila, a notable couple within the Pauline circle, probably sustained in a most decisive way the activity of St. Paul. The earliest reference to a deaconess is encountered in the Pauline Epistle to the Romans (16.1) and refers to Phoebe, a young sister from Kenchreae (near Corinth) whom Paul commends to the Romans. In the same chapter of his epistle, Paul refers to another nine women out of a whole of twenty-four notable people mentioned; among them, the above-mentioned Priscilla, the scholarly missionary and patron of the churches in Corinth and Ephesus. The notable female disciple Junia (mentioned together with Andronicus) is explicitly referred to as an Apostle; and she along with many other women (such as the explicitly named Mary, Tryphosa, Tryphaena, Persis, and so on) recall for us the early, apostolic, Christian environment where women played a vital role in the life of the church and its proclamatory mission. It seems that the role of the deaconess designated an ordained member of the church with specific duties and obligations. Sixty-four inscriptions from the Eastern Roman Empire testify to the existence of ordained deaconesses, while a few others refer to female presbyters (the meaning of which is not entirely clear).

Part of the body of Christian texts which did not find their way into the New Testament, such as the apocryphal *Acts of Paul and Thecla*, recount the fascination of the young betrothed virgin who for three days and three nights, without eating or drinking, remained fastened to the window like a spider listening to the words of Paul (Kraemer 1988; Lipsius and Bonnet 1891). According to the *Acts*, Thecla followed Paul and when thrown to the lions she was miraculously saved. It is interesting that when Paul declined to baptize her, Thecla baptized herself in a ditch of water. Although the events related are probably legendary, it

remains significant that the icon of Thecla as a leading female apostle was still convincing, and was set out in this literature to encourage Christian disciples in the post-apostolic generation. The place where Thecla is said to have spent the last years of her life, in Seleucia of Asia Minor, became the focal point of her cult which – as surviving ampullae found in the area show – was very popular and attracted large numbers of pilgrims from all over the Mediterranean. The Emperor Zeno built a large basilica there in 476. The remains of the basilica are surrounded by a large number of monastic dwellings, which further testify to the popularity of her cult and her continuing role as a patron of female ascetics. In the mid-4th century it was a place to which Gregory the Theologian retired for a time to prepare his ministry in Constantinople when he preached the Five Theological Orations.

The cessation of persecutions and the foundation of Constantinople, the capital of the Eastern Roman Empire that was to survive from the 4th to the 15th centuries, were times and events also marked by a distinguished female figure, namely the Empress Helena, mother of the first Christian emperor, Constantine the Great. The two were celebrated together as saints of the church on their Feastday of May 21. Empress Helena through her patronage of church life in Jerusalem became the one who discovered the True Cross of the Lord, in 326. Following this event the empress ordered a church to be built at the site of the discovery: it was the Church of the Holy Anastasis (Holy Sepulchre, as it is known in the West), which was consecrated in 335. The event is still commemorated every September 14, the Feast of the Elevation of the True Cross, and it represents one of the most important festivals of the Orthodox Church.

The 4th century is also marked by the Cappadocian fathers, who faithfully combined Christian doctrine with Greek thought. More important for our present purposes is the fact that they molded the profile of the women of their entourage in a way that greatly influenced Christian *mentalités* regarding the role and activity of women at home and society. Macrina, the eldest child of Basil of Caesarea and Gregory of Nyssa's family became the subject of a *Vita* written by St. Gregory of Nyssa in the form of a letter addressed to the monk Olympius. Macrina became the higumen of a monastery at the banks of the river Iris (a place of outstanding beauty) even before her brother St. Basil the Great had started his monastic settlement nearby after visiting Pachomius' coenobitic monastery at Tabennisi, in Egypt. In this same convent lived the mother of Macrina, Aemilia, with whom the saint, as it is said in the *Life*, had decided never to separate after the death of the young man to whom her parents had betrothed her. Macrina had a reputation as an ascetic that led many contemporaries to compare her to Thecla herself. The *Vita* tells that at the hour of Macrina's birth, Aemilia had a dream in which a radiant figure addressed the child she was carrying by the name of Thecla. The life and works of Macrina are narrated by her brother Gregory most vividly and the figure of the saint is fashioned on a hagiographical model, so as to be held up for emulation by future generations. Rarely had female figures been ever held up in this way in previous Greek literature. In doing this the Cappadocian fathers set out a new basis and status of Christian women in society. St. Gregory the Theologian does much the same in relation to his sister Gorgonia, using her funeral oration to elevate her as an ascetic example. The virtues that led Macrina to sanctity include chastity, the mortification of her body, obedience to her mother, humility in all respects, poverty, and almsgiving to everybody in need. Macrina's *Life* shows the way in which in the 4th century, martyrdom is being replaced by the new martyrly witness of virginity. Later in life and while higumen at her convent, Macrina acquired the power of healing, the casting out of demons, and also prophecy. There are also stories of how her giving of food to the poor miraculously did not cause her monastery's store of supplies to be diminished. Macrina's virtues echo the expectations of Orthodox Byzantine society of women. In the first Christian centuries, the renunciation of the body became a central issue in the practice of Christianity and undoubtedly it is linked to the rise of monasticism (both in its eremitic form initiated by Antony the Great (ca. 290–346) and in the coenobitic form propounded first by Pachomius and then by Basil the Great).

Women of authority had a massive influence over the development of Orthodoxy in its history. Christian empresses exercised their power carefully and wisely on many occasions for the benefit of the church (Holum 1982; Connor 2004). One of the most characteristic examples was the Augusta Pulcheria, who acted as a regent to her younger brother Theodosius II, who later married Athinais Eudocia. Pulcheria took vows of chastity and according to the sources transformed the imperial palace almost into a convent. She opposed fervently the doctrines of Nestorius and Eutyches, and was a passionate advocate for the title Theotokos, seeing in the Virgin Mary a powerful advocate for all humankind. She modeled herself on the intercessory role of the Blessed Virgin, a fact which Nestorius objected to, as well as to her defense of the Theotokos title (McGuckin 1994).

Almost a century later, the reign of Justinian, the most noteworthy emperor of the early Byzantine era, was enhanced by the role of his wife, the Empress Theodora, who (although of lowly origins, according to the historian Procopius) is probably the only woman of the Byzantine Empire that a non-specialist might have heard of. Theodora's Miaphysite christological sympathies influenced the theological developments of the 6th century, and were behind Justinian's regular efforts to reconcile the Egyptian and Syrian anti-Chalcedonian parties after her death, not least his desire to reconcile the schism definitively at the Council of Constantinople II in 553. Similarly, the presence of empresses during the Iconoclastic era immeasurably assisted the cause of the Iconophiles during the century-long debate over the veneration of images. The issue of the relationship between women and the veneration of icons is still an open field of discourse in modern scholarship. Two figures need to be mentioned at this point: first, the Empress Irene who put an end to the first phase of the Iconoclastic controversy; and secondly, the Empress Theodora. Irene, the wife of Emperor Leo IV, acted as regent to her son Constantine VI when the emperor died in 780. Irene, with the support of Patriarch Tarasius, summoned the Seventh Ecumenical Council, which ratified the cult of icons and the relics of the saints. Similarly, Theodora, the wife and later widow of Emperor Theophilus, in 843, who acted as regent to her son Michael, reinstated the cult of images which was celebrated as the Triumph of Orthodoxy (still celebrated in the Orthodox Church every first Sunday of Lent). St. Theodora is portrayed along with her young son at the upper register of the prototype icon of the Triumph of Orthodoxy (two examples of this iconographic type survive today, one at the British Museum in London and another at the Benaki Museum in Athens). In subsequent centuries, one should add to this list women of the imperial court like Anna Comnene, the daughter of Alexius I Comnenos, but also Zoe and innumerable other Byzantine aristocratic women who used their ability to be involved in societal life (because of their gifts of wealth, talent, and education) in ways that greatly advanced the life and mission of the church.

Another example of female talent used to powerful theological ends is the 9th-century poet Cassia, a legendary figure most commonly associated with her troparion on the repentant harlot which is still sung in the Orthodox Church on Tuesday in the Holy Week. Cassia's biographical details have not been established with any certainty but, judging from her surviving works, she must have been of aristocratic descent. In her poetry, Cassia propounds the veneration of icons and exalts the role of women in the fight against Iconoclasm. She is one of the very few women whose poetry came down to us signed in her own name (Tsironis 2002).

In Orthodox hagiography, over a wide span of time, women appear in a number of capacities: as mothers, daughters, nuns and higumens, providers of charity, compassion, and philanthropy. In the narratives, they often give the impression they are transparent to the grace of God and to visions revealing divine grace. The earliest tales of martyrs from the first Christian centuries are followed in the history of hagiography by tales of "transvested" nuns and female saints in the 5th and 6th centuries, who dressed as men in order to assume the most severe forms of ascetical life (sometimes merging as unknown "beardless eunuchs" in the life of male communities). From the 6th century onwards we also encounter narratives focusing on coenobitic nuns and married laywomen, who dominate the scene through the 8th and 9th centuries. Starting from Mary of Egypt, the exemplary harlot whose repentance and total renunciation of the body led her to sanctity, to women of a domestic environment who attained sanctity through charity and endurance of many sorrows (one case records the abuse of husbands as a cause of martyrdom), Byzantine hagiography covers the whole range of paradigms of the multiple ways which may lead a woman disciple

to sanctity. Despite its ancient character and limited range of socially open roles, this suggests that the road to holiness is broad and wide for women disciples, just as it is for men; that they have equal challenges and capacities in their Christian lives. At the same time these texts reveal to the reader the multiple functions of women in the context of medieval society and the Orthodox Church of the time. The case of the transvested ascetic female saints is of great significance for understanding the challenges faced by women in Orthodoxy. The *Life* of St. Mary/ Marinos is not the first instance where a woman puts on men's clothing in order to escape societal expectations and pursue an ascetic life. St. Thecla is also reported in her *Life* to have put on men's clothes in order to continue her pursuit of St. Paul at Myra. Nicholas Constas, in his study of the cult of the Virgin in late Antiquity, analyzes the symbolism and the complex issues underlying this form of cross-dressing: "Through the medium of clothing, individuals could achieve relative autonomy or advantage in interaction with others" (2003: 353). Clothes were thought of as absorbing the qualities of the people wearing them and in this respect the otherwise deviant act of wearing male clothes was accepted as an action through which women negated the seductive nature of their sex in pursuit of the Kingdom of God. St. Mary/Marinos – venerated both in East and West – dressed like a man and entered a monastery together with her father, aiming to lead an ascetic life (see Constas, in Talbot 1996: 1–12). A similar pattern of seeking anonymity and freedom to follow God despite all accusations and challenges is encountered in the *Life* of St. Matrona of Perge, a fervent defender of Chalcedonian Orthodoxy against the Monophysite policy of the Emperor Anastasius I (491–518), who spent her early years in disguise in the monastery of Bassianos in Constantinople (*Acta Sanctorum Novembris* 3). More than ten lives of transvested nuns survive from the period from the 5th to the 9th centuries and they testify to the need of women to supersede gender boundaries, even by deception if necessary. As Judith Herrin puts it, in an essay entitled "In Search of Byzantine Women": "The monastic disguises adopted by women enabled them to simulate a holiness reserved by male ecclesiastical authorities to men only. To the church fathers, the very idea of a holy woman was a contradiction in terms, which women could only get round by pretending to be men" (Cameron and Kuhrt 1983: 179).

Byzantine hagiography gives us an insight into various other kinds of female sanctity. Ascetics and hermits like Mary of Egypt and Theoktiste of Lesbos attained to holiness through the renunciation of the body; coenobitic nuns like Elizabeth the Wonderworker and Athanasia of Aegina, through their miracles during their lifetime or after their death; housewives paid for their benevolence by suffering death from their husbands' violent hands, like Mary the Younger or Thomais of Lesbos (Talbot 1996). The women who became saints during this time were thus married or unmarried, pursued an ascetic way of life or not, defended the true dogma of the church or lived quiet lives, as the case may be. Sanctity thus follows no fixed recipe and women arrive to the state of holiness from many various paths and ways. Their lives provide an example which sustained women during the Byzantine and post-Byzantine era.

The period from 1453 to the present has not witnessed major new developments as far as the role of women in a male-dominated environment has been concerned. The dawn of the new millennium found the Orthodox Church relatively well behind Western Christian denominations, which had made considerable efforts to include women in the official, liturgical, and pastoral life of the church. However, Orthodox women continued as usual setting an example of Christian love and sacrifice within the church. The figure of Mother Maria Skobtsova (married, divorced, and with children before becoming an ascetic), who dedicated her life to the service of the poor and the persecuted, and who died in a Nazi concentration camp on the last day of German occupation at Ravensbruck, is not unique, even though it is exemplary (Hackel 2003). Her recent canonization by the Russian Orthodox Church has elevated a remarkable woman, the twists and turns in whose life were all raised up in the end by her complete dedication to God. In modern times Orthodox women still work for the glory of God and the spread of his kingdom, motivated by a deep belief in the royal priesthood of believers and in the responsibility of the creature towards its Creator. The place of women in the counsels of the church for the future; their place in its offices of authority, and its common social and missionary strategies for the centuries ahead, is something that remains to be worked out and something that calls to be worked out, for the newly ascendant education and professional eminence of so many modern women demands an extensive reconsideration of the role of women in the Orthodox Church worldwide. Such a discussion has been partially initiated in the modern era, but a long road lies ahead, demanding much Christian honesty and willingness in all the Orthodox communities – not only those that already have large numbers of professionally educated women, but also those (for historical reasons) with less.

SEE ALSO: Contemporary Orthodox Theology; Deaconess; Marriage; Monasticism; St. Elizaveta Feodorovna (1864–1918); Virgins; Widows

References and Suggested Readings

Cameron, A. and Kuhrt, A. (eds.) (1983) *Images of Women in Antiquity*. Detroit: Wayne State University Press.

Connor, C. (2004) *Women of Byzantium*. New Haven: Yale University Press.

Constas, N. (2003) *Proclus of Constantinople and the Cult of the Virgin in Late Antiquity*. Leiden: Brill.

Hackel, S. (2003) *Pearl of Great Price: The Life of Mother Maria Skobtsova 1891–1945*, Crestwood, NY: St. Vladimir's Seminary Press.

Holum, K. (1982) *Theodosian Empresses: Women and Imperial Dominion in Late Antiquity*. Berkeley: University of California Press.

Kraemer, R. (1988) *Maenads, Martyrs, Matrons, Monastics*. Philadelphia: Fortress Press.

Lipsius, R. A. and Bonnet, M. (1891) *Acta Apostolorum Apocrypha*. Leipzig: Mendelssohn.

McGuckin, J. A. (1994) *St. Cyril of Alexandria: The Christological Controversy*. Leiden: E. J. Brill.

Talbot, A. M. (1996) *Holy Women of Byzantium*. Washington, DC: Dumbarton Oaks.

Tsironis, N. (2002) *Κασσιανή Υμνωδός*. Athens.

World Religions, Orthodoxy and

TIMOTHY J. BECKER

The Orthodox Church understands itself as the full completion of the covenant with Israel. From the outset, Orthodoxy has claimed continuity with a Jewish past, and so has assumed its monotheism, Scriptures, and critique of idolatry. Yet it has also stood in significant discontinuity with that past heritage, orienting the Jewish dispensation according to Jesus Christ, whom it proclaims as the true goal of the Law and the Prophets, and who exceeds them all (cf. Mt. 12.6; 12.41–2).

However, most who became Orthodox Christians came from the nations surrounding Israel and, while accepting the Jewish critique of their cults, progressively resisted Jewish culture. This differentiation between cult and ethnic culture saw the emergence of the new and distinctive category of "religion," in which cult took precedence but no longer necessarily corresponded to a particular culture. Thus, Orthodoxy has encountered the world with a restricted cult but an unrestricted attachment to culture; in this sense every culture can house Orthodoxy, while Orthodoxy can house only one cult, which it offers to all nations as the fulfilment of their own cultures.

Nearly all the fathers of the church saw Judaism in a closely relational mode to Christianity. Even those hostile to it were hostile likely because of local tensions rather than systematic theological reasons. The religions of other nations around them, however, were not seen positively. St. Athanasius (296–373) taught that the pagan cults were failures (at a basic logical and moral level) at assessing the innate Image of God properly, which was a live possibility. In a very influential early 4th-century treatise on the pagan cults, he said that rather than worshipping their uncreated Master, humans were swayed by evil to establish created things as God. Evil, which lacks existence, is thus the cause of false gods, which also lack existence (*Contra Gentes* 1.8). For Athanasius, the religions are not just errors in religious style, they are metaphysically the undoing of the world, the deification of ontologically diminishing forms of existence. Athanasius is also clear that this practice is widespread, implicating, among others, the Phoenicians, Egyptians, Persians, Syrians, Indians, Arabs, Ethiopians, and Armenians (*Contra Gentes* 1.23).

Two centuries later, Pseudo-Dionysius (early 6th century) wrote that the religions of the nations derived from their rejection of angels. God had assigned an angel to each nation for oversight and divine illumination (*The Celestial Hierarchy* 9.2–4; cf.

Dan. 10.13–21), which for Pseudo-Dionysius, explains the priesthood of Melchizedek (see Gen. 14.18–20; Ps. 110.4; Heb. 5.6), in the sense that he was faithful to angelic revelation. However, the vast majority of the nations had wandered from their angelic overseers and turned to false gods. Only Israel remained faithful to their angel, Michael, and so received illumination. Thus, for both Athanasius and Pseudo-Dionysius, the religious state of the world was a result of free will. All the nations could have been endowed with the true worship which Israel accepted, but have chosen otherwise because of moral and intellectual failures.

What this false worship would entail for the pagans at the Judgment was a matter of some reflection among the early fathers. A general sentiment, witnessed in the Egyptian desert literature, is that all followers of the cults were eternally lost. John of Damascus (655–750) summed up this view, teaching that repentance was not possible after death (*On the Orthodox Faith* 2.4). Gregory of Nyssa (331–95), following Origen (186–255), held that all things would make eternal progress towards God; though this has always been a minority position within Orthodoxy and was formally condemned as a dogmatic proposition in the 6th century. Nevertheless, Isaac of Nineveh (7th century) wrote in his recently discovered treatises (*The Second Part*) that God's mercy was greater than could be imagined; and one is also reminded of the celebrated saying of Silouan the Athonite (1866–1938): "Lord stand me at the gates of Hell and I shall see no one ever enters."

While uniformly rejecting "false gods," "demons," and "idols," the Orthodox theologians, always within an active missionary and evangelistic awareness given to them by a vastly pluralistic ancient world, have generally sought to claim for themselves elements within other religions that they have regarded as culturally valuable, as partially "compatible" with Christian truth. Chief among these characteristics have always been a prevalence towards monotheistic worship, an attachment to a rational mode of life, and the elevation of moral standards that were akin to those of the church. So, Justin Martyr (d. 165) argued that all who lived reasonably throughout history were in a real sense partakers of the Word, Jesus Christ (*First Apology* 46) and, as such, partial knowers of Christ (*Second Apology* 10). Justin retrospectively claimed for

Christ the achievements of figures as prominent as Socrates and Heraclitus. In some Greek churches it is not unknown to see, occasionally, the great philosophical figures, Socrates and Plato, depicted in the frescoes of the Narthex, as some form of Hellenic preparation (*propaideusis*) for the gospel.

Orthodoxy after the 3rd century was active in deliberately reconfiguring the theological and metaphysical systems of the Greek philosophers, in order to harmonize elements of them with the scriptural teachings about God and the world. For instance, Platonism regarded God as an impersonal ultimate principle, with which the soul had a necessary kinship. While Orthodoxy drew on Platonic conceptual patterns, it thoroughly reworked them. For the patristic tradition, God was a Person, to whom the soul related as a creature with no natural bonding, only a connection by God's graceful mercy that bridged an otherwise impassable chasm between Creator and creature. Thus, the fundamental cultural distinction between the immaterial soul and material body had become one between the Uncreated Maker and everything else, which had been created out of nothing and which (without God's vivifying grace) would lapse back into nothing. Athanasius epitomized this insight when he argued in the *Contra Gentes* that idolatry involved the worship of anything other than the Uncreated Creator.

In the early centuries of the church, reflection on the "other religions" was heavily conditioned by the pluralistic cultic scene of the late Roman Empire. There were regular persecutions of the church by the imperial authorities in this period, attacks which the Christians attributed to the hostility of demons roused by the church's refusal to pay homage to them, and which local pagan communities also articulated in similar ways, from a slightly different angle, accusing the Christians of being worthy of death because of their "atheistic" rejection of the ancient cults. Such a context was not likely to lead towards much positive regard for alternative religious systems, and the positive reflections of the "philosophical fathers" probably did not carry much beyond the intellectual class.

Within a few centuries, the church had spread across the Mediterranean world and into Ethiopia, Arabia, Armenia, Persia, and India. By the 7th century the East Syrian Church had even reached China, where it survived active until the close of the 10th century. By the 9th century, Orthodoxy began its movement among the Eastern European tribes of the Slavs, Moravians, Bulgars, Serbs, and Rus. Thus, at the end of its first millennium, Orthodoxy, and Eastern Christianity more generally, had encountered tribal religions from Africa to Arabia to Europe as well as Judaism, Zoroastrianism, Platonism, Hinduism, Buddhism, and Islam. Each new religion it discovered was assessed with reference to its own classical past and long experience of evangelization in pluralistic environments.

Among all the religions, Orthodoxy's relationship to Islam is distinctive. Islam is the only religion to have politically superseded Orthodoxy in homelands where once it was a majority. Between the 7th and 15th centuries, Orthodoxy moved from a position of power to that of an oppressed minority in Egypt, Palestine, Syria, Persia, Armenia, and finally the Levant. In the times of the Byzantine ascendancy, Islam was generally regarded in a hostile way (Muhammad as a false prophet). In times when the church was subject to Islamic control, there were more attempts to have a sympathetic understanding, and some degree of accommodation could be witnessed (along the lines that Muhammad had brought monotheism to his people, together with a sense of reverence for Scripture, and a moral code – all of which spoke of elements of divine inspiration).

When Muslim Turks finally overcame the Byzantine Empire in the 15th century, the remaining Orthodox stronghold became Russia. Through the extending of the Russian Empire, the Orthodox eventually came into contact with the religiously plural Mongol Empire (before it became Muslim), as well as with Buddhism, Shintoism, and Shamanism in Alaska. And throughout the 20th century the Orthodox in Russia and much of Eastern Europe had to struggle with communism, an atheistic system with religious roots and characteristics.

The 20th century also saw the large-scale movement of Orthodox into an increasingly religiously plural West. This, together with its involvement in the Christian ecumenical world, is leading Orthodoxy to become aware of its minority status within the global religious climate. The Orthodox today are faced, even in traditionally Orthodox countries, with making the transition, once again, from a context of power to one of weakness. In the West they are also faced with large-scale problems of the loss of religious identities, and a vastly greater pluralism than they had hitherto imagined. There are many challenges for the Orthodox Church in terms of what its future response will be. One thing is clear: the old attitudes that relied on clichés about other religions will have to be replaced by a deeper and closer study of what these religions actually do and teach. Many resources exist for such an extension of *caritas*. Patristic theology set up terms of rapprochement based upon the common heritage of humanity (all men and women of all religions) as made in the Image and Likeness of the Divine Logos who is the center of the worship of the Orthodox Church: the selfsame Lord, with a desire to save all humanity. The church, however, is governed by its divine commission to evangelize (Mt. 28.18–20), and pluralism in the form of accepting other religions as "equal or valid" alongside Orthodoxy is not seen as a viable path forward, or as compatible with its fundamental mission in the world to bring all to Christ and to witness to all the authentic traditions of the gospel in its own lifestyle and Christian culture. The exact resolution of many of these issues of Orthodoxy's relations to other religions remains to be clarified in the future. What is unarguable, however, is that Orthodoxy has a vast experience of living in a religiously plural world from its earliest origins, and that its relations with Judaism will remain on a different basis from all others. However, Islam also constitutes a special, though lesser, case because of its own origins with so many Jewish and Christian influences in its foundational Scriptures.

SEE ALSO: Ecumenism, Orthodoxy and; Evangelism; Islam, Orthodoxy and; Judaism, Orthodoxy and

References and Suggested Readings

Boyarin, D. (2003) "Semantic Differences; or 'Judaism'/ 'Christianity,'" in A. H. Becker and A. Y. Reed (eds.) *The Ways That Never Parted: Jews and Christians in Late Antiquity and the Early Middle Ages*. Tübingen: J. C. B. Mohr (Paul Siebeck).

Griffith, S. H. (2008) *The Church in the Shadow of the Mosque: Christians and Muslims in the World of Islam*. Princeton: Princeton University Press.

Louth, A. (2007) *The Origins of the Christian Mystical Tradition: From Plato to Denys*, 2nd edn. Oxford: Oxford University Press.

McGuckin, J. A. (2008) *The Orthodox Church: An Introduction to Its History, Doctrine, and Spiritual Culture*. Oxford: Wiley-Blackwell.

Moffett, S. H. (2003) *A History of Christianity in Asia, Vol. 1: Beginnings to 1500*. Maryknoll, NY: Orbis.

Pospielovsky, D. (1998) *The Orthodox Church in the History of Russia*. Crestwood, NY: St. Vladimir's Seminary Press.

Sunquist, S. W. (ed.) (2001) *A Dictionary of Asian Christianity*. Grand Rapids, MI: Eerdmans.

Y

Yannaras, Christos (b. 1935)
see Contemporary Orthodox
Theology

The Concise Encyclopedia of Orthodox Christianity, First Edition. Edited by John Anthony McGuckin.
© 2014 John Wiley & Sons, Ltd. Published 2014 by John Wiley & Sons, Ltd.

Index

The Concise Encyclopedia of Orthodox Christianity, First Edition. Edited by John Anthony McGuckin.
© 2014 John Wiley & Sons, Ltd. Published 2014 by John Wiley & Sons, Ltd.